even used some of your explanations as information in interviewing contractors to help our team. I have found how much Java knowledge they have by asking them about things I have learned from reading your book (e.g., the difference between arrays and Vectors). Your book is great! **Steve Wilkinson, Senior Staff Specialist, MCI Telecommunications**

Great book. Best book on Java I have seen so far. **Jeff Sinclair, Software Engineer, Kestral Computing**

Thank you for *Thinking in Java*. It's time someone went beyond mere language description to a thoughtful, penetrating analytic tutorial that doesn't kowtow to The Manufacturers. I've read almost all the others—only yours and Patrick Winston's have found a place in my heart. I'm already recommending it to customers. Thanks again. **Richard Brooks, Java Consultant, Sun Professional Services, Dallas**

Bruce, your book is wonderful! Your explanations are clear and direct. Through your fantastic book I have gained a tremendous amount of Java knowledge. The exercises are also FANTASTIC and do an excellent job reinforcing the ideas explained throughout the chapters. I look forward to reading more books written by you. Thank you for the tremendous service that you are providing by writing such great books. My code will be much better after reading *Thinking in Java*. I thank you and I'm sure any programmers who will have to maintain my code are also grateful to you. **Yvonne Watkins, Java Artisan, Discover Technologies, Inc.**

Other books cover the WHAT of Java (describing the syntax and the libraries) or the HOW of Java (practical programming examples). *Thinking in Java* is the only book I know that explains the WHY of Java; why it was designed the way it was, why it works the way it does, why it sometimes doesn't work, why it's better than C++, why it's not. Although it also does a good job of teaching the what and how of the language, *Thinking in Java* is definitely the thinking person's choice in a Java book. **Robert S. Stephenson**

Thanks for writing a great book. The more I read it the better I like it. My students like it, too. **Chuck Iverson**

I just want to commend you for your work on *Thinking in Java*. It is people like you that dignify the future of the Internet and I just want to thank you for your effort. It is very much appreciated. **Patrick Barrell, Network Officer Mamco, QAF Mfg. Inc.**

I really, really appreciate your enthusiasm and your work. I download every revision of your online books and am looking into languages and exploring what I would never have dared (C#, C++, Python, and Ruby, as a side effect). I have at least 15 other Java books (I needed 3 to make both JavaScript and PHP viable!) and subscriptions to Dr. Dobbs, JavaPro, JDJ, JavaWorld, etc., as a result of my pursuit of Java (and Enterprise Java) and certification but I still keep your book in higher esteem. It truly is a thinking man's book. I subscribe to your newsletter and hope to one day sit down and solve some of the problems you extend for the solutions guides for you (I'll buy the guides!) in appreciation. But in the meantime, thanks a lot. **Joshua Long, www.starbuxman.com**

Most of the Java books out there are fine for a start, and most just have beginning stuff and a lot of the same examples. Yours is by far the best advanced thinking book I've seen. Please publish it soon! ... I also bought *Thinking in C++* just because I was so impressed with *Thinking in Java*. **George Laframboise, LightWorx Technology Consulting, Inc.**

I wrote to you earlier about my favorable impressions regarding your *Thinking in C++* (a book that stands prominently on my shelf here at work). And today I've been able to delve into Java with your e-book in my virtual hand, and I must say (in my best Chevy Chase from *Modern Problems*), "I like it!" Very informative and explanatory, without reading like a dry textbook. You cover the most important yet the least covered concepts of Java development: the whys. **Sean Brady**

I develop in both Java and C++, and both of your books have been lifesavers for me. If I am stumped about a particular concept, I know that I can count on your books to a) explain the thought to me clearly and b) have solid examples that pertain to what I am trying to accomplish. I have yet to find another author that I continually whole-heartedly recommend to anyone who is willing to listen. **Josh Asbury, A^3 Software Consulting, Cincinnati, Ohio**

Your examples are clear and easy to understand. You took care of many important details of Java that can't be found easily in the weak Java documentation. And you don't waste the reader's time with the basic facts a programmer already knows. **Kai Engert, Innovative Software, Germany**

Comments from readers:

Thinking In Java should be read cover to cover by every Java programmer, then kept close at hand for frequent reference. The exercises are challenging, and the chapter on Collections is superb! Not only did this book help me to pass the Sun Certified Java Programmer exam; it's also the first book I turn to whenever I have a Java question. **Jim Pleger, Loudoun County (Virginia) Government**

Much better than any other Java book I've seen. Make that "by an order of magnitude"... very complete, with excellent right-to-the-point examples and intelligent, not dumbed-down, explanations ... In contrast to many other Java books I found it to be unusually mature, consistent, intellectually honest, well-written and precise. IMHO, an ideal book for studying Java. **Anatoly Vorobey, Technion University, Haifa, Israel**

One of the absolutely best programming tutorials I've seen for any language. **Joakim Ziegler, FIX sysop**

Thank you for your wonderful, wonderful book on Java. **Dr. Gavin Pillay, Registrar, King Edward VIII Hospital, South Africa**

Thank you again for your awesome book. I was really floundering (being a non-C programmer), but your book has brought me up to speed as fast as I could read it. It's really cool to be able to understand the underlying principles and concepts from the start, rather than having to try to build that conceptual model through trial and error. Hopefully I will be able to attend your seminar in the not-too-distant future. **Randall R. Hawley, Automation Technician, Eli Lilly & Co.**

The best computer book writing I have seen. **Tom Holland**

This is one of the best books I've read about a programming language... The best book ever written on Java. **Ravindra Pai, Oracle Corporation, SUNOS product line**

This is the best book on Java that I have ever found! You have done a great job. Your depth is amazing. I will be purchasing the book when it is published. I have been learning Java since October 96. I have read a few books, and consider yours a "MUST READ." These past few months we have been focused on a product written entirely in Java. Your book has helped solidify topics I was shaky on and has expanded my knowledge base. I have

Thinking
in
Java

Fourth Edition

Bruce Eckel
President, MindView, Inc.

I'm a great fan of your *Thinking in C++* and have recommended it to associates. As I go through the electronic version of your Java book, I'm finding that you've retained the same high level of writing. Thank you! **Peter R. Neuwald**

VERY well-written Java book...I think you've done a GREAT job on it. As the leader of a Chicago-area Java special interest group, I've favorably mentioned your book and Web site several times at our recent meetings. I would like to use *Thinking in Java* as the basis for a part of each monthly SIG meeting, in which we review and discuss each chapter in succession. **Mark Ertes**

By the way, printed TIJ2 in Russian is still selling great, and remains bestseller. Learning Java became synonym of reading TIJ2, isn't that nice? **Ivan Porty, translator and publisher of *Thinking in Java 2nd Edition* in Russian**

I really appreciate your work and your book is good. I recommend it here to our users and Ph.D. students. **Hugues Leroy // Irisa-Inria Rennes France, Head of Scientific Computing and Industrial Tranfert**

OK, I've only read about 40 pages of *Thinking in Java*, but I've already found it to be the most clearly written and presented programming book I've come across...and I'm a writer, myself, so I am probably a little critical. I have *Thinking in C++* on order and can't wait to crack it—I'm fairly new to programming and am hitting learning curves head-on everywhere. So this is just a quick note to say thanks for your excellent work. I had begun to burn a little low on enthusiasm from slogging through the mucky, murky prose of most computer books—even ones that came with glowing recommendations. I feel a whole lot better now. **Glenn Becker, Educational Theatre Association**

Thank you for making your wonderful book available. I have found it immensely useful in finally understanding what I experienced as confusing in Java and C++. Reading your book has been very satisfying. **Felix Bizaoui, Twin Oaks Industries, Louisa, Va.**

I must congratulate you on an excellent book. I decided to have a look at *Thinking in Java* based on my experience with *Thinking in C++*, and I was not disappointed. **Jaco van der Merwe, Software Specialist, DataFusion Systems Ltd, Stellenbosch, South Africa**

This has to be one of the best Java books I've seen. **E.F. Pritchard, Senior Software Engineer, Cambridge Animation Systems Ltd., United Kingdom**

Your book makes all the other Java books I've read or flipped through seem doubly useless and insulting. **Brett Porter, Senior Programmer, Art & Logic**

I have been reading your book for a week or two and compared to the books I have read earlier on Java, your book seems to have given me a great start. I have recommended this book to a lot of my friends and they have rated it excellent. Please accept my congratulations for coming out with an excellent book. **Rama Krishna Bhupathi, Software Engineer, TCSI Corporation, San Jose**

Just wanted to say what a "brilliant" piece of work your book is. I've been using it as a major reference for in-house Java work. I find that the table of contents is just right for quickly locating the section that is required. It's also nice to see a book that is not just a rehash of the API nor treats the programmer like a dummy. **Grant Sayer, Java Components Group Leader, Ceedata Systems Pty Ltd, Australia**

Wow! A readable, in-depth Java book. There are a lot of poor (and admittedly a couple of good) Java books out there, but from what I've seen yours is definitely one of the best. **John Root, Web Developer, Department of Social Security, London**

I've *just* started *Thinking in Java*. I expect it to be very good because I really liked *Thinking in C++* (which I read as an experienced C++ programmer, trying to stay ahead of the curve) ... You are a wonderful author. **Kevin K. Lewis, Technologist, ObjectSpace, Inc.**

I think it's a great book. I learned all I know about Java from this book. Thank you for making it available for free over the Internet. If you wouldn't have I'd know nothing about Java at all. But the best thing is that your book isn't a commercial brochure for Java. It also shows the bad sides of Java. YOU have done a great job here. **Frederik Fix, Belgium**

I have been hooked to your books all the time. A couple of years ago, when I wanted to start with C++, it was *C++ Inside & Out* which took me around the fascinating world of C++. It helped me in getting better opportunities in life. Now, in pursuit of more knowledge and when I wanted to learn Java, I bumped into *Thinking in Java*—no doubts in my mind as to whether I need some other book. Just fantastic. It is more like rediscovering myself as I get along with the book. It is just a month since I started with Java, and heartfelt thanks to you, I am understanding it better now. **Anand Kumar S., Software Engineer, Computervision, India**

Your book stands out as an excellent general introduction. **Peter Robinson, University of Cambridge Computer Laboratory**

It's by far the best material I have come across to help me learn Java and I just want you to know how lucky I feel to have found it. THANKS! **Chuck Peterson, Product Leader, Internet Product Line, IVIS International**

The book is great. It's the third book on Java I've started and I'm about two-thirds of the way through it now. I plan to finish this one. I found out about it because it is used in some internal classes at Lucent Technologies and a friend told me the book was on the Net. Good work. **Jerry Nowlin, MTS, Lucent Technologies**

Of the six or so Java books I've accumulated to date, your *Thinking in Java* is by far the best and clearest. **Michael Van Waas, Ph.D., President, TMR Associates**

I just want to say thanks for *Thinking in Java*. What a wonderful book you've made here! Not to mention downloadable for free! As a student I find your books invaluable (I have a copy of *C++ Inside Out*, another great book about C++), because they not only teach me the how-to, but also the whys, which are of course very important in building a strong foundation in languages such as C++ or Java. I have quite a lot of friends here who love programming just as I do, and I've told them about your books. They think it's great! Thanks again! By the way, I'm Indonesian and I live in Java. **Ray Frederick Djajadinata, Student at Trisakti University, Jakarta**

The mere fact that you have made this work free over the Net puts me into shock. I thought I'd let you know how much I appreciate and respect what you're doing. **Shane LeBouthillier, Computer Engineering student, University of Alberta, Canada**

I have to tell you how much I look forward to reading your monthly column. As a newbie to the world of object oriented programming, I appreciate the time and thoughtfulness that you give to even the most elementary topic. I have downloaded your book, but you can bet that I will purchase the hard copy when it is published. Thanks for all of your help. **Dan Cashmer, B. C. Ziegler & Co.**

Just want to congratulate you on a job well done. First I stumbled upon the PDF version of *Thinking in Java*. Even before I finished reading it, I ran to the store and found *Thinking in C++*. Now, I have been in the computer business for over eight years, as a consultant, software engineer, teacher/trainer, and recently as self-employed, so I'd like to think that I have seen enough (not "have seen it all," mind you, but enough). However, these books cause my girlfriend to call me a "geek." Not that I have anything against the concept—it is just that I thought this phase was well beyond me. But I find myself truly enjoying both books, like no other computer book I have touched or bought so far. Excellent writing style, very nice introduction of every new topic, and lots of wisdom in the books. Well done. **Simon Goland, simonsez@smartt.com, Simon Says Consulting, Inc.**

I must say that your *Thinking in Java* is great! That is exactly the kind of documentation I was looking for. Especially the sections about good and poor software design using Java. **Dirk Duehr, Lexikon Verlag, Bertelsmann AG, Germany**

Thank you for writing two great books (*Thinking in C++*, *Thinking in Java*). You have helped me immensely in my progression to object oriented programming. **Donald Lawson, DCL Enterprises**

Thank you for taking the time to write a really helpful book on Java. If teaching makes you understand something, by now you must be pretty pleased with yourself. **Dominic Turner, GEAC Support**

It's the best Java book I have ever read—and I read some. **Jean-Yves MENGANT, Chief Software Architect NAT-SYSTEM, Paris, France**

Thinking in Java gives the best coverage and explanation. Very easy to read, and I mean the code fragments as well. **Ron Chan, Ph.D., Expert Choice, Inc., Pittsburgh, Pa.**

Your book is great. I have read lots of programming books and your book still adds insights to programming in my mind. **Ningjian Wang, Information System Engineer, The Vanguard Group**

About *Thinking in C++*:

Winner of the 1995 Software Development Magazine Jolt Award for Best Book of the Year

"This book is a tremendous achievement. You owe it to yourself to have a copy on your shelf. The chapter on iostreams is the most comprehensive and understandable treatment of that subject I've seen to date."

Al Stevens
Contributing Editor, *Doctor Dobbs Journal*

"Eckel's book is the only one to so clearly explain how to rethink program construction for object orientation. That the book is also an excellent tutorial on the ins and outs of C++ is an added bonus."

Andrew Binstock
Editor, *Unix Review*

"Bruce continues to amaze me with his insight into C++, and *Thinking in C++* is his best collection of ideas yet. If you want clear answers to difficult questions about C++, buy this outstanding book."

Gary Entsminger
Author, *The Tao of Objects*

"*Thinking in C++* patiently and methodically explores the issues of when and how to use inlines, references, operator overloading, inheritance, and dynamic objects, as well as advanced topics such as the proper use of templates, exceptions and multiple inheritance. The entire effort is woven in a fabric that includes Eckel's own philosophy of object and program design. A must for every C++ developer's bookshelf, *Thinking in C++* is the one C++ book you must have if you're doing serious development with C++."

Richard Hale Shaw
Contributing Editor, *PC Magazine*

Thinking
in
Java

Fourth Edition

Bruce Eckel
President, MindView, Inc.

PRENTICE
HALL

Upper Saddle River, NJ • Boston • Indianapolis • San Francisco
New York • Toronto • Montreal • London • Munich • Paris
Madrid • Capetown • Sydney • Tokyo • Singapore • Mexico City

Many of the designations used by manufacturers and sellers to distinguish their products are claimed as trademarks. Where those designations appear in this book, and the publisher was aware of a trademark claim, the designations have been printed with initial capital letters or in all capitals.

Java is a trademark of Sun Microsystems, Inc. Windows 95, Windows NT, Windows 2000, and Windows XP are trademarks of Microsoft Corporation. All other product names and company names mentioned herein are the property of their respective owners.

The author and publisher have taken care in the preparation of this book, but make no expressed or implied warranty of any kind and assume no responsibility for errors or omissions. No liability is assumed for incidental or consequential damages in connection with or arising out of the use of the information or programs contained herein.

The publisher offers excellent discounts on this book when ordered in quantity for bulk purchases or special sales, which may include custom covers and/or content particular to your business, training goals, marketing focus, and branding interests. For more information, please contact:

> U.S. Corporate and Government Sales
> (800) 382-3419
> corpsales@pearsontechgroup.com

For sales outside the U.S., please contact:

> International Sales
> international@pearsoned.com

Visit us on the Web: www.prenhallprofessional.com

Cover design and interior design by Daniel Will-Harris, www.Will-Harris.com

Library of Congress Cataloging-in-Publication Data:

Eckel, Bruce.
  Thinking in Java / Bruce Eckel.—4th ed.
    p. cm.
  Includes bibliographical references and index.
  ISBN 0-13-187248-6 (pbk. : alk. paper)
    1. Java (Computer program language) I. Title.
  QA76.73.J38E25 2006
  005.13'3—dc22

                          2005036339

ISBN 0-13-187248-6

Text printed in the United States on recycled paper at Courier in Westford, Massachusetts.
Twelfth printing, May 2013

www.mindview.net

exceptional learning experiences

Seminars and Consulting

**Bruce Eckel
and his associates
are available for training in:**

- Object-oriented design
- Java
- Design patterns

Consulting:

- Starting your OO design process
- Design reviews
- Code reviews
- Problem analysis

Public seminars are periodically held on various topics for individuals and small-staff training; check the calendar and seminar section at **www.MindView.net** for more information.

Dedication

To Dawn

Overview

What's Inside

Preface

I originally approached Java as "just another programming language," which in many senses it is.

But as time passed and I studied it more deeply, I began to see that the fundamental intent of this language was different from other languages I had seen up to that point.

Programming is about managing complexity: the complexity of the problem you want to solve, laid upon the complexity of the machine in which it is solved. Because of this complexity, most of our programming projects fail. And yet, of all the programming languages of which I am aware, almost none have gone all out and decided that their *main* design goal would be to conquer the complexity of developing and maintaining programs.[1] Of course, many language design decisions were made with complexity in mind, but at some point there were always other issues that were considered essential to be added into the mix. Inevitably, those other issues are what cause programmers to eventually "hit the wall" with that language. For example, C++ had to be backwards-compatible with C (to allow easy migration for C programmers), as well as efficient. Those are both very useful goals and account for much of the success of C++, but they also expose extra complexity that prevents some projects from being finished (certainly, you can blame programmers and management, but if a language can help by catching your mistakes, why shouldn't it?). As another example, Visual BASIC (VB) was tied to BASIC, which wasn't really designed to be an extensible language, so all the extensions piled upon VB have produced some truly unmaintainable syntax. Perl is backwards-compatible with awk, sed, grep, and other Unix tools it was meant to replace, and as a result it is often accused of producing "write-only code" (that is, after a while you can't read it). On the other hand, C++, VB, Perl, and other languages like Smalltalk had *some* of their design efforts focused on the issue of complexity and as a result are remarkably successful in solving certain types of problems.

---

[1] However, I believe that the Python language comes closest to doing exactly that. See *www.Python.org*.

What has impressed me most as I have come to understand Java is that somewhere in the mix of Sun's design objectives, it seems that there was a goal of reducing complexity *for the programmer*. As if to say, "We care about reducing the time and difficulty of producing robust code." In the early days, this goal resulted in code that didn't run very fast (although this has improved over time), but it has indeed produced amazing reductions in development time—half or less of the time that it takes to create an equivalent C++ program. This result alone can save incredible amounts of time and money, but Java doesn't stop there. It goes on to wrap many of the complex tasks that have become important, such as multithreading and network programming, in language features or libraries that can at times make those tasks easy. And finally, it tackles some really big complexity problems: cross-platform programs, dynamic code changes, and even security, each of which can fit on your complexity spectrum anywhere from "impediment" to "show-stopper." So despite the performance problems that we've seen, the promise of Java is tremendous: It can make us significantly more productive programmers.

In all ways—creating the programs, working in teams, building user interfaces to communicate with the user, running the programs on different types of machines, and easily writing programs that communicate across the Internet—Java increases the communication bandwidth *between people*.

I think that the results of the communication revolution may not be seen from the effects of moving large quantities of bits around. We shall see the true revolution because we will all communicate with each other more easily: one-on-one, but also in groups and as a planet. I've heard it suggested that the next revolution is the formation of a kind of global mind that results from enough people and enough interconnectedness. Java may or may not be the tool that foments that revolution, but at least the possibility has made me feel like I'm doing something meaningful by attempting to teach the language.

Java SE5 and SE6

This edition of the book benefits greatly from the improvements made to the Java language in what Sun originally called JDK 1.5, and then later changed to JDK5 or J2SE5, then finally they dropped the outdated "2" and changed it to Java SE5. Many of the Java SE5 language changes were designed to improve the experience of the programmer. As you shall see, the Java language designers did not completely succeed at this task, but in general they made large steps in the right direction.

One of the important goals of this edition is to completely absorb the improvements of Java SE5/6, and to introduce and use them throughout this book. This means that this edition takes the somewhat bold step of being "Java SE5/6-only," and much of the code in the book will not compile with earlier versions of Java; the build system will complain and stop if you try. However, I think the benefits are worth the risk.

If you are somehow fettered to earlier versions of Java, I have covered the bases by providing free downloads of previous editions of this book via *www.MindView.net*. For various reasons, I have decided not to provide the current edition of the book in free electronic form, but only the prior editions.

Java SE6

This book was a monumental, time-consuming project, and before it was published, Java SE6 (code-named *mustang*) appeared in beta form. Although there were a few minor changes in Java SE6 that improved some of the examples in the book, for the most part the focus of Java SE6 did not affect the content of this book; the features were primarily speed improvements and library features that were outside the purview of this text.

The code in this book was successfully tested with a release candidate of Java SE6, so I do not expect any changes that will affect the content of this book. If there are any important changes by the time Java SE6 is officially released, these will be reflected in the book's source code, which is downloadable from *www.MindView.net*.

The cover indicates that this book is for "Java SE5/6," which means "written for Java SE5 and the very significant changes that version introduced into the language, but is equally applicable to Java SE6."

The 4th edition

The satisfaction of doing a new edition of a book is in getting things "right," according to what I have learned since the last edition came out. Often these insights are in the nature of the saying "A learning experience is what you get when you don't get what you want," and my opportunity is to fix something embarrassing or simply tedious. Just as often, creating the next edition

---

produces fascinating new ideas, and the embarrassment is far outweighed by the delight of discovery and the ability to express ideas in a better form than what I have previously achieved.

There is also the challenge that whispers in the back of my brain, that of making the book something that owners of previous editions will want to buy. This presses me to improve, rewrite and reorganize everything that I can, to make the book a new and valuable experience for dedicated readers.

Changes

The CD-ROM that has traditionally been packaged as part of this book is not part of this edition. The essential part of that CD, the *Thinking in C* multimedia seminar (created for MindView by Chuck Allison), is now available as a downloadable Flash presentation. The goal of that seminar is to prepare those who are not familiar enough with C syntax to understand the material presented in this book. Although two of the chapters in this book give decent introductory syntax coverage, they may not be enough for people without an adequate background, and *Thinking in C* is intended to help those people get to the necessary level.

The *Concurrency* chapter (formerly called "Multithreading") has been completely rewritten to match the major changes in the Java SE5 concurrency libraries, but it still gives you a basic foundation in the core ideas of concurrency. Without that core, it's hard to understand more complex issues of threading. I spent many months working on this, immersed in that netherworld called "concurrency," and in the end the chapter is something that not only provides a basic foundation but also ventures into more advanced territory.

There is a new chapter on every significant new Java SE5 language feature, and the other new features have been woven into modifications made to the existing material. Because of my continuing study of design patterns, more patterns have been introduced throughout the book as well.

The book has undergone significant reorganization. Much of this has come from the teaching process together with a realization that, perhaps, my perception of what a "chapter" was could stand some rethought. I have tended towards an unconsidered belief that a topic had to be "big enough" to justify being a chapter. But especially while teaching design patterns, I find that seminar attendees do best if I introduce a single pattern and then we immediately do an exercise, even if it means I only speak for a brief time (I discovered that this pace was also more enjoyable for me as a teacher). So in this version of the book I've tried to break chapters up by topic, and not worry about the resulting length of the chapters. I think it has been an improvement.

I have also come to realize the importance of code testing. Without a built-in test framework with tests that are run every time you do a build of your system, you have no way of knowing if your code is reliable or not. To accomplish this in the book, I created a test framework to display and validate the output of each program. (The framework was written in Python; you can find it in the downloadable code for this book at *www.MindView.net*.) Testing in general is covered in the supplement you will find at *http://MindView.net/Books/BetterJava*, which introduces what I now believe are fundamental skills that all programmers should have in their basic toolkit.

In addition, I've gone over every single example in the book and asked myself, "Why did I do it this way?" In most cases I have done some modification and improvement, both to make the examples more consistent within themselves and also to demonstrate what I consider to be best practices in Java coding (at least, within the limitations of an introductory text). Many of the existing examples have had very significant redesign and reimplementation. Examples that no longer made sense to me were removed, and new examples have been added.

Readers have made many, many wonderful comments about the first three editions of this book, which has naturally been very pleasant for me. However, every now and then, someone will have complaints, and for some reason one complaint that comes up periodically is "The book is too big." In my mind it is faint damnation indeed if "too many pages" is your only gripe. (One is reminded of the Emperor of Austria's complaint about Mozart's work: "Too many notes!" Not that I am in any way trying to compare myself to Mozart.) In addition, I can only assume that such a complaint comes from someone who is yet to be acquainted with the vastness of the Java language itself and has not seen the rest of the books on the subject. Despite this, one of the things I have attempted to do in this edition is trim out the portions that have become obsolete, or at least nonessential. In general, I've tried to go over everything, remove what is no longer necessary, include changes, and improve everything I could. I feel comfortable removing portions because the original material remains on the Web site (*www.MindView.net*), in the form of the freely downloadable 1st through 3rd editions of the book, and in the downloadable supplements for this book.

For those of you who still can't stand the size of the book, I do apologize. Believe it or not, I have worked hard to keep the size down.

Note on the cover design

The cover of *Thinking in Java* is inspired by the American Arts & Crafts Movement that began near the turn of the century and reached its zenith between 1900 and 1920. It began in England as a reaction to both the machine production of the Industrial Revolution and the highly ornamental style of the Victorian era. Arts & Crafts emphasized spare design, the forms of nature as seen in the art nouveau movement, hand-crafting, and the importance of the individual craftsperson, and yet it did not eschew the use of modern tools. There are many echoes with the situation we have today: the turn of the century, the evolution from the raw beginnings of the computer revolution to something more refined and meaningful, and the emphasis on software craftsmanship rather than just manufacturing code.

I see Java in this same way: as an attempt to elevate the programmer away from an operating system mechanic and toward being a "software craftsman."

Both the author and the book/cover designer (who have been friends since childhood) find inspiration in this movement, and both own furniture, lamps, and other pieces that are either original or inspired by this period.

The other theme in this cover suggests a collection box that a naturalist might use to display the insect specimens that he or she has preserved. These insects are objects that are placed within the box objects. The box objects are themselves placed within the "cover object," which illustrates the fundamental concept of aggregation in object-oriented programming. Of course, a programmer cannot help but make the association with "bugs," and here the bugs have been captured and presumably killed in a specimen jar, and finally confined within a small display box, as if to imply Java's ability to find, display, and subdue bugs (which is truly one of its most powerful attributes).

In this edition, I created the watercolor painting that you see as the cover background.

Acknowledgements

First, thanks to associates who have worked with me to give seminars, provide consulting, and develop teaching projects: Dave Bartlett, Bill Venners, Chuck Allison, Jeremy Meyer, and Jamie King. I appreciate your patience as I continue to try to develop the best model for independent folks like us to work together.

Recently, no doubt because of the Internet, I have become associated with a surprisingly large number of people who assist me in my endeavors, usually working from their own home offices. In the past, I would have had to pay for a pretty big office space to accommodate all these folks, but because of the Net, FedEx, and the telephone, I'm able to benefit from their help without the extra costs. In my attempts to learn to "play well with others," you have all been very helpful, and I hope to continue learning how to make my own work better through the efforts of others. Paula Steuer has been invaluable in taking over my haphazard business practices and making them sane (thanks for prodding me when I don't want to do something, Paula). Jonathan Wilcox, Esq., has sifted through my corporate structure and turned over every possible rock that might hide scorpions, and frog-marched us through the process of putting everything straight, legally. Thanks for your care and persistence. Sharlynn Cobaugh has made herself an expert in sound processing and an essential part of creating the multimedia training experiences, as well as tackling other problems. Thanks for your perseverance when faced with intractable computer problems. The folks at Amaio in Prague have helped me out with several projects. Daniel Will-Harris was the original work-by-Internet inspiration, and he is of course fundamental to all my graphic design solutions.

Over the years, through his conferences and workshops, Gerald Weinberg has become my unofficial coach and mentor, for which I thank him.

Ervin Varga was exceptionally helpful with technical corrections on the 4th edition—although other people helped on various chapters and examples, Ervin was my primary technical reviewer for the book, and he also took on the task of rewriting the solution guide for the 4th edition. Ervin found errors and made improvements to the book that were invaluable additions to this text. His thoroughness and attention to detail are amazing, and he's far and away the best technical reader I've ever had. Thanks, Ervin.

My weblog on Bill Venners' *www.Artima.com* has been a source of assistance when I've needed to bounce ideas around. Thanks to the readers that have helped me clarify concepts by submitting comments, including James Watson, Howard Lovatt, Michael Barker, and others, in particular those who helped with generics.

Thanks to Mark Welsh for his continuing assistance.

Evan Cofsky continues to be very supportive by knowing off the top of his head all the arcane details of setting up and maintaining Linux-based Web servers, and keeping the MindView server tuned and secure.

A special thanks to my new friend, coffee, who generated nearly boundless enthusiasm for this project. Camp4 Coffee in Crested Butte, Colorado, has become the standard hangout when people have come up to take MindView seminars, and during seminar breaks it is the best catering I've ever had. Thanks to my buddy Al Smith for creating it and making it such a great place, and for being such an interesting and entertaining part of the Crested Butte experience. And to all the Camp4 barristas who so cheerfully dole out beverages.

Thanks to the folks at Prentice Hall for continuing to give me what I want, putting up with all my special requirements, and for going out of their way to make things run smoothly for me.

Certain tools have proved invaluable during my development process and I am very grateful to the creators every time I use these. Cygwin (*www.cygwin.com*) has solved innumerable problems for me that Windows can't/won't and I become more attached to it each day (if I only had this 15 years ago when my brain was still hard-wired with Gnu Emacs). IBM's Eclipse (*www.eclipse.org*) is a truly wonderful contribution to the development community, and I expect to see great things from it as it continues to evolve (how did IBM become hip? I must have missed a memo). JetBrains IntelliJ Idea continues to forge creative new paths in development tools.

I began using Enterprise Architect from Sparxsystems on this book, and it has rapidly become my UML tool of choice. Marco Hunsicker's Jalopy code formatter (*www.triemax.com*) came in handy on numerous occasions, and Marco was very helpful in configuring it to my particular needs. I've also found Slava Pestov's JEdit and plug-ins to be helpful at times (*www.jedit.org*) and it's quite a reasonable beginner's editor for seminars.

And of course, if I don't say it enough everywhere else, I use Python (*www.Python.org*) constantly to solve problems, the brainchild of my buddy Guido Van Rossum and the gang of goofy geniuses with whom I spent a few great days sprinting (Tim Peters, I've now framed that mouse you borrowed, officially named the "TimBotMouse"). You guys need to find healthier places to eat lunch. (Also, thanks to the entire Python community, an amazing bunch of people.)

Lots of people sent in corrections and I am indebted to them all, but particular thanks go to (for the 1st edition): Kevin Raulerson (found tons of great bugs), Bob Resendes (simply incredible), John Pinto, Joe Dante, Joe Sharp (all three were fabulous), David Combs (many grammar and clarification corrections), Dr. Robert Stephenson, John Cook, Franklin Chen, Zev Griner, David Karr, Leander A. Stroschein, Steve Clark, Charles A. Lee, Austin Maher, Dennis P. Roth, Roque Oliveira, Douglas Dunn, Dejan Ristic, Neil Galarneau, David B. Malkovsky, Steve Wilkinson, and a host of others. Prof. Ir. Marc Meurrens put in a great deal of effort to publicize and make the electronic version of the 1st edition of the book available in Europe.

Thanks to those who helped me rewrite the examples to use the Swing library (for the 2nd edition), and for other assistance: Jon Shvarts, Thomas Kirsch, Rahim Adatia, Rajesh Jain, Ravi Manthena, Banu Rajamani, Jens Brandt, Nitin Shivaram, Malcolm Davis, and everyone who expressed support.

In the 4th edition, Chris Grindstaff was very helpful during the development of the SWT section, and Sean Neville wrote the first draft of the Flex section for me.

Every time I think I understand concurrent programming, another door opens and I've got a new mountain to climb. Thanks to Brian Goetz for helping me through the obstacles in the new version of the Concurrency chapter, and for finding all the bugs (I hope!).

It's not that much of a surprise to me that understanding Delphi helped me understand Java, since there are many concepts and language design decisions in common. My Delphi friends provided assistance by helping me gain insight into that marvelous programming environment. They are Marco Cantu (another Italian—perhaps being steeped in Latin gives one aptitude for

---

programming languages?), Neil Rubenking (who used to do the yoga/vegetarian/Zen thing until he discovered computers), and of course Zack Urlocker (the original Delphi product manager), a long-time pal whom I've traveled the world with. We're all indebted to the brilliance of Anders Hejlsberg, who continues to toil away at C# (which, as you'll learn in this book, was a major inspiration for Java SE5).

My friend Richard Hale Shaw's insights and support have been very helpful (and Kim's, too). Richard and I spent many months giving seminars together and trying to work out the perfect learning experience for the attendees.

The book design, cover design, and cover photo were created by my friend Daniel Will-Harris, noted author and designer (*www.Will-Harris.com*), who used to play with rub-on letters in junior high school while he awaited the invention of computers and desktop publishing, and complained of me mumbling over my algebra problems. However, I produced the camera-ready pages myself, so the typesetting errors are mine. Microsoft® Word XP for Windows was used to write the book and to create camera-ready pages in Adobe Acrobat; the book was created directly from the Acrobat PDF files. As a tribute to the electronic age, I happened to be overseas when I produced the final versions of the 1st and 2nd editions of the book—the 1st edition was sent from Cape Town, South Africa, and the 2nd edition was posted from Prague. The 3rd and 4th came from Crested Butte, Colorado. The body typeface is *Georgia* and the headlines are in *Verdana*. The cover typeface is *ITC Rennie Mackintosh*.

A special thanks to all my teachers and all my students (who are my teachers as well).

Molly the cat often sat in my lap while I worked on this edition, and thus offered her own kind of warm, furry support.

The supporting cast of friends includes, but is not limited to: Patty Gast (Masseuse extraordinaire), Andrew Binstock, Steve Sinofsky, JD Hildebrandt, Tom Keffer, Brian McElhinney, Brinkley Barr, Bill Gates at *Midnight Engineering Magazine*, Larry Constantine and Lucy Lockwood, Gene Wang, Dave Mayer, David Intersimone, Chris and Laura Strand, the Almquists, Brad Jerbic, Marilyn Cvitanic, Mark Mabry, the Robbins families, the Moelter families (and the McMillans), Michael Wilk, Dave Stoner, the Cranstons, Larry Fogg, Mike Sequeira, Gary Entsminger, Kevin and Sonda Donovan, Joe Lordi, Dave and Brenda Bartlett, Patti Gast, Blake, Annette & Jade, the

Rentschlers, the Sudeks, Dick, Patty, and Lee Eckel, Lynn and Todd, and their families. And of course, Mom and Dad.

Introduction

"He gave man speech, and speech created thought, Which is the measure of the Universe"—*Prometheus Unbound*, Shelley

> *Human beings ... are very much at the mercy of the particular language which has become the medium of expression for their society. It is quite an illusion to imagine that one adjusts to reality essentially without the use of language and that language is merely an incidental means of solving specific problems of communication and reflection. The fact of the matter is that the "real world" is to a large extent unconsciously built up on the language habits of the group.*

> *The Status of Linguistics as a Science*, 1929, Edward Sapir

Like any human language, Java provides a way to express concepts. If successful, this medium of expression will be significantly easier and more flexible than the alternatives as problems grow larger and more complex.

You can't look at Java as just a collection of features—some of the features make no sense in isolation. You can use the sum of the parts only if you are thinking about *design*, not simply coding. And to understand Java in this way, you must understand the problems with the language and with programming in general. This book discusses programming problems, why they are problems, and the approach Java has taken to solve them. Thus, the set of features that I explain in each chapter are based on the way I scc a particular type of problem being solved with the language. In this way I hope to move you, a little at a time, to the point where the Java mindset becomes your native tongue.

Throughout, I'll be taking the attitude that you want to build a model in your head that allows you to develop a deep understanding of the language; if you encounter a puzzle, you'll feed it to your model and deduce the answer.

Prerequisites

This book assumes that you have some programming familiarity: You understand that a program is a collection of statements, the idea of a subroutine/function/macro, control statements such as "if" and looping constructs such as "while," etc. However, you might have learned this in many places, such as programming with a macro language or working with a tool like Perl. As long as you've programmed to the point where you feel comfortable with the basic ideas of programming, you'll be able to work through this book. Of course, the book will be *easier* for C programmers and more so for C++ programmers, but don't count yourself out if you're not experienced with those languages—however, come willing to work hard. Also, the *Thinking in C* multimedia seminar that you can download from *www.MindView.net* will bring you up to speed in the fundamentals necessary to learn Java. However, I will be introducing the concepts of object-oriented programming (OOP) and Java's basic control mechanisms.

Although references may be made to C and C++ language features, these are not intended to be insider comments, but instead to help all programmers put Java in perspective with those languages, from which, after all, Java is descended. I will attempt to make these references simple and to explain anything that I think a non-C/C++ programmer would not be familiar with.

Learning Java

At about the same time that my first book, *Using C++* (Osborne/McGraw-Hill, 1989), came out, I began teaching that language. Teaching programming ideas has become my profession; I've seen nodding heads, blank faces, and puzzled expressions in audiences all over the world since 1987. As I began giving in-house training with smaller groups of people, I discovered something during the exercises. Even those people who were smiling and nodding were confused about many issues. I found out, by creating and chairing the C++ track at the Software Development Conference for a number of years (and later creating and chairing the Java track), that I and other speakers tended to give the typical audience too many topics too quickly. So eventually, through both variety in the audience level and the way that I presented the material, I would end up losing some portion of the audience. Maybe it's asking too much, but because I am one of those people resistant to traditional lecturing (and for most people, I believe, such resistance results from boredom), I wanted to try to keep everyone up to speed.

For a time, I was creating a number of different presentations in fairly short order. Thus, I ended up learning by experiment and iteration (a technique that also works well in program design). Eventually, I developed a course using everything I had learned from my teaching experience. My company, MindView, Inc., now gives this as the public and in-house *Thinking in Java* seminar; this is our main introductory seminar that provides the foundation for our more advanced seminars. You can find details at *www.MindView.net*. (The introductory seminar is also available as the *Hands-On Java* CD ROM. Information is available at the same Web site.)

The feedback that I get from each seminar helps me change and refocus the material until I think it works well as a teaching medium. But this book isn't just seminar notes; I tried to pack as much information as I could within these pages, and structured it to draw you through into the next subject. More than anything, the book is designed to serve the solitary reader who is struggling with a new programming language.

Goals

Like my previous book, *Thinking in C++*, this book was designed with one thing in mind: the way people learn a language. When I think of a chapter in the book, I think in terms of what makes a good lesson during a seminar. Seminar audience feedback helped me understand the difficult parts that needed illumination. In the areas where I got ambitious and included too many features all at once, I came to know—through the process of presenting the material—that if you include a lot of new features, you need to explain them all, and this easily compounds the student's confusion.

Each chapter tries to teach a single feature, or a small group of associated features, without relying on concepts that haven't been introduced yet. That way you can digest each piece in the context of your current knowledge before moving on.

My goals in this book are to:

1. Present the material one simple step at a time so that you can easily digest each idea before moving on. Carefully sequence the presentation of features so that you're exposed to a topic before you see it in use. Of course, this isn't always possible; in those situations, a brief introductory description is given.

2. Use examples that are as simple and short as possible. This sometimes prevents me from tackling "real world" problems, but I've found that beginners are usually happier when they can understand every detail of an example rather than being impressed by the scope of the problem it solves. Also, there's a severe limit to the amount of code that can be absorbed in a classroom situation. For this I will no doubt receive criticism for using "toy examples," but I'm willing to accept that in favor of producing something pedagogically useful.

3. Give you what I think is important for you to understand about the language, rather than everything that I know. I believe there is an information importance hierarchy, and that there are some facts that 95 percent of programmers will never need to know—details that just confuse people and increase their perception of the complexity of the language. To take an example from C, if you memorize the operator precedence table (I never did), you can write clever code. But if you need to think about it, it will also confuse the reader/maintainer of that code. So forget about precedence, and use parentheses when things aren't clear.

4. Keep each section focused enough so that the lecture time—and the time between exercise periods—is small. Not only does this keep the audience's minds more active and involved during a hands-on seminar, but it gives the reader a greater sense of accomplishment.

5. Provide you with a solid foundation so that you can understand the issues well enough to move on to more difficult coursework and books.

Teaching from this book

The original edition of this book evolved from a one-week seminar which was, when Java was in its infancy, enough time to cover the language. As Java grew and continued to encompass more and more features and libraries, I stubbornly tried to teach it all in one week. At one point, a customer asked me to teach "just the fundamentals," and in doing so I discovered that trying to cram everything into a single week had become painful for both myself and for seminarians. Java was no longer a "simple" language that could be taught in a week.

That experience and realization drove much of the reorganization of this book, which is now designed to support a two-week seminar or a two-term college course. The introductory portion ends with the *Error Handling with Exceptions* chapter, but you may also want to supplement this with an introduction to JDBC, Servlets and JSPs. This provides a foundation course, and is the core of the *Hands-On Java* CD ROM. The remainder of the book comprises an intermediate-level course, and is the material covered in the *Intermediate Thinking in Java* CD ROM. Both of these CD ROMs are for sale at *www.MindView.net*.

Contact Prentice-Hall at *www.prenhallprofessional.com* for information about professor support materials for this book.

JDK HTML documentation

The Java language and libraries from Sun Microsystems (a free download from *http://java.sun.com*) come with documentation in electronic form, readable using a Web browser. Many books published on Java have duplicated this documentation. So you either already have it or you can download it, and unless necessary, this book will not repeat that documentation, because it's usually much faster if you find the class descriptions with your Web browser than if you look them up in a book (and the online documentation is probably more up-to-date). You'll simply be referred to "the JDK documentation." This book will provide extra descriptions of the classes only when it's necessary to supplement that documentation so you can understand a particular example.

Exercises

I've discovered that simple exercises are exceptionally useful to complete a student's understanding during a seminar, so you'll find a set at the end of each chapter.

Most exercises are designed to be easy enough that they can be finished in a reasonable amount of time in a classroom situation while the instructor observes, making sure that all the students are absorbing the material. Some are more challenging, but none present major challenges.

Solutions to selected exercises can be found in the electronic document *The Thinking in Java Annotated Solution Guide*, available for sale from *www.MindView.net*.

Foundations for Java

Another bonus with this edition is the free multimedia seminar that you can download from *www.MindView.net*. This is the *Thinking in C* seminar that gives you an introduction to the C syntax, operators, and functions that Java syntax is based upon. In previous editions of the book this was in the *Foundations for Java* CD that was packaged with the book, but now the seminar may be freely downloaded.

I originally commissioned Chuck Allison to create *Thinking in C* as a standalone product, but decided to include it with the 2nd edition of *Thinking in C++* and 2nd and 3rd editions of *Thinking in Java* because of the consistent experience of having people come to seminars without an adequate background in basic C syntax. The thinking apparently goes "I'm a smart programmer and I don't want to learn C, but rather C++ or Java, so I'll just skip C and go directly to C++/Java." After arriving at the seminar, it slowly dawns on folks that the prerequisite of understanding C syntax is there for a very good reason.

Technologies have changed, and it made more sense to rework *Thinking in C* as a downloadable Flash presentation rather than including it as a CD. By providing this seminar online, I can ensure that everyone can begin with adequate preparation.

The *Thinking in C* seminar also allows the book to appeal to a wider audience. Even though the *Operators* and *Controlling Execution* chapters do cover the fundamental parts of Java that come from C, the online seminar is a gentler introduction, and assumes even less about the student's programming background than does the book.

Source code

All the source code for this book is available as copyrighted freeware, distributed as a single package, by visiting the Web site *www.MindView.net*. To make sure that you get the most current version, this is the official code distribution site. You may distribute the code in classroom and other educational situations.

The primary goal of the copyright is to ensure that the source of the code is properly cited, and to prevent you from republishing the code in print media without permission. (As long as the source is cited, using examples from the book in most media is generally not a problem.)

In each source-code file you will find a reference to the following copyright notice:

understands that the Source Code was developed for research
and instructional purposes and is advised not to rely
exclusively for any reason on the Source Code or any
program that includes the Source Code. Should the Source
Code or any resulting software prove defective, the user
assumes the cost of all necessary servicing, repair, or
correction.

5. IN NO EVENT SHALL MINDVIEW, INC., OR ITS PUBLISHER BE
LIABLE TO ANY PARTY UNDER ANY LEGAL THEORY FOR DIRECT,
INDIRECT, SPECIAL, INCIDENTAL, OR CONSEQUENTIAL DAMAGES,
INCLUDING LOST PROFITS, BUSINESS INTERRUPTION, LOSS OF
BUSINESS INFORMATION, OR ANY OTHER PECUNIARY LOSS, OR FOR
PERSONAL INJURIES, ARISING OUT OF THE USE OF THIS SOURCE
CODE AND ITS DOCUMENTATION, OR ARISING OUT OF THE INABILITY
TO USE ANY RESULTING PROGRAM, EVEN IF MINDVIEW, INC., OR
ITS PUBLISHER HAS BEEN ADVISED OF THE POSSIBILITY OF SUCH
DAMAGE. MINDVIEW, INC. SPECIFICALLY DISCLAIMS ANY
WARRANTIES, INCLUDING, BUT NOT LIMITED TO, THE IMPLIED
WARRANTIES OF MERCHANTABILITY AND FITNESS FOR A PARTICULAR
PURPOSE. THE SOURCE CODE AND DOCUMENTATION PROVIDED
HEREUNDER IS ON AN "AS IS" BASIS, WITHOUT ANY ACCOMPANYING
SERVICES FROM MINDVIEW, INC., AND MINDVIEW, INC. HAS NO
OBLIGATIONS TO PROVIDE MAINTENANCE, SUPPORT, UPDATES,
ENHANCEMENTS, OR MODIFICATIONS.

Please note that MindView, Inc. maintains a Web site which
is the sole distribution point for electronic copies of the
Source Code, http://www.MindView.net (and official mirror
sites), where it is freely available under the terms stated
above.

If you think you've found an error in the Source Code,
please submit a correction using the feedback system that
you will find at http://www.MindView.net.
///:~

You may use the code in your projects and in the classroom (including your
presentation materials) as long as the copyright notice that appears in each
source file is retained.

Coding standards

In the text of this book, identifiers (methods, variables, and class names) are set in **bold**. Most keywords are also set in bold, except for those keywords that are used so much that the bolding can become tedious, such as "class."

I use a particular coding style for the examples in this book. As much as possible, this follows the style that Sun itself uses in virtually all of the code you will find at its site (see *http://java.sun.com/docs/codeconv/index.html*), and seems to be supported by most Java development environments. If you've read my other works, you'll also notice that Sun's coding style coincides with mine—this pleases me, although I had nothing (that I know of) to do with it. The subject of formatting style is good for hours of hot debate, so I'll just say I'm not trying to dictate correct style via my examples; I have my own motivation for using the style that I do. Because Java is a free-form programming language, you can continue to use whatever style you're comfortable with. One solution to the coding style issue is to use a tool like *Jalopy* (*www.triemax.com*), which assisted me in developing this book, to change formatting to that which suits you.

The code files printed in the book are tested with an automated system, and should all work without compiler errors.

This book focuses on and is tested with Java SE5/6. If you need to learn about earlier releases of the language that are not covered in this edition, the 1st through 3rd editions of the book are freely downloadable at *www.MindView.net*.

Errors

No matter how many tools a writer uses to detect errors, some always creep in and these often leap off the page for a fresh reader. If you discover anything you believe to be an error, please use the link you will find for this book at *www.MindView.net* to submit the error along with your suggested correction. Your help is appreciated.

Introduction
to Objects

"We cut nature up, organize it into concepts, and ascribe significances as we do, largely because we are parties to an agreement that holds throughout our speech community and is codified in the patterns of our language ... we cannot talk at all except by subscribing to the organization and classification of data which the agreement decrees."
Benjamin Lee Whorf (1897-1941)

The genesis of the computer revolution was in a machine. The genesis of our programming languages thus tends to look like that machine.

But computers are not so much machines as they are mind amplification tools ("bicycles for the mind," as Steve Jobs is fond of saying) and a different kind of expressive medium. As a result, the tools are beginning to look less like machines and more like parts of our minds, and also like other forms of expression such as writing, painting, sculpture, animation, and filmmaking. Object-oriented programming (OOP) is part of this movement toward using the computer as an expressive medium.

This chapter will introduce you to the basic concepts of OOP, including an overview of development methods. This chapter, and this book, assumes that you have some programming experience, although not necessarily in C. If you think you need more preparation in programming before tackling this book, you should work through the *Thinking in C* multimedia seminar, downloadable from *www.MindView.net*.

This chapter is background and supplementary material. Many people do not feel comfortable wading into object-oriented programming without understanding the big picture first. Thus, there are many concepts that are introduced here to give you a solid overview of OOP. However, other people may not get the big picture concepts until they've seen some of the mechanics first; these people may become bogged down and lost without some code to get their hands on. If you're part of this latter group and are eager to get to the specifics of the language, feel free to jump past this chapter—skipping it at this point will not prevent you from writing programs or learning the language. However, you will want to come back here eventually to fill in your knowledge so you can understand why objects are important and how to design with them.

The progress of abstraction

All programming languages provide abstractions. It can be argued that the complexity of the problems you're able to solve is directly related to the kind and quality of abstraction. By "kind" I mean, "What is it that you are abstracting?" Assembly language is a small abstraction of the underlying machine. Many so-called "imperative" languages that followed (such as FORTRAN, BASIC, and C) were abstractions of assembly language. These languages are big improvements over assembly language, but their primary abstraction still requires you to think in terms of the structure of the computer rather than the structure of the problem you are trying to solve. The programmer must establish the association between the machine model (in the "solution space," which is the place where you're implementing that solution, such as a computer) and the model of the problem that is actually being solved (in the "problem space," which is the place where the problem exists, such as a business). The effort required to perform this mapping, and the fact that it is extrinsic to the programming language, produces programs that are difficult to write and expensive to maintain, and as a side effect created the entire "programming methods" industry.

The alternative to modeling the machine is to model the problem you're trying to solve. Early languages such as LISP and APL chose particular views of the world ("All problems are ultimately lists" or "All problems are algorithmic," respectively). Prolog casts all problems into chains of decisions. Languages have been created for constraint-based programming and for programming exclusively by manipulating graphical symbols. (The latter proved to be too restrictive.) Each of these approaches may be a good solution to the particular class of problem they're designed to solve, but when you step outside of that domain they become awkward.

The object-oriented approach goes a step further by providing tools for the programmer to represent elements in the problem space. This representation is general enough that the programmer is not constrained to any particular type of problem. We refer to the elements in the problem space and their representations in the solution space as "objects." (You will also need other objects that don't have problem-space analogs.) The idea is that the program is allowed to adapt itself to the lingo of the problem by adding new types of objects, so when you read the code describing the solution, you're reading words that also express the problem. This is a more flexible and powerful language abstraction than what we've had before.[1] Thus, OOP allows you to describe the problem in terms of the problem, rather than in terms of the computer where the solution will run. There's still a connection back to the computer: Each object looks quite a bit like a little computer—it has a state, and it has operations that you can ask it to perform. However, this doesn't seem like such a bad analogy to objects in the real world—they all have characteristics and behaviors.

Alan Kay summarized five basic characteristics of Smalltalk, the first successful object-oriented language and one of the languages upon which Java is based. These characteristics represent a pure approach to object-oriented programming:

1. **Everything is an object.** Think of an object as a fancy variable; it stores data, but you can "make requests" to that object, asking it to perform operations on itself. In theory, you can take any conceptual component in the problem you're trying to solve (dogs, buildings, services, etc.) and represent it as an object in your program.

2. **A program is a bunch of objects telling each other what to do by sending messages**. To make a request of an object, you "send a message" to that object. More concretely, you can think of a message as a request to call a method that belongs to a particular object.

3. **Each object has its own memory made up of other objects**. Put another way, you create a new kind of object by

---

[1] Some language designers have decided that object-oriented programming by itself is not adequate to easily solve all programming problems, and advocate the combination of various approaches into *multiparadigm* programming languages. See *Multiparadigm Programming in Leda* by Timothy Budd (Addison-Wesley, 1995).

making a package containing existing objects. Thus, you can build complexity into a program while hiding it behind the simplicity of objects.

4. **Every object has a type**. Using the parlance, each object is an *instance* of a *class*, in which "class" is synonymous with "type." The most important distinguishing characteristic of a class is "What messages can you send to it?"

5. **All objects of a particular type can receive the same messages**. This is actually a loaded statement, as you will see later. Because an object of type "circle" is also an object of type "shape," a circle is guaranteed to accept shape messages. This means you can write code that talks to shapes and automatically handle anything that fits the description of a shape. This *substitutability* is one of the powerful concepts in OOP.

Booch offers an even more succinct description of an object:

An object has state, behavior and identity.

This means that an object can have internal data (which gives it state), methods (to produce behavior), and each object can be uniquely distinguished from every other object—to put this in a concrete sense, each object has a unique address in memory.[2]

An object has an interface

Aristotle was probably the first to begin a careful study of the concept of *type;* he spoke of "the class of fishes and the class of birds." The idea that all objects, while being unique, are also part of a class of objects that have characteristics and behaviors in common was used directly in the first object-oriented language, Simula-67, with its fundamental keyword **class** that introduces a new type into a program.

Simula, as its name implies, was created for developing simulations such as the classic "bank teller problem." In this, you have numerous tellers,

---

[2] This is actually a bit restrictive, since objects can conceivably exist in different machines and address spaces, and they can also be stored on disk. In these cases, the identity of the object must be determined by something other than memory address.

customers, accounts, transactions, and units of money—a lot of "objects." Objects that are identical except for their state during a program's execution are grouped together into "classes of objects," and that's where the keyword **class** came from. Creating abstract data types (classes) is a fundamental concept in object-oriented programming. Abstract data types work almost exactly like built-in types: You can create variables of a type (called *objects* or *instances* in object-oriented parlance) and manipulate those variables (called *sending messages* or *requests;* you send a message and the object figures out what to do with it). The members (elements) of each class share some commonality: Every account has a balance, every teller can accept a deposit, etc. At the same time, each member has its own state: Each account has a different balance, each teller has a name. Thus, the tellers, customers, accounts, transactions, etc., can each be represented with a unique entity in the computer program. This entity is the object, and each object belongs to a particular class that defines its characteristics and behaviors.

So, although what we really do in object-oriented programming is create new data types, virtually all object-oriented programming languages use the "class" keyword. When you see the word "type" think "class" and vice versa.[3]

Since a class describes a set of objects that have identical characteristics (data elements) and behaviors (functionality), a class is really a data type because a floating point number, for example, also has a set of characteristics and behaviors. The difference is that a programmer defines a class to fit a problem rather than being forced to use an existing data type that was designed to represent a unit of storage in a machine. You extend the programming language by adding new data types specific to your needs. The programming system welcomes the new classes and gives them all the care and type checking that it gives to built-in types.

The object-oriented approach is not limited to building simulations. Whether or not you agree that any program is a simulation of the system you're designing, the use of OOP techniques can easily reduce a large set of problems to a simple solution.

Once a class is established, you can make as many objects of that class as you like, and then manipulate those objects as if they are the elements that exist

---

[3] Some people make a distinction, stating that type determines the interface while class is a particular implementation of that interface.

in the problem you are trying to solve. Indeed, one of the challenges of object-oriented programming is to create a one-to-one mapping between the elements in the problem space and objects in the solution space.

But how do you get an object to do useful work for you? There needs to be a way to make a request of the object so that it will do something, such as complete a transaction, draw something on the screen, or turn on a switch. And each object can satisfy only certain requests. The requests you can make of an object are defined by its *interface*, and the type is what determines the interface. A simple example might be a representation of a light bulb:

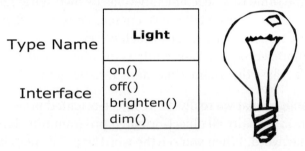

| Type Name | **Light** |
| Interface | on()
off()
brighten()
dim() |

```
Light lt = new Light();
lt.on();
```

The interface determines the requests that you can make for a particular object. However, there must be code somewhere to satisfy that request. This, along with the hidden data, comprises the *implementation*. From a procedural programming standpoint, it's not that complicated. A type has a method associated with each possible request, and when you make a particular request to an object, that method is called. This process is usually summarized by saying that you "send a message" (make a request) to an object, and the object figures out what to do with that message (it executes code).

Here, the name of the type/class is **Light**, the name of this particular **Light** object is **lt**, and the requests that you can make of a **Light** object are to turn it on, turn it off, make it brighter, or make it dimmer. You create a **Light** object by defining a "reference" (**lt**) for that object and calling **new** to request a new object of that type. To send a message to the object, you state the name of the object and connect it to the message request with a period (dot). From the standpoint of the user of a predefined class, that's pretty much all there is to programming with objects.

The preceding diagram follows the format of the *Unified Modeling Language* (UML). Each class is represented by a box, with the type name in the top portion of the box, any *data members* that you care to describe in the middle portion of the box, and the *methods* (the functions that belong to this object, which receive any messages you send to that object) in the bottom portion of the box. Often, only the name of the class and the public methods are shown in UML design diagrams, so the middle portion is not shown, as in this case. If you're interested only in the class name, then the bottom portion doesn't need to be shown, either.

An object provides services

While you're trying to develop or understand a program design, one of the best ways to think about objects is as "service providers." Your program itself will provide services to the user, and it will accomplish this by using the services offered by other objects. Your goal is to produce (or even better, locate in existing code libraries) a set of objects that provide the ideal services to solve your problem.

A way to start doing this is to ask, "If I could magically pull them out of a hat, what objects would solve my problem right away?" For example, suppose you are creating a bookkeeping program. You might imagine some objects that contain pre-defined bookkeeping input screens, another set of objects that perform bookkeeping calculations, and an object that handles printing of checks and invoices on all different kinds of printers. Maybe some of these objects already exist, and for the ones that don't, what would they look like? What services would *those* objects provide, and what objects would *they* need to fulfill their obligations? If you keep doing this, you will eventually reach a point where you can say either, "That object seems simple enough to sit down and write" or "I'm sure that object must exist already." This is a reasonable way to decompose a problem into a set of objects.

Thinking of an object as a service provider has an additional benefit: It helps to improve the cohesiveness of the object. *High cohesion* is a fundamental quality of software design: It means that the various aspects of a software component (such as an object, although this could also apply to a method or a library of objects) "fit together" well. One problem people have when designing objects is cramming too much functionality into one object. For example, in your check printing module, you may decide you need an object that knows all about formatting and printing. You'll probably discover that this is too much for one object, and that what you need is three or more objects. One object might be a catalog of all the possible check layouts, which can be queried for information about how to print a check. One object or set of objects can be a generic printing interface that knows all about different kinds of printers (but nothing about bookkeeping—this one is a candidate for buying rather than writing yourself). And a third object could use the services of the other two to accomplish the task. Thus, each object has a cohesive set of services it offers. In a good object-oriented design, each object does one thing well, but doesn't try to do too much. This not only allows the discovery of objects that might be purchased (the printer interface object), but it also produces new objects that might be reused somewhere else (the catalog of check layouts).

Treating objects as service providers is a great simplifying tool. This is useful not only during the design process, but also when someone else is trying to understand your code or reuse an object. If they can see the value of the object based on what service it provides, it makes it much easier to fit it into the design.

The hidden implementation

It is helpful to break up the playing field into *class creators* (those who create new data types) and *client programmers*[4] (the class consumers who use the data types in their applications). The goal of the client programmer is to collect a toolbox full of classes to use for rapid application development. The goal of the class creator is to build a class that exposes only what's necessary to the client programmer and keeps everything else hidden. Why? Because if it's hidden, the client programmer can't access it, which means that the class creator can change the hidden portion at will without worrying about the impact on anyone else. The hidden portion usually represents the tender insides of an object that could easily be corrupted by a careless or uninformed client programmer, so hiding the implementation reduces program bugs.

In any relationship it's important to have boundaries that are respected by all parties involved. When you create a library, you establish a relationship with the client programmer, who is also a programmer, but one who is putting together an application by using your library, possibly to build a bigger

---

4 I'm indebted to my friend Scott Meyers for this term.

library. If all the members of a class are available to everyone, then the client programmer can do anything with that class and there's no way to enforce rules. Even though you might really prefer that the client programmer not directly manipulate some of the members of your class, without access control there's no way to prevent it. Everything's naked to the world.

So the first reason for access control is to keep client programmers' hands off portions they shouldn't touch—parts that are necessary for the internal operation of the data type but not part of the interface that users need in order to solve their particular problems. This is actually a service to client programmers because they can easily see what's important to them and what they can ignore.

The second reason for access control is to allow the library designer to change the internal workings of the class without worrying about how it will affect the client programmer. For example, you might implement a particular class in a simple fashion to ease development, and then later discover that you need to rewrite it in order to make it run faster. If the interface and implementation are clearly separated and protected, you can accomplish this easily.

Java uses three explicit keywords to set the boundaries in a class: **public**, **private**, and **protected**. These *access specifiers* determine who can use the definitions that follow. **public** means the following element is available to everyone. The **private** keyword, on the other hand, means that no one can access that element except you, the creator of the type, inside methods of that type. **private** is a brick wall between you and the client programmer. Someone who tries to access a **private** member will get a compile-time error. The **protected** keyword acts like **private**, with the exception that an inheriting class has access to **protected** members, but not **private** members. Inheritance will be introduced shortly.

Java also has a "default" access, which comes into play if you don't use one of the aforementioned specifiers. This is usually called *package access* because classes can access the members of other classes in the same *package* (library component), but outside of the package those same members appear to be **private**.

Reusing the implementation

Once a class has been created and tested, it should (ideally) represent a useful unit of code. It turns out that this reusability is not nearly so easy to achieve as many would hope; it takes experience and insight to produce a reusable object design. But once you have such a design, it begs to be reused. Code reuse is one of the greatest advantages that object-oriented programming languages provide.

The simplest way to reuse a class is to just use an object of that class directly, but you can also place an object of that class inside a new class. We call this "creating a member object." Your new class can be made up of any number and type of other objects, in any combination that you need to achieve the functionality desired in your new class. Because you are composing a new class from existing classes, this concept is called *composition* (if the composition happens dynamically, it's usually called *aggregation*). Composition is often referred to as a "has-a" relationship, as in "A car has an engine."

(This UML diagram indicates composition with the filled diamond, which states there is one car. I will typically use a simpler form: just a line, without the diamond, to indicate an association.[5])

Composition comes with a great deal of flexibility. The member objects of your new class are typically private, making them inaccessible to the client programmers who are using the class. This allows you to change those members without disturbing existing client code. You can also change the member objects at run time, to dynamically change the behavior of your program. Inheritance, which is described next, does not have this flexibility since the compiler must place compile-time restrictions on classes created with inheritance.

---

[5] This is usually enough detail for most diagrams, and you don't need to get specific about whether you're using aggregation or composition.

Because inheritance is so important in object-oriented programming, it is often highly emphasized, and the new programmer can get the idea that inheritance should be used everywhere. This can result in awkward and overly complicated designs. Instead, you should first look to composition when creating new classes, since it is simpler and more flexible. If you take this approach, your designs will be cleaner. Once you've had some experience, it will be reasonably obvious when you need inheritance.

Inheritance

By itself, the idea of an object is a convenient tool. It allows you to package data and functionality together by *concept*, so you can represent an appropriate problem-space idea rather than being forced to use the idioms of the underlying machine. These concepts are expressed as fundamental units in the programming language by using the **class** keyword.

It seems a pity, however, to go to all the trouble to create a class and then be forced to create a brand new one that might have similar functionality. It's nicer if we can take the existing class, clone it, and then make additions and modifications to the clone. This is effectively what you get with *inheritance*, with the exception that if the original class (called the *base class* or *superclass* or *parent class*) is changed, the modified "clone" (called the *derived class* or *inherited class* or *subclass* or *child class*) also reflects those changes.

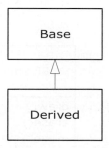

(The arrow in this UML diagram points from the derived class to the base class. As you will see, there is commonly more than one derived class.)

A type does more than describe the constraints on a set of objects; it also has a relationship with other types. Two types can have characteristics and behaviors in common, but one type may contain more characteristics than another and may also handle more messages (or handle them differently).

Inheritance expresses this similarity between types by using the concept of base types and derived types. A base type contains all of the characteristics and behaviors that are shared among the types derived from it. You create a base type to represent the core of your ideas about some objects in your system. From the base type, you derive other types to express the different ways that this core can be realized.

For example, a trash-recycling machine sorts pieces of trash. The base type is "trash," and each piece of trash has a weight, a value, and so on, and can be shredded, melted, or decomposed. From this, more specific types of trash are derived that may have additional characteristics (a bottle has a color) or behaviors (an aluminum can may be crushed, a steel can is magnetic). In addition, some behaviors may be different (the value of paper depends on its type and condition). Using inheritance, you can build a type hierarchy that expresses the problem you're trying to solve in terms of its types.

A second example is the classic "shape" example, perhaps used in a computer-aided design system or game simulation. The base type is "shape," and each shape has a size, a color, a position, and so on. Each shape can be drawn, erased, moved, colored, etc. From this, specific types of shapes are derived (inherited)—circle, square, triangle, and so on—each of which may have additional characteristics and behaviors. Certain shapes can be flipped, for example. Some behaviors may be different, such as when you want to calculate the area of a shape. The type hierarchy embodies both the similarities and differences between the shapes.

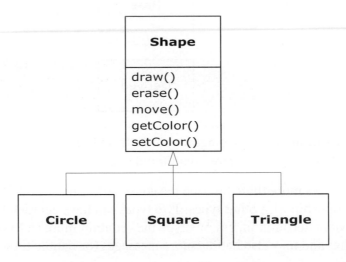

Casting the solution in the same terms as the problem is very useful because you don't need a lot of intermediate models to get from a description of the problem to a description of the solution. With objects, the type hierarchy is the primary model, so you go directly from the description of the system in the real world to the description of the system in code. Indeed, one of the difficulties people have with object-oriented design is that it's too simple to get from the beginning to the end. A mind trained to look for complex solutions can initially be stumped by this simplicity.

When you inherit from an existing type, you create a new type. This new type contains not only all the members of the existing type (although the **private** ones are hidden away and inaccessible), but more importantly it duplicates the interface of the base class. That is, all the messages you can send to objects of the base class you can also send to objects of the derived class. Since we know the type of a class by the messages we can send to it, this means that the derived class *is the same type as the base class*. In the previous example, "A circle is a shape." This type equivalence via inheritance is one of the fundamental gateways in understanding the meaning of object-oriented programming.

Since both the base class and derived class have the same fundamental interface, there must be some implementation to go along with that interface. That is, there must be some code to execute when an object receives a particular message. If you simply inherit a class and don't do anything else, the methods from the base-class interface come right along into the derived class. That means objects of the derived class have not only the same type, they also have the same behavior, which isn't particularly interesting.

You have two ways to differentiate your new derived class from the original base class. The first is quite straightforward: You simply add brand new methods to the derived class. These new methods are not part of the base-class interface. This means that the base class simply didn't do as much as you wanted it to, so you added more methods. This simple and primitive use for inheritance is, at times, the perfect solution to your problem. However, you should look closely for the possibility that your base class might also need these additional methods. This process of discovery and iteration of your design happens regularly in object-oriented programming.

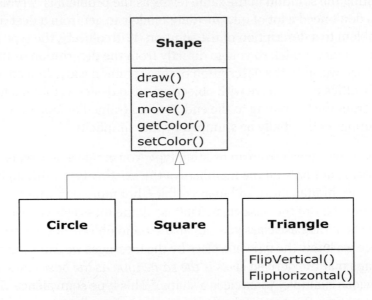

Although inheritance may sometimes imply (especially in Java, where the keyword for inheritance is **extends**) that you are going to add new methods to the interface, that's not necessarily true. The second and more important way to differentiate your new class is to *change* the behavior of an existing base-class method. This is referred to as *overriding* that method.

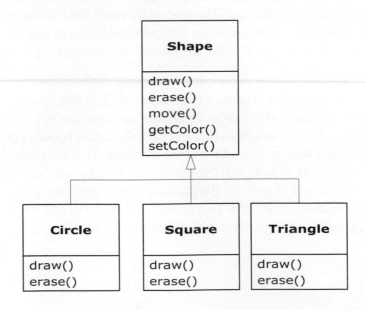

To override a method, you simply create a new definition for the method in the derived class. You're saying, "I'm using the same interface method here, but I want it to do something different for my new type."

Is-a vs. is-like-a relationships

There's a certain debate that can occur about inheritance: Should inheritance override *only* base-class methods (and not add new methods that aren't in the base class)? This would mean that the derived class is *exactly* the same type as the base class since it has exactly the same interface. As a result, you can exactly substitute an object of the derived class for an object of the base class. This can be thought of as *pure substitution*, and it's often referred to as the *substitution principle*. In a sense, this is the ideal way to treat inheritance. We often refer to the relationship between the base class and derived classes in this case as an *is-a* relationship, because you can say, "A circle *is a* shape." A test for inheritance is to determine whether you can state the is-a relationship about the classes and have it make sense.

There are times when you must add new interface elements to a derived type, thus extending the interface. The new type can still be substituted for the base type, but the substitution isn't perfect because your new methods are not accessible from the base type. This can be described as an *is-like-a* relationship (my term). The new type has the interface of the old type but it also contains other methods, so you can't really say it's exactly the same. For example, consider an air conditioner. Suppose your house is wired with all the controls for cooling; that is, it has an interface that allows you to control cooling. Imagine that the air conditioner breaks down and you replace it with a heat pump, which can both heat and cool. The heat pump *is-like-an* air conditioner, but it can do more. Because the control system of your house is designed only to control cooling, it is restricted to communication with the cooling part of the new object. The interface of the new object has been extended, and the existing system doesn't know about anything except the original interface.

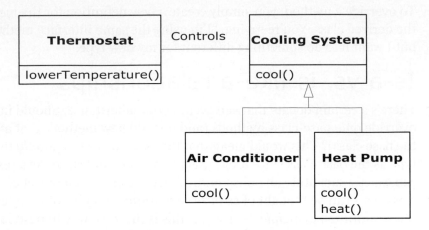

Of course, once you see this design it becomes clear that the base class "cooling system" is not general enough, and should be renamed to "temperature control system" so that it can also include heating—at which point the substitution principle will work. However, this diagram is an example of what can happen with design in the real world.

When you see the substitution principle it's easy to feel like this approach (pure substitution) is the only way to do things, and in fact it *is* nice if your design works out that way. But you'll find that there are times when it's equally clear that you must add new methods to the interface of a derived class. With inspection both cases should be reasonably obvious.

Interchangeable objects
with polymorphism

When dealing with type hierarchies, you often want to treat an object not as the specific type that it is, but instead as its base type. This allows you to write code that doesn't depend on specific types. In the shape example, methods manipulate generic shapes, unconcerned about whether they're circles, squares, triangles, or some shape that hasn't even been defined yet. All shapes can be drawn, erased, and moved, so these methods simply send a message to a shape object; they don't worry about how the object copes with the message.

Such code is unaffected by the addition of new types, and adding new types is the most common way to extend an object-oriented program to handle new situations. For example, you can derive a new subtype of shape called pentagon without modifying the methods that deal only with generic shapes. This ability to easily extend a design by deriving new subtypes is one of the essential ways to encapsulate change. This greatly improves designs while reducing the cost of software maintenance.

There's a problem, however, with attempting to treat derived-type objects as their generic base types (circles as shapes, bicycles as vehicles, cormorants as birds, etc.). If a method is going to tell a generic shape to draw itself, or a generic vehicle to steer, or a generic bird to move, the compiler cannot know at compile time precisely what piece of code will be executed. That's the whole point—when the message is sent, the programmer doesn't *want* to know what piece of code will be executed; the draw method can be applied equally to a circle, a square, or a triangle, and the object will execute the proper code depending on its specific type.

If you don't have to know what piece of code will be executed, then when you add a new subtype, the code it executes can be different without requiring changes to the method that calls it. Therefore, the compiler cannot know precisely what piece of code is executed, so what does it do? For example, in the following diagram the **BirdController** object just works with generic **Bird** objects and does not know what exact type they are. This is convenient from **BirdController**'s perspective because it doesn't have to write special code to determine the exact type of **Bird** it's working with or that **Bird**'s behavior. So how does it happen that, when **move( )** is called while ignoring the specific type of **Bird**, the right behavior will occur (a **Goose** walks, flies, or swims, and a **Penguin** walks or swims)?

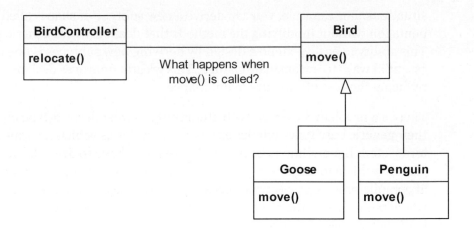

The answer is the primary twist in object-oriented programming: The compiler cannot make a function call in the traditional sense. The function call generated by a non-OOP compiler causes what is called *early binding*, a term you may not have heard before because you've never thought about it any other way. It means the compiler generates a call to a specific function name, and the runtime system resolves this call to the absolute address of the code to be executed. In OOP, the program cannot determine the address of the code until run time, so some other scheme is necessary when a message is sent to a generic object.

To solve the problem, object-oriented languages use the concept of *late binding*. When you send a message to an object, the code being called isn't determined until run time. The compiler does ensure that the method exists and performs type checking on the arguments and return value, but it doesn't know the exact code to execute.

To perform late binding, Java uses a special bit of code in lieu of the absolute call. This code calculates the address of the method body, using information stored in the object (this process is covered in great detail in the *Polymorphism* chapter). Thus, each object can behave differently according to the contents of that special bit of code. When you send a message to an object, the object actually does figure out what to do with that message.

In some languages you must explicitly state that you want a method to have the flexibility of late-binding properties (C++ uses the **virtual** keyword to do this). In these languages, by default, methods are *not* dynamically bound. In

Java, dynamic binding is the default behavior and you don't need to remember to add any extra keywords in order to get polymorphism.

Consider the shape example. The family of classes (all based on the same uniform interface) was diagrammed earlier in this chapter. To demonstrate polymorphism, we want to write a single piece of code that ignores the specific details of type and talks only to the base class. That code is *decoupled* from type-specific information and thus is simpler to write and easier to understand. And, if a new type—a **Hexagon**, for example—is added through inheritance, the code you write will work just as well for the new type of **Shape** as it did on the existing types. Thus, the program is *extensible*.

If you write a method in Java (as you will soon learn how to do):

```java
void doSomething(Shape shape) {
  shape.erase();
  // ...
  shape.draw();
}
```

This method speaks to any **Shape**, so it is independent of the specific type of object that it's drawing and erasing. If some other part of the program uses the **doSomething( )** method:

```java
Circle circle = new Circle();
Triangle triangle = new Triangle();
Line line = new Line();
doSomething(circle);
doSomething(triangle);
doSomething(line);
```

The calls to **doSomething( )** automatically work correctly, regardless of the exact type of the object.

This is a rather amazing trick. Consider the line:

```java
doSomething(circle);
```

What's happening here is that a **Circle** is being passed into a method that's expecting a **Shape**. Since a **Circle** *is* a **Shape** it can be treated as one by **doSomething( )**. That is, any message that **doSomething( )** can send to a **Shape**, a **Circle** can accept. So it is a completely safe and logical thing to do.

We call this process of treating a derived type as though it were its base type *upcasting*. The name *cast* is used in the sense of casting into a mold and the *up* comes from the way the inheritance diagram is typically arranged, with the base type at the top and the derived classes fanning out downward. Thus, casting to a base type is moving up the inheritance diagram: "upcasting."

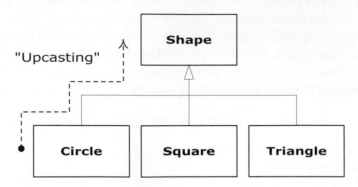

An object-oriented program contains some upcasting somewhere, because that's how you decouple yourself from knowing about the exact type you're working with. Look at the code in **doSomething( )**:

```
shape.erase();
// ...
shape.draw();
```

Notice that it doesn't say, "If you're a **Circle**, do this, if you're a **Square**, do that, etc." If you write that kind of code, which checks for all the possible types that a **Shape** can actually be, it's messy and you need to change it every time you add a new kind of **Shape**. Here, you just say, "You're a shape, I know you can **erase( )** and **draw( )** yourself, do it, and take care of the details correctly."

What's impressive about the code in **doSomething( )** is that, somehow, the right thing happens. Calling **draw( )** for **Circle** causes different code to be executed than when calling **draw( )** for a **Square** or a **Line**, but when the **draw( )** message is sent to an anonymous **Shape**, the correct behavior occurs based on the actual type of the **Shape**. This is amazing because, as mentioned earlier, when the Java compiler is compiling the code for **doSomething( )**, it cannot know exactly what types it is dealing with. So ordinarily, you'd expect it to end up calling the version of **erase( )** and **draw( )** for the base class **Shape**, and not for the specific **Circle**, **Square**, or **Line**. And yet the right thing happens because of polymorphism. The compiler and runtime system handle the details; all you need to know right now is that it does happen, and more importantly, how to design with it. When you send a message to an object, the object will do the right thing, even when upcasting is involved.

The singly rooted hierarchy

One of the issues in OOP that has become especially prominent since the introduction of C++ is whether all classes should ultimately be inherited from a single base class. In Java (as with virtually all other OOP languages *except* for C++) the answer is yes, and the name of this ultimate base class is simply **Object**. It turns out that the benefits of the singly rooted hierarchy are many.

All objects in a singly rooted hierarchy have an interface in common, so they are all ultimately the same fundamental type. The alternative (provided by C++) is that you don't know that everything is the same basic type. From a backward-compatibility standpoint this fits the model of C better and can be thought of as less restrictive, but when you want to do full-on object-oriented programming you must then build your own hierarchy to provide the same convenience that's built into other OOP languages. And in any new class library you acquire, some other incompatible interface will be used. It requires effort (and possibly multiple inheritance) to work the new interface into your design. Is the extra "flexibility" of C++ worth it? If you need it—if you have a large investment in C—it's quite valuable. If you're starting from scratch, other alternatives such as Java can often be more productive.

All objects in a singly rooted hierarchy can be guaranteed to have certain functionality. You know you can perform certain basic operations on every object in your system. All objects can easily be created on the heap, and argument passing is greatly simplified.

A singly rooted hierarchy makes it much easier to implement a *garbage collector*, which is one of the fundamental improvements of Java over C++. And since information about the type of an object is guaranteed to be in all objects, you'll never end up with an object whose type you cannot determine. This is especially important with system-level operations, such as exception handling, and to allow greater flexibility in programming.

Containers

In general, you don't know how many objects you're going to need to solve a particular problem, or how long they will last. You also don't know how to store those objects. How can you know how much space to create if that information isn't known until run time?

The solution to most problems in object-oriented design seems flippant: You create another type of object. The new type of object that solves this particular problem holds references to other objects. Of course, you can do the same thing with an *array*, which is available in most languages. But this new object, generally called a *container* (also called a *collection*, but the Java library uses that term in a different sense so this book will use "container"), will expand itself whenever necessary to accommodate everything you place inside it. So you don't need to know how many objects you're going to hold in a container. Just create a container object and let it take care of the details.

Fortunately, a good OOP language comes with a set of containers as part of the package. In C++, it's part of the Standard C++ Library and is often called the *Standard Template Library* (STL). Smalltalk has a very complete set of containers. Java also has numerous containers in its standard library. In some libraries, one or two generic containers is considered good enough for all needs, and in others (Java, for example) the library has different types of containers for different needs: several different kinds of **List** classes (to hold sequences), **Map**s (also known as *associative arrays*, to associate objects with other objects), **Set**s (to hold one of each type of object), and more components such as queues, trees, stacks, etc.

From a design standpoint, all you really want is a container that can be manipulated to solve your problem. If a single type of container satisfied all of your needs, there'd be no reason to have different kinds. There are two reasons that you need a choice of containers. First, containers provide different types of interfaces and external behavior. A stack has a different interface and behavior than a queue, which is different from a set or a list. One of these might provide a more flexible solution to your problem than the other. Second, different containers have different efficiencies for certain operations. For example, there are two basic types of **List**: **ArrayList** and **LinkedList**. Both are simple sequences that can have identical interfaces and external behaviors. But certain operations can have significantly different costs. Randomly accessing elements in an **ArrayList** is a constant-time operation; it takes the same amount of time regardless of the element you select. However, in a **LinkedList** it is expensive to move through the list to randomly select an element, and it takes longer to find an element that is farther down the list. On the other hand, if you want to insert an element in the middle of a sequence, it's cheaper in a **LinkedList** than in an **ArrayList**. These and other operations have different efficiencies depending on the underlying structure of the sequence. You might start building your program with a **LinkedList** and, when tuning for performance, change to an **ArrayList**. Because of the abstraction via the interface **List**, you can change from one to the other with minimal impact on your code.

Parameterized types (generics)

Before Java SE5, containers held the one universal type in Java: **Object**. The singly rooted hierarchy means that everything is an **Object**, so a container that holds **Object**s can hold anything.[6] This made containers easy to reuse.

To use such a container, you simply add object references to it and later ask for them back. But, since the container held only **Object**s, when you added an object reference into the container it was upcast to **Object**, thus losing its character. When fetching it back, you got an **Object** reference, and not a reference to the type that you put in. So how do you turn it back into something that has the specific type of the object that you put into the container?

Here, the cast is used again, but this time you're not casting up the inheritance hierarchy to a more general type. Instead, you cast down the hierarchy to a more specific type. This manner of casting is called *downcasting*. With upcasting, you know, for example, that a **Circle** is a type of **Shape** so it's safe to upcast, but you don't know that an **Object** is necessarily a **Circle** or a **Shape** so it's hardly safe to downcast unless you know exactly what you're dealing with.

It's not completely dangerous, however, because if you downcast to the wrong thing you'll get a runtime error called an *exception*, which will be described shortly. When you fetch object references from a container, though, you must

---

[6] They do not hold primitives, but Java SE5 *autoboxing* makes this restriction almost a non-issue. This is discussed in detail later in the book.

have some way to remember exactly what they are so you can perform a proper downcast.

Downcasting and the runtime checks require extra time for the running program and extra effort from the programmer. Wouldn't it make sense to somehow create the container so that it knows the types that it holds, eliminating the need for the downcast and a possible mistake? The solution is called a *parameterized type* mechanism. A parameterized type is a class that the compiler can automatically customize to work with particular types. For example, with a parameterized container, the compiler could customize that container so that it would accept only **Shape**s and fetch only **Shape**s.

One of the big changes in Java SE5 is the addition of parameterized types, called *generics* in Java. You'll recognize the use of generics by the angle brackets with types inside; for example, an **ArrayList** that holds **Shape** can be created like this:

```java
ArrayList<Shape> shapes = new ArrayList<Shape>();
```

There have also been changes to many of the standard library components in order to take advantage of generics. As you will see, generics have an impact on much of the code in this book.

Object creation & lifetime

One critical issue when working with objects is the way they are created and destroyed. Each object requires resources, most notably memory, in order to exist. When an object is no longer needed it must be cleaned up so that these resources are released for reuse. In simple programming situations the question of how an object is cleaned up doesn't seem too challenging: You create the object, use it for as long as it's needed, and then it should be destroyed. However, it's not hard to encounter situations that are more complex.

Suppose, for example, you are designing a system to manage air traffic for an airport. (The same model might also work for managing crates in a warehouse, or a video rental system, or a kennel for boarding pets.) At first it seems simple: Make a container to hold airplanes, then create a new airplane and place it in the container for each airplane that enters the air-traffic-control zone. For cleanup, simply clean up the appropriate airplane object when a plane leaves the zone.

But perhaps you have some other system to record data about the planes; perhaps data that doesn't require such immediate attention as the main controller function. Maybe it's a record of the flight plans of all the small planes that leave the airport. So you have a second container of small planes, and whenever you create a plane object you also put it in this second container if it's a small plane. Then some background process performs operations on the objects in this container during idle moments.

Now the problem is more difficult: How can you possibly know when to destroy the objects? When you're done with the object, some other part of the system might not be. This same problem can arise in a number of other situations, and in programming systems (such as C++) in which you must explicitly delete an object when you're done with it this can become quite complex.

Where is the data for an object and how is the lifetime of the object controlled? C++ takes the approach that control of efficiency is the most important issue, so it gives the programmer a choice. For maximum runtime speed, the storage and lifetime can be determined while the program is being written, by placing the objects on the stack (these are sometimes called *automatic* or *scoped* variables) or in the static storage area. This places a priority on the speed of storage allocation and release, and this control can be very valuable in some situations. However, you sacrifice flexibility because you must know the exact quantity, lifetime, and type of objects while you're writing the program. If you are trying to solve a more general problem such as computer-aided design, warehouse management, or air-traffic control, this is too restrictive.

The second approach is to create objects dynamically in a pool of memory called the heap. In this approach, you don't know until run time how many objects you need, what their lifetime is, or what their exact type is. Those are determined at the spur of the moment while the program is running. If you need a new object, you simply make it on the heap at the point that you need it. Because the storage is managed dynamically, at run time, the amount of time required to allocate storage on the heap can be noticeably longer than the time to create storage on the stack. Creating storage on the stack is often a single assembly instruction to move the stack pointer down and another to move it back up. The time to create heap storage depends on the design of the storage mechanism.

The dynamic approach makes the generally logical assumption that objects tend to be complicated, so the extra overhead of finding storage and releasing that storage will not have an important impact on the creation of an object. In addition, the greater flexibility is essential to solve the general programming problem.

Java uses dynamic memory allocation, exclusively.[7] Every time you want to create an object, you use the **new** operator to build a dynamic instance of that object.

There's another issue, however, and that's the lifetime of an object. With languages that allow objects to be created on the stack, the compiler determines how long the object lasts and can automatically destroy it. However, if you create it on the heap the compiler has no knowledge of its lifetime. In a language like C++, you must determine programmatically when to destroy the object, which can lead to memory leaks if you don't do it correctly (and this is a common problem in C++ programs). Java provides a feature called a *garbage collector* that automatically discovers when an object is no longer in use and destroys it. A garbage collector is much more convenient because it reduces the number of issues that you must track and the code you must write. More importantly, the garbage collector provides a much higher level of insurance against the insidious problem of memory leaks, which has brought many a C++ project to its knees.

With Java, the garbage collector is designed to take care of the problem of releasing the memory (although this doesn't include other aspects of cleaning up an object). The garbage collector "knows" when an object is no longer in use, and it then automatically releases the memory for that object. This, combined with the fact that all objects are inherited from the single root class **Object** and that you can create objects only one way—on the heap—makes the process of programming in Java much simpler than programming in C++. You have far fewer decisions to make and hurdles to overcome.

---

[7] Primitive types, which you'll learn about later, are a special case.

Exception handling: dealing with errors

Ever since the beginning of programming languages, error handling has been a particularly difficult issue. Because it's so hard to design a good error-handling scheme, many languages simply ignore the issue, passing the problem on to library designers who come up with halfway measures that work in many situations but that can easily be circumvented, generally by just ignoring them. A major problem with most error-handling schemes is that they rely on programmer vigilance in following an agreed-upon convention that is not enforced by the language. If the programmer is not vigilant—often the case if they are in a hurry—these schemes can easily be forgotten.

Exception handling wires error handling directly into the programming language and sometimes even the operating system. An exception is an object that is "thrown" from the site of the error and can be "caught" by an appropriate exception handler designed to handle that particular type of error. It's as if exception handling is a different, parallel path of execution that can be taken when things go wrong. And because it uses a separate execution path, it doesn't need to interfere with your normally executing code. This tends to make that code simpler to write because you aren't constantly forced to check for errors. In addition, a thrown exception is unlike an error value that's returned from a method or a flag that's set by a method in order to indicate an error condition—these can be ignored. An exception cannot be ignored, so it's guaranteed to be dealt with at some point. Finally, exceptions provide a way to reliably recover from a bad situation. Instead of just exiting the program, you are often able to set things right and restore execution, which produces much more robust programs.

Java's exception handling stands out among programming languages, because in Java, exception handling was wired in from the beginning and you're forced to use it. It is the single acceptable way to report errors. If you don't write your code to properly handle exceptions, you'll get a compile-time error message. This guaranteed consistency can sometimes make error handling much easier.

It's worth noting that exception handling isn't an object-oriented feature, although in object-oriented languages the exception is normally represented by an object. Exception handling existed before object-oriented languages.

Concurrent programming

A fundamental concept in computer programming is the idea of handling more than one task at a time. Many programming problems require that the program stop what it's doing, deal with some other problem, and then return to the main process. The solution has been approached in many ways. Initially, programmers with low-level knowledge of the machine wrote interrupt service routines, and the suspension of the main process was initiated through a hardware interrupt. Although this worked well, it was difficult and non-portable, so it made moving a program to a new type of machine slow and expensive.

Sometimes, interrupts are necessary for handling time-critical tasks, but there's a large class of problems in which you're simply trying to partition the problem into separately running pieces (tasks) so that the whole program can be more responsive. Within a program, these separately running pieces are called *threads*, and the general concept is called *concurrency*. A common example of concurrency is the user interface. By using tasks, a user can press a button and get a quick response rather than being forced to wait until the program finishes its current task.

Ordinarily, tasks are just a way to allocate the time of a single processor. But if the operating system supports multiple processors, each task can be assigned to a different processor, and they can truly run in parallel. One of the convenient features of concurrency at the language level is that the programmer doesn't need to worry about whether there are many processors or just one. The program is logically divided into tasks, and if the machine has more than one processor, then the program runs faster, without any special adjustments.

All this makes concurrency sound pretty simple. There is a catch: shared resources. If you have more than one task running that's expecting to access the same resource, you have a problem. For example, two processes can't simultaneously send information to a printer. To solve the problem, resources that can be shared, such as the printer, must be locked while they are being used. So a task locks a resource, completes its task, and then releases the lock so that someone else can use the resource.

Java's concurrency is built into the language, and Java SE5 has added significant additional library support.

Java and the Internet

If Java is, in fact, yet another computer programming language, you may question why it is so important and why it is being promoted as a revolutionary step in computer programming. The answer isn't immediately obvious if you're coming from a traditional programming perspective. Although Java is very useful for solving traditional standalone programming problems, it is also important because it solves programming problems for the World Wide Web.

What is the Web?

The Web can seem a bit of a mystery at first, with all this talk of "surfing," "presence," and "home pages." It's helpful to step back and see what it really is, but to do this you must understand client/server systems, another aspect of computing that's full of confusing issues.

Client/server computing

The primary idea of a client/server system is that you have a central repository of information—some kind of data, usually in a database—that you want to distribute on demand to some set of people or machines. A key to the client/server concept is that the repository of information is centrally located so that it can be changed and so that those changes will propagate out to the information consumers. Taken together, the information repository, the software that distributes the information, and the machine(s) where the information and software reside are called "the server." The software that resides on the consumer machine, communicates with the server, fetches the information, processes it, and then displays it on the consumer machine is called the *client*.

The basic concept of client/server computing, then, is not so complicated. The problems arise because you have a single server trying to serve many clients at once. Generally, a database management system is involved, so the designer "balances" the layout of data into tables for optimal use. In addition, systems often allow a client to insert new information into a server. This means you must ensure that one client's new data doesn't walk over another client's new data, or that data isn't lost in the process of adding it to the database (this is called transaction processing). As client software changes, it must be built, debugged, and installed on the client machines, which turns out to be more complicated and expensive than you might think. It's especially problematic to support multiple types of computers and operating systems. Finally, there's the all-important performance issue: You might have hundreds of clients making requests of your server at any moment, so a small delay can be critical. To minimize latency, programmers work hard to offload processing tasks, often to the client machine, but sometimes to other machines at the server site, using so-called *middleware*. (Middleware is also used to improve maintainability.)

The simple idea of distributing information has so many layers of complexity that the whole problem can seem hopelessly enigmatic. And yet it's crucial: Client/server computing accounts for roughly half of all programming activities. It's responsible for everything from taking orders and credit-card transactions to the distribution of any kind of data—stock market, scientific, government, you name it. What we've come up with in the past is individual solutions to individual problems, inventing a new solution each time. These were hard to create and hard to use, and the user had to learn a new interface for each one. The entire client/server problem needed to be solved in a big way.

The Web as a giant server

The Web is actually one giant client/server system. It's a bit worse than that, since you have all the servers and clients coexisting on a single network at once. You don't need to know that, because all you care about is connecting to and interacting with one server at a time (even though you might be hopping around the world in your search for the correct server).

Initially it was a simple one-way process. You made a request of a server and it handed you a file, which your machine's browser software (i.e., the client) would interpret by formatting onto your local machine. But in short order people began wanting to do more than just deliver pages from a server. They wanted full client/server capability so that the client could feed information back to the server, for example, to do database lookups on the server, to add new information to the server, or to place an order (which requires special security measures). These are the changes we've been seeing in the development of the Web.

The Web browser was a big step forward: the concept that one piece of information can be displayed on any type of computer without change. However, the original browsers were still rather primitive and rapidly bogged down by the demands placed on them. They weren't particularly interactive, and tended to clog up both the server and the Internet because whenever you needed to do something that required programming you had to send information back to the server to be processed. It could take many seconds or minutes to find out you had misspelled something in your request. Since the browser was just a viewer it couldn't perform even the simplest computing tasks. (On the other hand, it was safe, because it couldn't execute any programs on your local machine that might contain bugs or viruses.)

To solve this problem, different approaches have been taken. To begin with, graphics standards have been enhanced to allow better animation and video within browsers. The remainder of the problem can be solved only by incorporating the ability to run programs on the client end, under the browser. This is called *client-side programming*.

Client-side programming

The Web's initial server-browser design provided for interactive content, but the interactivity was completely provided by the server. The server produced static pages for the client browser, which would simply interpret and display them. Basic *HyperText Markup Language* (HTML) contains simple mechanisms for data gathering: text-entry boxes, check boxes, radio boxes, lists and drop-down lists, as well as a button that could only be programmed to reset the data on the form or "submit" the data on the form back to the server. This submission passes through the *Common Gateway Interface* (CGI) provided on all Web servers. The text within the submission tells CGI what to do with it. The most common action is to run a program located on the server in a directory that's typically called "cgi-bin." (If you watch the address window at the top of your browser when you push a button on a Web page, you can sometimes see "cgi-bin" within all the gobbledygook there.) These programs can be written in most languages. Perl has been a common choice because it is designed for text manipulation and is interpreted, so it can be installed on any server regardless of processor or operating system. However, Python (*www.Python.org*) has been making inroads because of its greater power and simplicity.

Many powerful Web sites today are built strictly on CGI, and you can in fact do nearly anything with CGI. However, Web sites built on CGI programs can rapidly become overly complicated to maintain, and there is also the problem of response time. The response of a CGI program depends on how much data must be sent, as well as the load on both the server and the Internet. (On top of this, starting a CGI program tends to be slow.) The initial designers of the

Web did not foresee how rapidly this bandwidth would be exhausted for the kinds of applications people developed. For example, any sort of dynamic graphing is nearly impossible to perform with consistency because a *Graphics Interchange Format* (GIF) file must be created and moved from the server to the client for each version of the graph. In addition, you've no doubt experienced the process of data validation for a Web input form. You press the submit button on a page; the data is shipped back to the server; the server starts a CGI program that discovers an error, formats an HTML page informing you of the error, and then sends the page back to you; you must then back up a page and try again. Not only is this slow, it's inelegant.

The solution is client-side programming. Most desktop computers that run Web browsers are powerful engines capable of doing vast work, and with the original static HTML approach they are sitting there, just idly waiting for the server to dish up the next page. Client-side programming means that the Web browser is harnessed to do whatever work it can, and the result for the user is a much speedier and more interactive experience at your Web site.

The problem with discussions of client-side programming is that they aren't very different from discussions of programming in general. The parameters are almost the same, but the platform is different; a Web browser is like a limited operating system. In the end, you must still program, and this accounts for the dizzying array of problems and solutions produced by client-side programming. The rest of this section provides an overview of the issues and approaches in client-side programming.

Plug-ins

One of the most significant steps forward in client-side programming is the development of the plug-in. This is a way for a programmer to add new functionality to the browser by downloading a piece of code that plugs itself into the appropriate spot in the browser. It tells the browser, "From now on you can perform this new activity." (You need to download the plug-in only once.) Some fast and powerful behavior is added to browsers via plug-ins, but writing a plug-in is not a trivial task, and isn't something you'd want to do as part of the process of building a particular site. The value of the plug-in for client-side programming is that it allows an expert programmer to develop extensions and add those extensions to a browser without the permission of the browser manufacturer. Thus, plug-ins provide a "back door" that allows the creation of new client-side programming languages (although not all languages are implemented as plug-ins).

Scripting languages

Plug-ins resulted in the development of browser scripting languages. With a scripting language, you embed the source code for your client-side program directly into the HTML page, and the plug-in that interprets that language is automatically activated while the HTML page is being displayed. Scripting languages tend to be reasonably easy to understand and, because they are simply text that is part of an HTML page, they load very quickly as part of the single server hit required to procure that page. The trade-off is that your code is exposed for everyone to see (and steal). Generally, however, you aren't doing amazingly sophisticated things with scripting languages, so this is not too much of a hardship.

One scripting language that you can expect a Web browser to support *without* a plug-in is JavaScript (this has only a passing resemblance to Java and you'll have to climb an additional learning curve to use it. It was named that way just to grab some of Java's marketing momentum). Unfortunately, most Web browsers originally implemented JavaScript in a different way from the other Web browsers, and even from other versions of themselves. The standardization of JavaScript in the form of *ECMAScript* has helped, but it has taken a long time for the various browsers to catch up (and it didn't help that Microsoft was pushing its own agenda in the form of VBScript, which also had vague similarities to JavaScript). In general, you must program in a kind of least-common-denominator form of JavaScript in order to be able to run on all browsers. Dealing with errors and debugging JavaScript can only be described as a mess. As proof of its difficulty, only recently has anyone created a truly complex piece of JavaScript (Google, in GMail), and that required excessive dedication and expertise.

This points out that the scripting languages used inside Web browsers are really intended to solve specific types of problems, primarily the creation of richer and more interactive graphical user interfaces (GUIs). However, a scripting language might solve 80 percent of the problems encountered in client-side programming. Your problems might very well fit completely within that 80 percent, and since scripting languages can allow easier and faster development, you should probably consider a scripting language before looking at a more involved solution such as Java programming.

Java

If a scripting language can solve 80 percent of the client-side programming problems, what about the other 20 percent—the "really hard stuff"? Java is a popular solution for this. Not only is it a powerful programming language built to be secure, cross-platform, and international, but Java is being continually extended to provide language features and libraries that elegantly handle problems that are difficult in traditional programming languages, such as concurrency, database access, network programming, and distributed computing. Java allows client-side programming via the *applet* and with *Java Web Start*.

An applet is a mini-program that will run only under a Web browser. The applet is downloaded automatically as part of a Web page (just as, for example, a graphic is automatically downloaded). When the applet is activated, it executes a program. This is part of its beauty—it provides you with a way to automatically distribute the client software from the server at the time the user needs the client software, and no sooner. The user gets the latest version of the client software without fail and without difficult reinstallation. Because of the way Java is designed, the programmer needs to create only a single program, and that program automatically works with all computers that have browsers with built-in Java interpreters. (This safely includes the vast majority of machines.) Since Java is a full-fledged programming language, you can do as much work as possible on the client before and after making requests of the server. For example, you won't need to send a request form across the Internet to discover that you've gotten a date or some other parameter wrong, and your client computer can quickly do the work of plotting data instead of waiting for the server to make a plot and ship a graphic image back to you. Not only do you get the immediate win of speed and responsiveness, but the general network traffic and load on servers can be reduced, preventing the entire Internet from slowing down.

Alternatives

To be honest, Java applets have not particularly lived up to their initial fanfare. When Java first appeared, what everyone seemed most excited about was applets, because these would finally allow serious client-side programmability, to increase responsiveness and decrease bandwidth requirements for Internet-based applications. People envisioned vast possibilities.

Indeed, you can find some very clever applets on the Web. But the overwhelming move to applets never happened. The biggest problem was probably that the 10 MB download necessary to install the Java Runtime Environment (JRE) was too scary for the average user. The fact that Microsoft chose not to include the JRE with Internet Explorer may have sealed its fate. In any event, Java applets didn't happen on a large scale.

Nonetheless, applets and *Java Web Start* applications are still valuable in some situations. Anytime you have control over user machines, for example within a corporation, it is reasonable to distribute and update client applications using these technologies, and this can save considerable time, effort, and money, especially if you need to do frequent updates.

In the *Graphical User Interfaces* chapter, we will look at one promising new technology, Macromedia's *Flex*, which allows you to create Flash-based applet-equivalents. Because the Flash Player is available on upwards of 98 percent of all Web browsers (including Windows, Linux and the Mac) it can be considered an accepted standard. Installing or upgrading the Flash Player is quick and easy. The ActionScript language is based on ECMAScript so it is reasonably familiar, but Flex allows you to program without worrying about browser specifics—thus it is far more attractive than JavaScript. For client-side programming, this is an alternative worth considering.

.NET and C#

For a while, the main competitor to Java applets was Microsoft's ActiveX, although that required that the client be running Windows. Since then, Microsoft has produced a full competitor to Java in the form of the .NET platform and the C# programming language. The .NET platform is roughly the same as the *Java Virtual Machine* (JVM; the software platform on which Java programs execute) and Java libraries, and C# bears unmistakable similarities to Java. This is certainly the best work that Microsoft has done in the arena of programming languages and programming environments. Of course, they had the considerable advantage of being able to see what worked well and what didn't work so well in Java, and build upon that, but build they have. This is the first time since its inception that Java has had any real competition. As a result, the Java designers at Sun have taken a hard look at C# and why programmers might want to move to it, and have responded by making fundamental improvements to Java in Java SE5.

Currently, the main vulnerability and important question concerning .NET is whether Microsoft will allow it to be *completely* ported to other platforms. They claim there's no problem doing this, and the Mono project (*www.go-mono.com*) has a partial implementation of .NET working on Linux, but until the implementation is complete and Microsoft has not decided to squash any part of it, .NET as a cross-platform solution is still a risky bet.

Internet vs. intranet

The Web is the most general solution to the client/server problem, so it makes sense to use the same technology to solve a subset of the problem, in particular the classic client/server problem *within* a company. With traditional client/server approaches you have the problem of multiple types of client computers, as well as the difficulty of installing new client software, both of which are handily solved with Web browsers and client-side programming. When Web technology is used for an information network that is restricted to a particular company, it is referred to as an intranet. Intranets provide much greater security than the Internet, since you can physically control access to the servers within your company. In terms of training, it seems that once people understand the general concept of a browser it's much easier for them to deal with differences in the way pages and applets look, so the learning curve for new kinds of systems seems to be reduced.

The security problem brings us to one of the divisions that seems to be automatically forming in the world of client-side programming. If your program is running on the Internet, you don't know what platform it will be working under, and you want to be extra careful that you don't disseminate buggy code. You need something cross-platform and secure, like a scripting language or Java.

If you're running on an intranet, you might have a different set of constraints. It's not uncommon that your machines could all be Intel/Windows platforms. On an intranet, you're responsible for the quality of your own code and can repair bugs when they're discovered. In addition, you might already have a body of legacy code that you've been using in a more traditional client/server approach, whereby you must physically install client programs every time you do an upgrade. The time wasted in installing upgrades is the most compelling reason to move to browsers, because upgrades are invisible and automatic (Java Web Start is also a solution to this problem). If you are involved in such an intranet, the most sensible approach to take is the shortest path that allows you to use your existing code base, rather than trying to recode your programs in a new language.

When faced with this bewildering array of solutions to the client-side programming problem, the best plan of attack is a cost-benefit analysis. Consider the constraints of your problem and what would be the shortest path to your solution. Since client-side programming is still programming, it's always a good idea to take the fastest development approach for your particular situation. This is an aggressive stance to prepare for inevitable encounters with the problems of program development.

Server-side programming

This whole discussion has ignored the issue of server-side programming, which is arguably where Java has had its greatest success. What happens when you make a request of a server? Most of the time the request is simply "Send me this file." Your browser then interprets the file in some appropriate fashion: as an HTML page, a graphic image, a Java applet, a script program, etc.

A more complicated request to a server generally involves a database transaction. A common scenario involves a request for a complex database search, which the server then formats into an HTML page and sends to you as the result. (Of course, if the client has more intelligence via Java or a scripting language, the raw data can be sent and formatted at the client end, which will be faster and less load on the server.) Or you might want to register your name in a database when you join a group or place an order, which will involve changes to that database. These database requests must be processed via some code on the server side, which is generally referred to as server-side programming. Traditionally, server-side programming has been performed using Perl, Python, C++, or some other language to create CGI programs, but more sophisticated systems have since appeared. These include Java-based Web servers that allow you to perform all your server-side programming in Java by writing what are called *servlets*. Servlets and their offspring, JSPs, are two of the most compelling reasons that companies that develop Web sites are moving to Java, especially because they eliminate the problems of dealing with differently abled browsers. Server-side programming topics are covered in *Thinking in Enterprise Java* at *www.MindView.net*.

Despite all this talk about Java on the Internet, it is a general-purpose programming language that can solve the kinds of problems that you can solve with other languages. Here, Java's strength is not only in its portability, but also its programmability, its robustness, its large, standard library and the numerous third-party libraries that are available and that continue to be developed.

Summary

You know what a procedural program looks like: data definitions and function calls. To find the meaning of such a program, you must work at it, looking through the function calls and low-level concepts to create a model in your mind. This is the reason we need intermediate representations when designing procedural programs—by themselves, these programs tend to be confusing because the terms of expression are oriented more toward the computer than to the problem you're solving.

Because OOP adds many new concepts on top of what you find in a procedural language, your natural assumption may be that the resulting Java program will be far more complicated than the equivalent procedural program. Here, you'll be pleasantly surprised: A well-written Java program is generally far simpler and much easier to understand than a procedural program. What you'll see are the definitions of the objects that represent concepts in your problem space (rather than the issues of the computer representation) and messages sent to those objects to represent the activities in that space. One of the delights of object-oriented programming is that, with a well-designed program, it's easy to understand the code by reading it. Usually, there's a lot less code as well, because many of your problems will be solved by reusing existing library code.

OOP and Java may not be for everyone. It's important to evaluate your own needs and decide whether Java will optimally satisfy those needs, or if you might be better off with another programming system (including the one you're currently using). If you know that your needs will be very specialized for the foreseeable future and if you have specific constraints that may not be satisfied by Java, then you owe it to yourself to investigate the alternatives (in particular, I recommend looking at Python; see *www.Python.org*). If you still choose Java as your language, you'll at least understand what the options were and have a clear vision of why you took that direction.

Everything
Is an Object

"If we spoke a different language, we would perceive a
somewhat different world."
   Ludwig Wittgenstein (1889-1951)

Although it is based on C++, Java is more of a "pure"
object-oriented language.

Both C++ and Java are hybrid languages, but in Java the designers felt that
the hybridization was not as important as it was in C++. A hybrid language
allows multiple programming styles; the reason C++ is hybrid is to support
backward compatibility with the C language. Because C++ is a superset of the
C language, it includes many of that language's undesirable features, which
can make some aspects of C++ overly complicated.

The Java language assumes that you want to do only object-oriented
programming. This means that before you can begin you must shift your
mindset into an object-oriented world (unless it's already there). The benefit
of this initial effort is the ability to program in a language that is simpler to
learn and to use than many other OOP languages. In this chapter you'll see
the basic components of a Java program and learn that (almost) everything in
Java is an object.

You manipulate objects
with references

Each programming language has its own means of manipulating elements in
memory. Sometimes the programmer must be constantly aware of what type
of manipulation is going on. Are you manipulating the element directly, or
are you dealing with some kind of indirect representation (a pointer in C or
C++) that must be treated with a special syntax?

All this is simplified in Java. You treat everything as an object, using a single consistent syntax. Although you *treat* everything as an object, the identifier you manipulate is actually a "reference" to an object.[1] You might imagine a television (the object) and a remote control (the reference). As long as you're holding this reference, you have a connection to the television, but when someone says, "Change the channel" or "Lower the volume," what you're manipulating is the reference, which in turn modifies the object. If you want to move around the room and still control the television, you take the remote/reference with you, not the television.

Also, the remote control can stand on its own, with no television. That is, just because you have a reference doesn't mean there's necessarily an object connected to it. So if you want to hold a word or sentence, you create a **String** reference:

```
String s;
```

But here you've created *only* the reference, not an object. If you decided to send a message to **s** at this point, you'll get an error because **s** isn't actually attached to anything (there's no television). A safer practice, then, is always to initialize a reference when you create it:

```
String s = "asdf";
```

---

[1] This can be a flashpoint. There are those who say, "Clearly, it's a pointer," but this presumes an underlying implementation. Also, Java references are much more akin to C++ references than to pointers in their syntax. In the 1st edition of this book, I chose to invent a new term, "handle," because C++ references and Java references have some important differences. I was coming out of C++ and did not want to confuse the C++ programmers whom I assumed would be the largest audience for Java. In the 2nd edition, I decided that "reference" was the more commonly used term, and that anyone changing from C++ would have a lot more to cope with than the terminology of references, so they might as well jump in with both feet. However, there are people who disagree even with the term "reference." I read in one book where it was "completely wrong to say that Java supports pass by reference," because Java object identifiers (according to that author) are *actually* "object references." And (he goes on) everything is *actually* pass by value. So you're not passing by reference, you're "passing an object reference by value." One could argue for the precision of such convoluted explanations, but I think my approach simplifies the understanding of the concept without hurting anything (well, the language lawyers may claim that I'm lying to you, but I'll say that I'm providing an appropriate abstraction).

However, this uses a special Java feature: Strings can be initialized with quoted text. Normally, you must use a more general type of initialization for objects.

You must create all the objects

When you create a reference, you want to connect it with a new object. You do so, in general, with the **new** operator. The keyword **new** says, "Make me a new one of these objects." So in the preceding example, you can say:

```
String s = new String("asdf");
```

Not only does this mean "Make me a new **String**," but it also gives information about *how* to make the **String** by supplying an initial character string.

Of course, Java comes with a plethora of ready-made types in addition to **String**. What's more important is that you can create your own types. In fact, creating new types is the fundamental activity in Java programming, and it's what you'll be learning about in the rest of this book.

Where storage lives

It's useful to visualize some aspects of how things are laid out while the program is running—in particular how memory is arranged. There are five different places to store data:

1. **Registers**. This is the fastest storage because it exists in a place different from that of other storage: inside the processor. However, the number of registers is severely limited, so registers are allocated as they are needed. You don't have direct control, nor do you see any evidence in your programs that registers even exist (C & C++, on the other hand, allow you to suggest register allocation to the compiler).

2. **The stack**. This lives in the general random-access memory (RAM) area, but has direct support from the processor via its *stack pointer*. The stack pointer is moved down to create new memory and moved up to release that memory. This is an extremely fast and efficient way to allocate storage, second only to registers. The

Java system must know, while it is creating the program, the exact lifetime of all the items that are stored on the stack. This constraint places limits on the flexibility of your programs, so while some Java storage exists on the stack—in particular, object references—Java objects themselves are not placed on the stack.

3.   **The heap**. This is a general-purpose pool of memory (also in the RAM area) where all Java objects live. The nice thing about the heap is that, unlike the stack, the compiler doesn't need to know how long that storage must stay on the heap. Thus, there's a great deal of flexibility in using storage on the heap. Whenever you need an object, you simply write the code to create it by using **new**, and the storage is allocated on the heap when that code is executed. Of course there's a price you pay for this flexibility: It may take more time to allocate and clean up heap storage than stack storage (if you even *could* create objects on the stack in Java, as you can in C++).

4.   **Constant storage**. Constant values are often placed directly in the program code, which is safe since they can never change. Sometimes constants are cordoned off by themselves so that they can be optionally placed in read-only memory (ROM), in embedded systems.[2]

5.   **Non-RAM storage**. If data lives completely outside a program, it can exist while the program is not running, outside the control of the program. The two primary examples of this are *streamed objects,* in which objects are turned into streams of bytes, generally to be sent to another machine, and *persistent objects,* in which the objects are placed on disk so they will hold their state even when the program is terminated. The trick with these types of storage is turning the objects into something that can exist on the other medium, and yet can be resurrected into a regular RAM-based object when necessary. Java provides support for *lightweight persistence*, and mechanisms such as JDBC and

---

[2] An example of this is the string pool. All literal strings and string-valued constant expressions are interned automatically and put into special static storage.

Hibernate provide more sophisticated support for storing and retrieving object information in databases.

Special case: primitive types

One group of types, which you'll use quite often in your programming, gets special treatment. You can think of these as "primitive" types. The reason for the special treatment is that to create an object with **new**—especially a small, simple variable—isn't very efficient, because **new** places objects on the heap. For these types Java falls back on the approach taken by C and C++. That is, instead of creating the variable by using **new**, an "automatic" variable is created that is *not a reference*. The variable holds the value directly, and it's placed on the stack, so it's much more efficient.

Java determines the size of each primitive type. These sizes don't change from one machine architecture to another as they do in most languages. This size invariance is one reason Java programs are more portable than programs in most other languages.

Primitive type	Size	Minimum	Maximum	Wrapper type
boolean	—	—	—	Boolean
char	16 bits	Unicode 0	Unicode $2^{16}-1$	Character
byte	8 bits	-128	+127	Byte
short	16 bits	-2^{15}	$+2^{15}-1$	Short
int	32 bits	-2^{31}	$+2^{31}-1$	Integer
long	64 bits	-2^{63}	$+2^{63}-1$	Long
float	32 bits	IEEE754	IEEE754	Float
double	64 bits	IEEE754	IEEE754	Double
void	—	—	—	Void

All numeric types are signed, so don't look for unsigned types.

The size of the **boolean** type is not explicitly specified; it is only defined to be able to take the literal values **true** or **false**.

The "wrapper" classes for the primitive data types allow you to make a non-primitive object on the heap to represent that primitive type. For example:

```
char c = 'x';
```

```
Character ch = new Character(c);
```

Or you could also use:

```
Character ch = new Character('x');
```

Java SE5 *autoboxing* will automatically convert from a primitive to a wrapper type:

```
Character ch = 'x';
```

and back:

```
char c = ch;
```

The reasons for wrapping primitives will be shown in a later chapter.

High-precision numbers

Java includes two classes for performing high-precision arithmetic: **BigInteger** and **BigDecimal**. Although these approximately fit into the same category as the "wrapper" classes, neither one has a primitive analogue.

Both classes have methods that provide analogues for the operations that you perform on primitive types. That is, you can do anything with a **BigInteger** or **BigDecimal** that you can with an **int** or **float**, it's just that you must use method calls instead of operators. Also, since there's more involved, the operations will be slower. You're exchanging speed for accuracy.

BigInteger supports arbitrary-precision integers. This means that you can accurately represent integral values of any size without losing any information during operations.

BigDecimal is for arbitrary-precision fixed-point numbers; you can use these for accurate monetary calculations, for example.

Consult the JDK documentation for details about the constructors and methods you can call for these two classes.

Arrays in Java

Virtually all programming languages support some kind of arrays. Using arrays in C and C++ is perilous because those arrays are only blocks of memory. If a program accesses the array outside of its memory block or uses the memory before initialization (common programming errors), there will be unpredictable results.

One of the primary goals of Java is safety, so many of the problems that plague programmers in C and C++ are not repeated in Java. A Java array is guaranteed to be initialized and cannot be accessed outside of its range. The range checking comes at the price of having a small amount of memory overhead on each array as well as verifying the index at run time, but the assumption is that the safety and increased productivity are worth the expense (and Java can sometimes optimize these operations).

When you create an array of objects, you are really creating an array of references, and each of those references is automatically initialized to a special value with its own keyword: **null**. When Java sees **null**, it recognizes that the reference in question isn't pointing to an object. You must assign an object to each reference before you use it, and if you try to use a reference that's still **null**, the problem will be reported at run time. Thus, typical array errors are prevented in Java.

You can also create an array of primitives. Again, the compiler guarantees initialization because it zeroes the memory for that array.

Arrays will be covered in detail in later chapters.

You never need to destroy an object

In most programming languages, the concept of the lifetime of a variable occupies a significant portion of the programming effort. How long does the variable last? If you are supposed to destroy it, when should you? Confusion over variable lifetimes can lead to a lot of bugs, and this section shows how Java greatly simplifies the issue by doing all the cleanup work for you.

Scoping

Most procedural languages have the concept of *scope*. This determines both the visibility and lifetime of the names defined within that scope. In C, C++, and Java, scope is determined by the placement of curly braces **{}**. So for example:

```
{
```

```
    int x = 12;
    // Only x available
    {
      int q = 96;
      // Both x & q available
    }
    // Only x available
    // q is "out of scope"
}
```

A variable defined within a scope is available only to the end of that scope.

Any text after a '//' to the end of a line is a comment.

Indentation makes Java code easier to read. Since Java is a free-form language, the extra spaces, tabs, and carriage returns do not affect the resulting program.

You *cannot* do the following, even though it is legal in C and C++:

```
{
  int x = 12;
  {
    int x = 96; // Illegal
  }
}
```

The compiler will announce that the variable **x** has already been defined. Thus the C and C++ ability to "hide" a variable in a larger scope is not allowed, because the Java designers thought that it led to confusing programs.

Scope of objects

Java objects do not have the same lifetimes as primitives. When you create a Java object using **new**, it hangs around past the end of the scope. Thus if you use:

```
{
  String s = new String("a string");
} // End of scope
```

the reference **s** vanishes at the end of the scope. However, the **String** object that **s** was pointing to is still occupying memory. In this bit of code, there is no way to access the object after the end of the scope, because the only reference to it is out of scope. In later chapters you'll see how the reference to the object can be passed around and duplicated during the course of a program.

It turns out that because objects created with **new** stay around for as long as you want them, a whole slew of C++ programming problems simply vanish in Java. In C++ you must not only make sure that the objects stay around for as long as you need them, you must also destroy the objects when you're done with them.

That brings up an interesting question. If Java leaves the objects lying around, what keeps them from filling up memory and halting your program? This is exactly the kind of problem that would occur in C++. This is where a bit of magic happens. Java has a *garbage collector*, which looks at all the objects that were created with **new** and figures out which ones are not being referenced anymore. Then it releases the memory for those objects, so the memory can be used for new objects. This means that you never need to worry about reclaiming memory yourself. You simply create objects, and when you no longer need them, they will go away by themselves. This eliminates a certain class of programming problem: the so-called "memory leak," in which a programmer forgets to release memory.

Creating new data types: **class**

If everything is an object, what determines how a particular class of object looks and behaves? Put another way, what establishes the *type* of an object? You might expect there to be a keyword called "type," and that certainly would have made sense. Historically, however, most object-oriented languages have used the keyword **class** to mean "I'm about to tell you what a new type of object looks like." The **class** keyword (which is so common that it will not usually be bold-faced throughout this book) is followed by the name of the new type. For example:

```
class ATypeName { /* Class body goes here */ }
```

This introduces a new type, although the class body consists only of a comment (the stars and slashes and what is inside, which will be discussed later in this chapter), so there is not too much that you can do with it. However, you can create an object of this type using **new**:

```
ATypeName a = new ATypeName();
```

But you cannot tell it to do much of anything (that is, you cannot send it any interesting messages) until you define some methods for it.

Fields and methods

When you define a class (and all you do in Java is define classes, make objects of those classes, and send messages to those objects), you can put two types of elements in your class: *fields* (sometimes called *data members*), and *methods* (sometimes called *member functions*). A field is an object of any type that you can talk to via its reference, or a primitive type. If it is a reference to an object, you must initialize that reference to connect it to an actual object (using **new**, as seen earlier).

Each object keeps its own storage for its fields; ordinary fields are not shared among objects. Here is an example of a class with some fields:

```
class DataOnly {
  int i;
  double d;
  boolean b;
}
```

This class doesn't *do* anything except hold data. But you can create an object like this:

```
DataOnly data = new DataOnly();
```

You can assign values to the fields, but you must first know how to refer to a member of an object. This is accomplished by stating the name of the object reference, followed by a period (dot), followed by the name of the member inside the object:

```
objectReference.member
```

For example:

```
data.i = 47;
data.d = 1.1;
data.b = false;
```

It is also possible that your object might contain other objects that contain data you'd like to modify. For this, you just keep "connecting the dots." For example:

```
myPlane.leftTank.capacity = 100;
```

The **DataOnly** class cannot do much of anything except hold data, because it has no methods. To understand how those work, you must first understand *arguments* and *return values*, which will be described shortly.

Default values for primitive members

When a primitive data type is a member of a class, it is guaranteed to get a default value if you do not initialize it:

Primitive type	Default
boolean	false
char	'\uoooo' (null)
byte	(byte)o
short	(short)o
int	o
long	oL
float	o.of
double	o.od

The default values are only what Java guarantees when the variable is used *as a member of a class*. This ensures that member variables of primitive types will always be initialized (something C++ doesn't do), reducing a source of bugs. However, this initial value may not be correct or even legal for the program you are writing. It's best to always explicitly initialize your variables.

This guarantee doesn't apply to *local variables*—those that are not fields of a class. Thus, if within a method definition you have:

```
int x;
```

Then **x** will get some arbitrary value (as in C and C++); it will not automatically be initialized to zero. You are responsible for assigning an appropriate value before you use **x**. If you forget, Java definitely improves on C++: You get a compile-time error telling you the variable might not have been initialized. (Many C++ compilers will warn you about uninitialized variables, but in Java these are errors.)

Methods, arguments, and return values

In many languages (like C and C++), the term *function* is used to describe a named subroutine. The term that is more commonly used in Java is *method*, as in "a way to do something." If you want, you can continue thinking in terms of functions. It's really only a syntactic difference, but this book follows the common Java usage of the term "method."

Methods in Java determine the messages an object can receive. The fundamental parts of a method are the name, the arguments, the return type, and the body. Here is the basic form:

```
ReturnType methodName( /* Argument list */ ) {
  /* Method body */
}
```

The return type describes the value that comes back from the method after you call it. The argument list gives the types and names for the information that you want to pass into the method. The method name and argument list (which is called the *signature* of the method) uniquely identify that method.

Methods in Java can be created only as part of a class. A method can be called only for an object,[3] and that object must be able to perform that method call. If you try to call the wrong method for an object, you'll get an error message at compile time. You call a method for an object by naming the object followed by a period (dot), followed by the name of the method and its argument list, like this:

```
objectName.methodName(arg1, arg2, arg3);
```

For example, suppose you have a method **f( )** that takes no arguments and returns a value of type **int**. Then, if you have an object called **a** for which **f( )** can be called, you can say this:

```
int x = a.f();
```

The type of the return value must be compatible with the type of **x**.

---

[3] **static** methods, which you'll learn about soon, can be called *for the class*, without an object.

This act of calling a method is commonly referred to as *sending a message to an object*. In the preceding example, the message is **f( )** and the object is **a**. Object-oriented programming is often summarized as simply "sending messages to objects."

The argument list

The method argument list specifies what information you pass into the method. As you might guess, this information—like everything else in Java—takes the form of objects. So, what you must specify in the argument list are the types of the objects to pass in and the name to use for each one. As in any situation in Java where you seem to be handing objects around, you are actually passing references.[4] The type of the reference must be correct, however. If the argument is supposed to be a **String**, you must pass in a **String** or the compiler will give an error.

Consider a method that takes a **String** as its argument. Here is the definition, which must be placed within a class definition for it to be compiled:

```
int storage(String s) {
  return s.length() * 2;
}
```

This method tells you how many bytes are required to hold the information in a particular **String**. (The size of each **char** in a **String** is 16 bits, or two bytes, to support Unicode characters.) The argument is of type **String** and is called **s**. Once **s** is passed into the method, you can treat it just like any other object. (You can send messages to it.) Here, the **length( )** method is called, which is one of the methods for **String**s; it returns the number of characters in a string.

You can also see the use of the **return** keyword, which does two things. First, it means "Leave the method, I'm done." Second, if the method produces a value, that value is placed right after the **return** statement. In this case, the return value is produced by evaluating the expression **s.length( ) * 2**.

---

[4] With the usual exception of the aforementioned "special" data types **boolean, char, byte, short, int, long, float**, and **double**. In general, though, you pass objects, which really means you pass references to objects.

You can return any type you want, but if you don't want to return anything at all, you do so by indicating that the method returns **void**. Here are some examples:

```
boolean flag() { return true; }
double naturalLogBase() { return 2.718; }
void nothing() { return; }
void nothing2() {}
```

When the return type is **void**, then the **return** keyword is used only to exit the method, and is therefore unnecessary when you reach the end of the method. You can return from a method at any point, but if you've given a non-**void** return type, then the compiler will force you (with error messages) to return the appropriate type of value regardless of where you return.

At this point, it can look like a program is just a bunch of objects with methods that take other objects as arguments and send messages to those other objects. That is indeed much of what goes on, but in the following chapter you'll learn how to do the detailed low-level work by making decisions within a method. For this chapter, sending messages will suffice.

Building a Java program

There are several other issues you must understand before seeing your first Java program.

Name visibility

A problem in any programming language is the control of names. If you use a name in one module of the program, and another programmer uses the same name in another module, how do you distinguish one name from another and prevent the two names from "clashing?" In C this is a particular problem because a program is often an unmanageable sea of names. C++ classes (on which Java classes are based) nest functions within classes so they cannot clash with function names nested within other classes. However, C++ still allows global data and global functions, so clashing is still possible. To solve this problem, C++ introduced *namespaces* using additional keywords.

Java was able to avoid all of this by taking a fresh approach. To produce an unambiguous name for a library, the Java creators want you to use your Internet domain name in reverse since domain names are guaranteed to be unique. Since my domain name is **MindView.net**, my utility library of foibles would be named **net.mindview.utility.foibles**. After your reversed domain name, the dots are intended to represent subdirectories.

In Java 1.0 and Java 1.1 the domain extensions **com**, **edu**, **org**, **net**, etc., were capitalized by convention, so the library would appear: **NET.mindview.utility.foibles**. Partway through the development of Java 2, however, it was discovered that this caused problems, so now the entire package name is lowercase.

This mechanism means that all of your files automatically live in their own namespaces, and each class within a file must have a unique identifier—the language prevents name clashes for you.

Using other components

Whenever you want to use a predefined class in your program, the compiler must know how to locate it. Of course, the class might already exist in the same source-code file that it's being called from. In that case, you simply use the class—even if the class doesn't get defined until later in the file (Java eliminates the so-called "forward referencing" problem).

What about a class that exists in some other file? You might think that the compiler should be smart enough to simply go and find it, but there is a problem. Imagine that you want to use a class with a particular name, but more than one definition for that class exists (presumably these are different definitions). Or worse, imagine that you're writing a program, and as you're building it you add a new class to your library that conflicts with the name of an existing class.

To solve this problem, you must eliminate all potential ambiguities. This is accomplished by telling the Java compiler exactly what classes you want by using the **import** keyword. **import** tells the compiler to bring in a package, which is a library of classes. (In other languages, a library could consist of functions and data as well as classes, but remember that all code in Java must be written inside a class.)

Most of the time you'll be using components from the standard Java libraries that come with your compiler. With these, you don't need to worry about long, reversed domain names; you just say, for example:

```
import java.util.ArrayList;
```

to tell the compiler that you want to use Java's **ArrayList** class. However, **util** contains a number of classes, and you might want to use several of them without declaring them all explicitly. This is easily accomplished by using '*' to indicate a wild card:

```
import java.util.*;
```

It is more common to import a collection of classes in this manner than to import classes individually.

The **static** keyword

Ordinarily, when you create a class you are describing how objects of that class look and how they will behave. You don't actually get an object until you create one using **new**, and at that point storage is allocated and methods become available.

There are two situations in which this approach is not sufficient. One is if you want to have only a single piece of storage for a particular field, regardless of how many objects of that class are created, or even if no objects are created. The other is if you need a method that isn't associated with any particular object of this class. That is, you need a method that you can call even if no objects are created.

You can achieve both of these effects with the **static** keyword. When you say something is **static**, it means that particular field or method is not tied to any particular object instance of that class. So even if you've never created an object of that class you can call a **static** method or access a **static** field. With ordinary, non-**static** fields and methods, you must create an object and use that object to access the field or method, since non-**static** fields and methods must know the particular object they are working with.[5]

Some object-oriented languages use the terms *class data* and *class methods*, meaning that the data and methods exist only for the class as a whole, and not for any particular objects of the class. Sometimes the Java literature uses these terms too.

---

[5] Of course, since **static** methods don't need any objects to be created before they are used, they cannot *directly* access non-**static** members or methods by simply calling those other members without referring to a named object (since non-**static** members and methods must be tied to a particular object).

To make a field or method **static**, you simply place the keyword before the definition. For example, the following produces a **static** field and initializes it:

```
class StaticTest {
  static int i = 47;
}
```

Now even if you make two **StaticTest** objects, there will still be only one piece of storage for **StaticTest.i.** Both objects will share the same **i.** Consider:

```
StaticTest st1 = new StaticTest();
StaticTest st2 = new StaticTest();
```

At this point, both **st1.i** and **st2.i** have the same value of 47 since they refer to the same piece of memory.

There are two ways to refer to a **static** variable. As the preceding example indicates, you can name it via an object, by saying, for example, **st2.i**. You can also refer to it directly through its class name, something you cannot do with a non-**static** member.

```
StaticTest.i++;
```

The **++** operator adds one to the variable. At this point, both **st1.i** and **st2.i** will have the value 48.

Using the class name is the preferred way to refer to a **static** variable. Not only does it emphasize that variable's **static** nature, but in some cases it gives the compiler better opportunities for optimization.

Similar logic applies to **static** methods. You can refer to a **static** method either through an object as you can with any method, or with the special additional syntax **ClassName.method( )**. You define a **static** method in a similar way:

```
class Incrementable {
  static void increment() { StaticTest.i++; }
}
```

You can see that the **Incrementable** method **increment( )** increments the **static** data **i** using the **++** operator. You can call **increment( )** in the typical way, through an object:

```
Incrementable sf = new Incrementable();
sf.increment();
```

Or, because **increment( )** is a **static** method, you can call it directly through its class:

```
Incrementable.increment();
```

Although **static**, when applied to a field, definitely changes the way the data is created (one for each class versus the non-**static** one for each object), when applied to a method it's not so dramatic. An important use of **static** for methods is to allow you to call that method without creating an object. This is essential, as you will see, in defining the **main( )** method that is the entry point for running an application.

Your first Java program

Finally, here's the first complete program. It starts by printing a string, and then the date, using the **Date** class from the Java standard library.

```
// HelloDate.java
import java.util.*;

public class HelloDate {
  public static void main(String[] args) {
    System.out.println("Hello, it's: ");
    System.out.println(new Date());
  }
}
```

At the beginning of each program file, you must place any necessary **import** statements to bring in extra classes you'll need for the code in that file. Note that I say "extra." That's because there's a certain library of classes that are automatically brought into every Java file: **java.lang**. Start up your Web browser and look at the documentation from Sun. (If you haven't downloaded the JDK documentation from *http://java.sun.com*, do so now.[6] Note that this documentation doesn't come packed with the JDK; you must do a separate download to get it.) If you look at the list of the packages, you'll see all the

---

[6] The Java compiler and documentation from Sun tend to change regularly, and the best place to get them is directly from Sun. By downloading it yourself, you will get the most recent version.

different class libraries that come with Java. Select **java.lang**. This will bring up a list of all the classes that are part of that library. Since **java.lang** is implicitly included in every Java code file, these classes are automatically available. There's no **Date** class listed in **java.lang**, which means you must import another library to use that. If you don't know the library where a particular class is, or if you want to see all of the classes, you can select "Tree" in the Java documentation. Now you can find every single class that comes with Java. Then you can use the browser's "find" function to find **Date**. When you do you'll see it listed as **java.util.Date**, which lets you know that it's in the **util** library and that you must **import java.util.*** in order to use **Date**.

If you go back to the beginning, select **java.lang** and then **System**, you'll see that the **System** class has several fields, and if you select **out**, you'll discover that it's a **static PrintStream** object. Since it's **static**, you don't need to create anything with **new**. The **out** object is always there, and you can just use it. What you can do with this **out** object is determined by its type: **PrintStream**. Conveniently, **PrintStream** is shown in the description as a hyperlink, so if you click on that, you'll see a list of all the methods you can call for **PrintStream**. There are quite a few, and these will be covered later in the book. For now all we're interested in is **println( )**, which in effect means "Print what I'm giving you out to the console and end with a newline." Thus, in any Java program you write you can write something like this:

```
System.out.println("A String of things");
```

whenever you want to display information to the console.

The name of the class is the same as the name of the file. When you're creating a standalone program such as this one, one of the classes in the file must have the same name as the file. (The compiler complains if you don't do this.) That class must contain a method called **main( )** with this signature and return type:

```
public static void main(String[] args) {
```

The **public** keyword means that the method is available to the outside world (described in detail in the *Access Control* chapter). The argument to **main( )** is an array of **String** objects. The **args** won't be used in this program, but the Java compiler insists that they be there because they hold the arguments from the command line.

The line that prints the date is quite interesting:

```
System.out.println(new Date());
```

The argument is a **Date** object that is being created just to send its value (which is automatically converted to a **String**) to **println( )**. As soon as this statement is finished, that **Date** is unnecessary, and the garbage collector can come along and get it anytime. We don't need to worry about cleaning it up.

When you look at the JDK documentation from *http://java.sun.com*, you will see that **System** has many other methods that allow you to produce interesting effects (one of Java's most powerful assets is its large set of standard libraries). For example:

```
//: object/ShowProperties.java

public class ShowProperties {
  public static void main(String[] args) {
    System.getProperties().list(System.out);
    System.out.println(System.getProperty("user.name"));
    System.out.println(
      System.getProperty("java.library.path"));
  }
} ///:~
```

The first line in **main( )** displays all of the "properties" from the system where you are running the program, so it gives you environment information. The **list( )** method sends the results to its argument, **System.out**. You will see later in the book that you can send the results elsewhere, to a file, for example. You can also ask for a specific property—in this case, the user name and **java.library.path**. (The unusual comments at the beginning and end will be explained a little later.)

Compiling and running

To compile and run this program, and all the other programs in this book, you must first have a Java programming environment. There are a number of third-party development environments, but in this book I will assume that you are using the Java Developer's Kit (JDK) from Sun, which is free. If you are using another development system,[7] you will need to look in the

---

[7] IBM's "jikes" compiler is a common alternative, as it is significantly faster than Sun's javac (although if you're building groups of files using *Ant*, there's not too much of a difference). There are also open-source projects to create Java compilers, runtime environments, and libraries.

documentation for that system to determine how to compile and run programs.

Get on the Internet and go to *http://java.sun.com*. There you will find information and links that will lead you through the process of downloading and installing the JDK for your particular platform.

Once the JDK is installed, and you've set up your computer's path information so that it will find **javac** and **java**, download and unpack the source code for this book (you can find it at *www.MindView.net*). This will create a subdirectory for each chapter in this book. Move to the subdirectory named **object** and type:

```
javac HelloDate.java
```

This command should produce no response. If you get any kind of an error message, it means you haven't installed the JDK properly and you need to investigate those problems.

On the other hand, if you just get your command prompt back, you can type:

```
java HelloDate
```

and you'll get the message and the date as output.

This is the process you can use to compile and run each of the programs in this book. However, you will see that the source code for this book also has a file called **build.xml** in each chapter, and this contains "Ant" commands for automatically building the files for that chapter. Buildfiles and Ant (including where to download it) are described more fully in the supplement you will find at *http://MindView.net/Books/BetterJava*, but once you have Ant installed (from *http://jakarta.apache.org/ant*) you can just type '**ant**' at the command prompt to compile and run the programs in each chapter. If you haven't installed Ant yet, you can just type the **javac** and **java** commands by hand.

Comments and embedded documentation

There are two types of comments in Java. The first is the traditional C-style comment that was inherited by C++. These comments begin with a /* and continue, possibly across many lines, until a */. Note that many programmers will begin each line of a continued comment with a *, so you'll often see:

```
/* This is a comment
 * that continues
 * across lines
 */
```

Remember, however, that everything inside the /* and */ is ignored, so there's no difference in saying:

```
/* This is a comment that
continues across lines */
```

The second form of comment comes from C++. It is the single-line comment, which starts with a // and continues until the end of the line. This type of comment is convenient and commonly used because it's easy. You don't need to hunt on the keyboard to find / and then * (instead, you just press the same key twice), and you don't need to close the comment. So you will often see:

```
// This is a one-line comment
```

Comment documentation

Possibly the biggest problem with documenting code has been maintaining that documentation. If the documentation and the code are separate, it becomes tedious to change the documentation every time you change the code. The solution seems simple: Link the code to the documentation. The easiest way to do this is to put everything in the same file. To complete the picture, however, you need a special comment syntax to mark the documentation and a tool to extract those comments and put them in a useful form. This is what Java has done.

The tool to extract the comments is called *Javadoc*, and it is part of the JDK installation. It uses some of the technology from the Java compiler to look for special comment tags that you put in your programs. It not only extracts the information marked by these tags, but it also pulls out the class name or method name that adjoins the comment. This way you can get away with the minimal amount of work to generate decent program documentation.

The output of Javadoc is an HTML file that you can view with your Web browser. Thus, Javadoc allows you to create and maintain a single source file and automatically generate useful documentation. Because of Javadoc, you have a straightforward standard for creating documentation, so you can expect or even demand documentation with all Java libraries.

In addition, you can write your own Javadoc handlers, called *doclets*, if you want to perform special operations on the information processed by Javadoc (to produce output in a different format, for example). Doclets are introduced in the supplement at *http://MindView.net/Books/BetterJava*.

What follows is only an introduction and overview of the basics of Javadoc. A thorough description can be found in the JDK documentation. When you unpack the documentation, look in the "tooldocs" subdirectory (or follow the "tooldocs" link).

Syntax

All of the Javadoc commands occur only within /** comments. The comments end with */ as usual. There are two primary ways to use Javadoc: Embed HTML or use "doc tags." *Standalone doc tags* are commands that start with an '@' and are placed at the beginning of a comment line. (A leading '*', however, is ignored.) *Inline doc tags* can appear anywhere within a Javadoc comment and also start with an '@' but are surrounded by curly braces.

There are three "types" of comment documentation, which correspond to the element the comment precedes: class, field, or method. That is, a class comment appears right before the definition of a class, a field comment appears right in front of the definition of a field, and a method comment appears right in front of the definition of a method. As a simple example:

```
//: object/Documentation1.java
/** A class comment */
public class Documentation1 {
  /** A field comment */
  public int i;
  /** A method comment */
  public void f() {}
} ///:~
```

Note that Javadoc will process comment documentation for only **public** and **protected** members. Comments for **private** and package-access members (see the *Access Control* chapter) are ignored, and you'll see no output. (However, you can use the **-private** flag to include **private** members as well.) This makes sense, since only **public** and **protected** members are available outside the file, which is the client programmer's perspective.

The output for the preceding code is an HTML file that has the same standard format as all the rest of the Java documentation, so users will be comfortable with the format and can easily navigate your classes. It's worth entering the preceding code, sending it through Javadoc, and viewing the resulting HTML file to see the results.

Embedded HTML

Javadoc passes HTML commands through to the generated HTML document. This allows you full use of HTML; however, the primary motive is to let you format code, such as:

```
//: object/Documentation2.java
/**
* <pre>
* System.out.println(new Date());
* </pre>
*/
public class Documentation2 {}
///:~
```

You can also use HTML just as you would in any other Web document to format the regular text in your descriptions:

```
//: object/Documentation3.java
/**
* You can <em>even</em> insert a list:
* <ol>
* <li> Item one
* <li> Item two
* <li> Item three
* </ol>
*/
public class Documentation3 {}
///:~
```

Note that within the documentation comment, asterisks at the beginning of a line are thrown away by Javadoc, along with leading spaces. Javadoc reformats everything so that it conforms to the standard documentation appearance. Don't use headings such as **<h1>** or **<hr>** as embedded HTML, because Javadoc inserts its own headings and yours will interfere with them.

All types of comment documentation—class, field, and method—can support embedded HTML.

Some example tags

Here are some of the Javadoc tags available for code documentation. Before trying to do anything serious using Javadoc, you should consult the Javadoc reference in the JDK documentation to learn all the different ways that you can use Javadoc.

@see

This tag allows you to refer to the documentation in other classes. Javadoc will generate HTML with the **@see** tags hyperlinked to the other documentation. The forms are:

```
@see classname
@see fully-qualified-classname
@see fully-qualified-classname#method-name
```

Each one adds a hyperlinked "See Also" entry to the generated documentation. Javadoc will not check the hyperlinks you give it to make sure they are valid.

{@link *package.class#member label*}

Very similar to **@see**, except that it can be used inline and uses the *label* as the hyperlink text rather than "See Also."

{@docRoot}

Produces the relative path to the documentation root directory. Useful for explicit hyperlinking to pages in the documentation tree.

{@inheritDoc}

Inherits the documentation from the nearest base class of this class into the current doc comment.

@version

This is of the form:

```
@version version-information
```

in which **version-information** is any significant information you see fit to include. When the **-version** flag is placed on the Javadoc command line, the version information will be called out specially in the generated HTML documentation.

@author

This is of the form:

```
@author author-information
```

in which **author-information** is, presumably, your name, but it could also include your email address or any other appropriate information. When the **-author** flag is placed on the Javadoc command line, the author information will be called out specially in the generated HTML documentation.

You can have multiple author tags for a list of authors, but they must be placed consecutively. All the author information will be lumped together into a single paragraph in the generated HTML.

@since

This tag allows you to indicate the version of this code that began using a particular feature. You'll see it appearing in the HTML Java documentation to indicate what version of the JDK is used.

@param

This is used for method documentation, and is of the form:

```
@param parameter-name description
```

in which **parameter-name** is the identifier in the method parameter list, and **description** is text that can continue on subsequent lines. The description is considered finished when a new documentation tag is encountered. You can have any number of these, presumably one for each parameter.

@return

This is used for method documentation, and looks like this:

```
@return description
```

in which **description** gives you the meaning of the return value. It can continue on subsequent lines.

@throws

Exceptions will be demonstrated in the *Error Handling with Exceptions* chapter. Briefly, they are objects that can be "thrown" out of a method if that method fails. Although only one exception object can emerge when you call a method, a particular method might produce any number of different types of exceptions, all of which need descriptions. So the form for the exception tag is:

```
@throws fully-qualified-class-name description
```

in which *fully-qualified-class-name* gives an unambiguous name of an exception class that's defined somewhere, and *description* (which can continue on subsequent lines) tells you why this particular type of exception can emerge from the method call.

@deprecated

This is used to indicate features that were superseded by an improved feature. The deprecated tag is a suggestion that you no longer use this particular feature, since sometime in the future it is likely to be removed. A method that is marked **@deprecated** causes the compiler to issue a warning if it is used. In Java SE5, the **@deprecated** Javadoc tag has been superseded by the **@Deprecated** *annotation* (you'll learn about these in the *Annotations* chapter).

Documentation example

Here is the first Java program again, this time with documentation comments added:

```
//: object/HelloDate.java
import java.util.*;

/** The first Thinking in Java example program.
 * Displays a string and today's date.
 * @author Bruce Eckel
 * @author www.MindView.net
 * @version 4.0
*/
public class HelloDate {
  /** Entry point to class & application.
   * @param args array of string arguments
   * @throws exceptions No exceptions thrown
```

```
    */
    public static void main(String[] args) {
        System.out.println("Hello, it's: ");
        System.out.println(new Date());
    }
} /* Output: (55% match)
Hello, it's:
Wed Oct 05 14:39:36 MDT 2005
*///:~
```

The first line of the file uses my own technique of putting a '//:' as a special marker for the comment line containing the source file name. That line contains the path information to the file (**object** indicates this chapter) followed by the file name. The last line also finishes with a comment, and this one ('///:~') indicates the end of the source code listing, which allows it to be automatically updated into the text of this book after being checked with a compiler and executed.

The /* **Output:** tag indicates the beginning of the output that will be generated by this file. In this form, it can be automatically tested to verify its accuracy. In this case, the **(55% match)** indicates to the testing system that the output will be fairly different from one run to the next so it should only expect a 55 percent correlation with the output shown here. Most examples in this book that produce output will contain the output in this commented form, so you can see the output and know that it is correct.

Coding style

The style described in the *Code Conventions for the Java Programming Language*[8] is to capitalize the first letter of a class name. If the class name consists of several words, they are run together (that is, you don't use underscores to separate the names), and the first letter of each embedded word is capitalized, such as:

```
class AllTheColorsOfTheRainbow { // ...
```

This is sometimes called "camel-casing." For almost everything else— methods, fields (member variables), and object reference names—the

---

[8] *http://java.sun.com/docs/codeconv/index.html*. To preserve space in this book and seminar presentations, not all of these guidelines could be followed, but you'll see that the style I use here matches the Java standard as much as possible.

accepted style is just as it is for classes *except* that the first letter of the identifier is lowercase. For example:

```java
class AllTheColorsOfTheRainbow {
  int anIntegerRepresentingColors;
  void changeTheHueOfTheColor(int newHue) {
    // ...
  }
  // ...
}
```

The user must also type all these long names, so be merciful.

The Java code you will see in the Sun libraries also follows the placement of open-and-close curly braces that you see used in this book.

Summary

The goal of this chapter is just enough Java to understand how to write a simple program. You've also gotten an overview of the language and some of its basic ideas. However, the examples so far have all been of the form "Do this, then do that, then do something else." The next two chapters will introduce the basic operators used in Java programming, and then show you how to control the flow of your program.

Exercises

Normally, exercises will be distributed throughout the chapters, but in this chapter you were learning how to write basic programs so all the exercises were delayed until the end.

The number in parentheses after each exercise number is an indicator of how difficult the exercise is, in a ranking from 1-10.

Solutions to selected exercises can be found in the electronic document *The Thinking in Java Annotated Solution Guide*, available for sale from *www.MindView.net*.

Exercise 1: (2) Create a class containing an **int** and a **char** that are not initialized, and print their values to verify that Java performs default initialization.

Exercise 2: (1) Following the **HelloDate.java** example in this chapter, create a "hello, world" program that simply displays that statement. You need only a single method in your class (the "main" one that gets executed when the program starts). Remember to make it **static** and to include the argument list, even though you don't use the argument list. Compile the program with **javac** and run it using **java**. If you are using a different development environment than the JDK, learn how to compile and run programs in that environment.

Exercise 3: (1) Find the code fragments involving **ATypeName** and turn them into a program that compiles and runs.

Exercise 4: (1) Turn the **DataOnly** code fragments into a program that compiles and runs.

Exercise 5: (1) Modify the previous exercise so that the values of the data in **DataOnly** are assigned to and printed in **main( )**.

Exercise 6: (2) Write a program that includes and calls the **storage( )** method defined as a code fragment in this chapter.

Exercise 7: (1) Turn the **Incrementable** code fragments into a working program.

Exercise 8: (3) Write a program that demonstrates that, no matter how many objects you create of a particular class, there is only one instance of a particular **static** field in that class.

Exercise 9: (2) Write a program that demonstrates that autoboxing works for all the primitive types and their wrappers.

Exercise 10: (2) Write a program that prints three arguments taken from the command line. To do this, you'll need to index into the command-line array of **String**s.

Exercise 11: (1) Turn the **AllTheColorsOfTheRainbow** example into a program that compiles and runs.

Exercise 12: (2) Find the code for the second version of **HelloDate.java**, which is the simple comment documentation example. Execute **Javadoc** on the file and view the results with your Web browser.

Exercise 13: (1) Run **Documentation1.java**, **Documentation2.java**, and **Documentation3.java** through **Javadoc**. Verify the resulting documentation with your Web browser.

Exercise 14: (1) Add an HTML list of items to the documentation in the previous exercise.

Exercise 15: (1) Take the program in Exercise 2 and add comment documentation to it. Extract this comment documentation into an HTML file using **Javadoc** and view it with your Web browser.

Exercise 16: (1) In the *Initialization & Cleanup* chapter, locate the **Overloading.java** example and add Javadoc documentation. Extract this comment documentation into an HTML file using **Javadoc** and view it with your Web browser.

Operators

At the lowest level, data in Java is manipulated using operators.

Because Java was inherited from C++, most of these operators will be familiar to C and C++ programmers. Java has also added some improvements and simplifications.

If you're familiar with C or C++ syntax, you can skim through this chapter and the next, looking for places where Java is different from those languages. However, if you find yourself floundering a bit in these two chapters, make sure you go through the multimedia seminar *Thinking in C*, freely downloadable from *www.MindView.net*. It contains audio lectures, slides, exercises, and solutions specifically designed to bring you up to speed with the fundamentals necessary to learn Java.

Simpler print statements

In the previous chapter, you were introduced to the Java print statement:

```
System.out.println("Rather a lot to type");
```

You may observe that this is not only a lot to type (and thus many redundant tendon hits), but also rather noisy to read. Most languages before and after Java have taken a much simpler approach to such a commonly used statement.

The *Access Control* chapter introduces the concept of the *static import* that was added to Java SE5, and creates a tiny library to simplify writing print statements. However, you don't need to know those details in order to begin using that library. We can rewrite the program from the last chapter using this new library:

```
//: operators/HelloDate.java
import java.util.*;
import static net.mindview.util.Print.*;

public class HelloDate {
```

```
  public static void main(String[] args) {
    print("Hello, it's: ");
    print(new Date());
  }
} /* Output: (55% match)
Hello, it's:
Wed Oct 05 14:39:05 MDT 2005
*///:~
```

The results are much cleaner. Notice the insertion of the **static** keyword in the second **import** statement.

In order to use this library, you must download this book's code package from *www.MindView.net* or one of its mirrors. Unzip the code tree and add the root directory of that code tree to your computer's CLASSPATH environment variable. (You'll eventually get a full introduction to the classpath, but you might as well get used to struggling with it early. Alas, it is one of the more common battles you will have with Java.)

Although the use of **net.mindview.util.Print** nicely simplifies most code, it is not justifiable everywhere. If there are only a small number of print statements in a program, I forego the **import** and write out the full **System.out.println( )**.

Exercise 1: (1) Write a program that uses the "short" and normal form of print statement.

Using Java operators

An operator takes one or more arguments and produces a new value. The arguments are in a different form than ordinary method calls, but the effect is the same. Addition and unary plus (+), subtraction and unary minus (-), multiplication (*), division (/), and assignment (=) all work much the same in any programming language.

All operators produce a value from their operands. In addition, some operators change the value of an operand. This is called a *side effect*. The most common use for operators that modify their operands is to generate the side effect, but you should keep in mind that the value produced is available for your use, just as in operators without side effects.

Thinking in Java   *Bruce Eckel*

Almost all operators work only with primitives. The exceptions are '=', '=='
and '!=', which work with all objects (and are a point of confusion for
objects). In addition, the **String** class supports '+' and '+='.

Precedence

Operator precedence defines how an expression evaluates when several
operators are present. Java has specific rules that determine the order of
evaluation. The easiest one to remember is that multiplication and division
happen before addition and subtraction. Programmers often forget the other
precedence rules, so you should use parentheses to make the order of
evaluation explicit. For example, look at statements **(1)** and **(2)**:

```
//: operators/Precedence.java

public class Precedence {
  public static void main(String[] args) {
    int x = 1, y = 2, z = 3;
    int a = x + y - 2/2 + z;          // (1)
    int b = x + (y - 2)/(2 + z);      // (2)
    System.out.println("a = " + a + " b = " + b);
  }
} /* Output:
a = 5 b = 1
*///:~
```

These statements look roughly the same, but from the output you can see that
they have very different meanings which depend on the use of parentheses.

Notice that the **System.out.println( )** statement involves the '+' operator.
In this context, '+' means "string concatenation" and, if necessary, "string
conversion." When the compiler sees a **String** followed by a '+' followed by a
non-**String**, it attempts to convert the non-**String** into a **String**. As you can
see from the output, it successfully converts from **int** into **String** for **a** and **b**.

Assignment

Assignment is performed with the operator =. It means "Take the value of the
right-hand side (often called the *rvalue*) and copy it into the left-hand side
(often called the *lvalue*)." An rvalue is any constant, variable, or expression
that produces a value, but an lvalue must be a distinct, named variable. (That

is, there must be a physical space to store the value.) For instance, you can assign a constant value to a variable:

```
a = 4;
```

but you cannot assign anything to a constant value—it cannot be an lvalue. (You can't say **4 = a;**.)

Assignment of primitives is quite straightforward. Since the primitive holds the actual value and not a reference to an object, when you assign primitives, you copy the contents from one place to another. For example, if you say **a = b** for primitives, then the contents of **b** are copied into **a**. If you then go on to modify **a**, **b** is naturally unaffected by this modification. As a programmer, this is what you can expect for most situations.

When you assign objects, however, things change. Whenever you manipulate an object, what you're manipulating is the reference, so when you assign "from one object to another," you're actually copying a reference from one place to another. This means that if you say **c = d** for objects, you end up with both **c** and **d** pointing to the object that, originally, only **d** pointed to. Here's an example that demonstrates this behavior:

```
//: operators/Assignment.java
// Assignment with objects is a bit tricky.
import static net.mindview.util.Print.*;

class Tank {
  int level;
}

public class Assignment {
  public static void main(String[] args) {
    Tank t1 = new Tank();
    Tank t2 = new Tank();
    t1.level = 9;
    t2.level = 47;
    print("1: t1.level: " + t1.level +
          ", t2.level: " + t2.level);
    t1 = t2;
    print("2: t1.level: " + t1.level +
          ", t2.level: " + t2.level);
    t1.level = 27;
    print("3: t1.level: " + t1.level +
          ", t2.level: " + t2.level);
```

```
    }
} /* Output:
1: t1.level: 9, t2.level: 47
2: t1.level: 47, t2.level: 47
3: t1.level: 27, t2.level: 27
*///:~
```

The **Tank** class is simple, and two instances (**t1** and **t2**) are created within
main( ). The **level** field within each **Tank** is given a different value, and
then **t2** is assigned to **t1**, and **t1** is changed. In many programming languages
you expect **t1** and **t2** to be independent at all times, but because you've
assigned a reference, changing the **t1** object appears to change the **t2** object
as well! This is because both **t1** and **t2** contain the same reference, which is
pointing to the same object. (The original reference that was in **t1**, that
pointed to the object holding a value of 9, was overwritten during the
assignment and effectively lost; its object will be cleaned up by the garbage
collector.)

This phenomenon is often called *aliasing*, and it's a fundamental way that
Java works with objects. But what if you don't want aliasing to occur in this
case? You could forego the assignment and say:

```
t1.level = t2.level;
```

This retains the two separate objects instead of discarding one and tying **t1**
and **t2** to the same object. You'll soon realize that manipulating the fields
within objects is messy and goes against good object-oriented design
principles. This is a nontrivial topic, so you should keep in mind that
assignment for objects can add surprises.

Exercise 2: (1) Create a class containing a **float** and use it to demonstrate
aliasing.

Aliasing during method calls

Aliasing will also occur when you pass an object into a method:

```
//: operators/PassObject.java
// Passing objects to methods may not be
// what you're used to.
import static net.mindview.util.Print.*;

class Letter {
  char c;
```

```
    }

public class PassObject {
  static void f(Letter y) {
    y.c = 'z';
  }
  public static void main(String[] args) {
    Letter x = new Letter();
    x.c = 'a';
    print("1: x.c: " + x.c);
    f(x);
    print("2: x.c: " + x.c);
  }
} /* Output:
1: x.c: a
2: x.c: z
*///:~
```

In many programming languages, the method **f( )** would appear to be making a copy of its argument **Letter y** inside the scope of the method. But once again a reference is being passed, so the line

```
y.c = 'z';
```

is actually changing the object outside of **f( )**.

Aliasing and its solution is a complex issue which is covered in one of the online supplements for this book. However, you should be aware of it at this point so you can watch for pitfalls.

Exercise 3: (1) Create a class containing a **float** and use it to demonstrate aliasing during method calls.

Mathematical operators

The basic mathematical operators are the same as the ones available in most programming languages: addition (+), subtraction (-), division (/), multiplication (*) and modulus (%, which produces the remainder from division). Integer division truncates, rather than rounds, the result.

Java also uses the shorthand notation from C/C++ that performs an operation and an assignment at the same time. This is denoted by an operator followed by an equal sign, and is consistent with all the operators in the language (whenever it makes sense). For example, to add 4 to the variable **x** and assign the result to **x**, use: **x += 4**.

This example shows the use of the mathematical operators:

```java
//: operators/MathOps.java
// Demonstrates the mathematical operators.
import java.util.*;
import static net.mindview.util.Print.*;

public class MathOps {
  public static void main(String[] args) {
    // Create a seeded random number generator:
    Random rand = new Random(47);
    int i, j, k;
    // Choose value from 1 to 100:
    j = rand.nextInt(100) + 1;
    print("j : " + j);
    k = rand.nextInt(100) + 1;
    print("k : " + k);
    i = j + k;
    print("j + k : " + i);
    i = j - k;
    print("j - k : " + i);
    i = k / j;
    print("k / j : " + i);
    i = k * j;
    print("k * j : " + i);
    i = k % j;
    print("k % j : " + i);
    j %= k;
    print("j %= k : " + j);
    // Floating-point number tests:
    float u, v, w; // Applies to doubles, too
    v = rand.nextFloat();
    print("v : " + v);
    w = rand.nextFloat();
    print("w : " + w);
    u = v + w;
    print("v + w : " + u);
    u = v - w;
    print("v - w : " + u);
    u = v * w;
    print("v * w : " + u);
    u = v / w;
```

```
        print("v / w : " + u);
        // The following also works for char,
        // byte, short, int, long, and double:
        u += v;
        print("u += v : " + u);
        u -= v;
        print("u -= v : " + u);
        u *= v;
        print("u *= v : " + u);
        u /= v;
        print("u /= v : " + u);
    }
} /* Output:
j : 59
k : 56
j + k : 115
j - k : 3
k / j : 0
k * j : 3304
k % j : 56
j %= k : 3
v : 0.5309454
w : 0.0534122
v + w : 0.5843576
v - w : 0.47753322
v * w : 0.028358962
v / w : 9.940527
u += v : 10.471473
u -= v : 9.940527
u *= v : 5.2778773
u /= v : 9.940527
*///:~
```

To generate numbers, the program first creates a **Random** object. If you
create a **Random** object with no arguments, Java uses the current time as a
seed for the random number generator, and will thus produce different
output for each execution of the program. However, in the examples in this
book, it is important that the output shown at the end of the examples be as
consistent as possible, so that this output can be verified with external tools.
By providing a *seed* (an initialization value for the random number generator
that will always produce the same sequence for a particular seed value) when
creating the **Random** object, the same random numbers will be generated

each time the program is executed, so the output is verifiable.[1] To generate more varying output, feel free to remove the seed in the examples in the book.

The program generates a number of different types of random numbers with the **Random** object simply by calling the methods **nextInt( )** and **nextFloat( )** (you can also call **nextLong( )** or **nextDouble( )**). The argument to **nextInt( )** sets the upper bound on the generated number. The lower bound is zero, which we don't want because of the possibility of a divide-by-zero, so the result is offset by one.

Exercise 4: (2) Write a program that calculates velocity using a constant distance and a constant time.

Unary minus and plus operators

The unary minus (-) and unary plus (+) are the same operators as binary minus and plus. The compiler figures out which use is intended by the way you write the expression. For instance, the statement

```
x = -a;
```

has an obvious meaning. The compiler is able to figure out:

```
x = a * -b;
```

but the reader might get confused, so it is sometimes clearer to say:

```
x = a * (-b);
```

Unary minus inverts the sign on the data. Unary plus provides symmetry with unary minus, but its only effect is to promote smaller-type operands to **int**.

Auto increment and decrement

Java, like C, has a number of shortcuts. Shortcuts can make code much easier to type, and either easier or harder to read.

Two of the nicer shortcuts are the increment and decrement operators (often referred to as the auto-increment and auto-decrement operators). The decrement operator is -- and means "decrease by one unit." The increment operator is ++ and means "increase by one unit." If **a** is an **int**, for example,

---

[1] The number 47 was considered a "magic number" at a college I attended, and it stuck.

the expression **++a** is equivalent to (**a = a + 1**). Increment and decrement operators not only modify the variable, but also produce the value of the variable as a result.

There are two versions of each type of operator, often called the *prefix* and *postfix* versions. *Pre-increment* means the **++** operator appears before the variable, and *post-increment* means the **++** operator appears after the variable. Similarly, *pre-decrement* means the **--** operator appears before the variable, and *post-decrement* means the **--** operator appears after the variable. For pre-increment and pre-decrement (i.e., **++a** or **--a**), the operation is performed and the value is produced. For post-increment and post-decrement (i.e., **a++** or **a--**), the value is produced, then the operation is performed. As an example:

```
//: operators/AutoInc.java
// Demonstrates the ++ and -- operators.
import static net.mindview.util.Print.*;

public class AutoInc {
  public static void main(String[] args) {
    int i = 1;
    print("i : " + i);
    print("++i : " + ++i); // Pre-increment
    print("i++ : " + i++); // Post-increment
    print("i : " + i);
    print("--i : " + --i); // Pre-decrement
    print("i-- : " + i--); // Post-decrement
    print("i : " + i);
  }
} /* Output:
i : 1
++i : 2
i++ : 2
i : 3
--i : 2
i-- : 2
i : 1
*///:~
```

You can see that for the prefix form, you get the value after the operation has been performed, but with the postfix form, you get the value before the operation is performed. These are the only operators, other than those involving assignment, that have side effects—they change the operand rather than using just its value.

The increment operator is one explanation for the name C++, implying "one step beyond C." In an early Java speech, Bill Joy (one of the Java creators), said that "Java=C++--" (C plus plus minus minus), suggesting that Java is C++ with the unnecessary hard parts removed, and therefore a much simpler language. As you progress in this book, you'll see that many parts are simpler, and yet in other ways Java isn't much easier than C++.

Relational operators

Relational operators generate a **boolean** result. They evaluate the relationship between the values of the operands. A relational expression produces **true** if the relationship is true, and **false** if the relationship is untrue. The relational operators are less than (<), greater than (>), less than or equal to (<=), greater than or equal to (>=), equivalent (==) and not equivalent (!=). Equivalence and nonequivalence work with all primitives, but the other comparisons won't work with type **boolean**. Because **boolean** values can only be **true** or **false**, "greater than" and "less than" doesn't make sense.

Testing object equivalence

The relational operators == and != also work with all objects, but their meaning often confuses the first-time Java programmer. Here's an example:

```
//: operators/Equivalence.java

public class Equivalence {
  public static void main(String[] args) {
    Integer n1 = new Integer(47);
    Integer n2 = new Integer(47);
    System.out.println(n1 == n2);
    System.out.println(n1 != n2);
  }
} /* Output:
false
true
*///:~
```

The statement **Systcm.out.println(n1 == n2)** will print the result of the **boolean** comparison within it. Surely the output should be "true" and then

---

"false," since both **Integer** objects are the same. But while the *contents* of the objects are the same, the references are not the same. The operators == and != compare object references, so the output is actually "false" and then "true." Naturally, this surprises people at first.

What if you want to compare the actual contents of an object for equivalence? You must use the special method **equals( )** that exists for all objects (not primitives, which work fine with == and !=). Here's how it's used:

```
//: operators/EqualsMethod.java

public class EqualsMethod {
  public static void main(String[] args) {
    Integer n1 = new Integer(47);
    Integer n2 = new Integer(47);
    System.out.println(n1.equals(n2));
  }
} /* Output:
true
*///:~
```

The result is now what you expect. Ah, but it's not as simple as that. If you create your own class, like this:

```
//: operators/EqualsMethod2.java
// Default equals() does not compare contents.

class Value {
  int i;
}

public class EqualsMethod2 {
  public static void main(String[] args) {
    Value v1 = new Value();
    Value v2 = new Value();
    v1.i = v2.i = 100;
    System.out.println(v1.equals(v2));
  }
} /* Output:
false
*///:~
```

things are confusing again: The result is **false**. This is because the default behavior of **equals( )** is to compare references. So unless you *override* equals( ) in your new class you won't get the desired behavior. Unfortunately, you won't learn about overriding until the *Reusing Classes* chapter and about the proper way to define **equals( )** until the *Containers in Depth* chapter, but being aware of the way **equals( )** behaves might save you some grief in the meantime.

Most of the Java library classes implement **equals( )** so that it compares the contents of objects instead of their references.

Exercise 5: (2) Create a class called **Dog** containing two **Strings**: **name** and **says**. In **main( )**, create two dog objects with names "spot" (who says, "Ruff!") and "scruffy" (who says, "Wurf!"). Then display their names and what they say.

Exercise 6: (3) Following Exercise 5, create a new **Dog** reference and assign it to spot's object. Test for comparison using == and **equals( )** for all references.

Logical operators

Each of the logical operators AND (**&&**), OR (**||**) and NOT (**!**) produces a **boolean** value of **true** or **false** based on the logical relationship of its arguments. This example uses the relational and logical operators:

```
//: operators/Bool.java
// Relational and logical operators.
import java.util.*;
import static net.mindview.util.Print.*;

public class Bool {
  public static void main(String[] args) {
    Random rand = new Random(47);
    int i = rand.nextInt(100);
    int j = rand.nextInt(100);
    print("i = " + i);
    print("j = " + j);
    print("i > j is " + (i > j));
    print("i < j is " + (i < j));
    print("i >= j is " + (i >= j));
    print("i <= j is " + (i <= j));
    print("i == j is " + (i == j));
    print("i != j is " + (i != j));
    // Treating an int as a boolean is not legal Java:
//! print("i && j is " + (i && j));
```

```
//! print("i || j is " + (i || j));
//! print("!i is " + !i);
    print("(i < 10) && (j < 10) is "
        + ((i < 10) && (j < 10)) );
    print("(i < 10) || (j < 10) is "
        + ((i < 10) || (j < 10)) );
  }
} /* Output:
i = 58
j = 55
i > j is true
i < j is false
i >= j is true
i <= j is false
i == j is false
i != j is true
(i < 10) && (j < 10) is false
(i < 10) || (j < 10) is false
*///:~
```

You can apply AND, OR, or NOT to **boolean** values only. You can't use a non-**boolean** as if it were a **boolean** in a logical expression as you can in C and C++. You can see the failed attempts at doing this commented out with a '//!' (this comment syntax enables automatic removal of comments to facilitate testing). The subsequent expressions, however, produce **boolean** values using relational comparisons, then use logical operations on the results.

Note that a **boolean** value is automatically converted to an appropriate text form if it is used where a **String** is expected.

You can replace the definition for **int** in the preceding program with any other primitive data type except **boolean**. Be aware, however, that the comparison of floating point numbers is very strict. A number that is the tiniest fraction different from another number is still "not equal." A number that is the tiniest bit above zero is still nonzero.

Exercise 7: (3) Write a program that simulates coin-flipping.

Short-circuiting

When dealing with logical operators, you run into a phenomenon called "short-circuiting." This means that the expression will be evaluated only *until* the truth or falsehood of the entire expression can be unambiguously determined. As a result, the latter parts of a logical expression might not be evaluated. Here's an example that demonstrates short-circuiting:

```java
//: operators/ShortCircuit.java
// Demonstrates short-circuiting behavior
// with logical operators.
import static net.mindview.util.Print.*;

public class ShortCircuit {
  static boolean test1(int val) {
    print("test1(" + val + ")");
    print("result: " + (val < 1));
    return val < 1;
  }
  static boolean test2(int val) {
    print("test2(" + val + ")");
    print("result: " + (val < 2));
    return val < 2;
  }
  static boolean test3(int val) {
    print("test3(" + val + ")");
    print("result: " + (val < 3));
    return val < 3;
  }
  public static void main(String[] args) {
    boolean b = test1(0) && test2(2) && test3(2);
    print("expression is " + b);
  }
} /* Output:
test1(0)
result: true
test2(2)
result: false
expression is false
*///:~
```

Each test performs a comparison against the argument and returns **true** or **false**. It also prints information to show you that it's being called. The tests are used in the expression:

```java
test1(0) && test2(2) && test3(2)
```

You might naturally think that all three tests would be executed, but the output shows otherwise. The first test produced a **true** result, so the expression evaluation continues. However, the second test produced a **false** result. Since this means that the whole expression must be **false**, why continue evaluating the rest of the expression? It might be expensive. The reason for short-circuiting, in fact, is that you can get a potential performance increase if all the parts of a logical expression do not need to be evaluated.

Literals

Ordinarily, when you insert a literal value into a program, the compiler knows exactly what type to make it. Sometimes, however, the type is ambiguous. When this happens, you must guide the compiler by adding some extra information in the form of characters associated with the literal value. The following code shows these characters:

```
//: operators/Literals.java
import static net.mindview.util.Print.*;

public class Literals {
  public static void main(String[] args) {
    int i1 = 0x2f; // Hexadecimal (lowercase)
    print("i1: " + Integer.toBinaryString(i1));
    int i2 = 0X2F; // Hexadecimal (uppercase)
    print("i2: " + Integer.toBinaryString(i2));
    int i3 = 0177; // Octal (leading zero)
    print("i3: " + Integer.toBinaryString(i3));
    char c = 0xffff; // max char hex value
    print("c: " + Integer.toBinaryString(c));
    byte b = 0x7f; // max byte hex value
    print("b: " + Integer.toBinaryString(b));
    short s = 0x7fff; // max short hex value
    print("s: " + Integer.toBinaryString(s));
    long n1 = 200L; // long suffix
    long n2 = 200l; // long suffix (but can be confusing)
    long n3 = 200;
    float f1 = 1;
    float f2 = 1F; // float suffix
    float f3 = 1f; // float suffix
    double d1 = 1d; // double suffix
    double d2 = 1D; // double suffix
    // (Hex and Octal also work with long)
  }
} /* Output:
i1: 101111
i2: 101111
```

```
i3: 1111111
c: 1111111111111111
b: 1111111
s: 111111111111111
*///:~
```

A trailing character after a literal value establishes its type. Uppercase or lowercase **L** means **long** (however, using a lowercase l is confusing because it can look like the number one). Uppercase or lowercase **F** means **float**. Uppercase or lowercase **D** means **double**.

Hexadecimal (base 16), which works with all the integral data types, is denoted by a leading **0x** or **0X** followed by **0-9** or **a-f** either in uppercase or lowercase. If you try to initialize a variable with a value bigger than it can hold (regardless of the numerical form of the value), the compiler will give you an error message. Notice in the preceding code the maximum possible hexadecimal values for **char**, **byte**, and **short**. If you exceed these, the compiler will automatically make the value an **int** and tell you that you need a narrowing *cast* for the assignment (casts are defined later in this chapter). You'll know you've stepped over the line.

Octal (base 8) is denoted by a leading zero in the number and digits from 0-7.

There is no literal representation for binary numbers in C, C++, or Java. However, when working with hexadecimal and octal notation, it's useful to display the binary form of the results. This is easily accomplished with the **static toBinaryString( )** methods from the **Integer** and **Long** classes. Notice that when passing smaller types to **Integer.toBinaryString( )**, the type is automatically converted to an **int**.

Exercise 8: (2) Show that hex and octal notations work with long values. Use **Long.toBinaryString( )** to display the results.

Exponential notation

Exponents use a notation that I've always found rather dismaying:

```
//: operators/Exponents.java
// "e" means "10 to the power."

public class Exponents {
  public static void main(String[] args) {
    // Uppercase and lowercase 'e' are the same:
    float expFloat = 1.39e-43f;
```

```
    expFloat = 1.39E-43f;
    System.out.println(expFloat);
    double expDouble = 47e47d; // 'd' is optional
    double expDouble2 = 47e47; // Automatically double
    System.out.println(expDouble);
  }
} /* Output:
1.39E-43
4.7E48
*///:~
```

In science and engineering, 'e' refers to the base of natural logarithms, approximately 2.718. (A more precise **double** value is available in Java as **Math.E**.) This is used in exponentiation expressions such as $1.39 \times e^{-43}$, which means 1.39×2.718^{-43}. However, when the FORTRAN programming language was invented, they decided that **e** would mean "ten to the power," which is an odd decision because FORTRAN was designed for science and engineering, and one would think its designers would be sensitive about introducing such an ambiguity.[2] At any rate, this custom was followed in C, C++ and now Java. So if you're used to thinking in terms of **e** as the base of natural logarithms, you must do a mental translation when you see an expression such as **1.39 e-43f** in Java; it means 1.39×10^{-43}.

Note that you don't need to use the trailing character when the compiler can figure out the appropriate type. With

```
long n3 = 200;
```

there's no ambiguity, so an **L** after the 200 would be superfluous. However, with

---

[2] John Kirkham writes, "I started computing in 1962 using FORTRAN II on an IBM 1620. At that time, and throughout the 1960s and into the 1970s, FORTRAN was an all uppercase language. This probably started because many of the early input devices were old teletype units that used 5 bit Baudot code, which had no lowercase capability. The 'E' in the exponential notation was also always uppercase and was never confused with the natural logarithm base 'e', which is always lowercase. The 'E' simply stood for exponential, which was for the base of the number system used—usually 10. At the time octal was also widely used by programmers. Although I never saw it used, if I had seen an octal number in exponential notation I would have considered it to be base 8. The first time I remember seeing an exponential using a lowercase 'e' was in the late 1970s and I also found it confusing. The problem arose as lowercase crept into FORTRAN, not at its beginning. We actually had functions to use if you really wanted to use the natural logarithm base, but they were all uppercase."

```
float f4 = 1e-43f; // 10 to the power
```

the compiler normally takes exponential numbers as doubles, so without the trailing **f**, it will give you an error telling you that you must use a cast to convert **double** to **float**.

Exercise 9: (1) Display the largest and smallest numbers for both **float** and **double** exponential notation.

Bitwise operators

The bitwise operators allow you to manipulate individual bits in an integral primitive data type. Bitwise operators perform Boolean algebra on the corresponding bits in the two arguments to produce the result.

The bitwise operators come from C's low-level orientation, where you often manipulate hardware directly and must set the bits in hardware registers. Java was originally designed to be embedded in TV set-top boxes, so this low-level orientation still made sense. However, you probably won't use the bitwise operators much.

The bitwise AND operator (**&**) produces a one in the output bit if both input bits are one; otherwise, it produces a zero. The bitwise OR operator (**|**) produces a one in the output bit if either input bit is a one and produces a zero only if both input bits are zero. The bitwise EXCLUSIVE OR, or XOR (**^**), produces a one in the output bit if one or the other input bit is a one, but not both. The bitwise NOT (**~**, also called the *ones complement* operator) is a unary operator; it takes only one argument. (All other bitwise operators are binary operators.) Bitwise NOT produces the opposite of the input bit—a one if the input bit is zero, a zero if the input bit is one.

The bitwise operators and logical operators use the same characters, so it is helpful to have a mnemonic device to help you remember the meanings: Because bits are "small," there is only one character in the bitwise operators.

Bitwise operators can be combined with the = sign to unite the operation and assignment: **&=**, **|=** and **^=** are all legitimate. (Since **~** is a unary operator, it cannot be combined with the = sign.)

The **boolean** type is treated as a one-bit value, so it is somewhat different. You can perform a bitwise AND, OR, and XOR, but you can't perform a bitwise NOT (presumably to prevent confusion with the logical NOT). For

---

booleans, the bitwise operators have the same effect as the logical operators except that they do not short circuit. Also, bitwise operations on **boolean**s include an XOR logical operator that is not included under the list of "logical" operators. You cannot use **boolean**s in shift expressions, which are described next.

Exercise 10: (3) Write a program with two constant values, one with alternating binary ones and zeroes, with a zero in the least-significant digit, and the second, also alternating, with a one in the least-significant digit (hint: It's easiest to use hexadecimal constants for this). Take these two values and combine them in all possible ways using the bitwise operators, and display the results using **Integer.toBinaryString( )**.

Shift operators

The shift operators also manipulate bits. They can be used solely with primitive, integral types. The left-shift operator (`<<`) produces the operand to the left of the operator after it has been shifted to the left by the number of bits specified to the right of the operator (inserting zeroes at the lower-order bits). The signed right-shift operator (`>>`) produces the operand to the left of the operator after it has been shifted to the right by the number of bits specified to the right of the operator. The signed right shift `>>` uses *sign extension*: If the value is positive, zeroes are inserted at the higher-order bits; if the value is negative, ones are inserted at the higher-order bits. Java has also added the unsigned right shift `>>>`, which uses *zero extension*: Regardless of the sign, zeroes are inserted at the higher-order bits. This operator does not exist in C or C++.

If you shift a **char**, **byte**, or **short**, it will be promoted to **int** before the shift takes place, and the result will be an **int**. Only the five low-order bits of the right-hand side will be used. This prevents you from shifting more than the number of bits in an **int**. If you're operating on a **long**, you'll get a **long** result. Only the six low-order bits of the right-hand side will be used, so you can't shift more than the number of bits in a **long**.

Shifts can be combined with the equal sign (`<<=` or `>>=` or `>>>=`). The lvalue is replaced by the lvalue shifted by the rvalue. There is a problem, however, with the unsigned right shift combined with assignment. If you use it with **byte** or **short**, you don't get the correct results. Instead, these are promoted to **int** and right shifted, but then truncated as they are assigned back into their variables, so you get **-1** in those cases. The following example demonstrates this:

```
//: operators/URShift.java
// Test of unsigned right shift.
import static net.mindview.util.Print.*;

public class URShift {
  public static void main(String[] args) {
    int i = -1;
    print(Integer.toBinaryString(i));
    i >>>= 10;
    print(Integer.toBinaryString(i));
    long l = -1;
    print(Long.toBinaryString(l));
    l >>>= 10;
    print(Long.toBinaryString(l));
    short s = -1;
    print(Integer.toBinaryString(s));
    s >>>= 10;
    print(Integer.toBinaryString(s));
    byte b = -1;
    print(Integer.toBinaryString(b));
    b >>>= 10;
    print(Integer.toBinaryString(b));
    b = -1;
    print(Integer.toBinaryString(b));
    print(Integer.toBinaryString(b>>>10));
  }
} /* Output:
11111111111111111111111111111111
1111111111111111111111
11111111111111111111111111111111111111111111111111111111111111111
11111111111111111111111111111111111111111111111111111111111111
11111111111111111111111111111111
11111111111111111111111111111111
11111111111111111111111111111111
11111111111111111111111111111111
11111111111111111111111111111111
1111111111111111111111
*///:~
```

In the last shift, the resulting value is not assigned back into **b**, but is printed directly, so the correct behavior occurs.

Here's an example that demonstrates the use of all the operators involving bits:

```
//: operators/BitManipulation.java
// Using the bitwise operators.
import java.util.*;
import static net.mindview.util.Print.*;

public class BitManipulation {
  public static void main(String[] args) {
    Random rand = new Random(47);
    int i = rand.nextInt();
    int j = rand.nextInt();
    printBinaryInt("-1", -1);
    printBinaryInt("+1", +1);
    int maxpos = 2147483647;
    printBinaryInt("maxpos", maxpos);
    int maxneg = -2147483648;
    printBinaryInt("maxneg", maxneg);
    printBinaryInt("i", i);
    printBinaryInt("~i", ~i);
    printBinaryInt("-i", -i);
    printBinaryInt("j", j);
    printBinaryInt("i & j", i & j);
    printBinaryInt("i | j", i | j);
    printBinaryInt("i ^ j", i ^ j);
    printBinaryInt("i << 5", i << 5);
    printBinaryInt("i >> 5", i >> 5);
    printBinaryInt("(~i) >> 5", (~i) >> 5);
    printBinaryInt("i >>> 5", i >>> 5);
    printBinaryInt("(~i) >>> 5", (~i) >>> 5);

    long l = rand.nextLong();
    long m = rand.nextLong();
    printBinaryLong("-1L", -1L);
    printBinaryLong("+1L", +1L);
    long ll = 9223372036854775807L;
    printBinaryLong("maxpos", ll);
    long lln = -9223372036854775808L;
    printBinaryLong("maxneg", lln);
    printBinaryLong("l", l);
    printBinaryLong("~l", ~l);
    printBinaryLong("-l", -l);
    printBinaryLong("m", m);
```

```
      printBinaryLong("l & m", l & m);
      printBinaryLong("l | m", l | m);
      printBinaryLong("l ^ m", l ^ m);
      printBinaryLong("l << 5", l << 5);
      printBinaryLong("l >> 5", l >> 5);
      printBinaryLong("(~l) >> 5", (~l) >> 5);
      printBinaryLong("l >>> 5", l >>> 5);
      printBinaryLong("(~l) >>> 5", (~l) >>> 5);
  }
  static void printBinaryInt(String s, int i) {
    print(s + ", int: " + i + ", binary:\n    " +
      Integer.toBinaryString(i));
  }
  static void printBinaryLong(String s, long l) {
    print(s + ", long: " + l + ", binary:\n    " +
      Long.toBinaryString(l));
  }
} /* Output:
-1, int: -1, binary:
    11111111111111111111111111111111
+1, int: 1, binary:
    1
maxpos, int: 2147483647, binary:
    1111111111111111111111111111111
maxneg, int: -2147483648, binary:
    10000000000000000000000000000000
i, int: -1172028779, binary:
    10111010001001000100001010010101
~i, int: 1172028778, binary:
    1000101110110111011110101101010
-i, int: 1172028779, binary:
    1000101110110111011110101101011
j, int: 1717241110, binary:
    1100110010110110000010100010110
i & j, int: 570425364, binary:
    100010000000000000000000010100
i | j, int: -25213033, binary:
    11111110011111110100011110010111
i ^ j, int: -595638397, binary:
    11011100011111101000111100000011
i << 5, int: 1149784736, binary:
    1000100100010000101001010100000
i >> 5, int: -36625900, binary:
    11111101110100010010001000010100
```

```
(~i) >> 5, int: 36625899, binary:
    10001011101101110111101011
i >>> 5, int: 97591828, binary:
    101110100010010001000010100
(~i) >>> 5, int: 36625899, binary:
    10001011101101110111101011
. . .
*///:~
```

The two methods at the end, **printBinaryInt( )** and **printBinaryLong( )**, take an **int** or a **long**, respectively, and print it out in binary format along with a descriptive string. As well as demonstrating the effect of all the bitwise operators for **int** and **long**, this example also shows the minimum, maximum, +1, and -1 values for **int** and **long** so you can see what they look like. Note that the high bit represents the sign: 0 means positive and 1 means negative. The output for the **int** portion is displayed above.

The binary representation of the numbers is referred to as *signed twos complement*.

Exercise 11: (3) Start with a number that has a binary one in the most significant position (hint: Use a hexadecimal constant). Using the signed right-shift operator, right shift it all the way through all of its binary positions, each time displaying the result using **Integer.toBinaryString( )**.

Exercise 12: (3) Start with a number that is all binary ones. Left shift it, then use the unsigned right-shift operator to right shift through all of its binary positions, each time displaying the result using **Integer.toBinaryString( )**.

Exercise 13: (1) Write a method that displays **char** values in binary form. Demonstrate it using several different characters.

Ternary **if-else** operator

The *ternary* operator, also called the *conditional* operator, is unusual because it has three operands. It is truly an operator because it produces a value, unlike the ordinary **if-else** statement that you'll see in the next section of this chapter. The expression is of the form:

```
boolean-exp ? value0 : value1
```

If *boolean-exp* evaluates to **true**, *valueo* is evaluated, and its result becomes the value produced by the operator. If *boolean-exp* is **false**, *value1* is evaluated and its result becomes the value produced by the operator.

Of course, you could use an ordinary **if-else** statement (described later), but the ternary operator is much terser. Although C (where this operator originated) prides itself on being a terse language, and the ternary operator might have been introduced partly for efficiency, you should be somewhat wary of using it on an everyday basis—it's easy to produce unreadable code.

The conditional operator is different from **if-else** because it produces a value. Here's an example comparing the two:

```
//: operators/TernaryIfElse.java
import static net.mindview.util.Print.*;

public class TernaryIfElse {
  static int ternary(int i) {
    return i < 10 ? i * 100 : i * 10;
  }
  static int standardIfElse(int i) {
    if(i < 10)
      return i * 100;
    else
      return i * 10;
  }
  public static void main(String[] args) {
    print(ternary(9));
    print(ternary(10));
    print(standardIfElse(9));
    print(standardIfElse(10));
  }
} /* Output:
900
100
900
100
*///:~
```

You can see that this code in **ternary( )** is more compact than what you'd need to write without the ternary operator, in **standardIfElse( )**. However, **standardIfElse( )** is easier to understand, and doesn't require a lot more typing. So be sure to ponder your reasons when choosing the ternary

---

operator—it's generally warranted when you're setting a variable to one of two values.

String operator + and +=

There's one special usage of an operator in Java: The + and += operators can be used to concatenate strings, as you've already seen. It seems a natural use of these operators even though it doesn't fit with the traditional way that they are used.

This capability seemed like a good idea in C++, so *operator overloading* was added to C++ to allow the C++ programmer to add meanings to almost any operator. Unfortunately, operator overloading combined with some of the other restrictions in C++ turns out to be a fairly complicated feature for programmers to design into their classes. Although operator overloading would have been much simpler to implement in Java than it was in C++ (as has been demonstrated in the C# language, which *does* have straightforward operator overloading), this feature was still considered too complex, so Java programmers cannot implement their own overloaded operators like C++ and C# programmers can.

The use of the **String** operators has some interesting behavior. If an expression begins with a **String**, then all operands that follow must be **String**s (remember that the compiler automatically turns a double-quoted sequence of characters into a **String**):

```
//: operators/StringOperators.java
import static net.mindview.util.Print.*;

public class StringOperators {
  public static void main(String[] args) {
    int x = 0, y = 1, z = 2;
    String s = "x, y, z ";
    print(s + x + y + z);
    print(x + " " + s); // Converts x to a String
    s += "(summed) = "; // Concatenation operator
    print(s + (x + y + z));
    print("" + x); // Shorthand for Integer.toString()
  }
} /* Output:
x, y, z 012
0 x, y, z
x, y, z (summed) = 3
```

```
0
*///:~
```

Note that the output from the first print statement is '**012**' instead of just '**3**', which is what you'd get if it was summing the integers. This is because the Java compiler converts **x**, **y**, and **z** into their **String** representations and concatenates those strings, instead of adding them together first. The second print statement converts the leading variable into a **String**, so the string conversion does not depend on what comes first. Finally, you see the use of the **+=** operator to append a string to **s**, and the use of parentheses to control the order of evaluation of the expression so that the **int**s are actually summed before they are displayed.

Notice the last example in **main( )**: you will sometimes see an empty **String** followed by a + and a primitive as a way to perform the conversion without calling the more cumbersome explicit method (**Integer.toString( )**, in this case).

Common pitfalls when using operators

One of the pitfalls when using operators is attempting to leave out the parentheses when you are even the least bit uncertain about how an expression will evaluate. This is still true in Java.

An extremely common error in C and C++ looks like this:

```
while(x = y) {
  // ....
}
```

The programmer was clearly trying to test for equivalence (==) rather than do an assignment. In C and C++ the result of this assignment will always be **true** if **y** is nonzero, and you'll probably get an infinite loop. In Java, the result of this expression is not a **boolean**, but the compiler expects a **boolean** and won't convert from an **int**, so it will conveniently give you a compile-time error and catch the problem before you ever try to run the program. So the pitfall never happens in Java. (The only time you won't get a compile-time error is when **x** and **y** are **boolean**, in which case **x = y** is a legal expression, and in the preceding example, probably an error.)

A similar problem in C and C++ is using bitwise AND and OR instead of the logical versions. Bitwise AND and OR use one of the characters (**&** or **|**) while logical AND and OR use two (**&&** and **||**). Just as with = and ==, it's easy to type just one character instead of two. In Java, the compiler again prevents this, because it won't let you cavalierly use one type where it doesn't belong.

Casting operators

The word *cast* is used in the sense of "casting into a mold." Java will automatically change one type of data into another when appropriate. For instance, if you assign an integral value to a floating point variable, the compiler will automatically convert the **int** to a **float**. Casting allows you to make this type conversion explicit, or to force it when it wouldn't normally happen.

To perform a cast, put the desired data type inside parentheses to the left of any value. You can see this in the following example:

```
//: operators/Casting.java

public class Casting {
  public static void main(String[] args) {
    int i = 200;
    long lng = (long)i;
    lng = i; // "Widening," so cast not really required
    long lng2 = (long)200;
    lng2 = 200;
    // A "narrowing conversion":
    i = (int)lng2; // Cast required
  }
} ///:~
```

As you can see, it's possible to perform a cast on a numeric value as well as on a variable. Notice that you can introduce superfluous casts; for example, the compiler will automatically promote an **int** value to a **long** when necessary. However, you are allowed to use superfluous casts to make a point or to clarify your code. In other situations, a cast may be essential just to get the code to compile.

In C and C++, casting can cause some headaches. In Java, casting is safe, with the exception that when you perform a so-called *narrowing conversion* (that is, when you go from a data type that can hold more information to one that doesn't hold as much), you run the risk of losing information. Here the compiler forces you to use a cast, in effect saying, "This can be a dangerous thing to do—if you want me to do it anyway you must make the cast explicit." With a *widening conversion* an explicit cast is not needed, because the new type will more than hold the information from the old type so that no information is ever lost.

Java allows you to cast any primitive type to any other primitive type, except for **boolean**, which doesn't allow any casting at all. Class types do not allow casting. To convert one to the other, there must be special methods. (You'll find out later in this book that objects can be cast within a *family* of types; an **Oak** can be cast to a **Tree** and vice versa, but not to a foreign type such as a **Rock**.)

Truncation and rounding

When you are performing narrowing conversions, you must pay attention to issues of truncation and rounding. For example, if you cast from a floating point value to an integral value, what does Java do? For example, if you have the value 29.7 and you cast it to an **int**, is the resulting value 30 or 29? The answer to this can be seen in this example:

```
//: operators/CastingNumbers.java
// What happens when you cast a float
// or double to an integral value?
import static net.mindview.util.Print.*;

public class CastingNumbers {
  public static void main(String[] args) {
    double above = 0.7, below = 0.4;
    float fabove = 0.7f, fbelow = 0.4f;
    print("(int)above: " + (int)above);
    print("(int)below: " + (int)below);
    print("(int)fabove: " + (int)fabove);
    print("(int)fbelow: " + (int)fbelow);
  }
} /* Output:
(int)above: 0
(int)below: 0
(int)fabove: 0
(int)fbelow: 0
*///:~
```

So the answer is that casting from a **float** or **double** to an integral value always truncates the number. If instead you want the result to be rounded, use the **round( )** methods in **java.lang.Math**:

```
//: operators/RoundingNumbers.java
// Rounding floats and doubles.
import static net.mindview.util.Print.*;

public class RoundingNumbers {
  public static void main(String[] args) {
    double above = 0.7, below = 0.4;
    float fabove = 0.7f, fbelow = 0.4f;
    print("Math.round(above): " + Math.round(above));
    print("Math.round(below): " + Math.round(below));
    print("Math.round(fabove): " + Math.round(fabove));
    print("Math.round(fbelow): " + Math.round(fbelow));
  }
} /* Output:
Math.round(above): 1
Math.round(below): 0
Math.round(fabove): 1
Math.round(fbelow): 0
*///:~
```

Since the **round( )** is part of **java.lang**, you don't need an extra import to use it.

Promotion

You'll discover that if you perform any mathematical or bitwise operations on primitive data types that are smaller than an **int** (that is, **char**, **byte**, or **short**), those values will be promoted to **int** before performing the operations, and the resulting value will be of type **int**. So if you want to assign back into the smaller type, you must use a cast. (And, since you're assigning back into a smaller type, you might be losing information.) In general, the largest data type in an expression is the one that determines the size of the result of that expression; if you multiply a **float** and a **double**, the result will be **double**; if you add an **int** and a **long**, the result will be **long**.

Java has no "sizeof"

In C and C++, the **sizeof( )** operator tells you the number of bytes allocated for data items. The most compelling reason for **sizeof( )** in C and C++ is for portability. Different data types might be different sizes on different machines, so the programmer must discover how big those types are when performing operations that are sensitive to size. For example, one computer might store integers in 32 bits, whereas another might store integers as 16 bits. Programs could store larger values in integers on the first machine. As you might imagine, portability is a huge headache for C and C++ programmers.

Java does not need a **sizeof( )** operator for this purpose, because all the data types are the same size on all machines. You do not need to think about portability on this level—it is designed into the language.

A compendium of operators

The following example shows which primitive data types can be used with particular operators. Basically, it is the same example repeated over and over, but using different primitive data types. The file will compile without error because the lines that fail are commented out with a //!.

```
//: operators/AllOps.java
// Tests all the operators on all the primitive data types
// to show which ones are accepted by the Java compiler.

public class AllOps {
  // To accept the results of a boolean test:
  void f(boolean b) {}
  void boolTest(boolean x, boolean y) {
    // Arithmetic operators:
    //! x = x * y;
    //! x = x / y;
    //! x = x % y;
    //! x = x + y;
    //! x = x - y;
    //! x++;
    //! x--;
    //! x = +y;
    //! x = -y;
    // Relational and logical:
    //! f(x > y);
    //! f(x >= y);
    //! f(x < y);
    //! f(x <= y);
    f(x == y);
```

```
    f(x != y);
    f(!y);
    x = x && y;
    x = x || y;
    // Bitwise operators:
    //! x = ~y;
    x = x & y;
    x = x | y;
    x = x ^ y;
    //! x = x << 1;
    //! x = x >> 1;
    //! x = x >>> 1;
    // Compound assignment:
    //! x += y;
    //! x -= y;
    //! x *= y;
    //! x /= y;
    //! x %= y;
    //! x <<= 1;
    //! x >>= 1;
    //! x >>>= 1;
    x &= y;
    x ^= y;
    x |= y;
    // Casting:
    //! char c = (char)x;
    //! byte b = (byte)x;
    //! short s = (short)x;
    //! int i = (int)x;
    //! long l = (long)x;
    //! float f = (float)x;
    //! double d = (double)x;
  }
  void charTest(char x, char y) {
    // Arithmetic operators:
    x = (char)(x * y);
    x = (char)(x / y);
    x = (char)(x % y);
    x = (char)(x + y);
    x = (char)(x - y);
    x++;
    x--;
    x = (char)+y;
    x = (char)-y;
```

```
    // Relational and logical:
    f(x > y);
    f(x >= y);
    f(x < y);
    f(x <= y);
    f(x == y);
    f(x != y);
    //! f(!x);
    //! f(x && y);
    //! f(x || y);
    // Bitwise operators:
    x= (char)~y;
    x = (char)(x & y);
    x  = (char)(x | y);
    x = (char)(x ^ y);
    x = (char)(x << 1);
    x = (char)(x >> 1);
    x = (char)(x >>> 1);
    // Compound assignment:
    x += y;
    x -= y;
    x *= y;
    x /= y;
    x %= y;
    x <<= 1;
    x >>= 1;
    x >>>= 1;
    x &= y;
    x ^= y;
    x |= y;
    // Casting:
    //! boolean bl = (boolean)x;
    byte b = (byte)x;
    short s = (short)x;
    int i = (int)x;
    long l = (long)x;
    float f = (float)x;
    double d = (double)x;
  }
  void byteTest(byte x, byte y) {
    // Arithmetic operators:
    x = (byte)(x* y);
    x = (byte)(x / y);
    x = (byte)(x % y);
```

```
x = (byte)(x + y);
x = (byte)(x - y);
x++;
x--;
x = (byte)+ y;
x = (byte)- y;
// Relational and logical:
f(x > y);
f(x >= y);
f(x < y);
f(x <= y);
f(x == y);
f(x != y);
//! f(!x);
//! f(x && y);
//! f(x || y);
// Bitwise operators:
x = (byte)~y;
x = (byte)(x & y);
x = (byte)(x | y);
x = (byte)(x ^ y);
x = (byte)(x << 1);
x = (byte)(x >> 1);
x = (byte)(x >>> 1);
// Compound assignment:
x += y;
x -= y;
x *= y;
x /= y;
x %= y;
x <<= 1;
x >>= 1;
x >>>= 1;
x &= y;
x ^= y;
x |= y;
// Casting:
//! boolean bl = (boolean)x;
char c = (char)x;
short s = (short)x;
int i = (int)x;
long l = (long)x;
float f = (float)x;
double d = (double)x;
```

```
}
void shortTest(short x, short y) {
  // Arithmetic operators:
  x = (short)(x * y);
  x = (short)(x / y);
  x = (short)(x % y);
  x = (short)(x + y);
  x = (short)(x - y);
  x++;
  x--;
  x = (short)+y;
  x = (short)-y;
  // Relational and logical:
  f(x > y);
  f(x >= y);
  f(x < y);
  f(x <= y);
  f(x == y);
  f(x != y);
  //! f(!x);
  //! f(x && y);
  //! f(x || y);
  // Bitwise operators:
  x = (short)~y;
  x = (short)(x & y);
  x = (short)(x | y);
  x = (short)(x ^ y);
  x = (short)(x << 1);
  x = (short)(x >> 1);
  x = (short)(x >>> 1);
  // Compound assignment:
  x += y;
  x -= y;
  x *= y;
  x /= y;
  x %= y;
  x <<= 1;
  x >>= 1;
  x >>>= 1;
  x &= y;
  x ^= y;
  x |= y;
  // Casting:
  //! boolean bl = (boolean)x;
```

```
    char c = (char)x;
    byte b = (byte)x;
    int i = (int)x;
    long l = (long)x;
    float f = (float)x;
    double d = (double)x;
  }
  void intTest(int x, int y) {
    // Arithmetic operators:
    x = x * y;
    x = x / y;
    x = x % y;
    x = x + y;
    x = x - y;
    x++;
    x--;
    x = +y;
    x = -y;
    // Relational and logical:
    f(x > y);
    f(x >= y);
    f(x < y);
    f(x <= y);
    f(x == y);
    f(x != y);
    //! f(!x);
    //! f(x && y);
    //! f(x || y);
    // Bitwise operators:
    x = ~y;
    x = x & y;
    x = x | y;
    x = x ^ y;
    x = x << 1;
    x = x >> 1;
    x = x >>> 1;
    // Compound assignment:
    x += y;
    x -= y;
    x *= y;
    x /= y;
    x %= y;
    x <<= 1;
    x >>= 1;
```

```
    x >>>= 1;
    x &= y;
    x ^= y;
    x |= y;
    // Casting:
    //! boolean bl = (boolean)x;
    char c = (char)x;
    byte b = (byte)x;
    short s = (short)x;
    long l = (long)x;
    float f = (float)x;
    double d = (double)x;
  }
  void longTest(long x, long y) {
    // Arithmetic operators:
    x = x * y;
    x = x / y;
    x = x % y;
    x = x + y;
    x = x - y;
    x++;
    x--;
    x = +y;
    x = -y;
    // Relational and logical:
    f(x > y);
    f(x >= y);
    f(x < y);
    f(x <= y);
    f(x == y);
    f(x != y);
    //! f(!x);
    //! f(x && y);
    //! f(x || y);
    // Bitwise operators:
    x = ~y;
    x = x & y;
    x = x | y;
    x = x ^ y;
    x = x << 1;
    x = x >> 1;
    x = x >>> 1;
    // Compound assignment:
    x += y;
```

```
      x -= y;
      x *= y;
      x /= y;
      x %= y;
      x <<= 1;
      x >>= 1;
      x >>>= 1;
      x &= y;
      x ^= y;
      x |= y;
      // Casting:
      //! boolean bl = (boolean)x;
      char c = (char)x;
      byte b = (byte)x;
      short s = (short)x;
      int i = (int)x;
      float f = (float)x;
      double d = (double)x;
    }
    void floatTest(float x, float y) {
      // Arithmetic operators:
      x = x * y;
      x = x / y;
      x = x % y;
      x = x + y;
      x = x - y;
      x++;
      x--;
      x = +y;
      x = -y;
      // Relational and logical:
      f(x > y);
      f(x >= y);
      f(x < y);
      f(x <= y);
      f(x == y);
      f(x != y);
      //! f(!x);
      //! f(x && y);
      //! f(x || y);
      // Bitwise operators:
      //! x = ~y;
      //! x = x & y;
      //! x = x | y;
```

```
    //! x = x ^ y;
    //! x = x << 1;
    //! x = x >> 1;
    //! x = x >>> 1;
    // Compound assignment:
    x += y;
    x -= y;
    x *= y;
    x /= y;
    x %= y;
    //! x <<= 1;
    //! x >>= 1;
    //! x >>>= 1;
    //! x &= y;
    //! x ^= y;
    //! x |= y;
    // Casting:
    //! boolean bl = (boolean)x;
    char c = (char)x;
    byte b = (byte)x;
    short s = (short)x;
    int i = (int)x;
    long l = (long)x;
    double d = (double)x;
  }
  void doubleTest(double x, double y) {
    // Arithmetic operators:
    x = x * y;
    x = x / y;
    x = x % y;
    x = x + y;
    x = x - y;
    x++;
    x--;
    x = +y;
    x = -y;
    // Relational and logical:
    f(x > y);
    f(x >= y);
    f(x < y);
    f(x <= y);
    f(x == y);
    f(x != y);
    //! f(!x);
```

```
//! f(x && y);
//! f(x || y);
// Bitwise operators:
//! x = ~y;
//! x = x & y;
//! x = x | y;
//! x = x ^ y;
//! x = x << 1;
//! x = x >> 1;
//! x = x >>> 1;
// Compound assignment:
x += y;
x -= y;
x *= y;
x /= y;
x %= y;
//! x <<= 1;
//! x >>= 1;
//! x >>>= 1;
//! x &= y;
//! x ^= y;
//! x |= y;
// Casting:
//! boolean bl = (boolean)x;
char c = (char)x;
byte b = (byte)x;
short s = (short)x;
int i = (int)x;
long l = (long)x;
float f = (float)x;
  }
} ///:~
```

Note that **boolean** is quite limited. You can assign to it the values **true** and **false**, and you can test it for truth or falsehood, but you cannot add booleans or perform any other type of operation on them.

In **char**, **byte**, and **short**, you can see the effect of promotion with the arithmetic operators. Each arithmetic operation on any of those types produces an **int** result, which must be explicitly cast back to the original type (a narrowing conversion that might lose information) to assign back to that type. With **int** values, however, you do not need to cast, because everything is already an **int**. Don't be lulled into thinking everything is safe, though. If you multiply two **int**s that are big enough, you'll overflow the result. The following example demonstrates this:

```
//: operators/Overflow.java
// Surprise! Java lets you overflow.

public class Overflow {
  public static void main(String[] args) {
    int big = Integer.MAX_VALUE;
    System.out.println("big = " + big);
    int bigger = big * 4;
    System.out.println("bigger = " + bigger);
  }
} /* Output:
big = 2147483647
bigger = -4
*///:~
```

You get no errors or warnings from the compiler, and no exceptions at run time. Java is good, but it's not *that* good.

Compound assignments do *not* require casts for **char**, **byte**, or **short**, even though they are performing promotions that have the same results as the direct arithmetic operations. On the other hand, the lack of the cast certainly simplifies the code.

You can see that, with the exception of **boolean**, any primitive type can be cast to any other primitive type. Again, you must be aware of the effect of a narrowing conversion when casting to a smaller type; otherwise, you might unknowingly lose information during the cast.

Exercise 14: (3) Write a method that takes two **String** arguments and uses all the **boolean** comparisons to compare the two **String**s and print the results. For the == and !=, also perform the **equals( )** test. In **main( )**, call your method with some different **String** objects.

Summary

If you've had experience with any languages that use C-like syntax, you can see that the operators in Java are so similar that there is virtually no learning curve. If you found this chapter challenging, make sure you view the multimedia presentation *Thinking in C*, available at *www.MindView.net*.

Solutions to selected exercises can be found in the electronic document *The Thinking in Java Annotated Solution Guide*, available for sale from *www.MindView.net*.

Controlling
Execution

Like a sentient creature, a program must manipulate its world and make choices during execution. In Java you make choices with execution control statements.

Java uses all of C's execution control statements, so if you've programmed with C or C++, then most of what you see will be familiar. Most procedural programming languages have some kind of control statements, and there is often overlap among languages. In Java, the keywords include **if-else**, **while**, **do-while**, **for**, **return**, **break**, and a selection statement called **switch**. Java does not, however, support the much-maligned **goto** (which can still be the most expedient way to solve certain types of problems). You can still do a **goto**-like jump, but it is much more constrained than a typical **goto**.

true and false

All conditional statements use the truth or falsehood of a conditional expression to determine the execution path. An example of a conditional expression is **a == b**. This uses the conditional operator **==** to see if the value of **a** is equivalent to the value of **b**. The expression returns **true** or **false**. Any of the relational operators you've seen in the previous chapter can be used to produce a conditional statement. Note that Java doesn't allow you to use a number as a **boolean**, even though it's allowed in C and C++ (where truth is nonzero and falsehood is zero). If you want to use a non-**boolean** in a **boolean** test, such as **if(a)**, you must first convert it to a **boolean** value by using a conditional expression, such as **if(a != 0)**.

if-else

The **if-else** statement is the most basic way to control program flow. The **else** is optional, so you can use **if** in two forms:

```
if(Boolean-expression)
  statement
```

or

```
if(Boolean-expression)
  statement
else
  statement
```

The *Boolean-expression* must produce a **boolean** result. The *statement* is either a simple statement terminated by a semicolon, or a compound statement, which is a group of simple statements enclosed in braces. Whenever the word "*statement*" is used, it always implies that the statement can be simple or compound.

As an example of **if-else**, here is a **test( )** method that will tell you whether a guess is above, below, or equivalent to a target number:

```
//: control/IfElse.java
import static net.mindview.util.Print.*;

public class IfElse {
  static int result = 0;
  static void test(int testval, int target) {
    if(testval > target)
      result = +1;
    else if(testval < target)
      result = -1;
    else
      result = 0; // Match
  }
  public static void main(String[] args) {
    test(10, 5);
    print(result);
    test(5, 10);
    print(result);
    test(5, 5);
    print(result);
  }
} /* Output:
1
-1
0
*///:~
```

In the middle of **test( )**, you'll also see an "**else if**," which is not a new keyword but just an **else** followed by a new **if** statement.

Although Java, like C and C++ before it, is a "free-form" language, it is conventional to indent the body of a control flow statement so the reader can easily determine where it begins and ends.

Iteration

Looping is controlled by **while**, **do-while** and **for**, which are sometimes classified as *iteration statements*. A statement repeats until the controlling *Boolean-expression* evaluates to **false**. The form for a **while** loop is:

```
while(Boolean-expression)
  statement
```

The *Boolean-expression* is evaluated once at the beginning of the loop and again before each further iteration of the statement.

Here's a simple example that generates random numbers until a particular condition is met:

```
//: control/WhileTest.java
// Demonstrates the while loop.

public class WhileTest {
  static boolean condition() {
    boolean result = Math.random() < 0.99;
    System.out.print(result + ", ");
    return result;
  }
  public static void main(String[] args) {
    while(condition())
      System.out.println("Inside 'while'");
    System.out.println("Exited 'while'");
  }
} /* (Execute to see output) *///:~
```

The **condition( )** method uses the **static** method **random( )** in the **Math** library, which generates a **double** value between 0 and 1. (It includes 0, but not 1.) The **result** value comes from the comparison operator <, which produces a **boolean** result. If you print a **boolean** value, you automatically get the appropriate string "true" or "false." The conditional expression for the

---

while says: "repeat the statements in the body as long as **condition( )** returns **true**."

do-while

The form for **do-while** is

```
do
  statement
while(Boolean-expression);
```

The sole difference between **while** and **do-while** is that the statement of the **do-while** always executes at least once, even if the expression evaluates to **false** the first time. In a **while**, if the conditional is **false** the first time the statement never executes. In practice, **do-while** is less common than **while**.

for

A **for** loop is perhaps the most commonly used form of iteration. This loop performs initialization before the first iteration. Then it performs conditional testing and, at the end of each iteration, some form of "stepping." The form of the **for** loop is:

```
for(initialization; Boolean-expression; step)
  statement
```

Any of the expressions *initialization*, *Boolean-expression* or *step* can be empty. The expression is tested before each iteration, and as soon as it evaluates to **false**, execution will continue at the line following the **for** statement. At the end of each loop, the *step* executes.

for loops are usually used for "counting" tasks:

```
//: control/ListCharacters.java
// Demonstrates "for" loop by listing
// all the lowercase ASCII letters.

public class ListCharacters {
  public static void main(String[] args) {
    for(char c = 0; c < 128; c++)
      if(Character.isLowerCase(c))
        System.out.println("value: " + (int)c +
          " character: " + c);
  }
} /* Output:
```

```
value: 97 character: a
value: 98 character: b
value: 99 character: c
value: 100 character: d
value: 101 character: e
value: 102 character: f
value: 103 character: g
value: 104 character: h
value: 105 character: i
value: 106 character: j
...
*///:~
```

Note that the variable **c** is defined at the point where it is used, inside the control expression of the **for** loop, rather than at the beginning of **main( )**. The scope of **c** is the statement controlled by the **for**.

This program also uses the **java.lang.Character** "wrapper" class, which not only wraps the primitive **char** type in an object, but also provides other utilities. Here, the **static isLowerCase( )** method is used to detect whether the character in question is a lowercase letter.

Traditional procedural languages like C require that all variables be defined at the beginning of a block so that when the compiler creates a block, it can allocate space for those variables. In Java and C++, you can spread your variable declarations throughout the block, defining them at the point that you need them. This allows a more natural coding style and makes code easier to understand.

Exercise 1: (1) Write a program that prints values from 1 to 100.

Exercise 2: (2) Write a program that generates 25 random **int** values. For each value, use an **if-else** statement to classify it as greater than, less than, or equal to a second randomly generated value.

Exercise 3: (1) Modify Exercise 2 so that your code is surrounded by an "infinite" **while** loop. It will then run until you interrupt it from the keyboard (typically by pressing Control-C).

Exercise 4: (3) Write a program that uses two nested **for** loops and the modulus operator (%) to detect and print prime numbers (integral numbers that are not evenly divisible by any other numbers except for themselves and 1).

Exercise 5: (4) Repeat Exercise 10 from the previous chapter, using the ternary operator and a bitwise test to display the ones and zeroes, instead of **Integer.toBinaryString( )**.

The comma operator

The comma *operator* (not the comma *separator*, which is used to separate definitions and method arguments) has only one use in Java: in the control expression of a **for** loop. In both the initialization and step portions of the control expression, you can have a number of statements separated by commas, and those statements will be evaluated sequentially.

Using the comma operator, you can define multiple variables within a **for** statement, but they must be of the same type:

```
//: control/CommaOperator.java

public class CommaOperator {
  public static void main(String[] args) {
    for(int i = 1, j = i + 10; i < 5; i++, j = i * 2) {
      System.out.println("i = " + i + " j = " + j);
    }
  }
} /* Output:
i = 1 j = 11
i = 2 j = 4
i = 3 j = 6
i = 4 j = 8
*///:~
```

The **int** definition in the **for** statement covers both **i** and **j**. The initialization portion can have any number of definitions *of one type*. The ability to define variables in a control expression is limited to the **for** loop. You cannot use this approach with any of the other selection or iteration statements.

You can see that in both the initialization and step portions, the statements are evaluated in sequential order.

Foreach syntax

Java SE5 introduces a new and more succinct **for** syntax, for use with arrays and containers (you'll learn more about these in the *Arrays* and *Containers* *in Depth* chapter). This is often called the *foreach syntax*, and it means that you don't have to create an **int** to count through a sequence of items—the foreach produces each item for you, automatically.

For example, suppose you have an array of **float** and you'd like to select each element in that array:

```
//: control/ForEachFloat.java
import java.util.*;

public class ForEachFloat {
  public static void main(String[] args) {
    Random rand = new Random(47);
    float f[] = new float[10];
    for(int i = 0; i < 10; i++)
      f[i] = rand.nextFloat();
    for(float x : f)
      System.out.println(x);
  }
} /* Output:
0.72711575
0.39982635
0.5309454
0.0534122
0.16020656
0.57799757
0.18847865
0.4170137
0.51660204
0.73734957
*///:~
```

The array is populated using the old **for** loop, because it must be accessed with an index. You can see the foreach syntax in the line:

```
    for(float x : f) {
```

This defines a variable **x** of type **float** and sequentially assigns each element of **f** to **x**.

Any method that returns an array is a candidate for use with foreach. For example, the **String** class has a method **toCharArray( )** that returns an array of **char**, so you can easily iterate through the characters in a string:

```
//: control/ForEachString.java
```

```
public class ForEachString {
  public static void main(String[] args) {
    for(char c : "An African Swallow".toCharArray() )
      System.out.print(c + " ");
  }
} /* Output:
A n   A f r i c a n   S w a l l o w
*///:~
```

As you'll see in the *Holding Your Objects* chapter, foreach will also work with any object that is **Iterable**.

Many **for** statements involve stepping through a sequence of integral values, like this:

```
for(int i = 0; i < 100; i++)
```

For these, the foreach syntax won't work unless you want to create an array of **int** first. To simplify this task, I've created a method called **range( )** in **net.mindview.util.Range** that automatically generates the appropriate array. My intent is for **range( )** to be used as a **static** import:

```
//: control/ForEachInt.java
import static net.mindview.util.Range.*;
import static net.mindview.util.Print.*;

public class ForEachInt {
  public static void main(String[] args) {
    for(int i : range(10)) // 0..9
      printnb(i + " ");
    print();
    for(int i : range(5, 10)) // 5..9
      printnb(i + " ");
    print();
    for(int i : range(5, 20, 3)) // 5..20 step 3
      printnb(i + " ");
    print();
  }
} /* Output:
0 1 2 3 4 5 6 7 8 9
5 6 7 8 9
5 8 11 14 17
*///:~
```

The **range( )** method has been *overloaded*, which means the same method name can be used with different argument lists (you'll learn about overloading soon). The first overloaded form of **range( )** just starts at zero and produces values up to but not including the top end of the range. The second form starts at the first value and goes until one less than the second, and the third form has a step value so it increases by that value. **range( )** is a very simple version of what's called a *generator*, which you'll see later in the book.

Note that although **range( )** allows the use of the foreach syntax in more places, and thus arguably increases readability, it is a little less efficient, so if you are tuning for performance you may want to use a *profiler*, which is a tool that measures the performance of your code.

You'll note the use of **printnb( )** in addition to **print( )**. The **printnb( )** method does not emit a newline, so it allows you to output a line in pieces.

The foreach syntax not only saves time when typing in code. More importantly, it is far easier to read and says *what* you are trying to do (get each element of the array) rather than giving the details of *how* you are doing it ("I'm creating this index so I can use it to select each of the array elements."). The foreach syntax will be used whenever possible in this book.

return

Several keywords represent *unconditional branching*, which simply means that the branch happens without any test. These include **return, break, continue**, and a way to jump to a labeled statement which is similar to the **goto** in other languages.

The **return** keyword has two purposes: It specifies what value a method will return (if it doesn't have a **void** return value) and it causes the current method to exit, returning that value. The preceding **test( )** method can be rewritten to take advantage of this:

```
//: control/IfElse2.java
import static net.mindview.util.Print.*;

public class IfElse2 {
  static int test(int testval, int target) {
    if(testval > target)
      return +1;
```

```
      else if(testval < target)
        return -1;
      else
        return 0; // Match
    }
  public static void main(String[] args) {
    print(test(10, 5));
    print(test(5, 10));
    print(test(5, 5));
    }
} /* Output:
1
-1
0
*///:~
```

There's no need for **else**, because the method will not continue after executing a **return**.

If you do not have a **return** statement in a method that returns **void**, there's an implicit **return** at the end of that method, so it's not always necessary to include a **return** statement. However, if your method states it will return anything other than **void**, you must ensure every code path will return a value.

Exercise 6: (2) Modify the two **test( )** methods in **IfElse.java** and **IfElse2.java** so that they take two extra arguments, **begin** and **end**, and so that **testval** is tested to see if it is within the range between (and including) **begin** and **end**.

break and **continue**

You can also control the flow of the loop inside the body of any of the iteration statements by using **break** and **continue**. **break** quits the loop without executing the rest of the statements in the loop. **continue** stops the execution of the current iteration and goes back to the beginning of the loop to begin the next iteration.

This program shows examples of **break** and **continue** within **for** and **while** loops:

```
//: control/BreakAndContinue.java
// Demonstrates break and continue keywords.
import static net.mindview.util.Range.*;
```

```
public class BreakAndContinue {
  public static void main(String[] args) {
    for(int i = 0; i < 100; i++) {
      if(i == 74) break; // Out of for loop
      if(i % 9 != 0) continue; // Next iteration
      System.out.print(i + " ");
    }
    System.out.println();
    // Using foreach:
    for(int i : range(100)) {
      if(i == 74) break; // Out of for loop
      if(i % 9 != 0) continue; // Next iteration
      System.out.print(i + " ");
    }
    System.out.println();
    int i = 0;
    // An "infinite loop":
    while(true) {
      i++;
      int j = i * 27;
      if(j == 1269) break; // Out of loop
      if(i % 10 != 0) continue; // Top of loop
      System.out.print(i + " ");
    }
  }
} /* Output:
0 9 18 27 36 45 54 63 72
0 9 18 27 36 45 54 63 72
10 20 30 40
*///:~
```

In the **for** loop, the value of **i** never gets to 100 because the **break** statement breaks out of the loop when **i** is 74. Normally, you'd use a **break** like this only if you didn't know when the terminating condition was going to occur. The **continue** statement causes execution to go back to the top of the iteration loop (thus incrementing **i**) whenever **i** is not evenly divisible by 9. When it is, the value is printed.

The second **for** loop shows the use of foreach, and that it produces the same results.

Finally, you see an "infinite" **while** loop that would, in theory, continue forever. However, inside the loop there is a **break** statement that will break out of the loop. In addition, you'll see that the **continue** statement moves control back to the top of the loop without completing anything after that **continue** statement. (Thus printing happens in the second loop only when the value of **i** is divisible by 10.) In the output, the value 0 is printed, because 0 % 9 produces 0.

Another form of the infinite loop is **for(;;)**. The compiler treats both **while(true)** and **for(;;)** in the same way, so whichever one you use is a matter of programming taste.

Exercise 7: Modify Exercise 1 so that the program exits by using the **break** keyword at value 99. Try using **return** instead.

The infamous "goto"

The **goto** keyword has been present in programming languages from the beginning. Indeed, **goto** was the genesis of program control in assembly language: "If condition A, then jump here; otherwise, jump there." If you read the assembly code that is ultimately generated by virtually any compiler, you'll see that program control contains many jumps (the Java compiler produces its own "assembly code," but this code is run by the Java Virtual Machine rather than directly on a hardware CPU).

A **goto** is a jump at the source-code level, and that's what brought it into disrepute. If a program will always jump from one point to another, isn't there some way to reorganize the code so the flow of control is not so jumpy? **goto** fell into true disfavor with the publication of the famous "Goto considered harmful" paper by Edsger Dijkstra, and since then **goto**-bashing has been a popular sport, with advocates of the cast-out keyword scurrying for cover.

As is typical in situations like this, the middle ground is the most fruitful. The problem is not the use of **goto**, but the overuse of **goto**; in rare situations **goto** is actually the best way to structure control flow.

Although **goto** is a reserved word in Java, it is not used in the language; Java has no **goto**. However, it does have something that looks a bit like a jump tied in with the **break** and **continue** keywords. It's not a jump but rather a way to break out of an iteration statement. The reason it's often thrown in with discussions of **goto** is because it uses the same mechanism: a label.

A label is an identifier followed by a colon, like this:

```
label1:
```

The *only* place a label is useful in Java is right before an iteration statement. And that means *right* before—it does no good to put any other statement between the label and the iteration. And the sole reason to put a label before an iteration is if you're going to nest another iteration or a **switch** (which you'll learn about shortly) inside it. That's because the **break** and **continue** keywords will normally interrupt only the current loop, but when used with a label, they'll interrupt the loops up to where the label exists:

```
label1:
outer-iteration {
  inner-iteration {
    //...
    break; // (1)
    //...
    continue;  // (2)
    //...
    continue label1; // (3)
    //...
    break label1;  // (4)
  }
}
```

In **(1)**, the **break** breaks out of the inner iteration and you end up in the outer iteration. In **(2)**, the **continue** moves back to the beginning of the inner iteration. But in **(3)**, the **continue label1** breaks out of the inner iteration *and* the outer iteration, all the way back to **label1**. Then it does in fact continue the iteration, but starting at the outer iteration. In **(4)**, the **break label1** also breaks all the way out to **label1**, but it does not reenter the iteration. It actually does break out of both iterations.

Here is an example using **for** loops:

```
//: control/LabeledFor.java
// For loops with "labeled break" and "labeled continue."
import static net.mindview.util.Print.*;

public class LabeledFor {
  public static void main(String[] args) {
    int i = 0;
    outer: // Can't have statements here
    for(; true ;) { // infinite loop
      inner: // Can't have statements here
```

```java
    for(; i < 10; i++) {
      print("i = " + i);
      if(i == 2) {
        print("continue");
        continue;
      }
      if(i == 3) {
        print("break");
        i++; // Otherwise i never
             // gets incremented.
        break;
      }
      if(i == 7) {
        print("continue outer");
        i++; // Otherwise i never
             // gets incremented.
        continue outer;
      }
      if(i == 8) {
        print("break outer");
        break outer;
      }
      for(int k = 0; k < 5; k++) {
        if(k == 3) {
          print("continue inner");
          continue inner;
        }
      }
    }
  }
  // Can't break or continue to labels here
  }
} /* Output:
i = 0
continue inner
i = 1
continue inner
i = 2
continue
i = 3
break
i = 4
continue inner
i = 5
```

```
continue inner
i = 6
continue inner
i = 7
continue outer
i = 8
break outer
*///:~
```

Note that **break** breaks out of the **for** loop, and that the increment expression doesn't occur until the end of the pass through the **for** loop. Since **break** skips the increment expression, the increment is performed directly in the case of **i == 3**. The **continue outer** statement in the case of **i == 7** also goes to the top of the loop and also skips the increment, so it too is incremented directly.

If not for the **break outer** statement, there would be no way to get out of the outer loop from within an inner loop, since **break** by itself can break out of only the innermost loop. (The same is true for **continue**.)

Of course, in the cases where breaking out of a loop will also exit the method, you can simply use a **return**.

Here is a demonstration of labeled **break** and **continue** statements with **while** loops:

```
//: control/LabeledWhile.java
// While loops with "labeled break" and "labeled continue."
import static net.mindview.util.Print.*;

public class LabeledWhile {
  public static void main(String[] args) {
    int i = 0;
    outer:
    while(true) {
      print("Outer while loop");
      while(true) {
        i++;
        print("i = " + i);
        if(i == 1) {
          print("continue");
          continue;
        }
        if(i == 3) {
```

```
            print("continue outer");
            continue outer;
        }
        if(i == 5) {
            print("break");
            break;
        }
        if(i == 7) {
            print("break outer");
            break outer;
        }
    }
}
} /* Output:
Outer while loop
i = 1
continue
i = 2
i = 3
continue outer
Outer while loop
i = 4
i = 5
break
Outer while loop
i = 6
i = 7
break outer
*///:~
```

The same rules hold true for **while**:

1. A plain **continue** goes to the top of the innermost loop and continues.

2. A labeled **continue** goes to the label and reenters the loop right after that label.

3. A **break** "drops out of the bottom" of the loop.

4. A labeled **break** drops out of the bottom of the end of the loop denoted by the label.

Thinking in Java Bruce Eckel

It's important to remember that the *only* reason to use labels in Java is when you have nested loops and you want to **break** or **continue** through more than one nested level.

In Dijkstra's "Goto considered harmful" paper, what he specifically objected to was the labels, not the **goto**. He observed that the number of bugs seems to increase with the number of labels in a program, and that labels and **goto**s make programs difficult to analyze. Note that Java labels don't suffer from this problem, since they are constrained in their placement and can't be used to transfer control in an ad hoc manner. It's also interesting to note that this is a case where a language feature is made more useful by restricting the power of the statement.

switch

The **switch** is sometimes called a *selection statement*. The **switch** statement selects from among pieces of code based on the value of an integral expression. Its general form is:

```
switch(integral-selector) {
  case integral-value1 : statement; break;
  case integral-value2 : statement; break;
  case integral-value3 : statement; break;
  case integral-value4 : statement; break;
  case integral-value5 : statement; break;
  // ...
  default: statement;
}
```

Integral-selector is an expression that produces an integral value. The **switch** compares the result of *integral-selector* to each *integral-value*. If it finds a match, the corresponding *statement* (a single statement or multiple statements; braces are not required) executes. If no match occurs, the **default** *statement* executes.

You will notice in the preceding definition that each **case** ends with a **break**, which causes execution to jump to the end of the **switch** body. This is the conventional way to build a **switch** statement, but the **break** is optional. If it is missing, the code for the following **case** statements executes until a **break** is encountered. Although you don't usually want this kind of behavior, it can be useful to an experienced programmer. Note that the last statement, following the **default**, doesn't have a **break** because the execution just falls through to where the **break** would have taken it anyway. You could put a **break** at the end of the **default** statement with no harm if you considered it important for style's sake.

The **switch** statement is a clean way to implement multiway selection (i.e., selecting from among a number of different execution paths), but it requires a selector that evaluates to an integral value, such as **int** or **char**. If you want to use, for example, a string or a floating point number as a selector, it won't work in a **switch** statement. For non-integral types, you must use a series of **if** statements. At the end of the next chapter, you'll see that Java SE5's new **enum** feature helps ease this restriction, as **enum**s are designed to work nicely with **switch**.

Here's an example that creates letters randomly and determines whether they're vowels or consonants:

```
//: control/VowelsAndConsonants.java
// Demonstrates the switch statement.
import java.util.*;
import static net.mindview.util.Print.*;

public class VowelsAndConsonants {
  public static void main(String[] args) {
    Random rand = new Random(47);
    for(int i = 0; i < 100; i++) {
      int c = rand.nextInt(26) + 'a';
      printnb((char)c + ", " + c + ": ");
      switch(c) {
        case 'a':
        case 'e':
        case 'i':
        case 'o':
        case 'u': print("vowel");
                  break;
        case 'y':
        case 'w': print("Sometimes a vowel");
                  break;
        default:  print("consonant");
      }
    }
  }
} /* Output:
y, 121: Sometimes a vowel
n, 110: consonant
```

```
z, 122: consonant
b, 98: consonant
r, 114: consonant
n, 110: consonant
y, 121: Sometimes a vowel
g, 103: consonant
c, 99: consonant
f, 102: consonant
o, 111: vowel
w, 119: Sometimes a vowel
z, 122: consonant
...
*///:~
```

Since **Random.nextInt(26)** generates a value between 0 and 25, you need only add an offset of '**a**' to produce the lowercase letters. The single-quoted characters in the **case** statements also produce integral values that are used for comparison.

Notice how the **case**s can be "stacked" on top of each other to provide multiple matches for a particular piece of code. You should also be aware that it's essential to put the **break** statement at the end of a particular case; otherwise, control will simply drop through and continue processing on the next case.

In the statement:

```
int c = rand.nextInt(26) + 'a';
```

Random.nextInt( ) produces a random **int** value from 0 to 25, which is added to the value of '**a**'. This means that '**a**' is automatically converted to an **int** to perform the addition.

In order to print **c** as a character, it must be cast to **char**; otherwise, you'll produce integral output.

Exercise 8: (2) Create a **switch** statement that prints a message for each **case**, and put the **switch** inside a **for** loop that tries each **case**. Put a **break** after each **case** and test it, then remove the **break**s and see what happens.

Exercise 9: (4) A *Fibonacci sequence* is the sequence of numbers 1, 1, 2, 3, 5, 8, 13, 21, 34, and so on, where each number (from the third on) is the sum of the previous two. Create a method that takes an integer as an argument and displays that many Fibonacci numbers starting from the beginning, e.g.,

---

If you run **java Fibonacci 5** (where **Fibonacci** is the name of the class) the output will be: 1, 1, 2, 3, 5.

Exercise 10: (5) A *vampire number* has an even number of digits and is formed by multiplying a pair of numbers containing half the number of digits of the result. The digits are taken from the original number in any order. Pairs of trailing zeroes are not allowed. Examples include:

$1260 = 21 * 60$
$1827 = 21 * 87$
$2187 = 27 * 81$

Write a program that finds all the 4-digit vampire numbers. (Suggested by Dan Forhan.)

Summary

This chapter concludes the study of fundamental features that appear in most programming languages: calculation, operator precedence, type casting, and selection and iteration. Now you're ready to begin taking steps that move you closer to the world of object-oriented programming. The next chapter will cover the important issues of initialization and cleanup of objects, followed in the subsequent chapter by the essential concept of implementation hiding.

Solutions to selected exercises can be found in the electronic document *The Thinking in Java Annotated Solution Guide*, available for sale from *www.MindView.net*.

Initialization
& Cleanup

As the computer revolution progresses, "unsafe" programming has become one of the major culprits that makes programming expensive.

Two of these safety issues are *initialization* and *cleanup*. Many C bugs occur when the programmer forgets to initialize a variable. This is especially true with libraries when users don't know how to initialize a library component, or even that they must. Cleanup is a special problem because it's easy to forget about an element when you're done with it, since it no longer concerns you. Thus, the resources used by that element are retained and you can easily end up running out of resources (most notably, memory).

C++ introduced the concept of a *constructor*, a special method automatically called when an object is created. Java also adopted the constructor, and in addition has a garbage collector that automatically releases memory resources when they're no longer being used. This chapter examines the issues of initialization and cleanup, and their support in Java.

Guaranteed initialization
with the constructor

You can imagine creating a method called **initialize( )** for every class you write. The name is a hint that it should be called before using the object. Unfortunately, this means the user must remember to call that method. In Java, the class designer can guarantee initialization of every object by providing a constructor. If a class has a constructor, Java automatically calls that constructor when an object is created, before users can even get their hands on it. So initialization is guaranteed.

The next challenge is what to name this method. There are two issues. The first is that any name you use could clash with a name you might like to use as a member in the class. The second is that because the compiler is responsible for calling the constructor, it must always know which method to call. The C++ solution seems the easiest and most logical, so it's also used in Java: The name of the constructor is the same as the name of the class. It makes sense that such a method will be called automatically during initialization.

Here's a simple class with a constructor:

```
//: initialization/SimpleConstructor.java
// Demonstration of a simple constructor.

class Rock {
  Rock() { // This is the constructor
    System.out.print("Rock ");
  }
}

public class SimpleConstructor {
  public static void main(String[] args) {
    for(int i = 0; i < 10; i++)
      new Rock();
  }
} /* Output:
Rock Rock Rock Rock Rock Rock Rock Rock Rock Rock
*///:~
```

Now, when an object is created:

```
new Rock();
```

storage is allocated and the constructor is called. It is guaranteed that the object will be properly initialized before you can get your hands on it.

Note that the coding style of making the first letter of all methods lowercase does not apply to constructors, since the name of the constructor must match the name of the class *exactly*.

A constructor that takes no arguments is called the *default constructor*. The Java documents typically use the term *no-arg* constructor, but "default constructor" has been in use for many years before Java appeared, so I will tend to use that. But like any method, the constructor can also have arguments to allow you to specify *how* an object is created. The preceding example can easily be changed so the constructor takes an argument:

```
//: initialization/SimpleConstructor2.java
// Constructors can have arguments.

class Rock2 {
  Rock2(int i) {
    System.out.print("Rock " + i + " ");
  }
}

public class SimpleConstructor2 {
  public static void main(String[] args) {
    for(int i = 0; i < 8; i++)
      new Rock2(i);
  }
} /* Output:
Rock 0 Rock 1 Rock 2 Rock 3 Rock 4 Rock 5 Rock 6 Rock 7
*///:~
```

Constructor arguments provide you with a way to provide parameters for the initialization of an object. For example, if the class **Tree** has a constructor that takes a single integer argument denoting the height of the tree, you create a **Tree** object like this:

```
Tree t = new Tree(12);  // 12-foot tree
```

If **Tree(int)** is your only constructor, then the compiler won't let you create a **Tree** object any other way.

Constructors eliminate a large class of problems and make the code easier to read. In the preceding code fragment, for example, you don't see an explicit call to some **initialize( )** method that is conceptually separate from creation. In Java, creation and initialization are unified concepts—you can't have one without the other.

The constructor is an unusual type of method because it has no return value. This is distinctly different from a **void** return value, in which the method returns nothing but you still have the option to make it return something else. Constructors return nothing and you don't have an option (the **new** expression does return a reference to the newly created object, but the constructor itself has no return value). If there were a return value, and if you could select your own, the compiler would somehow need to know what to do with that return value.

Exercise 1: (1) Create a class containing an uninitialized **String** reference. Demonstrate that this reference is initialized by Java to **null**.

Exercise 2: (2) Create a class with a **String** field that is initialized at the point of definition, and another one that is initialized by the constructor. What is the difference between the two approaches?

Method overloading

One of the important features in any programming language is the use of names. When you create an object, you give a name to a region of storage. A method is a name for an action. You refer to all objects and methods by using names. Well-chosen names create a system that is easier for people to understand and change. It's a lot like writing prose—the goal is to communicate with your readers.

A problem arises when mapping the concept of nuance in human language onto a programming language. Often, the same word expresses a number of different meanings—it's *overloaded*. This is useful, especially when it comes to trivial differences. You say, "Wash the shirt," "Wash the car," and "Wash the dog." It would be silly to be forced to say, "shirtWash the shirt," "carWash the car," and "dogWash the dog" just so the listener doesn't need to make any distinction about the action performed. Most human languages are redundant, so even if you miss a few words, you can still determine the meaning. You don't need unique identifiers—you can deduce meaning from context.

Most programming languages (C in particular) require you to have a unique identifier for each method (often called *functions* in those languages). So you could *not* have one function called **print( )** for printing integers and another called **print( )** for printing floats—each function requires a unique name.

In Java (and C++), another factor forces the overloading of method names: the constructor. Because the constructor's name is predetermined by the name of the class, there can be only one constructor name. But what if you want to create an object in more than one way? For example, suppose you build a class that can initialize itself in a standard way or by reading information from a file. You need two constructors, the default constructor and one that takes a **String** as an argument, which is the name of the file from which to initialize the object. Both are constructors, so they must have the same name—the name of the class. Thus, *method overloading* is essential to allow the same method name to be used with different argument types. And although method overloading is a must for constructors, it's a general convenience and can be used with any method.

Here's an example that shows both overloaded constructors and overloaded methods:

```java
//: initialization/Overloading.java
// Demonstration of both constructor
// and ordinary method overloading.
import static net.mindview.util.Print.*;

class Tree {
  int height;
  Tree() {
    print("Planting a seedling");
    height = 0;
  }
  Tree(int initialHeight) {
    height = initialHeight;
    print("Creating new Tree that is " +
      height + " feet tall");
  }
  void info() {
    print("Tree is " + height + " feet tall");
  }
  void info(String s) {
    print(s + ": Tree is " + height + " feet tall");
  }
}

public class Overloading {
  public static void main(String[] args) {
    for(int i = 0; i < 5; i++) {
      Tree t = new Tree(i);
      t.info();
      t.info("overloaded method");
    }
    // Overloaded constructor:
    new Tree();
  }
} /* Output:
Creating new Tree that is 0 feet tall
Tree is 0 feet tall
```

```
overloaded method: Tree is 0 feet tall
Creating new Tree that is 1 feet tall
Tree is 1 feet tall
overloaded method: Tree is 1 feet tall
Creating new Tree that is 2 feet tall
Tree is 2 feet tall
overloaded method: Tree is 2 feet tall
Creating new Tree that is 3 feet tall
Tree is 3 feet tall
overloaded method: Tree is 3 feet tall
Creating new Tree that is 4 feet tall
Tree is 4 feet tall
overloaded method: Tree is 4 feet tall
Planting a seedling
*///:~
```

A **Tree** object can be created either as a seedling, with no argument, or as a
plant grown in a nursery, with an existing height. To support this, there is a
default constructor, and one that takes the existing height.

You might also want to call the **info( )** method in more than one way. For
example, if you have an extra message you want printed, you can use
info(String), and **info( )** if you have nothing more to say. It would seem
strange to give two separate names to what is obviously the same concept.
Fortunately, method overloading allows you to use the same name for both.

Distinguishing overloaded methods

If the methods have the same name, how can Java know which method you
mean? There's a simple rule: Each overloaded method must take a unique list
of argument types.

If you think about this for a second, it makes sense. How else could a
programmer tell the difference between two methods that have the same
name, other than by the types of their arguments?

Even differences in the ordering of arguments are sufficient to distinguish
two methods, although you don't normally want to take this approach
because it produces difficult-to-maintain code:

```
//: initialization/OverloadingOrder.java
// Overloading based on the order of the arguments.
import static net.mindview.util.Print.*;
```

```java
public class OverloadingOrder {
  static void f(String s, int i) {
    print("String: " + s + ", int: " + i);
  }
  static void f(int i, String s) {
    print("int: " + i + ", String: " + s);
  }
  public static void main(String[] args) {
    f("String first", 11);
    f(99, "Int first");
  }
} /* Output:
String: String first, int: 11
int: 99, String: Int first
*///:~
```

The two **f( )** methods have identical arguments, but the order is different, and that's what makes them distinct.

Overloading with primitives

A primitive can be automatically promoted from a smaller type to a larger one, and this can be slightly confusing in combination with overloading. The following example demonstrates what happens when a primitive is handed to an overloaded method:

```java
//: initialization/PrimitiveOverloading.java
// Promotion of primitives and overloading.
import static net.mindview.util.Print.*;

public class PrimitiveOverloading {
  void f1(char x) { printnb("f1(char) "); }
  void f1(byte x) { printnb("f1(byte) "); }
  void f1(short x) { printnb("f1(short) "); }
  void f1(int x) { printnb("f1(int) "); }
  void f1(long x) { printnb("f1(long) "); }
  void f1(float x) { printnb("f1(float) "); }
  void f1(double x) { printnb("f1(double) "); }

  void f2(byte x) { printnb("f2(byte) "); }
  void f2(short x) { printnb("f2(short) "); }
  void f2(int x) { printnb("f2(int) "); }
  void f2(long x) { printnb("f2(long) "); }
  void f2(float x) { printnb("f2(float) "); }
```

```
void f2(double x) { printnb("f2(double) "); }

void f3(short x) { printnb("f3(short) "); }
void f3(int x) { printnb("f3(int) "); }
void f3(long x) { printnb("f3(long) "); }
void f3(float x) { printnb("f3(float) "); }
void f3(double x) { printnb("f3(double) "); }

void f4(int x) { printnb("f4(int) "); }
void f4(long x) { printnb("f4(long) "); }
void f4(float x) { printnb("f4(float) "); }
void f4(double x) { printnb("f4(double) "); }

void f5(long x) { printnb("f5(long) "); }
void f5(float x) { printnb("f5(float) "); }
void f5(double x) { printnb("f5(double) "); }

void f6(float x) { printnb("f6(float) "); }
void f6(double x) { printnb("f6(double) "); }

void f7(double x) { printnb("f7(double) "); }

void testConstVal() {
  printnb("5: ");
  f1(5);f2(5);f3(5);f4(5);f5(5);f6(5);f7(5); print();
}
void testChar() {
  char x = 'x';
  printnb("char: ");
  f1(x);f2(x);f3(x);f4(x);f5(x);f6(x);f7(x); print();
}
void testByte() {
  byte x = 0;
  printnb("byte: ");
  f1(x);f2(x);f3(x);f4(x);f5(x);f6(x);f7(x); print();
}
void testShort() {
  short x = 0;
  printnb("short: ");
  f1(x);f2(x);f3(x);f4(x);f5(x);f6(x);f7(x); print();
}
void testInt() {
  int x = 0;
  printnb("int: ");
```

```
      f1(x);f2(x);f3(x);f4(x);f5(x);f6(x);f7(x); print();
    }
    void testLong() {
      long x = 0;
      printnb("long: ");
      f1(x);f2(x);f3(x);f4(x);f5(x);f6(x);f7(x); print();
    }
    void testFloat() {
      float x = 0;
      printnb("float: ");
      f1(x);f2(x);f3(x);f4(x);f5(x);f6(x);f7(x); print();
    }
    void testDouble() {
      double x = 0;
      printnb("double: ");
      f1(x);f2(x);f3(x);f4(x);f5(x);f6(x);f7(x); print();
    }
    public static void main(String[] args) {
      PrimitiveOverloading p =
        new PrimitiveOverloading();
      p.testConstVal();
      p.testChar();
      p.testByte();
      p.testShort();
      p.testInt();
      p.testLong();
      p.testFloat();
      p.testDouble();
    }
} /* Output:
5: f1(int) f2(int) f3(int) f4(int) f5(long) f6(float)
f7(double)
char: f1(char) f2(int) f3(int) f4(int) f5(long) f6(float)
f7(double)
byte: f1(byte) f2(byte) f3(short) f4(int) f5(long)
f6(float) f7(double)
short: f1(short) f2(short) f3(short) f4(int) f5(long)
f6(float) f7(double)
int: f1(int) f2(int) f3(int) f4(int) f5(long) f6(float)
f7(double)
long: f1(long) f2(long) f3(long) f4(long) f5(long)
f6(float) f7(double)
float: f1(float) f2(float) f3(float) f4(float) f5(float)
f6(float) f7(double)
```

```
double: f1(double) f2(double) f3(double) f4(double)
f5(double) f6(double) f7(double)
*///:~
```

You can see that the constant value 5 is treated as an **int**, so if an overloaded method is available that takes an **int**, it is used. In all other cases, if you have a data type that is smaller than the argument in the method, that data type is promoted. **char** produces a slightly different effect, since if it doesn't find an exact **char** match, it is promoted to **int**.

What happens if your argument is *bigger* than the argument expected by the overloaded method? A modification of the preceding program gives the answer:

```
//: initialization/Demotion.java
// Demotion of primitives and overloading.
import static net.mindview.util.Print.*;

public class Demotion {
  void f1(char x) { print("f1(char)"); }
  void f1(byte x) { print("f1(byte)"); }
  void f1(short x) { print("f1(short)"); }
  void f1(int x) { print("f1(int)"); }
  void f1(long x) { print("f1(long)"); }
  void f1(float x) { print("f1(float)"); }
  void f1(double x) { print("f1(double)"); }

  void f2(char x) { print("f2(char)"); }
  void f2(byte x) { print("f2(byte)"); }
  void f2(short x) { print("f2(short)"); }
  void f2(int x) { print("f2(int)"); }
  void f2(long x) { print("f2(long)"); }
  void f2(float x) { print("f2(float)"); }

  void f3(char x) { print("f3(char)"); }
  void f3(byte x) { print("f3(byte)"); }
  void f3(short x) { print("f3(short)"); }
  void f3(int x) { print("f3(int)"); }
  void f3(long x) { print("f3(long)"); }

  void f4(char x) { print("f4(char)"); }
  void f4(byte x) { print("f4(byte)"); }
  void f4(short x) { print("f4(short)"); }
  void f4(int x) { print("f4(int)"); }
```

```java
    void f5(char x) { print("f5(char)"); }
    void f5(byte x) { print("f5(byte)"); }
    void f5(short x) { print("f5(short)"); }

    void f6(char x) { print("f6(char)"); }
    void f6(byte x) { print("f6(byte)"); }

    void f7(char x) { print("f7(char)"); }

    void testDouble() {
      double x = 0;
      print("double argument:");
      f1(x);f2((float)x);f3((long)x);f4((int)x);
      f5((short)x);f6((byte)x);f7((char)x);
    }
    public static void main(String[] args) {
      Demotion p = new Demotion();
      p.testDouble();
    }
} /* Output:
double argument:
f1(double)
f2(float)
f3(long)
f4(int)
f5(short)
f6(byte)
f7(char)
*///:~
```

Here, the methods take narrower primitive values. If your argument is wider, then you must perform a narrowing conversion with a cast. If you don't do this, the compiler will issue an error message.

Overloading on return values

It is common to wonder, "Why only class names and method argument lists? Why not distinguish between methods based on their return values?" For example, these two methods, which have the same name and arguments, are easily distinguished from each other:

```java
void f() {}
int f() { return 1; }
```

This might work fine as long as the compiler could unequivocally determine the meaning from the context, as in **int x = f( )**. However, you can also call a method and ignore the return value. This is often referred to as *calling a method for its side effect*, since you don't care about the return value, but instead want the other effects of the method call. So if you call the method this way:

```
f();
```

how can Java determine which **f( )** should be called? And how could someone reading the code see it? Because of this sort of problem, you cannot use return value types to distinguish overloaded methods.

Default constructors

As mentioned previously, a default constructor (a.k.a. a "no-arg" constructor) is one without arguments that is used to create a "default object." If you create a class that has no constructors, the compiler will automatically create a default constructor for you. For example:

```
//: initialization/DefaultConstructor.java

class Bird {}

public class DefaultConstructor {
  public static void main(String[] args) {
    Bird b = new Bird(); // Default!
  }
} ///:~
```

The expression

```
new Bird()
```

creates a new object and calls the default constructor, even though one was not explicitly defined. Without it, you would have no method to call to build the object. However, if you define any constructors (with or without arguments), the compiler will *not* synthesize one for you:

```
//: initialization/NoSynthesis.java

class Bird2 {
  Bird2(int i) {}
  Bird2(double d) {}
```

```
    }

public class NoSynthesis {
  public static void main(String[] args) {
    //! Bird2 b = new Bird2(); // No default
    Bird2 b2 = new Bird2(1);
    Bird2 b3 = new Bird2(1.0);
  }
} ///:~
```

If you say:

```
new Bird2()
```

the compiler will complain that it cannot find a constructor that matches. When you don't put in any constructors, it's as if the compiler says, "You are bound to need *some* constructor, so let me make one for you." But if you write a constructor, the compiler says, "You've written a constructor so you know what you're doing; if you didn't put in a default it's because you meant to leave it out."

Exercise 3: (1) Create a class with a default constructor (one that takes no arguments) that prints a message. Create an object of this class.

Exercise 4: (1) Add an overloaded constructor to the previous exercise that takes a **String** argument and prints it along with your message.

Exercise 5: (2) Create a class called **Dog** with an overloaded **bark( )** method. This method should be overloaded based on various primitive data types, and print different types of barking, howling, etc., depending on which overloaded version is called. Write a **main( )** that calls all the different versions.

Exercise 6: (1) Modify the previous exercise so that two of the overloaded methods have two arguments (of two different types), but in reversed order relative to each other. Verify that this works.

Exercise 7: (1) Create a class without a constructor, and then create an object of that class in **main( )** to verify that the default constructor is automatically synthesized.

The **this** keyword

If you have two objects of the same type called **a** and **b**, you might wonder how it is that you can call a method **peel( )** for both those objects:

```
//: initialization/BananaPeel.java

class Banana { void peel(int i) { /* ... */ } }

public class BananaPeel {
  public static void main(String[] args) {
    Banana a = new Banana(),
           b = new Banana();
    a.peel(1);
    b.peel(2);
  }
} ///:~
```

If there's only one method called **peel( )**, how can that method know whether it's being called for the object **a** or **b**?

To allow you to write the code in a convenient object-oriented syntax in which you "send a message to an object," the compiler does some undercover work for you. There's a secret first argument passed to the method **peel( )**, and that argument is the reference to the object that's being manipulated. So the two method calls become something like:

```
Banana.peel(a, 1);
Banana.peel(b, 2);
```

This is internal and you can't write these expressions and get the compiler to accept them, but it gives you an idea of what's happening.

Suppose you're inside a method and you'd like to get the reference to the current object. Since that reference is passed *secretly* by the compiler, there's no identifier for it. However, for this purpose there's a keyword: **this**. The **this** keyword—which can be used only inside a non-**static** method—produces the reference to the object that the method has been called for. You can treat the reference just like any other object reference. Keep in mind that if you're calling a method of your class from within another method of your class, you don't need to use **this**. You simply call the method. The current **this** reference is automatically used for the other method. Thus you can say:

```
//: initialization/Apricot.java
public class Apricot {
  void pick() { /* ... */ }
  void pit() { pick(); /* ... */ }
} ///:~
```

Inside **pit( )**, you *could* say **this.pick( )** but there's no need to.[1] The compiler does it for you automatically. The **this** keyword is used only for those special cases in which you need to explicitly use the reference to the current object. For example, it's often used in **return** statements when you want to return the reference to the current object:

```
//: initialization/Leaf.java
// Simple use of the "this" keyword.

public class Leaf {
  int i = 0;
  Leaf increment() {
    i++;
    return this;
  }
  void print() {
    System.out.println("i = " + i);
  }
  public static void main(String[] args) {
    Leaf x = new Leaf();
    x.increment().increment().increment().print();
  }
} /* Output:
i = 3
*///:~
```

Because **increment( )** returns the reference to the current object via the **this** keyword, multiple operations can easily be performed on the same object.

The **this** keyword is also useful for passing the current object to another method:

```
//: initialization/PassingThis.java

class Person {
```

---

[1] Some people will obsessively put **this** in front of every method call and field reference, arguing that it makes it "clearer and more explicit." Don't do it. There's a reason that we use high-level languages: They do things for us. If you put **this** in when it's not necessary, you will confuse and annoy everyone who reads your code, since all the rest of the code they've read *won't* use **this** everywhere. People expect **this** to be used only when it is necessary. Following a consistent and straightforward coding style saves time and money.

```
  public void eat(Apple apple) {
    Apple peeled = apple.getPeeled();
    System.out.println("Yummy");
  }
}

class Peeler {
  static Apple peel(Apple apple) {
    // ... remove peel
    return apple; // Peeled
  }
}

class Apple {
  Apple getPeeled() { return Peeler.peel(this); }
}

public class PassingThis {
  public static void main(String[] args) {
    new Person().eat(new Apple());
  }
} /* Output:
Yummy
*///:~
```

Apple needs to call **Peeler.peel( )**, which is a foreign utility method that performs an operation that, for some reason, needs to be external to **Apple** (perhaps the external method can be applied across many different classes, and you don't want to repeat the code). To pass itself to the foreign method, it must use **this**.

Exercise 8: (1) Create a class with two methods. Within the first method, call the second method twice: the first time without using **this**, and the second time using **this**—just to see it working; you should not use this form in practice.

Calling constructors from constructors

When you write several constructors for a class, there are times when you'd like to call one constructor from another to avoid duplicating code. You can make such a call by using the **this** keyword.

Normally, when you say **this**, it is in the sense of "this object" or "the current object," and by itself it produces the reference to the current object. In a constructor, the **this** keyword takes on a different meaning when you give it an argument list. It makes an explicit call to the constructor that matches that argument list. Thus you have a straightforward way to call other constructors:

```
//: initialization/Flower.java
// Calling constructors with "this"
import static net.mindview.util.Print.*;

public class Flower {
  int petalCount = 0;
  String s = "initial value";
  Flower(int petals) {
    petalCount = petals;
    print("Constructor w/ int arg only, petalCount= "
      + petalCount);
  }
  Flower(String ss) {
    print("Constructor w/ String arg only, s = " + ss);
    s = ss;
  }
  Flower(String s, int petals) {
    this(petals);
//!    this(s); // Can't call two!
    this.s = s; // Another use of "this"
    print("String & int args");
  }
  Flower() {
    this("hi", 47);
    print("default constructor (no args)");
  }
  void printPetalCount() {
//! this(11); // Not inside non-constructor!
    print("petalCount = " + petalCount + " s = "+ s);
  }
  public static void main(String[] args) {
    Flower x = new Flower();
    x.printPetalCount();
  }
} /* Output:
Constructor w/ int arg only, petalCount= 47
String & int args
default constructor (no args)
petalCount = 47 s = hi
*///:~
```

The constructor **Flower(String s, int petals)** shows that, while you can call one constructor using **this**, you cannot call two. In addition, the constructor call must be the first thing you do, or you'll get a compiler error message.

This example also shows another way you'll see **this** used. Since the name of the argument **s** and the name of the member data **s** are the same, there's an ambiguity. You can resolve it using **this.s**, to say that you're referring to the member data. You'll often see this form used in Java code, and it's used in numerous places in this book.

In **printPetalCount( )** you can see that the compiler won't let you call a constructor from inside any method other than a constructor.

Exercise 9: (1) Create a class with two (overloaded) constructors. Using **this**, call the second constructor inside the first one.

The meaning of **static**

With the **this** keyword in mind, you can more fully understand what it means to make a method **static**. It means that there is no **this** for that particular method. You cannot call non-**static** methods from inside **static** methods[2] (although the reverse is possible), and you can call a **static** method for the class itself, without any object. In fact, that's primarily what a **static** method is for. It's as if you're creating the equivalent of a global method. However, global methods are not permitted in Java, and putting the **static** method inside a class allows it access to other **static** methods and to **static** fields.

Some people argue that **static** methods are not object-oriented, since they do have the semantics of a global method; with a **static** method, you don't send a message to an object, since there's no **this**. This is probably a fair argument, and if you find yourself using a *lot* of **static** methods, you should probably rethink your strategy. However, **static**s are pragmatic, and there are times when you genuinely need them, so whether or not they are "proper OOP" should be left to the theoreticians.

---

[2] The one case in which this is possible occurs if you pass a reference to an object into the **static** method (the **static** method could also create its own object). Then, via the reference (which is now effectively **this**), you can call non-**static** methods and access non-**static** fields. But typically, if you want to do something like this, you'll just make an ordinary, non-**static** method.

Cleanup: finalization and garbage collection

Programmers know about the importance of initialization, but often forget the importance of cleanup. After all, who needs to clean up an **int**? But with libraries, simply "letting go" of an object once you're done with it is not always safe. Of course, Java has the garbage collector to reclaim the memory of objects that are no longer used. Now consider an unusual case: Suppose your object allocates "special" memory without using **new**. The garbage collector only knows how to release memory allocated *with* **new**, so it won't know how to release the object's "special" memory. To handle this case, Java provides a method called **finalize( )** that you can define for your class. Here's how it's *supposed* to work. When the garbage collector is ready to release the storage used for your object, it will first call **finalize( )**, and only on the next garbage-collection pass will it reclaim the object's memory. So if you choose to use **finalize( )**, it gives you the ability to perform some important cleanup *at the time of garbage collection*.

This is a potential programming pitfall because some programmers, especially C++ programmers, might initially mistake **finalize( )** for the *destructor* in C++, which is a function that is *always* called when an object is destroyed. It is important to distinguish between C++ and Java here, because in C++, *objects always get destroyed* (in a bug-free program), whereas in Java, objects do not always get garbage collected. Or, put another way:

1. Your objects might not get garbage collected.

2. Garbage collection is not destruction.

If you remember this, you will stay out of trouble. What it means is that if there is some activity that must be performed before you no longer need an object, you must perform that activity yourself. Java has no destructor or similar concept, so you must create an ordinary method to perform this cleanup. For example, suppose that in the process of creating your object, it draws itself on the screen. If you don't explicitly erase its image from the screen, it might never get cleaned up. If you put some kind of erasing functionality inside **finalize( )**, then if an object is garbage collected and **finalize( )** is called (and there's no guarantee this will happen), then the image will first be removed from the screen, but if it isn't, the image will remain.

You might find that the storage for an object never gets released because your program never nears the point of running out of storage. If your program completes and the garbage collector never gets around to releasing the storage for any of your objects, that storage will be returned to the operating system *en masse* as the program exits. This is a good thing, because garbage collection has some overhead, and if you never do it, you never incur that expense.

What is **finalize()** for?

So, if you should not use **finalize( )** as a general-purpose cleanup method, what good is it?

A third point to remember is:

3. Garbage collection is only about memory.

That is, the sole reason for the existence of the garbage collector is to recover memory that your program is no longer using. So any activity that is associated with garbage collection, most notably your **finalize( )** method, must also be only about memory and its deallocation.

Does this mean that if your object contains other objects, **finalize( )** should explicitly release those objects? Well, no—the garbage collector takes care of the release of all object memory regardless of how the object is created. It turns out that the need for **finalize( )** is limited to special cases in which your object can allocate storage in some way other than creating an object. But, you might observe, everything in Java is an object, so how can this be?

It would seem that **finalize( )** is in place because of the possibility that you'll do something C-like by allocating memory using a mechanism other than the normal one in Java. This can happen primarily through *native methods*, which are a way to call non-Java code from Java. (Native methods are covered in Appendix B in the electronic 2nd edition of this book, available at *www.MindView.net*.) C and C++ are the only languages currently supported by native methods, but since they can call subprograms in other languages, you can effectively call anything. Inside the non-Java code, C's **malloc( )** family of functions might be called to allocate storage, and unless you call **free( )**, that storage will not be released, causing a memory leak. Of course,

free( ) is a C and C++ function, so you'd need to call it in a native method inside your **finalize( )**.

After reading this, you probably get the idea that you won't use **finalize( )** much.[3] You're correct; it is not the appropriate place for normal cleanup to occur. So where should normal cleanup be performed?

You must perform cleanup

To clean up an object, the user of that object must call a cleanup method at the point the cleanup is desired. This sounds pretty straightforward, but it collides a bit with the C++ concept of the destructor. In C++, all objects are destroyed. Or rather, all objects *should be* destroyed. If the C++ object is created as a local (i.e., on the stack—not possible in Java), then the destruction happens at the closing curly brace of the scope in which the object was created. If the object was created using **new** (like in Java), the destructor is called when the programmer calls the C++ operator **delete** (which doesn't exist in Java). If the C++ programmer forgets to call **delete**, the destructor is never called, and you have a memory leak, plus the other parts of the object never get cleaned up. This kind of bug can be very difficult to track down, and is one of the compelling reasons to move from C++ to Java.

In contrast, Java doesn't allow you to create local objects—you must always use **new**. But in Java, there's no "delete" for releasing the object, because the garbage collector releases the storage for you. So from a simplistic standpoint, you could say that because of garbage collection, Java has no destructor. You'll see as this book progresses, however, that the presence of a garbage collector does not remove the need for or the utility of destructors. (And you should never call **finalize( )** directly, so that's not a solution.) If you want some kind of cleanup performed other than storage release, you must *still* explicitly call an appropriate method in Java, which is the equivalent of a C++ destructor without the convenience.

Remember that neither garbage collection nor finalization is guaranteed. If the JVM isn't close to running out of memory, then it might not waste time recovering memory through garbage collection.

---

[3] Joshua Bloch goes further in his section titled "avoid finalizers": "Finalizers are unpredictable, often dangerous, and generally unnecessary." *Effective Java™ Programming Language Guide*, p. 20 (Addison-Wesley, 2001).

The termination condition

In general, you can't rely on **finalize( )** being called, and you must create separate "cleanup" methods and call them explicitly. So it appears that **finalize( )** is only useful for obscure memory cleanup that most programmers will never use. However, there is an interesting use of **finalize( )** that does not rely on it being called every time. This is the verification of the *termination condition*[4] of an object.

At the point that you're no longer interested in an object—when it's ready to be cleaned up—that object should be in a state whereby its memory can be safely released. For example, if the object represents an open file, that file should be closed by the programmer before the object is garbage collected. If any portions of the object are not properly cleaned up, then you have a bug in your program that can be very difficult to find. **finalize( )** can be used to eventually discover this condition, even if it isn't always called. If one of the finalizations happens to reveal the bug, then you discover the problem, which is all you really care about.

Here's a simple example of how you might use it:

```
//: initialization/TerminationCondition.java
// Using finalize() to detect an object that
// hasn't been properly cleaned up.

class Book {
  boolean checkedOut = false;
  Book(boolean checkOut) {
    checkedOut = checkOut;
  }
  void checkIn() {
    checkedOut = false;
  }
  protected void finalize() {
    if(checkedOut)
      System.out.println("Error: checked out");
    // Normally, you'll also do this:
    // super.finalize(); // Call the base-class version
  }
```

---

[4] A term coined by Bill Venners (*www.Artima.com*) during a seminar that he and I were giving together.

```
    }

public class TerminationCondition {
  public static void main(String[] args) {
    Book novel = new Book(true);
    // Proper cleanup:
    novel.checkIn();
    // Drop the reference, forget to clean up:
    new Book(true);
    // Force garbage collection & finalization:
    System.gc();
  }
} /* Output:
Error: checked out
*///:~
```

The termination condition is that all **Book** objects are supposed to be checked in before they are garbage collected, but in **main( )**, a programmer error doesn't check in one of the books. Without **finalize( )** to verify the termination condition, this can be a difficult bug to find.

Note that **System.gc( )** is used to force finalization. But even if it isn't, it's highly probable that the errant **Book** will eventually be discovered through repeated executions of the program (assuming the program allocates enough storage to cause the garbage collector to execute).

You should generally assume that the base-class version of **finalize( )** will also be doing something important, and call it using **super**, as you can see in **Book.finalize( )**. In this case, it is commented out because it requires exception handling, which we haven't covered yet.

Exercise 10: (2) Create a class with a **finalize( )** method that prints a message. In **main( )**, create an object of your class. Explain the behavior of your program.

Exercise 11: (4) Modify the previous exercise so that your **finalize( )** will always be called.

Exercise 12: (4) Create a class called **Tank** that can be filled and emptied, and has a *termination condition* that it must be empty when the object is cleaned up. Write a **finalize( )** that verifies this termination condition. In **main( )**, test the possible scenarios that can occur when your **Tank** is used.

How a garbage collector works

If you come from a programming language where allocating objects on the heap is expensive, you may naturally assume that Java's scheme of allocating everything (except primitives) on the heap is also expensive. However, it turns out that the garbage collector can have a significant impact on *increasing* the speed of object creation. This might sound a bit odd at first— that storage release affects storage allocation—but it's the way some JVMs work, and it means that allocating storage for heap objects in Java can be nearly as fast as creating storage *on the stack* in other languages.

For example, you can think of the C++ heap as a yard where each object stakes out its own piece of turf. This real estate can become abandoned sometime later and must be reused. In some JVMs, the Java heap is quite different; it's more like a conveyor belt that moves forward every time you allocate a new object. This means that object storage allocation is remarkably rapid. The "heap pointer" is simply moved forward into virgin territory, so it's effectively the same as C++'s stack allocation. (Of course, there's a little extra overhead for bookkeeping, but it's nothing like searching for storage.)

You might observe that the heap isn't in fact a conveyor belt, and if you treat it that way, you'll start paging memory—moving it on and off disk, so that you can appear to have more memory than you actually do. Paging significantly impacts performance. Eventually, after you create enough objects, you'll run out of memory. The trick is that the garbage collector steps in, and while it collects the garbage it compacts all the objects in the heap so that you've effectively moved the "heap pointer" closer to the beginning of the conveyor belt and farther away from a page fault. The garbage collector rearranges things and makes it possible for the high-speed, infinite-free-heap model to be used while allocating storage.

To understand garbage collection in Java, it's helpful to learn how garbage-collection schemes work in other systems. A simple but slow garbage-collection technique is called *reference counting*. This means that each object contains a reference counter, and every time a reference is attached to that object, the reference count is increased. Every time a reference goes out of scope or is set to **null**, the reference count is decreased. Thus, managing reference counts is a small but constant overhead that happens throughout the lifetime of your program. The garbage collector moves through the entire list of objects, and when it finds one with a reference count of zero it releases that storage (however, reference counting schemes often release an object as soon as the count goes to zero). The one drawback is that if objects circularly refer to each other they can have nonzero reference counts while still being garbage. Locating such self-referential groups requires significant extra work for the garbage collector. Reference counting is commonly used to explain one kind of garbage collection, but it doesn't seem to be used in any JVM implementations.

In faster schemes, garbage collection is not based on reference counting. Instead, it is based on the idea that any non-dead object must ultimately be traceable back to a reference that lives either on the stack or in static storage. The chain might go through several layers of objects. Thus, if you start in the stack and in the static storage area and walk through all the references, you'll find all the live objects. For each reference that you find, you must trace into the object that it points to and then follow all the references in *that* object, tracing into the objects they point to, etc., until you've moved through the entire Web that originated with the reference on the stack or in static storage. Each object that you move through must still be alive. Note that there is no problem with detached self-referential groups—these are simply not found, and are therefore automatically garbage.

In the approach described here, the JVM uses an *adaptive* garbage-collection scheme, and what it does with the live objects that it locates depends on the variant currently being used. One of these variants is *stop-and-copy*. This means that—for reasons that will become apparent—the program is first stopped (this is not a background collection scheme). Then, each live object is copied from one heap to another, leaving behind all the garbage. In addition, as the objects are copied into the new heap, they are packed end-to-end, thus compacting the new heap (and allowing new storage to simply be reeled off the end as previously described).

Of course, when an object is moved from one place to another, all references that point at the object must be changed. The reference that goes from the stack or the static storage area to the object can be changed right away, but there can be other references pointing to this object that will be encountered later during the "walk." These are fixed up as they are found (you could imagine a table that maps old addresses to new ones).

There are two issues that make these so-called "copy collectors" inefficient. The first is the idea that you have two heaps and you slosh all the memory back and forth between these two separate heaps, maintaining twice as much memory as you actually need. Some JVMs deal with this by allocating the heap in chunks as needed and simply copying from one chunk to another.

The second issue is the copying process itself. Once your program becomes stable, it might be generating little or no garbage. Despite that, a copy collector will still copy all the memory from one place to another, which is wasteful. To prevent this, some JVMs detect that no new garbage is being generated and switch to a different scheme (this is the "adaptive" part). This other scheme is called *mark-and-sweep*, and it's what earlier versions of Sun's JVM used all the time. For general use, mark-and-sweep is fairly slow, but when you know you're generating little or no garbage, it's fast.

Mark-and-sweep follows the same logic of starting from the stack and static storage, and tracing through all the references to find live objects. However, each time it finds a live object, that object is marked by setting a flag in it, but the object isn't collected yet. Only when the marking process is finished does the sweep occur. During the sweep, the dead objects are released. However, no copying happens, so if the collector chooses to compact a fragmented heap, it does so by shuffling objects around.

"Stop-and-copy" refers to the idea that this type of garbage collection is *not* done in the background; instead, the program is stopped while the garbage collection occurs. In the Sun literature you'll find many references to garbage collection as a low-priority background process, but it turns out that the garbage collection was not implemented that way in earlier versions of the Sun JVM. Instead, the Sun garbage collector stopped the program when memory got low. Mark-and-sweep also requires that the program be stopped.

As previously mentioned, in the JVM described here memory is allocated in big blocks. If you allocate a large object, it gets its own block. Strict stop-and-copy requires copying every live object from the source heap to a new heap before you can free the old one, which translates to lots of memory. With blocks, the garbage collection can typically copy objects to dead blocks as it collects. Each block has a *generation count* to keep track of whether it's alive. In the normal case, only the blocks created since the last garbage collection are compacted; all other blocks get their generation count bumped if they have been referenced from somewhere. This handles the normal case of lots of short-lived temporary objects. Periodically, a full sweep is made—large objects are still not copied (they just get their generation count bumped), and blocks containing small objects are copied and compacted. The JVM monitors the efficiency of garbage collection and if it becomes a waste of time because all objects are long-lived, then it switches to mark-and-sweep. Similarly, the JVM keeps track of how successful mark-and-sweep is, and if the heap starts to become fragmented, it switches back to stop-and-copy. This is where the "adaptive" part comes in, so you end up with a mouthful: "Adaptive generational stop-and-copy mark-and-sweep."

There are a number of additional speedups possible in a JVM. An especially important one involves the operation of the loader and what is called a *just-in-time* (JIT) compiler. A JIT compiler partially or fully converts a program into native machine code so that it doesn't need to be interpreted by the JVM and thus runs much faster. When a class must be loaded (typically, the first time you want to create an object of that class), the **.class** file is located, and the bytecodes for that class are brought into memory. At this point, one approach is to simply JIT compile all the code, but this has two drawbacks: It takes a little more time, which, compounded throughout the life of the program, can add up; and it increases the size of the executable (bytecodes are significantly more compact than expanded JIT code), and this might cause paging, which definitely slows down a program. An alternative approach is *lazy evaluation,* which means that the code is not JIT compiled until necessary. Thus, code that never gets executed might never be JIT compiled. The Java HotSpot technologies in recent JDKs take a similar approach by increasingly optimizing a piece of code each time it is executed, so the more the code is executed, the faster it gets.

Member initialization

Java goes out of its way to guarantee that variables are properly initialized before they are used. In the case of a method's local variables, this guarantee comes in the form of a compile-time error. So if you say:

```
void f() {
  int i;
  i++; // Error -- i not initialized
}
```

you'll get an error message that says that **i** might not have been initialized. Of course, the compiler could have given **i** a default value, but an uninitialized local variable is probably a programmer error, and a default value would have covered that up. Forcing the programmer to provide an initialization value is more likely to catch a bug.

If a primitive is a field in a class, however, things are a bit different. As you saw in the *Everything Is an Object* chapter, each primitive field of a class is guaranteed to get an initial value. Here's a program that verifies this, and shows the values:

```java
//: initialization/InitialValues.java
// Shows default initial values.
import static net.mindview.util.Print.*;

public class InitialValues {
  boolean t;
  char c;
  byte b;
  short s;
  int i;
  long l;
  float f;
  double d;
  InitialValues reference;
  void printInitialValues() {
    print("Data type      Initial value");
    print("boolean      " + t);
    print("char         [" + c + "]");
    print("byte         " + b);
    print("short        " + s);
    print("int          " + i);
    print("long         " + l);
    print("float        " + f);
    print("double       " + d);
    print("reference    " + reference);
  }
  public static void main(String[] args) {
    InitialValues iv = new InitialValues();
    iv.printInitialValues();
    /* You could also say:
    new InitialValues().printInitialValues();
    */
  }
} /* Output:
Data type      Initial value
boolean        false
char           [ ]
byte           0
short          0
```

```
int            0
long           0
float          0.0
double         0.0
reference      null
*///:~
```

You can see that even though the values are not specified, they automatically get initialized (the **char** value is a zero, which prints as a space). So at least there's no threat of working with uninitialized variables.

When you define an object reference inside a class without initializing it to a new object, that reference is given a special value of **null**.

Specifying initialization

What happens if you want to give a variable an initial value? One direct way to do this is simply to assign the value at the point you define the variable in the class. (Notice you cannot do this in C++, although C++ novices always try.) Here the field definitions in class **InitialValues** are changed to provide initial values:

```
//: initialization/InitialValues2.java
// Providing explicit initial values.

public class InitialValues2 {
  boolean bool = true;
  char ch = 'x';
  byte b = 47;
  short s = 0xff;
  int i = 999;
  long lng = 1;
  float f = 3.14f;
  double d = 3.14159;
} ///:~
```

You can also initialize non-primitive objects in this same way. If **Depth** is a class, you can create a variable and initialize it like so:

```
//: initialization/Measurement.java
class Depth {}

public class Measurement {
  Depth d = new Depth();
  // ...
```

```
} ///:~
```

If you haven't given **d** an initial value and you try to use it anyway, you'll get a runtime error called an *exception* (covered in the *Error Handling with Exceptions* chapter).

You can even call a method to provide an initialization value:

```
//: initialization/MethodInit.java
public class MethodInit {
  int i = f();
  int f() { return 11; }
} ///:~
```

This method can have arguments, of course, but those arguments cannot be other class members that haven't been initialized yet. Thus, you can do this:

```
//: initialization/MethodInit2.java
public class MethodInit2 {
  int i = f();
  int j = g(i);
  int f() { return 11; }
  int g(int n) { return n * 10; }
} ///:~
```

But you cannot do this:

```
//: initialization/MethodInit3.java
public class MethodInit3 {
  //! int j = g(i); // Illegal forward reference
  int i = f();
  int f() { return 11; }
  int g(int n) { return n * 10; }
} ///:~
```

This is one place in which the compiler, appropriately, *does* complain about forward referencing, since this has to do with the order of initialization and not the way the program is compiled.

This approach to initialization is simple and straightforward. It has the limitation that *every* object of type **InitialValues** will get these same initialization values. Sometimes this is exactly what you need, but at other times you need more flexibility.

Constructor initialization

The constructor can be used to perform initialization, and this gives you greater flexibility in your programming because you can call methods and perform actions at run time to determine the initial values. There's one thing to keep in mind, however: You aren't precluding the automatic initialization, which happens before the constructor is entered. So, for example, if you say:

```
//: initialization/Counter.java
public class Counter {
  int i;
  Counter() { i = 7; }
  // ...
} ///:~
```

then **i** will first be initialized to 0, then to 7. This is true with all the primitive types and with object references, including those that are given explicit initialization at the point of definition. For this reason, the compiler doesn't try to force you to initialize elements in the constructor at any particular place, or before they are used—initialization is already guaranteed.

Order of initialization

Within a class, the order of initialization is determined by the order that the variables are defined within the class. The variable definitions may be scattered throughout and in between method definitions, but the variables are initialized before any methods can be called—even the constructor. For example:

```
//: initialization/OrderOfInitialization.java
// Demonstrates initialization order.
import static net.mindview.util.Print.*;

// When the constructor is called to create a
// Window object, you'll see a message:
class Window {
  Window(int marker) { print("Window(" + marker + ")"); }
}

class House {
  Window w1 = new Window(1); // Before constructor
  House() {
    // Show that we're in the constructor:
```

```
      print("House()");
      w3 = new Window(33); // Reinitialize w3
   }
   Window w2 = new Window(2); // After constructor
   void f() { print("f()"); }
   Window w3 = new Window(3); // At end
}

public class OrderOfInitialization {
   public static void main(String[] args) {
      House h = new House();
      h.f(); // Shows that construction is done
   }
} /* Output:
Window(1)
Window(2)
Window(3)
House()
Window(33)
f()
*///:~
```

In **House**, the definitions of the **Window** objects are intentionally scattered about to prove that they'll all get initialized before the constructor is entered or anything else can happen. In addition, **w3** is reinitialized inside the constructor.

From the output, you can see that the **w3** reference gets initialized twice: once before and once during the constructor call. (The first object is dropped, so it can be garbage collected later.) This might not seem efficient at first, but it guarantees proper initialization—what would happen if an overloaded constructor were defined that did *not* initialize **w3** and there wasn't a "default" initialization for **w3** in its definition?

static data initialization

There's only a single piece of storage for a **static**, regardless of how many objects are created. You can't apply the **static** keyword to local variables, so it only applies to fields. If a field is a **static** primitive and you don't initialize it, it gets the standard initial value for its type. If it's a reference to an object, the default initialization value is **null**.

If you want to place initialization at the point of definition, it looks the same as for non-**static**s.

To see *when* the **static** storage gets initialized, here's an example:

```
//: initialization/StaticInitialization.java
// Specifying initial values in a class definition.
import static net.mindview.util.Print.*;

class Bowl {
  Bowl(int marker) {
    print("Bowl(" + marker + ")");
  }
  void f1(int marker) {
    print("f1(" + marker + ")");
  }
}

class Table {
  static Bowl bowl1 = new Bowl(1);
  Table() {
    print("Table()");
    bowl2.f1(1);
  }
  void f2(int marker) {
    print("f2(" + marker + ")");
  }
  static Bowl bowl2 = new Bowl(2);
}

class Cupboard {
  Bowl bowl3 = new Bowl(3);
  static Bowl bowl4 = new Bowl(4);
  Cupboard() {
    print("Cupboard()");
    bowl4.f1(2);
  }
  void f3(int marker) {
    print("f3(" + marker + ")");
  }
  static Bowl bowl5 = new Bowl(5);
}

public class StaticInitialization {
  public static void main(String[] args) {
```

```
    print("Creating new Cupboard() in main");
    new Cupboard();
    print("Creating new Cupboard() in main");
    new Cupboard();
    table.f2(1);
    cupboard.f3(1);
  }
  static Table table = new Table();
  static Cupboard cupboard = new Cupboard();
} /* Output:
Bowl(1)
Bowl(2)
Table()
f1(1)
Bowl(4)
Bowl(5)
Bowl(3)
Cupboard()
f1(2)
Creating new Cupboard() in main
Bowl(3)
Cupboard()
f1(2)
Creating new Cupboard() in main
Bowl(3)
Cupboard()
f1(2)
f2(1)
f3(1)
*///:~
```

Bowl allows you to view the creation of a class, and **Table** and **Cupboard** have **static** members of **Bowl** scattered through their class definitions. Note that **Cupboard** creates a non-**static Bowl bowl3** prior to the **static** definitions.

From the output, you can see that the **static** initialization occurs only if it's necessary. If you don't create a **Table** object and you never refer to **Table.bowl1** or **Table.bowl2**, the **static Bowl bowl1** and **bowl2** will never be created. They are initialized only when the *first* **Table** object is created (or the first **static** access occurs). After that, the **static** objects are not reinitialized.

The order of initialization is **static**s first, if they haven't already been initialized by a previous object creation, and then the non-**static** objects. You can see the evidence of this in the output. To execute **main( )** (a **static** method), the **StaticInitialization** class must be loaded, and its **static** fields **table** and **cupboard** are then initialized, which causes *those* classes to be loaded, and since they both contain **static Bowl** objects, **Bowl** is then loaded. Thus, all the classes in this particular program get loaded before **main( )** starts. This is usually not the case, because in typical programs you won't have everything linked together by **static**s as you do in this example.

To summarize the process of creating an object, consider a class called **Dog**:

1. Even though it doesn't explicitly use the **static** keyword, the constructor is actually a **static** method. So the first time an object of type **Dog** is created, *or* the first time a **static** method or **static** field of class **Dog** is accessed, the Java interpreter must locate **Dog.class**, which it does by searching through the classpath.

2. As **Dog.class** is loaded (creating a **Class** object, which you'll learn about later), all of its **static** initializers are run. Thus, **static** initialization takes place only once, as the **Class** object is loaded for the first time.

3. When you create a **new Dog( )**, the construction process for a **Dog** object first allocates enough storage for a **Dog** object on the heap.

4. This storage is wiped to zero, automatically setting all the primitives in that **Dog** object to their default values (zero for numbers and the equivalent for **boolean** and **char**) and the references to **null**.

5. Any initializations that occur at the point of field definition are executed.

6. Constructors are executed. As you shall see in the *Reusing Classes* chapter, this might actually involve a fair amount of activity, especially when inheritance is involved.

Explicit **static** initialization

Java allows you to group other **static** initializations inside a special "**static** clause" (sometimes called a *static block*) in a class. It looks like this:

```
//: initialization/Spoon.java
public class Spoon {
  static int i;
  static {
    i = 47;
  }
} ///:~
```

It appears to be a method, but it's just the **static** keyword followed by a block of code. This code, like other **static** initializations, is executed only once: the first time you make an object of that class *or* the first time you access a **static** member of that class (even if you never make an object of that class). For example:

```
//: initialization/ExplicitStatic.java
// Explicit static initialization with the "static" clause.
import static net.mindview.util.Print.*;

class Cup {
  Cup(int marker) {
    print("Cup(" + marker + ")");
  }
  void f(int marker) {
    print("f(" + marker + ")");
  }
}

class Cups {
  static Cup cup1;
  static Cup cup2;
  static {
    cup1 = new Cup(1);
    cup2 = new Cup(2);
  }
  Cups() {
    print("Cups()");
  }
}
```

```
public class ExplicitStatic {
  public static void main(String[] args) {
    print("Inside main()");
    Cups.cup1.f(99);   // (1)
  }
  // static Cups cups1 = new Cups();   // (2)
  // static Cups cups2 = new Cups();   // (2)
} /* Output:
Inside main()
Cup(1)
Cup(2)
f(99)
*///:~
```

The **static** initializers for **Cups** run when either the access of the **static** object **cup1** occurs on the line marked **(1)**, or if line **(1)** is commented out and the lines marked **(2)** are uncommented. If both **(1)** and **(2)** are commented out, the **static** initialization for **Cups** never occurs, as you can see from the output. Also, it doesn't matter if one or both of the lines marked **(2)** are uncommented; the static initialization only occurs once.

Exercise 13: (1) Verify the statements in the previous paragraph.

Exercise 14: (1) Create a class with a **static String** field that is initialized at the point of definition, and another one that is initialized by the **static** block. Add a **static** method that prints both fields and demonstrates that they are both initialized before they are used.

Non-**static** instance initialization

Java provides a similar syntax, called *instance initialization*, for initializing non-**static** variables for each object. Here's an example:

```
//: initialization/Mugs.java
// Java "Instance Initialization."
import static net.mindview.util.Print.*;

class Mug {
  Mug(int marker) {
    print("Mug(" + marker + ")");
  }
  void f(int marker) {
    print("f(" + marker + ")");
  }
}
```

```java
public class Mugs {
  Mug mug1;
  Mug mug2;
  {
    mug1 = new Mug(1);
    mug2 = new Mug(2);
    print("mug1 & mug2 initialized");
  }
  Mugs() {
    print("Mugs()");
  }
  Mugs(int i) {
    print("Mugs(int)");
  }
  public static void main(String[] args) {
    print("Inside main()");
    new Mugs();
    print("new Mugs() completed");
    new Mugs(1);
    print("new Mugs(1) completed");
  }
} /* Output:
Inside main()
Mug(1)
Mug(2)
mug1 & mug2 initialized
Mugs()
new Mugs() completed
Mug(1)
Mug(2)
mug1 & mug2 initialized
Mugs(int)
new Mugs(1) completed
*///:~
```

You can see that the instance initialization clause:

```java
  {
    mug1 = new Mug(1);
    mug2 = new Mug(2);
    print("mug1 & mug2 initialized");
  }
```

looks exactly like the static initialization clause except for the missing **static** keyword. This syntax is necessary to support the initialization of *anonymous inner classes* (see the *Inner Classes* chapter), but it also allows you to guarantee that certain operations occur regardless of which explicit constructor is called. From the output, you can see that the instance initialization clause is executed before either one of the constructors.

Exercise 15:   (1) Create a class with a **String** that is initialized using instance initialization.

Array initialization

An array is simply a sequence of either objects or primitives that are all the same type and are packaged together under one identifier name. Arrays are defined and used with the square-brackets *indexing operator* **[ ]**. To define an array reference, you simply follow your type name with empty square brackets:

```
int[] a1;
```

You can also put the square brackets after the identifier to produce exactly the same meaning:

```
int a1[];
```

This conforms to expectations from C and C++ programmers. The former style, however, is probably a more sensible syntax, since it says that the type is "an **int** array." That style will be used in this book.

The compiler doesn't allow you to tell it how big the array is. This brings us back to that issue of "references." All that you have at this point is a reference to an array (you've allocated enough storage for that reference), and there's been no space allocated for the array object itself. To create storage for the array, you must write an initialization expression. For arrays, initialization can appear anywhere in your code, but you can also use a special kind of initialization expression that must occur at the point where the array is created. This special initialization is a set of values surrounded by curly braces. The storage allocation (the equivalent of using **new**) is taken care of by the compiler in this case. For example:

```
int[] a1 = { 1, 2, 3, 4, 5 };
```

So why would you ever define an array reference without an array?

```
int[] a2;
```

Well, it's possible to assign one array to another in Java, so you can say:

```
a2 = a1;
```

What you're really doing is copying a reference, as demonstrated here:

```
//: initialization/ArraysOfPrimitives.java
import static net.mindview.util.Print.*;

public class ArraysOfPrimitives {
  public static void main(String[] args) {
    int[] a1 = { 1, 2, 3, 4, 5 };
    int[] a2;
    a2 = a1;
    for(int i = 0; i < a2.length; i++)
      a2[i] = a2[i] + 1;
    for(int i = 0; i < a1.length; i++)
      print("a1[" + i + "] = " + a1[i]);
  }
} /* Output:
a1[0] = 2
a1[1] = 3
a1[2] = 4
a1[3] = 5
a1[4] = 6
*///:~
```

You can see that **a1** is given an initialization value but **a2** is not; **a2** is assigned later—in this case, to another array. Since **a2** and **a1** are then aliased to the same array, the changes made via **a2** are seen in **a1**.

All arrays have an intrinsic member (whether they're arrays of objects or arrays of primitives) that you can query—but not change—to tell you how many elements there are in the array. This member is **length**. Since arrays in Java, like C and C++, start counting from element zero, the largest element you can index is **length - 1**. If you go out of bounds, C and C++ quietly accept this and allow you to stomp all over your memory, which is the source of many infamous bugs. However, Java protects you against such problems by causing a runtime error (an *exception*) if you step out of bounds.[5]

What if you don't know how many elements you're going to need in your array while you're writing the program? You simply use **new** to create the elements in the array. Here, **new** works even though it's creating an array of primitives (**new** won't create a non-array primitive):

```
//: initialization/ArrayNew.java
// Creating arrays with new.
import java.util.*;
import static net.mindview.util.Print.*;

public class ArrayNew {
  public static void main(String[] args) {
    int[] a;
    Random rand = new Random(47);
    a = new int[rand.nextInt(20)];
    print("length of a = " + a.length);
    print(Arrays.toString(a));
  }
} /* Output:
length of a = 18
[0, 0, 0, 0, 0, 0, 0, 0, 0, 0, 0, 0, 0, 0, 0, 0, 0, 0]
*///:~
```

The size of the array is chosen at random by using the **Random.nextInt( )** method, which produces a value between zero and that of its argument. Because of the randomness, it's clear that array creation is actually happening at run time. In addition, the output of this program shows that array elements of primitive types are automatically initialized to "empty" values. (For numerics and **char**, this is zero, and for **boolean**, it's **false**.)

The **Arrays.toString( )** method, which is part of the standard **java.util** library, produces a printable version of a one-dimensional array.

---

[5] Of course, checking every array access costs time and code and there's no way to turn it off, which means that array accesses might be a source of inefficiency in your program if they occur at a critical juncture. For Internet security and programmer productivity, the Java designers saw that this was a worthwhile trade-off. Although you may be tempted to write code that you think might make array accesses more efficient, this is a waste of time because automatic compile-time and runtime optimizations will speed array accesses.

Of course, in this case the array could also have been defined and initialized in the same statement:

```
int[] a = new int[rand.nextInt(20)];
```

This is the preferred way to do it, if you can.

If you create a non-primitive array, you create an array of references. Consider the wrapper type **Integer**, which is a class and not a primitive:

```
//: initialization/ArrayClassObj.java
// Creating an array of nonprimitive objects.
import java.util.*;
import static net.mindview.util.Print.*;

public class ArrayClassObj {
  public static void main(String[] args) {
    Random rand = new Random(47);
    Integer[] a = new Integer[rand.nextInt(20)];
    print("length of a = " + a.length);
    for(int i = 0; i < a.length; i++)
      a[i] = rand.nextInt(500); // Autoboxing
    print(Arrays.toString(a));
  }
} /* Output: (Sample)
length of a = 18
[55, 193, 361, 461, 429, 368, 200, 22, 207, 288, 128, 51,
89, 309, 278, 498, 361, 20]
*///:~
```

Here, even after **new** is called to create the array:

```
Integer[] a = new Integer[rand.nextInt(20)];
```

it's only an array of references, and the initialization is not complete until the reference itself is initialized by creating a new **Integer** object (via autoboxing, in this case):

```
a[i] = rand.nextInt(500);
```

If you forget to create the object, however, you'll get an exception at run time when you try to use the empty array location.

It's also possible to initialize arrays of objects by using the curly brace-enclosed list. There are two forms:

```
//: initialization/ArrayInit.java
// Array initialization.
import java.util.*;

public class ArrayInit {
  public static void main(String[] args) {
    Integer[] a = {
      new Integer(1),
      new Integer(2),
      3, // Autoboxing
    };
    Integer[] b = new Integer[]{
      new Integer(1),
      new Integer(2),
      3, // Autoboxing
    };
    System.out.println(Arrays.toString(a));
    System.out.println(Arrays.toString(b));
  }
} /* Output:
[1, 2, 3]
[1, 2, 3]
*///:~
```

In both cases, the final comma in the list of initializers is optional. (This feature makes for easier maintenance of long lists.)

Although the first form is useful, it's more limited because it can only be used at the point where the array is defined. You can use the second and third forms anywhere, even inside a method call. For example, you could create an array of **String** objects to pass to the **main( )** of another class, to provide alternate command-line arguments to that **main( )**:

```
//: initialization/DynamicArray.java
// Array initialization.

public class DynamicArray {
  public static void main(String[] args) {
    Other.main(new String[]{ "fiddle", "de", "dum" });
  }
}

class Other {
  public static void main(String[] args) {
```

```
    for(String s : args)
      System.out.print(s + " ");
  }
} /* Output:
fiddle de dum
*///:~
```

The array created for the argument of **Other.main( )** is created at the point
of the method call, so you can even provide alternate arguments at the time of
the call.

Exercise 16: (1) Create an array of **String** objects and assign a **String** to
each element. Print the array by using a **for** loop.

Exercise 17: (2) Create a class with a constructor that takes a **String**
argument. During construction, print the argument. Create an array of object
references to this class, but don't actually create objects to assign into the
array. When you run the program, notice whether the initialization messages
from the constructor calls are printed.

Exercise 18: (1) Complete the previous exercise by creating objects to
attach to the array of references.

Variable argument lists

The second form provides a convenient syntax to create and call methods that
can produce an effect similar to C's *variable argument lists* (known as
"varargs" in C). These can include unknown quantities of arguments as well
as unknown types. Since all classes are ultimately inherited from the common
root class **Object** (a subject you will learn more about as this book
progresses), you can create a method that takes an array of **Object** and call it
like this:

```
//: initialization/VarArgs.java
// Using array syntax to create variable argument lists.

class A {}

public class VarArgs {
  static void printArray(Object[] args) {
    for(Object obj : args)
      System.out.print(obj + " ");
    System.out.println();
  }
```

```
    public static void main(String[] args) {
      printArray(new Object[]{
        new Integer(47), new Float(3.14), new Double(11.11)
      });
      printArray(new Object[]{"one", "two", "three" });
      printArray(new Object[]{new A(), new A(), new A()});
    }
} /* Output: (Sample)
47 3.14 11.11
one two three
A@1a46e30 A@3e25a5 A@19821f
*///:~
```

You can see that **printArray( )** takes an array of **Object**, then steps through the array using the foreach syntax and prints each one. The standard Java library classes produce sensible output, but the objects of the classes created here print the class name, followed by an '@' sign and hexadecimal digits. Thus, the default behavior (if you don't define a **toString( )** method for your class, which will be described later in the book) is to print the class name and the address of the object.

You may see pre-Java SE5 code written like the above in order to produce variable argument lists. In Java SE5, however, this long-requested feature was finally added, so you can now use ellipses to define a variable argument list, as you can see in **printArray( )**:

```
//: initialization/NewVarArgs.java
// Using array syntax to create variable argument lists.

public class NewVarArgs {
  static void printArray(Object... args) {
    for(Object obj : args)
      System.out.print(obj + " ");
    System.out.println();
  }
  public static void main(String[] args) {
    // Can take individual elements:
    printArray(new Integer(47), new Float(3.14),
      new Double(11.11));
    printArray(47, 3.14F, 11.11);
    printArray("one", "two", "three");
    printArray(new A(), new A(), new A());
    // Or an array:
    printArray((Object[])new Integer[]{ 1, 2, 3, 4 });
```

```
      printArray(); // Empty list is OK
  }
} /* Output: (75% match)
47 3.14 11.11
47 3.14 11.11
one two three
A@1bab50a A@c3c749 A@150bd4d
1 2 3 4
*///:~
```

With varargs, you no longer have to explicitly write out the array syntax—the compiler will actually fill it in for you when you specify varargs. You're still getting an array, which is why **printArray( )** is able to use foreach to iterate through the array. However, it's more than just an automatic conversion from a list of elements to an array. Notice the second-to-last line in the program, where an array of **Integer** (created using autoboxing) is cast to an **Object** array (to remove a compiler warning) and passed to **printArray( )**. Clearly, the compiler sees that this is already an array and performs no conversion on it. So if you have a group of items you can pass them in as a list, and if you already have an array it will accept that as the variable argument list.

The last line of the program shows that it's possible to pass zero arguments to a vararg list. This is helpful when you have optional trailing arguments:

```
//: initialization/OptionalTrailingArguments.java

public class OptionalTrailingArguments {
  static void f(int required, String... trailing) {
    System.out.print("required: " + required + " ");
    for(String s : trailing)
      System.out.print(s + " ");
    System.out.println();
  }
  public static void main(String[] args) {
    f(1, "one");
    f(2, "two", "three");
    f(0);
  }
} /* Output:
required: 1 one
required: 2 two three
required: 0
*///:~
```

This also shows how you can use varargs with a specified type other than **Object**. Here, all the varargs must be **String** objects. It's possible to use any type of argument in varargs, including a primitive type. The following example also shows that the vararg list becomes an array, and if there's nothing in the list it's an array of size zero:

```
//: initialization/VarargType.java

public class VarargType {
  static void f(Character... args) {
    System.out.print(args.getClass());
    System.out.println(" length " + args.length);
  }
  static void g(int... args) {
    System.out.print(args.getClass());
    System.out.println(" length " + args.length);
  }
  public static void main(String[] args) {
    f('a');
    f();
    g(1);
    g();
    System.out.println("int[]: " + new int[0].getClass());
  }
} /* Output:
class [Ljava.lang.Character; length 1
class [Ljava.lang.Character; length 0
class [I length 1
class [I length 0
int[]: class [I
*///:~
```

The **getClass( )** method is part of **Object**, and will be explored fully in the *Type Information* chapter. It produces the class of an object, and when you print this class, you see an encoded string representing the class type. The leading '**[**' indicates that this is an array of the type that follows. The '**I**' is for a primitive **int**; to double-check, I created an array of **int** in the last line and printed its type. This verifies that using varargs does not depend on autoboxing, but that it actually uses the primitive types.

Varargs do work in harmony with autoboxing, however. For example:

```
//: initialization/AutoboxingVarargs.java
```

```
public class AutoboxingVarargs {
  public static void f(Integer... args) {
    for(Integer i : args)
      System.out.print(i + " ");
    System.out.println();
  }
  public static void main(String[] args) {
    f(new Integer(1), new Integer(2));
    f(4, 5, 6, 7, 8, 9);
    f(10, new Integer(11), 12);
  }
} /* Output:
1 2
4 5 6 7 8 9
10 11 12
*///:~
```

Notice that you can mix the types together in a single argument list, and autoboxing selectively promotes the **int** arguments to **Integer**.

Varargs complicate the process of overloading, although it seems safe enough at first:

```
//: initialization/OverloadingVarargs.java

public class OverloadingVarargs {
  static void f(Character... args) {
    System.out.print("first");
    for(Character c : args)
      System.out.print(" " + c);
    System.out.println();
  }
  static void f(Integer... args) {
    System.out.print("second");
    for(Integer i : args)
      System.out.print(" " + i);
    System.out.println();
  }
  static void f(Long... args) {
    System.out.println("third");
  }
  public static void main(String[] args) {
    f('a', 'b', 'c');
    f(1);
    f(2, 1);
```

```
    f(0);
    f(0L);
    //! f(); // Won't compile -- ambiguous
  }
} /* Output:
first a b c
second 1
second 2 1
second 0
third
*///:~
```

In each case, the compiler is using autoboxing to match the overloaded method, and it calls the most specifically matching method.

But when you call **f( )** without arguments, it has no way of knowing which one to call. Although this error is understandable, it will probably surprise the client programmer.

You might try solving the problem by adding a non-vararg argument to one of the methods:

```
//: initialization/OverloadingVarargs2.java
// {CompileTimeError} (Won't compile)

public class OverloadingVarargs2 {
  static void f(float i, Character... args) {
    System.out.println("first");
  }
  static void f(Character... args) {
    System.out.print("second");
  }
  public static void main(String[] args) {
    f(1, 'a');
    f('a', 'b');
  }
} ///:~
```

The **{CompileTimeError}** comment tag excludes the file from this book's Ant build. If you compile it by hand you'll see the error message:

> *reference to f is ambiguous, both method f(float,java.lang.Character...) in OverloadingVarargs2 and method f(java.lang.Character...) in OverloadingVarargs2 match*

If you give *both* methods a non-vararg argument, it works:

```
//: initialization/OverloadingVarargs3.java

public class OverloadingVarargs3 {
  static void f(float i, Character... args) {
    System.out.println("first");
  }
  static void f(char c, Character... args) {
    System.out.println("second");
  }
  public static void main(String[] args) {
    f(1, 'a');
    f('a', 'b');
  }
} /* Output:
first
second
*///:~
```

You should generally only use a variable argument list on one version of an overloaded method. Or consider not doing it at all.

Exercise 19: (2) Write a method that takes a vararg **String** array. Verify that you can pass either a comma-separated list of **String**s or a **String[]** into this method.

Exercise 20: (1) Create a **main( )** that uses varargs instead of the ordinary **main( )** syntax. Print all the elements in the resulting **args** array. Test it with various numbers of command-line arguments.

Enumerated types

An apparently small addition in Java SE5 is the **enum** keyword, which makes your life much easier when you need to group together and use a set of *enumerated types*. In the past you would have created a set of constant integral values, but these do not naturally restrict themselves to your set and thus are riskier and more difficult to use. Enumerated types are a common enough need that C, C++, and a number of other languages have always had them. Before Java SE5, Java programmers were forced to know a lot and be quite careful when they wanted to properly produce the **enum** effect. Now Java has **enum**, too, and it's much more full-featured than what you find in C/C++. Here's a simple example:

```
//: initialization/Spiciness.java
public enum Spiciness {
  NOT, MILD, MEDIUM, HOT, FLAMING
} ///:~
```

This creates an enumerated type called **Spiciness** with five named values. Because the instances of enumerated types are constants, they are in all capital letters by convention (if there are multiple words in a name, they are separated by underscores).

To use an **enum**, you create a reference of that type and assign it to an instance:

```
//: initialization/SimpleEnumUse.java
public class SimpleEnumUse {
  public static void main(String[] args) {
    Spiciness howHot = Spiciness.MEDIUM;
    System.out.println(howHot);
  }
} /* Output:
MEDIUM
*///:~
```

The compiler automatically adds useful features when you create an **enum**. For example, it creates a **toString( )** so that you can easily display the name of an **enum** instance, which is how the print statement above produced its output. The compiler also creates an **ordinal( )** method to indicate the declaration order of a particular **enum** constant, and a **static values( )** method that produces an array of values of the **enum** constants in the order that they were declared:

```
//: initialization/EnumOrder.java
public class EnumOrder {
  public static void main(String[] args) {
    for(Spiciness s : Spiciness.values())
      System.out.println(s + ", ordinal " + s.ordinal());
  }
} /* Output:
NOT, ordinal 0
MILD, ordinal 1
MEDIUM, ordinal 2
HOT, ordinal 3
FLAMING, ordinal 4
*///:~
```

Although **enum**s appear to be a new data type, the keyword only produces some compiler behavior while generating a class for the **enum**, so in many ways you can treat an **enum** as if it were any other class. In fact, **enum**s *are* classes and have their own methods.

An especially nice feature is the way that **enum**s can be used inside **switch** statements:

```
//: initialization/Burrito.java

public class Burrito {
  Spiciness degree;
  public Burrito(Spiciness degree) { this.degree = degree;}
  public void describe() {
    System.out.print("This burrito is ");
    switch(degree) {
      case NOT:     System.out.println("not spicy at all.");
                    break;
      case MILD:
      case MEDIUM:  System.out.println("a little hot.");
                    break;
      case HOT:
      case FLAMING:
      default:      System.out.println("maybe too hot.");
    }
  }
  public static void main(String[] args) {
    Burrito
      plain = new Burrito(Spiciness.NOT),
      greenChile = new Burrito(Spiciness.MEDIUM),
      jalapeno = new Burrito(Spiciness.HOT);
    plain.describe();
    greenChile.describe();
    jalapeno.describe();
  }
} /* Output:
This burrito is not spicy at all.
This burrito is a little hot.
This burrito is maybe too hot.
*///:~
```

Since a **switch** is intended to select from a limited set of possibilities, it's an ideal match for an **enum**. Notice how the **enum** names can produce a much clearer indication of what the program means to do.

In general you can use an **enum** as if it were another way to create a data type, and then just put the results to work. That's the point, so you don't have to think too hard about them. Before the introduction of **enum** in Java SE5, you had to go to a lot of effort to make an equivalent enumerated type that was safe to use.

This is enough for you to understand and use basic **enum**s, but we'll look more deeply at them later in the book—they have their own chapter: *Enumerated Types*.

Exercise 21: (1) Create an **enum** of the least-valuable six types of paper currency. Loop through the **values( )** and print each value and its **ordinal( )**.

Exercise 22: (2) Write a **switch** statement for the **enum** in the previous example. For each **case**, output a description of that particular currency.

Summary

This seemingly elaborate mechanism for initialization, the constructor, should give you a strong hint about the critical importance placed on initialization in the language. As Bjarne Stroustrup, the inventor of C++, was designing that language, one of the first observations he made about productivity in C was that improper initialization of variables causes a significant portion of programming problems. These kinds of bugs are hard to find, and similar issues apply to improper cleanup. Because constructors allow you to *guarantee* proper initialization and cleanup (the compiler will not allow an object to be created without the proper constructor calls), you get complete control and safety.

In C++, destruction is quite important because objects created with **new** must be explicitly destroyed. In Java, the garbage collector automatically releases the memory for all objects, so the equivalent cleanup method in Java isn't necessary much of the time (but when it is, you must do it yourself). In cases where you don't need destructor-like behavior, Java's garbage collector greatly simplifies programming and adds much-needed safety in managing memory. Some garbage collectors can even clean up other resources like graphics and file handles. However, the garbage collector does add a runtime cost, the expense of which is difficult to put into perspective because of the historical slowness of Java interpreters. Although Java has had significant performance increases over time, the speed problem has taken its toll on the adoption of the language for certain types of programming problems.

Because of the guarantee that all objects will be constructed, there's actually more to the constructor than what is shown here. In particular, when you create new classes using either *composition* or *inheritance,* the guarantee of construction also holds, and some additional syntax is necessary to support this. You'll learn about composition, inheritance, and how they affect constructors in future chapters.

Solutions to selected exercises can be found in the electronic document *The Thinking in Java Annotated Solution Guide*, available for sale from *www.MindView.net.*

Access Control

Access control (or *implementation hiding*) is about "not getting it right the first time."

All good writers—including those who write software—know that a piece of work isn't good until it's been rewritten, often many times. If you leave a piece of code in a drawer for a while and come back to it, you may see a much better way to do it. This is one of the prime motivations for *refactoring*, which rewrites working code in order to make it more readable, understandable, and thus maintainable.[1]

There is a tension, however, in this desire to change and improve your code. There are often consumers (*client programmers*) who rely on some aspect of your code staying the same. So you want to change it; they want it to stay the same. Thus a primary consideration in object-oriented design is to "separate the things that change from the things that stay the same."

This is particularly important for libraries. Consumers of that library must rely on the part they use, and know that they won't need to rewrite code if a new version of the library comes out. On the flip side, the library creator must have the freedom to make modifications and improvements with the certainty that the client code won't be affected by those changes.

This can be achieved through convention. For example, the library programmer must agree not to remove existing methods when modifying a class in the library, since that would break the client programmer's code. The reverse situation is thornier, however. In the case of a field, how can the library creator know which fields have been accessed by client programmers? This is also true with methods that are only part of the implementation of a class, and not meant to be used directly by the client programmer. What if the

---

[1] See *Refactoring: Improving the Design of Existing Code*, by Martin Fowler, et al. (Addison-Wesley, 1999). Occasionally someone will argue against refactoring, suggesting that code which works is perfectly good and it's a waste of time to refactor it. The problem with this way of thinking is that the lion's share of a project's time and money is not in the initial writing of the code, but in maintaining it. Making code easier to understand translates into very significant dollars.

library creator wants to rip out an old implementation and put in a new one? Changing any of those members might break a client programmer's code. Thus the library creator is in a strait jacket and can't change anything.

To solve this problem, Java provides *access specifiers* to allow the library creator to say what is available to the client programmer and what is not. The levels of access control from "most access" to "least access" are **public**, **protected**, package access (which has no keyword), and **private**. From the previous paragraph you might think that, as a library designer, you'll want to keep everything as "private" as possible, and expose only the methods that you want the client programmer to use. This is exactly right, even though it's often counterintuitive for people who program in other languages (especially C) and who are used to accessing everything without restriction. By the end of this chapter you should be convinced of the value of access control in Java.

The concept of a library of components and the control over who can access the components of that library is not complete, however. There's still the question of how the components are bundled together into a cohesive library unit. This is controlled with the **package** keyword in Java, and the access specifiers are affected by whether a class is in the same package or in a separate package. So to begin this chapter, you'll learn how library components are placed into packages. Then you'll be able to understand the complete meaning of the access specifiers.

package: the library unit

A package contains a group of classes, organized together under a single *namespace*.

For example, there's a utility library that's part of the standard Java distribution, organized under the namespace **java.util**. One of the classes in **java.util** is called **ArrayList**. One way to use an **ArrayList** is to specify the full name **java.util.ArrayList**.

```
//: access/FullQualification.java

public class FullQualification {
  public static void main(String[] args) {
    java.util.ArrayList list = new java.util.ArrayList();
  }
} ///:~
```

This rapidly becomes tedious, so you'll probably want to use the **import** keyword instead. If you want to import a single class, you can name that class in the **import** statement:

```
//: access/SingleImport.java
import java.util.ArrayList;

public class SingleImport {
  public static void main(String[] args) {
    ArrayList list = new ArrayList();
  }
} ///:~
```

Now you can use **ArrayList** with no qualification. However, none of the other classes in **java.util** are available. To import everything, you simply use the '*' as you've been seeing in the rest of the examples in this book:

```
import java.util.*;
```

The reason for all this importing is to provide a mechanism to manage namespaces. The names of all your class members are insulated from each other. A method **f( )** inside a class **A** will not clash with an **f( )** that has the same signature in class **B**. But what about the class names? Suppose you create a **Stack** class that is installed on a machine that already has a **Stack** class that's written by someone else? This potential clashing of names is why it's important to have complete control over the namespaces in Java, and to create a unique identifier combination for each class.

Most of the examples thus far in this book have existed in a single file and have been designed for local use, so they haven't bothered with package names. These examples have actually been in packages: the "unnamed" or *default package*. This is certainly an option, and for simplicity's sake this approach will be used whenever possible throughout the rest of this book. However, if you're planning to create libraries or programs that are friendly to other Java programs on the same machine, you must think about preventing class name clashes.

When you create a source-code file for Java, it's commonly called a *compilation unit* (sometimes a *translation unit*). Each compilation unit must have a name ending in **.java**, and inside the compilation unit there can be a **public** class that must have the same name as the file (including capitalization, but excluding the **.java** file name extension). There can be only *one* **public** class in each compilation unit; otherwise, the compiler will complain. If there are additional classes in that compilation unit, they are hidden from the world outside that package because they're *not* **public**, and they comprise "support" classes for the main **public** class.

Code organization

When you compile a **.java** file, you get an output file *for each class in the* **.java** file. Each output file has the name of a class in the **.java** file, but with an extension of **.class**. Thus you can end up with quite a few **.class** files from a small number of **.java** files. If you've programmed with a compiled language, you might be used to the compiler spitting out an intermediate form (usually an "obj" file) that is then packaged together with others of its kind using a linker (to create an executable file) or a librarian (to create a library). That's not how Java works. A working program is a bunch of **.class** files, which can be packaged and compressed into a Java ARchive (JAR) file (using Java's **jar** archiver). The Java interpreter is responsible for finding, loading, and interpreting[2] these files.

A library is a group of these class files. Each source file usually has a **public** class and any number of non-**public** classes, so there's one **public** component for each source file. If you want to say that all these components (each in its own separate **.java** and **.class** files) belong together, that's where the **package** keyword comes in.

If you use a **package** statement, it *must* appear as the first non-comment in the file. When you say:

```
package access;
```

you're stating that this compilation unit is part of a library named **access**. Put another way, you're saying that the **public** class name within this compilation unit is under the umbrella of the name **access**, and anyone who wants to use that name must either fully specify the name or use the **import** keyword in combination with **access**, using the choices given previously. (Note that the convention for Java package names is to use all lowercase letters, even for intermediate words.)

---

[2] There's nothing in Java that forces the use of an interpreter. There exist native-code Java compilers that generate a single executable file.

For example, suppose the name of the file is **MyClass.java**. This means there can be one and only one **public** class in that file, and the name of that class must be **MyClass** (including the capitalization):

```
//: access/mypackage/MyClass.java
package access.mypackage;

public class MyClass {
  // ...
} ///:~
```

Now, if someone wants to use **MyClass** or, for that matter, any of the other **public** classes in **acccss**, they must use the **import** keyword to make the name or names in **access** available. The alternative is to give the fully qualified name:

```
//: access/QualifiedMyClass.java

public class QualifiedMyClass {
  public static void main(String[] args) {
    access.mypackage.MyClass m =
      new access.mypackage.MyClass();
  }
} ///:~
```

The **import** keyword can make this much cleaner:

```
//: access/ImportedMyClass.java
import access.mypackage.*;

public class ImportedMyClass {
  public static void main(String[] args) {
    MyClass m = new MyClass();
  }
} ///:~
```

It's worth keeping in mind that what the **package** and **import** keywords allow you to do, as a library designer, is to divide up the single global namespace so you won't have clashing names, no matter how many people get on the Internet and start writing classes in Java.

Creating unique package names

You might observe that, since a package never really gets "packaged" into a single file, a package can be made up of many **.class** files, and things could

---

get a bit cluttered. To prevent this, a logical thing to do is to place all the **.class** files for a particular package into a single directory; that is, use the hierarchical file structure of the operating system to your advantage. This is one way that Java references the problem of clutter; you'll see the other way later when the **jar** utility is introduced.

Collecting the package files into a single subdirectory solves two other problems: creating unique package names, and finding those classes that might be buried in a directory structure someplace. This is accomplished by encoding the path of the location of the **.class** file into the name of the **package**. By convention, the first part of the **package** name is the reversed Internet domain name of the creator of the class. Since Internet domain names are guaranteed to be unique, *if* you follow this convention, your **package** name will be unique and you'll never have a name clash. (That is, until you lose the domain name to someone else who starts writing Java code with the same path names as you did.) Of course, if you don't have your own domain name, then you must fabricate an unlikely combination (such as your first and last name) to create unique package names. If you've decided to start publishing Java code, it's worth the relatively small effort to get a domain name.

The second part of this trick is resolving the **package** name into a directory on your machine, so that when the Java program runs and it needs to load the **.class** file, it can locate the directory where the **.class** file resides.

The Java interpreter proceeds as follows. First, it finds the environment variable CLASSPATH[3] (set via the operating system, and sometimes by the installation program that installs Java or a Java-based tool on your machine). CLASSPATH contains one or more directories that are used as roots in a search for **.class** files. Starting at that root, the interpreter will take the package name and replace each dot with a slash to generate a path name off of the CLASSPATH root (so **package foo.bar.baz** becomes **foo\bar\baz** or **foo/bar/baz** or possibly something else, depending on your operating system). This is then concatenated to the various entries in the CLASSPATH. That's where it looks for the **.class** file with the name corresponding to the class you're trying to create. (It also searches some standard directories relative to where the Java interpreter resides.)

---

[3] When referring to the environment variable, capital letters will be used (CLASSPATH).

To understand this, consider my domain name, which is **MindView.net**. By reversing this and making it all lowercase, **net.mindview** establishes my unique global name for my classes. (The com, edu, org, etc., extensions were formerly capitalized in Java packages, but this was changed in Java 2 so the entire package name is lowercase.) I can further subdivide this by deciding that I want to create a library named **simple**, so I'll end up with a package name:

```
package net.mindview.simple;
```

Now this package name can be used as an umbrella namespace for the following two files:

```
//: net/mindview/simple/Vector.java
// Creating a package.
package net.mindview.simple;

public class Vector {
  public Vector() {
    System.out.println("net.mindview.simple.Vector");
  }
} ///:~
```

As mentioned before, the **package** statement must be the first non-comment code in the file. The second file looks much the same:

```
//: net/mindview/simple/List.java
// Creating a package.
package net.mindview.simple;

public class List {
  public List() {
    System.out.println("net.mindview.simple.List");
  }
} ///:~
```

Both of these files are placed in the subdirectory on my system:

```
C:\DOC\JavaT\net\mindview\simple
```

(Notice that the first comment line in every file in this book establishes the directory location of that file in the source-code tree—this is used by the automatic code-extraction tool for this book.)

If you walk back through this path, you can see the package name **net.mindview.simple**, but what about the first portion of the path? That's taken care of by the CLASSPATH environment variable, which is, on my machine:

```
CLASSPATH=.;D:\JAVA\LIB;C:\DOC\JavaT
```

You can see that the CLASSPATH can contain a number of alternative search paths.

There's a variation when using JAR files, however. You must put the actual name of the JAR file in the classpath, not just the path where it's located. So for a JAR named **grape.jar** your classpath would include:

```
CLASSPATH=.;D:\JAVA\LIB;C:\flavors\grape.jar
```

Once the classpath is set up properly, the following file can be placed in any directory:

```
//: access/LibTest.java
// Uses the library.
import net.mindview.simple.*;

public class LibTest {
  public static void main(String[] args) {
    Vector v = new Vector();
    List l = new List();
  }
} /* Output:
net.mindview.simple.Vector
net.mindview.simple.List
*///:~
```

When the compiler encounters the **import** statement for the **simple** library, it begins searching at the directories specified by CLASSPATH, looking for subdirectory **net/mindview/simple**, then seeking the compiled files of the appropriate names (**Vector.class** for **Vector**, and **List.class** for **List**). Note that both the classes and the desired methods in **Vector** and **List** must be **public**.

Setting the CLASSPATH has been such a trial for beginning Java users (it was for me, when I started) that Sun made the JDK in later versions of Java a bit smarter. You'll find that when you install it, even if you don't set the CLASSPATH, you'll be able to compile and run basic Java programs. To compile and run the source-code package for this book (available at *www.MindView.net*), however, you will need to add the base directory of the book's code tree to your CLASSPATH.

Exercise 1: (1) Create a class in a package. Create an instance of your class outside of that package.

Collisions

What happens if two libraries are imported via '*' and they include the same names? For example, suppose a program does this:

```
import net.mindview.simple.*;
import java.util.*;
```

Since **java.util.*** also contains a **Vector** class, this causes a potential collision. However, as long as you don't write the code that actually causes the collision, everything is OK—this is good, because otherwise you might end up doing a lot of typing to prevent collisions that would never happen.

The collision *does* occur if you now try to make a **Vector**:

```
Vector v = new Vector();
```

Which **Vector** class does this refer to? The compiler can't know, and the reader can't know either. So the compiler complains and forces you to be explicit. If I want the standard Java **Vector**, for example, I must say:

```
java.util.Vector v = new java.util.Vector();
```

Since this (along with the CLASSPATH) completely specifies the location of that **Vector**, there's no need for the **import java.util.*** statement unless I'm using something else from **java.util**.

Alternatively, you can use the single-class import form to prevent clashes—as long as you don't use both colliding names in the same program (in which case you must fall back to fully specifying the names).

Exercise 2: (1) Take the code fragments in this section and turn them into a program, and verify that collisions do in fact occur.

A custom tool library

With this knowledge, you can now create your own libraries of tools to reduce or eliminate duplicate code. Consider, for example, the alias we've been using for **System.out.println( )**, to reduce typing. This can be part of a class called **Print** so that you end up with a readable **static import**:

```
//: net/mindview/util/Print.java
// Print methods that can be used without
// qualifiers, using Java SE5 static imports:
package net.mindview.util;
import java.io.*;

public class Print {
  // Print with a newline:
  public static void print(Object obj) {
    System.out.println(obj);
  }
  // Print a newline by itself:
  public static void print() {
    System.out.println();
  }
  // Print with no line break:
  public static void printnb(Object obj) {
    System.out.print(obj);
  }
  // The new Java SE5 printf() (from C):
  public static PrintStream
  printf(String format, Object... args) {
    return System.out.printf(format, args);
  }
} ///:~
```

You can use the printing shorthand to print anything, either with a newline (**print( )**) or without a newline (**printnb( )**).

You can guess that the location of this file must be in a directory that starts at one of the CLASSPATH locations, then continues into **net/mindview**. After compiling, the **static print( )** and **printnb( )** methods can be used anywhere on your system with an **import static** statement:

```
//: access/PrintTest.java
// Uses the static printing methods in Print.java.
import static net.mindview.util.Print.*;

public class PrintTest {
  public static void main(String[] args) {
    print("Available from now on!");
    print(100);
```

```
    print(100L);
    print(3.14159);
  }
} /* Output:
Available from now on!
100
100
3.14159
*///:~
```

A second component of this library can be the **range( )** methods, introduced in the *Controlling Execution* chapter, that allow the use of the foreach syntax for simple integer sequences:

```
//: net/mindview/util/Range.java
// Array creation methods that can be used without
// qualifiers, using Java SE5 static imports:
package net.mindview.util;

public class Range {
  // Produce a sequence [0..n)
  public static int[] range(int n) {
    int[] result = new int[n];
    for(int i = 0; i < n; i++)
      result[i] = i;
    return result;
  }
  // Produce a sequence [start..end)
  public static int[] range(int start, int end) {
    int sz = end - start;
    int[] result = new int[sz];
    for(int i = 0; i < sz; i++)
      result[i] = start + i;
    return result;
  }
  // Produce a sequence [start..end) incrementing by step
  public static int[] range(int start, int end, int step) {
    int sz = (end - start)/step;
    int[] result = new int[sz];
    for(int i = 0; i < sz; i++)
      result[i] = start + (i * step);
    return result;
  }
} ///:~
```

From now on, whenever you come up with a useful new utility, you can add it to your own library. You'll see more components added to the **net.mindview.util** library throughout the book.

Using imports to change behavior

A feature that is missing from Java is C's *conditional compilation*, which allows you to change a switch and get different behavior without changing any other code. The reason such a feature was left out of Java is probably because it is most often used in C to solve cross-platform issues: Different portions of the code are compiled depending on the target platform. Since Java is intended to be automatically cross-platform, such a feature should not be necessary.

However, there are other valuable uses for conditional compilation. A very common use is for debugging code. The debugging features are enabled during development and disabled in the shipping product. You can accomplish this by changing the **package** that's imported in order to change the code used in your program from the debug version to the production version. This technique can be used for any kind of conditional code.

Exercise 3: (2) Create two packages: **debug** and **debugoff**, containing an identical class with a **debug( )** method. The first version displays its **String** argument to the console, the second does nothing. Use a **static import** line to import the class into a test program, and demonstrate the conditional compilation effect.

Package caveat

It's worth remembering that anytime you create a package, you implicitly specify a directory structure when you give the package a name. The package *must* live in the directory indicated by its name, which must be a directory that is searchable starting from the CLASSPATH. Experimenting with the **package** keyword can be a bit frustrating at first, because unless you adhere to the package-name to directory-path rule, you'll get a lot of mysterious runtime messages about not being able to find a particular class, even if that class is sitting there in the same directory. If you get a message like this, try commenting out the **package** statement, and if it runs, you'll know where the problem lies.

Note that compiled code is often placed in a different directory than source code, but the path to the compiled code must still be found by the JVM using the CLASSPATH.

Java access specifiers

The Java access specifiers **public**, **protected**, and **private** are placed in front of each definition for each member in your class, whether it's a field or a method. Each access specifier only controls the access for that particular definition.

If you don't provide an access specifier, it means "package access." So one way or another, everything has some kind of access control. In the following sections, you'll learn about the various types of access.

Package access

All the examples before this chapter used no access specifiers. The default access has no keyword, but it is commonly referred to as *package access* (and sometimes "friendly"). It means that all the other classes in the current package have access to that member, but to all the classes outside of this package, the member appears to be **private**. Since a compilation unit—a file—can belong only to a single package, all the classes within a single compilation unit are automatically available to each other via package access.

Package access allows you to group related classes together in a package so that they can easily interact with each other. When you put classes together in a package, thus granting mutual access to their package-access members, you "own" the code in that package. It makes sense that only code that you own should have package access to other code that you own. You could say that package access gives a meaning or a reason for grouping classes together in a package. In many languages the way you organize your definitions in files can be arbitrary, but in Java you're compelled to organize them in a sensible fashion. In addition, you'll probably want to exclude classes that shouldn't have access to the classes being defined in the current package.

The class controls the code that has access to its members. Code from another package can't just come around and say, "Hi, I'm a friend of **Bob**'s!" and expect to be shown the **protected**, package-access, and **private** members of **Bob**. The only way to grant access to a member is to:

1. Make the member **public**. Then everybody, everywhere, can access it.

2. Give the member package access by leaving off any access specifier, and put the other classes in the same package. Then the other classes in that package can access the member.

3. As you'll see in the *Reusing Classes* chapter, when inheritance is introduced, an inherited class can access a **protected** member as well as a **public** member (but not **private** members). It can access package-access members only if the two classes are in the same package. But don't worry about inheritance and **protected** right now.

4. Provide "accessor/mutator" methods (also known as "get/set" methods) that read and change the value. This is the most civilized approach in terms of OOP, and it is fundamental to JavaBeans, as you'll see in the *Graphical User Interfaces* chapter.

public: interface access

When you use the **public** keyword, it means that the member declaration that immediately follows **public** is available to everyone, in particular to the client programmer who uses the library. Suppose you define a package **dessert** containing the following compilation unit:

```
//: access/dessert/Cookie.java
// Creates a library.
package access.dessert;

public class Cookie {
  public Cookie() {
    System.out.println("Cookie constructor");
  }
  void bite() { System.out.println("bite"); }
} ///:~
```

Remember, the class file produced by **Cookie.java** must reside in a subdirectory called **dessert**, in a directory under **access** (indicating the *Access Control* chapter of this book) that must be under one of the CLASSPATH directories. Don't make the mistake of thinking that Java will always look at the current directory as one of the starting points for searching. If you don't have a '.' as one of the paths in your CLASSPATH, Java won't look there.

Now if you create a program that uses **Cookie**:

```
//: access/Dinner.java
// Uses the library.
import access.dessert.*;

public class Dinner {
  public static void main(String[] args) {
    Cookie x = new Cookie();
    //! x.bite(); // Can't access
  }
} /* Output:
Cookie constructor
*///:~
```

you can create a **Cookie** object, since its constructor is **public** and the class is **public**. (We'll look more at the concept of a **public** class later.) However, the **bite( )** member is inaccessible inside **Dinner.java** since **bite( )** provides access only within package **dessert**, so the compiler prevents you from using it.

The default package

You might be surprised to discover that the following code compiles, even though it would appear that it breaks the rules:

```
//: access/Cake.java
// Accesses a class in a separate compilation unit.

class Cake {
  public static void main(String[] args) {
    Pie x = new Pie();
    x.f();
  }
} /* Output:
Pie.f()
*///:~
```

In a second file in the same directory:

```
//: access/Pie.java
// The other class.
```

```
class Pie {
  void f() { System.out.println("Pie.f()"); }
} ///:~
```

You might initially view these as completely foreign files, and yet **Cake** is able to create a **Pie** object and call its **f( )** method. (Note that you must have '.' in your CLASSPATH in order for the files to compile.) You'd typically think that **Pie** and **f( )** have package access and are therefore not available to **Cake**. They *do* have package access—that part is correct. The reason that they are available in **Cake.java** is because they are in the same directory and have no explicit package name. Java treats files like this as implicitly part of the "default package" for that directory, and thus they provide package access to all the other files in that directory.

private: you can't touch that!

The **private** keyword means that no one can access that member except the class that contains that member, inside methods of that class. Other classes in the same package cannot access **private** members, so it's as if you're even insulating the class against yourself. On the other hand, it's not unlikely that a package might be created by several people collaborating together, so **private** allows you to freely change that member without concern that it will affect another class in the same package.

The default package access often provides an adequate amount of hiding; remember, a package-access member is inaccessible to the client programmer using the class. This is nice, since the default access is the one that you normally use (and the one that you'll get if you forget to add any access control). Thus, you'll typically think about access for the members that you explicitly want to make **public** for the client programmer, and as a result, you might initially think that you won't use the **private** keyword very often, since it's tolerable to get away without it. However, it turns out that the consistent use of **private** is very important, especially where multithreading is concerned. (As you'll see in the *Concurrency* chapter.)

Here's an example of the use of **private**:

```
//: access/IceCream.java
// Demonstrates "private" keyword.

class Sundae {
```

```
    private Sundae() {}
    static Sundae makeASundae() {
      return new Sundae();
    }
}

public class IceCream {
  public static void main(String[] args) {
    //! Sundae x = new Sundae();
    Sundae x = Sundae.makeASundae();
  }
} ///:~
```

This shows an example in which **private** comes in handy: You might want to control how an object is created and prevent someone from directly accessing a particular constructor (or all of them). In the preceding example, you cannot create a **Sundae** object via its constructor; instead, you must call the **makeASundae( )** method to do it for you.[4]

Any method that you're certain is only a "helper" method for that class can be made **private**, to ensure that you don't accidentally use it elsewhere in the package and thus prohibit yourself from changing or removing the method. Making a method **private** guarantees that you retain this option.

The same is true for a **private** field inside a class. Unless you must expose the underlying implementation (which is less likely than you might think), you should make all fields **private**. However, just because a reference to an object is **private** inside a class doesn't mean that some other object can't have a **public** reference to the same object. (See the online supplements for this book to learn about aliasing issues.)

protected: inheritance access

Understanding the **protected** access specifier requires a jump ahead. First, you should be aware that you don't need to understand this section to continue through this book up through inheritance (the *Reusing Classes* chapter). But for completeness, here is a brief description and example using **protected**.

---

[4] There's another effect in this case: Since the default constructor is the only one defined, and it's **private**, it will prevent inheritance of this class. (A subject that will be introduced later.)

The **protected** keyword deals with a concept called *inheritance*, which takes an existing class—which we refer to as the *base class*—and adds new members to that class without touching the existing class. You can also change the behavior of existing members of the class. To inherit from a class, you say that your new class **extends** an existing class, like this:

```
class Foo extends Bar {
```

The rest of the class definition looks the same.

If you create a new package and inherit from a class in another package, the only members you have access to are the **public** members of the original package. (Of course, if you perform the inheritance in the *same* package, you can manipulate all the members that have package access.) Sometimes the creator of the base class would like to take a particular member and grant access to derived classes but not the world in general. That's what **protected** does. **protected** also gives package access—that is, other classes in the same package may access **protected** elements.

If you refer back to the file **Cookie.java**, the following class *cannot* call the package-access member **bite( )**:

```
//: access/ChocolateChip.java
// Can't use package-access member from another package.
import access.dessert.*;

public class ChocolateChip extends Cookie {
  public ChocolateChip() {
    System.out.println("ChocolateChip constructor");
  }
  public void chomp() {
    //! bite(); // Can't access bite
  }
  public static void main(String[] args) {
    ChocolateChip x = new ChocolateChip();
    x.chomp();
  }
} /* Output:
Cookie constructor
ChocolateChip constructor
*///:~
```

One of the interesting things about inheritance is that if a method **bite( )** exists in class **Cookie**, then it also exists in any class inherited from **Cookie**.

Thinking in Java Bruce Eckel

But since **bite( )** has package access and is in a foreign package, it's unavailable to us in this one. Of course, you could make it **public**, but then everyone would have access, and maybe that's not what you want. If you change the class **Cookie** as follows:

```
//: access/cookie2/Cookie.java
package access.cookie2;

public class Cookie {
  public Cookie() {
    System.out.println("Cookie constructor");
  }
  protected void bite() {
    System.out.println("bite");
  }
} ///:~
```

now **bite( )** becomes accessible to anyone inheriting from **Cookie**:

```
//: access/ChocolateChip2.java
import access.cookie2.*;

public class ChocolateChip2 extends Cookie {
  public ChocolateChip2() {
    System.out.println("ChocolateChip2 constructor");
  }
  public void chomp() { bite(); } // Protected method
  public static void main(String[] args) {
    ChocolateChip2 x = new ChocolateChip2();
    x.chomp();
  }
} /* Output:
Cookie constructor
ChocolateChip2 constructor
bite
*///:~
```

Note that, although **bite( )** also has package access, it is *not* **public**.

Exercise 4: (2) Show that **protected** methods have package access but are not **public**.

Exercise 5: (2) Create a class with **public**, **private**, **protected**, and package-access fields and method members. Create an object of this class and see what kind of compiler messages you get when you try to access all the class members. Be aware that classes in the same directory are part of the "default" package.

Exercise 6: (1) Create a class with **protected** data. Create a second class in the same file with a method that manipulates the **protected** data in the first class.

Interface and implementation

Access control is often referred to as *implementation hiding*. Wrapping data and methods within classes in combination with implementation hiding is often called *encapsulation*.[5] The result is a data type with characteristics and behaviors.

Access control puts boundaries within a data type for two important reasons. The first is to establish what the client programmers can and can't use. You can build your internal mechanisms into the structure without worrying that the client programmers will accidentally treat the internals as part of the interface that they should be using.

This feeds directly into the second reason, which is to separate the interface from the implementation. If the structure is used in a set of programs, but client programmers can't do anything but send messages to the **public** interface, then you are free to change anything that's *not* **public** (e.g., package access, **protected**, or **private**) without breaking client code.

For clarity, you might prefer a style of creating classes that puts the **public** members at the beginning, followed by the **protected**, package-access, and **private** members. The advantage is that the user of the class can then read down from the top and see first what's important to them (the **public** members, because they can be accessed outside the file), and stop reading when they encounter the non-**public** members, which are part of the internal implementation:

```
//: access/OrganizedByAccess.java

public class OrganizedByAccess {
  public void pub1() { /* ... */ }
  public void pub2() { /* ... */ }
```

---

[5] However, people often refer to implementation hiding alone as encapsulation.

```
   public void pub3() { /* ... */ }
   private void priv1() { /* ... */ }
   private void priv2() { /* ... */ }
   private void priv3() { /* ... */ }
   private int i;
   // ...
} ///:~
```

This will make it only partially easier to read, because the interface and implementation are still mixed together. That is, you still see the source code—the implementation—because it's right there in the class. In addition, the comment documentation supported by Javadoc lessens the importance of code readability by the client programmer. Displaying the interface to the consumer of a class is really the job of the *class browser*, a tool whose job is to look at all the available classes and show you what you can do with them (i.e., what members are available) in a useful fashion. In Java, viewing the JDK documentation with a Web browser gives you the same effect as a class browser.

Class access

In Java, the access specifiers can also be used to determine which classes *within* a library will be available to the users of that library. If you want a class to be available to a client programmer, you use the **public** keyword on the entire class definition. This controls whether the client programmer can even create an object of the class.

To control the access of a class, the specifier must appear before the keyword **class**. Thus you can say:

```
public class Widget {
```

Now if the name of your library is **access**, any client programmer can access **Widget** by saying

```
import access.Widget;
```

or

```
import access.*;
```

However, there's an extra set of constraints:

---

1. There can be only one **public** class per compilation unit (file). The idea is that each compilation unit has a single public interface represented by that **public** class. It can have as many supporting package-access classes as you want. If you have more than one **public** class inside a compilation unit, the compiler will give you an error message.

2. The name of the **public** class must exactly match the name of the file containing the compilation unit, including capitalization. So for **Widget**, the name of the file must be **Widget.java**, not **widget.java** or **WIDGET.java**. Again, you'll get a compile-time error if they don't agree.

3. It is possible, though not typical, to have a compilation unit with no **public** class at all. In this case, you can name the file whatever you like (although naming it arbitrarily will be confusing to people reading and maintaining the code).

What if you've got a class inside **access** that you're only using to accomplish the tasks performed by **Widget** or some other **public** class in **access**? You don't want to go to the bother of creating documentation for the client programmer, and you think that sometime later you might want to completely change things and rip out your class altogether, substituting a different one. To give you this flexibility, you need to ensure that no client programmers become dependent on your particular implementation details hidden inside **access**. To accomplish this, you just leave the **public** keyword off the class, in which case it has package access. (That class can be used only within that package.)

Exercise 7: (1) Create the library according to the code fragments describing **access** and **Widget**. Create a **Widget** in a class that is not part of the **access** package.

When you create a package-access class, it still makes sense to make the fields of the class **private**—you should always make fields as **private** as possible—but it's generally reasonable to give the methods the same access as the class (package access). Since a package-access class is usually used only within the package, you only need to make the methods of such a class **public** if you're forced to, and in those cases, the compiler will tell you.

Note that a class cannot be **private** (that would make it inaccessible to anyone but the class) or **protected**.[6] So you have only two choices for class access: package access or **public**. If you don't want anyone else to have access to that class, you can make all the constructors **private**, thereby preventing anyone but you, inside a **static** member of the class, from creating an object of that class. Here's an example:

```
//: access/Lunch.java
// Demonstrates class access specifiers. Make a class
// effectively private with private constructors:

class Soup1 {
  private Soup1() {}
  // (1) Allow creation via static method:
  public static Soup1 makeSoup() {
    return new Soup1();
  }
}

class Soup2 {
  private Soup2() {}
  // (2) Create a static object and return a reference
  // upon request.(The "Singleton" pattern):
  private static Soup2 ps1 = new Soup2();
  public static Soup2 access() {
    return ps1;
  }
  public void f() {}
}

// Only one public class allowed per file:
public class Lunch {
  void testPrivate() {
    // Can't do this! Private constructor:
    //! Soup1 soup = new Soup1();
  }
  void testStatic() {
    Soup1 soup = Soup1.makeSoup();
  }
```

---

[6] Actually, an *inner class* can be private or protected, but that's a special case. These will be introduced in the *Inner Classes* chapter.

```
  void testSingleton() {
    Soup2.access().f();
  }
} ///:~
```

Up to now, most of the methods have been returning either **void** or a
primitive type, so the definition:

```
public static Soup1 makeSoup() {
  return new Soup1();
}
```

might look a little confusing at first. The word **Soup1** before the method
name (**makeSoup**) tells what the method returns. So far in this book, this
has usually been **void**, which means it returns nothing. But you can also
return a reference to an object, which is what happens here. This method
returns a reference to an object of class **Soup1**.

The classes **Soup1** and **Soup2** show how to prevent direct creation of a class
by making all the constructors **private**. Remember that if you don't explicitly
create at least one constructor, the default constructor (a constructor with no
arguments) will be created for you. By writing the default constructor, it
won't be created automatically. By making it **private**, no one can create an
object of that class. But now how does anyone use this class? The preceding
example shows two options. In **Soup1**, a **static** method is created that
creates a new **Soup1** and returns a reference to it. This can be useful if you
want to do some extra operations on the **Soup1** before returning it, or if you
want to keep count of how many **Soup1** objects to create (perhaps to restrict
their population).

Soup2 uses what's called a *design pattern*, which is covered in *Thinking in
Patterns (with Java)* at *www.MindView.net*. This particular pattern is called
a *Singleton*, because it allows only a single object to ever be created. The
object of class **Soup2** is created as a **static private** member of **Soup2**, so
there's one and only one, and you can't get at it except through the **public**
method **access( )**.

As previously mentioned, if you don't put an access specifier for class access,
it defaults to package access. This means that an object of that class can be
created by any other class in the package, but not outside the package.
(Remember, all the files within the same directory that don't have explicit

package declarations are implicitly part of the default package for that directory.)

Exercise 8: (4) Following the form of the example **Lunch.java**, create a class called **ConnectionManager** that manages a fixed array of **Connection** objects. The client programmer must not be able to explicitly create **Connection** objects, but can only get them via a **static** method in **ConnectionManager**. When the **ConnectionManager** runs out of objects, it returns a **null** reference. Test the classes in **main( )**.

Exercise 9: (2) Create the following file in the **access/local** directory (presumably in your CLASSPATH):

```
// access/local/PackagedClass.java
package access.local;

class PackagedClass {
  public PackagedClass() {
    System.out.println("Creating a packaged class");
  }
}
```

Then create the following file in a directory other than **access/local**:

```
// access/foreign/Foreign.java
package access.foreign;
import access.local.*;

public class Foreign {
    public static void main(String[] args) {
        PackagedClass pc = new PackagedClass();
    }
}
```

Explain why the compiler generates an error. Would making the **Foreign** class part of the **access.local** package change anything?

Summary

In any relationship it's important to have boundaries that are respected by all parties involved. When you create a library, you establish a relationship with the user of that library—the client programmer—who is another programmer, but one using your library to build an application or a bigger library.

Without rules, client programmers can do anything they want with all the members of a class, even if you might prefer they don't directly manipulate some of the members. Everything's naked to the world.

This chapter looked at how classes are built to form libraries: first, the way a group of classes is packaged within a library, and second, the way the class controls access to its members.

It is estimated that a C programming project begins to break down somewhere between 50K and 100K lines of code because C has a single namespace, and names begin to collide, causing extra management overhead. In Java, the **package** keyword, the package naming scheme, and the **import** keyword give you complete control over names, so the issue of name collision is easily avoided.

There are two reasons for controlling access to members. The first is to keep users' hands off portions that they shouldn't touch. These pieces are necessary for the internal operations of the class, but not part of the interface that the client programmer needs. So making methods and fields **private** is a service to client programmers, because they can easily see what's important to them and what they can ignore. It simplifies their understanding of the class.

The second and most important reason for access control is to allow the library designer to change the internal workings of the class without worrying about how it will affect the client programmer. You might, for example, build a class one way at first, and then discover that restructuring your code will provide much greater speed. If the interface and implementation are clearly separated and protected, you can accomplish this without forcing client programmers to rewrite their code. Access control ensures that no client programmer becomes dependent on any part of the underlying implementation of a class.

When you have the ability to change the underlying implementation, you not only have the freedom to improve your design, you also have the freedom to make mistakes. No matter how carefully you plan and design, you'll make mistakes. Knowing that it's relatively safe to make these mistakes means you'll be more experimental, you'll learn more quickly, and you'll finish your project sooner.

The public interface to a class is what the user *does* see, so that is the most important part of the class to get "right" during analysis and design. Even that allows you some leeway for change. If you don't get the interface right the first time, you can *add* more methods, as long as you don't remove any that client programmers have already used in their code.

Notice that access control focuses on a relationship—and a kind of communication—between a library creator and the external clients of that library. There are many situations where this is not the case. For example, you are writing all the code yourself, or you are working in close quarters with a small team and everything goes into the same package. These situations have a different kind of communication, and rigid adherence to access rules may not be optimal. Default (package) access may be just fine.

Solutions to selected exercises can be found in the electronic document *The Thinking in Java Annotated Solution Guide*, available for sale from *www.MindView.net*.

Reusing Classes

One of the most compelling features about Java is code reuse. But to be revolutionary, you've got to be able to do a lot more than copy code and change it.

That's the approach used in procedural languages like C, and it hasn't worked very well. Like everything in Java, the solution revolves around the class. You reuse code by creating new classes, but instead of creating them from scratch, you use existing classes that someone has already built and debugged.

The trick is to use the classes without soiling the existing code. In this chapter you'll see two ways to accomplish this. The first is quite straightforward: You simply create objects of your existing class inside the new class. This is called *composition,* because the new class is composed of objects of existing classes. You're simply reusing the functionality of the code, not its form.

The second approach is more subtle. It creates a new class as a *type of* an existing class. You literally take the form of the existing class and add code to it without modifying the existing class. This technique is called *inheritance,* and the compiler does most of the work. Inheritance is one of the cornerstones of object-oriented programming, and has additional implications that will be explored in the *Polymorphism* chapter.

It turns out that much of the syntax and behavior are similar for both composition and inheritance (which makes sense because they are both ways of making new types from existing types). In this chapter, you'll learn about these code reuse mechanisms.

Composition syntax

Composition has been used quite frequently up to this point in the book. You simply place object references inside new classes. For example, suppose you'd like an object that holds several **String** objects, a couple of primitives, and an object of another class. For the non-primitive objects, you put references inside your new class, but you define the primitives directly:

```
//: reusing/SprinklerSystem.java
```

```
// Composition for code reuse.

class WaterSource {
  private String s;
  WaterSource() {
    System.out.println("WaterSource()");
    s = "Constructed";
  }
  public String toString() { return s; }
}

public class SprinklerSystem {
  private String valve1, valve2, valve3, valve4;
  private WaterSource source = new WaterSource();
  private int i;
  private float f;
  public String toString() {
    return
      "valve1 = " + valve1 + " " +
      "valve2 = " + valve2 + " " +
      "valve3 = " + valve3 + " " +
      "valve4 = " + valve4 + "\n" +
      "i = " + i + " " + "f = " + f + " " +
      "source = " + source;
  }
  public static void main(String[] args) {
    SprinklerSystem sprinklers = new SprinklerSystem();
    System.out.println(sprinklers);
  }
} /* Output:
WaterSource()
valve1 = null valve2 = null valve3 = null valve4 = null
i = 0 f = 0.0 source = Constructed
*///:~
```

One of the methods defined in both classes is special: **toString( )**. Every non-primitive object has a **toString( )** method, and it's called in special situations when the compiler wants a **String** but it has an object. So in the expression in **SprinklerSystem.toString( )**:

```
"source = " + source;
```

the compiler sees you trying to add a **String** object ("**source = **") to a **WaterSource**. Because you can only "add" a **String** to another **String**, it says, "I'll turn **source** into a **String** by calling **toString( )**!" After doing this it can combine the two **String**s and pass the resulting **String** to **System.out.println( )** (or equivalently, this book's **print( )** and **printnb( ) static** methods). Anytime you want to allow this behavior with a class you create, you need only write a **toString( )** method.

Primitives that are fields in a class are automatically initialized to zero, as noted in the *Everything Is an Object* chapter. But the object references are initialized to **null**, and if you try to call methods for any of them, you'll get an exception—a runtime error. Conveniently, you can still print a **null** reference without throwing an exception.

It makes sense that the compiler doesn't just create a default object for every reference, because that would incur unnecessary overhead in many cases. If you want the references initialized, you can do it:

1. At the point the objects are defined. This means that they'll always be initialized before the constructor is called.

2. In the constructor for that class.

3. Right before you actually need to use the object. This is often called *lazy initialization*. It can reduce overhead in situations where object creation is expensive and the object doesn't need to be created every time.

4. Using *instance initialization*.

All four approaches are shown here:

```
//: reusing/Bath.java
// Constructor initialization with composition.
import static net.mindview.util.Print.*;

class Soap {
  private String s;
  Soap() {
    print("Soap()");
    s = "Constructed";
  }
  public String toString() { return s; }
}

public class Bath {
  private String // Initializing at point of definition:
```

```
      s1 = "Happy",
      s2 = "Happy",
      s3, s4;
    private Soap castille;
    private int i;
    private float toy;
    public Bath() {
      print("Inside Bath()");
      s3 = "Joy";
      toy = 3.14f;
      castille = new Soap();
    }
    // Instance initialization:
    { i = 47; }
    public String toString() {
      if(s4 == null) // Delayed initialization:
        s4 = "Joy";
      return
        "s1 = " + s1 + "\n" +
        "s2 = " + s2 + "\n" +
        "s3 = " + s3 + "\n" +
        "s4 = " + s4 + "\n" +
        "i = " + i + "\n" +
        "toy = " + toy + "\n" +
        "castille = " + castille;
    }
    public static void main(String[] args) {
      Bath b = new Bath();
      print(b);
    }
} /* Output:
Inside Bath()
Soap()
s1 = Happy
s2 = Happy
s3 = Joy
s4 = Joy
i = 47
toy = 3.14
castille = Constructed
*///:~
```

Note that in the **Bath** constructor, a statement is executed before any of the initializations take place. When you don't initialize at the point of definition, there's still no guarantee that you'll perform any initialization before you send a message to an object reference—except for the inevitable runtime exception.

When **toString( )** is called it fills in **s4** so that all the fields are properly initialized by the time they are used.

Exercise 1: (2) Create a simple class. Inside a second class, define a reference to an object of the first class. Use lazy initialization to instantiate this object.

Inheritance syntax

Inheritance is an integral part of Java (and all OOP languages). It turns out that you're always doing inheritance when you create a class, because unless you explicitly inherit from some other class, you implicitly inherit from Java's standard root class **Object**.

The syntax for composition is obvious, but inheritance uses a special syntax. When you inherit, you say, "This new class is like that old class." You state this in code before the opening brace of the class body, using the keyword **extends** followed by the name of the *base class*. When you do this, you automatically get all the fields and methods in the base class. Here's an example:

```
//: reusing/Detergent.java
// Inheritance syntax & properties.
import static net.mindview.util.Print.*;

class Cleanser {
  private String s = "Cleanser";
  public void append(String a) { s += a; }
  public void dilute() { append(" dilute()"); }
  public void apply() { append(" apply()"); }
  public void scrub() { append(" scrub()"); }
  public String toString() { return s; }
  public static void main(String[] args) {
    Cleanser x = new Cleanser();
    x.dilute(); x.apply(); x.scrub();
    print(x);
  }
}

public class Detergent extends Cleanser {
```

```
    // Change a method:
    public void scrub() {
      append(" Detergent.scrub()");
      super.scrub(); // Call base-class version
    }
    // Add methods to the interface:
    public void foam() { append(" foam()"); }
    // Test the new class:
    public static void main(String[] args) {
      Detergent x = new Detergent();
      x.dilute();
      x.apply();
      x.scrub();
      x.foam();
      print(x);
      print("Testing base class:");
      Cleanser.main(args);
    }
} /* Output:
Cleanser dilute() apply() Detergent.scrub() scrub() foam()
Testing base class:
Cleanser dilute() apply() scrub()
*///:~
```

This demonstrates a number of features. First, in the **Cleanser append( )**
method, **String**s are concatenated to **s** using the += operator, which is one of
the operators (along with '+') that the Java designers "overloaded" to work
with **String**s.

Second, both **Cleanser** and **Detergent** contain a **main( )** method. You can
create a **main( )** for each one of your classes; this technique of putting a
main( ) in each class allows easy testing for each class. And you don't need
to remove the **main( )** when you're finished; you can leave it in for later
testing.

Even if you have a lot of classes in a program, only the **main( )** for the class
invoked on the command line will be called. So in this case, when you say
java Detergent, **Detergent.main( )** will be called. But you can also say
java Cleanser to invoke **Cleanser.main( )**, even though **Cleanser** is not a
public class. Even if a class has package access, a **public main( )** is
accessible.

Here, you can see that **Detergent.main( )** calls **Cleanser.main( )** explicitly, passing it the same arguments from the command line (however, you could pass it any **String** array).

It's important that all of the methods in **Cleanser** are **public**. Remember that if you leave off any access specifier, the member defaults to package access, which allows access only to package members. Thus, *within this package*, anyone could use those methods if there were no access specifier. **Detergent** would have no trouble, for example. However, if a class from some other package were to inherit from **Cleanser**, it could access only **public** members. So to allow for inheritance, as a general rule make all fields **private** and all methods **public**. (**protected** members also allow access by derived classes; you'll learn about this later.) Of course, in particular cases you must make adjustments, but this is a useful guideline.

Cleanser has a set of methods in its interface: **append( )**, **dilute( )**, **apply( )**, **scrub( )**, and **toString( )**. Because **Detergent** is *derived from* **Cleanser** (via the **extends** keyword), it automatically gets all these methods in its interface, even though you don't see them all explicitly defined in **Detergent**. You can think of inheritance, then, as reusing the class.

As seen in **scrub( )**, it's possible to take a method that's been defined in the base class and modify it. In this case, you might want to call the method from the base class inside the new version. But inside **scrub( )**, you cannot simply call **scrub( )**, since that would produce a recursive call, which isn't what you want. To solve this problem, Java's **super** keyword refers to the "superclass" that the current class inherits. Thus the expression **super.scrub( )** calls the base-class version of the method **scrub( )**.

When inheriting, you're not restricted to using the methods of the base class. You can also add new methods to the derived class exactly the way you add any method to a class: Just define it. The method **foam( )** is an example of this.

In **Detergent.main( )** you can see that for a **Detergent** object, you can call all the methods that are available in **Cleanser** as well as in **Detergent** (i.e., **foam( )**).

Exercise 2: (2) Inherit a new class from class **Detergent**. Override **scrub( )** and add a new method called **sterilize( )**.

Initializing the base class

Since there are now two classes involved—the base class and the derived class—instead of just one, it can be a bit confusing to try to imagine the resulting object produced by a derived class. From the outside, it looks like the new class has the same interface as the base class and maybe some additional methods and fields. But inheritance doesn't just copy the interface of the base class. When you create an object of the derived class, it contains within it a *subobject* of the base class. This subobject is the same as if you had created an object of the base class by itself. It's just that from the outside, the subobject of the base class is wrapped within the derived-class object.

Of course, it's essential that the base-class subobject be initialized correctly, and there's only one way to guarantee this: Perform the initialization in the constructor by calling the base-class constructor, which has all the appropriate knowledge and privileges to perform the base-class initialization. Java automatically inserts calls to the base-class constructor in the derived-class constructor. The following example shows this working with three levels of inheritance:

```
//: reusing/Cartoon.java
// Constructor calls during inheritance.
import static net.mindview.util.Print.*;

class Art {
  Art() { print("Art constructor"); }
}

class Drawing extends Art {
  Drawing() { print("Drawing constructor"); }
}

public class Cartoon extends Drawing {
  public Cartoon() { print("Cartoon constructor"); }
  public static void main(String[] args) {
    Cartoon x = new Cartoon();
  }
} /* Output:
Art constructor
Drawing constructor
Cartoon constructor
*///:~
```

You can see that the construction happens from the base "outward," so the base class is initialized before the derived-class constructors can access it. Even if you don't create a constructor for **Cartoon( )**, the compiler will synthesize a default constructor for you that calls the base-class constructor.

Exercise 3: (2) Prove the previous sentence.

Exercise 4: (2) Prove that base-class constructors are (a) always called and (b) called before derived-class constructors.

Exercise 5: (1) Create two classes, **A** and **B**, with default constructors (empty argument lists) that announce themselves. Inherit a new class called **C** from **A**, and create a member of class **B** inside **C**. Do not create a constructor for **C**. Create an object of class **C** and observe the results.

Constructors with arguments

The preceding example has default constructors; that is, they don't have any arguments. It's easy for the compiler to call these because there's no question about what arguments to pass. If there is no default base-class constructor, or if you want to call a base-class constructor that has arguments, you must explicitly write a call to the base-class constructor using the **super** keyword and the appropriate argument list:

```
//: reusing/Chess.java
// Inheritance, constructors and arguments.
import static net.mindview.util.Print.*;

class Game {
  Game(int i) {
    print("Game constructor");
  }
}

class BoardGame extends Game {
  BoardGame(int i) {
    super(i);
    print("BoardGame constructor");
  }
}

public class Chess extends BoardGame {
  Chess() {
    super(11);
```

```
    print("Chess constructor");
  }
  public static void main(String[] args) {
    Chess x = new Chess();
  }
} /* Output:
Game constructor
BoardGame constructor
Chess constructor
*///:~
```

If you don't call the base-class constructor in **BoardGame( )**, the compiler will complain that it can't find a constructor of the form **Game( )**. In addition, the call to the base-class constructor *must* be the first thing you do in the derived-class constructor. (The compiler will remind you if you get it wrong.)

Exercise 6: (1) Using **Chess.java**, prove the statements in the previous paragraph.

Exercise 7: (1) Modify Exercise 5 so that **A** and **B** have constructors with arguments instead of default constructors. Write a constructor for **C** and perform all initialization within **C**'s constructor.

Exercise 8: (1) Create a base class with only a non-default constructor, and a derived class with both a default (no-arg) and non-default constructor. In the derived-class constructors, call the base-class constructor.

Exercise 9: (2) Create a class called **Root** that contains an instance of each of the classes (that you also create) named **Component1**, **Component2**, and **Component3**. Derive a class **Stem** from **Root** that also contains an instance of each "component." All classes should have default constructors that print a message about that class.

Exercise 10: (1) Modify the previous exercise so that each class only has non-default constructors.

Delegation

A third relationship, which is not directly supported by Java, is called *delegation*. This is midway between inheritance and composition, because you place a member object in the class you're building (like composition), but at the same time you expose all the methods from the member object in your new class (like inheritance). For example, a spaceship needs a control module:

```
//: reusing/SpaceShipControls.java

public class SpaceShipControls {
  void up(int velocity) {}
  void down(int velocity) {}
  void left(int velocity) {}
  void right(int velocity) {}
  void forward(int velocity) {}
  void back(int velocity) {}
  void turboBoost() {}
} ///:~
```

One way to build a spaceship is to use inheritance:

```
//: reusing/SpaceShip.java

public class SpaceShip extends SpaceShipControls {
  private String name;
  public SpaceShip(String name) { this.name = name; }
  public String toString() { return name; }
  public static void main(String[] args) {
    SpaceShip protector = new SpaceShip("NSEA Protector");
    protector.forward(100);
  }
} ///:~
```

However, a **SpaceShip** isn't really "a type of" **SpaceShipControls**, even if, for example, you "tell" a **SpaceShip** to go **forward( )**. It's more accurate to say that a **SpaceShip** *contains* **SpaceShipControls**, and at the same time all the methods in **SpaceShipControls** are exposed in a **SpaceShip**. Delegation solves the dilemma:

```
//: reusing/SpaceShipDelegation.java

public class SpaceShipDelegation {
  private String name;
  private SpaceShipControls controls =
    new SpaceShipControls();
  public SpaceShipDelegation(String name) {
    this.name = name;
  }
  // Delegated methods:
```

```java
    public void back(int velocity) {
      controls.back(velocity);
    }
    public void down(int velocity) {
      controls.down(velocity);
    }
    public void forward(int velocity) {
      controls.forward(velocity);
    }
    public void left(int velocity) {
      controls.left(velocity);
    }
    public void right(int velocity) {
      controls.right(velocity);
    }
    public void turboBoost() {
      controls.turboBoost();
    }
    public void up(int velocity) {
      controls.up(velocity);
    }
    public static void main(String[] args) {
      SpaceShipDelegation protector =
        new SpaceShipDelegation("NSEA Protector");
      protector.forward(100);
    }
} ///:~
```

You can see how the methods are forwarded to the underlying **controls** object, and the interface is thus the same as it is with inheritance. However, you have more control with delegation because you can choose to provide only a subset of the methods in the member object.

Although the Java language doesn't support delegation, development tools often do. The above example, for instance, was automatically generated using the JetBrains Idea IDE.

Exercise 11: (3) Modify **Detergent.java** so that it uses delegation.

Combining composition and inheritance

It is very common to use composition and inheritance together. The following example shows the creation of a more complex class, using both inheritance and composition, along with the necessary constructor initialization:

```
//: reusing/PlaceSetting.java
// Combining composition & inheritance.
import static net.mindview.util.Print.*;

class Plate {
  Plate(int i) {
    print("Plate constructor");
  }
}

class DinnerPlate extends Plate {
  DinnerPlate(int i) {
    super(i);
    print("DinnerPlate constructor");
  }
}

class Utensil {
  Utensil(int i) {
    print("Utensil constructor");
  }
}

class Spoon extends Utensil {
  Spoon(int i) {
    super(i);
    print("Spoon constructor");
  }
}

class Fork extends Utensil {
  Fork(int i) {
    super(i);
    print("Fork constructor");
  }
}
```

```java
class Knife extends Utensil {
  Knife(int i) {
    super(i);
    print("Knife constructor");
  }
}

// A cultural way of doing something:
class Custom {
  Custom(int i) {
    print("Custom constructor");
  }
}

public class PlaceSetting extends Custom {
  private Spoon sp;
  private Fork frk;
  private Knife kn;
  private DinnerPlate pl;
  public PlaceSetting(int i) {
    super(i + 1);
    sp = new Spoon(i + 2);
    frk = new Fork(i + 3);
    kn = new Knife(i + 4);
    pl = new DinnerPlate(i + 5);
    print("PlaceSetting constructor");
  }
  public static void main(String[] args) {
    PlaceSetting x = new PlaceSetting(9);
  }
} /* Output:
Custom constructor
Utensil constructor
Spoon constructor
Utensil constructor
Fork constructor
Utensil constructor
Knife constructor
Plate constructor
DinnerPlate constructor
PlaceSetting constructor
*///:~
```

Although the compiler forces you to initialize the base classes, and requires that you do it right at the beginning of the constructor, it doesn't watch over you to make sure that you initialize the member objects, so you must remember to pay attention to that.

It's rather amazing how cleanly the classes are separated. You don't even need the source code for the methods in order to reuse the code. At most, you just import a package. (This is true for both inheritance and composition.)

Guaranteeing proper cleanup

Java doesn't have the C++ concept of a *destructor,* a method that is automatically called when an object is destroyed. The reason is probably that in Java, the practice is simply to forget about objects rather than to destroy them, allowing the garbage collector to reclaim the memory as necessary.

Often this is fine, but there are times when your class might perform some activities during its lifetime that require cleanup. As mentioned in the *Initialization & Cleanup* chapter, you can't know when the garbage collector will be called, or if it will be called. So if you want something cleaned up for a class, you must explicitly write a special method to do it, and make sure that the client programmer knows that they must call this method. On top of this—as described in the *Error Handling with Exceptions* chapter—you must guard against an exception by putting such cleanup in a **finally** clause.

Consider an example of a computer-aided design system that draws pictures on the screen:

```
//: reusing/CADSystem.java
// Ensuring proper cleanup.
package reusing;
import static net.mindview.util.Print.*;

class Shape {
  Shape(int i) { print("Shape constructor"); }
  void dispose() { print("Shape dispose"); }
}

class Circle extends Shape {
  Circle(int i) {
    super(i);
    print("Drawing Circle");
  }
```

```java
  void dispose() {
    print("Erasing Circle");
    super.dispose();
  }
}

class Triangle extends Shape {
  Triangle(int i) {
    super(i);
    print("Drawing Triangle");
  }
  void dispose() {
    print("Erasing Triangle");
    super.dispose();
  }
}

class Line extends Shape {
  private int start, end;
  Line(int start, int end) {
    super(start);
    this.start = start;
    this.end = end;
    print("Drawing Line: " + start + ", " + end);
  }
  void dispose() {
    print("Erasing Line: " + start + ", " + end);
    super.dispose();
  }
}

public class CADSystem extends Shape {
  private Circle c;
  private Triangle t;
  private Line[] lines = new Line[3];
  public CADSystem(int i) {
    super(i + 1);
    for(int j = 0; j < lines.length; j++)
      lines[j] = new Line(j, j*j);
    c = new Circle(1);
    t = new Triangle(1);
    print("Combined constructor");
  }
  public void dispose() {
```

```
      print("CADSystem.dispose()");
      // The order of cleanup is the reverse
      // of the order of initialization:
      t.dispose();
      c.dispose();
      for(int i = lines.length - 1; i >= 0; i--)
        lines[i].dispose();
      super.dispose();
    }
  public static void main(String[] args) {
    CADSystem x = new CADSystem(47);
    try {
      // Code and exception handling...
    } finally {
      x.dispose();
    }
  }
} /* Output:
Shape constructor
Shape constructor
Drawing Line: 0, 0
Shape constructor
Drawing Line: 1, 1
Shape constructor
Drawing Line: 2, 4
Shape constructor
Drawing Circle
Shape constructor
Drawing Triangle
Combined constructor
CADSystem.dispose()
Erasing Triangle
Shape dispose
Erasing Circle
Shape dispose
Erasing Line: 2, 4
Shape dispose
Erasing Line: 1, 1
Shape dispose
Erasing Line: 0, 0
Shape dispose
Shape dispose
*///:~
```

Everything in this system is some kind of **Shape** (which is itself a kind of **Object**, since it's implicitly inherited from the root class). Each class overrides **Shape**'s **dispose( )** method in addition to calling the base-class version of that method using **super**. The specific **Shape** classes—**Circle**, **Triangle**, and **Line**—all have constructors that "draw," although any method called during the lifetime of the object can be responsible for doing something that needs cleanup. Each class has its own **dispose( )** method to restore non-memory things back to the way they were before the object existed.

In **main( )**, there are two keywords that you haven't seen before, and won't be explained in detail until the *Error Handling with Exceptions* chapter: **try** and **finally**. The **try** keyword indicates that the block that follows (delimited by curly braces) is a *guarded region*, which means that it is given special treatment. One of these special treatments is that the code in the **finally** clause following this guarded region is *always* executed, no matter how the **try** block exits. (With exception handling, it's possible to leave a **try** block in a number of non-ordinary ways.) Here, the **finally** clause is saying, "Always call **dispose( )** for **x**, no matter what happens."

In your cleanup method (**dispose( )**, in this case), you must also pay attention to the calling order for the base-class and member-object cleanup methods in case one subobject depends on another. In general, you should follow the same form that is imposed by a C++ compiler on its destructors: First perform all of the cleanup work specific to your class, in the reverse order of creation. (In general, this requires that base-class elements still be viable.) Then call the base-class cleanup method, as demonstrated here.

There are many cases in which the cleanup issue is not a problem; you just let the garbage collector do the work. But when you must perform explicit cleanup, diligence and attention are required, because there's not much you can rely on when it comes to garbage collection. The garbage collector might never be called. If it is, it can reclaim objects in any order it wants. You can't rely on garbage collection for anything but memory reclamation. If you want cleanup to take place, make your own cleanup methods and don't use **finalize( )**.

Exercise 12: (3) Add a proper hierarchy of **dispose( )** methods to all the classes in Exercise 9.

Name hiding

If a Java base class has a method name that's overloaded several times, redefining that method name in the derived class will *not* hide any of the base-class versions (unlike C++). Thus overloading works regardless of whether the method was defined at this level or in a base class:

```
//: reusing/Hide.java
// Overloading a base-class method name in a derived
// class does not hide the base-class versions.
import static net.mindview.util.Print.*;

class Homer {
  char doh(char c) {
    print("doh(char)");
    return 'd';
  }
  float doh(float f) {
    print("doh(float)");
    return 1.0f;
  }
}

class Milhouse {}

class Bart extends Homer {
  void doh(Milhouse m) {
    print("doh(Milhouse)");
  }
}

public class Hide {
  public static void main(String[] args) {
    Bart b = new Bart();
    b.doh(1);
    b.doh('x');
    b.doh(1.0f);
    b.doh(new Milhouse());
  }
} /* Output:
doh(float)
doh(char)
doh(float)
doh(Milhouse)
```

```
*///:~
```

You can see that all the overloaded methods of **Homer** are available in **Bart**, even though **Bart** introduces a new overloaded method (doing this in C++ would hide the base-class methods). As you'll see in the next chapter, it's far more common to override methods of the same name, using exactly the same signature and return type as in the base class. It can be confusing otherwise (which is why C++ disallows it—so you don't make what is probably a mistake).

Java SE5 has added the **@Override** annotation, which is not a keyword but can be used as if it were. When you mean to override a method, you can choose to add this annotation and the compiler will produce an error message if you accidentally overload instead of overriding:

```
//: reusing/Lisa.java
// {CompileTimeError} (Won't compile)

class Lisa extends Homer {
  @Override void doh(Milhouse m) {
    System.out.println("doh(Milhouse)");
  }
} ///:~
```

The **{CompileTimeError}** tag excludes the file from this book's Ant build, but if you compile it by hand you'll see the error message:

```
method does not override a method from its superclass
```

The **@Override** annotation will thus prevent you from accidentally overloading when you don't mean to.

Exercise 13: (2) Create a class with a method that is overloaded three times. Inherit a new class, add a new overloading of the method, and show that all four methods are available in the derived class.

Choosing composition vs. inheritance

Both composition and inheritance allow you to place subobjects inside your new class (composition explicitly does this—with inheritance it's implicit). You might wonder about the difference between the two, and when to choose one over the other.

Composition is generally used when you want the functionality of an existing class inside your new class, but not its interface. That is, you embed an object so that you can use it to implement features in your new class, but the user of your new class sees the interface you've defined for the new class rather than the interface from the embedded object. For this effect, you embed **private** objects of existing classes inside your new class.

Sometimes it makes sense to allow the class user to directly access the composition of your new class; that is, to make the member objects **public**. The member objects use implementation hiding themselves, so this is a safe thing to do. When the user knows you're assembling a bunch of parts, it makes the interface easier to understand. A **car** object is a good example:

```
//: reusing/Car.java
// Composition with public objects.

class Engine {
  public void start() {}
  public void rev() {}
  public void stop() {}
}

class Wheel {
  public void inflate(int psi) {}
}

class Window {
  public void rollup() {}
  public void rolldown() {}
}

class Door {
  public Window window = new Window();
  public void open() {}
  public void close() {}
}

public class Car {
  public Engine engine = new Engine();
  public Wheel[] wheel = new Wheel[4];
  public Door
    left = new Door(),
    right = new Door(); // 2-door
  public Car() {
```

```
      for(int i = 0; i < 4; i++)
        wheel[i] = new Wheel();
    }
    public static void main(String[] args) {
      Car car = new Car();
      car.left.window.rollup();
      car.wheel[0].inflate(72);
    }
  } ///:~
```

Because in this case the composition of a car is part of the analysis of the problem (and not simply part of the underlying design), making the members **public** assists the client programmer's understanding of how to use the class and requires less code complexity for the creator of the class. However, keep in mind that this is a special case, and that in general you should make fields **private**.

When you inherit, you take an existing class and make a special version of it. In general, this means that you're taking a general-purpose class and specializing it for a particular need. With a little thought, you'll see that it would make no sense to compose a car using a vehicle object—a car doesn't contain a vehicle, it *is* a vehicle. The *is-a* relationship is expressed with inheritance, and the *has-a* relationship is expressed with composition.

Exercise 14: (1) In **Car.java** add a **service( )** method to **Engine** and call this method in **main( )**.

protected

Now that you've been introduced to inheritance, the keyword **protected** finally has meaning. In an ideal world, the **private** keyword would be enough. In real projects, there are times when you want to make something hidden from the world at large and yet allow access for members of derived classes.

The **protected** keyword is a nod to pragmatism. It says, "This is **private** as far as the class user is concerned, but available to anyone who inherits from this class or anyone else in the same package." (**protected** also provides package access.)

Although it's possible to create **protected** fields, the best approach is to leave the fields **private**; you should always preserve your right to change the underlying implementation. You can then allow controlled access to inheritors of your class through **protected** methods:

```
//: reusing/Orc.java
// The protected keyword.
import static net.mindview.util.Print.*;

class Villain {
  private String name;
  protected void set(String nm) { name = nm; }
  public Villain(String name) { this.name = name; }
  public String toString() {
    return "I'm a Villain and my name is " + name;
  }
}

public class Orc extends Villain {
  private int orcNumber;
  public Orc(String name, int orcNumber) {
    super(name);
    this.orcNumber = orcNumber;
  }
  public void change(String name, int orcNumber) {
    set(name); // Available because it's protected
    this.orcNumber = orcNumber;
  }
  public String toString() {
    return "Orc " + orcNumber + ": " + super.toString();
  }
  public static void main(String[] args) {
    Orc orc = new Orc("Limburger", 12);
    print(orc);
    orc.change("Bob", 19);
    print(orc);
  }
} /* Output:
Orc 12: I'm a Villain and my name is Limburger
Orc 19: I'm a Villain and my name is Bob
*///:~
```

You can see that **change( )** has access to **set( )** because it's **protected**. Also note the way that **Orc**'s **toString( )** method is defined in terms of the base-class version of **toString( )**.

Exercise 15: (2) Create a class inside a package. Your class should contain a **protected** method. Outside of the package, try to call the **protected** method and explain the results. Now inherit from your class and call the **protected** method from inside a method of your derived class.

Upcasting

The most important aspect of inheritance is not that it provides methods for the new class. It's the relationship expressed between the new class and the base class. This relationship can be summarized by saying, "The new class *is a type of* the existing class."

This description is not just a fanciful way of explaining inheritance—it's supported directly by the language. As an example, consider a base class called **Instrument** that represents musical instruments, and a derived class called **Wind**. Because inheritance guarantees that all of the methods in the base class are also available in the derived class, any message you can send to the base class can also be sent to the derived class. If the **Instrument** class has a **play( )** method, so will **Wind** instruments. This means that you can accurately say that a **Wind** object is also a type of **Instrument**. The following example shows how the compiler supports this notion:

```
//: reusing/Wind.java
// Inheritance & upcasting.

class Instrument {
  public void play() {}
  static void tune(Instrument i) {
    // ...
    i.play();
  }
}

// Wind objects are instruments
// because they have the same interface:
public class Wind extends Instrument {
  public static void main(String[] args) {
    Wind flute = new Wind();
    Instrument.tune(flute); // Upcasting
  }
} ///:~
```

What's interesting in this example is the **tune( )** method, which accepts an **Instrument** reference. However, in **Wind.main( )** the **tune( )** method is handed a **Wind** reference. Given that Java is particular about type checking, it seems strange that a method that accepts one type will readily accept another type, until you realize that a **Wind** object is also an **Instrument** object, and there's no method that **tune( )** could call for an **Instrument** that isn't also in **Wind**. Inside **tune( )**, the code works for **Instrument** and anything derived from **Instrument**, and the act of converting a **Wind** reference into an **Instrument** reference is called *upcasting*.

Why "upcasting"?

The term is based on the way that class inheritance diagrams have traditionally been drawn: with the root at the top of the page, growing downward. (Of course, you can draw your diagrams any way you find helpful.) The inheritance diagram for **Wind.java** is then:

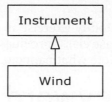

Casting from a derived type to a base type moves *up* on the inheritance diagram, so it's commonly referred to as *upcasting*. Upcasting is always safe because you're going from a more specific type to a more general type. That is, the derived class is a superset of the base class. It might contain more methods than the base class, but it must contain *at least* the methods in the base class. The only thing that can occur to the class interface during the upcast is that it can lose methods, not gain them. This is why the compiler allows upcasting without any explicit casts or other special notation.

You can also perform the reverse of upcasting, called *downcasting*, but this involves a dilemma that will be examined further in the next chapter, and in the *Type Information* chapter.

Composition vs. inheritance revisited

In object-oriented programming, the most likely way that you'll create and use code is by simply packaging data and methods together into a class, and using objects of that class. You'll also use existing classes to build new classes with composition. Less frequently, you'll use inheritance. So although inheritance gets a lot of emphasis when teaching OOP, it doesn't mean that you should use it everywhere you possibly can. On the contrary, you should use it sparingly, only when it's clear that inheritance is useful. One of the clearest ways to determine whether you should use composition or inheritance is to ask whether you'll ever need to upcast from your new class to the base class. If you must upcast, then inheritance is necessary, but if you don't need to upcast, then you should look closely at whether you need inheritance. The *Polymorphism* chapter provides one of the most compelling reasons for upcasting, but if you remember to ask, "Do I need to upcast?" you'll have a good tool for deciding between composition and inheritance.

Exercise 16: (2) Create a class called **Amphibian**. From this, inherit a class called **Frog**. Put appropriate methods in the base class. In **main( )**, create a **Frog** and upcast it to **Amphibian**, and demonstrate that all the methods still work.

Exercise 17: (1) Modify Exercise 16 so that **Frog** overrides the method definitions from the base class (provides new definitions using the same method signatures). Note what happens in **main( )**.

The **final** keyword

Java's **final** keyword has slightly different meanings depending on the context, but in general it says, "This cannot be changed." You might want to prevent changes for two reasons: design or efficiency. Because these two reasons are quite different, it's possible to misuse the **final** keyword.

The following sections discuss the three places where **final** can be used: for data, methods, and classes.

final data

Many programming languages have a way to tell the compiler that a piece of data is "constant." A constant is useful for two reasons:

1.   It can be a *compile-time constant* that won't ever change.

2.   It can be a value initialized at run time that you don't want changed.

In the case of a compile-time constant, the compiler is allowed to "fold" the constant value into any calculations in which it's used; that is, the calculation can be performed at compile time, eliminating some runtime overhead. In Java, these sorts of constants must be primitives and are expressed with the **final** keyword. A value must be given at the time of definition of such a constant.

A field that is both **static** and **final** has only one piece of storage that cannot be changed.

When **final** is used with object references rather than primitives, the meaning can be confusing. With a primitive, **final** makes the *value* a constant, but with an object reference, **final** makes the *reference* a constant. Once the reference is initialized to an object, it can never be changed to point to another object. However, the object itself can be modified; Java does not provide a way to make any arbitrary object a constant. (You can, however, write your class so that objects have the effect of being constant.) This restriction includes arrays, which are also objects.

Here's an example that demonstrates **final** fields. Note that by convention, fields that are both **static** and **final** (that is, compile-time constants) are capitalized and use underscores to separate words.

```
//: reusing/FinalData.java
// The effect of final on fields.
import java.util.*;
import static net.mindview.util.Print.*;

class Value {
  int i; // Package access
  public Value(int i) { this.i = i; }
}

public class FinalData {
  private static Random rand = new Random(47);
  private String id;
  public FinalData(String id) { this.id = id; }
  // Can be compile-time constants:
  private final int valueOne = 9;
  private static final int VALUE_TWO = 99;
  // Typical public constant:
  public static final int VALUE_THREE = 39;
  // Cannot be compile-time constants:
  private final int i4 = rand.nextInt(20);
  static final int INT_5 = rand.nextInt(20);
```

```
    private Value v1 = new Value(11);
    private final Value v2 = new Value(22);
    private static final Value VAL_3 = new Value(33);
    // Arrays:
    private final int[] a = { 1, 2, 3, 4, 5, 6 };
    public String toString() {
      return id + ": " + "i4 = " + i4 + ", INT_5 = " + INT_5;
    }
    public static void main(String[] args) {
      FinalData fd1 = new FinalData("fd1");
      //! fd1.valueOne++; // Error: can't change value
      fd1.v2.i++; // Object isn't constant!
      fd1.v1 = new Value(9); // OK -- not final
      for(int i = 0; i < fd1.a.length; i++)
        fd1.a[i]++; // Object isn't constant!
      //! fd1.v2 = new Value(0); // Error: Can't
      //! fd1.VAL_3 = new Value(1); // change reference
      //! fd1.a = new int[3];
      print(fd1);
      print("Creating new FinalData");
      FinalData fd2 = new FinalData("fd2");
      print(fd1);
      print(fd2);
    }
} /* Output:
fd1: i4 = 15, INT_5 = 18
Creating new FinalData
fd1: i4 = 15, INT_5 = 18
fd2: i4 = 13, INT_5 = 18
*///:~
```

Since **valueOne** and **VALUE_TWO** are **final** primitives with compile-time
values, they can both be used as compile-time constants and are not different
in any important way. **VALUE_THREE** is the more typical way you'll see
such constants defined: **public** so they're usable outside the package, **static**
to emphasize that there's only one, and **final** to say that it's a constant. Note
that **final static** primitives with constant initial values (that is, compile-time
constants) are named with all capitals by convention, with words separated
by underscores. (This is just like C constants, which is where the convention
originated.)

Just because something is **final** doesn't mean that its value is known at
compile time. This is demonstrated by initializing **i4** and **INT_5** at run time
using randomly generated numbers. This portion of the example also shows

the difference between making a **final** value **static** or non-**static**. This difference shows up only when the values are initialized at run time, since the compile-time values are treated the same by the compiler. (And presumably optimized out of existence.) The difference is shown when you run the program. Note that the values of **i4** for **fd1** and **fd2** are unique, but the value for **INT_5** is not changed by creating the second **FinalData** object. That's because it's **static** and is initialized once upon loading and not each time a new object is created.

The variables **v1** through **VAL_3** demonstrate the meaning of a **final** reference. As you can see in **main( )**, just because **v2** is **final** doesn't mean that you can't change its value. Because it's a reference, **final** means that you cannot rebind **v2** to a new object. You can also see that the same meaning holds true for an array, which is just another kind of reference. (There is no way that I know of to make the array references themselves **final**.) Making references **final** seems less useful than making primitives **final**.

Exercise 18: (2) Create a class with a **static final** field and a **final** field and demonstrate the difference between the two.

Blank **final**s

Java allows the creation of *blank finals*, which are fields that are declared as **final** but are not given an initialization value. In all cases, the blank **final** *must* be initialized before it is used, and the compiler ensures this. However, blank **final**s provide much more flexibility in the use of the **final** keyword since, for example, a **final** field inside a class can now be different for each object, and yet it retains its immutable quality. Here's an example:

```
//: reusing/BlankFinal.java
// "Blank" final fields.

class Poppet {
  private int i;
  Poppet(int ii) { i = ii; }
}

public class BlankFinal {
  private final int i = 0; // Initialized final
  private final int j; // Blank final
  private final Poppet p; // Blank final reference
  // Blank finals MUST be initialized in the constructor:
  public BlankFinal() {
```

```
    j = 1; // Initialize blank final
    p = new Poppet(1); // Initialize blank final reference
  }
  public BlankFinal(int x) {
    j = x; // Initialize blank final
    p = new Poppet(x); // Initialize blank final reference
  }
  public static void main(String[] args) {
    new BlankFinal();
    new BlankFinal(47);
  }
} ///:~
```

You're forced to perform assignments to **final**s either with an expression at the point of definition of the field or in every constructor. That way it's guaranteed that the **final** field is always initialized before use.

Exercise 19: (2) Create a class with a blank **final** reference to an object. Perform the initialization of the blank **final** inside all constructors. Demonstrate the guarantee that the **final** must be initialized before use, and that it cannot be changed once initialized.

final arguments

Java allows you to make arguments **final** by declaring them as such in the argument list. This means that inside the method you cannot change what the argument reference points to:

```
//: reusing/FinalArguments.java
// Using "final" with method arguments.

class Gizmo {
  public void spin() {}
}

public class FinalArguments {
  void with(final Gizmo g) {
    //! g = new Gizmo(); // Illegal -- g is final
  }
  void without(Gizmo g) {
    g = new Gizmo(); // OK -- g not final
    g.spin();
  }
  // void f(final int i) { i++; } // Can't change
  // You can only read from a final primitive:
```

```
    int g(final int i) { return i + 1; }
    public static void main(String[] args) {
      FinalArguments bf = new FinalArguments();
      bf.without(null);
      bf.with(null);
    }
} ///:~
```

The methods **f( )** and **g( )** show what happens when primitive arguments are **final**: You can read the argument, but you can't change it. This feature is primarily used to pass data to anonymous inner classes, which you'll learn about in the *Inner Classes* chapter.

final methods

There are two reasons for **final** methods. The first is to put a "lock" on the method to prevent any inheriting class from changing its meaning. This is done for design reasons when you want to make sure that a method's behavior is retained during inheritance and cannot be overridden.

The second reason **final** methods have been suggested in the past is efficiency. In earlier implementations of Java, if you made a method **final**, you allowed the compiler to turn any calls to that method into *inline* calls. When the compiler saw a **final** method call, it could (at its discretion) skip the normal approach of inserting code to perform the method call mechanism (push arguments on the stack, hop over to the method code and execute it, hop back and clean off the stack arguments, and deal with the return value) and instead replace the method call with a copy of the actual code in the method body. This eliminated the overhead of the method call. Of course, if a method is big, then your code begins to bloat, and you probably wouldn't see any performance gains from inlining, since any improvements were dwarfed by the amount of time spent inside the method.

In more recent versions of Java, the virtual machine (in particular, the hotspot technologies) can detect these situations and optimize away the extra indirection, so it is no longer necessary—in fact, it is now generally discouraged—to use **final** to try to help the optimizer. With Java SE5/6, you should let the compiler and JVM handle efficiency issues and make a method **final** only if you want to explicitly prevent overriding.[1]

final and private

Any **private** methods in a class are implicitly **final**. Because you can't access a **private** method, you can't override it. You can add the **final** specifier to a **private** method, but it doesn't give that method any extra meaning.

This issue can cause confusion, because if you try to override a **private** method (which is implicitly **final**), it seems to work, and the compiler doesn't give an error message:

```
//: reusing/FinalOverridingIllusion.java
// It only looks like you can override
// a private or private final method.
import static net.mindview.util.Print.*;

class WithFinals {
  // Identical to "private" alone:
  private final void f() { print("WithFinals.f()"); }
  // Also automatically "final":
  private void g() { print("WithFinals.g()"); }
}

class OverridingPrivate extends WithFinals {
  private final void f() {
    print("OverridingPrivate.f()");
  }
  private void g() {
    print("OverridingPrivate.g()");
  }
}

class OverridingPrivate2 extends OverridingPrivate {
  public final void f() {
    print("OverridingPrivate2.f()");
  }
}
```

---

[1] Don't fall prey to the urge to prematurely optimize. If you get your system working and it's too slow, it's doubtful that you can fix it with the **final** keyword. *http://MindView.net/Books/BetterJava* has information about profiling, which *can* be helpful in speeding up your program.

```
    public void g() {
      print("OverridingPrivate2.g()");
    }
}

public class FinalOverridingIllusion {
  public static void main(String[] args) {
    OverridingPrivate2 op2 = new OverridingPrivate2();
    op2.f();
    op2.g();
    // You can upcast:
    OverridingPrivate op = op2;
    // But you can't call the methods:
    //! op.f();
    //! op.g();
    // Same here:
    WithFinals wf = op2;
    //! wf.f();
    //! wf.g();
  }
} /* Output:
OverridingPrivate2.f()
OverridingPrivate2.g()
*///:~
```

"Overriding" can only occur if something is part of the base-class interface. That is, you must be able to upcast an object to its base type and call the same method (the point of this will become clear in the next chapter). If a method is **private**, it isn't part of the base-class interface. It is just some code that's hidden away inside the class, and it just happens to have that name, but if you create a **public**, **protected**, or package-access method with the same name in the derived class, there's no connection to the method that might happen to have that name in the base class. You haven't overridden the method; you've just created a new method. Since a **private** method is unreachable and effectively invisible, it doesn't factor into anything except for the code organization of the class for which it was defined.

Exercise 20: (1) Show that the **@Override** annotation solves the problem in this section.

Exercise 21: (1) Create a class with a **final** method. Inherit from that class and attempt to override that method.

final classes

When you say that an entire class is **final** (by preceding its definition with the **final** keyword), you state that you don't want to inherit from this class or allow anyone else to do so. In other words, for some reason the design of your class is such that there is never a need to make any changes, or for safety or security reasons you don't want subclassing.

```
//: reusing/Jurassic.java
// Making an entire class final.

class SmallBrain {}

final class Dinosaur {
  int i = 7;
  int j = 1;
  SmallBrain x = new SmallBrain();
  void f() {}
}

//! class Further extends Dinosaur {}
// error: Cannot extend final class 'Dinosaur'

public class Jurassic {
  public static void main(String[] args) {
    Dinosaur n = new Dinosaur();
    n.f();
    n.i = 40;
    n.j++;
  }
} ///:~
```

Note that the fields of a **final** class can be **final** or not, as you choose. The same rules apply to **final** for fields regardless of whether the class is defined as **final**. However, because it prevents inheritance, all *methods* in a **final** class are implicitly **final**, since there's no way to override them. You can add the **final** specifier to a method in a **final** class, but it doesn't add any meaning.

Exercise 22: (1) Create a **final** class and attempt to inherit from it.

Thinking in Java   *Bruce Eckel*

final caution

It can seem to be sensible to make a method **final** while you're designing a class. You might feel that no one could possibly want to override your methods. Sometimes this is true.

But be careful with your assumptions. In general, it's difficult to anticipate how a class can be reused, especially a general-purpose class. If you define a method as **final**, you might prevent the possibility of reusing your class through inheritance in some other programmer's project simply because you couldn't imagine it being used that way.

The standard Java library is a good example of this. In particular, the Java 1.0/1.1 **Vector** class was commonly used and might have been even more useful if, in the name of efficiency (which was almost certainly an illusion), all the methods hadn't been made **final**. It's easily conceivable that you might want to inherit and override with such a fundamentally useful class, but the designers somehow decided this wasn't appropriate. This is ironic for two reasons. First, **Stack** is inherited from **Vector**, which says that a **Stack** *is* a **Vector**, which isn't really true from a logical standpoint. Nonetheless, it's a case where the Java designers themselves inherited **Vector**. At the point they created **Stack** this way, they should have realized that **final** methods were too restrictive.

Second, many of the most important methods of **Vector**, such as **addElement( )** and **elementAt( )**, are **synchronized**. As you will see in the *Concurrency* chapter, this imposes a significant performance overhead that probably wipes out any gains provided by **final**. This lends credence to the theory that programmers are consistently bad at guessing where optimizations should occur. It's just too bad that such a clumsy design made it into the standard library, where everyone had to cope with it. (Fortunately, the modern Java container library replaces **Vector** with **ArrayList**, which behaves much more civilly. Unfortunately, there's still new code being written that uses the old container library.)

It's also interesting to note that **Hashtable**, another important Java 1.0/1.1 standard library class, does *not* have any **final** methods. As mentioned elsewhere in this book, it's quite obvious that some classes were designed by completely different people than others. (You'll see that the method names in **Hashtable** are much briefer compared to those in **Vector**, another piece of evidence.) This is precisely the sort of thing that should *not* be obvious to consumers of a class library. When things are inconsistent, it just makes more work for the user—yet another paean to the value of design and code walkthroughs. (Note that the modern Java container library replaces **Hashtable** with **HashMap**.)

Initialization and class loading

In more traditional languages, programs are loaded all at once, as part of the startup process. This is followed by initialization, and then the program begins. The process of initialization in these languages must be carefully controlled so that the order of initialization of **static**s doesn't cause trouble. C++, for example, has problems if one **static** expects another **static** to be valid before the second one has been initialized.

Java doesn't have this problem because it takes a different approach to loading. This is one of the activities that become easier because everything in Java is an object. Remember that the compiled code for each class exists in its own separate file. That file isn't loaded until the code is needed. In general, you can say that "class code is loaded at the point of first use." This is usually when the first object of that class is constructed, but loading also occurs when a **static** field or **static** method is accessed.[2]

The point of first use is also where the **static** initialization takes place. All the **static** objects and the **static** code block will be initialized in textual order (that is, the order that you write them down in the class definition) at the point of loading. The **static**s, of course, are initialized only once.

Initialization with inheritance

It's helpful to look at the whole initialization process, including inheritance, to get a full picture of what happens. Consider the following example:

```
//: reusing/Beetle.java
// The full process of initialization.
import static net.mindview.util.Print.*;
```

---

[2] The constructor is also a **static** method even though the **static** keyword is not explicit. So to be precise, a class is first loaded when any one of its **static** members is accessed.

```
class Insect {
  private int i = 9;
  protected int j;
  Insect() {
    print("i = " + i + ", j = " + j);
    j = 39;
  }
  private static int x1 =
    printInit("static Insect.x1 initialized");
  static int printInit(String s) {
    print(s);
    return 47;
  }
}

public class Beetle extends Insect {
  private int k = printInit("Beetle.k initialized");
  public Beetle() {
    print("k = " + k);
    print("j = " + j);
  }
  private static int x2 =
    printInit("static Beetle.x2 initialized");
  public static void main(String[] args) {
    print("Beetle constructor");
    Beetle b = new Beetle();
  }
} /* Output:
static Insect.x1 initialized
static Beetle.x2 initialized
Beetle constructor
i = 9, j = 0
Beetle.k initialized
k = 47
j = 39
*///:~
```

The first thing that happens when you run Java on **Beetle** is that you try to
access **Beetle.main( )** (a **static** method), so the loader goes out and finds
the compiled code for the **Beetle** class (in a file called **Beetle.class**). In the
process of loading it, the loader notices that it has a base class (that's what the
extends keyword says), which it then loads. This will happen whether or not
you're going to make an object of that base class. (Try commenting out the
object creation to prove it to yourself.)

If the base class has its own base class, that second base class would then be loaded, and so on. Next, the **static** initialization in the root base class (in this case, **Insect**) is performed, and then the next derived class, and so on. This is important because the derived-class **static** initialization might depend on the base-class member being initialized properly.

At this point, the necessary classes have all been loaded so the object can be created. First, all the primitives in this object are set to their default values and the object references are set to **null**—this happens in one fell swoop by setting the memory in the object to binary zero. Then the base-class constructor will be called. In this case the call is automatic, but you can also specify the base-class constructor call (as the first operation in the **Beetle( )** constructor) by using **super**. The base-class constructor goes through the same process in the same order as the derived-class constructor. After the base-class constructor completes, the instance variables are initialized in textual order. Finally, the rest of the body of the constructor is executed.

Exercise 23: (2) Prove that class loading takes place only once. Prove that loading may be caused by either the creation of the first instance of that class or by the access of a **static** member.

Exercise 24: (2) In **Beetle.java**, inherit a specific type of beetle from class **Beetle**, following the same format as the existing classes. Trace and explain the output.

Summary

Both inheritance and composition allow you to create new types from existing types. Composition reuses existing types as part of the underlying implementation of the new type, and inheritance reuses the interface.

With inheritance, the derived class has the base-class interface, so it can be *upcast* to the base, which is critical for polymorphism, as you'll see in the next chapter.

Despite the strong emphasis on inheritance in object-oriented programming, when you start a design you should generally prefer composition (or possibly delegation) during the first cut and use inheritance only when it is clearly necessary. Composition tends to be more flexible. In addition, by using the added artifice of inheritance with your member type, you can change the exact type, and thus the behavior, of those member objects at run time. Therefore, you can change the behavior of the composed object at run time.

When designing a system, your goal is to find or create a set of classes in which each class has a specific use and is neither too big (encompassing so much functionality that it's unwieldy to reuse) nor annoyingly small (you can't use it by itself or without adding functionality). If your designs become too complex, it's often helpful to add more objects by breaking down existing ones into smaller parts.

When you set out to design a system, it's important to realize that program development is an incremental process, just like human learning. It relies on experimentation; you can do as much analysis as you want, but you still won't know all the answers when you set out on a project. You'll have much more success—and more immediate feedback—if you start out to "grow" your project as an organic, evolutionary creature, rather than constructing it all at once like a glass-box skyscraper. Inheritance and composition are two of the most fundamental tools in object-oriented programming that allow you to perform such experiments.

Solutions to selected exercises can be found in the electronic document *The Thinking in Java Annotated Solution Guide*, available for sale from *www.MindView.net*.

Polymorphism

"I have been asked, 'Pray, Mr. Babbage, if you put into the machine wrong figures, will the right answers come out?' I am not able to rightly apprehend the kind of confusion of ideas that could provoke such a question." Charles Babbage (1791-1871)

Polymorphism is the third essential feature of an object-oriented programming language, after data abstraction and inheritance.

It provides another dimension of separation of interface from implementation, to decouple *what* from *how*. Polymorphism allows improved code organization and readability as well as the creation of *extensible* programs that can be "grown" not only during the original creation of the project, but also when new features are desired.

Encapsulation creates new data types by combining characteristics and behaviors. Implementation hiding separates the interface from the implementation by making the details **private**. This sort of mechanical organization makes ready sense to someone with a procedural programming background. But polymorphism deals with decoupling in terms of *types*. In the last chapter, you saw how inheritance allows the treatment of an object as its own type *or* its base type. This ability is critical because it allows many types (derived from the same base type) to be treated as if they were one type, and a single piece of code to work on all those different types equally. The polymorphic method call allows one type to express its distinction from another, similar type, as long as they're both derived from the same base type. This distinction is expressed through differences in behavior of the methods that you can call through the base class.

In this chapter, you'll learn about polymorphism (also called *dynamic binding* or *late binding* or *runtime binding*) starting from the basics, with simple examples that strip away everything but the polymorphic behavior of the program.

Upcasting revisited

In the last chapter you saw how an object can be used as its own type or as an object of its base type. Taking an object reference and treating it as a reference to its base type is called *upcasting* because of the way inheritance trees are drawn with the base class at the top.

You also saw a problem arise, which is embodied in the following example about musical instruments.

First, since several of these examples play **Note**s, we should create a separate **Note** enumeration, in a package:

```
//: polymorphism/music/Note.java
// Notes to play on musical instruments.
package polymorphism.music;

public enum Note {
    MIDDLE_C, C_SHARP, B_FLAT; // Etc.
} ///:~
```

enums were introduced in the *Initialization & Cleanup* chapter.

Here, **Wind** is a type of **Instrument**; therefore, **Wind** is inherited from **Instrument**:

```
//: polymorphism/music/Instrument.java
package polymorphism.music;
import static net.mindview.util.Print.*;

class Instrument {
  public void play(Note n) {
    print("Instrument.play()");
  }
}
 ///:~
```

```
//: polymorphism/music/Wind.java
package polymorphism.music;

// Wind objects are instruments
// because they have the same interface:
public class Wind extends Instrument {
  // Redefine interface method:
  public void play(Note n) {
```

```
      System.out.println("Wind.play() " + n);
    }
} ///:~
```

```
//: polymorphism/music/Music.java
// Inheritance & upcasting.
package polymorphism.music;

public class Music {
  public static void tune(Instrument i) {
    // ...
    i.play(Note.MIDDLE_C);
  }
  public static void main(String[] args) {
    Wind flute = new Wind();
    tune(flute); // Upcasting
  }
} /* Output:
Wind.play() MIDDLE_C
*///:~
```

The method **Music.tune( )** accepts an **Instrument** reference, but also anything derived from **Instrument**. In **main( )**, you can see this happening as a **Wind** reference is passed to **tune( )**, with no cast necessary. This is acceptable—the interface in **Instrument** must exist in **Wind**, because **Wind** is inherited from **Instrument**. Upcasting from **Wind** to **Instrument** may "narrow" that interface, but it cannot make it anything less than the full interface to **Instrument**.

Forgetting the object type

Music.java might seem strange to you. Why should anyone intentionally *forget* the type of an object? This is what happens when you upcast, and it seems like it might be much more straightforward if **tune( )** simply takes a **Wind** reference as its argument. This brings up an essential point: If you did that, you'd need to write a new **tune( )** for every type of **Instrument** in your system. Suppose you follow this reasoning and add **Stringed** and **Brass** instruments:

```
//: polymorphism/music/Music2.java
// Overloading instead of upcasting.
package polymorphism.music;
import static net.mindview.util.Print.*;
```

```java
class Stringed extends Instrument {
  public void play(Note n) {
    print("Stringed.play() " + n);
  }
}

class Brass extends Instrument {
  public void play(Note n) {
    print("Brass.play() " + n);
  }
}

public class Music2 {
  public static void tune(Wind i) {
    i.play(Note.MIDDLE_C);
  }
  public static void tune(Stringed i) {
    i.play(Note.MIDDLE_C);
  }
  public static void tune(Brass i) {
    i.play(Note.MIDDLE_C);
  }
  public static void main(String[] args) {
    Wind flute = new Wind();
    Stringed violin = new Stringed();
    Brass frenchHorn = new Brass();
    tune(flute); // No upcasting
    tune(violin);
    tune(frenchHorn);
  }
} /* Output:
Wind.play() MIDDLE_C
Stringed.play() MIDDLE_C
Brass.play() MIDDLE_C
*///:~
```

This works, but there's a major drawback: You must write type-specific methods for each new **Instrument** class you add. This means more programming in the first place, but it also means that if you want to add a new method like **tune( )** or a new type of **Instrument**, you've got a lot of work to do. Add the fact that the compiler won't give you any error messages if you forget to overload one of your methods, and the whole process of working with types becomes unmanageable.

Wouldn't it be much nicer if you could just write a single method that takes the base class as its argument, and not any of the specific derived classes? That is, wouldn't it be nice if you could forget that there are derived classes, and write your code to talk only to the base class?

That's exactly what polymorphism allows you to do. However, most programmers who come from a procedural programming background have a bit of trouble with the way polymorphism works.

Exercise 1: (2) Create a **Cycle** class, with subclasses **Unicycle**, **Bicycle** and **Tricycle**. Demonstrate that an instance of each type can be upcast to **Cycle** via a **ride( )** method.

The twist

The difficulty with **Music.java** can be seen by running the program. The output is **Wind.play( )**. This is clearly the desired output, but it doesn't seem to make sense that it would work that way. Look at the **tune( )** method:

```
public static void tune(Instrument i) {
  // ...
  i.play(Note.MIDDLE_C);
}
```

It receives an **Instrument** reference. So how can the compiler possibly know that this **Instrument** reference points to a **Wind** in this case and not a **Brass** or **Stringed**? The compiler can't. To get a deeper understanding of the issue, it's helpful to examine the subject of *binding*.

Method-call binding

Connecting a method call to a method body is called *binding*. When binding is performed before the program is run (by the compiler and linker, if there is one), it's called *early binding*. You might not have heard the term before because it has never been an option with procedural languages. C, for example, has only one kind of method call, and that's early binding.

The confusing part of the preceding program revolves around early binding, because the compiler cannot know the correct method to call when it has only an **Instrument** reference.

The solution is called *late binding*, which means that the binding occurs at run time, based on the type of object. Late binding is also called *dynamic binding* or *runtime binding*. When a language implements late binding, there must be some mechanism to determine the type of the object at run time and to call the appropriate method. That is, the compiler still doesn't know the object type, but the method-call mechanism finds out and calls the correct method body. The late-binding mechanism varies from language to language, but you can imagine that some sort of type information must be installed in the objects.

All method binding in Java uses late binding unless the method is **static** or **final** (**private** methods are implicitly **final**). This means that ordinarily you don't need to make any decisions about whether late binding will occur—it happens automatically.

Why would you declare a method **final**? As noted in the last chapter, it prevents anyone from overriding that method. Perhaps more important, it effectively "turns off" dynamic binding, or rather it tells the compiler that dynamic binding isn't necessary. This allows the compiler to generate slightly more efficient code for **final** method calls. However, in most cases it won't make any overall performance difference in your program, so it's best to only use **final** as a design decision, and not as an attempt to improve performance.

Producing the right behavior

Once you know that all method binding in Java happens polymorphically via late binding, you can write your code to talk to the base class and know that all the derived-class cases will work correctly using the same code. Or to put it another way, you "send a message to an object and let the object figure out the right thing to do."

The classic example in OOP is the "shape" example. This is commonly used because it is easy to visualize, but unfortunately it can confuse novice programmers into thinking that OOP is just for graphics programming, which is of course not the case.

The shape example has a base class called **Shape** and various derived types: **Circle**, **Square**, **Triangle**, etc. The reason the example works so well is that it's easy to say, "A circle is a type of shape" and be understood. The inheritance diagram shows the relationships:

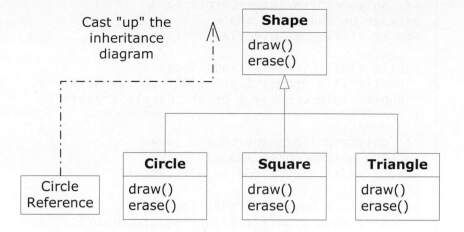

The upcast could occur in a statement as simple as:

```
Shape s = new Circle();
```

Here, a **Circle** object is created, and the resulting reference is immediately assigned to a **Shape**, which would seem to be an error (assigning one type to another); and yet it's fine because a **Circle** *is* a **Shape** by inheritance. So the compiler agrees with the statement and doesn't issue an error message.

Suppose you call one of the base-class methods (that have been overridden in the derived classes):

```
s.draw();
```

Again, you might expect that **Shape**'s **draw( )** is called because this is, after all, a **Shape** reference—so how could the compiler know to do anything else? And yet the proper **Circle.draw( )** is called because of late binding (polymorphism).

The following example puts it a slightly different way. First, let's create a reusable library of **Shape** types:

```
//: polymorphism/shape/Shape.java
package polymorphism.shape;

public class Shape {
  public void draw() {}
  public void erase() {}
} ///:~
```

```java
//: polymorphism/shape/Circle.java
package polymorphism.shape;
import static net.mindview.util.Print.*;

public class Circle extends Shape {
  public void draw() { print("Circle.draw()"); }
  public void erase() { print("Circle.erase()"); }
} ///:~
```

```java
//: polymorphism/shape/Square.java
package polymorphism.shape;
import static net.mindview.util.Print.*;

public class Square extends Shape {
  public void draw() { print("Square.draw()"); }
  public void erase() { print("Square.erase()"); }
} ///:~
```

```java
//: polymorphism/shape/Triangle.java
package polymorphism.shape;
import static net.mindview.util.Print.*;

public class Triangle extends Shape {
  public void draw() { print("Triangle.draw()"); }
  public void erase() { print("Triangle.erase()"); }
} ///:~
```

```java
//: polymorphism/shape/RandomShapeGenerator.java
// A "factory" that randomly creates shapes.
package polymorphism.shape;
import java.util.*;

public class RandomShapeGenerator {
  private Random rand = new Random(47);
  public Shape next() {
    switch(rand.nextInt(3)) {
      default:
      case 0: return new Circle();
      case 1: return new Square();
      case 2: return new Triangle();
    }
  }
} ///:~
```

```java
//: polymorphism/Shapes.java
// Polymorphism in Java.
```

```
import polymorphism.shape.*;

public class Shapes {
  private static RandomShapeGenerator gen =
    new RandomShapeGenerator();
  public static void main(String[] args) {
    Shape[] s = new Shape[9];
    // Fill up the array with shapes:
    for(int i = 0; i < s.length; i++)
      s[i] = gen.next();
    // Make polymorphic method calls:
    for(Shape shp : s)
      shp.draw();
  }
} /* Output:
Triangle.draw()
Triangle.draw()
Square.draw()
Triangle.draw()
Square.draw()
Triangle.draw()
Square.draw()
Triangle.draw()
Circle.draw()
*///:~
```

The base class **Shape** establishes the common interface to anything inherited from **Shape**—that is, all shapes can be drawn and erased. The derived classes override these definitions to provide unique behavior for each specific type of shape.

RandomShapeGenerator is a kind of "factory" that produces a reference to a randomly selected **Shape** object each time you call its **next( )** method. Note that the upcasting happens in the **return** statements, each of which takes a reference to a **Circle**, **Square**, or **Triangle** and sends it out of **next( )** as the return type, **Shape**. So whenever you call **next( )**, you never get a chance to see what specific type it is, since you always get back a plain **Shape** reference.

main( ) contains an array of **Shape** references filled through calls to **RandomShapeGenerator.next( )**. At this point you know you have **Shape**s, but you don't know anything more specific than that (and neither does the compiler). However, when you step through this array and call

draw( ) for each one, the correct type-specific behavior magically occurs, as you can see from the output when you run the program.

The point of creating the shapes randomly is to drive home the understanding that the compiler can have no special knowledge that allows it to make the correct calls at compile time. All the calls to **draw( )** must be made through dynamic binding.

Exercise 2: (1) Add the **@Override** annotation to the shapes example.

Exercise 3: (1) Add a new method in the base class of **Shapes.java** that prints a message, but don't override it in the derived classes. Explain what happens. Now override it in one of the derived classes but not the others, and see what happens. Finally, override it in all the derived classes.

Exercise 4: (2) Add a new type of **Shape** to **Shapes.java** and verify in **main( )** that polymorphism works for your new type as it does in the old types.

Exercise 5: (1) Starting from Exercise 1, add a **wheels( )** method in **Cycle**, which returns the number of wheels. Modify **ride( )** to call **wheels( )** and verify that polymorphism works.

Extensibility

Now let's return to the musical instrument example. Because of polymorphism, you can add as many new types as you want to the system without changing the **tune( )** method. In a well-designed OOP program, most or all of your methods will follow the model of **tune( )** and communicate only with the base-class interface. Such a program is *extensible* because you can add new functionality by inheriting new data types from the common base class. The methods that manipulate the base-class interface will not need to be changed at all to accommodate the new classes.

Consider what happens if you take the instrument example and add more methods in the base class and a number of new classes. Here's the diagram:

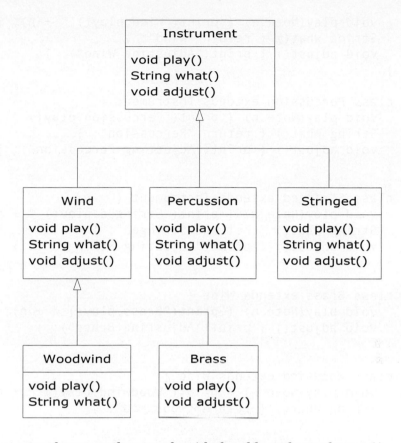

All these new classes work correctly with the old, unchanged **tune( )** method. Even if **tune( )** is in a separate file and new methods are added to the interface of **Instrument**, **tune( )** will still work correctly, even without recompiling it. Here is the implementation of the diagram:

```
//: polymorphism/music3/Music3.java
// An extensible program.
package polymorphism.music3;
import polymorphism.music.Note;
import static net.mindview.util.Print.*;

class Instrument {
  void play(Note n) { print("Instrument.play() " + n); }
  String what() { return "Instrument"; }
  void adjust() { print("Adjusting Instrument"); }
}

class Wind extends Instrument {
```

```java
  void play(Note n) { print("Wind.play() " + n); }
  String what() { return "Wind"; }
  void adjust() { print("Adjusting Wind"); }
}

class Percussion extends Instrument {
  void play(Note n) { print("Percussion.play() " + n); }
  String what() { return "Percussion"; }
  void adjust() { print("Adjusting Percussion"); }
}

class Stringed extends Instrument {
  void play(Note n) { print("Stringed.play() " + n); }
  String what() { return "Stringed"; }
  void adjust() { print("Adjusting Stringed"); }
}

class Brass extends Wind {
  void play(Note n) { print("Brass.play() " + n); }
  void adjust() { print("Adjusting Brass"); }
}

class Woodwind extends Wind {
  void play(Note n) { print("Woodwind.play() " + n); }
  String what() { return "Woodwind"; }
}

public class Music3 {
  // Doesn't care about type, so new types
  // added to the system still work right:
  public static void tune(Instrument i) {
    // ...
    i.play(Note.MIDDLE_C);
  }
  public static void tuneAll(Instrument[] e) {
    for(Instrument i : e)
      tune(i);
  }
  public static void main(String[] args) {
    // Upcasting during addition to the array:
    Instrument[] orchestra = {
      new Wind(),
      new Percussion(),
      new Stringed(),
```

```
        new Brass(),
        new Woodwind()
    };
    tuneAll(orchestra);
  }
} /* Output:
Wind.play() MIDDLE_C
Percussion.play() MIDDLE_C
Stringed.play() MIDDLE_C
Brass.play() MIDDLE_C
Woodwind.play() MIDDLE_C
*///:~
```

The new methods are **what( )**, which returns a **String** reference with a description of the class, and **adjust( )**, which provides some way to adjust each instrument.

In **main( )**, when you place something inside the **orchestra** array, you automatically upcast to **Instrument**.

You can see that the **tune( )** method is blissfully ignorant of all the code changes that have happened around it, and yet it works correctly. This is exactly what polymorphism is supposed to provide. Changes in your code don't cause damage to parts of the program that should not be affected. Put another way, polymorphism is an important technique for the programmer to "separate the things that change from the things that stay the same."

Exercise 6: (1) Change **Music3.java** so that **what( )** becomes the root **Object** method **toString( )**. Try printing the **Instrument** objects using **System.out.println( )** (without any casting).

Exercise 7: (2) Add a new type of **Instrument** to **Music3.java** and verify that polymorphism works for your new type.

Exercise 8: (2) Modify **Music3.java** so that it randomly creates **Instrument** objects the way **Shapes.java** does.

Exercise 9: (3) Create an inheritance hierarchy of **Rodent**: **Mouse**, **Gerbil**, **Hamster**, etc. In the base class, provide methods that are common to all **Rodent**s, and override these in the derived classes to perform different behaviors depending on the specific type of **Rodent**. Create an array of **Rodent**, fill it with different specific types of **Rodent**s, and call your base-class methods to see what happens.

Exercise 10: (3) Create a base class with two methods. In the first method, call the second method. Inherit a class and override the second method. Create an object of the derived class, upcast it to the base type, and call the first method. Explain what happens.

Pitfall: "overriding" **private** methods

Here's something you might innocently try to do:

```
//: polymorphism/PrivateOverride.java
// Trying to override a private method.
package polymorphism;
import static net.mindview.util.Print.*;

public class PrivateOverride {
  private void f() { print("private f()"); }
  public static void main(String[] args) {
    PrivateOverride po = new Derived();
    po.f();
  }
}

class Derived extends PrivateOverride {
  public void f() { print("public f()"); }
} /* Output:
private f()
*///:~
```

You might reasonably expect the output to be "**public f( )**", but a **private** method is automatically **final**, and is also hidden from the derived class. So **Derived**'s **f( )** in this case is a brand new method; it's not even overloaded, since the base-class version of **f( )** isn't visible in **Derived**.

The result of this is that only non-**private** methods may be overridden, but you should watch out for the appearance of overriding **private** methods, which generates no compiler warnings, but doesn't do what you might expect. To be clear, you should use a different name from a **private** base-class method in your derived class.

Pitfall: fields and **static** methods

Once you learn about polymorphism, you can begin to think that everything happens polymorphically. However, only ordinary method calls can be polymorphic. For example, if you access a field directly, that access will be resolved at compile time, as the following example demonstrates:[1]

```java
//: polymorphism/FieldAccess.java
// Direct field access is determined at compile time.

class Super {
  public int field = 0;
  public int getField() { return field; }
}

class Sub extends Super {
  public int field = 1;
  public int getField() { return field; }
  public int getSuperField() { return super.field; }
}

public class FieldAccess {
  public static void main(String[] args) {
    Super sup = new Sub(); // Upcast
    System.out.println("sup.field = " + sup.field +
      ", sup.getField() = " + sup.getField());
    Sub sub = new Sub();
    System.out.println("sub.field = " +
      sub.field + ", sub.getField() = " +
      sub.getField() +
      ", sub.getSuperField() = " +
      sub.getSuperField());
  }
} /* Output:
sup.field = 0, sup.getField() = 1
sub.field = 1, sub.getField() = 1, sub.getSuperField() = 0
*///:~
```

When a **Sub** object is upcast to a **Super** reference, any field accesses are resolved by the compiler, and are thus not polymorphic. In this example, different storage is allocated for **Super.field** and **Sub.field**. Thus, **Sub** actually contains two fields called **field**: its own and the one that it gets from **Super**. However, the **Super** version is not the default that is produced when

---

[1] Thanks to Randy Nichols for asking this question.

you refer to **field** in **Sub**; in order to get the **Super field** you must explicitly say **super.field**.

Although this seems like it could be a confusing issue, in practice it virtually never comes up. For one thing, you'll generally make all fields **private** and so you won't access them directly, but only as side effects of calling methods. In addition, you probably won't give the same name to a base-class field and a derived-class field, because it is confusing.

If a method is **static**, it doesn't behave polymorphically:

```
//: polymorphism/StaticPolymorphism.java
// Static methods are not polymorphic.

class StaticSuper {
  public static String staticGet() {
    return "Base staticGet()";
  }
  public String dynamicGet() {
    return "Base dynamicGet()";
  }
}

class StaticSub extends StaticSuper {
  public static String staticGet() {
    return "Derived staticGet()";
  }
  public String dynamicGet() {
    return "Derived dynamicGet()";
  }
}

public class StaticPolymorphism {
  public static void main(String[] args) {
    StaticSuper sup = new StaticSub(); // Upcast
    System.out.println(sup.staticGet());
    System.out.println(sup.dynamicGet());
  }
} /* Output:
Base staticGet()
Derived dynamicGet()
*///:~
```

static methods are associated with the class, and not the individual objects.

Constructors and polymorphism

As usual, constructors are different from other kinds of methods. This is also true when polymorphism is involved. Even though constructors are not polymorphic (they're actually **static** methods, but the **static** declaration is implicit), it's important to understand the way constructors work in complex hierarchies and with polymorphism. This understanding will help you avoid unpleasant entanglements.

Order of constructor calls

The order of constructor calls was briefly discussed in the *Initialization & Cleanup* chapter and again in the *Reusing Classes* chapter, but that was before polymorphism was introduced.

A constructor for the base class is always called during the construction process for a derived class. This call automatically moves up the inheritance hierarchy so that a constructor for every base class is called. This makes sense because the constructor has a special job: to see that the object is built properly. Since fields are usually **private**, you must generally assume that a derived class has access to its own members only, and not to those of the base class. Only the base-class constructor has the proper knowledge and access to initialize its own elements. Therefore, it's essential that all constructors get called; otherwise, the entire object wouldn't be constructed. That's why the compiler enforces a constructor call for every portion of a derived class. It will silently call the default constructor if you don't explicitly call a base-class constructor in the derived-class constructor body. If there is no default constructor, the compiler will complain. (In the case where a class has no constructors, the compiler will automatically synthesize a default constructor.)

Let's take a look at an example that shows the effects of composition, inheritance, and polymorphism on the order of construction:

```
//: polymorphism/Sandwich.java
// Order of constructor calls.
package polymorphism;
import static net.mindview.util.Print.*;

class Meal {
  Meal() { print("Meal()"); }
}
```

```java
class Bread {
  Bread() { print("Bread()"); }
}

class Cheese {
  Cheese() { print("Cheese()"); }
}

class Lettuce {
  Lettuce() { print("Lettuce()"); }
}

class Lunch extends Meal {
  Lunch() { print("Lunch()"); }
}

class PortableLunch extends Lunch {
  PortableLunch() { print("PortableLunch()");}
}

public class Sandwich extends PortableLunch {
  private Bread b = new Bread();
  private Cheese c = new Cheese();
  private Lettuce l = new Lettuce();
  public Sandwich() { print("Sandwich()"); }
  public static void main(String[] args) {
    new Sandwich();
  }
} /* Output:
Meal()
Lunch()
PortableLunch()
Bread()
Cheese()
Lettuce()
Sandwich()
*///:~
```

This example creates a complex class out of other classes, and each class has a constructor that announces itself. The important class is **Sandwich**, which reflects three levels of inheritance (four, if you count the implicit inheritance from **Object**) and three member objects. You can see the output when a **Sandwich** object is created in **main( )**. This means that the order of constructor calls for a complex object is as follows:

1. The base-class constructor is called. This step is repeated recursively such that the root of the hierarchy is constructed first, followed by the next-derived class, etc., until the most-derived class is reached.

2. Member initializers are called in the order of declaration.

3. The body of the derived-class constructor is called.

The order of the constructor calls is important. When you inherit, you know all about the base class and can access any **public** and **protected** members of the base class. This means that you must be able to assume that all the members of the base class are valid when you're in the derived class. In a normal method, construction has already taken place, so all the members of all parts of the object have been built. Inside the constructor, however, you must be able to know that all members that you use have been built. The only way to guarantee this is for the base-class constructor to be called first. Then when you're in the derived-class constructor, all the members you can access in the base class have been initialized. Knowing that all members are valid inside the constructor is also the reason that, whenever possible, you should initialize all member objects (that is, objects placed in the class using composition) at their point of definition in the class (e.g., **b**, **c**, and **l** in the preceding example). If you follow this practice, you will help ensure that all base-class members *and* member objects of the current object have been initialized. Unfortunately, this doesn't handle every case, as you will see in the next section.

Exercise 11: (1) Add class **Pickle** to **Sandwich.java**.

Inheritance and cleanup

When using composition and inheritance to create a new class, most of the time you won't have to worry about cleaning up; subobjects can usually be left to the garbage collector. If you do have cleanup issues, you must be diligent and create a **dispose( )** method (the name I have chosen to use here; you may come up with something better) for your new class. And with inheritance, you must override **dispose( )** in the derived class if you have any special cleanup that must happen as part of garbage collection. When you override **dispose( )** in an inherited class, it's important to remember to call the base-class version of **dispose( )**, since otherwise the base-class cleanup will not happen. The following example demonstrates this:

```
//: polymorphism/Frog.java
// Cleanup and inheritance.
package polymorphism;
import static net.mindview.util.Print.*;

class Characteristic {
  private String s;
  Characteristic(String s) {
    this.s = s;
    print("Creating Characteristic " + s);
  }
  protected void dispose() {
    print("disposing Characteristic " + s);
  }
}

class Description {
  private String s;
  Description(String s) {
    this.s = s;
    print("Creating Description " + s);
  }
  protected void dispose() {
    print("disposing Description " + s);
  }
}

class LivingCreature {
  private Characteristic p =
    new Characteristic("is alive");
  private Description t =
    new Description("Basic Living Creature");
  LivingCreature() {
    print("LivingCreature()");
  }
  protected void dispose() {
    print("LivingCreature dispose");
    t.dispose();
    p.dispose();
  }
}

class Animal extends LivingCreature {
  private Characteristic p =
```

```
        new Characteristic("has heart");
    private Description t =
      new Description("Animal not Vegetable");
    Animal() { print("Animal()"); }
    protected void dispose() {
      print("Animal dispose");
      t.dispose();
      p.dispose();
      super.dispose();
    }
  }

class Amphibian extends Animal {
  private Characteristic p =
    new Characteristic("can live in water");
  private Description t =
    new Description("Both water and land");
  Amphibian() {
    print("Amphibian()");
  }
  protected void dispose() {
    print("Amphibian dispose");
    t.dispose();
    p.dispose();
    super.dispose();
  }
}

public class Frog extends Amphibian {
  private Characteristic p = new Characteristic("Croaks");
  private Description t = new Description("Eats Bugs");
  public Frog() { print("Frog()"); }
  protected void dispose() {
    print("Frog dispose");
    t.dispose();
    p.dispose();
    super.dispose();
  }
  public static void main(String[] args) {
    Frog frog = new Frog();
    print("Bye!");
    frog.dispose();
  }
} /* Output:
```

```
Creating Characteristic is alive
Creating Description Basic Living Creature
LivingCreature()
Creating Characteristic has heart
Creating Description Animal not Vegetable
Animal()
Creating Characteristic can live in water
Creating Description Both water and land
Amphibian()
Creating Characteristic Croaks
Creating Description Eats Bugs
Frog()
Bye!
Frog dispose
disposing Description Eats Bugs
disposing Characteristic Croaks
Amphibian dispose
disposing Description Both water and land
disposing Characteristic can live in water
Animal dispose
disposing Description Animal not Vegetable
disposing Characteristic has heart
LivingCreature dispose
disposing Description Basic Living Creature
disposing Characteristic is alive
*///:~
```

Each class in the hierarchy also contains member objects of types
Characteristic and **Description**, which must also be disposed. The order
of disposal should be the reverse of the order of initialization, in case one
subobject is dependent on another. For fields, this means the reverse of the
order of declaration (since fields are initialized in declaration order). For base
classes (following the form that's used in C++ for destructors), you should
perform the derived-class cleanup first, then the base-class cleanup. That's
because the derived-class cleanup could call some methods in the base class
that require the base-class components to be alive, so you must not destroy
them prematurely. From the output you can see that all parts of the **Frog**
object are disposed in reverse order of creation.

From this example, you can see that although you don't always need to
perform cleanup, when you do, the process requires care and awareness.

Exercise 12: (3) Modify Exercise 9 so that it demonstrates the order of
initialization of the base classes and derived classes. Now add member

objects to both the base and derived classes, and show the order in which their initialization occurs during construction.

Also note that in the above example, a **Frog** object "owns" its member objects. It creates them, and it knows how long they should live (as long as the **Frog** does), so it knows when to **dispose( )** the member objects. However, if one of these member objects is shared with one or more other objects, the problem becomes more complex and you cannot simply assume that you can call **dispose( )**. In this case, *reference counting* may be necessary to keep track of the number of objects that are still accessing a shared object. Here's what it looks like:

```
//: polymorphism/ReferenceCounting.java
// Cleaning up shared member objects.
import static net.mindview.util.Print.*;

class Shared {
  private int refcount = 0;
  private static long counter = 0;
  private final long id = counter++;
  public Shared() {
    print("Creating " + this);
  }
  public void addRef() { refcount++; }
  protected void dispose() {
    if(--refcount == 0)
      print("Disposing " + this);
  }
  public String toString() { return "Shared " + id; }
}

class Composing {
  private Shared shared;
  private static long counter = 0;
  private final long id = counter++;
  public Composing(Shared shared) {
    print("Creating " + this);
    this.shared = shared;
    this.shared.addRef();
  }
  protected void dispose() {
    print("disposing " + this);
    shared.dispose();
  }
```

```java
    public String toString() { return "Composing " + id; }
}

public class ReferenceCounting {
  public static void main(String[] args) {
    Shared shared = new Shared();
    Composing[] composing = { new Composing(shared),
      new Composing(shared), new Composing(shared),
      new Composing(shared), new Composing(shared) };
    for(Composing c : composing)
      c.dispose();
  }
} /* Output:
Creating Shared 0
Creating Composing 0
Creating Composing 1
Creating Composing 2
Creating Composing 3
Creating Composing 4
disposing Composing 0
disposing Composing 1
disposing Composing 2
disposing Composing 3
disposing Composing 4
Disposing Shared 0
*///:~
```

The **static long counter** keeps track of the number of instances of **Shared** that are created, and it also provides a value for **id**. The type of **counter** is **long** rather than **int**, to prevent overflow (this is just good practice; overflowing such a counter is not likely to happen in any of the examples in this book). The **id** is **final** because we do not expect it to change its value during the lifetime of the object.

When you attach a shared object to your class, you must remember to call **addRef( )**, but the **dispose( )** method will keep track of the reference count and decide when to actually perform the cleanup. This technique requires extra diligence to use, but if you are sharing objects that require cleanup you don't have much choice.

Exercise 13:   (3) Add a **finalize( )** method to **ReferenceCounting.java** to verify the *termination condition* (see the *Initialization & Cleanup* chapter).

Exercise 14: (4) Modify Exercise 12 so that one of the member objects is a shared object with reference counting, and demonstrate that it works properly.

Behavior of polymorphic methods inside constructors

The hierarchy of constructor calls brings up an interesting dilemma. What happens if you're inside a constructor and you call a dynamically bound method of the object that's being constructed?

Inside an ordinary method, the dynamically bound call is resolved at run time, because the object cannot know whether it belongs to the class that the method is in or some class derived from it.

If you call a dynamically bound method inside a constructor, the overridden definition for that method is also used. However, the effect of this call can be rather unexpected because the overridden method will be called before the object is fully constructed. This can conceal some difficult-to-find bugs.

Conceptually, the constructor's job is to bring the object into existence (which is hardly an ordinary feat). Inside any constructor, the entire object might be only partially formed—you can only know that the base-class objects have been initialized. If the constructor is only one step in building an object of a class that's been derived from that constructor's class, the derived parts have not yet been initialized at the time that the current constructor is being called. A dynamically bound method call, however, reaches "outward" into the inheritance hierarchy. It calls a method in a derived class. If you do this inside a constructor, you can call a method that might manipulate members that haven't been initialized yet—a sure recipe for disaster.

You can see the problem in the following example:

```
//: polymorphism/PolyConstructors.java
// Constructors and polymorphism
// don't produce what you might expect.
import static net.mindview.util.Print.*;

class Glyph {
  void draw() { print("Glyph.draw()"); }
  Glyph() {
    print("Glyph() before draw()");
```

```
      draw();
      print("Glyph() after draw()");
    }
}

class RoundGlyph extends Glyph {
  private int radius = 1;
  RoundGlyph(int r) {
    radius = r;
    print("RoundGlyph.RoundGlyph(), radius = " + radius);
  }
  void draw() {
    print("RoundGlyph.draw(), radius = " + radius);
  }
}

public class PolyConstructors {
  public static void main(String[] args) {
    new RoundGlyph(5);
  }
} /* Output:
Glyph() before draw()
RoundGlyph.draw(), radius = 0
Glyph() after draw()
RoundGlyph.RoundGlyph(), radius = 5
*///:~
```

Glyph.draw( ) is designed to be overridden, which happens in
RoundGlyph. But the **Glyph** constructor calls this method, and the call
ends up in **RoundGlyph.draw( )**, which would seem to be the intent. But if
you look at the output, you can see that when **Glyph**'s constructor calls
draw( ), the value of **radius** isn't even the default initial value 1. It's 0. This
would probably result in either a dot or nothing at all being drawn on the
screen, and you'd be left staring, trying to figure out why the program won't
work.

The order of initialization described in the earlier section isn't quite complete,
and that's the key to solving the mystery. The actual process of initialization
is:

1.   The storage allocated for the object is initialized to binary zero
      before anything else happens.

2. The base-class constructors are called as described previously. At this point, the overridden **draw( )** method is called (yes, *before* the **RoundGlyph** constructor is called), which discovers a **radius** value of zero, due to Step 1.

3. Member initializers are called in the order of declaration.

4. The body of the derived-class constructor is called.

There's an upside to this, which is that everything is at least initialized to zero (or whatever zero means for that particular data type) and not just left as garbage. This includes object references that are embedded inside a class via composition, which become **null**. So if you forget to initialize that reference, you'll get an exception at run time. Everything else gets zero, which is usually a telltale value when you are looking at output.

On the other hand, you should be pretty horrified at the outcome of this program. You've done a perfectly logical thing, and yet the behavior is mysteriously wrong, with no complaints from the compiler. (C++ produces more rational behavior in this situation.) Bugs like this could easily be buried and take a long time to discover.

As a result, a good guideline for constructors is "Do as little as possible to set the object into a good state, and if you can possibly avoid it, don't call any other methods in this class." The only safe methods to call inside a constructor are those that are **final** in the base class. (This also applies to **private** methods, which are automatically **final**.) These cannot be overridden and thus cannot produce this kind of surprise. You may not always be able to follow this guideline, but it's something to strive towards.

Exercise 15: (2) Add a **RectangularGlyph** to **PolyConstructors.java** and demonstrate the problem described in this section.

Covariant return types

Java SE5 adds *covariant return types*, which means that an overridden method in a derived class can return a type derived from the type returned by the base-class method:

```
//: polymorphism/CovariantReturn.java

class Grain {
  public String toString() { return "Grain"; }
```

```
  }

class Wheat extends Grain {
  public String toString() { return "Wheat"; }
}

class Mill {
  Grain process() { return new Grain(); }
}

class WheatMill extends Mill {
  Wheat process() { return new Wheat(); }
}

public class CovariantReturn {
  public static void main(String[] args) {
    Mill m = new Mill();
    Grain g = m.process();
    System.out.println(g);
    m = new WheatMill();
    g = m.process();
    System.out.println(g);
  }
} /* Output:
Grain
Wheat
*///:~
```

The key difference between Java SE5 and earlier versions of Java is that the earlier versions would force the overridden version of **process( )** to return **Grain**, rather than **Wheat**, even though **Wheat** is derived from **Grain** and thus is still a legitimate return type. Covariant return types allow the more specific **Wheat** return type.

Designing with inheritance

Once you learn about polymorphism, it can seem that everything ought to be inherited, because polymorphism is such a clever tool. This can burden your designs; in fact, if you choose inheritance first when you're using an existing class to make a new class, things can become needlessly complicated.

A better approach is to choose composition first, especially when it's not obvious which one you should use. Composition does not force a design into an inheritance hierarchy. But composition is also more flexible since it's possible to dynamically choose a type (and thus behavior) when using composition, whereas inheritance requires that an exact type be known at compile time. The following example illustrates this:

```
//: polymorphism/Transmogrify.java
// Dynamically changing the behavior of an object
// via composition (the "State" design pattern).
import static net.mindview.util.Print.*;

class Actor {
  public void act() {}
}

class HappyActor extends Actor {
  public void act() { print("HappyActor"); }
}

class SadActor extends Actor {
  public void act() { print("SadActor"); }
}

class Stage {
  private Actor actor = new HappyActor();
  public void change() { actor = new SadActor(); }
  public void performPlay() { actor.act(); }
}

public class Transmogrify {
  public static void main(String[] args) {
    Stage stage = new Stage();
    stage.performPlay();
    stage.change();
    stage.performPlay();
  }
} /* Output:
HappyActor
SadActor
*///:~
```

A **Stage** object contains a reference to an **Actor**, which is initialized to a **HappyActor** object. This means **performPlay( )** produces a particular behavior. But since a reference can be re-bound to a different object at run time, a reference for a **SadActor** object can be substituted in **actor**, and then the behavior produced by **performPlay( )** changes. Thus you gain dynamic flexibility at run time. (This is also called the *State pattern*. See *Thinking in Patterns (with Java)* at *www.MindView.net*.) In contrast, you can't decide to inherit differently at run time; that must be completely determined at compile time.

A general guideline is "Use inheritance to express differences in behavior, and fields to express variations in state." In the preceding example, both are used; two different classes are inherited to express the difference in the **act( )** method, and **Stage** uses composition to allow its state to be changed. In this case, that change in state happens to produce a change in behavior.

Exercise 16:   (3) Following the example in **Transmogrify.java**, create a **Starship** class containing an **AlertStatus** reference that can indicate three different states. Include methods to change the states.

Substitution vs. extension

It would seem that the cleanest way to create an inheritance hierarchy is to take the "pure" approach. That is, only methods that have been established in the base class are overridden in the derived class, as seen in this diagram:

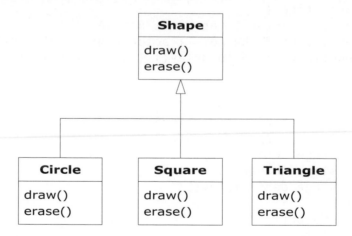

This can be called a pure "is-a" relationship because the interface of a class establishes what it is. Inheritance guarantees that any derived class will have the interface of the base class and nothing less. If you follow this diagram, derived classes will also have *no more* than the base-class interface.

This can be thought of as *pure substitution*, because derived class objects can be perfectly substituted for the base class, and you never need to know any extra information about the subclasses when you're using them:

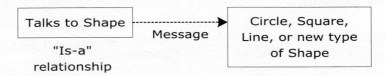

That is, the base class can receive any message you can send to the derived class because the two have exactly the same interface. All you need to do is upcast from the derived class and never look back to see what exact type of object you're dealing with. Everything is handled through polymorphism.

When you see it this way, it seems like a pure is-a relationship is the only sensible way to do things, and any other design indicates muddled thinking and is by definition broken. This too is a trap. As soon as you start thinking this way, you'll turn around and discover that extending the interface (which, unfortunately, the keyword **extends** seems to encourage) is the perfect solution to a particular problem. This can be termed an "is-like-a" relationship, because the derived class is *like* the base class—it has the same fundamental interface—but it has other features that require additional methods to implement:

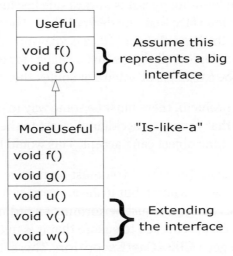

While this is also a useful and sensible approach (depending on the situation), it has a drawback. The extended part of the interface in the derived class is not available from the base class, so once you upcast, you can't call the new methods:

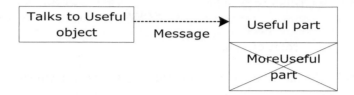

If you're not upcasting in this case, it won't bother you, but often you'll get into a situation in which you need to rediscover the exact type of the object so you can access the extended methods of that type. The following section shows how this is done.

Downcasting and runtime type information

Since you lose the specific type information via an *upcast* (moving up the inheritance hierarchy), it makes sense that to retrieve the type information—that is, to move back down the inheritance hierarchy—you use a *downcast*. However, you know an upcast is always safe because the base class cannot have a bigger interface than the derived class. Therefore, every message you send through the base-class interface is guaranteed to be accepted. But with a downcast, you don't really know that a shape (for example) is actually a circle. It could also be a triangle or square or some other type.

To solve this problem, there must be some way to guarantee that a downcast is correct, so that you won't accidentally cast to the wrong type and then send a message that the object can't accept. This would be quite unsafe.

In some languages (like C++) you must perform a special operation in order to get a type-safe downcast, but in Java, *every* cast is checked! So even though it looks like you're just performing an ordinary parenthesized cast, at run time this cast is checked to ensure that it is in fact the type you think it is. If it isn't, you get a **ClassCastException**. This act of checking types at run time is called *runtime type information* (RTTI). The following example demonstrates the behavior of RTTI:

```
//: polymorphism/RTTI.java
```

```
// Downcasting & Runtime type information (RTTI).
// {ThrowsException}

class Useful {
  public void f() {}
  public void g() {}
}

class MoreUseful extends Useful {
  public void f() {}
  public void g() {}
  public void u() {}
  public void v() {}
  public void w() {}
}

public class RTTI {
  public static void main(String[] args) {
    Useful[] x = {
      new Useful(),
      new MoreUseful()
    };
    x[0].f();
    x[1].g();
    // Compile time: method not found in Useful:
    //! x[1].u();
    ((MoreUseful)x[1]).u(); // Downcast/RTTI
    ((MoreUseful)x[0]).u(); // Exception thrown
  }
} ///:~
```

As in the previous diagram, **MoreUseful** extends the interface of **Useful**. But since it's inherited, it can also be upcast to a **Useful**. You can see this happening in the initialization of the array **x** in **main( )**. Since both objects in the array are of class **Useful**, you can send the **f( )** and **g( )** methods to both, and if you try to call **u( )** (which exists only in **MoreUseful**), you'll get a compile-time error message.

If you want to access the extended interface of a **MoreUseful** object, you can try to downcast. If it's the correct type, it will be successful. Otherwise, you'll get a **ClassCastException**. You don't need to write any special code for this exception, since it indicates a programmer error that could happen anywhere in a program. The **{ThrowsException}** comment tag tells this book's build system to expect this program to throw an exception when it executes.

There's more to RTTI than a simple cast. For example, there's a way to see what type you're dealing with *before* you try to downcast it. All of the *Type Information* chapter is devoted to the study of different aspects of Java runtime type information.

Exercise 17:   (2) Using the **Cycle** hierarchy from Exercise 1, add a **balance( )** method to **Unicycle** and **Bicycle**, but not to **Tricycle**. Create instances of all three types and upcast them to an array of **Cycle**. Try to call **balance( )** on each element of the array and observe the results. Downcast and call **balance( )** and observe what happens.

Summary

Polymorphism means "different forms." In object-oriented programming, you have the same interface from the base class, and different forms using that interface: the different versions of the dynamically bound methods.

You've seen in this chapter that it's impossible to understand, or even create, an example of polymorphism without using data abstraction and inheritance. Polymorphism is a feature that cannot be viewed in isolation (like a **switch** statement can, for example), but instead works only in concert, as part of the larger picture of class relationships.

To use polymorphism—and thus object-oriented techniques—effectively in your programs, you must expand your view of programming to include not just members and messages of an individual class, but also the commonality among classes and their relationships with each other. Although this requires significant effort, it's a worthy struggle. The results are faster program development, better code organization, extensible programs, and easier code maintenance.

Solutions to selected exercises can be found in the electronic document *The Thinking in Java Annotated Solution Guide*, available for sale from *www.MindView.net*.

Interfaces

Interfaces and abstract classes provide a more structured way to separate interface from implementation.

Such mechanisms are not that common in programming languages. C++, for example, only has indirect support for these concepts. The fact that language keywords exist in Java indicates that these ideas were considered important enough to provide direct support.

First, we'll look at the *abstract class*, which is a kind of midway step between an ordinary class and an interface. Although your first impulse will be to create an interface, the abstract class is an important and necessary tool for building classes that have some unimplemented methods. You can't always use a pure interface.

Abstract classes and methods

In all the "instrument" examples in the previous chapter, the methods in the base class **Instrument** were always "dummy" methods. If these methods are ever called, you've done something wrong. That's because the intent of **Instrument** is to create a *common interface* for all the classes derived from it.

In those examples, the only reason to establish this common interface is so that it can be expressed differently for each different subtype. It establishes a basic form, so that you can say what's common for all the derived classes. Another way of saying this is to call **Instrument** an *abstract base class*, or simply an *abstract class*.

If you have an abstract class like **Instrument**, objects of that specific class almost always have no meaning. You create an abstract class when you want to manipulate a set of classes through its common interface. Thus, **Instrument** is meant to express only the interface, and not a particular implementation, so creating an **Instrument** object makes no sense, and you'll probably want to prevent the user from doing it. This can be accomplished by making all the methods in **Instrument** generate errors, but that delays the information until run time and requires reliable exhaustive testing on the user's part. It's usually better to catch problems at compile time.

Java provides a mechanism for doing this called the *abstract method*.[1] This is a method that is incomplete; it has only a declaration and no method body. Here is the syntax for an abstract method declaration:

```
abstract void f();
```

A class containing abstract methods is called an *abstract class*. If a class contains one or more abstract methods, the class itself must be qualified as **abstract**. (Otherwise, the compiler gives you an error message.)

If an abstract class is incomplete, what is the compiler supposed to do when someone tries to make an object of that class? It cannot safely create an object of an abstract class, so you get an error message from the compiler. This way, the compiler ensures the purity of the abstract class, and you don't need to worry about misusing it.

If you inherit from an abstract class and you want to make objects of the new type, you must provide method definitions for all the abstract methods in the base class. If you don't (and you may choose not to), then the derived class is also abstract, and the compiler will force you to qualify *that* class with the **abstract** keyword.

It's possible to make a class **abstract** without including any **abstract** methods. This is useful when you've got a class in which it doesn't make sense to have any **abstract** methods, and yet you want to prevent any instances of that class.

The **Instrument** class from the previous chapter can easily be turned into an **abstract** class. Only some of the methods will be **abstract**, since making a class abstract doesn't force you to make all the methods **abstract**. Here's what it looks like:

---

[1] For C++ programmers, this is the analogue of C++'s *pure virtual function*.

Thinking in Java *Bruce Eckel*

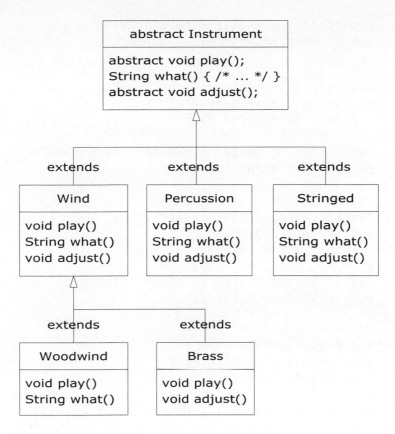

Here's the orchestra example modified to use **abstract** classes and methods:

```
//: interfaces/music4/Music4.java
// Abstract classes and methods.
package interfaces.music4;
import polymorphism.music.Note;
import static net.mindview.util.Print.*;

abstract class Instrument {
  private int i; // Storage allocated for each
  public abstract void play(Note n);
  public String what() { return "Instrument"; }
  public abstract void adjust();
}

class Wind extends Instrument {
  public void play(Note n) {
    print("Wind.play() " + n);
  }
```

```java
    public String what() { return "Wind"; }
    public void adjust() {}
}

class Percussion extends Instrument {
  public void play(Note n) {
    print("Percussion.play() " + n);
  }
  public String what() { return "Percussion"; }
  public void adjust() {}
}

class Stringed extends Instrument {
  public void play(Note n) {
    print("Stringed.play() " + n);
  }
  public String what() { return "Stringed"; }
  public void adjust() {}
}

class Brass extends Wind {
  public void play(Note n) {
    print("Brass.play() " + n);
  }
  public void adjust() { print("Brass.adjust()"); }
}

class Woodwind extends Wind {
  public void play(Note n) {
    print("Woodwind.play() " + n);
  }
  public String what() { return "Woodwind"; }
}

public class Music4 {
  // Doesn't care about type, so new types
  // added to the system still work right:
  static void tune(Instrument i) {
    // ...
    i.play(Note.MIDDLE_C);
  }
  static void tuneAll(Instrument[] e) {
    for(Instrument i : e)
      tune(i);
```

```
  }
  public static void main(String[] args) {
    // Upcasting during addition to the array:
    Instrument[] orchestra = {
      new Wind(),
      new Percussion(),
      new Stringed(),
      new Brass(),
      new Woodwind()
    };
    tuneAll(orchestra);
  }
} /* Output:
Wind.play() MIDDLE_C
Percussion.play() MIDDLE_C
Stringed.play() MIDDLE_C
Brass.play() MIDDLE_C
Woodwind.play() MIDDLE_C
*///:~
```

You can see that there's really no change except in the base class.

It's helpful to create **abstract** classes and methods because they make the abstractness of a class explicit, and tell both the user and the compiler how it was intended to be used. Abstract classes are also useful refactoring tools, since they allow you to easily move common methods up the inheritance hierarchy.

Exercise 1: (1) Modify Exercise 9 in the previous chapter so that **Rodent** is an **abstract** class. Make the methods of **Rodent** abstract whenever possible.

Exercise 2: (1) Create a class as **abstract** without including any **abstract** methods, and verify that you cannot create any instances of that class.

Exercise 3: (2) Create a base class with an **abstract print( )** method that is overridden in a derived class. The overridden version of the method prints the value of an **int** variable defined in the derived class. At the point of definition of this variable, give it a nonzero value. In the base-class constructor, call this method. In **main( )**, create an object of the derived type, and then call its **print( )** method. Explain the results.

Exercise 4: (3) Create an **abstract** class with no methods. Derive a class and add a method. Create a **static** method that takes a reference to the base class, downcasts it to the derived class, and calls the method. In **main( )**, demonstrate that it works. Now put the **abstract** declaration for the method in the base class, thus eliminating the need for the downcast.

Interfaces

The **interface** keyword takes the concept of abstractness one step further. The **abstract** keyword allows you to create one or more undefined methods in a class—you provide part of the interface without providing a corresponding implementation (however, an abstract class can still contain fields). The implementation is provided by inheritors. The **interface** keyword produces a completely abstract class, one that provides no implementation at all. It allows the creator to determine method names, argument lists, and return types, but no method bodies. An interface provides only a form, but no implementation.

An interface says, "All classes that *implement* this particular interface will look like this." Thus, any code that uses a particular interface knows what methods might be called for that interface, and that's all. So the interface is used to establish a "protocol" between classes. (Some object-oriented programming languages have a keyword called *protocol* to do the same thing.)

However, an interface is more than just an abstract class taken to the extreme, since it allows you to perform a variation of "multiple inheritance" by creating a class that can be upcast to more than one base type.

To create an interface, use the **interface** keyword instead of the **class** keyword. As with a class, you can add the **public** keyword before the **interface** keyword (but only if that interface is defined in a file of the same name). If you leave off the **public** keyword, you get package access, so the interface is only usable within the same package. An interface can also contain fields, but these are implicitly **static** and **final**.

To make a class that conforms to a particular interface (or group of interfaces), use the **implements** keyword, which says, "The interface is what it looks like, but now I'm going to say how it *works*." Other than that, it looks like inheritance. The diagram for the instrument example shows this:

Thinking in Java Bruce Eckel

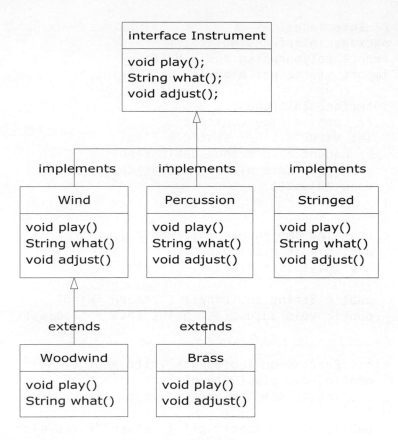

You can see from the **Woodwind** and **Brass** classes that once you've implemented an interface, that implementation becomes an ordinary class that can be extended in the regular way.

You can choose to explicitly declare the methods in an interface as **public**, but they are **public** even if you don't say it. So when you **implement** an interface, the methods from the interface *must* be defined as **public**. Otherwise, they would default to package access, and you'd be reducing the accessibility of a method during inheritance, which is not allowed by the Java compiler.

You can see this in the modified version of the **Instrument** example. Note that every method in the interface is strictly a declaration, which is the only thing the compiler allows. In addition, none of the methods in **Instrument** are declared as **public**, but they're automatically **public** anyway:

```
//: interfaces/music5/Music5.java
```

```java
// Interfaces.
package interfaces.music5;
import polymorphism.music.Note;
import static net.mindview.util.Print.*;

interface Instrument {
  // Compile-time constant:
  int VALUE = 5; // static & final
  // Cannot have method definitions:
  void play(Note n); // Automatically public
  void adjust();
}

class Wind implements Instrument {
  public void play(Note n) {
    print(this + ".play() " + n);
  }
  public String toString() { return "Wind"; }
  public void adjust() { print(this + ".adjust()"); }
}

class Percussion implements Instrument {
  public void play(Note n) {
    print(this + ".play() " + n);
  }
  public String toString() { return "Percussion"; }
  public void adjust() { print(this + ".adjust()"); }
}

class Stringed implements Instrument {
  public void play(Note n) {
    print(this + ".play() " + n);
  }
  public String toString() { return "Stringed"; }
  public void adjust() { print(this + ".adjust()"); }
}

class Brass extends Wind {
  public String toString() { return "Brass"; }
}

class Woodwind extends Wind {
  public String toString() { return "Woodwind"; }
}
```

```
public class Music5 {
  // Doesn't care about type, so new types
  // added to the system still work right:
  static void tune(Instrument i) {
    // ...
    i.play(Note.MIDDLE_C);
  }
  static void tuneAll(Instrument[] e) {
    for(Instrument i : e)
      tune(i);
  }
  public static void main(String[] args) {
    // Upcasting during addition to the array:
    Instrument[] orchestra = {
      new Wind(),
      new Percussion(),
      new Stringed(),
      new Brass(),
      new Woodwind()
    };
    tuneAll(orchestra);
  }
} /* Output:
Wind.play() MIDDLE_C
Percussion.play() MIDDLE_C
Stringed.play() MIDDLE_C
Brass.play() MIDDLE_C
Woodwind.play() MIDDLE_C
*///:~
```

One other change has been made to this version of the example: The **what( )** method has been changed to **toString( )**, since that was how the method was being used. Since **toString( )** is part of the root class **Object**, it doesn't need to appear in the interface.

The rest of the code works the same. Notice that it doesn't matter if you are upcasting to a "regular" class called **Instrument**, an **abstract** class called **Instrument**, or to an interface called **Instrument**. The behavior is the same. In fact, you can see in the **tune( )** method that there isn't any evidence about whether **Instrument** is a "regular" class, an **abstract** class, or an interface.

Exercise 5: (2) Create an interface containing three methods, in its own **package**. Implement the interface in a different **package**.

Exercise 6: (2) Prove that all the methods in an interface are automatically **public**.

Exercise 7: (1) Change Exercise 9 in the *Polymorphism* chapter so that **Rodent** is an interface.

Exercise 8: (2) In **polymorphism.Sandwich.java**, create an interface called **FastFood** (with appropriate methods) and change **Sandwich** so that it also implements **FastFood**.

Exercise 9: (3) Refactor **Music5.java** by moving the common methods in **Wind**, **Percussion** and **Stringed** into an **abstract** class.

Exercise 10: (3) Modify **Music5.java** by adding a **Playable** interface. Move the **play( )** declaration from **Instrument** to **Playable**. Add **Playable** to the derived classes by including it in the **implements** list. Change **tune( )** so that it takes a **Playable** instead of an **Instrument**.

Complete decoupling

Whenever a method works with a class instead of an interface, you are limited to using that class or its subclasses. If you would like to apply the method to a class that isn't in that hierarchy, you're out of luck. An interface relaxes this constraint considerably. As a result, it allows you to write more reusable code.

For example, suppose you have a **Processor** class that has a **name( )** and a **process( )** method that takes input, modifies it and produces output. The base class is extended to create different types of **Processor**. In this case, the **Processor** subtypes modify **String** objects (note that the return types can be covariant, but not the argument types):

```
//: interfaces/classprocessor/Apply.java
package interfaces.classprocessor;
import java.util.*;
import static net.mindview.util.Print.*;

class Processor {
  public String name() {
    return getClass().getSimpleName();
  }
  Object process(Object input) { return input; }
```

```
}

class Upcase extends Processor {
  String process(Object input) { // Covariant return
    return ((String)input).toUpperCase();
  }
}

class Downcase extends Processor {
  String process(Object input) {
    return ((String)input).toLowerCase();
  }
}

class Splitter extends Processor {
  String process(Object input) {
    // The split() argument divides a String into pieces:
    return Arrays.toString(((String)input).split(" "));
  }
}

public class Apply {
  public static void process(Processor p, Object s) {
    print("Using Processor " + p.name());
    print(p.process(s));
  }
  public static String s =
    "Disagreement with beliefs is by definition incorrect";
  public static void main(String[] args) {
    process(new Upcase(), s);
    process(new Downcase(), s);
    process(new Splitter(), s);
  }
} /* Output:
Using Processor Upcase
DISAGREEMENT WITH BELIEFS IS BY DEFINITION INCORRECT
Using Processor Downcase
disagreement with beliefs is by definition incorrect
Using Processor Splitter
[Disagreement, with, beliefs, is, by, definition,
incorrect]
*///:~
```

The **Apply.process( )** method takes any kind of **Processor** and applies it to an **Object**, then prints the results. Creating a method that behaves

---

differently depending on the argument object that you pass it is called the
Strategy design pattern. The method contains the fixed part of the algorithm
to be performed, and the Strategy contains the part that varies. The Strategy
is the object that you pass in, and it contains code to be executed. Here, the
Processor object is the Strategy, and in **main( )** you can see three different
Strategies applied to the **String s**.

The **split( )** method is part of the **String** class. It takes the **String** object and
splits it using the argument as a boundary, and returns a **String[]**. It is used
here as a shorter way of creating an array of **String**.

Now suppose you discover a set of electronic filters that seem like they could
fit into your **Apply.process( )** method:

```
//: interfaces/filters/Waveform.java
package interfaces.filters;

public class Waveform {
  private static long counter;
  private final long id = counter++;
  public String toString() { return "Waveform " + id; }
} ///:~
```

```
//: interfaces/filters/Filter.java
package interfaces.filters;

public class Filter {
  public String name() {
    return getClass().getSimpleName();
  }
  public Waveform process(Waveform input) { return input; }
} ///:~
```

```
//: interfaces/filters/LowPass.java
package interfaces.filters;

public class LowPass extends Filter {
  double cutoff;
  public LowPass(double cutoff) { this.cutoff = cutoff; }
  public Waveform process(Waveform input) {
    return input; // Dummy processing
  }
} ///:~
```

```
//: interfaces/filters/HighPass.java
```

```
package interfaces.filters;

public class HighPass extends Filter {
  double cutoff;
  public HighPass(double cutoff) { this.cutoff = cutoff; }
  public Waveform process(Waveform input) { return input; }
} ///:~

//: interfaces/filters/BandPass.java
package interfaces.filters;

public class BandPass extends Filter {
  double lowCutoff, highCutoff;
  public BandPass(double lowCut, double highCut) {
    lowCutoff = lowCut;
    highCutoff = highCut;
  }
  public Waveform process(Waveform input) { return input; }
} ///:~
```

Filter has the same interface elements as **Processor**, but because it isn't inherited from **Processor**—because the creator of the **Filter** class had no clue you might want to use it as a **Processor**—you can't use a **Filter** with the **Apply.process( )** method, even though it would work fine. Basically, the coupling between **Apply.process( )** and **Processor** is stronger than it needs to be, and this prevents the **Apply.process( )** code from being reused when it ought to be. Also notice that the inputs and outputs are both **Waveform**s.

If **Processor** is an interface, however, the constraints are loosened enough that you can reuse an **Apply.process( )** that takes that interface. Here are the modified versions of **Processor** and **Apply**:

```
//: interfaces/interfaceprocessor/Processor.java
package interfaces.interfaceprocessor;

public interface Processor {
  String name();
  Object process(Object input);
} ///:~

//: interfaces/interfaceprocessor/Apply.java
package interfaces.interfaceprocessor;
import static net.mindview.util.Print.*;
```

```
public class Apply {
  public static void process(Processor p, Object s) {
    print("Using Processor " + p.name());
    print(p.process(s));
  }
} ///:~
```

The first way you can reuse code is if client programmers can write their classes to conform to the interface, like this:

```
//: interfaces/interfaceprocessor/StringProcessor.java
package interfaces.interfaceprocessor;
import java.util.*;

public abstract class StringProcessor implements Processor{
  public String name() {
    return getClass().getSimpleName();
  }
  public abstract String process(Object input);
  public static String s =
    "If she weighs the same as a duck, she's made of wood";
  public static void main(String[] args) {
    Apply.process(new Upcase(), s);
    Apply.process(new Downcase(), s);
    Apply.process(new Splitter(), s);
  }
}

class Upcase extends StringProcessor {
  public String process(Object input) { // Covariant return
    return ((String)input).toUpperCase();
  }
}

class Downcase extends StringProcessor {
  public String process(Object input) {
    return ((String)input).toLowerCase();
  }
}

class Splitter extends StringProcessor {
  public String process(Object input) {
    return Arrays.toString(((String)input).split(" "));
  }
} /* Output:
```

```
Using Processor Upcase
IF SHE WEIGHS THE SAME AS A DUCK, SHE'S MADE OF WOOD
Using Processor Downcase
if she weighs the same as a duck, she's made of wood
Using Processor Splitter
[If, she, weighs, the, same, as, a, duck,, she's, made, of,
wood]
*///:~
```

However, you are often in the situation of not being able to modify the classes
that you want to use. In the case of the electronic filters, for example, the
library was discovered rather than created. In these cases, you can use the
Adapter design pattern. In Adapter, you write code to take the interface that
you have and produce the interface that you need, like this:

```
//: interfaces/interfaceprocessor/FilterProcessor.java
package interfaces.interfaceprocessor;
import interfaces.filters.*;

class FilterAdapter implements Processor {
  Filter filter;
  public FilterAdapter(Filter filter) {
    this.filter = filter;
  }
  public String name() { return filter.name(); }
  public Waveform process(Object input) {
    return filter.process((Waveform)input);
  }
}

public class FilterProcessor {
  public static void main(String[] args) {
    Waveform w = new Waveform();
    Apply.process(new FilterAdapter(new LowPass(1.0)), w);
    Apply.process(new FilterAdapter(new HighPass(2.0)), w);
    Apply.process(
      new FilterAdapter(new BandPass(3.0, 4.0)), w);
  }
} /* Output:
Using Processor LowPass
Waveform 0
Using Processor HighPass
Waveform 0
Using Processor BandPass
```

```
Waveform 0
*///:~
```

In this approach to Adapter, the **FilterAdapter** constructor takes the interface that you have—**Filter**—and produces an object that has the **Processor** interface that you need. You may also notice delegation in the **FilterAdapter** class.

Decoupling interface from implementation allows an interface to be applied to multiple different implementations, and thus your code is more reusable.

Exercise 11:   (4) Create a class with a method that takes a **String** argument and produces a result that swaps each pair of characters in that argument. Adapt the class so that it works with **interfaceprocessor.Apply.process( )**.

"Multiple inheritance" in Java

Because an interface has no implementation at all—that is, there is no storage associated with an interface—there's nothing to prevent many interfaces from being combined. This is valuable because there are times when you need to say, "An **x** is an **a** *and* a **b** *and* a **c**." In C++, this act of combining multiple class interfaces is called *multiple inheritance,* and it carries some rather sticky baggage because each class can have an implementation. In Java, you can perform the same act, but only one of the classes can have an implementation, so the C++ problems do not occur with Java when combining multiple interfaces:

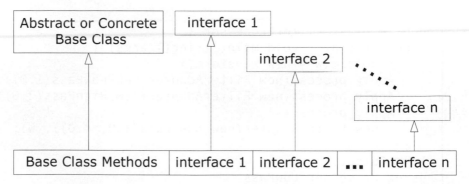

In a derived class, you aren't forced to have a base class that is either **abstract** or "concrete" (one with no **abstract** methods). If you *do* inherit from a non-interface, you can inherit from only one. All the rest of the base

elements must be interfaces. You place all the interface names after the
implements keyword and separate them with commas. You can have as
many interfaces as you want. You can upcast to each interface, because each
interface is an independent type. The following example shows a concrete
class combined with several interfaces to produce a new class:

```
//: interfaces/Adventure.java
// Multiple interfaces.

interface CanFight {
  void fight();
}

interface CanSwim {
  void swim();
}

interface CanFly {
  void fly();
}

class ActionCharacter {
  public void fight() {}
}

class Hero extends ActionCharacter
    implements CanFight, CanSwim, CanFly {
  public void swim() {}
  public void fly() {}
}

public class Adventure {
  public static void t(CanFight x) { x.fight(); }
  public static void u(CanSwim x) { x.swim(); }
  public static void v(CanFly x) { x.fly(); }
  public static void w(ActionCharacter x) { x.fight(); }
  public static void main(String[] args) {
    Hero h = new Hero();
    t(h); // Treat it as a CanFight
    u(h); // Treat it as a CanSwim
    v(h); // Treat it as a CanFly
    w(h); // Treat it as an ActionCharacter
  }
} ///:~
```

You can see that **Hero** combines the concrete class **ActionCharacter** with the interfaces **CanFight**, **CanSwim**, and **CanFly**. When you combine a concrete class with interfaces this way, the concrete class must come first, then the interfaces. (The compiler gives an error otherwise.)

The signature for **fight( )** is the same in the interface **CanFight** and the class **ActionCharacter**, and that **fight( )** is *not* provided with a definition in **Hero**. You can extend an interface, but then you've got another interface. When you want to create an object, all the definitions must first exist. Even though **Hero** does not explicitly provide a definition for **fight( )**, the definition comes along with **ActionCharacter**; thus, it's possible to create **Hero** objects.

In class **Adventure**, you can see that there are four methods that take arguments of the various interfaces and of the concrete class. When a **Hero** object is created, it can be passed to any of these methods, which means it is being upcast to each interface in turn. Because of the way interfaces are designed in Java, this works without any particular effort on the part of the programmer.

Keep in mind that one of the core reasons for interfaces is shown in the preceding example: to upcast to more than one base type (and the flexibility that this provides). However, a second reason for using interfaces is the same as using an **abstract** base class: to prevent the client programmer from making an object of this class and to establish that it is only an interface.

This brings up a question: Should you use an interface or an **abstract** class? If it's possible to create your base class without any method definitions or member variables, you should always prefer interfaces to **abstract** classes. In fact, if you know something is going to be a base class, you can consider making it an interface (this subject will be revisited in the chapter summary).

Exercise 12: (2) In **Adventure.java**, add an interface called **CanClimb**, following the form of the other interfaces.

Exercise 13: (2) Create an interface, and inherit two new interfaces from that interface. Multiply inherit a third interface from the second two.[2]

---

[2] This shows how interfaces prevent the "diamond problem" that occurs with C++ multiple inheritance.

Extending an interface
with inheritance

You can easily add new method declarations to an interface by using inheritance, and you can also combine several interfaces into a new interface with inheritance. In both cases you get a new interface, as seen in this example:

```
//: interfaces/HorrorShow.java
// Extending an interface with inheritance.

interface Monster {
  void menace();
}

interface DangerousMonster extends Monster {
  void destroy();
}

interface Lethal {
  void kill();
}

class DragonZilla implements DangerousMonster {
  public void menace() {}
  public void destroy() {}
}

interface Vampire extends DangerousMonster, Lethal {
  void drinkBlood();
}

class VeryBadVampire implements Vampire {
  public void menace() {}
  public void destroy() {}
  public void kill() {}
  public void drinkBlood() {}
}

public class HorrorShow {
  static void u(Monster b) { b.menace(); }
  static void v(DangerousMonster d) {
    d.menace();
```

```
    d.destroy();
  }
  static void w(Lethal l) { l.kill(); }
  public static void main(String[] args) {
    DangerousMonster barney = new DragonZilla();
    u(barney);
    v(barney);
    Vampire vlad = new VeryBadVampire();
    u(vlad);
    v(vlad);
    w(vlad);
  }
} ///:~
```

DangerousMonster is a simple extension to **Monster** that produces a new
interface. This is implemented in **DragonZilla**.

The syntax used in **Vampire** works *only* when inheriting interfaces.
Normally, you can use **extends** with only a single class, but **extends** can
refer to multiple base interfaces when building a new interface. As you can
see, the interface names are simply separated with commas.

Exercise 14:   (2) Create three interfaces, each with two methods. Inherit a
new interface that combines the three, adding a new method. Create a class
by implementing the new interface and also inheriting from a concrete class.
Now write four methods, each of which takes one of the four interfaces as an
argument. In **main( )**, create an object of your class and pass it to each of the
methods.

Exercise 15:   (2) Modify the previous exercise by creating an **abstract**
class and inheriting that into the derived class.

Name collisions when combining interfaces

You can encounter a small pitfall when implementing multiple interfaces. In
the preceding example, both **CanFight** and **ActionCharacter** have
identical **void fight( )** methods. An identical method is not a problem, but
what if the method differs by signature or return type? Here's an example:

```
//: interfaces/InterfaceCollision.java
package interfaces;

interface I1 { void f(); }
```

```
interface I2 { int f(int i); }
interface I3 { int f(); }
class C { public int f() { return 1; } }

class C2 implements I1, I2 {
  public void f() {}
  public int f(int i) { return 1; } // overloaded
}

class C3 extends C implements I2 {
  public int f(int i) { return 1; } // overloaded
}

class C4 extends C implements I3 {
  // Identical, no problem:
  public int f() { return 1; }
}

// Methods differ only by return type:
//! class C5 extends C implements I1 {}
//! interface I4 extends I1, I3 {} ///:~
```

The difficulty occurs because overriding, implementation, and overloading get unpleasantly mixed together. Also, overloaded methods cannot differ only by return type. When the last two lines are uncommented, the error messages say it all:

InterfaceCollision.java:23: f( ) in C cannot implement f( ) in I1; attempting to use incompatible return type
found : int
required: void
InterfaceCollision.java:24: Interfaces I3 and I1 are incompatible; both define f( ), but with different return type

Using the same method names in different interfaces that are intended to be combined generally causes confusion in the readability of the code, as well. Strive to avoid it.

Adapting to an interface

One of the most compelling reasons for interfaces is to allow multiple implementations for the same interface. In simple cases this is in the form of a method that accepts an interface, leaving it up to you to implement that interface and pass your object to the method.

Thus, a common use for interfaces is the aforementioned *Strategy* design pattern. You write a method that performs certain operations, and that method takes an interface that you also specify. You're basically saying, "You can use my method with any object you like, as long as your object conforms to my interface." This makes your method more flexible, general and reusable.

For example, the constructor for the Java SE5 **Scanner** class (which you'll learn more about in the *Strings* chapter) takes a **Readable** interface. You'll find that **Readable** is not an argument for any other method in the Java standard library—it was created solely for **Scanner**, so that **Scanner** doesn't have to constrain its argument to be a particular class. This way, **Scanner** can be made to work with more types. If you create a new class and you want it to be usable with **Scanner**, you make it **Readable**, like this:

```
//: interfaces/RandomWords.java
// Implementing an interface to conform to a method.
import java.nio.*;
import java.util.*;

public class RandomWords implements Readable {
  private static Random rand = new Random(47);
  private static final char[] capitals =
    "ABCDEFGHIJKLMNOPQRSTUVWXYZ".toCharArray();
  private static final char[] lowers =
    "abcdefghijklmnopqrstuvwxyz".toCharArray();
  private static final char[] vowels =
    "aeiou".toCharArray();
  private int count;
  public RandomWords(int count) { this.count = count; }
  public int read(CharBuffer cb) {
    if(count-- == 0)
      return -1; // Indicates end of input
    cb.append(capitals[rand.nextInt(capitals.length)]);
    for(int i = 0; i < 4; i++) {
      cb.append(vowels[rand.nextInt(vowels.length)]);
      cb.append(lowers[rand.nextInt(lowers.length)]);
    }
    cb.append(" ");
    return 10; // Number of characters appended
```

```
      }
   public static void main(String[] args) {
      Scanner s = new Scanner(new RandomWords(10));
      while(s.hasNext())
         System.out.println(s.next());
   }
} /* Output:
Yazeruyac
Fowenucor
Goeazimom
Raeuuacio
Nuoadesiw
Hageaikux
Ruqicibui
Numasetih
Kuuuuozog
Waqizeyoy
*///:~
```

The **Readable** interface only requires the implementation of a **read( )**
method. Inside **read( )**, you add to the **CharBuffer** argument (there are
several ways to do this; see the **CharBuffer** documentation), or return -1
when you have no more input.

Suppose you have a class that does not already implement **Readable**—how
do you make it work with **Scanner**? Here's an example of a class that
produces random floating point numbers:

```
//: interfaces/RandomDoubles.java
import java.util.*;

public class RandomDoubles {
   private static Random rand = new Random(47);
   public double next() { return rand.nextDouble(); }
   public static void main(String[] args) {
      RandomDoubles rd = new RandomDoubles();
      for(int i = 0; i < 7; i ++)
         System.out.print(rd.next() + " ");
   }
} /* Output:
0.7271157860730044 0.5309454508634242 0.16020656493302599
0.18847866977771732 0.5166020801268457 0.2678662084200585
0.2613610344283964
*///:~
```

Again, we can use the Adapter pattern, but in this case the adapted class can be created by inheriting and implementing the **Readable** interface. So, using the pseudo multiple inheritance provided by the **interface** keyword, we produce a new class which is both **RandomDoubles** and **Readable**:

```
//: interfaces/AdaptedRandomDoubles.java
// Creating an adapter with inheritance.
import java.nio.*;
import java.util.*;

public class AdaptedRandomDoubles extends RandomDoubles
implements Readable {
  private int count;
  public AdaptedRandomDoubles(int count) {
    this.count = count;
  }
  public int read(CharBuffer cb) {
    if(count-- == 0)
      return -1;
    String result = Double.toString(next()) + " ";
    cb.append(result);
    return result.length();
  }
  public static void main(String[] args) {
    Scanner s = new Scanner(new AdaptedRandomDoubles(7));
    while(s.hasNextDouble())
      System.out.print(s.nextDouble() + " ");
  }
} /* Output:
0.7271157860730044 0.5309454508634242 0.16020656493302599
0.18847866977771732 0.5166020801268457 0.2678662084200585
0.2613610344283964
*///:~
```

Because you can add an interface onto any existing class in this way, it means that a method that takes an interface provides a way for any class to be adapted to work with that method. This is the power of using interfaces instead of classes.

Exercise 16: (3) Create a class that produces a sequence of **char**s. Adapt this class so that it can be an input to a **Scanner** object.

Fields in interfaces

Because any fields you put into an interface are automatically **static** and **final**, the interface is a convenient tool for creating groups of constant values. Before Java SE5, this was the only way to produce the same effect as an **enum** in C or C++. So you will see pre-Java SE5 code like this:

```
//: interfaces/Months.java
// Using interfaces to create groups of constants.
package interfaces;

public interface Months {
  int
    JANUARY = 1, FEBRUARY = 2, MARCH = 3,
    APRIL = 4, MAY = 5, JUNE = 6, JULY = 7,
    AUGUST = 8, SEPTEMBER = 9, OCTOBER = 10,
    NOVEMBER = 11, DECEMBER = 12;
} ///:~
```

Notice the Java style of using all uppercase letters (with underscores to separate multiple words in a single identifier) for **static finals** that have constant initializers. The fields in an interface are automatically **public**, so that is not explicitly specified.

With Java SE5, you now have the much more powerful and flexible **enum** keyword, so it rarely makes sense to use interfaces for constants anymore. However, you will probably run across the old idiom on many occasions when reading legacy code (the supplements for this book at *www.MindView.net* contain a complete description of the pre-Java SE5 approach to producing enumerated types using interfaces). You can find more details about using **enum**s in the *Enumerated Types* chapter.

Exercise 17:   (2) Prove that the fields in an interface are implicitly **static** and **final**.

Initializing fields in interfaces

Fields defined in interfaces cannot be "blank **finals**," but they can be initialized with non-constant expressions. For example:

```
//: interfaces/RandVals.java
// Initializing interface fields with
// non-constant initializers.
```

```
import java.util.*;

public interface RandVals {
  Random RAND = new Random(47);
  int RANDOM_INT = RAND.nextInt(10);
  long RANDOM_LONG = RAND.nextLong() * 10;
  float RANDOM_FLOAT = RAND.nextLong() * 10;
  double RANDOM_DOUBLE = RAND.nextDouble() * 10;
} ///:~
```

Since the fields are **static**, they are initialized when the class is first loaded, which happens when any of the fields are accessed for the first time. Here's a simple test:

```
//: interfaces/TestRandVals.java
import static net.mindview.util.Print.*;

public class TestRandVals {
  public static void main(String[] args) {
    print(RandVals.RANDOM_INT);
    print(RandVals.RANDOM_LONG);
    print(RandVals.RANDOM_FLOAT);
    print(RandVals.RANDOM_DOUBLE);
  }
} /* Output:
8
-32032247016559954
-8.5939291E18
5.779976127815049
*///:~
```

The fields, of course, are not part of the interface. The values are stored in the static storage area for that interface.

Nesting interfaces

Interfaces may be nested within classes and within other interfaces.[3] This reveals a number of interesting features:

```
//: interfaces/nesting/NestingInterfaces.java
package interfaces.nesting;
```

---

[3] Thanks to Martin Danner for asking about this during a seminar.

```
class A {
  interface B {
    void f();
  }
  public class BImp implements B {
    public void f() {}
  }
  private class BImp2 implements B {
    public void f() {}
  }
  public interface C {
    void f();
  }
  class CImp implements C {
    public void f() {}
  }
  private class CImp2 implements C {
    public void f() {}
  }
  private interface D {
    void f();
  }
  private class DImp implements D {
    public void f() {}
  }
  public class DImp2 implements D {
    public void f() {}
  }
  public D getD() { return new DImp2(); }
  private D dRef;
  public void receiveD(D d) {
    dRef = d;
    dRef.f();
  }
}

interface E {
  interface G {
    void f();
  }
  // Redundant "public":
  public interface H {
    void f();
```

```
  }
  void g();
  // Cannot be private within an interface:
  //! private interface I {}
}

public class NestingInterfaces {
  public class BImp implements A.B {
    public void f() {}
  }
  class CImp implements A.C {
    public void f() {}
  }
  // Cannot implement a private interface except
  // within that interface's defining class:
  //! class DImp implements A.D {
  //!   public void f() {}
  //! }
  class EImp implements E {
    public void g() {}
  }
  class EGImp implements E.G {
    public void f() {}
  }
  class EImp2 implements E {
    public void g() {}
    class EG implements E.G {
      public void f() {}
    }
  }
  public static void main(String[] args) {
    A a = new A();
    // Can't access A.D:
    //! A.D ad = a.getD();
    // Doesn't return anything but A.D:
    //! A.DImp2 di2 = a.getD();
    // Cannot access a member of the interface:
    //! a.getD().f();
    // Only another A can do anything with getD():
    A a2 = new A();
    a2.receiveD(a.getD());
  }
} ///:~
```

The syntax for nesting an interface within a class is reasonably obvious. Just like non-nested interfaces, these can have **public** or package-access visibility.

As an added twist, interfaces can also be **private**, as seen in **A.D** (the same qualification syntax is used for nested interfaces as for nested classes). What good is a **private** nested interface? You might guess that it can only be implemented as a **private** inner class as in **DImp**, but **A.DImp2** shows that it can also be implemented as a **public** class. However, **A.DImp2** can only be used as itself. You are not allowed to mention the fact that it implements the **private** interface **D**, so implementing a **private** interface is a way to force the definition of the methods in that interface without adding any type information (that is, without allowing any upcasting).

The method **getD( )** produces a further quandary concerning the **private** interface: It's a **public** method that returns a reference to a **private** interface. What can you do with the return value of this method? In **main( )**, you can see several attempts to use the return value, all of which fail. The only thing that works is if the return value is handed to an object that has permission to use it—in this case, another **A**, via the **receiveD( )** method.

Interface **E** shows that interfaces can be nested within each other. However, the rules about interfaces—in particular, that all interface elements must be **public**—are strictly enforced here, so an interface nested within another interface is automatically **public** and cannot be made **private**.

NestingInterfaces shows the various ways that nested interfaces can be implemented. In particular, notice that when you implement an interface, you are not required to implement any interfaces nested within. Also, **private** interfaces cannot be implemented outside of their defining classes.

Initially, these features may seem like they are added strictly for syntactic consistency, but I generally find that once you know about a feature, you often discover places where it is useful.

Interfaces and factories

An interface is intended to be a gateway to multiple implementations, and a typical way to produce objects that fit the interface is the *Factory Method* design pattern. Instead of calling a constructor directly, you call a creation method on a factory object which produces an implementation of the interface—this way, in theory, your code is completely isolated from the implementation of the interface, thus making it possible to transparently swap one implementation for another. Here's a demonstration showing the structure of the Factory Method:

```
//: interfaces/Factories.java
import static net.mindview.util.Print.*;

interface Service {
  void method1();
  void method2();
}

interface ServiceFactory {
  Service getService();
}

class Implementation1 implements Service {
  Implementation1() {} // Package access
  public void method1() {print("Implementation1 method1");}
  public void method2() {print("Implementation1 method2");}
}

class Implementation1Factory implements ServiceFactory {
  public Service getService() {
    return new Implementation1();
  }
}

class Implementation2 implements Service {
  Implementation2() {} // Package access
  public void method1() {print("Implementation2 method1");}
  public void method2() {print("Implementation2 method2");}
}

class Implementation2Factory implements ServiceFactory {
  public Service getService() {
    return new Implementation2();
  }
}

public class Factories {
  public static void serviceConsumer(ServiceFactory fact) {
    Service s = fact.getService();
    s.method1();
```

```
      s.method2();
    }
  public static void main(String[] args) {
    serviceConsumer(new Implementation1Factory());
    // Implementations are completely interchangeable:
    serviceConsumer(new Implementation2Factory());
    }
} /* Output:
Implementation1 method1
Implementation1 method2
Implementation2 method1
Implementation2 method2
*///:~
```

Without the Factory Method, your code would somewhere have to specify the exact type of **Service** being created, so that it could call the appropriate constructor.

Why would you want to add this extra level of indirection? One common reason is to create a framework. Suppose you are creating a system to play games; for example, to play both chess and checkers on the same board:

```
//: interfaces/Games.java
// A Game framework using Factory Methods.
import static net.mindview.util.Print.*;

interface Game { boolean move(); }
interface GameFactory { Game getGame(); }

class Checkers implements Game {
  private int moves = 0;
  private static final int MOVES = 3;
  public boolean move() {
    print("Checkers move " + moves);
    return ++moves != MOVES;
  }
}

class CheckersFactory implements GameFactory {
  public Game getGame() { return new Checkers(); }
}

class Chess implements Game {
  private int moves = 0;
  private static final int MOVES = 4;
```

```
      public boolean move() {
        print("Chess move " + moves);
        return ++moves != MOVES;
      }
    }

    class ChessFactory implements GameFactory {
      public Game getGame() { return new Chess(); }
    }

    public class Games {
      public static void playGame(GameFactory factory) {
        Game s = factory.getGame();
        while(s.move())
          ;
      }
      public static void main(String[] args) {
        playGame(new CheckersFactory());
        playGame(new ChessFactory());
      }
    } /* Output:
    Checkers move 0
    Checkers move 1
    Checkers move 2
    Chess move 0
    Chess move 1
    Chess move 2
    Chess move 3
    *///:~
```

If the **Games** class represents a complex piece of code, this approach allows you to reuse that code with different types of games. You can imagine more elaborate games that can benefit from this pattern.

In the next chapter, you'll see a more elegant way to implement the factories using anonymous inner classes.

Exercise 18: (2) Create a **Cycle interface**, with implementations **Unicycle**, **Bicycle** and **Tricycle**. Create factories for each type of **Cycle**, and code that uses these factories.

Exercise 19: (3) Create a framework using Factory Methods that performs both coin tossing and dice tossing.

Summary

It is tempting to decide that interfaces are good, and therefore you should always choose interfaces over concrete classes. Of course, almost anytime you create a class, you could instead create an interface and a factory.

Many people have fallen to this temptation, creating interfaces and factories wherever it's possible. The logic seems to be that you might need to use a different implementation, so you should always add that abstraction. It has become a kind of premature design optimization.

Any abstraction should be motivated by a real need. Interfaces should be something you refactor to when necessary, rather than installing the extra level of indirection everywhere, along with the extra complexity. That extra complexity is significant, and if you make someone work through that complexity only to realize that you've added interfaces "just in case" and for no compelling reason—well, if I see such a thing I begin to question all the designs that this particular person has done.

An appropriate guideline is to *prefer classes to interfaces*. Start with classes, and if it becomes clear that interfaces are necessary, then refactor. Interfaces are a great tool, but they can easily be overused.

Solutions to selected exercises can be found in the electronic document *The Thinking in Java Annotated Solution Guide*, available for sale from *www.MindView.net*.

Inner Classes

It's possible to place a class definition within another class definition. This is called an *inner class*.

The inner class is a valuable feature because it allows you to group classes that logically belong together and to control the visibility of one within the other. However, it's important to understand that inner classes are distinctly different from composition.

At first, inner classes look like a simple code-hiding mechanism: You place classes inside other classes. You'll learn, however, that the inner class does more than that—it knows about and can communicate with the surrounding class—and the kind of code you can write with inner classes is more elegant and clear, although there's certainly no guarantee of this.

Initially, inner classes may seem odd, and it will take some time to become comfortable using them in your designs. The need for inner classes isn't always obvious, but after the basic syntax and semantics of inner classes have been described, the section "Why inner classes?" should begin to make clear the benefits of inner classes.

After that section, the remainder of the chapter contains more detailed explorations of the syntax of inner classes. These features are provided for language completeness, but you might not need to use them, at least not at first. So the initial parts of the chapter might be all you need for now, and you can leave the more detailed explorations as reference material.

Creating inner classes

You create an inner class just as you'd expect—by placing the class definition inside a surrounding class:

```
//: innerclasses/Parcel1.java
// Creating inner classes.

public class Parcel1 {
  class Contents {
    private int i = 11;
```

```
      public int value() { return i; }
    }
    class Destination {
      private String label;
      Destination(String whereTo) {
        label = whereTo;
      }
      String readLabel() { return label; }
    }
    // Using inner classes looks just like
    // using any other class, within Parcel1:
    public void ship(String dest) {
      Contents c = new Contents();
      Destination d = new Destination(dest);
      System.out.println(d.readLabel());
    }
    public static void main(String[] args) {
      Parcel1 p = new Parcel1();
      p.ship("Tasmania");
    }
} /* Output:
Tasmania
*///:~
```

The inner classes used inside **ship( )** look just like ordinary classes. Here, the only practical difference is that the names are nested within **Parcel1**. You'll see in a while that this isn't the only difference.

More typically, an outer class will have a method that returns a reference to an inner class, as you can see in the **to( )** and **contents( )** methods:

```
//: innerclasses/Parcel2.java
// Returning a reference to an inner class.

public class Parcel2 {
  class Contents {
    private int i = 11;
    public int value() { return i; }
  }
  class Destination {
    private String label;
    Destination(String whereTo) {
      label = whereTo;
    }
    String readLabel() { return label; }
```

```
    }
    public Destination to(String s) {
      return new Destination(s);
    }
    public Contents contents() {
      return new Contents();
    }
    public void ship(String dest) {
      Contents c = contents();
      Destination d = to(dest);
      System.out.println(d.readLabel());
    }
    public static void main(String[] args) {
      Parcel2 p = new Parcel2();
      p.ship("Tasmania");
      Parcel2 q = new Parcel2();
      // Defining references to inner classes:
      Parcel2.Contents c = q.contents();
      Parcel2.Destination d = q.to("Borneo");
    }
} /* Output:
Tasmania
*///:~
```

If you want to make an object of the inner class anywhere except from within a non-**static** method of the outer class, you must specify the type of that object as *OuterClassName.InnerClassName*, as seen in **main( )**.

Exercise 1: (1) Write a class named **Outer** that contains an inner class named **Inner**. Add a method to **Outer** that returns an object of type **Inner**. In **main( )**, create and initialize a reference to an **Inner**.

The link to the outer class

So far, it appears that inner classes are just a name-hiding and code organization scheme, which is helpful but not totally compelling. However, there's another twist. When you create an inner class, an object of that inner class has a *link to the enclosing object that made it*, and so it can access the members of that enclosing object—without any special qualifications. In addition, inner classes have access rights to all the elements in the enclosing class.[1] The following example demonstrates this:

```java
//: innerclasses/Sequence.java
// Holds a sequence of Objects.

interface Selector {
  boolean end();
  Object current();
  void next();
}

public class Sequence {
  private Object[] items;
  private int next = 0;
  public Sequence(int size) { items = new Object[size]; }
  public void add(Object x) {
    if(next < items.length)
      items[next++] = x;
  }
  private class SequenceSelector implements Selector {
    private int i = 0;
    public boolean end() { return i == items.length; }
    public Object current() { return items[i]; }
    public void next() { if(i < items.length) i++; }
  }
  public Selector selector() {
    return new SequenceSelector();
  }
  public static void main(String[] args) {
    Sequence sequence = new Sequence(10);
    for(int i = 0; i < 10; i++)
      sequence.add(Integer.toString(i));
    Selector selector = sequence.selector();
    while(!selector.end()) {
      System.out.print(selector.current() + " ");
      selector.next();
    }
  }
}
```

---

[1] This is very different from the design of *nested classes* in C++, which is simply a name-hiding mechanism. There is no link to an enclosing object and no implied permissions in C++.

Thinking in Java Bruce Eckel

```
} /* Output:
0 1 2 3 4 5 6 7 8 9
*///:~
```

The **Sequence** is simply a fixed-sized array of **Object** with a class wrapped around it. You call **add( )** to add a new **Object** to the end of the sequence (if there's room left). To fetch each of the objects in a **Sequence**, there's an interface called **Selector**. This is an example of the *Iterator* design pattern that you shall learn more about later in the book. A **Selector** allows you to see if you're at the **end( )**, to access the **current( ) Object**, and to move to the **next( ) Object** in the **Sequence**. Because **Selector** is an interface, other classes can implement the interface in their own ways, and other methods can take the interface as an argument, in order to create more general-purpose code.

Here, the **SequenceSelector** is a **private** class that provides **Selector** functionality. In **main( )**, you can see the creation of a **Sequence**, followed by the addition of a number of **String** objects. Then, a **Selector** is produced with a call to **selector( )**, and this is used to move through the **Sequence** and select each item.

At first, the creation of **SequenceSelector** looks like just another inner class. But examine it closely. Note that each of the methods—**end( )**, **current( )**, and **next( )**—refers to **items**, which is a reference that isn't part of **SequenceSelector**, but is instead a **private** field in the enclosing class. However, the inner class can access methods and fields from the enclosing class as if it owned them. This turns out to be very convenient, as you can see in the preceding example.

So an inner class has automatic access to the members of the enclosing class. How can this happen? The inner class secretly captures a reference to the particular object of the enclosing class that was responsible for creating it. Then, when you refer to a member of the enclosing class, that reference is used to select that member. Fortunately, the compiler takes care of all these details for you, but now you can see that an object of an inner class can be created only in association with an object of the enclosing class (when, as you shall see, the inner class is non-**static**). Construction of the inner-class object requires the reference to the object of the enclosing class, and the compiler will complain if it cannot access that reference. Most of the time this occurs without any intervention on the part of the programmer.

Exercise 2: (1) Create a class that holds a **String**, and has a **toString( )** method that displays this **String**. Add several instances of your new class to a **Sequence** object, then display them.

Exercise 3: (1) Modify Exercise 1 so that **Outer** has a **private String** field (initialized by the constructor), and **Inner** has a **toString( )** that displays this field. Create an object of type **Inner** and display it.

Using **.this** and **.new**

If you need to produce the reference to the outer-class object, you name the outer class followed by a dot and **this**. The resulting reference is automatically the correct type, which is known and checked at compile time, so there is no runtime overhead. Here's an example that shows how to use **.this**:

```
//: innerclasses/DotThis.java
// Qualifying access to the outer-class object.

public class DotThis {
  void f() { System.out.println("DotThis.f()"); }
  public class Inner {
    public DotThis outer() {
      return DotThis.this;
      // A plain "this" would be Inner's "this"
    }
  }
  public Inner inner() { return new Inner(); }
  public static void main(String[] args) {
    DotThis dt = new DotThis();
    DotThis.Inner dti = dt.inner();
    dti.outer().f();
  }
} /* Output:
DotThis.f()
*///:~
```

Sometimes you want to tell some other object to create an object of one of its inner classes. To do this you must provide a reference to the other outer-class object in the **new** expression, using the **.new** syntax, like this:

```
//: innerclasses/DotNew.java
// Creating an inner class directly using the .new syntax.
```

```
public class DotNew {
  public class Inner {}
  public static void main(String[] args) {
    DotNew dn = new DotNew();
    DotNew.Inner dni = dn.new Inner();
  }
} ///:~
```

To create an object of the inner class directly, you don't follow the same form and refer to the outer class name **DotNew** as you might expect, but instead you must use an *object* of the outer class to make an object of the inner class, as you can see above. This also resolves the name scoping issues for the inner class, so you don't say (indeed, you *can't* say) **dn.new DotNew.Inner( )**.

It's not possible to create an object of the inner class unless you already have an object of the outer class. This is because the object of the inner class is quietly connected to the object of the outer class that it was made from. However, if you make a *nested class* (a **static** inner class), then it doesn't need a reference to the outer-class object.

Here, you see the use of **.new** applied to the "Parcel" example:

```
//: innerclasses/Parcel3.java
// Using .new to create instances of inner classes.

public class Parcel3 {
  class Contents {
    private int i = 11;
    public int value() { return i; }
  }
  class Destination {
    private String label;
    Destination(String whereTo) { label = whereTo; }
    String readLabel() { return label; }
  }
  public static void main(String[] args) {
    Parcel3 p = new Parcel3();
    // Must use instance of outer class
    // to create an instance of the inner class:
    Parcel3.Contents c = p.new Contents();
    Parcel3.Destination d = p.new Destination("Tasmania");
  }
} ///:~
```

Exercise 4: (2) Add a method to the class **Sequence.SequenceSelector** that produces the reference to the outer class **Sequence**.

Exercise 5: (1) Create a class with an inner class. In a separate class, make an instance of the inner class.

Inner classes and upcasting

Inner classes really come into their own when you start upcasting to a base class, and in particular to an interface. (The effect of producing an interface reference from an object that implements it is essentially the same as upcasting to a base class.) That's because the inner class—the implementation of the interface—can then be unseen and unavailable, which is convenient for hiding the implementation. All you get back is a reference to the base class or the interface.

We can create interfaces for the previous examples:

```
//: innerclasses/Destination.java
public interface Destination {
  String readLabel();
} ///:~
```

```
//: innerclasses/Contents.java
public interface Contents {
  int value();
} ///:~
```

Now **Contents** and **Destination** represent interfaces available to the client programmer. Remember that an **interface** automatically makes all of its members **public**.

When you get a reference to the base class or the interface, it's possible that you can't even find out the exact type, as shown here:

```
//: innerclasses/TestParcel.java

class Parcel4 {
  private class PContents implements Contents {
    private int i = 11;
    public int value() { return i; }
  }
  protected class PDestination implements Destination {
```

Thinking in Java Bruce Eckel

```
    private String label;
    private PDestination(String whereTo) {
      label = whereTo;
    }
    public String readLabel() { return label; }
  }
  public Destination destination(String s) {
    return new PDestination(s);
  }
  public Contents contents() {
    return new PContents();
  }
}

public class TestParcel {
  public static void main(String[] args) {
    Parcel4 p = new Parcel4();
    Contents c = p.contents();
    Destination d = p.destination("Tasmania");
    // Illegal -- can't access private class:
    //! Parcel4.PContents pc = p.new PContents();
  }
} ///:~
```

In **Parcel4**, something new has been added: The inner class **PContents** is **private**, so nothing but **Parcel4** can access it. Normal (non-inner) classes cannot be made **private** or **protected**; they may only be given **public** or package access. **PDestination** is **protected**, so nothing but **Parcel4**, classes in the same package (since **protected** also gives package access), and the inheritors of **Parcel4** can access **PDestination**. This means that the client programmer has restricted knowledge and access to these members. In fact, you can't even downcast to a **private** inner class (or a **protected** inner class unless you're an inheritor), because you can't access the name, as you can see in **class TestParcel**. Thus, the **private** inner class provides a way for the class designer to completely prevent any type-coding dependencies and to completely hide details about implementation. In addition, extension of an interface is useless from the client programmer's perspective since the client programmer cannot access any additional methods that aren't part of the **public** interface. This also provides an opportunity for the Java compiler to generate more efficient code.

Exercise 6: (2) Create an interface with at least one method, in its own package. Create a class in a separate package. Add a **protected** inner class

---

that implements the interface. In a third package, inherit from your class and, inside a method, return an object of the **protected** inner class, upcasting to the interface during the return.

Exercise 7: (2) Create a class with a **private** field and a **private** method. Create an inner class with a method that modifies the outer-class field and calls the outer-class method. In a second outer-class method, create an object of the inner class and call its method, then show the effect on the outer-class object.

Exercise 8: (2) Determine whether an outer class has access to the **private** elements of its inner class.

Inner classes
in methods and scopes

What you've seen so far encompasses the typical use for inner classes. In general, the code that you'll write and read involving inner classes will be "plain" inner classes that are simple and easy to understand. However, the syntax for inner classes covers a number of other, more obscure techniques. Inner classes can be created within a method or even an arbitrary scope. There are two reasons for doing this:

1. As shown previously, you're implementing an interface of some kind so that you can create and return a reference.

2. You're solving a complicated problem and you want to create a class to aid in your solution, but you don't want it publicly available.

In the following examples, the previous code will be modified to use:

1. A class defined within a method

2. A class defined within a scope inside a method

3. An *anonymous* class implementing an interface

4. An anonymous class extending a class that has a non-default constructor

5. An anonymous class that performs field initialization

6. An anonymous class that performs construction using instance initialization (anonymous inner classes cannot have constructors)

The first example shows the creation of an entire class within the scope of a method (instead of the scope of another class). This is called a *local inner class*:

```
//: innerclasses/Parcel5.java
// Nesting a class within a method.

public class Parcel5 {
  public Destination destination(String s) {
    class PDestination implements Destination {
      private String label;
      private PDestination(String whereTo) {
        label = whereTo;
      }
      public String readLabel() { return label; }
    }
    return new PDestination(s);
  }
  public static void main(String[] args) {
    Parcel5 p = new Parcel5();
    Destination d = p.destination("Tasmania");
  }
} ///:~
```

The class **PDestination** is part of **destination( )** rather than being part of **Parcel5**. Therefore, **PDestination** cannot be accessed outside of **destination( )**. Notice the upcasting that occurs in the **return** statement— nothing comes out of **destination( )** except a reference to a **Destination** interface. Of course, the fact that the name of the class **PDestination** is placed inside **destination( )** doesn't mean that **PDestination** is not a valid object once **destination( )** returns.

You could use the class identifier **PDestination** for an inner class inside each class in the same subdirectory without a name clash.

The next example shows how you can nest an inner class within any arbitrary scope:

```
//: innerclasses/Parcel6.java
// Nesting a class within a scope.
```

```
public class Parcel6 {
  private void internalTracking(boolean b) {
    if(b) {
      class TrackingSlip {
        private String id;
        TrackingSlip(String s) {
          id = s;
        }
        String getSlip() { return id; }
      }
      TrackingSlip ts = new TrackingSlip("slip");
      String s = ts.getSlip();
    }
    // Can't use it here! Out of scope:
    //! TrackingSlip ts = new TrackingSlip("x");
  }
  public void track() { internalTracking(true); }
  public static void main(String[] args) {
    Parcel6 p = new Parcel6();
    p.track();
  }
} ///:~
```

The class **TrackingSlip** is nested inside the scope of an **if** statement. This does not mean that the *class* is conditionally created—it gets compiled along with everything else. However, it's not available outside the scope in which it is defined. Other than that, it looks just like an ordinary class.

Exercise 9: (1) Create an interface with at least one method, and implement that interface by defining an inner class within a method, which returns a reference to your interface.

Exercise 10: (1) Repeat the previous exercise but define the inner class within a scope within a method.

Exercise 11: (2) Create a **private** inner class that implements a **public** interface. Write a method that returns a reference to an instance of the **private** inner class, upcast to the interface. Show that the inner class is completely hidden by trying to downcast to it.

Anonymous inner classes

The next example looks a little odd:

```
//: innerclasses/Parcel7.java
```

```
// Returning an instance of an anonymous inner class.

public class Parcel7 {
  public Contents contents() {
    return new Contents() { // Insert a class definition
      private int i = 11;
      public int value() { return i; }
    }; // Semicolon required in this case
  }
  public static void main(String[] args) {
    Parcel7 p = new Parcel7();
    Contents c = p.contents();
  }
} ///:~
```

The **contents( )** method combines the creation of the return value with the definition of the class that represents that return value! In addition, the class is *anonymous*; it has no name. To make matters a bit worse, it looks like you're starting out to create a **Contents** object, But then, before you get to the semicolon, you say, "But wait, I think I'll slip in a class definition."

What this strange syntax means is "Create an object of an anonymous class that's inherited from **Contents**." The reference returned by the **new** expression is automatically upcast to a **Contents** reference. The anonymous inner-class syntax is a shorthand for:

```
//: innerclasses/Parcel7b.java
// Expanded version of Parcel7.java

public class Parcel7b {
  class MyContents implements Contents {
    private int i = 11;
    public int value() { return i; }
  }
  public Contents contents() { return new MyContents(); }
  public static void main(String[] args) {
    Parcel7b p = new Parcel7b();
    Contents c = p.contents();
  }
} ///:~
```

In the anonymous inner class, **Contents** is created by using a default constructor.

The following code shows what to do if your base class needs a constructor with an argument:

```
//: innerclasses/Parcel8.java
// Calling the base-class constructor.

public class Parcel8 {
  public Wrapping wrapping(int x) {
    // Base constructor call:
    return new Wrapping(x) { // Pass constructor argument.
      public int value() {
        return super.value() * 47;
      }
    }; // Semicolon required
  }
  public static void main(String[] args) {
    Parcel8 p = new Parcel8();
    Wrapping w = p.wrapping(10);
  }
} ///:~
```

That is, you simply pass the appropriate argument to the base-class constructor, seen here as the **x** passed in **new Wrapping(x)**. Although it's an ordinary class with an implementation, **Wrapping** is also being used as a common "interface" to its derived classes:

```
//: innerclasses/Wrapping.java
public class Wrapping {
  private int i;
  public Wrapping(int x) { i = x; }
  public int value() { return i; }
} ///:~
```

You'll notice that **Wrapping** has a constructor that requires an argument, to make things a bit more interesting.

The semicolon at the end of the anonymous inner class doesn't mark the end of the class body. Instead, it marks the end of the expression that happens to contain the anonymous class. Thus, it's identical to the use of the semicolon everywhere else.

You can also perform initialization when you define fields in an anonymous class:

```
//: innerclasses/Parcel9.java
```

```
// An anonymous inner class that performs
// initialization. A briefer version of Parcel5.java.

public class Parcel9 {
  // Argument must be final to use inside
  // anonymous inner class:
  public Destination destination(final String dest) {
    return new Destination() {
      private String label = dest;
      public String readLabel() { return label; }
    };
  }
  public static void main(String[] args) {
    Parcel9 p = new Parcel9();
    Destination d = p.destination("Tasmania");
  }
} ///:~
```

If you're defining an anonymous inner class and want to use an object that's defined outside the anonymous inner class, the compiler requires that the argument reference be **final**, as you see in the argument to **destination( )**. If you forget, you'll get a compile-time error message.

As long as you're simply assigning a field, the approach in this example is fine. But what if you need to perform some constructor-like activity? You can't have a named constructor in an anonymous class (since there's no name!), but with *instance initialization*, you can, in effect, create a constructor for an anonymous inner class, like this:

```
//: innerclasses/AnonymousConstructor.java
// Creating a constructor for an anonymous inner class.
import static net.mindview.util.Print.*;

abstract class Base {
  public Base(int i) {
    print("Base constructor, i = " + i);
  }
  public abstract void f();
}

public class AnonymousConstructor {
  public static Base getBase(int i) {
    return new Base(i) {
      { print("Inside instance initializer"); }
```

```
      public void f() {
        print("In anonymous f()");
      }
    };
  }
  public static void main(String[] args) {
    Base base = getBase(47);
    base.f();
  }
} /* Output:
Base constructor, i = 47
Inside instance initializer
In anonymous f()
*///:~
```

In this case, the variable **i** did *not* have to be final. While **i** is passed to the base constructor of the anonymous class, it is never directly used *inside* the anonymous class.

Here's the "parcel" theme with instance initialization. Note that the arguments to **destination( )** must be final since they are used within the anonymous class:

```
//: innerclasses/Parcel10.java
// Using "instance initialization" to perform
// construction on an anonymous inner class.

public class Parcel10 {
  public Destination
  destination(final String dest, final float price) {
    return new Destination() {
      private int cost;
      // Instance initialization for each object:
      {
        cost = Math.round(price);
        if(cost > 100)
          System.out.println("Over budget!");
      }
      private String label = dest;
      public String readLabel() { return label; }
    };
  }
  public static void main(String[] args) {
    Parcel10 p = new Parcel10();
    Destination d = p.destination("Tasmania", 101.395F);
```

```
  }
} /* Output:
Over budget!
*///:~
```

Inside the instance initializer you can see code that couldn't be executed as part of a field initializer (that is, the **if** statement). So in effect, an instance initializer is the constructor for an anonymous inner class. Of course, it's limited; you can't overload instance initializers, so you can have only one of these constructors.

Anonymous inner classes are somewhat limited compared to regular inheritance, because they can either extend a class or implement an interface, but not both. And if you do implement an interface, you can only implement one.

Exercise 12: (1) Repeat Exercise 7 using an anonymous inner class.

Exercise 13: (1) Repeat Exercise 9 using an anonymous inner class.

Exercise 14: (1) Modify **interfaces/HorrorShow.java** to implement **DangerousMonster** and **Vampire** using anonymous classes.

Exercise 15: (2) Create a class with a non-default constructor (one with arguments) and no default constructor (no "no-arg" constructor). Create a second class that has a method that returns a reference to an object of the first class. Create the object that you return by making an anonymous inner class that inherits from the first class.

Factory Method revisited

Look at how much nicer the **interfaces/Factories.java** example comes out when you use anonymous inner classes:

```
//: innerclasses/Factories.java
import static net.mindview.util.Print.*;

interface Service {
  void method1();
  void method2();
}

interface ServiceFactory {
  Service getService();
}
```

```java
class Implementation1 implements Service {
  private Implementation1() {}
  public void method1() {print("Implementation1 method1");}
  public void method2() {print("Implementation1 method2");}
  public static ServiceFactory factory =
    new ServiceFactory() {
      public Service getService() {
        return new Implementation1();
      }
    };
}

class Implementation2 implements Service {
  private Implementation2() {}
  public void method1() {print("Implementation2 method1");}
  public void method2() {print("Implementation2 method2");}
  public static ServiceFactory factory =
    new ServiceFactory() {
      public Service getService() {
        return new Implementation2();
      }
    };
}

public class Factories {
  public static void serviceConsumer(ServiceFactory fact) {
    Service s = fact.getService();
    s.method1();
    s.method2();
  }
  public static void main(String[] args) {
    serviceConsumer(Implementation1.factory);
    // Implementations are completely interchangeable:
    serviceConsumer(Implementation2.factory);
  }
} /* Output:
Implementation1 method1
Implementation1 method2
Implementation2 method1
Implementation2 method2
*///:~
```

Now the constructors for **Implementation1** and **Implementation2** can be **private**, and there's no need to create a named class as the factory. In addition, you often only need a single factory object, and so here it has been created as a **static** field in the **Service** implementation. The resulting syntax is more meaningful, as well.

The **interfaces/Games.java** example can also be improved with anonymous inner classes:

```
//: innerclasses/Games.java
// Using anonymous inner classes with the Game framework.
import static net.mindview.util.Print.*;

interface Game { boolean move(); }
interface GameFactory { Game getGame(); }

class Checkers implements Game {
  private Checkers() {}
  private int moves = 0;
  private static final int MOVES = 3;
  public boolean move() {
    print("Checkers move " + moves);
    return ++moves != MOVES;
  }
  public static GameFactory factory = new GameFactory() {
    public Game getGame() { return new Checkers(); }
  };
}

class Chess implements Game {
  private Chess() {}
  private int moves = 0;
  private static final int MOVES = 4;
  public boolean move() {
    print("Chess move " + moves);
    return ++moves != MOVES;
  }
  public static GameFactory factory = new GameFactory() {
    public Game getGame() { return new Chess(); }
  };
}

public class Games {
  public static void playGame(GameFactory factory) {
    Game s = factory.getGame();
    while(s.move())
```

```
      ;
    }
  public static void main(String[] args) {
    playGame(Checkers.factory);
    playGame(Chess.factory);
  }
} /* Output:
Checkers move 0
Checkers move 1
Checkers move 2
Chess move 0
Chess move 1
Chess move 2
Chess move 3
*///:~
```

Remember the advice given at the end of the last chapter: *Prefer classes to interfaces*. If your design demands an interface, you'll know it. Otherwise, don't put it in until you are forced to.

Exercise 16: (1) Modify the solution to Exercise 18 from the *Interfaces* chapter to use anonymous inner classes.

Exercise 17: (1) Modify the solution to Exercise 19 from the *Interfaces* chapter to use anonymous inner classes.

Nested classes

If you don't need a connection between the inner-class object and the outer-class object, then you can make the inner class **static**. This is commonly called a *nested class*.[2] To understand the meaning of **static** when applied to inner classes, you must remember that the object of an ordinary inner class implicitly keeps a reference to the object of the enclosing class that created it. This is not true, however, when you say an inner class is **static**. A nested class means:

  1.   You don't need an outer-class object in order to create an object of a nested class.

---

[2] Roughly similar to nested classes in C++, except that those classes cannot access private members as they can in Java.

2.   You can't access a non-**static** outer-class object from an object of a
      nested class.

Nested classes are different from ordinary inner classes in another way, as
well. Fields and methods in ordinary inner classes can only be at the outer
level of a class, so ordinary inner classes cannot have **static** data, **static**
fields, or nested classes. However, nested classes can have all of these:

```
//: innerclasses/Parcel11.java
// Nested classes (static inner classes).

public class Parcel11 {
  private static class ParcelContents implements Contents {
    private int i = 11;
    public int value() { return i; }
  }
  protected static class ParcelDestination
  implements Destination {
    private String label;
    private ParcelDestination(String whereTo) {
      label = whereTo;
    }
    public String readLabel() { return label; }
    // Nested classes can contain other static elements:
    public static void f() {}
    static int x = 10;
    static class AnotherLevel {
      public static void f() {}
      static int x = 10;
    }
  }
  public static Destination destination(String s) {
    return new ParcelDestination(s);
  }
  public static Contents contents() {
    return new ParcelContents();
  }
  public static void main(String[] args) {
    Contents c = contents();
    Destination d = destination("Tasmania");
  }
} ///:~
```

In **main( )**, no object of **Parcel11** is necessary; instead, you use the normal syntax for selecting a **static** member to call the methods that return references to **Contents** and **Destination**.

As you've seen earlier in this chapter, in an ordinary (non-**static**) inner class, the link to the outer-class object is achieved with a special **this** reference. A nested class does not have a special **this** reference, which makes it analogous to a **static** method.

Exercise 18: (1) Create a class containing a nested class. In **main( )**, create an instance of the nested class.

Exercise 19: (2) Create a class containing an inner class that itself contains an inner class. Repeat this using nested classes. Note the names of the **.class** files produced by the compiler.

Classes inside interfaces

Normally, you can't put any code inside an interface, but a nested class *can* be part of an interface. Any class you put inside an interface is automatically **public** and **static**. Since the class is **static**, it doesn't violate the rules for interfaces—the nested class is only placed inside the namespace of the interface. You can even implement the surrounding interface in the inner class, like this:

```
//: innerclasses/ClassInInterface.java
// {main: ClassInInterface$Test}

public interface ClassInInterface {
  void howdy();
  class Test implements ClassInInterface {
    public void howdy() {
      System.out.println("Howdy!");
    }
    public static void main(String[] args) {
      new Test().howdy();
    }
  }
} /* Output:
Howdy!
*///:~
```

Thinking in Java

It's convenient to nest a class inside an interface when you want to create some common code to be used with all different implementations of that interface.

Earlier in this book I suggested putting a **main( )** in every class to act as a test bed for that class. One drawback to this is the amount of extra compiled code you must carry around. If this is a problem, you can use a nested class to hold your test code:

```
//: innerclasses/TestBed.java
// Putting test code in a nested class.
// {main: TestBed$Tester}

public class TestBed {
  public void f() { System.out.println("f()"); }
  public static class Tester {
    public static void main(String[] args) {
      TestBed t = new TestBed();
      t.f();
    }
  }
} /* Output:
f()
*///:~
```

This generates a separate class called **TestBed$Tester** (to run the program, you say **java TestBed$Tester**, but you must escape the '**$**' under Unix/Linux systems). You can use this class for testing, but you don't need to include it in your shipping product; you can simply delete **TestBed$Tester.class** before packaging things up.

Exercise 20: (1) Create an interface containing a nested class. Implement this interface and create an instance of the nested class.

Exercise 21: (2) Create an interface that contains a nested class that has a **static** method that calls the methods of your interface and displays the results. Implement your interface and pass an instance of your implementation to the method.

Reaching outward from a multiply nested class

It doesn't matter how deeply an inner class may be nested—it can transparently access all of the members of all the classes it is nested within, as seen here:[3]

```
//: innerclasses/MultiNestingAccess.java
// Nested classes can access all members of all
// levels of the classes they are nested within.

class MNA {
  private void f() {}
  class A {
    private void g() {}
    public class B {
      void h() {
        g();
        f();
      }
    }
  }
}

public class MultiNestingAccess {
  public static void main(String[] args) {
    MNA mna = new MNA();
    MNA.A mnaa = mna.new A();
    MNA.A.B mnaab = mnaa.new B();
    mnaab.h();
  }
} ///:~
```

You can see that in **MNA.A.B**, the methods **g( )** and **f( )** are callable without any qualification (despite the fact that they are **private**). This example also demonstrates the syntax necessary to create objects of multiply nested inner classes when you create the objects in a different class. The ".**new**" syntax produces the correct scope, so you do not have to qualify the class name in the constructor call.

---

[3] Thanks again to Martin Danner.

Why inner classes?

At this point you've seen a lot of syntax and semantics describing the way inner classes work, but this doesn't answer the question of why they exist. Why did the Java designers go to so much trouble to add this fundamental language feature?

Typically, the inner class inherits from a class or implements an interface, and the code in the inner class manipulates the outer-class object that it was created within. So you could say that an inner class provides a kind of window into the outer class.

A question that cuts to the heart of inner classes is this: If I just need a reference to an interface, why don't I just make the outer class implement that interface? The answer is "If that's all you need, then that's how you should do it." So what is it that distinguishes an inner class implementing an interface from an outer class implementing the same interface? The answer is that you can't always have the convenience of interfaces—sometimes you're working with implementations. So the most compelling reason for inner classes is:

> *Each inner class can independently inherit from an implementation. Thus, the inner class is not limited by whether the outer class is already inheriting from an implementation.*

Without the ability that inner classes provide to inherit—in effect—from more than one concrete or **abstract** class, some design and programming problems would be intractable. So one way to look at the inner class is as the rest of the solution of the multiple-inheritance problem. Interfaces solve part of the problem, but inner classes effectively allow "multiple implementation inheritance." That is, inner classes effectively allow you to inherit from more than one non-interface.

To see this in more detail, consider a situation in which you have two interfaces that must somehow be implemented within a class. Because of the flexibility of interfaces, you have two choices: a single class or an inner class.

```
//: innerclasses/MultiInterfaces.java
// Two ways that a class can implement multiple interfaces.
package innerclasses;

interface A {}
```

```
interface B {}

class X implements A, B {}

class Y implements A {
  B makeB() {
    // Anonymous inner class:
    return new B() {};
  }
}

public class MultiInterfaces {
  static void takesA(A a) {}
  static void takesB(B b) {}
  public static void main(String[] args) {
    X x = new X();
    Y y = new Y();
    takesA(x);
    takesA(y);
    takesB(x);
    takesB(y.makeB());
  }
} ///:~
```

Of course, this assumes that the structure of your code makes logical sense either way. However, you'll ordinarily have some kind of guidance from the nature of the problem about whether to use a single class or an inner class. But without any other constraints, the approach in the preceding example doesn't really make much difference from an implementation standpoint. Both of them work.

However, if you have **abstract** or concrete classes instead of interfaces, you are suddenly limited to using inner classes if your class must somehow implement both of the others:

```
//: innerclasses/MultiImplementation.java
// With concrete or abstract classes, inner
// classes are the only way to produce the effect
// of "multiple implementation inheritance."
package innerclasses;

class D {}
abstract class E {}
```

```
class Z extends D {
  E makeE() { return new E() {}; }
}

public class MultiImplementation {
  static void takesD(D d) {}
  static void takesE(E e) {}
  public static void main(String[] args) {
    Z z = new Z();
    takesD(z);
    takesE(z.makeE());
  }
} ///:~
```

If you didn't need to solve the "multiple implementation inheritance" problem, you could conceivably code around everything else without the need for inner classes. But with inner classes you have these additional features:

1.   The inner class can have multiple instances, each with its own state information that is independent of the information in the outer-class object.

2.   In a single outer class you can have several inner classes, each of which implements the same interface or inherits from the same class in a different way. An example of this will be shown shortly.

3.   The point of creation of the inner-class object is not tied to the creation of the outer-class object.

4.   There is no potentially confusing "is-a" relationship with the inner class; it's a separate entity.

As an example, if **Sequence.java** did not use inner classes, you'd have to say, "A **Sequence** is a **Selector**," and you'd only be able to have one **Selector** in existence for a particular **Sequence**. You can easily have a second method, **reverseSelector( )**, that produces a **Selector** that moves backward through the sequence. This kind of flexibility is only available with inner classes.

Exercise 22: (2) Implement **reverseSelector( )** in **Sequence.java**.

Exercise 23: (4) Create an interface **U** with three methods. Create a class **A** with a method that produces a reference to a **U** by building an anonymous inner class. Create a second class **B** that contains an array of **U**. **B** should have one method that accepts and stores a reference to a **U** in the array, a second method that sets a reference in the array (specified by the method argument) to **null**, and a third method that moves through the array and calls the methods in **U**. In **main( )**, create a group of **A** objects and a single **B**. Fill the **B** with **U** references produced by the **A** objects. Use the **B** to call back into all the **A** objects. Remove some of the **U** references from the **B**.

Closures & callbacks

A *closure* is a callable object that retains information from the scope in which it was created. From this definition, you can see that an inner class is an object-oriented closure, because it doesn't just contain each piece of information from the outer-class object ("the scope in which it was created"), but it automatically holds a reference back to the whole outer-class object, where it has permission to manipulate all the members, even **private** ones.

One of the most compelling arguments made to include some kind of pointer mechanism in Java was to allow *callbacks*. With a callback, some other object is given a piece of information that allows it to call back into the originating object at some later point. This is a very powerful concept, as you will see later in the book. If a callback is implemented using a pointer, however, you must rely on the programmer to behave properly and not misuse the pointer. As you've seen by now, Java tends to be more careful than that, so pointers were not included in the language.

The closure provided by the inner class is a good solution—more flexible and far safer than a pointer. Here's an example:

```
//: innerclasses/Callbacks.java
// Using inner classes for callbacks
package innerclasses;
import static net.mindview.util.Print.*;

interface Incrementable {
  void increment();
}

// Very simple to just implement the interface:
class Callee1 implements Incrementable {
  private int i = 0;
  public void increment() {
    i++;
    print(i);
```

```
    }
}

class MyIncrement {
  public void increment() { print("Other operation"); }
  static void f(MyIncrement mi) { mi.increment(); }
}

// If your class must implement increment() in
// some other way, you must use an inner class:
class Callee2 extends MyIncrement {
  private int i = 0;
  public void increment() {
    super.increment();
    i++;
    print(i);
  }
  private class Closure implements Incrementable {
    public void increment() {
      // Specify outer-class method, otherwise
      // you'd get an infinite recursion:
      Callee2.this.increment();
    }
  }
  Incrementable getCallbackReference() {
    return new Closure();
  }
}

class Caller {
  private Incrementable callbackReference;
  Caller(Incrementable cbh) { callbackReference = cbh; }
  void go() { callbackReference.increment(); }
}

public class Callbacks {
  public static void main(String[] args) {
    Callee1 c1 = new Callee1();
    Callee2 c2 = new Callee2();
    MyIncrement.f(c2);
    Caller caller1 = new Caller(c1);
    Caller caller2 = new Caller(c2.getCallbackReference());
    caller1.go();
    caller1.go();
```

```
      caller2.go();
      caller2.go();
    }
  } /* Output:
Other operation
1
1
2
Other operation
2
Other operation
3
*///:~
```

This also shows a further distinction between implementing an interface in an outer class versus doing so in an inner class. **Callee1** is clearly the simpler solution in terms of the code. **Callee2** inherits from **MyIncrement**, which already has a different **increment( )** method that does something unrelated to the one expected by the **Incrementable** interface. When **MyIncrement** is inherited into **Callee2**, **increment( )** can't be overridden for use by **Incrementable**, so you're forced to provide a separate implementation using an inner class. Also note that when you create an inner class, you do not add to or modify the interface of the outer class.

Everything except **getCallbackReference( )** in **Callee2** is **private**. To allow *any* connection to the outside world, the interface **Incrementable** is essential. Here you can see how **interface**s allow for a complete separation of interface from implementation.

The inner class **Closure** implements **Incrementable** to provide a hook back into **Callee2**—but a safe hook. Whoever gets the **Incrementable** reference can, of course, only call **increment( )** and has no other abilities (unlike a pointer, which would allow you to run wild).

Caller takes an **Incrementable** reference in its constructor (although the capturing of the callback reference could happen at any time) and then, sometime later, uses the reference to "call back" into the **Callee** class.

The value of the callback is in its flexibility; you can dynamically decide what methods will be called at run time. The benefit of this will become more evident in the *Graphical User Interfaces* chapter, where callbacks are used everywhere to implement GUI functionality.

Inner classes & control frameworks

A more concrete example of the use of inner classes can be found in something that I will refer to here as a *control framework*.

An *application framework* is a class or a set of classes that's designed to solve a particular type of problem. To apply an application framework, you typically inherit from one or more classes and override some of the methods. The code that you write in the overridden methods customizes the general solution provided by that application framework in order to solve your specific problem. This is an example of the *Template Method* design pattern (see *Thinking in Patterns (with Java)* at *www.MindView.net*). The Template Method contains the basic structure of the algorithm, and it calls one or more overrideable methods to complete the action of that algorithm. A design pattern separates things that change from things that stay the same, and in this case the Template Method is the part that stays the same, and the overrideable methods are the things that change.

A control framework is a particular type of application framework dominated by the need to respond to events. A system that primarily responds to events is called an *event-driven system*. A common problem in application programming is the graphical user interface (GUI), which is almost entirely event-driven. As you will see in the *Graphical User Interfaces* chapter, the Java Swing library is a control framework that elegantly solves the GUI problem and that heavily uses inner classes.

To see how inner classes allow the simple creation and use of control frameworks, consider a control framework whose job is to execute events whenever those events are "ready." Although "ready" could mean anything, in this case it will be based on clock time. What follows is a control framework that contains no specific information about what it's controlling. That information is supplied during inheritance, when the **action( )** portion of the algorithm is implemented.

First, here is the interface that describes any control event. It's an **abstract** class instead of an actual interface because the default behavior is to perform the control based on time. Thus, some of the implementation is included here:

```
//: innerclasses/controller/Event.java
// The common methods for any control event.
package innerclasses.controller;
```

```java
public abstract class Event {
  private long eventTime;
  protected final long delayTime;
  public Event(long delayTime) {
    this.delayTime = delayTime;
    start();
  }
  public void start() { // Allows restarting
    eventTime = System.nanoTime() + delayTime;
  }
  public boolean ready() {
    return System.nanoTime() >= eventTime;
  }
  public abstract void action();
} ///:~
```

The constructor captures the time (measured from the time of creation of the object) when you want the **Event** to run, and then calls **start( )**, which takes the current time and adds the delay time to produce the time when the event will occur. Rather than being included in the constructor, **start( )** is a separate method. This way, you can restart the timer after the event has run out, so the **Event** object can be reused. For example, if you want a repeating event, you can simply call **start( )** inside your **action( )** method.

ready( ) tells you when it's time to run the **action( )** method. Of course, **ready( )** can be overridden in a derived class to base the **Event** on something other than time.

The following file contains the actual control framework that manages and fires events. The **Event** objects are held inside a container object of type **List<Event>** (pronounced "List of Event"), which you'll learn more about in the *Holding Your Objects* chapter. For now, all you need to know is that **add( )** will append an **Event** to the end of the **List**, **size( )** produces the number of entries in the **List**, the foreach syntax fetches successive **Event**s from the **List**, and **remove( )** removes the specified **Event** from the **List**.

```java
//: innerclasses/controller/Controller.java
// The reusable framework for control systems.
package innerclasses.controller;
import java.util.*;

public class Controller {
```

```
   // A class from java.util to hold Event objects:
   private List<Event> eventList = new ArrayList<Event>();
   public void addEvent(Event c) { eventList.add(c); }
   public void run() {
     while(eventList.size() > 0)
       // Make a copy so you're not modifying the list
       // while you're selecting the elements in it:
       for(Event e : new ArrayList<Event>(eventList))
         if(e.ready()) {
           System.out.println(e);
           e.action();
           eventList.remove(e);
         }
   }
 } ///:~
```

The **run( )** method loops through a copy of the **eventList**, hunting for an **Event** object that's **ready( )** to run. For each one it finds **ready( )**, it prints information using the object's **toString( )** method, calls the **action( )** method, and then removes the **Event** from the list.

Note that so far in this design you know nothing about exactly *what* an **Event** does. And this is the crux of the design—how it "separates the things that change from the things that stay the same." Or, to use my term, the "vector of change" is the different actions of the various kinds of **Event** objects, and you express different actions by creating different **Event** subclasses.

This is where inner classes come into play. They allow two things:

1.   The entire implementation of a control framework is created in a single class, thereby encapsulating everything that's unique about that implementation. Inner classes are used to express the many different kinds of **action( )** necessary to solve the problem.

2.   Inner classes keep this implementation from becoming awkward, since you're able to easily access any of the members in the outer class. Without this ability the code might become unpleasant enough that you'd end up seeking an alternative.

Consider a particular implementation of the control framework designed to control greenhouse functions.[4] Each action is entirely different: turning lights, water, and thermostats on and off, ringing bells, and restarting the system. But the control framework is designed to easily isolate this different code. Inner classes allow you to have multiple derived versions of the same base class, **Event**, within a single class. For each type of action, you inherit a new **Event** inner class, and write the control code in the **action( )** implementation.

As is typical with an application framework, the class **GreenhouseControls** is inherited from **Controller**:

```
//: innerclasses/GreenhouseControls.java
// This produces a specific application of the
// control system, all in a single class. Inner
// classes allow you to encapsulate different
// functionality for each type of event.
import innerclasses.controller.*;

public class GreenhouseControls extends Controller {
  private boolean light = false;
  public class LightOn extends Event {
    public LightOn(long delayTime) { super(delayTime); }
    public void action() {
      // Put hardware control code here to
      // physically turn on the light.
      light = true;
    }
    public String toString() { return "Light is on"; }
  }
  public class LightOff extends Event {
    public LightOff(long delayTime) { super(delayTime); }
    public void action() {
      // Put hardware control code here to
      // physically turn off the light.
      light = false;
    }
    public String toString() { return "Light is off"; }
  }
```

---

[4] For some reason this has always been a pleasing problem for me to solve; it came from my earlier book *C++ Inside & Out*, but Java allows a more elegant solution.

```java
    private boolean water = false;
    public class WaterOn extends Event {
      public WaterOn(long delayTime) { super(delayTime); }
      public void action() {
        // Put hardware control code here.
        water = true;
      }
      public String toString() {
        return "Greenhouse water is on";
      }
    }
    public class WaterOff extends Event {
      public WaterOff(long delayTime) { super(delayTime); }
      public void action() {
        // Put hardware control code here.
        water = false;
      }
      public String toString() {
        return "Greenhouse water is off";
      }
    }
    private String thermostat = "Day";
    public class ThermostatNight extends Event {
      public ThermostatNight(long delayTime) {
        super(delayTime);
      }
      public void action() {
        // Put hardware control code here.
        thermostat = "Night";
      }
      public String toString() {
        return "Thermostat on night setting";
      }
    }
    public class ThermostatDay extends Event {
      public ThermostatDay(long delayTime) {
        super(delayTime);
      }
      public void action() {
        // Put hardware control code here.
        thermostat = "Day";
      }
      public String toString() {
        return "Thermostat on day setting";
```

```
      }
    }
    // An example of an action() that inserts a
    // new one of itself into the event list:
    public class Bell extends Event {
      public Bell(long delayTime) { super(delayTime); }
      public void action() {
        addEvent(new Bell(delayTime));
      }
      public String toString() { return "Bing!"; }
    }
    public class Restart extends Event {
      private Event[] eventList;
      public Restart(long delayTime, Event[] eventList) {
        super(delayTime);
        this.eventList = eventList;
        for(Event e : eventList)
          addEvent(e);
      }
      public void action() {
        for(Event e : eventList) {
          e.start(); // Rerun each event
          addEvent(e);
        }
        start(); // Rerun this Event
        addEvent(this);
      }
      public String toString() {
        return "Restarting system";
      }
    }
  public static class Terminate extends Event {
    public Terminate(long delayTime) { super(delayTime); }
    public void action() { System.exit(0); }
    public String toString() { return "Terminating";  }
  }
} ///:~
```

Note that **light**, **water**, and **thermostat** belong to the outer class
GreenhouseControls, and yet the inner classes can access those fields
without qualification or special permission. Also, the **action( )** methods
usually involve some sort of hardware control.

Most of the **Event** classes look similar, but **Bell** and **Restart** are special. **Bell** rings and then adds a new **Bell** object to the event list, so it will ring again later. Notice how inner classes *almost* look like multiple inheritance: **Bell** and **Restart** have all the methods of **Event** and also appear to have all the methods of the outer class **GreenhouseControls**.

Restart is given an array of **Event** objects that it adds to the controller. Since **Restart( )** is just another **Event** object, you can also add a **Restart** object within **Restart.action( )** so that the system regularly restarts itself.

The following class configures the system by creating a **GreenhouseControls** object and adding various kinds of **Event** objects. This is an example of the *Command* design pattern—each object in **eventList** is a request encapsulated as an object:

```
//: innerclasses/GreenhouseController.java
// Configure and execute the greenhouse system.
// {Args: 5000}
import innerclasses.controller.*;

public class GreenhouseController {
  public static void main(String[] args) {
    GreenhouseControls gc = new GreenhouseControls();
    // Instead of hard-wiring, you could parse
    // configuration information from a text file here:
    gc.addEvent(gc.new Bell(900));
    Event[] eventList = {
      gc.new ThermostatNight(0),
      gc.new LightOn(200),
      gc.new LightOff(400),
      gc.new WaterOn(600),
      gc.new WaterOff(800),
      gc.new ThermostatDay(1400)
    };
    gc.addEvent(gc.new Restart(2000, eventList));
    if(args.length == 1)
      gc.addEvent(
        new GreenhouseControls.Terminate(
          new Integer(args[0])));
    gc.run();
  }
} /* Output:
Bing!
Thermostat on night setting
```

```
Light is on
Light is off
Greenhouse water is on
Greenhouse water is off
Thermostat on day setting
Restarting system
Terminating
*///:~
```

This class initializes the system, so it adds all the appropriate events. The **Restart** event is repeatedly run, and it loads the **eventList** into the **GreenhouseControls** object each time. If you provide a command-line argument indicating milliseconds, it will terminate the program after that many milliseconds (this is used for testing).

Of course, it's more flexible to read the events from a file instead of hard-coding them. An exercise in the *I/O* chapter asks you to modify this example to do just that.

This example should move you toward an appreciation of the value of inner classes, especially when used within a control framework. However, in the *Graphical User Interfaces* chapter you'll see how elegantly inner classes are used to describe the actions of a graphical user interface. By the time you finish that chapter, you should be fully convinced.

Exercise 24: (2) In **GreenhouseControls.java**, add **Event** inner classes that turn fans on and off. Configure **GreenhouseController.java** to use these new **Event** objects.

Exercise 25: (3) Inherit from **GreenhouseControls** in **GreenhouseControls.java** to add **Event** inner classes that turn water mist generators on and off. Write a new version of **GreenhouseController.java** to use these new **Event** objects.

Inheriting from inner classes

Because the inner-class constructor must attach to a reference of the enclosing class object, things are slightly complicated when you inherit from an inner class. The problem is that the "secret" reference to the enclosing class object *must* be initialized, and yet in the derived class there's no longer a default object to attach to. You must use a special syntax to make the association explicit:

```
//: innerclasses/InheritInner.java
// Inheriting an inner class.

class WithInner {
  class Inner {}
}

public class InheritInner extends WithInner.Inner {
  //! InheritInner() {} // Won't compile
  InheritInner(WithInner wi) {
    wi.super();
  }
  public static void main(String[] args) {
    WithInner wi = new WithInner();
    InheritInner ii = new InheritInner(wi);
  }
} ///:~
```

You can see that **InheritInner** is extending only the inner class, not the outer one. But when it comes time to create a constructor, the default one is no good, and you can't just pass a reference to an enclosing object. In addition, you must use the syntax

```
enclosingClassReference.super();
```

inside the constructor. This provides the necessary reference, and the program will then compile.

Exercise 26: (2) Create a class with an inner class that has a non-default constructor (one that takes arguments). Create a second class with an inner class that inherits from the first inner class.

Can inner classes be overridden?

What happens when you create an inner class, then inherit from the enclosing class and redefine the inner class? That is, is it possible to "override" the entire inner class? This seems like it would be a powerful concept, but "overriding" an inner class as if it were another method of the outer class doesn't really do anything:

```
//: innerclasses/BigEgg.java
// An inner class cannot be overriden like a method.
import static net.mindview.util.Print.*;
```

```
class Egg {
  private Yolk y;
  protected class Yolk {
    public Yolk() { print("Egg.Yolk()"); }
  }
  public Egg() {
    print("New Egg()");
    y = new Yolk();
  }
}

public class BigEgg extends Egg {
  public class Yolk {
    public Yolk() { print("BigEgg.Yolk()"); }
  }
  public static void main(String[] args) {
    new BigEgg();
  }
} /* Output:
New Egg()
Egg.Yolk()
*///:~
```

The default constructor is synthesized automatically by the compiler, and this calls the base-class default constructor. You might think that since a **BigEgg** is being created, the "overridden" version of **Yolk** would be used, but this is not the case, as you can see from the output.

This example shows that there isn't any extra inner-class magic going on when you inherit from the outer class. The two inner classes are completely separate entities, each in its own namespace. However, it's still possible to explicitly inherit from the inner class:

```
//: innerclasses/BigEgg2.java
// Proper inheritance of an inner class.
import static net.mindview.util.Print.*;

class Egg2 {
  protected class Yolk {
    public Yolk() { print("Egg2.Yolk()"); }
    public void f() { print("Egg2.Yolk.f()");}
  }
  private Yolk y = new Yolk();
  public Egg2() { print("New Egg2()"); }
```

```
    public void insertYolk(Yolk yy) { y = yy; }
    public void g() { y.f(); }
}

public class BigEgg2 extends Egg2 {
    public class Yolk extends Egg2.Yolk {
        public Yolk() { print("BigEgg2.Yolk()"); }
        public void f() { print("BigEgg2.Yolk.f()"); }
    }
    public BigEgg2() { insertYolk(new Yolk()); }
    public static void main(String[] args) {
        Egg2 e2 = new BigEgg2();
        e2.g();
    }
} /* Output:
Egg2.Yolk()
New Egg2()
Egg2.Yolk()
BigEgg2.Yolk()
BigEgg2.Yolk.f()
*///:~
```

Now **BigEgg2.Yolk** explicitly **extends Egg2.Yolk** and overrides its methods. The method **insertYolk( )** allows **BigEgg2** to upcast one of its own **Yolk** objects into the **y** reference in **Egg2**, so when **g( )** calls **y.f( )**, the overridden version of **f( )** is used. The second call to **Egg2.Yolk( )** is the base-class constructor call of the **BigEgg2.Yolk** constructor. You can see that the overridden version of **f( )** is used when **g( )** is called.

Local inner classes

As noted earlier, inner classes can also be created inside code blocks, typically inside the body of a method. A local inner class cannot have an access specifier because it isn't part of the outer class, but it does have access to the final variables in the current code block and all the members of the enclosing class. Here's an example comparing the creation of a local inner class with an anonymous inner class:

```
//: innerclasses/LocalInnerClass.java
// Holds a sequence of Objects.
import static net.mindview.util.Print.*;

interface Counter {
```

```
    int next();
}

public class LocalInnerClass {
  private int count = 0;
  Counter getCounter(final String name) {
    // A local inner class:
    class LocalCounter implements Counter {
      public LocalCounter() {
        // Local inner class can have a constructor
        print("LocalCounter()");
      }
      public int next() {
        printnb(name); // Access local final
        return count++;
      }
    }
    return new LocalCounter();
  }
  // The same thing with an anonymous inner class:
  Counter getCounter2(final String name) {
    return new Counter() {
      // Anonymous inner class cannot have a named
      // constructor, only an instance initializer:
      {
        print("Counter()");
      }
      public int next() {
        printnb(name); // Access local final
        return count++;
      }
    };
  }
  public static void main(String[] args) {
    LocalInnerClass lic = new LocalInnerClass();
    Counter
      c1 = lic.getCounter("Local inner "),
      c2 = lic.getCounter2("Anonymous inner ");
    for(int i = 0; i < 5; i++)
      print(c1.next());
    for(int i = 0; i < 5; i++)
      print(c2.next());
  }
} /* Output:
```

```
LocalCounter()
Counter()
Local inner 0
Local inner 1
Local inner 2
Local inner 3
Local inner 4
Anonymous inner 5
Anonymous inner 6
Anonymous inner 7
Anonymous inner 8
Anonymous inner 9
*///:~
```

Counter returns the next value in a sequence. It is implemented as both a local class and an anonymous inner class, both of which have the same behaviors and capabilities. Since the name of the local inner class is not accessible outside the method, the only justification for using a local inner class instead of an anonymous inner class is if you need a named constructor and/or an overloaded constructor, since an anonymous inner class can only use instance initialization.

Another reason to make a local inner class rather than an anonymous inner class is if you need to make more than one object of that class.

Inner-class identifiers

Since every class produces a **.class** file that holds all the information about how to create objects of this type (this information produces a "meta-class" called the **Class** object), you might guess that inner classes must also produce **.class** files to contain the information for *their* **Class** objects. The names of these files/classes have a strict formula: the name of the enclosing class, followed by a '**$**', followed by the name of the inner class. For example, the **.class** files created by **LocalInnerClass.java** include:

```
Counter.class
LocalInnerClass$1.class
LocalInnerClass$1LocalCounter.class
LocalInnerClass.class
```

If inner classes are anonymous, the compiler simply starts generating numbers as inner-class identifiers. If inner classes are nested within inner classes, their names are simply appended after a '**$**' and the outer-class identifier(s).

Although this scheme of generating internal names is simple and straightforward, it's also robust and handles most situations.[5] Since it is the standard naming scheme for Java, the generated files are automatically platform-independent. (Note that the Java compiler is changing your inner classes in all sorts of other ways in order to make them work.)

Summary

Interfaces and inner classes are more sophisticated concepts than what you'll find in many OOP languages; for example, there's nothing like them in C++. Together, they solve the same problem that C++ attempts to solve with its multiple inheritance (MI) feature. However, MI in C++ turns out to be rather difficult to use, whereas Java interfaces and inner classes are, by comparison, much more accessible.

Although the features themselves are reasonably straightforward, the use of these features is a design issue, much the same as polymorphism. Over time, you'll become better at recognizing situations where you should use an interface, or an inner class, or both. But at this point in this book, you should at least be comfortable with the syntax and semantics. As you see these language features in use, you'll eventually internalize them.

Solutions to selected exercises can be found in the electronic document *The Thinking in Java Annotated Solution Guide*, available for sale from *www.MindView.net*.

---

[5] On the other hand, '$' is a meta-character to the Unix shell and so you'll sometimes have trouble when listing the **.class** files. This is a bit strange coming from Sun, a Unix-based company. My guess is that they weren't considering this issue, but instead thought you'd naturally focus on the source-code files.

Holding Your Objects

It's a fairly simple program that only has a fixed quantity of objects with known lifetimes.

In general, your programs will always be creating new objects based on some criteria that will be known only at run time. Before then, you won't know the quantity or even the exact type of the objects you need. To solve the general programming problem, you need to create any number of objects, anytime, anywhere. So you can't rely on creating a named reference to hold each one of your objects:

```
MyType aReference;
```

since you'll never know how many of these you'll actually need.

Most languages provide some way to solve this essential problem. Java has several ways to hold objects (or rather, references to objects). The compiler-supported type is the array, which has been discussed before. An array is the most efficient way to hold a group of objects, and you're pointed towards this choice if you want to hold a group of primitives. But an array has a fixed size, and in the more general case, you won't know at the time you're writing the program how many objects you're going to need, or whether you need a more sophisticated way to store your objects—so the fixed-sized constraint of an array is too limiting.

The **java.util** library has a reasonably complete set of *container classes* to solve this problem, the basic types of which are **List**, **Set**, **Queue**, and **Map**. These types of objects are also known as *collection classes*, but because the Java library uses the name **Collection** to refer to a particular subset of the library, I shall use the more inclusive term "container." Containers provide sophisticated ways to hold your objects, and you can solve a surprising number of problems by using these tools.

Among their other characteristics—**Set**, for example, holds only one object of each value, and **Map** is an *associative array* that lets you associate objects with other objects—the Java container classes will automatically resize themselves. So, unlike with arrays, you can put in any number of objects and you don't need to worry about how big to make the container while you're writing the program.

Even though they don't have direct keyword support in Java,[1] container classes are fundamental tools that significantly increase your programming muscle. In this chapter you'll get a basic working knowledge of the Java container library, with an emphasis on typical usage. Here, we'll focus on the containers that you'll use in day-to-day programming. Later, in the *Containers in Depth* chapter, you'll learn about the rest of the containers and more details about their functionality and how to use them.

Generics and type-safe containers

One of the problems of using pre-Java SE5 containers was that the compiler allowed you to insert an incorrect type into a container. For example, consider a container of **Apple** objects, using the basic workhorse container, **ArrayList**. For now, you can think of **ArrayList** as "an array that automatically expands itself." Using an **ArrayList** is straightforward: Create one, insert objects using **add( )**, and access them with **get( )**, using an index—just as you do with an array, but without the square brackets.[2] **ArrayList** also has a method **size( )** to let you know how many elements have been added, so that you don't inadvertently index off the end and cause an error (by throwing a *runtime exception*; exceptions will be introduced in the chapter *Error Handling with Exceptions*).

In this example, **Apples** and **Orange**s are placed into the container, then pulled out. Normally, the Java compiler will give you a warning because the example does *not* use generics. Here, a special Java SE5 *annotation* is used to suppress the warning. Annotations start with an '@' sign, and can take an

---

[1] A number of languages, such as Perl, Python, and Ruby, have native support for containers.

[2] This is a place where operator overloading would have been nice. C++ and C# container classes produce a cleaner syntax using operator overloading.

argument; this one is **@SuppressWarnings** and the argument indicates that "unchecked" warnings only should be suppressed:

```
//: holding/ApplesAndOrangesWithoutGenerics.java
// Simple container example (produces compiler warnings).
// {ThrowsException}
import java.util.*;

class Apple {
  private static long counter;
  private final long id = counter++;
  public long id() { return id; }
}

class Orange {}

public class ApplesAndOrangesWithoutGenerics {
  @SuppressWarnings("unchecked")
  public static void main(String[] args) {
    ArrayList apples = new ArrayList();
    for(int i = 0; i < 3; i++)
      apples.add(new Apple());
    // Not prevented from adding an Orange to apples:
    apples.add(new Orange());
    for(int i = 0; i < apples.size(); i++)
      ((Apple)apples.get(i)).id();
      // Orange is detected only at run time
  }
} /* (Execute to see output) *///:~
```

You'll learn more about Java SE5 annotations in the *Annotations* chapter.

The classes **Apple** and **Orange** are distinct; they have nothing in common except that they are both **Object**s. (Remember that if you don't explicitly say what class you're inheriting from, you automatically inherit from **Object**.) Since **ArrayList** holds **Object**s, you can not only add **Apple** objects into this container using the **ArrayList** method **add( )**, but you can also add **Orange** objects without complaint at either compile time or run time. When you go to fetch out what you think are **Apple** objects using the **ArrayList** method **get( )**, you get back a reference to an **Object** that you must cast to an **Apple**. Then you need to surround the entire expression with parentheses to force the evaluation of the cast before calling the **id( )** method for **Apple**; otherwise, you'll get a syntax error.

At run time, when you try to cast the **Orange** object to an **Apple**, you'll get an error in the form of the aforementioned exception.

In the *Generics* chapter, you'll learn that *creating* classes using Java generics can be complex. However, *applying* predefined generic classes is usually straightforward. For example, to define an **ArrayList** intended to hold **Apple** objects, you say **ArrayList<Apple>** instead of just **ArrayList**. The angle brackets surround the *type parameters* (there may be more than one), which specify the type(s) that can be held by that instance of the container.

With generics, you're prevented, *at compile time*, from putting the wrong type of object into a container.[3] Here's the example again, using generics:

```
//: holding/ApplesAndOrangesWithGenerics.java
import java.util.*;

public class ApplesAndOrangesWithGenerics {
  public static void main(String[] args) {
    ArrayList<Apple> apples = new ArrayList<Apple>();
    for(int i = 0; i < 3; i++)
      apples.add(new Apple());
    // Compile-time error:
    // apples.add(new Orange());
    for(int i = 0; i < apples.size(); i++)
      System.out.println(apples.get(i).id());
    // Using foreach:
    for(Apple c : apples)
      System.out.println(c.id());
  }
} /* Output:
0
1
2
0
1
2
*///:~
```

---

[3] At the end of the *Generics* chapter, you'll find a discussion about whether this is such a bad problem. However, the *Generics* chapter will also show you that Java generics are useful for more than just type-safe containers.

Now the compiler will prevent you from putting an **Orange** into **apples**, so it becomes a compile-time error rather than a runtime error.

Also notice that the cast is no longer necessary when fetching items back out from the **List**. Since the **List** knows what type it holds, it does the cast for you when you call **get( )**. Thus, with generics you not only know that the compiler will check the type of object that you put into a container, but you also get cleaner syntax when using the objects in the container.

The example also shows that, if you do not need to use the index of each element, you can use the foreach syntax to select each element in the **List**.

You are not limited to putting the exact type of object into a container when you specify that type as a generic parameter. Upcasting works the same with generics as it does with other types:

```
//: holding/GenericsAndUpcasting.java
import java.util.*;

class GrannySmith extends Apple {}
class Gala extends Apple {}
class Fuji extends Apple {}
class Braeburn extends Apple {}

public class GenericsAndUpcasting {
  public static void main(String[] args) {
    ArrayList<Apple> apples = new ArrayList<Apple>();
    apples.add(new GrannySmith());
    apples.add(new Gala());
    apples.add(new Fuji());
    apples.add(new Braeburn());
    for(Apple c : apples)
      System.out.println(c);
  }
} /* Output: (Sample)
GrannySmith@7d772e
Gala@11b86e7
Fuji@35ce36
Braeburn@757aef
*///:~
```

Thus, you can add a subtype of **Apple** to a container that is specified to hold **Apple** objects.

The output is produced from the default **toString( )** method of **Object**, which prints the class name followed by the unsigned hexadecimal representation of the *hash code* of the object (generated by the **hashCode( )** method). You'll learn about hash codes in detail in *Containers in Depth*.

Exercise 1: (2) Create a new class called **Gerbil** with an **int gerbilNumber** that's initialized in the constructor. Give it a method called **hop( )** that displays which gerbil number this is, and that it's hopping. Create an **ArrayList** and add **Gerbil** objects to the **List**. Now use the **get( )** method to move through the **List** and call **hop( )** for each **Gerbil**.

Basic concepts

The Java container library takes the idea of "holding your objects" and divides it into two distinct concepts, expressed as the basic interfaces of the library:

1. **Collection**: a sequence of individual elements with one or more rules applied to them. A **List** must hold the elements in the way that they were inserted, a **Set** cannot have duplicate elements, and a **Queue** *produces* the elements in the order determined by a *queuing discipline* (usually the same order in which they are inserted).

2. **Map**: a group of key-value object pairs, allowing you to look up a value using a key. An **ArrayList** allows you to look up an object using a number, so in a sense it associates numbers to objects. A *map* allows you to look up an object using *another object*. It's also called an *associative array*, because it associates objects with other objects, or a *dictionary*, because you look up a value object using a key object just like you look up a definition using a word. **Map**s are powerful programming tools.

Although it's not always possible, ideally you'll write most of your code to talk to these interfaces, and the only place where you'll specify the precise type you're using is at the point of creation. So you can create a **List** like this:

```
List<Apple> apples = new ArrayList<Apple>();
```

Notice that the **ArrayList** has been upcast to a **List**, in contrast to the way it was handled in the previous examples. The intent of using the interface is that if you decide you want to change your implementation, all you need to do is change it at the point of creation, like this:

```
List<Apple> apples = new LinkedList<Apple>();
```

Thus, you'll typically make an object of a concrete class, upcast it to the corresponding interface, and then use the interface throughout the rest of your code.

This approach won't always work, because some classes have additional functionality. For example, **LinkedList** has additional methods that are not in the **List** interface, and a **TreeMap** has methods that are not in the **Map** interface. If you need to use those methods, you won't be able to upcast to the more general interface.

The **Collection** interface generalizes the idea of a *sequence*—a way of holding a group of objects. Here's a simple example that fills a **Collection** (represented here with an **ArrayList**) with **Integer** objects and then prints each element in the resulting container:

```
//: holding/SimpleCollection.java
import java.util.*;

public class SimpleCollection {
  public static void main(String[] args) {
    Collection<Integer> c = new ArrayList<Integer>();
    for(int i = 0; i < 10; i++)
      c.add(i); // Autoboxing
    for(Integer i : c)
      System.out.print(i + ", ");
  }
} /* Output:
0, 1, 2, 3, 4, 5, 6, 7, 8, 9,
*///:~
```

Since this example only uses **Collection** methods, any object of a class inherited from **Collection** would work, but **ArrayList** is the most basic type of sequence.

The name of the **add( )** method suggests that it puts a new element in the **Collection**. However, the documentation carefully states that **add( )** "ensures that this **Collection** contains the specified element." This is to allow for the meaning of **Set**, which adds the element only if it isn't already there. With an **ArrayList**, or any sort of **List**, **add( )** always means "put it in," because **List**s don't care if there are duplicates.

All **Collection**s can be traversed using the foreach syntax, as shown here. Later in this chapter you'll learn about a more flexible concept called an *Iterator*.

Exercise 2: (1) Modify **SimpleCollection.java** to use a **Set** for **c**.

Exercise 3: (2) Modify **innerclasses/Sequence.java** so that you can add any number of elements to it.

Adding groups of elements

There are utility methods in both the **Arrays** and **Collections** classes in **java.util** that add groups of elements to a **Collection**. **Arrays.asList( )** takes either an array or a comma-separated list of elements (using varargs) and turns it into a **List** object. **Collections.addAll( )** takes a **Collection** object and either an array or a comma-separated list and adds the elements to the **Collection**. Here's an example that shows both methods, as well as the more conventional **addAll( )** method that's part of all **Collection** types:

```
//: holding/AddingGroups.java
// Adding groups of elements to Collection objects.
import java.util.*;

public class AddingGroups {
  public static void main(String[] args) {
    Collection<Integer> collection =
      new ArrayList<Integer>(Arrays.asList(1, 2, 3, 4, 5));
    Integer[] moreInts = { 6, 7, 8, 9, 10 };
    collection.addAll(Arrays.asList(moreInts));
    // Runs significantly faster, but you can't
    // construct a Collection this way:
    Collections.addAll(collection, 11, 12, 13, 14, 15);
    Collections.addAll(collection, moreInts);
    // Produces a list "backed by" an array:
    List<Integer> list = Arrays.asList(16, 17, 18, 19, 20);
    list.set(1, 99); // OK -- modify an element
    // list.add(21); // Runtime error because the
                     // underlying array cannot be resized.
  }
} ///:~
```

The constructor for a **Collection** can accept another **Collection** which it uses for initializing itself, so you can use **Arrays.asList( )** to produce input for the constructor. However, **Collections.addAll( )** runs much faster, and it's just as easy to construct the **Collection** with no elements and then call **Collections.addAll( )**, so this is the preferred approach.

The **Collection.addAll( )** member method can only take an argument of another **Collection** object, so it is not as flexible as **Arrays.asList( )** or **Collections.addAll( )**, which use variable argument lists.

It's also possible to use the output of **Arrays.asList( )** directly, as a **List**, but the underlying representation in this case is the array, which cannot be resized. If you try to **add( )** or **delete( )** elements in such a list, that would attempt to change the size of an array, so you'll get an "Unsupported Operation" error at run time.

A limitation of **Arrays.asList( )** is that it takes a best guess about the resulting type of the **List**, and doesn't pay attention to what you're assigning it to. Sometimes this can cause a problem:

```
//: holding/AsListInference.java
// Arrays.asList() makes its best guess about type.
import java.util.*;

class Snow {}
class Powder extends Snow {}
class Light extends Powder {}
class Heavy extends Powder {}
class Crusty extends Snow {}
class Slush extends Snow {}

public class AsListInference {
  public static void main(String[] args) {
    List<Snow> snow1 = Arrays.asList(
      new Crusty(), new Slush(), new Powder());

    // Won't compile:
    // List<Snow> snow2 = Arrays.asList(
    //    new Light(), new Heavy());
    // Compiler says:
    // found    : java.util.List<Powder>
    // required: java.util.List<Snow>
```

```
    // Collections.addAll() doesn't get confused:
    List<Snow> snow3 = new ArrayList<Snow>();
    Collections.addAll(snow3, new Light(), new Heavy());

    // Give a hint using an
    // explicit type argument specification:
    List<Snow> snow4 = Arrays.<Snow>asList(
      new Light(), new Heavy());
  }
} ///:~
```

When trying to create **snow2**, **Arrays.asList( )** only has types of **Powder**, so it creates a **List<Powder>** rather than a **List<Snow>**, whereas **Collections.addAll( )** works fine because it knows from the first argument what the target type is.

As you can see from the creation of **snow4**, it's possible to insert a "hint" in the middle of **Arrays.asList( )**, to tell the compiler what the actual target type should be for the resulting **List** type produced by **Arrays.asList( )**. This is called an *explicit type argument specification*.

Maps are more complex, as you'll see, and the Java standard library does not provide any way to automatically initialize them, except from the contents of another **Map**.

Printing containers

You must use **Arrays.toString( )** to produce a printable representation of an array, but the containers print nicely without any help. Here's an example that also introduces you to the basic Java containers:

```
//: holding/PrintingContainers.java
// Containers print themselves automatically.
import java.util.*;
import static net.mindview.util.Print.*;

public class PrintingContainers {
  static Collection fill(Collection<String> collection) {
    collection.add("rat");
    collection.add("cat");
    collection.add("dog");
    collection.add("dog");
    return collection;
  }
```

Thinking in Java Bruce Eckel

```java
  static Map fill(Map<String,String> map) {
    map.put("rat", "Fuzzy");
    map.put("cat", "Rags");
    map.put("dog", "Bosco");
    map.put("dog", "Spot");
    return map;
  }
  public static void main(String[] args) {
    print(fill(new ArrayList<String>()));
    print(fill(new LinkedList<String>()));
    print(fill(new HashSet<String>()));
    print(fill(new TreeSet<String>()));
    print(fill(new LinkedHashSet<String>()));
    print(fill(new HashMap<String,String>()));
    print(fill(new TreeMap<String,String>()));
    print(fill(new LinkedHashMap<String,String>()));
  }
} /* Output:
[rat, cat, dog, dog]
[rat, cat, dog, dog]
[dog, cat, rat]
[cat, dog, rat]
[rat, cat, dog]
{dog=Spot, cat=Rags, rat=Fuzzy}
{cat=Rags, dog=Spot, rat=Fuzzy}
{rat=Fuzzy, cat=Rags, dog=Spot}
*///:~
```

This shows the two primary categories in the Java container library. The distinction is based on the number of items that are held in each "slot" in the container. The **Collection** category only holds one item in each slot. It includes the **List**, which holds a group of items in a specified sequence, the **Set**, which only allows the addition of one identical item, and the **Queue**, which only allows you to insert objects at one "end" of the container and remove objects from the other "end" (for the purposes of this example, this is just another way of looking at a sequence and so it is not shown). A **Map** holds two objects, a *key* and an associated *value*, in each slot.

In the output, you can see that the default printing behavior (provided via each container's **toString( )** method) produces reasonably readable results. A **Collection** is printed surrounded by square brackets, with each element separated by a comma. A **Map** is surrounded by curly braces, with each key and value associated with an equal sign (keys on the left, values on the right).

Holding Your Objects

The first **fill( )** method works with all types of **Collection**, each of which implements the **add( )** method to include new elements.

ArrayList and **LinkedList** are both types of **List**, and you can see from the output that they both hold elements in the same order in which they are inserted. The difference between the two is not only performance for certain types of operations, but also that a **LinkedList** contains more operations than an **ArrayList**. These will be explored more fully later in this chapter.

HashSet, **TreeSet** and **LinkedHashSet** are types of **Set**. The output shows that a **Set** will only hold one of each identical item, but it also shows that the different **Set** implementations store the elements differently. The **HashSet** stores elements using a rather complex approach that will be explored in the *Containers in Depth* chapter—all you need to know at this point is that this technique is the fastest way to retrieve elements, and as a result the storage order can seem nonsensical (often, you only care whether something is a member of the **Set**, not the order in which it appears). If storage order is important, you can use a **TreeSet**, which keeps the objects in ascending comparison order, or a **LinkedHashSet**, which keeps the objects in the order in which they were added.

A **Map** (also called an *associative array*) allows you to look up an object using a *key*, like a simple database. The associated object is called a *value*. If you have a **Map** that associates states with their capitals and you want to know the capital of Ohio, you look it up using "Ohio" as the key—almost as if you were indexing into an array. Because of this behavior, a **Map** only accepts one of each key.

Map.put(key, value) adds a value (the thing you want) and associates it with a key (the thing you look it up with). **Map.get(key)** produces the value associated with that key. The above example only adds key-value pairs, and does not perform lookups. That will be shown later.

Notice that you don't have to specify (or think about) the size of the **Map** because it resizes itself automatically. Also, **Map**s know how to print themselves, showing the association with keys and values. The order that the keys and values are held inside the **Map** is not the insertion order because the **HashMap** implementation uses a very fast algorithm that controls the order.

The example uses the three basic flavors of **Map**: **HashMap**, **TreeMap** and **LinkedHashMap**. Like **HashSet**, **HashMap** provides the fastest lookup technique, and also doesn't hold its elements in any apparent order. A **TreeMap** keeps the keys sorted by ascending comparison order, and a **LinkedHashMap** keeps the keys in insertion order while retaining the lookup speed of the **HashMap**.

Exercise 4: (3) Create a *generator* class that produces character names (as **String** objects) from your favorite movie (you can use *Snow White* or *Star Wars* as a fallback) each time you call **next( )**, and loops around to the beginning of the character list when it runs out of names. Use this generator to fill an array, an **ArrayList**, a **LinkedList**, a **HashSet**, a **LinkedHashSet**, and a **TreeSet**, then print each container.

List

Lists promise to maintain elements in a particular sequence. The **List** interface adds a number of methods to **Collection** that allow insertion and removal of elements in the middle of a **List**.

There are two types of **List**:

- The basic **ArrayList**, which excels at randomly accessing elements, but is slower when inserting and removing elements in the middle of a **List**.

- The **LinkedList**, which provides optimal sequential access, with inexpensive insertions and deletions from the middle of the **List**. A **LinkedList** is relatively slow for random access, but it has a larger feature set than the **ArrayList**.

The following example reaches forward in the book to use a library from the *Type Information* chapter by importing **typeinfo.pets**. This is a library that contains a hierarchy of **Pet** classes along with some tools to randomly generate **Pet** objects. You don't need to know the full details at this point, just that (1) there's a **Pet** class and various subtypes of **Pet** and (2) the **static Pets.arrayList( )** method will return an **ArrayList** filled with randomly selected **Pet** objects:

```
//: holding/ListFeatures.java
import typeinfo.pets.*;
import java.util.*;
import static net.mindview.util.Print.*;
```

```
public class ListFeatures {
  public static void main(String[] args) {
    Random rand = new Random(47);
    List<Pet> pets = Pets.arrayList(7);
    print("1: " + pets);
    Hamster h = new Hamster();
    pets.add(h); // Automatically resizes
    print("2: " + pets);
    print("3: " + pets.contains(h));
    pets.remove(h); // Remove by object
    Pet p = pets.get(2);
    print("4: " +  p + " " + pets.indexOf(p));
    Pet cymric = new Cymric();
    print("5: " + pets.indexOf(cymric));
    print("6: " + pets.remove(cymric));
    // Must be the exact object:
    print("7: " + pets.remove(p));
    print("8: " + pets);
    pets.add(3, new Mouse()); // Insert at an index
    print("9: " + pets);
    List<Pet> sub = pets.subList(1, 4);
    print("subList: " + sub);
    print("10: " + pets.containsAll(sub));
    Collections.sort(sub); // In-place sort
    print("sorted subList: " + sub);
    // Order is not important in containsAll():
    print("11: " + pets.containsAll(sub));
    Collections.shuffle(sub, rand); // Mix it up
    print("shuffled subList: " + sub);
    print("12: " + pets.containsAll(sub));
    List<Pet> copy = new ArrayList<Pet>(pets);
    sub = Arrays.asList(pets.get(1), pets.get(4));
    print("sub: " + sub);
    copy.retainAll(sub);
    print("13: " + copy);
    copy = new ArrayList<Pet>(pets); // Get a fresh copy
    copy.remove(2); // Remove by index
    print("14: " + copy);
    copy.removeAll(sub); // Only removes exact objects
    print("15: " + copy);
    copy.set(1, new Mouse()); // Replace an element
    print("16: " + copy);
    copy.addAll(2, sub); // Insert a list in the middle
```

```
        print("17: " + copy);
        print("18: " + pets.isEmpty());
        pets.clear(); // Remove all elements
        print("19: " + pets);
        print("20: " + pets.isEmpty());
        pets.addAll(Pets.arrayList(4));
        print("21: " + pets);
        Object[] o = pets.toArray();
        print("22: " + o[3]);
        Pet[] pa = pets.toArray(new Pet[0]);
        print("23: " + pa[3].id());
    }
} /* Output:
1: [Rat, Manx, Cymric, Mutt, Pug, Cymric, Pug]
2: [Rat, Manx, Cymric, Mutt, Pug, Cymric, Pug, Hamster]
3: true
4: Cymric 2
5: -1
6: false
7: true
8: [Rat, Manx, Mutt, Pug, Cymric, Pug]
9: [Rat, Manx, Mutt, Mouse, Pug, Cymric, Pug]
subList: [Manx, Mutt, Mouse]
10: true
sorted subList: [Manx, Mouse, Mutt]
11: true
shuffled subList: [Mouse, Manx, Mutt]
12: true
sub: [Mouse, Pug]
13: [Mouse, Pug]
14: [Rat, Mouse, Mutt, Pug, Cymric, Pug]
15: [Rat, Mutt, Cymric, Pug]
16: [Rat, Mouse, Cymric, Pug]
17: [Rat, Mouse, Mouse, Pug, Cymric, Pug]
18: false
19: []
20: true
21: [Manx, Cymric, Rat, EgyptianMau]
22: EgyptianMau
23: 14
*///:~
```

The print lines are numbered so the output can be related to the source code. The first output line shows the original **List** of **Pet**s. Unlike an array, a **List**

---

allows you to add elements after it has been created, or remove elements, and it resizes itself. That's its fundamental value: a modifiable sequence. You can see the result of adding a **Hamster** in output line 2—the object is appended to the end of the list.

You can find out whether an object is in the list using the **contains( )** method. If you want to remove an object, you can pass that object's reference to the **remove( )** method. Also, if you have a reference to an object, you can discover the index number where that object is located in the **List** using **indexOf( )**, as you can see in output line 4.

When deciding whether an element is part of a **List**, discovering the index of an element, and removing an element from a **List** by reference, the **equals( )** method (part of the root class **Object**) is used. Each **Pet** is defined to be a unique object, so even though there are two **Cymric**s in the list, if I create a new **Cymric** object and pass it to **indexOf( )**, the result will be **-1** (indicating it wasn't found), and attempts to **remove( )** the object will return **false**. For other classes, **equals( )** may be defined differently—**String**s, for example, are equal if the contents of two **String**s are identical. So to prevent surprises, it's important to be aware that **List** behavior changes depending on **equals( )** behavior.

In output lines 7 and 8, removing an object that exactly matches an object in the **List** is shown to be successful.

It's possible to insert an element in the middle of the **List**, as you can see in output line 9 and the code that precedes it, but this brings up an issue: for a **LinkedList**, insertion and removal in the middle of a list is a cheap operation (except for, in this case, the actual random access into the middle of the list), but for an **ArrayList** it is an expensive operation. Does this mean you should never insert elements in the middle of an **ArrayList**, and switch to a **LinkedList** if you do? No, it just means you should be aware of the issue, and if you start doing many insertions in the middle of an **ArrayList** *and* your program starts slowing down, that you might look at your **List** implementation as the possible culprit (the best way to discover such a bottleneck, as you will see in the supplement at *http://MindView.net/Books/BetterJava*, is to use a profiler). Optimization is a tricky issue, and the best policy is to leave it alone until you discover you need to worry about it (although understanding the issues is always a good idea).

The **subList( )** method allows you to easily create a slice out of a larger list, and this naturally produces a **true** result when passed to **containsAll( )** for that larger list. It's also interesting to note that order is unimportant—you can see in output lines 11 and 12 that calling the intuitively named **Collections.sort( )** and **Collections.shuffle( )** on **sub** doesn't affect the outcome of **containsAll( )**. **subList( )** produces a list backed by the original list. Therefore, changes in the returned list are reflected in the original list, and vice versa.

The **retainAll( )** method is effectively a "set intersection" operation, in this case keeping all the elements in **copy** that are also in **sub**. Again, the resulting behavior depends on the **equals( )** method.

Output line 14 shows the result of removing an element using its index number, which is more straightforward than removing it by object reference since you don't have to worry about **equals( )** behavior when using indexes.

The **removeAll( )** method also operates based on the **equals( )** method. As the name implies, it removes all the objects from the **List** that are in the argument **List**.

The **set( )** method is rather unfortunately named because of the potential confusion with the **Set** class—"replace" might have been a better name here, because it replaces the element at the index (the first argument) with the second argument.

Output line 17 shows that for **List**s, there's an overloaded **addAll( )** method that allows you to insert the new list in the middle of the original list, instead of just appending it to the end with the **addAll( )** that comes from **Collection**.

Output lines 18-20 show the effect of the **isEmpty( )** and **clear( )** methods.

Output lines 22 and 23 show how you can convert any **Collection** to an array using **toArray( )**. This is an overloaded method; the no-argument version returns an array of **Object**, but if you pass an array of the target type to the overloaded version, it will produce an array of the type specified (assuming it passes type checking). If the argument array is too small to hold all the objects in the **List** (as is the case here), **toArray( )** will create a new array of the appropriate size. **Pet** objects have an **id( )** method, which you can see is called on one of the objects in the resulting array.

Exercise 5: (3) Modify **ListFeatures.java** so that it uses **Integer**s (remember autoboxing!) instead of **Pet**s, and explain any difference in results.

Exercise 6: (2) Modify **ListFeatures.java** so that it uses **String**s instead of **Pet**s, and explain any difference in results.

Exercise 7: (3) Create a class, then make an initialized array of objects of your class. Fill a **List** from your array. Create a subset of your **List** by using **subList( )**, then remove this subset from your **List**.

Iterator

In any container, you must have a way to insert elements and fetch them out again. After all, that's the primary job of a container—to hold things. In a **List**, **add( )** is one way to insert elements, and **get( )** is one way to fetch elements.

If you want to start thinking at a higher level, there's a drawback: You need to program to the exact type of the container in order to use it. This might not seem bad at first, but what if you write code for a **List**, and later on you discover that it would be convenient to apply that same code to a **Set**? Or suppose you'd like to write, from the beginning, a piece of general-purpose code that doesn't know or care what type of container it's working with, so that it can be used on different types of containers without rewriting that code?

The concept of an *Iterator* (another design pattern) can be used to achieve this abstraction. An iterator is an object whose job is to move through a sequence and select each object in that sequence without the client programmer knowing or caring about the underlying structure of that sequence. In addition, an iterator is usually what's called a *lightweight object*: one that's cheap to create. For that reason, you'll often find seemingly strange constraints for iterators; for example, the Java **Iterator** can move in only one direction. There's not much you can do with an **Iterator** except:

1. Ask a **Collection** to hand you an **Iterator** using a method called **iterator( )**. That **Iterator** will be ready to return the first element in the sequence.

2. Get the next object in the sequence with **next( )**.

3. See if there are any more objects in the sequence with **hasNext( )**.

4.   Remove the last element returned by the iterator with **remove( )**.

To see how it works, we can again use the **Pet**s tools from the *Type Information* chapter:

```
//: holding/SimpleIteration.java
import typeinfo.pets.*;
import java.util.*;

public class SimpleIteration {
  public static void main(String[] args) {
    List<Pet> pets = Pets.arrayList(12);
    Iterator<Pet> it = pets.iterator();
    while(it.hasNext()) {
      Pet p = it.next();
      System.out.print(p.id() + ":" + p + " ");
    }
    System.out.println();
    // A simpler approach, when possible:
    for(Pet p : pets)
      System.out.print(p.id() + ":" + p + " ");
    System.out.println();
    // An Iterator can also remove elements:
    it = pets.iterator();
    for(int i = 0; i < 6; i++) {
      it.next();
      it.remove();
    }
    System.out.println(pets);
  }
} /* Output:
0:Rat 1:Manx 2:Cymric 3:Mutt 4:Pug 5:Cymric 6:Pug 7:Manx
8:Cymric 9:Rat 10:EgyptianMau 11:Hamster
0:Rat 1:Manx 2:Cymric 3:Mutt 4:Pug 5:Cymric 6:Pug 7:Manx
8:Cymric 9:Rat 10:EgyptianMau 11:Hamster
[Pug, Manx, Cymric, Rat, EgyptianMau, Hamster]
*///:~
```

With an **Iterator**, you don't need to worry about the number of elements in the container. That's taken care of for you by **hasNext( )** and **next( )**.

If you're simply moving forward through the **List** and not trying to modify the **List** object itself, you can see that the foreach syntax is more succinct.

An **Iterator** will also remove the last element produced by **next( )**, which means you must call **next( )** before you call **remove( )**.[4]

This idea of taking a container of objects and passing through it to perform an operation on each one is powerful and will be seen throughout this book.

Now consider the creation of a **display( )** method that is container-agnostic:

```
//: holding/CrossContainerIteration.java
import typeinfo.pets.*;
import java.util.*;

public class CrossContainerIteration {
  public static void display(Iterator<Pet> it) {
    while(it.hasNext()) {
      Pet p = it.next();
      System.out.print(p.id() + ":" + p + " ");
    }
    System.out.println();
  }
  public static void main(String[] args) {
    ArrayList<Pet> pets = Pets.arrayList(8);
    LinkedList<Pet> petsLL = new LinkedList<Pet>(pets);
    HashSet<Pet> petsHS = new HashSet<Pet>(pets);
    TreeSet<Pet> petsTS = new TreeSet<Pet>(pets);
    display(pets.iterator());
    display(petsLL.iterator());
    display(petsHS.iterator());
    display(petsTS.iterator());
  }
} /* Output:
0:Rat 1:Manx 2:Cymric 3:Mutt 4:Pug 5:Cymric 6:Pug 7:Manx
0:Rat 1:Manx 2:Cymric 3:Mutt 4:Pug 5:Cymric 6:Pug 7:Manx
4:Pug 6:Pug 3:Mutt 1:Manx 5:Cymric 7:Manx 2:Cymric 0:Rat
5:Cymric 2:Cymric 7:Manx 1:Manx 3:Mutt 6:Pug 4:Pug 0:Rat
*///:~
```

---

[4] **remove( )** is a so-called "optional" method (there are other such methods), which means that not all **Iterator** implementations must implement it. This topic is covered in the *Containers in Depth* chapter. The standard Java library containers implement **remove( )**, however, so you don't need to worry about it until that chapter.

Note that **display( )** contains no information about the type of sequence that it is traversing, and this shows the true power of the **Iterator**: the ability to separate the operation of traversing a sequence from the underlying structure of that sequence. For this reason, we sometimes say that iterators *unify access to containers*.

Exercise 8: (1) Modify Exercise 1 so it uses an **Iterator** to move through the **List** while calling **hop( )**.

Exercise 9: (4) Modify **innerclasses/Sequence.java** so that **Sequence** works with an **Iterator** instead of a **Selector**.

Exercise 10: (2) Change Exercise 9 in the *Polymorphism* chapter to use an **ArrayList** to hold the **Rodent**s and an **Iterator** to move through the sequence of **Rodent**s.

Exercise 11: (2) Write a method that uses an **Iterator** to step through a **Collection** and print the **toString( )** of each object in the container. Fill all the different types of **Collection**s with objects and apply your method to each container.

ListIterator

The **ListIterator** is a more powerful subtype of **Iterator** that is produced only by **List** classes. While **Iterator** can only move forward, **ListIterator** is bidirectional. It can also produce the indexes of the next and previous elements relative to where the iterator is pointing in the list, and it can replace the last element that it visited using the **set( )** method. You can produce a **ListIterator** that points to the beginning of the **List** by calling **listIterator( )**, and you can also create a **ListIterator** that starts out pointing to an index **n** in the list by calling **listIterator(n)**. Here's an example that demonstrates all these abilities:

```
//: holding/ListIteration.java
import typeinfo.pets.*;
import java.util.*;

public class ListIteration {
  public static void main(String[] args) {
    List<Pet> pets = Pets.arrayList(8);
    ListIterator<Pet> it = pets.listIterator();
    while(it.hasNext())
      System.out.print(it.next() + ", " + it.nextIndex() +
        ", " + it.previousIndex() + "; ");
```

```
    System.out.println();
    // Backwards:
    while(it.hasPrevious())
      System.out.print(it.previous().id() + " ");
    System.out.println();
    System.out.println(pets);
    it = pets.listIterator(3);
    while(it.hasNext()) {
      it.next();
      it.set(Pets.randomPet());
    }
    System.out.println(pets);
  }
} /* Output:
Rat, 1, 0; Manx, 2, 1; Cymric, 3, 2; Mutt, 4, 3; Pug, 5, 4;
Cymric, 6, 5; Pug, 7, 6; Manx, 8, 7;
7 6 5 4 3 2 1 0
[Rat, Manx, Cymric, Mutt, Pug, Cymric, Pug, Manx]
[Rat, Manx, Cymric, Cymric, Rat, EgyptianMau, Hamster,
EgyptianMau]
*///:~
```

The **Pets.randomPet( )** method is used to replace all the **Pet** objects in the
List from location 3 onward.

Exercise 12: (3) Create and populate a **List<Integer>**. Create a second
List<Integer> of the same size as the first, and use **ListIterator**s to read
elements from the first **List** and insert them into the second in reverse order.
(You may want to explore a number of different ways to solve this problem.)

LinkedList

The **LinkedList** also implements the basic **List** interface like **ArrayList**
does, but it performs certain operations (insertion and removal in the middle
of the **List**) more efficiently than does **ArrayList**. Conversely, it is less
efficient for random-access operations.

LinkedList also adds methods that allow it to be used as a stack, a **Queue**
or a double-ended queue (deque).

Some of these methods are aliases or slight variations of each other, to
produce names that are more familiar within the context of a particular usage
(**Queue**, in particular). For example, **getFirst( )** and **element( )** are
identical—they return the head (first element) of the list without removing it,

and throw **NoSuchElementException** if the **List** is empty. **peek( )** is a
slight variation of those two that returns **null** if the list is empty.

removeFirst( ) and **remove( )** are also identical—they remove and return
the head of the list, and throw **NoSuchElementException** for an empty
list, and **poll( )** is a slight variation that returns **null** if this list is empty.

addFirst( ) inserts an element at the beginning of the list.

offer( ) is the same as **add( )** and **addLast( )**. They all add an element to
the tail (end) of a list.

removeLast( ) removes and returns the last element of the list.

Here's an example that shows the basic similarity and differences between
these features. It doesn't repeat the behavior that was shown in
ListFeatures.java:

```
//: holding/LinkedListFeatures.java
import typeinfo.pets.*;
import java.util.*;
import static net.mindview.util.Print.*;

public class LinkedListFeatures {
  public static void main(String[] args) {
    LinkedList<Pet> pets =
      new LinkedList<Pet>(Pets.arrayList(5));
    print(pets);
    // Identical:
    print("pets.getFirst(): " + pets.getFirst());
    print("pets.element(): " + pets.element());
    // Only differs in empty-list behavior:
    print("pets.peek(): " + pets.peek());
    // Identical; remove and return the first element:
    print("pets.remove(): " + pets.remove());
    print("pets.removeFirst(): " + pets.removeFirst());
    // Only differs in empty-list behavior:
    print("pets.poll(): " + pets.poll());
    print(pets);
    pets.addFirst(new Rat());
    print("After addFirst(): " + pets);
    pets.offer(Pets.randomPet());
    print("After offer(): " + pets);
    pets.add(Pets.randomPet());
```

```
    print("After add(): " + pets);
    pets.addLast(new Hamster());
    print("After addLast(): " + pets);
    print("pets.removeLast(): " + pets.removeLast());
  }
} /* Output:
[Rat, Manx, Cymric, Mutt, Pug]
pets.getFirst(): Rat
pets.element(): Rat
pets.peek(): Rat
pets.remove(): Rat
pets.removeFirst(): Manx
pets.poll(): Cymric
[Mutt, Pug]
After addFirst(): [Rat, Mutt, Pug]
After offer(): [Rat, Mutt, Pug, Cymric]
After add(): [Rat, Mutt, Pug, Cymric, Pug]
After addLast(): [Rat, Mutt, Pug, Cymric, Pug, Hamster]
pets.removeLast(): Hamster
*///:~
```

The result of **Pets.arrayList( )** is handed to the **LinkedList** constructor in order to populate it. If you look at the **Queue** interface, you'll see the **element( )**, **offer( )**, **peek( )**, **poll( )** and **remove( )** methods that were added to **LinkedList** in order that it could be a **Queue** implementation. Full examples of **Queue**s will be given later in this chapter.

Exercise 13: (3) In the **innerclasses/GreenhouseController.java** example, the class **Controller** uses an **ArrayList**. Change the code to use a **LinkedList** instead, and use an **Iterator** to cycle through the set of events.

Exercise 14: (3) Create an empty **LinkedList<Integer>**. Using a **ListIterator**, add **Integer**s to the **List** by always inserting them in the middle of the **List**.

Stack

A stack is sometimes referred to as a "last-in, first-out" (LIFO) container. It's sometimes called a *pushdown stack*, because whatever you "push" on the stack last is the first item you can "pop" off of the stack. An often-used analogy is of cafeteria trays in a spring-loaded holder—the last ones that go in are the first ones that come out.

LinkedList has methods that directly implement stack functionality, so you can also just use a **LinkedList** rather than making a stack class. However, a stack class can sometimes tell the story better:

```
//: net/mindview/util/Stack.java
// Making a stack from a LinkedList.
package net.mindview.util;
import java.util.LinkedList;

public class Stack<T> {
  private LinkedList<T> storage = new LinkedList<T>();
  public void push(T v) { storage.addFirst(v); }
  public T peek() { return storage.getFirst(); }
  public T pop() { return storage.removeFirst(); }
  public boolean empty() { return storage.isEmpty(); }
  public String toString() { return storage.toString(); }
} ///:~
```

This introduces the simplest possible example of a class definition using generics. The **<T>** after the class name tells the compiler that this will be a *parameterized type*, and that the type parameter—the one that will be substituted with a real type when the class is used—is **T**. Basically, this says, "We're defining a **Stack** that holds objects of type **T**." The **Stack** is implemented using a **LinkedList**, and the **LinkedList** is also told that it is holding type **T**. Notice that **push( )** takes an object of type **T**, while **peek( )** and **pop( )** return an object of type **T**. The **peek( )** method provides you with the top element without removing it from the top of the stack, while **pop( )** removes and returns the top element.

If you want only stack behavior, inheritance is inappropriate here because it would produce a class with all the rest of the **LinkedList** methods (you'll see in the *Containers in Depth* chapter that this very mistake was made by the Java 1.0 designers when they created **java.util.Stack**).

Here's a simple demonstration of this new **Stack** class:

```
//: holding/StackTest.java
import net.mindview.util.*;

public class StackTest {
  public static void main(String[] args) {
    Stack<String> stack = new Stack<String>();
    for(String s : "My dog has fleas".split(" "))
      stack.push(s);
```

```
      while(!stack.empty())
        System.out.print(stack.pop() + " ");
    }
} /* Output:
fleas has dog My
*///:~
```

If you want to use this **Stack** class in your own code, you'll need to fully specify the package—or change the name of the class—when you create one; otherwise, you'll probably collide with the **Stack** in the **java.util** package. For example, if we **import java.util.*** into the above example, we must use package names in order to prevent collisions:

```
//: holding/StackCollision.java

public class StackCollision {
  public static void main(String[] args) {
    net.mindview.util.Stack<String> stack =
      new net.mindview.util.Stack<String>();
    for(String s : "My dog has fleas".split(" "))
      stack.push(s);
    while(!stack.empty())
      System.out.print(stack.pop() + " ");
    System.out.println();
    java.util.Stack<String> stack2 =
      new java.util.Stack<String>();
    for(String s : "My dog has fleas".split(" "))
      stack2.push(s);
    while(!stack2.empty())
      System.out.print(stack2.pop() + " ");
  }
} /* Output:
fleas has dog My
fleas has dog My
*///:~
```

The two **Stack** classes have the same interface, but there is no common **Stack** interface in **java.util**—probably because the original, poorly designed **java.util.Stack** class in Java 1.0 co-opted the name. Even though **java.util.Stack** exists, **LinkedList** produces a better **Stack** and so the **net.mindview.util.Stack** approach is preferable.

You can also control the selection of the "preferred" **Stack** implementation using an explicit import:

```
import net.mindview.util.Stack;
```

Now any reference to **Stack** will select the **net.mindview.util** version, and to select **java.util.Stack** you must use full qualification.

Exercise 15: (4) Stacks are often used to evaluate expressions in programming languages. Using **net.mindview.util.Stack**, evaluate the following expression, where '+' means "push the following letter onto the stack," and '-' means "pop the top of the stack and print it":
"+U+n+c---+e+r+t---+a-+i-+n+t+y---+ -+r+u--+l+e+s---"

Set

A **Set** refuses to hold more than one instance of each object value. If you try to add more than one instance of an equivalent object, the **Set** prevents duplication. The most common use for a **Set** is to test for membership, so that you can easily ask whether an object is in a **Set**. Because of this, lookup is typically the most important operation for a **Set**, so you'll usually choose a **HashSet** implementation, which is optimized for rapid lookup.

Set has the same interface as **Collection**, so there isn't any extra functionality like there is in the two different types of **List**. Instead, the **Set** is exactly a **Collection**—it just has different behavior. (This is the ideal use of inheritance and polymorphism: to express different behavior.) A **Set** determines membership based on the "value" of an object, a more complex topic that you will learn about in the *Containers in Depth* chapter.

Here's an example that uses a **HashSet** with **Integer** objects:

```
//: holding/SetOfInteger.java
import java.util.*;

public class SetOfInteger {
  public static void main(String[] args) {
    Random rand = new Random(47);
    Set<Integer> intset = new HashSet<Integer>();
    for(int i = 0; i < 10000; i++)
      intset.add(rand.nextInt(30));
    System.out.println(intset);
  }
} /* Output:
```

```
[15, 8, 23, 16, 7, 22, 9, 21, 6, 1, 29, 14, 24, 4, 19, 26,
11, 18, 3, 12, 27, 17, 2, 13, 28, 20, 25, 10, 5, 0]
*///:~
```

Ten thousand random numbers from 0 up to 29 are added to the **Set**, so you can imagine that each value has many duplications. And yet you can see that only one instance of each appears in the result.

You'll also notice that the output is in no discernible order. This is because a **HashSet** uses *hashing* for speed—hashing is covered in the *Containers in Depth* chapter. The order maintained by a **HashSet** is different from a **TreeSet** or a **LinkedHashSet**, since each implementation has a different way of storing elements. **TreeSet** keeps elements sorted into a red-black tree data structure, whereas **HashSet** uses the hashing function. **LinkedHashSet** also uses hashing for lookup speed, but *appears* to maintain elements in insertion order using a linked list.

If you want the results to be sorted, one approach is to use a **TreeSet** instead of a **HashSet**:

```
//: holding/SortedSetOfInteger.java
import java.util.*;

public class SortedSetOfInteger {
  public static void main(String[] args) {
    Random rand = new Random(47);
    SortedSet<Integer> intset = new TreeSet<Integer>();
    for(int i = 0; i < 10000; i++)
      intset.add(rand.nextInt(30));
    System.out.println(intset);
  }
} /* Output:
[0, 1, 2, 3, 4, 5, 6, 7, 8, 9, 10, 11, 12, 13, 14, 15, 16,
17, 18, 19, 20, 21, 22, 23, 24, 25, 26, 27, 28, 29]
*///:~
```

One of the most common operations you will perform is a test for set membership using **contains( )**, but there are also operations that will remind you of the Venn diagrams you may have been taught in elementary school:

```
//: holding/SetOperations.java
import java.util.*;
import static net.mindview.util.Print.*;
```

```
public class SetOperations {
  public static void main(String[] args) {
    Set<String> set1 = new HashSet<String>();
    Collections.addAll(set1,
      "A B C D E F G H I J K L".split(" "));
    set1.add("M");
    print("H: " + set1.contains("H"));
    print("N: " + set1.contains("N"));
    Set<String> set2 = new HashSet<String>();
    Collections.addAll(set2, "H I J K L".split(" "));
    print("set2 in set1: " + set1.containsAll(set2));
    set1.remove("H");
    print("set1: " + set1);
    print("set2 in set1: " + set1.containsAll(set2));
    set1.removeAll(set2);
    print("set2 removed from set1: " + set1);
    Collections.addAll(set1, "X Y Z".split(" "));
    print("'X Y Z' added to set1: " + set1);
  }
} /* Output:
H: true
N: false
set2 in set1: true
set1: [D, K, C, B, L, G, I, M, A, F, J, E]
set2 in set1: false
set2 removed from set1: [D, C, B, G, M, A, F, E]
'X Y Z' added to set1: [Z, D, C, B, G, M, A, F, Y, X, E]
*///:~
```

The method names are self-explanatory, and there are a few more that you will find in the JDK documentation.

Producing a list of unique elements can be quite useful. For example, suppose you'd like to list all the words in the file **SetOperations.java**, above. Using the **net.mindview.TextFile** utility that will be introduced later in the book, you can open and read a file into a **Set**:

```
//: holding/UniqueWords.java
import java.util.*;
import net.mindview.util.*;

public class UniqueWords {
  public static void main(String[] args) {
    Set<String> words = new TreeSet<String>(
```

```
       new TextFile("SetOperations.java", "\\W+"));
    System.out.println(words);
  }
} /* Output:
[A, B, C, Collections, D, E, F, G, H, HashSet, I, J, K, L,
M, N, Output, Print, Set, SetOperations, String, X, Y, Z,
add, addAll, added, args, class, contains, containsAll,
false, from, holding, import, in, java, main, mindview,
net, new, print, public, remove, removeAll, removed, set1,
set2, split, static, to, true, util, void]
*///:~
```

TextFile is inherited from **List<String>**. The **TextFile** constructor opens the file and breaks it into words according to the *regular expression* "\\W+", which means "one or more letters" (regular expressions are introduced in the *Strings* chapter). The result is handed to the **TreeSet** constructor, which adds the contents of the **List** to itself. Since it is a **TreeSet**, the result is sorted. In this case, the sorting is done *lexicographically* so that the uppercase and lowercase letters are in separate groups. If you'd like to sort it *alphabetically*, you can pass the **String.CASE_INSENSITIVE_ORDER Comparator** (a *comparator* is an object that establishes order) to the **TreeSet** constructor:

```
//: holding/UniqueWordsAlphabetic.java
// Producing an alphabetic listing.
import java.util.*;
import net.mindview.util.*;

public class UniqueWordsAlphabetic {
  public static void main(String[] args) {
    Set<String> words =
      new TreeSet<String>(String.CASE_INSENSITIVE_ORDER);
    words.addAll(
      new TextFile("SetOperations.java", "\\W+"));
    System.out.println(words);
  }
} /* Output:
[A, add, addAll, added, args, B, C, class, Collections,
contains, containsAll, D, E, F, false, from, G, H, HashSet,
holding, I, import, in, J, java, K, L, M, main, mindview,
N, net, new, Output, Print, public, remove, removeAll,
removed, Set, set1, set2, SetOperations, split, static,
String, to, true, util, void, X, Y, Z]
*///:~
```

Comparators will be explored in detail in the *Arrays* chapter.

Exercise 16: (5) Create a **Set** of the vowels. Working from **UniqueWords.java**, count and display the number of vowels in each input word, and also display the total number of vowels in the input file.

Map

The ability to map objects to other objects can be an immensely powerful way to solve programming problems. For example, consider a program to examine the randomness of Java's **Random** class. Ideally, **Random** would produce a perfect distribution of numbers, but to test this you need to generate many random numbers and count the ones that fall in the various ranges. A **Map** easily solves the problem; in this case, the key is the number produced by **Random**, and the value is the number of times that number appears:

```
//: holding/Statistics.java
// Simple demonstration of HashMap.
import java.util.*;

public class Statistics {
  public static void main(String[] args) {
    Random rand = new Random(47);
    Map<Integer,Integer> m =
      new HashMap<Integer,Integer>();
    for(int i = 0; i < 10000; i++) {
      // Produce a number between 0 and 20:
      int r = rand.nextInt(20);
      Integer freq = m.get(r);
      m.put(r, freq == null ? 1 : freq + 1);
    }
    System.out.println(m);
  }
} /* Output:
{15=497, 4=481, 19=464, 8=468, 11=531, 16=533, 18=478,
3=508, 7=471, 12=521, 17=509, 2=489, 13=506, 9=549, 6=519,
1=502, 14=477, 10=513, 5=503, 0=481}
*///:~
```

In **main( )**, autoboxing converts the randomly generated **int** into an **Integer** reference that can be used with the **HashMap** (you can't use primitives with containers). The **get( )** method returns **null** if the key is not already in the container (which means that this is the first time the number has been found). Otherwise, the **get( )** method produces the associated **Integer** value for the key, which is incremented (again, autoboxing simplifies the expression but there are actually conversions to and from **Integer** taking place).

Here's an example that allows you to use a **String** description to look up **Pet** objects. It also shows how you can test a **Map** to see if it contains a key or a value with **containsKey( )** and **containsValue( )**:

```
//: holding/PetMap.java
import typeinfo.pets.*;
import java.util.*;
import static net.mindview.util.Print.*;

public class PetMap {
  public static void main(String[] args) {
    Map<String,Pet> petMap = new HashMap<String,Pet>();
    petMap.put("My Cat", new Cat("Molly"));
    petMap.put("My Dog", new Dog("Ginger"));
    petMap.put("My Hamster", new Hamster("Bosco"));
    print(petMap);
    Pet dog = petMap.get("My Dog");
    print(dog);
    print(petMap.containsKey("My Dog"));
    print(petMap.containsValue(dog));
  }
} /* Output:
{My Cat=Cat Molly, My Hamster=Hamster Bosco, My Dog=Dog
Ginger}
Dog Ginger
true
true
*///:~
```

Maps, like arrays and **Collection**s, can easily be expanded to multiple dimensions; you simply make a **Map** whose values are **Map**s (and the values of *those* **Map**s can be other containers, even other **Map**s). Thus, it's quite easy to combine containers to quickly produce powerful data structures. For example, suppose you are keeping track of people who have multiple pets—all you need is a **Map<Person, List<Pet>>**:

```
//: holding/MapOfList.java
package holding;
```

```
import typeinfo.pets.*;
import java.util.*;
import static net.mindview.util.Print.*;

public class MapOfList {
  public static Map<Person, List<? extends Pet>>
    petPeople = new HashMap<Person, List<? extends Pet>>();
  static {
    petPeople.put(new Person("Dawn"),
      Arrays.asList(new Cymric("Molly"),new Mutt("Spot")));
    petPeople.put(new Person("Kate"),
      Arrays.asList(new Cat("Shackleton"),
        new Cat("Elsie May"), new Dog("Margrett")));
    petPeople.put(new Person("Marilyn"),
      Arrays.asList(
        new Pug("Louie aka Louis Snorkelstein Dupree"),
        new Cat("Stanford aka Stinky el Negro"),
        new Cat("Pinkola")));
    petPeople.put(new Person("Luke"),
      Arrays.asList(new Rat("Fuzzy"), new Rat("Fizzy")));
    petPeople.put(new Person("Isaac"),
      Arrays.asList(new Rat("Freckly")));
  }
  public static void main(String[] args) {
    print("People: " + petPeople.keySet());
    print("Pets: " + petPeople.values());
    for(Person person : petPeople.keySet()) {
      print(person + " has:");
      for(Pet pet : petPeople.get(person))
        print("    " + pet);
    }
  }
} /* Output:
People: [Person Luke, Person Marilyn, Person Isaac, Person
Dawn, Person Kate]
Pets: [[Rat Fuzzy, Rat Fizzy], [Pug Louie aka Louis
Snorkelstein Dupree, Cat Stanford aka Stinky el Negro, Cat
Pinkola], [Rat Freckly], [Cymric Molly, Mutt Spot], [Cat
Shackleton, Cat Elsie May, Dog Margrett]]
Person Luke has:
    Rat Fuzzy
    Rat Fizzy
Person Marilyn has:
    Pug Louie aka Louis Snorkelstein Dupree
```

```
    Cat Stanford aka Stinky el Negro
    Cat Pinkola
Person Isaac has:
    Rat Freckly
Person Dawn has:
    Cymric Molly
    Mutt Spot
Person Kate has:
    Cat Shackleton
    Cat Elsie May
    Dog Margrett
*///:~
```

A **Map** can return a **Set** of its keys, a **Collection** of its values, or a **Set** of its pairs. The **keySet( )** method produces a **Set** of all the keys in **petPeople**, which is used in the foreach statement to iterate through the **Map**.

Exercise 17:   (2) Take the **Gerbil** class in Exercise 1 and put it into a **Map** instead, associating each **Gerbil**'s name (e.g. "Fuzzy" or "Spot") as a **String** (the key) for each **Gerbil** (the value) you put in the table. Get an **Iterator** for the **keySet( )** and use it to move through the **Map**, looking up the **Gerbil** for each key and printing out the key and telling the **Gerbil** to **hop( )**.

Exercise 18:   (3) Fill a **HashMap** with key-value pairs. Print the results to show ordering by hash code. Extract the pairs, sort by key, and place the result into a **LinkedHashMap**. Show that the insertion order is maintained.

Exercise 19:   (2) Repeat the previous exercise with a **HashSet** and **LinkedHashSet**.

Exercise 20:   (3) Modify Exercise 16 so that you keep a count of the occurrence of each vowel.

Exercise 21:   (3) Using a **Map<String,Integer>**, follow the form of **UniqueWords.java** to create a program that counts the occurrence of words in a file. Sort the results using **Collections.sort( )** with a second argument of **String.CASE_INSENSITIVE_ORDER** (to produce an alphabetic sort), and display the result.

Exercise 22:   (5) Modify the previous exercise so that it uses a class containing a **String** and a count field to store each different word, and a **Set** of these objects to maintain the list of words.

Exercise 23: (4) Starting with **Statistics.java**, create a program that runs the test repeatedly and looks to see if any one number tends to appear more than the others in the results.

Exercise 24: (2) Fill a **LinkedHashMap** with **String** keys and objects of your choice. Now extract the pairs, sort them based on the keys, and reinsert them into the **Map**.

Exercise 25: (3) Create a **Map<String,ArrayList<Integer>>**. Use **net.mindview.TextFile** to open a text file and read it in a word at a time (use **"\\W+"** as the second argument to the **TextFile** constructor). Count the words as you read them in, and for each word in the file, record in the **ArrayList<Integer>** the word count associated with that word—this is, in effect, the location in the file where that word was found.

Exercise 26: (4) Take the resulting **Map** from the previous exercise and re-create the order of the words as they appeared in the original file.

Queue

A *queue* is typically a *"first-in, first-out"* (FIFO) container. That is, you put things in at one end and pull them out at the other, and the order in which you put them in will be the same order in which they come out. Queues are commonly used as a way to reliably transfer objects from one area of a program to another. Queues are especially important in concurrent programming, as you will see in the *Concurrency* chapter, because they safely transfer objects from one task to another.

LinkedList has methods to support queue behavior and it implements the **Queue** interface, so a **LinkedList** can be used as a **Queue** implementation. By upcasting a **LinkedList** to a **Queue**, this example uses the **Queue**-specific methods in the **Queue** interface:

```
//: holding/QueueDemo.java
// Upcasting to a Queue from a LinkedList.
import java.util.*;

public class QueueDemo {
  public static void printQ(Queue queue) {
    while(queue.peek() != null)
      System.out.print(queue.remove() + " ");
    System.out.println();
  }
  public static void main(String[] args) {
```

```
      Queue<Integer> queue = new LinkedList<Integer>();
      Random rand = new Random(47);
      for(int i = 0; i < 10; i++)
        queue.offer(rand.nextInt(i + 10));
      printQ(queue);
      Queue<Character> qc = new LinkedList<Character>();
      for(char c : "Brontosaurus".toCharArray())
        qc.offer(c);
      printQ(qc);
  }
} /* Output:
8 1 1 1 5 14 3 1 0 1
B r o n t o s a u r u s
*///:~
```

offer( ) is one of the **Queue**-specific methods; it inserts an element at the tail of the queue if it can, or returns **false**. Both **peek( )** and **element( )** return the head of the queue *without removing it*, but **peek( )** returns **null** if the queue is empty and **element( )** throws **NoSuchElementException**. Both **poll( )** and **remove( )** remove and return the head of the queue, but **poll( )** returns **null** if the queue is empty, while **remove( )** throws **NoSuchElementException**.

Autoboxing automatically converts the **int** result of **nextInt( )** into the **Integer** object required by **queue**, and the **char c** into the **Character** object required by **qc**. The **Queue** interface narrows access to the methods of **LinkedList** so that only the appropriate methods are available, and you are thus less tempted to use **LinkedList** methods (here, you could actually cast **queue** back to a **LinkedList**, but you are at least discouraged from doing so).

Notice that the **Queue**-specific methods provide complete and standalone functionality. That is, you can have a usable **Queue** without any of the methods that are in **Collection**, from which it is inherited.

Exercise 27: (2) Write a class called **Command** that contains a **String** and has a method **operation( )** that displays the **String**. Write a second class with a method that fills a **Queue** with **Command** objects and returns it. Pass the filled **Queue** to a method in a third class that consumes the objects in the **Queue** and calls their **operation( )** methods.

PriorityQueue

First-in, first-out (FIFO) describes the most typical *queuing discipline*. A queuing discipline is what decides, given a group of elements in the queue, which one goes next. First-in, first-out says that the next element should be the one that was waiting the longest.

A *priority queue* says that the element that goes next is the one with the greatest need (the highest priority). For example, in an airport, a customer might be pulled out of a queue if their plane is about to leave. If you build a messaging system, some messages will be more important than others, and should be dealt with sooner, regardless of when they arrive. The **PriorityQueue** was added in Java SE5 to provide an automatic implementation for this behavior.

When you **offer( )** an object onto a **PriorityQueue**, that object is sorted into the queue.[5] The default sorting uses the *natural order* of the objects in the queue, but you can modify the order by providing your own **Comparator**. The **PriorityQueue** ensures that when you call **peek( )**, **poll( )** or **remove( )**, the element you get will be the one with the highest priority.

It's trivial to make a **PriorityQueue** that works with built-in types like **Integer**, **String** or **Character**. In the following example, the first set of values are the identical random values from the previous example, so you can see that they emerge differently from the **PriorityQueue**:

```
//: holding/PriorityQueueDemo.java
import java.util.*;

public class PriorityQueueDemo {
  public static void main(String[] args) {
    PriorityQueue<Integer> priorityQueue =
      new PriorityQueue<Integer>();
    Random rand = new Random(47);
    for(int i = 0; i < 10; i++)
      priorityQueue.offer(rand.nextInt(i + 10));
```

---

[5] This actually depends on the implementation. Priority queue algorithms typically sort on insertion (maintaining a *heap*), but they may also perform the selection of the most important element upon removal. The choice of algorithm could be important if object priority can change while it is waiting in the queue.

```
        QueueDemo.printQ(priorityQueue);

        List<Integer> ints = Arrays.asList(25, 22, 20,
            18, 14, 9, 3, 1, 1, 2, 3, 9, 14, 18, 21, 23, 25);
        priorityQueue = new PriorityQueue<Integer>(ints);
        QueueDemo.printQ(priorityQueue);
        priorityQueue = new PriorityQueue<Integer>(
            ints.size(), Collections.reverseOrder());
        priorityQueue.addAll(ints);
        QueueDemo.printQ(priorityQueue);

        String fact = "EDUCATION SHOULD ESCHEW OBFUSCATION";
        List<String> strings = Arrays.asList(fact.split(""));
        PriorityQueue<String> stringPQ =
          new PriorityQueue<String>(strings);
        QueueDemo.printQ(stringPQ);
        stringPQ = new PriorityQueue<String>(
          strings.size(), Collections.reverseOrder());
        stringPQ.addAll(strings);
        QueueDemo.printQ(stringPQ);

        Set<Character> charSet = new HashSet<Character>();
        for(char c : fact.toCharArray())
          charSet.add(c); // Autoboxing
        PriorityQueue<Character> characterPQ =
          new PriorityQueue<Character>(charSet);
        QueueDemo.printQ(characterPQ);
    }
} /* Output:
0 1 1 1 1 1 3 5 8 14
1 1 2 3 3 9 9 14 14 18 18 20 21 22 23 25 25
25 25 23 22 21 20 18 18 14 14 9 9 3 3 2 1 1
      A A B C C C D D E E E F H H I I L N N O O O O S S
T T U U U W
W U U U T T S S S O O O O N N L I I H H F E E E D D C C C B
A A
  A B C D E F H I L N O S T U W
*///:~
```

You can see that duplicates are allowed, and the lowest values have the
highest priority (in the case of **String**, spaces also count as values and are
higher in priority than letters). To show how you can change the ordering by
providing your own **Comparator** object, the third constructor call to
PriorityQueue<Integer> and the second call to

PriorityQueue<String> use the reverse-order **Comparator** produced by **Collections.reverseOrder( )** (added in Java SE5).

The last section adds a **HashSet** to eliminate duplicate **Character**s, just to make things a little more interesting.

Integer, **String** and **Character** work with **PriorityQueue** because these classes already have natural ordering built in. If you want you use your own class in a **PriorityQueue**, you must include additional functionality to produce natural ordering, or provide your own **Comparator**. There's a more sophisticated example that demonstrates this in the *Containers in Depth* chapter.

Exercise 28: (2) Fill a **PriorityQueue** (using **offer( )**) with **Double** values created using **java.util.Random**, then remove the elements using **poll( )** and display them.

Exercise 29: (2) Create a simple class that inherits from **Object** and contains no members, and show that you cannot successfully add multiple elements of that class to a **PriorityQueue**. This issue will be fully explained in the *Containers in Depth* chapter.

Collection vs. Iterator

Collection is the root interface that describes what is common for all sequence containers. It might be thought of as an "incidental interface," one that appeared because of commonality between other interfaces. In addition, the **java.util.AbstractCollection** class provides a default implementation for a **Collection**, so that you can create a new subtype of **AbstractCollection** without unnecessary code duplication.

One argument for having an interface is that it allows you to create more generic code. By writing to an interface rather than an implementation, your code can be applied to more types of objects.[6] So if I write a method that takes a **Collection**, that method can be applied to any type that implements **Collection**—and this allows a new class to choose to implement **Collection**

---

[6] Some people advocate the automatic creation of an interface for every possible combination of methods in a class—sometimes for every single class. I believe that an interface should have more meaning than a mechanical duplication of method combinations, so I tend to wait until I see the value added by an interface before creating one.

---

in order to be used with my method. It's interesting to note, however, that the Standard C++ Library has no common base class for its containers—all commonality between containers is achieved through iterators. In Java, it might seem sensible to follow the C++ approach, and to express commonality between containers using an iterator rather than a **Collection**. However, the two approaches are bound together, since implementing **Collection** also means providing an **iterator( )** method:

```java
//: holding/InterfaceVsIterator.java
import typeinfo.pets.*;
import java.util.*;

public class InterfaceVsIterator {
  public static void display(Iterator<Pet> it) {
    while(it.hasNext()) {
      Pet p = it.next();
      System.out.print(p.id() + ":" + p + " ");
    }
    System.out.println();
  }
  public static void display(Collection<Pet> pets) {
    for(Pet p : pets)
      System.out.print(p.id() + ":" + p + " ");
    System.out.println();
  }
  public static void main(String[] args) {
    List<Pet> petList = Pets.arrayList(8);
    Set<Pet> petSet = new HashSet<Pet>(petList);
    Map<String,Pet> petMap =
      new LinkedHashMap<String,Pet>();
    String[] names = ("Ralph, Eric, Robin, Lacey, " +
      "Britney, Sam, Spot, Fluffy").split(", ");
    for(int i = 0; i < names.length; i++)
      petMap.put(names[i], petList.get(i));
    display(petList);
    display(petSet);
    display(petList.iterator());
    display(petSet.iterator());
    System.out.println(petMap);
    System.out.println(petMap.keySet());
    display(petMap.values());
    display(petMap.values().iterator());
  }
} /* Output:
```

```
0:Rat 1:Manx 2:Cymric 3:Mutt 4:Pug 5:Cymric 6:Pug 7:Manx
4:Pug 6:Pug 3:Mutt 1:Manx 5:Cymric 7:Manx 2:Cymric 0:Rat
0:Rat 1:Manx 2:Cymric 3:Mutt 4:Pug 5:Cymric 6:Pug 7:Manx
4:Pug 6:Pug 3:Mutt 1:Manx 5:Cymric 7:Manx 2:Cymric 0:Rat
{Ralph=Rat, Eric=Manx, Robin=Cymric, Lacey=Mutt,
Britney=Pug, Sam=Cymric, Spot=Pug, Fluffy=Manx}
[Ralph, Eric, Robin, Lacey, Britney, Sam, Spot, Fluffy]
0:Rat 1:Manx 2:Cymric 3:Mutt 4:Pug 5:Cymric 6:Pug 7:Manx
0:Rat 1:Manx 2:Cymric 3:Mutt 4:Pug 5:Cymric 6:Pug 7:Manx
*///:~
```

Both versions of **display( )** work with **Map** objects as well as with subtypes
of **Collection**, and both the **Collection** interface and the **Iterator** decouple
the **display( )** methods from knowing about the particular implementation
of the underlying container.

In this case the two approaches come up even. In fact, **Collection** pulls
ahead a bit because it is **Iterable**, and so in the implementation of
display(Collection) the foreach construct can be used, which makes the
code a little cleaner.

The use of **Iterator** becomes compelling when you implement a foreign
class, one that is not a **Collection**, in which it would be difficult or annoying
to make it implement the **Collection** interface. For example, if we create a
Collection implementation by inheriting from a class that holds **Pet** objects,
we must implement all the **Collection** methods, even if we don't need to use
them within the **display( )** method. Although this can easily be
accomplished by inheriting from **AbstractCollection**, you're forced to
implement **iterator( )** anyway, along with **size( )**, in order to provide the
methods that are not implemented by **AbstractCollection**, but that are
used by the other methods in **AbstractCollection**:

```
//: holding/CollectionSequence.java
import typeinfo.pets.*;
import java.util.*;

public class CollectionSequence
extends AbstractCollection<Pet> {
  private Pet[] pets = Pets.createArray(8);
  public int size() { return pets.length; }
  public Iterator<Pet> iterator() {
    return new Iterator<Pet>() {
      private int index = 0;
```

```
      public boolean hasNext() {
        return index < pets.length;
      }
      public Pet next() { return pets[index++]; }
      public void remove() { // Not implemented
        throw new UnsupportedOperationException();
      }
    };
  }
  public static void main(String[] args) {
    CollectionSequence c = new CollectionSequence();
    InterfaceVsIterator.display(c);
    InterfaceVsIterator.display(c.iterator());
  }
} /* Output:
0:Rat 1:Manx 2:Cymric 3:Mutt 4:Pug 5:Cymric 6:Pug 7:Manx
0:Rat 1:Manx 2:Cymric 3:Mutt 4:Pug 5:Cymric 6:Pug 7:Manx
*///:~
```

The **remove( )** method is an "optional operation," which you will learn about in the *Containers in Depth* chapter. Here, it's not necessary to implement it, and if you call it, it will throw an exception.

From this example, you can see that if you implement **Collection**, you also implement **iterator( )**, and just implementing **iterator( )** alone requires only slightly less effort than inheriting from **AbstractCollection**. However, if your class already inherits from another class, then you cannot also inherit from **AbstractCollection**. In that case, to implement **Collection** you'd have to implement all the methods in the interface. In this case it would be much easier to inherit and add the ability to create an iterator:

```
//: holding/NonCollectionSequence.java
import typeinfo.pets.*;
import java.util.*;

class PetSequence {
  protected Pet[] pets = Pets.createArray(8);
}

public class NonCollectionSequence extends PetSequence {
  public Iterator<Pet> iterator() {
    return new Iterator<Pet>() {
      private int index = 0;
      public boolean hasNext() {
```

```
            return index < pets.length;
        }
        public Pet next() { return pets[index++]; }
        public void remove() { // Not implemented
          throw new UnsupportedOperationException();
        }
      };
    }
    public static void main(String[] args) {
      NonCollectionSequence nc = new NonCollectionSequence();
      InterfaceVsIterator.display(nc.iterator());
    }
} /* Output:
0:Rat 1:Manx 2:Cymric 3:Mutt 4:Pug 5:Cymric 6:Pug 7:Manx
*///:~
```

Producing an **Iterator** is the least-coupled way of connecting a sequence to a method that consumes that sequence, and puts far fewer constraints on the sequence class than does implementing **Collection**.

Exercise 30: (5) Modify **CollectionSequence.java** so that it does not inherit from **AbstractCollection**, but instead implements **Collection**.

Foreach and iterators

So far, the foreach syntax has been primarily used with arrays, but it also works with any **Collection** object. You've actually seen a few examples of this using **ArrayList**, but here's a general proof:

```
//: holding/ForEachCollections.java
// All collections work with foreach.
import java.util.*;

public class ForEachCollections {
  public static void main(String[] args) {
    Collection<String> cs = new LinkedList<String>();
    Collections.addAll(cs,
      "Take the long way home".split(" "));
    for(String s : cs)
      System.out.print("'" + s + "' ");
  }
} /* Output:
'Take' 'the' 'long' 'way' 'home'
*///:~
```

Since **cs** is a **Collection**, this code shows that working with foreach is a characteristic of all **Collection** objects.

The reason that this works is that Java SE5 introduced a new interface called **Iterable** which contains an **iterator( )** method to produce an **Iterator**, and the **Iterable** interface is what foreach uses to move through a sequence. So if you create any class that implements **Iterable**, you can use it in a foreach statement:

```
//: holding/IterableClass.java
// Anything Iterable works with foreach.
import java.util.*;

public class IterableClass implements Iterable<String> {
  protected String[] words = ("And that is how " +
    "we know the Earth to be banana-shaped.").split(" ");
  public Iterator<String> iterator() {
    return new Iterator<String>() {
      private int index = 0;
      public boolean hasNext() {
        return index < words.length;
      }
      public String next() { return words[index++]; }
      public void remove() { // Not implemented
        throw new UnsupportedOperationException();
      }
    };
  }
  public static void main(String[] args) {
    for(String s : new IterableClass())
      System.out.print(s + " ");
  }
} /* Output:
And that is how we know the Earth to be banana-shaped.
*///:~
```

The **iterator( )** method returns an instance of an anonymous inner implementation of **Iterator<String>** which delivers each word in the array. In **main( )**, you can see that **IterableClass** does indeed work in a foreach statement.

In Java SE5, a number of classes have been made **Iterable**, primarily all **Collection** classes (but not **Map**s). For example, this code displays all the operating system environment variables:

```
//: holding/EnvironmentVariables.java
import java.util.*;

public class EnvironmentVariables {
  public static void main(String[] args) {
    for(Map.Entry entry: System.getenv().entrySet()) {
      System.out.println(entry.getKey() + ": " +
        entry.getValue());
    }
  }
} /* (Execute to see output) *///:~
```

System.getenv( )[7] returns a **Map**, **entrySet( )** produces a **Set** of
Map.Entry elements, and a **Set** is **Iterable** so it can be used in a foreach
loop.

A foreach statement works with an array or anything **Iterable**, but that
doesn't mean that an array is automatically an **Iterable**, nor is there any
autoboxing that takes place:

```
//: holding/ArrayIsNotIterable.java
import java.util.*;

public class ArrayIsNotIterable {
  static <T> void test(Iterable<T> ib) {
    for(T t : ib)
      System.out.print(t + " ");
  }
  public static void main(String[] args) {
    test(Arrays.asList(1, 2, 3));
    String[] strings = { "A", "B", "C" };
    // An array works in foreach, but it's not Iterable:
    //! test(strings);
    // You must explicitly convert it to an Iterable:
    test(Arrays.asList(strings));
  }
} /* Output:
1 2 3 A B C
*///:~
```

---

[7] This was not available before Java SE5, because it was thought to be too tightly coupled
to the operating system, and thus to violate "write once, run anywhere." The fact that it is
included now suggests that the Java designers are becoming more pragmatic.

Trying to pass an array as an **Iterable** argument fails. There is no automatic conversion to an **Iterable**; you must do it by hand.

Exercise 31: (3) Modify **polymorphism/shape/RandomShapeGenerator.java** to make it **Iterable**. You'll need to add a constructor that takes the number of elements that you want the iterator to produce before stopping. Verify that it works.

The *Adapter Method* idiom

What if you have an existing class that is **Iterable**, and you'd like to add one or more new ways to use this class in a foreach statement? For example, suppose you'd like to choose whether to iterate through a list of words in either a forward or reverse direction. If you simply inherit from the class and override the **iterator( )** method, you replace the existing method and you don't get a choice.

One solution is what I call the *Adapter Method* idiom. The "Adapter" part comes from design patterns, because you must provide a particular interface to satisfy the foreach statement. When you have one interface and you need another one, writing an adapter solves the problem. Here, I want to *add* the ability to produce a reverse iterator to the default forward iterator, so I can't override. Instead, I add a method that produces an **Iterable** object which can then be used in the foreach statement. As you see here, this allows us to provide multiple ways to use foreach:

```
//: holding/AdapterMethodIdiom.java
// The "Adapter Method" idiom allows you to use foreach
// with additional kinds of Iterables.
import java.util.*;

class ReversibleArrayList<T> extends ArrayList<T> {
  public ReversibleArrayList(Collection<T> c) { super(c); }
  public Iterable<T> reversed() {
    return new Iterable<T>() {
      public Iterator<T> iterator() {
        return new Iterator<T>() {
          int current = size() - 1;
          public boolean hasNext() { return current > -1; }
          public T next() { return get(current--); }
          public void remove() { // Not implemented
            throw new UnsupportedOperationException();
          }
```

```
        };
      }
    };
  }
}

public class AdapterMethodIdiom {
  public static void main(String[] args) {
    ReversibleArrayList<String> ral =
      new ReversibleArrayList<String>(
        Arrays.asList("To be or not to be".split(" ")));
    // Grabs the ordinary iterator via iterator():
    for(String s : ral)
      System.out.print(s + " ");
    System.out.println();
    // Hand it the Iterable of your choice
    for(String s : ral.reversed())
      System.out.print(s + " ");
  }
} /* Output:
To be or not to be
be to not or be To
*///:~
```

If you simply put the **ral** object in the foreach statement, you get the (default) forward iterator. But if you call **reversed( )** on the object, it produces different behavior.

Using this approach, I can add two adapter methods to the **IterableClass.java** example:

```
//: holding/MultiIterableClass.java
// Adding several Adapter Methods.
import java.util.*;

public class MultiIterableClass extends IterableClass {
  public Iterable<String> reversed() {
    return new Iterable<String>() {
      public Iterator<String> iterator() {
        return new Iterator<String>() {
          int current = words.length - 1;
          public boolean hasNext() { return current > -1; }
          public String next() { return words[current--]; }
          public void remove() { // Not implemented
            throw new UnsupportedOperationException();
```

```
          }
        };
      }
    };
  }
  public Iterable<String> randomized() {
    return new Iterable<String>() {
      public Iterator<String> iterator() {
        List<String> shuffled =
          new ArrayList<String>(Arrays.asList(words));
        Collections.shuffle(shuffled, new Random(47));
        return shuffled.iterator();
      }
    };
  }
  public static void main(String[] args) {
    MultiIterableClass mic = new MultiIterableClass();
    for(String s : mic.reversed())
      System.out.print(s + " ");
    System.out.println();
    for(String s : mic.randomized())
      System.out.print(s + " ");
    System.out.println();
    for(String s : mic)
      System.out.print(s + " ");
  }
} /* Output:
banana-shaped. be to Earth the know we how is that And
is banana-shaped. Earth that how the be And we know to
And that is how we know the Earth to be banana-shaped.
*///:~
```

Notice that the second method, **random( )**, doesn't create its own **Iterator** but simply returns the one from the shuffled **List**.

You can see from the output that the **Collections.shuffle( )** method doesn't affect the original array, but only shuffles the references in **shuffled**. This is only true because the **randomized( )** method wraps an **ArrayList** around the result of **Arrays.asList( )**. If the **List** produced by **Arrays.asList( )** is shuffled directly, it will modify the underlying array, as you can see here:

```
//: holding/ModifyingArraysAsList.java
import java.util.*;
```

```
public class ModifyingArraysAsList {
  public static void main(String[] args) {
    Random rand = new Random(47);
    Integer[] ia = { 1, 2, 3, 4, 5, 6, 7, 8, 9, 10 };
    List<Integer> list1 =
      new ArrayList<Integer>(Arrays.asList(ia));
    System.out.println("Before shuffling: " + list1);
    Collections.shuffle(list1, rand);
    System.out.println("After shuffling: " + list1);
    System.out.println("array: " + Arrays.toString(ia));

    List<Integer> list2 = Arrays.asList(ia);
    System.out.println("Before shuffling: " + list2);
    Collections.shuffle(list2, rand);
    System.out.println("After shuffling: " + list2);
    System.out.println("array: " + Arrays.toString(ia));
  }
} /* Output:
Before shuffling: [1, 2, 3, 4, 5, 6, 7, 8, 9, 10]
After shuffling: [4, 6, 3, 1, 8, 7, 2, 5, 10, 9]
array: [1, 2, 3, 4, 5, 6, 7, 8, 9, 10]
Before shuffling: [1, 2, 3, 4, 5, 6, 7, 8, 9, 10]
After shuffling: [9, 1, 6, 3, 7, 2, 5, 10, 4, 8]
array: [9, 1, 6, 3, 7, 2, 5, 10, 4, 8]
*///:~
```

In the first case, the output of **Arrays.asList( )** is handed to the
ArrayList( ) constructor, and this creates an **ArrayList** that references the
elements of **ia**. Shuffling these references doesn't modify the array. However,
if you use the result of **Arrays.asList(ia)** directly, shuffling modifies the
order of **ia**. It's important to be aware that **Arrays.asList( )** produces a **List**
object that uses the underlying array as its physical implementation. If you do
anything to that **List** that modifies it, and you don't want the original array
modified, you should make a copy into another container.

Exercise 32: (2) Following the example of **MultiIterableClass**, add
reversed( ) and **randomized( )** methods to
NonCollectionSequence.java, as well as making
NonCollectionSequence implement **Iterable**, and show that all the
approaches work in foreach statements.

Summary

Java provides a number of ways to hold objects:

---

1. An array associates numerical indexes to objects. It holds objects of a known type so that you don't have to cast the result when you're looking up an object. It can be multidimensional, and it can hold primitives. However, its size cannot be changed once you create it.

2. A **Collection** holds single elements, and a **Map** holds associated pairs. With Java generics, you specify the type of object to be held in the containers, so you can't put the wrong type into a container and you don't have to cast elements when you fetch them out of a container. Both **Collection**s and **Map**s automatically resize themselves as you add more elements. A container won't hold primitives, but autoboxing takes care of translating primitives back and forth to the wrapper types held in the container.

3. Like an array, a **List** also associates numerical indexes to objects— thus, arrays and **List**s are ordered containers.

4. Use an **ArrayList** if you're doing a lot of random accesses, but a **LinkedList** if you will be doing a lot of insertions and removals in the middle of the list.

5. The behavior of **Queue**s and stacks is provided via the **LinkedList**.

6. A **Map** is a way to associate not integral values, but *objects* with other objects. **HashMap**s are designed for rapid access, whereas a **TreeMap** keeps its keys in sorted order, and thus is not as fast as a **HashMap**. A **LinkedHashMap** keeps its elements in insertion order, but provides rapid access with hashing.

7. A **Set** only accepts one of each type of object. **HashSet**s provide maximally fast lookups, whereas **TreeSet**s keep the elements in sorted order. **LinkedHashSet**s keep elements in insertion order.

8. There's no need to use the legacy classes **Vector**, **Hashtable**, and **Stack** in new code.

It's helpful to look at a simplified diagram of the Java containers (without the abstract classes or legacy components). This only includes the interfaces and classes that you will encounter on a regular basis.

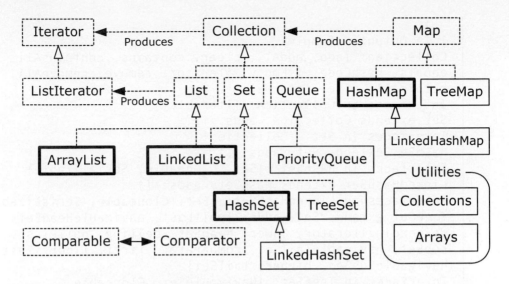

Simple Container Taxonomy

You'll see that there are really only four basic container components—**Map**, **List**, **Set**, and **Queue**—and only two or three implementations of each one (the **java.util.concurrent** implementations of **Queue** are not included in this diagram). The containers that you will use most often have heavy black lines around them.

The dotted boxes represent **interface**s, and the solid boxes are regular (concrete) classes. The dotted lines with hollow arrows indicate that a particular class is implementing an interface. The solid arrows show that a class can produce objects of the class the arrow is pointing to. For example, any **Collection** can produce an **Iterator**, and a **List** can produce a **ListIterator** (as well as an ordinary **Iterator**, since **List** is inherited from **Collection**).

Here's an example that shows the difference in methods between the various classes. The actual code is from the *Generics* chapter; I'm just calling it here to produce the output. The output also shows the interfaces that are implemented in each class or interface:

```
//: holding/ContainerMethods.java
import net.mindview.util.*;

public class ContainerMethods {
  public static void main(String[] args) {
    ContainerMethodDifferences.main(args);
```

```
    }
} /* Output: (Sample)
Collection: [add, addAll, clear, contains, containsAll,
equals, hashCode, isEmpty, iterator, remove, removeAll,
retainAll, size, toArray]
Interfaces in Collection: [Iterable]
Set extends Collection, adds: []
Interfaces in Set: [Collection]
HashSet extends Set, adds: []
Interfaces in HashSet: [Set, Cloneable, Serializable]
LinkedHashSet extends HashSet, adds: []
Interfaces in LinkedHashSet: [Set, Cloneable, Serializable]
TreeSet extends Set, adds: [pollLast, navigableHeadSet,
descendingIterator, lower, headSet, ceiling, pollFirst,
subSet, navigableTailSet, comparator, first, floor, last,
navigableSubSet, higher, tailSet]
Interfaces in TreeSet: [NavigableSet, Cloneable,
Serializable]
List extends Collection, adds: [listIterator, indexOf, get,
subList, set, lastIndexOf]
Interfaces in List: [Collection]
ArrayList extends List, adds: [ensureCapacity, trimToSize]
Interfaces in ArrayList: [List, RandomAccess, Cloneable,
Serializable]
LinkedList extends List, adds: [pollLast, offer,
descendingIterator, addFirst, peekLast, removeFirst,
peekFirst, removeLast, getLast, pollFirst, pop, poll,
addLast, removeFirstOccurrence, getFirst, element, peek,
offerLast, push, offerFirst, removeLastOccurrence]
Interfaces in LinkedList: [List, Deque, Cloneable,
Serializable]
Queue extends Collection, adds: [offer, element, peek,
poll]
Interfaces in Queue: [Collection]
PriorityQueue extends Queue, adds: [comparator]
Interfaces in PriorityQueue: [Serializable]
Map: [clear, containsKey, containsValue, entrySet, equals,
get, hashCode, isEmpty, keySet, put, putAll, remove, size,
values]
HashMap extends Map, adds: []
Interfaces in HashMap: [Map, Cloneable, Serializable]
LinkedHashMap extends HashMap, adds: []
Interfaces in LinkedHashMap: [Map]
```

```
SortedMap extends Map, adds: [subMap, comparator, firstKey,
lastKey, headMap, tailMap]
Interfaces in SortedMap: [Map]
TreeMap extends Map, adds: [descendingEntrySet, subMap,
pollLastEntry, lastKey, floorEntry, lastEntry, lowerKey,
navigableHeadMap, navigableTailMap, descendingKeySet,
tailMap, ceilingEntry, higherKey, pollFirstEntry,
comparator, firstKey, floorKey, higherEntry, firstEntry,
navigableSubMap, headMap, lowerEntry, ceilingKey]
Interfaces in TreeMap: [NavigableMap, Cloneable,
Serializable]
*///:~
```

You can see that all **Set**s except **TreeSet** have exactly the same interface as
Collection. **List** and **Collection** differ significantly, although **List** requires
methods that are in **Collection**. On the other hand, the methods in the
Queue interface stand alone; the **Collection** methods are not required to
create a functioning **Queue** implementation. Finally, the only intersection
between **Map** and **Collection** is the fact that a **Map** can produce
Collections using the **entrySet( )** and **values( )** methods.

Notice the tagging interface **java.util.RandomAccess**, which is attached to
ArrayList but not to **LinkedList**. This provides information for algorithms
that might want to dynamically change their behavior depending on the use
of a particular **List**.

It's true that this organization is somewhat odd, as object-oriented
hierarchies go. However, as you learn more about the containers in **java.util**
(in particular, in the *Containers in Depth* chapter), you'll see that there are
more issues than just a slightly odd inheritance structure. Container libraries
have always been difficult design problems—solving these problems involves
satisfying a set of forces that often oppose each other. So you should be
prepared for some compromises here and there.

Despite these issues, the Java containers are fundamental tools that you can
use on a day-to-day basis to make your programs simpler, more powerful,
and more effective. It might take you a little while to get comfortable with
some aspects of the library, but I think you'll find yourself rapidly acquiring
and using the classes in this library.

Solutions to selected exercises can be found in the electronic document *The Thinking in Java
Annotated Solution Guide*, available for sale from *www.MindView.net*.

Error Handling
with Exceptions

The basic philosophy of Java is that "badly formed code
will not be run."

The ideal time to catch an error is at compile time, before you even try to run
the program. However, not all errors can be detected at compile time. The
rest of the problems must be handled at run time through some formality that
allows the originator of the error to pass appropriate information to a
recipient who will know how to handle the difficulty properly.

Improved error recovery is one of the most powerful ways that you can
increase the robustness of your code. Error recovery is a fundamental
concern for every program you write, but it's especially important in Java,
where one of the primary goals is to create program components for others to
use. *To create a robust system, each component must be robust.* By
providing a consistent error-reporting model using exceptions, Java allows
components to reliably communicate problems to client code.

The goals for exception handling in Java are to simplify the creation of large,
reliable programs using less code than currently possible, and to do so with
more confidence that your application doesn't have an unhandled error.
Exceptions are not terribly difficult to learn, and are one of those features
that provide immediate and significant benefits to your project.

Because exception handling is the only official way that Java reports errors,
and it is enforced by the Java compiler, there are only so many examples that
can be written in this book without learning about exception handling. This
chapter introduces you to the code that you need to write to properly handle
exceptions, and shows how you can generate your own exceptions if one of
your methods gets into trouble.

Concepts

C and other earlier languages often had multiple error-handling schemes, and these were generally established by convention and not as part of the programming language. Typically, you returned a special value or set a flag, and the recipient was supposed to look at the value or the flag and determine that something was amiss. However, as the years passed, it was discovered that programmers who use a library tend to think of themselves as invincible—as in "Yes, errors might happen to others, but not in *my* code." So, not too surprisingly, they wouldn't check for the error conditions (and sometimes the error conditions were too silly to check for[1]). If you *were* thorough enough to check for an error every time you called a method, your code could turn into an unreadable nightmare. Because programmers could still coax systems out of these languages, they were resistant to admitting the truth: that this approach to handling errors was a major limitation to creating large, robust, maintainable programs.

The solution is to take the casual nature out of error handling and to enforce formality. This actually has a long history, because implementations of *exception handling* go back to operating systems in the 1960s, and even to BASIC's "**on error goto**." But C++ exception handling was based on Ada, and Java's is based primarily on C++ (although it looks more like Object Pascal).

The word "exception" is meant in the sense of "I take exception to that." At the point where the problem occurs, you might not know what to do with it, but you do know that you can't just continue on merrily; you must stop, and somebody, somewhere, must figure out what to do. But you don't have enough information in the current context to fix the problem. So you hand the problem out to a higher context where someone is qualified to make the proper decision.

The other rather significant benefit of exceptions is that they tend to reduce the complexity of error-handling code. Without exceptions, you must check for a particular error and deal with it at multiple places in your program. With exceptions, you no longer need to check for errors at the point of the method call, since the exception will guarantee that someone catches it. You

---

[1] The C programmer can look up the return value of **printf( )** for an example of this.

only need to handle the problem in one place, in the so-called *exception handler*. This saves you code, and it separates the code that describes what you want to do during normal execution from the code that is executed when things go awry. In general, reading, writing, and debugging code becomes much clearer with exceptions than when using the old way of error handling.

Basic exceptions

An *exceptional condition* is a problem that prevents the continuation of the current method or scope. It's important to distinguish an exceptional condition from a normal problem, in which you have enough information in the current context to somehow cope with the difficulty. With an exceptional condition, you cannot continue processing because you don't have the information necessary to deal with the problem *in the current context*. All you can do is jump out of the current context and relegate that problem to a higher context. This is what happens when you throw an exception.

Division is a simple example. If you're about to divide by zero, it's worth checking for that condition. But what does it mean that the denominator is zero? Maybe you know, in the context of the problem you're trying to solve in that particular method, how to deal with a zero denominator. But if it's an unexpected value, you can't deal with it and so must throw an exception rather than continuing along that execution path.

When you throw an exception, several things happen. First, the exception object is created in the same way that any Java object is created: on the heap, with **new**. Then the current path of execution (the one you couldn't continue) is stopped and the reference for the exception object is ejected from the current context. At this point the exception-handling mechanism takes over and begins to look for an appropriate place to continue executing the program. This appropriate place is the *exception handler,* whose job is to recover from the problem so the program can either try another tack or just continue.

As a simple example of throwing an exception, consider an object reference called **t**. It's possible that you might be passed a reference that hasn't been initialized, so you might want to check before trying to call a method using that object reference. You can send information about the error into a larger context by creating an object representing your information and "throwing" it out of your current context. This is called *throwing an exception*. Here's what it looks like:

```
if(t == null)
   throw new NullPointerException();
```

This throws the exception, which allows you—in the current context—to abdicate responsibility for thinking about the issue further. It's just magically handled somewhere else. Precisely *where* will be shown shortly.

Exceptions allow you to think of everything that you do as a transaction, and the exceptions guard those transactions: "...the fundamental premise of transactions is that we needed exception handling in distributed computations. Transactions are the computer equivalent of contract law. If anything goes wrong, we'll just blow away the whole computation."[2] You can also think about exceptions as a built-in undo system, because (with some care) you can have various recovery points in your program. If a part of the program fails, the exception will "undo" back to a known stable point in the program.

One of the most important aspects of exceptions is that if something bad happens, they don't allow a program to continue along its ordinary path. This has been a real problem in languages like C and C++; especially C, which had no way to force a program to stop going down a path if a problem occurred, so it was possible to ignore problems for a long time and get into a completely inappropriate state. Exceptions allow you to (if nothing else) force the program to stop and tell you what went wrong, or (ideally) force the program to deal with the problem and return to a stable state.

Exception arguments

As with any object in Java, you always create exceptions on the heap using **new**, which allocates storage and calls a constructor. There are two constructors in all standard exceptions: The first is the default constructor, and the second takes a string argument so that you can place pertinent information in the exception:

```
throw new NullPointerException("t = null");
```

This string can later be extracted using various methods, as you'll see.

---

[2] Jim Gray, Turing Award winner for his team's contributions on transactions, in an interview on *www.acmqueue.org*.

The keyword **throw** produces a number of interesting results. After creating an exception object with **new**, you give the resulting reference to **throw**. The object is, in effect, "returned" from the method, even though that object type isn't normally what the method is designed to return. A simplistic way to think about exception handling is as a different kind of return mechanism, although you get into trouble if you take that analogy too far. You can also exit from ordinary scopes by throwing an exception. In either case, an exception object is returned, and the method or scope exits.

Any similarity to an ordinary return from a method ends here, because *where* you return is someplace completely different from where you return for a normal method call. (You end up in an appropriate exception handler that might be far away—many levels on the call stack—from where the exception was thrown.)

In addition, you can throw any type of **Throwable**, which is the exception root class. Typically, you'll throw a different class of exception for each different type of error. The information about the error is represented both inside the exception object and implicitly in the name of the exception class, so someone in the bigger context can figure out what to do with your exception. (Often, the only information is the type of exception, and nothing meaningful is stored within the exception object.)

Catching an exception

To see how an exception is caught, you must first understand the concept of a *guarded region*. This is a section of code that might produce exceptions and is followed by the code to handle those exceptions.

The **try** block

If you're inside a method and you throw an exception (or another method that you call within this method throws an exception), that method will exit in the process of throwing. If you don't want a **throw** to exit the method, you can set up a special block within that method to capture the exception. This is called the *try block* because you "try" your various method calls there. The **try** block is an ordinary scope preceded by the keyword **try**:

```
try {
  // Code that might generate exceptions
}
```

If you were checking for errors carefully in a programming language that didn't support exception handling, you'd have to surround every method call with setup and error-testing code, even if you call the same method several times. With exception handling, you put everything in a **try** block and capture all the exceptions in one place. This means your code is much easier to write and read because the goal of the code is not confused with the error checking.

Exception handlers

Of course, the thrown exception must end up someplace. This "place" is the *exception handler,* and there's one for every exception type you want to catch. Exception handlers immediately follow the **try** block and are denoted by the keyword **catch**:

```
try {
  // Code that might generate exceptions
} catch(Type1 id1) {
  // Handle exceptions of Type1
} catch(Type2 id2) {
  // Handle exceptions of Type2
} catch(Type3 id3) {
  // Handle exceptions of Type3
}

// etc...
```

Each **catch** clause (exception handler) is like a little method that takes one and only one argument of a particular type. The identifier (**id1**, **id2**, and so on) can be used inside the handler, just like a method argument. Sometimes you never use the identifier because the type of the exception gives you enough information to deal with the exception, but the identifier must still be there.

The handlers must appear directly after the **try** block. If an exception is thrown, the exception-handling mechanism goes hunting for the first handler with an argument that matches the type of the exception. Then it enters that **catch** clause, and the exception is considered handled. The search for handlers stops once the **catch** clause is finished. Only the matching **catch** clause executes; it's not like a **switch** statement in which you need a **break** after each **case** to prevent the remaining ones from executing.

Note that within the **try** block, a number of different method calls might generate the same exception, but you need only one handler.

Termination vs. resumption

There are two basic models in exception-handling theory. Java supports *termination*,[3] in which you assume that the error is so critical that there's no way to get back to where the exception occurred. Whoever threw the exception decided that there was no way to salvage the situation, and they don't *want* to come back.

The alternative is called *resumption*. It means that the exception handler is expected to do something to rectify the situation, and then the faulting method is retried, presuming success the second time. If you want resumption, it means you still hope to continue execution after the exception is handled.

If you want resumption-like behavior in Java, don't throw an exception when you encounter an error. Instead, call a method that fixes the problem. Alternatively, place your **try** block inside a **while** loop that keeps reentering the **try** block until the result is satisfactory.

Historically, programmers using operating systems that supported resumptive exception handling eventually ended up using termination-like code and skipping resumption. So although resumption sounds attractive at first, it isn't quite so useful in practice. The dominant reason is probably the coupling that results: A resumptive handler would need to be aware of where the exception is thrown, and contain non-generic code specific to the throwing location. This makes the code difficult to write and maintain, especially for large systems where the exception can be generated from many points.

Creating your own exceptions

You're not stuck using the existing Java exceptions. The Java exception hierarchy can't foresee all the errors you might want to report, so you can create your own to denote a special problem that your library might encounter.

---

[3] As do most languages, including C++, C#, Python, D, etc.

To create your own exception class, you must inherit from an existing exception class, preferably one that is close in meaning to your new exception (although this is often not possible). The most trivial way to create a new type of exception is just to let the compiler create the default constructor for you, so it requires almost no code at all:

```
//: exceptions/InheritingExceptions.java
// Creating your own exceptions.

class SimpleException extends Exception {}

public class InheritingExceptions {
  public void f() throws SimpleException {
    System.out.println("Throw SimpleException from f()");
    throw new SimpleException();
  }
  public static void main(String[] args) {
    InheritingExceptions sed = new InheritingExceptions();
    try {
      sed.f();
    } catch(SimpleException e) {
      System.out.println("Caught it!");
    }
  }
} /* Output:
Throw SimpleException from f()
Caught it!
*///:~
```

The compiler creates a default constructor, which automatically (and invisibly) calls the base-class default constructor. Of course, in this case you don't get a **SimpleException(String)** constructor, but in practice that isn't used much. As you'll see, the most important thing about an exception is the class name, so most of the time an exception like the one shown here is satisfactory.

Here, the result is printed to the console, where it is automatically captured and tested with this book's output-display system. However, you may want to send error output to the *standard error* stream by writing to **System.err**. This is usually a better place to send error information than **System.out**, which may be redirected. If you send output to **System.err**, it will not be redirected along with **System.out** so the user is more likely to notice it.

You can also create an exception class that has a constructor with a **String** argument:

```
//: exceptions/FullConstructors.java

class MyException extends Exception {
  public MyException() {}
  public MyException(String msg) { super(msg); }
}

public class FullConstructors {
  public static void f() throws MyException {
    System.out.println("Throwing MyException from f()");
    throw new MyException();
  }
  public static void g() throws MyException {
    System.out.println("Throwing MyException from g()");
    throw new MyException("Originated in g()");
  }
  public static void main(String[] args) {
    try {
      f();
    } catch(MyException e) {
      e.printStackTrace(System.out);
    }
    try {
      g();
    } catch(MyException e) {
      e.printStackTrace(System.out);
    }
  }
} /* Output:
Throwing MyException from f()
MyException
        at FullConstructors.f(FullConstructors.java:11)
        at FullConstructors.main(FullConstructors.java:19)
Throwing MyException from g()
MyException: Originated in g()
        at FullConstructors.g(FullConstructors.java:15)
        at FullConstructors.main(FullConstructors.java:24)
*///:~
```

The added code is small: two constructors that define the way **MyException** is created. In the second constructor, the base-class constructor with a **String** argument is explicitly invoked by using the **super** keyword.

In the handlers, one of the **Throwable** (from which **Exception** is inherited) methods is called: **printStackTrace( )**. As you can see from the output, this produces information about the sequence of methods that were called to get to the point where the exception happened. Here, the information is sent to **System.out**, and automatically captured and displayed in the output. However, if you call the default version:

```
e.printStackTrace();
```

the information goes to the standard error stream.

Exercise 1: (2) Create a class with a **main( )** that throws an object of class **Exception** inside a **try** block. Give the constructor for **Exception** a **String** argument. Catch the exception inside a **catch** clause and print the **String** argument. Add a **finally** clause and print a message to prove you were there.

Exercise 2: (1) Define an object reference and initialize it to **null**. Try to call a method through this reference. Now wrap the code in a **try-catch** clause to catch the exception.

Exercise 3: (1) Write code to generate and catch an **ArrayIndexOutOfBoundsException**.

Exercise 4: (2) Create your own exception class using the **extends** keyword. Write a constructor for this class that takes a **String** argument and stores it inside the object with a **String** reference. Write a method that displays the stored **String**. Create a **try-catch** clause to exercise your new exception.

Exercise 5: (3) Create your own resumption-like behavior using a **while** loop that repeats until an exception is no longer thrown.

Exceptions and logging

You may also want to *log* the output using the **java.util.logging** facility. Although full details of logging are introduced in the supplement at *http://MindView.net/Books/BetterJava*, basic logging is straightforward enough to be used here.

```
//: exceptions/LoggingExceptions.java
```

```
// An exception that reports through a Logger.
import java.util.logging.*;
import java.io.*;

class LoggingException extends Exception {
  private static Logger logger =
    Logger.getLogger("LoggingException");
  public LoggingException() {
    StringWriter trace = new StringWriter();
    printStackTrace(new PrintWriter(trace));
    logger.severe(trace.toString());
  }
}

public class LoggingExceptions {
  public static void main(String[] args) {
    try {
      throw new LoggingException();
    } catch(LoggingException e) {
      System.err.println("Caught " + e);
    }
    try {
      throw new LoggingException();
    } catch(LoggingException e) {
      System.err.println("Caught " + e);
    }
  }
} /* Output: (85% match)
Aug 30, 2005 4:02:31 PM LoggingException <init>
SEVERE: LoggingException
        at
LoggingExceptions.main(LoggingExceptions.java:19)

Caught LoggingException
Aug 30, 2005 4:02:31 PM LoggingException <init>
SEVERE: LoggingException
        at
LoggingExceptions.main(LoggingExceptions.java:24)

Caught LoggingException
*///:~
```

The **static Logger.getLogger( )** method creates a **Logger** object associated with the **String** argument (usually the name of the package and class that the errors are about) which sends its output to **System.err**. The easiest way to write to a **Logger** is just to call the method associated with the level of logging message; here, **severe( )** is used. To produce the **String** for the logging message, we'd like to have the stack trace where the exception is thrown, but **printStackTrace( )** doesn't produce a **String** by default. To get a **String**, we need to use the overloaded **printStackTrace( )** that takes a **java.io.PrintWriter** object as an argument (all of this will be fully explained in the *I/O* chapter). If we hand the **PrintWriter** constructor a **java.io.StringWriter** object, the output can be extracted as a **String** by calling **toString( )**.

Although the approach used by **LoggingException** is very convenient because it builds all the logging infrastructure into the exception itself, and thus it works automatically without client programmer intervention, it's more common that you will be catching and logging someone else's exception, so you must generate the log message in the exception handler:

```
//: exceptions/LoggingExceptions2.java
// Logging caught exceptions.
import java.util.logging.*;
import java.io.*;

public class LoggingExceptions2 {
  private static Logger logger =
    Logger.getLogger("LoggingExceptions2");
  static void logException(Exception e) {
    StringWriter trace = new StringWriter();
    e.printStackTrace(new PrintWriter(trace));
    logger.severe(trace.toString());
  }
  public static void main(String[] args) {
    try {
      throw new NullPointerException();
    } catch(NullPointerException e) {
      logException(e);
    }
  }
} /* Output: (90% match)
Aug 30, 2005 4:07:54 PM LoggingExceptions2 logException
SEVERE: java.lang.NullPointerException
        at
LoggingExceptions2.main(LoggingExceptions2.java:16)
*///:~
```

The process of creating your own exceptions can be taken further. You can add extra constructors and members:

```
//: exceptions/ExtraFeatures.java
// Further embellishment of exception classes.
import static net.mindview.util.Print.*;

class MyException2 extends Exception {
  private int x;
  public MyException2() {}
  public MyException2(String msg) { super(msg); }
  public MyException2(String msg, int x) {
    super(msg);
    this.x = x;
  }
  public int val() { return x; }
  public String getMessage() {
    return "Detail Message: "+ x + " "+ super.getMessage();
  }
}

public class ExtraFeatures {
  public static void f() throws MyException2 {
    print("Throwing MyException2 from f()");
    throw new MyException2();
  }
  public static void g() throws MyException2 {
    print("Throwing MyException2 from g()");
    throw new MyException2("Originated in g()");
  }
  public static void h() throws MyException2 {
    print("Throwing MyException2 from h()");
    throw new MyException2("Originated in h()", 47);
  }
  public static void main(String[] args) {
    try {
      f();
    } catch(MyException2 e) {
      e.printStackTrace(System.out);
    }
    try {
      g();
    } catch(MyException2 e) {
      e.printStackTrace(System.out);
```

```
        }
      try {
        h();
      } catch(MyException2 e) {
        e.printStackTrace(System.out);
        System.out.println("e.val() = " + e.val());
      }
    }
  }
} /* Output:
Throwing MyException2 from f()
MyException2: Detail Message: 0 null
        at ExtraFeatures.f(ExtraFeatures.java:22)
        at ExtraFeatures.main(ExtraFeatures.java:34)
Throwing MyException2 from g()
MyException2: Detail Message: 0 Originated in g()
        at ExtraFeatures.g(ExtraFeatures.java:26)
        at ExtraFeatures.main(ExtraFeatures.java:39)
Throwing MyException2 from h()
MyException2: Detail Message: 47 Originated in h()
        at ExtraFeatures.h(ExtraFeatures.java:30)
        at ExtraFeatures.main(ExtraFeatures.java:44)
e.val() = 47
*///:~
```

A field **x** has been added, along with a method that reads that value and an additional constructor that sets it. In addition, **Throwable.getMessage( )** has been overridden to produce a more interesting detail message. **getMessage( )** is something like **toString( )** for exception classes.

Since an exception is just another kind of object, you can continue this process of embellishing the power of your exception classes. Keep in mind, however, that all this dressing-up might be lost on the client programmers using your packages, since they might simply look for the exception to be thrown and nothing more. (That's the way most of the Java library exceptions are used.)

Exercise 6: (1) Create two exception classes, each of which performs its own logging automatically. Demonstrate that these work.

Exercise 7: (1) Modify Exercise 3 so that the **catch** clause logs the results.

The exception specification

In Java, you're encouraged to inform the client programmer, who calls your method, of the exceptions that might be thrown from your method. This is civilized, because the caller can then know exactly what code to write to catch all potential exceptions. Of course, if the source code is available, the client programmer could hunt through and look for **throw** statements, but a library might not come with sources. To prevent this from being a problem, Java provides syntax (and *forces* you to use that syntax) to allow you to politely tell the client programmer what exceptions this method throws, so the client programmer can handle them. This is the *exception specification* and it's part of the method declaration, appearing after the argument list.

The exception specification uses an additional keyword, **throws**, followed by a list of all the potential exception types. So your method definition might look like this:

```
void f() throws TooBig, TooSmall, DivZero { //...
```

However, if you say

```
void f() { // ...
```

it means that no exceptions are thrown from the method (*except* for the exceptions inherited from **RuntimeException**, which can be thrown anywhere without exception specifications—these will be described later).

You can't lie about an exception specification. If the code within your method causes exceptions, but your method doesn't handle them, the compiler will detect this and tell you that you must either handle the exception or indicate with an exception specification that it may be thrown from your method. By enforcing exception specifications from top to bottom, Java guarantees that a certain level of exception correctness can be ensured at compile time.

There is one place you can lie: You can claim to throw an exception that you really don't. The compiler takes your word for it, and forces the users of your method to treat it as if it really does throw that exception. This has the beneficial effect of being a placeholder for that exception, so you can actually start throwing the exception later without requiring changes to existing code. It's also important for creating **abstract** base classes and **interface**s whose derived classes or implementations may need to throw exceptions.

Exceptions that are checked and enforced at compile time are called *checked exceptions*.

Exercise 8: (1) Write a class with a method that throws an exception of the type created in Exercise 4. Try compiling it without an exception specification to see what the compiler says. Add the appropriate exception specification. Try out your class and its exception inside a **try-catch** clause.

Catching any exception

It is possible to create a handler that catches any type of exception. You do this by catching the base-class exception type **Exception** (there are other types of base exceptions, but **Exception** is the base that's pertinent to virtually all programming activities):

```
catch(Exception e) {
  System.out.println("Caught an exception");
}
```

This will catch any exception, so if you use it you'll want to put it at the *end* of your list of handlers to avoid preempting any exception handlers that might otherwise follow it.

Since the **Exception** class is the base of all the exception classes that are important to the programmer, you don't get much specific information about the exception, but you can call the methods that come from *its* base type **Throwable**:

String getMessage( )
String getLocalizedMessage( )
Gets the detail message, or a message adjusted for this particular locale.

String toString( )
Returns a short description of the **Throwable**, including the detail message if there is one.

void printStackTrace( )
void printStackTrace(PrintStream)
void printStackTrace(java.io.PrintWriter)
Prints the **Throwable** and the **Throwable**'s call stack trace. The call stack shows the sequence of method calls that brought you to the point at which the exception was thrown. The first version prints to standard error, the second

and third print to a stream of your choice (in the *I/O* chapter, you'll
understand why there are two types of streams).

Throwable fillInStackTrace( )
Records information within this **Throwable** object about the current state of
the stack frames. Useful when an application is rethrowing an error or
exception (more about this shortly).

In addition, you get some other methods from **Throwable**'s base type
Object (everybody's base type). The one that might come in handy for
exceptions is **getClass( )**, which returns an object representing the class of
this object. You can in turn query this **Class** object for its name with
getName( ), which includes package information, or **getSimpleName( )**,
which produces the class name alone.

Here's an example that shows the use of the basic **Exception** methods:

```
//: exceptions/ExceptionMethods.java
// Demonstrating the Exception Methods.
import static net.mindview.util.Print.*;

public class ExceptionMethods {
  public static void main(String[] args) {
    try {
      throw new Exception("My Exception");
    } catch(Exception e) {
      print("Caught Exception");
      print("getMessage():" + e.getMessage());
      print("getLocalizedMessage():" +
        e.getLocalizedMessage());
      print("toString():" + e);
      print("printStackTrace():");
      e.printStackTrace(System.out);
    }
  }
} /* Output:
Caught Exception
getMessage():My Exception
getLocalizedMessage():My Exception
toString():java.lang.Exception: My Exception
printStackTrace():
java.lang.Exception: My Exception
        at ExceptionMethods.main(ExceptionMethods.java:8)
*///:~
```

You can see that the methods provide successively more information—each is effectively a superset of the previous one.

Exercise 9: (2) Create three new types of exceptions. Write a class with a method that throws all three. In **main( )**, call the method but only use a single **catch** clause that will catch all three types of exceptions.

The stack trace

The information provided by **printStackTrace( )** can also be accessed directly using **getStackTrace( )**. This method returns an array of stack trace elements, each representing one stack frame. Element zero is the top of the stack, and is the last method invocation in the sequence (the point this **Throwable** was created and thrown). The last element of the array and the bottom of the stack is the first method invocation in the sequence. This program provides a simple demonstration:

```
//: exceptions/WhoCalled.java
// Programmatic access to stack trace information.

public class WhoCalled {
  static void f() {
    // Generate an exception to fill in the stack trace
    try {
      throw new Exception();
    } catch (Exception e) {
      for(StackTraceElement ste : e.getStackTrace())
        System.out.println(ste.getMethodName());
    }
  }
  static void g() { f(); }
  static void h() { g(); }
  public static void main(String[] args) {
    f();
    System.out.println("------------------------------");
    g();
    System.out.println("------------------------------");
    h();
  }
} /* Output:
f
main
------------------------------
f
```

```
g
main
-------------------------------
f
g
h
main
*///:~
```

Here, we just print the method name, but you can also print the entire **StackTraceElement**, which contains additional information.

Rethrowing an exception

Sometimes you'll want to rethrow the exception that you just caught, particularly when you use **Exception** to catch any exception. Since you already have the reference to the current exception, you can simply rethrow that reference:

```
catch(Exception e) {
  System.out.println("An exception was thrown");
  throw e;
}
```

Rethrowing an exception causes it to go to the exception handlers in the next-higher context. Any further **catch** clauses for the same **try** block are still ignored. In addition, everything about the exception object is preserved, so the handler at the higher context that catches the specific exception type can extract all the information from that object.

If you simply rethrow the current exception, the information that you print about that exception in **printStackTrace( )** will pertain to the exception's origin, not the place where you rethrow it. If you want to install new stack trace information, you can do so by calling **fillInStackTrace( )**, which returns a **Throwable** object that it creates by stuffing the current stack information into the old exception object. Here's what it looks like:

```
//: exceptions/Rethrowing.java
// Demonstrating fillInStackTrace()

public class Rethrowing {
  public static void f() throws Exception {
    System.out.println("originating the exception in f()");
    throw new Exception("thrown from f()");
```

```java
        }
        public static void g() throws Exception {
            try {
                f();
            } catch(Exception e) {
                System.out.println("Inside g(),e.printStackTrace()");
                e.printStackTrace(System.out);
                throw e;
            }
        }
        public static void h() throws Exception {
            try {
                f();
            } catch(Exception e) {
                System.out.println("Inside h(),e.printStackTrace()");
                e.printStackTrace(System.out);
                throw (Exception)e.fillInStackTrace();
            }
        }
        public static void main(String[] args) {
            try {
                g();
            } catch(Exception e) {
                System.out.println("main: printStackTrace()");
                e.printStackTrace(System.out);
            }
            try {
                h();
            } catch(Exception e) {
                System.out.println("main: printStackTrace()");
                e.printStackTrace(System.out);
            }
        }
} /* Output:
originating the exception in f()
Inside g(),e.printStackTrace()
java.lang.Exception: thrown from f()
        at Rethrowing.f(Rethrowing.java:7)
        at Rethrowing.g(Rethrowing.java:11)
        at Rethrowing.main(Rethrowing.java:29)
main: printStackTrace()
java.lang.Exception: thrown from f()
        at Rethrowing.f(Rethrowing.java:7)
        at Rethrowing.g(Rethrowing.java:11)
```

```
          at Rethrowing.main(Rethrowing.java:29)
originating the exception in f()
Inside h(),e.printStackTrace()
java.lang.Exception: thrown from f()
        at Rethrowing.f(Rethrowing.java:7)
        at Rethrowing.h(Rethrowing.java:20)
        at Rethrowing.main(Rethrowing.java:35)
main: printStackTrace()
java.lang.Exception: thrown from f()
        at Rethrowing.h(Rethrowing.java:24)
        at Rethrowing.main(Rethrowing.java:35)
*///:~
```

The line where **fillInStackTrace( )** is called becomes the new point of
origin of the exception.

It's also possible to rethrow a different exception from the one you caught. If
you do this, you get a similar effect as when you use **fillInStackTrace( )**—
the information about the original site of the exception is lost, and what
you're left with is the information pertaining to the new **throw**:

```
//: exceptions/RethrowNew.java
// Rethrow a different object from the one that was caught.

class OneException extends Exception {
  public OneException(String s) { super(s); }
}

class TwoException extends Exception {
  public TwoException(String s) { super(s); }
}

public class RethrowNew {
  public static void f() throws OneException {
    System.out.println("originating the exception in f()");
    throw new OneException("thrown from f()");
  }
  public static void main(String[] args) {
    try {
      try {
        f();
      } catch(OneException e) {
        System.out.println(
          "Caught in inner try, e.printStackTrace()");
        e.printStackTrace(System.out);
```

```
          throw new TwoException("from inner try");
        }
    } catch(TwoException e) {
      System.out.println(
        "Caught in outer try, e.printStackTrace()");
      e.printStackTrace(System.out);
    }
  }
} /* Output:
originating the exception in f()
Caught in inner try, e.printStackTrace()
OneException: thrown from f()
        at RethrowNew.f(RethrowNew.java:15)
        at RethrowNew.main(RethrowNew.java:20)
Caught in outer try, e.printStackTrace()
TwoException: from inner try
        at RethrowNew.main(RethrowNew.java:25)
*///:~
```

The final exception knows only that it came from the inner **try** block and not from **f( )**.

You never have to worry about cleaning up the previous exception, or any exceptions for that matter. They're all heap-based objects created with **new**, so the garbage collector automatically cleans them all up.

Exception chaining

Often you want to catch one exception and throw another, but still keep the information about the originating exception—this is called *exception chaining*. Prior to JDK 1.4, programmers had to write their own code to preserve the original exception information, but now all **Throwable** subclasses have the option to take a *cause* object in their constructor. The *cause* is intended to be the originating exception, and by passing it in you maintain the stack trace back to its origin, even though you're creating and throwing a new exception.

It's interesting to note that the only **Throwable** subclasses that provide the *cause* argument in the constructor are the three fundamental exception classes **Error** (used by the JVM to report system errors), **Exception**, and **RuntimeException**. If you want to chain any other exception types, you do it through the **initCause( )** method rather than the constructor.

Here's an example that allows you to dynamically add fields to a
DynamicFields object at run time:

```
//: exceptions/DynamicFields.java
// {ThrowsException}
// A Class that dynamically adds fields to itself.
// Demonstrates exception chaining.
import static net.mindview.util.Print.*;
class DynamicFieldsException extends Exception {}

public class DynamicFields {
  private Object[][] fields;
  public DynamicFields(int initialSize) {
    fields = new Object[initialSize][2];
    for(int i = 0; i < initialSize; i++)
      fields[i] = new Object[] { null, null };
  }
  public String toString() {
    StringBuilder result = new StringBuilder();
    for(Object[] obj : fields) {
      result.append(obj[0]);
      result.append(": ");
      result.append(obj[1]);
      result.append("\n");
    }
    return result.toString();
  }
  private int hasField(String id) {
    for(int i = 0; i < fields.length; i++)
      if(id.equals(fields[i][0]))
        return i;
    return -1;
  }
  private int
  getFieldNumber(String id) throws NoSuchFieldException {
    int fieldNum = hasField(id);
    if(fieldNum == -1)
      throw new NoSuchFieldException();
    return fieldNum;
  }
  private int makeField(String id) {
    for(int i = 0; i < fields.length; i++)
      if(fields[i][0] == null) {
        fields[i][0] = id;
```

```java
        return i;
      }
    // No empty fields. Add one:
    Object[][] tmp = new Object[fields.length + 1][2];
    for(int i = 0; i < fields.length; i++)
      tmp[i] = fields[i];
    for(int i = fields.length; i < tmp.length; i++)
      tmp[i] = new Object[] { null, null };
    fields = tmp;
    // Recursive call with expanded fields:
    return makeField(id);
  }
  public Object
  getField(String id) throws NoSuchFieldException {
    return fields[getFieldNumber(id)][1];
  }
  public Object setField(String id, Object value)
  throws DynamicFieldsException {
    if(value == null) {
      // Most exceptions don't have a "cause" constructor.
      // In these cases you must use initCause(),
      // available in all Throwable subclasses.
      DynamicFieldsException dfe =
        new DynamicFieldsException();
      dfe.initCause(new NullPointerException());
      throw dfe;
    }
    int fieldNumber = hasField(id);
    if(fieldNumber == -1)
      fieldNumber = makeField(id);
    Object result = null;
    try {
      result = getField(id); // Get old value
    } catch(NoSuchFieldException e) {
      // Use constructor that takes "cause":
      throw new RuntimeException(e);
    }
    fields[fieldNumber][1] = value;
    return result;
  }
  public static void main(String[] args) {
    DynamicFields df = new DynamicFields(3);
    print(df);
    try {
```

```
            df.setField("d", "A value for d");
            df.setField("number", 47);
            df.setField("number2", 48);
            print(df);
            df.setField("d", "A new value for d");
            df.setField("number3", 11);
            print("df: " + df);
            print("df.getField(\"d\") : " + df.getField("d"));
            Object field = df.setField("d", null); // Exception
        } catch(NoSuchFieldException e) {
            e.printStackTrace(System.out);
        } catch(DynamicFieldsException e) {
            e.printStackTrace(System.out);
        }
    }
} /* Output:
null: null
null: null
null: null

d: A value for d
number: 47
number2: 48

df: d: A new value for d
number: 47
number2: 48
number3: 11

df.getField("d") : A new value for d
DynamicFieldsException
        at DynamicFields.setField(DynamicFields.java:64)
        at DynamicFields.main(DynamicFields.java:94)
Caused by: java.lang.NullPointerException
        at DynamicFields.setField(DynamicFields.java:66)
        ... 1 more
*///:~
```

Each **DynamicFields** object contains an array of **Object-Object** pairs. The first object is the field identifier (a **String**), and the second is the field value, which can be any type except an unwrapped primitive. When you create the object, you make an educated guess about how many fields you need. When you call **setField( )**, it either finds the existing field by that name or creates a new one, and puts in your value. If it runs out of space, it adds new space by creating an array of length one longer and copying the old elements in. If you try to put in a **null** value, then it throws a **DynamicFieldsException** by creating one and using **initCause( )** to insert a **NullPointerException** as the cause.

As a return value, **setField( )** also fetches out the old value at that field location using **getField( )**, which could throw a **NoSuchFieldException**. If the client programmer calls **getField( )**, then they are responsible for handling **NoSuchFieldException**, but if this exception is thrown inside **setField( )**, it's a programming error, so the **NoSuchFieldException** is converted to a **RuntimeException** using the constructor that takes a *cause* argument.

You'll notice that **toString( )** uses a **StringBuilder** to create its result. You'll learn more about **StringBuilder** in the *Strings* chapter, but in general you'll want to use it whenever you're writing a **toString( )** that involves looping, as is the case here.

Exercise 10: (2) Create a class with two methods, **f( )** and **g( )**. In **g( )**, throw an exception of a new type that you define. In **f( )**, call **g( )**, catch its exception and, in the **catch** clause, throw a different exception (of a second type that you define). Test your code in **main( )**.

Exercise 11: (1) Repeat the previous exercise, but inside the **catch** clause, wrap **g( )**'s exception in a **RuntimeException**.

Standard Java exceptions

The Java class **Throwable** describes anything that can be thrown as an exception. There are two general types of **Throwable** objects ("types of" = "inherited from"). **Error** represents compile-time and system errors that you don't worry about catching (except in very special cases). **Exception** is the basic type that can be thrown from any of the standard Java library class methods and from your methods and runtime accidents. So the Java programmer's base type of interest is usually **Exception**.

The best way to get an overview of the exceptions is to browse the JDK documentation. It's worth doing this once just to get a feel for the various exceptions, but you'll soon see that there isn't anything special between one exception and the next except for the name. Also, the number of exceptions in Java keeps expanding; basically, it's pointless to print them in a book. Any new library you get from a third-party vendor will probably have its own exceptions as well. The important thing to understand is the concept and what you should do with the exceptions.

The basic idea is that the name of the exception represents the problem that occurred, and the exception name is intended to be relatively self-explanatory. The exceptions are not all defined in **java.lang**; some are created to support other libraries such as **util**, **net**, and **io**, which you can see from their full class names or what they are inherited from. For example, all I/O exceptions are inherited from **java.io.IOException**.

Special case: **RuntimeException**

The first example in this chapter was

```
if(t == null)
  throw new NullPointerException();
```

It can be a bit horrifying to think that you must check for **null** on every reference that is passed into a method (since you can't know if the caller has passed you a valid reference). Fortunately, you don't—this is part of the standard runtime checking that Java performs for you, and if any call is made to a **null** reference, Java will automatically throw a **NullPointerException**. So the above bit of code is always superfluous, although you may want to perform other checks in order to guard against the appearance of a **NullPointerException**.

There's a whole group of exception types that are in this category. They're always thrown automatically by Java and you don't need to include them in your exception specifications. Conveniently enough, they're all grouped together by putting them under a single base class called **RuntimeException**, which is a perfect example of inheritance: It establishes a family of types that have some characteristics and behaviors in common. Also, you never need to write an exception specification saying that a method might throw a **RuntimeException** (or any type inherited from **RuntimeException**), because they are *unchecked exceptions*. Because they indicate bugs, you don't usually catch a **RuntimeException**—it's dealt with automatically. If you were forced to check for **RuntimeException**s, your code could get too messy. Even though you don't typically catch **RuntimeExceptions**, in your own packages you might choose to throw some of the **RuntimeException**s.

What happens when you don't catch such exceptions? Since the compiler doesn't enforce exception specifications for these, it's quite plausible that a **RuntimeException** could percolate all the way out to your **main( )** method without being caught. To see what happens in this case, try the following example:

```
//: exceptions/NeverCaught.java
// Ignoring RuntimeExceptions.
// {ThrowsException}

public class NeverCaught {
  static void f() {
    throw new RuntimeException("From f()");
  }
  static void g() {
    f();
  }
  public static void main(String[] args) {
    g();
  }
} ///:~
```

You can already see that a **RuntimeException** (or anything inherited from it) is a special case, since the compiler doesn't require an exception specification for these types. The output is reported to **System.err**:

```
Exception in thread "main" java.lang.RuntimeException: From f()
        at NeverCaught.f(NeverCaught.java:7)
        at NeverCaught.g(NeverCaught.java:10)
        at NeverCaught.main(NeverCaught.java:13)
```

So the answer is: If a **RuntimeException** gets all the way out to **main( )** without being caught, **printStackTrace( )** is called for that exception as the program exits.

Keep in mind that only exceptions of type **RuntimeException** (and subclasses) can be ignored in your coding, since the compiler carefully enforces the handling of all checked exceptions. The reasoning is that a **RuntimeException** represents a programming error, which is:

1.   An error you cannot anticipate. For example, a **null** reference that is outside of your control.

2. An error that you, as a programmer, should have checked for in your code (such as **ArrayIndexOutOfBoundsException** where you should have paid attention to the size of the array). An exception that happens from point #1 often becomes an issue for point #2.

You can see what a tremendous benefit it is to have exceptions in this case, since they help in the debugging process.

It's interesting to notice that you cannot classify Java exception handling as a single-purpose tool. Yes, it is designed to handle those pesky runtime errors that will occur because of forces outside your code's control, but it's also essential for certain types of programming bugs that the compiler cannot detect.

Exercise 12: (3) Modify **innerclasses/Sequence.java** so that it throws an appropriate exception if you try to put in too many elements.

Performing cleanup
with **finally**

There's often some piece of code that you want to execute whether or not an exception is thrown within a **try** block. This usually pertains to some operation other than memory recovery (since that's taken care of by the garbage collector). To achieve this effect, you use a **finally** clause[4] at the end of all the exception handlers. The full picture of an exception-handling section is thus:

```
try {
  // The guarded region: Dangerous activities
  // that might throw A, B, or C
} catch(A a1) {
  // Handler for situation A
} catch(B b1) {
  // Handler for situation B
} catch(C c1) {
  // Handler for situation C
```

---

[4] C++ exception handling does not have the **finally** clause because it relies on destructors to accomplish this sort of cleanup.

```
  } finally {
    // Activities that happen every time
  }
```

To demonstrate that the **finally** clause always runs, try this program:

```
//: exceptions/FinallyWorks.java
// The finally clause is always executed.

class ThreeException extends Exception {}

public class FinallyWorks {
  static int count = 0;
  public static void main(String[] args) {
    while(true) {
      try {
        // Post-increment is zero first time:
        if(count++ == 0)
          throw new ThreeException();
        System.out.println("No exception");
      } catch(ThreeException e) {
        System.out.println("ThreeException");
      } finally {
        System.out.println("In finally clause");
        if(count == 2) break; // out of "while"
      }
    }
  }
} /* Output:
ThreeException
In finally clause
No exception
In finally clause
*///:~
```

From the output, you can see that the **finally** clause is executed whether or not an exception is thrown.

This program also gives a hint for how you can deal with the fact that exceptions in Java do not allow you to resume back to where the exception was thrown, as discussed earlier. If you place your **try** block in a loop, you can establish a condition that must be met before you continue the program. You can also add a **static** counter or some other device to allow the loop to try several different approaches before giving up. This way you can build a greater level of robustness into your programs.

What's **finally** for?

In a language without garbage collection *and* without automatic destructor calls,[5] **finally** is important because it allows the programmer to guarantee the release of memory regardless of what happens in the **try** block. But Java has garbage collection, so releasing memory is virtually never a problem. Also, it has no destructors to call. So when do you need to use **finally** in Java?

The **finally** clause is necessary when you need to set something *other* than memory back to its original state. This is some kind of cleanup like an open file or network connection, something you've drawn on the screen, or even a switch in the outside world, as modeled in the following example:

```
//: exceptions/Switch.java
import static net.mindview.util.Print.*;

public class Switch {
  private boolean state = false;
  public boolean read() { return state; }
  public void on() { state = true; print(this); }
  public void off() { state = false; print(this); }
  public String toString() { return state ? "on" : "off"; }
} ///:~
```

```
//: exceptions/OnOffException1.java
public class OnOffException1 extends Exception {} ///:~
```

```
//: exceptions/OnOffException2.java
public class OnOffException2 extends Exception {} ///:~
```

```
//: exceptions/OnOffSwitch.java
// Why use finally?

public class OnOffSwitch {
  private static Switch sw = new Switch();
```

---

[5] A destructor is a function that's always called when an object becomes unused. You always know exactly where and when the destructor gets called. C++ has automatic destructor calls, and C# (which is much more like Java) has a way that automatic destruction can occur.

```
      public static void f()
      throws OnOffException1,OnOffException2 {}
      public static void main(String[] args) {
        try {
          sw.on();
          // Code that can throw exceptions...
          f();
          sw.off();
        } catch(OnOffException1 e) {
          System.out.println("OnOffException1");
          sw.off();
        } catch(OnOffException2 e) {
          System.out.println("OnOffException2");
          sw.off();
        }
      }
    } /* Output:
    on
    off
    *///:~
```

The goal here is to make sure that the switch is off when **main( )** is completed, so **sw.off( )** is placed at the end of the **try** block and at the end of each exception handler. But it's possible that an exception might be thrown that isn't caught here, so **sw.off( )** would be missed. However, with **finally** you can place the cleanup code from a **try** block in just one place:

```
//: exceptions/WithFinally.java
// Finally Guarantees cleanup.

public class WithFinally {
  static Switch sw = new Switch();
  public static void main(String[] args) {
    try {
      sw.on();
      // Code that can throw exceptions...
      OnOffSwitch.f();
    } catch(OnOffException1 e) {
      System.out.println("OnOffException1");
    } catch(OnOffException2 e) {
      System.out.println("OnOffException2");
    } finally {
      sw.off();
    }
  }
```

```
  }
} /* Output:
on
off
*///:~
```

Here the **sw.off( )** has been moved to just one place, where it's guaranteed to
run no matter what happens.

Even in cases in which the exception is not caught in the current set of **catch**
clauses, **finally** will be executed before the exception-handling mechanism
continues its search for a handler at the next higher level:

```
//: exceptions/AlwaysFinally.java
// Finally is always executed.
import static net.mindview.util.Print.*;

class FourException extends Exception {}

public class AlwaysFinally {
  public static void main(String[] args) {
    print("Entering first try block");
    try {
      print("Entering second try block");
      try {
        throw new FourException();
      } finally {
        print("finally in 2nd try block");
      }
    } catch(FourException e) {
      System.out.println(
        "Caught FourException in 1st try block");
    } finally {
      System.out.println("finally in 1st try block");
    }
  }
} /* Output:
Entering first try block
Entering second try block
finally in 2nd try block
Caught FourException in 1st try block
finally in 1st try block
*///:~
```

The **finally** statement will also be executed in situations in which **break** and **continue** statements are involved. Note that, along with the labeled **break** and labeled **continue**, **finally** eliminates the need for a **goto** statement in Java.

Exercise 13: (2) Modify Exercise 9 by adding a **finally** clause. Verify that your **finally** clause is executed, even if a **NullPointerException** is thrown.

Exercise 14: (2) Show that **OnOffSwitch.java** can fail by throwing a **RuntimeException** inside the **try** block.

Exercise 15: (2) Show that **WithFinally.java** doesn't fail by throwing a **RuntimeException** inside the **try** block.

Using **finally** during **return**

Because a **finally** clause is always executed, it's possible to return from multiple points within a method and still guarantee that important cleanup will be performed:

```
//: exceptions/MultipleReturns.java
import static net.mindview.util.Print.*;

public class MultipleReturns {
  public static void f(int i) {
    print("Initialization that requires cleanup");
    try {
      print("Point 1");
      if(i == 1) return;
      print("Point 2");
      if(i == 2) return;
      print("Point 3");
      if(i == 3) return;
      print("End");
      return;
    } finally {
      print("Performing cleanup");
    }
  }
  public static void main(String[] args) {
    for(int i = 1; i <= 4; i++)
      f(i);
  }
} /* Output:
```

Thinking in Java   Bruce Eckel

```
Initialization that requires cleanup
Point 1
Performing cleanup
Initialization that requires cleanup
Point 1
Point 2
Performing cleanup
Initialization that requires cleanup
Point 1
Point 2
Point 3
Performing cleanup
Initialization that requires cleanup
Point 1
Point 2
Point 3
End
Performing cleanup
*///:~
```

You can see from the output that it doesn't matter where you return from inside the **finally** class.

Exercise 16: (2) Modify **reusing/CADSystem.java** to demonstrate that **return**ing from the middle of a **try-finally** will still perform proper cleanup.

Exercise 17: (3) Modify **polymorphism/Frog.java** so that it uses **try-finally** to guarantee proper cleanup, and show that this works even if you **return** from the middle of the **try-finally**.

Pitfall: the lost exception

Unfortunately, there's a flaw in Java's exception implementation. Although exceptions are an indication of a crisis in your program and should never be ignored, it's possible for an exception to simply be lost. This happens with a particular configuration using a **finally** clause:

```
//: exceptions/LostMessage.java
// How an exception can be lost.

class VeryImportantException extends Exception {
  public String toString() {
    return "A very important exception!";
  }
```

```
    }

class HoHumException extends Exception {
  public String toString() {
    return "A trivial exception";
  }
}

public class LostMessage {
  void f() throws VeryImportantException {
    throw new VeryImportantException();
  }
  void dispose() throws HoHumException {
    throw new HoHumException();
  }
  public static void main(String[] args) {
    try {
      LostMessage lm = new LostMessage();
      try {
        lm.f();
      } finally {
        lm.dispose();
      }
    } catch(Exception e) {
      System.out.println(e);
    }
  }
} /* Output:
A trivial exception
*///:~
```

You can see from the output that there's no evidence of the
VeryImportantException, which is simply replaced by the
HoHumException in the **finally** clause. This is a rather serious pitfall,
since it means that an exception can be completely lost, and in a far more
subtle and difficult-to-detect fashion than the preceding example. In contrast,
C++ treats the situation in which a second exception is thrown before the first
one is handled as a dire programming error. Perhaps a future version of Java
will repair this problem (on the other hand, you will typically wrap any
method that throws an exception, such as **dispose( )** in the example above,
inside a **try-catch** clause).

An even simpler way to lose an exception is just to **return** from inside a
finally clause:

```
//: exceptions/ExceptionSilencer.java

public class ExceptionSilencer {
  public static void main(String[] args) {
    try {
      throw new RuntimeException();
    } finally {
      // Using 'return' inside the finally block
      // will silence any thrown exception.
      return;
    }
  }
} ///:~
```

If you run this program you'll see that it produces no output, even though an exception is thrown.

Exercise 18: (3) Add a second level of exception loss to **LostMessage.java** so that the **HoHumException** is itself replaced by a third exception.

Exercise 19: (2) Repair the problem in **LostMessage.java** by guarding the call in the **finally** clause.

Exception restrictions

When you override a method, you can throw only the exceptions that have been specified in the base-class version of the method. This is a useful restriction, since it means that code that works with the base class will automatically work with any object derived from the base class (a fundamental OOP concept, of course), including exceptions.

This example demonstrates the kinds of restrictions imposed (at compile time) for exceptions:

```
//: exceptions/StormyInning.java
// Overridden methods may throw only the exceptions
// specified in their base-class versions, or exceptions
// derived from the base-class exceptions.

class BaseballException extends Exception {}
class Foul extends BaseballException {}
class Strike extends BaseballException {}
```

```
abstract class Inning {
  public Inning() throws BaseballException {}
  public void event() throws BaseballException {
    // Doesn't actually have to throw anything
  }
  public abstract void atBat() throws Strike, Foul;
  public void walk() {} // Throws no checked exceptions
}

class StormException extends Exception {}
class RainedOut extends StormException {}
class PopFoul extends Foul {}

interface Storm {
  public void event() throws RainedOut;
  public void rainHard() throws RainedOut;
}

public class StormyInning extends Inning implements Storm {
  // OK to add new exceptions for constructors, but you
  // must deal with the base constructor exceptions:
  public StormyInning()
    throws RainedOut, BaseballException {}
  public StormyInning(String s)
    throws Foul, BaseballException {}
  // Regular methods must conform to base class:
//! void walk() throws PopFoul {} //Compile error
  // Interface CANNOT add exceptions to existing
  // methods from the base class:
//! public void event() throws RainedOut {}
  // If the method doesn't already exist in the
  // base class, the exception is OK:
  public void rainHard() throws RainedOut {}
  // You can choose to not throw any exceptions,
  // even if the base version does:
  public void event() {}
  // Overridden methods can throw inherited exceptions:
  public void atBat() throws PopFoul {}
  public static void main(String[] args) {
    try {
      StormyInning si = new StormyInning();
      si.atBat();
    } catch(PopFoul e) {
      System.out.println("Pop foul");
```

```
      } catch(RainedOut e) {
        System.out.println("Rained out");
      } catch(BaseballException e) {
        System.out.println("Generic baseball exception");
      }
      // Strike not thrown in derived version.
      try {
        // What happens if you upcast?
        Inning i = new StormyInning();
        i.atBat();
        // You must catch the exceptions from the
        // base-class version of the method:
      } catch(Strike e) {
        System.out.println("Strike");
      } catch(Foul e) {
        System.out.println("Foul");
      } catch(RainedOut e) {
        System.out.println("Rained out");
      } catch(BaseballException e) {
        System.out.println("Generic baseball exception");
      }
    }
} ///:~
```

In **Inning**, you can see that both the constructor and the **event( )** method say that they will throw an exception, but they never do. This is legal because it allows you to force the user to catch any exceptions that might be added in overridden versions of **event( )**. The same idea holds for **abstract** methods, as seen in **atBat( )**.

The interface **Storm** is interesting because it contains one method (**event( )**) that is defined in **Inning**, and one method that isn't. Both methods throw a new type of exception, **RainedOut**. When **StormyInning extends Inning** and **implements Storm**, you'll see that the **event( )** method in **Storm** *cannot* change the exception interface of **event( )** in **Inning**. Again, this makes sense because otherwise you'd never know if you were catching the correct thing when working with the base class. Of course, if a method described in an interface is not in the base class, such as **rainHard( )**, then there's no problem if it throws exceptions.

The restriction on exceptions does not apply to constructors. You can see in **StormyInning** that a constructor can throw anything it wants, regardless of what the base-class constructor throws. However, since a base-class constructor must always be called one way or another (here, the default constructor is called automatically), the derived-class constructor must declare any base-class constructor exceptions in its exception specification.

A derived-class constructor cannot catch exceptions thrown by its base-class constructor.

The reason **StormyInning.walk( )** will not compile is that it throws an exception, but **Inning.walk( )** does not. If this were allowed, then you could write code that called **Inning.walk( )** and that didn't have to handle any exceptions, but then when you substituted an object of a class derived from **Inning**, exceptions would be thrown so your code would break. By forcing the derived-class methods to conform to the exception specifications of the base-class methods, substitutability of objects is maintained.

The overridden **event( )** method shows that a derived-class version of a method may choose not to throw any exceptions, even if the base-class version does. Again, this is fine since it doesn't break code that is written assuming the base-class version throws exceptions. Similar logic applies to **atBat( )**, which throws **PopFoul**, an exception that is derived from **Foul** thrown by the base-class version of **atBat( )**. This way, if you write code that works with **Inning** and calls **atBat( )**, you must catch the **Foul** exception. Since **PopFoul** is derived from **Foul**, the exception handler will also catch **PopFoul**.

The last point of interest is in **main( )**. Here, you can see that if you're dealing with exactly a **StormyInning** object, the compiler forces you to catch only the exceptions that are specific to that class, but if you upcast to the base type, then the compiler (correctly) forces you to catch the exceptions for the base type. All these constraints produce much more robust exception-handling code.[6]

Although exception specifications are enforced by the compiler during inheritance, the exception specifications are not part of the type of a method, which comprises only the method name and argument types. Therefore, you cannot overload methods based on exception specifications. In addition, just

---

[6] ISO C++ added similar constraints that require derived-method exceptions to be the same as, or derived from, the exceptions thrown by the base-class method. This is one case in which C++ is actually able to check exception specifications at compile time.

---

because an exception specification exists in a base-class version of a method doesn't mean that it must exist in the derived-class version of the method. This is quite different from inheritance rules, where a method in the base class must also exist in the derived class. Put another way, the "exception specification interface" for a particular method may narrow during inheritance and overriding, but it may not widen—this is precisely the opposite of the rule for the class interface during inheritance.

Exercise 20: (3) Modify **StormyInning.java** by adding an **UmpireArgument** exception type and methods that throw this exception. Test the modified hierarchy.

Constructors

It's important that you always ask, "If an exception occurs, will everything be properly cleaned up?" Most of the time you're fairly safe, but with constructors there's a problem. The constructor puts the object into a safe starting state, but it might perform some operation—such as opening a file— that doesn't get cleaned up until the user is finished with the object and calls a special cleanup method. If you throw an exception from inside a constructor, these cleanup behaviors might not occur properly. This means that you must be especially diligent while you write your constructor.

You might think that **finally** is the solution. But it's not quite that simple, because **finally** performs the cleanup code *every time*. If a constructor fails partway through its execution, it might not have successfully created some part of the object that will be cleaned up in the **finally** clause.

In the following example, a class called **InputFile** is created that opens a file and allows you to read it one line at a time. It uses the classes **FileReader** and **BufferedReader** from the Java standard I/O library that will be discussed in the *I/O* chapter. These classes are simple enough that you probably won't have any trouble understanding their basic use:

```
//: exceptions/InputFile.java
// Paying attention to exceptions in constructors.
import java.io.*;

public class InputFile {
  private BufferedReader in;
  public InputFile(String fname) throws Exception {
    try {
```

```
      in = new BufferedReader(new FileReader(fname));
      // Other code that might throw exceptions
    } catch(FileNotFoundException e) {
      System.out.println("Could not open " + fname);
      // Wasn't open, so don't close it
      throw e;
    } catch(Exception e) {
      // All other exceptions must close it
      try {
        in.close();
      } catch(IOException e2) {
        System.out.println("in.close() unsuccessful");
      }
      throw e; // Rethrow
    } finally {
      // Don't close it here!!!
    }
  }
  public String getLine() {
    String s;
    try {
      s = in.readLine();
    } catch(IOException e) {
      throw new RuntimeException("readLine() failed");
    }
    return s;
  }
  public void dispose() {
    try {
      in.close();
      System.out.println("dispose() successful");
    } catch(IOException e2) {
      throw new RuntimeException("in.close() failed");
    }
  }
} ///:~
```

The constructor for **InputFile** takes a **String** argument, which is the name
of the file you want to open. Inside a **try** block, it creates a **FileReader** using
the file name. A **FileReader** isn't particularly useful until you use it to create
a **BufferedReader**. One of the benefits of **InputFile** is that it combines
these two actions.

If the **FileReader** constructor is unsuccessful, it throws a **FileNotFoundException**. This is the one case in which you don't want to close the file, because it wasn't successfully opened. Any *other* **catch** clauses must close the file because it *was* opened by the time those **catch** clauses are entered. (Of course, this gets trickier if more than one method can throw a **FileNotFoundException**. In that case, you'll usually have to break things into several **try** blocks.) The **close( )** method might throw an exception so it is tried and caught even though it's within the block of another **catch** clause—it's just another pair of curly braces to the Java compiler. After performing local operations, the exception is rethrown, which is appropriate because this constructor failed, and you don't want the calling method to assume that the object has been properly created and is valid.

In this example, the **finally** clause is definitely *not* the place to **close( )** the file, since that would close it every time the constructor completed. We want the file to be open for the useful lifetime of the **InputFile** object.

The **getLine( )** method returns a **String** containing the next line in the file. It calls **readLine( )**, which can throw an exception, but that exception is caught so that **getLine( )** doesn't throw any exceptions. One of the design issues with exceptions is whether to handle an exception completely at this level, to handle it partially and pass the same exception (or a different one) on, or whether to simply pass it on. Passing it on, when appropriate, can certainly simplify coding. In this situation, the **getLine( )** method *converts* the exception to a **RuntimeException** to indicate a programming error.

The **dispose( )** method must be called by the user when the **InputFile** object is no longer needed. This will release the system resources (such as file handles) that are used by the **BufferedReader** and/or **FileReader** objects. You don't want to do this until you're finished with the **InputFile** object. You might think of putting such functionality into a **finalize( )** method, but as mentioned in the *Initialization & Cleanup* chapter, you can't always be sure that **finalize( )** will be called (even if you *can* be sure that it will be called, you don't know *when*). This is one of the downsides to Java: All cleanup— other than memory cleanup—doesn't happen automatically, so you must inform the client programmers that they are responsible.

The safest way to use a class which might throw an exception during construction and which requires cleanup is to use nested **try** blocks:

```
//: exceptions/Cleanup.java
```

```
// Guaranteeing proper cleanup of a resource.

public class Cleanup {
  public static void main(String[] args) {
    try {
      InputFile in = new InputFile("Cleanup.java");
      try {
        String s;
        int i = 1;
        while((s = in.getLine()) != null)
          ; // Perform line-by-line processing here...
      } catch(Exception e) {
        System.out.println("Caught Exception in main");
        e.printStackTrace(System.out);
      } finally {
        in.dispose();
      }
    } catch(Exception e) {
      System.out.println("InputFile construction failed");
    }
  }
} /* Output:
dispose() successful
*///:~
```

Look carefully at the logic here: The construction of the **InputFile** object is
effectively in its own **try** block. If that construction fails, the outer **catch**
clause is entered and **dispose( )** is not called. However, if construction
succeeds then you want to make sure the object is cleaned up, so immediately
after construction you create a new **try** block. The **finally** that performs
cleanup is associated with the *inner* **try** block; this way, the **finally** clause is
not executed if construction fails, and it is *always* executed if construction
succeeds.

This general cleanup idiom should still be used if the constructor throws no
exceptions. The basic rule is: Right after you create an object that requires
cleanup, begin a **try-finally**:

```
//: exceptions/CleanupIdiom.java
// Each disposable object must be followed by a try-finally

class NeedsCleanup { // Construction can't fail
  private static long counter = 1;
  private final long id = counter++;
```

```java
  public void dispose() {
    System.out.println("NeedsCleanup " + id + " disposed");
  }
}

class ConstructionException extends Exception {}

class NeedsCleanup2 extends NeedsCleanup {
  // Construction can fail:
  public NeedsCleanup2() throws ConstructionException {}
}

public class CleanupIdiom {
  public static void main(String[] args) {
    // Section 1:
    NeedsCleanup nc1 = new NeedsCleanup();
    try {
      // ...
    } finally {
      nc1.dispose();
    }

    // Section 2:
    // If construction cannot fail you can group objects:
    NeedsCleanup nc2 = new NeedsCleanup();
    NeedsCleanup nc3 = new NeedsCleanup();
    try {
      // ...
    } finally {
      nc3.dispose(); // Reverse order of construction
      nc2.dispose();
    }

    // Section 3:
    // If construction can fail you must guard each one:
    try {
      NeedsCleanup2 nc4 = new NeedsCleanup2();
      try {
        NeedsCleanup2 nc5 = new NeedsCleanup2();
        try {
          // ...
        } finally {
          nc5.dispose();
        }
```

```
      } catch(ConstructionException e) { // nc5 constructor
        System.out.println(e);
      } finally {
        nc4.dispose();
      }
    } catch(ConstructionException e) { // nc4 constructor
      System.out.println(e);
    }
  }
} /* Output:
NeedsCleanup 1 disposed
NeedsCleanup 3 disposed
NeedsCleanup 2 disposed
NeedsCleanup 5 disposed
NeedsCleanup 4 disposed
*///:~
```

In **main( )**, section 1 is fairly straightforward: You follow a disposable object with a **try-finally**. If the object construction cannot fail, no **catch** is necessary. In section 2, you can see that objects with constructors that cannot fail can be grouped together for both construction and cleanup.

Section 3 shows how to deal with objects whose constructors can fail *and* which need cleanup. To properly handle this situation, things get messy, because you must surround each construction with its own **try-catch**, and each object construction must be followed by a **try-finally** to guarantee cleanup.

The messiness of exception handling in this case is a strong argument for creating constructors that cannot fail, although this is not always possible.

Note that if **dispose( )** can throw an exception you might need additional **try** blocks. Basically, you must think carefully about all the possibilities and guard for each one.

Exercise 21: (2) Demonstrate that a derived-class constructor cannot catch exceptions thrown by its base-class constructor.

Exercise 22: (2) Create a class called **FailingConstructor** with a constructor that might fail partway through the construction process and throw an exception. In **main( )**, write code that properly guards against this failure.

Exercise 23: (4) Add a class with a **dispose( )** method to the previous exercise. Modify **FailingConstructor** so that the constructor creates one of these disposable objects as a member object, after which the constructor might throw an exception, after which it creates a second disposable member object. Write code to properly guard against failure, and in **main( )** verify that all possible failure situations are covered.

Exercise 24: (3) Add a **dispose( )** method to the **FailingConstructor** class and write code to properly use this class.

Exception matching

When an exception is thrown, the exception-handling system looks through the "nearest" handlers in the order they are written. When it finds a match, the exception is considered handled, and no further searching occurs.

Matching an exception doesn't require a perfect match between the exception and its handler. A derived-class object will match a handler for the base class, as shown in this example:

```
//: exceptions/Human.java
// Catching exception hierarchies.

class Annoyance extends Exception {}
class Sneeze extends Annoyance {}

public class Human {
  public static void main(String[] args) {
    // Catch the exact type:
    try {
      throw new Sneeze();
    } catch(Sneeze s) {
      System.out.println("Caught Sneeze");
    } catch(Annoyance a) {
      System.out.println("Caught Annoyance");
    }
    // Catch the base type:
    try {
      throw new Sneeze();
    } catch(Annoyance a) {
      System.out.println("Caught Annoyance");
    }
  }
} /* Output:
```

```
Caught Sneeze
Caught Annoyance
*///:~
```

The **Sneeze** exception will be caught by the first **catch** clause that it matches, which is the first one, of course. However, if you remove the first **catch** clause, leaving only the **catch** clause for **Annoyance**, the code still works because it's catching the base class of **Sneeze**. Put another way, **catch(Annoyance a)** will catch an **Annoyance** *or any class derived from it*. This is useful because if you decide to add more derived exceptions to a method, then the client programmer's code will not need changing as long as the client catches the base-class exceptions.

If you try to "mask" the derived-class exceptions by putting the base-class **catch** clause first, like this:

```
try {
  throw new Sneeze();
} catch(Annoyance a) {
  // ...
} catch(Sneeze s) {
  // ...
}
```

the compiler will give you an error message, since it sees that the **Sneeze** **catch** clause can never be reached.

Exercise 25: (2) Create a three-level hierarchy of exceptions. Now create a base-class **A** with a method that throws an exception at the base of your hierarchy. Inherit **B** from **A** and override the method so it throws an exception at level two of your hierarchy. Repeat by inheriting class **C** from **B**. In **main( )**, create a **C** and upcast it to **A**, then call the method.

Alternative approaches

An exception-handling system is a trapdoor that allows your program to abandon execution of the normal sequence of statements. The trapdoor is used when an "exceptional condition" occurs, such that normal execution is no longer possible or desirable. Exceptions represent conditions that the current method is unable to handle. The reason exception-handling systems were developed is because the approach of dealing with each possible error condition produced by each function call was too onerous, and programmers simply weren't doing it. As a result, they were ignoring the errors. It's worth observing that the issue of programmer convenience in handling errors was a prime motivation for exceptions in the first place.

One of the important guidelines in exception handling is "Don't catch an exception unless you know what to do with it." In fact, one of the important *goals* of exception handling is to move the error-handling code away from the point where the errors occur. This allows you to focus on what you want to accomplish in one section of your code, and how you're going to deal with problems in a distinct separate section of your code. As a result, your mainline code is not cluttered with error-handling logic, and it's much easier to understand and maintain. Exception handling also tends to reduce the amount of error-handling code, by allowing one handler to deal with many error sites.

Checked exceptions complicate this scenario a bit, because they force you to add **catch** clauses in places where you may not be ready to handle an error. This results in the "harmful if swallowed" problem:

```
try {
  // ... to do something useful
} catch(ObligatoryException e) {} // Gulp!
```

Programmers (myself included, in the 1st edition of this book) would just do the simplest thing, and "swallow" the exception—often unintentionally, but once you do it, the compiler has been satisfied, so unless you remember to revisit and correct the code, the exception will be lost. The exception happens, but it vanishes completely when swallowed. Because the compiler forces you to write code right away to handle the exception, this seems like the easiest solution even though it's probably the worst thing you can do.

Horrified upon realizing that I had done this, in the 2nd edition I "fixed" the problem by printing the stack trace inside the handler (as is still seen—appropriately—in a number of examples in this chapter). While this is useful to trace the behavior of exceptions, it still indicates that you don't really know what to do with the exception at that point in your code. In this section you'll learn about some of the issues and complications arising from checked exceptions, and options that you have when dealing with them.

This topic seems simple. But it is not only complicated, it is also an issue of some volatility. There are people who are staunchly rooted on either side of the fence and who feel that the correct answer (theirs) is blatantly obvious. I believe the reason for one of these positions is the distinct benefit seen in going from a poorly typed language like pre-ANSI C to a strong, statically typed language (that is, checked at compile time) like C++ or Java. When you make that transition (as I did), the benefits are so dramatic that it can seem like static type checking is always the best answer to most problems. My hope is to relate a little bit of my own evolution that has brought the *absolute* value of static type checking into question; clearly, it's very helpful much of the time, but there's a fuzzy line we cross when it begins to get in the way and become a hindrance (one of my favorite quotes is "All models are wrong. Some are useful.").

History

Exception handling originated in systems like PL/1 and Mesa, and later appeared in CLU, Smalltalk, Modula-3, Ada, Eiffel, C++, Python, Java, and the post-Java languages Ruby and C#. The Java design is similar to C++, except in places where the Java designers felt that the C++ approach caused problems.

To provide programmers with a framework that they were more likely to use for error handling and recovery, exception handling was added to C++ rather late in the standardization process, promoted by Bjarne Stroustrup, the language's original author. The model for C++ exceptions came primarily from CLU. However, other languages existed at that time that also supported exception handling: Ada, Smalltalk (both of these had exceptions but no exception specifications) and Modula-3 (which included both exceptions and specifications).

In their seminal paper[7] on the subject, Liskov and Snyder observe that a major defect of languages like C, which report errors in a transient fashion, is that:

> *"...every invocation must be followed by a conditional test to determine what the outcome was. This requirement leads to programs that are difficult to read, and probably inefficient as well, thus discouraging programmers from signaling and handling exceptions."*

---

7 Barbara Liskov and Alan Snyder, *Exception Handling in CLU*, IEEE Transactions on Software Engineering, Vol. SE-5, No. 6, November 1979. This paper is not available on the Internet, only in print form, so you'll have to contact a library to get a copy.

Thus one of the original motivations of exception handling was to prevent this requirement, but with checked exceptions in Java we commonly see exactly this kind of code. They go on to say:

> *"...requiring that the text of a handler be attached to the invocation that raises the exception would lead to unreadable programs in which expressions were broken up with handlers."*

Following the CLU approach when designing C++ exceptions, Stroustrup stated that the goal was to reduce the amount of code required to recover from errors. I believe that he was observing that programmers were typically not writing error-handling code in C because the amount and placement of such code was daunting and distracting. As a result, they were used to doing it the C way, ignoring errors in code and using debuggers to track down problems. To use exceptions, these C programmers had to be convinced to write "additional" code that they weren't normally writing. Thus, to draw them into a better way of handling errors, the amount of code they would need to "add" must not be onerous. I think it's important to keep this goal in mind when looking at the effects of checked exceptions in Java.

C++ brought an additional idea over from CLU: the exception specification, to programmatically state in the method signature the exceptions that could result from calling that method. The exception specification really has two purposes. It can say, "I'm originating this exception in my code; you handle it." But it can also mean, "I'm ignoring this exception that can occur as a result of my code; you handle it." We've been focusing on the "you handle it" part when looking at the mechanics and syntax of exceptions, but here I'm particularly interested in the fact that we often ignore exceptions and that's what the exception specification can state.

In C++ the exception specification is not part of the type information of a function. The only compile-time checking is to ensure that exception specifications are used consistently; for example, if a function or method throws exceptions, then the overloaded or derived versions must also throw those exceptions. Unlike Java, however, no compile-time checking occurs to determine whether or not the function or method will actually throw that exception, or whether the exception specification is complete (that is, whether it accurately describes all exceptions that may be thrown). That validation does happen, but only at run time. If an exception is thrown that violates the exception specification, the C++ program will call the standard library function **unexpected( )**.

It is interesting to note that, because of the use of templates, exception specifications are not used at all in the Standard C++ Library. In Java, there are restrictions on the way that Java generics can be used with exception specifications.

Perspectives

First, it's worth noting that Java effectively invented the checked exception (clearly inspired by C++ exception specifications and the fact that C++ programmers typically don't bother with them). However, it was an experiment which no subsequent language has chosen to duplicate.

Secondly, checked exceptions appear to be an "obvious good thing" when seen in introductory examples and in small programs. It has been suggested that the subtle difficulties begin to appear when programs start to get large. Of course, largeness usually doesn't happen overnight; it creeps. Languages that may not be suited for large-scale projects are used for small projects. These projects grow, and at some point we realize that things have gone from "manageable" to "difficult." This is what I'm suggesting may be the case with too much type checking; in particular, with checked exceptions.

The scale of the program seems to be a significant issue. This is a problem because most discussions tend to use small programs as demonstrations. One of the C# designers observed that:

> "Examination of small programs leads to the conclusion that requiring exception specifications could both enhance developer productivity and enhance code quality, but experience with large software projects suggests a different result—decreased productivity and little or no increase in code quality." [8]

In reference to uncaught exceptions, the CLU creators stated:

> "We felt it was unrealistic to require the programmer to provide handlers in situations where no meaningful action can be taken." [9]

---

[8] *http://discuss.develop.com/archives/wa.exe?A2=ind0011A&L=DOTNET&P=R32820*

[9] *Exception Handling in CLU*, Liskov & Snyder.

When explaining why a function declaration with no specification means that it can throw *any* exception, rather than *no* exceptions, Stroustrup states:

> *"However, that would require exception specifications for essentially every function, would be a significant cause for recompilation, and would inhibit cooperation with software written in other languages. This would encourage programmers to subvert the exception-handling mechanisms and to write spurious code to suppress exceptions. It would provide a false sense of security to people who failed to notice the exception."* [10]

We see this very behavior—subverting the exceptions—happening with checked exceptions in Java.

Martin Fowler (author of *UML Distilled*, *Refactoring*, and *Analysis Patterns*) wrote the following to me:

> *"...on the whole I think that exceptions are good, but Java checked exceptions are more trouble than they are worth."*

I now think that Java's important step was to unify the error-reporting model, so that all errors are *reported* using exceptions. This wasn't happening with C++, because for backward compatibility with C the old model of just ignoring errors was still available. But if you have consistent reporting with exceptions, then exceptions can be used if desired, and if not, they will propagate out to the highest level (the console or other container program). When Java modified the C++ model so that exceptions were the only way to report errors, the extra enforcement of checked exceptions may have become less necessary.

In the past, I have been a strong believer that both checked exceptions and static type checking were essential to robust program development. However, both anecdotal and direct experience [11] with languages that are more dynamic than static has led me to think that the great benefits actually come from:

---

[10] Bjarne Stroustrup, *The C++ Programming Language*, 3rd Edition (Addison-Wesley, 1997), p. 376.

[11] Indirectly with Smalltalk via conversations with many experienced programmers in that language; directly with Python (*www.Python.org*).

1. A unified error-reporting model via exceptions, regardless of whether the programmer is forced by the compiler to handle them.

2. Type checking, regardless of *when* it takes place. That is, as long as proper use of a type is enforced, it often doesn't matter if it happens at compile time or run time.

On top of this, there are very significant productivity benefits to reducing the compile-time constraints upon the programmer. Indeed, *reflection* and *generics* are required to compensate for the overconstraining nature of static typing, as you shall see in a number of examples throughout the book.

I've already been told by some that what I say here constitutes blasphemy, and by uttering these words my reputation will be destroyed, civilizations will fall, and a higher percentage of programming projects will fail. The belief that the compiler can save your project by pointing out errors at compile time runs strong, but it's even more important to realize the limitation of what the compiler is able to do; in the supplement you will find at *http://MindView.net/Books/BetterJava*, I emphasize the value of an automated build process and unit testing, which give you far more leverage than you get by trying to turn everything into a syntax error. It's worth keeping in mind that:

> *"A good programming language is one that helps programmers write good programs. No programming language will prevent its users from writing bad programs."* [12]

In any event, the likelihood of checked exceptions ever being removed from Java seems dim. It would be too radical of a language change, and proponents within Sun appear to be quite strong. Sun has a history and policy of absolute backwards compatibility—to give you a sense of this, virtually all Sun software runs on all Sun hardware, no matter how old. However, if you find that some checked exceptions are getting in your way, or especially if you find yourself being forced to catch exceptions, but you don't know what to do with them, there are some alternatives.

---

[12] Kees Koster, designer of the CDL language, as quoted by Bertrand Meyer, designer of the Eiffel language, *www.elj.com/elj/v1/n1/bm/right/*.

Passing exceptions to the console

In simple programs, like many of those in this book, the easiest way to preserve the exceptions without writing a lot of code is to pass them out of **main( )** to the console. For example, if you want to open a file for reading (something you'll learn about in detail in the *I/O* chapter), you must open and close a **FileInputStream**, which throws exceptions. For a simple program, you can do this (you'll see this approach used in numerous places throughout this book):

```
//: exceptions/MainException.java
import java.io.*;

public class MainException {
  // Pass all exceptions to the console:
  public static void main(String[] args) throws Exception {
    // Open the file:
    FileInputStream file =
      new FileInputStream("MainException.java");
    // Use the file ...
    // Close the file:
    file.close();
  }
} ///:~
```

Note that **main( )** is also a method that may have an exception specification, and here the type of exception is **Exception**, the root class of all checked exceptions. By passing it out to the console, you are relieved from writing **try-catch** clauses within the body of **main( )**. (Unfortunately, file I/O is significantly more complex than it would appear to be from this example, so don't get too excited until after you've read the *I/O* chapter).

Exercise 26: (1) Change the file name string in **MainException.java** to name a file that doesn't exist. Run the program and note the result.

Converting checked to unchecked exceptions

Throwing an exception from **main( )** is convenient when you're writing simple programs for your own consumption, but is not generally useful. The real problem is when you are writing an ordinary method body, and you call another method and realize, "I have no idea what to do with this exception here, but I don't want to swallow it or print some banal message." With chained exceptions, a new and simple solution presents itself. You simply "wrap" a checked exception inside a **RuntimeException** by passing it to the **RuntimeException** constructor, like this:

```
try {
  // ... to do something useful
} catch(IDontKnowWhatToDoWithThisCheckedException e) {
  throw new RuntimeException(e);
}
```

This seems to be an ideal solution if you want to "turn off" the checked exception—you don't swallow it, and you don't have to put it in your method's exception specification, but because of exception chaining you don't lose any information from the original exception.

This technique provides the option to ignore the exception and let it bubble up the call stack without being required to write **try-catch** clauses and/or exception specifications. However, you may still catch and handle the specific exception by using **getCause( )**, as seen here:

```
//: exceptions/TurnOffChecking.java
// "Turning off" Checked exceptions.
import java.io.*;
import static net.mindview.util.Print.*;

class WrapCheckedException {
  void throwRuntimeException(int type) {
    try {
      switch(type) {
        case 0: throw new FileNotFoundException();
        case 1: throw new IOException();
        case 2: throw new RuntimeException("Where am I?");
        default: return;
      }
    } catch(Exception e) { // Adapt to unchecked:
      throw new RuntimeException(e);
    }
  }
}

class SomeOtherException extends Exception {}

public class TurnOffChecking {
```

```java
  public static void main(String[] args) {
    WrapCheckedException wce = new WrapCheckedException();
    // You can call throwRuntimeException() without a try
    // block, and let RuntimeExceptions leave the method:
    wce.throwRuntimeException(3);
    // Or you can choose to catch exceptions:
    for(int i = 0; i < 4; i++)
      try {
        if(i < 3)
          wce.throwRuntimeException(i);
        else
          throw new SomeOtherException();
      } catch(SomeOtherException e) {
          print("SomeOtherException: " + e);
      } catch(RuntimeException re) {
        try {
          throw re.getCause();
        } catch(FileNotFoundException e) {
          print("FileNotFoundException: " + e);
        } catch(IOException e) {
          print("IOException: " + e);
        } catch(Throwable e) {
          print("Throwable: " + e);
        }
      }
  }
} /* Output:
FileNotFoundException: java.io.FileNotFoundException
IOException: java.io.IOException
Throwable: java.lang.RuntimeException: Where am I?
SomeOtherException: SomeOtherException
*///:~
```

WrapCheckedException.throwRuntimeException( ) contains code that generates different types of exceptions. These are caught and wrapped inside **RuntimeException** objects, so they become the "cause" of those exceptions.

In **TurnOffChecking,** you can see that it's possible to call **throwRuntimeException( )** with no **try** block because the method does not throw any checked exceptions. However, when you're ready to catch exceptions, you still have the ability to catch any exception you want by putting your code inside a **try** block. You start by catching all the exceptions you explicitly know might emerge from the code in your **try** block—in this case, **SomeOtherException** is caught first. Lastly, you catch **RuntimeException** and **throw** the result of **getCause( )** (the wrapped exception). This extracts the originating exceptions, which can then be handled in their own **catch** clauses.

The technique of wrapping a checked exception in a **RuntimeException** will be used when appropriate throughout the rest of this book. Another solution is to create your own subclass of **RuntimeException**. This way, it doesn't need to be caught, but someone can catch it if they want to.

Exercise 27: (1) Modify Exercise 3 to convert the exception to a **RuntimeException**.

Exercise 28: (1) Modify Exercise 4 so that the custom exception class inherits from **RuntimeException**, and show that the compiler allows you to leave out the **try** block.

Exercise 29: (1) Modify all the exception types in **StormyInning.java** so that they **extend RuntimeException**, and show that no exception specifications or **try** blocks are necessary. Remove the '//!' comments and show how the methods can be compiled without specifications.

Exercise 30: (2) Modify **Human.java** so that the exceptions inherit from **RuntimeException**. Modify **main( )** so that the technique in **TurnOffChecking.java** is used to handle the different types of exceptions.

Exception guidelines

Use exceptions to:

1. Handle problems at the appropriate level. (Avoid catching exceptions unless you know what to do with them.)

2. Fix the problem and call the method that caused the exception again.

3. Patch things up and continue without retrying the method.

4. Calculate some alternative result instead of what the method was supposed to produce.

5. Do whatever you can in the current context and rethrow the *same* exception to a higher context.

6.   Do whatever you can in the current context and throw a *different* exception to a higher context.

7.   Terminate the program.

8.   Simplify. (If your exception scheme makes things more complicated, then it is painful and annoying to use.)

9.   Make your library and program safer. (This is a short-term investment for debugging, and a long-term investment for application robustness.)

Summary

Exceptions are integral to programming with Java; you can accomplish only so much without knowing how to work with them. For that reason, exceptions are introduced at this point in the book—there are many libraries (like I/O, mentioned earlier) that you can't use without handling exceptions.

One of the advantages of exception handling is that it allows you to concentrate on the problem you're trying to solve in one place, and then deal with the errors from that code in another place. And although exceptions are generally explained as tools that allow you to *report* and *recover from* errors at run time, I have come to wonder how often the "recovery" aspect is implemented, or even possible. My perception is that it is less than 10 percent of the time, and even then it probably amounts to unwinding the stack to a known stable state rather than actually performing any kind of resumptive behavior. Whether or not this is true, I have come to believe that the "reporting" function is where the essential value of exceptions lie. The fact that Java effectively insists that all errors be reported in the form of exceptions is what gives it a great advantage over languages like C++, which allow you to report errors in a number of different ways, or not at all. A consistent error-reporting system means that you no longer have to ask the question "Are errors slipping through the cracks?" with each piece of code you write (as long as you don't "swallow" the exceptions, that is!).

As you will see in future chapters, by laying this question to rest—even if you do so by throwing a **RuntimeException**—your design and implementation efforts can be focused on more interesting and challenging issues.

Solutions to selected exercises can be found in the electronic document *The Thinking in Java Annotated Solution Guide*, available for sale from *www.MindView.net*.

Strings

String manipulation is arguably one of the most common activities in computer programming.

This is especially true in Web systems, where Java is heavily used. In this chapter, we'll look more deeply at what is certainly the most commonly used class in the language, **String**, along with some of its associated classes and utilities.

Immutable **String**s

Objects of the **String** class are immutable. If you examine the JDK documentation for the **String** class, you'll see that every method in the class that appears to modify a **String** actually creates and returns a brand new **String** object containing the modification. The original **String** is left untouched.

Consider the following code:

```
//: strings/Immutable.java
import static net.mindview.util.Print.*;

public class Immutable {
  public static String upcase(String s) {
    return s.toUpperCase();
  }
  public static void main(String[] args) {
    String q = "howdy";
    print(q); // howdy
    String qq = upcase(q);
    print(qq); // HOWDY
    print(q); // howdy
  }
} /* Output:
howdy
HOWDY
howdy
*///:~
```

When **q** is passed in to **upcase( )** it's actually a copy of the reference to **q**. The object this reference is connected to stays in a single physical location. The references are copied as they are passed around.

Looking at the definition for **upcase( )**, you can see that the reference that's passed in has the name **s**, and it exists for only as long as the body of **upcase( )** is being executed. When **upcase( )** completes, the local reference **s** vanishes. **upcase( )** returns the result, which is the original string with all the characters set to uppercase. Of course, it actually returns a reference to the result. But it turns out that the reference that it returns is for a new object, and the original **q** is left alone.

This behavior is usually what you want. Suppose you say:

```
String s = "asdf";
String x = Immutable.upcase(s);
```

Do you really want the **upcase( )** method to *change* the argument? To the reader of the code, an argument usually looks like a piece of information provided to the method, not something to be modified. This is an important guarantee, since it makes code easier to write and understand.

Overloading '+' vs. **StringBuilder**

Since **String** objects are immutable, you can alias to a particular **String** as many times as you want. Because a **String** is read-only, there's no possibility that one reference will change something that will affect the other references.

Immutability can have efficiency issues. A case in point is the operator '+' that has been overloaded for **String** objects. Overloading means that an operation has been given an extra meaning when used with a particular class. (The '+' and '+=' for **String** are the only operators that are overloaded in Java, and Java does not allow the programmer to overload any others.)[1]

---

[1] C++ allows the programmer to overload operators at will. Because this can often be a complicated process (see Chapter 10 of *Thinking in C++, 2nd Edition,* Prentice Hall, 2000), the Java designers deemed it a "bad" feature that shouldn't be included in Java. It wasn't so bad that they didn't end up doing it themselves, and ironically enough, operator overloading would be much easier to use in Java than in C++. This can be seen in Python (see *www.Python.org*) and C#, which have garbage collection and straightforward operator overloading.

The '+' operator allows you to concatenate **Strings**:

```
//: strings/Concatenation.java

public class Concatenation {
  public static void main(String[] args) {
    String mango = "mango";
    String s = "abc" + mango + "def" + 47;
    System.out.println(s);
  }
} /* Output:
abcmangodef47
*///:~
```

You could imagine how this *might* work. The **String** "abc" could have a method **append( )** that creates a new **String** object containing "abc" concatenated with the contents of **mango**. The new **String** object would then create another new **String** that added "def," and so on.

This would certainly work, but it requires the creation of a lot of **String** objects just to put together this new **String**, and then you have a bunch of intermediate **String** objects that need to be garbage collected. I suspect that the Java designers tried this approach first (which is a lesson in software design—you don't really know anything about a system until you try it out in code and get something working). I also suspect that they discovered it delivered unacceptable performance.

To see what really happens, you can decompile the above code using the **javap** tool that comes as part of the JDK. Here's the command line:

```
javap -c Concatenation
```

The **-c** flag will produce the JVM bytecodes. After we strip out the parts we're not interested in and do a bit of editing, here are the relevant bytecodes:

```
public static void main(java.lang.String[]);
  Code:
   Stack=2, Locals=3, Args_size=1
    0:    ldc #2; //String mango
    2:    astore_1
    3:    new #3; //class StringBuilder
    6:    dup
    7:    invokespecial #4; //StringBuilder."<init>":()
    10:   ldc #5; //String abc
```

```
12:     invokevirtual #6; //StringBuilder.append:(String)
15:     aload_1
16:     invokevirtual #6; //StringBuilder.append:(String)
19:     ldc #7; //String def
21:     invokevirtual #6; //StringBuilder.append:(String)
24:     bipush 47
26:     invokevirtual #8; //StringBuilder.append:(I)
29:     invokevirtual #9; //StringBuilder.toString:()
32:     astore_2
33:     getstatic #10; //Field System.out:PrintStream;
36:     aload_2
37:     invokevirtual #11; // PrintStream.println:(String)
40:     return
```

If you've had experience with assembly language, this may look familiar to you—statements like **dup** and **invokevirtual** are the Java Virtual Machine (JVM) equivalent of assembly language. If you've never seen assembly language, don't worry about it—the important part to notice is the introduction by the compiler of the **java.lang.StringBuilder** class. There was no mention of **StringBuilder** in the source code, but the compiler decided to use it anyway, because it is much more efficient.

In this case, the compiler creates a **StringBuilder** object to build the **String** **s**, and calls **append( )** four times, one for each of the pieces. Finally, it calls **toString( )** to produce the result, which it stores (with **astore_2**) as **s**.

Before you assume that you should just use **String**s everywhere and that the compiler will make everything efficient, let's look a little more closely at what the compiler is doing. Here's an example that produces a **String** result in two ways: using **String**s, and by hand-coding with **StringBuilder**:

```
//: strings/WhitherStringBuilder.java

public class WhitherStringBuilder {
  public String implicit(String[] fields) {
    String result = "";
    for(int i = 0; i < fields.length; i++)
      result += fields[i];
    return result;
  }
  public String explicit(String[] fields) {
    StringBuilder result = new StringBuilder();
    for(int i = 0; i < fields.length; i++)
      result.append(fields[i]);
```

Thinking in Java *Bruce Eckel*

```
        return result.toString();
    }
} ///:~
```

Now if you run **javap -c WitherStringBuilder**, you can see the (simplified) code for the two different methods. First, **implicit( )**:

```
public java.lang.String implicit(java.lang.String[]);
  Code:
   0:     ldc #2; //String
   2:     astore_2
   3:     iconst_0
   4:     istore_3
   5:     iload_3
   6:     aload_1
   7:     arraylength
   8:     if_icmpge 38
   11:    new #3; //class StringBuilder
   14:    dup
   15:    invokespecial #4; // StringBuilder."<init>":()
   18:    aload_2
   19:    invokevirtual #5; // StringBuilder.append:()
   22:    aload_1
   23:    iload_3
   24:    aaload
   25:    invokevirtual #5; // StringBuilder.append:()
   28:    invokevirtual #6; // StringBuilder.toString:()
   31:    astore_2
   32:    iinc 3, 1
   35:    goto 5
   38:    aload_2
   39:    areturn
```

Notice **8:** and **35:**, which together form a loop. **8:** does an "integer compare greater than or equal to" of the operands on the stack and jumps to **38:** when the loop is done. **35:** is a goto back to the beginning of the loop, at **5:**. The important thing to note is that the **StringBuilder** construction happens *inside* this loop, which means you're going to get a new **StringBuilder** object every time you pass through the loop.

Here are the bytecodes for **explicit( )**:

```
public java.lang.String explicit(java.lang.String[]);
  Code:
   0:     new #3; //class StringBuilder
```

```
3:      dup
4:      invokespecial #4; // StringBuilder."<init>":()
7:      astore_2
8:      iconst_0
9:      istore_3
10:     iload_3
11:     aload_1
12:     arraylength
13:     if_icmpge 30
16:     aload_2
17:     aload_1
18:     iload_3
19:     aaload
20:     invokevirtual #5; // StringBuilder.append:()
23:     pop
24:     iinc 3, 1
27:     goto 10
30:     aload_2
31:     invokevirtual #6; // StringBuilder.toString:()
34:     areturn
```

Not only is the loop code shorter and simpler, the method only creates a single **StringBuilder** object. Creating an explicit **StringBuilder** also allows you to preallocate its size if you have extra information about how big it might need to be, so that it doesn't need to constantly reallocate the buffer.

Thus, when you create a **toString( )** method, if the operations are simple ones that the compiler can figure out on its own, you can generally rely on the compiler to build the result in a reasonable fashion. But if looping is involved, you should explicitly use a **StringBuilder** in your **toString( )**, like this:

```
//: strings/UsingStringBuilder.java
import java.util.*;

public class UsingStringBuilder {
  public static Random rand = new Random(47);
  public String toString() {
    StringBuilder result = new StringBuilder("[");
    for(int i = 0; i < 25; i++) {
      result.append(rand.nextInt(100));
      result.append(", ");
    }
    result.delete(result.length()-2, result.length());
    result.append("]");
```

```
      return result.toString();
  }
  public static void main(String[] args) {
    UsingStringBuilder usb = new UsingStringBuilder();
    System.out.println(usb);
  }
} /* Output:
[58, 55, 93, 61, 61, 29, 68, 0, 22, 7, 88, 28, 51, 89, 9,
78, 98, 61, 20, 58, 16, 40, 11, 22, 4]
*///:~
```

Notice that each piece of the result is added with an **append( )** statement. If you try to take shortcuts and do something like **append(a + ": " + c)**, the compiler will jump in and start making more **StringBuilder** objects again.

If you are in doubt about which approach to use, you can always run **javap** to double-check.

Although **StringBuilder** has a full complement of methods, including **insert( )**, **replace( )**, **substring( )** and even **reverse( )**, the ones you will generally use are **append( )** and **toString( )**. Note the use of **delete( )** to remove the last comma and space before adding the closing square bracket.

StringBuilder was introduced in Java SE5. Prior to this, Java used **StringBuffer**, which ensured thread safety (see the *Concurrency* chapter) and so was significantly more expensive. Thus, string operations in Java SE5/6 should be faster.

Exercise 1: (2) Analyze **SprinklerSystem.toString( )** in **reusing/SprinklerSystem.java** to discover whether writing the **toString( )** with an explicit **StringBuilder** will save any **StringBuilder** creations.

Unintended recursion

Because (like every other class) the Java standard containers are ultimately inherited from **Object**, they contain a **toString( )** method. This has been overridden so that they can produce a **String** representation of themselves, including the objects they hold. **ArrayList.toString( )**, for example, steps through the elements of the **ArrayList** and calls **toString( )** for each one:

```
//: strings/ArrayListDisplay.java
import generics.coffee.*;
import java.util.*;
```

```
public class ArrayListDisplay {
  public static void main(String[] args) {
    ArrayList<Coffee> coffees = new ArrayList<Coffee>();
    for(Coffee c : new CoffeeGenerator(10))
      coffees.add(c);
    System.out.println(coffees);
  }
} /* Output:
[Americano 0, Latte 1, Americano 2, Mocha 3, Mocha 4, Breve
5, Americano 6, Latte 7, Cappuccino 8, Cappuccino 9]
*///:~
```

Suppose you'd like your **toString( )** to print the address of your class. It seems to make sense to simply refer to **this**:

```
//: strings/InfiniteRecursion.java
// Accidental recursion.
// {RunByHand}
import java.util.*;

public class InfiniteRecursion {
  public String toString() {
    return " InfiniteRecursion address: " + this + "\n";
  }
  public static void main(String[] args) {
    List<InfiniteRecursion> v =
      new ArrayList<InfiniteRecursion>();
    for(int i = 0; i < 10; i++)
      v.add(new InfiniteRecursion());
    System.out.println(v);
  }
} ///:~
```

If you create an **InfiniteRecursion** object and then print it, you'll get a very long sequence of exceptions. This is also true if you place the **InfiniteRecursion** objects in an **ArrayList** and print that **ArrayList** as shown here. What's happening is automatic type conversion for **String**s. When you say:

```
"InfiniteRecursion address: " + this
```

The compiler sees a **String** followed by a '+' and something that's not a **String**, so it tries to convert **this** to a **String**. It does this conversion by calling **toString( )**, which produces a recursive call.

If you really do want to print the address of the object, the solution is to call the **Object toString( )** method, which does just that. So instead of saying **this**, you'd say **super.toString( )**.

Exercise 2: (1) Repair **InfiniteRecursion.java**.

Operations on **String**s

Here are some of the basic methods available for **String** objects. Methods that are overloaded are summarized in a single row:

Method	Arguments, Overloading	Use
Constructor	Overloaded: default, **String**, **StringBuilder**, **StringBuffer**, **char** arrays, **byte** arrays.	Creating **String** objects.
length( )		Number of characters in the **String**.
charAt( )	**int** Index	The **char** at a location in the **String**.
getChars( ), **getBytes( )**	The beginning and end from which to copy, the array to copy into, an index into the destination array.	Copy **char**s or **byte**s into an external array.
toCharArray( )		Produces a **char[]** containing the characters in the **String**.
equals( ), **equals-IgnoreCase( )**	A **String** to compare with.	An equality check on the contents of the two **String**s.
compareTo( )	A **String** to compare with.	Result is negative, zero, or positive depending on the lexicographical ordering of the **String** and the argument. Uppercase and lowercase are not equal!

Method	Arguments, Overloading	Use
contains( )	A **CharSequence** to search for.	Result is **true** if the argument is contained in the **String**.
contentEquals( )	A **CharSequence** or **StringBuffer** to compare to.	Result is **true** if there's an exact match with the argument.
equalsIgnoreCase( )	A **String** to compare with.	Result is **true** if the contents are equal, ignoring case.
regionMatches( )	Offset into this **String**, the other **String** and its offset and length to compare. Overload adds "ignore case."	**boolean** result indicates whether the region matches.
startsWith( )	**String** that it might start with. Overload adds offset into argument.	**boolean** result indicates whether the **String** starts with the argument.
endsWith( )	**String** that might be a suffix of this **String**.	**boolean** result indicates whether the argument is a suffix.
indexOf( ), **lastIndexOf( )**	Overloaded: **char**, **char** and starting index, **String**, **String** and starting index.	Returns -1 if the argument is not found within this **String**; otherwise, returns the index where the argument starts. **lastIndexOf( )** searches backward from end.
substring( ) (also **subSequence( )**)	Overloaded: starting index; starting index + ending index.	Returns a new **String** object containing the specified character set.
concat( )	The **String** to concatenate.	Returns a new **String** object containing the original **String**'s characters followed by the characters in the

Method	Arguments, Overloading	Use
		argument.
replace( )	The old character to search for, the new character to replace it with. Can also replace a **CharSequence** with a **CharSequence**.	Returns a new **String** object with the replacements made. Uses the old **String** if no match is found.
toLowerCase( ) toUpperCase( )		Returns a new **String** object with the case of all letters changed. Uses the old **String** if no changes need to be made.
trim( )		Returns a new **String** object with the whitespace removed from each end. Uses the old **String** if no changes need to be made.
valueOf( )	Overloaded: **Object**, **char[]**, **char[]** and offset and count, **boolean**, **char**, **int**, **long**, **float**, **double**.	Returns a **String** containing a character representation of the argument.
intern( )		Produces one and only one **String** reference per unique character sequence.

You can see that every **String** method carefully returns a new **String** object when it's necessary to change the contents. Also notice that if the contents don't need changing, the method will just return a reference to the original **String**. This saves storage and overhead.

The **String** methods involving *regular expressions* will be explained later in this chapter.

Formatting output

One of the long-awaited features that has finally appeared in Java SE5 is output formatting in the style of C's **printf( )** statement. Not only does this allow for simplified output code, but it also gives Java developers powerful control over output formatting and alignment.[2]

printf( )

C's **printf( )** doesn't assemble strings the way Java does, but takes a single *format string* and inserts values into it, formatting as it goes. Instead of using the overloaded '+' operator (which C doesn't overload) to concatenate quoted text and variables, **printf( )** uses special placeholders to show where the data should go. The arguments that are inserted into the format string follow in a comma-separated list.

For example:

```
printf("Row 1: [%d %f]\n", x, y);
```

At run time, the value of **x** is inserted into **%d** and the value of **y** is inserted into **%f**. These placeholders are called *format specifiers* and, in addition to telling where to insert the value, they also tell what kind of variable is to be inserted and how to format it. For instance, the '**%d**' above says that **x** is an integer and the '**%f**' says **y** is a floating point value (a **float** or **double**).

System.out.format( )

Java SE5 introduced the **format( )** method, available to **PrintStream** or **PrintWriter** objects (which you'll learn more about in the *I/O* chapter), which includes **System.out**. The **format( )** method is modeled after C's **printf( )**. There's even a convenience **printf( )** method that you can use if you're feeling nostalgic, which just calls **format( )**. Here's a simple example:

```
//: strings/SimpleFormat.java

public class SimpleFormat {
  public static void main(String[] args) {
    int x = 5;
```

---

[2] Mark Welsh assisted in the creation of this section, and the "Scanning input" section.

```
    double y = 5.332542;
    // The old way:
    System.out.println("Row 1: [" + x + " " + y + "]");
    // The new way:
    System.out.format("Row 1: [%d %f]\n", x, y);
    // or
    System.out.printf("Row 1: [%d %f]\n", x, y);
  }
} /* Output:
Row 1: [5 5.332542]
Row 1: [5 5.332542]
Row 1: [5 5.332542]
*///:~
```

You can see that **format( )** and **printf( )** are equivalent. In both cases, there's only a single format string, followed by one argument for each format specifier.

The **Formatter** class

All of Java's new formatting functionality is handled by the **Formatter** class in the **java.util** package. You can think of **Formatter** as a translator that converts your format string and data into the desired result. When you create a **Formatter** object, you tell it where you want this result to go by passing that information to the constructor:

```
//: strings/Turtle.java
import java.io.*;
import java.util.*;

public class Turtle {
  private String name;
  private Formatter f;
  public Turtle(String name, Formatter f) {
    this.name = name;
    this.f = f;
  }
  public void move(int x, int y) {
    f.format("%s The Turtle is at (%d,%d)\n", name, x, y);
  }
  public static void main(String[] args) {
    PrintStream outAlias = System.out;
    Turtle tommy = new Turtle("Tommy",
      new Formatter(System.out));
    Turtle terry = new Turtle("Terry",
```

```
        new Formatter(outAlias));
    tommy.move(0,0);
    terry.move(4,8);
    tommy.move(3,4);
    terry.move(2,5);
    tommy.move(3,3);
    terry.move(3,3);
  }
} /* Output:
Tommy The Turtle is at (0,0)
Terry The Turtle is at (4,8)
Tommy The Turtle is at (3,4)
Terry The Turtle is at (2,5)
Tommy The Turtle is at (3,3)
Terry The Turtle is at (3,3)
*///:~
```

All the **tommy** output goes to **System.out** and all the **terry** output goes to an alias of **System.out**. The constructor is overloaded to take a range of output locations, but the most useful are **PrintStream**s (as above), **OutputStream**s, and **File**s. You'll learn more about these in the *I/O* chapter.

Exercise 3: (1) Modify **Turtle.java** so that it sends all output to **System.err**.

The previous example uses a new format specifier, '**%s**'. This indicates a **String** argument and is an example of the simplest kind of format specifier—one that has only a conversion type.

Format specifiers

To control spacing and alignment when data is inserted, you need more elaborate format specifiers. Here's the general syntax:

```
%[argument_index$][flags][width][.precision]conversion
```

Often, you'll need to control the minimum size of a field. This can be accomplished by specifying a *width*. The **Formatter** guarantees that a field is at least a certain number of characters wide by padding it with spaces if necessary. By default, the data is right justified, but this can be overridden by including a '-' in the flags section.

The opposite of *width* is *precision*, which is used to specify a maximum. Unlike the *width*, which is applicable to all of the data conversion types and behaves the same with each, *precision* has a different meaning for different types. For **String**s, the *precision* specifies the maximum number of characters from the **String** to print. For floating point numbers, *precision* specifies the number of decimal places to display (the default is 6), rounding if there are too many or adding trailing zeroes if there are too few. Since integers have no fractional part, *precision* isn't applicable to them and you'll get an exception if you use precision with an integer conversion type.

This example uses format specifiers to print a shopping receipt:

```
//: strings/Receipt.java
import java.util.*;

public class Receipt {
  private double total = 0;
  private Formatter f = new Formatter(System.out);
  public void printTitle() {
    f.format("%-15s %5s %10s\n", "Item", "Qty", "Price");
    f.format("%-15s %5s %10s\n", "----", "---", "-----");
  }
  public void print(String name, int qty, double price) {
    f.format("%-15.15s %5d %10.2f\n", name, qty, price);
    total += price * qty;
  }
  public void printTotal() {
    f.format("%-15s %5s %10.2f\n", "Tax", "", total*0.06);
    f.format("%-15s %5s %10s\n", "", "", "-----");
    f.format("%-15s %5s %10.2f\n", "Total", "",
      total * 1.06);
  }
  public static void main(String[] args) {
    Receipt receipt = new Receipt();
    receipt.printTitle();
    receipt.print("Jack's Magic Beans", 4, 4.25);
    receipt.print("Princess Peas", 3, 5.1);
    receipt.print("Three Bears Porridge", 1, 14.29);
    receipt.printTotal();
  }
} /* Output:
Item              Qty      Price
----              ---      -----
Jack's Magic Be     4       4.25
```

```
Princess Peas         3        5.10
Three Bears Por       1       14.29
Tax                            2.80
                             - - - - -
Total                         49.39
*///:~
```

As you can see, the **Formatter** provides powerful control over spacing and alignment with fairly concise notation. Here, the format strings are simply copied in order to produce the appropriate spacing.

Exercise 4: (3) Modify **Receipt.java** so that the widths are all controlled by a single set of constant values. The goal is to allow you to easily change a width by changing a single value in one place.

Formatter conversions

These are the conversions you'll come across most frequently:

Conversion Characters	
d	Integral (as decimal)
c	Unicode character
b	Boolean value
s	String
f	Floating point (as decimal)
e	Floating point (in scientific notation)
x	Integral (as hex)
h	Hash code (as hex)
%	Literal "%"

Here's an example that shows these conversions in action:

```
//: strings/Conversion.java
import java.math.*;
import java.util.*;
```

```java
public class Conversion {
  public static void main(String[] args) {
    Formatter f = new Formatter(System.out);

    char u = 'a';
    System.out.println("u = 'a'");
    f.format("s: %s\n", u);
    // f.format("d: %d\n", u);
    f.format("c: %c\n", u);
    f.format("b: %b\n", u);
    // f.format("f: %f\n", u);
    // f.format("e: %e\n", u);
    // f.format("x: %x\n", u);
    f.format("h: %h\n", u);

    int v = 121;
    System.out.println("v = 121");
    f.format("d: %d\n", v);
    f.format("c: %c\n", v);
    f.format("b: %b\n", v);
    f.format("s: %s\n", v);
    // f.format("f: %f\n", v);
    // f.format("e: %e\n", v);
    f.format("x: %x\n", v);
    f.format("h: %h\n", v);

    BigInteger w = new BigInteger("50000000000000");
    System.out.println(
      "w = new BigInteger(\"50000000000000\")");
    f.format("d: %d\n", w);
    // f.format("c: %c\n", w);
    f.format("b: %b\n", w);
    f.format("s: %s\n", w);
    // f.format("f: %f\n", w);
    // f.format("e: %e\n", w);
    f.format("x: %x\n", w);
    f.format("h: %h\n", w);

    double x = 179.543;
    System.out.println("x = 179.543");
    // f.format("d: %d\n", x);
    // f.format("c: %c\n", x);
    f.format("b: %b\n", x);
    f.format("s: %s\n", x);
```

```
        f.format("f: %f\n", x);
        f.format("e: %e\n", x);
        // f.format("x: %x\n", x);
        f.format("h: %h\n", x);

        Conversion y = new Conversion();
        System.out.println("y = new Conversion()");
        // f.format("d: %d\n", y);
        // f.format("c: %c\n", y);
        f.format("b: %b\n", y);
        f.format("s: %s\n", y);
        // f.format("f: %f\n", y);
        // f.format("e: %e\n", y);
        // f.format("x: %x\n", y);
        f.format("h: %h\n", y);

        boolean z = false;
        System.out.println("z = false");
        // f.format("d: %d\n", z);
        // f.format("c: %c\n", z);
        f.format("b: %b\n", z);
        f.format("s: %s\n", z);
        // f.format("f: %f\n", z);
        // f.format("e: %e\n", z);
        // f.format("x: %x\n", z);
        f.format("h: %h\n", z);
    }
} /* Output: (Sample)
u = 'a'
s: a
c: a
b: true
h: 61
v = 121
d: 121
c: y
b: true
s: 121
x: 79
h: 79
w = new BigInteger("50000000000000")
d: 50000000000000
b: true
s: 50000000000000
```

```
x:  2d79883d2000
h:  8842a1a7
x = 179.543
b:  true
s:  179.543
f:  179.543000
e:  1.795430e+02
h:  1ef462c
y = new Conversion()
b:  true
s:  Conversion@9cab16
h:  9cab16
z = false
b:  false
s:  false
h:  4d5
*///:~
```

The commented lines show conversions that are invalid for that particular
variable type; executing them will trigger an exception.

Notice that the 'b' conversion works for each variable above. Although it's
valid for any argument type, it might not behave as you'd expect. For
boolean primitives or **Boolean** objects, the result will be **true** or **false**,
accordingly. However, for any other argument, as long as the argument type
is not **null** the result is always **true**. Even the numeric value of zero, which is
synonymous with **false** in many languages (including C), will produce **true**,
so be careful when using this conversion with non-boolean types.

There are more obscure conversion types and other format specifier options.
You can read about these in the JDK documentation for the **Formatter**
class.

Exercise 5: (5) For each of the basic conversion types in the above table,
write the most complex formatting expression possible. That is, use all the
possible format specifiers available for that conversion type.

String.format()

Java SE5 also took a cue from C's **sprintf( )**, which is used to create **String**s.
String.format( ) is a **static** method which takes all the same arguments as
Formatter's **format( )** but returns a **String**. It can come in handy when
you only need to call **format( )** once:

```
//: strings/DatabaseException.java

public class DatabaseException extends Exception {
  public DatabaseException(int transactionID, int queryID,
    String message) {
    super(String.format("(t%d, q%d) %s", transactionID,
      queryID, message));
  }
  public static void main(String[] args) {
    try {
      throw new DatabaseException(3, 7, "Write failed");
    } catch(Exception e) {
      System.out.println(e);
    }
  }
} /* Output:
DatabaseException: (t3, q7) Write failed
*///:~
```

Under the hood, all **String.format( )** does is instantiate a **Formatter** and pass your arguments to it, but using this convenience method can often be clearer and easier than doing it by hand.

A hex dump tool

As a second example, often you want to look at the bytes inside a binary file using hex format. Here's a small utility that displays a binary array of bytes in a readable hex format, using **String.format( )**:

```
//: net/mindview/util/Hex.java
package net.mindview.util;
import java.io.*;

public class Hex {
  public static String format(byte[] data) {
    StringBuilder result = new StringBuilder();
    int n = 0;
    for(byte b : data) {
      if(n % 16 == 0)
        result.append(String.format("%05X: ", n));
      result.append(String.format("%02X ", b));
      n++;
      if(n % 16 == 0) result.append("\n");
    }
    result.append("\n");
```

```
      return result.toString();
    }
  public static void main(String[] args) throws Exception {
    if(args.length == 0)
      // Test by displaying this class file:
      System.out.println(
        format(BinaryFile.read("Hex.class")));
    else
      System.out.println(
        format(BinaryFile.read(new File(args[0]))));
  }
} /* Output: (Sample)
00000: CA FE BA BE 00 00 00 31 00 52 0A 00 05 00 22 07
00010: 00 23 0A 00 02 00 22 08 00 24 07 00 25 0A 00 26
00020: 00 27 0A 00 28 00 29 0A 00 02 00 2A 08 00 2B 0A
00030: 00 2C 00 2D 08 00 2E 0A 00 02 00 2F 09 00 30 00
00040: 31 08 00 32 0A 00 33 00 34 0A 00 15 00 35 0A 00
00050: 36 00 37 07 00 38 0A 00 12 00 39 0A 00 33 00 3A
. . .
*///:~
```

To open and read the binary file, this uses another utility that will be introduced in the *I/O* chapter: **net.mindview.util.BinaryFile**. The **read( )** method returns the entire file as a **byte** array.

Exercise 6: (2) Create a class that contains **int**, **long**, **float** and **double** fields. Create a **toString( )** method for this class that uses **String.format( )**, and demonstrate that your class works correctly.

Regular expressions

Regular expressions have long been integral to standard Unix utilities like sed and awk, and languages like Python and Perl (some would argue that they are the predominant reason for Perl's success). String manipulation tools were previously delegated to the **String**, **StringBuffer**, and **StringTokenizer** classes in Java, which had relatively simple facilities compared to regular expressions.

Regular expressions are powerful and flexible text-processing tools. They allow you to specify, programmatically, complex patterns of text that can be discovered in an input string. Once you discover these patterns, you can then react to them any way you want. Although the syntax of regular expressions can be intimidating at first, they provide a compact and dynamic language that can be employed to solve all sorts of string processing, matching and selection, editing, and verification problems in a completely general way.

Basics

A regular expression is a way to describe strings in general terms, so that you can say, "If a string has these things in it, then it matches what I'm looking for." For example, to say that a number might or might not be preceded by a minus sign, you put in the minus sign followed by a question mark, like this:

```
-?
```

To describe an integer, you say that it's one or more digits. In regular expressions, a digit is described by saying '\d'. If you have any experience with regular expressions in other languages, you'll immediately notice a difference in the way backslashes are handled. In other languages, '\\' means "I want to insert a plain old (literal) backslash in the regular expression. Don't give it any special meaning." In Java, '\\' means "I'm inserting a regular expression backslash, so that the following character has special meaning." For example, if you want to indicate a digit, your regular expression string will be '\\d'. If you want to insert a literal backslash, you say '\\\\'. However, things like newlines and tabs just use a single backslash: '\n\t'.

To indicate "one or more of the preceding expression," you use a '+'. So to say, "possibly a minus sign, followed by one or more digits," you write:

```
-?\\d+
```

The simplest way to use regular expressions is to use the functionality built into the **String** class. For example, we can see whether a **String** matches the regular expression above:

```
//: strings/IntegerMatch.java

public class IntegerMatch {
  public static void main(String[] args) {
    System.out.println("-1234".matches("-?\\d+"));
    System.out.println("5678".matches("-?\\d+"));
    System.out.println("+911".matches("-?\\d+"));
    System.out.println("+911".matches("(-|\\+)?\\d+"));
  }
} /* Output:
true
true
```

```
false
true
*///:~
```

The first two expressions match, but the third one starts with a '+', which is a legitimate sign but means the number doesn't match the regular expression. So we need a way to say, "may start with a + or a -." In regular expressions, parentheses have the effect of grouping an expression, and the vertical bar '|' means OR. So

```
(-|\\+)?
```

means that this part of the string may be either a '-' or a '+' or nothing (because of the '?'). Because the '+' character has special meaning in regular expressions, it must be escaped with a '\\' in order to appear as an ordinary character in the expression.

A useful regular expression tool that's built into **String** is **split( )**, which means, "Split this string around matches of the given regular expression."

```
//: strings/Splitting.java
import java.util.*;

public class Splitting {
  public static String knights =
    "Then, when you have found the shrubbery, you must " +
    "cut down the mightiest tree in the forest... " +
    "with... a herring!";
  public static void split(String regex) {
    System.out.println(
      Arrays.toString(knights.split(regex)));
  }
  public static void main(String[] args) {
    split(" "); // Doesn't have to contain regex chars
    split("\\W+"); // Non-word characters
    split("n\\W+"); // 'n' followed by non-word characters
  }
} /* Output:
[Then,, when, you, have, found, the, shrubbery,, you, must,
cut, down, the, mightiest, tree, in, the, forest...,
with..., a, herring!]
[Then, when, you, have, found, the, shrubbery, you, must,
cut, down, the, mightiest, tree, in, the, forest, with, a,
herring]
```

```
[The, whe, you have found the shrubbery, you must cut dow,
the mightiest tree i, the forest... with... a herring!]
*///:~
```

First, note that you may use ordinary characters as regular expressions—a regular expression doesn't have to contain special characters, as you can see in the first call to **split( )**, which just splits on whitespace.

The second and third calls to **split( )** use '\W', which means a non-word character (the lowercase version, '\w', means a word character)—you can see that the punctuation has been removed in the second case. The third call to **split( )** says, "the letter **n** followed by one or more non-word characters." You can see that the split patterns do not appear in the result.

An overloaded version of **String.split( )** allows you to limit the number of splits that occur.

The final regular expression tool built into **String** is replacement. You can either replace the first occurrence, or all of them:

```
//: strings/Replacing.java
import static net.mindview.util.Print.*;

public class Replacing {
  static String s = Splitting.knights;
  public static void main(String[] args) {
    print(s.replaceFirst("f\\w+", "located"));
    print(s.replaceAll("shrubbery|tree|herring","banana"));
  }
} /* Output:
Then, when you have located the shrubbery, you must cut
down the mightiest tree in the forest... with... a herring!
Then, when you have found the banana, you must cut down the
mightiest banana in the forest... with... a banana!
*///:~
```

The first expression matches the letter **f** followed by one or more word characters (note that the **w** is lowercase this time). It only replaces the first match that it finds, so the word "found" is replaced by the word "located."

The second expression matches any of the three words separated by the OR vertical bars, and it replaces all matches that it finds.

You'll see that the non-**String** regular expressions have more powerful replacement tools—for example, you can call methods to perform replacements. Non-**String** regular expressions are also significantly more efficient if you need to use the regular expression more than once.

Exercise 7: (5) Using the documentation for **java.util.regex.Pattern** as a resource, write and test a regular expression that checks a sentence to see that it begins with a capital letter and ends with a period.

Exercise 8: (2) Split the string **Splitting.knights** on the words "the" or "you."

Exercise 9: (4) Using the documentation for **java.util.regex.Pattern** as a resource, replace all the vowels in **Splitting.knights** with underscores.

Creating regular expressions

You can begin learning regular expressions with a subset of the possible constructs. A complete list of constructs for building regular expressions can be found in the JDK documentation for the **Pattern** class for package **java.util.regex**.

Characters	
B	The specific character **B**
\xhh	Character with hex value **oxhh**
\uhhhh	The Unicode character with hex representation **oxhhhh**
\t	Tab
\n	Newline
\r	Carriage return
\f	Form feed
\e	Escape

The power of regular expressions begins to appear when you are defining character classes. Here are some typical ways to create character classes, and some predefined classes:

Character Classes	
.	Any character
[abc]	Any of the characters **a**, **b**, or **c** (same as

	a|b|c)
[^abc]	Any character except **a**, **b**, and **c** (negation)
[a-zA-Z]	Any character **a** through **z** or **A** through **Z** (range)
[abc[hij]]	Any of **a,b,c,h,i,j** (same as **a|b|c|h|i|j**) (union)
[a-z&&[hij]]	Either **h**, **i**, or **j** (intersection)
\s	A whitespace character (space, tab, newline, form feed, carriage return)
\S	A non-whitespace character (**[^\s]**)
\d	A numeric digit **[0-9]**
\D	A non-digit **[^0-9]**
\w	A word character **[a-zA-Z_0-9]**
\W	A non-word character **[^\w]**

What's shown here is only a sample; you'll want to bookmark the JDK documentation page for **java.util.regex.Pattern** so you can easily access all the possible regular expression patterns.

Logical Operators	
XY	X followed by Y
X|Y	X or Y
(X)	A *capturing group*. You can refer to the *i*th captured group later in the expression with \i.

Boundary Matchers	
^	Beginning of a line
$	End of a line
\b	Word boundary
\B	Non-word boundary
\G	End of the previous match

As an example, each of the following successfully matches the character sequence "Rudolph":

```
//: strings/Rudolph.java

public class Rudolph {
  public static void main(String[] args) {
    for(String pattern : new String[]{ "Rudolph",
      "[rR]udolph", "[rR][aeiou][a-z]ol.*", "R.*" })
      System.out.println("Rudolph".matches(pattern));
  }
} /* Output:
true
true
true
true
*///:~
```

Of course, your goal should not be to create the most obfuscated regular expression, but rather the simplest one necessary to do the job. You'll find that, once you start writing regular expressions, you'll often use your code as a reference when writing new regular expressions.

Quantifiers

A *quantifier* describes the way that a pattern absorbs input text:

- *Greedy*: Quantifiers are greedy unless otherwise altered. A greedy expression finds as many possible matches for the pattern as possible. A typical cause of problems is to assume that your pattern will only match the first possible group of characters, when it's actually greedy and will keep going until it's matched the largest possible string.

- *Reluctant*: Specified with a question mark, this quantifier matches the minimum number of characters necessary to satisfy the pattern. Also called *lazy, minimal matching, non-greedy,* or *ungreedy.*

- *Possessive*: Currently this is only available in Java (not in other languages) and is more advanced, so you probably won't use it right away. As a regular expression is applied to a string, it generates many states so that it can backtrack if the match fails. Possessive quantifiers do not keep those intermediate states, and thus prevent backtracking. They can be used to prevent a regular expression from running away and also to make it execute more efficiently.

Greedy	Reluctant	Possessive	Matches

Greedy	Reluctant	Possessive	Matches
X?	X??	X?+	X, one or none
X*	X*?	X*+	X, zero or more
X+	X+?	X++	X, one or more
X{n}	X{n}?	X{n}+	X, exactly n times
X{n,}	X{n,}?	X{n,}+	X, at least n times
X{n,m}	X{n,m}?	X{n,m}+	X, at least n but not more than m times

Keep in mind that the expression 'X' will often need to be surrounded in parentheses for it to work the way you desire. For example:

```
abc+
```

might seem like it would match the sequence 'abc' one or more times, and if you apply it to the input string 'abcabcabc', you will in fact get three matches. However, the expression *actually* says, "Match 'ab' followed by one or more occurrences of 'c'." To match the entire string 'abc' one or more times, you must say:

```
(abc)+
```

You can easily be fooled when using regular expressions; it's an orthogonal language, on top of Java.

CharSequence

The interface called **CharSequence** establishes a generalized definition of a character sequence abstracted from the **CharBuffer**, **String**, **StringBuffer**, or **StringBuilder** classes:

```
interface CharSequence {
  char charAt(int i);
  int length();
  CharSequence subSequence(int start, int end);
  String toString();
}
```

The aforementioned classes implement this interface. Many regular expression operations take **CharSequence** arguments.

Pattern and Matcher

In general, you'll compile regular expression objects rather than using the fairly limited **String** utilities. To do this, you import **java.util.regex**, then compile a regular expression by using the **static Pattern.compile( )** method. This produces a **Pattern** object based on its **String** argument. You use the **Pattern** by calling the **matcher( )** method, passing the string that you want to search. The **matcher( )** method produces a **Matcher** object, which has a set of operations to choose from (you can see all of these in the JDK documentation for **java.util.regex.Matcher**). For example, the **replaceAll( )** method replaces all the matches with its argument.

As a first example, the following class can be used to test regular expressions against an input string. The first command-line argument is the input string to match against, followed by one or more regular expressions to be applied to the input. Under Unix/Linux, the regular expressions must be quoted on the command line. This program can be useful in testing regular expressions as you construct them to see that they produce your intended matching behavior.

```
//: strings/TestRegularExpression.java
// Allows you to easily try out regular expressions.
// {Args: abcabcabcdefabc "abc+" "(abc)+" "(abc){2,}" }
import java.util.regex.*;
import static net.mindview.util.Print.*;

public class TestRegularExpression {
  public static void main(String[] args) {
    if(args.length < 2) {
      print("Usage:\njava TestRegularExpression " +
        "characterSequence regularExpression+");
      System.exit(0);
    }
    print("Input: \"" + args[0] + "\"");
    for(String arg : args) {
      print("Regular expression: \"" + arg + "\"");
      Pattern p = Pattern.compile(arg);
      Matcher m = p.matcher(args[0]);
      while(m.find()) {
        print("Match \"" + m.group() + "\" at positions " +
```

```
                    m.start() + "-" + (m.end() - 1));
        }
      }
    }
  }
} /* Output:
Input: "abcabcabcdefabc"
Regular expression: "abcabcabcdefabc"
Match "abcabcabcdefabc" at positions 0-14
Regular expression: "abc+"
Match "abc" at positions 0-2
Match "abc" at positions 3-5
Match "abc" at positions 6-8
Match "abc" at positions 12-14
Regular expression: "(abc)+"
Match "abcabcabc" at positions 0-8
Match "abc" at positions 12-14
Regular expression: "(abc){2,}"
Match "abcabcabc" at positions 0-8
*///:~
```

A **Pattern** object represents the compiled version of a regular expression. As seen in the preceding example, you can use the **matcher( )** method and the input string to produce a **Matcher** object from the compiled **Pattern** object. **Pattern** also has a **static** method:

```
static boolean matches(String regex, CharSequence input)
```

to check whether **regex** matches the entire **input CharSequence**, and a **split( )** method that produces an array of **String** that has been broken around matches of the **regex**.

A **Matcher** object is generated by calling **Pattern.matcher( )** with the input string as an argument. The **Matcher** object is then used to access the results, using methods to evaluate the success or failure of different types of matches:

```
boolean matches()
boolean lookingAt()
boolean find()
boolean find(int start)
```

The **matches( )** method is successful if the pattern matches the entire input string, while **lookingAt( )** is successful if the input string, starting at the beginning, is a match to the pattern.

Exercise 10: (2) For the phrase "Java now has regular expressions" evaluate whether the following expressions will find a match:

```
^Java
\Breg.*
n.w\s+h(a|i)s
s?
s*
s+
s{4}
s{1}.
s{0,3}
```

Exercise 11: (2) Apply the regular expression

```
(?i)((^[aeiou])|(\s+[aeiou]))\w+?[aeiou]\b
```

to

```
"Arline ate eight apples and one orange while Anita hadn't
any"
```

find()

Matcher.find( ) can be used to discover multiple pattern matches in the **CharSequence** to which it is applied. For example:

```
//: strings/Finding.java
import java.util.regex.*;
import static net.mindview.util.Print.*;

public class Finding {
  public static void main(String[] args) {
    Matcher m = Pattern.compile("\\w+")
      .matcher("Evening is full of the linnet's wings");
    while(m.find())
      printnb(m.group() + " ");
    print();
    int i = 0;
    while(m.find(i)) {
      printnb(m.group() + " ");
      i++;
    }
  }
} /* Output:
Evening is full of the linnet s wings
```

```
Evening vening ening ning ing ng g is is s full full ull ll
l of of f the the he e linnet linnet innet nnet net et t s
s wings wings ings ngs gs s
*///:~
```

The pattern '\\w+' splits the input into words. **find( )** is like an iterator, moving forward through the input string. However, the second version of **find( )** can be given an integer argument that tells it the character position for the beginning of the search—this version resets the search position to the value of the argument, as you can see from the output.

Groups

Groups are regular expressions set off by parentheses that can be called up later with their group number. Group 0 indicates the whole expression match, group 1 is the first parenthesized group, etc. Thus in

```
A(B(C))D
```

there are three groups: Group 0 is **ABCD**, group 1 is **BC**, and group 2 is **C**.

The **Matcher** object has methods to give you information about groups:

public int groupCount( ) returns the number of groups in this matcher's pattern. Group 0 is not included in this count.

public String group( ) returns group 0 (the entire match) from the previous match operation (**find( )**, for example).

public String group(int i) returns the given group number during the previous match operation. If the match was successful, but the group specified failed to match any part of the input string, then **null** is returned.

public int start(int group) returns the start index of the group found in the previous match operation.

public int end(int group) returns the index of the last character, plus one, of the group found in the previous match operation.

Here's an example:

```
//: strings/Groups.java
import java.util.regex.*;
import static net.mindview.util.Print.*;
```

```java
public class Groups {
  static public final String POEM =
    "Twas brillig, and the slithy toves\n" +
    "Did gyre and gimble in the wabe.\n" +
    "All mimsy were the borogoves,\n" +
    "And the mome raths outgrabe.\n\n" +
    "Beware the Jabberwock, my son,\n" +
    "The jaws that bite, the claws that catch.\n" +
    "Beware the Jubjub bird, and shun\n" +
    "The frumious Bandersnatch.";
  public static void main(String[] args) {
    Matcher m =
      Pattern.compile("(?m)(\\S+)\\s+((\\S+)\\s+(\\S+))$")
        .matcher(POEM);
    while(m.find()) {
      for(int j = 0; j <= m.groupCount(); j++)
        printnb("[" + m.group(j) + "]");
      print();
    }
  }
} /* Output:
[the slithy toves][the][slithy toves][slithy][toves]
[in the wabe.][in][the wabe.][the][wabe.]
[were the borogoves,][were][the
borogoves,][the][borogoves,]
[mome raths outgrabe.][mome][raths
outgrabe.][raths][outgrabe.]
[Jabberwock, my son,][Jabberwock,][my son,][my][son,]
[claws that catch.][claws][that catch.][that][catch.]
[bird, and shun][bird,][and shun][and][shun]
[The frumious Bandersnatch.][The][frumious
Bandersnatch.][frumious][Bandersnatch.]
*///:~
```

The poem is the first part of Lewis Carroll's "Jabberwocky," from *Through the Looking Glass*. You can see that the regular expression pattern has a number of parenthesized groups, consisting of any number of non-whitespace characters ('\S+') followed by any number of whitespace characters ('\s+'). The goal is to capture the last three words on each line; the end of a line is delimited by '$'. However, the normal behavior is to match '$' with the end of the entire input sequence, so you must explicitly tell the regular expression to pay attention to newlines within the input. This is accomplished with the '(?m)' pattern flag at the beginning of the sequence (pattern flags will be shown shortly).

Exercise 12: (5) Modify **Groups.java** to count all of the unique words that do not start with a capital letter.

start() and end()

Following a successful matching operation, **start( )** returns the start index of the previous match, and **end( )** returns the index of the last character matched, plus one. Invoking either **start( )** or **end( )** following an unsuccessful matching operation (or before attempting a matching operation) produces an **IllegalStateException**. The following program also demonstrates **matches( )** and **lookingAt( )**:[3]

```
//: strings/StartEnd.java
import java.util.regex.*;
import static net.mindview.util.Print.*;

public class StartEnd {
  public static String input =
    "As long as there is injustice, whenever a\n" +
    "Targathian baby cries out, wherever a distress\n" +
    "signal sounds among the stars ... We'll be there.\n" +
    "This fine ship, and this fine crew ...\n" +
    "Never give up! Never surrender!";
  private static class Display {
    private boolean regexPrinted = false;
    private String regex;
    Display(String regex) { this.regex = regex; }
    void display(String message) {
      if(!regexPrinted) {
        print(regex);
        regexPrinted = true;
      }
      print(message);
    }
  }
  static void examine(String s, String regex) {
    Display d = new Display(regex);
    Pattern p = Pattern.compile(regex);
    Matcher m = p.matcher(s);
    while(m.find())
      d.display("find() '" + m.group() +
```

---

[3] Quote from one of Commander Taggart's speeches on *Galaxy Quest*.

```
                     "' start = "+ m.start() + " end = " + m.end());
        if(m.lookingAt()) // No reset() necessary
          d.display("lookingAt() start = "
            + m.start() + " end = " + m.end());
        if(m.matches()) // No reset() necessary
          d.display("matches() start = "
            + m.start() + " end = " + m.end());
      }
    public static void main(String[] args) {
      for(String in : input.split("\n")) {
        print("input : " + in);
        for(String regex : new String[]{"\\w*ere\\w*",
          "\\w*ever", "T\\w+", "Never.*?!"})
          examine(in, regex);
      }
    }
} /* Output:
input : As long as there is injustice, whenever a
\w*ere\w*
find() 'there' start = 11 end = 16
\w*ever
find() 'whenever' start = 31 end = 39
input : Targathian baby cries out, wherever a distress
\w*ere\w*
find() 'wherever' start = 27 end = 35
\w*ever
find() 'wherever' start = 27 end = 35
T\w+
find() 'Targathian' start = 0 end = 10
lookingAt() start = 0 end = 10
input : signal sounds among the stars ... We'll be there.
\w*ere\w*
find() 'there' start = 43 end = 48
input : This fine ship, and this fine crew ...
T\w+
find() 'This' start = 0 end = 4
lookingAt() start = 0 end = 4
input : Never give up! Never surrender!
\w*ever
find() 'Never' start = 0 end = 5
find() 'Never' start = 15 end = 20
lookingAt() start = 0 end = 5
Never.*?!
find() 'Never give up!' start = 0 end = 14
```

```
find() 'Never surrender!' start = 15 end = 31
lookingAt() start = 0 end = 14
matches() start = 0 end = 31
*///:~
```

Notice that **find( )** will locate the regular expression anywhere in the input, but **lookingAt( )** and **matches( )** only succeed if the regular expression starts matching at the very beginning of the input. While **matches( )** only succeeds if the *entire* input matches the regular expression, **lookingAt( )**[4] succeeds if only the first part of the input matches.

Exercise 13: (2) Modify **StartEnd.java** so that it uses **Groups.POEM** as input, but still produces positive outputs for **find( )**, **lookingAt( )** and **matches( )**.

Pattern flags

An alternative **compile( )** method accepts flags that affect matching behavior:

```
Pattern Pattern.compile(String regex, int flag)
```

where **flag** is drawn from among the following **Pattern** class constants:

Compile Flag	Effect
Pattern.CANON_EQ	Two characters will be considered to match if, and only if, their full canonical decompositions match. The expression '\u003F', for example, will match the string '?' when this flag is specified. By default, matching does not take canonical equivalence into account.
Pattern.CASE_INSENSITIVE (?i)	By default, case-insensitive matching assumes that only characters in the US-ASCII character set are being matched.

---

[4] I have no idea how they came up with this method name, or what it's supposed to refer to. But it's reassuring to know that whoever comes up with nonintuitive method names is still employed at Sun. And that their apparent policy of not reviewing code designs is still in place. Sorry for the sarcasm, but this kind of thing gets tiresome after a few years.

	This flag allows your pattern to match without regard to case (upper or lower). Unicode-aware case-insensitive matching can be enabled by specifying the **UNICODE_CASE** flag in conjunction with this flag.
Pattern.COMMENTS **(?x)**	In this mode, whitespace is ignored, and embedded comments starting with # are ignored until the end of a line. Unix lines mode can also be enabled via the embedded flag expression.
Pattern.DOTALL **(?s)**	In dotall mode, the expression '**.**' matches any character, including a line terminator. By default, the '**.**' expression does not match line terminators.
Pattern.MULTILINE **(?m)**	In multiline mode, the expressions '**^**' and '**$**' match the beginning and ending of a line, respectively. '**^**' also matches the beginning of the input string, and '**$**' also matches the end of the input string. By default, these expressions only match at the beginning and the end of the entire input string.
Pattern.UNICODE_CASE **(?u)**	Case-insensitive matching, when enabled by the **CASE_INSENSITIVE** flag, is done in a manner consistent with the Unicode Standard. By default, case-insensitive matching assumes that only characters in the US-ASCII character set are being matched.
Pattern.UNIX_LINES **(?d)**	In this mode, only the '**\n**' line terminator is recognized in the behavior of '**.**', '**^**', and '**$**'.

Particularly useful among these flags are **Pattern.CASE_INSENSITIVE**, **Pattern.MULTILINE**, and **Pattern.COMMENTS** (which is helpful for clarity and/or documentation). Note that the behavior of most of the flags can also be obtained by inserting the parenthesized characters, shown beneath the flags in the table, into your regular expression preceding the place where you want the mode to take effect.

You can combine the effect of these and other flags through an "OR" ('|') operation:

```
//: strings/ReFlags.java
import java.util.regex.*;

public class ReFlags {
  public static void main(String[] args) {
    Pattern p =  Pattern.compile("^java",
      Pattern.CASE_INSENSITIVE | Pattern.MULTILINE);
    Matcher m = p.matcher(
      "java has regex\nJava has regex\n" +
      "JAVA has pretty good regular expressions\n" +
      "Regular expressions are in Java");
    while(m.find())
      System.out.println(m.group());
  }
} /* Output:
java
Java
JAVA
*///:~
```

This creates a pattern that will match lines starting with "java," "Java," "JAVA," etc., and attempt a match for each line within a multiline set (matches starting at the beginning of the character sequence and following each line terminator within the character sequence). Note that the **group( )** method only produces the matched portion.

split( )

split( ) divides an input string into an array of **String** objects, delimited by the regular expression.

```
String[] split(CharSequence input)
String[] split(CharSequence input, int limit)
```

This is a handy way to break input text on a common boundary:

```
//: strings/SplitDemo.java
import java.util.regex.*;
import java.util.*;
import static net.mindview.util.Print.*;

public class SplitDemo {
  public static void main(String[] args) {
    String input =
      "This!!unusual use!!of exclamation!!points";
    print(Arrays.toString(
      Pattern.compile("!!").split(input)));
    // Only do the first three:
    print(Arrays.toString(
      Pattern.compile("!!").split(input, 3)));
  }
} /* Output:
[This, unusual use, of exclamation, points]
[This, unusual use, of exclamation!!points]
*///:~
```

The second form of **split( )** limits the number of splits that occur.

Exercise 14: (1) Rewrite **SplitDemo** using **String.split( )**.

Replace operations

Regular expressions are especially useful to replace text. Here are the available methods:

replaceFirst(String replacement) replaces the first matching part of the input string with **replacement**.

replaceAll(String replacement) replaces every matching part of the input string with **replacement**.

appendReplacement(StringBuffer sbuf, String replacement) performs step-by-step replacements into **sbuf**, rather than replacing only the first one or all of them, as in **replaceFirst( )** and **replaceAll( )**, respectively. This is a *very* important method, because it allows you to call methods and perform other processing in order to produce **replacement** (**replaceFirst( )** and **replaceAll( )** are only able to put in fixed strings).

With this method, you can programmatically pick apart the groups and create powerful replacements.

appendTail(StringBuffer sbuf) is invoked after one or more invocations of the **appendReplacement( )** method in order to copy the remainder of the input string.

Here's an example that shows the use of all the replace operations. The block of commented text at the beginning is extracted and processed with regular expressions for use as input in the rest of the example:

```
//: strings/TheReplacements.java
import java.util.regex.*;
import net.mindview.util.*;
import static net.mindview.util.Print.*;

/*! Here's a block of text to use as input to
    the regular expression matcher. Note that we'll
    first extract the block of text by looking for
    the special delimiters, then process the
    extracted block. !*/

public class TheReplacements {
  public static void main(String[] args) throws Exception {
    String s = TextFile.read("TheReplacements.java");
    // Match the specially commented block of text above:
    Matcher mInput =
      Pattern.compile("/\\*!(.*)!\\*/", Pattern.DOTALL)
        .matcher(s);
    if(mInput.find())
      s = mInput.group(1); // Captured by parentheses
    // Replace two or more spaces with a single space:
    s = s.replaceAll(" {2,}", " ");
    // Replace one or more spaces at the beginning of each
    // line with no spaces. Must enable MULTILINE mode:
    s = s.replaceAll("(?m)^ +", "");
    print(s);
    s = s.replaceFirst("[aeiou]", "(VOWEL1)");
    StringBuffer sbuf = new StringBuffer();
    Pattern p = Pattern.compile("[aeiou]");
    Matcher m = p.matcher(s);
    // Process the find information as you
    // perform the replacements:
    while(m.find())
```

```
        m.appendReplacement(sbuf, m.group().toUpperCase());
      // Put in the remainder of the text:
      m.appendTail(sbuf);
      print(sbuf);
    }
} /* Output:
Here's a block of text to use as input to
the regular expression matcher. Note that we'll
first extract the block of text by looking for
the special delimiters, then process the
extracted block.
H(VOWEL1)rE's A blOck Of tExt tO UsE As InpUt tO
thE rEgUlAr ExprEssIOn mAtchEr. NOtE thAt wE'll
fIrst ExtrAct thE blOck Of tExt by lOOkIng fOr
thE spEcIAl dElImItErs, thEn prOcEss thE
ExtrActEd blOck.
*///:~
```

The file is opened and read using the **TextFile** class in the **net.mindview.util** library (the code for this will be shown in the *I/O* chapter). The **static read( )** method reads the entire file and returns it as a **String**. **mInput** is created to match all the text (notice the grouping parentheses) between '/*!' and '!*/'. Then, more than two spaces are reduced to a single space, and any space at the beginning of each line is removed (in order to do this on all lines and not just the beginning of the input, multiline mode must be enabled). These two replacements are performed with the equivalent (but more convenient, in this case) **replaceAll( )** that's part of **String**. Note that since each replacement is only used once in the program, there's no extra cost to doing it this way rather than precompiling it as a **Pattern**.

replaceFirst( ) only performs the first replacement that it finds. In addition, the replacement strings in **replaceFirst( )** and **replaceAll( )** are just literals, so if you want to perform some processing on each replacement, they don't help. In that case, you need to use **appendReplacement( )**, which allows you to write any amount of code in the process of performing the replacement. In the preceding example, a **group( )** is selected and processed—in this situation, setting the vowel found by the regular expression to uppercase—as the resulting **sbuf** is being built. Normally, you step through and perform all the replacements and then call **appendTail( )**, but if you want to simulate **replaceFirst( )** (or "replace n"), you just do the replacement one time and then call **appendTail( )** to put the rest into **sbuf**.

appendReplacement( ) also allows you to refer to captured groups directly in the replacement string by saying "$g", where 'g' is the group number. However, this is for simpler processing and wouldn't give you the desired results in the preceding program.

reset( )

An existing **Matcher** object can be applied to a new character sequence using the **reset( )** methods:

```
//: strings/Resetting.java
import java.util.regex.*;

public class Resetting {
  public static void main(String[] args) throws Exception {
    Matcher m = Pattern.compile("[frb][aiu][gx]")
      .matcher("fix the rug with bags");
    while(m.find())
      System.out.print(m.group() + " ");
    System.out.println();
    m.reset("fix the rig with rags");
    while(m.find())
      System.out.print(m.group() + " ");
  }
} /* Output:
fix rug bag
fix rig rag
*///:~
```

reset( ) without any arguments sets the **Matcher** to the beginning of the current sequence.

Regular expressions and Java I/O

Most of the examples so far have shown regular expressions applied to static strings. The following example shows one way to apply regular expressions to search for matches in a file. Inspired by Unix's *grep*, **JGrep.java** takes two arguments: a file name and the regular expression that you want to match. The output shows each line where a match occurs and the match position(s) within the line.

```
//: strings/JGrep.java
// A very simple version of the "grep" program.
// {Args: JGrep.java "\\b[Ssct]\\w+"}
```

```java
import java.util.regex.*;
import net.mindview.util.*;

public class JGrep {
  public static void main(String[] args) throws Exception {
    if(args.length < 2) {
      System.out.println("Usage: java JGrep file regex");
      System.exit(0);
    }
    Pattern p = Pattern.compile(args[1]);
    // Iterate through the lines of the input file:
    int index = 0;
    Matcher m = p.matcher("");
    for(String line : new TextFile(args[0])) {
      m.reset(line);
      while(m.find())
        System.out.println(index++ + ": " +
          m.group() + ": " + m.start());
    }
  }
} /* Output: (Sample)
0: strings: 4
1: simple: 10
2: the: 28
3: Ssct: 26
4: class: 7
5: static: 9
6: String: 26
7: throws: 41
8: System: 6
9: System: 6
10: compile: 24
11: through: 15
12: the: 23
13: the: 36
14: String: 8
15: System: 8
16: start: 31
*///:~
```

The file is opened as a **net.mindview.util.TextFile** object (which will be shown in the *I/O* chapter), which reads the lines of the file into an **ArrayList**. This means that the foreach syntax can iterate through the lines in the **TextFile** object.

Although it's possible to create a new **Matcher** object within the **for** loop, it is slightly more optimal to create an empty **Matcher** object outside the loop and use the **reset( )** method to assign each line of the input to the **Matcher**. The result is scanned with **find( )**.

The test arguments open the **JGrep.java** file to read as input, and search for words starting with **[Ssct]**.

You can learn much more about regular expressions in *Mastering Regular Expressions, 2nd Edition*, by Jeffrey E. F. Friedl (O'Reilly, 2002). There are also numerous introductions to regular expressions on the Internet, and you can often find helpful information in the documentation for languages like Perl and Python.

Exercise 15:   (5) Modify **JGrep.java** to accept flags as arguments (e.g., **Pattern.CASE_INSENSITIVE**, **Pattern.MULTILINE**).

Exercise 16:   (5) Modify **JGrep.java** to accept a directory name or a file name as argument (if a directory is provided, search should include all files in the directory). Hint: You can generate a list of file names with:

```
File[] files = new File(".").listFiles();
```

Exercise 17:   (8) Write a program that reads a Java source-code file (you provide the file name on the command line) and displays all the comments.

Exercise 18:   (8) Write a program that reads a Java source-code file (you provide the file name on the command line) and displays all the string literals in the code.

Exercise 19:   (8) Building on the previous two exercises, write a program that examines Java source code and produces all the class names used in a particular program.

Scanning input

Until now it has been relatively painful to read data from a human-readable file or from standard input. The usual solution is to read in a line of text, tokenize it, and then use the various parse methods of **Integer**, **Double**, etc., to parse the data:

```
//: strings/SimpleRead.java
import java.io.*;
```

```java
public class SimpleRead {
  public static BufferedReader input = new BufferedReader(
    new StringReader("Sir Robin of Camelot\n22 1.61803"));
  public static void main(String[] args) {
    try {
      System.out.println("What is your name?");
      String name = input.readLine();
      System.out.println(name);
      System.out.println(
        "How old are you? What is your favorite double?");
      System.out.println("(input: <age> <double>)");
      String numbers = input.readLine();
      System.out.println(numbers);
      String[] numArray = numbers.split(" ");
      int age = Integer.parseInt(numArray[0]);
      double favorite = Double.parseDouble(numArray[1]);
      System.out.format("Hi %s.\n", name);
      System.out.format("In 5 years you will be %d.\n",
        age + 5);
      System.out.format("My favorite double is %f.",
        favorite / 2);
    } catch(IOException e) {
      System.err.println("I/O exception");
    }
  }
} /* Output:
What is your name?
Sir Robin of Camelot
How old are you? What is your favorite double?
(input: <age> <double>)
22 1.61803
Hi Sir Robin of Camelot.
In 5 years you will be 27.
My favorite double is 0.809015.
*///:~
```

The **input** field uses classes from **java.io**, which will not officially be introduced until the *I/O* chapter. A **StringReader** turns a **String** into a readable stream, and this object is used to create a **BufferedReader** because **BufferedReader** has a **readLine( )** method. The result is that the **input** object can be read a line at a time, just as if it were standard input from the console.

readLine( ) is used to get the **String** for each line of input. It's fairly straightforward when you want to get one input for each line of data, but if two input values are on a single line, things get messy—the line must be split so we can parse each input separately. Here, the splitting takes place when creating **numArray**, but note that the **split( )** method was introduced in J2SE1.4, so before that you had to do something else.

The **Scanner** class, added in Java SE5, relieves much of the burden of scanning input:

```
//: strings/BetterRead.java
import java.util.*;

public class BetterRead {
  public static void main(String[] args) {
    Scanner stdin = new Scanner(SimpleRead.input);
    System.out.println("What is your name?");
    String name = stdin.nextLine();
    System.out.println(name);
    System.out.println(
      "How old are you? What is your favorite double?");
    System.out.println("(input: <age> <double>)");
    int age = stdin.nextInt();
    double favorite = stdin.nextDouble();
    System.out.println(age);
    System.out.println(favorite);
    System.out.format("Hi %s.\n", name);
    System.out.format("In 5 years you will be %d.\n",
      age + 5);
    System.out.format("My favorite double is %f.",
      favorite / 2);
  }
} /* Output:
What is your name?
Sir Robin of Camelot
How old are you? What is your favorite double?
(input: <age> <double>)
22
1.61803
Hi Sir Robin of Camelot.
In 5 years you will be 27.
My favorite double is 0.809015.
*///:~
```

The **Scanner** constructor can take just about any kind of input object, including a **File** object (which will also be covered in the *I/O* chapter), an **InputStream**, a **String**, or in this case a **Readable**, which is an interface introduced in Java SE5 to describe "something that has a **read( )** method." The **BufferedReader** from the previous example falls into this category.

With **Scanner**, the input, tokenizing, and parsing are all ensconced in various different kinds of "next" methods. A plain **next( )** returns the next **String** token, and there are "next" methods for all the primitive types (except **char**) as well as for **BigDecimal** and **BigInteger**. All of the "next" methods *block*, meaning they will return only after a complete data token is available for input. There are also corresponding "hasNext" methods that return **truc** if the next input token is of the correct type.

An interesting difference between the two previous examples above is the lack of a **try** block for **IOException**s in **BetterRead.java**. One of the assumptions made by the **Scanner** is that an **IOException** signals the end of input, and so these are swallowed by the **Scanner**. However, the most recent exception is available through the **ioException( )** method, so you are able to examine it if necessary.

Exercise 20: (2) Create a class that contains **int**, **long**, **float** and **double** and **String** fields. Create a constructor for this class that takes a single **String** argument, and scans that string into the various fields. Add a **toString( )** method and demonstrate that your class works correctly.

Scanner delimiters

By default, a **Scanner** splits input tokens along whitespace, but you can also specify your own delimiter pattern in the form of a regular expression:

```
//: strings/ScannerDelimiter.java
import java.util.*;

public class ScannerDelimiter {
  public static void main(String[] args) {
    Scanner scanner = new Scanner("12, 42, 78, 99, 42");
    scanner.useDelimiter("\\s*,\\s*");
    while(scanner.hasNextInt())
      System.out.println(scanner.nextInt());
  }
} /* Output:
12
```

```
42
78
99
42
*///:~
```

This example uses commas (surrounded by arbitrary amounts of whitespace) as the delimiter when reading from the given **String**. This same technique can be used to read from comma-delimited files. In addition to **useDelimiter( )** for setting the delimiter pattern, there is also **delimiter( )**, which returns the current **Pattern** being used as a delimiter.

Scanning with regular expressions

In addition to scanning for predefined primitive types, you can also scan for your own user-defined patterns, which is helpful when scanning more complex data. This example scans threat data from a log like your firewall might produce:

```
//: strings/ThreatAnalyzer.java
import java.util.regex.*;
import java.util.*;

public class ThreatAnalyzer {
  static String threatData =
    "58.27.82.161@02/10/2005\n" +
    "204.45.234.40@02/11/2005\n" +
    "58.27.82.161@02/11/2005\n" +
    "58.27.82.161@02/12/2005\n" +
    "58.27.82.161@02/12/2005\n" +
    "[Next log section with different data format]";
  public static void main(String[] args) {
    Scanner scanner = new Scanner(threatData);
    String pattern = "(\\d+[.]\\d+[.]\\d+[.]\\d+)@" +
      "(\\d{2}/\\d{2}/\\d{4})";
    while(scanner.hasNext(pattern)) {
      scanner.next(pattern);
      MatchResult match = scanner.match();
      String ip = match.group(1);
      String date = match.group(2);
      System.out.format("Threat on %s from %s\n", date, ip);
    }
  }
} /* Output:
```

```
Threat on 02/10/2005 from 58.27.82.161
Threat on 02/11/2005 from 204.45.234.40
Threat on 02/11/2005 from 58.27.82.161
Threat on 02/12/2005 from 58.27.82.161
Threat on 02/12/2005 from 58.27.82.161
*///:~
```

When you use **next( )** with a specific pattern, that pattern is matched against the next input token. The result is made available by the **match( )** method, and as you can see above, it works just like the regular expression matching you saw earlier.

There's one caveat when scanning with regular expressions. The pattern is matched against the next input token only, so if your pattern contains a delimiter it will never be matched.

StringTokenizer

Before regular expressions (in J2SE1.4) or the **Scanner** class (in Java SE5), the way to split a string into parts was to "tokenize" it with **StringTokenizer**. But now it's much easier and more succinct to do the same thing with regular expressions or the **Scanner** class. Here's a simple comparison of **StringTokenizer** to the other two techniques:

```
//: strings/ReplacingStringTokenizer.java
import java.util.*;

public class ReplacingStringTokenizer {
  public static void main(String[] args) {
    String input = "But I'm not dead yet! I feel happy!";
    StringTokenizer stoke = new StringTokenizer(input);
    while(stoke.hasMoreElements())
      System.out.print(stoke.nextToken() + " ");
    System.out.println();
    System.out.println(Arrays.toString(input.split(" ")));
    Scanner scanner = new Scanner(input);
    while(scanner.hasNext())
      System.out.print(scanner.next() + " ");
  }
} /* Output:
But I'm not dead yet! I feel happy!
[But, I'm, not, dead, yet!, I, feel, happy!]
But I'm not dead yet! I feel happy!
*///:~
```

With regular expressions or **Scanner** objects, you can also split a string into parts using more complex patterns—something that's difficult with **StringTokenizer**. It seems safe to say that the **StringTokenizer** is obsolete.

Summary

In the past, Java support for string manipulation was rudimentary, but in recent editions of the language we've seen far more sophisticated support adopted from other languages. At this point, the support for strings is reasonably complete, although you must sometimes pay attention to efficiency details such as the appropriate use of **StringBuilder**.

Solutions to selected exercises can be found in the electronic document *The Thinking in Java Annotated Solution Guide*, available for sale from *www.MindView.net*.

Type Information

Runtime type information (RTTI) allows you to discover and use type information while a program is running.

It frees you from the constraint of doing type-oriented things only at compile time, and can enable some very powerful programs. The need for RTTI uncovers a plethora of interesting (and often perplexing) OO design issues, and raises fundamental questions about how you should structure your programs.

This chapter looks at the ways that Java allows you to discover information about objects and classes at run time. This takes two forms: "traditional" RTTI, which assumes that you have all the types available at compile time, and the *reflection* mechanism, which allows you to discover and use class information solely at run time.

The need for RTTI

Consider the now-familiar example of a class hierarchy that uses polymorphism. The generic type is the base class **Shape**, and the specific derived types are **Circle**, **Square**, and **Triangle**:

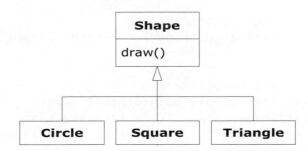

This is a typical class hierarchy diagram, with the base class at the top and the derived classes growing downward. The normal goal in object-oriented programming is for your code to manipulate references to the base type (**Shape**, in this case), so if you decide to extend the program by adding a new class (such as **Rhomboid**, derived from **Shape**), the bulk of the code is not affected. In this example, the dynamically bound method in the **Shape**

interface is **draw( )**, so the intent is for the client programmer to call **draw( )** through a generic **Shape** reference. In all of the derived classes, **draw( )** is overridden, and because it is a dynamically bound method, the proper behavior will occur even though it is called through a generic **Shape** reference. That's polymorphism.

Thus, you generally create a specific object (**Circle**, **Square**, or **Triangle**), upcast it to a **Shape** (forgetting the specific type of the object), and use that anonymous **Shape** reference in the rest of the program.

You might code the **Shape** hierarchy as follows:

```
//: typeinfo/Shapes.java
import java.util.*;

abstract class Shape {
  void draw() { System.out.println(this + ".draw()"); }
  abstract public String toString();
}

class Circle extends Shape {
  public String toString() { return "Circle"; }
}

class Square extends Shape {
  public String toString() { return "Square"; }
}

class Triangle extends Shape {
  public String toString() { return "Triangle"; }
}

public class Shapes {
  public static void main(String[] args) {
    List<Shape> shapeList = Arrays.asList(
      new Circle(), new Square(), new Triangle()
    );
    for(Shape shape : shapeList)
      shape.draw();
  }
} /* Output:
Circle.draw()
Square.draw()
Triangle.draw()
```

```
*///:~
```

The base class contains a **draw( )** method that indirectly uses **toString( )** to print an identifier for the class by passing **this** to **System.out.println( )** (notice that **toString( )** is declared **abstract** to force inheritors to override it, and to prevent the instantiation of a plain **Shape**). If an object appears in a string concatenation expression (involving '+' and **String** objects), the **toString( )** method is automatically called to produce a **String** representation for that object. Each of the derived classes overrides the **toString( )** method (from **Object**) so that **draw( )** ends up (polymorphically) printing something different in each case.

In this example, the upcast occurs when the shape is placed into the **List<Shape>**. During the upcast to **Shape**, the fact that the objects are *specific types* of **Shape** is lost. To the array, they are just **Shape**s.

At the point that you fetch an element out of the array, the container—which is actually holding everything as an **Object**—automatically casts the result back to a **Shape**. This is the most basic form of RTTI, because all casts are checked at run time for correctness. That's what RTTI means: At run time, the type of an object is identified.

In this case, the RTTI cast is only partial: The **Object** is cast to a **Shape**, and not all the way to a **Circle**, **Square**, or **Triangle**. That's because the only thing you *know* at this point is that the **List<Shape>** is full of **Shape**s. At compile time, this is enforced by the container and the Java generic system, but at run time the cast ensures it.

Now polymorphism takes over and the exact code that's executed for the **Shape** is determined by whether the reference is for a **Circle**, **Square**, or **Triangle**. And in general, this is how it should be; you want the bulk of your code to know as little as possible about *specific* types of objects, and to just deal with the general representation of a family of objects (in this case, **Shape**). As a result, your code will be easier to write, read, and maintain, and your designs will be easier to implement, understand, and change. So polymorphism is a general goal in object-oriented programming.

But what if you have a special programming problem that's easiest to solve if you know the exact type of a generic reference? For example, suppose you want to allow your users to highlight all the shapes of any particular type by turning them a special color. This way, they can find all the triangles on the screen by highlighting them. Or perhaps your method needs to "rotate" a list of shapes, but it makes no sense to rotate a circle so you'd like to skip the circles. With RTTI, you can ask a **Shape** reference the exact type that it's referring to, and thus select and isolate special cases.

The **Class** object

To understand how RTTI works in Java, you must first know how type information is represented at run time. This is accomplished through a special kind of object called the *Class object,* which contains information about the class. In fact, the **Class** object is used to create all of the "regular" objects of your class. Java performs its RTTI using the **Class** object, even if you're doing something like a cast. The class **Class** also has a number of other ways you can use RTTI.

There's one **Class** object for each class that is part of your program. That is, each time you write and compile a new class, a single **Class** object is also created (and stored, appropriately enough, in an identically named **.class** file). To make an object of that class, the Java Virtual Machine (JVM) that's executing your program uses a subsystem called a *class loader*.

The class loader subsystem can actually comprise a chain of class loaders, but there's only one *primordial class loader*, which is part of the JVM implementation. The primordial class loader loads so-called *trusted classes*, including Java API classes, typically from the local disk. It's usually not necessary to have additional class loaders in the chain, but if you have special needs (such as loading classes in a special way to support Web server applications, or downloading classes across a network), then you have a way to hook in additional class loaders.

All classes are loaded into the JVM dynamically, upon the first use of a class. This happens when the program makes the first reference to a **static** member of that class. It turns out that the constructor is also a **static** method of a class, even though the **static** keyword is not used for a constructor. Therefore, creating a new object of that class using the **new** operator also counts as a reference to a **static** member of the class.

Thus, a Java program isn't completely loaded before it begins, but instead pieces of it are loaded when necessary. This is different from many traditional languages. Dynamic loading enables behavior that is difficult or impossible to duplicate in a statically loaded language like C++.

The class loader first checks to see if the **Class** object for that type is loaded. If not, the default class loader finds the **.class** file with that name (an add-on class loader might, for example, look for the bytecodes in a database instead). As the bytes for the class are loaded, they are *verified* to ensure that they have not been corrupted and that they do not comprise bad Java code (this is one of the lines of defense for security in Java).

Once the **Class** object for that type is in memory, it is used to create all objects of that type. Here's a program to prove it:

```java
//: typeinfo/SweetShop.java
// Examination of the way the class loader works.
import static net.mindview.util.Print.*;

class Candy {
  static { print("Loading Candy"); }
}

class Gum {
  static { print("Loading Gum"); }
}

class Cookie {
  static { print("Loading Cookie"); }
}

public class SweetShop {
  public static void main(String[] args) {
    print("inside main");
    new Candy();
    print("After creating Candy");
    try {
      Class.forName("Gum");
    } catch(ClassNotFoundException e) {
      print("Couldn't find Gum");
    }
    print("After Class.forName(\"Gum\")");
    new Cookie();
    print("After creating Cookie");
  }
} /* Output:
inside main
Loading Candy
After creating Candy
```

```
Loading Gum
After Class.forName("Gum")
Loading Cookie
After creating Cookie
*///:~
```

Each of the classes **Candy**, **Gum**, and **Cookie** has a **static** clause that is executed as the class is loaded for the first time. Information will be printed to tell you when loading occurs for that class. In **main( )**, the object creations are spread out between print statements to help detect the time of loading.

You can see from the output that each **Class** object is loaded only when it's needed, and the **static** initialization is performed upon class loading.

A particularly interesting line is:

```
Class.forName("Gum");
```

All **Class** objects belong to the class **Class**. A **Class** object is like any other object, so you can get and manipulate a reference to it (that's what the loader does). One of the ways to get a reference to the **Class** object is the **static forName( )** method, which takes a **String** containing the textual name (watch the spelling and capitalization!) of the particular class you want a reference for. It returns a **Class** reference, which is being ignored here; the call to **forName( )** is being made for its side effect, which is to load the class **Gum** if it isn't already loaded. In the process of loading, **Gum**'s **static** clause is executed.

In the preceding example, if **Class.forName( )** fails because it can't find the class you're trying to load, it will throw a **ClassNotFoundException**. Here, we simply report the problem and move on, but in more sophisticated programs, you might try to fix the problem inside the exception handler.

Anytime you want to use type information at run time, you must first get a reference to the appropriate **Class** object. **Class.forName( )** is one convenient way to do this, because you don't need an object of that type in order to get the **Class** reference. However, if you already have an object of the type you're interested in, you can fetch the **Class** reference by calling a method that's part of the **Object** root class: **getClass( )**. This returns the **Class** reference representing the actual type of the object. **Class** has many interesting methods; here are a few of them:

```
//: typeinfo/toys/ToyTest.java
```

```
// Testing class Class.
package typeinfo.toys;
import static net.mindview.util.Print.*;

interface HasBatteries {}
interface Waterproof {}
interface Shoots {}

class Toy {
  // Comment out the following default constructor
  // to see NoSuchMethodError from (*1*)
  Toy() {}
  Toy(int i) {}
}

class FancyToy extends Toy
implements HasBatteries, Waterproof, Shoots {
  FancyToy() { super(1); }
}

public class ToyTest {
  static void printInfo(Class cc) {
    print("Class name: " + cc.getName() +
      " is interface? [" + cc.isInterface() + "]");
    print("Simple name: " + cc.getSimpleName());
    print("Canonical name : " + cc.getCanonicalName());
  }
  public static void main(String[] args) {
    Class c = null;
    try {
      c = Class.forName("typeinfo.toys.FancyToy");
    } catch(ClassNotFoundException e) {
      print("Can't find FancyToy");
      System.exit(1);
    }
    printInfo(c);
    for(Class face : c.getInterfaces())
      printInfo(face);
    Class up = c.getSuperclass();
    Object obj = null;
    try {
      // Requires default constructor:
      obj = up.newInstance();
    } catch(InstantiationException e) {
```

```
        print("Cannot instantiate");
        System.exit(1);
      } catch(IllegalAccessException e) {
        print("Cannot access");
        System.exit(1);
      }
      printInfo(obj.getClass());
    }
} /* Output:
Class name: typeinfo.toys.FancyToy is interface? [false]
Simple name: FancyToy
Canonical name : typeinfo.toys.FancyToy
Class name: typeinfo.toys.HasBatteries is interface? [true]
Simple name: HasBatteries
Canonical name : typeinfo.toys.HasBatteries
Class name: typeinfo.toys.Waterproof is interface? [true]
Simple name: Waterproof
Canonical name : typeinfo.toys.Waterproof
Class name: typeinfo.toys.Shoots is interface? [true]
Simple name: Shoots
Canonical name : typeinfo.toys.Shoots
Class name: typeinfo.toys.Toy is interface? [false]
Simple name: Toy
Canonical name : typeinfo.toys.Toy
*///:~
```

FancyToy inherits from **Toy** and **implements** the **interface**s
HasBatteries, **Waterproof**, and **Shoots**. In **main( )**, a **Class** reference is
created and initialized to the **FancyToy Class** using **forName( )** inside an
appropriate **try** block. Notice that you must use the fully qualified name
(including the package name) in the string that you pass to **forName( )**.

printInfo( ) uses **getName( )** to produce the fully qualified class name, and
getSimpleName( ) and **getCanonicalName( )** (introduced in Java SE5)
to produce the name without the package, and the fully qualified name,
respectively. As its name implies, **isInterface( )** tells you whether this **Class**
object represents an interface. Thus, with the **Class** object you can find out
just about everything you want to know about a type.

The **Class.getInterfaces( )** method called in **main( )** returns an array of
Class objects representing the interfaces that are contained in the **Class**
object of interest.

If you have a **Class** object, you can also ask it for its direct base class using **getSuperclass( )**. This returns a **Class** reference that you can further query. Thus you can discover an object's entire class hierarchy at run time.

The **newInstance( )** method of **Class** is a way to implement a "virtual constructor," which allows you to say, "I don't know exactly what type you are, but create yourself properly anyway." In the preceding example, **up** is just a **Class** reference with no further type information known at compile time. And when you create a new instance, you get back an **Object** reference. But that reference is pointing to a **Toy** object. Of course, before you can send any messages other than those accepted by **Object**, you must investigate it a bit and do some casting. In addition, the class that's being created with **newInstance( )** must have a default constructor. Later in this chapter, you'll see how to dynamically create objects of classes using any constructor, with the Java *reflection* API.

Exercise 1: (1) In **ToyTest.java**, comment out **Toy**'s default constructor and explain what happens.

Exercise 2: (2) Incorporate a new kind of interface into **ToyTest.java** and verify that it is detected and displayed properly.

Exercise 3: (2) Add **Rhomboid** to **Shapes.java**. Create a **Rhomboid**, upcast it to a **Shape**, then downcast it back to a **Rhomboid**. Try downcasting to a **Circle** and see what happens.

Exercise 4: (2) Modify the previous exercise so that it uses **instanceof** to check the type before performing the downcast.

Exercise 5: (3) Implement a **rotate(Shape)** method in **Shapes.java**, such that it checks to see if it is rotating a **Circle** (and, if so, doesn't perform the operation).

Exercise 6: (4) Modify **Shapes.java** so that it can "highlight" (set a flag in) all shapes of a particular type. The **toString( )** method for each derived **Shape** should indicate whether that **Shape** is "highlighted."

Exercise 7: (3) Modify **SweetShop.java** so that each type of object creation is controlled by a command-line argument. That is, if your command line is "**java SweetShop Candy**," then only the **Candy** object is created. Notice how you can control which **Class** objects are loaded via the command-line argument.

Exercise 8: (5) Write a method that takes an object and recursively prints all the classes in that object's hierarchy.

Exercise 9: (5) Modify the previous exercise so that it uses **Class.getDeclaredFields( )** to also display information about the fields in a class.

Exercise 10: (3) Write a program to determine whether an array of **char** is a primitive type or a true **Object**.

Class literals

Java provides a second way to produce the reference to the **Class** object: the *class literal*. In the preceding program this would look like:

```
FancyToy.class;
```

which is not only simpler, but also safer since it's checked at compile time (and thus does not need to be placed in a **try** block). Because it eliminates the **forName( )** method call, it's also more efficient.

Class literals work with regular classes as well as interfaces, arrays, and primitive types. In addition, there's a standard field called **TYPE** that exists for each of the primitive wrapper classes. The **TYPE** field produces a reference to the **Class** object for the associated primitive type, such that:

... is equivalent to ...	
boolean.class	**Boolean.TYPE**
char.class	**Character.TYPE**
byte.class	**Byte.TYPE**
short.class	**Short.TYPE**
int.class	**Integer.TYPE**
long.class	**Long.TYPE**
float.class	**Float.TYPE**
double.class	**Double.TYPE**
void.class	**Void.TYPE**

My preference is to use the ".class" versions if you can, since they're more consistent with regular classes.

It's interesting to note that creating a reference to a **Class** object using ".class" doesn't automatically initialize the **Class** object. There are actually three steps in preparing a class for use:

1. *Loading*, which is performed by the class loader. This finds the bytecodes (usually, but not necessarily, on your disk in your classpath) and creates a **Class** object from those bytecodes.

2. *Linking*. The link phase verifies the bytecodes in the class, allocates storage for **static** fields, and if necessary, resolves all references to other classes made by this class.

3. *Initialization*. If there's a superclass, initialize that. Execute **static** initializers and **static** initialization blocks.

Initialization is delayed until the first reference to a **static** method (the constructor is implicitly **static**) or to a non-constant **static** field:

```
//: typeinfo/ClassInitialization.java
import java.util.*;

class Initable {
  static final int staticFinal = 47;
  static final int staticFinal2 =
    ClassInitialization.rand.nextInt(1000);
  static {
    System.out.println("Initializing Initable");
  }
}

class Initable2 {
  static int staticNonFinal = 147;
  static {
    System.out.println("Initializing Initable2");
  }
}

class Initable3 {
  static int staticNonFinal = 74;
  static {
    System.out.println("Initializing Initable3");
```

```
    }
  }

public class ClassInitialization {
  public static Random rand = new Random(47);
  public static void main(String[] args) throws Exception {
    Class initable = Initable.class;
    System.out.println("After creating Initable ref");
    // Does not trigger initialization:
    System.out.println(Initable.staticFinal);
    // Does trigger initialization:
    System.out.println(Initable.staticFinal2);
    // Does trigger initialization:
    System.out.println(Initable2.staticNonFinal);
    Class initable3 = Class.forName("Initable3");
    System.out.println("After creating Initable3 ref");
    System.out.println(Initable3.staticNonFinal);
  }
} /* Output:
After creating Initable ref
47
Initializing Initable
258
Initializing Initable2
147
Initializing Initable3
After creating Initable3 ref
74
*///:~
```

Effectively, initialization is "as lazy as possible." From the creation of the
initable reference, you can see that just using the **.class** syntax to get a
reference to the class doesn't cause initialization. However,
Class.forName( ) initializes the class immediately in order to produce the
Class reference, as you can see in the creation of **initable3**.

If a **static final** value is a "compile-time constant," such as
Initable.staticFinal, that value can be read without causing the **Initable**
class to be initialized. Making a field **static** and **final**, however, does not
guarantee this behavior: accessing **Initable.staticFinal2** forces class
initialization because it cannot be a compile-time constant.

If a **static** field is not **final**, accessing it always requires linking (to allocate storage for the field) and initialization (to initialize that storage) before it can be read, as you can see in the access to **Initable2.staticNonFinal**.

Generic class references

A **Class** reference points to a **Class** object, which manufactures instances of classes and contains all the method code for those instances. It also contains the **static**s for that class. So a **Class** reference really does indicate the exact type of what it's pointing to: an object of the class **Class**.

However, the designers of Java SE5 saw an opportunity to make this a bit more specific by allowing you to constrain the type of **Class** object that the **Class** reference is pointing to, using the generic syntax. In the following example, both syntaxes are correct:

```
//: typeinfo/GenericClassReferences.java

public class GenericClassReferences {
  public static void main(String[] args) {
    Class intClass = int.class;
    Class<Integer> genericIntClass = int.class;
    genericIntClass = Integer.class; // Same thing
    intClass = double.class;
    // genericIntClass = double.class; // Illegal
  }
} ///:~
```

The ordinary class reference does not produce a warning. However, you can see that the ordinary class reference can be reassigned to any other **Class** object, whereas the generic class reference can only be assigned to its declared type. By using the generic syntax, you allow the compiler to enforce extra type checking.

What if you'd like to loosen the constraint a little? Initially, it seems like you ought to be able to do something like:

```
Class<Number> genericNumberClass = int.class;
```

This would seem to make sense because **Integer** is inherited from **Number**. But this doesn't work, because the **Integer Class** object is not a subclass of the **Number Class** object (this may seem like a subtle distinction; we'll look into it more deeply in the *Generics* chapter).

To loosen the constraints when using generic **Class** references, I employ the *wildcard*, which is part of Java generics. The wildcard symbol is '**?**', and it indicates "anything." So we can add wildcards to the ordinary **Class** reference in the above example and produce the same results:

```
//: typeinfo/WildcardClassReferences.java

public class WildcardClassReferences {
  public static void main(String[] args) {
    Class<?> intClass = int.class;
    intClass = double.class;
  }
} ///:~
```

In Java SE5, **Class<?>** is preferred over plain **Class**, even though they are equivalent and the plain **Class**, as you saw, doesn't produce a compiler warning. The benefit of **Class<?>** is that it indicates that you aren't just using a non-specific class reference by accident, or out of ignorance. You *chose* the non-specific version.

In order to create a **Class** reference that is constrained to a type *or any subtype*, you combine the wildcard with the **extends** keyword to create a *bound*. So instead of just saying **Class<Number>**, you say:

```
//: typeinfo/BoundedClassReferences.java

public class BoundedClassReferences {
  public static void main(String[] args) {
    Class<? extends Number> bounded = int.class;
    bounded = double.class;
    bounded = Number.class;
    // Or anything else derived from Number.
  }
} ///:~
```

The reason for adding the generic syntax to **Class** references is only to provide compile-time type checking, so that if you do something wrong you find out about it a little sooner. You can't actually go astray with ordinary **Class** references, but if you make a mistake you won't find out until run time, which can be inconvenient.

Here's an example that uses the generic class syntax. It stores a class reference, and later produces a **List** filled with objects that it generates using **newInstance( )**:

```
//: typeinfo/FilledList.java
import java.util.*;

class CountedInteger {
  private static long counter;
  private final long id = counter++;
  public String toString() { return Long.toString(id); }
}

public class FilledList<T> {
  private Class<T> type;
  public FilledList(Class<T> type) { this.type = type; }
  public List<T> create(int nElements) {
    List<T> result = new ArrayList<T>();
    try {
      for(int i = 0; i < nElements; i++)
        result.add(type.newInstance());
    } catch(Exception e) {
      throw new RuntimeException(e);
    }
    return result;
  }
  public static void main(String[] args) {
    FilledList<CountedInteger> fl =
      new FilledList<CountedInteger>(CountedInteger.class);
    System.out.println(fl.create(15));
  }
} /* Output:
[0, 1, 2, 3, 4, 5, 6, 7, 8, 9, 10, 11, 12, 13, 14]
*///:~
```

Notice that this class must assume that any type that it works with has a default constructor (one without arguments), and you'll get an exception if that isn't the case. The compiler does not issue any warnings for this program.

An interesting thing happens when you use the generic syntax for **Class** objects: **newInstance( )** will return the exact type of the object, rather than just a basic **Object** as you saw in **ToyTest.java**. This is somewhat limited:

```
//: typeinfo/toys/GenericToyTest.java
// Testing class Class.
package typeinfo.toys;
```

```
public class GenericToyTest {
  public static void main(String[] args) throws Exception {
    Class<FancyToy> ftClass = FancyToy.class;
    // Produces exact type:
    FancyToy fancyToy = ftClass.newInstance();
    Class<? super FancyToy> up = ftClass.getSuperclass();
    // This won't compile:
    // Class<Toy> up2 = ftClass.getSuperclass();
    // Only produces Object:
    Object obj = up.newInstance();
  }
} ///:~
```

If you get the superclass, the compiler will only allow you to say that the superclass reference is "some class that is a superclass of **FancyToy**" as seen in the expression **Class<? super FancyToy>**. It will not accept a declaration of **Class<Toy>**. This seems a bit strange because **getSuperclass( )** returns the base *class* (not interface) and the compiler knows what that class is at compile time—in this case, **Toy.class**, not just "some superclass of **FancyToy**." In any event, because of the vagueness, the return value of **up.newInstance( )** is not a precise type, but just an **Object**.

New cast syntax

Java SE5 also adds a casting syntax for use with **Class** references, which is the **cast( )** method:

```
//: typeinfo/ClassCasts.java

class Building {}
class House extends Building {}

public class ClassCasts {
  public static void main(String[] args) {
    Building b = new House();
    Class<House> houseType = House.class;
    House h = houseType.cast(b);
    h = (House)b; // ... or just do this.
  }
} ///:~
```

The **cast( )** method takes the argument object and casts it to the type of the **Class** reference. Of course, if you look at the above code it seems like a lot of extra work compared to the last line in **main( )**, which does the same thing.

The new casting syntax is useful for situations where you *can't* just use an ordinary cast. This usually happens when you're writing generic code (which you'll learn about in the *Generics* chapter), and you've stored a **Class** reference that you want to use to cast with at a later time. It turns out to be a rare thing—I found only one instance where **cast( )** was used in the entire Java SE5 library (it was in **com.sun.mirror.util.DeclarationFilter**).

Another new feature had *no* usage in the Java SE5 library: **Class.asSubclass( )**. This allows you to cast the class object to a more specific type.

Checking before a cast

So far, you've seen forms of RTTI, including:

1. The classic cast; e.g., "**(Shape)**," which uses RTTI to make sure the cast is correct. This will throw a **ClassCastException** if you've performed a bad cast.

2. The **Class** object representing the type of your object. The **Class** object can be queried for useful runtime information.

In C++, the classic cast "**(Shape)**" does *not* perform RTTI. It simply tells the compiler to treat the object as the new type. In Java, which does perform the type check, this cast is often called a "type-safe downcast." The reason for the term "downcast" is the historical arrangement of the class hierarchy diagram. If casting a **Circle** to a **Shape** is an upcast, then casting a **Shape** to a **Circle** is a downcast. However, because it knows that a **Circle** is also a **Shape**, the compiler freely allows an upcast assignment, without requiring any explicit cast syntax. The compiler *cannot* know, given a **Shape**, what that **Shape** actually is—it could be exactly a **Shape**, or it could be a subtype of **Shape**, such as a **Circle**, **Square**, **Triangle** or some other type. At compile time, the compiler only sees a **Shape**. Thus, it won't allow you to perform a downcast assignment without using an explicit cast, to tell it that you have extra information that allows you to know that it is a particular type (the compiler *will* check to see if that downcast is reasonable, so it won't let you downcast to a type that's not actually a subclass).

There's a third form of RTTI in Java. This is the keyword **instanceof**, which tells you if an object is an instance of a particular type. It returns a **boolean** so you use it in the form of a question, like this:

```
if(x instanceof Dog)
  ((Dog)x).bark();
```

The **if** statement checks to see if the object **x** belongs to the class **Dog** *before* casting **x** to a **Dog**. It's important to use **instanceof** before a downcast when you don't have other information that tells you the type of the object; otherwise, you'll end up with a **ClassCastException**.

Ordinarily, you might be hunting for one type (triangles to turn purple, for example), but you can easily tally *all* of the objects by using **instanceof**. For example, suppose you have a family of classes to describe **Pet**s (and their people, a feature which will come in handy in a later example). Each **Individual** in the hierarchy has an **id** and an optional name. Although the classes that follow inherit from **Individual**, there are some complexities in the **Individual** class, so that code will be shown and explained in the *Containers in Depth* chapter. As you can see, it's not really necessary to see the code for **Individual** at this point—you only need to know that you can create it with or without a name, and that each **Individual** has a method **id( )** that returns a unique identifier (created by counting each object). There's also a **toString( )** method; if you don't provide a name for an **Individual**, **toString( )** only produces the simple type name.

Here is the class hierarchy that inherits from **Individual**:

```
//: typeinfo/pets/Person.java
package typeinfo.pets;

public class Person extends Individual {
  public Person(String name) { super(name); }
} ///:~

//: typeinfo/pets/Pet.java
package typeinfo.pets;

public class Pet extends Individual {
  public Pet(String name) { super(name); }
  public Pet() { super(); }
} ///:~

//: typeinfo/pets/Dog.java
package typeinfo.pets;

public class Dog extends Pet {
  public Dog(String name) { super(name); }
```

```
    public Dog() { super(); }
} ///:~

//: typeinfo/pets/Mutt.java
package typeinfo.pets;

public class Mutt extends Dog {
  public Mutt(String name) { super(name); }
  public Mutt() { super(); }
} ///:~

//: typeinfo/pets/Pug.java
package typeinfo.pets;

public class Pug extends Dog {
  public Pug(String name) { super(name); }
  public Pug() { super(); }
} ///:~

//: typeinfo/pets/Cat.java
package typeinfo.pets;

public class Cat extends Pet {
  public Cat(String name) { super(name); }
  public Cat() { super(); }
} ///:~

//: typeinfo/pets/EgyptianMau.java
package typeinfo.pets;

public class EgyptianMau extends Cat {
  public EgyptianMau(String name) { super(name); }
  public EgyptianMau() { super(); }
} ///:~

//: typeinfo/pets/Manx.java
package typeinfo.pets;

public class Manx extends Cat {
  public Manx(String name) { super(name); }
  public Manx() { super(); }
} ///:~

//: typeinfo/pets/Cymric.java
package typeinfo.pets;

public class Cymric extends Manx {
```

```
    public Cymric(String name) { super(name); }
    public Cymric() { super(); }
} ///:~

//: typeinfo/pets/Rodent.java
package typeinfo.pets;

public class Rodent extends Pet {
    public Rodent(String name) { super(name); }
    public Rodent() { super(); }
} ///:~

//: typeinfo/pets/Rat.java
package typeinfo.pets;

public class Rat extends Rodent {
    public Rat(String name) { super(name); }
    public Rat() { super(); }
} ///:~

//: typeinfo/pets/Mouse.java
package typeinfo.pets;

public class Mouse extends Rodent {
    public Mouse(String name) { super(name); }
    public Mouse() { super(); }
} ///:~

//: typeinfo/pets/Hamster.java
package typeinfo.pets;

public class Hamster extends Rodent {
    public Hamster(String name) { super(name); }
    public Hamster() { super(); }
} ///:~
```

Next, we need a way to randomly create different types of pets, and for convenience, to create arrays and **List**s of pets. To allow this tool to evolve through several different implementations, we'll define it as an abstract class:

```
//: typeinfo/pets/PetCreator.java
// Creates random sequences of Pets.
package typeinfo.pets;
import java.util.*;

public abstract class PetCreator {
```

```
    private Random rand = new Random(47);
    // The List of the different types of Pet to create:
    public abstract List<Class<? extends Pet>> types();
    public Pet randomPet() { // Create one random Pet
      int n = rand.nextInt(types().size());
      try {
        return types().get(n).newInstance();
      } catch(InstantiationException e) {
        throw new RuntimeException(e);
      } catch(IllegalAccessException e) {
        throw new RuntimeException(e);
      }
    }
  public Pet[] createArray(int size) {
    Pet[] result = new Pet[size];
    for(int i = 0; i < size; i++)
      result[i] = randomPet();
    return result;
  }
  public ArrayList<Pet> arrayList(int size) {
    ArrayList<Pet> result = new ArrayList<Pet>();
    Collections.addAll(result, createArray(size));
    return result;
  }
} ///:~
```

The **abstract types( )** method defers to a derived class to get the **List** of
Class objects (this is a variation of the *Template Method* design pattern).
Notice that the type of class is specified to be "anything derived from **Pet**," so
that **newInstance( )** produces a **Pet** without requiring a cast.
randomPet( ) randomly indexes into the **List** and uses the selected **Class**
object to generate a new instance of that class with **Class.newInstancc( )**.
The **createArray( )** method uses **randomPet( )** to fill an array, and
arrayList( ) uses **createArray( )** in turn.

You can get two kinds of exceptions when calling **newInstance( )**. You can
see these handled in the **catch** clauses following the **try** block. Again, the
names of the exceptions are relatively useful explanations of what went
wrong (**IllegalAccessException** relates to a violation of the Java security
mechanism, in this case if the default constructor is **private**).

When you derive a subclass of **PetCreator**, the only thing you need to supply
is the **List** of the types of pet that you want to create using **randomPet( )**

---

and the other methods. The **types( )** method will normally just return a reference to a static **List**. Here's an implementation using **forName( )**:

```
//: typeinfo/pets/ForNameCreator.java
package typeinfo.pets;
import java.util.*;

public class ForNameCreator extends PetCreator {
  private static List<Class<? extends Pet>> types =
    new ArrayList<Class<? extends Pet>>();
  // Types that you want to be randomly created:
  private static String[] typeNames = {
    "typeinfo.pets.Mutt",
    "typeinfo.pets.Pug",
    "typeinfo.pets.EgyptianMau",
    "typeinfo.pets.Manx",
    "typeinfo.pets.Cymric",
    "typeinfo.pets.Rat",
    "typeinfo.pets.Mouse",
    "typeinfo.pets.Hamster"
  };
  @SuppressWarnings("unchecked")
  private static void loader() {
    try {
      for(String name : typeNames)
        types.add(
          (Class<? extends Pet>)Class.forName(name));
    } catch(ClassNotFoundException e) {
      throw new RuntimeException(e);
    }
  }
  static { loader(); }
  public List<Class<? extends Pet>> types() {return types;}
} ///:~
```

The **loader( )** method creates the **List** of **Class** objects using **Class.forName( )**. This may generate a **ClassNotFoundException**, which makes sense since you're passing it a **String** which cannot be validated at compile time. Since the **Pet** objects are in package **typeinfo**, the package name must be used when referring to the classes.

In order to produce a typed **List** of **Class** objects, a cast is required, which produces a compile-time warning. The **loader( )** method is defined separately and then placed inside a static initialization clause because the

@SuppressWarnings annotation cannot be placed directly onto the static initialization clause.

To count **Pet**s, we need a tool that keeps track of the quantities of various different types of **Pet**s. A **Map** is perfect for this; the keys are the **Pet** type names and the values are **Integer**s to hold the **Pet** quantities. This way, you can say, "How many **Hamster** objects are there?" We can use **instanceof** to count **Pet**s:

```java
//: typeinfo/PetCount.java
// Using instanceof.
import typeinfo.pets.*;
import java.util.*;
import static net.mindview.util.Print.*;

public class PetCount {
  static class PetCounter extends HashMap<String,Integer> {
    public void count(String type) {
      Integer quantity = get(type);
      if(quantity == null)
        put(type, 1);
      else
        put(type, quantity + 1);
    }
  }
  public static void
  countPets(PetCreator creator) {
    PetCounter counter= new PetCounter();
    for(Pet pet : creator.createArray(20)) {
      // List each individual pet:
      printnb(pet.getClass().getSimpleName() + " ");
      if(pet instanceof Pet)
        counter.count("Pet");
      if(pet instanceof Dog)
        counter.count("Dog");
      if(pet instanceof Mutt)
        counter.count("Mutt");
      if(pet instanceof Pug)
        counter.count("Pug");
      if(pet instanceof Cat)
        counter.count("Cat");
      if(pet instanceof EgyptianMau)
        counter.count("EgyptianMau");
      if(pet instanceof Manx)
```

```
        counter.count("Manx");
      if(pet instanceof Cymric)
        counter.count("Cymric");
      if(pet instanceof Rodent)
        counter.count("Rodent");
      if(pet instanceof Rat)
        counter.count("Rat");
      if(pet instanceof Mouse)
        counter.count("Mouse");
      if(pet instanceof Hamster)
        counter.count("Hamster");
    }
    // Show the counts:
    print();
    print(counter);
  }
  public static void main(String[] args) {
    countPets(new ForNameCreator());
  }
} /* Output:
Rat Manx Cymric Mutt Pug Cymric Pug Manx Cymric Rat
EgyptianMau Hamster EgyptianMau Mutt Mutt Cymric Mouse Pug
Mouse Cymric
{Rat=2, Cymric=5, Cat=9, Pet=20, Dog=6, Manx=7,
EgyptianMau=2, Pug=3, Mouse=2, Rodent=5, Hamster=1, Mutt=3}
*///:~
```

In **countPets( )**, an array is randomly filled with **Pet**s using a **PetCreator**. Then each **Pet** in the array is tested and counted using **instanceof**.

There's a rather narrow restriction on **instanceof**: You can compare it to a named type only, and not to a **Class** object. In the preceding example you might feel that it's tedious to write out all of those **instanceof** expressions, and you're right. But there is no way to cleverly automate **instanceof** by creating an array of **Class** objects and comparing it to those instead (stay tuned—you'll see an alternative). This isn't as great a restriction as you might think, because you'll eventually understand that your design is probably flawed if you end up writing a lot of **instanceof** expressions.

Using class literals

If we reimplement the **PetCreator** using class literals, the result is cleaner in many ways:

```
//: typeinfo/pets/LiteralPetCreator.java
// Using class literals.
package typeinfo.pets;
import java.util.*;

public class LiteralPetCreator extends PetCreator {
  // No try block needed.
  @SuppressWarnings("unchecked")
  public static final List<Class<? extends Pet>> allTypes =
    Collections.unmodifiableList(Arrays.asList(
      Pet.class, Dog.class, Cat.class,  Rodent.class,
      Mutt.class, Pug.class, EgyptianMau.class, Manx.class,
      Cymric.class, Rat.class, Mouse.class,Hamster.class));
  // Types for random creation:
  private static final List<Class<? extends Pet>> types =
    allTypes.subList(allTypes.indexOf(Mutt.class),
      allTypes.size());
  public List<Class<? extends Pet>> types() {
    return types;
  }
  public static void main(String[] args) {
    System.out.println(types);
  }
} /* Output:
[class typeinfo.pets.Mutt, class typeinfo.pets.Pug, class
typeinfo.pets.EgyptianMau, class typeinfo.pets.Manx, class
typeinfo.pets.Cymric, class typeinfo.pets.Rat, class
typeinfo.pets.Mouse, class typeinfo.pets.Hamster]
*///:~
```

In the upcoming **PetCount3.java** example, we need to pre-load a **Map** with all the **Pet** types (not just the ones that are to be randomly generated), so the **allTypes List** is necessary. The **types** list is the portion of **allTypes** (created using **List.subList( )**) that includes the exact pet types, so it is used for random **Pet** generation.

This time, the creation of **types** does not need to be surrounded by a **try** block since it's evaluated at compile time and thus won't throw any exceptions, unlike **Class.forName( )**.

We now have two implementations of **PetCreator** in the **typeinfo.pets** library. In order to provide the second one as a default implementation, we can create a *Façade* that utilizes **LiteralPetCreator**:

```
//: typeinfo/pets/Pets.java
// Facade to produce a default PetCreator.
package typeinfo.pets;
import java.util.*;

public class Pets {
  public static final PetCreator creator =
    new LiteralPetCreator();
  public static Pet randomPet() {
    return creator.randomPet();
  }
  public static Pet[] createArray(int size) {
    return creator.createArray(size);
  }
  public static ArrayList<Pet> arrayList(int size) {
    return creator.arrayList(size);
  }
} ///:~
```

This also provides indirection to **randomPet( )**, **createArray( )** and **arrayList( )**.

Because **PetCount.countPets( )** takes a **PetCreator** argument, we can easily test the **LiteralPetCreator** (via the above Façade):

```
//: typeinfo/PetCount2.java
import typeinfo.pets.*;

public class PetCount2 {
  public static void main(String[] args) {
    PetCount.countPets(Pets.creator);
  }
} /* (Execute to see output) *///:~
```

The output is the same as that of **PetCount.java**.

A dynamic **instanceof**

The **Class.isInstance( )** method provides a way to dynamically test the type of an object. Thus, all those tedious **instanceof** statements can be removed from **PetCount.java**:

```
//: typeinfo/PetCount3.java
// Using isInstance()
import typeinfo.pets.*;
```

```java
import java.util.*;
import net.mindview.util.*;
import static net.mindview.util.Print.*;

public class PetCount3 {
  static class PetCounter
  extends LinkedHashMap<Class<? extends Pet>,Integer> {
    public PetCounter() {
      super(MapData.map(LiteralPetCreator.allTypes, 0));
    }
    public void count(Pet pet) {
      // Class.isInstance() eliminates instanceofs:
      for(Map.Entry<Class<? extends Pet>,Integer> pair
          : entrySet())
        if(pair.getKey().isInstance(pet))
          put(pair.getKey(), pair.getValue() + 1);
    }
    public String toString() {
      StringBuilder result = new StringBuilder("{");
      for(Map.Entry<Class<? extends Pet>,Integer> pair
          : entrySet()) {
        result.append(pair.getKey().getSimpleName());
        result.append("=");
        result.append(pair.getValue());
        result.append(", ");
      }
      result.delete(result.length()-2, result.length());
      result.append("}");
      return result.toString();
    }
  }
  public static void main(String[] args) {
    PetCounter petCount = new PetCounter();
    for(Pet pet : Pets.createArray(20)) {
      printnb(pet.getClass().getSimpleName() + " ");
      petCount.count(pet);
    }
    print();
    print(petCount);
  }
} /* Output:
Rat Manx Cymric Mutt Pug Cymric Pug Manx Cymric Rat
EgyptianMau Hamster EgyptianMau Mutt Mutt Cymric Mouse Pug
Mouse Cymric
```

```
{Pet=20, Dog=6, Cat=9, Rodent=5, Mutt=3, Pug=3,
EgyptianMau=2, Manx=7, Cymric=5, Rat=2, Mouse=2, Hamster=1}
*///:~
```

In order to count all the different types of **Pet**, the **PetCounter Map** is pre-loaded with the types from **LiteralPetCreator.allTypes**. This uses the **net.mindview.util.MapData** class, which takes an **Iterable** (the **allTypes List**) and a constant value (zero, in this case), and fills the **Map** with keys taken from **allTypes** and values of zero). Without pre-loading the **Map**, you would only end up counting the types that are randomly generated, and not the base types like **Pet** and **Cat**.

You can see that the **isInstance( )** method has eliminated the need for the **instanceof** expressions. In addition, this means that you can add new types of **Pet** simply by changing the **LiteralPetCreator.types** array; the rest of the program does not need modification (as it did when using the **instanceof** expressions).

The **toString( )** method has been overloaded for easier-to-read output that still matches the typical output that you see when printing a **Map**.

Counting recursively

The **Map** in **PetCount3.PetCounter** was pre-loaded with all the different **Pet** classes. Instead of pre-loading the map, we can use **Class.isAssignableFrom( )** and create a general-purpose tool that is not limited to counting **Pet**s:

```
//: net/mindview/util/TypeCounter.java
// Counts instances of a type family.
package net.mindview.util;
import java.util.*;

public class TypeCounter extends HashMap<Class<?>,Integer>{
  private Class<?> baseType;
  public TypeCounter(Class<?> baseType) {
    this.baseType = baseType;
  }
  public void count(Object obj) {
    Class<?> type = obj.getClass();
    if(!baseType.isAssignableFrom(type))
      throw new RuntimeException(obj + " incorrect type: "
        + type + ", should be type or subtype of "
```

```
      + baseType);
    countClass(type);
  }
  private void countClass(Class<?> type) {
    Integer quantity = get(type);
    put(type, quantity == null ? 1 : quantity + 1);
    Class<?> superClass = type.getSuperclass();
    if(superClass != null &&
       baseType.isAssignableFrom(superClass))
      countClass(superClass);
  }
  public String toString() {
    StringBuilder result = new StringBuilder("{");
    for(Map.Entry<Class<?>,Integer> pair : entrySet()) {
      result.append(pair.getKey().getSimpleName());
      result.append("=");
      result.append(pair.getValue());
      result.append(", ");
    }
    result.delete(result.length()-2, result.length());
    result.append("}");
    return result.toString();
  }
} ///:~
```

The **count( )** method gets the **Class** of its argument, and uses
isAssignableFrom( ) to perform a runtime check to verify that the object
that you've passed actually belongs to the hierarchy of interest.
countClass( ) first counts the exact type of the class. Then, if **baseType** is
assignable from the superclass, **countClass( )** is called recursively on the
superclass.

```
//: typeinfo/PetCount4.java
import typeinfo.pets.*;
import net.mindview.util.*;
import static net.mindview.util.Print.*;

public class PetCount4 {
  public static void main(String[] args) {
    TypeCounter counter = new TypeCounter(Pet.class);
    for(Pet pet : Pets.createArray(20)) {
      printnb(pet.getClass().getSimpleName() + " ");
      counter.count(pet);
    }
```

```
      print();
      print(counter);
    }
  } /* Output: (Sample)
Rat Manx Cymric Mutt Pug Cymric Pug Manx Cymric Rat
EgyptianMau Hamster EgyptianMau Mutt Mutt Cymric Mouse Pug
Mouse Cymric
{Mouse=2, Dog=6, Manx=7, EgyptianMau=2, Rodent=5, Pug=3,
Mutt=3, Cymric=5, Cat=9, Hamster=1, Pet=20, Rat=2}
*///:~
```

As you can see from the output, both base types as well as exact types are counted.

Exercise 11:   (2) Add **Gerbil** to the **typeinfo.pets** library and modify all the examples in this chapter to adapt to this new class.

Exercise 12:   (3) Use **TypeCounter** with the **CoffeeGenerator.java** class in the *Generics* chapter.

Exercise 13:   (3) Use **TypeCounter** with the **RegisteredFactories.java** example in this chapter.

Registered factories

A problem with generating objects of the **Pet**s hierarchy is the fact that every time you add a new type of **Pet** to the hierarchy you must remember to add it to the entries in **LiteralPetCreator.java**. In a system where you add more classes on a regular basis this can become problematic.

You might think of adding a static initializer to each subclass, so that the initializer would add its class to a list somewhere. Unfortunately, static initializers are only called when the class is first loaded, so you have a chicken-and-egg problem: The generator doesn't have the class in its list, so it can never create an object of that class, so the class won't get loaded and placed in the list.

Basically, you're forced to create the list yourself, by hand (unless you want to write a tool that searches through and analyzes your source code, then creates and compiles the list). So the best you can probably do is to put the list in one central, obvious place. The base class for the hierarchy of interest is probably the best place.

The other change we'll make here is to defer the creation of the object to the class itself, using the *Factory Method* design pattern. A factory method can be called polymorphically, and creates an object of the appropriate type for you. In this very simple version, the factory method is the **create( )** method in the **Factory** interface:

```
//: typeinfo/factory/Factory.java
package typeinfo.factory;
public interface Factory<T> { T create(); } ///:~
```

The generic parameter **T** allows **create( )** to return a different type for each implementation of **Factory**. This also makes use of covariant return types.

In this example, the base class **Part** contains a **List** of factory objects. Factories for types that should be produced by the **createRandom( )** method are "registered" with the base class by adding them to the **partFactories List**:

```
//: typeinfo/RegisteredFactories.java
// Registering Class Factories in the base class.
import typeinfo.factory.*;
import java.util.*;

class Part {
  public String toString() {
    return getClass().getSimpleName();
  }
  static List<Factory<? extends Part>> partFactories =
    new ArrayList<Factory<? extends Part>>();
  static {
    // Collections.addAll() gives an "unchecked generic
    // array creation ... for varargs parameter" warning.
    partFactories.add(new FuelFilter.Factory());
    partFactories.add(new AirFilter.Factory());
    partFactories.add(new CabinAirFilter.Factory());
    partFactories.add(new OilFilter.Factory());
    partFactories.add(new FanBelt.Factory());
    partFactories.add(new PowerSteeringBelt.Factory());
    partFactories.add(new GeneratorBelt.Factory());
  }
  private static Random rand = new Random(47);
  public static Part createRandom() {
    int n = rand.nextInt(partFactories.size());
    return partFactories.get(n).create();
```

```java
    }
  }

  class Filter extends Part {}

  class FuelFilter extends Filter {
    // Create a Class Factory for each specific type:
    public static class Factory
    implements typeinfo.factory.Factory<FuelFilter> {
      public FuelFilter create() { return new FuelFilter(); }
    }
  }

  class AirFilter extends Filter {
    public static class Factory
    implements typeinfo.factory.Factory<AirFilter> {
      public AirFilter create() { return new AirFilter(); }
    }
  }

  class CabinAirFilter extends Filter {
    public static class Factory
    implements typeinfo.factory.Factory<CabinAirFilter> {
      public CabinAirFilter create() {
        return new CabinAirFilter();
      }
    }
  }

  class OilFilter extends Filter {
    public static class Factory
    implements typeinfo.factory.Factory<OilFilter> {
      public OilFilter create() { return new OilFilter(); }
    }
  }

  class Belt extends Part {}

  class FanBelt extends Belt {
    public static class Factory
    implements typeinfo.factory.Factory<FanBelt> {
      public FanBelt create() { return new FanBelt(); }
    }
  }
```

```
class GeneratorBelt extends Belt {
  public static class Factory
  implements typeinfo.factory.Factory<GeneratorBelt> {
    public GeneratorBelt create() {
      return new GeneratorBelt();
    }
  }
}

class PowerSteeringBelt extends Belt {
  public static class Factory
  implements typeinfo.factory.Factory<PowerSteeringBelt> {
    public PowerSteeringBelt create() {
      return new PowerSteeringBelt();
    }
  }
}

public class RegisteredFactories {
  public static void main(String[] args) {
    for(int i = 0; i < 10; i++)
      System.out.println(Part.createRandom());
  }
} /* Output:
GeneratorBelt
CabinAirFilter
GeneratorBelt
AirFilter
PowerSteeringBelt
CabinAirFilter
FuelFilter
PowerSteeringBelt
PowerSteeringBelt
FuelFilter
*///:~
```

Not all classes in the hierarchy should be instantiated; in this case **Filter** and **Belt** are just classifiers so you do not create an instance of either one, but only of their subclasses. If a class *should* be created by **createRandom( )**, it contains an inner **Factory** class. The only way to reuse the name **Factory** as seen above is by qualifying **typeinfo.factory.Factory**.

Although you can use **Collections.addAll( )** to add the factories to the list, the compiler expresses its unhappiness with a warning about a "generic array creation" (which is supposed to be impossible, as you'll see in the *Generics* chapter), so I reverted to calling **add( )**. The **createRandom( )** method randomly selects a factory object from **partFactories** and calls its **create( )** to produce a new **Part**.

Exercise 14: (4) A constructor is a kind of factory method. Modify **RegisteredFactories.java** so that instead of using an explicit factory, the class object is stored in the **List**, and **newInstance( )** is used to create each object.

Exercise 15: (4) Implement a new **PetCreator** using Registered Factories, and modify the **Pets** Façade so that it uses this one instead of the other two. Ensure that the rest of the examples that use **Pets.java** still work correctly.

Exercise 16: (4) Modify the **Coffee** hierarchy in the *Generics* chapter to use Registered Factories.

instanceof vs. Class equivalence

When you are querying for type information, there's an important difference between either form of **instanceof** (that is, **instanceof** or **isInstance( )**, which produce equivalent results) and the direct comparison of the **Class** objects. Here's an example that demonstrates the difference:

```
//: typeinfo/FamilyVsExactType.java
// The difference between instanceof and class
package typeinfo;
import static net.mindview.util.Print.*;

class Base {}
class Derived extends Base {}

public class FamilyVsExactType {
  static void test(Object x) {
    print("Testing x of type " + x.getClass());
    print("x instanceof Base " + (x instanceof Base));
    print("x instanceof Derived "+ (x instanceof Derived));
    print("Base.isInstance(x) "+ Base.class.isInstance(x));
    print("Derived.isInstance(x) " +
      Derived.class.isInstance(x));
    print("x.getClass() == Base.class " +
```

```
          (x.getClass() == Base.class));
      print("x.getClass() == Derived.class " +
          (x.getClass() == Derived.class));
      print("x.getClass().equals(Base.class)) "+
          (x.getClass().equals(Base.class)));
      print("x.getClass().equals(Derived.class)) " +
          (x.getClass().equals(Derived.class)));
    }
    public static void main(String[] args) {
      test(new Base());
      test(new Derived());
    }
} /* Output:
Testing x of type class typeinfo.Base
x instanceof Base true
x instanceof Derived false
Base.isInstance(x) true
Derived.isInstance(x) false
x.getClass() == Base.class true
x.getClass() == Derived.class false
x.getClass().equals(Base.class) true
x.getClass().equals(Derived.class) false
Testing x of type class typeinfo.Derived
x instanceof Base true
x instanceof Derived true
Base.isInstance(x) true
Derived.isInstance(x) true
x.getClass() == Base.class false
x.getClass() == Derived.class true
x.getClass().equals(Base.class) false
x.getClass().equals(Derived.class) true
*///:~
```

The **test( )** method performs type checking with its argument using both
forms of **instanceof**. It then gets the **Class** reference and uses == and
equals( ) to test for equality of the **Class** objects. Reassuringly, **instanceof**
and **isInstance( )** produce exactly the same results, as do **equals( )** and ==.
But the tests themselves draw different conclusions. In keeping with the
concept of type, **instanceof** says, "Are you this class, or a class derived from
this class?" On the other hand, if you compare the actual **Class** objects using
==, there is no concern with inheritance—it's either the exact type or it isn't.

Reflection: runtime class information

If you don't know the precise type of an object, RTTI will tell you. However, there's a limitation: The type must be known at compile time in order for you to detect it using RTTI and to do something useful with the information. Put another way, the compiler must know about all the classes you're working with.

This doesn't seem like that much of a limitation at first, but suppose you're given a reference to an object that's not in your program space. In fact, the class of the object isn't even available to your program at compile time. For example, suppose you get a bunch of bytes from a disk file or from a network connection, and you're told that those bytes represent a class. Since this class shows up long after the compiler generates the code for your program, how can you possibly use such a class?

In a traditional programming environment, this seems like a far-fetched scenario. But as we move into a larger programming world, there are important cases in which this happens. The first is component-based programming, in which you build projects using *Rapid Application Development* (RAD) in an Application Builder *Integrated Development Environment*, which I shall refer to simply as an *IDE*. This is a visual approach to creating a program by moving icons that represent components onto a form. These components are then configured by setting some of their values at program time. This design-time configuration requires that any component be instantiable, that it exposes parts of itself, and that it allows its properties to be read and modified. In addition, components that handle *Graphical User Interface* (GUI) events must expose information about appropriate methods so that the IDE can assist the programmer in overriding these event-handling methods. Reflection provides the mechanism to detect the available methods and produce the method names. Java provides a structure for component-based programming through JavaBeans (described in the *Graphical User Interfaces* chapter).

Another compelling motivation for discovering class information at run time is to provide the ability to create and execute objects on remote platforms, across a network. This is called *Remote Method Invocation* (RMI), and it allows a Java program to have objects distributed across many machines.

This distribution can happen for a number of reasons. For example, perhaps you're doing a computation-intensive task, and in order to speed things up, you want to break it up and put pieces on machines that are idle. In other situations you might want to place code that handles particular types of tasks (e.g., "Business Rules" in a multitier client/server architecture) on a particular machine, so the machine becomes a common repository describing those actions, and it can be easily changed to affect everyone in the system. (This is an interesting development, since the machine exists solely to make software changes easy!) Along these lines, distributed computing also supports specialized hardware that might be good at a particular task—matrix inversions, for example—but inappropriate or too expensive for general-purpose programming.

The class **Class** supports the concept of *reflection*, along with the **java.lang.reflect** library which contains the classes **Field**, **Method**, and **Constructor** (each of which implements the **Member** interface). Objects of these types are created by the JVM at run time to represent the corresponding member in the unknown class. You can then use the **Constructor**s to create new objects, the **get( )** and **set( )** methods to read and modify the fields associated with **Field** objects, and the **invoke( )** method to call a method associated with a **Method** object. In addition, you can call the convenience methods **getFields( )**, **getMethods( )**, **getConstructors( )**, etc., to return arrays of the objects representing the fields, methods, and constructors. (You can find out more by looking up the class **Class** in the JDK documentation.) Thus, the class information for anonymous objects can be completely determined at run time, and nothing need be known at compile time.

It's important to realize that there's nothing magic about reflection. When you're using reflection to interact with an object of an unknown type, the JVM will simply look at the object and see that it belongs to a particular class (just like ordinary RTTI). Before anything can be done with it, the **Class** object must be loaded. Thus, the **.class** file for that particular type must still be available to the JVM, either on the local machine or across the network. So the true difference between RTTI and reflection is that with RTTI, the compiler opens and examines the **.class** file at compile time. Put another way, you can call all the methods of an object in the "normal" way. With reflection, the **.class** file is unavailable at compile time; it is opened and examined by the runtime environment.

A class method extractor

Normally you won't need to use the reflection tools directly, but they can be helpful when you need to create more dynamic code. Reflection is in the language to support other Java features, such as object serialization and JavaBeans (both covered later in the book). However, there are times when it's quite useful to dynamically extract information about a class.

Consider a class method extractor. Looking at a class definition source code or JDK documentation shows only the methods that are defined or overridden *within that class definition*. But there might be dozens more available to you that have come from base classes. To locate these is both tedious and time consuming.[1] Fortunately, reflection provides a way to write a simple tool that will automatically show you the entire interface. Here's the way it works:

```
//: typeinfo/ShowMethods.java
// Using reflection to show all the methods of a class,
// even if the methods are defined in the base class.
// {Args: ShowMethods}
import java.lang.reflect.*;
import java.util.regex.*;
import static net.mindview.util.Print.*;

public class ShowMethods {
  private static String usage =
    "usage:\n" +
    "ShowMethods qualified.class.name\n" +
    "To show all methods in class or:\n" +
    "ShowMethods qualified.class.name word\n" +
    "To search for methods involving 'word'";
  private static Pattern p = Pattern.compile("\\w+\\.");
  public static void main(String[] args) {
    if(args.length < 1) {
      print(usage);
      System.exit(0);
    }
    int lines = 0;
    try {
```

---

[1] Especially in the past. However, Sun has greatly improved its HTML Java documentation so that it's easier to see base-class methods.

```
        Class<?> c = Class.forName(args[0]);
        Method[] methods = c.getMethods();
        Constructor[] ctors = c.getConstructors();
        if(args.length == 1) {
          for(Method method : methods)
            print(
              p.matcher(method.toString()).replaceAll(""));
          for(Constructor ctor : ctors)
            print(p.matcher(ctor.toString()).replaceAll(""));
          lines = methods.length + ctors.length;
        } else {
          for(Method method : methods)
            if(method.toString().indexOf(args[1]) != -1) {
              print(
                p.matcher(method.toString()).replaceAll(""));
              lines++;
            }
          for(Constructor ctor : ctors)
            if(ctor.toString().indexOf(args[1]) != -1) {
              print(p.matcher(
                ctor.toString()).replaceAll(""));
              lines++;
            }
        }
    } catch(ClassNotFoundException e) {
      print("No such class: " + e);
    }
  }
} /* Output:
public static void main(String[])
public native int hashCode()
public final native Class getClass()
public final void wait(long,int) throws
InterruptedException
public final void wait() throws InterruptedException
public final native void wait(long) throws
InterruptedException
public boolean equals(Object)
public String toString()
public final native void notify()
public final native void notifyAll()
public ShowMethods()
*///:~
```

The **Class** methods **getMethods( )** and **getConstructors( )** return an array of **Method** and array of **Constructor**, respectively. Each of these classes has further methods to dissect the names, arguments, and return values of the methods they represent. But you can also just use **toString( )**, as is done here, to produce a **String** with the entire method signature. The rest of the code extracts the command-line information, determines if a particular signature matches your target string (using **indexOf( )**), and strips off the name qualifiers using regular expressions (introduced in the *Strings* chapter).

The result produced by **Class.forName( )** cannot be known at compile time, and therefore all the method signature information is being extracted at run time. If you investigate the JDK reflection documentation, you'll see that there is enough support to actually set up and make a method call on an object that's totally unknown at compile time (there will be examples of this later in this book). Although initially this is something you may not think you'll ever need, the value of full reflection can be quite surprising.

The output above is produced from the command line:

```
java ShowMethods ShowMethods
```

You can see that the output includes a **public** default constructor, even though no constructor was defined. The constructor you see is the one that's automatically synthesized by the compiler. If you then make **ShowMethods** a non-**public** class (that is, package access), the synthesized default constructor no longer shows up in the output. The synthesized default constructor is automatically given the same access as the class.

Another interesting experiment is to invoke **java ShowMethods java.lang.String** with an extra argument of **char**, **int**, **String**, etc.

This tool can be a real time-saver while you're programming, when you can't remember if a class has a particular method and you don't want to go hunting through the index or class hierarchy in the JDK documentation, or if you don't know whether that class can do anything with, for example, **Color** objects.

The *Graphical User Interfaces* chapter contains a GUI version of this program (customized to extract information for Swing components) so you can leave it running while you're writing code, to allow quick lookups.

Exercise 17: (2) Modify the regular expression in **ShowMethods.java** to additionally strip off the keywords **native** and **final** (hint: use the OR operator '|').

Exercise 18: (1) Make **ShowMethods** a non-**public** class and verify that the synthesized default constructor no longer shows up in the output.

Exercise 19: (4) In **ToyTest.java**, use reflection to create a **Toy** object using the non-default constructor.

Exercise 20: (5) Look up the interface for **java.lang.Class** in the JDK documentation from *http://java.sun.com*. Write a program that takes the name of a class as a command-line argument, then uses the **Class** methods to dump all the information available for that class. Test your program with a standard library class and a class you create.

Dynamic proxies

Proxy is one of the basic design patterns. It is an object that you insert in place of the "real" object in order to provide additional or different operations—these usually involve communication with a "real" object, so a proxy typically acts as a go-between. Here's a trivial example to show the structure of a proxy:

```
//: typeinfo/SimpleProxyDemo.java
import static net.mindview.util.Print.*;

interface Interface {
  void doSomething();
  void somethingElse(String arg);
}

class RealObject implements Interface {
  public void doSomething() { print("doSomething"); }
  public void somethingElse(String arg) {
    print("somethingElse " + arg);
  }
}

class SimpleProxy implements Interface {
  private Interface proxied;
  public SimpleProxy(Interface proxied) {
    this.proxied = proxied;
  }
```

```
  public void doSomething() {
    print("SimpleProxy doSomething");
    proxied.doSomething();
  }
  public void somethingElse(String arg) {
    print("SimpleProxy somethingElse " + arg);
    proxied.somethingElse(arg);
  }
}

class SimpleProxyDemo {
  public static void consumer(Interface iface) {
    iface.doSomething();
    iface.somethingElse("bonobo");
  }
  public static void main(String[] args) {
    consumer(new RealObject());
    consumer(new SimpleProxy(new RealObject()));
  }
} /* Output:
doSomething
somethingElse bonobo
SimpleProxy doSomething
doSomething
SimpleProxy somethingElse bonobo
somethingElse bonobo
*///:~
```

Because **consumer( )** accepts an **Interface**, it can't know if it's getting a
RealObject or a **SimpleProxy**, because both implement **Interface**. But
the **SimpleProxy** inserted between the client and the **RealObject** performs
operations and then calls the identical method on a **RealObject**.

A proxy can be helpful anytime you'd like to separate extra operations into a
different place than the "real object," and especially when you want to easily
change from not using the extra operations to using them, and vice versa (the
point of design patterns is to encapsulate change—so you need to be changing
things in order to justify the pattern). For example, what if you wanted to
track calls to the methods in the **RealObject**, or to measure the overhead of
such calls? This is not code you want to have incorporated in your
application, so a proxy allows you to add and remove it easily.

Java's *dynamic proxy* takes the idea of a proxy one step further, by both
creating the proxy object dynamically and handling calls to the proxied

methods dynamically. All calls made on a dynamic proxy are redirected to a single *invocation handler*, which has the job of discovering what the call is and deciding what to do about it. Here's **SimpleProxyDemo.java** rewritten to use a dynamic proxy:

```java
//: typeinfo/SimpleDynamicProxy.java
import java.lang.reflect.*;

class DynamicProxyHandler implements InvocationHandler {
  private Object proxied;
  public DynamicProxyHandler(Object proxied) {
    this.proxied = proxied;
  }
  public Object
  invoke(Object proxy, Method method, Object[] args)
  throws Throwable {
    System.out.println("**** proxy: " + proxy.getClass() +
      ", method: " + method + ", args: " + args);
    if(args != null)
      for(Object arg : args)
        System.out.println("  " + arg);
    return method.invoke(proxied, args);
  }
}

class SimpleDynamicProxy {
  public static void consumer(Interface iface) {
    iface.doSomething();
    iface.somethingElse("bonobo");
  }
  public static void main(String[] args) {
    RealObject real = new RealObject();
    consumer(real);
    // Insert a proxy and call again:
    Interface proxy = (Interface)Proxy.newProxyInstance(
      Interface.class.getClassLoader(),
      new Class[]{ Interface.class },
      new DynamicProxyHandler(real));
    consumer(proxy);
  }
} /* Output: (95% match)
doSomething
somethingElse bonobo
```

```
**** proxy: class $Proxy0, method: public abstract void
Interface.doSomething(), args: null
doSomething
**** proxy: class $Proxy0, method: public abstract void
Interface.somethingElse(java.lang.String), args:
[Ljava.lang.Object;@42e816
  bonobo
somethingElse bonobo
*///:~
```

You create a dynamic proxy by calling the **static** method
Proxy.newProxyInstance( ), which requires a class loader (you can
generally just hand it a class loader from an object that has already been
loaded), a list of interfaces (not classes or abstract classes) that you wish the
proxy to implement, and an implementation of the interface
InvocationHandler. The dynamic proxy will redirect all calls to the
invocation handler, so the constructor for the invocation handler is usually
given the reference to the "real" object so that it can forward requests once it
performs its intermediary task.

The **invoke( )** method is handed the proxy object, in case you need to
distinguish where the request came from—but in many cases you won't care.
However, be careful when calling methods on the proxy inside **invoke( )**,
because calls through the interface are redirected through the proxy.

In general you will perform the proxied operation and then use
Method.invoke( ) to forward the request to the proxied object, passing the
necessary arguments. This may initially seem limiting, as if you can only
perform generic operations. However, you can filter for certain method calls,
while passing others through:

```
//: typeinfo/SelectingMethods.java
// Looking for particular methods in a dynamic proxy.
import java.lang.reflect.*;
import static net.mindview.util.Print.*;

class MethodSelector implements InvocationHandler {
  private Object proxied;
  public MethodSelector(Object proxied) {
    this.proxied = proxied;
  }
  public Object
  invoke(Object proxy, Method method, Object[] args)
```

```
        throws Throwable {
      if(method.getName().equals("interesting"))
        print("Proxy detected the interesting method");
      return method.invoke(proxied, args);
    }
}

interface SomeMethods {
  void boring1();
  void boring2();
  void interesting(String arg);
  void boring3();
}

class Implementation implements SomeMethods {
  public void boring1() { print("boring1"); }
  public void boring2() { print("boring2"); }
  public void interesting(String arg) {
    print("interesting " + arg);
  }
  public void boring3() { print("boring3"); }
}

class SelectingMethods {
  public static void main(String[] args) {
    SomeMethods proxy= (SomeMethods)Proxy.newProxyInstance(
      SomeMethods.class.getClassLoader(),
      new Class[]{ SomeMethods.class },
      new MethodSelector(new Implementation()));
    proxy.boring1();
    proxy.boring2();
    proxy.interesting("bonobo");
    proxy.boring3();
  }
} /* Output:
boring1
boring2
Proxy detected the interesting method
interesting bonobo
boring3
*///:~
```

Here, we are just looking for method names, but you could also be looking for other aspects of the method signature, and you could even search for particular argument values.

The dynamic proxy is not a tool that you'll use every day, but it can solve certain types of problems very nicely. You can learn more about *Proxy* and other design patterns in *Thinking in Patterns* (see *www.MindView.net*) and *Design Patterns*, by Erich Gamma et al. (Addison-Wesley, 1995).

Exercise 21: (3) Modify **SimpleProxyDemo.java** so that it measures method-call times.

Exercise 22: (3) Modify **SimpleDynamicProxy.java** so that it measures method-call times.

Exercise 23: (3) Inside **invoke( )** in **SimpleDynamicProxy.java**, try to print the **proxy** argument and explain what happens.

Project:[2] Write a system using dynamic proxies to implement *transactions*, where the proxy performs a *commit* if the proxied call is successful (doesn't throw any exceptions) and a *rollback* if it fails. Your commit and rollback should work on an external text file, which is outside the control of Java exceptions. You will have to pay attention to the *atomicity* of operations.

Null Objects

When you use the built-in **null** to indicate the absence of an object, you must test a reference for **null**-ness every time you use it. This can get very tedious and produce ponderous code. The problem is that **null** has no behavior of its own except for producing a **NullPointerException** if you try to do anything with it. Sometimes it is useful to introduce the idea of a *Null Object*[3] that will accept messages for the object that it's "standing in" for, but will return values indicating that no "real" object is actually there. This way, you can

---

[2] Projects are suggestions to be used (for example) as term projects. Solutions to projects are not included in the solution guide.

[3] Discovered by Bobby Woolf and Bruce Anderson. This can be seen as a special case of the *Strategy* pattern. A variant of *Null Object* is the *Null Iterator* pattern, which makes iteration over the nodes in a composite hierarchy transparent to the client (the client can then use the same logic for iterating over the composite and leaf nodes).

assume that all objects are valid and you don't have to waste programming time checking for **null** (and reading the resulting code).

Although it's fun to imagine a programming language that would automatically create Null Objects for you, in practice it doesn't make sense to use them everywhere—sometimes checking for **null** is fine, and sometimes you can reasonably assume that you won't encounter **null**, and sometimes even detecting aberrations via **NullPointerException** is acceptable. The place where Null Objects seem to be most useful is "closer to the data," with objects that represent entities in the problem space. As a simple example, many systems will have a **Person** class, and there are situations in the code where you don't have an actual person (or you do, but you don't have all the information about that person yet), so traditionally you'd use a **null** reference and test for it. Instead, we can make a Null Object. But even though the Null Object will respond to all messages that the "real" object will respond to, you still need a way to test for nullness. The simplest way to do this is to create a tagging interface:

```
//: net/mindview/util/Null.java
package net.mindview.util;
public interface Null {} ///:~
```

This allows **instanceof** to detect the Null Object, and more importantly, does not require you to add an **isNull( )** method to all your classes (which would be, after all, just a different way of performing RTTI—why not use the built-in facility instead?).

```
//: typeinfo/Person.java
// A class with a Null Object.
import net.mindview.util.*;

class Person {
  public final String first;
  public final String last;
  public final String address;
  // etc.
  public Person(String first, String last, String address){
    this.first = first;
    this.last = last;
    this.address = address;
  }
  public String toString() {
    return "Person: " + first + " " + last + " " + address;
```

```
    }
    public static class NullPerson
    extends Person implements Null {
      private NullPerson() { super("None", "None", "None"); }
      public String toString() { return "NullPerson"; }
    }
    public static final Person NULL = new NullPerson();
  } ///:~
```

In general, the Null Object will be a Singleton, so here it is created as a **static final** instance. This works because **Person** is *immutable*—you can only set the values in the constructor, and then read those values, but you can't modify them (because **String**s themselves are inherently immutable). If you want to change a **NullPerson**, you can only replace it with a new **Person** object. Notice that you have the option of detecting the generic **Null** or the more specific **NullPerson** using **instanceof**, but with the Singleton approach you can also just use **equals( )** or even == to compare to **Person.NULL**.

Now suppose you're back in the high-flying days of Internet startups and you've been given a big pile of venture funding for your Amazing Idea. You're ready to staff up, but while you're waiting for positions to be filled, you can use **Person** Null Objects as placeholders for each **Position**:

```
//: typeinfo/Position.java

class Position {
  private String title;
  private Person person;
  public Position(String jobTitle, Person employee) {
    title = jobTitle;
    person = employee;
    if(person == null)
      person = Person.NULL;
  }
  public Position(String jobTitle) {
    title = jobTitle;
    person = Person.NULL;
  }
  public String getTitle() { return title; }
  public void setTitle(String newTitle) {
    title = newTitle;
  }
  public Person getPerson() { return person; }
```

```
  public void setPerson(Person newPerson) {
    person = newPerson;
    if(person == null)
      person = Person.NULL;
  }
  public String toString() {
    return "Position: " + title + " " + person;
  }
} ///:~
```

With **Position**, we don't need to make a Null Object because the existence of
Person.NULL implies a null **Position** (it's possible that, later, you'll
discover the need to add an explicit Null Object for **Position**, but YAGNI[4]
(*You Aren't Going to Need It*) says to try "the simplest thing that could
possibly work" for your first draft, and to wait until some aspect of the
program requires you to add in the extra feature, rather than assuming it's
necessary).

The **Staff** class can now look for Null Objects when you are filling positions:

```
//: typeinfo/Staff.java
import java.util.*;

public class Staff extends ArrayList<Position> {
  public void add(String title, Person person) {
    add(new Position(title, person));
  }
  public void add(String... titles) {
    for(String title : titles)
      add(new Position(title));
  }
  public Staff(String... titles) { add(titles); }
  public boolean positionAvailable(String title) {
    for(Position position : this)
      if(position.getTitle().equals(title) &&
         position.getPerson() == Person.NULL)
        return true;
    return false;
  }
  public void fillPosition(String title, Person hire) {
```

---

[4] A tenet of *Extreme Programming* (XP), as is "Do the simplest thing that could possibly
work."

```
      for(Position position : this)
        if(position.getTitle().equals(title) &&
          position.getPerson() == Person.NULL) {
          position.setPerson(hire);
          return;
        }
      throw new RuntimeException(
        "Position " + title + " not available");
    }
    public static void main(String[] args) {
      Staff staff = new Staff("President", "CTO",
        "Marketing Manager", "Product Manager",
        "Project Lead", "Software Engineer",
        "Software Engineer", "Software Engineer",
        "Software Engineer", "Test Engineer",
        "Technical Writer");
      staff.fillPosition("President",
        new Person("Me", "Last", "The Top, Lonely At"));
      staff.fillPosition("Project Lead",
        new Person("Janet", "Planner", "The Burbs"));
      if(staff.positionAvailable("Software Engineer"))
        staff.fillPosition("Software Engineer",
          new Person("Bob", "Coder", "Bright Light City"));
      System.out.println(staff);
    }
} /* Output:
[Position: President Person: Me Last The Top, Lonely At,
Position: CTO NullPerson, Position: Marketing Manager
NullPerson, Position: Product Manager NullPerson, Position:
Project Lead Person: Janet Planner The Burbs, Position:
Software Engineer Person: Bob Coder Bright Light City,
Position: Software Engineer NullPerson, Position: Software
Engineer NullPerson, Position: Software Engineer
NullPerson, Position: Test Engineer NullPerson, Position:
Technical Writer NullPerson]
*///:~
```

Notice that you must still test for Null Objects in some places, which is not that different from checking for **null**, but in other places (such as **toString( )** conversions, in this case), you don't have to perform extra tests; you can just assume that all object references are valid.

If you are working with interfaces instead of concrete classes, it's possible to use a **DynamicProxy** to automatically create the Null Objects. Suppose we

have a **Robot** interface that defines a name, model, and a **List<Operation>**
that describes what the **Robot** is capable of doing. **Operation** contains a
description and a command (it's a type of *Command* pattern):

```
//: typeinfo/Operation.java

public interface Operation {
  String description();
  void command();
} ///:~
```

You can access a **Robot**'s services by calling **operations( )**:

```
//: typeinfo/Robot.java
import java.util.*;
import net.mindview.util.*;

public interface Robot {
  String name();
  String model();
  List<Operation> operations();
  class Test {
    public static void test(Robot r) {
      if(r instanceof Null)
        System.out.println("[Null Robot]");
      System.out.println("Robot name: " + r.name());
      System.out.println("Robot model: " + r.model());
      for(Operation operation : r.operations()) {
        System.out.println(operation.description());
        operation.command();
      }
    }
  }
} ///:~
```

This also incorporates a nested class to perform tests.

We can now create a **Robot** that removes snow:

```
//: typeinfo/SnowRemovalRobot.java
import java.util.*;

public class SnowRemovalRobot implements Robot {
  private String name;
  public SnowRemovalRobot(String name) {this.name = name;}
```

```java
    public String name() { return name; }
    public String model() { return "SnowBot Series 11"; }
    public List<Operation> operations() {
      return Arrays.asList(
        new Operation() {
          public String description() {
            return name + " can shovel snow";
          }
          public void command() {
            System.out.println(name + " shoveling snow");
          }
        },
        new Operation() {
          public String description() {
            return name + " can chip ice";
          }
          public void command() {
            System.out.println(name + " chipping ice");
          }
        },
        new Operation() {
          public String description() {
            return name + " can clear the roof";
          }
          public void command() {
            System.out.println(name + " clearing roof");
          }
        }
      );
    }
    public static void main(String[] args) {
      Robot.Test.test(new SnowRemovalRobot("Slusher"));
    }
} /* Output:
Robot name: Slusher
Robot model: SnowBot Series 11
Slusher can shovel snow
Slusher shoveling snow
Slusher can chip ice
Slusher chipping ice
Slusher can clear the roof
Slusher clearing roof
*///:~
```

There will presumably be many different types of **Robot**, and we'd like to have each Null Object do something special for each **Robot** type—in this case, incorporate information about the exact type of **Robot** the Null Object is standing for. This information will be captured by the dynamic proxy:

```
//: typeinfo/NullRobot.java
// Using a dynamic proxy to create a Null Object.
import java.lang.reflect.*;
import java.util.*;
import net.mindview.util.*;

class NullRobotProxyHandler implements InvocationHandler {
  private String nullName;
  private Robot proxied = new NRobot();
  NullRobotProxyHandler(Class<? extends Robot> type) {
    nullName = type.getSimpleName() + " NullRobot";
  }
  private class NRobot implements Null, Robot {
    public String name() { return nullName; }
    public String model() { return nullName; }
    public List<Operation> operations() {
      return Collections.emptyList();
    }
  }
  public Object
  invoke(Object proxy, Method method, Object[] args)
  throws Throwable {
    return method.invoke(proxied, args);
  }
}

public class NullRobot {
  public static Robot
  newNullRobot(Class<? extends Robot> type) {
    return (Robot)Proxy.newProxyInstance(
      NullRobot.class.getClassLoader(),
      new Class[]{ Null.class, Robot.class },
      new NullRobotProxyHandler(type));
  }
  public static void main(String[] args) {
    Robot[] bots = {
      new SnowRemovalRobot("SnowBee"),
      newNullRobot(SnowRemovalRobot.class)
    };
```

```
      for(Robot bot : bots)
        Robot.Test.test(bot);
    }
} /* Output:
Robot name: SnowBee
Robot model: SnowBot Series 11
SnowBee can shovel snow
SnowBee shoveling snow
SnowBee can chip ice
SnowBee chipping ice
SnowBee can clear the roof
SnowBee clearing roof
[Null Robot]
Robot name: SnowRemovalRobot NullRobot
Robot model: SnowRemovalRobot NullRobot
*///:~
```

Whenever you need a null **Robot** object, you just call **newNullRobot( )**, passing the type of **Robot** you want a proxy for. The proxy fulfills the requirements of the **Robot** and **Null** interfaces, and provides the specific name of the type that it proxies.

Mock Objects & Stubs

Logical variations of the Null Object are the *Mock Object* and the *Stub*. Like Null Object, both of these are stand-ins for the "real" object that will be used in the finished program. However, both Mock Object and Stub pretend to be live objects that deliver real information, rather than being a more intelligent placeholder for **null**, as Null Object is.

The distinction between Mock Object and Stub is one of degree. Mock Objects tend to be lightweight and self-testing, and usually many of them are created to handle various testing situations. Stubs just return stubbed data, are typically heavyweight and are often reused between tests. Stubs can be configured to change depending on how they are called. So a Stub is a sophisticated object that does lots of things, whereas you usually create lots of small, simple Mock Objects if you need to do many things.

Exercise 24: (4) Add Null Objects to **RegisteredFactories.java**.

Interfaces and type information

An important goal of the **interface** keyword is to allow the programmer to isolate components, and thus reduce coupling. If you write to interfaces, you accomplish this, but with type information it's possible to get around that—interfaces are not airtight guarantees of decoupling. Here's an example, starting with an interface:

```
//: typeinfo/interfacea/A.java
package typeinfo.interfacea;

public interface A {
  void f();
} ///:~
```

This interface is then implemented, and you can see how to sneak around to the actual implementation type:

```
//: typeinfo/InterfaceViolation.java
// Sneaking around an interface.
import typeinfo.interfacea.*;

class B implements A {
  public void f() {}
  public void g() {}
}

public class InterfaceViolation {
  public static void main(String[] args) {
    A a = new B();
    a.f();
    // a.g(); // Compile error
    System.out.println(a.getClass().getName());
    if(a instanceof B) {
      B b = (B)a;
      b.g();
    }
  }
} /* Output:
B
*///:~
```

Using RTTI, we discover that **a** has been implemented as a **B**. By casting to **B**, we can call a method that's not in **A**.

This is perfectly legal and acceptable, but you may not want client programmers to do this, because it gives them an opportunity to couple more closely to your code than you'd like. That is, you may think that the **interface** keyword is protecting you, but it isn't, and the fact that you're using **B** to implement **A** in this case is effectively a matter of public record.[5]

One solution is to simply say that programmers are on their own if they decide to use the actual class rather than the interface. This is probably reasonable in many cases, but if "probably" isn't enough, you might want to apply more stringent controls.

The easiest approach is to use package access for the implementation, so that clients outside the package may not see it:

```
//: typeinfo/packageaccess/HiddenC.java
package typeinfo.packageaccess;
import typeinfo.interfacea.*;
import static net.mindview.util.Print.*;

class C implements A {
  public void f() { print("public C.f()"); }
  public void g() { print("public C.g()"); }
  void u() { print("package C.u()"); }
  protected void v() { print("protected C.v()"); }
  private void w() { print("private C.w()"); }
}

public class HiddenC {
  public static A makeA() { return new C(); }
} ///:~
```

The only **public** part of this package, **HiddenC**, produces an **A** interface when you call it. What's interesting about this is that even if you were to return a **C** from **makeA( )**, you still couldn't use anything but an **A** from outside the package, since you cannot name **C** outside the package.

---

[5] The most famous case of this is the Windows operating system, which had a published API that you were supposed to write to, and an unpublished but visible set of functions that you could discover and call. To solve problems, programmers used the hidden API functions, which forced Microsoft to maintain them as if they were part of the public API. This became a source of great cost and effort for the company.

Now if you try to downcast to **C**, you can't do it because there is no 'C' type available outside the package:

```
//: typeinfo/HiddenImplementation.java
// Sneaking around package access.
import typeinfo.interfacea.*;
import typeinfo.packageaccess.*;
import java.lang.reflect.*;

public class HiddenImplementation {
  public static void main(String[] args) throws Exception {
    A a = HiddenC.makeA();
    a.f();
    System.out.println(a.getClass().getName());
    // Compile error: cannot find symbol 'C':
    /* if(a instanceof C) {
      C c = (C)a;
      c.g();
    } */
    // Oops! Reflection still allows us to call g():
    callHiddenMethod(a, "g");
    // And even methods that are less accessible!
    callHiddenMethod(a, "u");
    callHiddenMethod(a, "v");
    callHiddenMethod(a, "w");
  }
  static void callHiddenMethod(Object a, String methodName)
  throws Exception {
    Method g = a.getClass().getDeclaredMethod(methodName);
    g.setAccessible(true);
    g.invoke(a);
  }
} /* Output:
public C.f()
typeinfo.packageaccess.C
public C.g()
package C.u()
protected C.v()
private C.w()
*///:~
```

As you can see, it's still possible to reach in and call *all* of the methods using reflection, even **private** methods! If you know the name of the method, you can call **setAccessible(true)** on the **Method** object to make it callable, as seen in **callHiddenMethod( )**.

You may think that you can prevent this by only distributing compiled code, but that's no solution. All you must do is run **javap**, which is the decompiler that comes with the JDK. Here's the command line:

```
javap -private C
```

The **-private** flag indicates that all members should be displayed, even private ones. Here's the output:

```
class typeinfo.packageaccess.C extends
java.lang.Object implements typeinfo.interfacea.A {
    typeinfo.packageaccess.C();
    public void f();
    public void g();
    void u();
    protected void v();
    private void w();
}
```

So anyone can get the names and signatures of your most private methods, and call them.

What if you implement the interface as a private inner class? Here's what it looks like:

```
//: typeinfo/InnerImplementation.java
// Private inner classes can't hide from reflection.
import typeinfo.interfacea.*;
import static net.mindview.util.Print.*;

class InnerA {
  private static class C implements A {
    public void f() { print("public C.f()"); }
    public void g() { print("public C.g()"); }
    void u() { print("package C.u()"); }
    protected void v() { print("protected C.v()"); }
    private void w() { print("private C.w()"); }
  }
  public static A makeA() { return new C(); }
}

public class InnerImplementation {
```

```
    public static void main(String[] args) throws Exception {
      A a = InnerA.makeA();
      a.f();
      System.out.println(a.getClass().getName());
      // Reflection still gets into the private class:
      HiddenImplementation.callHiddenMethod(a, "g");
      HiddenImplementation.callHiddenMethod(a, "u");
      HiddenImplementation.callHiddenMethod(a, "v");
      HiddenImplementation.callHiddenMethod(a, "w");
    }
} /* Output:
public C.f()
InnerA$C
public C.g()
package C.u()
protected C.v()
private C.w()
*///:~
```

That didn't hide anything from reflection. What about an anonymous class?

```
//: typeinfo/AnonymousImplementation.java
// Anonymous inner classes can't hide from reflection.
import typeinfo.interfacea.*;
import static net.mindview.util.Print.*;

class AnonymousA {
  public static A makeA() {
    return new A() {
      public void f() { print("public C.f()"); }
      public void g() { print("public C.g()"); }
      void u() { print("package C.u()"); }
      protected void v() { print("protected C.v()"); }
      private void w() { print("private C.w()"); }
    };
  }
}

public class AnonymousImplementation {
  public static void main(String[] args) throws Exception {
    A a = AnonymousA.makeA();
    a.f();
    System.out.println(a.getClass().getName());
    // Reflection still gets into the anonymous class:
    HiddenImplementation.callHiddenMethod(a, "g");
```

```
    HiddenImplementation.callHiddenMethod(a, "u");
    HiddenImplementation.callHiddenMethod(a, "v");
    HiddenImplementation.callHiddenMethod(a, "w");
  }
} /* Output:
public C.f()
AnonymousA$1
public C.g()
package C.u()
protected C.v()
private C.w()
*///:~
```

There doesn't seem to be any way to prevent reflection from reaching in and calling methods that have non-public access. This is also true for fields, even **private** fields:

```
//: typeinfo/ModifyingPrivateFields.java
import java.lang.reflect.*;

class WithPrivateFinalField {
  private int i = 1;
  private final String s = "I'm totally safe";
  private String s2 = "Am I safe?";
  public String toString() {
    return "i = " + i + ", " + s + ", " + s2;
  }
}

public class ModifyingPrivateFields {
  public static void main(String[] args) throws Exception {
    WithPrivateFinalField pf = new WithPrivateFinalField();
    System.out.println(pf);
    Field f = pf.getClass().getDeclaredField("i");
    f.setAccessible(true);
    System.out.println("f.getInt(pf): " + f.getInt(pf));
    f.setInt(pf, 47);
    System.out.println(pf);
    f = pf.getClass().getDeclaredField("s");
    f.setAccessible(true);
    System.out.println("f.get(pf): " + f.get(pf));
    f.set(pf, "No, you're not!");
    System.out.println(pf);
    f = pf.getClass().getDeclaredField("s2");
    f.setAccessible(true);
```

```
            System.out.println("f.get(pf): " + f.get(pf));
            f.set(pf, "No, you're not!");
            System.out.println(pf);
        }
    }
} /* Output:
i = 1, I'm totally safe, Am I safe?
f.getInt(pf): 1
i = 47, I'm totally safe, Am I safe?
f.get(pf): I'm totally safe
i = 47, I'm totally safe, Am I safe?
f.get(pf): Am I safe?
i = 47, I'm totally safe, No, you're not!
*///:~
```

However, **final** fields are actually safe from change. The runtime system accepts any attempts at change without complaint, but nothing actually happens.

In general, all these access violations are not the worst thing in the world. If someone uses such a technique to call methods that you marked with **private** or package access (thus clearly indicating they should not call them), then it's difficult for them to complain if you change some aspect of those methods. On the other hand, the fact that you always have a back door into a class may allow you to solve certain types of problems that could otherwise be difficult or impossible, and the benefits of reflection in general are undeniable.

Exercise 25: (2) Create a class containing **private**, **protected** and package-access methods. Write code to access these methods from outside of the class's package.

Summary

RTTI allows you to discover type information from an anonymous base-class reference. Thus, it's ripe for misuse by the novice, since it might make sense before polymorphic method calls do. For people coming from a procedural background, it's difficult not to organize programs into sets of **switch** statements. You can accomplish this with RTTI and thus lose the important value of polymorphism in code development and maintenance. The intent of OO programming is to use polymorphic method calls everywhere you can, and RTTI only when you must.

However, using polymorphic method calls as they are intended requires that you have control of the base-class definition, because at some point in the extension of your program you might discover that the base class doesn't include the method you need. If the base class comes from someone else's library, one solution is RTTI: You can inherit a new type and add your extra method. Elsewhere in the code you can detect your particular type and call that special method. This doesn't destroy the polymorphism and extensibility of the program, because adding a new type will not require you to hunt for **switch** statements in your program. However, when you add code that requires your new feature, you must use RTTI to detect your particular type.

Putting a feature in a base class might mean that, for the benefit of one particular class, all of the other classes derived from that base require some meaningless stub of a method. This makes the interface less clear and annoys those who must override abstract methods when they derive from that base class. For example, consider a class hierarchy representing musical instruments. Suppose you want to clear the spit valves of all the appropriate instruments in your orchestra. One option is to put a **clearSpitValve( )** method in the base class **Instrument**, but this is confusing because it implies that **Percussion**, **Stringed** and **Electronic** instruments also have spit valves. RTTI provides a much more reasonable solution because you can place the method in the specific class where it's appropriate (**Wind**, in this case). At the same time, you may discover that there's a more sensible solution—here, a **prepareInstrument( )** method in the base class. However, you might not see such a solution when you're first solving the problem and could mistakenly assume that you must use RTTI.

Finally, RTTI will sometimes solve efficiency problems. Suppose your code nicely uses polymorphism, but it turns out that one of your objects reacts to this general-purpose code in a horribly inefficient way. You can pick out that type using RTTI and write case-specific code to improve the efficiency. Be wary, however, of programming for efficiency too soon. It's a seductive trap. It's best to get the program working *first*, then decide if it's running fast enough, and only then should you attack efficiency issues—with a profiler (see the supplement at *http://MindView.net/Books/BetterJava*).

We've also seen that reflection opens up a new world of programming possibilities by allowing a much more dynamic style of programming. There are some for whom the dynamic nature of reflection is disturbing. The fact that you can do things that can only be checked at run time and reported with exceptions seems, to a mind grown comfortable with the security of static type checking, to be the wrong direction. Some people go so far as to say that introducing the possibility of a runtime exception is a clear indicator that such code should be avoided. I find that this sense of security is an illusion— there are always things that can happen at run time and throw exceptions, even in a program that contains no **try** blocks or exception specifications. Instead, I think that the existence of a consistent error-reporting model *empowers* us to write dynamic code using reflection. Of course it's worth trying to write code that can be statically checked ... when you can. But I believe that dynamic code is one of the important facilities that separate Java from languages like C++.

Exercise 26: (3) Implement **clearSpitValve( )** as described in the summary.

Solutions to selected exercises can be found in the electronic document *The Thinking in Java Annotated Solution Guide*, available for sale from *www.MindView.net*.

Generics

Ordinary classes and methods work with specific types: either primitives or class types. If you are writing code that might be used across more types, this rigidity can be overconstraining.[1]

One way that object-oriented languages allow generalization is through polymorphism. You can write (for example) a method that takes a base class object as an argument, and then use that method with any class derived from that base class. Now your method is a little more general and can be used in more places. The same is true within classes—anyplace you use a specific type, a base type provides more flexibility. Of course, anything but a **final** class[2] can be extended, so this flexibility is automatic much of the time.

Sometimes, being constrained to a single hierarchy is too limiting. If a method argument is an interface instead of a class, the limitations are loosened to include anything that implements the interface—including classes that haven't been created yet. This gives the client programmer the option of implementing an interface in order to conform to your class or method. So interfaces allow you to cut across class hierarchies, as long as you have the option to create a new class in order to do so.

Sometimes even an interface is too restrictive. An interface still requires that your code work with that particular interface. You could write even more general code if you could say that your code works with "some unspecified type," rather than a specific interface or class.

This is the concept of generics, one of the more significant changes in Java SE5. Generics implement the concept of *parameterized types*, which allow

---

[1] Angelika Langer's *Java Generics FAQ* (see *www.angelikalanger.com/GenericsFAQ/JavaGenericsFAQ.html*) as well as her other writings (together with Klaus Kreft) have been invaluable during the preparation of this chapter.

[2] Or a class with all **private** constructors.

multiple types. The term "generic" means "pertaining or appropriate to large groups of classes." The original intent of generics in programming languages was to allow the programmer the greatest amount of expressiveness possible when writing classes or methods, by loosening the constraints on the types that those classes or methods work with. As you will see in this chapter, the Java implementation of generics is not that broad reaching—indeed, you may question whether the term "generic" is even appropriate for this feature.

If you've never seen any kind of parameterized type mechanism before, Java generics will probably seem like a convenient addition to the language. When you create an instance of a parameterized type, casts will be taken care of for you and the type correctness will be ensured at compile time. This seems like an improvement.

However, if you've had experience with a parameterized type mechanism, in C++, for example, you will find that you can't do everything that you might expect when using Java generics. While using someone else's generic type is fairly easy, when creating your own you will encounter a number of surprises. One of the things I shall try to explain is how the feature came to be like it is.

This is not to say that Java generics are useless. In many cases they make code more straightforward and even elegant. But if you're coming from a language that has implemented a more pure version of generics, you may be disappointed. In this chapter, we will examine both the strengths and the limitations of Java generics so that you can use this new feature more effectively.

Comparison with C++

The Java designers stated that much of the inspiration for the language came as a reaction to C++. Despite this, it is possible to teach Java largely without reference to C++, and I have endeavored to do so except when the comparison will give you greater depth of understanding.

Generics require more comparison with C++ for two reasons. First, understanding certain aspects of C++ *templates* (the main inspiration for generics, including the basic syntax) will help you understand the foundations of the concept, as well as—and this is very important—the limitations of what you can do with Java generics and why. The ultimate goal is to give you a clear understanding of where the boundaries lie, because my experience is that by understanding the boundaries, you become a more powerful programmer. By knowing what you can't do, you can make better use of what you can do (partly because you don't waste time bumping up against walls).

The second reason is that there is significant misunderstanding in the Java community about C++ templates, and this misunderstanding may further confuse you about the intent of generics.

So although I will introduce a few C++ template examples in this chapter, I will keep them to a minimum.

Simple generics

One of the most compelling initial motivations for generics is to create *container classes*, which you saw in the *Holding Your Objects* chapter (you'll learn more about these in the *Containers in Depth* chapter). A container is a place to hold objects while you're working with them. Although this is also true of arrays, containers tend to be more flexible and have different characteristics than simple arrays. Virtually all programs require that you hold a group of objects while you use them, so containers are one of the most reusable of class libraries.

Let's look at a class that holds a single object. Of course, the class could specify the exact type of the object, like this:

```
//: generics/Holder1.java

class Automobile {}

public class Holder1 {
  private Automobile a;
  public Holder1(Automobile a) { this.a = a; }
  Automobile get() { return a; }
} ///:~
```

But this is not a very reusable tool, since it can't be used to hold anything else. We would prefer not to write a new one of these for every type we encounter.

Before Java SE5, we would simply make it hold an **Object**:

```
//: generics/Holder2.java

public class Holder2 {
  private Object a;
```

```
    public Holder2(Object a) { this.a = a; }
    public void set(Object a) { this.a = a; }
    public Object get() { return a; }
    public static void main(String[] args) {
      Holder2 h2 = new Holder2(new Automobile());
      Automobile a = (Automobile)h2.get();
      h2.set("Not an Automobile");
      String s = (String)h2.get();
      h2.set(1); // Autoboxes to Integer
      Integer x = (Integer)h2.get();
    }
} ///:~
```

Now a **Holder2** can hold anything—and in this example, a single **Holder2** holds three different types of objects.

There are some cases where you want a container to hold multiple types of objects, but typically you only put one type of object into a container. One of the primary motivations for generics is to specify what type of object a container holds, and to have that specification backed up by the compiler.

So instead of **Object**, we'd like to use an unspecified type, which can be decided at a later time. To do this, you put a *type parameter* inside angle brackets after the class name, and then substitute an actual type when you use the class. For the "holder" class, it looks like this, where **T** is the type parameter:

```
//: generics/Holder3.java

public class Holder3<T> {
  private T a;
  public Holder3(T a) { this.a = a; }
  public void set(T a) { this.a = a; }
  public T get() { return a; }
  public static void main(String[] args) {
    Holder3<Automobile> h3 =
      new Holder3<Automobile>(new Automobile());
    Automobile a = h3.get(); // No cast needed
    // h3.set("Not an Automobile"); // Error
    // h3.set(1); // Error
  }
} ///:~
```

Now when you create a **Holder3**, you must specify what type you want to put into it using the same angle-bracket syntax, as you can see in **main( )**. You are only allowed to put objects of that type (or a subtype, since the substitution principle still works with generics) into the holder. And when you get a value out, it is automatically the right type.

That's the core idea of Java generics: You tell it what type you want to use, and it takes care of the details.

In general, you can treat generics as if they are any other type—they just happen to have type parameters. But as you'll see, you can use generics just by naming them along with their type argument list.

Exercise 1: (1) Use **Holder3** with the **typeinfo.pets** library to show that a **Holder3** that is specified to hold a base type can also hold a derived type.

Exercise 2: (1) Create a holder class that holds three objects of the same type, along with the methods to store and fetch those objects and a constructor to initialize all three.

A tuple library

One of the things you often want to do is return multiple objects from a method call. The **return** statement only allows you to specify a single object, so the answer is to create an object that holds the multiple objects that you want to return. Of course, you can write a special class every time you encounter the situation, but with generics it's possible to solve the problem once and save yourself the effort in the future. At the same time, you are ensuring compile-time type safety.

This concept is called a *tuple*, and it is simply a group of objects wrapped together into a single object. The recipient of the object is allowed to read the elements but not put new ones in. (This concept is also called a *Data Transfer Object* (or *Messenger*.)

Tuples can typically be any length, but each object in the tuple can be of a different type. However, we want to specify the type of each object and ensure that when the recipient reads the value, they get the right type. To deal with the problem of multiple lengths, we create multiple different tuples. Here's one that holds two objects:

```
//: net/mindview/util/TwoTuple.java
package net.mindview.util;
```

```java
public class TwoTuple<A,B> {
  public final A first;
  public final B second;
  public TwoTuple(A a, B b) { first = a; second = b; }
  public String toString() {
    return "(" + first + ", " + second + ")";
  }
} ///:~
```

The constructor captures the object to be stored, and **toString( )** is a convenience function to display the values in a list. Note that a tuple implicitly keeps its elements in order.

Upon first reading, you may think that this could violate common safety principles of Java programming. Shouldn't **first** and **second** be **private**, and only accessed with methods named **getFirst( )** and **getSecond( )**? Consider the safety that you would get in that case: Clients could still read the objects and do whatever they want with them, but they could not assign **first** or **second** to anything else. The **final** declaration buys you the same safety, but the above form is shorter and simpler.

Another design observation is that you might *want* to allow a client programmer to point **first** or **second** to another object. However, it's safer to leave it in the above form, and just force the user to create a new **TwoTuple** if they want one that has different elements.

The longer-length tuples can be created with inheritance. You can see that adding more type parameters is a simple matter:

```java
//: net/mindview/util/ThreeTuple.java
package net.mindview.util;

public class ThreeTuple<A,B,C> extends TwoTuple<A,B> {
  public final C third;
  public ThreeTuple(A a, B b, C c) {
    super(a, b);
    third = c;
  }
  public String toString() {
    return "(" + first + ", " + second + ", " + third +")";
  }
} ///:~
```

A stack class

Let's look at something slightly more complicated: the traditional pushdown stack. In the *Holding Your Objects* chapter, you saw this implemented using a **LinkedList** as the **net.mindview.util.Stack** class (page 412). In that example, you can see that a **LinkedList** already has the necessary methods to create a stack. The **Stack** was constructed by composing one generic class (**Stack<T>**) with another generic class (**LinkedList<T>**). In that example, notice that (with a few exceptions that we shall look at later) a generic type is just another type.

Instead of using **LinkedList**, we can implement our own internal linked storage mechanism.

```
//: generics/LinkedStack.java
// A stack implemented with an internal linked structure.

public class LinkedStack<T> {
  private static class Node<U> {
    U item;
    Node<U> next;
    Node() { item = null; next = null; }
    Node(U item, Node<U> next) {
      this.item = item;
      this.next = next;
    }
    boolean end() { return item == null && next == null; }
  }
  private Node<T> top = new Node<T>(); // End sentinel
  public void push(T item) {
    top = new Node<T>(item, top);
  }
  public T pop() {
    T result = top.item;
    if(!top.end())
      top = top.next;
    return result;
  }
  public static void main(String[] args) {
    LinkedStack<String> lss = new LinkedStack<String>();
    for(String s : "Phasers on stun!".split(" "))
      lss.push(s);
    String s;
    while((s = lss.pop()) != null)
```

```
      System.out.println(s);
  }
} /* Output:
stun!
on
Phasers
*///:~
```

The inner class **Node** is also a generic, and has its own type parameter.

This example makes use of an *end sentinel* to determine when the stack is empty. The end sentinel is created when the **LinkedStack** is constructed, and each time you call **push( )** a new **Node<T>** is created and linked to the previous **Node<T>**. When you call **pop( )**, you always return the **top.item**, and then you discard the current **Node<T>** and move to the next one—except when you hit the end sentinel, in which case you don't move. That way, if the client keeps calling **pop( )**, they keep getting **null** back to indicate that the stack is empty.

Exercise 5: (2) Remove the type parameter on the **Node** class and modify the rest of the code in **LinkedStack.java** to show that an inner class has access to the generic type parameters of its outer class.

RandomList

For another example of a holder, suppose you'd like a special type of list that randomly selects one of its elements each time you call **select( )**. When doing this you want to build a tool that works with all objects, so you use generics:

```java
//: generics/RandomList.java
import java.util.*;

public class RandomList<T> {
  private ArrayList<T> storage = new ArrayList<T>();
  private Random rand = new Random(47);
  public void add(T item) { storage.add(item); }
  public T select() {
    return storage.get(rand.nextInt(storage.size()));
  }
  public static void main(String[] args) {
    RandomList<String> rs = new RandomList<String>();
    for(String s: ("The quick brown fox jumped over " +
        "the lazy brown dog").split(" "))
      rs.add(s);
```

```
    for(int i = 0; i < 11; i++)
      System.out.print(rs.select() + " ");
  }
} /* Output:
brown over fox quick quick dog brown The brown lazy brown
*///:~
```

Exercise 6: (1) Use **RandomList** with two more types in addition to the one shown in **main( )**.

Generic interfaces

Generics also work with interfaces. For example, a *generator* is a class that creates objects. It's actually a specialization of the *Factory Method* design pattern, but when you ask a generator for new object, you don't pass it any arguments, whereas you typically do pass arguments to a Factory Method. The generator knows how to create new objects without any extra information.

Typically, a generator just defines one method, the method that produces new objects. Here, we'll call it **next( )**, and include it in the standard utilities:

```
//: net/mindview/util/Generator.java
// A generic interface.
package net.mindview.util;
public interface Generator<T> { T next(); } ///:~
```

The return type of **next( )** is parameterized to **T**. As you can see, using generics with interfaces is no different than using generics with classes.

To demonstrate the implementation of a **Generator**, we'll need some classes. Here's a coffee hierarchy:

```
//: generics/coffee/Coffee.java
package generics.coffee;

public class Coffee {
  private static long counter = 0;
  private final long id = counter++;
  public String toString() {
    return getClass().getSimpleName() + " " + id;
  }
} ///:~
```

```
//: generics/coffee/Latte.java
```

```
package generics.coffee;
public class Latte extends Coffee {} ///:~

//: generics/coffee/Mocha.java
package generics.coffee;
public class Mocha extends Coffee {} ///:~

//: generics/coffee/Cappuccino.java
package generics.coffee;
public class Cappuccino extends Coffee {} ///:~

//: generics/coffee/Americano.java
package generics.coffee;
public class Americano extends Coffee {} ///:~

//: generics/coffee/Breve.java
package generics.coffee;
public class Breve extends Coffee {} ///:~
```

Now we can implement a **Generator<Coffee>** that produces random different types of **Coffee** objects:

```
//: generics/coffee/CoffeeGenerator.java
// Generate different types of Coffee:
package generics.coffee;
import java.util.*;
import net.mindview.util.*;

public class CoffeeGenerator
implements Generator<Coffee>, Iterable<Coffee> {
  private Class<?>[] types = { Latte.class, Mocha.class,
    Cappuccino.class, Americano.class, Breve.class, };
  private static Random rand = new Random(47);
  public CoffeeGenerator() {}
  // For iteration:
  private int size = 0;
  public CoffeeGenerator(int sz) { size = sz; }
  public Coffee next() {
    try {
      return (Coffee)
        types[rand.nextInt(types.length)].newInstance();
      // Report programmer errors at run time:
    } catch(Exception e) {
      throw new RuntimeException(e);
    }
  }
```

```java
  class CoffeeIterator implements Iterator<Coffee> {
    int count = size;
    public boolean hasNext() { return count > 0; }
    public Coffee next() {
      count--;
      return CoffeeGenerator.this.next();
    }
    public void remove() { // Not implemented
      throw new UnsupportedOperationException();
    }
  };
  public Iterator<Coffee> iterator() {
    return new CoffeeIterator();
  }
  public static void main(String[] args) {
    CoffeeGenerator gen = new CoffeeGenerator();
    for(int i = 0; i < 5; i++)
      System.out.println(gen.next());
    for(Coffee c : new CoffeeGenerator(5))
      System.out.println(c);
  }
} /* Output:
Americano 0
Latte 1
Americano 2
Mocha 3
Mocha 4
Breve 5
Americano 6
Latte 7
Cappuccino 8
Cappuccino 9
*///:~
```

The parameterized **Generator** interface ensures that **next( )** returns the parameter type. **CoffeeGenerator** also implements the **Iterable** interface, so it can be used in a foreach statement. However, it requires an "end sentinel" to know when to stop, and this is produced using the second constructor.

Here's a second implementation of **Generator<T>**, this time to produce Fibonacci numbers:

```java
//: generics/Fibonacci.java
```

```
// Generate a Fibonacci sequence.
import net.mindview.util.*;

public class Fibonacci implements Generator<Integer> {
  private int count = 0;
  public Integer next() { return fib(count++); }
  private int fib(int n) {
    if(n < 2) return 1;
    return fib(n-2) + fib(n-1);
  }
  public static void main(String[] args) {
    Fibonacci gen = new Fibonacci();
    for(int i = 0; i < 18; i++)
      System.out.print(gen.next() + " ");
  }
} /* Output:
1 1 2 3 5 8 13 21 34 55 89 144 233 377 610 987 1597 2584
*///:~
```

Although we are working with **int**s both inside and outside the class, the type parameter is **Integer**. This brings up one of the limitations of Java generics: You cannot use primitives as type parameters. However, Java SE5 conveniently added autoboxing and autounboxing to convert from primitive types to wrapper types and back. You can see the effect here because **int**s are seamlessly used and produced by the class.

We can go one step further and make an **Iterable** Fibonacci generator. One option is to reimplement the class and add the **Iterable** interface, but you don't always have control of the original code, and you don't want to rewrite when you don't have to. Instead, we can create an *adapter* to produce the desired interface—this design pattern was introduced earlier in the book.

Adapters can be implemented in multiple ways. For example, you could use inheritance to generate the adapted class:

```
//: generics/IterableFibonacci.java
// Adapt the Fibonacci class to make it Iterable.
import java.util.*;

public class IterableFibonacci
extends Fibonacci implements Iterable<Integer> {
  private int n;
  public IterableFibonacci(int count) { n = count; }
  public Iterator<Integer> iterator() {
```

```
      return new Iterator<Integer>() {
        public boolean hasNext() { return n > 0; }
        public Integer next() {
          n--;
          return IterableFibonacci.this.next();
        }
        public void remove() { // Not implemented
          throw new UnsupportedOperationException();
        }
      };
    }
    public static void main(String[] args) {
      for(int i : new IterableFibonacci(18))
        System.out.print(i + " ");
    }
} /* Output:
1 1 2 3 5 8 13 21 34 55 89 144 233 377 610 987 1597 2584
*///:~
```

To use **IterableFibonacci** in a foreach statement, you give the constructor a boundary so that **hasNext( )** can know when to return **false**.

Exercise 7: (2) Use composition instead of inheritance to adapt **Fibonacci** to make it **Iterable**.

Exercise 8: (2) Following the form of the **Coffee** example, create a hierarchy of **StoryCharacter**s from your favorite movie, dividing them into **GoodGuys** and **BadGuys**. Create a generator for **StoryCharacter**s, following the form of **CoffeeGenerator**.

Generic methods

So far we've looked at parameterizing entire classes. You can also parameterize methods within a class. The class itself may or may not be generic—this is independent of whether you have a generic method.

A generic method allows the method to vary independently of the class. As a guideline, you should use generic methods "whenever you can." That is, if it's possible to make a method generic rather than the entire class, it's probably going to be clearer to do so. In addition, if a method is **static**, it has no access to the generic type parameters of the class, so if it needs to use genericity it must be a generic method.

To define a generic method, you simply place a generic parameter list before the return value, like this:

```
//: generics/GenericMethods.java

public class GenericMethods {
  public <T> void f(T x) {
    System.out.println(x.getClass().getName());
  }
  public static void main(String[] args) {
    GenericMethods gm = new GenericMethods();
    gm.f("");
    gm.f(1);
    gm.f(1.0);
    gm.f(1.0F);
    gm.f('c');
    gm.f(gm);
  }
} /* Output:
java.lang.String
java.lang.Integer
java.lang.Double
java.lang.Float
java.lang.Character
GenericMethods
*///:~
```

The class **GenericMethods** is not parameterized, although both a class and its methods may be parameterized at the same time. But in this case, only the method **f( )** has a type parameter, indicated by the parameter list before the method's return type.

Notice that with a generic class, you must specify the type parameters when you instantiate the class. But with a generic method, you don't usually have to specify the parameter types, because the compiler can figure that out for you. This is called *type argument inference*. So calls to **f( )** look like normal method calls, and it appears that **f( )** has been infinitely overloaded. It will even take an argument of the type **GenericMethods**.

For the calls to **f( )** that use primitive types, autoboxing comes into play, automatically wrapping the primitive types in their associated objects. In fact, generic methods and autoboxing can eliminate some code that previously required hand conversion.

Exercise 9: (1) Modify **GenericMethods.java** so that **f( )** accepts three arguments, all of which are of a different parameterized type.

Exercise 10: (1) Modify the previous exercise so that one of **f( )**'s arguments is non-parameterized.

Leveraging type argument inference

One of the complaints about generics is that it adds even more text to your code. Consider **holding/MapOfList.java** from the *Holding Your Objects* chapter. The creation of the **Map** of **List** looks like this:

```
Map<Person, List<? extends Pet>> petPeople =
  new HashMap<Person, List<? extends Pet>>();
```

(This use of **extends** and the question marks will be explained later in this chapter.) It appears that you are repeating yourself, and that the compiler should figure out one of the generic argument lists from the other. Alas, it cannot, but type argument inference in a generic method can produce some simplification. For example, we can create a utility containing various **static** methods, which produces the most commonly used implementations of the various containers:

```
//: net/mindview/util/New.java
// Utilities to simplify generic container creation
// by using type argument inference.
package net.mindview.util;
import java.util.*;

public class New {
  public static <K,V> Map<K,V> map() {
    return new HashMap<K,V>();
  }
  public static <T> List<T> list() {
    return new ArrayList<T>();
  }
  public static <T> LinkedList<T> lList() {
    return new LinkedList<T>();
  }
  public static <T> Set<T> set() {
    return new HashSet<T>();
  }
  public static <T> Queue<T> queue() {
    return new LinkedList<T>();
```

```
    }
    // Examples:
    public static void main(String[] args) {
        Map<String, List<String>> sls = New.map();
        List<String> ls = New.list();
        LinkedList<String> lls = New.lList();
        Set<String> ss = New.set();
        Queue<String> qs = New.queue();
    }
} ///:~
```

In **main( )** you can see examples of how this is used—type argument inference eliminates the need to repeat the generic parameter list. This can be applied to **holding/MapOfList.java**:

```
//: generics/SimplerPets.java
import typeinfo.pets.*;
import java.util.*;
import net.mindview.util.*;

public class SimplerPets {
    public static void main(String[] args) {
        Map<Person, List<? extends Pet>> petPeople = New.map();
        // Rest of the code is the same...
    }
} ///:~
```

Although this is an interesting example of type argument inference, it's difficult to say how much it actually buys you. The person reading the code is required to parse and understand this additional library and its implications, so it might be just as productive to leave the original (admittedly repetitious) definition in place—ironically, for simplicity. However, if the standard Java library were to add something like the **New.java** utility above, it would make sense to use it.

Type inference doesn't work for anything other than assignment. If you pass the result of a method call such as **New.map( )** as an argument to another method, the compiler will *not* try to perform type inference. Instead it will treat the method call as though the return value is assigned to a variable of type **Object**. Here's an example that fails:

```
//: generics/LimitsOfInference.java
import typeinfo.pets.*;
import java.util.*;
```

```
public class LimitsOfInference {
  static void
  f(Map<Person, List<? extends Pet>> petPeople) {}
  public static void main(String[] args) {
    // f(New.map()); // Does not compile
  }
} ///:~
```

Exercise 11:   (1) Test **New.java** by creating your own classes and ensuring that **New** will work properly with them.

Explicit type specification

It is possible to explicitly specify the type in a generic method, although the syntax is rarely needed. To do so, you place the type in angle brackets after the dot and immediately preceding the method name. When calling a method from within the same class, you must use **this** before the dot, and when working with **static** methods, you must use the class name before the dot. The problem shown in **LimitsOfInference.java** can be solved using this syntax:

```
//: generics/ExplicitTypeSpecification.java
import typeinfo.pets.*;
import java.util.*;
import net.mindview.util.*;

public class ExplicitTypeSpecification {
  static void f(Map<Person, List<Pet>> petPeople) {}
  public static void main(String[] args) {
    f(New.<Person, List<Pet>>map());
  }
} ///:~
```

Of course, this eliminates the benefit of using the **New** class to reduce the amount of typing, but the extra syntax is only required when you are not writing an assignment statement.

Exercise 12:   (1) Repeat the previous exercise using explicit type specification.

Varargs and generic methods

Generic methods and variable argument lists coexist nicely:

```
//: generics/GenericVarargs.java
import java.util.*;

public class GenericVarargs {
  public static <T> List<T> makeList(T... args) {
    List<T> result = new ArrayList<T>();
    for(T item : args)
      result.add(item);
    return result;
  }
  public static void main(String[] args) {
    List<String> ls = makeList("A");
    System.out.println(ls);
    ls = makeList("A", "B", "C");
    System.out.println(ls);
    ls = makeList("ABCDEFFHIJKLMNOPQRSTUVWXYZ".split(""));
    System.out.println(ls);
  }
} /* Output:
[A]
[A, B, C]
[, A, B, C, D, E, F, F, H, I, J, K, L, M, N, O, P, Q, R, S,
T, U, V, W, X, Y, Z]
*///:~
```

The **makeList( )** method shown here produces the same functionality as the standard library's **java.util.Arrays.asList( )** method.

A generic method to use with **Generator**s

It is convenient to use a generator to fill a **Collection**, and it makes sense to "generify" this operation:

```
//: generics/Generators.java
// A utility to use with Generators.
import generics.coffee.*;
import java.util.*;
import net.mindview.util.*;

public class Generators {
  public static <T> Collection<T>
  fill(Collection<T> coll, Generator<T> gen, int n) {
    for(int i = 0; i < n; i++)
```

```
      coll.add(gen.next());
    return coll;
  }
  public static void main(String[] args) {
    Collection<Coffee> coffee = fill(
      new ArrayList<Coffee>(), new CoffeeGenerator(), 4);
    for(Coffee c : coffee)
      System.out.println(c);
    Collection<Integer> fnumbers = fill(
      new ArrayList<Integer>(), new Fibonacci(), 12);
    for(int i : fnumbers)
      System.out.print(i + ", ");
  }
} /* Output:
Americano 0
Latte 1
Americano 2
Mocha 3
1, 1, 2, 3, 5, 8, 13, 21, 34, 55, 89, 144,
*///:~
```

Notice how the generic method **fill( )** can be transparently applied to both **Coffee** and **Integer** containers and generators.

Exercise 13: (4) Overload the **fill( )** method so that the arguments and return types are the specific subtypes of **Collection**: **List**, **Queue** and **Set**. This way, you don't lose the type of container. Can you overload to distinguish between **List** and **LinkedList**?

A general-purpose **Generator**

Here's a class that produces a **Generator** for any class that has a default constructor. To reduce typing, it also includes a generic method to produce a **BasicGenerator**:

```
//: net/mindview/util/BasicGenerator.java
// Automatically create a Generator, given a class
// with a default (no-arg) constructor.
package net.mindview.util;

public class BasicGenerator<T> implements Generator<T> {
  private Class<T> type;
  public BasicGenerator(Class<T> type){ this.type = type; }
  public T next() {
    try {
```

```
      // Assumes type is a public class:
      return type.newInstance();
    } catch(Exception e) {
      throw new RuntimeException(e);
    }
  }
  // Produce a Default generator given a type token:
  public static <T> Generator<T> create(Class<T> type) {
    return new BasicGenerator<T>(type);
  }
} ///:~
```

This class provides a basic implementation that will produce objects of a class that (1) is **public** (because **BasicGenerator** is in a separate package, the class in question must have **public** and not just package access) and (2) has a default constructor (one that takes no arguments). To create one of these **BasicGenerator** objects, you call the **create( )** method and pass it the type token for the type you want generated. The generic **create( )** method allows you to say **BasicGenerator.create(MyType.class)** instead of the more awkward **new BasicGenerator<MyType>(MyType.class)**.

For example, here's a simple class that has a default constructor:

```
//: generics/CountedObject.java

public class CountedObject {
  private static long counter = 0;
  private final long id = counter++;
  public long id() { return id; }
  public String toString() { return "CountedObject " + id;}
} ///:~
```

The **CountedObject** class keeps track of how many instances of itself have been created, and reports these in its **toString( )**.

Using **BasicGenerator**, you can easily create a **Generator** for **CountedObject**:

```
//: generics/BasicGeneratorDemo.java
import net.mindview.util.*;

public class BasicGeneratorDemo {
  public static void main(String[] args) {
    Generator<CountedObject> gen =
      BasicGenerator.create(CountedObject.class);
```

```
      for(int i = 0; i < 5; i++)
        System.out.println(gen.next());
    }
} /* Output:
CountedObject 0
CountedObject 1
CountedObject 2
CountedObject 3
CountedObject 4
*///:~
```

You can see how the generic method reduces the amount of typing necessary to produce the **Generator** object. Java generics force you to pass in the **Class** object anyway, so you might as well use it for type inference in the **create( )** method.

Exercise 14: (1) Modify **BasicGeneratorDemo.java** to use the explicit form of creation for the **Generator** (that is, use the explicit constructor instead of the generic **create( )** method).

Simplifying tuple use

Type argument inference, together with **static** imports, allows the tuples we saw earlier to be rewritten into a more general-purpose library. Here, tuples can be created using an overloaded **static** method:

```
//: net/mindview/util/Tuple.java
// Tuple library using type argument inference.
package net.mindview.util;

public class Tuple {
  public static <A,B> TwoTuple<A,B> tuple(A a, B b) {
    return new TwoTuple<A,B>(a, b);
  }
  public static <A,B,C> ThreeTuple<A,B,C>
  tuple(A a, B b, C c) {
    return new ThreeTuple<A,B,C>(a, b, c);
  }
  public static <A,B,C,D> FourTuple<A,B,C,D>
  tuple(A a, B b, C c, D d) {
    return new FourTuple<A,B,C,D>(a, b, c, d);
  }
  public static <A,B,C,D,E>
  FiveTuple<A,B,C,D,E> tuple(A a, B b, C c, D d, E e) {
    return new FiveTuple<A,B,C,D,E>(a, b, c, d, e);
```

```
    }
} ///:~
```

Here's a modification of **TupleTest.java** to test **Tuple.java**:

```
//: generics/TupleTest2.java
import net.mindview.util.*;
import static net.mindview.util.Tuple.*;

public class TupleTest2 {
  static TwoTuple<String,Integer> f() {
    return tuple("hi", 47);
  }
  static TwoTuple f2() { return tuple("hi", 47); }
  static ThreeTuple<Amphibian,String,Integer> g() {
    return tuple(new Amphibian(), "hi", 47);
  }
  static
  FourTuple<Vehicle,Amphibian,String,Integer> h() {
    return tuple(new Vehicle(), new Amphibian(), "hi", 47);
  }
  static
  FiveTuple<Vehicle,Amphibian,String,Integer,Double> k() {
    return tuple(new Vehicle(), new Amphibian(),
      "hi", 47, 11.1);
  }
  public static void main(String[] args) {
    TwoTuple<String,Integer> ttsi = f();
    System.out.println(ttsi);
    System.out.println(f2());
    System.out.println(g());
    System.out.println(h());
    System.out.println(k());
  }
} /* Output: (80% match)
(hi, 47)
(hi, 47)
(Amphibian@7d772e, hi, 47)
(Vehicle@757aef, Amphibian@d9f9c3, hi, 47)
(Vehicle@1a46e30, Amphibian@3e25a5, hi, 47, 11.1)
*///:~
```

Notice that **f( )** returns a parameterized **TwoTuple** object, while **f2( )** returns an unparameterized **TwoTuple** object. The compiler doesn't warn about **f2( )** in this case because the return value is not being used in a parameterized fashion; in a sense, it is being "upcast" to an unparameterized **TwoTuple**. However, if you were to try to capture the result of **f2( )** into a parameterized **TwoTuple**, the compiler would issue a warning.

Exercise 15: (1) Verify the previous statement.

Exercise 16: (2) Add a **SixTuple** to **Tuple.java**, and test it in **TupleTest2.java**.

A **Set** utility

For another example of the use of generic methods, consider the mathematical relationships that can be expressed using **Set**s. These can be conveniently defined as generic methods, to be used with all different types:

```java
//: net/mindview/util/Sets.java
package net.mindview.util;
import java.util.*;

public class Sets {
  public static <T> Set<T> union(Set<T> a, Set<T> b) {
    Set<T> result = new HashSet<T>(a);
    result.addAll(b);
    return result;
  }
  public static <T>
  Set<T> intersection(Set<T> a, Set<T> b) {
    Set<T> result = new HashSet<T>(a);
    result.retainAll(b);
    return result;
  }
  // Subtract subset from superset:
  public static <T> Set<T>
  difference(Set<T> superset, Set<T> subset) {
    Set<T> result = new HashSet<T>(superset);
    result.removeAll(subset);
    return result;
  }
  // Reflexive--everything not in the intersection:
  public static <T> Set<T> complement(Set<T> a, Set<T> b) {
    return difference(union(a, b), intersection(a, b));
  }
} ///:~
```

The first three methods duplicate the first argument by copying its references into a new **HashSet** object, so the argument **Set**s are not directly modified. The return value is thus a new **Set** object.

The four methods represent mathematical set operations: **union( )** returns a **Set** containing the combination of the two arguments, **intersection( )** returns a **Set** containing the common elements between the two arguments, **difference( )** performs a subtraction of the **subset** elements from the **superset**, and **complement( )** returns a **Set** of all the elements that are not in the intersection. To create a simple example showing the effects of these methods, here's an **enum** containing different names of watercolors:

```
//: generics/watercolors/Watercolors.java
package generics.watercolors;

public enum Watercolors {
  ZINC, LEMON_YELLOW, MEDIUM_YELLOW, DEEP_YELLOW, ORANGE,
  BRILLIANT_RED, CRIMSON, MAGENTA, ROSE_MADDER, VIOLET,
  CERULEAN_BLUE_HUE, PHTHALO_BLUE, ULTRAMARINE,
  COBALT_BLUE_HUE, PERMANENT_GREEN, VIRIDIAN_HUE,
  SAP_GREEN, YELLOW_OCHRE, BURNT_SIENNA, RAW_UMBER,
  BURNT_UMBER, PAYNES_GRAY, IVORY_BLACK
} ///:~
```

For convenience (so that all the names don't have to be qualified), this is imported statically into the following example. This example uses the **EnumSet**, which is a Java SE5 tool for easy creation of **Set**s from **enum**s. (You'll learn more about **EnumSet** in the *Enumerated Types* chapter.) Here, the **static** method **EnumSet.range( )** is given the first and last elements of the range to create in the resulting **Set**:

```
//: generics/WatercolorSets.java
import generics.watercolors.*;
import java.util.*;
import static net.mindview.util.Print.*;
import static net.mindview.util.Sets.*;
import static generics.watercolors.Watercolors.*;

public class WatercolorSets {
  public static void main(String[] args) {
    Set<Watercolors> set1 =
      EnumSet.range(BRILLIANT_RED, VIRIDIAN_HUE);
    Set<Watercolors> set2 =
      EnumSet.range(CERULEAN_BLUE_HUE, BURNT_UMBER);
```

```
        print("set1: " + set1);
        print("set2: " + set2);
        print("union(set1, set2): " + union(set1, set2));
        Set<Watercolors> subset = intersection(set1, set2);
        print("intersection(set1, set2): " + subset);
        print("difference(set1, subset): " +
          difference(set1, subset));
        print("difference(set2, subset): " +
          difference(set2, subset));
        print("complement(set1, set2): " +
          complement(set1, set2));
    }
} /* Output: (Sample)
set1: [BRILLIANT_RED, CRIMSON, MAGENTA, ROSE_MADDER,
VIOLET, CERULEAN_BLUE_HUE, PHTHALO_BLUE, ULTRAMARINE,
COBALT_BLUE_HUE, PERMANENT_GREEN, VIRIDIAN_HUE]
set2: [CERULEAN_BLUE_HUE, PHTHALO_BLUE, ULTRAMARINE,
COBALT_BLUE_HUE, PERMANENT_GREEN, VIRIDIAN_HUE, SAP_GREEN,
YELLOW_OCHRE, BURNT_SIENNA, RAW_UMBER, BURNT_UMBER]
union(set1, set2): [SAP_GREEN, ROSE_MADDER, YELLOW_OCHRE,
PERMANENT_GREEN, BURNT_UMBER, COBALT_BLUE_HUE, VIOLET,
BRILLIANT_RED, RAW_UMBER, ULTRAMARINE, BURNT_SIENNA,
CRIMSON, CERULEAN_BLUE_HUE, PHTHALO_BLUE, MAGENTA,
VIRIDIAN_HUE]
intersection(set1, set2): [ULTRAMARINE, PERMANENT_GREEN,
COBALT_BLUE_HUE, PHTHALO_BLUE, CERULEAN_BLUE_HUE,
VIRIDIAN_HUE]
difference(set1, subset): [ROSE_MADDER, CRIMSON, VIOLET,
MAGENTA, BRILLIANT_RED]
difference(set2, subset): [RAW_UMBER, SAP_GREEN,
YELLOW_OCHRE, BURNT_SIENNA, BURNT_UMBER]
complement(set1, set2): [SAP_GREEN, ROSE_MADDER,
YELLOW_OCHRE, BURNT_UMBER, VIOLET, BRILLIANT_RED,
RAW_UMBER, BURNT_SIENNA, CRIMSON, MAGENTA]
*///:~
```

You can see the results of each operation from the output.

The following example uses **Sets.difference( )** to show the method differences between various **Collection** and **Map** classes in **java.util**:

```
//: net/mindview/util/ContainerMethodDifferences.java
package net.mindview.util;
import java.lang.reflect.*;
import java.util.*;
```

```java
public class ContainerMethodDifferences {
  static Set<String> methodSet(Class<?> type) {
    Set<String> result = new TreeSet<String>();
    for(Method m : type.getMethods())
      result.add(m.getName());
    return result;
  }
  static void interfaces(Class<?> type) {
    System.out.print("Interfaces in " +
      type.getSimpleName() + ": ");
    List<String> result = new ArrayList<String>();
    for(Class<?> c : type.getInterfaces())
      result.add(c.getSimpleName());
    System.out.println(result);
  }
  static Set<String> object = methodSet(Object.class);
  static { object.add("clone"); }
  static void
  difference(Class<?> superset, Class<?> subset) {
    System.out.print(superset.getSimpleName() +
      " extends " + subset.getSimpleName() + ", adds: ");
    Set<String> comp = Sets.difference(
      methodSet(superset), methodSet(subset));
    comp.removeAll(object); // Don't show 'Object' methods
    System.out.println(comp);
    interfaces(superset);
  }
  public static void main(String[] args) {
    System.out.println("Collection: " +
      methodSet(Collection.class));
    interfaces(Collection.class);
    difference(Set.class, Collection.class);
    difference(HashSet.class, Set.class);
    difference(LinkedHashSet.class, HashSet.class);
    difference(TreeSet.class, Set.class);
    difference(List.class, Collection.class);
    difference(ArrayList.class, List.class);
    difference(LinkedList.class, List.class);
    difference(Queue.class, Collection.class);
    difference(PriorityQueue.class, Queue.class);
    System.out.println("Map: " + methodSet(Map.class));
    difference(HashMap.class, Map.class);
    difference(LinkedHashMap.class, HashMap.class);
```

```
    difference(SortedMap.class, Map.class);
    difference(TreeMap.class, Map.class);
  }
} ///:~
```

The output of this program was used in the "Summary" section of the
Holding Your Objects chapter.

Exercise 17:   (4) Study the JDK documentation for **EnumSet**. You'll see
that there's a **clone( )** method defined. However, you cannot **clone( )** from
the reference to the **Set** interface passed in **Sets.java**. Can you modify
Sets.java to handle both the general case of a **Set** interface as shown, and
the special case of an **EnumSet**, using **clone( )** instead of creating a new
HashSet?

Anonymous inner classes

Generics can also be used with inner classes and anonymous inner classes.
Here's an example that implements the **Generator** interface using
anonymous inner classes:

```
//: generics/BankTeller.java
// A very simple bank teller simulation.
import java.util.*;
import net.mindview.util.*;

class Customer {
  private static long counter = 1;
  private final long id = counter++;
  private Customer() {}
  public String toString() { return "Customer " + id; }
  // A method to produce Generator objects:
  public static Generator<Customer> generator() {
    return new Generator<Customer>() {
      public Customer next() { return new Customer(); }
    };
  }
}

class Teller {
  private static long counter = 1;
  private final long id = counter++;
  private Teller() {}
  public String toString() { return "Teller " + id; }
```

```
  // A single Generator object:
  public static Generator<Teller> generator =
    new Generator<Teller>() {
      public Teller next() { return new Teller(); }
    };
}

public class BankTeller {
  public static void serve(Teller t, Customer c) {
    System.out.println(t + " serves " + c);
  }
  public static void main(String[] args) {
    Random rand = new Random(47);
    Queue<Customer> line = new LinkedList<Customer>();
    Generators.fill(line, Customer.generator(), 15);
    List<Teller> tellers = new ArrayList<Teller>();
    Generators.fill(tellers, Teller.generator, 4);
    for(Customer c : line)
      serve(tellers.get(rand.nextInt(tellers.size())), c);
  }
} /* Output:
Teller 3 serves Customer 1
Teller 2 serves Customer 2
Teller 3 serves Customer 3
Teller 1 serves Customer 4
Teller 1 serves Customer 5
Teller 3 serves Customer 6
Teller 1 serves Customer 7
Teller 2 serves Customer 8
Teller 3 serves Customer 9
Teller 3 serves Customer 10
Teller 2 serves Customer 11
Teller 4 serves Customer 12
Teller 2 serves Customer 13
Teller 1 serves Customer 14
Teller 1 serves Customer 15
*///:~
```

Both **Customer** and **Teller** have **private** constructors, thereby forcing you to use **Generator** objects. **Customer** has a **generator( )** method that produces a new **Generator<Customer>** object each time you call it. You may not need multiple **Generator** objects, and **Teller** creates a single public **generator** object. You can see both of these approaches used in the **fill( )** methods in **main( )**.

Since both the **generator( )** method in **Customer** and the **Generator** object in **Teller** are **static**, they cannot be part of an interface, so there is no way to "generify" this particular idiom. Despite that, it works reasonably well with the **fill( )** method.

We'll look at other versions of this queuing problem in the *Concurrency* chapter.

Exercise 18: (3) Following the form of **BankTeller.java**, create an example where **BigFish** eat **LittleFish** in the **Ocean**.

Building complex models

An important benefit of generics is the ability to simply and safely create complex models. For example, we can easily create a **List** of tuples:

```
//: generics/TupleList.java
// Combining generic types to make complex generic types.
import java.util.*;
import net.mindview.util.*;

public class TupleList<A,B,C,D>
extends ArrayList<FourTuple<A,B,C,D>> {
  public static void main(String[] args) {
    TupleList<Vehicle, Amphibian, String, Integer> tl =
      new TupleList<Vehicle, Amphibian, String, Integer>();
    tl.add(TupleTest.h());
    tl.add(TupleTest.h());
    for(FourTuple<Vehicle,Amphibian,String,Integer> i: tl)
      System.out.println(i);
  }
} /* Output: (75% match)
(Vehicle@11b86e7, Amphibian@35ce36, hi, 47)
(Vehicle@757aef, Amphibian@d9f9c3, hi, 47)
*///:~
```

Although it gets somewhat verbose (especially the creation of the iterator), you end up with a fairly powerful data structure without too much code.

Here's another example showing how straightforward it is to build complex models using generic types. Even though each class is created as a building block, the total has many parts. In this case, the model is a retail store with aisles, shelves and products:

```
//: generics/Store.java
// Building up a complex model using generic containers.
import java.util.*;
import net.mindview.util.*;

class Product {
  private final int id;
  private String description;
  private double price;
  public Product(int IDnumber, String descr, double price){
    id = IDnumber;
    description = descr;
    this.price = price;
    System.out.println(toString());
  }
  public String toString() {
    return id + ": " + description + ", price: $" + price;
  }
  public void priceChange(double change) {
    price += change;
  }
  public static Generator<Product> generator =
    new Generator<Product>() {
      private Random rand = new Random(47);
      public Product next() {
        return new Product(rand.nextInt(1000), "Test",
          Math.round(rand.nextDouble() * 1000.0) + 0.99);
      }
    };
}

class Shelf extends ArrayList<Product> {
  public Shelf(int nProducts) {
    Generators.fill(this, Product.generator, nProducts);
  }
}

class Aisle extends ArrayList<Shelf> {
  public Aisle(int nShelves, int nProducts) {
    for(int i = 0; i < nShelves; i++)
      add(new Shelf(nProducts));
  }
}
```

```java
class CheckoutStand {}
class Office {}

public class Store extends ArrayList<Aisle> {
  private ArrayList<CheckoutStand> checkouts =
    new ArrayList<CheckoutStand>();
  private Office office = new Office();
  public Store(int nAisles, int nShelves, int nProducts) {
    for(int i = 0; i < nAisles; i++)
      add(new Aisle(nShelves, nProducts));
  }
  public String toString() {
    StringBuilder result = new StringBuilder();
    for(Aisle a : this)
      for(Shelf s : a)
        for(Product p : s) {
          result.append(p);
          result.append("\n");
        }
    return result.toString();
  }
  public static void main(String[] args) {
    System.out.println(new Store(14, 5, 10));
  }
} /* Output:
258: Test, price: $400.99
861: Test, price: $160.99
868: Test, price: $417.99
207: Test, price: $268.99
551: Test, price: $114.99
278: Test, price: $804.99
520: Test, price: $554.99
140: Test, price: $530.99
...
*///:~
```

As you can see in **Store.toString( )**, the result is many layers of containers that are nonetheless type-safe and manageable. What's impressive is that it is not intellectually prohibitive to assemble such a model.

Exercise 19: (2) Following the form of **Store.java**, build a model of a containerized cargo ship.

The mystery of erasure

As you begin to delve more deeply into generics, there are a number of things that won't initially make sense. For example, although you can say **ArrayList.class**, you cannot say **ArrayList<Integer>.class**. And consider the following:

```
//: generics/ErasedTypeEquivalence.java
import java.util.*;

public class ErasedTypeEquivalence {
  public static void main(String[] args) {
    Class c1 = new ArrayList<String>().getClass();
    Class c2 = new ArrayList<Integer>().getClass();
    System.out.println(c1 == c2);
  }
} /* Output:
true
*///:~
```

ArrayList<String> and **ArrayList<Integer>** could easily be argued to be distinct types. Different types behave differently, and if you try, for example, to put an **Integer** into an **ArrayList<String>**, you get different behavior (it fails) than if you put an **Integer** into an **ArrayList<Integer>** (it succeeds). And yet the above program suggests that they are the same type.

Here's an example that adds to this puzzle:

```
//: generics/LostInformation.java
import java.util.*;

class Frob {}
class Fnorkle {}
class Quark<Q> {}
class Particle<POSITION,MOMENTUM> {}

public class LostInformation {
  public static void main(String[] args) {
    List<Frob> list = new ArrayList<Frob>();
    Map<Frob,Fnorkle> map = new HashMap<Frob,Fnorkle>();
    Quark<Fnorkle> quark = new Quark<Fnorkle>();
    Particle<Long,Double> p = new Particle<Long,Double>();
    System.out.println(Arrays.toString(
      list.getClass().getTypeParameters()));
```

```
        System.out.println(Arrays.toString(
          map.getClass().getTypeParameters()));
        System.out.println(Arrays.toString(
          quark.getClass().getTypeParameters()));
        System.out.println(Arrays.toString(
          p.getClass().getTypeParameters()));
    }
} /* Output:
[E]
[K, V]
[Q]
[POSITION, MOMENTUM]
*///:~
```

According to the JDK documentation, **Class.getTypeParameters( )** "returns an array of **TypeVariable** objects that represent the type variables declared by the generic declaration..." This seems to suggest that you might be able to find out what the parameter types are. However, as you can see from the output, all you find out is the identifiers that are used as the parameter placeholders, which is not such an interesting piece of information.

The cold truth is:

> *There's no information about generic parameter types available inside generic code.*

Thus, you can know things like the identifier of the type parameter and the bounds of the generic type—you just can't know the actual type parameter(s) used to create a particular instance. This fact, which is especially frustrating if you're coming from C++, is the most fundamental issue that you must deal with when working with Java generics.

Java generics are implemented using *erasure*. This means that any specific type information is erased when you use a generic. Inside the generic, the only thing that you know is that you're using an object. So **List<String>** and **List<Integer>** *are*, in fact, the same type at run time. Both forms are "erased" to their *raw type*, **List**. Understanding erasure and how you must deal with it will be one of the biggest hurdles you will face when learning Java generics, and that's what we'll explore in this section.

The C++ approach

Here's a C++ example which uses *templates*. You'll notice that the syntax for parameterized types is quite similar, because Java took inspiration from C++:

```
//: generics/Templates.cpp
#include <iostream>
using namespace std;

template<class T> class Manipulator {
  T obj;
public:
  Manipulator(T x) { obj = x; }
  void manipulate() { obj.f(); }
};

class HasF {
public:
  void f() { cout << "HasF::f()" << endl; }
};

int main() {
  HasF hf;
  Manipulator<HasF> manipulator(hf);
  manipulator.manipulate();
} /* Output:
HasF::f()
///:~
```

The **Manipulator** class stores an object of type **T**. What's interesting is the **manipulate( )** method, which calls a method **f( )** on **obj**. How can it know that the **f( )** method exists for the type parameter **T**? The C++ compiler checks when you instantiate the template, so at the point of instantiation of **Manipulator<HasF>**, it sees that **HasF** has a method **f( )**. If it were not the case, you'd get a compile-time error, and thus type safety is preserved.

Writing this kind of code in C++ is straightforward because when a template is instantiated, the template code knows the type of its template parameters. Java generics are different. Here's the translation of **HasF**:

```
//: generics/HasF.java

public class HasF {
  public void f() { System.out.println("HasF.f()"); }
```

```
} ///:~
```

If we take the rest of the example and translate it to Java, it won't compile:

```
//: generics/Manipulation.java
// {CompileTimeError} (Won't compile)

class Manipulator<T> {
  private T obj;
  public Manipulator(T x) { obj = x; }
  // Error: cannot find symbol: method f():
  public void manipulate() { obj.f(); }
}

public class Manipulation {
  public static void main(String[] args) {
    HasF hf = new HasF();
    Manipulator<HasF> manipulator =
      new Manipulator<HasF>(hf);
    manipulator.manipulate();
  }
} ///:~
```

Because of erasure, the Java compiler can't map the requirement that **manipulate( )** must be able to call **f( )** on **obj** to the fact that **HasF** has a method **f( )**. In order to call **f( )**, we must assist the generic class by giving it a *bound* that tells the compiler to only accept types that conform to that bound. This reuses the **extends** keyword. Because of the bound, the following compiles:

```
//: generics/Manipulator2.java

class Manipulator2<T extends HasF> {
  private T obj;
  public Manipulator2(T x) { obj = x; }
  public void manipulate() { obj.f(); }
} ///:~
```

The bound **<T extends HasF>** says that **T** must be of type **HasF** or something derived from **HasF**. If this is true, then it is safe to call **f( )** on **obj**.

We say that a generic type parameter *erases to its first bound* (it's possible to have multiple bounds, as you shall see later). We also talk about the *erasure of the type parameter*. The compiler actually replaces the type parameter

---

Generics   653

with its erasure, so in the above case, **T** erases to **HasF**, which is the same as replacing **T** with **HasF** in the class body.

You may correctly observe that in **Manipulation2.java**, generics do not contribute anything. You could just as easily perform the erasure yourself and produce a class without generics:

```
//: generics/Manipulator3.java

class Manipulator3 {
  private HasF obj;
  public Manipulator3(HasF x) { obj = x; }
  public void manipulate() { obj.f(); }
} ///:~
```

This brings up an important point: Generics are only useful when you want to use type parameters that are more "generic" than a specific type (and all its subtypes)—that is, when you want code to work across multiple classes. As a result, the type parameters and their application in useful generic code will usually be more complex than simple class replacement. However, you can't just say that anything of the form **<T extends HasF>** is therefore flawed. For example, if a class has a method that returns **T**, then generics are helpful, because they will then return the exact type:

```
//: generics/ReturnGenericType.java

class ReturnGenericType<T extends HasF> {
  private T obj;
  public ReturnGenericType(T x) { obj = x; }
  public T get() { return obj; }
} ///:~
```

You have to look at all the code and understand whether it is "complex enough" to warrant the use of generics.

We'll look at bounds in more detail later in the chapter.

Exercise 20: (1) Create an interface with two methods, and a class that implements that interface and adds another method. In another class, create a generic method with an argument type that is bounded by the interface, and show that the methods in the interface are callable inside this generic method. In **main( )**, pass an instance of the implementing class to the generic method.

Migration compatibility

To allay any potential confusion about erasure, you must clearly understand that it is *not* a language feature. It is a compromise in the implementation of Java generics, necessary because generics were not made part of the language from the beginning. This compromise will cause you pain, so you need to get used to it early and to understand why it's there.

If generics had been part of Java 1.0, the feature would not have been implemented using erasure—it would have used *reification* to retain the type parameters as first-class entities, so you would have been able to perform type-based language and reflective operations on type parameters. You'll see later in this chapter that erasure reduces the "genericity" of generics. Generics are still useful in Java, just not as useful as they could be, and the reason is erasure.

In an erasure-based implementation, generic types are treated as second-class types that cannot be used in some important contexts. The generic types are present only during static type checking, after which every generic type in the program is erased by replacing it with a non-generic upper bound. For example, type annotations such as **List<T>** are erased to **List**, and ordinary type variables are erased to **Object** unless a bound is specified.

The core motivation for erasure is that it allows generified clients to be used with non-generified libraries, and vice versa. This is often called *migration compatibility*. In the ideal world, we would have had a single day when everything was generified at once. In reality, even if programmers are only writing generic code, they will have to deal with non-generic libraries that were written before Java SE5. The authors of those libraries may never have the incentive to generify their code, or they may just take their time in getting to it.

So Java generics not only must support *backwards compatibility*—existing code and class files are still legal, and continue to mean what they meant before—but also must support migration compatibility, so that libraries can become generic at their own pace, and when a library does become generic, it doesn't break code and applications that depend upon it. After deciding that this was the goal, the Java designers and the various groups working on the problem decided that erasure was the only feasible solution. Erasure enables this migration towards generics by allowing non-generic code to coexist with generic code.

For example, suppose an application uses two libraries, **X** and **Y**, and **Y** uses library **Z**. With the advent of Java SE5, the creators of this application and these libraries will probably, eventually, want to migrate to generics. Each of them, however, will have different motivations and constraints as to when that migration happens. To achieve migration compatibility, each library and application must be independent of all the others regarding whether generics are used. Thus, they must not be able to detect whether other libraries are or are not using generics. Ergo, the evidence that a particular library is using generics must be "erased."

Without some kind of migration path, all the libraries that had been built up over time stood the chance of being cut off from the developers that chose to move to Java generics. Libraries are arguably the part of a programming language that has the greatest productivity impact, so this was not an acceptable cost. Whether or not erasure was the best or only migration path is something that only time will tell.

The problem with erasure

So the primary justification for erasure is the transition process from non-generified code to generified code, and to incorporate generics into the language without breaking existing libraries. Erasure allows existing non-generic client code to continue to be used without change, until clients are ready to rewrite code for generics. This is a noble motivation, because it doesn't suddenly break all existing code.

The cost of erasure is significant. Generic types cannot be used in operations that explicitly refer to runtime types, such as casts, **instanceof** operations, and **new** expressions. Because all the type information about the parameters is lost, whenever you're writing generic code you must constantly be reminding yourself that it only *appears* that you have type information about a parameter. So when you write a piece of code like this:

```
class Foo<T> {
  T var;
}
```

it appears that when you create an instance of **Foo**:

```
Foo<Cat> f = new Foo<Cat>();
```

the code in **class Foo** ought to know that it is now working with a **Cat**. The syntax strongly suggests that the type **T** is being substituted everywhere throughout the class. But it isn't, and you must remind yourself, "No, it's just an **Object**," whenever you're writing the code for the class.

In addition, erasure and migration compatibility mean that the use of generics is not enforced when you might want it to be:

```
//: generics/ErasureAndInheritance.java

class GenericBase<T> {
  private T element;
  public void set(T arg) { element = arg; }
  public T get() { return element; }
}

class Derived1<T> extends GenericBase<T> {}

class Derived2 extends GenericBase {} // No warning

// class Derived3 extends GenericBase<?> {}
// Strange error:
//    unexpected type found : ?
//    required: class or interface without bounds

public class ErasureAndInheritance {
  @SuppressWarnings("unchecked")
  public static void main(String[] args) {
    Derived2 d2 = new Derived2();
    Object obj = d2.get();
    d2.set(obj); // Warning here!
  }
} ///:~
```

Derived2 inherits from **GenericBase** with no generic parameters, and the compiler doesn't issue a warning. The warning doesn't occur until **set( )** is called.

To turn off the warning, Java provides an annotation, the one that you see in the listing (this annotation was not supported in earlier releases of Java SE5):

```
@SuppressWarnings("unchecked")
```

Notice that this is placed on the method that generates the warning, rather than the entire class. It's best to be as "focused" as possible when you turn off a warning, so that you don't accidentally cloak a real problem by turning off warnings too broadly.

Presumably, the error produced by **Derived3** means that the compiler expects a raw base class.

Add to this the extra effort of managing bounds when you want to treat your type parameter as more than just an **Object**, and you have far more effort for much less payoff than you get in parameterized types in languages like C++, Ada or Eiffel. This is not to say that those languages in general buy you more than Java does for the majority of programming problems, but rather that their parameterized type mechanisms are more flexible and powerful than Java's.

The action at the boundaries

Because of erasure, I find that the most confusing aspect of generics is the fact that you can represent things that have no meaning. For example:

```
//: generics/ArrayMaker.java
import java.lang.reflect.*;
import java.util.*;

public class ArrayMaker<T> {
  private Class<T> kind;
  public ArrayMaker(Class<T> kind) { this.kind = kind; }
  @SuppressWarnings("unchecked")
  T[] create(int size) {
    return (T[])Array.newInstance(kind, size);
  }
  public static void main(String[] args) {
    ArrayMaker<String> stringMaker =
      new ArrayMaker<String>(String.class);
    String[] stringArray = stringMaker.create(9);
    System.out.println(Arrays.toString(stringArray));
  }
} /* Output:
[null, null, null, null, null, null, null, null, null]
*///:~
```

Even though **kind** is stored as **Class<T>**, erasure means that it is actually just being stored as a **Class**, with no parameter. So, when you do something with it, as in creating an array, **Array.newInstance( )** doesn't actually have the type information that's implied in **kind**; so it cannot produce the specific result, which must therefore be cast, which produces a warning that you cannot satisfy.

Note that using **Array.newInstance( )** is the recommended approach for creating arrays in generics.

If we create a container instead of an array, things are different:

```
//: generics/ListMaker.java
import java.util.*;

public class ListMaker<T> {
  List<T> create() { return new ArrayList<T>(); }
  public static void main(String[] args) {
    ListMaker<String> stringMaker= new ListMaker<String>();
    List<String> stringList = stringMaker.create();
  }
} ///:~
```

The compiler gives no warnings, even though we know (from erasure) that the **<T>** in **new ArrayList<T>( )** inside **create( )** is removed—at run time there's no **<T>** inside the class, so it seems meaningless. But if you follow this idea and change the expression to **new ArrayList( )**, the compiler gives a warning.

Is it really meaningless in this case? What if you were to put some objects in the **list** before returning it, like this:

```
//: generics/FilledListMaker.java
import java.util.*;

public class FilledListMaker<T> {
  List<T> create(T t, int n) {
    List<T> result = new ArrayList<T>();
    for(int i = 0; i < n; i++)
      result.add(t);
    return result;
  }
  public static void main(String[] args) {
    FilledListMaker<String> stringMaker =
      new FilledListMaker<String>();
    List<String> list = stringMaker.create("Hello", 4);
    System.out.println(list);
  }
} /* Output:
[Hello, Hello, Hello, Hello]
*///:~
```

Even though the compiler is unable to know anything about **T** inside **create( )**, it can still ensure—at compile time—that what you put into **result** is of type **T**, so that it agrees with **ArrayList<T>**. Thus, even though erasure removes the information about the actual type inside a method or class, the compiler can still ensure internal consistency in the way that the type is used within the method or class.

Because erasure removes type information in the body of a method, what matters at run time is the *boundaries*: the points where objects enter and leave a method. These are the points at which the compiler performs type checks at compile time, and inserts casting code. Consider the following non-generic example:

```
//: generics/SimpleHolder.java

public class SimpleHolder {
  private Object obj;
  public void set(Object obj) { this.obj = obj; }
  public Object get() { return obj; }
  public static void main(String[] args) {
    SimpleHolder holder = new SimpleHolder();
    holder.set("Item");
    String s = (String)holder.get();
  }
} ///:~
```

If we decompile the result with **javap -c SimpleHolder**, we get (after editing):

```
public void set(java.lang.Object);
   0:    aload_0
   1:    aload_1
   2:    putfield #2; //Field obj:Object;
   5:    return

public java.lang.Object get();
   0:    aload_0
   1:    getfield #2; //Field obj:Object;
   4:    areturn

public static void main(java.lang.String[]);
   0:    new #3; //class SimpleHolder
   3:    dup
   4:    invokespecial #4; //Method "<init>":()V
```

```
7:    astore_1
8:    aload_1
9:    ldc #5; //String Item
11:   invokevirtual #6; //Method set:(Object;)V
14:   aload_1
15:   invokevirtual #7; //Method get:()Object;
18:   checkcast #8; //class java/lang/String
21:   astore_2
22:   return
```

The **set( )** and **get( )** methods simply store and produce the value, and the cast is checked at the point of the call to **get( )**.

Now incorporate generics into the above code:

```
//: generics/GenericHolder.java

public class GenericHolder<T> {
  private T obj;
  public void set(T obj) { this.obj = obj; }
  public T get() { return obj; }
  public static void main(String[] args) {
    GenericHolder<String> holder =
      new GenericHolder<String>();
    holder.set("Item");
    String s = holder.get();
  }
} ///:~
```

The need for the cast from **get( )** has disappeared, but we also know that the value passed to **set( )** is being type-checked at compile time. Here are the relevant bytecodes:

```
public void set(java.lang.Object);
  0:    aload_0
  1:    aload_1
  2:    putfield #2; //Field obj:Object;
  5:    return

public java.lang.Object get();
  0:    aload_0
  1:    getfield #2; //Field obj:Object;
  4:    areturn

public static void main(java.lang.String[]);
```

```
 0:      new #3; //class GenericHolder
 3:      dup
 4:      invokespecial #4; //Method "<init>":()V
 7:      astore_1
 8:      aload_1
 9:      ldc #5; //String Item
11:      invokevirtual #6; //Method set:(Object;)V
14:      aload_1
15:      invokevirtual #7; //Method get:()Object;
18:      checkcast #8; //class java/lang/String
21:      astore_2
22:      return
```

The resulting code is identical. The extra work of checking the incoming type in **set( )** is free, because it is performed by the compiler. And the cast for the outgoing value of **get( )** is still there, but it's no less than you'd have to do yourself—and it's automatically inserted by the compiler, so the code you write (and read) is less noisy.

Since **get( )** and **set( )** produce the same bytecodes, all the action in generics happens at the boundaries—the extra compile-time check for incoming values, and the inserted cast for outgoing values. It helps to counter the confusion of erasure to remember that "the boundaries are where the action takes place."

Compensating for erasure

As we've seen, erasure loses the ability to perform certain operations in generic code. Anything that requires the knowledge of the exact type at run time won't work:

```
//: generics/Erased.java
// {CompileTimeError} (Won't compile)

public class Erased<T> {
  private final int SIZE = 100;
  public static void f(Object arg) {
    if(arg instanceof T) {}          // Error
    T var = new T();                 // Error
    T[] array = new T[SIZE];         // Error
    T[] array = (T)new Object[SIZE]; // Unchecked warning
  }
} ///:~
```

Occasionally you can program around these issues, but sometimes you must compensate for erasure by introducing a *type tag*. This means you explicitly pass in the **Class** object for your type so that you can use it in type expressions.

For example, the attempt to use **instanceof** in the previous program fails because the type information has been erased. If you introduce a type tag, a dynamic **isInstance( )** can be used instead:

```
//: generics/ClassTypeCapture.java

class Building {}
class House extends Building {}

public class ClassTypeCapture<T> {
  Class<T> kind;
  public ClassTypeCapture(Class<T> kind) {
    this.kind = kind;
  }
  public boolean f(Object arg) {
    return kind.isInstance(arg);
  }
  public static void main(String[] args) {
    ClassTypeCapture<Building> ctt1 =
      new ClassTypeCapture<Building>(Building.class);
    System.out.println(ctt1.f(new Building()));
    System.out.println(ctt1.f(new House()));
    ClassTypeCapture<House> ctt2 =
      new ClassTypeCapture<House>(House.class);
    System.out.println(ctt2.f(new Building()));
    System.out.println(ctt2.f(new House()));
  }
} /* Output:
true
true
false
true
*///:~
```

The compiler ensures that the type tag matches the generic argument.

Exercise 21: (4) Modify **ClassTypeCapture.java** by adding a **Map<String,Class<?>>**, a method **addType(String typename, Class<?> kind)**, and a method **createNew(String typename)**.

---

createNew( ) will either produce a new instance of the class associated with its argument string, or produce an error message.

Creating instances of types

The attempt to create a **new T( )** in **Erased.java** won't work, partly because of erasure, and partly because the compiler cannot verify that **T** has a default (no-arg) constructor. But in C++ this operation is natural, straightforward, and safe (it's checked at compile time):

```
//: generics/InstantiateGenericType.cpp
// C++, not Java!

template<class T> class Foo {
  T x; // Create a field of type T
  T* y; // Pointer to T
public:
  // Initialize the pointer:
  Foo() { y = new T(); }
};

class Bar {};

int main() {
  Foo<Bar> fb;
  Foo<int> fi; // ... and it works with primitives
} ///:~
```

The solution in Java is to pass in a factory object, and use that to make the new instance. A convenient factory object is just the **Class** object, so if you use a type tag, you can use **newInstance( )** to create a new object of that type:

```
//: generics/InstantiateGenericType.java
import static net.mindview.util.Print.*;

class ClassAsFactory<T> {
  T x;
  public ClassAsFactory(Class<T> kind) {
    try {
      x = kind.newInstance();
    } catch(Exception e) {
      throw new RuntimeException(e);
    }
  }
}
```

```
    }

class Employee {}

public class InstantiateGenericType {
  public static void main(String[] args) {
    ClassAsFactory<Employee> fe =
      new ClassAsFactory<Employee>(Employee.class);
    print("ClassAsFactory<Employee> succeeded");
    try {
      ClassAsFactory<Integer> fi =
        new ClassAsFactory<Integer>(Integer.class);
    } catch(Exception e) {
      print("ClassAsFactory<Integer> failed");
    }
  }
} /* Output:
ClassAsFactory<Employee> succeeded
ClassAsFactory<Integer> failed
*///:~
```

This compiles, but fails with **ClassAsFactory<Integer>** because **Integer** has no default constructor. Because the error is not caught at compile time, this approach is frowned upon by the Sun folks. They suggest instead that you use an explicit factory and constrain the type so that it only takes a class that implements this factory:

```
//: generics/FactoryConstraint.java

interface FactoryI<T> {
  T create();
}

class Foo2<T> {
  private T x;
  public <F extends FactoryI<T>> Foo2(F factory) {
    x = factory.create();
  }
  // ...
}

class IntegerFactory implements FactoryI<Integer> {
  public Integer create() {
    return new Integer(0);
```

```
      }
    }

    class Widget {
      public static class Factory implements FactoryI<Widget> {
        public Widget create() {
          return new Widget();
        }
      }
    }

    public class FactoryConstraint {
      public static void main(String[] args) {
        new Foo2<Integer>(new IntegerFactory());
        new Foo2<Widget>(new Widget.Factory());
      }
    } ///:~
```

Note that this is really just a variation of passing **Class<T>**. Both approaches pass factory objects; **Class<T>** happens to be the built-in factory object, whereas the above approach creates an explicit factory object. But you get compile-time checking.

Another approach is the *Template Method* design pattern. In the following example, **get( )** is the Template Method, and **create( )** is defined in the subclass to produce an object of that type:

```
//: generics/CreatorGeneric.java

abstract class GenericWithCreate<T> {
  final T element;
  GenericWithCreate() { element = create(); }
  abstract T create();
}

class X {}

class Creator extends GenericWithCreate<X> {
  X create() { return new X(); }
  void f() {
    System.out.println(element.getClass().getSimpleName());
  }
}
```

```
public class CreatorGeneric {
  public static void main(String[] args) {
    Creator c = new Creator();
    c.f();
  }
} /* Output:
X
*///:~
```

Exercise 22: (6) Use a type tag along with reflection to create a method that uses the argument version of **newInstance( )** to create an object of a class with a constructor that has arguments.

Exercise 23: (1) Modify **FactoryConstraint.java** so that **create( )** takes an argument.

Exercise 24: (3) Modify Exercise 21 so that factory objects are held in the **Map** instead of **Class<?>**.

Arrays of generics

As you saw in **Erased.java**, you can't create arrays of generics. The general solution is to use an **ArrayList** everywhere that you are tempted to create an array of generics:

```
//: generics/ListOfGenerics.java
import java.util.*;

public class ListOfGenerics<T> {
  private List<T> array = new ArrayList<T>();
  public void add(T item) { array.add(item); }
  public T get(int index) { return array.get(index); }
} ///:~
```

Here you get the behavior of an array but the compile-time type safety afforded by generics.

At times, you will still want to create an array of generic types (the **ArrayList**, for example, uses arrays internally). Interestingly enough, you can define a *reference* in a way that makes the compiler happy. For example:

```
//: generics/ArrayOfGenericReference.java

class Generic<T> {}
```

```
public class ArrayOfGenericReference {
  static Generic<Integer>[] gia;
} ///:~
```

The compiler accepts this without producing warnings. But you can never create an array of that exact type (including the type parameters), so it's a little confusing. Since all arrays have the same structure (size of each array slot and array layout) regardless of the type they hold, it seems that you should be able to create an array of **Object** and cast that to the desired array type. This does in fact compile, but it won't run; it produces a **ClassCastException**:

```
//: generics/ArrayOfGeneric.java

public class ArrayOfGeneric {
  static final int SIZE = 100;
  static Generic<Integer>[] gia;
  @SuppressWarnings("unchecked")
  public static void main(String[] args) {
    // Compiles; produces ClassCastException:
    //! gia = (Generic<Integer>[])new Object[SIZE];
    // Runtime type is the raw (erased) type:
    gia = (Generic<Integer>[])new Generic[SIZE];
    System.out.println(gia.getClass().getSimpleName());
    gia[0] = new Generic<Integer>();
    //! gia[1] = new Object(); // Compile-time error
    // Discovers type mismatch at compile time:
    //! gia[2] = new Generic<Double>();
  }
} /* Output:
Generic[]
*///:~
```

The problem is that arrays keep track of their actual type, and that type is established at the point of creation of the array. So even though **gia** has been cast to a **Generic<Integer>[]**, that information only exists at compile time (and without the **@SuppressWarnings** annotation, you'd get a warning for that cast). At run time, it's still an array of **Object**, and that causes problems. The only way to successfully create an array of a generic type is to create a new array of the erased type, and cast that.

Let's look at a slightly more sophisticated example. Consider a simple generic wrapper around an array:

```
//: generics/GenericArray.java

public class GenericArray<T> {
  private T[] array;
  @SuppressWarnings("unchecked")
  public GenericArray(int sz) {
    array = (T[])new Object[sz];
  }
  public void put(int index, T item) {
    array[index] = item;
  }
  public T get(int index) { return array[index]; }
  // Method that exposes the underlying representation:
  public T[] rep() { return array; }
  public static void main(String[] args) {
    GenericArray<Integer> gai =
      new GenericArray<Integer>(10);
    // This causes a ClassCastException:
    //! Integer[] ia = gai.rep();
    // This is OK:
    Object[] oa = gai.rep();
  }
} ///:~
```

As before, we can't say **T[] array = new T[sz]**, so we create an array of objects and cast it.

The **rep( )** method returns a **T[]**, which in **main( )** should be an **Integer[]** for **gai**, but if you call it and try to capture the result as an **Integer[]** reference, you get a **ClassCastException**, again because the actual runtime type is **Object[]**.

If you compile **GenericArray.java** after commenting out the **@SuppressWarnings** annotation, the compiler produces a warning:

```
Note: GenericArray.java uses unchecked or unsafe operations.
Note: Recompile with -Xlint:unchecked for details.
```

In this case, we've gotten a single warning, and we believe that it's about the cast. But if you really want to make sure, you should compile with **-Xlint:unchecked**:

```
GenericArray.java:7: warning: [unchecked] unchecked cast
found    : java.lang.Object[]
required: T[]
```

```
    array = (T[])new Object[sz];
                ^
1 warning
```

It is indeed complaining about that cast. Because warnings become noise, the best thing we could possibly do, once we verify that a particular warning is expected, is to turn it off using **@SuppressWarnings**. That way, when a warning does appear, we'll actually investigate it.

Because of erasure, the runtime type of the array can only be **Object[]**. If we immediately cast it to **T[]**, then at compile time the actual type of the array is lost, and the compiler may miss out on some potential error checks. Because of this, it's better to use an **Object[]** inside the collection, and add a cast to **T** when you use an array element. Let's see how that would look with the **GenericArray.java** example:

```java
//: generics/GenericArray2.java

public class GenericArray2<T> {
  private Object[] array;
  public GenericArray2(int sz) {
    array = new Object[sz];
  }
  public void put(int index, T item) {
    array[index] = item;
  }
  @SuppressWarnings("unchecked")
  public T get(int index) { return (T)array[index]; }
  @SuppressWarnings("unchecked")
  public T[] rep() {
    return (T[])array; // Warning: unchecked cast
  }
  public static void main(String[] args) {
    GenericArray2<Integer> gai =
      new GenericArray2<Integer>(10);
    for(int i = 0; i < 10; i ++)
      gai.put(i, i);
    for(int i = 0; i < 10; i ++)
      System.out.print(gai.get(i) + " ");
    System.out.println();
    try {
      Integer[] ia = gai.rep();
    } catch(Exception e) { System.out.println(e); }
  }
```

```
} /* Output: (Sample)
0 1 2 3 4 5 6 7 8 9
java.lang.ClassCastException: [Ljava.lang.Object; cannot be
cast to [Ljava.lang.Integer;
*///:~
```

Initially, this doesn't look very different, just that the cast has been moved. Without the **@SuppressWarnings** annotations, you will still get "unchecked" warnings. However, the internal representation is now **Object[]** rather than **T[]**. When **get( )** is called, it casts the object to **T**, which is in fact the correct type, so that is safe. However, if you call **rep( )**, it again attempts to cast the **Object[]** to a **T[]**, which is still incorrect, and produces a warning at compile time and an exception at run time. Thus there's no way to subvert the type of the underlying array, which can only be **Object[]**. The advantage of treating **array** internally as **Object[]** instead of **T[]** is that it's less likely that you'll forget the runtime type of the array and accidentally introduce a bug (although the majority, and perhaps all, of such bugs would be rapidly detected at run time).

For new code, you should pass in a type token. In that case, the **GenericArray** looks like this:

```
//: generics/GenericArrayWithTypeToken.java
import java.lang.reflect.*;

public class GenericArrayWithTypeToken<T> {
  private T[] array;
  @SuppressWarnings("unchecked")
  public GenericArrayWithTypeToken(Class<T> type, int sz) {
    array = (T[])Array.newInstance(type, sz);
  }
  public void put(int index, T item) {
    array[index] = item;
  }
  public T get(int index) { return array[index]; }
  // Expose the underlying representation:
  public T[] rep() { return array; }
  public static void main(String[] args) {
    GenericArrayWithTypeToken<Integer> gai =
      new GenericArrayWithTypeToken<Integer>(
        Integer.class, 10);
    // This now works:
    Integer[] ia = gai.rep();
  }
```

```
} ///:~
```

The type token **Class<T>** is passed into the constructor in order to recover from the erasure, so that we can create the actual type of array that we need, although the warning from the cast must be suppressed with **@SuppressWarnings**. Once we do get the actual type, we can return it and get the desired results, as you see in **main( )**. The runtime type of the array is the exact type **T[]**.

Unfortunately, if you look at the source code in the Java SE5 standard libraries, you'll see there are casts from **Object** arrays to parameterized types everywhere. For example, here's the copy-**ArrayList**-from-**Collection** constructor, after cleaning up and simplifying:

```java
public ArrayList(Collection c) {
  size = c.size();
  elementData = (E[])new Object[size];
  c.toArray(elementData);
}
```

If you look through **ArrayList.java**, you'll find plenty of these casts. And what happens when we compile it?

```
Note: ArrayList.java uses unchecked or unsafe operations.
Note: Recompile with -Xlint:unchecked for details.
```

Sure enough, the standard libraries produce lots of warnings. If you've worked with C, especially pre-ANSI C, you remember a particular effect of warnings: When you discover you can ignore them, you do. For that reason, it's best to not issue any kind of message from the compiler unless the programmer must do something about it.

In his weblog,[3] Neal Gafter (one of the lead developers for Java SE5) points out that he was lazy when rewriting the Java libraries, and that we should not do what he did. Neal also points out that he could not fix some of the Java library code without breaking the existing interface. So even if certain idioms appear in the Java library sources, that's not necessarily the right way to do it. When you look at library code, you cannot assume that it's an example that you should follow in your own code.

----

[3] *http://gafter.blogspot.com/2004/09/puzzling-through-erasure-answer.html*

Bounds

Bounds were briefly introduced earlier in the chapter (see page 652). Bounds allow you to place constraints on the parameter types that can be used with generics. Although this allows you to enforce rules about the types that your generics can be applied to, a potentially more important effect is that you can call methods that are in your bound types.

Because erasure removes type information, the only methods you can call for an unbounded generic parameter are those available for **Object**. If, however, you are able to constrain that parameter to be a subset of types, then you can call the methods in that subset. To perform this constraint, Java generics reuse the **extends** keyword. It's important for you to understand that **extends** has a significantly different meaning in the context of generic bounds than it does ordinarily. This example shows the basics of bounds:

```
//: generics/BasicBounds.java

interface HasColor { java.awt.Color getColor(); }

class Colored<T extends HasColor> {
  T item;
  Colored(T item) { this.item = item; }
  T getItem() { return item; }
  // The bound allows you to call a method:
  java.awt.Color color() { return item.getColor(); }
}

class Dimension { public int x, y, z; }

// This won't work -- class must be first, then interfaces:
// class ColoredDimension<T extends HasColor & Dimension> {

// Multiple bounds:
class ColoredDimension<T extends Dimension & HasColor> {
  T item;
  ColoredDimension(T item) { this.item = item; }
  T getItem() { return item; }
  java.awt.Color color() { return item.getColor(); }
  int getX() { return item.x; }
  int getY() { return item.y; }
  int getZ() { return item.z; }
}
```

Generics

```
interface Weight { int weight(); }

// As with inheritance, you can have only one
// concrete class but multiple interfaces:
class Solid<T extends Dimension & HasColor & Weight> {
  T item;
  Solid(T item) { this.item = item; }
  T getItem() { return item; }
  java.awt.Color color() { return item.getColor(); }
  int getX() { return item.x; }
  int getY() { return item.y; }
  int getZ() { return item.z; }
  int weight() { return item.weight(); }
}

class Bounded
extends Dimension implements HasColor, Weight {
  public java.awt.Color getColor() { return null; }
  public int weight() { return 0; }
}

public class BasicBounds {
  public static void main(String[] args) {
    Solid<Bounded> solid =
      new Solid<Bounded>(new Bounded());
    solid.color();
    solid.getY();
    solid.weight();
  }
} ///:~
```

You might observe that **BasicBounds.java** seems to contain redundancies that could be eliminated through inheritance. Here, you can see how each level of inheritance also adds bounds constraints:

```
//: generics/InheritBounds.java

class HoldItem<T> {
  T item;
  HoldItem(T item) { this.item = item; }
  T getItem() { return item; }
}

class Colored2<T extends HasColor> extends HoldItem<T> {
```

```
    Colored2(T item) { super(item); }
    java.awt.Color color() { return item.getColor(); }
}

class ColoredDimension2<T extends Dimension & HasColor>
extends Colored2<T> {
    ColoredDimension2(T item) {  super(item); }
    int getX() { return item.x; }
    int getY() { return item.y; }
    int getZ() { return item.z; }
}

class Solid2<T extends Dimension & HasColor & Weight>
extends ColoredDimension2<T> {
    Solid2(T item) {  super(item); }
    int weight() { return item.weight(); }
}

public class InheritBounds {
    public static void main(String[] args) {
        Solid2<Bounded> solid2 =
            new Solid2<Bounded>(new Bounded());
        solid2.color();
        solid2.getY();
        solid2.weight();
    }
} ///:~
```

HoldItem simply holds an object, so this behavior is inherited into **Colored2**, which also requires that its parameter conforms to **HasColor**. **ColoredDimension2** and **Solid2** further extend the hierarchy and add bounds at each level. Now the methods are inherited and they don't have to be repeated in each class.

Here's an example with more layers:

```
//: generics/EpicBattle.java
// Demonstrating bounds in Java generics.
import java.util.*;

interface SuperPower {}
interface XRayVision extends SuperPower {
    void seeThroughWalls();
}
interface SuperHearing extends SuperPower {
```

```java
    void hearSubtleNoises();
}
interface SuperSmell extends SuperPower {
  void trackBySmell();
}

class SuperHero<POWER extends SuperPower> {
  POWER power;
  SuperHero(POWER power) { this.power = power; }
  POWER getPower() { return power; }
}

class SuperSleuth<POWER extends XRayVision>
extends SuperHero<POWER> {
  SuperSleuth(POWER power) { super(power); }
  void see() { power.seeThroughWalls(); }
}

class CanineHero<POWER extends SuperHearing & SuperSmell>
extends SuperHero<POWER> {
  CanineHero(POWER power) { super(power); }
  void hear() { power.hearSubtleNoises(); }
  void smell() { power.trackBySmell(); }
}

class SuperHearSmell implements SuperHearing, SuperSmell {
  public void hearSubtleNoises() {}
  public void trackBySmell() {}
}

class DogBoy extends CanineHero<SuperHearSmell> {
  DogBoy() { super(new SuperHearSmell()); }
}

public class EpicBattle {
  // Bounds in generic methods:
  static <POWER extends SuperHearing>
  void useSuperHearing(SuperHero<POWER> hero) {
    hero.getPower().hearSubtleNoises();
  }
  static <POWER extends SuperHearing & SuperSmell>
  void superFind(SuperHero<POWER> hero) {
    hero.getPower().hearSubtleNoises();
    hero.getPower().trackBySmell();
```

```
    }
    public static void main(String[] args) {
      DogBoy dogBoy = new DogBoy();
      useSuperHearing(dogBoy);
      superFind(dogBoy);
      // You can do this:
      List<? extends SuperHearing> audioBoys;
      // But you can't do this:
      // List<? extends SuperHearing & SuperSmell> dogBoys;
    }
} ///:~
```

Notice that wildcards (which we shall study next) are limited to a single bound.

Exercise 25: (2) Create two interfaces and a class that implements both. Create two generic methods, one whose argument parameter is bounded by the first interface and one whose argument parameter is bounded by the second interface. Create an instance of the class that implements both interfaces, and show that it can be used with both generic methods.

Wildcards

You've already seen some simple uses of *wildcards*—question marks in generic argument expressions—in the *Holding Your Objects* chapter and more in the *Type Information* chapter. This section will explore the issue more deeply.

We'll start with an example that shows a particular behavior of arrays: You can assign an array of a derived type to an array reference of the base type:

```
//: generics/CovariantArrays.java

class Fruit {}
class Apple extends Fruit {}
class Jonathan extends Apple {}
class Orange extends Fruit {}

public class CovariantArrays {
  public static void main(String[] args) {
    Fruit[] fruit = new Apple[10];
    fruit[0] = new Apple(); // OK
    fruit[1] = new Jonathan(); // OK
    // Runtime type is Apple[], not Fruit[] or Orange[]:
```

```
    try {
      // Compiler allows you to add Fruit:
      fruit[0] = new Fruit(); // ArrayStoreException
    } catch(Exception e) { System.out.println(e); }
    try {
      // Compiler allows you to add Oranges:
      fruit[0] = new Orange(); // ArrayStoreException
    } catch(Exception e) { System.out.println(e); }
  }
} /* Output:
java.lang.ArrayStoreException: Fruit
java.lang.ArrayStoreException: Orange
*///:~
```

The first line in **main( )** creates an array of **Apple** and assigns it to a reference to an array of **Fruit**. This makes sense—an **Apple** is a kind of **Fruit**, so an array of **Apple** should also be an array of **Fruit**.

However, if the actual array type is **Apple[]**, you should only be able to place an **Apple** or a subtype of **Apple** into the array, which in fact works at both compile time and run time. But notice that the compiler allows you to place a **Fruit** object into the array. This makes sense to the compiler, because it has a **Fruit[]** reference—why shouldn't it allow a **Fruit** object, or anything descended from **Fruit**, such as **Orange**, to be placed into the array? So at compile time, this is allowed. The runtime array mechanism, however, knows that it's dealing with an **Apple[]** and throws an exception when a foreign type is placed into the array.

"Upcast" is actually rather a misnomer here. What you're really doing is assigning one array to another. The array behavior is that it holds other objects, but because we are able to upcast, it's clear that the array objects can preserve the rules about the type of objects they contain. It's as if the arrays are conscious of what they are holding, so between the compile-time checks and the runtime checks, you can't abuse them.

This arrangement for arrays is not so terrible, because you *do* find out at run time that you've inserted an improper type. But one of the primary goals of generics is to move such error detection to compile time. So what happens when we try to use generic containers instead of arrays?

```
//: generics/NonCovariantGenerics.java
// {CompileTimeError} (Won't compile)
import java.util.*;
```

```
public class NonCovariantGenerics {
  // Compile Error: incompatible types:
  List<Fruit> flist = new ArrayList<Apple>();
} ///:~
```

Although you may at first read this as saying, "You can't assign a container of **Apple** to a container of **Fruit**," remember that generics are not just about containers. What it's really saying is, "You can't assign a generic *involving* **Apple**s to a generic *involving* **Fruit**." If, as in the case of arrays, the compiler knew enough about the code to determine that containers were involved, perhaps it could give some leeway. But it doesn't know anything like that, so it refuses to allow the "upcast." But it really isn't an "upcast" anyway—a **List** of **Apple** is not a **List** of **Fruit**. A **List** of **Apple** will hold **Apple**s and subtypes of **Apple**, and a **List** of **Fruit** will hold any kind of **Fruit**. Yes, including **Apple**s, but that doesn't make it a **List** of **Apple**; it's still a **List** of **Fruit**. A **List** of **Apple** is not type-equivalent to a **List** of **Fruit**, even if an **Apple** is a type of **Fruit**.

The real issue is that we are talking about the type of the container, rather than the type that the container is holding. Unlike arrays, generics do not have built-in covariance. This is because arrays are completely defined in the language and can thus have both compile-time and runtime checks built in, but with generics, the compiler and runtime system cannot know what you want to do with your types and what the rules should be.

Sometimes, however, you'd like to establish some kind of upcasting relationship between the two. This is what wildcards allow.

```
//: generics/GenericsAndCovariance.java
import java.util.*;

public class GenericsAndCovariance {
  public static void main(String[] args) {
    // Wildcards allow covariance:
    List<? extends Fruit> flist = new ArrayList<Apple>();
    // Compile Error: can't add any type of object:
    // flist.add(new Apple());
    // flist.add(new Fruit());
    // flist.add(new Object());
    flist.add(null); // Legal but uninteresting
    // We know that it returns at least Fruit:
    Fruit f = flist.get(0);
```

```
    }
} ///:~
```

The type of **flist** is now **List<? extends Fruit>**, which you can read as "a list of any type that's inherited from **Fruit**." This doesn't actually mean that the **List** will hold any type of **Fruit**, however. The wildcard refers to a definite type, so it means "some specific type which the **flist** reference doesn't specify." So the **List** that's assigned has to be holding some specified type such as **Fruit** or **Apple**, but in order to upcast to **flist**, that type is a "don't actually care."

If the only constraint is that the **List** hold a specific **Fruit** or subtype of **Fruit**, but you don't actually care what it is, then what can you do with such a **List**? If you don't know what type the **List** is holding, how can you safely add an object? Just as with the "upcast" array in **CovariantArrays.java**, you can't, except that the compiler prevents it from happening rather than the runtime system. You discover the problem sooner.

You might argue that things have gone a bit overboard, because now you can't even add an **Apple** to a **List** that you just said would hold **Apple**s. Yes, but the compiler doesn't know that. A **List<? extends Fruit>** could legally point to a **List<Orange>**. Once you do this kind of "upcast," you lose the ability to pass anything in, even an **Object**.

On the other hand, if you call a method that returns **Fruit**, that's safe because you know that anything in the **List** must at least be of type **Fruit**, so the compiler allows it.

Exercise 26: (2) Demonstrate array covariance using **Number**s and **Integer**s.

Exercise 27: (2) Show that covariance doesn't work with **List**s, using **Number**s and **Integer**s, then introduce wildcards.

How smart is the compiler?

Now, you might guess that you are prevented from calling any methods that take arguments, but consider this:

```
//: generics/CompilerIntelligence.java
import java.util.*;

public class CompilerIntelligence {
```

```
  public static void main(String[] args) {
    List<? extends Fruit> flist =
      Arrays.asList(new Apple());
    Apple a = (Apple)flist.get(0); // No warning
    flist.contains(new Apple()); // Argument is 'Object'
    flist.indexOf(new Apple()); // Argument is 'Object'
  }
} ///:~
```

You can see calls to **contains( )** and **indexOf( )** that take **Apple** objects as arguments, and those are just fine. Does this mean that the compiler actually examines the code to see if a particular method modifies its object?

By looking at the documentation for **ArrayList**, we find that the compiler is not that smart. While **add( )** takes an argument of the generic parameter type, **contains( )** and **indexOf( )** take arguments of type **Object**. So when you specify an **ArrayList<? extends Fruit>**, the argument for **add( )** becomes '**? extends Fruit**'. From that description, the compiler cannot know which specific subtype of **Fruit** is required there, so it won't accept any type of **Fruit**. It doesn't matter if you upcast the **Apple** to a **Fruit** first—the compiler simply refuses to call a method (such as **add( )**) if a wildcard is involved in the argument list.

With **contains( )** and **indexOf( )**, the arguments are of type **Object**, so there are no wildcards involved and the compiler allows the call. This means that it's up to the generic class designer to decide which calls are "safe," and to use **Object** types for their arguments. To disallow a call when the type is used with wildcards, use the type parameter in the argument list.

You can see this in a very simple **Holder** class:

```
//: generics/Holder.java

public class Holder<T> {
  private T value;
  public Holder() {}
  public Holder(T val) { value = val; }
  public void set(T val) { value = val; }
  public T get() { return value; }
  public boolean equals(Object obj) {
    return value.equals(obj);
  }
  public static void main(String[] args) {
    Holder<Apple> Apple = new Holder<Apple>(new Apple());
```

```
      Apple d = Apple.get();
      Apple.set(d);
      // Holder<Fruit> Fruit = Apple; // Cannot upcast
      Holder<? extends Fruit> fruit = Apple; // OK
      Fruit p = fruit.get();
      d = (Apple)fruit.get(); // Returns 'Object'
      try {
        Orange c = (Orange)fruit.get(); // No warning
      } catch(Exception e) { System.out.println(e); }
      // fruit.set(new Apple()); // Cannot call set()
      // fruit.set(new Fruit()); // Cannot call set()
      System.out.println(fruit.equals(d)); // OK
    }
} /* Output: (Sample)
java.lang.ClassCastException: Apple cannot be cast to
Orange
true
*///:~
```

Holder has a **set( )** which takes a **T**, a **get( )** which returns a **T**, and an **equals( )** that takes an **Object**. As you've already seen, if you create a **Holder<Apple>**, you cannot upcast it to a **Holder<Fruit>**, but you can upcast to a **Holder<? extends Fruit>**. If you call **get( )**, it only returns a **Fruit**—that's as much as it knows given the "anything that extends **Fruit**" bound. If you know more about what's there, you can cast to a specific type of **Fruit** and there won't be any warning about it, but you risk a **ClassCastException**. The **set( )** method won't work with either an **Apple** or a **Fruit**, because the **set( )** argument is also "**? Extends Fruit**," which means it can be anything and the compiler can't verify type safety for "anything."

However, the **equals( )** method works fine because it takes an **Object** instead of a **T** as an argument. Thus, the compiler is only paying attention to the types of objects that are passed and returned. It is not analyzing the code to see if you perform any actual writes or reads.

Contravariance

It's also possible to go the other way, and use *supertype wildcards*. Here, you say that the wildcard is bounded by any base class of a particular class, by specifying **<? super MyClass>** or even using a type parameter: **<? super T>** (although you cannot give a generic parameter a supertype bound; that is, you cannot say **<T super MyClass>**). This allows you to safely pass a typed object into a generic type. Thus, with supertype wildcards you can write into a **Collection**:

```
//: generics/SuperTypeWildcards.java
import java.util.*;

public class SuperTypeWildcards {
  static void writeTo(List<? super Apple> apples) {
    apples.add(new Apple());
    apples.add(new Jonathan());
    // apples.add(new Fruit()); // Error
  }
} ///:~
```

The argument **apples** is a **List** of some type that is the base type of **Apple**; thus you know that it is safe to add an **Apple** or a subtype of **Apple**. Since the *lower bound* is **Apple**, however, you don't know that it is safe to add **Fruit** to such a **List**, because that would allow the **List** to be opened up to the addition of non-**Apple** types, which would violate static type safety.

You can thus begin to think of subtype and supertype bounds in terms of how you can "write" (pass into a method) to a generic type, and "read" (return from a method) from a generic type.

Supertype bounds relax the constraints on what you can pass into a method:

```
//: generics/GenericWriting.java
import java.util.*;

public class GenericWriting {
  static <T> void writeExact(List<T> list, T item) {
    list.add(item);
  }
  static List<Apple> apples = new ArrayList<Apple>();
  static List<Fruit> fruit = new ArrayList<Fruit>();
  static void f1() {
    writeExact(apples, new Apple());
    writeExact(fruit, new Apple()); // Error JDK5, OK in 6
    // Was: Incompatible types: found Fruit, required Apple
  }
  static <T> void
  writeWithWildcard(List<? super T> list, T item) {
    list.add(item);
  }
```

```
  static void f2() {
    writeWithWildcard(apples, new Apple());
    writeWithWildcard(fruit, new Apple());
  }
  public static void main(String[] args) { f1(); f2(); }
} ///:~
```

The **writeExact( )** method uses an exact parameter type (no wildcards). In **f1( )** you can see that this works fine—as long as you only put an **Apple** into a **List<Apple>**. However, **writeExact( )** does not allow you to put an **Apple** into a **List<Fruit>**, even though you know that should be possible.

In **writeWithWildcard( )**, the argument is now a **List<? super T>**, so the **List** holds a specific type that is derived from **T**; thus it is safe to pass a **T** or anything derived from **T** as an argument to **List** methods. You can see this in **f2( )**, where it's still possible to put an **Apple** into a **List<Apple>**, as before, but it is now also possible to put an **Apple** into a **List<Fruit>**, as you expect.

We can perform this same type of analysis as a review of covariance and wildcards:

```
//: generics/GenericReading.java
import java.util.*;

public class GenericReading {
  static <T> T readExact(List<T> list) {
    return list.get(0);
  }
  static List<Apple> apples = Arrays.asList(new Apple());
  static List<Fruit> fruit = Arrays.asList(new Fruit());
  // A static method adapts to each call:
  static void f1() {
    Apple a = readExact(apples);
    Fruit f = readExact(fruit);
    f = readExact(apples);
  }
  // If, however, you have a class, then its type is
  // established when the class is instantiated:
  static class Reader<T> {
    T readExact(List<T> list) { return list.get(0); }
  }
  static void f2() {
    Reader<Fruit> fruitReader = new Reader<Fruit>();
```

```
      Fruit f = fruitReader.readExact(fruit);
      // Fruit a = fruitReader.readExact(apples); // Error:
      // readExact(List<Fruit>) cannot be
      // applied to (List<Apple>).
    }
  static class CovariantReader<T> {
    T readCovariant(List<? extends T> list) {
      return list.get(0);
    }
  }
  static void f3() {
    CovariantReader<Fruit> fruitReader =
      new CovariantReader<Fruit>();
    Fruit f = fruitReader.readCovariant(fruit);
    Fruit a = fruitReader.readCovariant(apples);
  }
  public static void main(String[] args) {
    f1(); f2(); f3();
  }
} ///:~
```

As before, the first method **readExact( )** uses the precise type. So if you use the precise type with no wildcards, you can both write and read that precise type into and out of a **List**. In addition, for the return value, the **static** generic method **readExact( )** effectively "adapts" to each method call, and returns an **Apple** from a **List<Apple>** and a **Fruit** from a **List<Fruit>**, as you can see in **f1( )**. Thus, if you can get away with a **static** generic method, you don't necessarily need covariance if you're just reading.

If you have a generic class, however, the parameter is established for the class when you make an instance of that class. As you can see in **f2( )**, the **fruitReader** instance can read a piece of **Fruit** from a **List<Fruit>**, since that is its exact type. But a **List<Apple>** should also produce **Fruit** objects, and the **fruitReader** doesn't allow this.

To fix the problem, the **CovariantReader.readCovariant( )** method takes a **List<? extends T>**, and so it's safe to read a **T** from that list (you know that everything in that list is at least a **T**, and possibly something derived from a **T**). In **f3( )** you can see that it's now possible to read a **Fruit** from a **List<Apple>**.

Exercise 28: (4) Create a generic class **Generic1<T>** with a single method that takes an argument of type **T**. Create a second generic class

Generic2<T> with a single method that returns an argument of type **T**. Write a generic method with a contravariant argument of the first generic class that calls its method. Write a second generic method with a covariant argument of the second generic class that calls its method. Test using the **typeinfo.pets** library.

Unbounded wildcards

The *unbounded wildcard* **<?>** appears to mean "anything," and so using an unbounded wildcard seems equivalent to using a raw type. Indeed, the compiler seems at first to agree with this assessment:

```
//: generics/UnboundedWildcards1.java
import java.util.*;

public class UnboundedWildcards1 {
  static List list1;
  static List<?> list2;
  static List<? extends Object> list3;
  static void assign1(List list) {
    list1 = list;
    list2 = list;
    // list3 = list; // Warning: unchecked conversion
    // Found: List, Required: List<? extends Object>
  }
  static void assign2(List<?> list) {
    list1 = list;
    list2 = list;
    list3 = list;
  }
  static void assign3(List<? extends Object> list) {
    list1 = list;
    list2 = list;
    list3 = list;
  }
  public static void main(String[] args) {
    assign1(new ArrayList());
    assign2(new ArrayList());
    // assign3(new ArrayList()); // Warning:
    // Unchecked conversion. Found: ArrayList
    // Required: List<? extends Object>
    assign1(new ArrayList<String>());
    assign2(new ArrayList<String>());
    assign3(new ArrayList<String>());
    // Both forms are acceptable as List<?>:
```

```
        List<?> wildList = new ArrayList();
        wildList = new ArrayList<String>();
        assign1(wildList);
        assign2(wildList);
        assign3(wildList);
    }
} ///:~
```

There are many cases like the ones you see here where the compiler could care less whether you use a raw type or **<?>**. In those cases, **<?>** can be thought of as a decoration; and yet it is valuable because, in effect, it says, "I wrote this code with Java generics in mind, and I don't mean here that I'm using a raw type, but that in this case the generic parameter can hold any type."

A second example shows an important use of unbounded wildcards. When you are dealing with multiple generic parameters, it's sometimes important to allow one parameter to be any type while establishing a particular type for the other parameter:

```
//: generics/UnboundedWildcards2.java
import java.util.*;

public class UnboundedWildcards2 {
    static Map map1;
    static Map<?,?> map2;
    static Map<String,?> map3;
    static void assign1(Map map) { map1 = map; }
    static void assign2(Map<?,?> map) { map2 = map; }
    static void assign3(Map<String,?> map) { map3 = map; }
    public static void main(String[] args) {
        assign1(new HashMap());
        assign2(new HashMap());
        // assign3(new HashMap()); // Warning:
        // Unchecked conversion. Found: HashMap
        // Required: Map<String,?>
        assign1(new HashMap<String,Integer>());
        assign2(new HashMap<String,Integer>());
        assign3(new HashMap<String,Integer>());
    }
} ///:~
```

But again, when you have all unbounded wildcards, as seen in **Map<?,?>**, the compiler doesn't seem to distinguish it from a raw **Map**. In addition,

UnboundedWildcards1.java shows that the compiler treats **List<?>** and **List<? extends Object>** differently.

What's confusing is that the compiler doesn't always care about the difference between, for example, **List** and **List<?>**, so they can seem like the same thing. Indeed, since a generic argument erases to its first bound, **List<?>** would seem to be equivalent to **List<Object>**, and **List** is effectively **List<Object>** as well—except neither of those statements is exactly true. **List** actually means "a raw **List** that holds any **Object** type," whereas **List<?>** means "a non-raw **List** of *some specific type*, but we just don't know what that type is."

When does the compiler actually care about the difference between raw types and types involving unbounded wildcards? The following example uses the previously defined **Holder<T>** class. It contains methods that take **Holder** as an argument, but in various forms: as a raw type, with a specific type parameter, and with an unbounded wildcard parameter:

```
//: generics/Wildcards.java
// Exploring the meaning of wildcards.

public class Wildcards {
  // Raw argument:
  static void rawArgs(Holder holder, Object arg) {
    // holder.set(arg); // Warning:
    //   Unchecked call to set(T) as a
    //   member of the raw type Holder
    // holder.set(new Wildcards()); // Same warning

    // Can't do this; don't have any 'T':
    // T t = holder.get();

    // OK, but type information has been lost:
    Object obj = holder.get();
  }
  // Similar to rawArgs(), but errors instead of warnings:
  static void unboundedArg(Holder<?> holder, Object arg) {
    // holder.set(arg); // Error:
    //   set(capture of ?) in Holder<capture of ?>
    //   cannot be applied to (Object)
    // holder.set(new Wildcards()); // Same error

    // Can't do this; don't have any 'T':
```

```
    // T t = holder.get();

    // OK, but type information has been lost:
    Object obj = holder.get();
  }
  static <T> T exact1(Holder<T> holder) {
    T t = holder.get();
    return t;
  }
  static <T> T exact2(Holder<T> holder, T arg) {
    holder.set(arg);
    T t = holder.get();
    return t;
  }
  static <T>
  T wildSubtype(Holder<? extends T> holder, T arg) {
    // holder.set(arg); // Error:
    //     set(capture of ? extends T) in
    //     Holder<capture of ? extends T>
    //     cannot be applied to (T)
    T t = holder.get();
    return t;
  }
  static <T>
  void wildSupertype(Holder<? super T> holder, T arg) {
    holder.set(arg);
    // T t = holder.get();   // Error:
    //    Incompatible types: found Object, required T

    // OK, but type information has been lost:
    Object obj = holder.get();
  }
  public static void main(String[] args) {
    Holder raw = new Holder<Long>();
    // Or:
    raw = new Holder();
    Holder<Long> qualified = new Holder<Long>();
    Holder<?> unbounded = new Holder<Long>();
    Holder<? extends Long> bounded = new Holder<Long>();
    Long lng = 1L;

    rawArgs(raw, lng);
    rawArgs(qualified, lng);
    rawArgs(unbounded, lng);
```

```
        rawArgs(bounded, lng);

        unboundedArg(raw, lng);
        unboundedArg(qualified, lng);
        unboundedArg(unbounded, lng);
        unboundedArg(bounded, lng);

        // Object r1 = exact1(raw); // Warnings:
        //   Unchecked conversion from Holder to Holder<T>
        //   Unchecked method invocation: exact1(Holder<T>)
        //   is applied to (Holder)
        Long r2 = exact1(qualified);
        Object r3 = exact1(unbounded); // Must return Object
        Long r4 = exact1(bounded);

        // Long r5 = exact2(raw, lng); // Warnings:
        //   Unchecked conversion from Holder to Holder<Long>
        //   Unchecked method invocation: exact2(Holder<T>,T)
        //   is applied to (Holder,Long)
        Long r6 = exact2(qualified, lng);
        // Long r7 = exact2(unbounded, lng); // Error:
        //   exact2(Holder<T>,T) cannot be applied to
        //   (Holder<capture of ?>,Long)
        // Long r8 = exact2(bounded, lng); // Error:
        //   exact2(Holder<T>,T) cannot be applied
        //   to (Holder<capture of ? extends Long>,Long)

        // Long r9 = wildSubtype(raw, lng); // Warnings:
        //   Unchecked conversion from Holder
        //   to Holder<? extends Long>
        //   Unchecked method invocation:
        //   wildSubtype(Holder<? extends T>,T) is
        //   applied to (Holder,Long)
        Long r10 = wildSubtype(qualified, lng);
        // OK, but can only return Object:
        Object r11 = wildSubtype(unbounded, lng);
        Long r12 = wildSubtype(bounded, lng);

        // wildSupertype(raw, lng); // Warnings:
        //   Unchecked conversion from Holder
        //   to Holder<? super Long>
        //   Unchecked method invocation:
        //   wildSupertype(Holder<? super T>,T)
        //   is applied to (Holder,Long)
```

```
    wildSupertype(qualified, lng);
    // wildSupertype(unbounded, lng); // Error:
    //    wildSupertype(Holder<? super T>,T) cannot be
    //    applied to (Holder<capture of ?>,Long)
    // wildSupertype(bounded, lng); // Error:
    //    wildSupertype(Holder<? super T>,T) cannot be
    //  applied to (Holder<capture of ? extends Long>,Long)
  }
} ///:~
```

In **rawArgs( )**, the compiler knows that **Holder** is a generic type, so even though it is expressed as a raw type here, the compiler knows that passing an **Object** to **set( )** is unsafe. Since it's a raw type, you can pass an object of any type into **set( )**, and that object is upcast to **Object**. So anytime you have a raw type, you give up compile-time checking. The call to **get( )** shows the same issue: There's no **T**, so the result can only be an **Object**.

It's easy to start thinking that a raw **Holder** and a **Holder<?>** are roughly the same thing. But **unboundedArg( )** emphasizes that they are different—it discovers the same kind of problems, but reports them as errors rather than warnings, because the raw **Holder** will hold a combination of any types, whereas a **Holder<?>** holds a homogeneous collection of *some specific type*, and thus you can't just pass in an **Object**.

In **exact1( )** and **exact2( )**, you see the exact generic parameters used—no wildcards. You'll see that **exact2( )** has different limitations than **exact1( )**, because of the extra argument.

In **wildSubtype( )**, the constraints on the type of **Holder** are relaxed to include a **Holder** of anything that **extends T**. Again, this means that **T** could be **Fruit**, while **holder** could legitimately be a **Holder<Apple>**. To prevent putting an **Orange** in a **Holder<Apple>**, the call to **set( )** (or any method that takes an argument of the type parameter) is disallowed. However, you still know that anything that comes out of a **Holder<? extends Fruit>** will at least be **Fruit**, so **get( )** (or any method that produces a return value of the type parameter) is allowed.

Supertype wildcards are shown in **wildSupertype( )**, which shows the opposite behavior of **wildSubtype( )**: **holder** can be a container that holds any type that's a base class of **T**. Thus, **set( )** can accept a **T**, since anything that works with a base type will polymorphically work with a derived type (thus a **T**). However, trying to call **get( )** is not helpful, because the type held by **holder** can be any supertype at all, so the only safe one is **Object**.

This example also shows the limitations on what you can and can't do with an unbounded parameter in **unbounded( )**: You can't **get( )** or **set( )** a **T** because you don't have a **T**.

In **main( )** you can see which of these methods can accept which types of arguments without errors and warnings. For migration compatibility, **rawArgs( )** will take all the different variations of **Holder** without producing warnings. The **unboundedArg( )** method is equally accepting of all types, although, as previously noted, it handles them differently inside the body of the method.

If you pass a raw **Holder** reference into a method that takes an "exact" generic type (no wildcards), you get a warning because the exact argument is expecting information that doesn't exist in the raw type. And if you pass an unbounded reference to **exact1( )**, there's no type information to establish the return type.

You can see that **exact2( )** has the most constraints, since it wants exactly a **Holder<T>** and an argument of type **T**, and because of this it generates errors or warnings unless you give it the exact arguments. Sometimes this is OK, but if it's overconstraining, then you can use wildcards, depending on whether you want to get typed return values from your generic argument (as seen in **wildSubtype( )**) or you want to pass typed arguments to your generic argument (as seen in **wildSupertype( )**).

Thus, the benefit of using exact types instead of wildcard types is that you can do more with the generic parameters. But using wildcards allows you to accept a broader range of parameterized types as arguments. You must decide which trade-off is more appropriate for your needs on a case-by-case basis.

Capture conversion

One situation in particular *requires* the use of **<?>** rather than a raw type. If you pass a raw type to a method that uses **<?>**, it's possible for the compiler to infer the actual type parameter, so that the method can turn around and call another method that uses the exact type. The following example demonstrates the technique, which is called *capture conversion* because the unspecified wildcard type is captured and converted to an exact type. Here,

---

Thinking in Java   *Bruce Eckel*

the comments about warnings only take effect when the
@SuppressWarnings annotation is removed:

```
//: generics/CaptureConversion.java

public class CaptureConversion {
  static <T> void f1(Holder<T> holder) {
    T t = holder.get();
    System.out.println(t.getClass().getSimpleName());
  }
  static void f2(Holder<?> holder) {
    f1(holder); // Call with captured type
  }
  @SuppressWarnings("unchecked")
  public static void main(String[] args) {
    Holder raw = new Holder<Integer>(1);
    // f1(raw); // Produces warnings
    f2(raw); // No warnings
    Holder rawBasic = new Holder();
    rawBasic.set(new Object()); // Warning
    f2(rawBasic); // No warnings
    // Upcast to Holder<?>, still figures it out:
    Holder<?> wildcarded = new Holder<Double>(1.0);
    f2(wildcarded);
  }
} /* Output:
Integer
Object
Double
*///:~
```

The type parameters in **f1( )** are all exact, without wildcards or bounds. In **f2( )**, the **Holder** parameter is an unbounded wildcard, so it would seem to be effectively unknown. However, within **f2( )**, **f1( )** is called and **f1( )** requires a known parameter. What's happening is that the parameter type is captured in the process of calling **f2( )**, so it can be used in the call to **f1( )**.

You might wonder if this technique could be used for writing, but that would require you to pass a specific type along with the **Holder<?>**. Capture conversion only works in situations where, within the method, you need to work with the exact type. Notice that you can't return **T** from **f2( )**, because **T** is unknown for **f2( )**. Capture conversion is interesting, but quite limited.

Exercise 29: (5) Create a generic method that takes as an argument a **Holder<List<?>>**. Determine what methods you can and can't call for the **Holder** and for the **List**. Repeat for an argument of **List<Holder<?>>**.

Issues

This section addresses an assorted set of issues that appear when you are using Java generics.

No primitives as type parameters

As mentioned earlier in this chapter, one of the limitations you will discover in Java generics is that you cannot use primitives as type parameters. So you cannot, for example, create an **ArrayList<int>**.

The solution is to use the primitive wrapper classes in conjunction with Java SE5 autoboxing. If you create an **ArrayList<Integer>** and use primitive **int**s with this container, you'll discover that autoboxing does the conversion to and from **Integer** automatically—so it's almost as if you have an **ArrayList<int>**:

```
//: generics/ListOfInt.java
// Autoboxing compensates for the inability to use
// primitives in generics.
import java.util.*;

public class ListOfInt {
  public static void main(String[] args) {
    List<Integer> li = new ArrayList<Integer>();
    for(int i = 0; i < 5; i++)
      li.add(i);
    for(int i : li)
      System.out.print(i + " ");
  }
} /* Output:
0 1 2 3 4
*///:~
```

Note that autoboxing even allows the foreach syntax to produce **int**s.

In general this solution works fine—you're able to successfully store and retrieve **int**s. There happen to be some conversions going on but these are hidden from you. However, if performance is a problem, you can use a specialized version of the containers adapted for primitive types; one open-source version of this is **org.apache.commons.collections.primitives**.

Here's another approach, which creates a **Set** of **Byte**s:

```
//: generics/ByteSet.java
import java.util.*;

public class ByteSet {
  Byte[] possibles = { 1,2,3,4,5,6,7,8,9 };
  Set<Byte> mySet =
    new HashSet<Byte>(Arrays.asList(possibles));
  // But you can't do this:
  // Set<Byte> mySet2 = new HashSet<Byte>(
  //   Arrays.<Byte>asList(1,2,3,4,5,6,7,8,9));
} ///:~
```

Notice that autoboxing solves some problems, but not all. The following example shows a generic **Generator** interface that specifies a **next( )** that returns an object of the parameter type. The **FArray** class contains a generic method that uses a generator to fill an array with objects (making the *class* generic wouldn't work in this case because the method is **static**). The **Generator** implementations come from the *Arrays* chapter, and in **main( )** you can see **FArray.fill( )** used to fill arrays with objects:

```
//: generics/PrimitiveGenericTest.java
import net.mindview.util.*;

// Fill an array using a generator:
class FArray {
  public static <T> T[] fill(T[] a, Generator<T> gen) {
    for(int i = 0; i < a.length; i++)
      a[i] = gen.next();
    return a;
  }
}

public class PrimitiveGenericTest {
  public static void main(String[] args) {
    String[] strings = FArray.fill(
      new String[7], new RandomGenerator.String(10));
    for(String s : strings)
      System.out.println(s);
    Integer[] integers = FArray.fill(
```

```
        new Integer[7], new RandomGenerator.Integer());
    for(int i: integers)
      System.out.println(i);
    // Autoboxing won't save you here. This won't compile:
    // int[] b =
    //    FArray.fill(new int[7], new RandIntGenerator());
  }
} /* Output:
YNzbrnyGcF
OWZnTcQrGs
eGZMmJMRoE
suEcUOneOE
dLsmwHLGEa
hKcxrEqUCB
bkInaMesbt
7052
6665
2654
3909
5202
2209
5458
*///:~
```

Since **RandomGenerator.Integer** implements **Generator<Integer>**, my hope was that autoboxing would automatically convert the value of **next( )** from **Integer** to **int**. However, autoboxing doesn't apply to arrays, so this won't work.

Exercise 30: (2) Create a **Holder** for each of the primitive wrapper types, and show that autoboxing and autounboxing works for the **set( )** and **get( )** methods of each instance.

Implementing parameterized interfaces

A class cannot implement two variants of the same generic interface. Because of erasure, these are both the same interface. Here's a situation where this clash occurs:

```
//: generics/MultipleInterfaceVariants.java
// {CompileTimeError} (Won't compile)

interface Payable<T> {}

class Employee implements Payable<Employee> {}
```

```
class Hourly extends Employee
  implements Payable<Hourly> {} ///:~
```

Hourly won't compile because erasure reduces **Payable<Employee>** and **Payable<Hourly>** to the same class, **Payable**, and the above code would mean that you'd be implementing the same interface twice. Interestingly enough, if you remove the generic parameters from both uses of **Payable**—as the compiler does during erasure—the code compiles.

This issue can become annoying when you are working with some of the more fundamental Java interfaces, such as **Comparable<T>**, as you'll see a little later in this section.

Exercise 31: (1) Remove all the generics from **MultipleInterfaceVariants.java** and modify the code so that the example compiles.

Casting and warnings

Using a cast or **instanceof** with a generic type parameter doesn't have any effect. The following container stores values internally as **Object**s and casts them back to **T** when you fetch them:

```
//: generics/GenericCast.java

class FixedSizeStack<T> {
  private int index = 0;
  private Object[] storage;
  public FixedSizeStack(int size) {
    storage = new Object[size];
  }
  public void push(T item) { storage[index++] = item; }
  @SuppressWarnings("unchecked")
  public T pop() { return (T)storage[--index]; }
}

public class GenericCast {
  public static final int SIZE = 10;
  public static void main(String[] args) {
    FixedSizeStack<String> strings =
      new FixedSizeStack<String>(SIZE);
    for(String s : "A B C D E F G H I J".split(" "))
      strings.push(s);
    for(int i = 0; i < SIZE; i++) {
```

```
        String s = strings.pop();
        System.out.print(s + " ");
    }
  }
} /* Output:
J I H G F E D C B A
*///:~
```

Without the **@SuppressWarnings** annotation, the compiler will produce
an "unchecked cast" warning for **pop( )**. Because of erasure, it can't know
whether the cast is safe, and the **pop( )** method doesn't actually do any
casting. **T** is erased to its first bound, which is **Object** by default, so **pop( )** is
actually just casting an **Object** to an **Object**.

There are times when generics do not eliminate the need to cast, and this
generates a warning by the compiler which is inappropriate. For example:

```
//: generics/NeedCasting.java
import java.io.*;
import java.util.*;

public class NeedCasting {
  @SuppressWarnings("unchecked")
  public void f(String[] args) throws Exception {
    ObjectInputStream in = new ObjectInputStream(
      new FileInputStream(args[0]));
    List<Widget> shapes = (List<Widget>)in.readObject();
  }
} ///:~
```

As you'll learn in the next chapter, **readObject( )** cannot know what it is
reading, so it returns an object that must be cast. But when you comment out
the **@SuppressWarnings** annotation and compile the program, you get a
warning:

```
Note: NeedCasting.java uses unchecked or unsafe operations.
Note: Recompile with -Xlint:unchecked for details.
```

And if you follow the instructions and recompile with **-Xlint:unchecked**:

```
NeedCasting.java:12: warning: [unchecked] unchecked cast
found    : java.lang.Object
required: java.util.List<Widget>
    List<Shape> shapes = (List<Widget>)in.readObject();
```

You're forced to cast, and yet you're told you shouldn't. To solve the problem, you must use a new form of cast introduced in Java SE5, the cast via a generic class:

```
//: generics/ClassCasting.java
import java.io.*;
import java.util.*;

public class ClassCasting {
  @SuppressWarnings("unchecked")
  public void f(String[] args) throws Exception {
    ObjectInputStream in = new ObjectInputStream(
      new FileInputStream(args[0]));
    // Won't Compile:
//    List<Widget> lw1 =
//    List<Widget>.class.cast(in.readObject());
    List<Widget> lw2 = List.class.cast(in.readObject());
  }
} ///:~
```

However, you can't cast to the actual type (**List<Widget>**). That is, you can't say

```
List<Widget>.class.cast(in.readObject())
```

and even if you add another cast like this:

```
(List<Widget>)List.class.cast(in.readObject())
```

you'll still get a warning.

Exercise 32: (1) Verify that **FixedSizeStack** in **GenericCast.java** generates exceptions if you try to go out of its bounds. Does this mean that bounds-checking code is not required?

Exercise 33: (3) Repair **GenericCast.java** using an **ArrayList**.

Overloading

This won't compile, even though it's a reasonable thing to try:

```
//: generics/UseList.java
// {CompileTimeError} (Won't compile)
import java.util.*;

public class UseList<W,T> {
```

```
  void f(List<T> v) {}
  void f(List<W> v) {}
} ///:~
```

Overloading the method produces the identical type signature because of erasure.

Instead, you must provide distinct method names when the erased arguments do not produce a unique argument list:

```
//: generics/UseList2.java
import java.util.*;

public class UseList2<W,T> {
  void f1(List<T> v) {}
  void f2(List<W> v) {}
} ///:~
```

Fortunately, this kind of problem is detected by the compiler.

Base class hijacks an interface

Suppose you have a **Pet** class that is **Comparable** to other **Pet** objects:

```
//: generics/ComparablePet.java

public class ComparablePet
implements Comparable<ComparablePet> {
  public int compareTo(ComparablePet arg) { return 0; }
} ///:~
```

It makes sense to try to narrow the type that a subclass of **ComparablePet** can be compared to. For example, a **Cat** should only be **Comparable** with other **Cat**s:

```
//: generics/HijackedInterface.java
// {CompileTimeError} (Won't compile)

class Cat extends ComparablePet implements Comparable<Cat>{
  // Error: Comparable cannot be inherited with
  // different arguments: <Cat> and <Pet>
  public int compareTo(Cat arg) { return 0; }
} ///:~
```

Unfortunately, this won't work. Once the **ComparablePet** argument is established for **Comparable**, no other implementing class can ever be compared to anything but a **ComparablePet**:

```
//: generics/RestrictedComparablePets.java

class Hamster extends ComparablePet
implements Comparable<ComparablePet> {
  public int compareTo(ComparablePet arg) { return 0; }
}

// Or just:

class Gecko extends ComparablePet {
  public int compareTo(ComparablePet arg) { return 0; }
} ///:~
```

Hamster shows that it is possible to reimplement the same interface that is in **ComparablePet**, as long as it is exactly the same, including the parameter types. However, this is the same as just overriding the methods in the base class, as seen in **Gecko**.

Self-bounded types

There's one rather mind-bending idiom that appears periodically in Java generics. Here's what it looks like:

```
class SelfBounded<T extends SelfBounded<T>> { // ...
```

This has the dizzying effect of two mirrors pointed at each other, a kind of infinite reflection. The class **SelfBounded** takes a generic argument **T**, **T** is constrained by a bound, and that bound is **SelfBounded**, with **T** as an argument.

This is difficult to parse when you first see it, and it emphasizes that the **extends** keyword, when used with bounds, is definitely different than when it is used to create subclasses.

Curiously recurring generics

To understand what a self-bounded type means, let's start with a simpler version of the idiom, without the self-bound.

You can't inherit directly from a generic parameter. However, you *can* inherit from a class that uses that generic parameter in its own definition. That is, you can say:

```
//: generics/CuriouslyRecurringGeneric.java

class GenericType<T> {}

public class CuriouslyRecurringGeneric
  extends GenericType<CuriouslyRecurringGeneric> {} ///:~
```

This could be called *curiously recurring generics* (CRG) after Jim Coplien's *Curiously Recurring Template Pattern* in C++. The "curiously recurring" part refers to the fact that your class appears, rather curiously, in its own base class.

To understand what this means, try saying it aloud: "I'm creating a new class that inherits from a generic type that takes my class name as its parameter." What can the generic base type accomplish when given the derived class name? Well, generics in Java are about arguments and return types, so it can produce a base class that uses the derived type for its arguments and return types. It can also use the derived type for field types, even though those will be erased to **Object**. Here's a generic class that expresses this:

```
//: generics/BasicHolder.java

public class BasicHolder<T> {
  T element;
  void set(T arg) { element = arg; }
  T get() { return element; }
  void f() {
    System.out.println(element.getClass().getSimpleName());
  }
} ///:~
```

It's an ordinary generic type with methods that both accept and produce objects of the parameter type, along with a method that operates on the stored field (although it only performs **Object** operations on that field).

We can use **BasicHolder** in a curiously recurring generic:

```
//: generics/CRGWithBasicHolder.java

class Subtype extends BasicHolder<Subtype> {}
```

```
public class CRGWithBasicHolder {
  public static void main(String[] args) {
    Subtype st1 = new Subtype(), st2 = new Subtype();
    st1.set(st2);
    Subtype st3 = st1.get();
    st1.f();
  }
} /* Output:
Subtype
*///:~
```

Notice something important here: The new class **Subtype** takes arguments and returns values of **Subtype**, not just the base class **BasicHolder**. This is the essence of CRG: *The base class substitutes the derived class for its parameters*. This means that the generic base class becomes a kind of template for common functionality for all its derived classes, but this functionality will use the derived type for all of its arguments and return values. That is, the exact type instead of the base type will be used in the resulting class. So in **Subtype**, both the argument to **set( )** and the return type of **get( )** are exactly **Subtype**s.

Self-bounding

The **BasicHolder** can use any type as its generic parameter, as seen here:

```
//: generics/Unconstrained.java

class Other {}
class BasicOther extends BasicHolder<Other> {}

public class Unconstrained {
  public static void main(String[] args) {
    BasicOther b = new BasicOther(), b2 = new BasicOther();
    b.set(new Other());
    Other other = b.get();
    b.f();
  }
} /* Output:
Other
*///:~
```

Self-bounding takes the extra step of *forcing* the generic to be used as its own bound argument. Look at how the resulting class can and can't be used:

Generics

```
//: generics/SelfBounding.java

class SelfBounded<T extends SelfBounded<T>> {
  T element;
  SelfBounded<T> set(T arg) {
    element = arg;
    return this;
  }
  T get() { return element; }
}

class A extends SelfBounded<A> {}
class B extends SelfBounded<A> {} // Also OK

class C extends SelfBounded<C> {
  C setAndGet(C arg) { set(arg); return get(); }
}

class D {}
// Can't do this:
// class E extends SelfBounded<D> {}
// Compile error: Type parameter D is not within its bound

// Alas, you can do this, so you can't force the idiom:
class F extends SelfBounded {}

public class SelfBounding {
  public static void main(String[] args) {
    A a = new A();
    a.set(new A());
    a = a.set(new A()).get();
    a = a.get();
    C c = new C();
    c = c.setAndGet(new C());
  }
} ///:~
```

What self-bounding does is require the use of the class in an inheritance relationship like this:

```
class A extends SelfBounded<A> {}
```

This forces you to pass the class that you are defining as a parameter to the base class.

What's the added value in self-bounding the parameter? The type parameter must be the same as the class being defined. As you can see in the definition of class **B**, you can also derive from a **SelfBounded** that uses a parameter of another **SelfBounded**, although the predominant use seems to be the one that you see for class **A**. The attempt to define **E** shows that you cannot use a type parameter that is not a **SelfBounded**.

Unfortunately, **F** compiles without warnings, so the self-bounding idiom is not enforceable. If it's really important, it may require an external tool to ensure that raw types are not being used in place of parameterized types.

Notice that you can remove the constraint and all the classes will still compile, but **E** will also compile:

```
//: generics/NotSelfBounded.java

public class NotSelfBounded<T> {
  T element;
  NotSelfBounded<T> set(T arg) {
    element = arg;
    return this;
  }
  T get() { return element; }
}

class A2 extends NotSelfBounded<A2> {}
class B2 extends NotSelfBounded<A2> {}

class C2 extends NotSelfBounded<C2> {
  C2 setAndGet(C2 arg) { set(arg); return get(); }
}

class D2 {}
// Now this is OK:
class E2 extends NotSelfBounded<D2> {} ///:~
```

So clearly, the self-bounding constraint serves only to force the inheritance relationship. If you use self-bounding, you know that the type parameter used by the class will be the same basic type as the class that's using that parameter. It forces anyone using that class to follow that form.

It's also possible to use self-bounding for generic methods:

```
//: generics/SelfBoundingMethods.java
```

```
public class SelfBoundingMethods {
  static <T extends SelfBounded<T>> T f(T arg) {
    return arg.set(arg).get();
  }
  public static void main(String[] args) {
    A a = f(new A());
  }
} ///:~
```

This prevents the method from being applied to anything but a self-bounded argument of the form shown.

Argument covariance

The value of self-bounding types is that they produce *covariant argument types*—method argument types vary to follow the subclasses.

Although self-bounding types also produce return types that are the same as the subclass type, this is not so important because *covariant return types* were introduced in Java SE5:

```
//: generics/CovariantReturnTypes.java

class Base {}
class Derived extends Base {}

interface OrdinaryGetter {
  Base get();
}

interface DerivedGetter extends OrdinaryGetter {
  // Return type of overridden method is allowed to vary:
  Derived get();
}

public class CovariantReturnTypes {
  void test(DerivedGetter d) {
    Derived d2 = d.get();
  }
} ///:~
```

The **get( )** method in **DerivedGetter** overrides **get( )** in **OrdinaryGetter** *and* returns a type that is derived from the type returned by **OrdinaryGetter.get( )**. Although this is a perfectly logical thing to do—a derived type method should be able to return a more specific type than the base type method that it's overriding—it was illegal in earlier versions of Java.

A self-bounded generic does in fact produce the exact derived type as a return value, as seen here with **get( )**:

```
//: generics/GenericsAndReturnTypes.java

interface GenericGetter<T extends GenericGetter<T>> {
  T get();
}

interface Getter extends GenericGetter<Getter> {}

public class GenericsAndReturnTypes {
  void test(Getter g) {
    Getter result = g.get();
    GenericGetter gg = g.get(); // Also the base type
  }
} ///:~
```

Notice that this code would not have compiled unless covariant return types were included in Java SE5.

In non-generic code, however, the *argument* types cannot be made to vary with the subtypes:

```
//: generics/OrdinaryArguments.java

class OrdinarySetter {
  void set(Base base) {
    System.out.println("OrdinarySetter.set(Base)");
  }
}

class DerivedSetter extends OrdinarySetter {
  void set(Derived derived) {
    System.out.println("DerivedSetter.set(Derived)");
  }
}

public class OrdinaryArguments {
  public static void main(String[] args) {
    Base base = new Base();
    Derived derived = new Derived();
```

```
    DerivedSetter ds = new DerivedSetter();
    ds.set(derived);
    ds.set(base); // Compiles: overloaded, not overridden!
  }
} /* Output:
DerivedSetter.set(Derived)
OrdinarySetter.set(Base)
*///:~
```

Both **set(derived)** and **set(base)** are legal, so **DerivedSetter.set( )** is not overriding **OrdinarySetter.set( )**, but instead it is *overloading* that method. From the output, you can see that there are two methods in **DerivedSetter**, so the base-class version is still available, thus verifying that it has been overloaded.

However, with self-bounding types, there is only one method in the derived class, and that method takes the derived type as its argument, not the base type:

```
//: generics/SelfBoundingAndCovariantArguments.java

interface SelfBoundSetter<T extends SelfBoundSetter<T>> {
  void set(T arg);
}

interface Setter extends SelfBoundSetter<Setter> {}

public class SelfBoundingAndCovariantArguments {
  void testA(Setter s1, Setter s2, SelfBoundSetter sbs) {
    s1.set(s2);
    // s1.set(sbs); // Error:
    // set(Setter) in SelfBoundSetter<Setter>
    // cannot be applied to (SelfBoundSetter)
  }
} ///:~
```

The compiler doesn't recognize the attempt to pass in the base type as an argument to **set( )**, because there is no method with that signature. The argument has, in effect, been overridden.

Without self-bounding, the ordinary inheritance mechanism steps in, and you get overloading, just as with the non-generic case:

```
//: generics/PlainGenericInheritance.java
```

```
class GenericSetter<T> { // Not self-bounded
  void set(T arg){
    System.out.println("GenericSetter.set(Base)");
  }
}

class DerivedGS extends GenericSetter<Base> {
  void set(Derived derived){
    System.out.println("DerivedGS.set(Derived)");
  }
}

public class PlainGenericInheritance {
  public static void main(String[] args) {
    Base base = new Base();
    Derived derived = new Derived();
    DerivedGS dgs = new DerivedGS();
    dgs.set(derived);
    dgs.set(base); // Compiles: overloaded, not overridden!
  }
} /* Output:
DerivedGS.set(Derived)
GenericSetter.set(Base)
*///:~
```

This code mimics **OrdinaryArguments.java**; in that example,
DerivedSetter inherits from **OrdinarySetter** which contains a **set(Base)**.
Here, **DerivedGS** inherits from **GenericSetter<Base>** which also
contains a **set(Base)**, created by the generic. And just like
OrdinaryArguments.java, you can see from the output that **DerivedGS**
contains two overloaded versions of **set( )**. Without self-bounding, you
overload on argument types. If you use self-bounding, you only end up with
one version of a method, which takes the exact argument type.

Exercise 34: (4) Create a self-bounded generic type that contains an
abstract method that takes an argument of the generic type parameter and
produces a return value of the generic type parameter. In a non-**abstract**
method of the class, call the **abstract** method and return its result. Inherit
from the self-bounded type and test the resulting class.

Generics

Dynamic type safety

Because you can pass generic containers to pre-Java SE5 code, there's still the possibility that old-style code can corrupt your containers. Java SE5 has a set of utilities in **java.util.Collections** to solve the type-checking problem in this situation: the **static** methods **checkedCollection( )**, **checkedList( )**, **checkedMap( )**, **checkedSet( )**, **checkedSortedMap( )** and **checkedSortedSet( )**. Each of these takes the container you want to dynamically check as the first argument and the type that you want to enforce as the second argument.

A checked container will throw a **ClassCastException** at the point you try to *insert* an improper object, as opposed to a pre-generic (raw) container which would inform you that there was a problem when you pulled the object *out*. In the latter case, you know there's a problem but you don't know who the culprit is, but with checked containers you find out who tried to insert the bad object.

Let's look at the problem of "putting a cat in a list of dogs" using a checked container. Here, **oldStyleMethod( )** represents legacy code because it takes a raw **List**, and the **@SuppressWarnings("unchecked")** annotation is necessary to suppress the resulting warning:

```
//: generics/CheckedList.java
// Using Collection.checkedList().
import typeinfo.pets.*;
import java.util.*;

public class CheckedList {
  @SuppressWarnings("unchecked")
  static void oldStyleMethod(List probablyDogs) {
    probablyDogs.add(new Cat());
  }
  public static void main(String[] args) {
    List<Dog> dogs1 = new ArrayList<Dog>();
    oldStyleMethod(dogs1); // Quietly accepts a Cat
    List<Dog> dogs2 = Collections.checkedList(
      new ArrayList<Dog>(), Dog.class);
    try {
      oldStyleMethod(dogs2); // Throws an exception
    } catch(Exception e) {
      System.out.println("Expected: " + e);
    }
```

```
    // Derived types work fine:
    List<Pet> pets = Collections.checkedList(
      new ArrayList<Pet>(), Pet.class);
    pets.add(new Dog());
    pets.add(new Cat());
  }
} /* Output:
Expected: java.lang.ClassCastException: Attempt to insert
class typeinfo.pets.Cat element into collection with
element type class typeinfo.pets.Dog
*///:~
```

When you run the program you'll see that the insertion of a **Cat** goes unchallenged by **dogs1**, but **dogs2** immediately throws an exception upon the insertion of an incorrect type. You can also see that it's fine to put derived-type objects into a checked container that is checking for the base type.

Exercise 35: (1) Modify **CheckedList.java** so that it uses the **Coffee** classes defined in this chapter.

Exceptions

Because of erasure, the use of generics with exceptions is extremely limited. A **catch** clause cannot catch an exception of a generic type, because the exact type of the exception must be known at both compile time and run time. Also, a generic class can't directly or indirectly inherit from **Throwable** (this further prevents you from trying to define generic exceptions that can't be caught).

However, type parameters may be used in the **throws** clause of a method declaration. This allows you to write generic code that varies with the type of a checked exception:

```
//: generics/ThrowGenericException.java
import java.util.*;

interface Processor<T,E extends Exception> {
  void process(List<T> resultCollector) throws E;
}

class ProcessRunner<T,E extends Exception>
extends ArrayList<Processor<T,E>> {
  List<T> processAll() throws E {
```

```
      List<T> resultCollector = new ArrayList<T>();
      for(Processor<T,E> processor : this)
        processor.process(resultCollector);
      return resultCollector;
    }
}

class Failure1 extends Exception {}

class Processor1 implements Processor<String,Failure1> {
  static int count = 3;
  public void
  process(List<String> resultCollector) throws Failure1 {
    if(count-- > 1)
      resultCollector.add("Hep!");
    else
      resultCollector.add("Ho!");
    if(count < 0)
        throw new Failure1();
  }
}

class Failure2 extends Exception {}

class Processor2 implements Processor<Integer,Failure2> {
  static int count = 2;
  public void
  process(List<Integer> resultCollector) throws Failure2 {
    if(count-- == 0)
      resultCollector.add(47);
    else {
      resultCollector.add(11);
    }
    if(count < 0)
        throw new Failure2();
  }
}

public class ThrowGenericException {
  public static void main(String[] args) {
    ProcessRunner<String,Failure1> runner =
      new ProcessRunner<String,Failure1>();
    for(int i = 0; i < 3; i++)
      runner.add(new Processor1());
```

```
      try {
        System.out.println(runner.processAll());
      } catch(Failure1 e) {
        System.out.println(e);
      }

      ProcessRunner<Integer,Failure2> runner2 =
        new ProcessRunner<Integer,Failure2>();
      for(int i = 0; i < 3; i++)
        runner2.add(new Processor2());
      try {
        System.out.println(runner2.processAll());
      } catch(Failure2 e) {
        System.out.println(e);
      }
    }
  }
} ///:~
```

A **Processor** performs a **process( )** and may throw an exception of type **E**. The result of the **process( )** is stored in the **List<T> resultCollector** (this is called a *collecting parameter*). A **ProcessRunner** has a **processAll( )** method that executes every **Process** object that it holds, and returns the **resultCollector**.

If you could not parameterize the exceptions that are thrown, you would be unable to write this code generically because of the checked exceptions.

Exercise 36: (2) Add a second parameterized exception to the **Processor** class and demonstrate that the exceptions can vary independently.

Mixins

The term *mixin* seems to have acquired numerous meanings over time, but the fundamental concept is that of mixing in capabilities from multiple classes in order to produce a resulting class that represents all the types of the mixins. This is often something you do at the last minute, which makes it convenient to easily assemble classes.

One value of mixins is that they consistently apply characteristics and behaviors across multiple classes. As a bonus, if you want to change something in a mixin class, those changes are then applied across all the classes where the mixin is applied. Because of this, mixins have part of the flavor of *aspect-oriented programming* (AOP), and aspects are often suggested to solve the mixin problem.

Mixins in C++

One of the strongest arguments made for multiple inheritance in C++ is for the use of mixins. However, a more interesting and elegant approach to mixins is using parameterized types, whereby a mixin is a class that inherits from its type parameter. In C++, you can easily create mixins because C++ remembers the type of its template parameters.

Here's a C++ example with two mixin types: one that allows you to mix in the property of having a time stamp, and another that mixes in a serial number for each object instance:

```cpp
//: generics/Mixins.cpp
#include <string>
#include <ctime>
#include <iostream>
using namespace std;

template<class T> class TimeStamped : public T {
  long timeStamp;
public:
  TimeStamped() { timeStamp = time(0); }
  long getStamp() { return timeStamp; }
};

template<class T> class SerialNumbered : public T {
  long serialNumber;
  static long counter;
public:
  SerialNumbered() { serialNumber = counter++; }
  long getSerialNumber() { return serialNumber; }
};

// Define and initialize the static storage:
template<class T> long SerialNumbered<T>::counter = 1;

class Basic {
  string value;
public:
  void set(string val) { value = val; }
  string get() { return value; }
```

```
  };

int main() {
  TimeStamped<SerialNumbered<Basic> > mixin1, mixin2;
  mixin1.set("test string 1");
  mixin2.set("test string 2");
  cout << mixin1.get() << " " << mixin1.getStamp() <<
    " " << mixin1.getSerialNumber() << endl;
  cout << mixin2.get() << " " << mixin2.getStamp() <<
    " " << mixin2.getSerialNumber() << endl;
} /* Output: (Sample)
test string 1 1129840250 1
test string 2 1129840250 2
*///:~
```

In **main( )**, the resulting type of **mixin1** and **mixin2** has all the methods of
the mixed-in types. You can think of a mixin as a function that maps existing
classes to new subclasses. Notice how trivial it is to create a mixin using this
technique; basically, you just say, "Here's what I want," and it happens:

```
  TimeStamped<SerialNumbered<Basic> > mixin1, mixin2;
```

Unfortunately, Java generics don't permit this. Erasure forgets the base-class
type, so a generic class cannot inherit directly from a generic parameter.

Mixing with interfaces

A commonly suggested solution is to use interfaces to produce the effect of
mixins, like this:

```
//: generics/Mixins.java
import java.util.*;

interface TimeStamped { long getStamp(); }

class TimeStampedImp implements TimeStamped {
  private final long timeStamp;
  public TimeStampedImp() {
    timeStamp = new Date().getTime();
  }
  public long getStamp() { return timeStamp; }
}

interface SerialNumbered { long getSerialNumber(); }
```

```java
class SerialNumberedImp implements SerialNumbered {
  private static long counter = 1;
  private final long serialNumber = counter++;
  public long getSerialNumber() { return serialNumber; }
}

interface Basic {
  public void set(String val);
  public String get();
}

class BasicImp implements Basic {
  private String value;
  public void set(String val) { value = val; }
  public String get() { return value; }
}

class Mixin extends BasicImp
implements TimeStamped, SerialNumbered {
  private TimeStamped timeStamp = new TimeStampedImp();
  private SerialNumbered serialNumber =
    new SerialNumberedImp();
  public long getStamp() { return timeStamp.getStamp(); }
  public long getSerialNumber() {
    return serialNumber.getSerialNumber();
  }
}

public class Mixins {
  public static void main(String[] args) {
    Mixin mixin1 = new Mixin(), mixin2 = new Mixin();
    mixin1.set("test string 1");
    mixin2.set("test string 2");
    System.out.println(mixin1.get() + " " +
      mixin1.getStamp() +  " " + mixin1.getSerialNumber());
    System.out.println(mixin2.get() + " " +
      mixin2.getStamp() +  " " + mixin2.getSerialNumber());
  }
} /* Output: (Sample)
test string 1 1132437151359 1
test string 2 1132437151359 2
*///:~
```

The **Mixin** class is basically using *delegation*, so each mixed-in type requires a field in **Mixin**, and you must write all the necessary methods in **Mixin** to forward calls to the appropriate object. This example uses trivial classes, but with a more complex mixin the code grows rapidly.[4]

Exercise 37: (2) Add a new mixin class **Colored** to **Mixins.java**, mix it into **Mixin**, and show that it works.

Using the Decorator pattern

When you look at the way that it is used, the concept of a mixin seems closely related to the *Decorator* design pattern.[5] Decorators are often used when, in order to satisfy every possible combination, simple subclassing produces so many classes that it becomes impractical.

The Decorator pattern uses layered objects to dynamically and transparently add responsibilities to individual objects. Decorator specifies that all objects that wrap around your initial object have the same basic interface. Something is decoratable, and you layer on functionality by wrapping other classes around the decoratable. This makes the use of the decorators transparent— there are a set of common messages you can send to an object whether it has been decorated or not. A decorating class can also add methods, but as you shall see, this is limited.

Decorators are implemented using composition and formal structures (the decoratable/decorator hierarchy), whereas mixins are inheritance-based. So you could think of parameterized-type-based mixins as a generic decorator mechanism that does not require the inheritance structure of the Decorator design pattern.

The previous example can be recast using Decorator:

```
//: generics/decorator/Decoration.java
package generics.decorator;
import java.util.*;

class Basic {
```

---

[4] Note that some programming environments, such as Eclipse and IntelliJ Idea, will automatically generate delegation code.

[5] Patterns are the subject of *Thinking in Patterns (with Java)*, which you can find at *www.MindView.net*. See also *Design Patterns*, by Erich Gamma et al. (Addison-Wesley, 1995).

```java
    private String value;
    public void set(String val) { value = val; }
    public String get() { return value; }
}

class Decorator extends Basic {
    protected Basic basic;
    public Decorator(Basic basic) { this.basic = basic; }
    public void set(String val) { basic.set(val); }
    public String get() { return basic.get(); }
}

class TimeStamped extends Decorator {
    private final long timeStamp;
    public TimeStamped(Basic basic) {
        super(basic);
        timeStamp = new Date().getTime();
    }
    public long getStamp() { return timeStamp; }
}

class SerialNumbered extends Decorator {
    private static long counter = 1;
    private final long serialNumber = counter++;
    public SerialNumbered(Basic basic) { super(basic); }
    public long getSerialNumber() { return serialNumber; }
}

public class Decoration {
    public static void main(String[] args) {
        TimeStamped t = new TimeStamped(new Basic());
        TimeStamped t2 = new TimeStamped(
            new SerialNumbered(new Basic()));
        //! t2.getSerialNumber(); // Not available
        SerialNumbered s = new SerialNumbered(new Basic());
        SerialNumbered s2 = new SerialNumbered(
            new TimeStamped(new Basic()));
        //! s2.getStamp(); // Not available
    }
} ///:~
```

The class resulting from a mixin contains all the methods of interest, but the type of the object that results from using decorators is the last type that it was decorated with. That is, although it's *possible* to add more than one layer, the final layer is the actual type, so only the final layer's methods are visible, whereas the type of the mixin is *all* the types that have been mixed together. So a significant drawback to Decorator is that it only effectively works with one layer of decoration (the final one), and the mixin approach is arguably more natural. Thus, Decorator is only a limited solution to the problem addressed by mixins.

Exercise 38: (4) Create a simple Decorator system by starting with basic coffee, then providing decorators of steamed milk, foam, chocolate, caramel and whipped cream.

Mixins with dynamic proxies

It's possible to use a dynamic proxy to create a mechanism that more closely models mixins than does the Decorator (see the *Type Information* chapter for an explanation of how Java's dynamic proxies work). With a dynamic proxy, the *dynamic* type of the resulting class is the combined types that have been mixed in.

Because of the constraints of dynamic proxies, each class that is mixed in must be the implementation of an interface:

```
//: generics/DynamicProxyMixin.java
import java.lang.reflect.*;
import java.util.*;
import net.mindview.util.*;
import static net.mindview.util.Tuple.*;

class MixinProxy implements InvocationHandler {
  Map<String,Object> delegatesByMethod;
  public MixinProxy(TwoTuple<Object,Class<?>>... pairs) {
    delegatesByMethod = new HashMap<String,Object>();
    for(TwoTuple<Object,Class<?>> pair : pairs) {
      for(Method method : pair.second.getMethods()) {
        String methodName = method.getName();
        // The first interface in the map
        // implements the method.
        if (!delegatesByMethod.containsKey(methodName))
          delegatesByMethod.put(methodName, pair.first);
      }
    }
  }
  public Object invoke(Object proxy, Method method,
    Object[] args) throws Throwable {
```

```
      String methodName = method.getName();
      Object delegate = delegatesByMethod.get(methodName);
      return method.invoke(delegate, args);
    }
    @SuppressWarnings("unchecked")
    public static Object newInstance(TwoTuple... pairs) {
      Class[] interfaces = new Class[pairs.length];
      for(int i = 0; i < pairs.length; i++) {
        interfaces[i] = (Class)pairs[i].second;
      }
      ClassLoader cl =
        pairs[0].first.getClass().getClassLoader();
      return Proxy.newProxyInstance(
        cl, interfaces, new MixinProxy(pairs));
    }
}

public class DynamicProxyMixin {
  public static void main(String[] args) {
    Object mixin = MixinProxy.newInstance(
      tuple(new BasicImp(), Basic.class),
      tuple(new TimeStampedImp(), TimeStamped.class),
      tuple(new SerialNumberedImp(),SerialNumbered.class));
    Basic b = (Basic)mixin;
    TimeStamped t = (TimeStamped)mixin;
    SerialNumbered s = (SerialNumbered)mixin;
    b.set("Hello");
    System.out.println(b.get());
    System.out.println(t.getStamp());
    System.out.println(s.getSerialNumber());
  }
} /* Output: (Sample)
Hello
1132519137015
1
*///:~
```

Because only the dynamic type, and not the static type, includes all the mixed-in types, this is still not quite as nice as the C++ approach, because you're forced to downcast to the appropriate type before you can call methods for it. However, it is significantly closer to a true mixin.

There has been a fair amount of work done towards the support of mixins for Java, including the creation of at least one language add-on, the Jam language, specifically for supporting mixins.

Exercise 39: (1) Add a new mixin class **Colored** to **DynamicProxyMixin.java**, mix it into **mixin**, and show that it works.

Latent typing

The beginning of this chapter introduced the idea of writing code that can be applied as generally as possible. To do this, we need ways to loosen the constraints on the types that our code works with, without losing the benefits of static type checking. We are then able to write code that can be used in more situations without change—that is, more "generic" code.

Java generics appear to take a further step in this direction. When you are writing or using generics that simply hold objects, the code works with any type (except for primitives, although as you've seen, autoboxing smoothes this over). Or, put another way, "holder" generics are able to say, "I don't care what type you are." Code that doesn't care what type it works with can indeed be applied everywhere, and is thus quite "generic."

As you've also seen, a problem arises when you want to perform manipulations on generic types (other than calling **Object** methods), because erasure requires that you specify the bounds of the generic types that may be used, in order to safely call specific methods for the generic objects in your code. This is a significant limitation to the concept of "generic" because you must constrain your generic types so that they inherit from particular classes or implement particular interfaces. In some cases you might end up using an ordinary class or interface instead, because a bounded generic might be no different from specifying a class or interface.

One solution that some programming languages provide is called *latent typing* or *structural typing*. A more whimsical term is *duck typing*, as in, "If it walks like a duck and talks like a duck, you might as well treat it like a duck." Duck typing has become a fairly popular term, possibly because it doesn't carry the historical baggage that other terms do.

Generic code typically only calls a few methods on a generic type, and a language with latent typing loosens the constraint (and produces more generic code) by only requiring that a subset of methods be implemented, *not* a particular class or interface. Because of this, latent typing allows you to cut across class hierarchies, calling methods that are not part of a common interface. So a piece of code might say, in effect, "I don't care what type you are as long as you can **speak( )** and **sit( )**." By not requiring a specific type, your code can be more generic.

Latent typing is a code organization and reuse mechanism. With it you can write a piece of code that can be reused more easily than without it. Code organization and reuse are the foundational levers of all computer programming: Write it once, use it more than once, and keep the code in one place. Because I am not required to name an exact interface that my code operates upon, with latent typing I can write less code and apply it more easily in more places.

Two examples of languages that support latent typing are Python (freely downloadable from *www.Python.org*) and C++.[6] Python is a dynamically typed language (virtually all the type checking happens at run time) and C++ is a statically typed language (the type checking happens at compile time), so latent typing does not require either static or dynamic type checking.

If we take the above description and express it in Python, it looks like this:

```
#: generics/DogsAndRobots.py

class Dog:
    def speak(self):
        print "Arf!"
    def sit(self):
        print "Sitting"
    def reproduce(self):
        pass

class Robot:
    def speak(self):
        print "Click!"
    def sit(self):
        print "Clank!"
    def oilChange(self):
        pass
```

---

[6] The Ruby and Smalltalk languages also support latent typing.

```
def perform(anything):
    anything.speak()
    anything.sit()

a = Dog()
b = Robot()
perform(a)
perform(b)
#:~
```

Python uses indentation to determine scope (so no curly braces are needed), and a colon to begin a new scope. A '#' indicates a comment to the end of the line, like '//' in Java. The methods of a class explicitly specify the equivalent of the **this** reference as the first argument, called **self** by convention. Constructor calls do not require any sort of "**new**" keyword. And Python allows regular (non-member) functions, as evidenced by **perform( )**.

In **perform(anything)**, notice that there is no type for **anything**, and **anything** is just an identifier. It must be able to perform the operations that **perform( )** asks of it, so an interface is implied. But you never have to explicitly write out that interface—it's *latent*. **perform( )** doesn't care about the type of its argument, so I can pass any object to it as long as it supports the **speak( )** and **sit( )** methods. If you pass an object to **perform( )** that does not support these operations, you'll get a runtime exception.

We can produce the same effect in C++:

```
//: generics/DogsAndRobots.cpp

class Dog {
public:
  void speak() {}
  void sit() {}
  void reproduce() {}
};

class Robot {
public:
  void speak() {}
  void sit() {}
  void oilChange() {
};

template<class T> void perform(T anything) {
```

```
    anything.speak();
    anything.sit();
}

int main() {
  Dog d;
  Robot r;
  perform(d);
  perform(r);
} ///:~
```

In both Python and C++, **Dog** and **Robot** have nothing in common, other than that they happen to have two methods with identical signatures. From a type standpoint, they are completely distinct types. However, **perform( )** doesn't care about the specific type of its argument, and latent typing allows it to accept both types of object.

C++ ensures that it can actually send those messages. The compiler gives you an error message if you try to pass the wrong type (these error messages have historically been terrible and verbose, and are the primary reason that C++ templates have a poor reputation). Although they do it at different times— C++ at compile time, and Python at run time—both languages ensure that types cannot be misused and are thus considered to be *strongly typed*.[7] Latent typing does not compromise strong typing.

Because generics were added to Java late in the game, there was no chance that any kind of latent typing could be implemented, so Java has no support for this feature. As a result, it initially seems that Java's generic mechanism is "less generic" than a language that supports latent typing.[8] For instance, if we try to implement the above example in Java, we are forced to use a class or an interface and specify it in a bounds expression:

```
//: generics/Performs.java

public interface Performs {
```

---

[7] Because you can use casts, which effectively disable the type system, some people argue that C++ is weakly typed, but that's extreme. It's probably safer to say that C++ is "strongly typed with a trap door."

[8] The implementation of Java's generics using erasure is sometimes referred to as *second-class* generic types.

```
      void speak();
      void sit();
} ///:~
```

```
//: generics/DogsAndRobots.java
// No latent typing in Java
import typeinfo.pets.*;
import static net.mindview.util.Print.*;

class PerformingDog extends Dog implements Performs {
  public void speak() { print("Woof!"); }
  public void sit() { print("Sitting"); }
  public void reproduce() {}
}

class Robot implements Performs {
  public void speak() { print("Click!"); }
  public void sit() { print("Clank!"); }
  public void oilChange() {}
}

class Communicate {
  public static <T extends Performs>
  void perform(T performer) {
    performer.speak();
    performer.sit();
  }
}

public class DogsAndRobots {
  public static void main(String[] args) {
    PerformingDog d = new PerformingDog();
    Robot r = new Robot();
    Communicate.perform(d);
    Communicate.perform(r);
  }
} /* Output:
Woof!
Sitting
Click!
Clank!
*///:~
```

However, note that **perform( )** does not need to use generics in order to work. It can simply be specified to accept a **Performs** object:

```
//: generics/SimpleDogsAndRobots.java
// Removing the generic; code still works.

class CommunicateSimply {
  static void perform(Performs performer) {
    performer.speak();
    performer.sit();
  }
}

public class SimpleDogsAndRobots {
  public static void main(String[] args) {
    CommunicateSimply.perform(new PerformingDog());
    CommunicateSimply.perform(new Robot());
  }
} /* Output:
Woof!
Sitting
Click!
Clank!
*///:~
```

In this case, generics were simply not necessary, since the classes were already forced to implement the **Performs** interface.

Compensating for the lack of latent typing

Although Java does not support latent typing, it turns out that this does not mean that your bounded generic code cannot be applied across different type hierarchies. That is, it is still possible to create truly generic code, but it takes some extra effort.

Reflection

One approach you can use is reflection. Here's a **perform( )** method that uses latent typing:

```
//: generics/LatentReflection.java
// Using Reflection to produce latent typing.
import java.lang.reflect.*;
import static net.mindview.util.Print.*;
```

```
// Does not implement Performs:
class Mime {
  public void walkAgainstTheWind() {}
  public void sit() { print("Pretending to sit"); }
  public void pushInvisibleWalls() {}
  public String toString() { return "Mime"; }
}

// Does not implement Performs:
class SmartDog {
  public void speak() { print("Woof!"); }
  public void sit() { print("Sitting"); }
  public void reproduce() {}
}

class CommunicateReflectively {
  public static void perform(Object speaker) {
    Class<?> spkr = speaker.getClass();
    try {
      try {
        Method speak = spkr.getMethod("speak");
        speak.invoke(speaker);
      } catch(NoSuchMethodException e) {
        print(speaker + " cannot speak");
      }
      try {
        Method sit = spkr.getMethod("sit");
        sit.invoke(speaker);
      } catch(NoSuchMethodException e) {
        print(speaker + " cannot sit");
      }
    } catch(Exception e) {
      throw new RuntimeException(speaker.toString(), e);
    }
  }
}

public class LatentReflection {
  public static void main(String[] args) {
    CommunicateReflectively.perform(new SmartDog());
    CommunicateReflectively.perform(new Robot());
    CommunicateReflectively.perform(new Mime());
  }
} /* Output:
```

```
Woof!
Sitting
Click!
Clank!
Mime cannot speak
Pretending to sit
*///:~
```

Here, the classes are completely disjoint and have no base classes (other than **Object**) or interfaces in common. Through reflection, **CommunicateReflectively.perform( )** is able to dynamically establish whether the desired methods are available and call them. It is even able to deal with the fact that **Mime** only has one of the necessary methods, and partially fulfills its goal.

Applying a method to a sequence

Reflection provides some interesting possibilities, but it relegates all the type checking to run time, and is thus undesirable in many situations. If you can achieve compile-time type checking, that's usually more desirable. But is it possible to have compile-time type checking *and* latent typing?

Let's look at an example that explores the problem. Suppose you want to create an **apply( )** method that will apply any method to every object in a sequence. This is a situation where interfaces don't seem to fit. You want to apply any method to a collection of objects, and interfaces constrain you too much to describe "any method." How do you do this in Java?

Initially, we can solve the problem with reflection, which turns out to be fairly elegant because of Java SE5 varargs:

```
//: generics/Apply.java
// {main: ApplyTest}
import java.lang.reflect.*;
import java.util.*;
import static net.mindview.util.Print.*;

public class Apply {
  public static <T, S extends Iterable<? extends T>>
  void apply(S seq, Method f, Object... args) {
    try {
      for(T t: seq)
        f.invoke(t, args);
    } catch(Exception e) {
```

```
          // Failures are programmer errors
          throw new RuntimeException(e);
        }
    }
  }
}

class Shape {
  public void rotate() { print(this + " rotate"); }
  public void resize(int newSize) {
    print(this + " resize " + newSize);
  }
}

class Square extends Shape {}

class FilledList<T> extends ArrayList<T> {
  public FilledList(Class<? extends T> type, int size) {
    try {
      for(int i = 0; i < size; i++)
        // Assumes default constructor:
        add(type.newInstance());
    } catch(Exception e) {
      throw new RuntimeException(e);
    }
  }
}

class ApplyTest {
  public static void main(String[] args) throws Exception {
    List<Shape> shapes = new ArrayList<Shape>();
    for(int i = 0; i < 10; i++)
      shapes.add(new Shape());
    Apply.apply(shapes, Shape.class.getMethod("rotate"));
    Apply.apply(shapes,
      Shape.class.getMethod("resize", int.class), 5);
    List<Square> squares = new ArrayList<Square>();
    for(int i = 0; i < 10; i++)
      squares.add(new Square());
    Apply.apply(squares, Shape.class.getMethod("rotate"));
    Apply.apply(squares,
      Shape.class.getMethod("resize", int.class), 5);

    Apply.apply(new FilledList<Shape>(Shape.class, 10),
      Shape.class.getMethod("rotate"));
```

```
    Apply.apply(new FilledList<Shape>(Square.class, 10),
      Shape.class.getMethod("rotate"));

    SimpleQueue<Shape> shapeQ = new SimpleQueue<Shape>();
    for(int i = 0; i < 5; i++) {
      shapeQ.add(new Shape());
      shapeQ.add(new Square());
    }
    Apply.apply(shapeQ, Shape.class.getMethod("rotate"));
  }
} /* (Execute to see output) *///:~
```

In **Apply**, we get lucky because there happens to be an **Iterable** interface built into Java which is used by the Java containers library. Because of this, the **apply( )** method can accept anything that implements the **Iterable** interface, which includes all the **Collection** classes such as **List**. But it can also accept anything else, as long as you make it **Iterable**—for example, the **SimpleQueue** class defined here and used above in **main( )**:

```
//: generics/SimpleQueue.java
// A different kind of container that is Iterable
import java.util.*;

public class SimpleQueue<T> implements Iterable<T> {
  private LinkedList<T> storage = new LinkedList<T>();
  public void add(T t) { storage.offer(t); }
  public T get() { return storage.poll(); }
  public Iterator<T> iterator() {
    return storage.iterator();
  }
} ///:~
```

In **Apply.java**, exceptions are converted to **RuntimeException**s because there's not much of a way to recover from exceptions—they really do represent programmer errors in this case.

Note that I had to put in bounds and wildcards in order for **Apply** and **FilledList** to be used in all desired situations. You can experiment by taking these out, and you'll discover that some applications of **Apply** and **FilledList** will not work.

FilledList presents a bit of a quandary. In order for a type to be used, it must have a default (no-arg) constructor. Java has no way to assert such a thing at compile time, so it becomes a runtime issue. A common suggestion to ensure compile-time checking is to define a factory interface that has a method that generates objects; then **FilledList** would accept that interface rather than the "raw factory" of the type token. The problem with this is that all the classes you use in **FilledList** must then implement your factory interface. Alas, most classes are created without knowledge of your interface, and therefore do not implement it. Later, I'll show one solution using adapters.

But the approach shown, of using a type token, is perhaps a reasonable trade-off (at least as a first-cut solution). With this approach, using something like **FilledList** is just easy enough that it may be used rather than ignored. Of course, because errors are reported at run time, you need confidence that these errors will appear early in the development process.

Note that the type token technique is recommended in the Java literature, such as Gilad Bracha's paper *Generics in the Java Programming Language,*[9] where he notes, "It's an idiom that's used extensively in the new APIs for manipulating annotations, for example." However, I've discovered some inconsistency in people's comfort level with this technique; some people strongly prefer the factory approach, which was presented earlier in this chapter.

Also, as elegant as the Java solution turns out to be, we must observe that the use of reflection (although it has been improved significantly in recent versions of Java) may be slower than a non-reflection implementation, since so much is happening at run time. This should not stop you from using the solution, at least as a first cut (lest you fall sway to premature optimization), but it's certainly a distinction between the two approaches.

Exercise 40: (3) Add a **speak( )** method to all the pets in **typeinfo.pets**. Modify **Apply.java** to call the **speak( )** method for a heterogeneous collection of **Pet**.

When you don't happen to have the right interface

The above example benefited because the **Iterable** interface was already built in, and was exactly what we needed. But what about the general case,

---

9 See citation at the end of this chapter.

when there isn't an interface already in place that just happens to fit your needs?

For example, let's generalize the idea in **FilledList** and create a parameterized **fill( )** method that will take a sequence and fill it using a **Generator**. When we try to write this in Java, we run into a problem, because there is no convenient "**Addable**" interface as there was an **Iterable** interface in the previous example. So instead of saying, "anything that you can call **add( )** for," you must say, "subtype of **Collection**." The resulting code is not particularly generic, since it must be constrained to work with **Collection** implementations. If I try to use a class that doesn't implement **Collection**, my generic code won't work. Here's what it looks like:

```java
//: generics/Fill.java
// Generalizing the FilledList idea
// {main: FillTest}
import java.util.*;

// Doesn't work with "anything that has an add()." There is
// no "Addable" interface so we are narrowed to using a
// Collection. We cannot generalize using generics in
// this case.

public class Fill {
  public static <T> void fill(Collection<T> collection,
  Class<? extends T> classToken, int size) {
    for(int i = 0; i < size; i++)
      // Assumes default constructor:
      try {
        collection.add(classToken.newInstance());
      } catch(Exception e) {
        throw new RuntimeException(e);
      }
  }
}

class Contract {
  private static long counter = 0;
  private final long id = counter++;
  public String toString() {
    return getClass().getName() + " " + id;
  }
}
class TitleTransfer extends Contract {}
```

```
class FillTest {
  public static void main(String[] args) {
    List<Contract> contracts = new ArrayList<Contract>();
    Fill.fill(contracts, Contract.class, 3);
    Fill.fill(contracts, TitleTransfer.class, 2);
    for(Contract c: contracts)
      System.out.println(c);
    SimpleQueue<Contract> contractQueue =
      new SimpleQueue<Contract>();
    // Won't work. fill() is not generic enough:
    // Fill.fill(contractQueue, Contract.class, 3);
  }
} /* Output:
Contract 0
Contract 1
Contract 2
TitleTransfer 3
TitleTransfer 4
*///:~
```

This is where a parameterized type mechanism with latent typing is valuable, because you are not at the mercy of the past design decisions of any particular library creator, so you do not have to rewrite your code every time you encounter a new library that didn't take your situation into account (thus the code is truly "generic"). In the above case, because the Java designers (understandably) did not see the need for an "**Addable**" interface, we are constrained within the **Collection** hierarchy, and **SimpleQueue**, even though it has an **add( )** method, will not work. Because it is thus constrained to working with **Collection**, the code is not particularly "generic." With latent typing, this would not be the case.

Simulating latent typing with adapters

So Java generics don't have latent typing, and we need something like latent typing in order to write code that can be applied across class boundaries (that is, "generic" code). Is there some way to get around this limitation?

What would latent typing accomplish here? It means that you could write code saying, "I don't care what type I'm using here as long as it has these methods." In effect, latent typing creates an *implicit interface* containing the desired methods. So it follows that if we write the necessary interface by hand (since Java doesn't do it for us), that should solve the problem.

Writing code to produce an interface that we want from an interface that we have is an example of the Adapter design pattern. We can use adapters to adapt existing classes to produce the desired interface, with a relatively small amount of code. The solution, which uses the previously defined **Coffee** hierarchy, demonstrates different ways of writing adapters:

```java
//: generics/Fill2.java
// Using adapters to simulate latent typing.
// {main: Fill2Test}
import generics.coffee.*;
import java.util.*;
import net.mindview.util.*;
import static net.mindview.util.Print.*;

interface Addable<T> { void add(T t); }

public class Fill2 {
  // Classtoken version:
  public static <T> void fill(Addable<T> addable,
  Class<? extends T> classToken, int size) {
    for(int i = 0; i < size; i++)
      try {
        addable.add(classToken.newInstance());
      } catch(Exception e) {
        throw new RuntimeException(e);
      }
  }
  // Generator version:
  public static <T> void fill(Addable<T> addable,
  Generator<T> generator, int size) {
    for(int i = 0; i < size; i++)
      addable.add(generator.next());
  }
}

// To adapt a base type, you must use composition.
// Make any Collection Addable using composition:
class AddableCollectionAdapter<T> implements Addable<T> {
  private Collection<T> c;
  public AddableCollectionAdapter(Collection<T> c) {
    this.c = c;
  }
  public void add(T item) { c.add(item); }
}
```

```
// A Helper to capture the type automatically:
class Adapter {
  public static <T>
  Addable<T> collectionAdapter(Collection<T> c) {
    return new AddableCollectionAdapter<T>(c);
  }
}

// To adapt a specific type, you can use inheritance.
// Make a SimpleQueue Addable using inheritance:
class AddableSimpleQueue<T>
extends SimpleQueue<T> implements Addable<T> {
  public void add(T item) { super.add(item); }
}

class Fill2Test {
  public static void main(String[] args) {
    // Adapt a Collection:
    List<Coffee> carrier = new ArrayList<Coffee>();
    Fill2.fill(
      new AddableCollectionAdapter<Coffee>(carrier),
      Coffee.class, 3);
    // Helper method captures the type:
    Fill2.fill(Adapter.collectionAdapter(carrier),
      Latte.class, 2);
    for(Coffee c: carrier)
      print(c);
    print("----------------------");
    // Use an adapted class:
    AddableSimpleQueue<Coffee> coffeeQueue =
      new AddableSimpleQueue<Coffee>();
    Fill2.fill(coffeeQueue, Mocha.class, 4);
    Fill2.fill(coffeeQueue, Latte.class, 1);
    for(Coffee c: coffeeQueue)
      print(c);
  }
} /* Output:
Coffee 0
Coffee 1
Coffee 2
Latte 3
Latte 4
----------------------
```

```
Mocha 5
Mocha 6
Mocha 7
Mocha 8
Latte 9
*///:~
```

Fill2 doesn't require a **Collection** as **Fill** did. Instead, it only needs something that implements **Addable**, and **Addable** has been written just for **Fill**—it is a manifestation of the latent type that I wanted the compiler to make for me.

In this version, I've also added an overloaded **fill( )** that takes a **Generator** rather than a type token. The **Generator** is type-safe at compile time: The compiler ensures that you pass it a proper **Generator**, so no exceptions can be thrown.

The first adapter, **AddableCollectionAdapter**, works with the base type **Collection**, which means that any implementation of **Collection** can be used. This version simply stores the **Collection** reference and uses it to implement **add( )**.

If you have a specific type rather than the base class of a hierarchy, you can write somewhat less code when creating your adapter by using inheritance, as you can see in **AddableSimpleQueue**.

In **Fill2Test.main( )**, you can see the various types of adapters at work. First, a **Collection** type is adapted with **AddableCollectionAdapter**. A second version of this uses a generic helper method, and you can see how the generic method captures the type so it doesn't have to be explicitly written—this is a convenient trick that produces more elegant code.

Next, the pre-adapted **AddableSimpleQueue** is used. Note that in both cases the adapters allow the classes that previously didn't implement **Addable** to be used with **Fill2.fill( )**.

Using adapters like this would seem to compensate for the lack of latent typing, and thus allow you to write genuinely generic code. However, it's an extra step and something that must be understood both by the library creator and the library consumer, and the concept may not be grasped as readily by less experienced programmers. By removing the extra step, latent typing makes generic code easier to apply, and this is its value.

Exercise 41: (1) Modify **Fill2.java** to use the classes in **typeinfo.pets** instead of the **Coffee** classes.

Using function objects as strategies

This final example will create truly generic code using the adapter approach described in the previous section. The example began as an attempt to create a sum over a sequence of elements (of any type that can be summed), but evolved into performing general operations using a *functional* style of programming.

If you just look at the process of trying to add objects, you can see that this is a case where we have common operations across classes, but the operations are not represented in any base class that we can specify—sometimes you can even use a '+' operator, and other times there may be some kind of "add" method. This is generally the situation that you encounter when trying to write generic code, because you want the code to apply across multiple classes—especially, as in this case, multiple classes that already exist and that we have no ability to "fix." Even if you were to narrow this case to subclasses of **Number**, that superclass doesn't include anything about "addability."

The solution is to use the *Strategy* design pattern, which produces more elegant code because it completely isolates "the thing that changes" inside of a *function object*.[10] A function object is an object that in some way behaves like a function—typically, there's one method of interest (in languages that support operator overloading, you can make the call to this method *look* like an ordinary method call). The value of function objects is that, unlike an ordinary method, they can be passed around, and they can also have state that persists across calls. Of course, you can accomplish something like this with any method in a class, but (as with any design pattern) the function object is primarily distinguished by its intent. Here the intent is to create something that behaves like a single method that you can pass around; thus it is closely coupled with—and sometimes indistinguishable from—the Strategy design pattern.

---

[10] You will sometimes see these called *functors*. I will use the term *function object* rather than *functor*, as the term "functor" has a specific and different meaning in mathematics.

As I've found with a number of design patterns, the lines get kind of blurry here: We are creating function objects which perform adaptation, and they are being passed into methods to be used as strategies.

Taking this approach, I added the various kinds of generic methods that I had originally set out to create, and more. Here is the result:

```
//: generics/Functional.java
import java.math.*;
import java.util.concurrent.atomic.*;
import java.util.*;
import static net.mindview.util.Print.*;

// Different types of function objects:
interface Combiner<T> { T combine(T x, T y); }
interface UnaryFunction<R,T> { R function(T x); }
interface Collector<T> extends UnaryFunction<T,T> {
  T result(); // Extract result of collecting parameter
}
interface UnaryPredicate<T> { boolean test(T x); }

public class Functional {
  // Calls the Combiner object on each element to combine
  // it with a running result, which is finally returned:
  public static <T> T
  reduce(Iterable<T> seq, Combiner<T> combiner) {
    Iterator<T> it = seq.iterator();
    if(it.hasNext()) {
      T result = it.next();
      while(it.hasNext())
        result = combiner.combine(result, it.next());
      return result;
    }
    // If seq is the empty list:
    return null; // Or throw exception
  }
  // Take a function object and call it on each object in
  // the list, ignoring the return value. The function
  // object may act as a collecting parameter, so it is
  // returned at the end.
  public static <T> Collector<T>
  forEach(Iterable<T> seq, Collector<T> func) {
    for(T t : seq)
      func.function(t);
```

```
      return func;
    }
    // Creates a list of results by calling a
    // function object for each object in the list:
    public static <R,T> List<R>
    transform(Iterable<T> seq, UnaryFunction<R,T> func) {
      List<R> result = new ArrayList<R>();
      for(T t : seq)
        result.add(func.function(t));
      return result;
    }
    // Applies a unary predicate to each item in a sequence,
    // and returns a list of items that produced "true":
    public static <T> List<T>
    filter(Iterable<T> seq, UnaryPredicate<T> pred) {
      List<T> result = new ArrayList<T>();
      for(T t : seq)
        if(pred.test(t))
          result.add(t);
      return result;
    }
    // To use the above generic methods, we need to create
    // function objects to adapt to our particular needs:
    static class IntegerAdder implements Combiner<Integer> {
      public Integer combine(Integer x, Integer y) {
        return x + y;
      }
    }
    static class
    IntegerSubtracter implements Combiner<Integer> {
      public Integer combine(Integer x, Integer y) {
        return x - y;
      }
    }
    static class
    BigDecimalAdder implements Combiner<BigDecimal> {
      public BigDecimal combine(BigDecimal x, BigDecimal y) {
        return x.add(y);
      }
    }
    static class
    BigIntegerAdder implements Combiner<BigInteger> {
      public BigInteger combine(BigInteger x, BigInteger y) {
        return x.add(y);
```

```
      }
    }
    static class
    AtomicLongAdder implements Combiner<AtomicLong> {
      public AtomicLong combine(AtomicLong x, AtomicLong y) {
        // Not clear whether this is meaningful:
        return new AtomicLong(x.addAndGet(y.get()));
      }
    }
    // We can even make a UnaryFunction with an "ulp"
    // (Units in the last place):
    static class BigDecimalUlp
    implements UnaryFunction<BigDecimal,BigDecimal> {
      public BigDecimal function(BigDecimal x) {
        return x.ulp();
      }
    }
    static class GreaterThan<T extends Comparable<T>>
    implements UnaryPredicate<T> {
      private T bound;
      public GreaterThan(T bound) { this.bound = bound; }
      public boolean test(T x) {
        return x.compareTo(bound) > 0;
      }
    }
    static class MultiplyingIntegerCollector
    implements Collector<Integer> {
      private Integer val = 1;
      public Integer function(Integer x) {
        val *= x;
        return val;
      }
      public Integer result() { return val; }
    }
    public static void main(String[] args) {
      // Generics, varargs & boxing working together:
      List<Integer> li = Arrays.asList(1, 2, 3, 4, 5, 6, 7);
      Integer result = reduce(li, new IntegerAdder());
      print(result);

      result = reduce(li, new IntegerSubtracter());
      print(result);

      print(filter(li, new GreaterThan<Integer>(4)));
```

```
    print(forEach(li,
      new MultiplyingIntegerCollector()).result());

    print(forEach(filter(li, new GreaterThan<Integer>(4)),
      new MultiplyingIntegerCollector()).result());

    MathContext mc = new MathContext(7);
    List<BigDecimal> lbd = Arrays.asList(
      new BigDecimal(1.1, mc), new BigDecimal(2.2, mc),
      new BigDecimal(3.3, mc), new BigDecimal(4.4, mc));
    BigDecimal rbd = reduce(lbd, new BigDecimalAdder());
    print(rbd);

    print(filter(lbd,
      new GreaterThan<BigDecimal>(new BigDecimal(3))));

    // Use the prime-generation facility of BigInteger:
    List<BigInteger> lbi = new ArrayList<BigInteger>();
    BigInteger bi = BigInteger.valueOf(11);
    for(int i = 0; i < 11; i++) {
      lbi.add(bi);
      bi = bi.nextProbablePrime();
    }
    print(lbi);

    BigInteger rbi = reduce(lbi, new BigIntegerAdder());
    print(rbi);
    // The sum of this list of primes is also prime:
    print(rbi.isProbablePrime(5));

    List<AtomicLong> lal = Arrays.asList(
      new AtomicLong(11), new AtomicLong(47),
      new AtomicLong(74), new AtomicLong(133));
    AtomicLong ral = reduce(lal, new AtomicLongAdder());
    print(ral);

    print(transform(lbd,new BigDecimalUlp()));
  }
} /* Output:
28
-26
[5, 6, 7]
5040
```

```
210
11.000000
[3.300000, 4.400000]
[11, 13, 17, 19, 23, 29, 31, 37, 41, 43, 47]
311
true
265
[0.000001, 0.000001, 0.000001, 0.000001]
*///:~
```

I begin by defining interfaces for different types of function objects. These were created on demand, as I developed the different methods and discovered the need for each. The **Combiner** class was suggested by an anonymous contributor to one of the articles posted on my Web site. The **Combiner** abstracts away the specific detail of trying to add two objects, and just says that they are being combined somehow. As a result, you can see that **IntegerAdder** and **IntegerSubtracter** can be types of **Combiner**.

A **UnaryFunction** takes a single argument and produces a result; the argument and result need not be of the same type. A **Collector** is used as a "collecting parameter," and you can extract the result when you're finished. A **UnaryPredicate** produces a **boolean** result. There are other types of function objects that can be defined, but these are enough to make the point.

The **Functional** class contains a number of generic methods that apply function objects to sequences. **reduce( )** applies the function in a **Combiner** to each element of a sequence in order to produce a single result.

forEach( ) takes a **Collector** and applies its function to each element, ignoring the result of each function call. This can be called just for the side effect (which wouldn't be a "functional" style of programming but can still be useful), or the **Collector** can maintain internal state to become a collecting parameter, as is the case in this example.

transform( ) produces a list by calling a **UnaryFunction** on each object in the sequence and capturing the result.

Finally, **filter( )** applies a **UnaryPredicate** to each object in a sequence and stores the ones that produce **true** in a **List**, which it returns.

You can define additional generic functions. The C++ STL, for example, has lots of them. The problem has also been solved in some open-source libraries, such as the JGA (Generic Algorithms for Java).

Thinking in Java Bruce Eckel

In C++, latent typing takes care of matching up operations when you call functions, but in Java we need to write the function objects to adapt the generic methods to our particular needs. So the next part of the class shows various different implementations of the function objects. Note, for example, that **IntegerAdder** and **BigDecimalAdder** solve the same problem—adding two objects—by calling the appropriate operations for their particular type. So that's the Adapter pattern and Strategy pattern combined.

In **main( )**, you can see that in each method call, a sequence is passed along with the appropriate function object. Also, a number of the expressions can get fairly complex, such as:

```
forEach(filter(li, new GreaterThan(4)),
        new MultiplyingIntegerCollector()).result()
```

This produces a list by selecting all elements in **li** that are greater than 4, and then applies the **MultiplyingIntegerCollector( )** to the resulting list and extracts the **result( )**. I won't explain the details of the rest of the code other than to say that you can probably figure it out by walking through it.

Exercise 42: (5) Create two separate classes, with nothing in common. Each class should hold a value, and at least have methods that produce that value and perform a modification upon that value. Modify **Functional.java** so that it performs functional operations on collections of your classes (these operations do not have to be arithmetic as they are in **Functional.java**).

Summary: Is casting really so bad?

Having worked to explain C++ templates since their inception, I have probably been putting forward the following argument longer than most people. Only recently have I stopped to wonder how often this argument is valid—how many times does the problem I'm about to describe really slip through the cracks?

The argument goes like this. One of the most compelling places to use a generic type mechanism is with container classes such as the **List**s, **Set**s, **Map**s, etc. that you saw in *Holding Your Objects* and that you shall see more of in the *Containers in Depth* chapter. Before Java SE5, when you put an object into a container, it would be upcast to **Object**, so you'd lose the type information. When you wanted to pull it back out to do something with it, you had to cast it back down to the proper type. My example was a **List** of **Cat** (a variation of this using apples and oranges is shown at the beginning of the *Holding Your Objects* chapter). Without the Java SE5 generic version of the container, you put **Object**s in and you get **Object**s out, so it's easily possible to put a **Dog** in a **List** of **Cat**.

However, pre-generic Java wouldn't let you *misuse* the objects that you put into a container. If you threw a **Dog** into a container of **Cat**s and then tried to treat everything in the container as a **Cat**, you'd get a **RuntimeException** when you pulled the **Dog** reference out of the **Cat** container and tried to cast it to a **Cat**. You'd still discover the problem, but you discovered it at run time rather than compile time.

In previous editions of this book, I go on to say:

> *This is more than just an annoyance. It's something that can create difficult-to-find bugs. If one part (or several parts) of a program inserts objects into a container, and you discover only in a separate part of the program through an exception that a bad object was placed in the container, then you must find out where the bad insert occurred.*

However, upon further examination of the argument, I began to wonder about it. First, how often does it happen? I don't remember this kind of thing ever happening to me, and when I asked people at conferences, I didn't hear anyone say that it had happened to them. Another book used an example of a list called **files** that contained **String** objects—in this example it seemed perfectly natural to add a **File** object to **files**, so a better name for the object might have been **fileNames**. No matter how much type checking Java provides, it's still possible to write obscure programs, and a badly written program that compiles is still a badly written program. Perhaps most people use well-named containers such as "**cats**" that provide a visual warning to the programmer who would try to add a non-**Cat**. And even if it did happen, how long would such a thing really stay buried? It would seem that as soon as you started running tests with real data, you'd see an exception pretty quickly.

One author even asserted that such a bug could "remain buried for years." But I do not recall any deluge of reports of people having great difficulty finding "dog in cat list" bugs, or even producing them very often. Whereas you will see in the *Concurrency* chapter that with threads, it is very easy and common to have bugs that may appear extremely rarely, and only give you a vague idea of what's wrong. So is the "dog in cat list" argument really the reason that this very significant and fairly complex feature has been added to Java?

I believe the *intent* of the general-purpose language feature called "generics" (not necessarily Java's particular implementation of it) is *expressiveness*, not just creating type-safe containers. Type-safe containers come as a side effect of the ability to create more general-purpose code.

So even though the "dog in cat list" argument is often used to justify generics, it is questionable. And as I asserted at the beginning of the chapter, I do not believe that this is what the *concept* of generics is really about. Instead, generics are as their name implies—a way to write more "generic" code that is less constrained by the types it can work with, so a single piece of code can be applied to more types. As you have seen in this chapter, it is fairly easy to write truly generic "holder" classes (which the Java containers are), but to write generic code that manipulates its generic types requires extra effort, on the part of both the class creator *and* the class consumer, who must understand the concept and implementation of the Adapter design pattern. That extra effort reduces the ease of use of the feature, and may thus make it less applicable in places where it might otherwise have added value.

Also note that because generics were back-engineered into Java instead of being designed into the language from the start, some of the containers cannot be made as robust as they should be. For example, look at **Map**, in particular the methods **containsKey(Object key)** and **get(Object key)**. If these classes had been designed with pre-existing generics, these methods would have used parameterized types instead of **Object**, thus affording the compile-time checking that generics are supposed to provide. In C++ **map**s, for example, the key type is always checked at compile time.

One thing is very clear: Introducing any kind of generic mechanism in a later version of a language, after that language has come into general use, is a very, very messy proposition, and one that cannot be accomplished without pain. In C++, templates were introduced in the initial ISO version of the language (although even that caused some pain because there was an earlier non-template version in use before the first Standard C++ appeared), so in effect templates were *always* a part of the language. In Java, generics were not introduced until almost 10 years after the language was first released, so the issues of migrating to generics are quite considerable, and have made a significant impact on the design of generics. The result is that you, the programmer, will suffer because of the lack of vision exhibited by the Java designers when they created version 1.0. When Java was first being created, the designers, of course, knew about C++ templates, and they even considered including them in the language, but for one reason or another decided to leave them out (indications are that they were in a hurry). As a result, both the language and the programmers that use it will suffer. Only time will show the ultimate impact that Java's approach to generics will have on the language.

Some languages, notably *Nice* (see *http://nice.sourceforge.net*; this language generates Java bytecodes and works with existing Java libraries) and NextGen (see *http://japan.cs.rice.edu/nextgen*) have incorporated cleaner and less impactful approaches to parameterized types. It's not impossible to imagine such a language becoming a successor to Java, because it takes exactly the approach that C++ did with C: Use what's there and improve upon it.

Further reading

The introductory document for generics is *Generics in the Java Programming Language*, by Gilad Bracha, located at *http://java.sun.com/j2se/1.5/pdf/generics-tutorial.pdf*.

Angelika Langer's *Java Generics FAQs* is a very helpful resource, located at *www.angelikalanger.com/GenericsFAQ/JavaGenericsFAQ.html*.

You can find out more about wildcards in *Adding Wildcards to the Java Programming Language*, by Torgerson, Ernst, Hansen, von der Ahe, Bracha and Gafter, located at *www.jot.fm/issues/issue_2004_12/article5*.

Solutions to selected exercises can be found in the electronic document *The Thinking in Java Annotated Solution Guide*, available for sale from *www.MindView.net*.

Arrays

At the end of the *Initialization & Cleanup* chapter, you learned how to define and initialize an array.

The simple view of arrays is that you create and populate them, you select elements from them using **int** indexes, and they don't change their size. Most of the time that's all you need to know, but sometimes you need to perform more sophisticated operations on arrays, and you may also need to evaluate the use of an array vs. a more flexible container. This chapter will show you how to think about arrays in more depth.

Why arrays are special

There are a number of other ways to hold objects, so what makes an array special?

There are three issues that distinguish arrays from other types of containers: efficiency, type, and the ability to hold primitives. The array is Java's most efficient way to store and randomly access a sequence of object references. The array is a simple linear sequence, which makes element access fast. The cost of this speed is that the size of an array object is fixed and cannot be changed for the lifetime of that array. You might suggest an **ArrayList** (from *Holding Your Objects*), which will automatically allocate more space, creating a new one and moving all the references from the old one to the new one. Although you should generally prefer an **ArrayList** to an array, this flexibility has overhead, so an **ArrayList** is measurably less efficient than an array.

Both arrays and containers guarantee that you can't abuse them. Whether you're using an array or a container, you'll get a **RuntimeException** if you exceed the bounds, indicating a programmer error.

Before generics, the other container classes dealt with objects as if they had no specific type. That is, they treated them as type **Object**, the root class of all classes in Java. Arrays are superior to pre-generic containers because you create an array to hold a specific type. This means that you get compile-time type checking to prevent you from inserting the wrong type or mistaking the type that you're extracting. Of course, Java will prevent you from sending an inappropriate message to an object at either compile time or run time. So it's not riskier one way or the other; it's just nicer if the compiler points it out to you, and there's less likelihood that the end user will get surprised by an exception.

An array can hold primitives, whereas a pre-generic container could not. With generics, however, containers can specify and check the type of objects they hold, and with autoboxing containers can act as if they are able to hold primitives, since the conversion is automatic. Here's an example that compares arrays with generic containers:

```java
//: arrays/ContainerComparison.java
import java.util.*;
import static net.mindview.util.Print.*;

class BerylliumSphere {
  private static long counter;
  private final long id = counter++;
  public String toString() { return "Sphere " + id; }
}

public class ContainerComparison {
  public static void main(String[] args) {
    BerylliumSphere[] spheres = new BerylliumSphere[10];
    for(int i = 0; i < 5; i++)
      spheres[i] = new BerylliumSphere();
    print(Arrays.toString(spheres));
    print(spheres[4]);

    List<BerylliumSphere> sphereList =
      new ArrayList<BerylliumSphere>();
    for(int i = 0; i < 5; i++)
      sphereList.add(new BerylliumSphere());
    print(sphereList);
    print(sphereList.get(4));

    int[] integers = { 0, 1, 2, 3, 4, 5 };
    print(Arrays.toString(integers));
    print(integers[4]);

    List<Integer> intList = new ArrayList<Integer>(
      Arrays.asList(0, 1, 2, 3, 4, 5));
    intList.add(97);
```

```
        print(intList);
        print(intList.get(4));
    }
} /* Output:
[Sphere 0, Sphere 1, Sphere 2, Sphere 3, Sphere 4, null,
null, null, null, null]
Sphere 4
[Sphere 5, Sphere 6, Sphere 7, Sphere 8, Sphere 9]
Sphere 9
[0, 1, 2, 3, 4, 5]
4
[0, 1, 2, 3, 4, 5, 97]
4
*///:~
```

Both ways of holding objects are type-checked, and the only apparent difference is that arrays use **[ ]** for accessing elements, and a **List** uses methods such as **add( )** and **get( )**. The similarity between arrays and the **ArrayList** is intentional, so that it's conceptually easy to switch between the two. But as you saw in the *Holding Your Objects* chapter, containers have significantly more functionality than arrays.

With the advent of autoboxing, containers are nearly as easy to use for primitives as arrays. The only remaining advantage to arrays is efficiency. However, when you're solving a more general problem, arrays can be too restrictive, and in those cases you use a container class.

Arrays are first-class objects

Regardless of what type of array you're working with, the array identifier is actually a reference to a true object that's created on the heap. This is the object that holds the references to the other objects, and it can be created either implicitly, as part of the array initialization syntax, or explicitly with a **new** expression. Part of the array object (in fact, the only field or method you can access) is the read-only **length** member that tells you how many elements can be stored in that array object. The '**[ ]**' syntax is the only other access that you have to the array object.

The following example summarizes the various ways that an array can be initialized, and how the array references can be assigned to different array objects. It also shows that arrays of objects and arrays of primitives are almost identical in their use. The only difference is that arrays of objects hold references, but arrays of primitives hold the primitive values directly.

```java
//: arrays/ArrayOptions.java
// Initialization & re-assignment of arrays.
import java.util.*;
import static net.mindview.util.Print.*;

public class ArrayOptions {
  public static void main(String[] args) {
    // Arrays of objects:
    BerylliumSphere[] a; // Local uninitialized variable
    BerylliumSphere[] b = new BerylliumSphere[5];
    // The references inside the array are
    // automatically initialized to null:
    print("b: " + Arrays.toString(b));
    BerylliumSphere[] c = new BerylliumSphere[4];
    for(int i = 0; i < c.length; i++)
      if(c[i] == null) // Can test for null reference
        c[i] = new BerylliumSphere();
    // Aggregate initialization:
    BerylliumSphere[] d = { new BerylliumSphere(),
      new BerylliumSphere(), new BerylliumSphere()
    };
    // Dynamic aggregate initialization:
    a = new BerylliumSphere[]{
      new BerylliumSphere(), new BerylliumSphere(),
    };
    // (Trailing comma is optional in both cases)
    print("a.length = " + a.length);
    print("b.length = " + b.length);
    print("c.length = " + c.length);
    print("d.length = " + d.length);
    a = d;
    print("a.length = " + a.length);

    // Arrays of primitives:
    int[] e; // Null reference
    int[] f = new int[5];
    // The primitives inside the array are
    // automatically initialized to zero:
    print("f: " + Arrays.toString(f));
    int[] g = new int[4];
    for(int i = 0; i < g.length; i++)
```

```
        g[i] = i*i;
    int[] h = { 11, 47, 93 };
    // Compile error: variable e not initialized:
    //!print("e.length = " + e.length);
    print("f.length = " + f.length);
    print("g.length = " + g.length);
    print("h.length = " + h.length);
    e = h;
    print("e.length = " + e.length);
    e = new int[]{ 1, 2 };
    print("e.length = " + e.length);
  }
} /* Output:
b: [null, null, null, null, null]
a.length = 2
b.length = 5
c.length = 4
d.length = 3
a.length = 3
f: [0, 0, 0, 0, 0]
f.length = 5
g.length = 4
h.length = 3
e.length = 3
e.length = 2
*///:~
```

The array **a** is an uninitialized local variable, and the compiler prevents you
from doing anything with this reference until you've properly initialized it.
The array **b** is initialized to point to an array of **BerylliumSphere**
references, but no actual **BerylliumSphere** objects are ever placed in that
array. However, you can still ask what the size of the array is, since **b** is
pointing to a legitimate object. This brings up a slight drawback: You can't
find out how many elements are actually *in* the array, since **length** tells you
only how many elements *can* be placed in the array; that is, the size of the
array object, not the number of elements it actually holds. However, when an
array object is created, its references are automatically initialized to **null**, so
you can see whether a particular array slot has an object in it by checking to
see whether it's **null**. Similarly, an array of primitives is automatically
initialized to zero for numeric types, **(char)0** for **char**, and **false** for
boolean.

Array **c** shows the creation of the array object followed by the assignment of **BerylliumSphere** objects to all the slots in the array. Array **d** shows the "aggregate initialization" syntax that causes the array object to be created (implicitly with **new** on the heap, just like for array **c**) *and* initialized with **BerylliumSphere** objects, all in one statement.

The next array initialization can be thought of as a "dynamic aggregate initialization." The aggregate initialization used by **d** must be used at the point of **d**'s definition, but with the second syntax you can create and initialize an array object anywhere. For example, suppose **hide( )** is a method that takes an array of **BerylliumSphere** objects. You could call it by saying:

```
hide(d);
```

but you can also dynamically create the array you want to pass as the argument:

```
hide(new BerylliumSphere[]{ new BerylliumSphere(),
  new BerylliumSphere() });
```

In many situations this syntax provides a more convenient way to write code.

The expression:

```
a = d;
```

shows how you can take a reference that's attached to one array object and assign it to another array object, just as you can do with any other type of object reference. Now both **a** and **d** are pointing to the same array object on the heap.

The second part of **ArrayOptions.java** shows that primitive arrays work just like object arrays *except* that primitive arrays hold the primitive values directly.

Exercise 1: (2) Create a method that takes an array of **BerylliumSphere** as an argument. Call the method, creating the argument dynamically. Demonstrate that ordinary aggregate array initialization doesn't work in this case. Discover the only situations where ordinary aggregate array initialization works, and where dynamic aggregate initialization is redundant.

Returning an array

Suppose you're writing a method and you don't want to return just one thing, but a whole bunch of things. Languages like C and C++ make this difficult because you can't just return an array, only a pointer to an array. This introduces problems because it becomes messy to control the lifetime of the array, which leads to memory leaks.

In Java, you just return the array. You never worry about responsibility for that array—it will be around as long as you need it, and the garbage collector will clean it up when you're done.

As an example, consider returning an array of **String**:

```
//: arrays/IceCream.java
// Returning arrays from methods.
import java.util.*;

public class IceCream {
  private static Random rand = new Random(47);
  static final String[] FLAVORS = {
    "Chocolate", "Strawberry", "Vanilla Fudge Swirl",
    "Mint Chip", "Mocha Almond Fudge", "Rum Raisin",
    "Praline Cream", "Mud Pie"
  };
  public static String[] flavorSet(int n) {
    if(n > FLAVORS.length)
      throw new IllegalArgumentException("Set too big");
    String[] results = new String[n];
    boolean[] picked = new boolean[FLAVORS.length];
    for(int i = 0; i < n; i++) {
      int t;
      do
        t = rand.nextInt(FLAVORS.length);
      while(picked[t]);
      results[i] = FLAVORS[t];
      picked[t] = true;
    }
    return results;
  }
  public static void main(String[] args) {
    for(int i = 0; i < 7; i++)
      System.out.println(Arrays.toString(flavorSet(3)));
  }
```

```
} /* Output:
[Rum Raisin, Mint Chip, Mocha Almond Fudge]
[Chocolate, Strawberry, Mocha Almond Fudge]
[Strawberry, Mint Chip, Mocha Almond Fudge]
[Rum Raisin, Vanilla Fudge Swirl, Mud Pie]
[Vanilla Fudge Swirl, Chocolate, Mocha Almond Fudge]
[Praline Cream, Strawberry, Mocha Almond Fudge]
[Mocha Almond Fudge, Strawberry, Mint Chip]
*///:~
```

The method **flavorSet( )** creates an array of **String** called **results**. The size of this array is **n**, determined by the argument that you pass into the method. Then it proceeds to choose flavors randomly from the array **FLAVORS** and place them into **results**, which it returns. Returning an array is just like returning any other object—it's a reference. It's not important that the array was created within **flavorSet( )**, or that the array was created anyplace else, for that matter. The garbage collector takes care of cleaning up the array when you're done with it, and the array will persist for as long as you need it.

As an aside, notice that when **flavorSet( )** chooses flavors randomly, it ensures that a particular choice hasn't already been selected. This is performed in a **do** loop that keeps making random choices until it finds one not already in the **picked** array. (Of course, a **String** comparison also could have been performed to see if the random choice was already in the **results** array.) If it's successful, it adds the entry and finds the next one (**i** gets incremented).

You can see from the output that **flavorSet( )** chooses the flavors in a random order each time.

Exercise 2: (1) Write a method that takes an **int** argument and returns an array of that size, filled with **BerylliumSphere** objects.

Multidimensional arrays

You can easily create multidimensional arrays. For a multidimensional array of primitives, you delimit each vector in the array by using curly braces:

```
//: arrays/MultidimensionalPrimitiveArray.java
// Creating multidimensional arrays.
import java.util.*;

public class MultidimensionalPrimitiveArray {
```

```
    public static void main(String[] args) {
      int[][] a = {
        { 1, 2, 3, },
        { 4, 5, 6, },
      };
      System.out.println(Arrays.deepToString(a));
    }
} /* Output:
[[1, 2, 3], [4, 5, 6]]
*///:~
```

Each nested set of curly braces moves you into the next level of the array.

This example uses the Java SE5 **Arrays.deepToString( )** method, which turns multidimensional arrays into **String**s, as you can see from the output.

You can also allocate an array using **new**. Here's a three-dimensional array allocated in a **new** expression:

```
//: arrays/ThreeDWithNew.java
import java.util.*;

public class ThreeDWithNew {
  public static void main(String[] args) {
    // 3-D array with fixed length:
    int[][][] a = new int[2][2][4];
    System.out.println(Arrays.deepToString(a));
  }
} /* Output:
[[[0, 0, 0, 0], [0, 0, 0, 0]], [[0, 0, 0, 0], [0, 0, 0,
0]]]
*///:~
```

You can see that primitive array values are automatically initialized if you don't give them an explicit initialization value. Arrays of objects are initialized to **null**.

Each vector in the arrays that make up the matrix can be of any length (this is called a *ragged array*):

```
//: arrays/RaggedArray.java
import java.util.*;

public class RaggedArray {
  public static void main(String[] args) {
```

```
    Random rand = new Random(47);
    // 3-D array with varied-length vectors:
    int[][][] a = new int[rand.nextInt(7)][][];
    for(int i = 0; i < a.length; i++) {
      a[i] = new int[rand.nextInt(5)][];
      for(int j = 0; j < a[i].length; j++)
        a[i][j] = new int[rand.nextInt(5)];
    }
    System.out.println(Arrays.deepToString(a));
  }
} /* Output:
[[], [[0], [0], [0, 0, 0, 0]], [[], [0, 0], [0, 0]], [[0,
0, 0], [0], [0, 0, 0, 0]], [[0, 0, 0], [0, 0, 0], [0], []],
[[0], [], [0]]]
*///:~
```

The first **new** creates an array with a random-length first element and the rest undetermined. The second **new** inside the **for** loop fills out the elements but leaves the third index undetermined until you hit the third **new**.

You can deal with arrays of non-primitive objects in a similar fashion. Here, you can see how to collect many **new** expressions with curly braces:

```
//: arrays/MultidimensionalObjectArrays.java
import java.util.*;

public class MultidimensionalObjectArrays {
  public static void main(String[] args) {
    BerylliumSphere[][] spheres = {
      { new BerylliumSphere(), new BerylliumSphere() },
      { new BerylliumSphere(), new BerylliumSphere(),
        new BerylliumSphere(), new BerylliumSphere() },
      { new BerylliumSphere(), new BerylliumSphere(),
        new BerylliumSphere(), new BerylliumSphere(),
        new BerylliumSphere(), new BerylliumSphere(),
        new BerylliumSphere(), new BerylliumSphere() },
    };
    System.out.println(Arrays.deepToString(spheres));
  }
} /* Output:
[[Sphere 0, Sphere 1], [Sphere 2, Sphere 3, Sphere 4,
Sphere 5], [Sphere 6, Sphere 7, Sphere 8, Sphere 9, Sphere
10, Sphere 11, Sphere 12, Sphere 13]]
*///:~
```

You can see that **spheres** is another ragged array, where the length of each list of objects is different.

Autoboxing also works with array initializers:

```
//: arrays/AutoboxingArrays.java
import java.util.*;

public class AutoboxingArrays {
  public static void main(String[] args) {
    Integer[][] a = { // Autoboxing:
      { 1, 2, 3, 4, 5, 6, 7, 8, 9, 10 },
      { 21, 22, 23, 24, 25, 26, 27, 28, 29, 30 },
      { 51, 52, 53, 54, 55, 56, 57, 58, 59, 60 },
      { 71, 72, 73, 74, 75, 76, 77, 78, 79, 80 },
    };
    System.out.println(Arrays.deepToString(a));
  }
} /* Output:
[[1, 2, 3, 4, 5, 6, 7, 8, 9, 10], [21, 22, 23, 24, 25, 26,
27, 28, 29, 30], [51, 52, 53, 54, 55, 56, 57, 58, 59, 60],
[71, 72, 73, 74, 75, 76, 77, 78, 79, 80]]
*///:~
```

Here's how an array of non-primitive objects can be built up piece-by-piece:

```
//: arrays/AssemblingMultidimensionalArrays.java
// Creating multidimensional arrays.
import java.util.*;

public class AssemblingMultidimensionalArrays {
  public static void main(String[] args) {
    Integer[][] a;
    a = new Integer[3][];
    for(int i = 0; i < a.length; i++) {
      a[i] = new Integer[3];
      for(int j = 0; j < a[i].length; j++)
        a[i][j] = i * j; // Autoboxing
    }
    System.out.println(Arrays.deepToString(a));
  }
} /* Output:
[[0, 0, 0], [0, 1, 2], [0, 2, 4]]
*///:~
```

The **i*j** is only there to put an interesting value into the **Integer**.

The **Arrays.deepToString( )** method works with both primitive arrays and object arrays:

```
//: arrays/MultiDimWrapperArray.java
// Multidimensional arrays of "wrapper" objects.
import java.util.*;

public class MultiDimWrapperArray {
  public static void main(String[] args) {
    Integer[][] a1 = { // Autoboxing
      { 1, 2, 3, },
      { 4, 5, 6, },
    };
    Double[][][] a2 = { // Autoboxing
      { { 1.1, 2.2 }, { 3.3, 4.4 } },
      { { 5.5, 6.6 }, { 7.7, 8.8 } },
      { { 9.9, 1.2 }, { 2.3, 3.4 } },
    };
    String[][] a3 = {
      { "The", "Quick", "Sly", "Fox" },
      { "Jumped", "Over" },
      { "The", "Lazy", "Brown", "Dog", "and", "friend" },
    };
    System.out.println("a1: " + Arrays.deepToString(a1));
    System.out.println("a2: " + Arrays.deepToString(a2));
    System.out.println("a3: " + Arrays.deepToString(a3));
  }
} /* Output:
a1: [[1, 2, 3], [4, 5, 6]]
a2: [[[1.1, 2.2], [3.3, 4.4]], [[5.5, 6.6], [7.7, 8.8]],
[[9.9, 1.2], [2.3, 3.4]]]
a3: [[The, Quick, Sly, Fox], [Jumped, Over], [The, Lazy,
Brown, Dog, and, friend]]
*///:~
```

Again, in the **Integer** and **Double** arrays, Java SE5 autoboxing creates the wrapper objects for you.

Exercise 3: (4) Write a method that creates and initializes a two-dimensional array of **double**. The size of the array is determined by the arguments of the method, and the initialization values are a range determined by beginning and ending values that are also arguments of the method. Create a second method that will print the array generated by the first method. In **main( )** test the methods by creating and printing several different sizes of arrays.

Exercise 4: (2) Repeat the previous exercise for a three-dimensional array.

Exercise 5: (1) Demonstrate that multidimensional arrays of non-primitive types are automatically initialized to **null**.

Exercise 6: (1) Write a method that takes two **int** arguments, indicating the two sizes of a 2-D array. The method should create and fill a 2-D array of **BerylliumSphere** according to the size arguments.

Exercise 7: (1) Repeat the previous exercise for a 3-D array.

Arrays and generics

In general, arrays and generics do not mix well. You cannot instantiate arrays of parameterized types:

```
Peel<Banana>[] peels = new Peel<Banana>[10]; // Illegal
```

Erasure removes the parameter type information, and arrays must know the exact type that they hold, in order to enforce type safety.

However, you can parameterize the type of the array itself:

```
//: arrays/ParameterizedArrayType.java

class ClassParameter<T> {
  public T[] f(T[] arg) { return arg; }
}

class MethodParameter {
  public static <T> T[] f(T[] arg) { return arg; }
}

public class ParameterizedArrayType {
  public static void main(String[] args) {
    Integer[] ints = { 1, 2, 3, 4, 5 };
    Double[] doubles = { 1.1, 2.2, 3.3, 4.4, 5.5 };
    Integer[] ints2 =
      new ClassParameter<Integer>().f(ints);
    Double[] doubles2 =
      new ClassParameter<Double>().f(doubles);
```

```
      ints2 = MethodParameter.f(ints);
      doubles2 = MethodParameter.f(doubles);
  }
} ///:~
```

Note the convenience of using a parameterized method instead of a parameterized class: You don't have to instantiate a class with a parameter for each different type you need to apply it to, and you can make it **static**. Of course, you can't always choose to use a parameterized method instead of a parameterized class, but it can be preferable.

As it turns out, it's not precisely correct to say that you cannot create arrays of generic types. True, the compiler won't let you *instantiate* an array of a generic type. However, it will let you create a reference to such an array. For example:

```
    List<String>[] ls;
```

This passes through the compiler without complaint. And although you cannot create an actual array object that holds generics, you can create an array of the non-generified type and cast it:

```
//: arrays/ArrayOfGenerics.java
// It is possible to create arrays of generics.
import java.util.*;

public class ArrayOfGenerics {
  @SuppressWarnings("unchecked")
  public static void main(String[] args) {
    List<String>[] ls;
    List[] la = new List[10];
    ls = (List<String>[])la; // "Unchecked" warning
    ls[0] = new ArrayList<String>();
    // Compile-time checking produces an error:
    //! ls[1] = new ArrayList<Integer>();

    // The problem: List<String> is a subtype of Object
    Object[] objects = ls; // So assignment is OK
    // Compiles and runs without complaint:
    objects[1] = new ArrayList<Integer>();

    // However, if your needs are straightforward it is
    // possible to create an array of generics, albeit
    // with an "unchecked" warning:
```

```
    List<BerylliumSphere>[] spheres =
      (List<BerylliumSphere>[])new List[10];
    for(int i = 0; i < spheres.length; i++)
      spheres[i] = new ArrayList<BerylliumSphere>();
  }
} ///:~
```

Once you have a reference to a **List<String>[]**, you can see that you get some compile-time checking. The problem is that arrays are covariant, so a **List<String>[]** is also an **Object[]**, and you can use this to assign an **ArrayList<Integer>** into your array, with no error at either compile time or run time.

If you know you're not going to upcast and your needs are relatively simple, however, it is possible to create an array of generics, which will provide basic compile-time type checking. However, a generic container will virtually always be a better choice than an array of generics.

In general you'll find that generics are effective at the *boundaries* of a class or method. In the interiors, erasure usually makes generics unusable. So you cannot, for example, create an array of a generic type:

```
//: arrays/ArrayOfGenericType.java
// Arrays of generic types won't compile.

public class ArrayOfGenericType<T> {
  T[] array; // OK
  @SuppressWarnings("unchecked")
  public ArrayOfGenericType(int size) {
    //! array = new T[size]; // Illegal
    array = (T[])new Object[size]; // "unchecked" Warning
  }
  // Illegal:
  //! public <U> U[] makeArray() { return new U[10]; }
} ///:~
```

Erasure gets in the way again—this example attempts to create arrays of types that have been erased, and are thus unknown types. Notice that you *can* create an array of **Object**, and cast it, but without the **@SuppressWarnings** annotation you get an "unchecked" warning at compile time because the array doesn't really hold or dynamically check for type **T**. That is, if I create a **String[]**, Java will enforce at both compile time and run time that I can only place **String** objects in that array. However, if I create an **Object[]**, I can put anything into that array except primitive types.

Exercise 8: (1) Demonstrate the assertions in the previous paragraph.

Exercise 9: (3) Create the classes necessary for the **Peel<Banana>** example and show that the compiler doesn't accept it. Fix the problem using an **ArrayList**.

Exercise 10: (2) Modify **ArrayOfGenerics.java** to use containers instead of arrays. Show that you can eliminate the compile-time warnings.

Creating test data

When experimenting with arrays, and with programs in general, it's helpful to be able to easily generate arrays filled with test data. The tools in this section will fill an array with values or objects.

Arrays.fill()

The Java standard library **Arrays** class has a rather trivial **fill( )** method: It only duplicates a single value into each location, or in the case of objects, copies the same reference into each location. Here's an example:

```
//: arrays/FillingArrays.java
// Using Arrays.fill()
import java.util.*;
import static net.mindview.util.Print.*;

public class FillingArrays {
  public static void main(String[] args) {
    int size = 6;
    boolean[] a1 = new boolean[size];
    byte[] a2 = new byte[size];
    char[] a3 = new char[size];
    short[] a4 = new short[size];
    int[] a5 = new int[size];
    long[] a6 = new long[size];
    float[] a7 = new float[size];
    double[] a8 = new double[size];
    String[] a9 = new String[size];
    Arrays.fill(a1, true);
    print("a1 = " + Arrays.toString(a1));
    Arrays.fill(a2, (byte)11);
```

```
        print("a2 = " + Arrays.toString(a2));
        Arrays.fill(a3, 'x');
        print("a3 = " + Arrays.toString(a3));
        Arrays.fill(a4, (short)17);
        print("a4 = " + Arrays.toString(a4));
        Arrays.fill(a5, 19);
        print("a5 = " + Arrays.toString(a5));
        Arrays.fill(a6, 23);
        print("a6 = " + Arrays.toString(a6));
        Arrays.fill(a7, 29);
        print("a7 = " + Arrays.toString(a7));
        Arrays.fill(a8, 47);
        print("a8 = " + Arrays.toString(a8));
        Arrays.fill(a9, "Hello");
        print("a9 = " + Arrays.toString(a9));
        // Manipulating ranges:
        Arrays.fill(a9, 3, 5, "World");
        print("a9 = " + Arrays.toString(a9));
    }
} /* Output:
a1 = [true, true, true, true, true, true]
a2 = [11, 11, 11, 11, 11, 11]
a3 = [x, x, x, x, x, x]
a4 = [17, 17, 17, 17, 17, 17]
a5 = [19, 19, 19, 19, 19, 19]
a6 = [23, 23, 23, 23, 23, 23]
a7 = [29.0, 29.0, 29.0, 29.0, 29.0, 29.0]
a8 = [47.0, 47.0, 47.0, 47.0, 47.0, 47.0]
a9 = [Hello, Hello, Hello, Hello, Hello, Hello]
a9 = [Hello, Hello, Hello, World, World, Hello]
*///:~
```

You can either fill the entire array or, as the last two statements show, fill a range of elements. But since you can only call **Arrays.fill( )** with a single data value, the results are not especially useful.

Data **Generator**s

To create more interesting arrays of data, but in a flexible fashion, we'll use the **Generator** concept that was introduced in the *Generics* chapter. If a tool uses a **Generator**, you can produce any kind of data via your choice of

Generator (this is an example of the *Strategy* design pattern—each different **Generator** represents a different strategy[1]).

This section will supply some **Generator**s, and as you've seen before, you can easily define your own.

First, here's a basic set of counting generators for all primitive wrapper types, and for **String**s. The generator classes are nested within the **CountingGenerator** class so that they may use the same name as the object types they are generating; for example, a generator that creates **Integer** objects would be created with the expression **new CountingGenerator.Integer( )**:

```
//: net/mindview/util/CountingGenerator.java
// Simple generator implementations.
package net.mindview.util;

public class CountingGenerator {
  public static class
  Boolean implements Generator<java.lang.Boolean> {
    private boolean value = false;
    public java.lang.Boolean next() {
      value = !value; // Just flips back and forth
      return value;
    }
  }
  public static class
  Byte implements Generator<java.lang.Byte> {
    private byte value = 0;
    public java.lang.Byte next() { return value++; }
  }
  static char[] chars = ("abcdefghijklmnopqrstuvwxyz" +
    "ABCDEFGHIJKLMNOPQRSTUVWXYZ").toCharArray();
  public static class
  Character implements Generator<java.lang.Character> {
    int index = -1;
    public java.lang.Character next() {
      index = (index + 1) % chars.length;
```

---

[1] Although this is a place where things are a bit fuzzy. You could also make an argument that a **Generator** represents the *Command* pattern. However, I think that the task is to fill an array, and the **Generator** fulfills part of that task, so it's more strategy-like than command-like.

```
      return chars[index];
    }
  }
  public static class
  String implements Generator<java.lang.String> {
    private int length = 7;
    Generator<java.lang.Character> cg = new Character();
    public String() {}
    public String(int length) { this.length = length; }
    public java.lang.String next() {
      char[] buf = new char[length];
      for(int i = 0; i < length; i++)
        buf[i] = cg.next();
      return new java.lang.String(buf);
    }
  }
  public static class
  Short implements Generator<java.lang.Short> {
    private short value = 0;
    public java.lang.Short next() { return value++; }
  }
  public static class
  Integer implements Generator<java.lang.Integer> {
    private int value = 0;
    public java.lang.Integer next() { return value++; }
  }
  public static class
  Long implements Generator<java.lang.Long> {
    private long value = 0;
    public java.lang.Long next() { return value++; }
  }
  public static class
  Float implements Generator<java.lang.Float> {
    private float value = 0;
    public java.lang.Float next() {
      float result = value;
      value += 1.0;
      return result;
    }
  }
  public static class
  Double implements Generator<java.lang.Double> {
    private double value = 0.0;
    public java.lang.Double next() {
```

```
        double result = value;
        value += 1.0;
        return result;
    }
  }
} ///:~
```

Each class implements some meaning of "counting." In the case of **CountingGenerator.Character**, this is just the upper and lowercase letters repeated over and over. The **CountingGenerator.String** class uses **CountingGenerator.Character** to fill an array of characters, which is then turned into a **String**. The size of the array is determined by the constructor argument. Notice that **CountingGenerator.String** uses a basic **Generator<java.lang.Character>** instead of a specific reference to **CountingGenerator.Character**. Later, this generator can be replaced to produce **RandomGenerator.String** in **RandomGenerator.java**.

Here's a test tool that uses reflection with the nested **Generator** idiom, so that it can be used to test any set of **Generator**s that follow this form:

```
//: arrays/GeneratorsTest.java
import net.mindview.util.*;

public class GeneratorsTest {
  public static int size = 10;
  public static void test(Class<?> surroundingClass) {
    for(Class<?> type : surroundingClass.getClasses()) {
      System.out.print(type.getSimpleName() + ": ");
      try {
        Generator<?> g = (Generator<?>)type.newInstance();
        for(int i = 0; i < size; i++)
          System.out.printf(g.next() + " ");
        System.out.println();
      } catch(Exception e) {
        throw new RuntimeException(e);
      }
    }
  }
  public static void main(String[] args) {
    test(CountingGenerator.class);
  }
} /* Output:
Double: 0.0 1.0 2.0 3.0 4.0 5.0 6.0 7.0 8.0 9.0
Float: 0.0 1.0 2.0 3.0 4.0 5.0 6.0 7.0 8.0 9.0
```

```
Long: 0 1 2 3 4 5 6 7 8 9
Integer: 0 1 2 3 4 5 6 7 8 9
Short: 0 1 2 3 4 5 6 7 8 9
String: abcdefg hijklmn opqrstu vwxyzAB CDEFGHI JKLMNOP
QRSTUVW XYZabcd efghijk lmnopqr
Character: a b c d e f g h i j
Byte: 0 1 2 3 4 5 6 7 8 9
Boolean: true false true false true false true false true
false
*///:~
```

This assumes that the class under test contains a set of nested **Generator** objects, each of which has a default constructor (one without arguments). The reflection method **getClasses( )** produces all the nested classes. The **test( )** method then creates an instance of each of these generators, and prints the result produced by calling **next( )** ten times.

Here is a set of **Generator**s that use the random number generator. Because the **Random** constructor is initialized with a constant value, the output is repeatable each time you run a program using one of these **Generator**s:

```
//: net/mindview/util/RandomGenerator.java
// Generators that produce random values.
package net.mindview.util;
import java.util.*;

public class RandomGenerator {
  private static Random r = new Random(47);
  public static class
  Boolean implements Generator<java.lang.Boolean> {
    public java.lang.Boolean next() {
      return r.nextBoolean();
    }
  }
  public static class
  Byte implements Generator<java.lang.Byte> {
    public java.lang.Byte next() {
      return (byte)r.nextInt();
    }
  }
  public static class
  Character implements Generator<java.lang.Character> {
    public java.lang.Character next() {
      return CountingGenerator.chars[
```

```java
          r.nextInt(CountingGenerator.chars.length)];
    }
  }
  public static class
  String extends CountingGenerator.String {
    // Plug in the random Character generator:
    { cg = new Character(); } // Instance initializer
    public String() {}
    public String(int length) { super(length); }
  }
  public static class
  Short implements Generator<java.lang.Short> {
    public java.lang.Short next() {
      return (short)r.nextInt();
    }
  }
  public static class
  Integer implements Generator<java.lang.Integer> {
    private int mod = 10000;
    public Integer() {}
    public Integer(int modulo) { mod = modulo; }
    public java.lang.Integer next() {
      return r.nextInt(mod);
    }
  }
  public static class
  Long implements Generator<java.lang.Long> {
    private int mod = 10000;
    public Long() {}
    public Long(int modulo) { mod = modulo; }
    public java.lang.Long next() {
      return new java.lang.Long(r.nextInt(mod));
    }
  }
  public static class
  Float implements Generator<java.lang.Float> {
    public java.lang.Float next() {
      // Trim all but the first two decimal places:
      int trimmed = Math.round(r.nextFloat() * 100);
      return ((float)trimmed) / 100;
    }
  }
  public static class
  Double implements Generator<java.lang.Double> {
```

```
      public java.lang.Double next() {
        long trimmed = Math.round(r.nextDouble() * 100);
        return ((double)trimmed) / 100;
      }
    }
  } ///:~
```

You can see that **RandomGenerator.String** inherits from **CountingGenerator.String** and simply plugs in the new **Character** generator.

To generate numbers that aren't too large, **RandomGenerator.Integer** defaults to a modulus of 10,000, but the overloaded constructor allows you to choose a smaller value. The same approach is used for **RandomGenerator.Long**. For the **Float** and **Double Generator**s, the values after the decimal point are trimmed.

We can reuse **GeneratorsTest** to test **RandomGenerator**:

```
//: arrays/RandomGeneratorsTest.java
import net.mindview.util.*;

public class RandomGeneratorsTest {
  public static void main(String[] args) {
    GeneratorsTest.test(RandomGenerator.class);
  }
} /* Output:
Double: 0.73 0.53 0.16 0.19 0.52 0.27 0.26 0.05 0.8 0.76
Float: 0.53 0.16 0.53 0.4 0.49 0.25 0.8 0.11 0.02 0.8
Long: 7674 8804 8950 7826 4322 896 8033 2984 2344 5810
Integer: 8303 3141 7138 6012 9966 8689 7185 6992 5746 3976
Short: 3358 20592 284 26791 12834 -8092 13656 29324 -1423
5327
String: bkInaMe sbtWHkj UrUkZPg wsqPzDy CyRFJQA HxxHvHq
XumcXZJ oogoYWM NvqeuTp nXsgqia
Character: x x E A J J m z M s
Byte: -60 -17 55 -14 -5 115 39 -37 79 115
Boolean: false true false false true true true true true
true
*///:~
```

You can change the number of values produced by changing the **GeneratorsTest.size** value, which is **public**.

Creating arrays from **Generator**s

In order to take a **Generator** and produce an array, we need two conversion tools. The first one uses any **Generator** to produce an array of **Object** subtypes. To cope with the problem of primitives, the second tool takes any array of primitive wrapper types and produces the associated array of primitives.

The first tool has two options, represented by an overloaded **static** method, **array( )**. The first version of the method takes an existing array and fills it using a **Generator**, and the second version takes a **Class** object, a **Generator**, and the desired number of elements, and creates a new array, again filling it using the **Generator**. Notice that this tool only produces arrays of **Object** subtypes and cannot create primitive arrays:

```
//: net/mindview/util/Generated.java
package net.mindview.util;

public class Generated {
  // Fill an existing array:
  public static <T> T[] array(T[] a, Generator<T> gen) {
    return new CollectionData<T>(gen, a.length).toArray(a);
  }
  // Create a new array:
  @SuppressWarnings("unchecked")
  public static <T> T[] array(Class<T> type,
      Generator<T> gen, int size) {
    T[] a =
      (T[])java.lang.reflect.Array.newInstance(type, size);
    return new CollectionData<T>(gen, size).toArray(a);
  }
} ///:~
```

The **CollectionData** class will be defined in the *Containers in Depth* chapter. It creates a **Collection** object filled with elements produced by the **Generator gen**. The number of elements is determined by the second constructor argument. All **Collection** subtypes have a **toArray( )** method that will fill the argument array with the elements from the **Collection**.

The second method uses reflection to dynamically create a new array of the appropriate type and size. This is then filled using the same technique as the first method.

We can test **Generated** using one of the **CountingGenerator** classes defined in the previous section:

```
//: arrays/TestGenerated.java
import java.util.*;
import net.mindview.util.*;

public class TestGenerated {
  public static void main(String[] args) {
    Integer[] a = { 9, 8, 7, 6 };
    System.out.println(Arrays.toString(a));
    a = Generated.array(a,new CountingGenerator.Integer());
    System.out.println(Arrays.toString(a));
    Integer[] b = Generated.array(Integer.class,
        new CountingGenerator.Integer(), 15);
    System.out.println(Arrays.toString(b));
  }
} /* Output:
[9, 8, 7, 6]
[0, 1, 2, 3]
[0, 1, 2, 3, 4, 5, 6, 7, 8, 9, 10, 11, 12, 13, 14]
*///:~
```

Even though the array **a** is initialized, those values are overwritten by passing it through **Generated.array( )**, which replaces the values (but leaves the original array in place). The initialization of **b** shows how you can create a filled array from scratch.

Generics don't work with primitives, and we want to use the generators to fill primitive arrays. To solve the problem, we create a converter that takes any array of wrapper objects and converts it to an array of the associated primitive types. Without this tool, we would have to create special case generators for all the primitives.

```
//: net/mindview/util/ConvertTo.java
package net.mindview.util;

public class ConvertTo {
  public static boolean[] primitive(Boolean[] in) {
    boolean[] result = new boolean[in.length];
    for(int i = 0; i < in.length; i++)
      result[i] = in[i]; // Autounboxing
    return result;
  }
```

```java
  public static char[] primitive(Character[] in) {
    char[] result = new char[in.length];
    for(int i = 0; i < in.length; i++)
      result[i] = in[i];
    return result;
  }
  public static byte[] primitive(Byte[] in) {
    byte[] result = new byte[in.length];
    for(int i = 0; i < in.length; i++)
      result[i] = in[i];
    return result;
  }
  public static short[] primitive(Short[] in) {
    short[] result = new short[in.length];
    for(int i = 0; i < in.length; i++)
      result[i] = in[i];
    return result;
  }
  public static int[] primitive(Integer[] in) {
    int[] result = new int[in.length];
    for(int i = 0; i < in.length; i++)
      result[i] = in[i];
    return result;
  }
  public static long[] primitive(Long[] in) {
    long[] result = new long[in.length];
    for(int i = 0; i < in.length; i++)
      result[i] = in[i];
    return result;
  }
  public static float[] primitive(Float[] in) {
    float[] result = new float[in.length];
    for(int i = 0; i < in.length; i++)
      result[i] = in[i];
    return result;
  }
  public static double[] primitive(Double[] in) {
    double[] result = new double[in.length];
    for(int i = 0; i < in.length; i++)
      result[i] = in[i];
    return result;
  }
} ///:~
```

Each version of **primitive( )** creates an appropriate primitive array of the correct length, then copies the elements from the **in** array of wrapper types. Notice that autounboxing takes place in the expression:

```
result[i] = in[i];
```

Here's an example that shows how you can use **ConvertTo** with both versions of **Generated.array( )**:

```
//: arrays/PrimitiveConversionDemonstration.java
import java.util.*;
import net.mindview.util.*;

public class PrimitiveConversionDemonstration {
  public static void main(String[] args) {
    Integer[] a = Generated.array(Integer.class,
        new CountingGenerator.Integer(), 15);
    int[] b = ConvertTo.primitive(a);
    System.out.println(Arrays.toString(b));
    boolean[] c = ConvertTo.primitive(
      Generated.array(Boolean.class,
        new CountingGenerator.Boolean(), 7));
    System.out.println(Arrays.toString(c));
  }
} /* Output:
[0, 1, 2, 3, 4, 5, 6, 7, 8, 9, 10, 11, 12, 13, 14]
[true, false, true, false, true, false, true]
*///:~
```

Finally, here's a program that tests the array generation tools using **RandomGenerator** classes:

```
//: arrays/TestArrayGeneration.java
// Test the tools that use generators to fill arrays.
import java.util.*;
import net.mindview.util.*;
import static net.mindview.util.Print.*;

public class TestArrayGeneration {
  public static void main(String[] args) {
    int size = 6;
    boolean[] a1 = ConvertTo.primitive(Generated.array(
      Boolean.class, new RandomGenerator.Boolean(), size));
    print("a1 = " + Arrays.toString(a1));
    byte[] a2 = ConvertTo.primitive(Generated.array(
```

```
      Byte.class, new RandomGenerator.Byte(), size));
    print("a2 = " + Arrays.toString(a2));
    char[] a3 = ConvertTo.primitive(Generated.array(
      Character.class,
      new RandomGenerator.Character(), size));
    print("a3 = " + Arrays.toString(a3));
    short[] a4 = ConvertTo.primitive(Generated.array(
      Short.class, new RandomGenerator.Short(), size));
    print("a4 = " + Arrays.toString(a4));
    int[] a5 = ConvertTo.primitive(Generated.array(
      Integer.class, new RandomGenerator.Integer(), size));
    print("a5 = " + Arrays.toString(a5));
    long[] a6 = ConvertTo.primitive(Generated.array(
      Long.class, new RandomGenerator.Long(), size));
    print("a6 = " + Arrays.toString(a6));
    float[] a7 = ConvertTo.primitive(Generated.array(
      Float.class, new RandomGenerator.Float(), size));
    print("a7 = " + Arrays.toString(a7));
    double[] a8 = ConvertTo.primitive(Generated.array(
      Double.class, new RandomGenerator.Double(), size));
    print("a8 = " + Arrays.toString(a8));
  }
} /* Output:
a1 = [true, false, true, false, false, true]
a2 = [104, -79, -76, 126, 33, -64]
a3 = [Z, n, T, c, Q, r]
a4 = [-13408, 22612, 15401, 15161, -28466, -12603]
a5 = [7704, 7383, 7706, 575, 8410, 6342]
a6 = [7674, 8804, 8950, 7826, 4322, 896]
a7 = [0.01, 0.2, 0.4, 0.79, 0.27, 0.45]
a8 = [0.16, 0.87, 0.7, 0.66, 0.87, 0.59]
*///:~
```

This also ensures that each version of **ConvertTo.primitive( )** works correctly.

Exercise 11:   (2) Show that autoboxing doesn't work with arrays.

Exercise 12:   (1) Create an initialized array of **double** using **CountingGenerator**. Print the results.

Exercise 13:   (2) Fill a **String** using **CountingGenerator.Character**.

Exercise 14:   (6) Create an array of each primitive type, then fill each array by using **CountingGenerator**. Print each array.

Exercise 15: (2) Modify **ContainerComparison.java** by creating a **Generator** for **BerylliumSphere**, and change **main( )** to use that **Generator** with **Generated.array( )**.

Exercise 16: (3) Starting with **CountingGenerator.java**, create a **SkipGenerator** class that produces new values by incrementing according to a constructor argument. Modify **TestArrayGeneration.java** to show that your new class works correctly.

Exercise 17: (5) Create and test a **Generator** for **BigDecimal**, and ensure that it works with the **Generated** methods.

Arrays utilities

In **java.util**, you'll find the **Arrays** class, which holds a set of **static** utility methods for arrays. There are six basic methods: **equals( )**, to compare two arrays for equality (and a **deepEquals( )** for multidimensional arrays); **fill( )**, which you've seen earlier in this chapter; **sort( )**, to sort an array; **binarySearch( )**, to find an element in a sorted array; **toString( )**, to produce a **String** representation for an array; and **hashCode( )**, to produce the hash value of an array (you'll learn what this means in the *Containers in Depth* chapter). All of these methods are overloaded for all the primitive types and **Object**s. In addition, **Arrays.asList( )** takes any sequence or array and turns it into a **List** container—this method was covered in the *Holding Your Objects* chapter.

Before discussing the **Arrays** methods, there's one other useful method that isn't part of **Arrays**.

Copying an array

The Java standard library provides a **static** method, **System.arraycopy( )**, which can copy arrays far more quickly than if you use a **for** loop to perform the copy by hand. **System.arraycopy( )** is overloaded to handle all types. Here's an example that manipulates arrays of **int**:

```
//: arrays/CopyingArrays.java
// Using System.arraycopy()
import java.util.*;
import static net.mindview.util.Print.*;

public class CopyingArrays {
  public static void main(String[] args) {
```

```
    int[] i = new int[7];
    int[] j = new int[10];
    Arrays.fill(i, 47);
    Arrays.fill(j, 99);
    print("i = " + Arrays.toString(i));
    print("j = " + Arrays.toString(j));
    System.arraycopy(i, 0, j, 0, i.length);
    print("j = " + Arrays.toString(j));
    int[] k = new int[5];
    Arrays.fill(k, 103);
    System.arraycopy(i, 0, k, 0, k.length);
    print("k = " + Arrays.toString(k));
    Arrays.fill(k, 103);
    System.arraycopy(k, 0, i, 0, k.length);
    print("i = " + Arrays.toString(i));
    // Objects:
    Integer[] u = new Integer[10];
    Integer[] v = new Integer[5];
    Arrays.fill(u, new Integer(47));
    Arrays.fill(v, new Integer(99));
    print("u = " + Arrays.toString(u));
    print("v = " + Arrays.toString(v));
    System.arraycopy(v, 0, u, u.length/2, v.length);
    print("u = " + Arrays.toString(u));
  }
} /* Output:
i = [47, 47, 47, 47, 47, 47, 47]
j = [99, 99, 99, 99, 99, 99, 99, 99, 99, 99]
j = [47, 47, 47, 47, 47, 47, 47, 99, 99, 99]
k = [47, 47, 47, 47, 47]
i = [103, 103, 103, 103, 103, 47, 47]
u = [47, 47, 47, 47, 47, 47, 47, 47, 47, 47]
v = [99, 99, 99, 99, 99]
u = [47, 47, 47, 47, 47, 99, 99, 99, 99, 99]
*///:~
```

The arguments to **arraycopy( )** are the source array, the offset into the source array from whence to start copying, the destination array, the offset into the destination array where the copying begins, and the number of elements to copy. Naturally, any violation of the array boundaries will cause an exception.

The example shows that both primitive arrays and object arrays can be copied. However, if you copy arrays of objects, then only the references get copied—there's no duplication of the objects themselves. This is called a *shallow copy* (see the online supplements for this book for more details).

System.arraycopy( ) will not perform autoboxing or autounboxing—the two arrays must be of exactly the same type.

Exercise 18: (3) Create and fill an array of **BerylliumSphere**. Copy this array to a new array and show that it's a shallow copy.

Comparing arrays

Arrays provides the **equals( )** method to compare entire arrays for equality, which is overloaded for all the primitives and for **Object**. To be equal, the arrays must have the same number of elements, and each element must be equivalent to each corresponding element in the other array, using the **equals( )** for each element. (For primitives, that primitive's wrapper class **equals( )** is used; for example, **Integer.equals( )** for **int**.) For example:

```
//: arrays/ComparingArrays.java
// Using Arrays.equals()
import java.util.*;
import static net.mindview.util.Print.*;

public class ComparingArrays {
  public static void main(String[] args) {
    int[] a1 = new int[10];
    int[] a2 = new int[10];
    Arrays.fill(a1, 47);
    Arrays.fill(a2, 47);
    print(Arrays.equals(a1, a2));
    a2[3] = 11;
    print(Arrays.equals(a1, a2));
    String[] s1 = new String[4];
    Arrays.fill(s1, "Hi");
    String[] s2 = { new String("Hi"), new String("Hi"),
      new String("Hi"), new String("Hi") };
    print(Arrays.equals(s1, s2));
  }
} /* Output:
true
false
true
*///:~
```

Originally, **a1** and **a2** are exactly equal, so the output is "true," but then one of the elements is changed, which makes the result "false." In the last case, all the elements of **s1** point to the same object, but **s2** has four unique objects. However, array equality is based on contents (via **Object.equals( )**), so the result is "true."

Exercise 19:   (2) Create a class with an **int** field that's initialized from a constructor argument. Create two arrays of these objects, using identical initialization values for each array, and show that **Arrays.equals( )** says that they are unequal. Add an **equals( )** method to your class to fix the problem.

Exercise 20:   (4) Demonstrate **deepEquals( )** for multidimensional arrays.

Array element comparisons

Sorting must perform comparisons based on the actual type of the object. Of course, one approach is to write a different sorting method for every different type, but such code is not reusable for new types.

A primary goal of programming design is to "separate things that change from things that stay the same," and here, the code that stays the same is the general sort algorithm, but the thing that changes from one use to the next is the way objects are compared. So instead of placing the comparison code into many different sort routines, the *Strategy* design pattern is used.[2] With a Strategy, the part of the code that varies is encapsulated inside a separate class (the Strategy object). You hand a Strategy object to the code that's always the same, which uses the Strategy to fulfill its algorithm. That way, you can make different objects to express different ways of comparison and feed them to the same sorting code.

Java has two ways to provide comparison functionality. The first is with the "natural" comparison method that is imparted to a class by implementing the **java.lang.Comparable** interface. This is a very simple interface with a single method, **compareTo( )**. This method takes another object of the same type as an argument and produces a negative value if the current object is less

---

[2] *Design Patterns*, Erich Gamma et al. (Addison-Wesley, 1995). See *Thinking in Patterns (with Java)* at *www.MindView.net*.

than the argument, zero if the argument is equal, and a positive value if the current object is greater than the argument.

Here's a class that implements **Comparable** and demonstrates the comparability by using the Java standard library method **Arrays.sort( )**:

```
//: arrays/CompType.java
// Implementing Comparable in a class.
import java.util.*;
import net.mindview.util.*;
import static net.mindview.util.Print.*;

public class CompType implements Comparable<CompType> {
  int i;
  int j;
  private static int count = 1;
  public CompType(int n1, int n2) {
    i = n1;
    j = n2;
  }
  public String toString() {
    String result = "[i = " + i + ", j = " + j + "]";
    if(count++ % 3 == 0)
      result += "\n";
    return result;
  }
  public int compareTo(CompType rv) {
    return (i < rv.i ? -1 : (i == rv.i ? 0 : 1));
  }
  private static Random r = new Random(47);
  public static Generator<CompType> generator() {
    return new Generator<CompType>() {
      public CompType next() {
        return new CompType(r.nextInt(100),r.nextInt(100));
      }
    };
  }
  public static void main(String[] args) {
    CompType[] a =
      Generated.array(new CompType[12], generator());
    print("before sorting:");
    print(Arrays.toString(a));
    Arrays.sort(a);
    print("after sorting:");
```

```
     print(Arrays.toString(a));
  }
} /* Output:
before sorting:
[[i = 58, j = 55], [i = 93, j = 61], [i = 61, j = 29]
, [i = 68, j = 0], [i = 22, j = 7], [i = 88, j = 28]
, [i = 51, j = 89], [i = 9, j = 78], [i = 98, j = 61]
, [i = 20, j = 58], [i = 16, j = 40], [i = 11, j = 22]
]
after sorting:
[[i = 9, j = 78], [i = 11, j = 22], [i = 16, j = 40]
, [i = 20, j = 58], [i = 22, j = 7], [i = 51, j = 89]
, [i = 58, j = 55], [i = 61, j = 29], [i = 68, j = 0]
, [i = 88, j = 28], [i = 93, j = 61], [i = 98, j = 61]
]
*///:~
```

When you define the comparison method, you are responsible for deciding what it means to compare one of your objects to another. Here, only the **i** values are used in the comparison, and the **j** values are ignored.

The **generator( )** method produces an object that implements the **Generator** interface by creating an anonymous inner class. This builds **CompType** objects by initializing them with random values. In **main( )**, the generator is used to fill an array of **CompType**, which is then sorted. If **Comparable** hadn't been implemented, then you'd get a **ClassCastException** at run time when you tried to call **sort( )**. This is because **sort( )** casts its argument to **Comparable**.

Now suppose someone hands you a class that doesn't implement **Comparable**, or hands you this class that *does* implement **Comparable**, but you decide you don't like the way it works and would rather have a different comparison method for the type. To solve the problem, you create a separate class that implements an interface called **Comparator** (briefly introduced in the *Holding Your Objects* chapter). This is an example of the *Strategy* design pattern. It has two methods, **compare( )** and **equals( )**. However, you don't have to implement **equals( )** except for special performance needs, because anytime you create a class, it is implicitly inherited from **Object**, which has an **equals( )**. So you can just use the default **Object equals( )** and satisfy the contract imposed by the interface.

The **Collections** class (which we'll look at more in the next chapter) contains a method **reverseOrder( )** that produces a **Comparator** to reverse the natural sorting order. This can be applied to **CompType**:

```
//: arrays/Reverse.java
// The Collections.reverseOrder() Comparator
import java.util.*;
import net.mindview.util.*;
import static net.mindview.util.Print.*;

public class Reverse {
  public static void main(String[] args) {
    CompType[] a = Generated.array(
      new CompType[12], CompType.generator());
    print("before sorting:");
    print(Arrays.toString(a));
    Arrays.sort(a, Collections.reverseOrder());
    print("after sorting:");
    print(Arrays.toString(a));
  }
} /* Output:
before sorting:
[[i = 58, j = 55], [i = 93, j = 61], [i = 61, j = 29]
, [i = 68, j = 0], [i = 22, j = 7], [i = 88, j = 28]
, [i = 51, j = 89], [i = 9, j = 78], [i = 98, j = 61]
, [i = 20, j = 58], [i = 16, j = 40], [i = 11, j = 22]
]
after sorting:
[[i = 98, j = 61], [i = 93, j = 61], [i = 88, j = 28]
, [i = 68, j = 0], [i = 61, j = 29], [i = 58, j = 55]
, [i = 51, j = 89], [i = 22, j = 7], [i = 20, j = 58]
, [i = 16, j = 40], [i = 11, j = 22], [i = 9, j = 78]
]
*///:~
```

You can also write your own **Comparator**. This one compares **CompType** objects based on their **j** values rather than their **i** values:

```
//: arrays/ComparatorTest.java
// Implementing a Comparator for a class.
import java.util.*;
import net.mindview.util.*;
import static net.mindview.util.Print.*;

class CompTypeComparator implements Comparator<CompType> {
```

```
    public int compare(CompType o1, CompType o2) {
      return (o1.j < o2.j ? -1 : (o1.j == o2.j ? 0 : 1));
    }
}

public class ComparatorTest {
  public static void main(String[] args) {
    CompType[] a = Generated.array(
      new CompType[12], CompType.generator());
    print("before sorting:");
    print(Arrays.toString(a));
    Arrays.sort(a, new CompTypeComparator());
    print("after sorting:");
    print(Arrays.toString(a));
  }
} /* Output:
before sorting:
[[i = 58, j = 55], [i = 93, j = 61], [i = 61, j = 29]
, [i = 68, j = 0], [i = 22, j = 7], [i = 88, j = 28]
, [i = 51, j = 89], [i = 9, j = 78], [i = 98, j = 61]
, [i = 20, j = 58], [i = 16, j = 40], [i = 11, j = 22]
]
after sorting:
[[i = 68, j = 0], [i = 22, j = 7], [i = 11, j = 22]
, [i = 88, j = 28], [i = 61, j = 29], [i = 16, j = 40]
, [i = 58, j = 55], [i = 20, j = 58], [i = 93, j = 61]
, [i = 98, j = 61], [i = 9, j = 78], [i = 51, j = 89]
]
*///:~
```

Exercise 21: (3) Try to sort an array of the objects in Exercise 18. Implement **Comparable** to fix the problem. Now create a **Comparator** to sort the objects into reverse order.

Sorting an array

With the built-in sorting methods, you can sort any array of primitives, or any array of objects that either implements **Comparable** or has an associated **Comparator**.[3] Here's an example that generates random **String** objects and sorts them:

---

[3] Surprisingly, there was no support in Java 1.0 or 1.1 for sorting **String**s.

```
//: arrays/StringSorting.java
// Sorting an array of Strings.
import java.util.*;
import net.mindview.util.*;
import static net.mindview.util.Print.*;

public class StringSorting {
  public static void main(String[] args) {
    String[] sa = Generated.array(new String[20],
      new RandomGenerator.String(5));
    print("Before sort: " + Arrays.toString(sa));
    Arrays.sort(sa);
    print("After sort: " + Arrays.toString(sa));
    Arrays.sort(sa, Collections.reverseOrder());
    print("Reverse sort: " + Arrays.toString(sa));
    Arrays.sort(sa, String.CASE_INSENSITIVE_ORDER);
    print("Case-insensitive sort: " + Arrays.toString(sa));
  }
} /* Output:
Before sort: [YNzbr, nyGcF, OWZnT, cQrGs, eGZMm, JMRoE,
suEcU, OneOE, dLsmw, HLGEa, hKcxr, EqUCB, bkIna, Mesbt,
WHkjU, rUkZP, gwsqP, zDyCy, RFJQA, HxxHv]
After sort: [EqUCB, HLGEa, HxxHv, JMRoE, Mesbt, OWZnT,
OneOE, RFJQA, WHkjU, YNzbr, bkIna, cQrGs, dLsmw, eGZMm,
gwsqP, hKcxr, nyGcF, rUkZP, suEcU, zDyCy]
Reverse sort: [zDyCy, suEcU, rUkZP, nyGcF, hKcxr, gwsqP,
eGZMm, dLsmw, cQrGs, bkIna, YNzbr, WHkjU, RFJQA, OneOE,
OWZnT, Mesbt, JMRoE, HxxHv, HLGEa, EqUCB]
Case-insensitive sort: [bkIna, cQrGs, dLsmw, eGZMm, EqUCB,
gwsqP, hKcxr, HLGEa, HxxHv, JMRoE, Mesbt, nyGcF, OneOE,
OWZnT, RFJQA, rUkZP, suEcU, WHkjU, YNzbr, zDyCy]
*///:~
```

One thing you'll notice about the output in the **String** sorting algorithm is that it's *lexicographic*, so it puts all the words starting with uppercase letters first, followed by all the words starting with lowercase letters. (Telephone books are typically sorted this way.) If you want to group the words together regardless of case, use **String.CASE_INSENSITIVE_ORDER** as shown in the last call to **sort( )** in the above example.

The sorting algorithm that's used in the Java standard library is designed to be optimal for the particular type you're sorting—a Quicksort for primitives, and a stable merge sort for objects. You don't need to worry about performance unless your profiler points you to the sorting process as a bottleneck.

Searching a sorted array

Once an array is sorted, you can perform a fast search for a particular item by using **Arrays.binarySearch( )**. However, if you try to use **binarySearch( )** on an unsorted array the results will be unpredictable. The following example uses a **RandomGenerator.Integer** to fill an array, and then uses the same generator to produce search values:

```
//: arrays/ArraySearching.java
// Using Arrays.binarySearch().
import java.util.*;
import net.mindview.util.*;
import static net.mindview.util.Print.*;

public class ArraySearching {
  public static void main(String[] args) {
    Generator<Integer> gen =
      new RandomGenerator.Integer(1000);
    int[] a = ConvertTo.primitive(
      Generated.array(new Integer[25], gen));
    Arrays.sort(a);
    print("Sorted array: " + Arrays.toString(a));
    while(true) {
      int r = gen.next();
      int location = Arrays.binarySearch(a, r);
      if(location >= 0) {
        print("Location of " + r + " is " + location +
          ", a[" + location + "] = " + a[location]);
        break; // Out of while loop
      }
    }
  }
} /* Output:
Sorted array: [128, 140, 200, 207, 258, 258, 278, 288, 322,
429, 511, 520, 522, 551, 555, 589, 693, 704, 809, 861, 861,
868, 916, 961, 998]
Location of 322 is 8, a[8] = 322
*///:~
```

In the **while** loop, random values are generated as search items until one of them is found.

Arrays.binarySearch( ) produces a value greater than or equal to zero if the search item is found. Otherwise, it produces a negative value representing the place that the element should be inserted if you are maintaining the sorted array by hand. The value produced is

```
-(insertion point) - 1
```

The insertion point is the index of the first element greater than the key, or **a.size( )**, if all elements in the array are less than the specified key.

If an array contains duplicate elements, there is no guarantee which of those duplicates will be found. The search algorithm is not designed to support duplicate elements, but rather to tolerate them. If you need a sorted list of non-duplicated elements, use a **TreeSet** (to maintain sorted order) or **LinkedHashSet** (to maintain insertion order). These classes take care of all the details for you automatically. Only in cases of performance bottlenecks should you replace one of these classes with a hand-maintained array.

If you sort an object array using a **Comparator** (primitive arrays do not allow sorting with a **Comparator**), you must include that same **Comparator** when you perform a **binarySearch( )** (using the overloaded version of **binarySearch( )**). For example, the **StringSorting.java** program can be modified to perform a search:

```
//: arrays/AlphabeticSearch.java
// Searching with a Comparator.
import java.util.*;
import net.mindview.util.*;

public class AlphabeticSearch {
  public static void main(String[] args) {
    String[] sa = Generated.array(new String[30],
      new RandomGenerator.String(5));
    Arrays.sort(sa, String.CASE_INSENSITIVE_ORDER);
    System.out.println(Arrays.toString(sa));
    int index = Arrays.binarySearch(sa, sa[10],
      String.CASE_INSENSITIVE_ORDER);
    System.out.println("Index: "+ index + "\n"+ sa[index]);
  }
} /* Output:
[bkIna, cQrGs, cXZJo, dLsmw, eGZMm, EqUCB, gwsqP, hKcxr,
HLGEa, HqXum, HxxHv, JMRoE, JmzMs, Mesbt, MNvqe, nyGcF,
ogoYW, OneOE, OWZnT, RFJQA, rUkZP, sgqia, slJrL, suEcU,
uTpnX, vpfFv, WHkjU, xxEAJ, YNzbr, zDyCy]
```

```
Index: 10
HxxHv
*///:~
```

The **Comparator** must be passed to the overloaded **binarySearch( )** as the third argument. In this example, success is guaranteed because the search item is selected from the array itself.

Exercise 22: (2) Show that the results of performing a **binarySearch( )** on an unsorted array are unpredictable.

Exercise 23: (2) Create an array of **Integer**, fill it with random **int** values (using autoboxing), and sort it into reverse order using a **Comparator**.

Exercise 24: (3) Show that the class from Exercise 19 can be searched.

Summary

In this chapter, you've seen that Java provides reasonable support for fixed-sized, low-level arrays. This sort of array emphasizes performance over flexibility, just like the C and C++ array model. In the initial version of Java, fixed-sized, low-level arrays were absolutely necessary, not only because the Java designers chose to include primitive types (also for performance), but because the support for containers in that version was very minimal. Thus, in early versions of Java, it was always reasonable to choose arrays.

In subsequent versions of Java, container support improved significantly, and now containers tend to outshine arrays in all ways except for performance, and even then, the performance of containers has been significantly improved. As stated in other places in this book, performance problems are usually never where you imagine them to be, anyway.

With the addition of autoboxing and generics, holding primitives in containers has become effortless, which further encourages you to replace low-level arrays with containers. Because generics produce type-safe containers, arrays no long have an advantage on that front, either.

As noted in this chapter and as you'll see when you try to use them, generics are fairly hostile towards arrays. Often, even when you can get generics and arrays to work together in some form (as you'll see in the next chapter), you'll still end up with "unchecked" warnings during compilation.

On several occasions I have been told directly by Java language designers that I should be using containers instead of arrays, when we were discussing particular examples (I was using arrays to demonstrate specific techniques and so I did not have that option).

All of these issues indicate that you should "prefer containers to arrays" when programming in recent versions of Java. Only when it's proven that performance is an issue (and that switching to an array will make a difference) should you refactor to arrays.

This is a rather bold statement, but some languages have no fixed-sized, low-level arrays at all. They only have resizable containers with significantly more functionality than C/C++/Java-style arrays. Python,[4] for example, has a **list** type that uses basic array syntax, but has much greater functionality—you can even inherit from it:

```
#: arrays/PythonLists.py

aList = [1, 2, 3, 4, 5]
print type(aList) # <type 'list'>
print aList # [1, 2, 3, 4, 5]
print aList[4] # 5    Basic list indexing
aList.append(6) # lists can be resized
aList += [7, 8] # Add a list to a list
print aList # [1, 2, 3, 4, 5, 6, 7, 8]
aSlice = aList[2:4]
print aSlice # [3, 4]

class MyList(list): # Inherit from list
    # Define a method, 'this' pointer is explicit:
    def getReversed(self):
        reversed = self[:] # Copy list using slices
        reversed.reverse() # Built-in list method
        return reversed

list2 = MyList(aList) # No 'new' needed for object creation
print type(list2) # <class '__main__.MyList'>
print list2.getReversed() # [8, 7, 6, 5, 4, 3, 2, 1]
#:~
```

_____

4 See *www.Python.org*.

Basic Python syntax was introduced in the previous chapter. Here, a list is created by simply surrounding a comma-separated sequence of objects with square brackets. The result is an object with a runtime type of **list** (the output of the **print** statements is shown as comments on the same line). The result of printing a **list** is the same as that of using **Arrays.toString( )** in Java.

Creating a sub-sequence of a **list** is accomplished with "slicing," by placing the '**:**' operator inside the index operation. The **list** type has many more built-in operations.

MyList is a **class** definition; the base classes are placed within the parentheses. Inside the class, **def** statements produce methods, and the first argument to the method is automatically the equivalent of **this** in Java, except that in Python it's explicit and the identifier **self** is used by convention (it's not a keyword). Notice how the constructor is automatically inherited.

Although everything in Python really *is* an object (including integral and floating point types), you still have an escape hatch in that you can optimize performance-critical portions of your code by writing extensions in C, C++ or a special tool called Pyrex, which is designed to easily speed up your code. This way you can have object purity without being prevented from performance improvements.

The PHP language[5] goes even further by having only a single array type, which acts as both an **int**-indexed array and an associative array (a **Map**).

It's interesting to speculate, after this many years of Java evolution, whether the designers would put primitives and low-level arrays in the language if they were to start over again. If these were left out, it would be possible to make a truly pure object-oriented language (despite claims, Java is not a pure OO language, precisely because of the low-level detritus). The initial argument for efficiency always seems compelling, but over time we have seen an evolution away from this idea and towards the use of higher-level components like containers. Add to this the fact that if containers can be built into the core language as they are in some languages, then the compiler has a much better opportunity to optimize.

---

5 See *www.php.net*.

Green-fields speculation aside, we are certainly stuck with arrays, and you will see them when reading code. Containers, however, are almost always a better choice.

Exercise 25: (3) Rewrite **PythonLists.py** in Java.

Solutions to selected exercises can be found in the electronic document *The Thinking in Java Annotated Solution Guide*, available for sale from *www.MindView.net*.

Containers in Depth

The *Holding Your Objects* chapter introduced the ideas and basic functionality of the Java containers library, and is enough to get you started using containers. This chapter explores this important library more deeply.

In order to get full use of the containers library, you need to know more than what was introduced in *Holding Your Objects*, but this chapter relies on advanced material (like generics) so it was delayed until later in the book.

After a more complete overview of containers, you'll learn how hashing works, and how to write **hashCode( )** and **equals( )** to work with hashed containers. You'll learn why there are different versions of some containers and how to choose between them. The chapter finishes with an exploration of general-purpose utilities and special classes.

Full container taxonomy

The "Summary" section of the *Holding Your Objects* chapter showed a simplified diagram of the Java containers library. Here is a more complete diagram of the collections library, including abstract classes and legacy components (with the exception of **Queue** implementations):

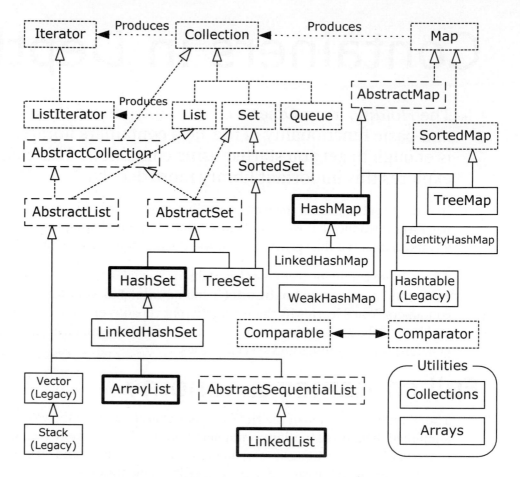

Full Container Taxonomy

Java SE5 adds:

- The **Queue** interface (which **LinkedList** has been modified to implement, as you saw in *Holding Your Objects*) and its implementations **PriorityQueue** and various flavors of **BlockingQueue** that will be shown in the *Concurrency* chapter.

- A **ConcurrentMap** interface and its implementation **ConcurrentHashMap**, also for use in threading and shown in the *Concurrency* chapter.

- **CopyOnWriteArrayList** and **CopyOnWriteArraySet**, also for concurrency.

- **EnumSet** and **EnumMap**, special implementations of **Set** and **Map** for use with **enum**s, and shown in the *Enumerated Types* chapter.

- Several utilities in the **Collections** class.

The long-dashed boxes represent **abstract** classes, and you can see a number of classes whose names begin with "**Abstract**." These can seem a bit confusing at first, but they are simply tools that partially implement a particular interface. If you were making your own **Set**, for example, you wouldn't start with the **Set** interface and implement all the methods; instead, you'd inherit from **AbstractSet** and do the minimal necessary work to make your new class. However, the containers library contains enough functionality to satisfy your needs virtually all the time, so you can usually ignore any class that begins with "**Abstract**."

Filling containers

Although the problem of printing containers is solved, filling containers suffers from the same deficiency as **java.util.Arrays**. Just as with **Arrays**, there is a companion class called **Collections** containing **static** utility methods, including one called **fill( )**. Like the **Arrays** version, this **fill( )** just duplicates a single object reference throughout the container. In addition, it only works for **List** objects, but the resulting list can be passed to a constructor or to an **addAll( )** method:

```
//: containers/FillingLists.java
// The Collections.fill() & Collections.nCopies() methods.
import java.util.*;

class StringAddress {
  private String s;
  public StringAddress(String s) { this.s = s; }
  public String toString() {
    return super.toString() + " " + s;
  }
}

public class FillingLists {
  public static void main(String[] args) {
    List<StringAddress> list= new ArrayList<StringAddress>(
      Collections.nCopies(4, new StringAddress("Hello")));
    System.out.println(list);
```

```
    Collections.fill(list, new StringAddress("World!"));
    System.out.println(list);
  }
} /* Output: (Sample)
[StringAddress@82ba41 Hello, StringAddress@82ba41 Hello,
StringAddress@82ba41 Hello, StringAddress@82ba41 Hello]
[StringAddress@923e30 World!, StringAddress@923e30 World!,
StringAddress@923e30 World!, StringAddress@923e30 World!]
*///:~
```

This example shows two ways to fill a **Collection** with references to a single object. The first, **Collections.nCopies( )**, creates a **List** which is passed to the constructor; this fills the **ArrayList**.

The **toString( )** method in **StringAddress** calls **Object.toString( )**, which produces the class name followed by the unsigned hexadecimal representation of the hash code of the object (generated by the **hashCode( )** method). You can see from the output that all the references are set to the same object, and this is also true after the second method, **Collections.fill( )**, is called. The **fill( )** method is made even less useful by the fact that it can only replace elements that are already in the **List** and will not add new elements.

A **Generator** solution

Virtually all **Collection** subtypes have a constructor that takes another **Collection** object, from which it can fill the new container. In order to easily create test data, then, all we need to do is build a class that takes constructor arguments of a **Generator** (defined in the *Generics* chapter and further explored in the *Arrays* chapter) and a **quantity** value:

```
//: net/mindview/util/CollectionData.java
// A Collection filled with data using a generator object.
package net.mindview.util;
import java.util.*;

public class CollectionData<T> extends ArrayList<T> {
  public CollectionData(Generator<T> gen, int quantity) {
    for(int i = 0; i < quantity; i++)
      add(gen.next());
  }
  // A generic convenience method:
  public static <T> CollectionData<T>
```

```
    list(Generator<T> gen, int quantity) {
      return new CollectionData<T>(gen, quantity);
    }
} ///:~
```

This uses the **Generator** to put as many objects into the container as you
need. The resulting container can then be passed to the constructor for any
Collection, and that constructor will copy the data into itself. The **addAll( )**
method that's part of every **Collection** subtype can also be used to populate
an existing **Collection**.

The generic convenience method reduces the amount of typing necessary
when using the class.

CollectionData is an example of the *Adapter* design pattern;[1] it adapts a
Generator to the constructor for a **Collection**.

Here's an example that initializes a **LinkedHashSet**:

```
//: containers/CollectionDataTest.java
import java.util.*;
import net.mindview.util.*;

class Government implements Generator<String> {
  String[] foundation = ("strange women lying in ponds " +
    "distributing swords is no basis for a system of " +
    "government").split(" ");
  private int index;
  public String next() { return foundation[index++]; }
}

public class CollectionDataTest {
  public static void main(String[] args) {
    Set<String> set = new LinkedHashSet<String>(
      new CollectionData<String>(new Government(), 15));
    // Using the convenience method:
    set.addAll(CollectionData.list(new Government(), 15));
    System.out.println(set);
  }
} /* Output:
```

---

[1] This may not be a strict definition of adapter as defined in the *Design Patterns* book, but
I think it meets the spirit of the idea.

```
[strange, women, lying, in, ponds, distributing, swords,
is, no, basis, for, a, system, of, government]
*///:~
```

The elements are in the same order in which they are inserted because a
LinkedHashSet maintains a linked list holding the insertion order.

All the generators defined in the *Arrays* chapter are now available via the
CollectionData adapter. Here's an example that uses two of them:

```
//: containers/CollectionDataGeneration.java
// Using the Generators defined in the Arrays chapter.
import java.util.*;
import net.mindview.util.*;

public class CollectionDataGeneration {
  public static void main(String[] args) {
    System.out.println(new ArrayList<String>(
      CollectionData.list( // Convenience method
        new RandomGenerator.String(9), 10)));
    System.out.println(new HashSet<Integer>(
      new CollectionData<Integer>(
        new RandomGenerator.Integer(), 10)));
  }
} /* Output:
[YNzbrnyGc, FOWZnTcQr, GseGZMmJM, RoEsuEcUO, neOEdLsmw,
HLGEahKcx, rEqUCBbkI, naMesbtWH, kjUrUkZPg, wsqPzDyCy]
[573, 4779, 871, 4367, 6090, 7882, 2017, 8037, 3455, 299]
*///:~
```

The **String** length produced by **RandomGenerator.String** is controlled
by the constructor argument.

Map generators

We can take the same approach for a **Map**, but that requires a **Pair** class
since a pair of objects (one key and one value) must be produced by each call
to a **Generator**'s **next( )** in order to populate a **Map**:

```
//: net/mindview/util/Pair.java
package net.mindview.util;

public class Pair<K,V> {
  public final K key;
  public final V value;
```

```
    public Pair(K k, V v) {
      key = k;
      value = v;
    }
} ///:~
```

The **key** and **value** fields are made **public** and **final** so that **Pair** becomes a read-only *Data Transfer Object* (or *Messenger.*

The **Map** adapter can now use various combinations of **Generator**s, **Iterable**s, and constant values to fill **Map** initialization objects:

```
//: net/mindview/util/MapData.java
// A Map filled with data using a generator object.
package net.mindview.util;
import java.util.*;

public class MapData<K,V> extends LinkedHashMap<K,V> {
  // A single Pair Generator:
  public MapData(Generator<Pair<K,V>> gen, int quantity) {
    for(int i = 0; i < quantity; i++) {
      Pair<K,V> p = gen.next();
      put(p.key, p.value);
    }
  }
  // Two separate Generators:
  public MapData(Generator<K> genK, Generator<V> genV,
      int quantity) {
    for(int i = 0; i < quantity; i++) {
      put(genK.next(), genV.next());
    }
  }
  // A key Generator and a single value:
  public MapData(Generator<K> genK, V value, int quantity){
    for(int i = 0; i < quantity; i++) {
      put(genK.next(), value);
    }
  }
  // An Iterable and a value Generator:
  public MapData(Iterable<K> genK, Generator<V> genV) {
    for(K key : genK) {
      put(key, genV.next());
    }
  }
  // An Iterable and a single value:
```

```
  public MapData(Iterable<K> genK, V value) {
    for(K key : genK) {
      put(key, value);
    }
  }
  // Generic convenience methods:
  public static <K,V> MapData<K,V>
  map(Generator<Pair<K,V>> gen, int quantity) {
    return new MapData<K,V>(gen, quantity);
  }
  public static <K,V> MapData<K,V>
  map(Generator<K> genK, Generator<V> genV, int quantity) {
    return new MapData<K,V>(genK, genV, quantity);
  }
  public static <K,V> MapData<K,V>
  map(Generator<K> genK, V value, int quantity) {
    return new MapData<K,V>(genK, value, quantity);
  }
  public static <K,V> MapData<K,V>
  map(Iterable<K> genK, Generator<V> genV) {
    return new MapData<K,V>(genK, genV);
  }
  public static <K,V> MapData<K,V>
  map(Iterable<K> genK, V value) {
    return new MapData<K,V>(genK, value);
  }
} ///:~
```

This gives you a choice of using a single **Generator<Pair<K,V>>**, two separate **Generators**, one **Generator** and a constant value, an **Iterable** (which includes any **Collection**) and a **Generator**, or an **Iterable** and a single value. The generic convenience methods reduce the amount of typing necessary when creating a **MapData** object.

Here's an example using **MapData**. The **Letters Generator** also implements **Iterable** by producing an **Iterator**; this way, it can be used to test the **MapData.map( )** methods that work with an **Iterable**:

```
//: containers/MapDataTest.java
import java.util.*;
import net.mindview.util.*;
import static net.mindview.util.Print.*;

class Letters implements Generator<Pair<Integer,String>>,
```

```
  Iterable<Integer> {
private int size = 9;
private int number = 1;
private char letter = 'A';
public Pair<Integer,String> next() {
  return new Pair<Integer,String>(
    number++, "" + letter++);
}
public Iterator<Integer> iterator() {
  return new Iterator<Integer>() {
    public Integer next() { return number++; }
    public boolean hasNext() { return number < size; }
    public void remove() {
      throw new UnsupportedOperationException();
    }
  };
}
}

public class MapDataTest {
  public static void main(String[] args) {
    // Pair Generator:
    print(MapData.map(new Letters(), 11));
    // Two separate generators:
    print(MapData.map(new CountingGenerator.Character(),
      new RandomGenerator.String(3), 8));
    // A key Generator and a single value:
    print(MapData.map(new CountingGenerator.Character(),
      "Value", 6));
    // An Iterable and a value Generator:
    print(MapData.map(new Letters(),
      new RandomGenerator.String(3)));
    // An Iterable and a single value:
    print(MapData.map(new Letters(), "Pop"));
  }
} /* Output:
{1=A, 2=B, 3=C, 4=D, 5=E, 6=F, 7=G, 8=H, 9=I, 10=J, 11=K}
{a=YNz, b=brn, c=yGc, d=FOW, e=ZnT, f=cQr, g=Gse, h=GZM}
{a=Value, b=Value, c=Value, d=Value, e=Value, f=Value}
{1=mJM, 2=RoE, 3=suE, 4=cUO, 5=neO, 6=EdL, 7=smw, 8=HLG}
{1=Pop, 2=Pop, 3=Pop, 4=Pop, 5=Pop, 6=Pop, 7=Pop, 8=Pop}
*///:~
```

This example also uses the generators from the *Arrays* chapter.

You can create any generated data set for **Map**s or **Collection**s using these tools, and then initialize a **Map** or **Collection** using the constructor or the **Map.putAll( )** or **Collection.addAll( )** methods.

Using **Abstract** classes

An alternative approach to the problem of producing test data for containers is to create custom **Collection** and **Map** implementations. Each **java.util** container has its own **Abstract** class that provides a partial implementation of that container, so all you must do is implement the necessary methods in order to produce the desired container. If the resulting container is read-only, as it typically is for test data, the number of methods you need to provide is minimized.

Although it isn't particularly necessary in this case, the following solution also provides the opportunity to demonstrate another design pattern: the *Flyweight*. You use a flyweight when the ordinary solution requires too many objects, or when producing normal objects takes up too much space. The Flyweight pattern externalizes part of the object so that, instead of everything in the object being contained within the object, some or all of the object is looked up in a more efficient external table (or produced through some other calculation that saves space).

An important point of this example is to demonstrate how relatively simple it is to create a custom **Map** and **Collection** by inheriting from the **java.util.Abstract** classes. In order to create a read-only **Map**, you inherit from **AbstractMap** and implement **entrySet( )**. In order to create a read-only **Set**, you inherit from **AbstractSet** and implement **iterator( )** and **size( )**.

The data set in this example is a **Map** of the countries of the world and their capitals.[2] The **capitals( )** method produces a **Map** of countries and capitals. The **names( )** method produces a **List** of the country names. In both cases you can get a partial listing by providing an **int** argument indicating the desired size:

```
//: net/mindview/util/Countries.java
```

---

[2] This data was found on the Internet. Various corrections have been submitted by readers over time.

```java
// "Flyweight" Maps and Lists of sample data.
package net.mindview.util;
import java.util.*;
import static net.mindview.util.Print.*;

public class Countries {
  public static final String[][] DATA = {
    // Africa
    {"ALGERIA","Algiers"}, {"ANGOLA","Luanda"},
    {"BENIN","Porto-Novo"}, {"BOTSWANA","Gaberone"},
    {"BURKINA FASO","Ouagadougou"},
    {"BURUNDI","Bujumbura"},
    {"CAMEROON","Yaounde"}, {"CAPE VERDE","Praia"},
    {"CENTRAL AFRICAN REPUBLIC","Bangui"},
    {"CHAD","N'djamena"}, {"COMOROS","Moroni"},
    {"CONGO","Brazzaville"}, {"DJIBOUTI","Dijibouti"},
    {"EGYPT","Cairo"}, {"EQUATORIAL GUINEA","Malabo"},
    {"ERITREA","Asmara"}, {"ETHIOPIA","Addis Ababa"},
    {"GABON","Libreville"}, {"THE GAMBIA","Banjul"},
    {"GHANA","Accra"}, {"GUINEA","Conakry"},
    {"BISSAU","Bissau"},
    {"COTE D'IVOIR (IVORY COAST)","Yamoussoukro"},
    {"KENYA","Nairobi"}, {"LESOTHO","Maseru"},
    {"LIBERIA","Monrovia"}, {"LIBYA","Tripoli"},
    {"MADAGASCAR","Antananarivo"}, {"MALAWI","Lilongwe"},
    {"MALI","Bamako"}, {"MAURITANIA","Nouakchott"},
    {"MAURITIUS","Port Louis"}, {"MOROCCO","Rabat"},
    {"MOZAMBIQUE","Maputo"}, {"NAMIBIA","Windhoek"},
    {"NIGER","Niamey"}, {"NIGERIA","Abuja"},
    {"RWANDA","Kigali"},
    {"SAO TOME E PRINCIPE","Sao Tome"},
    {"SENEGAL","Dakar"}, {"SEYCHELLES","Victoria"},
    {"SIERRA LEONE","Freetown"}, {"SOMALIA","Mogadishu"},
    {"SOUTH AFRICA","Pretoria/Cape Town"},
    {"SUDAN","Khartoum"},
    {"SWAZILAND","Mbabane"}, {"TANZANIA","Dodoma"},
    {"TOGO","Lome"}, {"TUNISIA","Tunis"},
    {"UGANDA","Kampala"},
    {"DEMOCRATIC REPUBLIC OF THE CONGO (ZAIRE)",
     "Kinshasa"},
    {"ZAMBIA","Lusaka"}, {"ZIMBABWE","Harare"},
    // Asia
    {"AFGHANISTAN","Kabul"}, {"BAHRAIN","Manama"},
    {"BANGLADESH","Dhaka"}, {"BHUTAN","Thimphu"},
```

```
{"BRUNEI","Bandar Seri Begawan"},
{"CAMBODIA","Phnom Penh"},
{"CHINA","Beijing"}, {"CYPRUS","Nicosia"},
{"INDIA","New Delhi"}, {"INDONESIA","Jakarta"},
{"IRAN","Tehran"}, {"IRAQ","Baghdad"},
{"ISRAEL","Jerusalem"}, {"JAPAN","Tokyo"},
{"JORDAN","Amman"}, {"KUWAIT","Kuwait City"},
{"LAOS","Vientiane"}, {"LEBANON","Beirut"},
{"MALAYSIA","Kuala Lumpur"}, {"THE MALDIVES","Male"},
{"MONGOLIA","Ulan Bator"},
{"MYANMAR (BURMA)","Rangoon"},
{"NEPAL","Katmandu"}, {"NORTH KOREA","P'yongyang"},
{"OMAN","Muscat"}, {"PAKISTAN","Islamabad"},
{"PHILIPPINES","Manila"}, {"QATAR","Doha"},
{"SAUDI ARABIA","Riyadh"}, {"SINGAPORE","Singapore"},
{"SOUTH KOREA","Seoul"}, {"SRI LANKA","Colombo"},
{"SYRIA","Damascus"},
{"TAIWAN (REPUBLIC OF CHINA)","Taipei"},
{"THAILAND","Bangkok"}, {"TURKEY","Ankara"},
{"UNITED ARAB EMIRATES","Abu Dhabi"},
{"VIETNAM","Hanoi"}, {"YEMEN","Sana'a"},
// Australia and Oceania
{"AUSTRALIA","Canberra"}, {"FIJI","Suva"},
{"KIRIBATI","Bairiki"},
{"MARSHALL ISLANDS","Dalap-Uliga-Darrit"},
{"MICRONESIA","Palikir"}, {"NAURU","Yaren"},
{"NEW ZEALAND","Wellington"}, {"PALAU","Koror"},
{"PAPUA NEW GUINEA","Port Moresby"},
{"SOLOMON ISLANDS","Honaira"}, {"TONGA","Nuku'alofa"},
{"TUVALU","Fongafale"}, {"VANUATU","< Port-Vila"},
{"WESTERN SAMOA","Apia"},
// Eastern Europe and former USSR
{"ARMENIA","Yerevan"}, {"AZERBAIJAN","Baku"},
{"BELARUS (BYELORUSSIA)","Minsk"},
{"BULGARIA","Sofia"}, {"GEORGIA","Tbilisi"},
{"KAZAKSTAN","Almaty"}, {"KYRGYZSTAN","Alma-Ata"},
{"MOLDOVA","Chisinau"}, {"RUSSIA","Moscow"},
{"TAJIKISTAN","Dushanbe"}, {"TURKMENISTAN","Ashkabad"},
{"UKRAINE","Kyiv"}, {"UZBEKISTAN","Tashkent"},
// Europe
{"ALBANIA","Tirana"}, {"ANDORRA","Andorra la Vella"},
{"AUSTRIA","Vienna"}, {"BELGIUM","Brussels"},
{"BOSNIA","-"}, {"HERZEGOVINA","Sarajevo"},
{"CROATIA","Zagreb"}, {"CZECH REPUBLIC","Prague"},
```

```
    {"DENMARK","Copenhagen"}, {"ESTONIA","Tallinn"},
    {"FINLAND","Helsinki"}, {"FRANCE","Paris"},
    {"GERMANY","Berlin"}, {"GREECE","Athens"},
    {"HUNGARY","Budapest"}, {"ICELAND","Reykjavik"},
    {"IRELAND","Dublin"}, {"ITALY","Rome"},
    {"LATVIA","Riga"}, {"LIECHTENSTEIN","Vaduz"},
    {"LITHUANIA","Vilnius"}, {"LUXEMBOURG","Luxembourg"},
    {"MACEDONIA","Skopje"}, {"MALTA","Valletta"},
    {"MONACO","Monaco"}, {"MONTENEGRO","Podgorica"},
    {"THE NETHERLANDS","Amsterdam"}, {"NORWAY","Oslo"},
    {"POLAND","Warsaw"}, {"PORTUGAL","Lisbon"},
    {"ROMANIA","Bucharest"}, {"SAN MARINO","San Marino"},
    {"SERBIA","Belgrade"}, {"SLOVAKIA","Bratislava"},
    {"SLOVENIA","Ljuijana"}, {"SPAIN","Madrid"},
    {"SWEDEN","Stockholm"}, {"SWITZERLAND","Berne"},
    {"UNITED KINGDOM","London"}, {"VATICAN CITY","---"},
    // North and Central America
    {"ANTIGUA AND BARBUDA","Saint John's"},
    {"BAHAMAS","Nassau"},
    {"BARBADOS","Bridgetown"}, {"BELIZE","Belmopan"},
    {"CANADA","Ottawa"}, {"COSTA RICA","San Jose"},
    {"CUBA","Havana"}, {"DOMINICA","Roseau"},
    {"DOMINICAN REPUBLIC","Santo Domingo"},
    {"EL SALVADOR","San Salvador"},
    {"GRENADA","Saint George's"},
    {"GUATEMALA","Guatemala City"},
    {"HAITI","Port-au-Prince"},
    {"HONDURAS","Tegucigalpa"}, {"JAMAICA","Kingston"},
    {"MEXICO","Mexico City"}, {"NICARAGUA","Managua"},
    {"PANAMA","Panama City"}, {"ST. KITTS","-"},
    {"NEVIS","Basseterre"}, {"ST. LUCIA","Castries"},
    {"ST. VINCENT AND THE GRENADINES","Kingstown"},
    {"UNITED STATES OF AMERICA","Washington, D.C."},
    // South America
    {"ARGENTINA","Buenos Aires"},
    {"BOLIVIA","Sucre (legal)/La Paz(administrative)"},
    {"BRAZIL","Brasilia"}, {"CHILE","Santiago"},
    {"COLOMBIA","Bogota"}, {"ECUADOR","Quito"},
    {"GUYANA","Georgetown"}, {"PARAGUAY","Asuncion"},
    {"PERU","Lima"}, {"SURINAME","Paramaribo"},
    {"TRINIDAD AND TOBAGO","Port of Spain"},
    {"URUGUAY","Montevideo"}, {"VENEZUELA","Caracas"},
};
// Use AbstractMap by implementing entrySet()
```

```java
      private static class FlyweightMap
      extends AbstractMap<String,String> {
        private static class Entry
        implements Map.Entry<String,String> {
          int index;
          Entry(int index) { this.index = index; }
          public boolean equals(Object o) {
            return DATA[index][0].equals(o);
          }
          public String getKey() { return DATA[index][0]; }
          public String getValue() { return DATA[index][1]; }
          public String setValue(String value) {
            throw new UnsupportedOperationException();
          }
          public int hashCode() {
            return DATA[index][0].hashCode();
          }
        }
        // Use AbstractSet by implementing size() & iterator()
        static class EntrySet
        extends AbstractSet<Map.Entry<String,String>> {
          private int size;
          EntrySet(int size) {
            if(size < 0)
              this.size = 0;
            // Can't be any bigger than the array:
            else if(size > DATA.length)
              this.size = DATA.length;
            else
              this.size = size;
          }
          public int size() { return size; }
          private class Iter
          implements Iterator<Map.Entry<String,String>> {
            // Only one Entry object per Iterator:
            private Entry entry = new Entry(-1);
            public boolean hasNext() {
              return entry.index < size - 1;
            }
            public Map.Entry<String,String> next() {
              entry.index++;
              return entry;
            }
            public void remove() {
```

```
          throw new UnsupportedOperationException();
        }
      }
      public
      Iterator<Map.Entry<String,String>> iterator() {
        return new Iter();
      }
    }
  }
  private static Set<Map.Entry<String,String>> entries =
    new EntrySet(DATA.length);
  public Set<Map.Entry<String,String>> entrySet() {
    return entries;
  }
}
// Create a partial map of 'size' countries:
static Map<String,String> select(final int size) {
  return new FlyweightMap() {
    public Set<Map.Entry<String,String>> entrySet() {
      return new EntrySet(size);
    }
  };
}
static Map<String,String> map = new FlyweightMap();
public static Map<String,String> capitals() {
  return map; // The entire map
}
public static Map<String,String> capitals(int size) {
  return select(size); // A partial map
}
static List<String> names =
  new ArrayList<String>(map.keySet());
// All the names:
public static List<String> names() { return names; }
// A partial list:
public static List<String> names(int size) {
  return new ArrayList<String>(select(size).keySet());
}
public static void main(String[] args) {
  print(capitals(10));
  print(names(10));
  print(new HashMap<String,String>(capitals(3)));
  print(new LinkedHashMap<String,String>(capitals(3)));
  print(new TreeMap<String,String>(capitals(3)));
  print(new Hashtable<String,String>(capitals(3)));
```

```
    print(new HashSet<String>(names(6)));
    print(new LinkedHashSet<String>(names(6)));
    print(new TreeSet<String>(names(6)));
    print(new ArrayList<String>(names(6)));
    print(new LinkedList<String>(names(6)));
    print(capitals().get("BRAZIL"));
  }
} /* Output:
{ALGERIA=Algiers, ANGOLA=Luanda, BENIN=Porto-Novo,
BOTSWANA=Gaberone, BULGARIA=Sofia, BURKINA
FASO=Ouagadougou, BURUNDI=Bujumbura, CAMEROON=Yaounde, CAPE
VERDE=Praia, CENTRAL AFRICAN REPUBLIC=Bangui}
[ALGERIA, ANGOLA, BENIN, BOTSWANA, BULGARIA, BURKINA FASO,
BURUNDI, CAMEROON, CAPE VERDE, CENTRAL AFRICAN REPUBLIC]
{BENIN=Porto-Novo, ANGOLA=Luanda, ALGERIA=Algiers}
{ALGERIA=Algiers, ANGOLA=Luanda, BENIN=Porto-Novo}
{ALGERIA=Algiers, ANGOLA=Luanda, BENIN=Porto-Novo}
{ALGERIA=Algiers, ANGOLA=Luanda, BENIN=Porto-Novo}
[BULGARIA, BURKINA FASO, BOTSWANA, BENIN, ANGOLA, ALGERIA]
[ALGERIA, ANGOLA, BENIN, BOTSWANA, BULGARIA, BURKINA FASO]
[ALGERIA, ANGOLA, BENIN, BOTSWANA, BULGARIA, BURKINA FASO]
[ALGERIA, ANGOLA, BENIN, BOTSWANA, BULGARIA, BURKINA FASO]
[ALGERIA, ANGOLA, BENIN, BOTSWANA, BULGARIA, BURKINA FASO]
Brasilia
*///:~
```

The two-dimensional array of **String DATA** is **public** so it can be used elsewhere. **FlyweightMap** must implement the **entrySet( )** method, which requires both a custom **Set** implementation and a custom **Map.Entry** class. Here's part of the flyweight: each **Map.Entry** object simply stores its index, rather than the actual key and value. When you call **getKey( )** or **getValue( )**, it uses the index to return the appropriate **DATA** element. The **EntrySet** ensures that its **size** is no bigger than **DATA**.

You can see the other part of the flyweight implemented in **EntrySet.Iterator**. Instead of creating a **Map.Entry** object for each data pair in **DATA**, there's only one **Map.Entry** object *per iterator*. The **Entry** object is used as a window into the data; it only contains an **index** into the static array of strings. Every time you call **next( )** for the iterator, the **index** in the **Entry** is incremented so that it points to the next element pair, and then that **Iterator**'s single **Entry** object is returned from **next( )**.[3]

The **select( )** method produces a **FlyweightMap** containing an **EntrySet** of the desired size, and this is used in the overloaded **capitals( )** and **names( )** methods that you see demonstrated in **main( )**.

For some tests, the limited size of **Countries** is a problem. We can take the same approach to produce initialized custom containers that have a data set of any size. This class is a **List** that can be any size, and is (effectively) pre-initialized with **Integer** data:

```
//: net/mindview/util/CountingIntegerList.java
// List of any length, containing sample data.
package net.mindview.util;
import java.util.*;

public class CountingIntegerList
extends AbstractList<Integer> {
  private int size;
  public CountingIntegerList(int size) {
    this.size = size < 0 ? 0 : size;
  }
  public Integer get(int index) {
    return Integer.valueOf(index);
  }
  public int size() { return size; }
  public static void main(String[] args) {
    System.out.println(new CountingIntegerList(30));
  }
} /* Output:
[0, 1, 2, 3, 4, 5, 6, 7, 8, 9, 10, 11, 12, 13, 14, 15, 16,
17, 18, 19, 20, 21, 22, 23, 24, 25, 26, 27, 28, 29]
*///:~
```

To create a read-only **List** from an **AbstractList**, you must implement **get( )** and **size( )**. Again, a flyweight solution is used: **get( )** produces the value when you ask for it, so the **List** doesn't actually have to be populated.

---

[3] The **Map**s in **java.util** perform bulk copies using **getKey( )** and **getValue( )** for **Map**s, so this works. If a custom **Map** were to simply copy the entire **Map.Entry** then this approach would cause a problem.

Here is a **Map** containing pre-initialized unique **Integer**s and **String**s; it can also be any size:

```
//: net/mindview/util/CountingMapData.java
// Unlimited-length Map containing sample data.
package net.mindview.util;
import java.util.*;

public class CountingMapData
extends AbstractMap<Integer,String> {
  private int size;
  private static String[] chars =
    "A B C D E F G H I J K L M N O P Q R S T U V W X Y Z"
    .split(" ");
  public CountingMapData(int size) {
    if(size < 0) this.size = 0;
    else this.size = size;
  }
  private static class Entry
  implements Map.Entry<Integer,String> {
    int index;
    Entry(int index) { this.index = index; }
    public boolean equals(Object o) {
      return Integer.valueOf(index).equals(o);
    }
    public Integer getKey() { return index; }
    public String getValue() {
      return
        chars[index % chars.length] +
        Integer.toString(index / chars.length);
    }
    public String setValue(String value) {
      throw new UnsupportedOperationException();
    }
    public int hashCode() {
      return Integer.valueOf(index).hashCode();
    }
  }
  public Set<Map.Entry<Integer,String>> entrySet() {
    // LinkedHashSet retains initialization order:
    Set<Map.Entry<Integer,String>> entries =
      new LinkedHashSet<Map.Entry<Integer,String>>();
    for(int i = 0; i < size; i++)
      entries.add(new Entry(i));
```

```
      return entries;
    }
    public static void main(String[] args) {
      System.out.println(new CountingMapData(60));
    }
} /* Output:
{0=A0, 1=B0, 2=C0, 3=D0, 4=E0, 5=F0, 6=G0, 7=H0, 8=I0,
9=J0, 10=K0, 11=L0, 12=M0, 13=N0, 14=O0, 15=P0, 16=Q0,
17=R0, 18=S0, 19=T0, 20=U0, 21=V0, 22=W0, 23=X0, 24=Y0,
25=Z0, 26=A1, 27=B1, 28=C1, 29=D1, 30=E1, 31=F1, 32=G1,
33=H1, 34=I1, 35=J1, 36=K1, 37=L1, 38=M1, 39=N1, 40=O1,
41=P1, 42=Q1, 43=R1, 44=S1, 45=T1, 46=U1, 47=V1, 48=W1,
49=X1, 50=Y1, 51=Z1, 52=A2, 53=B2, 54=C2, 55=D2, 56=E2,
57=F2, 58=G2, 59=H2}
*///:~
```

Here, a **LinkedHashSet** is used instead of creating a custom **Set** class, so
the flyweight is not fully implemented.

Exercise 1: (1) Create a **List** (try both **ArrayList** and **LinkedList**) and
fill it using **Countries**. Sort the list and print it, then apply
Collections.shuffle( ) to the list repeatedly, printing it each time so that
you can see how the **shuffle( )** method randomizes the list differently each
time.

Exercise 2: (2) Produce a **Map** and a **Set** containing all the countries that
begin with 'A'.

Exercise 3: (1) Using **Countries**, fill a **Set** multiple times with the same
data and verify that the **Set** ends up with only one of each instance. Try this
with **HashSet**, **LinkedHashSet**, and **TreeSet**.

Exercise 4: (2) Create a **Collection** initializer that opens a file and breaks
it into words using **TextFile**, and then uses the words as the source of data
for the resulting **Collection**. Demonstrate that it works.

Exercise 5: (3) Modify **CountingMapData.java** to fully implement the
flyweight by adding a custom **EntrySet** class like the one in
Countries.java.

Collection functionality

The following table shows everything you can do with a **Collection** (not
including the methods that automatically come through with **Object**), and
thus, everything you can do with a **Set** or a **List**. (**List** also has additional

functionality.) **Maps** are not inherited from **Collection** and will be treated separately.

boolean add(T)	Ensures that the container holds the argument which is of generic type **T**. Returns **false** if it doesn't add the argument. (This is an "optional" method, described in the next section.)
boolean addAll(Collection<? extends T>)	Adds all the elements in the argument. Returns **true** if any elements were added. ("Optional.")
void clear( )	Removes all the elements in the container. ("Optional.")
boolean contains(T)	**true** if the container holds the argument which is of generic type **T**.
Boolean containsAll(Collection<?>)	**true** if the container holds all the elements in the argument.
boolean isEmpty( )	**true** if the container has no elements.
Iterator<T> iterator( )	Returns an **Iterator<T>** that you can use to move through the elements in the container.
Boolean remove(Object)	If the argument is in the container, one instance of that element is removed. Returns **true** if a removal occurred. ("Optional.")
boolean removeAll(Collection<?>)	Removes all the elements that are contained in the argument. Returns **true** if any removals occurred. ("Optional.")
Boolean retainAll(Collection<?>)	Retains only elements that are contained in the argument (an "intersection," from set theory). Returns **true** if any changes occurred. ("Optional.")
int size( )	Returns the number of elements in the container.
Object[] toArray( )	Returns an array containing all the elements in the container.
<T> T[] toArray(T[] a)	Returns an array containing all the elements in the container. The runtime type of the result is that of the argument

Notice that there's no **get( )** method for random-access element selection. That's because **Collection** also includes **Set**, which maintains its own internal ordering (and thus makes random-access lookup meaningless). Thus, if you want to examine the elements of a **Collection**, you must use an iterator.

The following example demonstrates all of these methods. Although these methods work with anything that implements **Collection**, an **ArrayList** is used as a "least-common denominator":

```
//: containers/CollectionMethods.java
// Things you can do with all Collections.
import java.util.*;
import net.mindview.util.*;
import static net.mindview.util.Print.*;

public class CollectionMethods {
  public static void main(String[] args) {
    Collection<String> c = new ArrayList<String>();
    c.addAll(Countries.names(6));
    c.add("ten");
    c.add("eleven");
    print(c);
    // Make an array from the List:
    Object[] array = c.toArray();
    // Make a String array from the List:
    String[] str = c.toArray(new String[0]);
    // Find max and min elements; this means
    // different things depending on the way
    // the Comparable interface is implemented:
    print("Collections.max(c) = " + Collections.max(c));
    print("Collections.min(c) = " + Collections.min(c));
    // Add a Collection to another Collection
    Collection<String> c2 = new ArrayList<String>();
    c2.addAll(Countries.names(6));
    c.addAll(c2);
    print(c);
    c.remove(Countries.DATA[0][0]);
    print(c);
    c.remove(Countries.DATA[1][0]);
    print(c);
    // Remove all components that are
```

```java
    // in the argument collection:
    c.removeAll(c2);
    print(c);
    c.addAll(c2);
    print(c);
    // Is an element in this Collection?
    String val = Countries.DATA[3][0];
    print("c.contains(" + val  + ") = " + c.contains(val));
    // Is a Collection in this Collection?
    print("c.containsAll(c2) = " + c.containsAll(c2));
    Collection<String> c3 =
      ((List<String>)c).subList(3, 5);
    // Keep all the elements that are in both
    // c2 and c3 (an intersection of sets):
    c2.retainAll(c3);
    print(c2);
    // Throw away all the elements
    // in c2 that also appear in c3:
    c2.removeAll(c3);
    print("c2.isEmpty() = " +  c2.isEmpty());
    c = new ArrayList<String>();
    c.addAll(Countries.names(6));
    print(c);
    c.clear(); // Remove all elements
    print("after c.clear():" + c);
  }
} /* Output:
[ALGERIA, ANGOLA, BENIN, BOTSWANA, BULGARIA, BURKINA FASO,
ten, eleven]
Collections.max(c) = ten
Collections.min(c) = ALGERIA
[ALGERIA, ANGOLA, BENIN, BOTSWANA, BULGARIA, BURKINA FASO,
ten, eleven, ALGERIA, ANGOLA, BENIN, BOTSWANA, BULGARIA,
BURKINA FASO]
[ANGOLA, BENIN, BOTSWANA, BULGARIA, BURKINA FASO, ten,
eleven, ALGERIA, ANGOLA, BENIN, BOTSWANA, BULGARIA, BURKINA
FASO]
[BENIN, BOTSWANA, BULGARIA, BURKINA FASO, ten, eleven,
ALGERIA, ANGOLA, BENIN, BOTSWANA, BULGARIA, BURKINA FASO]
[ten, eleven]
[ten, eleven, ALGERIA, ANGOLA, BENIN, BOTSWANA, BULGARIA,
BURKINA FASO]
c.contains(BOTSWANA) = true
c.containsAll(c2) = true
```

```
[ANGOLA, BENIN]
c2.isEmpty() = true
[ALGERIA, ANGOLA, BENIN, BOTSWANA, BULGARIA, BURKINA FASO]
after c.clear():[]
*///:~
```

ArrayLists are created containing different sets of data and upcast to
Collection objects, so it's clear that nothing other than the **Collection**
interface is being used. **main( )** uses simple exercises to show all of the
methods in **Collection**.

Subsequent sections in this chapter describe the various implementations of
List, **Set**, and **Map** and indicate in each case (with an asterisk) which one
should be your default choice. Descriptions of the legacy classes **Vector**,
Stack, and **Hashtable** are delayed to the end of the chapter—although you
shouldn't use these classes, you will see them in old code.

Optional operations

The methods that perform various kinds of addition and removal are *optional
operations* in the **Collection** interface. This means that the implementing
class is not required to provide functioning definitions for these methods.

This is a very unusual way to define an interface. As you've seen, an interface
is a contract in object-oriented design. It says, "No matter how you choose to
implement this interface, I guarantee that you can send these messages to
this object."[4] But an "optional" operation violates this very fundamental
principle; it says that calling some methods will *not* perform meaningful
behavior. Instead, they will throw exceptions! It appears that compile-time
type safety is discarded.

It's not quite that bad. If an operation is optional, the compiler still restricts
you to calling only the methods in that interface. It's not like a dynamic
language, in which you can call any method for any object, and find out at run
time whether a particular call will work.[5] In addition, most methods that take

---

[4] I am using the term "interface" here to describe both the formal **interface** keyword and
the more general meaning of "the methods supported by any class or subclass."

[5] Although this sounds odd and possibly useless when I describe it this way, you've seen,
especially in the *Type Information* chapter, that this kind of dynamic behavior can be very
powerful.

---

a **Collection** as an argument only *read* from that **Collection**, and all the "read" methods of **Collection** are *not* optional.

Why would you define methods as "optional"? Doing so prevents an explosion of interfaces in the design. Other designs for container libraries always seem to end up with a confusing plethora of interfaces to describe each of the variations on the main theme. It's not even possible to capture all of the special cases in interfaces, because someone can always invent a new interface. The "unsupported operation" approach achieves an important goal of the Java containers library: The containers are simple to learn and use. Unsupported operations are a special case that can be delayed until necessary. For this approach to work, however:

1. The **UnsupportedOperationException** must be a rare event. That is, for most classes, all operations should work, and only in special cases should an operation be unsupported. This is true in the Java containers library, since the classes you'll use 99 percent of the time—**ArrayList**, **LinkedList**, **HashSet**, and **HashMap**, as well as the other concrete implementations—support all of the operations. The design does provide a "back door" if you want to create a new **Collection** without providing meaningful definitions for all the methods in the **Collection** interface, and yet still fit it into the existing library.

2. When an operation *is* unsupported, there should be reasonable likelihood that an **UnsupportedOperationException** will appear at implementation time, rather than after you've shipped the product to the customer. After all, it indicates a programming error: You've used an implementation incorrectly.

It's worth noting that unsupported operations are only detectable at run time, and therefore represent dynamic type checking. If you're coming from a statically typed language like C++, Java might appear to be just another statically typed language. Java certainly *has* static type checking, but it also has a significant amount of dynamic typing, so it's hard to say that it's exactly one type of language or another. Once you begin to notice this, you'll start to see other examples of dynamic type checking in Java.

Unsupported operations

A common source of unsupported operations involves a container backed by a fixed-sized data structure. You get such a container when you turn an array into a **List** with the **Arrays.asList( )** method. You can also *choose* to make any container (including a **Map**) throw **UnsupportedOperationException**s by using the "unmodifiable" methods in the **Collections** class. This example shows both cases:

```
//: containers/Unsupported.java
// Unsupported operations in Java containers.
import java.util.*;

public class Unsupported {
  static void test(String msg, List<String> list) {
    System.out.println("--- " + msg + " ---");
    Collection<String> c = list;
    Collection<String> subList = list.subList(1,8);
    // Copy of the sublist:
    Collection<String> c2 = new ArrayList<String>(subList);
    try { c.retainAll(c2); } catch(Exception e) {
      System.out.println("retainAll(): " + e);
    }
    try { c.removeAll(c2); } catch(Exception e) {
      System.out.println("removeAll(): " + e);
    }
    try { c.clear(); } catch(Exception e) {
      System.out.println("clear(): " + e);
    }
    try { c.add("X"); } catch(Exception e) {
      System.out.println("add(): " + e);
    }
    try { c.addAll(c2); } catch(Exception e) {
      System.out.println("addAll(): " + e);
    }
    try { c.remove("C"); } catch(Exception e) {
      System.out.println("remove(): " + e);
    }
    // The List.set() method modifies the value but
    // doesn't change the size of the data structure:
    try {
      list.set(0, "X");
    } catch(Exception e) {
      System.out.println("List.set(): " + e);
```

```
      }
    }
    public static void main(String[] args) {
      List<String> list =
        Arrays.asList("A B C D E F G H I J K L".split(" "));
      test("Modifiable Copy", new ArrayList<String>(list));
      test("Arrays.asList()", list);
      test("unmodifiableList()",
        Collections.unmodifiableList(
          new ArrayList<String>(list)));
    }
} /* Output:
--- Modifiable Copy ---
--- Arrays.asList() ---
retainAll(): java.lang.UnsupportedOperationException
removeAll(): java.lang.UnsupportedOperationException
clear(): java.lang.UnsupportedOperationException
add(): java.lang.UnsupportedOperationException
addAll(): java.lang.UnsupportedOperationException
remove(): java.lang.UnsupportedOperationException
--- unmodifiableList() ---
retainAll(): java.lang.UnsupportedOperationException
removeAll(): java.lang.UnsupportedOperationException
clear(): java.lang.UnsupportedOperationException
add(): java.lang.UnsupportedOperationException
addAll(): java.lang.UnsupportedOperationException
remove(): java.lang.UnsupportedOperationException
List.set(): java.lang.UnsupportedOperationException
*///:~
```

Because **Arrays.asList( )** produces a **List** that is backed by a fixed-size array, it makes sense that the only supported operations are the ones that don't change the *size* of the array. Any method that would cause a change to the size of the underlying data structure produces an **UnsupportedOperationException**, to indicate a call to an unsupported method (a programming error).

Note that you can always pass the result of **Arrays.asList( )** as a constructor argument to any **Collection** (or use the **addAll( )** method, or the **Collections.addAll( ) static** method) in order to create a regular container that allows the use of all the methods—this is shown in the first call to **test( )** in **main( )**. Such a call produces a new resizable underlying data structure.

The "unmodifiable" methods in the **Collections** class wrap the container in a proxy that produces an **UnsupportedOperationException** if you perform any operation that modifies the container in any way. The goal of using these methods is to produce a "constant" container object. The full list of "unmodifiable" **Collections** methods is described later.

The last **try** block in **test( )** examines the **set( )** method that's part of **List**. This is interesting, because you can see how the granularity of the "unsupported operation" technique comes in handy—the resulting "interface" can vary by one method between the object returned by **Arrays.asList( )** and that returned by **Collections.unmodifiableList( )**. **Arrays.asList( )** returns a fixed-sized **List**, whereas **Collections.unmodifiableList( )** produces a list that cannot be changed. As you can see from the output, it's OK to *modify* the elements in the **List** returned by **Arrays.asList( )**, because this would not violate the "fixed-sized" nature of that **List**. But clearly, the result of **unmodifiableList( )** should not be modifiable in any way. If interfaces were used, this would have required two additional interfaces, one with a working **set( )** method and one without. Additional interfaces would be required for various unmodifiable subtypes of **Collection**.

The documentation for a method that takes a container as an argument should specify which of the optional methods must be implemented.

Exercise 6: (2) Note that **List** has additional "optional" operations that are not included in **Collection**. Write a version of **Unsupported.java** that tests these additional optional operations.

List functionality

As you've seen, the basic **List** is quite simple to use: Most of the time you just call **add( )** to insert objects, use **get( )** to get them out one at a time, and call **iterator( )** to get an **Iterator** for the sequence.

The methods in the following example each cover a different group of activities: things that every **List** can do (**basicTest( )**), moving around with an **Iterator** (**iterMotion( )**) versus changing things with an **Iterator** (**iterManipulation( )**), seeing the effects of **List** manipulation (**testVisual( )**), and operations available only to **LinkedList**s:

```
//: containers/Lists.java
// Things you can do with Lists.
```

```java
import java.util.*;
import net.mindview.util.*;
import static net.mindview.util.Print.*;

public class Lists {
  private static boolean b;
  private static String s;
  private static int i;
  private static Iterator<String> it;
  private static ListIterator<String> lit;
  public static void basicTest(List<String> a) {
    a.add(1, "x"); // Add at location 1
    a.add("x"); // Add at end
    // Add a collection:
    a.addAll(Countries.names(25));
    // Add a collection starting at location 3:
    a.addAll(3, Countries.names(25));
    b = a.contains("1"); // Is it in there?
    // Is the entire collection in there?
    b = a.containsAll(Countries.names(25));
    // Lists allow random access, which is cheap
    // for ArrayList, expensive for LinkedList:
    s = a.get(1); // Get (typed) object at location 1
    i = a.indexOf("1"); // Tell index of object
    b = a.isEmpty(); // Any elements inside?
    it = a.iterator(); // Ordinary Iterator
    lit = a.listIterator(); // ListIterator
    lit = a.listIterator(3); // Start at loc 3
    i = a.lastIndexOf("1"); // Last match
    a.remove(1); // Remove location 1
    a.remove("3"); // Remove this object
    a.set(1, "y"); // Set location 1 to "y"
    // Keep everything that's in the argument
    // (the intersection of the two sets):
    a.retainAll(Countries.names(25));
    // Remove everything that's in the argument:
    a.removeAll(Countries.names(25));
    i = a.size(); // How big is it?
    a.clear(); // Remove all elements
  }
  public static void iterMotion(List<String> a) {
    ListIterator<String> it = a.listIterator();
    b = it.hasNext();
    b = it.hasPrevious();
```

```
        s = it.next();
        i = it.nextIndex();
        s = it.previous();
        i = it.previousIndex();
    }
    public static void iterManipulation(List<String> a) {
        ListIterator<String> it = a.listIterator();
        it.add("47");
        // Must move to an element after add():
        it.next();
        // Remove the element after the newly produced one:
        it.remove();
        // Must move to an element after remove():
        it.next();
        // Change the element after the deleted one:
        it.set("47");
    }
    public static void testVisual(List<String> a) {
        print(a);
        List<String> b = Countries.names(25);
        print("b = " + b);
        a.addAll(b);
        a.addAll(b);
        print(a);
        // Insert, remove, and replace elements
        // using a ListIterator:
        ListIterator<String> x = a.listIterator(a.size()/2);
        x.add("one");
        print(a);
        print(x.next());
        x.remove();
        print(x.next());
        x.set("47");
        print(a);
        // Traverse the list backwards:
        x = a.listIterator(a.size());
        while(x.hasPrevious())
            printnb(x.previous() + " ");
        print();
        print("testVisual finished");
    }
    // There are some things that only LinkedLists can do:
    public static void testLinkedList() {
        LinkedList<String> ll = new LinkedList<String>();
```

```
        ll.addAll(Countries.names(25));
        print(ll);
        // Treat it like a stack, pushing:
        ll.addFirst("one");
        ll.addFirst("two");
        print(ll);
        // Like "peeking" at the top of a stack:
        print(ll.getFirst());
        // Like popping a stack:
        print(ll.removeFirst());
        print(ll.removeFirst());
        // Treat it like a queue, pulling elements
        // off the tail end:
        print(ll.removeLast());
        print(ll);
    }
    public static void main(String[] args) {
        // Make and fill a new list each time:
        basicTest(
            new LinkedList<String>(Countries.names(25)));
        basicTest(
            new ArrayList<String>(Countries.names(25)));
        iterMotion(
            new LinkedList<String>(Countries.names(25)));
        iterMotion(
            new ArrayList<String>(Countries.names(25)));
        iterManipulation(
            new LinkedList<String>(Countries.names(25)));
        iterManipulation(
            new ArrayList<String>(Countries.names(25)));
        testVisual(
            new LinkedList<String>(Countries.names(25)));
        testLinkedList();
    }
} /* (Execute to see output) *///:~
```

In **basicTest( )** and **iterMotion( )** the calls are made in order to show the proper syntax, and although the return value is captured, it is not used. In some cases, the return value isn't captured at all. You should look up the full usage of each of these methods in the JDK documentation before you use them.

Exercise 7: (4) Create both an **ArrayList** and a **LinkedList**, and fill each using the **Countries.names( )** generator. Print each list using an ordinary **Iterator**, then insert one list into the other by using a **ListIterator**, inserting at every other location. Now perform the insertion starting at the end of the first list and moving backward.

Exercise 8: (7) Create a generic, singly linked list class called **SList**, which, to keep things simple, does *not* implement the **List** interface. Each **Link** object in the list should contain a reference to the next element in the list, but not the previous one (**LinkedList**, in contrast, is a doubly linked list, which means it maintains links in both directions). Create your own **SListIterator** which, again for simplicity, does not implement **ListIterator**. The only method in **SList** other than **toString( )** should be **iterator( )**, which produces an **SListIterator**. The only way to insert and remove elements from an **SList** is through **SListIterator**. Write code to demonstrate **SList**.

Sets and storage order

The **Set** examples in the *Holding Your Objects* chapter provide a good introduction to the operations that can be performed with basic **Set**s. However, those examples conveniently use predefined Java types such as **Integer** and **String**, which were designed to be usable inside containers. When creating your own types, be aware that a **Set** needs a way to maintain storage order. How the storage order is maintained varies from one implementation of **Set** to another. Thus, different **Set** implementations not only have different behaviors, they have different requirements for the type of object that you can put into a particular **Set**:

Set (interface)	Each element that you add to the **Set** must be unique; otherwise, the **Set** doesn't add the duplicate element. Elements added to a **Set** must at least define **equals( )** to establish object uniqueness. **Set** has exactly the same interface as **Collection**. The **Set** interface does not guarantee that it will maintain its elements in any particular order.
HashSet*	For **Set**s where fast lookup time is important. Elements must also define **hashCode( )**.
TreeSet	An ordered **Set** backed by a tree. This way, you can extract an ordered sequence from a **Set**. Elements must also implement the **Comparable** interface.
LinkedHashSet	Has the lookup speed of a **HashSet**, but

| | internally maintains the order in which you add the elements (the insertion order) using a linked list. Thus, when you iterate through the **Set**, the results appear in insertion order. Elements must also define **hashCode( )**. |

The asterisk on **HashSet** indicates that, in the absence of other constraints, this should be your default choice because it is optimized for speed.

Defining **hashCode( )** will be described later in this chapter. You must create an **equals( )** for both hashed and tree storage, but the **hashCode( )** is necessary only if the class will be placed in a **HashSet** (which is likely, since that should generally be your first choice as a **Set** implementation) or **LinkedHashSet**. However, for good programming style, you should always override **hashCode( )** when you override **equals( )**.

This example demonstrates the methods that must be defined in order to successfully use a type with a particular **Set** implementation:

```
//: containers/TypesForSets.java
// Methods necessary to put your own type in a Set.
import java.util.*;

class SetType {
  int i;
  public SetType(int n) { i = n; }
  public boolean equals(Object o) {
    return o instanceof SetType && (i == ((SetType)o).i);
  }
  public String toString() { return Integer.toString(i); }
}

class HashType extends SetType {
  public HashType(int n) { super(n); }
  public int hashCode() { return i; }
}

class TreeType extends SetType
implements Comparable<TreeType> {
  public TreeType(int n) { super(n); }
  public int compareTo(TreeType arg) {
    return (arg.i < i ? -1 : (arg.i == i ? 0 : 1));
  }
}
```

```java
public class TypesForSets {
  static <T> Set<T> fill(Set<T> set, Class<T> type) {
    try {
      for(int i = 0; i < 10; i++)
          set.add(
            type.getConstructor(int.class).newInstance(i));
    } catch(Exception e) {
      throw new RuntimeException(e);
    }
    return set;
  }
  static <T> void test(Set<T> set, Class<T> type) {
    fill(set, type);
    fill(set, type); // Try to add duplicates
    fill(set, type);
    System.out.println(set);
  }
  public static void main(String[] args) {
    test(new HashSet<HashType>(), HashType.class);
    test(new LinkedHashSet<HashType>(), HashType.class);
    test(new TreeSet<TreeType>(), TreeType.class);
    // Things that don't work:
    test(new HashSet<SetType>(), SetType.class);
    test(new HashSet<TreeType>(), TreeType.class);
    test(new LinkedHashSet<SetType>(), SetType.class);
    test(new LinkedHashSet<TreeType>(), TreeType.class);
    try {
      test(new TreeSet<SetType>(), SetType.class);
    } catch(Exception e) {
      System.out.println("Expected: " + e.getMessage());
    }
    try {
      test(new TreeSet<HashType>(), HashType.class);
    } catch(Exception e) {
      System.out.println("Expected: " + e.getMessage());
    }
  }
} /* Output: (Sample)
[2, 4, 9, 8, 6, 1, 3, 7, 5, 0]
[0, 1, 2, 3, 4, 5, 6, 7, 8, 9]
[9, 8, 7, 6, 5, 4, 3, 2, 1, 0]
[9, 9, 7, 5, 1, 2, 6, 3, 0, 7, 2, 4, 4, 7, 9, 1, 3, 6, 2,
4, 3, 0, 5, 0, 8, 8, 8, 6, 5, 1]
```

```
[0, 5, 5, 6, 5, 0, 3, 1, 9, 8, 4, 2, 3, 9, 7, 3, 4, 4, 0,
7, 1, 9, 6, 2, 1, 8, 2, 8, 6, 7]
[0, 1, 2, 3, 4, 5, 6, 7, 8, 9, 0, 1, 2, 3, 4, 5, 6, 7, 8,
9, 0, 1, 2, 3, 4, 5, 6, 7, 8, 9]
[0, 1, 2, 3, 4, 5, 6, 7, 8, 9, 0, 1, 2, 3, 4, 5, 6, 7, 8,
9, 0, 1, 2, 3, 4, 5, 6, 7, 8, 9]
Expected: java.lang.ClassCastException: SetType cannot be
cast to java.lang.Comparable
Expected: java.lang.ClassCastException: HashType cannot be
cast to java.lang.Comparable
*///:~
```

In order to prove which methods are necessary for a particular **Set** and at the same time to avoid code duplication, three classes are created. The base class, **SetType**, simply stores an **int**, and produces it via **toString( )**. Since all classes stored in **Set**s must have an **equals( )**, that method is also placed in the base class. Equality is based on the value of the **int i**.

HashType inherits from **SetType** and adds the **hashCode( )** method necessary for an object to be placed in a hashed implementation of a **Set**.

The **Comparable** interface, implemented by **TreeType**, is necessary if an object is to be used in any kind of sorted container, such as a **SortedSet** (of which **TreeSet** is the only implementation). In **compareTo( )**, note that I did *not* use the "simple and obvious" form **return i-i2**. Although this is a common programming error, it would only work properly if **i** and **i2** were "unsigned" **int**s (if Java *had* an "unsigned" keyword, which it does not). It breaks for Java's signed **int**, which is not big enough to represent the difference of two signed **int**s. If **i** is a large positive integer and **j** is a large negative integer, **i-j** will overflow and return a negative value, which will not work.

You'll usually want the **compareTo( )** method to produce a natural ordering that is consistent with the **equals( )** method. If **equals( )** produces **true** for a particular comparison, then **compareTo( )** should produce a zero result for that comparison, and if **equals( )** produces **false** for a comparison then **compareTo( )** should produce a nonzero result for that comparison.

In **TypesForSets**, both **fill( )** and **test( )** are defined using generics, in order to prevent code duplication. To verify the behavior of a **Set**, **test( )** calls **fill( )** on the test **set** three times, attempting to introduce duplicate objects. The **fill( )** method takes a **Set** of any type, and a **Class** object of the same type. It uses the **Class** object to discover the constructor that takes an **int** argument, and calls that constructor to add elements to the **Set**.

From the output, you can see that the **HashSet** keeps the elements in some mysterious order (which will be made clear later in the chapter), the **LinkedHashSet** keeps the elements in the order in which they were inserted, and the **TreeSet** maintains the elements in sorted order (because of the way that **compareTo( )** is implemented, this happens to be descending order).

If we try to use types that don't properly support the necessary operations with **Set**s that require those operations, things go very wrong. Placing a **SetType** or **TreeType** object, which doesn't include a redefined **hashCode( )** method, into any hashed implementations results in duplicate values, so the primary contract of the **Set** is violated. This is rather disturbing because there's not even a runtime error. However, the default **hashCode( )** is legitimate and so this is legal behavior, even if it's incorrect. The only reliable way to ensure the correctness of such a program is to incorporate unit tests into your build system (see the supplement at *http://MindView.net/Books/BetterJava* for more information).

If you try to use a type that doesn't implement **Comparable** in a **TreeSet**, you get a more definitive result: An exception is thrown when the **TreeSet** attempts to use the object as a **Comparable**.

SortedSet

The elements in a **SortedSet** are guaranteed to be in sorted order, which allows additional functionality to be provided with the following methods that are in the **SortedSet** interface:

Comparator comparator( ): Produces the **Comparator** used for this **Set**, or **null** for natural ordering.

Object first( ): Produces the lowest element.

Object last( ): Produces the highest element.

SortedSet subSet(fromElement, toElement): Produces a view of this **Set** with elements from **fromElement**, inclusive, to **toElement**, exclusive.

SortedSet headSet(toElement): Produces a view of this **Set** with elements less than **toElement**.

SortedSet tailSet(fromElement): Produces a view of this **Set** with
elements greater than or equal to **fromElement**.

Here's a simple demonstration:

```
//: containers/SortedSetDemo.java
// What you can do with a TreeSet.
import java.util.*;
import static net.mindview.util.Print.*;

public class SortedSetDemo {
  public static void main(String[] args) {
    SortedSet<String> sortedSet = new TreeSet<String>();
    Collections.addAll(sortedSet,
      "one two three four five six seven eight"
        .split(" "));
    print(sortedSet);
    String low = sortedSet.first();
    String high = sortedSet.last();
    print(low);
    print(high);
    Iterator<String> it = sortedSet.iterator();
    for(int i = 0; i <= 6; i++) {
      if(i == 3) low = it.next();
      if(i == 6) high = it.next();
      else it.next();
    }
    print(low);
    print(high);
    print(sortedSet.subSet(low, high));
    print(sortedSet.headSet(high));
    print(sortedSet.tailSet(low));
  }
} /* Output:
[eight, five, four, one, seven, six, three, two]
eight
two
one
two
[one, seven, six, three]
[eight, five, four, one, seven, six, three]
[one, seven, six, three, two]
*///:~
```

Note that **SortedSet** means "sorted according to the comparison function of the object," not "insertion order." Insertion order can be preserved using a **LinkedHashSet**.

Exercise 9: (2) Use **RandomGenerator.String** to fill a **TreeSet**, but use alphabetic ordering. Print the **TreeSet** to verify the sort order.

Exercise 10: (7) Using a **LinkedList** as your underlying implementation, define your own **SortedSet**.

Queues

Other than concurrency applications, the only two Java SE5 implementations of **Queue** are **LinkedList** and **PriorityQueue**, which are differentiated by ordering behavior rather than performance. Here's a basic example that involves most of the **Queue** implementations (not all of them will work in this example), including the concurrency-based **Queue**s. You place elements in one end and extract them from the other:

```
//: containers/QueueBehavior.java
// Compares the behavior of some of the queues
import java.util.concurrent.*;
import java.util.*;
import net.mindview.util.*;

public class QueueBehavior {
  private static int count = 10;
  static <T> void test(Queue<T> queue, Generator<T> gen) {
    for(int i = 0; i < count; i++)
      queue.offer(gen.next());
    while(queue.peek() != null)
      System.out.print(queue.remove() + " ");
    System.out.println();
  }
  static class Gen implements Generator<String> {
    String[] s = ("one two three four five six seven " +
      "eight nine ten").split(" ");
    int i;
    public String next() { return s[i++]; }
  }
  public static void main(String[] args) {
    test(new LinkedList<String>(), new Gen());
    test(new PriorityQueue<String>(), new Gen());
    test(new ArrayBlockingQueue<String>(count), new Gen());
```

```
      test(new ConcurrentLinkedQueue<String>(), new Gen());
      test(new LinkedBlockingQueue<String>(), new Gen());
      test(new PriorityBlockingQueue<String>(), new Gen());
  }
} /* Output:
one two three four five six seven eight nine ten
eight five four nine one seven six ten three two
one two three four five six seven eight nine ten
one two three four five six seven eight nine ten
one two three four five six seven eight nine ten
eight five four nine one seven six ten three two
*///:~
```

You can see that, with the exception of the priority queues, a **Queue** will produce elements in exactly the same order as they are placed in the **Queue**.

Priority queues

Priority queues were given a simple introduction in the *Holding Your Objects* chapter. A more interesting problem is a to-do list, where each object contains a string and a primary and secondary priority value. The ordering of this list is again controlled by implementing **Comparable**:

```
//: containers/ToDoList.java
// A more complex use of PriorityQueue.
import java.util.*;

class ToDoList extends PriorityQueue<ToDoList.ToDoItem> {
  static class ToDoItem implements Comparable<ToDoItem> {
    private char primary;
    private int secondary;
    private String item;
    public ToDoItem(String td, char pri, int sec) {
      primary = pri;
      secondary = sec;
      item = td;
    }
    public int compareTo(ToDoItem arg) {
      if(primary > arg.primary)
        return +1;
      if(primary == arg.primary)
        if(secondary > arg.secondary)
          return +1;
        else if(secondary == arg.secondary)
```

```
          return 0;
      return -1;
    }
    public String toString() {
      return Character.toString(primary) +
        secondary + ": " + item;
    }
  }
  public void add(String td, char pri, int sec) {
    super.add(new ToDoItem(td, pri, sec));
  }
  public static void main(String[] args) {
    ToDoList toDoList = new ToDoList();
    toDoList.add("Empty trash", 'C', 4);
    toDoList.add("Feed dog", 'A', 2);
    toDoList.add("Feed bird", 'B', 7);
    toDoList.add("Mow lawn", 'C', 3);
    toDoList.add("Water lawn", 'A', 1);
    toDoList.add("Feed cat", 'B', 1);
    while(!toDoList.isEmpty())
      System.out.println(toDoList.remove());
  }
} /* Output:
A1: Water lawn
A2: Feed dog
B1: Feed cat
B7: Feed bird
C3: Mow lawn
C4: Empty trash
*///:~
```

You can see how the ordering of the items happens automatically because of
the priority queue.

Exercise 11: (2) Create a class that contains an **Integer** that is initialized
to a value between 0 and 100 using **java.util.Random**. Implement
Comparable using this **Integer** field. Fill a **PriorityQueue** with objects of
your class, and extract the values using **poll( )** to show that it produces the
expected order.

Deques

A *deque* (double-ended queue) is like a queue, but you can add and remove
elements from either end. There are methods in **LinkedList** that support
deque operations, but there is no explicit interface for a deque in the Java

standard libraries. Thus, **LinkedList** cannot implement this interface and you cannot upcast to a **Deque** interface as you can to a **Queue** in the previous example. However, you can create a **Deque** class using composition, and simply expose the relevant methods from **LinkedList**:

```
//: net/mindview/util/Deque.java
// Creating a Deque from a LinkedList.
package net.mindview.util;
import java.util.*;

public class Deque<T> {
  private LinkedList<T> deque = new LinkedList<T>();
  public void addFirst(T e) { deque.addFirst(e); }
  public void addLast(T e) { deque.addLast(e); }
  public T getFirst() { return deque.getFirst(); }
  public T getLast() { return deque.getLast(); }
  public T removeFirst() { return deque.removeFirst(); }
  public T removeLast() { return deque.removeLast(); }
  public int size() { return deque.size(); }
  public String toString() { return deque.toString(); }
  // And other methods as necessary...
} ///:~
```

If you put this **Deque** to use in your own programs, you may discover that you need to add other methods in order to make it practical.

Here's a simple test of the **Deque** class:

```
//: containers/DequeTest.java
import net.mindview.util.*;
import static net.mindview.util.Print.*;

public class DequeTest {
  static void fillTest(Deque<Integer> deque) {
    for(int i = 20; i < 27; i++)
      deque.addFirst(i);
    for(int i = 50; i < 55; i++)
      deque.addLast(i);
  }
  public static void main(String[] args) {
    Deque<Integer> di = new Deque<Integer>();
    fillTest(di);
    print(di);
    while(di.size() != 0)
      printnb(di.removeFirst() + " ");
```

```
      print();
      fillTest(di);
      while(di.size() != 0)
        printnb(di.removeLast() + " ");
  }
} /* Output:
[26, 25, 24, 23, 22, 21, 20, 50, 51, 52, 53, 54]
26 25 24 23 22 21 20 50 51 52 53 54
54 53 52 51 50 20 21 22 23 24 25 26
*///:~
```

It's less likely that you'll put elements in and take them out at both ends, so **Deque** is not as commonly used as **Queue**.

Understanding **Map**s

As you learned in the *Holding Your Objects* chapter, the basic idea of a map (also called an *associative array*) is that it maintains key-value associations (pairs) so you can look up a value using a key. The standard Java library contains different basic implementations of **Map**s: **HashMap**, **TreeMap**, **LinkedHashMap**, **WeakHashMap**, **ConcurrentHashMap**, and **IdentityHashMap**. They all have the same basic **Map** interface, but they differ in behaviors including efficiency, the order in which the pairs are held and presented, how long the objects are held by the map, how the map works in multithreaded programs, and how key equality is determined. The number of implementations of the **Map** interface should tell you something about the importance of this tool.

So you can gain a deeper understanding of **Map**s, it is helpful to look at how an associative array is constructed. Here is an extremely simple implementation:

```
//: containers/AssociativeArray.java
// Associates keys with values.
import static net.mindview.util.Print.*;

public class AssociativeArray<K,V> {
  private Object[][] pairs;
  private int index;
  public AssociativeArray(int length) {
    pairs = new Object[length][2];
  }
  public void put(K key, V value) {
```

```java
      if(index >= pairs.length)
        throw new ArrayIndexOutOfBoundsException();
      pairs[index++] = new Object[]{ key, value };
    }
    @SuppressWarnings("unchecked")
    public V get(K key) {
      for(int i = 0; i < index; i++)
        if(key.equals(pairs[i][0]))
          return (V)pairs[i][1];
      return null; // Did not find key
    }
    public String toString() {
      StringBuilder result = new StringBuilder();
      for(int i = 0; i < index; i++) {
        result.append(pairs[i][0].toString());
        result.append(" : ");
        result.append(pairs[i][1].toString());
        if(i < index - 1)
          result.append("\n");
      }
      return result.toString();
    }
    public static void main(String[] args) {
      AssociativeArray<String,String> map =
        new AssociativeArray<String,String>(6);
      map.put("sky", "blue");
      map.put("grass", "green");
      map.put("ocean", "dancing");
      map.put("tree", "tall");
      map.put("earth", "brown");
      map.put("sun", "warm");
      try {
        map.put("extra", "object"); // Past the end
      } catch(ArrayIndexOutOfBoundsException e) {
        print("Too many objects!");
      }
      print(map);
      print(map.get("ocean"));
    }
  } /* Output:
Too many objects!
sky : blue
grass : green
ocean : dancing
```

```
tree : tall
earth : brown
sun : warm
dancing
*///:~
```

The essential methods in an associative array are **put( )** and **get( )**, but for easy display, **toString( )** has been overridden to print the key-value pairs. To show that it works, **main( )** loads an **AssociativeArray** with pairs of strings and prints the resulting map, followed by a **get( )** of one of the values.

To use the **get( )** method, you pass in the **key** that you want it to look up, and it produces the associated value as the result or returns **null** if it can't be found. The **get( )** method is using what is possibly the least efficient approach imaginable to locate the value: starting at the top of the array and using **equals( )** to compare keys. But the point here is simplicity, not efficiency.

So the above version is instructive, but it isn't very efficient and it has a fixed size, which is inflexible. Fortunately, the **Map**s in **java.util** do not have these problems and can be substituted into the above example.

Exercise 12: (1) Substitute a **HashMap**, a **TreeMap** and a **LinkedHashMap** in **AssociativeArray.java**'s **main( )**.

Exercise 13: (4) Use **AssociativeArray.java** to create a word-occurrence counter, mapping **String** to **Integer**. Using the **net.mindview.util.TextFile** utility in this book, open a text file and break up the words in that file using whitespace and punctuation, and count the occurrence of the words in that file.

Performance

Performance is a fundamental issue for maps, and it's very slow to use a linear search in **get( )** when hunting for a key. This is where **HashMap** speeds things up. Instead of a slow search for the key, it uses a special value called a *hash code*. The hash code is a way to take some information in the object in question and turn it into a "relatively unique" **int** for that object. **hashCode( )** is a method in the root class **Object**, so all Java objects can produce a hash code. A **HashMap** takes the **hashCode( )** of the object and uses it to quickly hunt for the key. This results in a dramatic performance improvement.[6]

Here are the basic **Map** implementations. The asterisk on **HashMap** indicates that, in the absence of other constraints, this should be your default choice because it is optimized for speed. The other implementations emphasize other characteristics, and are thus not as fast as **HashMap**.

HashMap*	Implementation based on a hash table. (Use this class instead of **Hashtable**.) Provides constant-time performance for inserting and locating pairs. Performance can be adjusted via constructors that allow you to set the *capacity* and *load factor* of the hash table.
LinkedHashMap	Like a **HashMap**, but when you iterate through it, you get the pairs in insertion order, or in least-recently-used (LRU) order. Only slightly slower than a **HashMap**, except when iterating, where it is faster due to the linked list used to maintain the internal ordering.
TreeMap	Implementation based on a red-black tree. When you view the keys or the pairs, they will be in sorted order (determined by **Comparable** or **Comparator**). The point of a **TreeMap** is that you get the results in sorted order. **TreeMap** is the only **Map** with the **subMap( )** method, which allows you to return a portion of the tree.
WeakHashMap	A map of *weak keys* that allow objects referred to by the map to be released; designed to solve certain types of

---

[6] If these speedups still don't meet your performance needs, you can further accelerate table lookup by writing your own **Map** and customizing it to your particular types to avoid delays due to casting to and from **Object**s. To reach even higher levels of performance, speed enthusiasts can use Donald Knuth's *The Art of Computer Programming, Volume 3: Sorting and Searching, Second Edition*, to replace overflow bucket lists with arrays that have two additional benefits: they can be optimized for disk storage characteristics and they can save most of the time of creating and garbage collecting individual records.

	problems. If no references to a particular key are held outside the map, that key may be garbage collected.
ConcurrentHashMap	A thread-safe **Map** which does not involve synchronization locking. This is discussed in the *Concurrency* chapter.
IdentityHashMap	A hash map that uses == instead of **equals( )** to compare keys. Only for solving special types of problems; not for general use.

Hashing is the most commonly used way to store elements in a map. Later, you'll learn how hashing works.

The requirements for the keys used in a **Map** are the same as for the elements in a **Set**. You saw these demonstrated in **TypesForSets.java**. Any key must have an **equals( )** method. If the key is used in a hashed **Map**, it must also have a proper **hashCode( )**. If the key is used in a **TreeMap**, it must implement **Comparable**.

The following example shows the operations available through the **Map** interface, using the previously defined **CountingMapData** test data set:

```
//: containers/Maps.java
// Things you can do with Maps.
import java.util.concurrent.*;
import java.util.*;
import net.mindview.util.*;
import static net.mindview.util.Print.*;

public class Maps {
  public static void printKeys(Map<Integer,String> map) {
    printnb("Size = " + map.size() + ", ");
    printnb("Keys: ");
    print(map.keySet()); // Produce a Set of the keys
  }
  public static void test(Map<Integer,String> map) {
    print(map.getClass().getSimpleName());
    map.putAll(new CountingMapData(25));
    // Map has 'Set' behavior for keys:
    map.putAll(new CountingMapData(25));
    printKeys(map);
    // Producing a Collection of the values:
```

```
      printnb("Values: ");
      print(map.values());
      print(map);
      print("map.containsKey(11): " + map.containsKey(11));
      print("map.get(11): " + map.get(11));
      print("map.containsValue(\"F0\"): "
        + map.containsValue("F0"));
      Integer key = map.keySet().iterator().next();
      print("First key in map: " + key);
      map.remove(key);
      printKeys(map);
      map.clear();
      print("map.isEmpty(): " + map.isEmpty());
      map.putAll(new CountingMapData(25));
      // Operations on the Set change the Map:
      map.keySet().removeAll(map.keySet());
      print("map.isEmpty(): " + map.isEmpty());
    }
  public static void main(String[] args) {
      test(new HashMap<Integer,String>());
      test(new TreeMap<Integer,String>());
      test(new LinkedHashMap<Integer,String>());
      test(new IdentityHashMap<Integer,String>());
      test(new ConcurrentHashMap<Integer,String>());
      test(new WeakHashMap<Integer,String>());
    }
} /* Output:
HashMap
Size = 25, Keys: [15, 8, 23, 16, 7, 22, 9, 21, 6, 1, 14,
24, 4, 19, 11, 18, 3, 12, 17, 2, 13, 20, 10, 5, 0]
Values: [P0, I0, X0, Q0, H0, W0, J0, V0, G0, B0, O0, Y0,
E0, T0, L0, S0, D0, M0, R0, C0, N0, U0, K0, F0, A0]
{15=P0, 8=I0, 23=X0, 16=Q0, 7=H0, 22=W0, 9=J0, 21=V0, 6=G0,
1=B0, 14=O0, 24=Y0, 4=E0, 19=T0, 11=L0, 18=S0, 3=D0, 12=M0,
17=R0, 2=C0, 13=N0, 20=U0, 10=K0, 5=F0, 0=A0}
map.containsKey(11): true
map.get(11): L0
map.containsValue("F0"): true
First key in map: 15
Size = 24, Keys: [8, 23, 16, 7, 22, 9, 21, 6, 1, 14, 24, 4,
19, 11, 18, 3, 12, 17, 2, 13, 20, 10, 5, 0]
map.isEmpty(): true
map.isEmpty(): true
...
```

```
*///:~
```

The **printKeys( )** method demonstrates how to produce a **Collection** view of a **Map**. The **keySet( )** method produces a **Set** backed by the keys in the **Map**. Because of improved printing support in Java SE5, you can simply print the result of the **values( )** method, which produces a **Collection** containing all the values in the **Map.** (Note that keys must be unique, but values may contain duplicates.) Since these **Collection**s are backed by the **Map**, any changes in a **Collection** will be reflected in the associated **Map**.

The rest of the program provides simple examples of each **Map** operation and tests each basic type of **Map**.

Exercise 14:   (3) Show that **java.util.Properties** works in the above program.

SortedMap

If you have a **SortedMap** (of which **TreeMap** is the only one available), the keys are guaranteed to be in sorted order, which allows additional functionality to be provided with these methods in the **SortedMap** interface:

Comparator comparator( ): Produces the comparator used for this **Map**, or **null** for natural ordering.

T firstKey( ): Produces the lowest key.

T lastKey( ): Produces the highest key.

SortedMap subMap(fromKey, toKey): Produces a view of this **Map** with keys from **fromKey**, inclusive, to **toKey**, exclusive.

SortedMap headMap(toKey): Produces a view of this **Map** with keys less than **toKey**.

SortedMap tailMap(fromKey): Produces a view of this **Map** with keys greater than or equal to **fromKey**.

Here's an example that's similar to **SortedSetDemo.java** and shows this additional behavior of **TreeMap**s:

```
//: containers/SortedMapDemo.java
// What you can do with a TreeMap.
import java.util.*;
import net.mindview.util.*;
import static net.mindview.util.Print.*;
```

```
public class SortedMapDemo {
  public static void main(String[] args) {
    TreeMap<Integer,String> sortedMap =
      new TreeMap<Integer,String>(new CountingMapData(10));
    print(sortedMap);
    Integer low = sortedMap.firstKey();
    Integer high = sortedMap.lastKey();
    print(low);
    print(high);
    Iterator<Integer> it = sortedMap.keySet().iterator();
    for(int i = 0; i <= 6; i++) {
      if(i == 3) low = it.next();
      if(i == 6) high = it.next();
      else it.next();
    }
    print(low);
    print(high);
    print(sortedMap.subMap(low, high));
    print(sortedMap.headMap(high));
    print(sortedMap.tailMap(low));
  }
} /* Output:
{0=A0, 1=B0, 2=C0, 3=D0, 4=E0, 5=F0, 6=G0, 7=H0, 8=I0,
9=J0}
0
9
3
7
{3=D0, 4=E0, 5=F0, 6=G0}
{0=A0, 1=B0, 2=C0, 3=D0, 4=E0, 5=F0, 6=G0}
{3=D0, 4=E0, 5=F0, 6=G0, 7=H0, 8=I0, 9=J0}
*///:~
```

Here, the pairs are stored by key-sorted order. Because there is a sense of order in the **TreeMap**, the concept of "location" makes sense, so you can have first and last elements and submaps.

LinkedHashMap

The **LinkedHashMap** hashes everything for speed, but also produces the pairs in insertion order during a traversal (**System.out.println( )** iterates through the map, so you see the results of traversal). In addition, a **LinkedHashMap** can be configured in the constructor to use a *least-recently-used* (LRU) algorithm based on accesses, so elements that haven't been accessed (and thus are candidates for removal) appear at the front of the list. This allows easy creation of programs that do periodic cleanup in order to save space. Here's a simple example showing both features:

```
//: containers/LinkedHashMapDemo.java
// What you can do with a LinkedHashMap.
import java.util.*;
import net.mindview.util.*;
import static net.mindview.util.Print.*;

public class LinkedHashMapDemo {
  public static void main(String[] args) {
    LinkedHashMap<Integer,String> linkedMap =
      new LinkedHashMap<Integer,String>(
        new CountingMapData(9));
    print(linkedMap);
    // Least-recently-used order:
    linkedMap =
      new LinkedHashMap<Integer,String>(16, 0.75f, true);
    linkedMap.putAll(new CountingMapData(9));
    print(linkedMap);
    for(int i = 0; i < 6; i++) // Cause accesses:
      linkedMap.get(i);
    print(linkedMap);
    linkedMap.get(0);
    print(linkedMap);
  }
} /* Output:
{0=A0, 1=B0, 2=C0, 3=D0, 4=E0, 5=F0, 6=G0, 7=H0, 8=I0}
{0=A0, 1=B0, 2=C0, 3=D0, 4=E0, 5=F0, 6=G0, 7=H0, 8=I0}
{6=G0, 7=H0, 8=I0, 0=A0, 1=B0, 2=C0, 3=D0, 4=E0, 5=F0}
{6=G0, 7=H0, 8=I0, 1=B0, 2=C0, 3=D0, 4=E0, 5=F0, 0=A0}
*///:~
```

You can see from the output that the pairs are indeed traversed in insertion order, even for the LRU version. However, after the first six items (only) are accessed in the LRU version, the last three items move to the front of the list. Then, when "**o**" is accessed again, it moves to the back of the list.

Hashing and hash codes

The examples in the *Holding Your Objects* chapter used predefined classes as **HashMap** keys. These examples worked because the predefined classes had all the necessary wiring to make them behave correctly as keys.

A common pitfall occurs when you create your own classes to be used as keys for **HashMap**s, and forget to put in the necessary wiring. For example, consider a weather predicting system that matches **Groundhog** objects to **Prediction** objects. This seems fairly straightforward—you create the two classes, and use **Groundhog** as the key and **Prediction** as the value:

```
//: containers/Groundhog.java
// Looks plausible, but doesn't work as a HashMap key.

public class Groundhog {
  protected int number;
  public Groundhog(int n) { number = n; }
  public String toString() {
    return "Groundhog #" + number;
  }
} ///:~
```

```
//: containers/Prediction.java
// Predicting the weather with groundhogs.
import java.util.*;

public class Prediction {
  private static Random rand = new Random(47);
  private boolean shadow = rand.nextDouble() > 0.5;
  public String toString() {
    if(shadow)
      return "Six more weeks of Winter!";
    else
      return "Early Spring!";
  }
} ///:~
```

```
//: containers/SpringDetector.java
// What will the weather be?
import java.lang.reflect.*;
import java.util.*;
import static net.mindview.util.Print.*;

public class SpringDetector {
  // Uses a Groundhog or class derived from Groundhog:
  public static <T extends Groundhog>
  void detectSpring(Class<T> type) throws Exception {
    Constructor<T> ghog = type.getConstructor(int.class);
    Map<Groundhog,Prediction> map =
      new HashMap<Groundhog,Prediction>();
```

```
    for(int i = 0; i < 10; i++)
      map.put(ghog.newInstance(i), new Prediction());
    print("map = " + map);
    Groundhog gh = ghog.newInstance(3);
    print("Looking up prediction for " + gh);
    if(map.containsKey(gh))
      print(map.get(gh));
    else
      print("Key not found: " + gh);
  }
  public static void main(String[] args) throws Exception {
    detectSpring(Groundhog.class);
  }
} /* Output:
map = {Groundhog #3=Early Spring!, Groundhog #7=Early
Spring!, Groundhog #5=Early Spring!, Groundhog #9=Six more
weeks of Winter!, Groundhog #8=Six more weeks of Winter!,
Groundhog #0=Six more weeks of Winter!, Groundhog #6=Early
Spring!, Groundhog #4=Six more weeks of Winter!, Groundhog
#1=Six more weeks of Winter!, Groundhog #2=Early Spring!}
Looking up prediction for Groundhog #3
Key not found: Groundhog #3
*///:~
```

Each **Groundhog** is given an identity number, so you can look up a
Prediction in the **HashMap** by saying, "Give me the **Prediction**
associated with **Groundhog** #3." The **Prediction** class contains a **boolean**
that is initialized using **java.util.random( )** and a **toString( )** that
interprets the result for you. The **detectSpring( )** method is created using
reflection to instantiate and use the **class Groundhog** or any class derived
from **Groundhog**. This will come in handy later, when we inherit a new type
of **Groundhog** to solve the problem demonstrated here.

A **HashMap** is filled with **Groundhog**s and their associated **Prediction**s.
The **HashMap** is printed so that you can see it has been filled. Then a
Groundhog with an identity number of 3 is used as a key to look up the
prediction for **Groundhog** #3 (which you can see must be in the **Map**).

It seems simple enough, but it doesn't work—it can't find the key for #3. The
problem is that **Groundhog** is automatically inherited from the common
root class **Object**, and it is **Object**'s **hashCode( )** method that is used to
generate the hash code for each object. By default this just uses the address of
its object. Thus, the first instance of **Groundhog(3)** does *not* produce a hash

code equal to the hash code for the second instance of **Groundhog(3)** that we tried to use as a lookup.

You might think that all you need to do is write an appropriate override for **hashCode( )**. But it still won't work until you've done one more thing: override the **equals( )** that is also part of **Object**. **equals( )** is used by the **HashMap** when trying to determine if your key is equal to any of the keys in the table.

A proper **equals( )** must satisfy the following five conditions:

1. Reflexive: For any **x**, **x.equals(x)** should return **true**.

2. Symmetric: For any **x** and **y**, **x.equals(y)** should return **true** if and only if **y.equals(x)** returns **true**.

3. Transitive: For any **x**, **y**, and **z**, if **x.equals(y)** returns **true** and **y.equals(z)** returns **true**, then **x.equals(z)** should return **true**.

4. Consistent: For any **x** and **y**, multiple invocations of **x.equals(y)** consistently return **true** or consistently return **false**, provided no information used in equals comparisons on the object is modified.

5. For any non-**null x**, **x.equals(null)** should return **false**.

Again, the default **Object.equals( )** simply compares object addresses, so one **Groundhog(3)** is not equal to another **Groundhog(3)**. Thus, to use your own classes as keys in a **HashMap**, you must override both **hashCode( )** and **equals( )**, as shown in the following solution to the groundhog problem:

```
//: containers/Groundhog2.java
// A class that's used as a key in a HashMap
// must override hashCode() and equals().

public class Groundhog2 extends Groundhog {
  public Groundhog2(int n) { super(n); }
  public int hashCode() { return number; }
  public boolean equals(Object o) {
    return o instanceof Groundhog2 &&
      (number == ((Groundhog2)o).number);
  }
} ///:~
```

```
//: containers/SpringDetector2.java
// A working key.

public class SpringDetector2 {
  public static void main(String[] args) throws Exception {
    SpringDetector.detectSpring(Groundhog2.class);
  }
} /* Output:
map = {Groundhog #2=Early Spring!, Groundhog #4=Six more
weeks of Winter!, Groundhog #9=Six more weeks of Winter!,
Groundhog #8=Six more weeks of Winter!, Groundhog #6=Early
Spring!, Groundhog #1=Six more weeks of Winter!, Groundhog
#3=Early Spring!, Groundhog #7=Early Spring!, Groundhog
#5=Early Spring!, Groundhog #0=Six more weeks of Winter!}
Looking up prediction for Groundhog #3
Early Spring!
*///:~
```

Groundhog2.hashCode( ) returns the groundhog number as a hash value.
In this example, the programmer is responsible for ensuring that no two
groundhogs exist with the same ID number. The **hashCode( )** is not
required to return a unique identifier (something you'll understand better
later in this chapter), but the **equals( )** method must strictly determine
whether two objects are equivalent. Here, **equals( )** is based on the
groundhog number, so if two **Groundhog2** objects exist as keys in the
HashMap with the same groundhog number, it will fail.

Even though it appears that the **equals( )** method is only checking to see
whether the argument is an instance of **Groundhog2** (using the **instanceof**
keyword, which was explained in the *Type Information* chapter), the
instanceof actually quietly does a second sanity check to see if the object is
null, since **instanceof** produces **false** if the left-hand argument is **null**.
Assuming it's the correct type and not **null**, the comparison is based on the
actual **number** values in each object. You can see from the output that the
behavior is now correct.

When creating your own class to use in a **HashSet**, you must pay attention to
the same issues as when it is used as a key in a **HashMap**.

Understanding **hashCode()**

The preceding example is only a start toward solving the problem correctly. It
shows that if you do not override **hashCode( )** and **equals( )** for your key,

the hashed data structure (**HashSet**, **HashMap**, **LinkedHashSet**, or **LinkedHashMap**) probably won't deal with your key properly. For a *good* solution to the problem, however, you need to understand what's going on inside the hashed data structure.

First, consider the motivation behind hashing: You want to look up an object using another object. But you can also accomplish this with a **TreeMap**, or you can even implement your own **Map**. In contrast to a hashed implementation, the following example implements a **Map** using a pair of **ArrayLists**. Unlike **AssociativeArray.java**, this includes a full implementation of the **Map** interface, which accounts for the **entrySet( )** method:

```
//: containers/SlowMap.java
// A Map implemented with ArrayLists.
import java.util.*;
import net.mindview.util.*;

public class SlowMap<K,V> extends AbstractMap<K,V> {
  private List<K> keys = new ArrayList<K>();
  private List<V> values = new ArrayList<V>();
  public V put(K key, V value) {
    V oldValue = get(key); // The old value or null
    if(!keys.contains(key)) {
      keys.add(key);
      values.add(value);
    } else
      values.set(keys.indexOf(key), value);
    return oldValue;
  }
  public V get(Object key) { // key is type Object, not K
    if(!keys.contains(key))
      return null;
    return values.get(keys.indexOf(key));
  }
  public Set<Map.Entry<K,V>> entrySet() {
    Set<Map.Entry<K,V>> set= new HashSet<Map.Entry<K,V>>();
    Iterator<K> ki = keys.iterator();
    Iterator<V> vi = values.iterator();
    while(ki.hasNext())
      set.add(new MapEntry<K,V>(ki.next(), vi.next()));
    return set;
  }
  public static void main(String[] args) {
```

```
        SlowMap<String,String> m= new SlowMap<String,String>();
        m.putAll(Countries.capitals(15));
        System.out.println(m);
        System.out.println(m.get("BULGARIA"));
        System.out.println(m.entrySet());
    }
} /* Output:
{CAMEROON=Yaounde, CHAD=N'djamena, CONGO=Brazzaville, CAPE
VERDE=Praia, ALGERIA=Algiers, COMOROS=Moroni, CENTRAL
AFRICAN REPUBLIC=Bangui, BOTSWANA=Gaberone,
BURUNDI=Bujumbura, BENIN=Porto-Novo, BULGARIA=Sofia,
EGYPT=Cairo, ANGOLA=Luanda, BURKINA FASO=Ouagadougou,
DJIBOUTI=Dijibouti}
Sofia
[CAMEROON=Yaounde, CHAD=N'djamena, CONGO=Brazzaville, CAPE
VERDE=Praia, ALGERIA=Algiers, COMOROS=Moroni, CENTRAL
AFRICAN REPUBLIC=Bangui, BOTSWANA=Gaberone,
BURUNDI=Bujumbura, BENIN=Porto-Novo, BULGARIA=Sofia,
EGYPT=Cairo, ANGOLA=Luanda, BURKINA FASO=Ouagadougou,
DJIBOUTI=Dijibouti]
*///:~
```

The **put( )** method simply places the keys and values in corresponding
ArrayLists. In accordance with the **Map** interface, it must return the old key
or **null** if there was no old key.

Also following the specifications for **Map**, **get( )** produces **null** if the key is
not in the **SlowMap**. If the key exists, it is used to look up the numerical
index indicating its location in the **keys List**, and this number is used as an
index to produce the associated value from the **values List**. Notice that the
type of **key** is **Object** in **get( )**, rather than the parameterized type **K** as you
might expect (and which was indeed used in **AssociativeArray.java**). This
is a result of the injection of generics into the Java language at such a late
date—if generics had been an original feature in the language, **get( )** could
have specified the type of its parameter.

The **Map.entrySet( )** method must produce a set of **Map.Entry** objects.
However, **Map.Entry** is an interface describing an implementation-
dependent structure, so if you want to make your own type of **Map**, you must
also define an implementation of **Map.Entry**:

```
//: containers/MapEntry.java
// A simple Map.Entry for sample Map implementations.
import java.util.*;
```

```
public class MapEntry<K,V> implements Map.Entry<K,V> {
  private K key;
  private V value;
  public MapEntry(K key, V value) {
    this.key = key;
    this.value = value;
  }
  public K getKey() { return key; }
  public V getValue() { return value; }
  public V setValue(V v) {
    V result = value;
    value = v;
    return result;
  }
  public int hashCode() {
    return (key==null ? 0 : key.hashCode()) ^
      (value==null ? 0 : value.hashCode());
  }
  public boolean equals(Object o) {
    if(!(o instanceof MapEntry)) return false;
    @SuppressWarnings("unchecked")
    MapEntry<K,V> me = (MapEntry<K,V>)o;
    return
      (key == null ?
       me.getKey() == null : key.equals(me.getKey())) &&
      (value == null ?
       me.getValue()== null : value.equals(me.getValue()));
  }
  public String toString() { return key + "=" + value; }
} ///:~
```

Here, a very simple class called **MapEntry** holds and retrieves the keys and values. This is used in **entrySet( )** to produce a **Set** of key-value pairs. Notice that **entrySet( )** uses a **HashSet** to hold the pairs, and **MapEntry** takes the simple approach of just using **key**'s **hashCode( )**. Although this solution is very simple, and appears to work in the trivial test in **SlowMap.main( )**, it is not a correct implementation because a copy of the keys and values is made. A correct implementation of **entrySet( )** will provide a *view* into the **Map**, rather than a copy, and this view will allow modification of the original map (which a copy doesn't). Exercise 16 provides the opportunity to repair the problem.

Note that the **equals( )** method in **MapEntry** must check both keys and values. The meaning of the **hashCode( )** method will be described shortly.

The **String** representation of the contents of the **SlowMap** is automatically produced by the **toString( )** method defined in **AbstractMap**.

In **SlowMap.main( )**, a **SlowMap** is loaded and then the contents are displayed. A call to **get( )** shows that it works.

Exercise 15:   (1) Repeat Exercise 13 using a **SlowMap**.

Exercise 16:   (7) Apply the tests in **Maps.java** to **SlowMap** to verify that it works. Fix anything in **SlowMap** that doesn't work correctly.

Exercise 17:   (2) Implement the rest of the **Map** interface for **SlowMap**.

Exercise 18:   (3) Using **SlowMap.java** for inspiration, create a **SlowSet**.

Hashing for speed

SlowMap.java shows that it's not that hard to produce a new type of **Map**. But as the name suggests, a **SlowMap** isn't very fast, so you probably wouldn't use it if you had an alternative available. The problem is in the lookup of the key; the keys are not kept in any particular order, so a simple linear search is used. A linear search is the slowest way to find something.

The whole point of hashing is speed: Hashing allows the lookup to happen quickly. Since the bottleneck is in the speed of the key lookup, one of the solutions to the problem is to keep the keys sorted and then use **Collections.binarySearch( )** to perform the lookup (an exercise will walk you through this process).

Hashing goes further by saying that all you want to do is to store the key *somewhere* in a way that it can be found quickly. The fastest structure in which to store a group of elements is an array, so that will be used for representing the key information (note that I said "key information," and not the key itself). But because an array cannot be resized, we have a problem: We want to store an indeterminate number of values in the **Map**, but if the number of keys is fixed by the array size, how can this be?

The answer is that the array will not hold the keys. From the key object, a number will be derived that will index into the array. This number is the *hash code*, produced by the **hashCode( )** method (in computer science parlance, this is the *hash function*) defined in **Object** and presumably overridden by your class.

To solve the problem of the fixed-size array, more than one key may produce the same index. That is, there may be *collisions*. Because of this, it doesn't matter how big the array is; any key object's hash code will land somewhere in that array.

So the process of looking up a value starts by computing the hash code and using it to index into the array. If you could guarantee that there were no collisions (which is possible if you have a fixed number of values), then you'd have a *perfect hashing function*, but that's a special case.[7] In all other cases, collisions are handled by *external chaining:* The array doesn't point directly to a value, but instead to a list of values. These values are searched in a linear fashion using the **equals( )** method. Of course, this aspect of the search is much slower, but if the hash function is good, there will only be a few values in each slot. So instead of searching through the entire list, you quickly jump to a slot where you only have to compare a few entries to find the value. This is much faster, which is why the **HashMap** is so quick.

Knowing the basics of hashing, you can implement a simple hashed **Map**:

```
//: containers/SimpleHashMap.java
// A demonstration hashed Map.
import java.util.*;
import net.mindview.util.*;

public class SimpleHashMap<K,V> extends AbstractMap<K,V> {
  // Choose a prime number for the hash table
  // size, to achieve a uniform distribution:
  static final int SIZE = 997;
  // You can't have a physical array of generics,
  // but you can upcast to one:
  @SuppressWarnings("unchecked")
  LinkedList<MapEntry<K,V>>[] buckets =
    new LinkedList[SIZE];
  public V put(K key, V value) {
    V oldValue = null;
    int index = Math.abs(key.hashCode()) % SIZE;
    if(buckets[index] == null)
      buckets[index] = new LinkedList<MapEntry<K,V>>();
```

---

[7] The case of a perfect hashing function is implemented in the Java SE5 **EnumMap** and **EnumSet**, because an **enum** defines a fixed number of instances. See the *Enumerated Types* chapter.

```
        LinkedList<MapEntry<K,V>> bucket = buckets[index];
        MapEntry<K,V> pair = new MapEntry<K,V>(key, value);
        boolean found = false;
        ListIterator<MapEntry<K,V>> it = bucket.listIterator();
        while(it.hasNext()) {
          MapEntry<K,V> iPair = it.next();
          if(iPair.getKey().equals(key)) {
            oldValue = iPair.getValue();
            it.set(pair); // Replace old with new
            found = true;
            break;
          }
        }
        if(!found)
          buckets[index].add(pair);
        return oldValue;
      }
      public V get(Object key) {
        int index = Math.abs(key.hashCode()) % SIZE;
        if(buckets[index] == null) return null;
        for(MapEntry<K,V> iPair : buckets[index])
          if(iPair.getKey().equals(key))
            return iPair.getValue();
        return null;
      }
      public Set<Map.Entry<K,V>> entrySet() {
        Set<Map.Entry<K,V>> set= new HashSet<Map.Entry<K,V>>();
        for(LinkedList<MapEntry<K,V>> bucket : buckets) {
          if(bucket == null) continue;
          for(MapEntry<K,V> mpair : bucket)
            set.add(mpair);
        }
        return set;
      }
      public static void main(String[] args) {
        SimpleHashMap<String,String> m =
          new SimpleHashMap<String,String>();
        m.putAll(Countries.capitals(25));
        System.out.println(m);
        System.out.println(m.get("ERITREA"));
        System.out.println(m.entrySet());
      }
    } /* Output:
```

```
{CAMEROON=Yaounde, CONGO=Brazzaville, CHAD=N'djamena, COTE
D'IVOIR (IVORY COAST)=Yamoussoukro, CENTRAL AFRICAN
REPUBLIC=Bangui, GUINEA=Conakry, BOTSWANA=Gaberone,
BISSAU=Bissau, EGYPT=Cairo, ANGOLA=Luanda, BURKINA
FASO=Ouagadougou, ERITREA=Asmara, THE GAMBIA=Banjul,
KENYA=Nairobi, GABON=Libreville, CAPE VERDE=Praia,
ALGERIA=Algiers, COMOROS=Moroni, EQUATORIAL GUINEA=Malabo,
BURUNDI=Bujumbura, BENIN=Porto-Novo, BULGARIA=Sofia,
GHANA=Accra, DJIBOUTI=Dijibouti, ETHIOPIA=Addis Ababa}
Asmara
[CAMEROON=Yaounde, CONGO=Brazzaville, CHAD=N'djamena, COTE
D'IVOIR (IVORY COAST)=Yamoussoukro, CENTRAL AFRICAN
REPUBLIC=Bangui, GUINEA=Conakry, BOTSWANA=Gaberone,
BISSAU=Bissau, EGYPT=Cairo, ANGOLA=Luanda, BURKINA
FASO=Ouagadougou, ERITREA=Asmara, THE GAMBIA=Banjul,
KENYA=Nairobi, GABON=Libreville, CAPE VERDE=Praia,
ALGERIA=Algiers, COMOROS=Moroni, EQUATORIAL GUINEA=Malabo,
BURUNDI=Bujumbura, BENIN=Porto-Novo, BULGARIA=Sofia,
GHANA=Accra, DJIBOUTI=Dijibouti, ETHIOPIA=Addis Ababa]
*///:~
```

Because the "slots" in a hash table are often referred to as *buckets,* the array that represents the actual table is called **buckets**. To promote even distribution, the number of buckets is typically a prime number.[8] Notice that it is an array of **LinkedList**, which automatically provides for collisions: Each new item is simply added to the end of the list in a particular bucket. Even though Java will not let you create an array of generics, it is possible to make a *reference* to such an array. Here, it is convenient to upcast to such an array, to prevent extra casting later in the code.

For a **put( )**, the **hashCode( )** is called for the key and the result is forced to a positive number. To fit the resulting number into the **buckets** array, the modulus operator is used with the size of that array. If that location is **null**, it means there are no elements that hash to that location, so a new **LinkedList** is created to hold the object that just did hash to that location. However, the

---

[8] As it turns out, a prime number is not actually the ideal size for hash buckets, and recent hashed implementations in Java use a power-of-two size (after extensive testing). Division or remainder is the slowest operation on a modern processor. With a power-of-two hash table length, masking can be used instead of division. Since **get( )** is by far the most common operation, the % is a large part of the cost, and the power-of-two approach eliminates this (but may also affect some **hashCode( )** methods).

normal process is to look through the list to see if there are duplicates, and if there are, the old value is put into **oldValue** and the new value replaces the old. The **found** flag keeps track of whether an old key-value pair was found and, if not, the new pair is appended to the end of the list.

The **get( )** calculates the index into the **buckets** array in the same fashion as **put( )** (this is important in order to guarantee that you end up in the same spot). If a **LinkedList** exists, it is searched for a match.

Note that this implementation is not meant to be tuned for performance; it is only intended to show the operations performed by a hash map. If you look at the source code for **java.util.HashMap**, you'll see a tuned implementation. Also, for simplicity **SimpleHashMap** uses the same approach to **entrySet( )** as did **SlowMap**, which is oversimplified and will not work for a general-purpose **Map**.

Exercise 19: (1) Repeat Exercise 13 using a **SimpleHashMap**.

Exercise 20: (3) Modify **SimpleHashMap** so that it reports collisions, and test this by adding the same data set twice so that you see collisions.

Exercise 21: (2) Modify **SimpleHashMap** so that it reports the number of "probes" necessary when collisions occur. That is, how many calls to **next( )** must be made on the **Iterator**s that walk the **LinkedList**s looking for matches?

Exercise 22: (4) Implement the **clear( )** and **remove( )** methods for **SimpleHashMap**.

Exercise 23: (3) Implement the rest of the **Map** interface for **SimpleHashMap**.

Exercise 24: (5) Following the example in **SimpleHashMap.java**, create and test a **SimpleHashSet**.

Exercise 25: (6) Instead of using a **ListIterator** for each bucket, modify **MapEntry** so that it is a self-contained singly linked list (each **MapEntry** should have a forward link to the next **MapEntry**). Modify the rest of the code in **SimpleHashMap.java** so that this new approach works correctly.

Overriding **hashCode()**

Now that you understand how hashing works, writing your own **hashCode( )** method will make more sense.

First of all, you don't control the creation of the actual value that's used to index into the array of buckets. That is dependent on the capacity of the particular **HashMap** object, and that capacity changes depending on how full the container is, and what the *load factor* is (this term will be described later). Thus, the value produced by your **hashCode( )** will be further processed in order to create the bucket index (in **SimpleHashMap**, the calculation is just a modulo by the size of the bucket array).

The most important factor in creating a **hashCode( )** is that, regardless of when **hashCode( )** is called, it produces the same value for a particular object every time it is called. If you end up with an object that produces one **hashCode( )** value when it is **put( )** into a **HashMap** and another during a **get( )**, you won't be able to retrieve the objects. So if your **hashCode( )** depends on mutable data in the object, the user must be made aware that changing the data will produce a different key because it generates a different **hashCode( )**.

In addition, you will probably *not* want to generate a **hashCode( )** that is based on unique object information—in particular, the value of **this** makes a bad **hashCode( )** because then you can't generate a new key identical to the one used to **put( )** the original key-value pair. This was the problem that occurred in **SpringDetector.java**, because the default implementation of **hashCode( )** *does* use the object address. So you'll want to use information in the object that identifies the object in a meaningful way.

One example can be seen in the **String** class. **String**s have the special characteristic that if a program has several **String** objects that contain identical character sequences, then those **String** objects all map to the same memory. So it makes sense that the **hashCode( )** produced by two separate instances of the **String "hello"** should be identical. You can see this in the following program:

```
//: containers/StringHashCode.java

public class StringHashCode {
  public static void main(String[] args) {
    String[] hellos = "Hello Hello".split(" ");
    System.out.println(hellos[0].hashCode());
    System.out.println(hellos[1].hashCode());
  }
} /* Output: (Sample)
69609650
```

```
69609650
*///:~
```

The **hashCode( )** for **String** is clearly based on the contents of the **String**.

So, for a **hashCode( )** to be effective, it must be fast and it must be meaningful; that is, it must generate a value based on the contents of the object. Remember that this value doesn't have to be unique—you should lean toward speed rather than uniqueness—but between **hashCode( )** and **equals( )**, the identity of the object must be completely resolved.

Because the **hashCode( )** is further processed before the bucket index is produced, the range of values is not important; it just needs to generate an **int**.

There's one other factor: A good **hashCode( )** should result in an even distribution of values. If the values tend to cluster, then the **HashMap** or **HashSet** will be more heavily loaded in some areas and will not be as fast as it can be with an evenly distributed hashing function.

In *Effective Java™ Programming Language Guide* (Addison-Wesley, 2001), Joshua Bloch gives a basic recipe for generating a decent **hashCode( )**:

1. Store some constant nonzero value, say 17, in an **int** variable called **result**.

2. For each significant field **f** in your object (that is, each field taken into account by the **equals( )** method), calculate an **int** hash code **c** for the field:

Field type	Calculation
boolean	c = (f ? 0 : 1)
byte, **char**, **short**, or **int**	c = (int)f
long	c = (int)(f ^ (f >>>32))
float	c = Float.floatToIntBits(f);
double	long l = Double.doubleToLongBits(f); c = (int)(l ^ (l >>> 32))

Object, where **equals( )** calls **equals( )** for this field	c = f.hashCode( )
Array	Apply above rules to each element

3. Combine the hash code(s) computed above:
   result = 37 * result + c;

4. Return **result**.

5. Look at the resulting **hashCode( )** and make sure that equal instances have equal hash codes.

Here's an example that follows these guidelines:

```
//: containers/CountedString.java
// Creating a good hashCode().
import java.util.*;
import static net.mindview.util.Print.*;

public class CountedString {
  private static List<String> created =
    new ArrayList<String>();
  private String s;
  private int id = 0;
  public CountedString(String str) {
    s = str;
    created.add(s);
    // id is the total number of instances
    // of this string in use by CountedString:
    for(String s2 : created)
      if(s2.equals(s))
        id++;
  }
  public String toString() {
    return "String: " + s + " id: " + id +
      " hashCode(): " + hashCode();
  }
  public int hashCode() {
    // The very simple approach:
    // return s.hashCode() * id;
    // Using Joshua Bloch's recipe:
```

```java
      int result = 17;
      result = 37 * result + s.hashCode();
      result = 37 * result + id;
      return result;
    }
    public boolean equals(Object o) {
      return o instanceof CountedString &&
        s.equals(((CountedString)o).s) &&
        id == ((CountedString)o).id;
    }
    public static void main(String[] args) {
      Map<CountedString,Integer> map =
        new HashMap<CountedString,Integer>();
      CountedString[] cs = new CountedString[5];
      for(int i = 0; i < cs.length; i++) {
        cs[i] = new CountedString("hi");
        map.put(cs[i], i); // Autobox int -> Integer
      }
      print(map);
      for(CountedString cstring : cs) {
        print("Looking up " + cstring);
        print(map.get(cstring));
      }
    }
} /* Output: (Sample)
{String: hi id: 4 hashCode(): 146450=3, String: hi id: 1
hashCode(): 146447=0, String: hi id: 3 hashCode():
146449=2, String: hi id: 5 hashCode(): 146451=4, String: hi
id: 2 hashCode(): 146448=1}
Looking up String: hi id: 1 hashCode(): 146447
0
Looking up String: hi id: 2 hashCode(): 146448
1
Looking up String: hi id: 3 hashCode(): 146449
2
Looking up String: hi id: 4 hashCode(): 146450
3
Looking up String: hi id: 5 hashCode(): 146451
4
*///:~
```

CountedString includes a **String** and an **id** that represents the number of **CountedString** objects that contain an identical **String**. The counting is accomplished in the constructor by iterating through the **static ArrayList** where all the **String**s are stored.

Both **hashCode( )** and **equals( )** produce results based on both fields; if they were just based on the **String** alone or the **id** alone, there would be duplicate matches for distinct values.

In **main( )**, several **CountedString** objects are created using the same **String**, to show that the duplicates create unique values because of the count **id**. The **HashMap** is displayed so that you can see how it is stored internally (no discernible orders), and then each key is looked up individually to demonstrate that the lookup mechanism is working properly.

As a second example, consider the **Individual** class that was used as the base class for the **typeinfo.pet** library defined in the *Type Information* chapter. The **Individual** class was used in that chapter but the definition has been delayed until this chapter so you could properly understand the implementation:

```java
//: typeinfo/pets/Individual.java
package typeinfo.pets;

public class Individual implements Comparable<Individual> {
  private static long counter = 0;
  private final long id = counter++;
  private String name;
  public Individual(String name) { this.name = name; }
  // 'name' is optional:
  public Individual() {}
  public String toString() {
    return getClass().getSimpleName() +
      (name == null ? "" : " " + name);
  }
  public long id() { return id; }
  public boolean equals(Object o) {
    return o instanceof Individual &&
      id == ((Individual)o).id;
  }
  public int hashCode() {
    int result = 17;
    if(name != null)
      result = 37 * result + name.hashCode();
    result = 37 * result + (int)id;
    return result;
```

```
    }
    public int compareTo(Individual arg) {
      // Compare by class name first:
      String first = getClass().getSimpleName();
      String argFirst = arg.getClass().getSimpleName();
      int firstCompare = first.compareTo(argFirst);
      if(firstCompare != 0)
      return firstCompare;
      if(name != null && arg.name != null) {
        int secondCompare = name.compareTo(arg.name);
        if(secondCompare != 0)
          return secondCompare;
      }
      return (arg.id < id ? -1 : (arg.id == id ? 0 : 1));
    }
} ///:~
```

The **compareTo( )** method has a hierarchy of comparisons, so that it will produce a sequence that is sorted first by actual type, then by **name** if there is one, and finally falls back to creation order. Here's an example that shows how it works:

```
//: containers/IndividualTest.java
import holding.MapOfList;
import typeinfo.pets.*;
import java.util.*;

public class IndividualTest {
  public static void main(String[] args) {
    Set<Individual> pets = new TreeSet<Individual>();
    for(List<? extends Pet> lp :
        MapOfList.petPeople.values())
      for(Pet p : lp)
        pets.add(p);
    System.out.println(pets);
  }
} /* Output:
[Cat Elsie May, Cat Pinkola, Cat Shackleton, Cat Stanford
aka Stinky el Negro, Cymric Molly, Dog Margrett, Mutt Spot,
Pug Louie aka Louis Snorkelstein Dupree, Rat Fizzy, Rat
Freckly, Rat Fuzzy]
*///:~
```

Since all of these pets have names, they are sorted first by type, then by name within their type.

Writing a proper **hashCode( )** and **equals( )** for a new class can be tricky. You can find tools to help you do this in Apache's "Jakarta Commons" project at *jakarta.apache.org/commons*, under "lang" (this project also has many other potentially useful libraries, and appears to be the Java community's answer to the C++ community's *www.boost.org*).

Exercise 26: (2) Add a **char** field to **CountedString** that is also initialized in the constructor, and modify the **hashCode( )** and **equals( )** methods to include the value of this **char**.

Exercise 27: (3) Modify the **hashCode( )** in **CountedString.java** by removing the combination with **id**, and demonstrate that **CountedString** still works as a key. What is the problem with this approach?

Exercise 28: (4) Modify **net/mindview/util/Tuple.java** to make it a general-purpose class by adding **hashCode( )**, **equals( )**, and implementing **Comparable** for each type of **Tuple**.

Choosing an implementation

By now you should understand that although there are only four fundamental container types—**Map**, **List**, **Set**, and **Queue**—there is more than one implementation of each interface. If you need to use the functionality offered by a particular interface, how do you decide which implementation to use?

Each different implementation has its own features, strengths, and weaknesses. For example, you can see in the figure at the beginning of this chapter that the "feature" of **Hashtable**, **Vector**, and **Stack** is that they are legacy classes, so that old code doesn't break (it's best if you don't use those for new code).

The different types of **Queue**s in the Java library are differentiated only by the way they accept and produce values (you'll see the importance of these in the *Concurrency* chapter).

The distinction between containers often comes down to what they are "backed by"—that is, the data structures that physically implement the desired interface. For example, because **ArrayList** and **LinkedList** implement the **List** interface, the *basic* **List** operations are the same regardless of which one you use. However, **ArrayList** is backed by an array, and **LinkedList** is implemented in the usual way for a doubly linked list, as individual objects each containing data along with references to the previous and next elements in the list. Because of this, if you want to do many insertions and removals in the middle of a list, a **LinkedList** is the appropriate choice. (**LinkedList** also has additional functionality that is established in **AbstractSequentialList**.) If not, an **ArrayList** is typically faster.

As another example, a **Set** can be implemented as either a **TreeSet**, a **HashSet**, or a **LinkedHashSet**.[9] Each one has different behaviors: **HashSet** is for typical use and provides raw speed on lookup, **LinkedHashSet** keeps pairs in insertion order, and **TreeSet** is backed by **TreeMap** and is designed to produce a constantly sorted set. You choose the implementation based on the behavior you need.

Sometimes different implementations of a particular container will have operations in common, but the performance of those operations will be different. In this case, you'll choose between implementations based on how often you use a particular operation, and how fast you need it to be. For cases like this, one way to look at the differences between container implementations is with a performance test.

A performance test framework

To prevent code duplication and to provide consistency among tests, I've put the basic functionality of the test process into a framework. The following code establishes a base class from which you create a list of anonymous inner classes, one for each different test. Each of these inner classes is called as part of the testing process. This approach allows you to easily add and remove new kinds of tests.

This is another example of the *Template Method* design pattern. Although you follow the typical Template Method approach of overriding the method **Test.test( )** for each particular test, in this case the core code (that doesn't change) is in a separate **Tester** class.[10] The type of container under test is the generic parameter **C**:

---

[9] Or as an **EnumSet** or **CopyOnWriteArraySet**, which are special cases. While acknowledging that there may be additional specialized implementations of various container interfaces, this section attempts to look at the more general cases.

[10] Krzysztof Sobolewski assisted me in figuring out the generics for this example.

```
//: containers/Test.java
// Framework for performing timed tests of containers.

public abstract class Test<C> {
  String name;
  public Test(String name) { this.name = name; }
  // Override this method for different tests.
  // Returns actual number of repetitions of test.
  abstract int test(C container, TestParam tp);
} ///:~
```

Each **Test** object stores the name of that test. When you call the **test( )** method, it must be given the container to be tested along with a "messenger" or "data transfer object" that holds the various parameters for that particular test. The parameters include **size**, indicating the number of elements in the container, and **loops**, which controls the number of iterations for that test. These parameters may or may not be used in every test.

Each container will undergo a sequence of calls to **test( )**, each with a different **TestParam**, so **TestParam** also contains **static array( )** methods that make it easy to create arrays of **TestParam** objects. The first version of **array( )** takes a variable argument list containing alternating **size** and **loops** values, and the second version takes the same kind of list except that the values are inside **String**s—this way, it can be used to parse command-line arguments:

```
//: containers/TestParam.java
// A "data transfer object."

public class TestParam {
  public final int size;
  public final int loops;
  public TestParam(int size, int loops) {
    this.size = size;
    this.loops = loops;
  }
  // Create an array of TestParam from a varargs sequence:
  public static TestParam[] array(int... values) {
    int size = values.length/2;
    TestParam[] result = new TestParam[size];
    int n = 0;
    for(int i = 0; i < size; i++)
      result[i] = new TestParam(values[n++], values[n++]);
    return result;
```

```
    }
    // Convert a String array to a TestParam array:
    public static TestParam[] array(String[] values) {
      int[] vals = new int[values.length];
      for(int i = 0; i < vals.length; i++)
        vals[i] = Integer.decode(values[i]);
      return array(vals);
    }
} ///:~
```

To use the framework, you pass the container to be tested along with a **List** of
Test objects to a **Tester.run( )** method (these are overloaded generic
convenience methods which reduce the amount of typing necessary to use
them). **Tester.run( )** calls the appropriate overloaded constructor, then calls
timedTest( ), which executes each test in the list for that container.
timedTest( ) repeats each test for each of the **TestParam** objects in
paramList. Because **paramList** is initialized from the static
defaultParams array, you can change the **paramList** for all tests by
reassigning **defaultParams**, or you can change the **paramList** for one test
by passing in a custom **paramList** for that test:

```
//: containers/Tester.java
// Applies Test objects to lists of different containers.
import java.util.*;

public class Tester<C> {
  public static int fieldWidth = 8;
  public static TestParam[] defaultParams= TestParam.array(
    10, 5000, 100, 5000, 1000, 5000, 10000, 500);
  // Override this to modify pre-test initialization:
  protected C initialize(int size) { return container; }
  protected C container;
  private String headline = "";
  private List<Test<C>> tests;
  private static String stringField() {
    return "%" + fieldWidth + "s";
  }
  private static String numberField() {
    return "%" + fieldWidth + "d";
  }
  private static int sizeWidth = 5;
  private static String sizeField = "%" + sizeWidth + "s";
  private TestParam[] paramList = defaultParams;
  public Tester(C container, List<Test<C>> tests) {
```

```
      this.container = container;
      this.tests = tests;
      if(container != null)
        headline = container.getClass().getSimpleName();
    }
    public Tester(C container, List<Test<C>> tests,
        TestParam[] paramList) {
      this(container, tests);
      this.paramList = paramList;
    }
    public void setHeadline(String newHeadline) {
      headline = newHeadline;
    }
    // Generic methods for convenience :
    public static <C> void run(C cntnr, List<Test<C>> tests){
      new Tester<C>(cntnr, tests).timedTest();
    }
    public static <C> void run(C cntnr,
        List<Test<C>> tests, TestParam[] paramList) {
      new Tester<C>(cntnr, tests, paramList).timedTest();
    }
    private void displayHeader() {
      // Calculate width and pad with '-':
      int width = fieldWidth * tests.size() + sizeWidth;
      int dashLength = width - headline.length() - 1;
      StringBuilder head = new StringBuilder(width);
      for(int i = 0; i < dashLength/2; i++)
        head.append('-');
      head.append(' ');
      head.append(headline);
      head.append(' ');
      for(int i = 0; i < dashLength/2; i++)
        head.append('-');
      System.out.println(head);
      // Print column headers:
      System.out.format(sizeField, "size");
      for(Test<C> test : tests)
        System.out.format(stringField(), test.name);
      System.out.println();
    }
    // Run the tests for this container:
    public void timedTest() {
      displayHeader();
      for(TestParam param : paramList) {
```

```
      System.out.format(sizeField, param.size);
      for(Test<C> test : tests) {
        C kontainer = initialize(param.size);
        long start = System.nanoTime();
        // Call the overriden method:
        int reps = test.test(kontainer, param);
        long duration = System.nanoTime() - start;
        long timePerRep = duration / reps; // Nanoseconds
        System.out.format(numberField(), timePerRep);
      }
      System.out.println();
    }
  }
} ///:~
```

The **stringField( )** and **numberField( )** methods produce formatting strings for outputting the results. The standard width for formatting can be changed by modifying the **static fieldWidth** value. The **displayHeader( )** method formats and prints the header information for each test.

If you need to perform special initialization, override the **initialize( )** method. This produces an initialized container object of the appropriate size—you can either modify the existing container object or create a new one. You can see in **test( )** that the result is captured in a local reference called **kontainer**, which allows you to replace the stored member **container** with a completely different initialized container.

The return value of each **Test.test( )** method must be the number of operations performed by that test, which is used to calculate the number of nanoseconds required for each operation. You should be aware that **System.nanoTime( )** typically produces values with a granularity that is greater than one (and this granularity will vary with machines and operating systems), and this will produce a certain amount of rattle in the results.

The results may vary from machine to machine; these tests are only intended to compare the performance of the different containers.

Choosing between **List**s

Here is a performance test for the most essential of the **List** operations. For comparison, it also shows the most important **Queue** operations. Two separate lists of tests are created for testing each class of container. In this case, **Queue** operations only apply to **LinkedLists**.

```
//: containers/ListPerformance.java
// Demonstrates performance differences in Lists.
// {Args: 100 500} Small to keep build testing short
import java.util.*;
import net.mindview.util.*;

public class ListPerformance {
  static Random rand = new Random();
  static int reps = 1000;
  static List<Test<List<Integer>>> tests =
    new ArrayList<Test<List<Integer>>>();
  static List<Test<LinkedList<Integer>>> qTests =
    new ArrayList<Test<LinkedList<Integer>>>();
  static {
    tests.add(new Test<List<Integer>>("add") {
      int test(List<Integer> list, TestParam tp) {
        int loops = tp.loops;
        int listSize = tp.size;
        for(int i = 0; i < loops; i++) {
          list.clear();
          for(int j = 0; j < listSize; j++)
            list.add(j);
        }
        return loops * listSize;
      }
    });
    tests.add(new Test<List<Integer>>("get") {
      int test(List<Integer> list, TestParam tp) {
        int loops = tp.loops * reps;
        int listSize = list.size();
        for(int i = 0; i < loops; i++)
          list.get(rand.nextInt(listSize));
        return loops;
      }
    });
    tests.add(new Test<List<Integer>>("set") {
      int test(List<Integer> list, TestParam tp) {
        int loops = tp.loops * reps;
        int listSize = list.size();
        for(int i = 0; i < loops; i++)
          list.set(rand.nextInt(listSize), 47);
        return loops;
      }
    });
```

```
tests.add(new Test<List<Integer>>("iteradd") {
  int test(List<Integer> list, TestParam tp) {
    final int LOOPS = 1000000;
    int half = list.size() / 2;
    ListIterator<Integer> it = list.listIterator(half);
    for(int i = 0; i < LOOPS; i++)
      it.add(47);
    return LOOPS;
  }
});
tests.add(new Test<List<Integer>>("insert") {
  int test(List<Integer> list, TestParam tp) {
    int loops = tp.loops;
    for(int i = 0; i < loops; i++)
      list.add(5, 47); // Minimize random-access cost
    return loops;
  }
});
tests.add(new Test<List<Integer>>("remove") {
  int test(List<Integer> list, TestParam tp) {
    int loops = tp.loops;
    int size = tp.size;
    for(int i = 0; i < loops; i++) {
      list.clear();
      list.addAll(new CountingIntegerList(size));
      while(list.size() > 5)
        list.remove(5); // Minimize random-access cost
    }
    return loops * size;
  }
});
// Tests for queue behavior:
qTests.add(new Test<LinkedList<Integer>>("addFirst") {
  int test(LinkedList<Integer> list, TestParam tp) {
    int loops = tp.loops;
    int size = tp.size;
    for(int i = 0; i < loops; i++) {
      list.clear();
      for(int j = 0; j < size; j++)
        list.addFirst(47);
    }
    return loops * size;
  }
});
```

```
      qTests.add(new Test<LinkedList<Integer>>("addLast") {
        int test(LinkedList<Integer> list, TestParam tp) {
          int loops = tp.loops;
          int size = tp.size;
          for(int i = 0; i < loops; i++) {
            list.clear();
            for(int j = 0; j < size; j++)
              list.addLast(47);
          }
          return loops * size;
        }
      });
      qTests.add(
        new Test<LinkedList<Integer>>("rmFirst") {
          int test(LinkedList<Integer> list, TestParam tp) {
            int loops = tp.loops;
            int size = tp.size;
            for(int i = 0; i < loops; i++) {
              list.clear();
              list.addAll(new CountingIntegerList(size));
              while(list.size() > 0)
                list.removeFirst();
            }
            return loops * size;
          }
        });
      qTests.add(new Test<LinkedList<Integer>>("rmLast") {
        int test(LinkedList<Integer> list, TestParam tp) {
          int loops = tp.loops;
          int size = tp.size;
          for(int i = 0; i < loops; i++) {
            list.clear();
            list.addAll(new CountingIntegerList(size));
            while(list.size() > 0)
              list.removeLast();
          }
          return loops * size;
        }
      });
    }
    static class ListTester extends Tester<List<Integer>> {
      public ListTester(List<Integer> container,
          List<Test<List<Integer>>> tests) {
        super(container, tests);
```

```
      }
      // Fill to the appropriate size before each test:
      @Override protected List<Integer> initialize(int size){
        container.clear();
        container.addAll(new CountingIntegerList(size));
        return container;
      }
      // Convenience method:
      public static void run(List<Integer> list,
          List<Test<List<Integer>>> tests) {
        new ListTester(list, tests).timedTest();
      }
    }
    public static void main(String[] args) {
      if(args.length > 0)
        Tester.defaultParams = TestParam.array(args);
      // Can only do these two tests on an array:
      Tester<List<Integer>> arrayTest =
        new Tester<List<Integer>>(null, tests.subList(1, 3)){
          // This will be called before each test. It
          // produces a non-resizeable array-backed list:
          @Override protected
          List<Integer> initialize(int size) {
            Integer[] ia = Generated.array(Integer.class,
              new CountingGenerator.Integer(), size);
            return Arrays.asList(ia);
          }
        };
      arrayTest.setHeadline("Array as List");
      arrayTest.timedTest();
      Tester.defaultParams= TestParam.array(
        10, 5000, 100, 5000, 1000, 1000, 10000, 200);
      if(args.length > 0)
        Tester.defaultParams = TestParam.array(args);
      ListTester.run(new ArrayList<Integer>(), tests);
      ListTester.run(new LinkedList<Integer>(), tests);
      ListTester.run(new Vector<Integer>(), tests);
      Tester.fieldWidth = 12;
      Tester<LinkedList<Integer>> qTest =
        new Tester<LinkedList<Integer>>(
          new LinkedList<Integer>(), qTests);
      qTest.setHeadline("Queue tests");
      qTest.timedTest();
    }
```

```
} /* Output: (Sample)
--- Array as List ---
  size    get      set
    10    130      183
   100    130      164
  1000    129      165
 10000    129      165
-------------------- ArrayList --------------------
  size    add      get    set iteradd  insert  remove
    10    121      139    191     435    3952     446
   100     72      141    191     247    3934     296
  1000     98      141    194     839    2202     923
 10000    122      144    190    6880   14042    7333
-------------------- LinkedList --------------------
  size    add      get    set iteradd  insert  remove
    10    182      164    198     658     366     262
   100    106      202    230     457     108     201
  1000    133     1289   1353     430     136     239
 10000    172    13648  13187     435     255     239
-------------------- Vector --------------------
  size    add      get    set iteradd  insert  remove
    10    129      145    187     290    3635     253
   100     72      144    190     263    3691     292
  1000     99      145    193     846    2162     927
 10000    108      145    186    6871   14730    7135
-------------------- Queue tests --------------------
  size  addFirst    addLast    rmFirst    rmLast
    10       199        163        251       253
   100        98         92        180       179
  1000        99         93        216       212
 10000       111        109        262       384
*///:~
```

Each test requires careful thought to ensure that you are producing
meaningful results. For example, the "**add**" test clears the **List** and then
refills it to the specified list size. The call to **clear( )** is thus part of the test,
and may have an impact on the time, especially for small tests. Although the
results here seem fairly reasonable, you could imagine rewriting the test
framework so that there is a call to a preparation method (which would, in
this case, include the **clear( )** call) *outside* of the timing loop.

Note that for each test, you must accurately calculate the number of
operations that occur and return that value from **test( )**, so the timing is
correct.

The "**get**" and "**set**" tests both use the random number generator to perform random accesses to the **List**. In the output, you can see that, for a **List** backed by an array and for an **ArrayList**, these accesses are fast and very consistent regardless of the list size, whereas for a **LinkedList**, the access times grow very significantly for larger lists. Clearly, linked lists are not a good choice if you will be performing many random accesses.

The "**iteradd**" test uses an iterator in the middle of the list to insert new elements. For an **ArrayList** this gets expensive as the list gets bigger, but for a **LinkedList** it is relatively cheap, and constant regardless of size. This makes sense because an **ArrayList** must create space and copy all its references forward during an insertion. This becomes expensive as the **ArrayList** gets bigger. A **LinkedList** only needs to link in a new element, and doesn't have to modify the rest of the list, so you expect the cost to be roughly the same regardless of the list size.

The "**insert**" and "**remove**" tests both use location number 5 as the point of insertion or removal, rather than either end of the **List**. A **LinkedList** treats the endpoints of the **List** specially—this improves the speed when using a **LinkedList** as a **Queue**. However, if you add or remove elements in the middle of the list, you include the cost of random access, which we've already seen varies with the different **List** implementations. By performing the insertions and removals at location 5, the cost of the random access should be negligible and we should see only the cost of insertion and removal, but we will not see any specialized optimization for the end of a **LinkedList**. You can see from the output that the cost of insertion and removal in a **LinkedList** is quite cheap and doesn't vary with the list size, but with an **ArrayList**, insertions especially are *very* expensive, and the cost increases with list size.

From the **Queue** tests, you can see how quickly a **LinkedList** can insert and remove elements from the endpoints of the list, which is optimal for **Queue** behavior.

Normally, you can just call **Tester.run( )**, passing the container and the **tests** list. Here, however, we must override the **initialize( )** method so that the **List** is cleared and refilled before each test—otherwise the **List** control over the size of the **List** would be lost during the various tests. **ListTester** inherits from **Tester** and performs this initialization using **CountingIntegerList**. The **run( )** convenience method is also overridden.

We'd also like to compare array access to container access (primarily against **ArrayList**). In the first test in **main( )**, a special **Test** object is created using an anonymous inner class. The **initialize( )** method is overridden to create a new object each time it is called (ignoring the stored **container** object, so **null** is the **container** argument for this **Tester** constructor). The new object is created using **Generated.array( )** (which was defined in the *Arrays* chapter) and **Arrays.asList( )**. Only two of the tests can be performed in this case, because you cannot insert or remove elements when using a **List** backed by an array, so the **List.subList( )** method is used to select the desired tests from the **tests** list.

For random-access **get( )** and **set( )** operations, a **List** backed by an array is slightly faster than an **ArrayList**, but the same operations are dramatically more expensive for a **LinkedList** because it is not designed for random-access operations.

Vector should be avoided; it's only in the library for legacy code support (the only reason it works in this program is because it was adapted to be a **List** for forward compatibility).

The best approach is probably to choose an **ArrayList** as your default and to change to a **LinkedList** if you need its extra functionality or you discover performance problems due to many insertions and removals from the middle of the list. If you are working with a fixed-sized group of elements, either use a **List** backed by an array (as produced by **Arrays.asList( )**), or if necessary, an actual array.

CopyOnWriteArrayList is a special implementation of **List** used in concurrent programming, and will be discussed in the *Concurrency* chapter.

Exercise 29:   (2) Modify **ListPerformance.java** so that the **List**s hold **String** objects instead of **Integer**s. Use a **Generator** from the *Arrays* chapter to create test values.

Exercise 30:   (3) Compare the performance of **Collections.sort( )** between an **ArrayList** and a **LinkedList**.

Exercise 31:   (5) Create a container that encapsulates an array of **String**, and that only allows adding **String**s and getting **String**s, so that there are no casting issues during use. If the internal array isn't big enough for the next add, your container should automatically resize it. In **main( )**, compare the performance of your container with an **ArrayList<String>**.

Exercise 32: (2) Repeat the previous exercise for a container of **int**, and compare the performance to an **ArrayList<Integer>**. In your performance comparison, include the process of incrementing each object in the container.

Exercise 33: (5) Create a **FastTraversalLinkedList** that internally uses a **LinkedList** for rapid insertions and removals, and an **ArrayList** for rapid traversals and **get( )** operations. Test it by modifying **ListPerformance.java**.

Microbenchmarking dangers

When writing so-called *microbenchmarks*, you must be careful not to assume too much, and to narrow your tests so that as much as possible they are only timing the items of interest. You must also be careful to ensure that your tests run long enough to produce interesting data, and take into account that some of the Java HotSpot technologies will only kick in when a program runs for a certain time (this is important to consider for short-running programs, as well).

Results will be different according to the computer and JVM you are using, so you should run these tests yourself to verify that the results are similar to those shown in this book. You should not be so concerned with absolute numbers as with the performance comparisons between one type of container and another.

Also, a *profiler* may do a better job of performance analysis than you can. Java comes with a profiler (see the supplement at *http://MindView.net/Books/BetterJava*) and there are third-party profilers available, both free/open-source and commercial.

A related example concerns **Math.random( )**. Does it produce a value from zero to one, inclusive or exclusive of the value "1"? In math lingo, is it (0,1), or [0,1], or (0,1] or [0,1)? (The square bracket means "includes," whereas the parenthesis means "doesn't include.") A test program *might* provide the answer:

```
//: containers/RandomBounds.java
// Does Math.random() produce 0.0 and 1.0?
// {RunByHand}
import static net.mindview.util.Print.*;

public class RandomBounds {
  static void usage() {
```

```
      print("Usage:");
      print("\tRandomBounds lower");
      print("\tRandomBounds upper");
      System.exit(1);
    }
  public static void main(String[] args) {
    if(args.length != 1) usage();
    if(args[0].equals("lower")) {
      while(Math.random() != 0.0)
        ; // Keep trying
      print("Produced 0.0!");
    }
    else if(args[0].equals("upper")) {
      while(Math.random() != 1.0)
        ; // Keep trying
      print("Produced 1.0!");
    }
    else
      usage();
  }
} ///:~
```

To run the program, you type a command line of either:

```
java RandomBounds lower
```

or

```
java RandomBounds upper
```

In both cases, you are forced to break out of the program manually, so it would appear that **Math.random( )** never produces either 0.0 or 1.0. But this is where such an experiment can be deceiving. If you consider that there are about 262 different double fractions between 0 and 1, the likelihood of reaching any one value experimentally might exceed the lifetime of one computer, or even one experimenter. It turns out that 0.0 *is* included in the output of **Math.random( )**. Or, in math lingo, it is [0,1). Thus, you must be careful to analyze your experiments and to understand their limitations.

Choosing between **Set**s

Depending on the behavior you desire, you can choose a **TreeSet**, a **HashSet**, or a **LinkedHashSet**. The following test program gives an indication of the performance trade-off between these implementations:

```
//: containers/SetPerformance.java
// Demonstrates performance differences in Sets.
// {Args: 100 5000} Small to keep build testing short
import java.util.*;

public class SetPerformance {
  static List<Test<Set<Integer>>> tests =
    new ArrayList<Test<Set<Integer>>>();
  static {
    tests.add(new Test<Set<Integer>>("add") {
      int test(Set<Integer> set, TestParam tp) {
        int loops = tp.loops;
        int size = tp.size;
        for(int i = 0; i < loops; i++) {
          set.clear();
          for(int j = 0; j < size; j++)
            set.add(j);
        }
        return loops * size;
      }
    });
    tests.add(new Test<Set<Integer>>("contains") {
      int test(Set<Integer> set, TestParam tp) {
        int loops = tp.loops;
        int span = tp.size * 2;
        for(int i = 0; i < loops; i++)
          for(int j = 0; j < span; j++)
            set.contains(j);
        return loops * span;
      }
    });
    tests.add(new Test<Set<Integer>>("iterate") {
      int test(Set<Integer> set, TestParam tp) {
        int loops = tp.loops * 10;
        for(int i = 0; i < loops; i++) {
          Iterator<Integer> it = set.iterator();
          while(it.hasNext())
            it.next();
        }
        return loops * set.size();
      }
    });
  }
  public static void main(String[] args) {
```

```
    if(args.length > 0)
      Tester.defaultParams = TestParam.array(args);
    Tester.fieldWidth = 10;
    Tester.run(new TreeSet<Integer>(), tests);
    Tester.run(new HashSet<Integer>(), tests);
    Tester.run(new LinkedHashSet<Integer>(), tests);
  }
} /* Output: (Sample)
------------- TreeSet -------------
  size       add   contains    iterate
    10       746        173         89
   100       501        264         68
  1000       714        410         69
 10000      1975        552         69
------------- HashSet -------------
  size       add   contains    iterate
    10       308         91         94
   100       178         75         73
  1000       216        110         72
 10000       711        215        100
---------- LinkedHashSet ----------
  size       add   contains    iterate
    10       350         65         83
   100       270         74         55
  1000       303        111         54
 10000      1615        256         58
*///:~
```

The performance of **HashSet** is generally superior to **TreeSet**, but
especially when adding elements and looking them up, which are the two
most important operations. **TreeSet** exists because it maintains its elements
in sorted order, so you use it only when you need a sorted **Set**. Because of the
internal structure necessary to support sorting *and* because iteration is
something you're more likely to do, iteration is usually faster with a **TreeSet**
than a **HashSet**.

Note that **LinkedHashSet** is more expensive for insertions than **HashSet**;
this is because of the extra cost of maintaining the linked list along with the
hashed container.

Exercise 34: (1) Modify **SetPerformance.java** so that the **Set**s hold
String objects instead of **Integer**s. Use a **Generator** from the *Arrays*
chapter to create test values.

Choosing between **Map**s

This program gives an indication of the trade-off between **Map** implementations:

```
//: containers/MapPerformance.java
// Demonstrates performance differences in Maps.
// {Args: 100 5000} Small to keep build testing short
import java.util.*;

public class MapPerformance {
  static List<Test<Map<Integer,Integer>>> tests =
    new ArrayList<Test<Map<Integer,Integer>>>();
  static {
    tests.add(new Test<Map<Integer,Integer>>("put") {
      int test(Map<Integer,Integer> map, TestParam tp) {
        int loops = tp.loops;
        int size = tp.size;
        for(int i = 0; i < loops; i++) {
          map.clear();
          for(int j = 0; j < size; j++)
            map.put(j, j);
        }
        return loops * size;
      }
    });
    tests.add(new Test<Map<Integer,Integer>>("get") {
      int test(Map<Integer,Integer> map, TestParam tp) {
        int loops = tp.loops;
        int span = tp.size * 2;
        for(int i = 0; i < loops; i++)
          for(int j = 0; j < span; j++)
            map.get(j);
        return loops * span;
      }
    });
    tests.add(new Test<Map<Integer,Integer>>("iterate") {
      int test(Map<Integer,Integer> map, TestParam tp) {
        int loops = tp.loops * 10;
        for(int i = 0; i < loops; i ++) {
          Iterator it = map.entrySet().iterator();
          while(it.hasNext())
            it.next();
        }
```

```
        return loops * map.size();
      }
    });
  }
  public static void main(String[] args) {
    if(args.length > 0)
      Tester.defaultParams = TestParam.array(args);
    Tester.run(new TreeMap<Integer,Integer>(), tests);
    Tester.run(new HashMap<Integer,Integer>(), tests);
    Tester.run(new LinkedHashMap<Integer,Integer>(),tests);
    Tester.run(
      new IdentityHashMap<Integer,Integer>(), tests);
    Tester.run(new WeakHashMap<Integer,Integer>(), tests);
    Tester.run(new Hashtable<Integer,Integer>(), tests);
  }
} /* Output: (Sample)
---------- TreeMap ----------
 size     put     get iterate
   10     748     168     100
  100     506     264      76
 1000     771     450      78
10000    2962     561      83
---------- HashMap ----------
 size     put     get iterate
   10     281      76      93
  100     179      70      73
 1000     267     102      72
10000    1305     265      97
------- LinkedHashMap -------
 size     put     get iterate
   10     354     100      72
  100     273      89      50
 1000     385     222      56
10000    2787     341      56
------ IdentityHashMap ------
 size     put     get iterate
   10     290     144     101
  100     204     287     132
 1000     508     336      77
10000     767     266      56
-------- WeakHashMap --------
 size     put     get iterate
   10     484     146     151
  100     292     126     117
```

```
 1000      411      136      152
10000     2165      138      555
--------- Hashtable ---------
 size      put      get iterate
   10      264      113      113
  100      181      105       76
 1000      260      201       80
10000     1245      134       77
*///:~
```

Insertions for all the **Map** implementations except for **IdentityHashMap** get significantly slower as the size of the **Map** gets large. In general, however, lookup is much cheaper than insertion, which is good because you'll typically be looking items up much more often than you insert them.

Hashtable performance is roughly the same as **HashMap**. Since **HashMap** is intended to replace **Hashtable**, and thus uses the same underlying storage and lookup mechanism (which you will learn about later), this is not too surprising.

A **TreeMap** is generally slower than a **HashMap**. As with **TreeSet**, a **TreeMap** is a way to create an ordered list. The behavior of a tree is such that it's always in order and doesn't have to be specially sorted. Once you fill a **TreeMap**, you can call **keySet( )** to get a **Set** view of the keys, then **toArray( )** to produce an array of those keys. You can then use the **static** method **Arrays.binarySearch( )** to rapidly find objects in your sorted array. Of course, this only makes sense if the behavior of a **HashMap** is unacceptable, since **HashMap** is designed to rapidly find keys. Also, you can easily create a **HashMap** from a **TreeMap** with a single object creation or call to **putAll( )**. In the end, when you're using a **Map**, your first choice should be **HashMap**, and only if you need a constantly sorted **Map** will you need **TreeMap**.

LinkedHashMap tends to be slower than **HashMap** for insertions because it maintains the linked list (to preserve insertion order) in addition to the hashed data structure. Because of this list, iteration is faster.

IdentityHashMap has different performance because it uses == rather than **equals( )** for comparisons. **WeakHashMap** is described later in this chapter.

Exercise 35: (1) Modify **MapPerformance.java** to include tests of **SlowMap**.

Exercise 36: (5) Modify **SlowMap** so that instead of two **ArrayList**s, it holds a single **ArrayList** of **MapEntry** objects. Verify that the modified version works correctly. Using **MapPerformance.java**, test the speed of your new **Map**. Now change the **put( )** method so that it performs a **sort( )** after each pair is entered, and modify **get( )** to use **Collections.binarySearch( )** to look up the key. Compare the performance of the new version with the old ones.

Exercise 37: (2) Modify **SimpleHashMap** to use **ArrayList**s instead of **LinkedList**s. Modify **MapPerformance.java** to compare the performance of the two implementations.

HashMap performance factors

It's possible to hand-tune a **HashMap** to increase its performance for your particular application. So that you can understand performance issues when tuning a **HashMap**, some terminology is necessary:

Capacity: The number of buckets in the table.

Initial capacity: The number of buckets when the table is created. **HashMap** and **HashSet** have constructors that allow you to specify the initial capacity.

Size: The number of entries currently in the table.

Load factor: Size/capacity. A load factor of 0 is an empty table, 0.5 is a half-full table, etc. A lightly loaded table will have few collisions and so is optimal for insertions and lookups (but will slow down the process of traversing with an iterator). **HashMap** and **HashSet** have constructors that allow you to specify the load factor, which means that when this load factor is reached, the container will automatically increase the capacity (the number of buckets) by roughly doubling it and will redistribute the existing objects into the new set of buckets (this is called *rehashing*).

The default load factor used by **HashMap** is 0.75 (it doesn't rehash until the table is three-fourths full). This seems to be a good trade-off between time and space costs. A higher load factor decreases the space required by the table but increases the lookup cost, which is important because lookup is what you do most of the time (including both **get( )** and **put( )**).

If you know that you'll be storing many entries in a **HashMap**, creating it with an appropriately large initial capacity will prevent the overhead of automatic rehashing.[11]

Exercise 38: (3) Look up the **HashMap** class in the JDK documentation. Create a **HashMap**, fill it with elements, and determine the load factor. Test the lookup speed with this map, then attempt to increase the speed by making a new **HashMap** with a larger initial capacity and copying the old map into the new one, then run your lookup speed test again on the new map.

Exercise 39: (6) Add a **private rehash( )** method to **SimpleHashMap** that is invoked when the load factor exceeds 0.75. During rehashing, double the number of buckets, then search for the first prime number greater than that to determine the new number of buckets.

Utilities

There are a number of standalone utilities for containers, expressed as **static** methods inside the **java.util.Collections** class. You've already seen some of these, such as **addAll( )**, **reverseOrder( )** and **binarySearch( )**. Here are the others (the **synchronized** and **unmodifiable** utilities will be covered in sections that follow). In this table, generics are used when they are relevant:

checkedCollection(**Collection<T>, Class<T> type)** **checkedList(** **List<T>, Class<T> type)** **checkedMap(Map<K,V>,** **Class<K> keyType,** **Class<V> valueType)** **checkedSet(Set<T>,**	Produces a *dynamically* type-safe view of a **Collection**, or a specific subtype of **Collection**. Use this when it's not possible to use the statically checked version. These were shown in the *Generics* chapter under the heading

---

[11] In a private message, Joshua Bloch wrote: "... I believe that we erred by allowing implementation details (such as hash table size and load factor) into our APIs. The client should perhaps tell us the maximum expected size of a collection, and we should take it from there. Clients can easily do more harm than good by choosing values for these parameters. As an extreme example, consider **Vector**'s **capacityIncrement**. No one should ever set this, and we shouldn't have provided it. If you set it to any nonzero value, the asymptotic cost of a sequence of appends goes from linear to quadratic. In other words, it destroys your performance. Over time, we're beginning to wise up about this sort of thing. If you look at **IdentityHashMap**, you'll see that it has no low-level tuning parameters."

Class<T> type) **checkedSortedMap(** **SortedMap<K,V>,** **Class<K> keyType,** **Class<V> valueType)** **checkedSortedSet(** **SortedSet<T>,** **Class<T> type)**	"Dynamic type safety."
max(Collection) **min(Collection)**	Produces the maximum or minimum element in the argument using the natural comparison method of the objects in the **Collection**.
max(Collection, Comparator) **min(Collection, Comparator)**	Produces the maximum or minimum element in the **Collection** using the **Comparator**.
indexOfSubList(List source, **List target)**	Produces starting index of the *first* place where **target** appears inside **source**, or -1 if none occurs.
lastIndexOfSubList(List **source, List target)**	Produces starting index of the *last* place where **target** appears inside **source**, or -1 if none occurs.
replaceAll(List<T>, **T oldVal, T newVal)**	Replaces all **oldVal** with **newVal**.
reverse(List)	Reverses all the elements in place.
reverseOrder( ) **reverseOrder(** **Comparator<T>)**	Returns a **Comparator** that reverses the natural ordering of a collection of objects that implement **Comparable<T>**. The second version reverses the order of the supplied **Comparator.**
rotate(List, int distance)	Moves all elements forward by **distance**, taking the ones off the end and placing them at the beginning.
shuffle(List) **shuffle(List, Random)**	Randomly permutes the specified list. The first form provides its own randomization source, or you may provide your own with the second

	form.
sort(List\<T\>) **sort(List\<T\>,** **Comparator\<? super T\> c)**	Sorts the **List\<T\>** using its natural ordering. The second form allows you to provide a **Comparator** for sorting.
copy(List\<? super T\> dest, **List\<? extends T\> src)**	Copies elements from **src** to **dest**.
swap(List, int i, int j)	Swaps elements at locations **i** and **j** in the **List**. Probably faster than what you'd write by hand.
fill(List\<? super T\>, T x)	Replaces all the elements of list with **x**.
nCopies(int n, T x)	Returns an immutable **List\<T\>** of size **n** whose references all point to **x**.
disjoint(Collection, Collection)	Returns **true** if the two collections have no elements in common.
frequency(Collection, Object x)	Returns the number of elements in the **Collection** equal to **x**.
emptyList( ) **emptyMap( )** **emptySet( )**	Returns an immutable empty **List**, **Map**, or **Set**. These are generic, so the resulting **Collection** will be parameterized to the desired type.
singleton(T x) **singletonList(T x)** **singletonMap(K key, V value)**	Produces an immutable **Set\<T\>**, **List\<T\>**, or **Map\<K,V\>** containing a single entry based on the given argument(s).
list(Enumeration\<T\> e)	Produces an **ArrayList\<T\>** containing the elements in the order in which they are returned by the (old-style) **Enumeration** (predecessor to the **Iterator**). For converting from legacy code.
enumeration(Collection\<T\>)	Produces an old-style **Enumeration\<T\>** for the argument.

Note that **min( )** and **max( )** work with **Collection** objects, not with **List**s, so you don't need to worry about whether the **Collection** should be sorted or

---

not. (As mentioned earlier, you *do* need to **sort( )** a **List** or an array before performing a **binarySearch( )**.)

Here's an example showing the basic use of most of the utilities in the above table:

```
//: containers/Utilities.java
// Simple demonstrations of the Collections utilities.
import java.util.*;
import static net.mindview.util.Print.*;

public class Utilities {
  static List<String> list = Arrays.asList(
    "one Two three Four five six one".split(" "));
  public static void main(String[] args) {
    print(list);
    print("'list' disjoint (Four)?: " +
      Collections.disjoint(list,
        Collections.singletonList("Four")));
    print("max: " + Collections.max(list));
    print("min: " + Collections.min(list));
    print("max w/ comparator: " + Collections.max(list,
      String.CASE_INSENSITIVE_ORDER));
    print("min w/ comparator: " + Collections.min(list,
      String.CASE_INSENSITIVE_ORDER));
    List<String> sublist =
      Arrays.asList("Four five six".split(" "));
    print("indexOfSubList: " +
      Collections.indexOfSubList(list, sublist));
    print("lastIndexOfSubList: " +
      Collections.lastIndexOfSubList(list, sublist));
    Collections.replaceAll(list, "one", "Yo");
    print("replaceAll: " + list);
    Collections.reverse(list);
    print("reverse: " + list);
    Collections.rotate(list, 3);
    print("rotate: " + list);
    List<String> source =
      Arrays.asList("in the matrix".split(" "));
    Collections.copy(list, source);
    print("copy: " + list);
    Collections.swap(list, 0, list.size() - 1);
    print("swap: " + list);
    Collections.shuffle(list, new Random(47));
```

```
      print("shuffled: " + list);
      Collections.fill(list, "pop");
      print("fill: " + list);
      print("frequency of 'pop': " +
        Collections.frequency(list, "pop"));
      List<String> dups = Collections.nCopies(3, "snap");
      print("dups: " + dups);
      print("'list' disjoint 'dups'?: " +
        Collections.disjoint(list, dups));
      // Getting an old-style Enumeration:
      Enumeration<String> e = Collections.enumeration(dups);
      Vector<String> v = new Vector<String>();
      while(e.hasMoreElements())
        v.addElement(e.nextElement());
      // Converting an old-style Vector
      // to a List via an Enumeration:
      ArrayList<String> arrayList =
        Collections.list(v.elements());
      print("arrayList: " + arrayList);
  }
} /* Output:
[one, Two, three, Four, five, six, one]
'list' disjoint (Four)?: false
max: three
min: Four
max w/ comparator: Two
min w/ comparator: five
indexOfSubList: 3
lastIndexOfSubList: 3
replaceAll: [Yo, Two, three, Four, five, six, Yo]
reverse: [Yo, six, five, Four, three, Two, Yo]
rotate: [three, Two, Yo, Yo, six, five, Four]
copy: [in, the, matrix, Yo, six, five, Four]
swap: [Four, the, matrix, Yo, six, five, in]
shuffled: [six, matrix, the, Four, Yo, five, in]
fill: [pop, pop, pop, pop, pop, pop, pop]
frequency of 'pop': 7
dups: [snap, snap, snap]
'list' disjoint 'dups'?: true
arrayList: [snap, snap, snap]
*///:~
```

The output explains the behavior of each utility method. Note the difference in **min( )** and **max( )** with the **String.CASE_INSENSITIVE_ORDER Comparator** because of capitalization.

Sorting and searching **List**s

Utilities to perform sorting and searching for **List**s have the same names and signatures as those for sorting arrays of objects, but are **static** methods of **Collections** instead of **Arrays**. Here's an example that uses the **list** data from **Utilities.java**:

```
//: containers/ListSortSearch.java
// Sorting and searching Lists with Collections utilities.
import java.util.*;
import static net.mindview.util.Print.*;

public class ListSortSearch {
  public static void main(String[] args) {
    List<String> list =
      new ArrayList<String>(Utilities.list);
    list.addAll(Utilities.list);
    print(list);
    Collections.shuffle(list, new Random(47));
    print("Shuffled: " + list);
    // Use a ListIterator to trim off the last elements:
    ListIterator<String> it = list.listIterator(10);
    while(it.hasNext()) {
      it.next();
      it.remove();
    }
    print("Trimmed: " + list);
    Collections.sort(list);
    print("Sorted: " + list);
    String key = list.get(7);
    int index = Collections.binarySearch(list, key);
    print("Location of " + key + " is " + index +
      ", list.get(" + index + ") = " + list.get(index));
    Collections.sort(list, String.CASE_INSENSITIVE_ORDER);
    print("Case-insensitive sorted: " + list);
    key = list.get(7);
    index = Collections.binarySearch(list, key,
      String.CASE_INSENSITIVE_ORDER);
    print("Location of " + key + " is " + index +
      ", list.get(" + index + ") = " + list.get(index));
```

```
  }
} /* Output:
[one, Two, three, Four, five, six, one, one, Two, three,
Four, five, six, one]
Shuffled: [Four, five, one, one, Two, six, six, three,
three, five, Four, Two, one, one]
Trimmed: [Four, five, one, one, Two, six, six, three,
three, five]
Sorted: [Four, Two, five, five, one, one, six, six, three,
three]
Location of six is 7, list.get(7) = six
Case-insensitive sorted: [five, five, Four, one, one, six,
six, three, three, Two]
Location of three is 7, list.get(7) = three
*///:~
```

Just as when searching and sorting with arrays, if you sort using a **Comparator**, you must **binarySearch( )** using the same **Comparator**.

This program also demonstrates the **shuffle( )** method in **Collections**, which randomizes the order of a **List**. A **ListIterator** is created at a particular location in the shuffled list, and used to remove the elements from that location until the end of the list.

Exercise 40: (5) Create a class containing two **String** objects and make it **Comparable** so that the comparison only cares about the first **String**. Fill an array and an **ArrayList** with objects of your class, using the **RandomGenerator** generator. Demonstrate that sorting works properly. Now make a **Comparator** that only cares about the second **String**, and demonstrate that sorting works properly. Also perform a binary search using your **Comparator**.

Exercise 41: (3) Modify the class in the previous exercise so that it will work with **HashSet**s and as a key in **HashMaps**.

Exercise 42: (2) Modify Exercise 40 so that an alphabetic sort is used.

Making a **Collection** or **Map** unmodifiable

Often it is convenient to create a read-only version of a **Collection** or **Map**. The **Collections** class allows you to do this by passing the original container into a method that hands back a read-only version. There are a number of variations on this method, for **Collection**s (if you can't treat a **Collection** as a more specific type), **List**s, **Set**s, and **Map**s. This example shows the proper way to build read-only versions of each:

```
//: containers/ReadOnly.java
// Using the Collections.unmodifiable methods.
import java.util.*;
import net.mindview.util.*;
import static net.mindview.util.Print.*;

public class ReadOnly {
  static Collection<String> data =
    new ArrayList<String>(Countries.names(6));
  public static void main(String[] args) {
    Collection<String> c =
      Collections.unmodifiableCollection(
        new ArrayList<String>(data));
    print(c); // Reading is OK
    //! c.add("one"); // Can't change it

    List<String> a = Collections.unmodifiableList(
        new ArrayList<String>(data));
    ListIterator<String> lit = a.listIterator();
    print(lit.next()); // Reading is OK
    //! lit.add("one"); // Can't change it

    Set<String> s = Collections.unmodifiableSet(
      new HashSet<String>(data));
    print(s); // Reading is OK
    //! s.add("one"); // Can't change it

    // For a SortedSet:
    Set<String> ss = Collections.unmodifiableSortedSet(
      new TreeSet<String>(data));

    Map<String,String> m = Collections.unmodifiableMap(
      new HashMap<String,String>(Countries.capitals(6)));
    print(m); // Reading is OK
    //! m.put("Ralph", "Howdy!");

    // For a SortedMap:
    Map<String,String> sm =
      Collections.unmodifiableSortedMap(
        new TreeMap<String,String>(Countries.capitals(6)));
  }
}
```

```
} /* Output:
[ALGERIA, ANGOLA, BENIN, BOTSWANA, BULGARIA, BURKINA FASO]
ALGERIA
[BULGARIA, BURKINA FASO, BOTSWANA, BENIN, ANGOLA, ALGERIA]
{BULGARIA=Sofia, BURKINA FASO=Ouagadougou,
BOTSWANA=Gaberone, BENIN=Porto-Novo, ANGOLA=Luanda,
ALGERIA=Algiers}
*///:~
```

Calling the "unmodifiable" method for a particular type does not cause compile-time checking, but once the transformation has occurred, any calls to methods that modify the contents of a particular container will produce an **UnsupportedOperationException**.

In each case, you must fill the container with meaningful data *before* you make it read-only. Once it is loaded, the best approach is to replace the existing reference with the reference that is produced by the "unmodifiable" call. That way, you don't run the risk of accidentally trying to change the contents once you've made it unmodifiable. On the other hand, this tool also allows you to keep a modifiable container as **private** within a class and to return a read-only reference to that container from a method call. So, you can change it from within the class, but everyone else can only read it.

Synchronizing a **Collection** or **Map**

The **synchronized** keyword is an important part of the subject of *multithreading*, a more complicated topic that will not be introduced until the *Concurrency* chapter. Here, I shall note only that the **Collections** class contains a way to automatically synchronize an entire container. The syntax is similar to the "unmodifiable" methods:

```
//: containers/Synchronization.java
// Using the Collections.synchronized methods.
import java.util.*;

public class Synchronization {
  public static void main(String[] args) {
    Collection<String> c =
      Collections.synchronizedCollection(
        new ArrayList<String>());
    List<String> list = Collections.synchronizedList(
      new ArrayList<String>());
    Set<String> s = Collections.synchronizedSet(
```

```
      new HashSet<String>());
    Set<String> ss = Collections.synchronizedSortedSet(
      new TreeSet<String>());
    Map<String,String> m = Collections.synchronizedMap(
      new HashMap<String,String>());
    Map<String,String> sm =
      Collections.synchronizedSortedMap(
        new TreeMap<String,String>());
  }
} ///:~
```

It is best to immediately pass the new container through the appropriate "synchronized" method, as shown above. That way, there's no chance of accidentally exposing the unsynchronized version.

Fail fast

The Java containers also have a mechanism to prevent more than one process from modifying the contents of a container. The problem occurs if you're in the middle of iterating through a container, and then some other process steps in and inserts, removes, or changes an object in that container. Maybe you've already passed that element in the container, maybe it's ahead of you, maybe the size of the container shrinks after you call **size( )**—there are many scenarios for disaster. The Java containers library uses a *fail-fast* mechanism that looks for any changes to the container other than the ones your process is personally responsible for. If it detects that someone else is modifying the container, it immediately produces a **ConcurrentModification-Exception**. This is the "fail-fast" aspect—it doesn't try to detect a problem later on using a more complex algorithm.

It's quite easy to see the fail-fast mechanism in operation—all you must do is create an iterator and then add something to the collection that the iterator is pointing to, like this:

```
//: containers/FailFast.java
// Demonstrates the "fail-fast" behavior.
import java.util.*;

public class FailFast {
  public static void main(String[] args) {
    Collection<String> c = new ArrayList<String>();
    Iterator<String> it = c.iterator();
    c.add("An object");
    try {
```

```
      String s = it.next();
    } catch(ConcurrentModificationException e) {
      System.out.println(e);
    }
  }
}
} /* Output:
java.util.ConcurrentModificationException
*///:~
```

The exception happens because something is placed in the container *after* the iterator is acquired from the container. The possibility that two parts of the program might modify the same container produces an uncertain state, so the exception notifies you that you should change your code—in this case, acquire the iterator *after* you have added all the elements to the container.

The **ConcurrentHashMap**, **CopyOnWriteArrayList**, and **CopyOnWriteArraySet** use techniques that avoid **ConcurrentModificationException**s.

Holding references

The **java.lang.ref** library contains a set of classes that allow greater flexibility in garbage collection. These classes are especially useful when you have large objects that may cause memory exhaustion. There are three classes inherited from the abstract class **Reference**: **SoftRcfcrcncc**, **WeakReference**, and **PhantomReference**. Each of these provides a different level of indirection for the garbage collector if the object in question is only reachable through one of these **Reference** objects.

If an object is *reachable*, it means that somewhere in your program the object can be found. This could mean that you have an ordinary reference on the stack that goes right to the object, but you might also have a reference to an object that has a reference to the object in question; there can be many intermediate links. If an object is reachable, the garbage collector cannot release it because it's still in use by your program. If an object isn't reachable, there's no way for your program to use it, so it's safe to garbage collect that object.

You use **Reference** objects when you want to continue to hold on to a reference to that object—you want to reach that object—but you also want to allow the garbage collector to release that object. Thus, you have a way to use the object, but if memory exhaustion is imminent, you allow that object to be released.

You accomplish this by using a **Reference** object as an intermediary (a *proxy*) between you and the ordinary reference. In addition, there must be no ordinary references to the object (ones that are not wrapped inside **Reference** objects). If the garbage collector discovers that an object is reachable through an ordinary reference, it will not release that object.

In the order of **SoftReference**, **WeakReference**, and **PhantomReference**, each one is "weaker" than the last and corresponds to a different level of reachability. Soft references are for implementing memory-sensitive caches. Weak references are for implementing "canonicalizing mappings"—where instances of objects can be simultaneously used in multiple places in a program, to save storage—that do not prevent their keys (or values) from being reclaimed. Phantom references are for scheduling pre-mortem cleanup actions in a more flexible way than is possible with the Java finalization mechanism.

With **SoftReference**s and **WeakReference**s, you have a choice about whether to place them on a **ReferenceQueue** (the device used for pre-mortem cleanup actions), but a **PhantomReference** can only be built on a **ReferenceQueue**. Here's a simple demonstration:

```
//: containers/References.java
// Demonstrates Reference objects
import java.lang.ref.*;
import java.util.*;

class VeryBig {
  private static final int SIZE = 10000;
  private long[] la = new long[SIZE];
  private String ident;
  public VeryBig(String id) { ident = id; }
  public String toString() { return ident; }
  protected void finalize() {
    System.out.println("Finalizing " + ident);
  }
}

public class References {
  private static ReferenceQueue<VeryBig> rq =
    new ReferenceQueue<VeryBig>();
```

```
public static void checkQueue() {
  Reference<? extends VeryBig> inq = rq.poll();
  if(inq != null)
    System.out.println("In queue: " + inq.get());
}
public static void main(String[] args) {
  int size = 10;
  // Or, choose size via the command line:
  if(args.length > 0)
    size = new Integer(args[0]);
  LinkedList<SoftReference<VeryBig>> sa =
    new LinkedList<SoftReference<VeryBig>>();
  for(int i = 0; i < size; i++) {
    sa.add(new SoftReference<VeryBig>(
      new VeryBig("Soft " + i), rq));
    System.out.println("Just created: " + sa.getLast());
    checkQueue();
  }
  LinkedList<WeakReference<VeryBig>> wa =
    new LinkedList<WeakReference<VeryBig>>();
  for(int i = 0; i < size; i++) {
    wa.add(new WeakReference<VeryBig>(
      new VeryBig("Weak " + i), rq));
    System.out.println("Just created: " + wa.getLast());
    checkQueue();
  }
  SoftReference<VeryBig> s =
    new SoftReference<VeryBig>(new VeryBig("Soft"));
  WeakReference<VeryBig> w =
    new WeakReference<VeryBig>(new VeryBig("Weak"));
  System.gc();
  LinkedList<PhantomReference<VeryBig>> pa =
    new LinkedList<PhantomReference<VeryBig>>();
  for(int i = 0; i < size; i++) {
    pa.add(new PhantomReference<VeryBig>(
      new VeryBig("Phantom " + i), rq));
    System.out.println("Just created: " + pa.getLast());
    checkQueue();
  }
}
} /* (Execute to see output) *///:~
```

When you run this program (you'll want to redirect the output into a text file so that you can view the output in pages), you'll see that the objects are

---

Containers in Depth   *891*

garbage collected, even though you still have access to them through the **Reference** object (to get the actual object reference, you use **get( )**). You'll also see that the **ReferenceQueue** always produces a **Reference** containing a **null** object. To use this, inherit from a particular **Reference** class and add more useful methods to the new class.

The **WeakHashMap**

The containers library has a special **Map** to hold weak references: the **WeakHashMap**. This class is designed to make the creation of canonicalized mappings easier. In such a mapping, you are saving storage by creating only one instance of a particular value. When the program needs that value, it looks up the existing object in the mapping and uses that (rather than creating one from scratch). The mapping may make the values as part of its initialization, but it's more likely that the values are made on demand.

Since this is a storage-saving technique, it's very convenient that the **WeakHashMap** allows the garbage collector to automatically clean up the keys and values. You don't have to do anything special to the keys and values you want to place in the **WeakHashMap**; these are automatically wrapped in **WeakReference**s by the map. The trigger to allow cleanup is that the key is no longer in use, as demonstrated here:

```
//: containers/CanonicalMapping.java
// Demonstrates WeakHashMap.
import java.util.*;

class Element {
  private String ident;
  public Element(String id) { ident = id; }
  public String toString() { return ident; }
  public int hashCode() { return ident.hashCode(); }
  public boolean equals(Object r) {
    return r instanceof Element &&
      ident.equals(((Element)r).ident);
  }
  protected void finalize() {
    System.out.println("Finalizing " +
      getClass().getSimpleName() + " " + ident);
  }
}

class Key extends Element {
```

```
      public Key(String id) { super(id); }
}

class Value extends Element {
   public Value(String id) { super(id); }
}

public class CanonicalMapping {
   public static void main(String[] args) {
      int size = 1000;
      // Or, choose size via the command line:
      if(args.length > 0)
        size = new Integer(args[0]);
      Key[] keys = new Key[size];
      WeakHashMap<Key,Value> map =
        new WeakHashMap<Key,Value>();
      for(int i = 0; i < size; i++) {
        Key k = new Key(Integer.toString(i));
        Value v = new Value(Integer.toString(i));
        if(i % 3 == 0)
          keys[i] = k; // Save as "real" references
        map.put(k, v);
      }
      System.gc();
   }
} /* (Execute to see output) *///:~
```

The **Key** class must have a **hashCode( )** and an **equals( )** since it is being
used as a key in a hashed data structure. The subject of **hashCode( )** was
described earlier in this chapter.

When you run the program, you'll see that the garbage collector will skip
every third key, because an ordinary reference to that key has also been
placed in the **keys** array, and thus those objects cannot be garbage collected.

Java 1.0/1.1 containers

Unfortunately, a lot of code was written using the Java 1.0/1.1 containers, and
even new code is sometimes written using these classes. So although you
should never use the old containers when writing new code, you'll still need
to be aware of them. However, the old containers were quite limited, so
there's not that much to say about them, and since they are anachronistic, I

will try to refrain from overemphasizing some of their hideous design decisions.

Vector & Enumeration

The only self-expanding sequence in Java 1.0/1.1 was the **Vector**, so it saw a lot of use. Its flaws are too numerous to describe here (see the 1st edition of this book, available as a free download from *www.MindView.net*). Basically, you can think of it as an **ArrayList** with long, awkward method names. In the revised Java container library, **Vector** was adapted so that it could work as a **Collection** and a **List**. This turns out to be a bit perverse, as it may confuse some people into thinking that **Vector** has gotten better, when it is actually included only to support older Java code.

The Java 1.0/1.1 version of the iterator chose to invent a new name, "enumeration," instead of using a term that everyone was already familiar with ("iterator"). The **Enumeration** interface is smaller than **Iterator**, with only two methods, and it uses longer method names: **boolean hasMoreElements( )** produces **true** if this enumeration contains more elements, and **Object nextElement( )** returns the next element of this enumeration if there are any more (otherwise it throws an exception).

Enumeration is only an interface, not an implementation, and even new libraries sometimes still use the old **Enumeration**, which is unfortunate but generally harmless. Even though you should always use **Iterator** when you can in your own code, you must be prepared for libraries that want to hand you an **Enumeration**.

In addition, you can produce an **Enumeration** for any **Collection** by using the **Collections.enumeration( )** method, as seen in this example:

```
//: containers/Enumerations.java
// Java 1.0/1.1 Vector and Enumeration.
import java.util.*;
import net.mindview.util.*;

public class Enumerations {
  public static void main(String[] args) {
    Vector<String> v =
      new Vector<String>(Countries.names(10));
    Enumeration<String> e = v.elements();
    while(e.hasMoreElements())
      System.out.print(e.nextElement() + ", ");
```

```
    // Produce an Enumeration from a Collection:
    e = Collections.enumeration(new ArrayList<String>());
  }
} /* Output:
ALGERIA, ANGOLA, BENIN, BOTSWANA, BULGARIA, BURKINA FASO,
BURUNDI, CAMEROON, CAPE VERDE, CENTRAL AFRICAN REPUBLIC,
*///:~
```

To produce an **Enumeration**, you call **elements( )**, then you can use it to perform a forward iteration.

The last line creates an **ArrayList** and uses **enumeration( )** to adapt an **Enumeration** from the **ArrayList Iterator**. Thus, if you have old code that wants an **Enumeration**, you can still use the new containers.

Hashtable

As you've seen in the performance comparison in this chapter, the basic **Hashtable** is very similar to the **HashMap**, even down to the method names. There's no reason to use **Hashtable** instead of **HashMap** in new code.

Stack

The concept of the stack was introduced earlier, with the **LinkedList**. What's rather odd about the Java 1.0/1.1 **Stack** is that instead of using a **Vector** with composition, **Stack** is *inherited* from **Vector**. So it has all of the characteristics and behaviors of a **Vector** plus some extra **Stack** behaviors. It's difficult to know whether the designers consciously thought that this was an especially useful way of doing things, or whether it was just a naïve design; in any event it was clearly not reviewed before it was rushed into distribution, so this bad design is *still* hanging around (but you shouldn't use it).

Here's a simple demonstration of **Stack** that pushes each **String** representation of an **enum**. It also shows how you can just as easily use a **LinkedList** as a stack, or the **Stack** class created in the *Holding Your Objects* chapter:

```
//: containers/Stacks.java
// Demonstration of Stack Class.
import java.util.*;
import static net.mindview.util.Print.*;
```

```
enum Month { JANUARY, FEBRUARY, MARCH, APRIL, MAY, JUNE,
  JULY, AUGUST, SEPTEMBER, OCTOBER, NOVEMBER }

public class Stacks {
  public static void main(String[] args) {
    Stack<String> stack = new Stack<String>();
    for(Month m : Month.values())
      stack.push(m.toString());
    print("stack = " + stack);
    // Treating a stack as a Vector:
    stack.addElement("The last line");
    print("element 5 = " + stack.elementAt(5));
    print("popping elements:");
    while(!stack.empty())
      printnb(stack.pop() + " ");

    // Using a LinkedList as a Stack:
    LinkedList<String> lstack = new LinkedList<String>();
    for(Month m : Month.values())
      lstack.addFirst(m.toString());
    print("lstack = " + lstack);
    while(!lstack.isEmpty())
      printnb(lstack.removeFirst() + " ");

    // Using the Stack class from
    // the Holding Your Objects Chapter:
    net.mindview.util.Stack<String> stack2 =
      new net.mindview.util.Stack<String>();
    for(Month m : Month.values())
      stack2.push(m.toString());
    print("stack2 = " + stack2);
    while(!stack2.empty())
      printnb(stack2.pop() + " ");

  }
} /* Output:
stack = [JANUARY, FEBRUARY, MARCH, APRIL, MAY, JUNE, JULY,
AUGUST, SEPTEMBER, OCTOBER, NOVEMBER]
element 5 = JUNE
popping elements:
The last line NOVEMBER OCTOBER SEPTEMBER AUGUST JULY JUNE
MAY APRIL MARCH FEBRUARY JANUARY lstack = [NOVEMBER,
OCTOBER, SEPTEMBER, AUGUST, JULY, JUNE, MAY, APRIL, MARCH,
FEBRUARY, JANUARY]
```

```
NOVEMBER OCTOBER SEPTEMBER AUGUST JULY JUNE MAY APRIL MARCH
FEBRUARY JANUARY stack2 = [NOVEMBER, OCTOBER, SEPTEMBER,
AUGUST, JULY, JUNE, MAY, APRIL, MARCH, FEBRUARY, JANUARY]
NOVEMBER OCTOBER SEPTEMBER AUGUST JULY JUNE MAY APRIL MARCH
FEBRUARY JANUARY
*///:~
```

A **String** representation is generated from the **Month enum** constants, inserted into the **Stack** with **push( )**, and later fetched from the top of the stack with a **pop( )**. To make a point, **Vector** operations are also performed on the **Stack** object. This is possible because, by virtue of inheritance, a **Stack** *is* a **Vector**. Thus, all operations that can be performed on a **Vector** can also be performed on a **Stack**, such as **elementAt( )**.

As mentioned earlier, you should use a **LinkedList** when you want stack behavior, or the **net.mindview.util.Stack** class created from the **LinkedList** class.

BitSet

A **BitSet** is used if you want to efficiently store a lot of on-off information. It's efficient only from the standpoint of size; if you're looking for efficient access, it is slightly slower than using a native array.

In addition, the minimum size of the **BitSet** is that of a **long**: 64 bits. This implies that if you're storing anything smaller, like 8 bits, a **BitSet** will be wasteful; you're better off creating your own class, or just an array, to hold your flags if size is an issue. (This will only be the case if you're creating a *lot* of objects containing lists of on-off information, and should only be decided based on profiling and other metrics. If you make this decision because you just think something is too big, you will end up creating needless complexity and wasting a lot of time.)

A normal container expands as you add more elements, and the **BitSet** does this as well. The following example shows how the **BitSet** works:

```
//: containers/Bits.java
// Demonstration of BitSet.
import java.util.*;
import static net.mindview.util.Print.*;

public class Bits {
  public static void printBitSet(BitSet b) {
```

```
    print("bits: " + b);
    StringBuilder bbits = new StringBuilder();
    for(int j = 0; j < b.size() ; j++)
      bbits.append(b.get(j) ? "1" : "0");
    print("bit pattern: " + bbits);
  }
  public static void main(String[] args) {
    Random rand = new Random(47);
    // Take the LSB of nextInt():
    byte bt = (byte)rand.nextInt();
    BitSet bb = new BitSet();
    for(int i = 7; i >= 0; i--)
      if(((1 << i) &  bt) != 0)
        bb.set(i);
      else
        bb.clear(i);
    print("byte value: " + bt);
    printBitSet(bb);

    short st = (short)rand.nextInt();
    BitSet bs = new BitSet();
    for(int i = 15; i >= 0; i--)
      if(((1 << i) &  st) != 0)
        bs.set(i);
      else
        bs.clear(i);
    print("short value: " + st);
    printBitSet(bs);

    int it = rand.nextInt();
    BitSet bi = new BitSet();
    for(int i = 31; i >= 0; i--)
      if(((1 << i) &  it) != 0)
        bi.set(i);
      else
        bi.clear(i);
    print("int value: " + it);
    printBitSet(bi);

    // Test bitsets >= 64 bits:
    BitSet b127 = new BitSet();
    b127.set(127);
    print("set bit 127: " + b127);
    BitSet b255 = new BitSet(65);
```

```
    b255.set(255);
    print("set bit 255: " + b255);
    BitSet b1023 = new BitSet(512);
    b1023.set(1023);
    b1023.set(1024);
    print("set bit 1023: " + b1023);
  }
} /* Output:
byte value: -107
bits: {0, 2, 4, 7}
bit pattern:
1010100100000000000000000000000000000000000000000000000000000
00000
short value: 1302
bits: {1, 2, 4, 8, 10}
bit pattern:
0110100010100000000000000000000000000000000000000000000000000
00000
int value: -2014573909
bits: {0, 1, 3, 5, 7, 9, 11, 18, 19, 21, 22, 23, 24, 25,
26, 31}
bit pattern:
1101010101010000001101111110000100000000000000000000000000000
00000
set bit 127: {127}
set bit 255: {255}
set bit 1023: {1023, 1024}
*///:~
```

The random number generator is used to create a random **byte**, **short**, and **int**, and each one is transformed into a corresponding bit pattern in a **BitSet**. This works fine because a **BitSet** is 64 bits, so none of these cause it to increase in size. Then larger **BitSet**s are created. You can see that the **BitSet** is expanded as necessary.

An **EnumSet** (see the *Enumerated Types* chapter) is usually a better choice than a **BitSet** if you have a fixed set of flags that you can name, because the **EnumSet** allows you to manipulate the names rather than numerical bit locations, and thus reduces errors. **EnumSet** also prevents you from accidentally adding new flag locations, which could cause some serious, difficult-to-find bugs. The only reasons you should use **BitSet** instead of **EnumSet** is if you don't know how many flags you will need until run time, or if it is unreasonable to assign names to the flags, or you need one of the

---

special operations in **BitSet** (see the JDK documentation for **BitSet** and **EnumSet**).

Summary

The containers library is arguably the most important library for an object-oriented language. Most programming will use containers more than any other library components. Some languages (Python, for example) even include the fundamental container components (lists, maps and sets) as built-ins.

As you saw in the *Holding Your Objects* chapter, it's possible to do a number of very interesting things using containers, without much effort. However, at some point you're forced to know more about containers in order to use them properly—in particular, you must know enough about hashing operations to write your own **hashCode( )** method (and you must know when it is necessary), and you must know enough about the various container implementations that you can choose the appropriate one for your needs. This chapter covered these concepts and discussed additional useful details about the container library. At this point you should be reasonably well prepared to use the Java containers in your everyday programming tasks.

The design of a containers library is difficult (this is true of most library design problems). In C++, the container classes covered the bases with many different classes. This was better than what was available prior to the C++ container classes (nothing), but it didn't translate well into Java. At the other extreme, I've seen a containers library that consists of a single class, "container," which acts like both a linear sequence and an associative array at the same time. The Java container library strikes a balance: the full functionality that you expect from a mature container library, but easier to learn and use than the C++ container classes and other similar container libraries. The result can seem a bit odd in places. Unlike some of the decisions made in the early Java libraries, these oddities were not accidents, but carefully considered decisions based on trade-offs in complexity.

Solutions to selected exercises can be found in the electronic document *The Thinking in Java Annotated Solution Guide*, available for sale from *www.MindView.net*.

I/O

Creating a good input/output (I/O) system is one of the more difficult tasks for a language designer. This is evidenced by the number of different approaches.

The challenge seems to be in covering all possibilities. Not only are there different sources and sinks of I/O that you want to communicate with (files, the console, network connections, etc.), but you need to talk to them in a wide variety of ways (sequential, random-access, buffered, binary, character, by lines, by words, etc.).

The Java library designers attacked this problem by creating lots of classes. In fact, there are so many classes for Java's I/O system that it can be intimidating at first (ironically, the Java I/O design actually prevents an explosion of classes). There was also a significant change in the I/O library after Java 1.0, when the original byte-oriented library was supplemented with **char**-oriented, Unicode-based I/O classes. The **nio** classes (for "new I/O," a name we'll still be using years from now even though they were introduced in JDK 1.4 and so are already "old") were added for improved performance and functionality. As a result, there are a fair number of classes to learn before you understand enough of Java's I/O picture that you can use it properly. In addition, it's rather important to understand the evolution of the I/O library, even if your first reaction is "Don't bother me with history, just show me how to use it!" The problem is that without the historical perspective, you will rapidly become confused with some of the classes and when you should and shouldn't use them.

This chapter will give you an introduction to the variety of I/O classes in the standard Java library and how to use them.

The **File** class

Before getting into the classes that actually read and write data to streams, we'll look at a library utility that assists you with file directory issues.

The **File** class has a deceiving name; you might think it refers to a file, but it doesn't. In fact, "FilePath" would have been a better name for the class. It can represent either the *name* of a particular file or the *names* of a set of files in a directory. If it's a set of files, you can ask for that set using the **list( )** method, which returns an array of **String**. It makes sense to return an array rather than one of the flexible container classes, because the number of elements is fixed, and if you want a different directory listing, you just create a different **File** object. This section shows an example of the use of this class, including the associated **FilenameFilter** interface.

A directory lister

Suppose you'd like to see a directory listing. The **File** object can be used in two ways. If you call **list( )** with no arguments, you'll get the full list that the **File** object contains. However, if you want a restricted list—for example, if you want all of the files with an extension of **.java**—then you use a "directory filter," which is a class that tells how to select the **File** objects for display.

Here's the example. Note that the result has been effortlessly sorted (alphabetically) using the **java.util.Arrays.sort( )** method and the **String.CASE_INSENSITIVE_ORDER Comparator**:

```
//: io/DirList.java
// Display a directory listing using regular expressions.
// {Args: "D.*\.java"}
import java.util.regex.*;
import java.io.*;
import java.util.*;

public class DirList {
  public static void main(String[] args) {
    File path = new File(".");
    String[] list;
    if(args.length == 0)
      list = path.list();
    else
      list = path.list(new DirFilter(args[0]));
    Arrays.sort(list, String.CASE_INSENSITIVE_ORDER);
    for(String dirItem : list)
      System.out.println(dirItem);
  }
}

class DirFilter implements FilenameFilter {
  private Pattern pattern;
```

```
   public DirFilter(String regex) {
     pattern = Pattern.compile(regex);
   }
   public boolean accept(File dir, String name) {
     return pattern.matcher(name).matches();
   }
} /* Output:
DirectoryDemo.java
DirList.java
DirList2.java
DirList3.java
*///:~
```

The **DirFilter** class implements the interface **FilenameFilter**. Notice how simple the **FilenameFilter** interface is:

```
public interface FilenameFilter {
  boolean accept(File dir, String name);
}
```

DirFilter's sole reason for existence is to provide the **accept( )** method to the **list( )** method so that **list( )** can "call back" **accept( )** to determine which file names should be included in the list. Thus, this structure is often referred to as a *callback*. More specifically, this is an example of the *Strategy* design pattern, because **list( )** implements basic functionality, and you provide the Strategy in the form of a **FilenameFilter** in order to complete the algorithm necessary for **list( )** to provide its service. Because **list( )** takes a **FilenameFilter** object as its argument, it means that you can pass an object of any class that implements **FilenameFilter** to choose (even at run time) how the **list( )** method will behave. The purpose of a Strategy is to provide flexibility in the behavior of code.

The **accept( )** method must accept a **File** object representing the directory that a particular file is found in, and a **String** containing the name of that file. Remember that the **list( )** method is calling **accept( )** for each of the file names in the directory object to see which one should be included; this is indicated by the **boolean** result returned by **accept( )**.

accept( ) uses a regular expression **matcher** object to see if the regular expression **regex** matches the name of the file. Using **accept( )**, the **list( )** method returns an array.

Anonymous inner classes

This example is ideal for rewriting using an anonymous inner class (described in *Inner Classes*). As a first cut, a method **filter( )** is created that returns a reference to a **FilenameFilter**:

```
//: io/DirList2.java
// Uses anonymous inner classes.
// {Args: "D.*\.java"}
import java.util.regex.*;
import java.io.*;
import java.util.*;

public class DirList2 {
  public static FilenameFilter filter(final String regex) {
    // Creation of anonymous inner class:
    return new FilenameFilter() {
      private Pattern pattern = Pattern.compile(regex);
      public boolean accept(File dir, String name) {
        return pattern.matcher(name).matches();
      }
    }; // End of anonymous inner class
  }
  public static void main(String[] args) {
    File path = new File(".");
    String[] list;
    if(args.length == 0)
      list = path.list();
    else
      list = path.list(filter(args[0]));
    Arrays.sort(list, String.CASE_INSENSITIVE_ORDER);
    for(String dirItem : list)
      System.out.println(dirItem);
  }
} /* Output:
DirectoryDemo.java
DirList.java
DirList2.java
DirList3.java
*///:~
```

Note that the argument to **filter( )** must be **final**. This is required by the anonymous inner class so that it can use an object from outside its scope.

This design is an improvement because the **FilenameFilter** class is now tightly bound to **DirList2**. However, you can take this approach one step further and define the anonymous inner class as an argument to **list( )**, in which case it's even smaller:

```
//: io/DirList3.java
// Building the anonymous inner class "in-place."
// {Args: "D.*\.java"}
import java.util.regex.*;
import java.io.*;
import java.util.*;

public class DirList3 {
  public static void main(final String[] args) {
    File path = new File(".");
    String[] list;
    if(args.length == 0)
      list = path.list();
    else
      list = path.list(new FilenameFilter() {
        private Pattern pattern = Pattern.compile(args[0]);
        public boolean accept(File dir, String name) {
          return pattern.matcher(name).matches();
        }
      });
    Arrays.sort(list, String.CASE_INSENSITIVE_ORDER);
    for(String dirItem : list)
      System.out.println(dirItem);
  }
} /* Output:
DirectoryDemo.java
DirList.java
DirList2.java
DirList3.java
*///:~
```

The argument to **main( )** is now **final**, since the anonymous inner class uses **args[0]** directly.

This shows you how anonymous inner classes allow the creation of specific, one-off classes to solve problems. One benefit of this approach is that it keeps the code that solves a particular problem isolated in one spot. On the other hand, it is not always as easy to read, so you must use it judiciously.

Exercise 1: (3) Modify **DirList.java** (or one of its variants) so that the **FilenameFilter** opens and reads each file (using the **net.mindview.util.TextFile** utility) and accepts the file based on whether any of the trailing arguments on the command line exist in that file.

Exercise 2: (2) Create a class called **SortedDirList** with a constructor that takes a **File** object and builds a sorted directory list from the files at that **File**. Add to this class two overloaded **list( )** methods: the first produces the whole list, and the second produces the subset of the list that matches its argument (which is a regular expression).

Exercise 3: (3) Modify **DirList.java** (or one of its variants) so that it sums up the file sizes of the selected files.

Directory utilities

A common task in programming is to perform operations on sets of files, either in the local directory or by walking the entire directory tree. It is useful to have a tool that will produce the set of files for you. The following utility class produces either an array of **File** objects in the local directory using the **local( )** method, or a **List<File>** of the entire directory tree starting at the given directory using **walk( )** (**File** objects are more useful than file names because **File** objects contain more information). The files are chosen based on the regular expression that you provide:

```
//: net/mindview/util/Directory.java
// Produce a sequence of File objects that match a
// regular expression in either a local directory,
// or by walking a directory tree.
package net.mindview.util;
import java.util.regex.*;
import java.io.*;
import java.util.*;

public final class Directory {
  public static File[]
  local(File dir, final String regex) {
    return dir.listFiles(new FilenameFilter() {
      private Pattern pattern = Pattern.compile(regex);
      public boolean accept(File dir, String name) {
        return pattern.matcher(
          new File(name).getName()).matches();
      }
    });
```

```
  }
  public static File[]
  local(String path, final String regex) { // Overloaded
    return local(new File(path), regex);
  }
  // A two-tuple for returning a pair of objects:
  public static class TreeInfo implements Iterable<File> {
    public List<File> files = new ArrayList<File>();
    public List<File> dirs = new ArrayList<File>();
    // The default iterable element is the file list:
    public Iterator<File> iterator() {
      return files.iterator();
    }
    void addAll(TreeInfo other) {
      files.addAll(other.files);
      dirs.addAll(other.dirs);
    }
    public String toString() {
      return "dirs: " + PPrint.pformat(dirs) +
        "\n\nfiles: " + PPrint.pformat(files);
    }
  }
  public static TreeInfo
  walk(String start, String regex) { // Begin recursion
    return recurseDirs(new File(start), regex);
  }
  public static TreeInfo
  walk(File start, String regex) { // Overloaded
    return recurseDirs(start, regex);
  }
  public static TreeInfo walk(File start) { // Everything
    return recurseDirs(start, ".*");
  }
  public static TreeInfo walk(String start) {
    return recurseDirs(new File(start), ".*");
  }
  static TreeInfo recurseDirs(File startDir, String regex){
    TreeInfo result = new TreeInfo();
    for(File item : startDir.listFiles()) {
      if(item.isDirectory()) {
        result.dirs.add(item);
        result.addAll(recurseDirs(item, regex));
      } else // Regular file
        if(item.getName().matches(regex))
```

```
        result.files.add(item);
    }
    return result;
}
// Simple validation test:
public static void main(String[] args) {
    if(args.length == 0)
        System.out.println(walk("."));
    else
        for(String arg : args)
            System.out.println(walk(arg));
}
} ///:~
```

The **local( )** method uses a variant of **File.list( )** called **listFiles( )** that produces an array of **File**. You can see that it also uses a **FilenameFilter**. If you need a **List** instead of an array, you can convert the result yourself using **Arrays.asList( )**.

The **walk( )** method converts the name of the starting directory into a **File** object and calls **recurseDirs( )**, which performs a recursive directory walk, collecting more information with each recursion. To distinguish ordinary files from directories, the return value is effectively a "tuple" of objects—a **List** holding ordinary files, and another holding directories. The fields are intentionally made **public** here, because the point of **TreeInfo** is simply to collect the objects together—if you were just returning a **List**, you wouldn't make it **private**, so just because you are returning a pair of objects, it doesn't mean you need to make them **private**. Note that **TreeInfo** implements **Iterable<File>**, which produces the files, so that you have a "default iteration" over the file list, whereas you can specify directories by saying ".**dirs**".

The **TreeInfo.toString( )** method uses a "pretty printer" class so that the output is easer to view. The default **toString( )** methods for containers print all the elements for a container on a single line. For large collections this can become difficult to read, so you may want to use an alternate formatting. Here's a tool that adds newlines and indents each element:

```
//: net/mindview/util/PPrint.java
// Pretty-printer for collections
package net.mindview.util;
import java.util.*;
```

```
public class PPrint {
  public static String pformat(Collection<?> c) {
    if(c.size() == 0) return "[]";
    StringBuilder result = new StringBuilder("[");
    for(Object elem : c) {
      if(c.size() != 1)
        result.append("\n  ");
      result.append(elem);
    }
    if(c.size() != 1)
      result.append("\n");
    result.append("]");
    return result.toString();
  }
  public static void pprint(Collection<?> c) {
    System.out.println(pformat(c));
  }
  public static void pprint(Object[] c) {
    System.out.println(pformat(Arrays.asList(c)));
  }
} ///:~
```

The **pformat( )** method produces a formatted **String** from a **Collection**,
and the **pprint( )** method uses **pformat( )** to do its job. Note that the
special cases of no elements and a single element are handled differently.
There's also a version of **pprint( )** for arrays.

The **Directory** utility is placed in the **net.mindview.util** package so that it
is easily available. Here's a sample of how you can use it:

```
//: io/DirectoryDemo.java
// Sample use of Directory utilities.
import java.io.*;
import net.mindview.util.*;
import static net.mindview.util.Print.*;

public class DirectoryDemo {
  public static void main(String[] args) {
    // All directories:
    PPrint.pprint(Directory.walk(".").dirs);
    // All files beginning with 'T'
    for(File file : Directory.local(".", "T.*"))
      print(file);
    print("----------------------");
    // All Java files beginning with 'T':
```

```
      for(File file : Directory.walk(".", "T.*\\.java"))
        print(file);
      print("======================");
      // Class files containing "Z" or "z":
      for(File file : Directory.walk(".",".*[Zz].*\\.class"))
        print(file);
  }
} /* Output: (Sample)
[.\xfiles]
.\TestEOF.class
.\TestEOF.java
.\TransferTo.class
.\TransferTo.java
----------------------
.\TestEOF.java
.\TransferTo.java
.\xfiles\ThawAlien.java
======================
.\FreezeAlien.class
.\GZIPcompress.class
.\ZipCompress.class
*///:~
```

You may need to refresh your knowledge of regular expressions from the
Strings chapter in order to understand the second arguments in **local( )** and
walk( ).

We can take this a step further and create a tool that will walk directories *and*
process the files within them according to a **Strategy** object (this is another
example of the *Strategy* design pattern):

```
//: net/mindview/util/ProcessFiles.java
package net.mindview.util;
import java.io.*;

public class ProcessFiles {
  public interface Strategy {
    void process(File file);
  }
  private Strategy strategy;
  private String ext;
  public ProcessFiles(Strategy strategy, String ext) {
    this.strategy = strategy;
    this.ext = ext;
  }
```

```java
    public void start(String[] args) {
      try {
        if(args.length == 0)
          processDirectoryTree(new File("."));
        else
          for(String arg : args) {
            File fileArg = new File(arg);
            if(fileArg.isDirectory())
              processDirectoryTree(fileArg);
            else {
              // Allow user to leave off extension:
              if(!arg.endsWith("." + ext))
                arg += "." + ext;
              strategy.process(
                new File(arg).getCanonicalFile());
            }
          }
      } catch(IOException e) {
        throw new RuntimeException(e);
      }
    }
    public void
    processDirectoryTree(File root) throws IOException {
      for(File file : Directory.walk(
          root.getAbsolutePath(), ".*\\." + ext))
        strategy.process(file.getCanonicalFile());
    }
    // Demonstration of how to use it:
    public static void main(String[] args) {
      new ProcessFiles(new ProcessFiles.Strategy() {
        public void process(File file) {
          System.out.println(file);
        }
      }, "java").start(args);
    }
} /* (Execute to see output) *///:~
```

The **Strategy** interface is nested within **ProcessFiles**, so that if you want to implement it you must **implement ProcessFiles.Strategy**, which provides more context for the reader. **ProcessFiles** does all the work of finding the files that have a particular extension (the **ext** argument to the constructor), and when it finds a matching file, it simply hands it to the **Strategy** object (which is also an argument to the constructor).

If you don't give it any arguments, **ProcessFiles** assumes that you want to traverse all the directories off of the current directory. You can also specify a particular file, with or without the extension (it will add the extension if necessary), or one or more directories.

In **main( )** you see a basic example of how to use the tool; it prints the names of all the Java source files according to the command line that you provide.

Exercise 4: (2) Use **Directory.walk( )** to sum the sizes of all files in a directory tree whose names match a particular regular expression.

Exercise 5: (1) Modify **ProcessFiles.java** so that it matches a regular expression rather than a fixed extension.

Checking for and creating directories

The **File** class is more than just a representation for an existing file or directory. You can also use a **File** object to create a new directory or an entire directory path if it doesn't exist. You can also look at the characteristics of files (size, last modification date, read/write), see whether a **File** object represents a file or a directory, and delete a file. The following example shows some of the other methods available with the **File** class (see the JDK documentation from *http://java.sun.com* for the full set):

```
//: io/MakeDirectories.java
// Demonstrates the use of the File class to
// create directories and manipulate files.
// {Args: MakeDirectoriesTest}
import java.io.*;

public class MakeDirectories {
  private static void usage() {
    System.err.println(
      "Usage:MakeDirectories path1 ...\n" +
      "Creates each path\n" +
      "Usage:MakeDirectories -d path1 ...\n" +
      "Deletes each path\n" +
      "Usage:MakeDirectories -r path1 path2\n" +
      "Renames from path1 to path2");
    System.exit(1);
  }
  private static void fileData(File f) {
    System.out.println(
      "Absolute path: " + f.getAbsolutePath() +
```

```
        "\n Can read: " + f.canRead() +
        "\n Can write: " + f.canWrite() +
        "\n getName: " + f.getName() +
        "\n getParent: " + f.getParent() +
        "\n getPath: " + f.getPath() +
        "\n length: " + f.length() +
        "\n lastModified: " + f.lastModified());
      if(f.isFile())
        System.out.println("It's a file");
      else if(f.isDirectory())
        System.out.println("It's a directory");
    }
    public static void main(String[] args) {
      if(args.length < 1) usage();
      if(args[0].equals("-r")) {
        if(args.length != 3) usage();
        File
          old = new File(args[1]),
          rname = new File(args[2]);
        old.renameTo(rname);
        fileData(old);
        fileData(rname);
        return; // Exit main
      }
      int count = 0;
      boolean del = false;
      if(args[0].equals("-d")) {
        count++;
        del = true;
      }
      count--;
      while(++count < args.length) {
        File f = new File(args[count]);
        if(f.exists()) {
          System.out.println(f + " exists");
          if(del) {
            System.out.println("deleting..." + f);
            f.delete();
          }
        }
        else { // Doesn't exist
          if(!del) {
            f.mkdirs();
            System.out.println("created " + f);
```

```
            }
        }
        fileData(f);
    }
  }
} /* Output: (80% match)
created MakeDirectoriesTest
Absolute path: d:\aaa-TIJ4\code\io\MakeDirectoriesTest
 Can read: true
 Can write: true
 getName: MakeDirectoriesTest
 getParent: null
 getPath: MakeDirectoriesTest
 length: 0
 lastModified: 1101690308831
It's a directory
*///:~
```

In **fileData( )** you can see various file investigation methods used to display information about the file or directory path.

The first method that's exercised by **main( )** is **renameTo( )**, which allows you to rename (or move) a file to an entirely new path represented by the argument, which is another **File** object. This also works with directories of any length.

If you experiment with the preceding program, you'll find that you can make a directory path of any complexity, because **mkdirs( )** will do all the work for you.

Exercise 6: (5) Use **ProcessFiles** to find all the Java source-code files in a particular directory subtree that have been modified after a particular date.

Input and output

Programming language I/O libraries often use the abstraction of a *stream*, which represents any data source or sink as an object capable of producing or receiving pieces of data. The stream hides the details of what happens to the data inside the actual I/O device.

The Java library classes for I/O are divided by input and output, as you can see by looking at the class hierarchy in the JDK documentation. Through inheritance, everything derived from the **InputStream** or **Reader** classes has basic methods called **read( )** for reading a single **byte** or an array of **byte**s. Likewise, everything derived from **OutputStream** or **Writer** classes has basic methods called **write( )** for writing a single **byte** or an array of **byte**s. However, you won't generally use these methods; they exist so that other classes can use them—these other classes provide a more useful interface. Thus, you'll rarely create your stream object by using a single class, but instead will layer multiple objects together to provide your desired functionality (this is the *Decorator* design pattern, as you shall see in this section). The fact that you create more than one object to produce a single stream is the primary reason that Java's I/O library is confusing.

It's helpful to categorize the classes by their functionality. In Java 1.0, the library designers started by deciding that all classes that had anything to do with input would be inherited from **InputStream**, and all classes that were associated with output would be inherited from **OutputStream**.

As is the practice in this book, I will attempt to provide an overview of the classes, but assume that you will use the JDK documentation to determine all the details, such as the exhaustive list of methods of a particular class.

Types of **InputStream**

InputStream's job is to represent classes that produce input from different sources. These sources can be:

1. An array of bytes.

2. A **String** object.

3. A file.

4. A "pipe," which works like a physical pipe: You put things in at one end and they come out the other.

5. A sequence of other streams, so you can collect them together into a single stream.

6. Other sources, such as an Internet connection. (This is covered in *Thinking in Enterprise Java*, available at *www.MindView.net.*)

Each of these has an associated subclass of **InputStream**. In addition, the **FilterInputStream** is also a type of **InputStream**, to provide a base class for "decorator" classes that attach attributes or useful interfaces to input streams. This is discussed later.

Table I/O-1. Types of InputStream

Class	Function	Constructor arguments
		How to use it
ByteArray-InputStream	Allows a buffer in memory to be used as an **InputStream**.	The buffer from which to extract the bytes.
		As a source of data: Connect it to a **FilterInputStream** object to provide a useful interface.
StringBuffer-InputStream	Converts a **String** into an **InputStream**.	A **String**. The underlying implementation actually uses a **StringBuffer**.
		As a source of data: Connect it to a **FilterInputStream** object to provide a useful interface.
File-InputStream	For reading information from a file.	A **String** representing the file name, or a **File** or **FileDescriptor** object.
		As a source of data: Connect it to a **FilterInputStream** object to provide a useful interface.
Piped-InputStream	Produces the data that's being written to the associated **PipedOutput-Stream**. Implements the "piping" concept.	**PipedOutputStream**
		As a source of data in multithreading: Connect it to a **FilterInputStream** object to provide a useful interface.
Sequence-InputStream	Converts two or more **InputStream** objects into a single	Two **InputStream** objects or an **Enumeration** for a container of **InputStream** objects.

Class	Function	Constructor arguments
		How to use it
	InputStream.	As a source of data: Connect it to a **FilterInputStream** object to provide a useful interface.
Filter-InputStream	Abstract class that is an interface for decorators that provide useful functionality to the other **InputStream** classes. See Table I/O-3.	See Table I/O-3.
		See Table I/O-3.

Types of **OutputStream**

This category includes the classes that decide where your output will go: an array of bytes (but not a **String**—presumably, you can create one using the array of bytes), a file, or a "pipe."

In addition, the **FilterOutputStream** provides a base class for "decorator" classes that attach attributes or useful interfaces to output streams. This is discussed later.

Table I/O-2. Types of OutputStream

Class	Function	Constructor arguments
		How to use it
ByteArray-OutputStream	Creates a buffer in memory. All the data that you send to the stream is placed in this buffer.	Optional initial size of the buffer.
		To designate the destination of your data: Connect it to a **FilterOutputStream** object to provide a useful interface.

Class	Function	Constructor arguments
		How to use it
File-OutputStream	For sending information to a file.	A **String** representing the file name, or a **File** or **FileDescriptor** object.
		To designate the destination of your data: Connect it to a **FilterOutputStream** object to provide a useful interface.
Piped-OutputStream	Any information you write to this automatically ends up as input for the associated **PipedInput-Stream**. Implements the "piping" concept.	**PipedInputStream**
		To designate the destination of your data for multithreading: Connect it to a **FilterOutputStream** object to provide a useful interface.
Filter-OutputStream	Abstract class that is an interface for decorators that provide useful functionality to the other **OutputStream** classes. See Table I/O-4.	See Table I/O-4.
		See Table I/O-4.

Adding attributes and useful interfaces

Decorators were introduced in the *Generics* chapter, on page 717. The Java I/O library requires many different combinations of features, and this is the justification for using the Decorator design pattern.[1] The reason for the

---

[1] It's not clear that this was a good design decision, especially compared to the simplicity of I/O libraries in other languages. But it's the justification for the decision.

---

existence of the "filter" classes in the Java I/O library is that the abstract "filter" class is the base class for all the decorators. A decorator must have the same interface as the object it decorates, but the decorator can also extend the interface, which occurs in several of the "filter" classes.

There is a drawback to Decorator, however. Decorators give you much more flexibility while you're writing a program (since you can easily mix and match attributes), but they add complexity to your code. The reason that the Java I/O library is awkward to use is that you must create many classes—the "core" I/O type plus all the decorators—in order to get the single I/O object that you want.

The classes that provide the decorator interface to control a particular **InputStream** or **OutputStream** are the **FilterInputStream** and **FilterOutputStream**, which don't have very intuitive names. **FilterInputStream** and **FilterOutputStream** are derived from the base classes of the I/O library, **InputStream** and **OutputStream**, which is a key requirement of the decorator (so that it provides the common interface to all the objects that are being decorated).

Reading from an **InputStream** with **FilterInputStream**

The **FilterInputStream** classes accomplish two significantly different things. **DataInputStream** allows you to read different types of primitive data as well as **String** objects. (All the methods start with "read," such as **readByte( )**, **readFloat( )**, etc.) This, along with its companion **DataOutputStream**, allows you to move primitive data from one place to another via a stream. These "places" are determined by the classes in Table I/O-1.

The remaining **FilterInputStream** classes modify the way an **InputStream** behaves internally: whether it's buffered or unbuffered, whether it keeps track of the lines it's reading (allowing you to ask for line numbers or set the line number), and whether you can push back a single character. The last two classes look a lot like support for building a compiler (they were probably added to support the experiment of "building a Java compiler in Java"), so you probably won't use them in general programming.

You'll need to buffer your input almost every time, regardless of the I/O device you're connecting to, so it would have made more sense for the I/O library to have a special case (or simply a method call) for unbuffered input rather than buffered input.

Table I/O-3. Types of FilterInputStream

Class	Function	Constructor arguments
		How to use it
Data-InputStream	Used in concert with **DataOutputStream**, so you can read primitives (**int**, **char**, **long**, etc.) from a stream in a portable fashion.	**InputStream**
		Contains a full interface to allow you to read primitive types.
Buffered-InputStream	Use this to prevent a physical read every time you want more data. You're saying, "Use a buffer."	**InputStream**, with optional buffer size.
		This doesn't provide an interface per se. It just adds buffering to the process. Attach an interface object.
LineNumber-InputStream	Keeps track of line numbers in the input stream; you can call **getLineNumber( )** and **setLineNumber(int)**.	**InputStream**
		This just adds line numbering, so you'll probably attach an interface object.
Pushback-InputStream	Has a one-byte push-back buffer so that you can push back the last character read.	**InputStream**
		Generally used in the scanner for a compiler. You probably won't use this.

Writing to an **OutputStream** with **FilterOutputStream**

The complement to **DataInputStream** is **DataOutputStream**, which formats each of the primitive types and **String** objects onto a stream in such a way that any **DataInputStream**, on any machine, can read them. All the methods start with "write," such as **writeByte( )**, **writeFloat( )**, etc.

The original intent of **PrintStream** was to print all of the primitive data types and **String** objects in a viewable format. This is different from **DataOutputStream**, whose goal is to put data elements on a stream in a way that **DataInputStream** can portably reconstruct them.

The two important methods in **PrintStream** are **print( )** and **println( )**, which are overloaded to print all the various types. The difference between **print( )** and **println( )** is that the latter adds a newline when it's done.

PrintStream can be problematic because it traps all **IOException**s (you must explicitly test the error status with **checkError( )**, which returns **true** if an error has occurred). Also, **PrintStream** doesn't internationalize properly. These problems are solved with **PrintWriter**, described later.

BufferedOutputStream is a modifier and tells the stream to use buffering so you don't get a physical write every time you write to the stream. You'll probably always want to use this when doing output.

Table I/O-4. Types of FilterOutputStream

Class	Function	Constructor arguments
		How to use it
Data-OutputStream	Used in concert with **DataInputStream** so you can write primitives (**int**, **char**, **long**, etc.) to a stream in a portable fashion.	**OutputStream**
		Contains a full interface to allow you to write primitive types.

Class	Function	Constructor arguments
		How to use it
PrintStream	For producing formatted output. While **DataOutputStream** handles the *storage* of data, **PrintStream** handles *display*.	**OutputStream**, with optional **boolean** indicating that the buffer is flushed with every newline.
		Should be the "final" wrapping for your **OutputStream** object. You'll probably use this a lot.
Buffered-OutputStream	Use this to prevent a physical write every time you send a piece of data. You're saying, "Use a buffer." You can call **flush( )** to flush the buffer.	**OutputStream**, with optional buffer size.
		This doesn't provide an interface per se. It just adds buffering to the process. Attach an interface object.

Readers & Writers

Java 1.1 made significant modifications to the fundamental I/O stream library. When you see the **Reader** and **Writer** classes, your first thought (like mine) might be that these were meant to replace the **InputStream** and **OutputStream** classes. But that's not the case. Although some aspects of the original streams library are deprecated (if you use them you will receive a warning from the compiler), the **InputStream** and **OutputStream** classes still provide valuable functionality in the form of byte-oriented I/O, whereas the **Reader** and **Writer** classes provide Unicode-compliant, character-based I/O. In addition:

1. Java 1.1 added new classes into the **InputStream** and **OutputStream** hierarchy, so it's obvious those hierarchies weren't being replaced.

2. There are times when you must use classes from the "byte" hierarchy *in combination* with classes in the "character" hierarchy. To accomplish this, there are "adapter" classes: **InputStreamReader** converts an **InputStream** to a **Reader**, and **OutputStreamWriter** converts an **OutputStream** to a **Writer**.

The most important reason for the **Reader** and **Writer** hierarchies is for internationalization. The old I/O stream hierarchy supports only 8-bit byte streams and doesn't handle the 16-bit Unicode characters well. Since Unicode is used for internationalization (and Java's native **char** is 16-bit Unicode), the **Reader** and **Writer** hierarchies were added to support Unicode in all I/O operations. In addition, the new libraries are designed for faster operations than the old.

Sources and sinks of data

Almost all of the original Java I/O stream classes have corresponding **Reader** and **Writer** classes to provide native Unicode manipulation. However, there are some places where the byte-oriented **InputStream**s and **OutputStream**s are the correct solution; in particular, the **java.util.zip** libraries are byte-oriented rather than **char**-oriented. So the most sensible approach to take is to *try* to use the **Reader** and **Writer** classes whenever you can. You'll discover the situations when you have to use the byte-oriented libraries because your code won't compile.

Here is a table that shows the correspondence between the sources and sinks of information (that is, where the data physically comes from or goes to) in the two hierarchies.

Sources & sinks: Java 1.0 class	Corresponding Java 1.1 class
InputStream	Reader adapter: InputStreamReader
OutputStream	Writer adapter: OutputStreamWriter
FileInputStream	FileReader
FileOutputStream	FileWriter

Sources & sinks: Java 1.0 class	Corresponding Java 1.1 class
StringBufferInputStream (deprecated)	**StringReader**
(no corresponding class)	**StringWriter**
ByteArrayInputStream	**CharArrayReader**
ByteArrayOutputStream	**CharArrayWriter**
PipedInputStream	**PipedReader**
PipedOutputStream	**PipedWriter**

In general, you'll find that the interfaces for the two different hierarchies are similar, if not identical.

Modifying stream behavior

For **InputStream**s and **OutputStream**s, streams were adapted for particular needs using "decorator" subclasses of **FilterInputStream** and **FilterOutputStream**. The **Reader** and **Writer** class hierarchies continue the use of this idea—but not exactly.

In the following table, the correspondence is a rougher approximation than in the previous table. The difference is because of the class organization; although **BufferedOutputStream** is a subclass of **FilterOutputStream**, **BufferedWriter** is *not* a subclass of **FilterWriter** (which, even though it is **abstract**, has no subclasses and so appears to have been put in either as a placeholder or simply so you don't wonder where it is). However, the interfaces to the classes are quite a close match.

Filters: Java 1.0 class	Corresponding Java 1.1 class
FilterInputStream	**FilterReader**
FilterOutputStream	**FilterWriter** (abstract class with no subclasses)
BufferedInputStream	**BufferedReader** (also has **readLine( )**)
BufferedOutputStream	**BufferedWriter**
DataInputStream	Use **DataInputStream** (except when you need to use

Filters: Java 1.0 class	Corresponding Java 1.1 class
	readLine( ), when you should use a BufferedReader)
PrintStream	PrintWriter
LineNumberInputStream (deprecated)	LineNumberReader
StreamTokenizer	StreamTokenizer (Use the constructor that takes a Reader instead)
PushbackInputStream	PushbackReader

There's one direction that's quite clear: Whenever you want to use
readLine( ), you shouldn't do it with a **DataInputStream** (this is met with
a deprecation message at compile time), but instead use a **BufferedReader**.
Other than this, **DataInputStream** is still a "preferred" member of the I/O
library.

To make the transition to using a **PrintWriter** easier, it has constructors
that take any **OutputStream** object as well as **Writer** objects.
PrintWriter's formatting interface is virtually the same as **PrintStream**.

In Java SE5, **PrintWriter** constructors were added to simplify the creation
of files when writing output, as you shall see shortly.

One **PrintWriter** constructor also has an option to perform automatic
flushing, which happens after every **println( )** if the constructor flag is set.

Unchanged classes

Some classes were left unchanged between Java 1.0 and Java 1.1:

Java 1.0 classes without corresponding Java 1.1 classes
DataOutputStream
File
RandomAccessFile
SequenceInputStream

DataOutputStream, in particular, is used without change, so for storing and retrieving data in a transportable format, you use the **InputStream** and **OutputStream** hierarchies.

Off by itself:
RandomAccessFile

RandomAccessFile is used for files containing records of known size so that you can move from one record to another using **seek( )**, then read or change the records. The records don't have to be the same size; you just have to determine how big they are and where they are placed in the file.

At first it's a little bit hard to believe that **RandomAccessFile** is not part of the **InputStream** or **OutputStream** hierarchy. However, it has no association with those hierarchies other than that it happens to implement the **DataInput** and **DataOutput** interfaces (which are also implemented by **DataInputStream** and **DataOutputStream**). It doesn't even use any of the functionality of the existing **InputStream** or **OutputStream** classes; it's a completely separate class, written from scratch, with all of its own (mostly native) methods. The reason for this may be that **RandomAccessFile** has essentially different behavior than the other I/O types, since you can move forward and backward within a file. In any event, it stands alone, as a direct descendant of **Object**.

Essentially, a **RandomAccessFile** works like a **DataInputStream** pasted together with a **DataOutputStream**, along with the methods **getFilePointer( )** to find out where you are in the file, **seek( )** to move to a new point in the file, and **length( )** to determine the maximum size of the file. In addition, the constructors require a second argument (identical to **fopen( )** in C) indicating whether you are just randomly reading ("**r**") or reading and writing ("**rw**"). There's no support for write-only files, which could suggest that **RandomAccessFile** might have worked well if it were inherited from **DataInputStream**.

The seeking methods are available only in **RandomAccessFile**, which works for files only. **BufferedInputStream** does allow you to **mark( )** a position (whose value is held in a single internal variable) and **reset( )** to that position, but this is limited and not very useful.

Most, if not all, of the **RandomAccessFile** functionality is superseded as of JDK 1.4 with the **nio** *memory-mapped files*, which will be described later in this chapter.

Typical uses of I/O streams

Although you can combine the I/O stream classes in many different ways, you'll probably just use a few combinations. The following examples can be used as a basic reference for typical I/O usage.

In these examples, exception handing will be simplified by passing exceptions out to the console, but this is appropriate only in small examples and utilities. In your code you'll want to consider more sophisticated error-handling approaches.

Buffered input file

To open a file for character input, you use a **FileReader** with a **String** or a **File** object as the file name. For speed, you'll want that file to be buffered so you give the resulting reference to the constructor for a **BufferedReader**. Since **BufferedReader** also provides the **readLine( )** method, this is your final object and the interface you read from. When **readLine( )** returns **null**, you're at the end of the file.

```
//: io/BufferedInputFile.java
import java.io.*;

public class BufferedInputFile {
  // Throw exceptions to console:
  public static String
  read(String filename) throws IOException {
    // Reading input by lines:
    BufferedReader in = new BufferedReader(
      new FileReader(filename));
    String s;
    StringBuilder sb = new StringBuilder();
    while((s = in.readLine())!= null)
      sb.append(s + "\n");
    in.close();
    return sb.toString();
  }
  public static void main(String[] args)
  throws IOException {
```

```
    System.out.print(read("BufferedInputFile.java"));
  }
} /* (Execute to see output) *///:~
```

The **StringBuilder sb** is used to accumulate the entire contents of the file (including newlines that must be added since **readLine( )** strips them off). Finally, **close( )** is called to close the file.[2]

Exercise 7: (2) Open a text file so that you can read the file one line at a time. Read each line as a **String** and place that **String** object into a **LinkedList**. Print all of the lines in the **LinkedList** in reverse order.

Exercise 8: (1) Modify Exercise 7 so that the name of the file you read is provided as a command-line argument.

Exercise 9: (1) Modify Exercise 8 to force all the lines in the **LinkedList** to uppercase and send the results to **System.out**.

Exercise 10: (2) Modify Exercise 8 to take additional command-line arguments of words to find in the file. Print all lines in which any of the words match.

Exercise 11: (2) In the **innerclasses/GreenhouseController.java** example, **GreenhouseController** contains a hard-coded set of events. Change the program so that it reads the events and their relative times from a text file. ((difficulty level 8): Use a *Factory Method* design pattern to build the events—see *Thinking in Patterns (with Java)* at *www.MindView.net*.)

Input from memory

Here, the **String** result from **BufferedInputFile.read( )** is used to create a **StringReader**. Then **read( )** is used to read each character one at a time and send it out to the console:

```
//: io/MemoryInput.java
import java.io.*;

public class MemoryInput {
```

---

[2] In the original design, **close( )** was supposed to be called when **finalize( )** ran, and you will see **finalize( )** defined this way for I/O classes. However, as is discussed elsewhere in this book, the **finalize( )** feature didn't work out the way the Java designers originally envisioned it (that is to say, it's irreparably broken), so the only safe approach is to explicitly call **close( )** for files.

```
    public static void main(String[] args)
    throws IOException {
      StringReader in = new StringReader(
        BufferedInputFile.read("MemoryInput.java"));
      int c;
      while((c = in.read()) != -1)
        System.out.print((char)c);
  }
} /* (Execute to see output) *///:~
```

Note that **read( )** returns the next character as an **int** and thus it must be cast to a **char** to print properly.

Formatted memory input

To read "formatted" data, you use a **DataInputStream**, which is a byte-oriented I/O class (rather than **char**-oriented). Thus you must use all **InputStream** classes rather than **Reader** classes. Of course, you can read anything (such as a file) as bytes using **InputStream** classes, but here a **String** is used:

```
//: io/FormattedMemoryInput.java
import java.io.*;

public class FormattedMemoryInput {
  public static void main(String[] args)
  throws IOException {
    try {
      DataInputStream in = new DataInputStream(
        new ByteArrayInputStream(
          BufferedInputFile.read(
            "FormattedMemoryInput.java").getBytes()));
      while(true)
        System.out.write((char)in.readByte());
    } catch(EOFException e) {
      System.err.println("End of stream");
    }
  }
} /* (Execute to see output) *///:~
```

A **ByteArrayInputStream** must be given an array of bytes. To produce this, **String** has a **getBytes( )** method. The resulting **ByteArrayInputStream** is an appropriate **InputStream** to hand to **DataInputStream**.

If you read the characters from a **DataInputStream** one **byte** at a time using **readByte( )**, any **byte** value is a legitimate result, so the return value cannot be used to detect the end of input. Instead, you can use the **available( )** method to find out how many more characters are available. Here's an example that shows how to read a file one **byte** at a time:

```
//: io/TestEOF.java
// Testing for end of file while reading a byte at a time.
import java.io.*;

public class TestEOF {
  public static void main(String[] args)
  throws IOException {
    DataInputStream in = new DataInputStream(
      new BufferedInputStream(
        new FileInputStream("TestEOF.java")));
    while(in.available() != 0)
      System.out.write(in.readByte());
  }
} /* (Execute to see output) *///:~
```

Note that **available( )** works differently depending on what sort of medium you're reading from; it's literally "the number of bytes that can be read *without blocking.*" With a file, this means the whole file, but with a different kind of stream this might not be true, so use it thoughtfully.

You could also detect the end of input in cases like these by catching an exception. However, the use of exceptions for control flow is considered a misuse of that feature.

Basic file output

A **FileWriter** object writes data to a file. You'll virtually always want to buffer the output by wrapping it in a **BufferedWriter** (try removing this wrapping to see the impact on the performance—buffering tends to dramatically increase performance of I/O operations). In this example, it's decorated as a **PrintWriter** to provide formatting. The data file created this way is readable as an ordinary text file:

```
//: io/BasicFileOutput.java
import java.io.*;

public class BasicFileOutput {
```

```
static String file = "BasicFileOutput.out";
public static void main(String[] args)
throws IOException {
  BufferedReader in = new BufferedReader(
    new StringReader(
      BufferedInputFile.read("BasicFileOutput.java")));
  PrintWriter out = new PrintWriter(
    new BufferedWriter(new FileWriter(file)));
  int lineCount = 1;
  String s;
  while((s = in.readLine()) != null )
    out.println(lineCount++ + ": " + s);
  out.close();
  // Show the stored file:
  System.out.println(BufferedInputFile.read(file));
  }
} /* (Execute to see output) *///:~
```

As the lines are written to the file, line numbers are added. Note that **LineNumberReader** is *not* used, because it's a silly class and you don't need it. You can see from this example that it's trivial to keep track of your own line numbers.

When the input stream is exhausted, **readLine( )** returns **null**. You'll see an explicit **close( )** for **out**, because if you don't call **close( )** for all your output files, you might discover that the buffers don't get flushed, so the file will be incomplete.

Text file output shortcut

Java SE5 added a helper constructor to **PrintWriter** so that you don't have to do all the decoration by hand every time you want to create a text file and write to it. Here's **BasicFileOutput.java** rewritten to use this shortcut:

```
//: io/FileOutputShortcut.java
import java.io.*;

public class FileOutputShortcut {
  static String file = "FileOutputShortcut.out";
  public static void main(String[] args)
  throws IOException {
    BufferedReader in = new BufferedReader(
      new StringReader(
        BufferedInputFile.read("FileOutputShortcut.java")));
    // Here's the shortcut:
```

```
      PrintWriter out = new PrintWriter(file);
      int lineCount = 1;
      String s;
      while((s = in.readLine()) != null )
        out.println(lineCount++ + ": " + s);
      out.close();
      // Show the stored file:
      System.out.println(BufferedInputFile.read(file));
    }
} /* (Execute to see output) *///:~
```

You still get buffering, you just don't have to do it yourself. Unfortunately, other commonly written tasks were not given shortcuts, so typical I/O will still involve a lot of redundant text. However, the **TextFile** utility that is used in this book, and which will be defined a little later in this chapter, does simplify these common tasks.

Exercise 12:   (3) Modify Exercise 8 to also open a text file so you can write text into it. Write the lines in the **LinkedList**, along with line numbers (do not attempt to use the "LineNumber" classes), out to the file.

Exercise 13:   (3) Modify **BasicFileOutput.java** so that it uses **LineNumberReader** to keep track of the line count. Note that it's much easier to just keep track programmatically.

Exercise 14:   (2) Starting with **BasicFileOutput.java**, write a program that compares the performance of writing to a file when using buffered and unbuffered I/O.

Storing and recovering data

A **PrintWriter** formats data so that it's readable by a human. However, to output data for recovery by another stream, you use a **DataOutputStream** to write the data and a **DataInputStream** to recover the data. Of course, these streams can be anything, but the following example uses a file, buffered for both reading and writing. **DataOutputStream** and **DataInputStream** are byte-oriented and thus require **InputStream**s and **OutputStream**s:

```
//: io/StoringAndRecoveringData.java
import java.io.*;

public class StoringAndRecoveringData {
  public static void main(String[] args)
  throws IOException {
```

```
    DataOutputStream out = new DataOutputStream(
      new BufferedOutputStream(
        new FileOutputStream("Data.txt")));
    out.writeDouble(3.14159);
    out.writeUTF("That was pi");
    out.writeDouble(1.41413);
    out.writeUTF("Square root of 2");
    out.close();
    DataInputStream in = new DataInputStream(
      new BufferedInputStream(
        new FileInputStream("Data.txt")));
    System.out.println(in.readDouble());
    // Only readUTF() will recover the
    // Java-UTF String properly:
    System.out.println(in.readUTF());
    System.out.println(in.readDouble());
    System.out.println(in.readUTF());
  }
} /* Output:
3.14159
That was pi
1.41413
Square root of 2
*///:~
```

If you use a **DataOutputStream** to write the data, then Java guarantees that you can accurately recover the data using a **DataInputStream**—regardless of what different platforms write and read the data. This is incredibly valuable, as anyone knows who has spent time worrying about platform-specific data issues. That problem vanishes if you have Java on both platforms.[3]

When you are using a **DataOutputStream**, the only reliable way to write a **String** so that it can be recovered by a **DataInputStream** is to use UTF-8 encoding, accomplished in this example using **writeUTF( )** and **readUTF( )**. UTF-8 is a multi-byte format, and the length of encoding varies according to the actual character set in use. If you're working with ASCII or mostly ASCII characters (which occupy only seven bits), Unicode is a

---

[3] XML is another way to solve the problem of moving data across different computing platforms, and does not depend on having Java on all platforms. XML is introduced later in this chapter.

---

tremendous waste of space and/or bandwidth, so UTF-8 encodes ASCII characters in a single byte, and non-ASCII characters in two or three bytes. In addition, the length of the string is stored in the first two bytes of the UTF-8 string. However, **writeUTF( )** and **readUTF( )** use a special variation of UTF-8 for Java (which is completely described in the JDK documentation for those methods), so if you read a string written with **writeUTF( )** using a non-Java program, you must write special code in order to read the string properly.

With **writeUTF( )** and **readUTF( )**, you can intermingle **String**s and other types of data using a **DataOutputStream**, with the knowledge that the **String**s will be properly stored as Unicode and will be easily recoverable with a **DataInputStream**.

The **writeDouble( )** method stores the **double** number to the stream, and the complementary **readDouble( )** method recovers it (there are similar methods for reading and writing the other types). But for any of the reading methods to work correctly, you must know the exact placement of the data item in the stream, since it would be equally possible to read the stored **double** as a simple sequence of bytes, or as a **char**, etc. So you must either have a fixed format for the data in the file, or extra information must be stored in the file that you parse to determine where the data is located. Note that object serialization or XML (both described later in this chapter) may be easier ways to store and retrieve complex data structures.

Exercise 15: (4) Look up **DataOutputStream** and **DataInputStream** in the JDK documentation. Starting with **StoringAndRecoveringData.java**, create a program that stores and then retrieves all the different possible types provided by the **DataOutputStream** and **DataInputStream** classes. Verify that the values are stored and retrieved accurately.

Reading and writing random-access files

Using a **RandomAccessFile** is like using a combined **DataInputStream** and **DataOutputStream** (because it implements the same interfaces: **DataInput** and **DataOutput**). In addition, you can use **seek( )** to move about in the file and change the values.

When using **RandomAccessFile**, you must know the layout of the file so that you can manipulate it properly. **RandomAccessFile** has specific methods to read and write primitives and UTF-8 strings. Here's an example:

```
//: io/UsingRandomAccessFile.java
import java.io.*;

public class UsingRandomAccessFile {
  static String file = "rtest.dat";
  static void display() throws IOException {
    RandomAccessFile rf = new RandomAccessFile(file, "r");
    for(int i = 0; i < 7; i++)
      System.out.println(
        "Value " + i + ": " + rf.readDouble());
    System.out.println(rf.readUTF());
    rf.close();
  }
  public static void main(String[] args)
  throws IOException {
    RandomAccessFile rf = new RandomAccessFile(file, "rw");
    for(int i = 0; i < 7; i++)
      rf.writeDouble(i*1.414);
    rf.writeUTF("The end of the file");
    rf.close();
    display();
    rf = new RandomAccessFile(file, "rw");
    rf.seek(5*8);
    rf.writeDouble(47.0001);
    rf.close();
    display();
  }
} /* Output:
Value 0: 0.0
Value 1: 1.414
Value 2: 2.828
Value 3: 4.242
Value 4: 5.656
Value 5: 7.069999999999999
Value 6: 8.484
The end of the file
Value 0: 0.0
Value 1: 1.414
Value 2: 2.828
Value 3: 4.242
```

```
Value 4: 5.656
Value 5: 47.0001
Value 6: 8.484
The end of the file
*///:~
```

The **display( )** method opens a file and displays seven elements within as **double** values. In **main( )**, the file is created, then opened and modified. Since a **double** is always eight bytes long, to **seek( )** to double number 5 you just multiply **5*8** to produce the seek value.

As previously noted, **RandomAccessFile** is effectively separate from the rest of the I/O hierarchy, save for the fact that it implements the **DataInput** and **DataOutput** interfaces. It doesn't support decoration, so you cannot combine it with any of the aspects of the **InputStream** and **OutputStream** subclasses. You must assume that a **RandomAccessFile** is properly buffered since you cannot add that.

The one option you have is in the second constructor argument: You can open a **RandomAccessFile** to read (**"r"**) or read and write (**"rw"**).

You may want to consider using **nio** memory-mapped files instead of **RandomAccessFile**.

Exercise 16: (2) Look up **RandomAccessFile** in the JDK documentation. Starting with **UsingRandomAccessFile.java**, create a program that stores and then retrieves all the different possible types provided by the **RandomAccessFile** class. Verify that the values are stored and retrieved accurately.

Piped streams

The **PipedInputStream**, **PipedOutputStream**, **PipedReader** and **PipedWriter** have been mentioned only briefly in this chapter. This is not to suggest that they aren't useful, but their value is not apparent until you begin to understand concurrency, since the piped streams are used to communicate between tasks. This is covered along with an example in the *Concurrency* chapter.

File reading & writing utilities

A very common programming task is to read a file into memory, modify it, and then write it out again. One of the problems with the Java I/O library is that it requires you to write quite a bit of code in order to perform these common operations—there are no basic helper functions to do them for you. What's worse, the decorators make it rather hard to remember how to open files. Thus, it makes sense to add helper classes to your library that will easily perform these basic tasks for you. Java SE5 has added a convenience constructor to **PrintWriter** so you can easily open a text file for writing. However, there are many other common tasks that you will want to do over and over, and it makes sense to eliminate the redundant code associated with those tasks.

Here's the **TextFile** class that has been used in previous examples in this book to simplify reading and writing files. It contains **static** methods to read and write text files as a single string, and you can create a **TextFile** object that holds the lines of the file in an **ArrayList** (so you have all the **ArrayList** functionality while manipulating the file contents):

```
//: net/mindview/util/TextFile.java
// Static functions for reading and writing text files as
// a single string, and treating a file as an ArrayList.
package net.mindview.util;
import java.io.*;
import java.util.*;

public class TextFile extends ArrayList<String> {
  // Read a file as a single string:
  public static String read(String fileName) {
    StringBuilder sb = new StringBuilder();
    try {
      BufferedReader in= new BufferedReader(new FileReader(
        new File(fileName).getAbsoluteFile()));
      try {
        String s;
        while((s = in.readLine()) != null) {
          sb.append(s);
          sb.append("\n");
        }
      } finally {
        in.close();
      }
    } catch(IOException e) {
      throw new RuntimeException(e);
    }
    return sb.toString();
```

```java
  }
  // Write a single file in one method call:
  public static void write(String fileName, String text) {
    try {
      PrintWriter out = new PrintWriter(
        new File(fileName).getAbsoluteFile());
      try {
        out.print(text);
      } finally {
        out.close();
      }
    } catch(IOException e) {
      throw new RuntimeException(e);
    }
  }
  // Read a file, split by any regular expression:
  public TextFile(String fileName, String splitter) {
    super(Arrays.asList(read(fileName).split(splitter)));
    // Regular expression split() often leaves an empty
    // String at the first position:
    if(get(0).equals("")) remove(0);
  }
  // Normally read by lines:
  public TextFile(String fileName) {
    this(fileName, "\n");
  }
  public void write(String fileName) {
    try {
      PrintWriter out = new PrintWriter(
        new File(fileName).getAbsoluteFile());
      try {
        for(String item : this)
          out.println(item);
      } finally {
        out.close();
      }
    } catch(IOException e) {
      throw new RuntimeException(e);
    }
  }
  // Simple test:
  public static void main(String[] args) {
    String file = read("TextFile.java");
    write("test.txt", file);
```

```
      TextFile text = new TextFile("test.txt");
      text.write("test2.txt");
      // Break into unique sorted list of words:
      TreeSet<String> words = new TreeSet<String>(
        new TextFile("TextFile.java", "\\W+"));
      // Display the capitalized words:
      System.out.println(words.headSet("a"));
    }
} /* Output:
[0, ArrayList, Arrays, Break, BufferedReader,
BufferedWriter, Clean, Display, File, FileReader,
FileWriter, IOException, Normally, Output, PrintWriter,
Read, Regular, RuntimeException, Simple, Static, String,
StringBuilder, System, TextFile, Tools, TreeSet, W, Write]
*///:~
```

read( ) appends each line to a **StringBuilder**, followed by a newline, because that is stripped out during reading. Then it returns a **String** containing the whole file. **write( )** opens and writes the text **String** to the file.

Notice that any code that opens a file guards the file's **close( )** call in a **finally** clause to guarantee that the file will be properly closed.

The constructor uses the **read( )** method to turn the file into a **String**, then uses **String.split( )** to divide the result into lines along newline boundaries (if you use this class a lot, you may want to rewrite this constructor to improve efficiency). Alas, there is no corresponding "join" method, so the non-**static write( )** method must write the lines out by hand.

Because this class is intended to trivialize the process of reading and writing files, all **IOException**s are converted to **RuntimeException**s, so the user doesn't have to use **try-catch** blocks. However, you may need to create another version that passes **IOException**s out to the caller.

In **main( )**, a basic test is performed to ensure that the methods work.

Although this utility did not require much code to create, using it can save a lot of time and make your life easier, as you'll see in some of the examples later in this chapter.

Another way to solve the problem of reading text files is to use the **java.util.Scanner** class introduced in Java SE5. However, this is only for reading files, not writing them, and that tool (which you'll notice is *not* in java.io) is primarily designed for creating programming-language scanners or "little languages."

Exercise 17: (4) Using **TextFile** and a **Map<Character,Integer>**, create a program that counts the occurrence of all the different characters in a file. (So if there are 12 occurrences of the letter 'a' in the file, the **Integer** associated with the **Character** containing 'a' in the **Map** contains '12').

Exercise 18: (1) Modify **TextFile.java** so that it passes **IOExceptions** out to the caller.

Reading binary files

This utility is similar to **TextFile.java** in that it simplifies the process of reading binary files:

```
//: net/mindview/util/BinaryFile.java
// Utility for reading files in binary form.
package net.mindview.util;
import java.io.*;

public class BinaryFile {
  public static byte[] read(File bFile) throws IOException{
    BufferedInputStream bf = new BufferedInputStream(
      new FileInputStream(bFile));
    try {
      byte[] data = new byte[bf.available()];
      bf.read(data);
      return data;
    } finally {
      bf.close();
    }
  }
  public static byte[]
  read(String bFile) throws IOException {
    return read(new File(bFile).getAbsoluteFile());
  }
} ///:~
```

One overloaded method takes a **File** argument; the second takes a **String** argument, which is the file name. Both return the resulting **byte** array.

The **available( )** method is used to produce the appropriate array size, and this particular version of the overloaded **read( )** method fills the array.

Exercise 19: (2) Using **BinaryFile** and a **Map<Byte,Integer>**, create a program that counts the occurrence of all the different bytes in a file.

Exercise 20: (4) Using **Directory.walk( )** and **BinaryFile**, verify that all **.class** files in a directory tree begin with the hex characters '**CAFEBABE**'.

Standard I/O

The term *standard I/O* refers to the Unix concept of a single stream of information that is used by a program (this idea is reproduced in some form in Windows and many other operating systems). All of the program's input can come from *standard input*, all of its output can go to *standard output*, and all of its error messages can be sent to *standard error*. The value of standard I/O is that programs can easily be chained together, and one program's standard output can become the standard input for another program. This is a powerful tool.

Reading from standard input

Following the standard I/O model, Java has **System.in**, **System.out**, and **System.err**. Throughout this book, you've seen how to write to standard output using **System.out**, which is already pre-wrapped as a **PrintStream** object. **System.err** is likewise a **PrintStream**, but **System.in** is a raw **InputStream** with no wrapping. This means that although you can use **System.out** and **System.err** right away, **System.in** must be wrapped before you can read from it.

You'll typically read input a line at a time using **readLine( )**. To do this, wrap **System.in** in a **BufferedReader**, which requires you to convert **System.in** to a **Reader** using **InputStreamReader**. Here's an example that simply echoes each line that you type in:

```
//: io/Echo.java
// How to read from standard input.
// {RunByHand}
import java.io.*;

public class Echo {
  public static void main(String[] args)
  throws IOException {
    BufferedReader stdin = new BufferedReader(
      new InputStreamReader(System.in));
    String s;
```

```
      while((s = stdin.readLine()) != null && s.length()!= 0)
        System.out.println(s);
      // An empty line or Ctrl-Z terminates the program
    }
} ///:~
```

The reason for the exception specification is that **readLine( )** can throw an **IOException**. Note that **System.in** should usually be buffered, as with most streams.

Exercise 21:   (1) Write a program that takes standard input and capitalizes all characters, then puts the results on standard output. Redirect the contents of a file into this program (the process of redirection will vary depending on your operating system).

Changing **System.out** to a **PrintWriter**

System.out is a **PrintStream**, which is an **OutputStream**. **PrintWriter** has a constructor that takes an **OutputStream** as an argument. Thus, if you want, you can convert **System.out** into a **PrintWriter** using that constructor:

```
//: io/ChangeSystemOut.java
// Turn System.out into a PrintWriter.
import java.io.*;

public class ChangeSystemOut {
  public static void main(String[] args) {
    PrintWriter out = new PrintWriter(System.out, true);
    out.println("Hello, world");
  }
} /* Output:
Hello, world
*///:~
```

It's important to use the two-argument version of the **PrintWriter** constructor and to set the second argument to **true** in order to enable automatic flushing; otherwise, you may not see the output.

Redirecting standard I/O

The Java **System** class allows you to redirect the standard input, output, and error I/O streams using simple **static** method calls:

---

setIn(InputStream)
setOut(PrintStream)
setErr(PrintStream)

Redirecting output is especially useful if you suddenly start creating a large amount of output on your screen, and it's scrolling past faster than you can read it.[4] Redirecting input is valuable for a command-line program in which you want to test a particular user-input sequence repeatedly. Here's a simple example that shows the use of these methods:

```
//: io/Redirecting.java
// Demonstrates standard I/O redirection.
import java.io.*;

public class Redirecting {
  public static void main(String[] args)
  throws IOException {
    PrintStream console = System.out;
    BufferedInputStream in = new BufferedInputStream(
      new FileInputStream("Redirecting.java"));
    PrintStream out = new PrintStream(
      new BufferedOutputStream(
        new FileOutputStream("test.out")));
    System.setIn(in);
    System.setOut(out);
    System.setErr(out);
    BufferedReader br = new BufferedReader(
      new InputStreamReader(System.in));
    String s;
    while((s = br.readLine()) != null)
      System.out.println(s);
    out.close(); // Remember this!
    System.setOut(console);
  }
} ///:~
```

This program attaches standard input to a file and redirects standard output and standard error to another file. Notice that it stores a reference to the

---

[4] The *Graphical User Interfaces* chapter shows an even more convenient solution for this: a GUI program with a scrolling text area.

---

original **System.out** object at the beginning of the program, and restores the system output to that object at the end.

I/O redirection manipulates streams of bytes, not streams of characters; thus, **InputStream**s and **OutputStream**s are used rather than **Reader**s and **Writer**s.

Process control

You will often need to execute other operating system programs from inside Java, and to control the input and output from such programs. The Java library provides classes to perform such operations.

A common task is to run a program and send the resulting output to the console. This section contains a utility to simplify this task.

Two types of errors can occur with this utility: the normal errors that result in exceptions—for these we will just rethrow a runtime exception—and errors from the execution of the process itself. We want to report these errors with a separate exception:

```
//: net/mindview/util/OSExecuteException.java
package net.mindview.util;

public class OSExecuteException extends RuntimeException {
  public OSExecuteException(String why) { super(why); }
} ///:~
```

To run a program, you pass **OSExecute.command( )** a **command** string, which is the same command that you would type to run the program on the console. This command is passed to the **java.lang.ProcessBuilder** constructor (which requires it as a sequence of **String** objects), and the resulting **ProcessBuilder** object is started:

```
//: net/mindview/util/OSExecute.java
// Run an operating system command
// and send the output to the console.
package net.mindview.util;
import java.io.*;

public class OSExecute {
  public static void command(String command) {
    boolean err = false;
    try {
```

```
      Process process =
        new ProcessBuilder(command.split(" ")).start();
      BufferedReader results = new BufferedReader(
        new InputStreamReader(process.getInputStream()));
      String s;
      while((s = results.readLine())!= null)
        System.out.println(s);
      BufferedReader errors = new BufferedReader(
        new InputStreamReader(process.getErrorStream()));
      // Report errors and return nonzero value
      // to calling process if there are problems:
      while((s = errors.readLine())!= null) {
        System.err.println(s);
        err = true;
      }
    } catch(Exception e) {
      // Compensate for Windows 2000, which throws an
      // exception for the default command line:
      if(!command.startsWith("CMD /C"))
        command("CMD /C " + command);
      else
        throw new RuntimeException(e);
    }
    if(err)
      throw new OSExecuteException("Errors executing " +
        command);
  }
} ///:~
```

To capture the standard output stream from the program as it executes, you call **getInputStream( )**. This is because an **InputStream** is something we can read from.

The results from the program arrive a line at a time, so they are read using **readLine( )**. Here the lines are simply printed, but you may also want to capture and return them from **command( )**.

The program's errors are sent to the standard error stream, and are captured by calling **getErrorStream( )**. If there are any errors, they are printed and an **OSExecuteException** is thrown so the calling program will handle the problem.

Here's an example that shows how to use **OSExecute**:

```
//: io/OSExecuteDemo.java
// Demonstrates standard I/O redirection.
import net.mindview.util.*;

public class OSExecuteDemo {
  public static void main(String[] args) {
    OSExecute.command("javap OSExecuteDemo");
  }
} /* Output:
Compiled from "OSExecuteDemo.java"
public class OSExecuteDemo extends java.lang.Object{
    public OSExecuteDemo();
    public static void main(java.lang.String[]);
}
*///:~
```

This uses the **javap** decompiler (that comes with the JDK) to decompile the program.

Exercise 22: (5) Modify **OSExecute.java** so that, instead of printing the standard output stream, it returns the results of executing the program as a **List** of **String**s. Demonstrate the use of this new version of the utility.

New I/O

The Java "new" I/O library, introduced in JDK 1.4 in the **java.nio.*** packages, has one goal: speed. In fact, the "old" I/O packages have been reimplemented using **nio** in order to take advantage of this speed increase, so you will benefit even if you don't explicitly write code with **nio**. The speed increase occurs both in file I/O, which is explored here, and in network I/O, which is covered in *Thinking in Enterprise Java*.

The speed comes from using structures that are closer to the operating system's way of performing I/O: *channels* and *buffers*. You could think of it as a coal mine; the channel is the mine containing the seam of coal (the data), and the buffer is the cart that you send into the mine. The cart comes back full of coal, and you get the coal from the cart. That is, you don't interact directly with the channel; you interact with the buffer and send the buffer into the channel. The channel either pulls data from the buffer, or puts data into the buffer.

The only kind of buffer that communicates directly with a channel is a **ByteBuffer**—that is, a buffer that holds raw bytes. If you look at the JDK documentation for **java.nio.ByteBuffer**, you'll see that it's fairly basic: You create one by telling it how much storage to allocate, and there are methods to put and get data, in either raw byte form or as primitive data types. But there's no way to put or get an object, or even a **String**. It's fairly low-level, precisely because this makes a more efficient mapping with most operating systems.

Three of the classes in the "old" I/O have been modified so that they produce a **FileChannel**: **FileInputStream**, **FileOutputStream**, and, for both reading and writing, **RandomAccessFile**. Notice that these are the byte manipulation streams, in keeping with the low-level nature of **nio**. The **Reader** and **Writer** character-mode classes do not produce channels, but the **java.nio.channels.Channels** class has utility methods to produce **Reader**s and **Writer**s from channels.

Here's a simple example that exercises all three types of stream to produce channels that are writeable, read/writeable, and readable:

```
//: io/GetChannel.java
// Getting channels from streams
import java.nio.*;
import java.nio.channels.*;
import java.io.*;
public class GetChannel {
  private static final int BSIZE = 1024;
  public static void main(String[] args) throws Exception {
    // Write a file:
    FileChannel fc =
      new FileOutputStream("data.txt").getChannel();
    fc.write(ByteBuffer.wrap("Some text ".getBytes()));
    fc.close();
    // Add to the end of the file:
    fc =
      new RandomAccessFile("data.txt", "rw").getChannel();
    fc.position(fc.size()); // Move to the end
    fc.write(ByteBuffer.wrap("Some more".getBytes()));
    fc.close();
    // Read the file:
    fc = new FileInputStream("data.txt").getChannel();
    ByteBuffer buff = ByteBuffer.allocate(BSIZE);
    fc.read(buff);
    buff.flip();
    while(buff.hasRemaining())
```

```
      System.out.write(buff.get());
    System.out.flush();
  }
} /* Output:
Some text Some more
*///:~
```

For any of the stream classes shown here, **getChannel( )** will produce a **FileChannel**. A channel is fairly basic: You can hand it a **ByteBuffer** for reading or writing, and you can lock regions of the file for exclusive access (this will be described later).

One way to put bytes into a **ByteBuffer** is to stuff them in directly using one of the "put" methods, to put one or more bytes, or values of primitive types. However, as seen here, you can also "wrap" an existing **byte** array in a **ByteBuffer** using the **wrap( )** method. When you do this, the underlying array is not copied, but instead is used as the storage for the generated **ByteBuffer**. We say that the **ByteBuffer** is "backed by" the array.

The **data.txt** file is reopened using a **RandomAccessFile**. Notice that you can move the **FileChannel** around in the file; here, it is moved to the end so that additional writes will be appended.

For read-only access, you must explicitly allocate a **ByteBuffer** using the **static allocate( )** method. The goal of **nio** is to rapidly move large amounts of data, so the size of the **ByteBuffer** should be significant—in fact, the 1K used here is probably quite a bit smaller than you'd normally want to use (you'll have to experiment with your working application to find the best size).

It's also possible to go for even more speed by using **allocateDirect( )** instead of **allocate( )** to produce a "direct" buffer that may have an even higher coupling with the operating system. However, the overhead in such an allocation is greater, and the actual implementation varies from one operating system to another, so again, you must experiment with your working application to discover whether direct buffers will buy you any advantage in speed.

Once you call **read( )** to tell the **FileChannel** to store bytes into the **ByteBuffer**, you must call **flip( )** on the buffer to tell it to get ready to have its bytes extracted (yes, this seems a bit crude, but remember that it's very low-level and is done for maximum speed). And if we were to use the buffer for further **read( )** operations, we'd also have to call **clear( )** to prepare it for each **read( )**. You can see this in a simple file-copying program:

```
//: io/ChannelCopy.java
// Copying a file using channels and buffers
// {Args: ChannelCopy.java test.txt}
import java.nio.*;
import java.nio.channels.*;
import java.io.*;

public class ChannelCopy {
  private static final int BSIZE = 1024;
  public static void main(String[] args) throws Exception {
    if(args.length != 2) {
      System.out.println("arguments: sourcefile destfile");
      System.exit(1);
    }
    FileChannel
      in = new FileInputStream(args[0]).getChannel(),
      out = new FileOutputStream(args[1]).getChannel();
    ByteBuffer buffer = ByteBuffer.allocate(BSIZE);
    while(in.read(buffer) != -1) {
      buffer.flip(); // Prepare for writing
      out.write(buffer);
      buffer.clear();  // Prepare for reading
    }
  }
} ///:~
```

You can see that one **FileChannel** is opened for reading, and one for writing. A **ByteBuffer** is allocated, and when **FileChannel.read( )** returns **-1** (a holdover, no doubt, from Unix and C), it means that you've reached the end of the input. After each **read( )**, which puts data into the buffer, **flip( )** prepares the buffer so that its information can be extracted by the **write( )**. After the **write( )**, the information is still in the buffer, and **clear( )** resets all the internal pointers so that it's ready to accept data during another **read( )**.

The preceding program is not the ideal way to handle this kind of operation, however. Special methods **transferTo( )** and **transferFrom( )** allow you to connect one channel directly to another:

```
//: io/TransferTo.java
// Using transferTo() between channels
// {Args: TransferTo.java TransferTo.txt}
```

```
import java.nio.channels.*;
import java.io.*;

public class TransferTo {
  public static void main(String[] args) throws Exception {
    if(args.length != 2) {
      System.out.println("arguments: sourcefile destfile");
      System.exit(1);
    }
    FileChannel
      in = new FileInputStream(args[0]).getChannel(),
      out = new FileOutputStream(args[1]).getChannel();
    in.transferTo(0, in.size(), out);
    // Or:
    // out.transferFrom(in, 0, in.size());
  }
} ///:~
```

You won't do this kind of thing very often, but it's good to know about.

Converting data

If you look back at **GetChannel.java**, you'll notice that, to print the information in the file, we are pulling the data out one **byte** at a time and casting each **byte** to a **char**. This seems a bit primitive—if you look at the **java.nio.CharBuffer** class, you'll see that it has a **toString( )** method that says, "Returns a string containing the characters in this buffer." Since a **ByteBuffer** can be viewed as a **CharBuffer** with the **asCharBuffer( )** method, why not use that? As you can see from the first line in the output statement below, this doesn't work out:

```
//: io/BufferToText.java
// Converting text to and from ByteBuffers
import java.nio.*;
import java.nio.channels.*;
import java.nio.charset.*;
import java.io.*;

public class BufferToText {
  private static final int BSIZE = 1024;
  public static void main(String[] args) throws Exception {
    FileChannel fc =
      new FileOutputStream("data2.txt").getChannel();
    fc.write(ByteBuffer.wrap("Some text".getBytes()));
```

```
        fc.close();
        fc = new FileInputStream("data2.txt").getChannel();
        ByteBuffer buff = ByteBuffer.allocate(BSIZE);
        fc.read(buff);
        buff.flip();
        // Doesn't work:
        System.out.println(buff.asCharBuffer());
        // Decode using this system's default Charset:
        buff.rewind();
        String encoding = System.getProperty("file.encoding");
        System.out.println("Decoded using " + encoding + ": "
          + Charset.forName(encoding).decode(buff));
        // Or, we could encode with something that will print:
        fc = new FileOutputStream("data2.txt").getChannel();
        fc.write(ByteBuffer.wrap(
          "Some text".getBytes("UTF-16BE")));
        fc.close();
        // Now try reading again:
        fc = new FileInputStream("data2.txt").getChannel();
        buff.clear();
        fc.read(buff);
        buff.flip();
        System.out.println(buff.asCharBuffer());
        // Use a CharBuffer to write through:
        fc = new FileOutputStream("data2.txt").getChannel();
        buff = ByteBuffer.allocate(24); // More than needed
        buff.asCharBuffer().put("Some text");
        fc.write(buff);
        fc.close();
        // Read and display:
        fc = new FileInputStream("data2.txt").getChannel();
        buff.clear();
        fc.read(buff);
        buff.flip();
        System.out.println(buff.asCharBuffer());
    }
} /* Output:
????
Decoded using Cp1252: Some text
Some text
Some text
*///:~
```

The buffer contains plain bytes, and to turn these into characters, we must
either *encode* them as we put them in (so that they will be meaningful when

they come out) or *decode* them as they come out of the buffer. This can be accomplished using the **java.nio.charset.Charset** class, which provides tools for encoding into many different types of character sets:

```
//: io/AvailableCharSets.java
// Displays Charsets and aliases
import java.nio.charset.*;
import java.util.*;
import static net.mindview.util.Print.*;

public class AvailableCharSets {
  public static void main(String[] args) {
    SortedMap<String,Charset> charSets =
      Charset.availableCharsets();
    Iterator<String> it = charSets.keySet().iterator();
    while(it.hasNext()) {
      String csName = it.next();
      printnb(csName);
      Iterator aliases =
        charSets.get(csName).aliases().iterator();
      if(aliases.hasNext())
        printnb(": ");
      while(aliases.hasNext()) {
        printnb(aliases.next());
        if(aliases.hasNext())
          printnb(", ");
      }
      print();
    }
  }
} /* Output:
Big5: csBig5
Big5-HKSCS: big5-hkscs, big5hk, big5-hkscs:unicode3.0,
big5hkscs, Big5_HKSCS
EUC-JP: eucjis, x-eucjp, csEUCPkdFmtjapanese, eucjp,
Extended_UNIX_Code_Packed_Format_for_Japanese, x-euc-jp,
euc_jp
EUC-KR: ksc5601, 5601, ksc5601_1987, ksc_5601, ksc5601-
1987, euc_kr, ks_c_5601-1987, euckr, csEUCKR
GB18030: gb18030-2000
GB2312: gb2312-1980, gb2312, EUC_CN, gb2312-80, euc-cn,
euccn, x-EUC-CN
GBK: windows-936, CP936
...
```

```
*///:~
```

So, returning to **BufferToText.java**, if you **rewind( )** the buffer (to go back to the beginning of the data) and then use that platform's default character set to **decode( )** the data, the resulting **CharBuffer** will print to the console just fine. To discover the default character set, use **System.getProperty("file.encoding")**, which produces the string that names the character set. Passing this to **Charset.forName( )** produces the **Charset** object that can be used to decode the string.

Another alternative is to **encode( )** using a character set that will result in something printable when the file is read, as you see in the third part of **BufferToText.java**. Here, UTF-16BE is used to write the text into the file, and when it is read, all you must do is convert it to a **CharBuffer**, and it produces the expected text.

Finally, you see what happens if you *write* to the **ByteBuffer** through a **CharBuffer** (you'll learn more about this later). Note that 24 bytes are allocated for the **ByteBuffer**. Since each **char** requires two bytes, this is enough for 12 **char**s, but "Some text" only has 9. The remaining zero bytes still appear in the representation of the **CharBuffer** produced by its **toString( )**, as you can see in the output.

Exercise 23: (6) Create and test a utility method to print the contents of a **CharBuffer** up to the point where the characters are no longer printable.

Fetching primitives

Although a **ByteBuffer** only holds bytes, it contains methods to produce each of the different types of primitive values from the bytes it contains. This example shows the insertion and extraction of various values using these methods:

```
//: io/GetData.java
// Getting different representations from a ByteBuffer
import java.nio.*;
import static net.mindview.util.Print.*;

public class GetData {
  private static final int BSIZE = 1024;
  public static void main(String[] args) {
    ByteBuffer bb = ByteBuffer.allocate(BSIZE);
    // Allocation automatically zeroes the ByteBuffer:
```

```
      int i = 0;
      while(i++ < bb.limit())
        if(bb.get() != 0)
          print("nonzero");
      print("i = " + i);
      bb.rewind();
      // Store and read a char array:
      bb.asCharBuffer().put("Howdy!");
      char c;
      while((c = bb.getChar()) != 0)
        printnb(c + " ");
      print();
      bb.rewind();
      // Store and read a short:
      bb.asShortBuffer().put((short)471142);
      print(bb.getShort());
      bb.rewind();
      // Store and read an int:
      bb.asIntBuffer().put(99471142);
      print(bb.getInt());
      bb.rewind();
      // Store and read a long:
      bb.asLongBuffer().put(99471142);
      print(bb.getLong());
      bb.rewind();
      // Store and read a float:
      bb.asFloatBuffer().put(99471142);
      print(bb.getFloat());
      bb.rewind();
      // Store and read a double:
      bb.asDoubleBuffer().put(99471142);
      print(bb.getDouble());
      bb.rewind();
    }
} /* Output:
i = 1025
H o w d y !
12390
99471142
99471142
9.9471144E7
9.9471142E7
*///:~
```

After a **ByteBuffer** is allocated, its values are checked to see whether buffer allocation automatically zeroes the contents—and it does. All 1,024 values are checked (up to the **limit( )** of the buffer), and all are zero.

The easiest way to insert primitive values into a **ByteBuffer** is to get the appropriate "view" on that buffer using **asCharBuffer( )**, **asShortBuffer( )**, etc., and then to use that view's **put( )** method. You can see this is the process used for each of the primitive data types. The only one of these that is a little odd is the **put( )** for the **ShortBuffer**, which requires a cast (note that the cast truncates and changes the resulting value). All the other view buffers do not require casting in their **put( )** methods.

View buffers

A "view buffer" allows you to look at an underlying **ByteBuffer** through the window of a particular primitive type. The **ByteBuffer** is still the actual storage that's "backing" the view, so any changes you make to the view are reflected in modifications to the data in the **ByteBuffer**. As seen in the previous example, this allows you to conveniently insert primitive types into a **ByteBuffer**. A view also allows you to read primitive values from a **ByteBuffer**, either one at a time (as **ByteBuffer** allows) or in batches (into arrays). Here's an example that manipulates **int**s in a **ByteBuffer** via an **IntBuffer**:

```
//: io/IntBufferDemo.java
// Manipulating ints in a ByteBuffer with an IntBuffer
import java.nio.*;

public class IntBufferDemo {
  private static final int BSIZE = 1024;
  public static void main(String[] args) {
    ByteBuffer bb = ByteBuffer.allocate(BSIZE);
    IntBuffer ib = bb.asIntBuffer();
    // Store an array of int:
    ib.put(new int[]{ 11, 42, 47, 99, 143, 811, 1016 });
    // Absolute location read and write:
    System.out.println(ib.get(3));
    ib.put(3, 1811);
    // Setting a new limit before rewinding the buffer.
    ib.flip();
    while(ib.hasRemaining()) {
      int i = ib.get();
      System.out.println(i);
```

```
      }
    }
} /* Output:
99
11
42
47
1811
143
811
1016
*///:~
```

The overloaded **put( )** method is first used to store an array of **int**. The following **get( )** and **put( )** method calls directly access an **int** location in the underlying **ByteBuffer**. Note that these absolute location accesses are available for primitive types by talking directly to a **ByteBuffer**, as well.

Once the underlying **ByteBuffer** is filled with **int**s or some other primitive type via a view buffer, then that **ByteBuffer** can be written directly to a channel. You can just as easily read from a channel and use a view buffer to convert everything to a particular type of primitive. Here's an example that interprets the same sequence of bytes as **short**, **int**, **float**, **long**, and **double** by producing different view buffers on the same **ByteBuffer**:

```
//: io/ViewBuffers.java
import java.nio.*;
import static net.mindview.util.Print.*;

public class ViewBuffers {
  public static void main(String[] args) {
    ByteBuffer bb = ByteBuffer.wrap(
      new byte[]{ 0, 0, 0, 0, 0, 0, 0, 'a' });
    bb.rewind();
    printnb("Byte Buffer ");
    while(bb.hasRemaining())
      printnb(bb.position()+ " -> " + bb.get() + ", ");
    print();
    CharBuffer cb =
      ((ByteBuffer)bb.rewind()).asCharBuffer();
    printnb("Char Buffer ");
    while(cb.hasRemaining())
      printnb(cb.position() + " -> " + cb.get() + ", ");
    print();
```

```
        FloatBuffer fb =
          ((ByteBuffer)bb.rewind()).asFloatBuffer();
        printnb("Float Buffer ");
        while(fb.hasRemaining())
          printnb(fb.position()+ " -> " + fb.get() + ", ");
        print();
        IntBuffer ib =
          ((ByteBuffer)bb.rewind()).asIntBuffer();
        printnb("Int Buffer ");
        while(ib.hasRemaining())
          printnb(ib.position()+ " -> " + ib.get() + ", ");
        print();
        LongBuffer lb =
          ((ByteBuffer)bb.rewind()).asLongBuffer();
        printnb("Long Buffer ");
        while(lb.hasRemaining())
          printnb(lb.position()+ " -> " + lb.get() + ", ");
        print();
        ShortBuffer sb =
          ((ByteBuffer)bb.rewind()).asShortBuffer();
        printnb("Short Buffer ");
        while(sb.hasRemaining())
          printnb(sb.position()+ " -> " + sb.get() + ", ");
        print();
        DoubleBuffer db =
          ((ByteBuffer)bb.rewind()).asDoubleBuffer();
        printnb("Double Buffer ");
        while(db.hasRemaining())
          printnb(db.position()+ " -> " + db.get() + ", ");
    }
} /* Output:
Byte Buffer 0 -> 0, 1 -> 0, 2 -> 0, 3 -> 0, 4 -> 0, 5 -> 0,
6 -> 0, 7 -> 97,
Char Buffer 0 ->  , 1 ->  , 2 ->  , 3 -> a,
Float Buffer 0 -> 0.0, 1 -> 1.36E-43,
Int Buffer 0 -> 0, 1 -> 97,
Long Buffer 0 -> 97,
Short Buffer 0 -> 0, 1 -> 0, 2 -> 0, 3 -> 97,
Double Buffer 0 -> 4.8E-322,
*///:~
```

The **ByteBuffer** is produced by "wrapping" an eight-**byte** array, which is then displayed via view buffers of all the different primitive types. You can see in the following diagram the way the data appears differently when read from the different types of buffers:

0	0	0	0	0	0	0	97	bytes
							a	chars
0		0		0		97		shorts
0				97				ints
0.0				1.36E-43				floats
97								longs
4.8E-322								doubles

This corresponds to the output from the program.

Exercise 24: (1) Modify **IntBufferDemo.java** to use **double**s.

Endians

Different machines may use different byte-ordering approaches to store data. "Big endian" places the most significant byte in the lowest memory address, and "little endian" places the most significant byte in the highest memory address. When storing a quantity that is greater than one **byte**, like **int**, **float**, etc., you may need to consider the byte ordering. A **ByteBuffer** stores data in big endian form, and data sent over a network always uses big endian order. You can change the endian-ness of a **ByteBuffer** using **order( )** with an argument of **ByteOrder.BIG_ENDIAN** or **ByteOrder.LITTLE_ENDIAN**.

Consider a **ByteBuffer** containing the following two bytes:

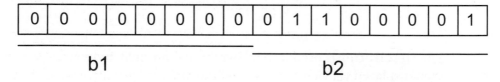

0	0	0	0	0	0	0	0	0	1	1	0	0	0	0	1

b1   b2

If you read the data as a **short (ByteBuffer.asShortBuffer( ))**, you will get the number 97 (00000000 01100001), but if you change to little endian, you will get the number 24832 (01100001 00000000).

Here's an example that shows how byte ordering is changed in characters depending on the endian setting:

```
//: io/Endians.java
// Endian differences and data storage.
import java.nio.*;
import java.util.*;
import static net.mindview.util.Print.*;

public class Endians {
  public static void main(String[] args) {
    ByteBuffer bb = ByteBuffer.wrap(new byte[12]);
    bb.asCharBuffer().put("abcdef");
    print(Arrays.toString(bb.array()));
    bb.rewind();
    bb.order(ByteOrder.BIG_ENDIAN);
    bb.asCharBuffer().put("abcdef");
    print(Arrays.toString(bb.array()));
    bb.rewind();
    bb.order(ByteOrder.LITTLE_ENDIAN);
    bb.asCharBuffer().put("abcdef");
    print(Arrays.toString(bb.array()));
  }
} /* Output:
[0, 97, 0, 98, 0, 99, 0, 100, 0, 101, 0, 102]
[0, 97, 0, 98, 0, 99, 0, 100, 0, 101, 0, 102]
[97, 0, 98, 0, 99, 0, 100, 0, 101, 0, 102, 0]
*///:~
```

The **ByteBuffer** is given enough space to hold all the bytes in **charArray** as an external buffer so that the **array( )** method can be called to display the underlying bytes. The **array( )** method is "optional," and you can only call it on a buffer that is backed by an array; otherwise, you'll get an **UnsupportedOperationException**.

charArray is inserted into the **ByteBuffer** via a **CharBuffer** view. When the underlying bytes are displayed, you can see that the default ordering is the same as the subsequent big endian order, whereas the little endian order swaps the bytes.

Data manipulation with buffers

The following diagram illustrates the relationships between the **nio** classes, so that you can see how to move and convert data. For example, if you wish to write a **byte** array to a file, then you wrap the **byte** array using the **ByteBuffer.wrap( )** method, open a channel on the **FileOutputStream** using the **getChannel( )** method, and then write data into **FileChannel** from this **ByteBuffer**.

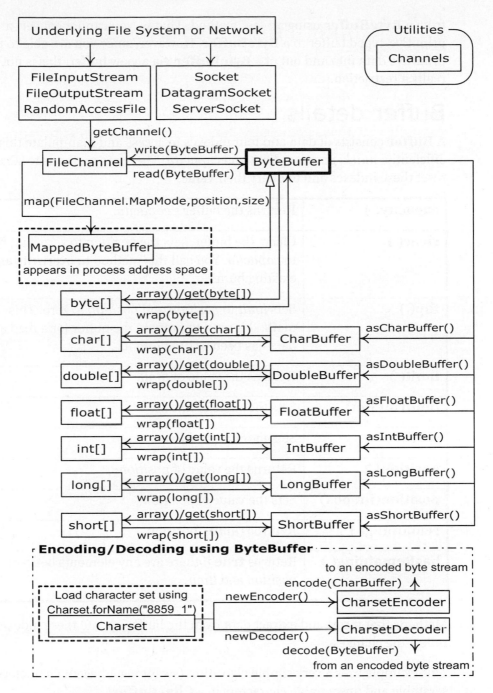

Note that **ByteBuffer** is the only way to move data into and out of channels, and that you can only create a standalone primitive-typed buffer, or get one from a **ByteBuffer** using an "as" method. That is, you cannot convert a primitive-typed buffer *to* a **ByteBuffer**. However, since you are able to move primitive data into and out of a **ByteBuffer** via a view buffer, this is not really a restriction.

Buffer details

A **Buffer** consists of data and four indexes to access and manipulate this data efficiently: *mark, position, limit* and *capacity*. There are methods to set and reset these indexes and to query their value.

capacity( )	Returns the buffer's *capacity*.
clear( )	Clears the buffer, sets the *position* to zero, and *limit* to *capacity*. You call this method to overwrite an existing buffer.
flip( )	Sets *limit* to *position* and *position* to zero. This method is used to prepare the buffer for a read after data has been written into it.
limit( )	Returns the value of *limit*.
limit(int lim)	Sets the value of *limit*.
mark( )	Sets *mark* at *position*.
position( )	Returns the value of *position*.
position(int pos)	Sets the value of *position*.
remaining( )	Returns (*limit - position*).
hasRemaining( )	Returns **true** if there are any elements between *position* and *limit*.

Methods that insert and extract data from the buffer update these indexes to reflect the changes.

This example uses a very simple algorithm (swapping adjacent characters) to scramble and unscramble characters in a **CharBuffer**:

```
//: io/UsingBuffers.java
```

```
import java.nio.*;
import static net.mindview.util.Print.*;

public class UsingBuffers {
  private static void symmetricScramble(CharBuffer buffer){
    while(buffer.hasRemaining()) {
      buffer.mark();
      char c1 = buffer.get();
      char c2 = buffer.get();
      buffer.reset();
      buffer.put(c2).put(c1);
    }
  }
  public static void main(String[] args) {
    char[] data = "UsingBuffers".toCharArray();
    ByteBuffer bb = ByteBuffer.allocate(data.length * 2);
    CharBuffer cb = bb.asCharBuffer();
    cb.put(data);
    print(cb.rewind());
    symmetricScramble(cb);
    print(cb.rewind());
    symmetricScramble(cb);
    print(cb.rewind());
  }
} /* Output:
UsingBuffers
sUniBgfuefsr
UsingBuffers
*///:~
```

Although you could produce a **CharBuffer** directly by calling **wrap( )** with a **char** array, an underlying **ByteBuffer** is allocated instead, and a **CharBuffer** is produced as a view on the **ByteBuffer**. This emphasizes that the goal is always to manipulate a **ByteBuffer**, since that is what interacts with a channel.

Here's what the buffer looks like at the entrance of the **symmetricScramble( )** method:

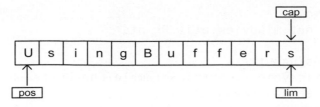

The *position* points to the first element in the buffer, and the *capacity* and *limit* point immediately after the last element.

In **symmetricScramble( )**, the **while** loop iterates until *position* is equivalent to *limit*. The *position* of the buffer changes when a relative **get( )** or **put( )** function is called on it. You can also call absolute **get( )** and **put( )** methods that include an index argument, which is the location where the **get( )** or **put( )** takes place. These methods do not modify the value of the buffer's *position*.

When the control enters the **while** loop, the value of *mark* is set using a **mark( )** call. The state of the buffer is then:

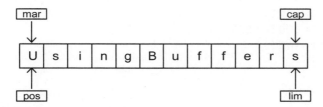

The two relative **get( )** calls save the value of the first two characters in variables **c1** and **c2**. After these two calls, the buffer looks like this:

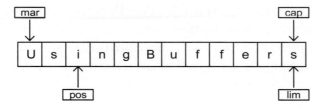

To perform the swap, we need to write **c2** at *position* = 0 and **c1** at *position* = 1. We can either use the absolute put method to achieve this, or set the value of *position* to *mark*, which is what **reset( )** does:

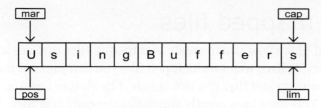

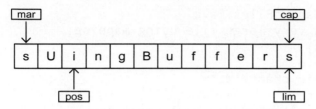

The two **put( )** methods write **c2** and then **c1**:

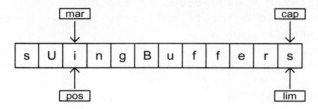

During the next iteration of the loop, *mark* is set to the current value of *position*:

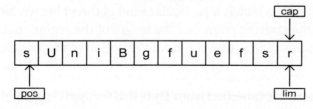

The process continues until the entire buffer is traversed. At the end of the **while** loop, *position* is at the end of the buffer. If you print the buffer, only the characters between the *position* and *limit* are printed. Thus, if you want to show the entire contents of the buffer, you must set *position* to the start of the buffer using **rewind( )**. Here is the state of buffer after the **rewind( )** call (the value of *mark* becomes undefined):

When the function **symmetricScramble( )** is called again, the **CharBuffer** undergoes the same process and is restored to its original state.

Memory-mapped files

Memory-mapped files allow you to create and modify files that are too big to bring into memory. With a memory-mapped file, you can pretend that the entire file is in memory and that you can access it by simply treating it as a very large array. This approach greatly simplifies the code you write in order to modify the file. Here's a small example:

```
//: io/LargeMappedFiles.java
// Creating a very large file using mapping.
// {RunByHand}
import java.nio.*;
import java.nio.channels.*;
import java.io.*;
import static net.mindview.util.Print.*;

public class LargeMappedFiles {
  static int length = 0x8000000; // 128 MB
  public static void main(String[] args) throws Exception {
    MappedByteBuffer out =
      new RandomAccessFile("test.dat", "rw").getChannel()
      .map(FileChannel.MapMode.READ_WRITE, 0, length);
    for(int i = 0; i < length; i++)
      out.put((byte)'x');
    print("Finished writing");
    for(int i = length/2; i < length/2 + 6; i++)
      printnb((char)out.get(i));
  }
} ///:~
```

To do both writing and reading, we start with a **RandomAccessFile**, get a channel for that file, and then call **map( )** to produce a **MappedByteBuffer**, which is a particular kind of direct buffer. Note that you must specify the starting point and the length of the region that you want to map in the file; this means that you have the option to map smaller regions of a large file.

MappedByteBuffer is inherited from **ByteBuffer**, so it has all of **ByteBuffer**'s methods. Only the very simple uses of **put( )** and **get( )** are shown here, but you can also use methods like **asCharBuffer( )**, etc.

The file created with the preceding program is 128 MB long, which is probably larger than your OS will allow in memory at one time. The file appears to be accessible all at once because only portions of it are brought into memory, and other parts are swapped out. This way a very large file (up to 2 GB) can easily be modified. Note that the file-mapping facilities of the underlying operating system are used to maximize performance.

Performance

Although the performance of "old" stream I/O has been improved by implementing it with **nio**, mapped file access tends to be dramatically faster. This program does a simple performance comparison:

```
//: io/MappedIO.java
import java.nio.*;
import java.nio.channels.*;
import java.io.*;

public class MappedIO {
  private static int numOfInts = 4000000;
  private static int numOfUbuffInts = 200000;
  private abstract static class Tester {
    private String name;
    public Tester(String name) { this.name = name; }
    public void runTest() {
      System.out.print(name + ": ");
      try {
        long start = System.nanoTime();
        test();
        double duration = System.nanoTime() - start;
        System.out.format("%.2f\n", duration/1.0e9);
      } catch(IOException e) {
        throw new RuntimeException(e);
      }
    }
    public abstract void test() throws IOException;
  }
  private static Tester[] tests = {
    new Tester("Stream Write") {
      public void test() throws IOException {
        DataOutputStream dos = new DataOutputStream(
          new BufferedOutputStream(
            new FileOutputStream(new File("temp.tmp"))));
        for(int i = 0; i < numOfInts; i++)
          dos.writeInt(i);
        dos.close();
```

```
          }
        },
        new Tester("Mapped Write") {
          public void test() throws IOException {
            FileChannel fc =
              new RandomAccessFile("temp.tmp", "rw")
              .getChannel();
            IntBuffer ib = fc.map(
              FileChannel.MapMode.READ_WRITE, 0, fc.size())
              .asIntBuffer();
            for(int i = 0; i < numOfInts; i++)
              ib.put(i);
            fc.close();
          }
        },
        new Tester("Stream Read") {
          public void test() throws IOException {
            DataInputStream dis = new DataInputStream(
              new BufferedInputStream(
                new FileInputStream("temp.tmp")));
            for(int i = 0; i < numOfInts; i++)
              dis.readInt();
            dis.close();
          }
        },
        new Tester("Mapped Read") {
          public void test() throws IOException {
            FileChannel fc = new FileInputStream(
              new File("temp.tmp")).getChannel();
            IntBuffer ib = fc.map(
              FileChannel.MapMode.READ_ONLY, 0, fc.size())
              .asIntBuffer();
            while(ib.hasRemaining())
              ib.get();
            fc.close();
          }
        },
        new Tester("Stream Read/Write") {
          public void test() throws IOException {
            RandomAccessFile raf = new RandomAccessFile(
              new File("temp.tmp"), "rw");
            raf.writeInt(1);
            for(int i = 0; i < numOfUbuffInts; i++) {
              raf.seek(raf.length() - 4);
```

```
          raf.writeInt(raf.readInt());
        }
        raf.close();
      }
    },
    new Tester("Mapped Read/Write") {
      public void test() throws IOException {
        FileChannel fc = new RandomAccessFile(
          new File("temp.tmp"), "rw").getChannel();
        IntBuffer ib = fc.map(
          FileChannel.MapMode.READ_WRITE, 0, fc.size())
          .asIntBuffer();
        ib.put(0);
        for(int i = 1; i < numOfUbuffInts; i++)
          ib.put(ib.get(i - 1));
        fc.close();
      }
    }
  };
  public static void main(String[] args) {
    for(Tester test : tests)
      test.runTest();
  }
} /* Output: (90% match)
Stream Write: 0.56
Mapped Write: 0.12
Stream Read: 0.80
Mapped Read: 0.07
Stream Read/Write: 5.32
Mapped Read/Write: 0.02
*///:~
```

As seen in earlier examples in this book, **runTest( )** is used by the *Template Method* to create a testing framework for various implementations of **test( )** defined in anonymous inner subclasses. Each of these subclasses performs one kind of test, so the **test( )** methods also give you a prototype for performing the various I/O activities.

Although a mapped write would seem to use a **FileOutputStream**, all output in file mapping must use a **RandomAccessFile**, just as read/write does in the preceding code.

Note that the **test( )** methods include the time for initialization of the various I/O objects, so even though the setup for mapped files can be expensive, the overall gain compared to stream I/O is significant.

Exercise 25: (6) Experiment with changing the **ByteBuffer.allocate( )** statements in the examples in this chapter to **ByteBuffer.allocateDirect( )**. Demonstrate performance differences, but also notice whether the startup time of the programs noticeably changes.

Exercise 26: (3) Modify **strings/JGrep.java** to use Java **nio** memory-mapped files.

File locking

File locking allows you to synchronize access to a file as a shared resource. However, two threads that contend for the same file may be in different JVMs, or one may be a Java thread and the other some native thread in the operating system. The file locks are visible to other operating system processes because Java file locking maps directly to the native operating system locking facility.

Here is a simple example of file locking.

```
//: io/FileLocking.java
import java.nio.channels.*;
import java.util.concurrent.*;
import java.io.*;

public class FileLocking {
  public static void main(String[] args) throws Exception {
    FileOutputStream fos= new FileOutputStream("file.txt");
    FileLock fl = fos.getChannel().tryLock();
    if(fl != null) {
      System.out.println("Locked File");
      TimeUnit.MILLISECONDS.sleep(100);
      fl.release();
      System.out.println("Released Lock");
    }
    fos.close();
  }
} /* Output:
Locked File
Released Lock
*///:~
```

You get a **FileLock** on the entire file by calling either **tryLock( )** or **lock( )** on a **FileChannel**. (**SocketChannel**, **DatagramChannel**, and **ServerSocketChannel** do not need locking since they are inherently single-process entities; you don't generally share a network socket between two processes.) **tryLock( )** is non-blocking. It tries to grab the lock, but if it cannot (when some other process already holds the same lock and it is not shared), it simply returns from the method call. **lock( )** blocks until the lock is acquired, or the thread that invoked **lock( )** is interrupted, or the channel on which the **lock( )** method is called is closed. A lock is released using **FileLock.release( )**.

It is also possible to lock a part of the file by using

```
tryLock(long position, long size, boolean shared)
```

or

```
lock(long position, long size, boolean shared)
```

which locks the region **(size - position)**. The third argument specifies whether this lock is shared.

Although the zero-argument locking methods adapt to changes in the size of a file, locks with a fixed size do not change if the file size changes. If a lock is acquired for a region from **position** to **position+size** and the file increases beyond **position+size**, then the section beyond **position+size** is not locked. The zero-argument locking methods lock the entire file, even if it grows.

Support for exclusive or shared locks must be provided by the underlying operating system. If the operating system does not support shared locks and a request is made for one, an exclusive lock is used instead. The type of lock (shared or exclusive) can be queried using **FileLock.isShared( )**.

Locking portions of a mapped file

As mentioned earlier, file mapping is typically used for very large files. You may need to lock portions of such a large file so that other processes may modify unlocked parts of the file. This is something that happens, for example, with a database, so that it can be available to many users at once.

Here's an example that has two threads, each of which locks a distinct portion of a file:

```
//: io/LockingMappedFiles.java
// Locking portions of a mapped file.
// {RunByHand}
import java.nio.*;
import java.nio.channels.*;
import java.io.*;

public class LockingMappedFiles {
  static final int LENGTH = 0x8FFFFFF; // 128 MB
  static FileChannel fc;
  public static void main(String[] args) throws Exception {
    fc =
      new RandomAccessFile("test.dat", "rw").getChannel();
    MappedByteBuffer out =
      fc.map(FileChannel.MapMode.READ_WRITE, 0, LENGTH);
    for(int i = 0; i < LENGTH; i++)
      out.put((byte)'x');
    new LockAndModify(out, 0, 0 + LENGTH/3);
    new LockAndModify(out, LENGTH/2, LENGTH/2 + LENGTH/4);
  }
  private static class LockAndModify extends Thread {
    private ByteBuffer buff;
    private int start, end;
    LockAndModify(ByteBuffer mbb, int start, int end) {
      this.start = start;
      this.end = end;
      mbb.limit(end);
      mbb.position(start);
      buff = mbb.slice();
      start();
    }
    public void run() {
      try {
        // Exclusive lock with no overlap:
        FileLock fl = fc.lock(start, end, false);
        System.out.println("Locked: "+ start +" to "+ end);
        // Perform modification:
        while(buff.position() < buff.limit() - 1)
          buff.put((byte)(buff.get() + 1));
        fl.release();
        System.out.println("Released: "+start+" to "+ end);
      } catch(IOException e) {
        throw new RuntimeException(e);
      }
```

```
        }
    }
} ///:~
```

The **LockAndModify** thread class sets up the buffer region and creates a **slice( )** to be modified, and in **run( )**, the lock is acquired on the file channel (you can't acquire a lock on the buffer—only the channel). The call to **lock( )** is very similar to acquiring a threading lock on an object—you now have a "critical section" with exclusive access to that portion of the file.[5]

The locks are automatically released when the JVM exits, or the channel on which it was acquired is closed, but you can also explicitly call **release( )** on the **FileLock** object, as shown here.

Compression

The Java I/O library contains classes to support reading and writing streams in a compressed format. You wrap these around other I/O classes to provide compression functionality.

These classes are not derived from the **Reader** and **Writer** classes, but instead are part of the **InputStream** and **OutputStream** hierarchies. This is because the compression library works with bytes, not characters. However, you might sometimes be forced to mix the two types of streams. (Remember that you can use **InputStreamReader** and **OutputStreamWriter** to provide easy conversion between one type and another.)

Compression class	Function
CheckedInputStream	**GetCheckSum( )** produces checksum for any **InputStream** (not just decompression).
CheckedOutputStream	**GetCheckSum( )** produces checksum for any **OutputStream** (not just compression).
DeflaterOutputStream	Base class for compression classes.
ZipOutputStream	A **DeflaterOutputStream** that

---

[5] More details about threads will be found in the *Concurrency* chapter.

Compression class	Function
	compresses data into the Zip file format.
GZIPOutputStream	A **DeflaterOutputStream** that compresses data into the GZIP file format.
InflaterInputStream	Base class for decompression classes.
ZipInputStream	An **InflaterInputStream** that decompresses data that has been stored in the Zip file format.
GZIPInputStream	An **InflaterInputStream** that decompresses data that has been stored in the GZIP file format.

Although there are many compression algorithms, Zip and GZIP are possibly the most commonly used. Thus you can easily manipulate your compressed data with the many tools available for reading and writing these formats.

Simple compression with GZIP

The GZIP interface is simple and thus is probably more appropriate when you have a single stream of data that you want to compress (rather than a container of dissimilar pieces of data). Here's an example that compresses a single file:

```
//: io/GZIPcompress.java
// {Args: GZIPcompress.java}
import java.util.zip.*;
import java.io.*;

public class GZIPcompress {
  public static void main(String[] args)
  throws IOException {
    if(args.length == 0) {
      System.out.println(
        "Usage: \nGZIPcompress file\n" +
        "\tUses GZIP compression to compress " +
        "the file to test.gz");
      System.exit(1);
    }
    InputStream in = new BufferedInputStream(
      new FileInputStream(args[0]));
    BufferedOutputStream out = new BufferedOutputStream(
      new GZIPOutputStream(
```

```
      new FileOutputStream("test.gz")));
    System.out.println("Writing file");
    int c;
    while((c = in.read()) != -1)
      out.write(c);
    in.close();
    out.close();
    System.out.println("Reading file");
    BufferedReader in2 = new BufferedReader(
      new InputStreamReader(new GZIPInputStream(
        new FileInputStream("test.gz"))));
    String s;
    while((s = in2.readLine()) != null)
      System.out.println(s);
  }
} /* (Execute to see output) *///:~
```

The use of the compression classes is straightforward; you simply wrap your output stream in a **GZIPOutputStream** or **ZipOutputStream**, and your input stream in a **GZIPInputStream** or **ZipInputStream**. All else is ordinary I/O reading and writing. This is an example of mixing the **char**-oriented streams with the byte-oriented streams; **in** uses the **Reader** classes, whereas **GZIPOutputStream**'s constructor can accept only an **OutputStream** object, not a **Writer** object. When the file is opened, the **GZIPInputStream** is converted to a **Reader**.

Multifile storage with Zip

The library that supports the Zip format is more extensive. With it you can easily store multiple files, and there's even a separate class to make the process of reading a Zip file easy. The library uses the standard Zip format so that it works seamlessly with all the Zip tools currently downloadable on the Internet. The following example has the same form as the previous example, but it handles as many command-line arguments as you want. In addition, it shows the use of the **Checksum** classes to calculate and verify the checksum for the file. There are two **Checksum** types: **Adler32** (which is faster) and **CRC32** (which is slower but slightly more accurate).

```
//: io/ZipCompress.java
// Uses Zip compression to compress any
// number of files given on the command line.
// {Args: ZipCompress.java}
import java.util.zip.*;
```

```
import java.io.*;
import java.util.*;
import static net.mindview.util.Print.*;

public class ZipCompress {
  public static void main(String[] args)
  throws IOException {
    FileOutputStream f = new FileOutputStream("test.zip");
    CheckedOutputStream csum =
      new CheckedOutputStream(f, new Adler32());
     ZipOutputStream zos = new ZipOutputStream(csum);
     BufferedOutputStream out =
      new BufferedOutputStream(zos);
    zos.setComment("A test of Java Zipping");
    // No corresponding getComment(), though.
    for(String arg : args) {
      print("Writing file " + arg);
      InputStream in = new BufferedInputStream(
          new FileInputStream(arg));
      zos.putNextEntry(new ZipEntry(arg));
      int c;
      while((c = in.read()) != -1)
        out.write(c);
      in.close();
      out.flush();
    }
    out.close();
    // Checksum valid only after the file has been closed!
    print("Checksum: " + csum.getChecksum().getValue());
    // Now extract the files:
    print("Reading file");
    FileInputStream fi = new FileInputStream("test.zip");
    CheckedInputStream csumi =
      new CheckedInputStream(fi, new Adler32());
    ZipInputStream in2 = new ZipInputStream(csumi);
    BufferedInputStream bis = new BufferedInputStream(in2);
    ZipEntry ze;
    while((ze = in2.getNextEntry()) != null) {
      print("Reading file " + ze);
      int x;
      while((x = bis.read()) != -1)
        System.out.write(x);
    }
    if(args.length == 1)
```

```
print("Checksum: " + csumi.getChecksum().getValue());
bis.close();
// Alternative way to open and read Zip files:
ZipFile zf = new ZipFile("test.zip");
Enumeration e = zf.entries();
while(e.hasMoreElements()) {
  ZipEntry ze2 = (ZipEntry)e.nextElement();
  print("File: " + ze2);
  // ... and extract the data as before
}
/* if(args.length == 1) */
  }
} /* (Execute to see output) *///:~
```

For each file to add to the archive, you must call **putNextEntry( )** and pass it a **ZipEntry** object. The **ZipEntry** object contains an extensive interface that allows you to get and set all the data available on that particular entry in your Zip file: name, compressed and uncompressed sizes, date, CRC checksum, extra field data, comment, compression method, and whether it's a directory entry. However, even though the Zip format has a way to set a password, this is not supported in Java's Zip library. And although **CheckedInputStream** and **CheckedOutputStream** support both **Adler32** and **CRC32** checksums, the **ZipEntry** class supports only an interface for CRC. This is a restriction of the underlying Zip format, but it might limit you from using the faster **Adler32**.

To extract files, **ZipInputStream** has a **getNextEntry( )** method that returns the next **ZipEntry** if there is one. As a more succinct alternative, you can read the file using a **ZipFile** object, which has a method **entries( )** to return an **Enumeration** to the **ZipEntries**.

In order to read the checksum, you must somehow have access to the associated **Checksum** object. Here, a reference to the **CheckedOutputStream** and **CheckedInputStream** objects is retained, but you could also just hold on to a reference to the **Checksum** object.

A baffling method in Zip streams is **setComment( )**. As shown in **ZipCompress.java**, you can set a comment when you're writing a file, but there's no way to recover the comment in the **ZipInputStream**. Comments appear to be supported fully on an entry-by-entry basis only via **ZipEntry**.

Of course, you are not limited to files when using the **GZIP** or **Zip** libraries—you can compress anything, including data to be sent through a network connection.

Java ARchives (JARs)

The Zip format is also used in the JAR (Java ARchive) file format, which is a way to collect a group of files into a single compressed file, just like Zip. However, like everything else in Java, JAR files are cross-platform, so you don't need to worry about platform issues. You can also include audio and image files as well as class files.

JAR files are particularly helpful when you deal with the Internet. Before JAR files, your Web browser would have to make repeated requests of a Web server in order to download all the files that made up an applet. In addition, each of these files was uncompressed. By combining all of the files for a particular applet into a single JAR file, only one server request is necessary and the transfer is faster because of compression. And each entry in a JAR file can be digitally signed for security.

A JAR file consists of a single file containing a collection of zipped files along with a "manifest" that describes them. (You can create your own manifest file; otherwise, the **jar** program will do it for you.) You can find out more about JAR manifests in the JDK documentation.

The **jar** utility that comes with Sun's JDK automatically compresses the files of your choice. You invoke it on the command line:

```
jar [options] destination [manifest] inputfile(s)
```

The options are simply a collection of letters (no hyphen or any other indicator is necessary). Unix/Linux users will note the similarity to the **tar** options. These are:

c	Creates a new or empty archive.
t	Lists the table of contents.
x	Extracts all files.
x file	Extracts the named file.
f	Says, "I'm going to give you the name of the file." If you don't use this, **jar** assumes that its input will come from standard input, or, if it is creating a file, its output will go to

	standard output.
m	Says that the first argument will be the name of the user-created manifest file.
v	Generates verbose output describing what **jar** is doing.
o	Only stores the files; doesn't compress the files (use to create a JAR file that you can put in your classpath).
M	Doesn't automatically create a manifest file.

If a subdirectory is included in the files to be put into the JAR file, that subdirectory is automatically added, including all of its subdirectories, etc. Path information is also preserved.

Here are some typical ways to invoke **jar**. The following command creates a JAR file called **myJarFile.jar** that contains all of the class files in the current directory, along with an automatically generated manifest file:

```
jar cf myJarFile.jar *.class
```

The next command is like the previous example, but it adds a user-created manifest file called **myManifestFile.mf**:

```
jar cmf myJarFile.jar myManifestFile.mf *.class
```

This produces a table of contents of the files in **myJarFile.jar**:

```
jar tf myJarFile.jar
```

This adds the "verbose" flag to give more detailed information about the files in **myJarFile.jar**:

```
jar tvf myJarFile.jar
```

Assuming **audio**, **classes**, and **image** are subdirectories, this combines all of the subdirectories into the file **myApp.jar**. The "verbose" flag is also included to give extra feedback while the **jar** program is working:

```
jar cvf myApp.jar audio classes image
```

If you create a JAR file using the **o** (zero) option, that file can be placed in your CLASSPATH:

```
CLASSPATH="lib1.jar;lib2.jar;"
```

Then Java can search **lib1.jar** and **lib2.jar** for class files.

The **jar** tool isn't as general-purpose as a **Zip** utility. For example, you can't add or update files to an existing JAR file; you can create JAR files only from scratch. Also, you can't move files into a JAR file, erasing them as they are moved. However, a JAR file created on one platform will be transparently readable by the **jar** tool on any other platform (a problem that sometimes plagues **Zip** utilities).

As you will see in the *Graphical User Interfaces* chapter, JAR files are also used to package JavaBeans.

Object serialization

When you create an object, it exists for as long as you need it, but under no circumstances does it exist when the program terminates. While this makes sense at first, there are situations in which it would be incredibly useful if an object could exist and hold its information even while the program wasn't running. Then, the next time you started the program, the object would be there and it would have the same information it had the previous time the program was running. Of course, you can get a similar effect by writing the information to a file or to a database, but in the spirit of making everything an object, it would be quite convenient to declare an object to be "persistent," and have all the details taken care of for you.

Java's *object serialization* allows you to take any object that implements the **Serializable** interface and turn it into a sequence of bytes that can later be fully restored to regenerate the original object. This is even true across a network, which means that the serialization mechanism automatically compensates for differences in operating systems. That is, you can create an object on a Windows machine, serialize it, and send it across the network to a Unix machine, where it will be correctly reconstructed. You don't have to worry about the data representations on the different machines, the byte ordering, or any other details.

By itself, object serialization is interesting because it allows you to implement *lightweight persistence*. Persistence means that an object's lifetime is not determined by whether a program is executing; the object lives *in between* invocations of the program. By taking a serializable object and writing it to disk, then restoring that object when the program is reinvoked, you're able to produce the effect of persistence. The reason it's called "lightweight" is that you can't simply define an object using some kind of "persistent" keyword and let the system take care of the details (perhaps this will happen in the future). Instead, you must explicitly serialize and deserialize the objects in your program. If you need a more serious persistence mechanism, consider a tool like Hibernate (*http://hibernate.sourceforge.net*). For details, see *Thinking in Enterprise Java*, downloadable from *www.MindView.net*.

Object serialization was added to the language to support two major features. Java's *Remote Method Invocation* (RMI) allows objects that live on other machines to behave as if they live on your machine. When messages are sent to remote objects, object serialization is necessary to transport the arguments and return values. RMI is discussed in *Thinking in Enterprise Java*.

Object serialization is also necessary for JavaBeans, described in the *Graphical User Interfaces* chapter. When a Bean is used, its state information is generally configured at design time. This state information must be stored and later recovered when the program is started; object serialization performs this task.

Serializing an object is quite simple as long as the object implements the **Serializable** interface (this is a tagging interface and has no methods). When serialization was added to the language, many standard library classes were changed to make them serializable, including all of the wrappers for the primitive types, all of the container classes, and many others. Even **Class** objects can be serialized.

To serialize an object, you create some sort of **OutputStream** object and then wrap it inside an **ObjectOutputStream** object. At this point you need only call **writeObject( )**, and your object is serialized and sent to the **OutputStream** (object serialization is byte-oriented, and thus uses the **InputStream** and **OutputStream** hierarchies). To reverse the process, you wrap an **InputStream** inside an **ObjectInputStream** and call **readObject( )**. What comes back is, as usual, a reference to an upcast **Object**, so you must downcast to set things straight.

A particularly clever aspect of object serialization is that it not only saves an image of your object, but it also follows all the references contained in your object and saves *those* objects, and follows all the references in each of those objects, etc. This is sometimes referred to as the "web of objects" that a single object can be connected to, and it includes arrays of references to objects as well as member objects. If you had to maintain your own object serialization scheme, maintaining the code to follow all these links could be mind-boggling. However, Java object serialization seems to pull it off flawlessly, no doubt using an optimized algorithm that traverses the web of objects. The following example tests the serialization mechanism by making a "worm" of linked objects, each of which has a link to the next segment in the worm as well as an array of references to objects of a different class, **Data**:

```
//: io/Worm.java
// Demonstrates object serialization.
import java.io.*;
import java.util.*;
import static net.mindview.util.Print.*;

class Data implements Serializable {
  private int n;
  public Data(int n) { this.n = n; }
  public String toString() { return Integer.toString(n); }
}

public class Worm implements Serializable {
  private static Random rand = new Random(47);
  private Data[] d = {
    new Data(rand.nextInt(10)),
    new Data(rand.nextInt(10)),
    new Data(rand.nextInt(10))
  };
  private Worm next;
  private char c;
  // Value of i == number of segments
  public Worm(int i, char x) {
    print("Worm constructor: " + i);
    c = x;
    if(--i > 0)
      next = new Worm(i, (char)(x + 1));
  }
  public Worm() {
    print("Default constructor");
  }
  public String toString() {
    StringBuilder result = new StringBuilder(":");
    result.append(c);
    result.append("(");
    for(Data dat : d)
      result.append(dat);
    result.append(")");
    if(next != null)
```

```
      result.append(next);
    return result.toString();
  }
  public static void main(String[] args)
  throws ClassNotFoundException, IOException {
    Worm w = new Worm(6, 'a');
    print("w = " + w);
    ObjectOutputStream out = new ObjectOutputStream(
      new FileOutputStream("worm.out"));
    out.writeObject("Worm storage\n");
    out.writeObject(w);
    out.close(); // Also flushes output
    ObjectInputStream in = new ObjectInputStream(
      new FileInputStream("worm.out"));
    String s = (String)in.readObject();
    Worm w2 = (Worm)in.readObject();
    print(s + "w2 = " + w2);
    ByteArrayOutputStream bout =
      new ByteArrayOutputStream();
    ObjectOutputStream out2 = new ObjectOutputStream(bout);
    out2.writeObject("Worm storage\n");
    out2.writeObject(w);
    out2.flush();
    ObjectInputStream in2 = new ObjectInputStream(
      new ByteArrayInputStream(bout.toByteArray()));
    s = (String)in2.readObject();
    Worm w3 = (Worm)in2.readObject();
    print(s + "w3 = " + w3);
  }
} /* Output:
Worm constructor: 6
Worm constructor: 5
Worm constructor: 4
Worm constructor: 3
Worm constructor: 2
Worm constructor: 1
w = :a(853):b(119):c(802):d(788):e(199):f(881)
Worm storage
w2 = :a(853):b(119):c(802):d(788):e(199):f(881)
Worm storage
w3 = :a(853):b(119):c(802):d(788):e(199):f(881)
*///:~
```

To make things interesting, the array of **Data** objects inside **Worm** are initialized with random numbers. (This way, you don't suspect the compiler of keeping some kind of meta-information.) Each **Worm** segment is labeled with a **char** that's automatically generated in the process of recursively generating the linked list of **Worm**s. When you create a **Worm**, you tell the constructor how long you want it to be. To make the **next** reference, it calls the **Worm** constructor with a length of one less, etc. The final **next** reference is left as **null**, indicating the end of the **Worm**.

The point of all this was to make something reasonably complex that couldn't easily be serialized. The act of serializing, however, is quite simple. Once the **ObjectOutputStream** is created from some other stream, **writeObject( )** serializes the object. Notice the call to **writeObject( )** for a **String**, as well. You can also write all the primitive data types using the same methods as **DataOutputStream** (they share the same interface).

There are two separate code sections that look similar. The first writes and reads a file, and the second, for variety, writes and reads a **ByteArray**. You can read and write an object using serialization to any **DataInputStream** or **DataOutputStream**, including, as you can see in *Thinking in Enterprise Java*, a network.

You can see from the output that the deserialized object really does contain all of the links that were in the original object.

Note that no constructor, not even the default constructor, is called in the process of deserializing a **Serializable** object. The entire object is restored by recovering data from the **InputStream**.

Exercise 27:   (1) Create a **Serializable** class containing a reference to an object of a second **Serializable** class. Create an instance of your class, serialize it to disk, then restore it and verify that the process worked correctly.

Finding the class

You might wonder what's necessary for an object to be recovered from its serialized state. For example, suppose you serialize an object and send it as a file or through a network to another machine. Could a program on the other machine reconstruct the object using only the contents of the file?

The best way to answer this question is (as usual) by performing an experiment. The following file goes in the subdirectory for this chapter:

```
//: io/Alien.java
// A serializable class.
```

```
import java.io.*;
public class Alien implements Serializable {} ///:~
```

The file that creates and serializes an **Alien** object goes in the same directory:

```
//: io/FreezeAlien.java
// Create a serialized output file.
import java.io.*;

public class FreezeAlien {
  public static void main(String[] args) throws Exception {
    ObjectOutput out = new ObjectOutputStream(
      new FileOutputStream("X.file"));
    Alien quellek = new Alien();
    out.writeObject(quellek);
  }
} ///:~
```

Rather than catching and handling exceptions, this program takes the quick-and-dirty approach of passing the exceptions out of **main( )**, so they'll be reported on the console.

Once the program is compiled and run, it produces a file called **X.file** in the **io** directory. The following code is in a subdirectory called **xfiles**:

```
//: io/xfiles/ThawAlien.java
// Try to recover a serialized file without the
// class of object that's stored in that file.
// {RunByHand}
import java.io.*;

public class ThawAlien {
  public static void main(String[] args) throws Exception {
    ObjectInputStream in = new ObjectInputStream(
      new FileInputStream(new File("..", "X.file")));
    Object mystery = in.readObject();
    System.out.println(mystery.getClass());
  }
} /* Output:
class Alien
*///:~
```

Even opening the file and reading in the object **mystery** requires the **Class** object for **Alien**; the JVM cannot find **Alien.class** (unless it happens to be in the classpath, which it shouldn't be in this example). You'll get a

ClassNotFoundException. (Once again, all evidence of alien life vanishes before proof of its existence can be verified!) The JVM must be able to find the associated **.class** file.

Controlling serialization

As you can see, the default serialization mechanism is trivial to use. But what if you have special needs? Perhaps you have special security issues and you don't want to serialize portions of your object, or perhaps it just doesn't make sense for one subobject to be serialized if that part needs to be created anew when the object is recovered.

You can control the process of serialization by implementing the **Externalizable** interface instead of the **Serializable** interface. The **Externalizable** interface extends the **Serializable** interface and adds two methods, **writeExternal( )** and **readExternal( )**, that are automatically called for your object during serialization and deserialization so that you can perform your special operations.

The following example shows simple implementations of the **Externalizable** interface methods. Note that **Blip1** and **Blip2** are nearly identical except for a subtle difference (see if you can discover it by looking at the code):

```
//: io/Blips.java
// Simple use of Externalizable & a pitfall.
import java.io.*;
import static net.mindview.util.Print.*;

class Blip1 implements Externalizable {
  public Blip1() {
    print("Blip1 Constructor");
  }
  public void writeExternal(ObjectOutput out)
      throws IOException {
    print("Blip1.writeExternal");
  }
  public void readExternal(ObjectInput in)
     throws IOException, ClassNotFoundException {
    print("Blip1.readExternal");
  }
}
```

```java
class Blip2 implements Externalizable {
  Blip2() {
    print("Blip2 Constructor");
  }
  public void writeExternal(ObjectOutput out)
      throws IOException {
    print("Blip2.writeExternal");
  }
  public void readExternal(ObjectInput in)
      throws IOException, ClassNotFoundException {
    print("Blip2.readExternal");
  }
}

public class Blips {
  public static void main(String[] args)
  throws IOException, ClassNotFoundException {
    print("Constructing objects:");
    Blip1 b1 = new Blip1();
    Blip2 b2 = new Blip2();
    ObjectOutputStream o = new ObjectOutputStream(
      new FileOutputStream("Blips.out"));
    print("Saving objects:");
    o.writeObject(b1);
    o.writeObject(b2);
    o.close();
    // Now get them back:
    ObjectInputStream in = new ObjectInputStream(
      new FileInputStream("Blips.out"));
    print("Recovering b1:");
    b1 = (Blip1)in.readObject();
    // OOPS! Throws an exception:
//! print("Recovering b2:");
//! b2 = (Blip2)in.readObject();
  }
} /* Output:
Constructing objects:
Blip1 Constructor
Blip2 Constructor
Saving objects:
Blip1.writeExternal
Blip2.writeExternal
Recovering b1:
Blip1 Constructor
```

```
Blip1.readExternal
*///:~
```

The reason that the **Blip2** object is not recovered is that trying to do so causes an exception. Can you see the difference between **Blip1** and **Blip2**? The constructor for **Blip1** is **public**, while the constructor for **Blip2** is not, and that causes the exception upon recovery. Try making **Blip2**'s constructor **public** and removing the //! comments to see the correct results.

When **b1** is recovered, the **Blip1** default constructor is called. This is different from recovering a **Serializable** object, in which the object is constructed entirely from its stored bits, with no constructor calls. With an **Externalizable** object, all the normal default construction behavior occurs (including the initializations at the point of field definition), and *then* **readExternal( )** is called. You need to be aware of this—in particular, the fact that all the default construction always takes place—to produce the correct behavior in your **Externalizable** objects.

Here's an example that shows what you must do to fully store and retrieve an **Externalizable** object:

```
//: io/Blip3.java
// Reconstructing an externalizable object.
import java.io.*;
import static net.mindview.util.Print.*;

public class Blip3 implements Externalizable {
  private int i;
  private String s; // No initialization
  public Blip3() {
    print("Blip3 Constructor");
    // s, i not initialized
  }
  public Blip3(String x, int a) {
    print("Blip3(String x, int a)");
    s = x;
    i = a;
    // s & i initialized only in non-default constructor.
  }
  public String toString() { return s + i; }
  public void writeExternal(ObjectOutput out)
  throws IOException {
    print("Blip3.writeExternal");
    // You must do this:
```

```
      out.writeObject(s);
      out.writeInt(i);
    }
    public void readExternal(ObjectInput in)
    throws IOException, ClassNotFoundException {
      print("Blip3.readExternal");
      // You must do this:
      s = (String)in.readObject();
      i = in.readInt();
    }
    public static void main(String[] args)
    throws IOException, ClassNotFoundException {
      print("Constructing objects:");
      Blip3 b3 = new Blip3("A String ", 47);
      print(b3);
      ObjectOutputStream o = new ObjectOutputStream(
        new FileOutputStream("Blip3.out"));
      print("Saving object:");
      o.writeObject(b3);
      o.close();
      // Now get it back:
      ObjectInputStream in = new ObjectInputStream(
        new FileInputStream("Blip3.out"));
      print("Recovering b3:");
      b3 = (Blip3)in.readObject();
      print(b3);
    }
} /* Output:
Constructing objects:
Blip3(String x, int a)
A String 47
Saving object:
Blip3.writeExternal
Recovering b3:
Blip3 Constructor
Blip3.readExternal
A String 47
*///:~
```

The fields **s** and **i** are initialized only in the second constructor, but not in the
default constructor. This means that if you don't initialize **s** and **i** in
readExternal( ), **s** will be **null** and **i** will be zero (since the storage for the
object gets wiped to zero in the first step of object creation). If you comment
out the two lines of code following the phrases "You must do this:" and run

the program, you'll see that when the object is recovered, **s** is **null** and **i** is zero.

If you are inheriting from an **Externalizable** object, you'll typically call the base-class versions of **writeExternal( )** and **readExternal( )** to provide proper storage and retrieval of the base-class components.

So to make things work correctly, you must not only write the important data from the object during the **writeExternal( )** method (there is no default behavior that writes any of the member objects for an **Externalizable** object), but you must also recover that data in the **readExternal( )** method. This can be a bit confusing at first because the default construction behavior for an **Externalizable** object can make it seem like some kind of storage and retrieval takes place automatically. It does not.

Exercise 28: (2) In **Blips.java**, copy the file and rename it to **BlipCheck.java** and rename the class **Blip2** to **BlipCheck** (making it **public** and removing the public scope from the class **Blips** in the process). Remove the //! marks in the file and execute the program, including the offending lines. Next, comment out the default constructor for **BlipCheck**. Run it and explain why it works. Note that after compiling, you must execute the program with "**java Blips**" because the **main( )** method is still in the class **Blips**.

Exercise 29: (2) In **Blip3.java**, comment out the two lines after the phrases "You must do this:" and run the program. Explain the result and why it differs from when the two lines are in the program.

The **transient** keyword

When you're controlling serialization, there might be a particular subobject that you don't want Java's serialization mechanism to automatically save and restore. This is commonly the case if that subobject represents sensitive information that you don't want to serialize, such as a password. Even if that information is **private** in the object, once it has been serialized, it's possible for someone to access it by reading a file or intercepting a network transmission.

One way to prevent sensitive parts of your object from being serialized is to implement your class as **Externalizable**, as shown previously. Then nothing is automatically serialized, and you can explicitly serialize only the necessary parts inside **writeExternal( )**.

If you're working with a **Serializable** object, however, all serialization happens automatically. To control this, you can turn off serialization on a field-by-field basis using the **transient** keyword, which says, "Don't bother saving or restoring this—I'll take care of it."

For example, consider a **Logon** object that keeps information about a particular login session. Suppose that, once you verify the login, you want to store the data, but without the password. The easiest way to do this is by implementing **Serializable** and marking the **password** field as **transient**. Here's what it looks like:

```java
//: io/Logon.java
// Demonstrates the "transient" keyword.
import java.util.concurrent.*;
import java.io.*;
import java.util.*;
import static net.mindview.util.Print.*;

public class Logon implements Serializable {
  private Date date = new Date();
  private String username;
  private transient String password;
  public Logon(String name, String pwd) {
    username = name;
    password = pwd;
  }
  public String toString() {
    return "logon info: \n   username: " + username +
      "\n   date: " + date + "\n   password: " + password;
  }
  public static void main(String[] args) throws Exception {
    Logon a = new Logon("Hulk", "myLittlePony");
    print("logon a = " + a);
    ObjectOutputStream o = new ObjectOutputStream(
      new FileOutputStream("Logon.out"));
    o.writeObject(a);
    o.close();
    TimeUnit.SECONDS.sleep(1); // Delay
    // Now get them back:
    ObjectInputStream in = new ObjectInputStream(
      new FileInputStream("Logon.out"));
    print("Recovering object at " + new Date());
    a = (Logon)in.readObject();
    print("logon a = " + a);
```

```
    }
} /* Output: (Sample)
logon a = logon info:
   username: Hulk
   date: Sat Nov 19 15:03:26 MST 2005
   password: myLittlePony
Recovering object at Sat Nov 19 15:03:28 MST 2005
logon a = logon info:
   username: Hulk
   date: Sat Nov 19 15:03:26 MST 2005
   password: null
*///:~
```

You can see that the **date** and **username** fields are ordinary (not **transient**), and thus are automatically serialized. However, the **password** is **transient**, so it is not stored to disk; also, the serialization mechanism makes no attempt to recover it. When the object is recovered, the **password** field is **null**. Note that while **toString( )** assembles a **String** object using the overloaded '+' operator, a **null** reference is automatically converted to the string "null."

You can also see that the **date** field is stored to and recovered from disk and not generated anew.

Since **Externalizable** objects do not store any of their fields by default, the **transient** keyword is for use with **Serializable** objects only.

An alternative to **Externalizable**

If you're not keen on implementing the **Externalizable** interface, there's another approach. You can implement the **Serializable** interface and *add* (notice I say "add" and not "override" or "implement") methods called **writeObject( )** and **readObject( )** that will automatically be called when the object is serialized and deserialized, respectively. That is, if you provide these two methods, they will be used instead of the default serialization.

The methods must have these exact signatures:

```
private void writeObject(ObjectOutputStream stream)
throws IOException;

private void readObject(ObjectInputStream stream)
throws IOException, ClassNotFoundException
```

From a design standpoint, things get really weird here. First of all, you might think that because these methods are not part of a base class or the **Serializable** interface, they ought to be defined in their own interface(s). But notice that they are defined as **private**, which means they are to be called only by other members of this class. However, you don't actually call them from other members of this class, but instead the **writeObject( )** and **readObject( )** methods of the **ObjectOutputStream** and **ObjectInputStream** objects call your object's **writeObject( )** and **readObject( )** methods. (Notice my tremendous restraint in not launching into a long diatribe about using the same method names here. In a word: confusing.) You might wonder how the **ObjectOutputStream** and **ObjectInputStream** objects have access to **private** methods of your class. We can only assume that this is part of the serialization magic.[6]

Anything defined in an interface is automatically **public**, so if **writeObject( )** and **readObject( )** must be **private**, then they can't be part of an interface. Since you must follow the signatures exactly, the effect is the same as if you're implementing an interface.

It would appear that when you call **ObjectOutputStream.writeObject( )**, the **Serializable** object that you pass it to is interrogated (using reflection, no doubt) to see if it implements its own **writeObject( )**. If so, the normal serialization process is skipped and the custom **writeObject( )** is called. The same situation exists for **readObject( )**.

There's one other twist. Inside your **writeObject( )**, you can choose to perform the default **writeObject( )** action by calling **defaultWriteObject( )**. Likewise, inside **readObject( )** you can call **defaultReadObject( )**. Here is a simple example that demonstrates how you can control the storage and retrieval of a **Serializable** object:

```
//: io/SerialCtl.java
// Controlling serialization by adding your own
// writeObject() and readObject() methods.
import java.io.*;

public class SerialCtl implements Serializable {
  private String a;
```

---

[6] The section "Interfaces and type information" at the end of the *Type Information* chapter shows how it's possible to access **private** methods from outside of the class.

```java
  private transient String b;
  public SerialCtl(String aa, String bb) {
    a = "Not Transient: " + aa;
    b = "Transient: " + bb;
  }
  public String toString() { return a + "\n" + b; }
  private void writeObject(ObjectOutputStream stream)
  throws IOException {
    stream.defaultWriteObject();
    stream.writeObject(b);
  }
  private void readObject(ObjectInputStream stream)
  throws IOException, ClassNotFoundException {
    stream.defaultReadObject();
    b = (String)stream.readObject();
  }
  public static void main(String[] args)
  throws IOException, ClassNotFoundException {
    SerialCtl sc = new SerialCtl("Test1", "Test2");
    System.out.println("Before:\n" + sc);
    ByteArrayOutputStream buf= new ByteArrayOutputStream();
    ObjectOutputStream o = new ObjectOutputStream(buf);
    o.writeObject(sc);
    // Now get it back:
    ObjectInputStream in = new ObjectInputStream(
      new ByteArrayInputStream(buf.toByteArray()));
    SerialCtl sc2 = (SerialCtl)in.readObject();
    System.out.println("After:\n" + sc2);
  }
} /* Output:
Before:
Not Transient: Test1
Transient: Test2
After:
Not Transient: Test1
Transient: Test2
*///:~
```

In this example, one **String** field is ordinary and the other is **transient**, to prove that the non-**transient** field is saved by the **defaultWriteObject( )** method and the **transient** field is saved and restored explicitly. The fields are initialized inside the constructor rather than at the point of definition to prove that they are not being initialized by some automatic mechanism during deserialization.

If you use the default mechanism to write the non-**transient** parts of your object, you must call **defaultWriteObject( )** as the first operation in **writeObject( )**, and **defaultReadObject( )** as the first operation in **readObject( )**. These are strange method calls. It would appear, for example, that you are calling **defaultWriteObject( )** for an **ObjectOutputStream** and passing it no arguments, and yet it somehow turns around and knows the reference to your object and how to write all the non-**transient** parts. Spooky.

The storage and retrieval of the **transient** objects uses more familiar code. And yet, think about what happens here. In **main( )**, a **SerialCtl** object is created, and then it's serialized to an **ObjectOutputStream.** (Notice in this case that a buffer is used instead of a file—it's all the same to the **ObjectOutputStream.**) The serialization occurs in the line:

```
o.writeObject(sc);
```

The **writeObject( )** method must be examining **sc** to see if it has its own **writeObject( )** method. (Not by checking the interface—there isn't one—or the class type, but by actually hunting for the method using reflection.) If it does, it uses that. A similar approach holds true for **readObject( )**. Perhaps this was the only practical way that they could solve the problem, but it's certainly strange.

Versioning

It's possible that you might want to change the version of a serializable class (objects of the original class might be stored in a database, for example). This is supported, but you'll probably do it only in special cases, and it requires an extra depth of understanding that we will not attempt to achieve here. The JDK documents downloadable from *http://java.sun.com* cover this topic quite thoroughly.

You will also notice in the JDK documentation many comments that begin with:

> **Warning:** *Serialized objects of this class will not be compatible with future Swing releases. The current serialization support is appropriate for short term storage or RMI between applications ...*

This is because the versioning mechanism is too simple to work reliably in all situations, especially with JavaBeans. They're working on a correction for the design, and that's what the warning is about.

Using persistence

It's quite appealing to use serialization technology to store some of the state of your program so that you can easily restore the program to the current state later. But before you can do this, some questions must be answered. What happens if you serialize two objects that both have a reference to a third object? When you restore those two objects from their serialized state, do you get only one occurrence of the third object? What if you serialize your two objects to separate files and deserialize them in different parts of your code?

Here's an example that shows the problem:

```
//: io/MyWorld.java
import java.io.*;
import java.util.*;
import static net.mindview.util.Print.*;

class House implements Serializable {}

class Animal implements Serializable {
  private String name;
  private House preferredHouse;
  Animal(String nm, House h) {
    name = nm;
    preferredHouse = h;
  }
  public String toString() {
    return name + "[" + super.toString() +
      "], " + preferredHouse + "\n";
  }
}

public class MyWorld {
  public static void main(String[] args)
  throws IOException, ClassNotFoundException {
    House house = new House();
    List<Animal> animals = new ArrayList<Animal>();
    animals.add(new Animal("Bosco the dog", house));
    animals.add(new Animal("Ralph the hamster", house));
    animals.add(new Animal("Molly the cat", house));
    print("animals: " + animals);
    ByteArrayOutputStream buf1 =
      new ByteArrayOutputStream();
    ObjectOutputStream o1 = new ObjectOutputStream(buf1);
```

```
      o1.writeObject(animals);
      o1.writeObject(animals); // Write a 2nd set
      // Write to a different stream:
      ByteArrayOutputStream buf2 =
        new ByteArrayOutputStream();
      ObjectOutputStream o2 = new ObjectOutputStream(buf2);
      o2.writeObject(animals);
      // Now get them back:
      ObjectInputStream in1 = new ObjectInputStream(
        new ByteArrayInputStream(buf1.toByteArray()));
      ObjectInputStream in2 = new ObjectInputStream(
        new ByteArrayInputStream(buf2.toByteArray()));
      List
        animals1 = (List)in1.readObject(),
        animals2 = (List)in1.readObject(),
        animals3 = (List)in2.readObject();
      print("animals1: " + animals1);
      print("animals2: " + animals2);
      print("animals3: " + animals3);
    }
} /* Output: (Sample)
animals: [Bosco the dog[Animal@addbf1], House@42e816
, Ralph the hamster[Animal@9304b1], House@42e816
, Molly the cat[Animal@190d11], House@42e816
]
animals1: [Bosco the dog[Animal@de6f34], House@156ee8e
, Ralph the hamster[Animal@47b480], House@156ee8e
, Molly the cat[Animal@19b49e6], House@156ee8e
]
animals2: [Bosco the dog[Animal@de6f34], House@156ee8e
, Ralph the hamster[Animal@47b480], House@156ee8e
, Molly the cat[Animal@19b49e6], House@156ee8e
]
animals3: [Bosco the dog[Animal@10d448], House@e0e1c6
, Ralph the hamster[Animal@6ca1c], House@e0e1c6
, Molly the cat[Animal@1bf216a], House@e0e1c6
]
*///:~
```

One thing that's interesting here is that it's possible to use object serialization to and from a **byte** array as a way of doing a "deep copy" of any object that's **Serializable.** (A deep copy means that you're duplicating the entire web of objects, rather than just the basic object and its references.) Object copying is covered in depth in the online supplements for this book.

Animal objects contain fields of type **House**. In **main( )**, a **List** of these **Animal**s is created and it is serialized twice to one stream and then again to a separate stream. When these are deserialized and printed, you see the output shown for one run (the objects will be in different memory locations each run).

Of course, you expect that the deserialized objects have different addresses from their originals. But notice that in **animals1** and **animals2**, the same addresses appear, including the references to the **House** object that both share. On the other hand, when **animals3** is recovered, the system has no way of knowing that the objects in this other stream are aliases of the objects in the first stream, so it makes a completely different web of objects.

As long as you're serializing everything to a single stream, you'll recover the same web of objects that you wrote, with no accidental duplication of objects. Of course, you can change the state of your objects in between the time you write the first and the last, but that's your responsibility; the objects will be written in whatever state they are in (and with whatever connections they have to other objects) at the time you serialize them.

The safest thing to do if you want to save the state of a system is to serialize as an "atomic" operation. If you serialize some things, do some other work, and serialize some more, etc., then you will not be storing the system safely. Instead, put all the objects that comprise the state of your system in a single container and simply write that container out in one operation. Then you can restore it with a single method call as well.

The following example is an imaginary computer-aided design (CAD) system that demonstrates the approach. In addition, it throws in the issue of **static** fields; if you look at the JDK documentation, you'll see that **Class** is **Serializable**, so it should be easy to store the **static** fields by simply serializing the **Class** object. That seems like a sensible approach, anyway.

```
//: io/StoreCADState.java
// Saving the state of a pretend CAD system.
import java.io.*;
import java.util.*;

abstract class Shape implements Serializable {
  public static final int RED = 1, BLUE = 2, GREEN = 3;
  private int xPos, yPos, dimension;
  private static Random rand = new Random(47);
```

```java
    private static int counter = 0;
    public abstract void setColor(int newColor);
    public abstract int getColor();
    public Shape(int xVal, int yVal, int dim) {
      xPos = xVal;
      yPos = yVal;
      dimension = dim;
    }
    public String toString() {
      return getClass() +
        "color[" + getColor() + "] xPos[" + xPos +
        "] yPos[" + yPos + "] dim[" + dimension + "]\n";
    }
    public static Shape randomFactory() {
      int xVal = rand.nextInt(100);
      int yVal = rand.nextInt(100);
      int dim = rand.nextInt(100);
      switch(counter++ % 3) {
        default:
        case 0: return new Circle(xVal, yVal, dim);
        case 1: return new Square(xVal, yVal, dim);
        case 2: return new Line(xVal, yVal, dim);
      }
    }
}

class Circle extends Shape {
  private static int color = RED;
  public Circle(int xVal, int yVal, int dim) {
    super(xVal, yVal, dim);
  }
  public void setColor(int newColor) { color = newColor; }
  public int getColor() { return color; }
}

class Square extends Shape {
  private static int color;
  public Square(int xVal, int yVal, int dim) {
    super(xVal, yVal, dim);
    color = RED;
  }
  public void setColor(int newColor) { color = newColor; }
  public int getColor() { return color; }
}
```

```
class Line extends Shape {
  private static int color = RED;
  public static void
  serializeStaticState(ObjectOutputStream os)
  throws IOException { os.writeInt(color); }
  public static void
  deserializeStaticState(ObjectInputStream os)
  throws IOException { color = os.readInt(); }
  public Line(int xVal, int yVal, int dim) {
    super(xVal, yVal, dim);
  }
  public void setColor(int newColor) { color = newColor; }
  public int getColor() { return color; }
}

public class StoreCADState {
  public static void main(String[] args) throws Exception {
    List<Class<? extends Shape>> shapeTypes =
      new ArrayList<Class<? extends Shape>>();
    // Add references to the class objects:
    shapeTypes.add(Circle.class);
    shapeTypes.add(Square.class);
    shapeTypes.add(Line.class);
    List<Shape> shapes = new ArrayList<Shape>();
    // Make some shapes:
    for(int i = 0; i < 10; i++)
      shapes.add(Shape.randomFactory());
    // Set all the static colors to GREEN:
    for(int i = 0; i < 10; i++)
      ((Shape)shapes.get(i)).setColor(Shape.GREEN);
    // Save the state vector:
    ObjectOutputStream out = new ObjectOutputStream(
      new FileOutputStream("CADState.out"));
    out.writeObject(shapeTypes);
    Line.serializeStaticState(out);
    out.writeObject(shapes);
    // Display the shapes:
    System.out.println(shapes);
  }
} /* Output:
[class Circlecolor[3] xPos[58] yPos[55] dim[93]
, class Squarecolor[3] xPos[61] yPos[61] dim[29]
, class Linecolor[3] xPos[68] yPos[0] dim[22]
```

```
,  class Circlecolor[3]  xPos[7]  yPos[88]  dim[28]
,  class Squarecolor[3]  xPos[51]  yPos[89]  dim[9]
,  class Linecolor[3]  xPos[78]  yPos[98]  dim[61]
,  class Circlecolor[3]  xPos[20]  yPos[58]  dim[16]
,  class Squarecolor[3]  xPos[40]  yPos[11]  dim[22]
,  class Linecolor[3]  xPos[4]  yPos[83]  dim[6]
,  class Circlecolor[3]  xPos[75]  yPos[10]  dim[42]
]
*///:~
```

The **Shape** class **implements Serializable**, so anything that is inherited from **Shape** is automatically **Serializable** as well. Each **Shape** contains data, and each derived **Shape** class contains a **static** field that determines the color of all of those types of **Shape**s. (Placing a **static** field in the base class would result in only one field, since **static** fields are not duplicated in derived classes.) Methods in the base class can be overridden to set the color for the various types (**static** methods are not dynamically bound, so these are normal methods). The **randomFactory( )** method creates a different **Shape** each time you call it, using random values for the **Shape** data.

Circle and **Square** are straightforward extensions of **Shape**; the only difference is that **Circle** initializes **color** at the point of definition and **Square** initializes it in the constructor. We'll leave the discussion of **Line** for later.

In **main( )**, one **ArrayList** is used to hold the **Class** objects and the other to hold the shapes.

Recovering the objects is fairly straightforward:

```
//: io/RecoverCADState.java
// Restoring the state of the pretend CAD system.
// {RunFirst: StoreCADState}
import java.io.*;
import java.util.*;

public class RecoverCADState {
  @SuppressWarnings("unchecked")
  public static void main(String[] args) throws Exception {
    ObjectInputStream in = new ObjectInputStream(
      new FileInputStream("CADState.out"));
    // Read in the same order they were written:
    List<Class<? extends Shape>> shapeTypes =
      (List<Class<? extends Shape>>)in.readObject();
```

```
        Line.deserializeStaticState(in);
        List<Shape> shapes = (List<Shape>)in.readObject();
        System.out.println(shapes);
    }
} /* Output:
[class Circlecolor[1] xPos[58] yPos[55] dim[93]
, class Squarecolor[0] xPos[61] yPos[61] dim[29]
, class Linecolor[3] xPos[68] yPos[0] dim[22]
, class Circlecolor[1] xPos[7] yPos[88] dim[28]
, class Squarecolor[0] xPos[51] yPos[89] dim[9]
, class Linecolor[3] xPos[78] yPos[98] dim[61]
, class Circlecolor[1] xPos[20] yPos[58] dim[16]
, class Squarecolor[0] xPos[40] yPos[11] dim[22]
, class Linecolor[3] xPos[4] yPos[83] dim[6]
, class Circlecolor[1] xPos[75] yPos[10] dim[42]
]
*///:~
```

You can see that the values of **xPos**, **yPos**, and **dim** were all stored and recovered successfully, but there's something wrong with the retrieval of the **static** information. It's all "3" going in, but it doesn't come out that way. **Circle**s have a value of 1 (**RED**, which is the definition), and **Square**s have a value of 0 (remember, they are initialized in the constructor). It's as if the **static**s didn't get serialized at all! That's right—even though class **Class** is **Serializable**, it doesn't do what you expect. So if you want to serialize **static**s, you must do it yourself.

This is what the **serializeStaticState( )** and **deserializeStaticState( )** **static** methods in **Line** are for. You can see that they are explicitly called as part of the storage and retrieval process. (Note that the order of writing to the serialize file and reading back from it must be maintained.) Thus to make these programs run correctly, you must:

1. Add a **serializeStaticState( )** and **deserializeStaticState( )** to the shapes.

2. Remove the **ArrayList shapeTypes** and all code related to it.

3. Add calls to the new serialize and deserialize **static** methods in the shapes.

Another issue you might have to think about is security, since serialization also saves **private** data. If you have a security issue, those fields should be marked as **transient**. But then you have to design a secure way to store that information so that when you do a restore, you can reset those **private** variables.

Exercise 30: (1) Repair the program **CADState.java** as described in the text.

XML

An important limitation of object serialization is that it is a Java-only solution: Only Java programs can deserialize such objects. A more interoperable solution is to convert data to XML format, which allows it to be consumed by a large variety of platforms and languages.

Because of its popularity, there are a confusing number of options for programming with XML, including the **javax.xml.** * libraries distributed with the JDK. I've chosen to use Elliotte Rusty Harold's open-source XOM library (downloads and documentation at *www.xom.nu*) because it seems to be the simplest and most straightforward way to produce and modify XML using Java. In addition, XOM emphasizes XML correctness.

As an example, suppose you have **Person** objects containing first and last names that you'd like to serialize into XML. The following **Person** class has a **getXML( )** method that uses XOM to produce the **Person** data converted to an XML **Element** object, and a constructor that takes an **Element** and extracts the appropriate **Person** data (notice that the XML examples are in their own subdirectory):

```
//: xml/Person.java
// Use the XOM library to write and read XML
// {Requires: nu.xom.Node; You must install
// the XOM library from http://www.xom.nu }
import nu.xom.*;
import java.io.*;
import java.util.*;

public class Person {
  private String first, last;
  public Person(String first, String last) {
    this.first = first;
    this.last = last;
  }
  // Produce an XML Element from this Person object:
```

```java
    public Element getXML() {
        Element person = new Element("person");
        Element firstName = new Element("first");
        firstName.appendChild(first);
        Element lastName = new Element("last");
        lastName.appendChild(last);
        person.appendChild(firstName);
        person.appendChild(lastName);
        return person;
    }
    // Constructor to restore a Person from an XML Element:
    public Person(Element person) {
        first= person.getFirstChildElement("first").getValue();
        last = person.getFirstChildElement("last").getValue();
    }
    public String toString() { return first + " " + last; }
    // Make it human-readable:
    public static void
    format(OutputStream os, Document doc) throws Exception {
        Serializer serializer= new Serializer(os,"ISO-8859-1");
        serializer.setIndent(4);
        serializer.setMaxLength(60);
        serializer.write(doc);
        serializer.flush();
    }
    public static void main(String[] args) throws Exception {
        List<Person> people = Arrays.asList(
            new Person("Dr. Bunsen", "Honeydew"),
            new Person("Gonzo", "The Great"),
            new Person("Phillip J.", "Fry"));
        System.out.println(people);
        Element root = new Element("people");
        for(Person p : people)
            root.appendChild(p.getXML());
        Document doc = new Document(root);
        format(System.out, doc);
        format(new BufferedOutputStream(new FileOutputStream(
            "People.xml")), doc);
    }
} /* Output:
[Dr. Bunsen Honeydew, Gonzo The Great, Phillip J. Fry]
<?xml version="1.0" encoding="ISO-8859-1"?>
<people>
    <person>
```

```
        <first>Dr. Bunsen</first>
        <last>Honeydew</last>
    </person>
    <person>
        <first>Gonzo</first>
        <last>The Great</last>
    </person>
    <person>
        <first>Phillip J.</first>
        <last>Fry</last>
    </person>
</people>
*///:~
```

The XOM methods are fairly self-explanatory and can be found in the XOM documentation.

XOM also contains a **Serializer** class that you can see used in the **format( )** method to turn the XML into a more readable form. If you just call **toXML( )** you'll get everything run together, so the **Serializer** is a convenient tool.

Deserializing **Person** objects from an XML file is also simple:

```
//: xml/People.java
// {Requires: nu.xom.Node; You must install
// the XOM library from http://www.xom.nu }
// {RunFirst: Person}
import nu.xom.*;
import java.util.*;

public class People extends ArrayList<Person> {
  public People(String fileName) throws Exception  {
    Document doc = new Builder().build(fileName);
    Elements elements =
      doc.getRootElement().getChildElements();
    for(int i = 0; i < elements.size(); i++)
      add(new Person(elements.get(i)));
  }
  public static void main(String[] args) throws Exception {
    People p = new People("People.xml");
    System.out.println(p);
  }
} /* Output:
[Dr. Bunsen Honeydew, Gonzo The Great, Phillip J. Fry]
*///:~
```

The **People** constructor opens and reads a file using XOM's
Builder.build( ) method, and the **getChildElements( )** method produces
an **Elements** list (not a standard Java **List**, but an object that only has a
size( ) and **get( )** method—Harold did not want to force people to use Java
SE5, but still wanted a type-safe container). Each **Element** in this list
represents a **Person** object, so it is handed to the second **Person**
constructor. Note that this requires that you know ahead of time the exact
structure of your XML file, but this is often true with these kinds of problems.
If the structure doesn't match what you expect, XOM will throw an exception.
It's also possible for you to write more complex code that will explore the
XML document rather than making assumptions about it, for cases when you
have less concrete information about the incoming XML structure.

In order to get these examples to compile, you will have to put the JAR files
from the XOM distribution into your classpath.

This has only been a brief introduction to XML programming with Java and
the XOM library; for more information see *www.xom.nu.*

Exercise 31:   (2) Add appropriate address information to **Person.java**
and **People.java**.

Exercise 32:   (4) Using a **Map<String,Integer>** and the
net.mindview.util.TextFile utility, write a program that counts the
occurrence of words in a file (use **"\\W+"** as the second argument to the
TextFile constructor). Store the results as an XML file.

Preferences

The *Preferences* API is much closer to persistence than it is to object
serialization, because it automatically stores and retrieves your information.
However, its use is restricted to small and limited data sets—you can only
hold primitives and **Strings**, and the length of each stored **String** can't be
longer than 8K (not tiny, but you don't want to build anything serious with it,
either). As the name suggests, the Preferences API is designed to store and
retrieve user preferences and program-configuration settings.

Preferences are key-value sets (like **Map**s) stored in a hierarchy of nodes.
Although the node hierarchy can be used to create complicated structures, it's
typical to create a single node named after your class and store the
information there. Here's a simple example:

```
//: io/PreferencesDemo.java
import java.util.prefs.*;
import static net.mindview.util.Print.*;

public class PreferencesDemo {
  public static void main(String[] args) throws Exception {
    Preferences prefs = Preferences
      .userNodeForPackage(PreferencesDemo.class);
    prefs.put("Location", "Oz");
    prefs.put("Footwear", "Ruby Slippers");
    prefs.putInt("Companions", 4);
    prefs.putBoolean("Are there witches?", true);
    int usageCount = prefs.getInt("UsageCount", 0);
    usageCount++;
    prefs.putInt("UsageCount", usageCount);
    for(String key : prefs.keys())
      print(key + ": "+ prefs.get(key, null));
    // You must always provide a default value:
    print("How many companions does Dorothy have? " +
      prefs.getInt("Companions", 0));
  }
} /* Output: (Sample)
Location: Oz
Footwear: Ruby Slippers
Companions: 4
Are there witches?: true
UsageCount: 53
How many companions does Dorothy have? 4
*///:~
```

Here, **userNodeForPackage( )** is used, but you could also choose
systemNodeForPackage( ); the choice is somewhat arbitrary, but the idea
is that "user" is for individual user preferences, and "system" is for general
installation configuration. Since **main( )** is **static**,
PreferencesDemo.class is used to identify the node, but inside a non-
static method, you'll usually use **getClass( )**. You don't need to use the
current class as the node identifier, but that's the usual practice.

Once you create the node, it's available for either loading or reading data.
This example loads the node with various types of items and then gets the
keys( ). These come back as a **String[]**, which you might not expect if you're
used to the **keys( )** method in the collections library. Notice the second
argument to **get( )**. This is the default value that is produced if there isn't any

entry for that key value. While iterating through a set of keys, you always know there's an entry, so using **null** as the default is safe, but normally you'll be fetching a named key, as in:

```
prefs.getInt("Companions", 0));
```

In the normal case, you'll want to provide a reasonable default value. In fact, a typical idiom is seen in the lines:

```
int usageCount = prefs.getInt("UsageCount", 0);
usageCount++;
prefs.putInt("UsageCount", usageCount);
```

This way, the first time you run the program, the **UsageCount** will be zero, but on subsequent invocations it will be nonzero.

When you run **PreferencesDemo.java** you'll see that the **UsageCount** does indeed increment every time you run the program, but where is the data stored? There's no local file that appears after the program is run the first time. The Preferences API uses appropriate system resources to accomplish its task, and these will vary depending on the OS. In Windows, the registry is used (since it's already a hierarchy of nodes with key-value pairs). But the whole point is that the information is magically stored for you so that you don't have to worry about how it works from one system to another.

There's more to the Preferences API than shown here. Consult the JDK documentation, which is fairly understandable, for further details.

Exercise 33: (2) Write a program that displays the current value of a directory called "base directory" and prompts you for a new value. Use the Preferences API to store the value.

Summary

The Java I/O stream library does satisfy the basic requirements: You can perform reading and writing with the console, a file, a block of memory, or even across the Internet. With inheritance, you can create new types of input and output objects. And you can even add a simple extensibility to the kinds of objects a stream will accept by redefining the **toString( )** method that's automatically called when you pass an object to a method that's expecting a **String** (Java's limited "automatic type conversion").

There are questions left unanswered by the documentation and design of the I/O stream library. For example, it would have been nice if you could say that you want an exception thrown if you try to overwrite a file when opening it for output—some programming systems allow you to specify that you want to open an output file, but only if it doesn't already exist. In Java, it appears that you are supposed to use a **File** object to determine whether a file exists, because if you open it as a **FileOutputStream** or **FileWriter**, it will always get overwritten.

The I/O stream library brings up mixed feelings; it does much of the job and it's portable. But if you don't already understand the Decorator design pattern, the design is not intuitive, so there's extra overhead in learning and teaching it. It's also incomplete; for example, I shouldn't have to write utilities like **TextFile** (the new Java SE5 **PrintWriter** is a step in the right direction here, but is only a partial solution). There has been a big improvement in Java SE5: They've finally added the kind of output formatting that virtually every other language has always supported.

Once you *do* understand the Decorator pattern and begin using the library in situations that require its flexibility, you can begin to benefit from this design, at which point its cost in extra lines of code may not bother you as much.

Solutions to selected exercises can be found in the electronic document *The Thinking in Java Annotated Solution Guide*, available for sale from *www.MindView.net*.

Enumerated Types

The **enum** keyword allows you to create a new type with a restricted set of named values, and to treat those values as regular program components. This turns out to be very useful. [1]

Enumerations were introduced briefly at the end of *Initialization & Cleanup*. However, now that you understand some of the deeper issues in Java, we can take a more detailed look at the Java SE5 enumeration feature. You'll see that there are some very interesting things that you can do with **enum**s, but this chapter should also give you more insight into other language features that you've now seen, such as generics and reflection. You'll also learn a few more design patterns.

Basic **enum** features

As shown in *Initialization & Cleanup*, you can step through the list of **enum** constants by calling **values( )** on the **enum**. The **values( )** method produces an array of the **enum** constants in the order in which they were declared, so you can use the resulting array in (for example) a foreach loop.

When you create an **enum**, an associated class is produced for you by the compiler. This class is automatically inherited from **java.lang.Enum**, which provides certain capabilities that you can see in this example:

```
//: enumerated/EnumClass.java
// Capabilities of the Enum class
import static net.mindview.util.Print.*;

enum Shrubbery { GROUND, CRAWLING, HANGING }

public class EnumClass {
  public static void main(String[] args) {
    for(Shrubbery s : Shrubbery.values()) {
```

---

[1] Joshua Bloch was extremely helpful in developing this chapter.

```
      print(s + " ordinal: " + s.ordinal());
      printnb(s.compareTo(Shrubbery.CRAWLING) + " ");
      printnb(s.equals(Shrubbery.CRAWLING) + " ");
      print(s == Shrubbery.CRAWLING);
      print(s.getDeclaringClass());
      print(s.name());
      print("----------------------");
    }
    // Produce an enum value from a string name:
    for(String s : "HANGING CRAWLING GROUND".split(" ")) {
      Shrubbery shrub = Enum.valueOf(Shrubbery.class, s);
      print(shrub);
    }
  }
} /* Output:
GROUND ordinal: 0
-1 false false
class Shrubbery
GROUND
----------------------
CRAWLING ordinal: 1
0 true true
class Shrubbery
CRAWLING
----------------------
HANGING ordinal: 2
1 false false
class Shrubbery
HANGING
----------------------
HANGING
CRAWLING
GROUND
*///:~
```

The **ordinal( )** method produces an **int** indicating the declaration order of each **enum** instance, starting from zero. You can always safely compare **enum** instances using ==, and **equals( )** and **hashCode( )** are automatically created for you. The **Enum** class is **Comparable**, so there's a **compareTo( )** method, and it is also **Serializable**.

If you call **getDeclaringClass( )** on an **enum** instance, you'll find out the enclosing **enum** class.

The **name( )** method produces the name exactly as it is declared, and this is what you get with **toString( )**, as well. **valueOf( )** is a **static** member of **Enum**, and produces the **enum** instance that corresponds to the **String** name you pass to it, or throws an exception if there's no match.

Using **static** imports with **enum**s

Consider a variation of **Burrito.java** from the *Initialization & Cleanup* chapter:

```
//: enumerated/Spiciness.java
package enumerated;

public enum Spiciness {
  NOT, MILD, MEDIUM, HOT, FLAMING
} ///:~
```

```
//: enumerated/Burrito.java
package enumerated;
import static enumerated.Spiciness.*;

public class Burrito {
  Spiciness degree;
  public Burrito(Spiciness degree) { this.degree = degree;}
  public String toString() { return "Burrito is "+ degree;}
  public static void main(String[] args) {
    System.out.println(new Burrito(NOT));
    System.out.println(new Burrito(MEDIUM));
    System.out.println(new Burrito(HOT));
  }
} /* Output:
Burrito is NOT
Burrito is MEDIUM
Burrito is HOT
*///:~
```

The **static import** brings all the **enum** instance identifiers into the local namespace, so they don't need to be qualified. Is this a good idea, or is it better to be explicit and qualify all **enum** instances? It probably depends on the complexity of your code. The compiler certainly won't let you use the wrong type, so your only concern is whether the code will be confusing to the reader. In many situations it will probably be fine but you should evaluate it on an individual basis.

Note that it is not possible to use this technique if the **enum** is defined in the same file or the default package (apparently there were some arguments within Sun about whether to allow this).

Adding methods to an **enum**

Except for the fact that you can't inherit from it, an **enum** can be treated much like a regular class. This means that you can add methods to an **enum**. It's even possible for an **enum** to have a **main( )**.

You may want to produce different descriptions for an enumeration than the default **toString( )**, which simply produces the name of that **enum** instance, as you've seen. To do this, you can provide a constructor to capture extra information, and additional methods to provide an extended description, like this:

```java
//: enumerated/OzWitch.java
// The witches in the land of Oz.
import static net.mindview.util.Print.*;

public enum OzWitch {
  // Instances must be defined first, before methods:
  WEST("Miss Gulch, aka the Wicked Witch of the West"),
  NORTH("Glinda, the Good Witch of the North"),
  EAST("Wicked Witch of the East, wearer of the Ruby " +
    "Slippers, crushed by Dorothy's house"),
  SOUTH("Good by inference, but missing");
  private String description;
  // Constructor must be package or private access:
  private OzWitch(String description) {
    this.description = description;
  }
  public String getDescription() { return description; }
  public static void main(String[] args) {
    for(OzWitch witch : OzWitch.values())
      print(witch + ": " + witch.getDescription());
  }
} /* Output:
WEST: Miss Gulch, aka the Wicked Witch of the West
NORTH: Glinda, the Good Witch of the North
EAST: Wicked Witch of the East, wearer of the Ruby
Slippers, crushed by Dorothy's house
SOUTH: Good by inference, but missing
```

```
*///:~
```

Notice that if you are going to define methods you must end the sequence of **enum** instances with a semicolon. Also, Java forces you to define the instances as the first thing in the **enum**. You'll get a compile-time error if you try to define them after any of the methods or fields.

The constructor and methods have the same form as a regular class, because with a few restrictions this *is* a regular class. So you can do pretty much anything you want with **enum**s (although you'll usually keep them pretty ordinary).

Although the constructor has been made **private** here as an example, it doesn't make much difference what access you use—the constructor can only be used to create the **enum** instances that you declare inside the **enum** definition; the compiler won't let you use it to create any new instances once the **enum** definition is complete.

Overriding **enum** methods

Here's another approach to producing different string values for enumerations. In this case, the instance names are OK but we want to reformat them for display. Overriding the **toString( )** method for an **enum** is the same as overriding it for a regular class:

```java
//: enumerated/SpaceShip.java
public enum SpaceShip {
  SCOUT, CARGO, TRANSPORT, CRUISER, BATTLESHIP, MOTHERSHIP;
  public String toString() {
    String id = name();
    String lower = id.substring(1).toLowerCase();
    return id.charAt(0) + lower;
  }
  public static void main(String[] args) {
    for(SpaceShip s : values()) {
      System.out.println(s);
    }
  }
} /* Output:
Scout
Cargo
Transport
Cruiser
Battleship
```

```
Mothership
*///:~
```

The **toString( )** method gets the **SpaceShip** name by calling **name( )**, and modifies the result so that only the first letter is capitalized.

enums in **switch** statements

One very convenient capability of **enum**s is the way that they can be used in **switch** statements. Ordinarily, a **switch** only works with an integral value, but since **enum**s have an established integral order and the order of an instance can be produced with the **ordinal( )** method (apparently the compiler does something like this), **enum**s can be used in **switch** statements.

Although normally you must qualify an **enum** instance with its type, you do not have to do this in a **case** statement. Here's an example that uses an **enum** to create a little state machine:

```
//: enumerated/TrafficLight.java
// Enums in switch statements.
import static net.mindview.util.Print.*;

// Define an enum type:
enum Signal { GREEN, YELLOW, RED, }

public class TrafficLight {
  Signal color = Signal.RED;
  public void change() {
    switch(color) {
      // Note that you don't have to say Signal.RED
      // in the case statement:
      case RED:    color = Signal.GREEN;
                   break;
      case GREEN:  color = Signal.YELLOW;
                   break;
      case YELLOW: color = Signal.RED;
                   break;
    }
  }
  public String toString() {
    return "The traffic light is " + color;
  }
  public static void main(String[] args) {
```

```
      TrafficLight t = new TrafficLight();
      for(int i = 0; i < 7; i++) {
        print(t);
        t.change();
      }
    }
  }
} /* Output:
The traffic light is RED
The traffic light is GREEN
The traffic light is YELLOW
The traffic light is RED
The traffic light is GREEN
The traffic light is YELLOW
The traffic light is RED
*///:~
```

The compiler does not complain that there is no **default** statement inside the **switch**, but that's not because it notices that you have **case** statements for each **Signal** instance. If you comment out one of the **case** statements it still won't complain. This means you will have to pay attention and ensure that you cover all the cases on your own. On the other hand, if you are calling **return** from **case** statements, the compiler *will* complain if you don't have a **default**—even if you've covered all the possible values of the **enum**.

Exercise 1: (2) Use a **static import** to modify **TrafficLight.java** so you don't have to qualify the **enum** instances.

The mystery of **values()**

As noted earlier, all **enum** classes are created for you by the compiler and extend the **Enum** class. However, if you look at **Enum**, you'll see that there is no **values( )** method, even though we've been using it. Are there any other "hidden" methods? We can write a small reflection program to find out:

```
//: enumerated/Reflection.java
// Analyzing enums using reflection.
import java.lang.reflect.*;
import java.util.*;
import net.mindview.util.*;
import static net.mindview.util.Print.*;

enum Explore { HERE, THERE }

public class Reflection {
```

```java
  public static Set<String> analyze(Class<?> enumClass) {
    print("----- Analyzing " + enumClass + " -----");
    print("Interfaces:");
    for(Type t : enumClass.getGenericInterfaces())
      print(t);
    print("Base: " + enumClass.getSuperclass());
    print("Methods: ");
    Set<String> methods = new TreeSet<String>();
    for(Method m : enumClass.getMethods())
      methods.add(m.getName());
    print(methods);
    return methods;
  }
  public static void main(String[] args) {
    Set<String> exploreMethods = analyze(Explore.class);
    Set<String> enumMethods = analyze(Enum.class);
    print("Explore.containsAll(Enum)? " +
      exploreMethods.containsAll(enumMethods));
    printnb("Explore.removeAll(Enum): ");
    exploreMethods.removeAll(enumMethods);
    print(exploreMethods);
    // Decompile the code for the enum:
    OSExecute.command("javap Explore");
  }
} /* Output:
----- Analyzing class Explore -----
Interfaces:
Base: class java.lang.Enum
Methods:
[compareTo, equals, getClass, getDeclaringClass, hashCode,
name, notify, notifyAll, ordinal, toString, valueOf,
values, wait]
----- Analyzing class java.lang.Enum -----
Interfaces:
java.lang.Comparable<E>
interface java.io.Serializable
Base: class java.lang.Object
Methods:
[compareTo, equals, getClass, getDeclaringClass, hashCode,
name, notify, notifyAll, ordinal, toString, valueOf, wait]
Explore.containsAll(Enum)? true
Explore.removeAll(Enum): [values]
Compiled from "Reflection.java"
final class Explore extends java.lang.Enum{
```

```
      public static final Explore HERE;
      public static final Explore THERE;
      public static final Explore[] values();
      public static Explore valueOf(java.lang.String);
      static {};
}
*///:~
```

So the answer is that **values( )** is a **static** method that is added by the
compiler. You can see that **valueOf( )** is also added to **Explore** in the
process of creating the **enum**. This is slightly confusing, because there's also
a **valueOf( )** that is part of the **Enum** class, but that method has two
arguments and the added method only has one. However, the use of the **Set**
method here is only looking at method names, and not signatures, so after
calling **Explore.removeAll(Enum)**, the only thing that remains is
[values].

In the output, you can see that **Explore** has been made **final** by the
compiler, so you cannot inherit from an **enum**. There's also a **static**
initialization clause, which as you'll see later can be redefined.

Because of erasure (described in the *Generics* chapter), the decompiler does
not have full information about **Enum**, so it shows the base class of **Explore**
as a raw **Enum** rather than the actual **Enum<Explore>**.

Because **values( )** is a **static** method inserted into the **enum** definition by
the compiler, if you upcast an **enum** type to **Enum**, the **values( )** method
will not be available. Notice, however, that there is a **getEnumConstants( )**
method in **Class**, so even if **values( )** is not part of the interface of **Enum**,
you can still get the **enum** instances via the **Class** object:

```
//: enumerated/UpcastEnum.java
// No values() method if you upcast an enum

enum Search { HITHER, YON }

public class UpcastEnum {
  public static void main(String[] args) {
    Search[] vals = Search.values();
    Enum e = Search.HITHER; // Upcast
    // e.values(); // No values() in Enum
    for(Enum en : e.getClass().getEnumConstants())
      System.out.println(en);
```

```
    }
} /* Output:
HITHER
YON
*///:~
```

Because **getEnumConstants( )** is a method of **Class**, you can call it for a class that has no enumerations:

```
//: enumerated/NonEnum.java

public class NonEnum {
  public static void main(String[] args) {
    Class<Integer> intClass = Integer.class;
    try {
      for(Object en : intClass.getEnumConstants())
        System.out.println(en);
    } catch(Exception e) {
      System.out.println("Expected: " + e);
    }
  }
} /* Output:
Expected: java.lang.NullPointerException
*///:~
```

However, the method returns **null**, so you get an exception if you try to use the result.

Implements, not inherits

We've established that all **enum**s extend **java.lang.Enum**. Since Java does not support multiple inheritance, this means that you cannot create an **enum** via inheritance:

```
enum NotPossible extends Pet { ... // Won't work
```

However, it *is* possible to create an **enum** that implements one or more interfaces:

```
//: enumerated/cartoons/EnumImplementation.java
// An enum can implement an interface
package enumerated.cartoons;
import java.util.*;
import net.mindview.util.*;
```

```
enum CartoonCharacter
implements Generator<CartoonCharacter> {
  SLAPPY, SPANKY, PUNCHY, SILLY, BOUNCY, NUTTY, BOB;
  private Random rand = new Random(47);
  public CartoonCharacter next() {
    return values()[rand.nextInt(values().length)];
  }
}

public class EnumImplementation {
  public static <T> void printNext(Generator<T> rg) {
    System.out.print(rg.next() + ", ");
  }
  public static void main(String[] args) {
    // Choose any instance:
    CartoonCharacter cc = CartoonCharacter.BOB;
    for(int i = 0; i < 10; i++)
      printNext(cc);
  }
} /* Output:
BOB, PUNCHY, BOB, SPANKY, NUTTY, PUNCHY, SLAPPY, NUTTY,
NUTTY, SLAPPY,
*///:~
```

The result is slightly odd, because to call a method you must have an instance of the **enum** to call it on. However, a **CartoonCharacter** can now be accepted by any method that takes a **Generator**; for example, **printNext( )**.

Exercise 2: (2) Instead of implementing an interface, make **next( )** a **static** method. What are the benefits and drawbacks of this approach?

Random selection

Many of the examples in this chapter require random selection from among **enum** instances, as you saw in **CartoonCharacter.next( )**. It's possible to generalize this task using generics and put the result in the common library:

```
//: net/mindview/util/Enums.java
package net.mindview.util;
import java.util.*;

public class Enums {
  private static Random rand = new Random(47);
  public static <T extends Enum<T>> T random(Class<T> ec) {
```

```
      return random(ec.getEnumConstants());
    }
    public static <T> T random(T[] values) {
      return values[rand.nextInt(values.length)];
    }
} ///:~
```

The rather odd syntax **<T extends Enum<T>>** describes **T** as an **enum** instance. By passing in **Class<T>**, we make the class object available, and the array of **enum** instances can thus be produced. The overloaded **random( )** method only needs to know that it is getting a **T[]** because it doesn't need to perform **Enum** operations; it only needs to select an array element at random. The return type is the exact type of the **enum**.

Here's a simple test of the **random( )** method:

```
//: enumerated/RandomTest.java
import net.mindview.util.*;

enum Activity { SITTING, LYING, STANDING, HOPPING,
  RUNNING, DODGING, JUMPING, FALLING, FLYING }

public class RandomTest {
  public static void main(String[] args) {
    for(int i = 0; i < 20; i++)
      System.out.print(Enums.random(Activity.class) + " ");
  }
} /* Output:
STANDING FLYING RUNNING STANDING RUNNING STANDING LYING
DODGING SITTING RUNNING HOPPING HOPPING HOPPING RUNNING
STANDING LYING FALLING RUNNING FLYING LYING
*///:~
```

Although **Enums** is a small class, you'll see that it prevents a fair amount of duplication in this chapter. Duplication tends to produce mistakes, so eliminating duplication is a useful pursuit.

Using interfaces for organization

The inability to inherit from an **enum** can be a bit frustrating at times. The motivation for inheriting from an **enum** comes partly from wanting to extend the number of elements in the original **enum**, and partly from wanting to create subcategories by using subtypes.

You can achieve categorization by grouping the elements together inside an interface and creating an enumeration based on that interface. For example, suppose you have different classes of food that you'd like to create as **enum**s, but you'd still like each one to be a type of **Food**. Here's what it looks like:

```
//: enumerated/menu/Food.java
// Subcategorization of enums within interfaces.
package enumerated.menu;

public interface Food {
  enum Appetizer implements Food {
    SALAD, SOUP, SPRING_ROLLS;
  }
  enum MainCourse implements Food {
    LASAGNE, BURRITO, PAD_THAI,
    LENTILS, HUMMOUS, VINDALOO;
  }
  enum Dessert implements Food {
    TIRAMISU, GELATO, BLACK_FOREST_CAKE,
    FRUIT, CREME_CARAMEL;
  }
  enum Coffee implements Food {
    BLACK_COFFEE, DECAF_COFFEE, ESPRESSO,
    LATTE, CAPPUCCINO, TEA, HERB_TEA;
  }
} ///:~
```

Since the only subtyping available for an **enum** is that of interface implementation, each nested **enum** implements the surrounding interface **Food**. Now it's possible to say that "everything is a type of **Food**" as you can see here:

```
//: enumerated/menu/TypeOfFood.java
package enumerated.menu;
import static enumerated.menu.Food.*;

public class TypeOfFood {
  public static void main(String[] args) {
    Food food = Appetizer.SALAD;
    food = MainCourse.LASAGNE;
    food = Dessert.GELATO;
    food = Coffee.CAPPUCCINO;
  }
} ///:~
```

The upcast to **Food** works for each **enum** type that **implements Food**, so they are all types of **Food**.

An interface, however, is not as useful as an **enum** when you want to deal with a set of types. If you want to have an "**enum** of **enum**s" you can create a surrounding **enum** with one instance for each **enum** in **Food**:

```
//: enumerated/menu/Course.java
package enumerated.menu;
import net.mindview.util.*;

public enum Course {
  APPETIZER(Food.Appetizer.class),
  MAINCOURSE(Food.MainCourse.class),
  DESSERT(Food.Dessert.class),
  COFFEE(Food.Coffee.class);
  private Food[] values;
  private Course(Class<? extends Food> kind) {
    values = kind.getEnumConstants();
  }
  public Food randomSelection() {
    return Enums.random(values);
  }
} ///:~
```

Each of the above **enum**s takes the corresponding **Class** object as a constructor argument, from which it can extract and store all the **enum** instances using **getEnumConstants( )**. These instances are later used in **randomSelection( )**, so now we can create a randomly generated meal by selecting one **Food** item from each **Course**:

```
//: enumerated/menu/Meal.java
package enumerated.menu;

public class Meal {
  public static void main(String[] args) {
    for(int i = 0; i < 5; i++) {
      for(Course course : Course.values()) {
        Food food = course.randomSelection();
        System.out.println(food);
      }
      System.out.println("---");
    }
  }
```

```
} /* Output:
SPRING_ROLLS
VINDALOO
FRUIT
DECAF_COFFEE
---
SOUP
VINDALOO
FRUIT
TEA
---
SALAD
BURRITO
FRUIT
TEA
---
SALAD
BURRITO
CREME_CARAMEL
LATTE
---
SOUP
BURRITO
TIRAMISU
ESPRESSO
---
*///:~
```

In this case, the value of creating an **enum** of **enum**s is to iterate through each **Course**. Later, in the **VendingMachine.java** example, you'll see another approach to categorization which is dictated by different constraints.

Another, more compact, approach to the problem of categorization is to nest **enum**s within **enum**s, like this:

```
//: enumerated/SecurityCategory.java
// More succinct subcategorization of enums.
import net.mindview.util.*;

enum SecurityCategory {
  STOCK(Security.Stock.class), BOND(Security.Bond.class);
  Security[] values;
  SecurityCategory(Class<? extends Security> kind) {
    values = kind.getEnumConstants();
  }
```

```
interface Security {
  enum Stock implements Security { SHORT, LONG, MARGIN }
  enum Bond implements Security { MUNICIPAL, JUNK }
}
public Security randomSelection() {
  return Enums.random(values);
}
public static void main(String[] args) {
  for(int i = 0; i < 10; i++) {
    SecurityCategory category =
      Enums.random(SecurityCategory.class);
    System.out.println(category + ": " +
      category.randomSelection());
  }
}
} /* Output:
BOND: MUNICIPAL
BOND: MUNICIPAL
STOCK: MARGIN
STOCK: MARGIN
BOND: JUNK
STOCK: SHORT
STOCK: LONG
STOCK: LONG
BOND: MUNICIPAL
BOND: JUNK
*///:~
```

The **Security** interface is necessary to collect the contained **enum**s together as a common type. These are then categorized into the **enum**s within **SecurityCategory**.

If we take this approach with the **Food** example, the result is:

```
//: enumerated/menu/Meal2.java
package enumerated.menu;
import net.mindview.util.*;

public enum Meal2 {
  APPETIZER(Food.Appetizer.class),
  MAINCOURSE(Food.MainCourse.class),
  DESSERT(Food.Dessert.class),
  COFFEE(Food.Coffee.class);
  private Food[] values;
  private Meal2(Class<? extends Food> kind) {
```

```
      values = kind.getEnumConstants();
  }
  public interface Food {
    enum Appetizer implements Food {
      SALAD, SOUP, SPRING_ROLLS;
    }
    enum MainCourse implements Food {
      LASAGNE, BURRITO, PAD_THAI,
      LENTILS, HUMMOUS, VINDALOO;
    }
    enum Dessert implements Food {
      TIRAMISU, GELATO, BLACK_FOREST_CAKE,
      FRUIT, CREME_CARAMEL;
    }
    enum Coffee implements Food {
      BLACK_COFFEE, DECAF_COFFEE, ESPRESSO,
      LATTE, CAPPUCCINO, TEA, HERB_TEA;
    }
  }
  public Food randomSelection() {
    return Enums.random(values);
  }
  public static void main(String[] args) {
    for(int i = 0; i < 5; i++) {
      for(Meal2 meal : Meal2.values()) {
        Food food = meal.randomSelection();
        System.out.println(food);
      }
      System.out.println("---");
    }
  }
} /* Same output as Meal.java *///:~
```

In the end, it's only a reorganization of the code but it may produce a clearer structure in some cases.

Exercise 3: (1) Add a new **Course** to **Course.java** and demonstrate that it works in **Meal.java**.

Exercise 4: (1) Repeat the above exercise for **Meal2.java**.

Exercise 5: (4) Modify **control/VowelsAndConsonants.java** so that it uses three **enum** types: **VOWEL**, **SOMETIMES_A_VOWEL**, and **CONSONANT**. The **enum** constructor should take the various letters that describe that particular category. Hint: Use varargs, and remember that varargs automatically creates an array for you.

Exercise 6: (3) Is there any special benefit in nesting **Appetizer**, **MainCourse**, **Dessert**, and **Coffee** inside **Food** rather than making them standalone **enum**s that just happen to implement **Food**?

Using **EnumSet** instead of flags

A **Set** is a kind of collection that only allows one of each type of object to be added. Of course, an **enum** requires that all its members be unique, so it would seem to have set behavior, but since you can't add or remove elements it's not very useful as a set. The **EnumSet** was added to Java SE5 to work in concert with **enum**s to create a replacement for traditional **int**-based "bit flags." Such flags are used to indicate some kind of on-off information, but you end up manipulating bits rather than concepts, so it's easy to write confusing code.

The **EnumSet** is designed for speed, because it must compete effectively with bit flags (operations will be typically much faster than a **HashSet**). Internally, it is represented by (if possible) a single **long** that is treated as a bit-vector, so it's extremely fast and efficient. The benefit is that you now have a much more expressive way to indicate the presence or absence of a binary feature, without having to worry about performance.

The elements of an **EnumSet** must come from a single **enum**. A possible example uses an **enum** of positions in a building where alarm sensors are present:

```
//: enumerated/AlarmPoints.java
package enumerated;
public enum AlarmPoints {
  STAIR1, STAIR2, LOBBY, OFFICE1, OFFICE2, OFFICE3,
  OFFICE4, BATHROOM, UTILITY, KITCHEN
} ///:~
```

The **EnumSet** can be used to keep track of the alarm status:

```
//: enumerated/EnumSets.java
// Operations on EnumSets
package enumerated;
import java.util.*;
import static enumerated.AlarmPoints.*;
import static net.mindview.util.Print.*;
```

```java
public class EnumSets {
  public static void main(String[] args) {
    EnumSet<AlarmPoints> points =
      EnumSet.noneOf(AlarmPoints.class); // Empty set
    points.add(BATHROOM);
    print(points);
    points.addAll(EnumSet.of(STAIR1, STAIR2, KITCHEN));
    print(points);
    points = EnumSet.allOf(AlarmPoints.class);
    points.removeAll(EnumSet.of(STAIR1, STAIR2, KITCHEN));
    print(points);
    points.removeAll(EnumSet.range(OFFICE1, OFFICE4));
    print(points);
    points = EnumSet.complementOf(points);
    print(points);
  }
} /* Output:
[BATHROOM]
[STAIR1, STAIR2, BATHROOM, KITCHEN]
[LOBBY, OFFICE1, OFFICE2, OFFICE3, OFFICE4, BATHROOM,
UTILITY]
[LOBBY, BATHROOM, UTILITY]
[STAIR1, STAIR2, OFFICE1, OFFICE2, OFFICE3, OFFICE4,
KITCHEN]
*///:~
```

A **static import** is used to simplify the use of the **enum** constants. The method names are fairly self-explanatory, and you can find the full details in the JDK documentation. When you look at this documentation, you'll see something interesting—the **of( )** method has been overloaded both with varargs and with individual methods taking two through five explicit arguments. This is an indication of the concern for performance with **EnumSet**, because a single **of( )** method using varargs could have solved the problem, but it's slightly less efficient than having explicit arguments. Thus, if you call **of( )** with two through five arguments you will get the explicit (slightly faster) method calls, but if you call it with one argument or more than five, you will get the varargs version of **of( )**. Notice that if you call it with one argument, the compiler will not construct the varargs array and so there is no extra overhead for calling that version with a single argument.

EnumSets are built on top of **long**s, a **long** is 64 bits, and each **enum** instance requires one bit to indicate presence or absence. This means you can

---

have an **EnumSet** for an **enum** of up to 64 elements without going beyond the use of a single **long**. What happens if you have more than 64 elements in your **enum**?

```
//: enumerated/BigEnumSet.java
import java.util.*;

public class BigEnumSet {
  enum Big { A0, A1, A2, A3, A4, A5, A6, A7, A8, A9, A10,
    A11, A12, A13, A14, A15, A16, A17, A18, A19, A20, A21,
    A22, A23, A24, A25, A26, A27, A28, A29, A30, A31, A32,
    A33, A34, A35, A36, A37, A38, A39, A40, A41, A42, A43,
    A44, A45, A46, A47, A48, A49, A50, A51, A52, A53, A54,
    A55, A56, A57, A58, A59, A60, A61, A62, A63, A64, A65,
    A66, A67, A68, A69, A70, A71, A72, A73, A74, A75 }
  public static void main(String[] args) {
    EnumSet<Big> bigEnumSet = EnumSet.allOf(Big.class);
    System.out.println(bigEnumSet);
  }
} /* Output:
[A0, A1, A2, A3, A4, A5, A6, A7, A8, A9, A10, A11, A12,
A13, A14, A15, A16, A17, A18, A19, A20, A21, A22, A23, A24,
A25, A26, A27, A28, A29, A30, A31, A32, A33, A34, A35, A36,
A37, A38, A39, A40, A41, A42, A43, A44, A45, A46, A47, A48,
A49, A50, A51, A52, A53, A54, A55, A56, A57, A58, A59, A60,
A61, A62, A63, A64, A65, A66, A67, A68, A69, A70, A71, A72,
A73, A74, A75]
*///:~
```

The **EnumSet** clearly has no problem with an **enum** that has more than 64 elements, so we may presume that it adds another **long** when necessary.

Exercise 7: (3) Find the source code for **EnumSet** and explain how it works.

Using **EnumMap**

An **EnumMap** is a specialized **Map** that requires that its keys be from a single **enum**. Because of the constraints on an **enum**, an **EnumMap** can be implemented internally as an array. Thus they are extremely fast, so you can freely use **EnumMap**s for **enum**-based lookups.

You can only call **put( )** for keys that are in your **enum**, but other than that it's like using an ordinary **Map**.

Here's an example that demonstrates the use of the *Command* design pattern. This pattern starts with an interface containing (typically) a single method, and creates multiple implementations with different behavior for that method. You install Command objects, and your program calls them when necessary:

```
//: enumerated/EnumMaps.java
// Basics of EnumMaps.
package enumerated;
import java.util.*;
import static enumerated.AlarmPoints.*;
import static net.mindview.util.Print.*;

interface Command { void action(); }

public class EnumMaps {
  public static void main(String[] args) {
    EnumMap<AlarmPoints,Command> em =
      new EnumMap<AlarmPoints,Command>(AlarmPoints.class);
    em.put(KITCHEN, new Command() {
      public void action() { print("Kitchen fire!"); }
    });
    em.put(BATHROOM, new Command() {
      public void action() { print("Bathroom alert!"); }
    });
    for(Map.Entry<AlarmPoints,Command> e : em.entrySet()) {
      printnb(e.getKey() + ": ");
      e.getValue().action();
    }
    try { // If there's no value for a particular key:
      em.get(UTILITY).action();
    } catch(Exception e) {
      print("Expected: " + e);
    }
  }
} /* Output:
BATHROOM: Bathroom alert!
KITCHEN: Kitchen fire!
Expected: java.lang.NullPointerException
*///:~
```

Just as with **EnumSet**, the order of elements in the **EnumMap** is determined by their order of definition in the **enum**.

The last part of **main( )** shows that there is always a key entry for each of the **enum**s, but the value is **null** unless you have called **put( )** for that key.

One advantage of **EnumMap** over *constant-specific methods* (described next) is that an **EnumMap** allows you to change the value objects, whereas you'll see that constant-specific methods are fixed at compile time.

As you'll see later in the chapter, **EnumMap**s can be used to perform *multiple dispatching* for situations where you have multiple types of **enum**s interacting with each other.

Constant-specific methods

Java **enum**s have a very interesting feature that allows you to give each **enum** instance different behavior by creating methods for each one. To do this, you define one or more **abstract** methods as part of the **enum**, then define the methods for each **enum** instance. For example:

```
//: enumerated/ConstantSpecificMethod.java
import java.util.*;
import java.text.*;

public enum ConstantSpecificMethod {
  DATE_TIME {
    String getInfo() {
      return
        DateFormat.getDateInstance().format(new Date());
    }
  },
  CLASSPATH {
    String getInfo() {
      return System.getenv("CLASSPATH");
    }
  },
  VERSION {
    String getInfo() {
      return System.getProperty("java.version");
    }
  };
  abstract String getInfo();
  public static void main(String[] args) {
    for(ConstantSpecificMethod csm : values())
      System.out.println(csm.getInfo());
  }
```

```
} /* (Execute to see output) *///:~
```

You can look up and call methods via their associated **enum** instance. This is often called *table-driven code* (and note the similarity to the aforementioned Command pattern).

In object-oriented programming, different behavior is associated with different classes. Because each instance of an **enum** can have its own behavior via constant-specific methods, this suggests that each instance is a distinct type. In the above example, each **enum** instance is being treated as the "base type" **ConstantSpecificMethod** but you get polymorphic behavior with the method call **getInfo( )**.

However, you can only take the similarity so far. You cannot treat **enum** instances as class types:

```
//: enumerated/NotClasses.java
// {Exec: javap -c LikeClasses}
import static net.mindview.util.Print.*;

enum LikeClasses {
  WINKEN { void behavior() { print("Behavior1"); } },
  BLINKEN { void behavior() { print("Behavior2"); } },
  NOD { void behavior() { print("Behavior3"); } };
  abstract void behavior();
}

public class NotClasses {
  // void f1(LikeClasses.WINKEN instance) {} // Nope
} /* Output:
Compiled from "NotClasses.java"
abstract class LikeClasses extends java.lang.Enum{
public static final LikeClasses WINKEN;

public static final LikeClasses BLINKEN;

public static final LikeClasses NOD;
...
*///:~
```

In **f1( )**, you can see that the compiler doesn't allow you to use an **enum** instance as a class type, which makes sense if you consider the code generated by the compiler—each **enum** element is a **static final** instance of **LikeClasses**.

Also, because they are **static**, **enum** instances of inner **enum**s do not behave like ordinary inner classes; you cannot access non-**static** fields or methods in the outer class.

As a more interesting example, consider a car wash. Each customer is given a menu of choices for their wash, and each option performs a different action. A constant-specific method can be associated with each option, and an **EnumSet** can be used to hold the customer's selections:

```
//: enumerated/CarWash.java
import java.util.*;
import static net.mindview.util.Print.*;

public class CarWash {
  public enum Cycle {
    UNDERBODY {
      void action() { print("Spraying the underbody"); }
    },
    WHEELWASH {
      void action() { print("Washing the wheels"); }
    },
    PREWASH {
      void action() { print("Loosening the dirt"); }
    },
    BASIC {
      void action() { print("The basic wash"); }
    },
    HOTWAX {
      void action() { print("Applying hot wax"); }
    },
    RINSE {
      void action() { print("Rinsing"); }
    },
    BLOWDRY {
      void action() { print("Blowing dry"); }
    };
    abstract void action();
  }
  EnumSet<Cycle> cycles =
    EnumSet.of(Cycle.BASIC, Cycle.RINSE);
  public void add(Cycle cycle) { cycles.add(cycle); }
  public void washCar() {
    for(Cycle c : cycles)
      c.action();
```

```
    }
    public String toString() { return cycles.toString(); }
    public static void main(String[] args) {
        CarWash wash = new CarWash();
        print(wash);
        wash.washCar();
        // Order of addition is unimportant:
        wash.add(Cycle.BLOWDRY);
        wash.add(Cycle.BLOWDRY); // Duplicates ignored
        wash.add(Cycle.RINSE);
        wash.add(Cycle.HOTWAX);
        print(wash);
        wash.washCar();
    }
} /* Output:
[BASIC, RINSE]
The basic wash
Rinsing
[BASIC, HOTWAX, RINSE, BLOWDRY]
The basic wash
Applying hot wax
Rinsing
Blowing dry
*///:~
```

The syntax for defining a constant-specific method is effectively that of an anonymous inner class, but more succinct.

This example also shows more characteristics of **EnumSet**s. Since it's a set, it will only hold one of each item, so duplicate calls to **add( )** with the same argument are ignored (this makes sense, since you can only flip a bit "on" once). Also, the order that you add **enum** instances is unimportant—the output order is determined by the declaration order of the **enum**.

Is it possible to override constant-specific methods, instead of implementing an **abstract** method? Yes, as you can see here:

```
//: enumerated/OverrideConstantSpecific.java
import static net.mindview.util.Print.*;

public enum OverrideConstantSpecific {
    NUT, BOLT,
    WASHER {
        void f() { print("Overridden method"); }
```

```
    };
    void f() { print("default behavior"); }
    public static void main(String[] args) {
      for(OverrideConstantSpecific ocs : values()) {
        printnb(ocs + ": ");
        ocs.f();
      }
    }
} /* Output:
NUT: default behavior
BOLT: default behavior
WASHER: Overridden method
*///:~
```

Although **enum**s do prevent certain types of code, in general you should experiment with them as if they were classes.

Chain of Responsibility with **enum**s

In the *Chain of Responsibility* design pattern, you create a number of different ways to solve a problem and chain them together. When a request occurs, it is passed along the chain until one of the solutions can handle the request.

You can easily implement a simple Chain of Responsibility with constant-specific methods. Consider a model of a post office, which tries to deal with each piece of mail in the most general way possible, but has to keep trying until it ends up treating the mail as a dead letter. Each attempt can be thought of as a *Strategy* (another design pattern), and the entire list together is a Chain of Responsibility.

We start by describing a piece of mail. All the different characteristics of interest can be expressed using **enum**s. Because the **Mail** objects will be randomly generated, the easiest way to reduce the probability of (for example) a piece of mail being given a **YES** for **GeneralDelivery** is to create more non-**YES** instances, so the **enum** definitions look a little funny at first.

Within **Mail**, you'll see **randomMail( )**, which creates random pieces of test mail. The **generator( )** method produces an **Iterable** object that uses **randomMail( )** to produce a number of mail objects, one each time you call **next( )** via the iterator. This construct allows the simple creation of a foreach loop by calling **Mail.generator( )**:

Thinking in Java   *Bruce Eckel*

```
//: enumerated/PostOffice.java
// Modeling a post office.
import java.util.*;
import net.mindview.util.*;
import static net.mindview.util.Print.*;

class Mail {
  // The NO's lower the probability of random selection:
  enum GeneralDelivery {YES,NO1,NO2,NO3,NO4,NO5}
  enum Scannability {UNSCANNABLE,YES1,YES2,YES3,YES4}
  enum Readability {ILLEGIBLE,YES1,YES2,YES3,YES4}
  enum Address {INCORRECT,OK1,OK2,OK3,OK4,OK5,OK6}
  enum ReturnAddress {MISSING,OK1,OK2,OK3,OK4,OK5}
  GeneralDelivery generalDelivery;
  Scannability scannability;
  Readability readability;
  Address address;
  ReturnAddress returnAddress;
  static long counter = 0;
  long id = counter++;
  public String toString() { return "Mail " + id; }
  public String details() {
    return toString() +
      ", General Delivery: " + generalDelivery +
      ", Address Scanability: " + scannability +
      ", Address Readability: " + readability +
      ", Address Address: " + address +
      ", Return address: " + returnAddress;
  }
  // Generate test Mail:
  public static Mail randomMail() {
    Mail m = new Mail();
    m.generalDelivery= Enums.random(GeneralDelivery.class);
    m.scannability = Enums.random(Scannability.class);
    m.readability = Enums.random(Readability.class);
    m.address = Enums.random(Address.class);
    m.returnAddress = Enums.random(ReturnAddress.class);
    return m;
  }
  public static Iterable<Mail> generator(final int count) {
    return new Iterable<Mail>() {
      int n = count;
      public Iterator<Mail> iterator() {
        return new Iterator<Mail>() {
```

```
              public boolean hasNext() { return n-- > 0; }
              public Mail next() { return randomMail(); }
              public void remove() { // Not implemented
                throw new UnsupportedOperationException();
              }
          };
        }
      };
    }
}

public class PostOffice {
  enum MailHandler {
    GENERAL_DELIVERY {
      boolean handle(Mail m) {
        switch(m.generalDelivery) {
          case YES:
            print("Using general delivery for " + m);
            return true;
          default: return false;
        }
      }
    },
    MACHINE_SCAN {
      boolean handle(Mail m) {
        switch(m.scannability) {
          case UNSCANNABLE: return false;
          default:
            switch(m.address) {
              case INCORRECT: return false;
              default:
                print("Delivering "+ m + " automatically");
                return true;
            }
        }
      }
    },
    VISUAL_INSPECTION {
      boolean handle(Mail m) {
        switch(m.readability) {
          case ILLEGIBLE: return false;
          default:
            switch(m.address) {
              case INCORRECT: return false;
```

```
                default:
                  print("Delivering " + m + " normally");
                  return true;
              }
          }
      }
    },
    RETURN_TO_SENDER {
      boolean handle(Mail m) {
        switch(m.returnAddress) {
          case MISSING: return false;
          default:
            print("Returning " + m + " to sender");
            return true;
        }
      }
    };
    abstract boolean handle(Mail m);
  }
  static void handle(Mail m) {
    for(MailHandler handler : MailHandler.values())
      if(handler.handle(m))
        return;
    print(m + " is a dead letter");
  }
  public static void main(String[] args) {
    for(Mail mail : Mail.generator(10)) {
      print(mail.details());
      handle(mail);
      print("*****");
    }
  }
} /* Output:
Mail 0, General Delivery: NO2, Address Scanability:
UNSCANNABLE, Address Readability: YES3, Address Address:
OK1, Return address: OK1
Delivering Mail 0 normally
*****
Mail 1, General Delivery: NO5, Address Scanability: YES3,
Address Readability: ILLEGIBLE, Address Address: OK5,
Return address: OK1
Delivering Mail 1 automatically
*****
```

```
Mail 2, General Delivery: YES, Address Scanability: YES3,
Address Readability: YES1, Address Address: OK1, Return
address: OK5
Using general delivery for Mail 2
*****
Mail 3, General Delivery: NO4, Address Scanability: YES3,
Address Readability: YES1, Address Address: INCORRECT,
Return address: OK4
Returning Mail 3 to sender
*****
Mail 4, General Delivery: NO4, Address Scanability:
UNSCANNABLE, Address Readability: YES1, Address Address:
INCORRECT, Return address: OK2
Returning Mail 4 to sender
*****
Mail 5, General Delivery: NO3, Address Scanability: YES1,
Address Readability: ILLEGIBLE, Address Address: OK4,
Return address: OK2
Delivering Mail 5 automatically
*****
Mail 6, General Delivery: YES, Address Scanability: YES4,
Address Readability: ILLEGIBLE, Address Address: OK4,
Return address: OK4
Using general delivery for Mail 6
*****
Mail 7, General Delivery: YES, Address Scanability: YES3,
Address Readability: YES4, Address Address: OK2, Return
address: MISSING
Using general delivery for Mail 7
*****
Mail 8, General Delivery: NO3, Address Scanability: YES1,
Address Readability: YES3, Address Address: INCORRECT,
Return address: MISSING
Mail 8 is a dead letter
*****
Mail 9, General Delivery: NO1, Address Scanability:
UNSCANNABLE, Address Readability: YES2, Address Address:
OK1, Return address: OK4
Delivering Mail 9 normally
*****
*///:~
```

The Chain of Responsibility is expressed in **enum MailHandler**, and the
order of the **enum** definitions determines the order in which the strategies

---

are attempted on each piece of mail. Each strategy is tried in turn until one succeeds or they all fail, in which case you have a dead letter.

Exercise 8: (6) Modify **PostOffice.java** so it has the ability to forward mail.

Exercise 9: (5) Modify **class PostOffice** so that it uses an **EnumMap**.

Project:[2] Specialized languages like Prolog use *backward chaining* in order to solve problems like this. Using **PostOffice.java** for inspiration, research such languages and develop a program that allows new "rules" to be easily added to the system.

State machines with **enum**s

Enumerated types can be ideal for creating *state machines*. A state machine can be in a finite number of specific states. The machine normally moves from one state to the next based on an input, but there are also *transient states*; the machine moves out of these as soon as their task is performed.

There are certain allowable inputs for each state, and different inputs change the state of the machine to different new states. Because **enum**s restrict the set of possible cases, they are quite useful for enumerating the different states and inputs.

Each state also typically has some kind of associated output.

A vending machine is a good example of a state machine. First, we define the various inputs in an **enum**:

```
//: enumerated/Input.java
package enumerated;
import java.util.*;

public enum Input {
  NICKEL(5), DIME(10), QUARTER(25), DOLLAR(100),
  TOOTHPASTE(200), CHIPS(75), SODA(100), SOAP(50),
  ABORT_TRANSACTION {
    public int amount() { // Disallow
      throw new RuntimeException("ABORT.amount()");
```

---

[2] Projects are suggestions to be used (for example) as term projects. Solutions to projects are not included in the solution guide.

```
        }
    },
    STOP { // This must be the last instance.
      public int amount() { // Disallow
        throw new RuntimeException("SHUT_DOWN.amount()");
      }
    };
    int value; // In cents
    Input(int value) { this.value = value; }
    Input() {}
    int amount() { return value; }; // In cents
    static Random rand = new Random(47);
    public static Input randomSelection() {
      // Don't include STOP:
      return values()[rand.nextInt(values().length - 1)];
    }
} ///:~
```

Note that two of the **Input**s have an associated amount, so **amount( )** is defined in the interface. However, it is inappropriate to call **amount( )** for the other two **Input** types, so they throw an exception if you call **amount( )**. Although this is a bit of an odd setup (define a method in an interface, then throw an exception if you call it for certain implementations), it is imposed upon us because of the constraints of **enum**s.

The **VendingMachine** will react to these inputs by first categorizing them via the **Category enum**, so that it can **switch** on the categories. This example shows how **enum**s make code clearer and easier to manage:

```
//: enumerated/VendingMachine.java
// {Args: VendingMachineInput.txt}
package enumerated;
import java.util.*;
import net.mindview.util.*;
import static enumerated.Input.*;
import static net.mindview.util.Print.*;

enum Category {
  MONEY(NICKEL, DIME, QUARTER, DOLLAR),
  ITEM_SELECTION(TOOTHPASTE, CHIPS, SODA, SOAP),
  QUIT_TRANSACTION(ABORT_TRANSACTION),
  SHUT_DOWN(STOP);
  private Input[] values;
  Category(Input... types) { values = types; }
```

```
    private static EnumMap<Input,Category> categories =
      new EnumMap<Input,Category>(Input.class);
    static {
      for(Category c : Category.class.getEnumConstants())
        for(Input type : c.values)
          categories.put(type, c);
    }
    public static Category categorize(Input input) {
      return categories.get(input);
    }
  }

public class VendingMachine {
  private static State state = State.RESTING;
  private static int amount = 0;
  private static Input selection = null;
  enum StateDuration { TRANSIENT } // Tagging enum
  enum State {
    RESTING {
      void next(Input input) {
        switch(Category.categorize(input)) {
          case MONEY:
            amount += input.amount();
            state = ADDING_MONEY;
            break;
          case SHUT_DOWN:
            state = TERMINAL;
          default:
        }
      }
    },
    ADDING_MONEY {
      void next(Input input) {
        switch(Category.categorize(input)) {
          case MONEY:
            amount += input.amount();
            break;
          case ITEM_SELECTION:
            selection = input;
            if(amount < selection.amount())
              print("Insufficient money for " + selection);
            else state = DISPENSING;
            break;
          case QUIT_TRANSACTION:
```

```
                  state = GIVING_CHANGE;
                  break;
                case SHUT_DOWN:
                  state = TERMINAL;
                default:
              }
            }
          },
        DISPENSING(StateDuration.TRANSIENT) {
          void next() {
            print("here is your " + selection);
            amount -= selection.amount();
            state = GIVING_CHANGE;
          }
        },
        GIVING_CHANGE(StateDuration.TRANSIENT) {
          void next() {
            if(amount > 0) {
              print("Your change: " + amount);
              amount = 0;
            }
            state = RESTING;
          }
        },
        TERMINAL { void output() { print("Halted"); } };
        private boolean isTransient = false;
        State() {}
        State(StateDuration trans) { isTransient = true; }
        void next(Input input) {
          throw new RuntimeException("Only call " +
            "next(Input input) for non-transient states");
        }
        void next() {
          throw new RuntimeException("Only call next() for " +
            "StateDuration.TRANSIENT states");
        }
        void output() { print(amount); }
      }
      static void run(Generator<Input> gen) {
        while(state != State.TERMINAL) {
          state.next(gen.next());
          while(state.isTransient)
            state.next();
          state.output();
```

```
    }
  }
  public static void main(String[] args) {
    Generator<Input> gen = new RandomInputGenerator();
    if(args.length == 1)
      gen = new FileInputGenerator(args[0]);
    run(gen);
  }
}

// For a basic sanity check:
class RandomInputGenerator implements Generator<Input> {
  public Input next() { return Input.randomSelection(); }
}

// Create Inputs from a file of ';'-separated strings:
class FileInputGenerator implements Generator<Input> {
  private Iterator<String> input;
  public FileInputGenerator(String fileName) {
    input = new TextFile(fileName, ";").iterator();
  }
  public Input next() {
    if(!input.hasNext())
      return null;
    return Enum.valueOf(Input.class, input.next().trim());
  }
} /* Output:
25
50
75
here is your CHIPS
0
100
200
here is your TOOTHPASTE
0
25
35
Your change: 35
0
25
35
Insufficient money for SODA
35
```

```
60
70
75
Insufficient money for SODA
75
Your change: 75
0
Halted
*///:~
```

Because selecting among **enum** instances is most often accomplished with a **switch** statement (notice the extra effort that the language goes to in order to make a **switch** on **enum**s easy), one of the most common questions to ask when you are organizing multiple **enum**s is "What do I want to **switch** on?" Here, it's easiest to work back from the **VendingMachine** by noting that in each **State**, you need to **switch** on the basic categories of input action: money being inserted, an item being selected, the transaction being aborted, and the machine being turned off. However, within those categories, you have different types of money that can be inserted and different items that can be selected. The **Category enum** groups the different types of **Input** so that the **categorize( )** method can produce the appropriate **Category** inside a **switch**. This method uses an **EnumMap** to efficiently and safely perform the lookup.

If you study **class VendingMachine**, you can see how each state is different, and responds differently to input. Also note the two transient states; in **run( )** the machine waits for an **Input** and doesn't stop moving through states until it is no longer in a transient state.

The **VendingMachine** can be tested in two ways, by using two different **Generator** objects. The **RandomInputGenerator** just keeps producing inputs, everything except **SHUT_DOWN**. By running this for a long time you get a kind of sanity check to help ensure that the machine will not wander into a bad state. The **FileInputGenerator** takes a file describing inputs in text form, turns them into **enum** instances, and creates **Input** objects. Here's the text file used to produce the output shown above:

```
//:! enumerated/VendingMachineInput.txt
QUARTER; QUARTER; QUARTER; CHIPS;
DOLLAR; DOLLAR; TOOTHPASTE;
QUARTER; DIME; ABORT_TRANSACTION;
QUARTER; DIME; SODA;
QUARTER; DIME; NICKEL; SODA;
```

```
ABORT_TRANSACTION;
STOP;
///:~
```

One limitation to this design is that the fields in **VendingMachine** that are accessed by **enum State** instances *must* be **static**, which means you can only have a single **VendingMachine** instance. This may not be that big of an issue if you think about an actual (embedded Java) implementation, since you are likely to have only one application per machine.

Exercise 10: (7) Modify **class VendingMachine** (only) using **EnumMap** so that one program can have multiple instances of **VendingMachine**.

Exercise 11: (7) In a real vending machine you will want to easily add and change the type of vended items, so the limits imposed by an **enum** on **Input** are impractical (remember that **enum**s are for a restricted set of types). Modify **VendingMachine.java** so that the vended items are represented by a **class** instead of being part of **Input**, and initialize an **ArrayList** of these objects from a text file (using **net.mindview.util.TextFile**).

Project:[3] Design the vending machine using internationalization, so that one machine can easily be adapted to all countries.

Multiple dispatching

When you are dealing with multiple interacting types, a program can get particularly messy. For example, consider a system that parses and executes mathematical expressions. You want to say **Number.plus(Number)**, **Number.multiply(Number)**, etc., where **Number** is the base class for a family of numerical objects. But when you say **a.plus(b)**, and you don't know the exact type of either **a** or **b**, how can you get them to interact properly?

The answer starts with something you probably don't think about: Java only performs *single dispatching*. That is, if you are performing an operation on more than one object whose type is unknown, Java can invoke the dynamic binding mechanism on only one of those types. This doesn't solve the

---

[3] Projects are suggestions to be used (for example) as term projects. Solutions to projects are not included in the solution guide.

problem described here, so you end up detecting some types manually and effectively producing your own dynamic binding behavior.

The solution is called *multiple dispatching*. (In this case, there will be only two dispatches, which is referred to as *double dispatching*.) Polymorphism can only occur via method calls, so if you want double dispatching, there must be two method calls: the first to determine the first unknown type, and the second to determine the second unknown type. With multiple dispatching, you must have a virtual call for each of the types—if you are working with two different type hierarchies that are interacting, you'll need a virtual call in each hierarchy. Generally, you'll set up a configuration such that a single method call produces more than one virtual method call and thus services more than one type in the process. To get this effect, you need to work with more than one method: You'll need a method call for each dispatch. The methods in the following example (which implements the "paper, scissors, rock" game, traditionally called *RoShamBo*) are called **compete( )** and **eval( )** and are both members of the same type. They produce one of three possible outcomes:[4]

```
//: enumerated/Outcome.java
package enumerated;
public enum Outcome { WIN, LOSE, DRAW } ///:~
```

```
//: enumerated/RoShamBo1.java
// Demonstration of multiple dispatching.
package enumerated;
import java.util.*;
import static enumerated.Outcome.*;

interface Item {
  Outcome compete(Item it);
  Outcome eval(Paper p);
  Outcome eval(Scissors s);
  Outcome eval(Rock r);
}

class Paper implements Item {
  public Outcome compete(Item it) { return it.eval(this); }
```

---

4 This example existed for a number of years in both C++ and Java (in *Thinking in Patterns*) on *www.MindView.net* before it appeared, without attribution, in a book by other authors.

```java
  public Outcome eval(Paper p) { return DRAW; }
  public Outcome eval(Scissors s) { return WIN; }
  public Outcome eval(Rock r) { return LOSE; }
  public String toString() { return "Paper"; }
}

class Scissors implements Item {
  public Outcome compete(Item it) { return it.eval(this); }
  public Outcome eval(Paper p) { return LOSE; }
  public Outcome eval(Scissors s) { return DRAW; }
  public Outcome eval(Rock r) { return WIN; }
  public String toString() { return "Scissors"; }
}

class Rock implements Item {
  public Outcome compete(Item it) { return it.eval(this); }
  public Outcome eval(Paper p) { return WIN; }
  public Outcome eval(Scissors s) { return LOSE; }
  public Outcome eval(Rock r) { return DRAW; }
  public String toString() { return "Rock"; }
}

public class RoShamBo1 {
  static final int SIZE = 20;
  private static Random rand = new Random(47);
  public static Item newItem() {
    switch(rand.nextInt(3)) {
      default:
      case 0: return new Scissors();
      case 1: return new Paper();
      case 2: return new Rock();
    }
  }
  public static void match(Item a, Item b) {
    System.out.println(
      a + " vs. " + b + ": " +  a.compete(b));
  }
  public static void main(String[] args) {
    for(int i = 0; i < SIZE; i++)
      match(newItem(), newItem());
  }
} /* Output:
Rock vs. Rock: DRAW
Paper vs. Rock: WIN
```

```
Paper vs. Rock: WIN
Paper vs. Rock: WIN
Scissors vs. Paper: WIN
Scissors vs. Scissors: DRAW
Scissors vs. Paper: WIN
Rock vs. Paper: LOSE
Paper vs. Paper: DRAW
Rock vs. Paper: LOSE
Paper vs. Scissors: LOSE
Paper vs. Scissors: LOSE
Rock vs. Scissors: WIN
Rock vs. Paper: LOSE
Paper vs. Rock: WIN
Scissors vs. Paper: WIN
Paper vs. Scissors: LOSE
Paper vs. Scissors: LOSE
Paper vs. Scissors: LOSE
Paper vs. Scissors: LOSE
*///:~
```

Item is the interface for the types that will be multiply dispatched.
RoShamBo1.match( ) takes two **Item** objects and begins the double-dispatching process by calling the **Item.compete( )** function. The virtual
mechanism determines the type of **a**, so it wakes up inside the **compete( )**
function of **a**'s concrete type. The **compete( )** function performs the second
dispatch by calling **eval( )** on the remaining type. Passing itself (**this**) as an
argument to **eval( )** produces a call to the overloaded **eval( )** function, thus
preserving the type information of the first dispatch. When the second
dispatch is completed, you know the exact types of both **Item** objects.

It requires a lot of ceremony to set up multiple dispatching, but keep in mind
that the benefit is the syntactic elegance achieved when making the call—
instead of writing awkward code to determine the type of one or more objects
during a call, you simply say, "You two! I don't care what types you are,
interact properly with each other!" Make sure this kind of elegance is
important to you before embarking on multiple dispatching, however.

Dispatching with **enum**s

Performing a straight translation of **RoShamBo1.java** into an **enum**-based
solution is problematic because **enum** instances are not types, so the
overloaded **eval( )** methods won't work—you can't use **enum** instances as

argument types. However, there are a number of different approaches to implementing multiple dispatching which benefit from **enum**s.

One approach uses a constructor to initialize each **enum** instance with a "row" of outcomes; taken together this produces a kind of lookup table:

```
//: enumerated/RoShamBo2.java
// Switching one enum on another.
package enumerated;
import static enumerated.Outcome.*;

public enum RoShamBo2 implements Competitor<RoShamBo2> {
  PAPER(DRAW, LOSE, WIN),
  SCISSORS(WIN, DRAW, LOSE),
  ROCK(LOSE, WIN, DRAW);
  private Outcome vPAPER, vSCISSORS, vROCK;
  RoShamBo2(Outcome paper,Outcome scissors,Outcome rock) {
    this.vPAPER = paper;
    this.vSCISSORS = scissors;
    this.vROCK = rock;
  }
  public Outcome compete(RoShamBo2 it) {
    switch(it) {
      default:
      case PAPER: return vPAPER;
      case SCISSORS: return vSCISSORS;
      case ROCK: return vROCK;
    }
  }
  public static void main(String[] args) {
    RoShamBo.play(RoShamBo2.class, 20);
  }
} /* Output:
ROCK vs. ROCK: DRAW
SCISSORS vs. ROCK: LOSE
SCISSORS vs. ROCK: LOSE
SCISSORS vs. ROCK: LOSE
PAPER vs. SCISSORS: LOSE
PAPER vs. PAPER: DRAW
PAPER vs. SCISSORS: LOSE
ROCK vs. SCISSORS: WIN
SCISSORS vs. SCISSORS: DRAW
ROCK vs. SCISSORS: WIN
SCISSORS vs. PAPER: WIN
```

```
SCISSORS vs. PAPER: WIN
ROCK vs. PAPER: LOSE
ROCK vs. SCISSORS: WIN
SCISSORS vs. ROCK: LOSE
PAPER vs. SCISSORS: LOSE
SCISSORS vs. PAPER: WIN
SCISSORS vs. PAPER: WIN
SCISSORS vs. PAPER: WIN
SCISSORS vs. PAPER: WIN
*///:~
```

Once both types have been determined in **compete( )**, the only action is the return of the resulting **Outcome**. However, you could also call another method, even (for example) via a *Command* object that was assigned in the constructor.

RoShamBo2.java is much smaller and more straightforward than the original example, and thus easier to keep track of. Notice that you're still using two dispatches to determine the type of both objects. In **RoShamBo1.java**, both dispatches were performed using virtual method calls, but here, only the first dispatch uses a virtual method call. The second dispatch uses a **switch**, but is safe because the **enum** limits the choices in the **switch** statement.

The code that drives the **enum** has been separated out so that it can be used in the other examples. First, the **Competitor** interface defines a type that competes with another **Competitor**:

```
//: enumerated/Competitor.java
// Switching one enum on another.
package enumerated;

public interface Competitor<T extends Competitor<T>> {
  Outcome compete(T competitor);
} ///:~
```

Then we define two **static** methods (**static** to avoid having to specify the parameter type explicitly). First, **match( )** calls **compete( )** for one **Competitor** vs. another, and you can see that in this case the type parameter only needs to be a **Competitor<T>**. But in **play( )**, the type parameter must be both an **Enum<T>** because it is used in **Enums.random( )**, and a **Competitor<T>** because it is passed to **match( )**:

```
//: enumerated/RoShamBo.java
```

```
// Common tools for RoShamBo examples.
package enumerated;
import net.mindview.util.*;

public class RoShamBo {
  public static <T extends Competitor<T>>
  void match(T a, T b) {
    System.out.println(
      a + " vs. " + b + ": " +  a.compete(b));
  }
  public static <T extends Enum<T> & Competitor<T>>
  void play(Class<T> rsbClass, int size) {
    for(int i = 0; i < size; i++)
      match(
        Enums.random(rsbClass),Enums.random(rsbClass));
  }
} ///:~
```

The **play( )** method does not have a return value that involves the type parameter **T**, so it seems like you might use wildcards inside the **Class<T>** type instead of using the leading parameter description. However, wildcards cannot extend more than one base type, so we must use the above expression.

Using constant-specific methods

Because constant-specific methods allow you to provide different method implementations for each **enum** instance, they might seem like a perfect solution for setting up multiple dispatching. But even though they can be given different behavior in this way, **enum** instances are not types, so you cannot use them as argument types in method signatures. The best you can do for this example is to set up a **switch** statement:

```
//: enumerated/RoShamBo3.java
// Using constant-specific methods.
package enumerated;
import static enumerated.Outcome.*;

public enum RoShamBo3 implements Competitor<RoShamBo3> {
  PAPER {
    public Outcome compete(RoShamBo3 it) {
      switch(it) {
        default: // To placate the compiler
        case PAPER: return DRAW;
        case SCISSORS: return LOSE;
```

```java
          case ROCK: return WIN;
      }
    }
  },
  SCISSORS {
    public Outcome compete(RoShamBo3 it) {
      switch(it) {
        default:
        case PAPER: return WIN;
        case SCISSORS: return DRAW;
        case ROCK: return LOSE;
      }
    }
  },
  ROCK {
    public Outcome compete(RoShamBo3 it) {
      switch(it) {
        default:
        case PAPER: return LOSE;
        case SCISSORS: return WIN;
        case ROCK: return DRAW;
      }
    }
  };
  public abstract Outcome compete(RoShamBo3 it);
  public static void main(String[] args) {
    RoShamBo.play(RoShamBo3.class, 20);
  }
} /* Same output as RoShamBo2.java *///:~
```

Although this is functional and not unreasonable, the solution of
RoShamBo2.java seems to require less code when adding a new type, and
thus seems more straightforward.

However, **RoShamBo3.java** can be simplified and compressed:

```java
//: enumerated/RoShamBo4.java
package enumerated;

public enum RoShamBo4 implements Competitor<RoShamBo4> {
  ROCK {
    public Outcome compete(RoShamBo4 opponent) {
      return compete(SCISSORS, opponent);
    }
  },
```

```
    SCISSORS {
      public Outcome compete(RoShamBo4 opponent) {
        return compete(PAPER, opponent);
      }
    },
    PAPER {
      public Outcome compete(RoShamBo4 opponent) {
        return compete(ROCK, opponent);
      }
    };
    Outcome compete(RoShamBo4 loser, RoShamBo4 opponent) {
      return ((opponent == this) ? Outcome.DRAW
          : ((opponent == loser) ? Outcome.WIN
                                 : Outcome.LOSE));
    }
    public static void main(String[] args) {
      RoShamBo.play(RoShamBo4.class, 20);
    }
} /* Same output as RoShamBo2.java *///:~
```

Here, the second dispatch is performed by the two-argument version of
compete( ), which performs a sequence of comparisons and is thus similar
to the action of a **switch**. It's smaller, but a bit confusing. For a large system
this confusion can become debilitating.

Dispatching with **EnumMap**s

It's possible to perform a "true" double dispatch using the **EnumMap** class,
which is specifically designed to work very efficiently with **enum**s. Since the
goal is to switch on two unknown types, an **EnumMap** of **EnumMap**s can
be used to produce the double dispatch:

```
//: enumerated/RoShamBo5.java
// Multiple dispatching using an EnumMap of EnumMaps.
package enumerated;
import java.util.*;
import static enumerated.Outcome.*;

enum RoShamBo5 implements Competitor<RoShamBo5> {
  PAPER, SCISSORS, ROCK;
  static EnumMap<RoShamBo5,EnumMap<RoShamBo5,Outcome>>
    table = new EnumMap<RoShamBo5,
      EnumMap<RoShamBo5,Outcome>>(RoShamBo5.class);
  static {
```

```
    for(RoShamBo5 it : RoShamBo5.values())
      table.put(it,
        new EnumMap<RoShamBo5,Outcome>(RoShamBo5.class));
    initRow(PAPER, DRAW, LOSE, WIN);
    initRow(SCISSORS, WIN, DRAW, LOSE);
    initRow(ROCK, LOSE, WIN, DRAW);
  }
  static void initRow(RoShamBo5 it,
    Outcome vPAPER, Outcome vSCISSORS, Outcome vROCK) {
    EnumMap<RoShamBo5,Outcome> row =
      RoShamBo5.table.get(it);
    row.put(RoShamBo5.PAPER, vPAPER);
    row.put(RoShamBo5.SCISSORS, vSCISSORS);
    row.put(RoShamBo5.ROCK, vROCK);
  }
  public Outcome compete(RoShamBo5 it) {
    return table.get(this).get(it);
  }
  public static void main(String[] args) {
    RoShamBo.play(RoShamBo5.class, 20);
  }
} /* Same output as RoShamBo2.java *////:~
```

The **EnumMap** is initialized using a **static** clause; you can see the table-like structure of the calls to **initRow( )**. Notice the **compete( )** method, where you can see both dispatches happening in a single statement.

Using a 2-D array

We can simplify the solution even more by noting that each **enum** instance has a fixed value (based on its declaration order) and that **ordinal( )** produces this value. A two-dimensional array mapping the competitors onto the outcomes produces the smallest and most straightforward solution (and possibly the fastest, although remember that **EnumMap** uses an internal array):

```
//: enumerated/RoShamBo6.java
// Enums using "tables" instead of multiple dispatch.
package enumerated;
import static enumerated.Outcome.*;

enum RoShamBo6 implements Competitor<RoShamBo6> {
  PAPER, SCISSORS, ROCK;
  private static Outcome[][] table = {
```

```
       { DRAW, LOSE, WIN }, // PAPER
       { WIN, DRAW, LOSE }, // SCISSORS
       { LOSE, WIN, DRAW }, // ROCK
    };
    public Outcome compete(RoShamBo6 other) {
      return table[this.ordinal()][other.ordinal()];
    }
    public static void main(String[] args) {
      RoShamBo.play(RoShamBo6.class, 20);
    }
} ///:~
```

The **table** has exactly the same order as the calls to **initRow( )** in the previous example.

The small size of this code holds great appeal over the previous examples, partly because it seems much easier to understand and modify but also because it just seems more straightforward. However, it's not quite as "safe" as the previous examples because it uses an array. With a larger array, you might get the size wrong, and if your tests do not cover all possibilities something could slip through the cracks.

All of these solutions are different types of tables, but it's worth exploring the expression of the tables to find the one that fits best. Note that even though the above solution is the most compact, it is also fairly rigid because it can only produce a constant output given constant inputs. However, there's nothing that prevents you from having **table** produce a function object. For certain types of problems, the concept of "table-driven code" can be very powerful.

Summary

Even though enumerated types are not terribly complex in themselves, this chapter was postponed until later in the book because of what you can do with **enum**s in combination with features like polymorphism, generics, and reflection.

Although they are significantly more sophisticated than **enum**s in C or C++, **enum**s are still a "small" feature, something the language has survived (a bit awkwardly) without for many years. And yet this chapter shows the valuable impact that a "small" feature can have—sometimes it gives you just the right leverage to solve a problem elegantly and clearly, and as I have been saying throughout this book, elegance is important, and clarity may make the difference between a successful solution and one that fails because others cannot understand it.

On the subject of clarity, an unfortunate source of confusion comes from the poor choice in Java 1.0 of the term "enumeration" instead of the common and well-accepted term "iterator" to indicate an object that selects each element of a sequence (as shown in *Collections*). Some languages even refer to enumerated data types as "enumerators!" This mistake has since been rectified in Java, but the **Enumeration** interface could not, of course, simply be removed and so is still hanging around in old (and sometimes new!) code, the library, and documentation.

Solutions to selected exercises can be found in the electronic document *The Thinking in Java Annotated Solution Guide*, available for sale from *www.MindView.net*.

Annotations

Annotations (also known as *metadata*) provide a formalized way to add information to your code so that you can easily use that data at some later point.[1]

Annotations are partly motivated by a general trend toward combining metadata with source-code files, instead of keeping it in external documents. They are also a response to feature pressure from other languages like C#.

Annotations are one of the fundamental language changes introduced in Java SE5. They provide information that you need to fully describe your program, but that cannot be expressed in Java. Thus, annotations allow you to store extra information about your program in a format that is tested and verified by the compiler. Annotations can be used to generate descriptor files or even new class definitions and help ease the burden of writing "boilerplate" code. Using annotations, you can keep this metadata in the Java source code, and have the advantage of cleaner looking code, compile-time type checking and the annotation API to help build processing tools for your annotations. Although a few types of metadata come predefined in Java SE5, in general the kind of annotations you add and what you do with them are entirely up to you.

The syntax of annotations is reasonably simple and consists mainly of the addition of the @ symbol to the language. Java SE5 contains three general-purpose built-in annotations, defined in **java.lang**:

- **@Override**, to indicate that a method definition is intended to override a method in the base class. This generates a compiler error if you accidentally misspell the method name or give an improper signature.[2]

---

[1] Jeremy Meyer came to Crested Butte and spent two weeks with me working on this chapter. His help was invaluable.

[2] This was no doubt inspired by a similar feature in C#. The C# feature is a keyword and not an annotation, and is enforced by the compiler. That is, when you override a method in

- **@Deprecated**, to produce a compiler warning if this element is used.

- **@SuppressWarnings**, to turn off inappropriate compiler warnings. This annotation is allowed but not supported in earlier releases of Java SE5 (it was ignored).

Four additional annotation types support the creation of new annotations; you will learn about these in this chapter.

Anytime you create descriptor classes or interfaces that involve repetitive work, you can usually use annotations to automate and simplify the process. Much of the extra work in *Enterprise JavaBeans* (EJBs), for example, is eliminated through the use of annotations in EJB3.0.

Annotations can replace existing systems like XDoclet, which is an independent doclet tool (see the supplement at *http://MindView.net/Books/BetterJava*) that is specifically designed for creating annotation-style doclets. In contrast, annotations are true language constructs and hence are structured, and are type-checked at compile time. Keeping all the information in the actual source code and not in comments makes the code neater and easier to maintain. By using and extending the annotation API and tools, or with external bytecode manipulation libraries as you will see in this chapter, you can perform powerful inspection and manipulation of your source code as well as the bytecode.

Basic syntax

In the example below, the method **testExecute( )** is annotated with **@Test**. This doesn't do anything by itself, but the compiler will ensure that you have a definition for the **@Test** annotation in your build path. As you will see later in the chapter, you can create a tool which runs this method for you via reflection.

```
//: annotations/Testable.java
package annotations;
import net.mindview.atunit.*;
```

C#, you must use the **override** keyword, whereas in Java the **@Override** annotation is optional.

```
public class Testable {
  public void execute() {
    System.out.println("Executing..");
  }
  @Test void testExecute() { execute(); }
} ///:~
```

Annotated methods are no different from other methods. The **@Test** annotation in this example can be used in combination with any of the modifiers like **public** or **static** or **void**. Syntactically, annotations are used in much the same way as modifiers.

Defining annotations

Here is the definition of the annotation above. You can see that annotation definitions look a lot like interface definitions. In fact, they compile to class files like any other Java interface:

```
//: net/mindview/atunit/Test.java
// The @Test tag.
package net.mindview.atunit;
import java.lang.annotation.*;

@Target(ElementType.METHOD)
@Retention(RetentionPolicy.RUNTIME)
public @interface Test {} ///:-
```

Apart from the @ symbol, the definition of **@Test** is much like that of an empty interface. An annotation definition also requires the *meta-annotations* **@Target** and **@Retention**. **@Target** defines where you can apply this annotation (a method or a field, for example). **@Retention** defines whether the annotations are available in the source code (**SOURCE**), in the class files (**CLASS**), or at run time (**RUNTIME**).

Annotations will usually contain *elements* to specify values in your annotations. A program or tool can use these parameters when processing your annotations. Elements look like interface methods, except that you can declare default values.

An annotation without any elements, such as **@Test** above, is called a *marker annotation*.

Here is a simple annotation that tracks use cases in a project. Programmers annotate each method or set of methods which fulfill the requirements of a

---

particular use case. A project manager can get an idea of project progress by counting the implemented use cases, and developers maintaining the project can easily find use cases if they need to update or debug business rules within the system.

```
//: annotations/UseCase.java
import java.lang.annotation.*;

@Target(ElementType.METHOD)
@Retention(RetentionPolicy.RUNTIME)
public @interface UseCase {
  public int id();
  public String description() default "no description";
} ///:~
```

Notice that **id** and **description** resemble method declarations. Because **id** is type-checked by the compiler, it is a reliable way of linking a tracking database to the use case document and the source code. The element **description** has a **default** value which is picked up by the annotation processor if no value is specified when a method is annotated.

Here is a class with three methods annotated as use cases:

```
//: annotations/PasswordUtils.java
import java.util.*;

public class PasswordUtils {
  @UseCase(id = 47, description =
  "Passwords must contain at least one numeric")
  public boolean validatePassword(String password) {
    return (password.matches("\\w*\\d\\w*"));
  }
  @UseCase(id = 48)
  public String encryptPassword(String password) {
   return new StringBuilder(password).reverse().toString();
  }
  @UseCase(id = 49, description =
  "New passwords can't equal previously used ones")
  public boolean checkForNewPassword(
    List<String> prevPasswords, String password) {
    return !prevPasswords.contains(password);
  }
} ///:~
```

The values of the annotation elements are expressed as name-value pairs in parentheses after the **@UseCase** declaration. The annotation for **encryptPassword( )** is not passed a value for the **description** element here, so the default value defined in the **@interface UseCase** will appear when the class is run through an annotation processor.

You could imagine using a system like this in order to "sketch" out your system, and then filling in the functionality as you build it.

Meta-annotations

There are currently only three standard annotations (described earlier) and four meta-annotations defined in the Java language. The meta-annotations are for annotating annotations:

@Target	Where this annotation can be applied. The possible **ElementType** arguments are: **CONSTRUCTOR**: Constructor declaration **FIELD**: Field declaration (includes **enum** constants) **LOCAL_VARIABLE**: Local variable declaration **METHOD**: Method declaration **PACKAGE**: Package declaration **PARAMETER**: Parameter declaration **TYPE**: Class, interface (including annotation type), or **enum** declaration
@Retention	How long the annotation information is kept. The possible **RetentionPolicy** arguments are: **SOURCE**: Annotations are discarded by the compiler. **CLASS**: Annotations are available in the class file by the compiler but can be discarded by the VM. **RUNTIME**: Annotations are retained by the VM at run time, so they may be read reflectively.
@Documented	Include this annotation in the Javadocs.
@Inherited	Allow subclasses to inherit parent annotations.

Most of the time, you will be defining your own annotations and writing your own processors to deal with them.

Writing annotation processors

Without tools to read them, annotations are hardly more useful than comments. An important part of the process of using annotations is to create and use *annotation processors*. Java SE5 provides extensions to the reflection API to help you create these tools. It also provides an external tool called **apt** to help you parse Java source code with annotations.

Here is a very simple annotation processor that reads the annotated **PasswordUtils** class and uses reflection to look for **@UseCase** tags. Given a list of **id** values, it lists the use cases it finds and reports any that are missing:

```
//: annotations/UseCaseTracker.java
import java.lang.reflect.*;
import java.util.*;

public class UseCaseTracker {
  public static void
  trackUseCases(List<Integer> useCases, Class<?> cl) {
    for(Method m : cl.getDeclaredMethods()) {
      UseCase uc = m.getAnnotation(UseCase.class);
      if(uc != null) {
        System.out.println("Found Use Case:" + uc.id() +
          " " + uc.description());
        useCases.remove(new Integer(uc.id()));
      }
    }
    for(int i : useCases) {
      System.out.println("Warning: Missing use case-" + i);
    }
  }
  public static void main(String[] args) {
    List<Integer> useCases = new ArrayList<Integer>();
    Collections.addAll(useCases, 47, 48, 49, 50);
    trackUseCases(useCases, PasswordUtils.class);
  }
} /* Output:
Found Use Case:47 Passwords must contain at least one
numeric
Found Use Case:48 no description
Found Use Case:49 New passwords can't equal previously used
ones
```

```
        Warning: Missing use case-50
        *///:~
```

This uses both the reflection method **getDeclaredMethods( )** and the method **getAnnotation( )**, which comes from the **AnnotatedElement** interface (classes like **Class**, **Method** and **Field** all implement this interface). This method returns the annotation object of the specified type, in this case "**UseCase**." If there are no annotations of that particular type on the annotated method, a **null** value is returned. The element values are extracted by calling **id( )** and **description( )**. Remember that no description was specified in the annotation for the **encryptPassword( )** method, so the processor above finds the default value "**no description**" when it calls the **description( )** method on that particular annotation.

Annotation elements

The **@UseCase** tag defined in **UseCase.java** contains the **int** element **id** and **String** element **description**. Here is a list of the allowed types for annotation elements:

- All primitives (**int**, **float**, **boolean** etc.)
- **String**
- **Class**
- **enum**s
- **Annotation**s
- Arrays of any of the above

The compiler will report an error if you try to use any other types. Note that you are not allowed to use any of the wrapper classes, but because of autoboxing this isn't really a limitation. You can also have elements that are themselves annotations. As you will see a bit later, nested annotations can be very helpful.

Default value constraints

The compiler is quite picky about default element values. No element can have an unspecified value. This means that elements must either have default values or values provided by the class that uses the annotation.

There is another restriction, which is that none of the non-primitive type elements are allowed to take **null** as a value, either when declared in the

---

source code or when defined as a default value in the annotation interface. This makes it hard to write a processor that acts on the presence or absence of an element, because every element is effectively present in every annotation declaration. You can get around this by checking for specific values, like empty strings or negative values:

```
//: annotations/SimulatingNull.java
import java.lang.annotation.*;

@Target(ElementType.METHOD)
@Retention(RetentionPolicy.RUNTIME)
public @interface SimulatingNull {
  public int id() default -1;
  public String description() default "";
} ///:~
```

This is a typical idiom in annotation definitions.

Generating external files

Annotations are especially useful when working with frameworks that require some sort of additional information to accompany your source code. Technologies like Enterprise JavaBeans (prior to EJB3) require numerous interfaces and deployment descriptors which are "boilerplate" code, defined in the same way for every bean. Web services, custom tag libraries and object/relational mapping tools like Toplink and Hibernate often require XML descriptors that are external to the code. After defining a Java class, the programmer must undergo the tedium of respecifying information like the name, package and so on—information that already exists in the original class. Whenever you use an external descriptor file, you end up with two separate sources of information about a class, which usually leads to code synchronization problems. This also requires that programmers working on the project must know about editing the descriptor as well as how to write Java programs.

Suppose you want to provide basic object/relational mapping functionality to automate the creation of a database table in order to store a JavaBean. You could use an XML descriptor file to specify the name of the class, each member, and information about its database mapping. Using annotations, however, you can keep all of the information in the JavaBean source file. To do this, you need annotations to define the name of the database table associated with the bean, the columns, and the SQL types to map to the bean's properties.

Here is an annotation for a bean that tells the annotation processor that it should create a database table:

```
//: annotations/database/DBTable.java
package annotations.database;
import java.lang.annotation.*;

@Target(ElementType.TYPE) // Applies to classes only
@Retention(RetentionPolicy.RUNTIME)
public @interface DBTable {
  public String name() default "";
} ///:~
```

Each **ElementType** that you specify in the **@Target** annotation is a restriction that tells the compiler that your annotation can only be applied to that particular type. You can specify a single value of the **enum ElementType**, or you can specify a comma-separated list of any combination of values. If you want to apply the annotation to any **ElementType**, you can leave out the **@Target** annotation altogether, although this is uncommon.

Note that **@DBTable** has a **name( )** element so that the annotation can supply a name for the database table that the processor will create.

Here are the annotations for the JavaBean fields:

```
//: annotations/database/Constraints.java
package annotations.database;
import java.lang.annotation.*;

@Target(ElementType.FIELD)
@Retention(RetentionPolicy.RUNTIME)
public @interface Constraints {
  boolean primaryKey() default false;
  boolean allowNull() default true;
  boolean unique() default false;
} ///:~

//: annotations/database/SQLString.java
package annotations.database;
import java.lang.annotation.*;
```

```
@Target(ElementType.FIELD)
@Retention(RetentionPolicy.RUNTIME)
public @interface SQLString {
  int value() default 0;
  String name() default "";
  Constraints constraints() default @Constraints;
} ///:~

//: annotations/database/SQLInteger.java
package annotations.database;
import java.lang.annotation.*;

@Target(ElementType.FIELD)
@Retention(RetentionPolicy.RUNTIME)
public @interface SQLInteger {
  String name() default "";
  Constraints constraints() default @Constraints;
} ///:~
```

The **@Constraints** annotation allows the processor to extract the metadata about the database table. This represents a small subset of the constraints generally offered by databases, but it gives you the general idea. The elements **primaryKey( )**, **allowNull( )** and **unique( )** are given sensible default values so that in most cases a user of the annotation won't have to type too much.

The other two **@interfaces** define SQL types. Again, for this framework to be more useful, you need to define an annotation for each additional SQL type. Here, two types will be enough.

These types each have a **name( )** element and a **constraints( )** element. The latter makes use of the nested annotation feature to embed the information about the column type's database constraints. Note that the default value for the **constraints( )** element is **@Constraints**. Since there are no element values specified in parentheses after this annotation type, the default value of **constraints( )** is actually an **@Constraints** annotation with its own default values set. To make a nested **@Constraints** annotation with uniqueness set to **true** by default, you can define its element like this:

```
//: annotations/database/Uniqueness.java
// Sample of nested annotations
package annotations.database;

public @interface Uniqueness {
```

```
    Constraints constraints()
       default @Constraints(unique=true);
} ///:~
```

Here is a simple bean that uses these annotations:

```
//: annotations/database/Member.java
package annotations.database;

@DBTable(name = "MEMBER")
public class Member {
  @SQLString(30) String firstName;
  @SQLString(50) String lastName;
  @SQLInteger Integer age;
  @SQLString(value = 30,
  constraints = @Constraints(primaryKey = true))
  String handle;
  static int memberCount;
  public String getHandle() { return handle; }
  public String getFirstName() { return firstName; }
  public String getLastName() { return lastName; }
  public String toString() { return handle; }
  public Integer getAge() { return age; }
} ///:~
```

The **@DBTable** class annotation is given the value "MEMBER", which will
be used as the table name. The bean properties, **firstName** and **lastName**,
are both annotated with **@SQLString**s and have element values of 30 and
50, respectively. These annotations are interesting for two reasons: First, they
use the default value on the nested **@Constraints** annotation, and second,
they use a shortcut feature. If you define an element on an annotation with
the name **value**, then as long as it is the only element type specified you don't
need to use the name-value pair syntax; you can just specify the value in
parentheses. This can be applied to any of the legal element types. Of course
this limits you to naming your element "value" but in the case above, it does
allow for the semantically meaningful and easy-to-read annotation
specification:

```
    @SQLString(30)
```

The processor will use this value to set the size of the SQL column that it will
create.

As neat as the default-value syntax is, it quickly becomes complex. Look at the annotation on the field **handle**. This has an **@SQLString** annotation, but it also needs to be a primary key on the database, so the element type **primaryKey** must be set on the nested **@Constraint** annotation. This is where it gets messy. You are now forced to use the rather long-winded name-value pair form for this nested annotation, respecifying the element name *and* the **@interface** name. But because the specially named element **value** is no longer the only element value being specified, you can't use the shortcut form. As you can see, the result is not pretty.

Alternative solutions

There are other ways of creating annotations for this task. You could, for example, have a single annotation class called **@TableColumn** with an **enum** element which defines values like STRING, INTEGER, FLOAT, etc. This eliminates the need for an **@interface** for each SQL type, but makes it impossible to qualify your types with additional elements like *size*, or *precision*, which is probably more useful.

You could also use a **String** element to describe the actual SQL type, e.g., "VARCHAR(30)" or "INTEGER". This does allow you to qualify the types, but it ties up the mapping from Java type to SQL type in your code, which is not good design. You don't want to have to recompile classes if you change databases; it would be more elegant just to tell your annotation processor that you are using a different "flavor" of SQL, and it let it take that into account when processing the annotations.

A third workable solution is to use two annotation types together, **@Constraints** and the relevant SQL type (for example, **@SQLInteger**), to annotate the desired field. This is slightly messy but the compiler allows as many different annotations as you like on an annotation target. Note that when using multiple annotations, you cannot use the same annotation twice.

Annotations don't support inheritance

You cannot use the **extends** keyword with **@interfaces**. This is a pity, because an elegant solution would have been to define an annotation **@TableColumn**, as suggested above, with a nested annotation of type **@SQLType**. That way, you could inherit all your SQL types, like **@SQLInteger** and **@SQLString**, from **@SQLType**. This would reduce typing and neaten the syntax. There doesn't seem to be any suggestion of annotations supporting inheritance in future releases, so the examples above seem to be the best you can do under the circumstances.

Implementing the processor

Here is an example of an annotation processor which reads in a class file, checks for its database annotations and generates the SQL command for making the database:

```
//: annotations/database/TableCreator.java
// Reflection-based annotation processor.
// {Args: annotations.database.Member}
package annotations.database;
import java.lang.annotation.*;
import java.lang.reflect.*;
import java.util.*;

public class TableCreator {
  public static void main(String[] args) throws Exception {
    if(args.length < 1) {
      System.out.println("arguments: annotated classes");
      System.exit(0);
    }
    for(String className : args) {
      Class<?> cl = Class.forName(className);
      DBTable dbTable = cl.getAnnotation(DBTable.class);
      if(dbTable == null) {
        System.out.println(
          "No DBTable annotations in class " + className);
        continue;
      }
      String tableName = dbTable.name();
      // If the name is empty, use the Class name:
      if(tableName.length() < 1)
        tableName = cl.getName().toUpperCase();
      List<String> columnDefs = new ArrayList<String>();
      for(Field field : cl.getDeclaredFields()) {
        String columnName = null;
        Annotation[] anns = field.getDeclaredAnnotations();
        if(anns.length < 1)
          continue; // Not a db table column
        if(anns[0] instanceof SQLInteger) {
          SQLInteger sInt = (SQLInteger) anns[0];
          // Use field name if name not specified
```

```
        if(sInt.name().length() < 1)
          columnName = field.getName().toUpperCase();
        else
          columnName = sInt.name();
        columnDefs.add(columnName + " INT" +
          getConstraints(sInt.constraints()));
      }
      if(anns[0] instanceof SQLString) {
        SQLString sString = (SQLString) anns[0];
        // Use field name if name not specified.
        if(sString.name().length() < 1)
          columnName = field.getName().toUpperCase();
        else
          columnName = sString.name();
        columnDefs.add(columnName + " VARCHAR(" +
          sString.value() + ")" +
          getConstraints(sString.constraints()));
      }
      StringBuilder createCommand = new StringBuilder(
        "CREATE TABLE " + tableName + "(");
      for(String columnDef : columnDefs)
        createCommand.append("\n    " + columnDef + ",");
      // Remove trailing comma
      String tableCreate = createCommand.substring(
        0, createCommand.length() - 1) + ");";
      System.out.println("Table Creation SQL for " +
        className + " is :\n" + tableCreate);
    }
  }
}
  private static String getConstraints(Constraints con) {
    String constraints = "";
    if(!con.allowNull())
      constraints += " NOT NULL";
    if(con.primaryKey())
      constraints += " PRIMARY KEY";
    if(con.unique())
      constraints += " UNIQUE";
    return constraints;
  }
} /* Output:
Table Creation SQL for annotations.database.Member is :
CREATE TABLE MEMBER(
    FIRSTNAME VARCHAR(30));
```

```
Table Creation SQL for annotations.database.Member is :
CREATE TABLE MEMBER(
    FIRSTNAME VARCHAR(30),
    LASTNAME VARCHAR(50));
Table Creation SQL for annotations.database.Member is :
CREATE TABLE MEMBER(
    FIRSTNAME VARCHAR(30),
    LASTNAME VARCHAR(50),
    AGE INT);
Table Creation SQL for annotations.database.Member is :
CREATE TABLE MEMBER(
    FIRSTNAME VARCHAR(30),
    LASTNAME VARCHAR(50),
    AGE INT,
    HANDLE VARCHAR(30) PRIMARY KEY);
*///:~
```

The **main( )** method cycles through each of the class names on the command line. Each class is loaded using **forName( )** and checked to see if it has the **@DBTable** annotation on it with **getAnnotation(DBTable.class)**. If it does, then the table name is found and stored. All of the fields in the class are then loaded and checked using **getDeclaredAnnotations( )**. This method returns an array of all of the defined annotations for a particular method. The **instanceof** operator is used to determine if these annotations are of type **@SQLInteger** and **@SQLString**, and in each case the relevant **String** fragment is then created with the name of the table column. Note that because there is no inheritance of annotation interfaces, using **getDeclaredAnnotations( )** is the only way you can approximate polymorphic behavior.

The nested @**Constraint** annotation is passed to the **getConstraints( )** which builds up a **String** containing the SQL constraints.

It is worth mentioning that the technique shown above is a somewhat naïve way of defining an object/relational mapping. Having an annotation of type **@DBTable** which takes the table name as a parameter forces you to recompile your Java code if you want to change the table name. This might not be desirable. There are many available frameworks for mapping objects to relational databases, and more and more of them are making use of annotations.

Exercise 1: (2) Implement more SQL types in the database example.

Project:[3] Modify the database example so that it connects and interacts with a real database using JDBC.

Project: Modify the database example so that it creates conformant XML files rather than writing SQL code.

Using **apt** to process annotations

The *annotation processing tool* **apt** is Sun's first version of a tool that aids the processing of annotations. Because it is an early incarnation, the tool is still a little primitive, but it has features which can make your life easier.

Like **javac**, **apt** is designed to be run on Java source files rather than compiled classes. By default, **apt** compiles the source files when it has finished processing them. This is useful if you are automatically creating new source files as part of your build process. In fact, **apt** checks newly created source files for annotations and compiles them all in the same pass.

When your annotation processor creates a new source file, that file is itself checked for annotations in a new *round* (as it is referred to in the documentation) of processing. The tool will continue round after round of processing until no more source files are being created. It then compiles all of the source files.

Each annotation you write will need its own processor, but the **apt** tool can easily group several annotation processors together. It allows you to specify multiple classes to be processed, which is a lot easier than having to iterate through **File** classes yourself. You can also add listeners to receive notification of when an annotation processing round is complete.

At the time of this writing, **apt** is not available as an Ant task (see the supplement at *http://MindView.net/Books/BetterJava*), but it can obviously be run as an external task from Ant in the meantime. In order to compile the annotation processors in this section you must have **tools.jar** in your classpath; this library also contains the the **com.sun.mirror.*** interfaces.

apt works by using an **AnnotationProcessorFactory** to create the right kind of annotation processor for each annotation it finds. When you run **apt**,

---

[3] Projects are suggestions to be used (for example) as term projects. Solutions to projects are not included in the solution guide.

you specify either a factory class or a classpath where it can find the factories it needs. If you don't do this, **apt** will embark on an arcane *discovery* process, the details of which can be found in the *Developing an Annotation Processor* section of Sun's documentation.

When you create an annotation processor for use with **apt**, you can't use the reflection features in Java because you are working with source code, not compiled classes.[4] The **mirror** API[5] solves this problem by allowing you to view methods, fields and types in uncompiled source code.

Here is an annotation that can be used to extract the public methods from a class and turn them into an interface:

```
//: annotations/ExtractInterface.java
// APT-based annotation processing.
package annotations;
import java.lang.annotation.*;

@Target(ElementType.TYPE)
@Retention(RetentionPolicy.SOURCE)
public @interface ExtractInterface {
  public String value();
} ///:~
```

The **RetentionPolicy** is **SOURCE** because there is no point in keeping this annotation in the class file after we have extracted the interface from the class. The following class provides a public method which can become part of a useful interface:

```
//: annotations/Multiplier.java
// APT-based annotation processing.
package annotations;

@ExtractInterface("IMultiplier")
public class Multiplier {
  public int multiply(int x, int y) {
    int total = 0;
    for(int i = 0; i < x; i++)
```

---

[4] However, using the non-standard **-XclassesAsDecls** option, you may work with annotations that are in compiled classes.

[5] The Java designers coyly suggest that a mirror is where you find a reflection.

```
      total = add(total, y);
    return total;
  }
  private int add(int x, int y) { return x + y; }
  public static void main(String[] args) {
    Multiplier m = new Multiplier();
    System.out.println("11*16 = " + m.multiply(11, 16));
  }
} /* Output:
11*16 = 176
*///:~
```

The **Multiplier** class (which only works with positive integers) has a
multiply( ) method which calls the private **add( )** method numerous times
to perform multiplication. The **add( )** method is not public, so is not part of
the interface. The annotation is given the value of **IMultiplier**, which is the
name of the interface to create.

Now you need a processor to do the extraction:

```
//: annotations/InterfaceExtractorProcessor.java
// APT-based annotation processing.
// {Exec: apt -factory
// annotations.InterfaceExtractorProcessorFactory
// Multiplier.java -s ../annotations}
package annotations;
import com.sun.mirror.apt.*;
import com.sun.mirror.declaration.*;
import java.io.*;
import java.util.*;

public class InterfaceExtractorProcessor
  implements AnnotationProcessor {
  private final AnnotationProcessorEnvironment env;
  private ArrayList<MethodDeclaration> interfaceMethods =
    new ArrayList<MethodDeclaration>();
  public InterfaceExtractorProcessor(
    AnnotationProcessorEnvironment env) { this.env = env; }
  public void process() {
    for(TypeDeclaration typeDecl :
      env.getSpecifiedTypeDeclarations()) {
      ExtractInterface annot =
        typeDecl.getAnnotation(ExtractInterface.class);
      if(annot == null)
        break;
```

```
       for(MethodDeclaration m : typeDecl.getMethods())
         if(m.getModifiers().contains(Modifier.PUBLIC) &&
            !(m.getModifiers().contains(Modifier.STATIC)))
           interfaceMethods.add(m);
       if(interfaceMethods.size() > 0) {
         try {
           PrintWriter writer =
             env.getFiler().createSourceFile(annot.value());
           writer.println("package " +
             typeDecl.getPackage().getQualifiedName() +";");
           writer.println("public interface " +
             annot.value() + " {");
           for(MethodDeclaration m : interfaceMethods) {
             writer.print("  public ");
             writer.print(m.getReturnType() + " ");
             writer.print(m.getSimpleName() + " (");
             int i = 0;
             for(ParameterDeclaration parm :
               m.getParameters()) {
               writer.print(parm.getType() + " " +
                 parm.getSimpleName());
               if(++i < m.getParameters().size())
                 writer.print(", ");
             }
             writer.println(");");
           }
           writer.println("}");
           writer.close();
         } catch(IOException ioe) {
           throw new RuntimeException(ioe);
         }
       }
     }
   }
 }
} ///:~
```

The **process( )** method is where all the work is done. The
MethodDeclaration class and its **getModifiers( )** method are used to
identify the **public** methods (but ignore the **static** ones) of the class being
processed. If any are found, they are stored in an **ArrayList** and used to
create the methods of a new interface definition in a **.java** file.

Notice that an **AnnotationProcessorEnvironment** object is passed into
the constructor. You can query this object for all of the types (class

definitions) that the **apt** tool is processing, and you can use it to get a **Messager** object and a **Filer** object. The **Messager** enables you to report messages to the user, e.g., any errors that might have occurred with the processing and where they are in the source code. The **Filer** is a kind of **PrintWriter** through which you will create new files. The main reason that you use a **Filer** object, rather than a plain **PrintWriter**, is that it allows **apt** to keep track of any new files that you create, so it can check them for annotations and compile them if it needs to.

You will also see that the method **createSourceFile( )** opens an ordinary output stream with the correct name for your Java class or interface. There isn't any support for creating Java language constructs, so you have to generate the Java source code using the somewhat primitive **print( )** and **println( )** methods. This means making sure that your brackets match up and that your code is syntactically correct.

process( ) is called by the **apt** tool, which needs a factory to provide the right processor:

```
//: annotations/InterfaceExtractorProcessorFactory.java
// APT-based annotation processing.
package annotations;
import com.sun.mirror.apt.*;
import com.sun.mirror.declaration.*;
import java.util.*;

public class InterfaceExtractorProcessorFactory
  implements AnnotationProcessorFactory {
  public AnnotationProcessor getProcessorFor(
    Set<AnnotationTypeDeclaration> atds,
    AnnotationProcessorEnvironment env) {
    return new InterfaceExtractorProcessor(env);
  }
  public Collection<String> supportedAnnotationTypes() {
    return
     Collections.singleton("annotations.ExtractInterface");
  }
  public Collection<String> supportedOptions() {
    return Collections.emptySet();
  }
} ///:~
```

There are only three methods on the **AnnotationProcessorFactory** interface. As you can see, the one which provides the processor is **getProcessorFor( )**, which takes a **Set** of type declarations (the Java classes that the **apt** tool is being run against), and the **AnnotationProcessorEnvironment** object, which you have already seen being passed through to the processor. The other two methods, **supportedAnnotationTypes( )** and **supportedOptions( )**, are there so you can check that you have processors for all of the annotations found by **apt** and that you support all options specified at the command prompt. The **getProcessorFor( )** method is particularly important because if you don't return the full class name of your annotation type in the **String** collection, **apt** will warn you that there is no relevant processor and exit without doing anything.

The processor and factory are in the package **annotations**, so for the directory structure above, the command line is embedded in the '**Exec**' comment tag at the beginning of **InterfaceExtractorProcessor.java**. This tells **apt** to use the factory class defined above and process the file **Multiplier.java**. The -**s** option specifies that any new files must be created in the directory **annotations**. The generated **IMultiplier.java** file, as you might guess by looking at the **println( )** statements in the processor above, looks like this:

```
package annotations;
public interface IMultiplier {
  public int multiply (int x, int y);
}
```

This file will also be compiled by **apt**, so you will see the file **IMultiplier.class** in the same directory.

Exercise 2: (3) Add support for division to the interface extractor.

Using the *Visitor* pattern with **apt**

Processing annotations can become complex. The example above is a relatively simple annotation processor and only interprets one annotation, but still requires a fair amount of complexity to make it work. To prevent the complexity from scaling up badly when you have more annotations and more processors, the **mirror** API provides classes to support the *Visitor* design pattern. Visitor is one of the classic design patterns from the book *Design*

Patterns by Gamma et al., and you can also find a more a detailed explanation in *Thinking in Patterns*.

A Visitor traverses a data structure or collection of objects, performing an operation on each one. The data structure need not be ordered, and the operation that you perform on each object will be specific to its type. This decouples the operations from the objects themselves, meaning that you can add new operations without adding methods to the class definitions.

This makes it useful for processing annotations, because a Java class can be thought of as a collection of objects such as **TypeDeclaration**s, **FieldDeclaration**s, **MethodDeclaration**s, and so on. When you use the **apt** tool with the Visitor pattern, you provide a **Visitor** class which has a method for handling each type of declaration that you visit. Thus you can implement appropriate behavior for annotations on methods, classes, fields and so on.

Here is the SQL table generator again, this time using a factory and a processor that makes use of the Visitor pattern:

```
//: annotations/database/TableCreationProcessorFactory.java
// The database example using Visitor.
// {Exec: apt -factory
// annotations.database.TableCreationProcessorFactory
// database/Member.java -s database}
package annotations.database;
import com.sun.mirror.apt.*;
import com.sun.mirror.declaration.*;
import com.sun.mirror.util.*;
import java.util.*;
import static com.sun.mirror.util.DeclarationVisitors.*;

public class TableCreationProcessorFactory
  implements AnnotationProcessorFactory {
  public AnnotationProcessor getProcessorFor(
    Set<AnnotationTypeDeclaration> atds,
    AnnotationProcessorEnvironment env) {
    return new TableCreationProcessor(env);
  }
  public Collection<String> supportedAnnotationTypes() {
    return Arrays.asList(
      "annotations.database.DBTable",
      "annotations.database.Constraints",
```

```
          "annotations.database.SQLString",
          "annotations.database.SQLInteger");
    }
    public Collection<String> supportedOptions() {
      return Collections.emptySet();
    }
    private static class TableCreationProcessor
      implements AnnotationProcessor {
      private final AnnotationProcessorEnvironment env;
      private String sql = "";
      public TableCreationProcessor(
        AnnotationProcessorEnvironment env) {
        this.env = env;
      }
      public void process() {
        for(TypeDeclaration typeDecl :
          env.getSpecifiedTypeDeclarations()) {
          typeDecl.accept(getDeclarationScanner(
            new TableCreationVisitor(), NO_OP));
          sql = sql.substring(0, sql.length() - 1) + ");";
          System.out.println("creation SQL is :\n" + sql);
          sql = "";
        }
      }
      private class TableCreationVisitor
        extends SimpleDeclarationVisitor {
        public void visitClassDeclaration(
          ClassDeclaration d) {
          DBTable dbTable = d.getAnnotation(DBTable.class);
          if(dbTable != null) {
            sql += "CREATE TABLE ";
            sql += (dbTable.name().length() < 1)
              ? d.getSimpleName().toUpperCase()
              : dbTable.name();
            sql += " (";
          }
        }
        public void visitFieldDeclaration(
          FieldDeclaration d) {
          String columnName = "";
          if(d.getAnnotation(SQLInteger.class) != null) {
            SQLInteger sInt = d.getAnnotation(
                SQLInteger.class);
            // Use field name if name not specified
```

```
          if(sInt.name().length() < 1)
            columnName = d.getSimpleName().toUpperCase();
          else
            columnName = sInt.name();
          sql += "\n     " + columnName + " INT" +
            getConstraints(sInt.constraints()) + ",";
        }
        if(d.getAnnotation(SQLString.class) != null) {
          SQLString sString = d.getAnnotation(
              SQLString.class);
          // Use field name if name not specified.
          if(sString.name().length() < 1)
            columnName = d.getSimpleName().toUpperCase();
          else
            columnName = sString.name();
          sql += "\n     " + columnName + " VARCHAR(" +
            sString.value() + ")" +
            getConstraints(sString.constraints()) + ",";
        }
      }
    }
    private String getConstraints(Constraints con) {
      String constraints = "";
      if(!con.allowNull())
        constraints += " NOT NULL";
      if(con.primaryKey())
        constraints += " PRIMARY KEY";
      if(con.unique())
        constraints += " UNIQUE";
      return constraints;
    }
  }
}
} ///:~
```

The output is identical to the previous **DBTable** example.

The processor and the visitor are inner classes in this example. Note that the **process( )** method only adds the visitor class and initializes the SQL string.

Both parameters of **getDeclarationScanner( )** are visitors; the first is used before each declaration is visited and the second is used afterwards. This processor only needs the pre-visit visitor, so **NO_OP** is given as the second parameter. This is a **static** field in the **DeclarationVisitor** interface, which is a **DeclarationVisitor** that doesn't do anything.

TableCreationVisitor extends **SimpleDeclarationVisitor**, overriding the two methods **visitClassDeclaration( )** and **visitFieldDeclaration( )**. The **SimpleDeclarationVisitor** is an adapter that implements all of the methods on the **DeclarationVisitor** interface, so you can concentrate on the ones you need. In **visitClassDeclaration( )**, the **ClassDeclaration** object is checked for the **DBTable** annotation, and if it is there, the first part of the SQL creation **String** is initialized. In **visitFieldDeclaration( )**, the field declaration is queried for its field annotations and the information is extracted in much the same way as it was in the original example, earlier in the chapter.

This may seem like a more complicated way of doing things, but it produces a more scalable solution. If the complexity of your annotation processor increases, then writing your own standalone processor as in the earlier example would soon become quite complicated.

Exercise 3: (2) Add support for more SQL types to **TableCreationProcessorFactory.java**.

Annotation-based unit testing

Unit testing is the practice of creating one or more tests for each method in a class, in order to regularly test the portions of a class for correct behavior. The most popular tool used for unit testing in Java is called *JUnit*; at the time of this writing, JUnit was in the process of being updated to JUnit version 4, in order to incorporate annotations.[6] One of the main problems with pre-annotation versions of JUnit is the amount of "ceremony" necessary in order to set up and run JUnit tests. This has been reduced over time, but annotations will move testing closer to "the simplest unit testing system that can possibly work."

With pre-annotation versions of JUnit, you must create a separate class to hold your unit tests. With annotations we can include the unit tests inside the class to be tested, and thus reduce the time and trouble of unit testing to a minimum. This approach has the additional benefit of being able to test **private** methods as easily as **public** ones.

---

[6] I originally had thoughts of making a "better JUnit" based on the design shown here. However, it appears that JUnit4 also includes many of the ideas presented here, so it remains easier to go along with that.

Since this example test framework is annotation-based, it's called **@Unit**. The most basic form of testing, and one which you will probably use much of the time, only needs the **@Test** annotation to indicate which methods should be tested. One option is for the test methods to take no arguments and return a **boolean** to indicate success or failure. You can use any name you like for test methods. Also, **@Unit** test methods can have any access that you'd like, including **private**.

To use **@Unit**, all you need to do is import **net.mindview.atunit**,[7] mark the appropriate methods and fields with **@Unit** test tags (which you'll learn about in the following examples) and then have your build system run **@Unit** on the resulting class. Here's a simple example:

```
//: annotations/AtUnitExample1.java
package annotations;
import net.mindview.atunit.*;
import net.mindview.util.*;

public class AtUnitExample1 {
  public String methodOne() {
    return "This is methodOne";
  }
  public int methodTwo() {
    System.out.println("This is methodTwo");
    return 2;
  }
  @Test boolean methodOneTest() {
    return methodOne().equals("This is methodOne");
  }
  @Test boolean m2() { return methodTwo() == 2; }
  @Test private boolean m3() { return true; }
  // Shows output for failure:
  @Test boolean failureTest() { return false; }
  @Test boolean anotherDisappointment() { return false; }
  public static void main(String[] args) throws Exception {
    OSExecute.command(
      "java net.mindview.atunit.AtUnit AtUnitExample1");
  }
} /* Output:
annotations.AtUnitExample1
```

---

[7] This library is part of this book's code package, available at *www.MindView.net.*

```
  . methodOneTest
  . m2 This is methodTwo

  . m3
  . failureTest (failed)
  . anotherDisappointment (failed)
(5 tests)

>>> 2 FAILURES <<<
  annotations.AtUnitExample1: failureTest
  annotations.AtUnitExample1: anotherDisappointment
*///:~
```

Classes to be **@Unit** tested must be placed in packages.

The **@Test** annotation preceding the methods **methodOneTest( )**, **m2( )**, **m3( )**, **failureTest( )** and **anotherDisappointment( )** tells @Unit to run these methods as unit tests. It will also ensure that those methods take no arguments and return a **boolean** or **void**. Your only responsibility when you write the unit test is to determine whether the test succeeds or fails and returns **true** or **false**, respectively (for methods that return **boolean**).

If you're familiar with JUnit, you'll also note **@Unit**'s more informative output—you can see the test that's currently being run so the output from that test is more useful, and at the end it tells you the classes and tests that caused failures.

You're not forced to embed test methods inside your classes, if that doesn't work for you. The easiest way to create non-embedded tests is with inheritance:

```
//: annotations/AtUnitExternalTest.java
// Creating non-embedded tests.
package annotations;
import net.mindview.atunit.*;
import net.mindview.util.*;

public class AtUnitExternalTest extends AtUnitExample1 {
  @Test boolean _methodOne() {
    return methodOne().equals("This is methodOne");
  }
  @Test boolean _methodTwo() { return methodTwo() == 2; }
  public static void main(String[] args) throws Exception {
    OSExecute.command(
```

```
      "java net.mindview.atunit.AtUnit AtUnitExternalTest");
  }
} /* Output:
annotations.AtUnitExternalTest
  . _methodOne
  . _methodTwo This is methodTwo

OK (2 tests)
*///:~
```

This example also demonstrates the value of flexible naming (in contrast to JUnit's requirement to start all your tests with the word "**test**"). Here, **@Test** methods that are directly testing another method are given the name of that method starting with an underscore (I'm not suggesting that this is an ideal style, just showing a possibility).

You can also use composition to create non-embedded tests:

```
//: annotations/AtUnitComposition.java
// Creating non-embedded tests.
package annotations;
import net.mindview.atunit.*;
import net.mindview.util.*;

public class AtUnitComposition {
  AtUnitExample1 testObject = new AtUnitExample1();
  @Test boolean _methodOne() {
    return
      testObject.methodOne().equals("This is methodOne");
  }
  @Test boolean _methodTwo() {
    return testObject.methodTwo() == 2;
  }
  public static void main(String[] args) throws Exception {
    OSExecute.command(
      "java net.mindview.atunit.AtUnit AtUnitComposition");
  }
} /* Output:
annotations.AtUnitComposition
  . _methodOne
  . _methodTwo This is methodTwo

OK (2 tests)
*///:~
```

A new member **testObject** is created for each test, since an
AtUnitComposition object is created for each test.

There are no special "assert" methods as there are in JUnit, but the second
form of the **@Test** method allows you to return **void** (or **boolean**, if you still
want to return **true** or **false** in this case). To test for success, you can use
Java **assert** statements. Java assertions normally have to be enabled with the
-ea flag on the **java** command line, but **@Unit** automatically enables them.
To indicate failure, you can even use an exception. One of the **@Unit** design
goals is to require as little additional syntax as possible, and Java's **assert**
and exceptions are all that is necessary to report errors. A failed **assert** or an
exception that emerges from the test method is treated as a failed test, but
@Unit does not halt in this case—it continues until all the tests are run.
Here's an example:

```
//: annotations/AtUnitExample2.java
// Assertions and exceptions can be used in @Tests.
package annotations;
import java.io.*;
import net.mindview.atunit.*;
import net.mindview.util.*;

public class AtUnitExample2 {
  public String methodOne() {
    return "This is methodOne";
  }
  public int methodTwo() {
    System.out.println("This is methodTwo");
    return 2;
  }
  @Test void assertExample() {
    assert methodOne().equals("This is methodOne");
  }
  @Test void assertFailureExample() {
    assert 1 == 2: "What a surprise!";
  }
  @Test void exceptionExample() throws IOException {
    new FileInputStream("nofile.txt"); // Throws
  }
  @Test boolean assertAndReturn() {
    // Assertion with message:
    assert methodTwo() == 2: "methodTwo must equal 2";
    return methodOne().equals("This is methodOne");
```

```
  }
  public static void main(String[] args) throws Exception {
    OSExecute.command(
      "java net.mindview.atunit.AtUnit AtUnitExample2");
  }
} /* Output:
annotations.AtUnitExample2
  . assertExample
  . assertFailureExample java.lang.AssertionError: What a
surprise!
(failed)
  . exceptionExample java.io.FileNotFoundException:
nofile.txt (The system cannot find the file specified)
(failed)
  . assertAndReturn This is methodTwo

(4 tests)

>>> 2 FAILURES <<<
  annotations.AtUnitExample2: assertFailureExample
  annotations.AtUnitExample2: exceptionExample
*///:~
```

Here's an example using non-embedded tests with assertions, performing some simple tests of **java.util.HashSet**:

```
//: annotations/HashSetTest.java
package annotations;
import java.util.*;
import net.mindview.atunit.*;
import net.mindview.util.*;

public class HashSetTest {
  HashSet<String> testObject = new HashSet<String>();
  @Test void initialization() {
    assert testObject.isEmpty();
  }
  @Test void _contains() {
    testObject.add("one");
    assert testObject.contains("one");
  }
  @Test void _remove() {
    testObject.add("one");
    testObject.remove("one");
    assert testObject.isEmpty();
```

```
      }
   public static void main(String[] args) throws Exception {
      OSExecute.command(
         "java net.mindview.atunit.AtUnit HashSetTest");
   }
} /* Output:
annotations.HashSetTest
   . initialization
   . _remove
   . _contains
OK (3 tests)
*///:~
```

The inheritance approach would seem to be simpler, in the absence of other constraints.

Exercise 4: (3) Verify that a new **testObject** is created before each test.

Exercise 5: (1) Modify the above example to use the inheritance approach.

Exercise 6: (1) Test **LinkedList** using the approach shown in **HashSetTest.java**.

Exercise 7: (1) Modify the previous exercise to use the inheritance approach.

For each unit test, **@Unit** creates an object of the class under test using the default constructor. The test is called for that object, and then the object is discarded to prevent side effects from leaking into other unit tests. This relies on the default constructor to create the objects. If you don't have a default constructor or you need more sophisticated construction for objects, you create a **static** method to build the object and attach the **@TestObjectCreate** annotation, like this:

```
//: annotations/AtUnitExample3.java
package annotations;
import net.mindview.atunit.*;
import net.mindview.util.*;

public class AtUnitExample3 {
   private int n;
   public AtUnitExample3(int n) { this.n = n; }
   public int getN() { return n; }
   public String methodOne() {
```

```
        return "This is methodOne";
    }
    public int methodTwo() {
      System.out.println("This is methodTwo");
      return 2;
    }
    @TestObjectCreate static AtUnitExample3 create() {
      return new AtUnitExample3(47);
    }
    @Test boolean initialization() { return n == 47; }
    @Test boolean methodOneTest() {
      return methodOne().equals("This is methodOne");
    }
    @Test boolean m2() { return methodTwo() == 2; }
    public static void main(String[] args) throws Exception {
      OSExecute.command(
        "java net.mindview.atunit.AtUnit AtUnitExample3");
    }
} /* Output:
annotations.AtUnitExample3
  . initialization
  . methodOneTest
  . m2 This is methodTwo

OK (3 tests)
*///:~
```

The **@TestObjectCreate** method must be **static** and must return an object
of the type that you're testing—the **@Unit** program will ensure that this is
true.

Sometimes you need additional fields to support your unit testing. The
@TestProperty annotation can be used to tag fields that are only used for
unit testing (so that they can be removed before you deliver the product to the
client). Here's an example that reads values from a **String** that is broken up
using the **String.split( )** method. This input is used to produce test objects:

```
//: annotations/AtUnitExample4.java
package annotations;
import java.util.*;
import net.mindview.atunit.*;
import net.mindview.util.*;
import static net.mindview.util.Print.*;
```

```
public class AtUnitExample4 {
  static String theory = "All brontosauruses " +
    "are thin at one end, much MUCH thicker in the " +
    "middle, and then thin again at the far end.";
  private String word;
  private Random rand = new Random(); // Time-based seed
  public AtUnitExample4(String word) { this.word = word; }
  public String getWord() { return word; }
  public String scrambleWord() {
    List<Character> chars = new ArrayList<Character>();
    for(Character c : word.toCharArray())
      chars.add(c);
    Collections.shuffle(chars, rand);
    StringBuilder result = new StringBuilder();
    for(char ch : chars)
      result.append(ch);
    return result.toString();
  }
  @TestProperty static List<String> input =
    Arrays.asList(theory.split(" "));
  @TestProperty
    static Iterator<String> words = input.iterator();
  @TestObjectCreate static AtUnitExample4 create() {
    if(words.hasNext())
      return new AtUnitExample4(words.next());
    else
      return null;
  }
  @Test boolean words() {
    print("'" + getWord() + "'");
    return getWord().equals("are");
  }
  @Test boolean scramble1() {
    // Change to a specific seed to get verifiable results:
    rand = new Random(47);
    print("'" + getWord() + "'");
    String scrambled = scrambleWord();
    print(scrambled);
    return scrambled.equals("lAl");
  }
  @Test boolean scramble2() {
    rand = new Random(74);
    print("'" + getWord() + "'");
    String scrambled = scrambleWord();
```

```
      print(scrambled);
      return scrambled.equals("tsaeborornussu");
    }
    public static void main(String[] args) throws Exception {
      System.out.println("starting");
      OSExecute.command(
        "java net.mindview.atunit.AtUnit AtUnitExample4");
    }
} /* Output:
starting
annotations.AtUnitExample4
  . scramble1 'All'
lAl

  . scramble2 'brontosauruses'
tsaeborornussu

  . words 'are'

OK (3 tests)
*///:~
```

@TestProperty can also be used to tag methods that may be used during testing, but are not tests themselves.

Note that this program relies on the execution order of the tests, which is in general not a good practice.

If your test object creation performs initialization that requires later cleanup, you can optionally add a **static @TestObjectCleanup** method to perform cleanup when you are finished with the test object. In this example, **@TestObjectCreate** opens a file to create each test object, so the file must be closed before the test object is discarded:

```
//: annotations/AtUnitExample5.java
package annotations;
import java.io.*;
import net.mindview.atunit.*;
import net.mindview.util.*;

public class AtUnitExample5 {
  private String text;
  public AtUnitExample5(String text) { this.text = text; }
  public String toString() { return text; }
```

```
@TestProperty static PrintWriter output;
@TestProperty static int counter;
@TestObjectCreate static AtUnitExample5 create() {
  String id = Integer.toString(counter++);
  try {
    output = new PrintWriter("Test" + id + ".txt");
  } catch(IOException e) {
    throw new RuntimeException(e);
  }
  return new AtUnitExample5(id);
}
@TestObjectCleanup static void
cleanup(AtUnitExample5 tobj) {
  System.out.println("Running cleanup");
  output.close();
}
@Test boolean test1() {
  output.print("test1");
  return true;
}
@Test boolean test2() {
  output.print("test2");
  return true;
}
@Test boolean test3() {
  output.print("test3");
  return true;
}
public static void main(String[] args) throws Exception {
  OSExecute.command(
    "java net.mindview.atunit.AtUnit AtUnitExample5");
}
} /* Output:
annotations.AtUnitExample5
  . test1
Running cleanup
  . test2
Running cleanup
  . test3
Running cleanup
OK (3 tests)
*///:~
```

You can see from the output that the cleanup method is automatically run
after each test.

Using @Unit with generics

Generics pose a special problem, because you can't "test generically." You must test for a specific type parameter or set of parameters. The solution is simple: Inherit a test class from a specified version of the generic class.

Here's a simple implementation of a stack:

```
//: annotations/StackL.java
// A stack built on a linkedList.
package annotations;
import java.util.*;

public class StackL<T> {
  private LinkedList<T> list = new LinkedList<T>();
  public void push(T v) { list.addFirst(v); }
  public T top() { return list.getFirst(); }
  public T pop() { return list.removeFirst(); }
} ///:~
```

To test a **String** version, inherit a test class from **StackL<String>**:

```
//: annotations/StackLStringTest.java
// Applying @Unit to generics.
package annotations;
import net.mindview.atunit.*;
import net.mindview.util.*;

public class StackLStringTest extends StackL<String> {
  @Test void _push() {
    push("one");
    assert top().equals("one");
    push("two");
    assert top().equals("two");
  }
  @Test void _pop() {
    push("one");
    push("two");
    assert pop().equals("two");
    assert pop().equals("one");
  }
  @Test void _top() {
    push("A");
    push("B");
    assert top().equals("B");
```

```
      assert top().equals("B");
  }
  public static void main(String[] args) throws Exception {
    OSExecute.command(
      "java net.mindview.atunit.AtUnit StackLStringTest");
  }
} /* Output:
annotations.StackLStringTest
  . _push
  . _pop
  . _top
OK (3 tests)
*///:~
```

The only potential drawback to inheritance is that you lose the ability to
access **private** methods in the class under test. If this is a problem, you can
either make the method in question **protected**, or add a non-private
@TestProperty method that calls the **private** method (the
@TestProperty method will then be stripped out of the production code by
the **AtUnitRemover** tool that is shown later in this chapter).

Exercise 8: (2) Create a class with a **private** method and add a non-
private @TestProperty method as described above. Call this method in
your test code.

Exercise 9: (2) Write basic **@Unit** tests for **HashMap**.

Exercise 10: (2) Select an example from elsewhere in the book and add
@Unit tests.

No "suites" necessary

One of the big advantages of **@Unit** over JUnit is that "suites" are
unnecessary. In JUnit, you need to somehow tell the unit testing tool what it
is that you need to test, and this requires the introduction of "suites" to group
tests together so that JUnit can find them and run the tests.

@Unit simply searches for class files containing the appropriate annotations,
and then executes the **@Test** methods. Much of my goal with the **@Unit**
testing system is to make it incredibly transparent, so that people can begin
using it by simply adding **@Test** methods, with no other special code or
knowledge like that required by JUnit and many other unit testing
frameworks. It's hard enough to write tests without adding any new hurdles,

so **@Unit** tries to make it trivial. This way, you're more likely to actually write the tests.

Implementing **@Unit**

First, we need to define all the annotation types. These are simple tags, and have no fields. The **@Test** tag was defined at the beginning of the chapter, and here are the rest of the annotations:

```
//: net/mindview/atunit/TestObjectCreate.java
// The @Unit @TestObjectCreate tag.
package net.mindview.atunit;
import java.lang.annotation.*;

@Target(ElementType.METHOD)
@Retention(RetentionPolicy.RUNTIME)
public @interface TestObjectCreate {} ///:~
```

```
//: net/mindview/atunit/TestObjectCleanup.java
// The @Unit @TestObjectCleanup tag.
package net.mindview.atunit;
import java.lang.annotation.*;

@Target(ElementType.METHOD)
@Retention(RetentionPolicy.RUNTIME)
public @interface TestObjectCleanup {} ///:~
```

```
//: net/mindview/atunit/TestProperty.java
// The @Unit @TestProperty tag.
package net.mindview.atunit;
import java.lang.annotation.*;

// Both fields and methods may be tagged as properties:
@Target({ElementType.FIELD, ElementType.METHOD})
@Retention(RetentionPolicy.RUNTIME)
public @interface TestProperty {} ///:~
```

All the tests have **RUNTIME** retention because the **@Unit** system must discover the tests in compiled code.

To implement the system that runs the tests, we use reflection to extract the annotations. The program uses this information to decide how to build the test objects and run tests on them. Because of annotations this is surprisingly small and straightforward:

```
//: net/mindview/atunit/AtUnit.java
// An annotation-based unit-test framework.
// {RunByHand}
package net.mindview.atunit;
import java.lang.reflect.*;
import java.io.*;
import java.util.*;
import net.mindview.util.*;
import static net.mindview.util.Print.*;

public class AtUnit implements ProcessFiles.Strategy {
  static Class<?> testClass;
  static List<String> failedTests= new ArrayList<String>();
  static long testsRun = 0;
  static long failures = 0;
  public static void main(String[] args) throws Exception {
    ClassLoader.getSystemClassLoader()
      .setDefaultAssertionStatus(true); // Enable asserts
    new ProcessFiles(new AtUnit(), "class").start(args);
    if(failures == 0)
      print("OK (" + testsRun + " tests)");
    else {
      print("(" + testsRun + " tests)");
      print("\n>>> " + failures + " FAILURE" +
        (failures > 1 ? "S" : "") + " <<<");
      for(String failed : failedTests)
        print("  " + failed);
    }
  }
  public void process(File cFile) {
    try {
      String cName = ClassNameFinder.thisClass(
        BinaryFile.read(cFile));
      if(!cName.contains("."))
        return; // Ignore unpackaged classes
      testClass = Class.forName(cName);
    } catch(Exception e) {
      throw new RuntimeException(e);
    }
    TestMethods testMethods = new TestMethods();
    Method creator = null;
    Method cleanup = null;
    for(Method m : testClass.getDeclaredMethods()) {
      testMethods.addIfTestMethod(m);
```

```java
      if(creator == null)
        creator = checkForCreatorMethod(m);
      if(cleanup == null)
        cleanup = checkForCleanupMethod(m);
    }
    if(testMethods.size() > 0) {
      if(creator == null)
        try {
          if(!Modifier.isPublic(testClass
            .getDeclaredConstructor().getModifiers())) {
            print("Error: " + testClass +
              " default constructor must be public");
            System.exit(1);
          }
        } catch(NoSuchMethodException e) {
          // Synthesized default constructor; OK
        }
      print(testClass.getName());
    }
    for(Method m : testMethods) {
      printnb("  . " + m.getName() + " ");
      try {
        Object testObject = createTestObject(creator);
        boolean success = false;
        try {
          if(m.getReturnType().equals(boolean.class))
            success = (Boolean)m.invoke(testObject);
          else {
            m.invoke(testObject);
            success = true; // If no assert fails
          }
        } catch(InvocationTargetException e) {
          // Actual exception is inside e:
          print(e.getCause());
        }
        print(success ? "" : "(failed)");
        testsRun++;
        if(!success) {
          failures++;
          failedTests.add(testClass.getName() +
            ": " + m.getName());
        }
        if(cleanup != null)
          cleanup.invoke(testObject, testObject);
```

```
        } catch(Exception e) {
          throw new RuntimeException(e);
        }
      }
    }
    static class TestMethods extends ArrayList<Method> {
      void addIfTestMethod(Method m) {
        if(m.getAnnotation(Test.class) == null)
          return;
        if(!(m.getReturnType().equals(boolean.class) ||
            m.getReturnType().equals(void.class)))
          throw new RuntimeException("@Test method" +
            " must return boolean or void");
        m.setAccessible(true); // In case it's private, etc.
        add(m);
      }
    }
    private static Method checkForCreatorMethod(Method m) {
      if(m.getAnnotation(TestObjectCreate.class) == null)
        return null;
      if(!m.getReturnType().equals(testClass))
        throw new RuntimeException("@TestObjectCreate " +
          "must return instance of Class to be tested");
      if((m.getModifiers() &
          java.lang.reflect.Modifier.STATIC) < 1)
        throw new RuntimeException("@TestObjectCreate " +
          "must be static.");
      m.setAccessible(true);
      return m;
    }
    private static Method checkForCleanupMethod(Method m) {
      if(m.getAnnotation(TestObjectCleanup.class) == null)
        return null;
      if(!m.getReturnType().equals(void.class))
        throw new RuntimeException("@TestObjectCleanup " +
          "must return void");
      if((m.getModifiers() &
          java.lang.reflect.Modifier.STATIC) < 1)
        throw new RuntimeException("@TestObjectCleanup " +
          "must be static.");
      if(m.getParameterTypes().length == 0 ||
        m.getParameterTypes()[0] != testClass)
        throw new RuntimeException("@TestObjectCleanup " +
          "must take an argument of the tested type.");
```

```
      m.setAccessible(true);
      return m;
    }
    private static Object createTestObject(Method creator) {
      if(creator != null) {
        try {
          return creator.invoke(testClass);
        } catch(Exception e) {
          throw new RuntimeException("Couldn't run " +
            "@TestObject (creator) method.");
        }
      } else { // Use the default constructor:
        try {
          return testClass.newInstance();
        } catch(Exception e) {
          throw new RuntimeException("Couldn't create a " +
            "test object. Try using a @TestObject method.");
        }
      }
    }
  }
} ///:~
```

AtUnit.java uses the **ProcessFiles** tool in **net.mindview.util**. The
AtUnit class implements **ProcessFiles.Strategy**, which comprises the
method **process( )**. This way, an instance of **AtUnit** can be passed to the
ProcessFiles constructor. The second constructor argument tells
ProcessFiles to look for all files that have "**class**" extensions.

If you do not provide a command-line argument, the program will traverse
the current directory tree. You may also provide multiple arguments which
can be either class files (with or without the **.class** extension) or directories.
Since **@Unit** will automatically find the testable classes and methods, no
"suite" mechanism is necessary.[8]

One of the problems that **AtUnit.java** must solve when it discovers class
files is that the actual qualified class name (including package) is not evident
from the class file name. In order to discover this information, the class file
must be analyzed, which is not trivial, but not impossible, either.[9] So the first

---

[8] It is not clear why the default constructor for the class under test must be **public**, but if
it isn't, the call to **newInstance( )** just hangs (doesn't throw an exception).

[9] Jeremy Meyer and I spent most of a day figuring this out.

thing that happens when a **.class** file is found is that it is opened and its binary data is read and handed to **ClassNameFinder.thisClass( )**. Here, we are moving into the realm of "bytecode engineering," because we are actually analyzing the contents of a class file:

```
//: net/mindview/atunit/ClassNameFinder.java
package net.mindview.atunit;
import java.io.*;
import java.util.*;
import net.mindview.util.*;
import static net.mindview.util.Print.*;

public class ClassNameFinder {
  public static String thisClass(byte[] classBytes) {
    Map<Integer,Integer> offsetTable =
      new HashMap<Integer,Integer>();
    Map<Integer,String> classNameTable =
      new HashMap<Integer,String>();
    try {
      DataInputStream data = new DataInputStream(
        new ByteArrayInputStream(classBytes));
      int magic = data.readInt();  // 0xcafebabe
      int minorVersion = data.readShort();
      int majorVersion = data.readShort();
      int constant_pool_count = data.readShort();
      int[] constant_pool = new int[constant_pool_count];
      for(int i = 1; i < constant_pool_count; i++) {
        int tag = data.read();
        int tableSize;
        switch(tag) {
          case 1: // UTF
            int length = data.readShort();
            char[] bytes = new char[length];
            for(int k = 0; k < bytes.length; k++)
              bytes[k] = (char)data.read();
            String className = new String(bytes);
            classNameTable.put(i, className);
            break;
          case 5: // LONG
          case 6: // DOUBLE
            data.readLong(); // discard 8 bytes
            i++; // Special skip necessary
            break;
          case 7: // CLASS
```

```
              int offset = data.readShort();
              offsetTable.put(i, offset);
              break;
            case 8: // STRING
              data.readShort(); // discard 2 bytes
              break;
            case 3:  // INTEGER
            case 4:  // FLOAT
            case 9:  // FIELD_REF
            case 10: // METHOD_REF
            case 11: // INTERFACE_METHOD_REF
            case 12: // NAME_AND_TYPE
              data.readInt(); // discard 4 bytes;
              break;
            default:
              throw new RuntimeException("Bad tag " + tag);
          }
        }
        short access_flags = data.readShort();
        int this_class = data.readShort();
        int super_class = data.readShort();
        return classNameTable.get(
          offsetTable.get(this_class)).replace('/', '.');
      } catch(Exception e) {
        throw new RuntimeException(e);
      }
    }
  }
  // Demonstration:
  public static void main(String[] args) throws Exception {
    if(args.length > 0) {
      for(String arg : args)
        print(thisClass(BinaryFile.read(new File(arg))));
    } else
      // Walk the entire tree:
      for(File klass : Directory.walk(".", ".*\\.class"))
        print(thisClass(BinaryFile.read(klass)));
  }
} ///:~
```

Although it's not possible to go into full detail here, each class file follows a particular format and I've tried to use meaningful field names for the pieces of data that are picked out of the **ByteArrayInputStream**; you can also see the size of each piece by the length of the read performed on the input stream. For example, the first 32 bits of any class file is always the "magic number" hex `0xcafebabe`,[10] and the next two **short**s are version information. The constant pool contains the constants for the program and so is of variable size; the next **short** tells how big it is, so that an appropriate-sized array can be allocated. Each entry in the constant pool may be a fixed-size or variable-sized value, so we must examine the tag that begins each one to find out what to do with it—that's the **switch** statement. Here, we are not trying to accurately analyze all the data in the class file, but merely to step through and store the pieces of interest, so you'll notice that a fair amount of data is discarded. Information about classes is stored in the **classNameTable** and the **offsetTable**. After the constant pool is read, the **this_class** information can be found, which is an index into the **offsetTable**, which produces an index into the **classNameTable**, which produces the class name.

Back in **AtUnit.java**, **process( )** now has the class name and can look to see if it contains a '.', which means it's in a package. Unpackaged classes are ignored. If a class is in a package, the standard class loader is used to load the class with **Class.forName( )**. Now the class can be analyzed for **@Unit** annotations.

We only need to look for three things: **@Test** methods, which are stored in a **TestMethods** list, and whether there's an **@TestObjectCreate** and **@TestObjectCleanup** method. These are discovered through the associated method calls that you see in the code, which look for the annotations.

If any **@Test** methods have been found, the name of the class is printed so the viewer can see what's happening, and then each test is executed. This means printing the method name, then calling **createTestObject( )**, which will use the **@TestObjectCreate** method if one exists, or will fall back to the default constructor otherwise. Once the test object has been created, the test method is invoked upon that object. If the test returns a **boolean**, the result is captured. If not, we assume success if there is no exception (which would happen in the case of a failed **assert** *or* any other kind of exception). If an exception is thrown, the exception information is printed to show the cause. If any failure occurs, the failure count is increased and the class name and

---

[10] Various legends surround the meaning of this, but since Java was created by nerds we can make a reasonable guess that it had something to do with fantasizing about a woman in a coffee shop.

method are added to **failedTests** so these can be reported at the end of the run.

Exercise 11:   (5) Add an **@TestNote** annotation to **@Unit**, so that the accompanying note is simply displayed during testing.

Removing test code

Although in many projects it won't make a difference if you leave the test code in the deliverable (especially if you make all the test methods **private**, which you can do if you like), in some cases you will want to strip out the test code either to keep the deliverable small or so that it is not exposed to the client.

This requires more sophisticated bytecode engineering than it is comfortable to do by hand. However, the open-source Javassist library[11] brings bytecode engineering into the realm of the possible. The following program takes an optional **-r** flag as its first argument; if you provide the flag it will remove the **@Test** annotations, and if you do not it will simply display the **@Test** annotations. **ProcessFiles** is also used here to traverse the files and directories of your choosing:

```
//: net/mindview/atunit/AtUnitRemover.java
// Displays @Unit annotations in compiled class files. If
// first argument is "-r", @Unit annotations are removed.
// {Args: ..}
// {Requires: javassist.bytecode.ClassFile;
// You must install the Javassist library from
// http://sourceforge.net/projects/jboss/ }
package net.mindview.atunit;
import javassist.*;
import javassist.bytecode.*;
import javassist.bytecode.annotation.*;
import java.io.*;
import net.mindview.util.*;
import static net.mindview.util.Print.*;
```

---

[11] Thanks to Dr. Shigeru Chiba for creating this library, and for all his help in developing **AtUnitRemover.java**.

```
public class AtUnitRemover
implements ProcessFiles.Strategy {
  private static boolean remove = false;
  public static void main(String[] args) throws Exception {
    if(args.length > 0 && args[0].equals("-r")) {
      remove = true;
      String[] nargs = new String[args.length - 1];
      System.arraycopy(args, 1, nargs, 0, nargs.length);
      args = nargs;
    }
    new ProcessFiles(
      new AtUnitRemover(), "class").start(args);
  }
  public void process(File cFile) {
    boolean modified = false;
    try {
      String cName = ClassNameFinder.thisClass(
        BinaryFile.read(cFile));
      if(!cName.contains("."))
        return; // Ignore unpackaged classes
      ClassPool cPool = ClassPool.getDefault();
      CtClass ctClass = cPool.get(cName);
      for(CtMethod method : ctClass.getDeclaredMethods()) {
        MethodInfo mi = method.getMethodInfo();
        AnnotationsAttribute attr = (AnnotationsAttribute)
          mi.getAttribute(AnnotationsAttribute.visibleTag);
        if(attr == null) continue;
        for(Annotation ann : attr.getAnnotations()) {
          if(ann.getTypeName()
              .startsWith("net.mindview.atunit")) {
            print(ctClass.getName() + " Method: "
              + mi.getName() + " " + ann);
            if(remove) {
              ctClass.removeMethod(method);
              modified = true;
            }
          }
        }
      }
      // Fields are not removed in this version (see text).
      if(modified)
        ctClass.toBytecode(new DataOutputStream(
          new FileOutputStream(cFile)));
      ctClass.detach();
```

```
    } catch(Exception e) {
      throw new RuntimeException(e);
    }
  }
} ///:~
```

The **ClassPool** is a kind of picture of all the classes in the system that you are modifying. It guarantees the consistency of all the modified classes. You must get each **CtClass** from the **ClassPool**, similar to the way the class loader and **Class.forName( )** load classes into the JVM.

The **CtClass** contains the bytecodes for a class object and allows you to produce information about the class and to manipulate the code in the class. Here, we call **getDeclaredMethods( )** (just like Java's reflection mechanism) and get a **MethodInfo** object from each **CtMethod** object. From this, we can look at the annotations. If a method has an annotation in the **net.mindview.atunit** package, that method is removed.

If the class has been modified, the original class file is overwritten with the new class.

At the time of this writing, the "remove" functionality in Javassist had recently been added,[12] and we discovered that removing **@TestProperty** fields turns out to be more complex than removing methods. Because there may be static initialization operations that refer to those fields, you cannot simply remove them. So the above version of the code only removes **@Unit** methods. However, you should check the Javassist Web site for updates; field removal should eventually be possible. In the meantime, note that the external testing method shown in **AtUnitExternalTest.java** allows all tests to be removed by simply deleting the class file created by the test code.

Summary

Annotations are a welcome addition to Java. They are a structured and type-checked means of adding metadata to your code without rendering it unreadable and messy. They can help remove the tedium of writing deployment descriptors and other generated files. The fact that the **@deprecated** Javadoc tag has been superseded by the **@Deprecated**

---

[12] Dr. Shigeru Chiba very nicely added the **CtClass.removeMethod( )** at our request.

---

annotation is just one indication of how much better suited annotations are for describing information about classes than are comments.

Only a small handful of annotations come with Java SE5. This means that, if you can't find a library elsewhere, you will be creating annotations and the associated logic to do this. With the **apt** tool, you can compile newly generated files in one step, easing the build process, but currently there is little more in the **mirror** API than some basic functionality to help you identify the elements of Java class definitions. As you've seen, Javassist can be used for bytecode engineering, or you can hand-code your own bytecode manipulation tools.

This situation will certainly improve, and providers of APIs and frameworks will start providing annotations as part of their toolkits. As you can imagine by seeing the **@Unit** system, it is very likely that annotations will cause significant changes in our Java programming experience.

Solutions to selected exercises can be found in the electronic document *The Thinking in Java Annotated Solution Guide*, available for sale from *www.MindView.net*.

Concurrency

Up to this point, you've been learning about *sequential programming*. Everything in a program happens one step at a time.

A large subset of programming problems can be solved using sequential programming. For some problems, however, it becomes convenient or even essential to execute several parts of a program in parallel, so that those portions either appear to be executing concurrently, or if multiple processors are available, actually do execute simultaneously.

Parallel programming can produce great improvements in program execution speed, provide an easier model for designing certain types of programs, or both. However, becoming adept at concurrent programming theory and techniques is a step up from everything you've learned so far in this book, and is an intermediate to advanced topic. This chapter can only serve as an introduction, and you should by no means consider yourself a good concurrent programmer even if you understand this chapter thoroughly.

As you shall see, the real problem with concurrency occurs when tasks that are executing in parallel begin to interfere with each other. This can happen in such a subtle and occasional manner that it's probably fair to say that concurrency is "arguably deterministic but effectively nondeterministic." That is, you can make an argument to conclude that it's possible to write concurrent programs that, through care and code inspection, work correctly. In practice, however, it's much easier to write concurrent programs that only appear to work, but given the right conditions, will fail. These conditions may never actually occur, or occur so infrequently that you never see them during testing. In fact, you may not be able to write test code that will generate failure conditions for your concurrent program. The resulting failures will often only occur occasionally, and as a result they appear in the form of customer complaints. This is one of the strongest arguments for studying concurrency: If you ignore it, you're likely to get bitten.

Concurrency thus seems fraught with peril, and if that makes you a bit fearful, this is probably a good thing. Although Java SE5 has made significant improvements in concurrency, there are still no safety nets like compile-time verification or checked exceptions to tell you when you make a mistake. With concurrency, you're on your own, and only by being both suspicious and aggressive can you write multithreaded code in Java that will be reliable.

People sometimes suggest that concurrency is too advanced to include in a book that introduces the language. They argue that concurrency is a discrete topic that can be treated independently, and the few cases where it appears in daily programming (such as graphical user interfaces) can be handled with special idioms. Why introduce such a complex topic if you can avoid it?

Alas, if only it were so. Unfortunately, you don't get to choose when threads will appear in your Java programs. Just because you never start a thread yourself doesn't mean you'll be able to avoid writing threaded code. For example, Web systems are one of the most common Java applications, and the basic Web library class, the servlet, is inherently multithreaded—this is essential because Web servers often contain multiple processors, and concurrency is an ideal way to utilize these processors. As simple as a servlet might seem, you must understand concurrency issues in order to use servlets properly. The same goes for graphical user interface programming, as you shall see in the *Graphical User Interfaces* chapter. Although the Swing and SWT libraries both have mechanisms for thread safety, it's hard to know how to use these properly without understanding concurrency.

Java is a multithreaded language, and concurrency issues are present whether you are aware of them or not. As a result, there are many Java programs in use that either just work by accident, or work most of the time and mysteriously break every now and again because of undiscovered concurrency flaws. Sometimes this breakage is benign, but sometimes it means the loss of valuable data, and if you aren't at least aware of concurrency issues, you may end up assuming the problem is somewhere else rather than in your software. These kinds of issues can also be exposed or amplified if a program is moved to a multiprocessor system. Basically, knowing about concurrency makes you aware that apparently correct programs can exhibit incorrect behavior.

Concurrent programming is like stepping into a new world and learning a new language, or at least a new set of language concepts. Understanding concurrent programming is on the same order of difficulty as understanding object-oriented programming. If you apply some effort, you can fathom the basic mechanism, but it generally takes deep study and understanding to develop a true grasp of the subject. The goal of this chapter is to give you a solid foundation in the basics of concurrency so that you can understand the concepts and write reasonable multithreaded programs. Be aware that you can easily become overconfident. If you are writing anything complex, you will need to study dedicated books on the topic.

The many faces of concurrency

A primary reason why concurrent programming can be confusing is that there is more than one problem to solve using concurrency, and more than one approach to implementing concurrency, and no clean mapping between the two issues (and often a blurring of the lines all around). As a result, you're forced to understand all issues and special cases in order to use concurrency effectively.

The problems that you solve with concurrency can be roughly classified as "speed" and "design manageability."

Faster execution

The speed issue sounds simple at first: If you want a program to run faster, break it into pieces and run each piece on a separate processor. Concurrency is a fundamental tool for multiprocessor programming. Now, with Moore's Law running out of steam (at least for conventional chips), speed improvements are appearing in the form of multicore processors rather than faster chips. To make your programs run faster, you'll have to learn to take advantage of those extra processors, and that's one thing that concurrency gives you.

If you have a multiprocessor machine, multiple tasks can be distributed across those processors, which can dramatically improve throughput. This is often the case with powerful multiprocessor Web servers, which can distribute large numbers of user requests across CPUs in a program that allocates one thread per request.

However, concurrency can often improve the performance of programs running on a *single* processor.

This can sound a bit counterintuitive. If you think about it, a concurrent program running on a single processor should actually have *more* overhead than if all the parts of the program ran sequentially, because of the added cost of the so-called *context switch* (changing from one task to another). On the surface, it would appear to be cheaper to run all the parts of the program as a single task and save the cost of context switching.

The issue that can make a difference is *blocking*. If one task in your program is unable to continue because of some condition outside of the control of the program (typically I/O), we say that the task or the thread *blocks*. Without concurrency, the whole program comes to a stop until the external condition changes. If the program is written using concurrency, however, the other tasks in the program can continue to execute when one task is blocked, so the program continues to move forward. In fact, from a performance standpoint, it makes no sense to use concurrency on a single-processor machine unless one of the tasks might block.

A very common example of performance improvements in single-processor systems is *event-driven programming*. Indeed, one of the most compelling reasons for using concurrency is to produce a responsive user interface. Consider a program that performs some long-running operation and thus ends up ignoring user input and being unresponsive. If you have a "quit" button, you don't want to be forced to poll it in every piece of code you write. This produces awkward code, without any guarantee that a programmer won't forget to perform the check. Without concurrency, the only way to produce a responsive user interface is for all tasks to periodically check for user input. By creating a separate thread of execution to respond to user input, even though this thread will be blocked most of the time, the program guarantees a certain level of responsiveness.

The program needs to continue performing its operations, and at the same time it needs to return control to the user interface so that the program can respond to the user. But a conventional method cannot continue performing its operations and at the same time return control to the rest of the program. In fact, this sounds like an impossibility, as if the CPU must be in two places at once, but this is precisely the illusion that concurrency provides (in the case of multiprocessor systems, this is more than just an illusion).

One very straightforward way to implement concurrency is at the operating system level, using *processes*. A process is a self-contained program running within its own address space. A *multitasking* operating system can run more than one process (program) at a time by periodically switching the CPU from one process to another, while making it look as if each process is chugging along on its own. Processes are very attractive because the operating system usually isolates one process from another so they cannot interfere with each other, which makes programming with processes relatively easy. In contrast, concurrent systems like the one used in Java share resources like memory and I/O, so the fundamental difficulty in writing multithreaded programs is coordinating the use of these resources between different thread-driven tasks, so that they cannot be accessed by more than one task at a time.

Here's a simple example that utilizes operating system processes. While writing a book, I regularly make multiple redundant backup copies of the current state of the book. I make a copy into a local directory, one onto a memory stick, one onto a Zip disk, and one onto a remote FTP site. To automate this process, I wrote a small program (in Python, but the concepts are the same) which zips the book into a file with a version number in the name and then performs the copies. Initially, I performed all the copies sequentially, waiting for each one to complete before starting the next one. But then I realized that each copy operation took a different amount of time depending on the I/O speed of the medium. Since I was using a multitasking operating system, I could start each copy operation as a separate process and let them run in parallel, which speeds up the execution of the entire program. While one process is blocked, another one can be moving forward.

This is an ideal example of concurrency. Each task executes as a process in its own address space, so there's no possibility of interference between tasks. More importantly, there's no *need* for the tasks to communicate with each other because they're all completely independent. The operating system minds all the details of ensuring proper file copying. As a result, there's no risk and you get a faster program, effectively for free.

Some people go so far as to advocate processes as the only reasonable approach to concurrency,[1] but unfortunately there are generally quantity and overhead limitations to processes that prevent their applicability across the concurrency spectrum.

Some programming languages are designed to isolate concurrent tasks from each other. These are generally called *functional languages*, where each function call produces no side effects (and so cannot interfere with other functions) and can thus be driven as an independent task. *Erlang* is one such

---

[1] Eric Raymond, for example, makes a strong case in *The Art of UNIX Programming* (Addison-Wesley, 2004).

language, and it includes safe mechanisms for one task to communicate with another. If you find that a portion of your program must make heavy use of concurrency and you are running into excessive problems trying to build that portion, you may want to consider creating that part of your program in a dedicated concurrency language like Erlang.

Java took the more traditional approach of adding support for threading on top of a sequential language.[2] Instead of forking external processes in a multitasking operating system, threading creates tasks *within* the single process represented by the executing program. One advantage that this provided was operating system transparency, which was an important design goal for Java. For example, the pre-OSX versions of the Macintosh operating system (a reasonably important target for the first versions of Java) did not support multitasking. Unless multithreading had been added to Java, any concurrent Java programs wouldn't have been portable to the Macintosh and similar platforms, thus breaking the "write once/run everywhere" requirement.[3]

Improving code design

A program that uses multiple tasks on a single-CPU machine is still just doing one thing at a time, so it must be theoretically possible to write the same program without using any tasks. However, concurrency provides an important organizational benefit: The design of your program can be greatly simplified. Some types of problems, such as simulation, are difficult to solve without support for concurrency.

Most people have seen at least one form of simulation, as either a computer game or computer-generated animations within movies. Simulations generally involve many interacting elements, each with "a mind of its own." Although you may observe that, on a single-processor machine, each simulation element is being driven forward by that one processor, from a

---

[2] It could be argued that trying to bolt concurrency onto a sequential language is a doomed approach, but you'll have to draw your own conclusions.

[3] This requirement was never completely fulfilled and is no longer so loudly touted by Sun. Ironically, one reason that "write once/run everywhere" didn't completely work may have resulted from problems in the threading system—which might actually be fixed in Java SE5.

programming standpoint it's much easier to pretend that each simulation element has its own processor and is an independent task.

A full-fledged simulation may involve a very large number of tasks, corresponding to the fact that each element in a simulation can act independently—this includes doors and rocks, not just elves and wizards. Multithreaded systems often have a relatively small size limit on the number of threads available, sometimes on the order of tens or hundreds. This number may vary outside the control of the program—it may depend on the platform, or in the case of Java, the version of the JVM. In Java, you can generally assume that you will not have enough threads available to provide one for each element in a large simulation.

A typical approach to solving this problem is the use of *cooperative* multithreading. Java's threading is *preemptive*, which means that a scheduling mechanism provides time slices for each thread, periodically interrupting a thread and context switching to another thread so that each one is given a reasonable amount of time to drive its task. In a cooperative system, each task voluntarily gives up control, which requires the programmer to consciously insert some kind of yielding statement into each task. The advantage to a cooperative system is twofold: Context switching is typically much cheaper than with a preemptive system, and there is theoretically no limit to the number of independent tasks that can be running at once. When you are dealing with a large number of simulation elements, this can be the ideal solution. Note, however, that some cooperative systems are not designed to distribute tasks across processors, which can be very limiting.

At the other extreme, concurrency is a very useful model—because it's what is actually happening—when you are working with modern *messaging* systems, which involve many independent computers distributed across a network. In this case, all the processes are running completely independently of each other, and there's not even an opportunity to share resources. However, you must still synchronize the information transfer between processes so that the entire messaging system doesn't lose information or incorporate information at incorrect times. Even if you don't plan to use concurrency very much in your immediate future, it's helpful to understand it just so you can grasp messaging architectures, which are becoming more predominant ways to create distributed systems.

Concurrency imposes costs, including complexity costs, but these are usually outweighed by improvements in program design, resource balancing, and user convenience. In general, threads enable you to create a more loosely coupled design; otherwise, parts of your code would be forced to pay explicit attention to tasks that would normally be handled by threads.

Basic threading

Concurrent programming allows you to partition a program into separate, independently running tasks. Using multithreading, each of these independent tasks (also called subtasks) is driven by a *thread of execution*. A *thread* is a single sequential flow of control within a process. A single process can thus have multiple concurrently executing tasks, but you program as if each task has the CPU to itself. An underlying mechanism divides up the CPU time for you, but in general, you don't need to think about it.

The threading model is a programming convenience to simplify juggling several operations at the same time within a single program: The CPU will pop around and give each task some of its time.[4] Each task has the consciousness of constantly having the CPU to itself, but the CPU's time is being sliced among all the tasks (except when the program is actually running on multiple CPUs). One of the great things about threading is that you are abstracted away from this layer, so your code does not need to know whether it is running on a single CPU or many. Thus, using threads is a way to create transparently scalable programs—if a program is running too slowly, you can easily speed it up by adding CPUs to your computer. Multitasking and multithreading tend to be the most reasonable ways to utilize multiprocessor systems.

Defining tasks

A thread drives a task, so you need a way to describe that task. This is provided by the **Runnable** interface. To define a task, simply implement **Runnable** and write a **run( )** method to make the task do your bidding.

---

[4] This is true when the system uses time slicing (Windows, for example). Solaris uses a FIFO concurrency model: Unless a higher-priority thread is awakened, the current thread runs until it blocks or terminates. That means that other threads with the same priority don't run until the current one gives up the processor.

For example, the following **LiftOff** task displays the countdown before liftoff:

```
//: concurrency/LiftOff.java
// Demonstration of the Runnable interface.

public class LiftOff implements Runnable {
  protected int countDown = 10; // Default
  private static int taskCount = 0;
  private final int id = taskCount++;
  public LiftOff() {}
  public LiftOff(int countDown) {
    this.countDown = countDown;
  }
  public String status() {
    return "#" + id + "(" +
      (countDown > 0 ? countDown : "Liftoff!") + "), ";
  }
  public void run() {
    while(countDown-- > 0) {
      System.out.print(status());
      Thread.yield();
    }
  }
} ///:~
```

The identifier **id** distinguishes between multiple instances of the task. It is **final** because it is not expected to change once it is initialized.

A task's **run( )** method usually has some kind of loop that continues until the task is no longer necessary, so you must establish the condition on which to break out of this loop (one option is to simply **return** from **run( )**). Often, **run( )** is cast in the form of an infinite loop, which means that, barring some factor that causes **run( )** to terminate, it will continue forever (later in the chapter you'll see how to safely terminate tasks).

The call to the **static** method **Thread.yield( )** inside **run( )** is a suggestion to the *thread scheduler* (the part of the Java threading mechanism that moves the CPU from one thread to the next) that says, "I've done the important parts of my cycle and this would be a good time to switch to another task for a while." It's completely optional, but it is used here because it tends to produce more interesting output in these examples: You're more likely to see evidence of tasks being swapped in and out.

In the following example, the task's **run( )** is not driven by a separate thread; it is simply called directly in **main( )** (actually, this *is* using a thread: the one that is always allocated for **main( )**):

```
//: concurrency/MainThread.java

public class MainThread {
  public static void main(String[] args) {
    LiftOff launch = new LiftOff();
    launch.run();
  }
} /* Output:
#0(9), #0(8), #0(7), #0(6), #0(5), #0(4), #0(3), #0(2),
#0(1), #0(Liftoff!),
*///:~
```

When a class is derived from **Runnable**, it must have a **run( )** method, but that's nothing special—it doesn't produce any innate threading abilities. To achieve threading behavior, you must explicitly attach a task to a thread.

The **Thread** class

The traditional way to turn a **Runnable** object into a working task is to hand it to a **Thread** constructor. This example shows how to drive a **LiftOff** object using a **Thread**:

```
//: concurrency/BasicThreads.java
// The most basic use of the Thread class.

public class BasicThreads {
  public static void main(String[] args) {
    Thread t = new Thread(new LiftOff());
    t.start();
    System.out.println("Waiting for LiftOff");
  }
} /* Output: (90% match)
Waiting for LiftOff
#0(9), #0(8), #0(7), #0(6), #0(5), #0(4), #0(3), #0(2),
#0(1), #0(Liftoff!),
*///:~
```

A **Thread** constructor only needs a **Runnable** object. Calling a **Thread** object's **start( )** will perform the necessary initialization for the thread and then call that **Runnable**'s **run( )** method to start the task in the new thread.

Even though **start( )** appears to be making a call to a long-running method, you can see from the output—the "Waiting for LiftOff" message appears before the countdown has completed—that **start( )** quickly returns. In effect, you have made a method call to **LiftOff.run( )**, and that method has not yet finished, but because **LiftOff.run( )** is being executed by a different thread, you can still pcrform other operations in the **main( )** thread. (This ability is not restricted to the **main( )** thread—any thread can start another thread.) Thus, the program is running two methods at once—**main( )** and **LiftOff.run( )**. **run( )** is the code that is executed "simultaneously" with the other threads in a program.

You can easily add more threads to drive more tasks. Here, you can see how all the tasks run in concert with one another:[5]

```
//: concurrency/MoreBasicThreads.java
// Adding more threads.

public class MoreBasicThreads {
  public static void main(String[] args) {
    for(int i = 0; i < 5; i++)
      new Thread(new LiftOff()).start();
    System.out.println("Waiting for LiftOff");
  }
} /* Output: (Sample)
Waiting for LiftOff
#0(9), #1(9), #2(9), #3(9), #4(9), #0(8), #1(8), #2(8),
#3(8), #4(8), #0(7), #1(7), #2(7), #3(7), #4(7), #0(6),
#1(6), #2(6), #3(6), #4(6), #0(5), #1(5), #2(5), #3(5),
#4(5), #0(4), #1(4), #2(4), #3(4), #4(4), #0(3), #1(3),
#2(3), #3(3), #4(3), #0(2), #1(2), #2(2), #3(2), #4(2),
#0(1), #1(1), #2(1), #3(1), #4(1), #0(Liftoff!),
#1(Liftoff!), #2(Liftoff!), #3(Liftoff!), #4(Liftoff!),
*///:~
```

The output shows that the execution of the different tasks is mixed together as the threads are swapped in and out. This swapping is automatically controlled by the thread scheduler. If you have multiple processors on your

---

[5] In this case, a single thread (**main( )**), is creating all the **LiftOff** threads. If you have multiple threads crcating **LiftOff** threads, however, it is possible for more than one **LiftOff** to have the same **id**. You'll learn why later in this chapter.

---

machine, the thread scheduler will quietly distribute the threads among the processors.[6]

The output for one run of this program will be different from that of another, because the thread-scheduling mechanism is not deterministic. In fact, you may see dramatic differences in the output of this simple program between one version of the JDK and the next. For example, an earlier JDK didn't time-slice very often, so thread 1 might loop to extinction first, then thread 2 would go through all of its loops, etc. This was virtually the same as calling a routine that would do all the loops at once, except that starting up all those threads is more expensive. Later JDKs seem to produce better time-slicing behavior, so each thread seems to get more regular service. Generally, these kinds of JDK behavioral changes have not been mentioned by Sun, so you cannot plan on any consistent threading behavior. The best approach is to be as conservative as possible while writing threaded code.

When **main( )** creates the **Thread** objects, it isn't capturing the references for any of them. With an ordinary object, this would make it fair game for garbage collection, but not with a **Thread**. Each **Thread** "registers" itself so there is actually a reference to it someplace, and the garbage collector can't clean it up until the task exits its **run( )** and dies. You can see from the output that the tasks are indeed running to conclusion, so a thread creates a separate thread of execution that persists after the call to **start( )** completes.

Exercise 1: (2) Implement a **Runnable**. Inside **run( )**, print a message, and then call **yield( )**. Repeat this three times, and then return from **run( )**. Put a startup message in the constructor and a shutdown message when the task terminates. Create a number of these tasks and drive them using threads.

Exercise 2: (2) Following the form of **generics/Fibonacci.java**, create a task that produces a sequence of **n** Fibonacci numbers, where **n** is provided to the constructor of the task. Create a number of these tasks and drive them using threads.

Using **Executor**s

Java SE5 **java.util.concurrent** *Executors* simplify concurrent programming by managing **Thread** objects for you. **Executor**s provide a layer of indirection between a client and the execution of a task; instead of a

---

[6] This was not true for some of the earliest versions of Java.

client executing a task directly, an intermediate object executes the task. **Executor**s allow you to manage the execution of asynchronous tasks without having to explicitly manage the lifecycle of threads. **Executor**s are the preferred method for starting tasks in Java SE5/6.

We can use an **Executor** instead of explicitly creating **Thread** objects in **MoreBasicThreads.java**. A **LiftOff** object knows how to run a specific task; like the *Command* design pattern, it exposes a single method to be executed. An **ExecutorService** (an **Executor** with a service lifecycle—e.g., shutdown) knows how to build the appropriate context to execute **Runnable** objects. In the following example, the **CachedThreadPool** creates one thread per task. Note that an **ExecutorService** object is created using a **static Executors** method which determines the kind of **Executor** it will be:

```
//: concurrency/CachedThreadPool.java
import java.util.concurrent.*;

public class CachedThreadPool {
  public static void main(String[] args) {
    ExecutorService exec = Executors.newCachedThreadPool();
    for(int i = 0; i < 5; i++)
      exec.execute(new LiftOff());
    exec.shutdown();
  }
} /* Output: (Sample)
#0(9), #0(8), #1(9), #2(9), #3(9), #4(9), #0(7), #1(8),
#2(8), #3(8), #4(8), #0(6), #1(7), #2(7), #3(7), #4(7),
#0(5), #1(6), #2(6), #3(6), #4(6), #0(4), #1(5), #2(5),
#3(5), #4(5), #0(3), #1(4), #2(4), #3(4), #4(4), #0(2),
#1(3), #2(3), #3(3), #4(3), #0(1), #1(2), #2(2), #3(2),
#4(2), #0(Liftoff!), #1(1), #2(1), #3(1), #4(1),
#1(Liftoff!), #2(Liftoff!), #3(Liftoff!), #4(Liftoff!),
*///:~
```

Very often, a single **Executor** can be used to create and manage all the tasks in your system.

The call to **shutdown( )** prevents new tasks from being submitted to that **Executor**. The current thread (in this case, the one driving **main( )**) will continue to run all tasks submitted before **shutdown( )** was called. The program will exit as soon as all the tasks in the **Executor** finish.

You can easily replace the **CachedThreadPool** in the previous example with a different type of **Executor**. A **FixedThreadPool** uses a limited set of threads to execute the submitted tasks:

```
//: concurrency/FixedThreadPool.java
import java.util.concurrent.*;

public class FixedThreadPool {
  public static void main(String[] args) {
    // Constructor argument is number of threads:
    ExecutorService exec = Executors.newFixedThreadPool(5);
    for(int i = 0; i < 5; i++)
      exec.execute(new LiftOff());
    exec.shutdown();
  }
} /* Output: (Sample)
#0(9), #0(8), #1(9), #2(9), #3(9), #4(9), #0(7), #1(8),
#2(8), #3(8), #4(8), #0(6), #1(7), #2(7), #3(7), #4(7),
#0(5), #1(6), #2(6), #3(6), #4(6), #0(4), #1(5), #2(5),
#3(5), #4(5), #0(3), #1(4), #2(4), #3(4), #4(4), #0(2),
#1(3), #2(3), #3(3), #4(3), #0(1), #1(2), #2(2), #3(2),
#4(2), #0(Liftoff!), #1(1), #2(1), #3(1), #4(1),
#1(Liftoff!), #2(Liftoff!), #3(Liftoff!), #4(Liftoff!),
*///:~
```

With the **FixedThreadPool**, you do expensive thread allocation once, up front, and you thus limit the number of threads. This saves time because you aren't constantly paying for thread creation overhead for every single task. Also, in an event-driven system, event handlers that require threads can be serviced as quickly as you want by simply fetching threads from the pool. You don't overrun the available resources because the **FixedThreadPool** uses a bounded number of **Thread** objects.

Note that in any of the thread pools, existing threads are automatically reused when possible.

Although this book will use **CachedThreadPool**s, consider using **FixedThreadPool**s in production code. A **CachedThreadPool** will generally create as many threads as it needs during the execution of a program and then will stop creating new threads as it recycles the old ones, so it's a reasonable first choice as an **Executor**. Only if this approach causes problems do you need to switch to a **FixedThreadPool**.

A **SingleThreadExecutor** is like a **FixedThreadPool** with a size of one thread.[7] This is useful for anything you want to run in another thread continually (a long-lived task), such as a task that listens to incoming socket connections. It is also handy for short tasks that you want to run in a thread—for example, small tasks that update a local or remote log, or for an event-dispatching thread.

If more than one task is submitted to a **SingleThreadExecutor**, the tasks will be queued and each task will run to completion before the next task is begun, all using the same thread. In the following example, you'll see each task completed, in the order in which it was submitted, before the next one is begun. Thus, a **SingleThreadExecutor** serializes the tasks that are submitted to it, and maintains its own (hidden) queue of pending tasks.

```
//: concurrency/SingleThreadExecutor.java
import java.util.concurrent.*;

public class SingleThreadExecutor {
  public static void main(String[] args) {
    ExecutorService exec =
      Executors.newSingleThreadExecutor();
    for(int i = 0; i < 5; i++)
      exec.execute(new LiftOff());
    exec.shutdown();
  }
} /* Output:
#0(9), #0(8), #0(7), #0(6), #0(5), #0(4), #0(3), #0(2),
#0(1), #0(Liftoff!), #1(9), #1(8), #1(7), #1(6), #1(5),
#1(4), #1(3), #1(2), #1(1), #1(Liftoff!), #2(9), #2(8),
#2(7), #2(6), #2(5), #2(4), #2(3), #2(2), #2(1),
#2(Liftoff!), #3(9), #3(8), #3(7), #3(6), #3(5), #3(4),
#3(3), #3(2), #3(1), #3(Liftoff!), #4(9), #4(8), #4(7),
#4(6), #4(5), #4(4), #4(3), #4(2), #4(1), #4(Liftoff!),
*///:~
```

As another example, suppose you have a number of threads running tasks that use the file system. You can run these tasks with a **SingleThreadExecutor** to ensure that only one task at a time is running

---

[7] It also offers an important concurrency guarantee that the others do not—no two tasks will be called concurrently. This changes the locking requirements for the tasks (you'll learn about locking later in the chapter).

from any thread. This way, you don't need to deal with synchronizing on the shared resource (and you won't clobber the file system in the meantime). Sometimes a better solution is to synchronize on the resource (which you'll learn about later in this chapter), but a **SingleThreadExecutor** lets you skip the trouble of getting coordinated properly just to prototype something. By serializing tasks, you can eliminate the need to serialize the objects.

Exercise 3: (1) Repeat Exercise 1 using the different types of executors shown in this section.

Exercise 4: (1) Repeat Exercise 2 using the different types of executors shown in this section.

Producing return values from tasks

A **Runnable** is a separate task that performs work, but it doesn't return a value. If you want the task to produce a value when it's done, you can implement the **Callable** interface rather than the **Runnable** interface. **Callable**, introduced in Java SE5, is a generic with a type parameter representing the return value from the method **call( )** (instead of **run( )**), and must be invoked using an **ExecutorService submit( )** method. Here's a simple example:

```
//: concurrency/CallableDemo.java
import java.util.concurrent.*;
import java.util.*;

class TaskWithResult implements Callable<String> {
  private int id;
  public TaskWithResult(int id) {
    this.id = id;
  }
  public String call() {
    return "result of TaskWithResult " + id;
  }
}

public class CallableDemo {
  public static void main(String[] args) {
    ExecutorService exec = Executors.newCachedThreadPool();
    ArrayList<Future<String>> results =
      new ArrayList<Future<String>>();
    for(int i = 0; i < 10; i++)
      results.add(exec.submit(new TaskWithResult(i)));
```

```
    for(Future<String> fs : results)
      try {
        // get() blocks until completion:
        System.out.println(fs.get());
      } catch(InterruptedException e) {
        System.out.println(e);
        return;
      } catch(FxecutionException e) {
        System.out.println(e);
      } finally {
        exec.shutdown();
      }
  }
} /* Output:
result of TaskWithResult 0
result of TaskWithResult 1
result of TaskWithResult 2
result of TaskWithResult 3
result of TaskWithResult 4
result of TaskWithResult 5
result of TaskWithResult 6
result of TaskWithResult 7
result of TaskWithResult 8
result of TaskWithResult 9
*///:~
```

The **submit( )** method produces a **Future** object, parameterized for the particular type of result returned by the **Callable**. You can query the **Future** with **isDone( )** to see if it has completed. When the task is completed and has a result, you can call **get( )** to fetch the result. You can simply call **get( )** without checking **isDone( )**, in which case **get( )** will block until the result is ready. You can also call **get( )** with a timeout, or **isDone( )** to see if the task has completed, before trying to call **get( )** to fetch the result.

The overloaded **Executors.callable( )** method takes a **Runnable** and produces a **Callable**. **ExecutorService** has some "invoke" methods that run collections of **Callable** objects.

Exercise 5: (2) Modify Exercise 2 so that the task is a **Callable** that sums the values of all the Fibonacci numbers. Create several tasks and display the results.

Sleeping

A simple way to affect the behavior of your tasks is by calling **sleep( )** to cease (block) the execution of that task for a given time. In the **LiftOff** class, if you replace the call to **yield( )** with a call to **sleep( )**, you get the following:

```
//: concurrency/SleepingTask.java
// Calling sleep() to pause for a while.
import java.util.concurrent.*;

public class SleepingTask extends LiftOff {
  public void run() {
    try {
      while(countDown-- > 0) {
        System.out.print(status());
        // Old-style:
        // Thread.sleep(100);
        // Java SE5/6-style:
        TimeUnit.MILLISECONDS.sleep(100);
      }
    } catch(InterruptedException e) {
      System.err.println("Interrupted");
    }
  }
  public static void main(String[] args) {
    ExecutorService exec = Executors.newCachedThreadPool();
    for(int i = 0; i < 5; i++)
      exec.execute(new SleepingTask());
    exec.shutdown();
  }
} /* Output:
#0(9), #1(9), #2(9), #3(9), #4(9), #0(8), #1(8), #2(8),
#3(8), #4(8), #0(7), #1(7), #2(7), #3(7), #4(7), #0(6),
#1(6), #2(6), #3(6), #4(6), #0(5), #1(5), #2(5), #3(5),
#4(5), #0(4), #1(4), #2(4), #3(4), #4(4), #0(3), #1(3),
#2(3), #3(3), #4(3), #0(2), #1(2), #2(2), #3(2), #4(2),
#0(1), #1(1), #2(1), #3(1), #4(1), #0(Liftoff!),
#1(Liftoff!), #2(Liftoff!), #3(Liftoff!), #4(Liftoff!),
*///:~
```

The call to **sleep( )** can throw an **InterruptedException**, and you can see that this is caught in **run( )**. Because exceptions won't propagate across threads back to **main( )**, you must locally handle any exceptions that arise within a task.

Java SE5 introduced the more explicit version of **sleep( )** as part of the **TimeUnit** class, as shown in the above example. This provides better readability by allowing you to specify the units of the **sleep( )** delay. **TimeUnit** can also be used to perform conversions, as you shall see later in the chapter.

Depending on your platform, you may notice that the tasks run in "perfectly distributed" order—zero through four, then back to zero again. This makes sense because, after each print statement, each task goes to sleep (it blocks), which allows the thread scheduler to switch to another thread, driving another task. However, the sequential behavior relies on the underlying threading mechanism, which is different from one operating system to another, so you cannot rely on it. If you must control the order of execution of tasks, your best bet is to use synchronization controls (described later) or, in some cases, not to use threads at all, but instead to write your own cooperative routines that hand control to each other in a specified order.

Exercise 6: (2) Create a task that sleeps for a random amount of time between 1 and 10 seconds, then displays its sleep time and exits. Create and run a quantity (given on the command line) of these tasks.

Priority

The *priority* of a thread conveys the importance of a thread to the scheduler. Although the order in which the CPU runs a set of threads is indeterminate, the scheduler will lean toward running the waiting thread with the highest priority first. However, this doesn't mean that threads with lower priority aren't run (so you can't get deadlocked because of priorities). Lower-priority threads just tend to run less often.

The vast majority of the time, all threads should run at the default priority. Trying to manipulate thread priorities is usually a mistake.

Here's an example that demonstrates priority levels. You can read the priority of an existing thread with **getPriority( )** and change it at any time with **setPriority( )**.

```
//: concurrency/SimplePriorities.java
// Shows the use of thread priorities.
import java.util.concurrent.*;

public class SimplePriorities implements Runnable {
  private int countDown = 5;
```

```java
  private volatile double d; // No optimization
  private int priority;
  public SimplePriorities(int priority) {
    this.priority = priority;
  }
  public String toString() {
    return Thread.currentThread() + ": " + countDown;
  }
  public void run() {
    Thread.currentThread().setPriority(priority);
    while(true) {
      // An expensive, interruptable operation:
      for(int i = 1; i < 100000; i++) {
        d += (Math.PI + Math.E) / (double)i;
        if(i % 1000 == 0)
          Thread.yield();
      }
      System.out.println(this);
      if(--countDown == 0) return;
    }
  }
  public static void main(String[] args) {
    ExecutorService exec = Executors.newCachedThreadPool();
    for(int i = 0; i < 5; i++)
      exec.execute(
        new SimplePriorities(Thread.MIN_PRIORITY));
    exec.execute(
      new SimplePriorities(Thread.MAX_PRIORITY));
    exec.shutdown();
  }
} /* Output: (70% match)
Thread[pool-1-thread-6,10,main]: 5
Thread[pool-1-thread-6,10,main]: 4
Thread[pool-1-thread-6,10,main]: 3
Thread[pool-1-thread-6,10,main]: 2
Thread[pool-1-thread-6,10,main]: 1
Thread[pool-1-thread-3,1,main]: 5
Thread[pool-1-thread-2,1,main]: 5
Thread[pool-1-thread-1,1,main]: 5
Thread[pool-1-thread-5,1,main]: 5
Thread[pool-1-thread-4,1,main]: 5
...
*///:~
```

toString( ) is overridden to use **Thread.toString( )**, which prints the thread name, the priority level, and the "thread group" that the thread belongs to. You can set the thread name yourself via the constructor; here it's automatically generated as **pool-1-thread-1**, **pool-1-thread-2**, etc. The overridden **toString( )** also shows the countdown value of the task. Notice that you can get a reference to the **Thread** object that is driving a task, inside that task, by calling **Thread.currentThread( )**.

You can see that the priority level of the last thread is at the highest level, and all the rest of the threads are at the lowest level. Note that the priority is set at the beginning of **run( )**; setting it in the constructor would do no good since the **Executor** has not begun the task at that point.

Inside **run( )**, 100,000 repetitions of a rather expensive floating point calculation are performed, involving **double** addition and division. The variable **d** is **volatile** to try to ensure that no compiler optimizations are performed. Without this calculation, you don't see the effect of setting the priority levels. (Try it: Comment out the **for** loop containing the **double** calculations.) With the calculation, you see that the thread with **MAX_PRIORITY** is given a higher preference by the thread scheduler. (At least, this was the behavior on a Windows XP machine.) Even though printing to the console is also an expensive behavior, you won't see the priority levels that way, because console printing doesn't get interrupted (otherwise, the console display would get garbled during threading), whereas the math calculation can be interrupted. The calculation takes long enough that the scheduling mechanism jumps in, swaps tasks, and pays attention to the priorities so that high-priority threads get preference. However, to ensure that a context switch occurs, **yield( )** statements are regularly called.

Although the JDK has 10 priority levels, this doesn't map well to many operating systems. For example, Windows has 7 priority levels that are not fixed, so the mapping is indeterminate. Sun's Solaris has 2^{31} levels. The only portable approach is to stick to **MAX_PRIORITY**, **NORM_PRIORITY**, and **MIN_PRIORITY** when you're adjusting priority levels.

Yielding

If you know that you've accomplished what you need to during one pass through a loop in your **run( )** method, you can give a hint to the thread-scheduling mechanism that you've done enough and that some other task might as well have the CPU. This hint (and it *is* a hint—there's no guarantee

your implementation will listen to it) takes the form of the **yield( )** method.
When you call **yield( )**, you are suggesting that other threads *of the same
priority* might be run.

LiftOff.java uses **yield( )** to produce well-distributed processing across the
various **LiftOff** tasks. Try commenting out the call to **Thread.yield( )** in
LiftOff.run( ) to see the difference. In general, however, you can't rely on
yield( ) for any serious control or tuning of your application. Indeed,
yield( ) is often used incorrectly.

Daemon threads

A "daemon" thread is intended to provide a general service in the background
as long as the program is running, but is not part of the essence of the
program. Thus, when all of the non-daemon threads complete, the program is
terminated, killing all daemon threads in the process. Conversely, if there are
any non-daemon threads still running, the program doesn't terminate. There
is, for instance, a non-daemon thread that runs **main( )**.

```
//: concurrency/SimpleDaemons.java
// Daemon threads don't prevent the program from ending.
import java.util.concurrent.*;
import static net.mindview.util.Print.*;

public class SimpleDaemons implements Runnable {
  public void run() {
    try {
      while(true) {
        TimeUnit.MILLISECONDS.sleep(100);
        print(Thread.currentThread() + " " + this);
      }
    } catch(InterruptedException e) {
      print("sleep() interrupted");
    }
  }
  public static void main(String[] args) throws Exception {
    for(int i = 0; i < 10; i++) {
      Thread daemon = new Thread(new SimpleDaemons());
      daemon.setDaemon(true); // Must call before start()
      daemon.start();
    }
    print("All daemons started");
    TimeUnit.MILLISECONDS.sleep(175);
```

```
  }
} /* Output: (Sample)
All daemons started
Thread[Thread-0,5,main] SimpleDaemons@530daa
Thread[Thread-1,5,main] SimpleDaemons@a62fc3
Thread[Thread-2,5,main] SimpleDaemons@89ae9e
Thread[Thread-3,5,main] SimpleDaemons@1270b73
Thread[Thread-4,5,main] SimpleDaemons@60aeb0
Thread[Thread-5,5,main] SimpleDaemons@16caf43
Thread[Thread-6,5,main] SimpleDaemons@66848c
Thread[Thread-7,5,main] SimpleDaemons@8813f2
Thread[Thread-8,5,main] SimpleDaemons@1d58aae
Thread[Thread-9,5,main] SimpleDaemons@83cc67

...
*///:~
```

You must set the thread to be a daemon by calling **setDaemon( )** before it is started.

There's nothing to keep the program from terminating once **main( )** finishes its job, since there are nothing but daemon threads running. So that you can see the results of starting all the daemon threads, the **main( )** thread is briefly put to sleep. Without this, you see only some of the results from the creation of the daemon threads. (Try **sleep( )** calls of various lengths to see this behavior.)

SimpleDaemons.java creates explicit **Thread** objects in order to set their daemon flag. It is possible to customize the attributes (daemon, priority, name) of threads created by **Executor**s by writing a custom **ThreadFactory**:

```
//: net/mindview/util/DaemonThreadFactory.java
package net.mindview.util;
import java.util.concurrent.*;

public class DaemonThreadFactory implements ThreadFactory {
  public Thread newThread(Runnable r) {
    Thread t = new Thread(r);
    t.setDaemon(true);
    return t;
  }
} ///:~
```

The only difference from an ordinary **ThreadFactory** is that this one sets the daemon status to **true**. You can now pass a new **DaemonThreadFactory** as an argument to **Executors.newCachedThreadPool( )**:

```
//: concurrency/DaemonFromFactory.java
// Using a Thread Factory to create daemons.
import java.util.concurrent.*;
import net.mindview.util.*;
import static net.mindview.util.Print.*;

public class DaemonFromFactory implements Runnable {
  public void run() {
    try {
      while(true) {
        TimeUnit.MILLISECONDS.sleep(100);
        print(Thread.currentThread() + " " + this);
      }
    } catch(InterruptedException e) {
      print("Interrupted");
    }
  }
  public static void main(String[] args) throws Exception {
    ExecutorService exec = Executors.newCachedThreadPool(
      new DaemonThreadFactory());
    for(int i = 0; i < 10; i++)
      exec.execute(new DaemonFromFactory());
    print("All daemons started");
    TimeUnit.MILLISECONDS.sleep(500); // Run for a while
  }
} /* (Execute to see output) *///:~
```

Each of the **static ExecutorService** creation methods is overloaded to take a **ThreadFactory** object that it will use to create new threads.

We can take this one step further and create a **DaemonThreadPoolExecutor** utility:

```
//: net/mindview/util/DaemonThreadPoolExecutor.java
package net.mindview.util;
import java.util.concurrent.*;

public class DaemonThreadPoolExecutor
extends ThreadPoolExecutor {
  public DaemonThreadPoolExecutor() {
```

```
      super(0, Integer.MAX_VALUE, 60L, TimeUnit.SECONDS,
        new SynchronousQueue<Runnable>(),
        new DaemonThreadFactory());
    }
} ///:~
```

To get the values for the constructor base-class call, I simply looked at the
Executors.java source code.

You can find out if a thread is a daemon by calling **isDaemon( )**. If a thread
is a daemon, then any threads it creates will automatically be daemons, as the
following example demonstrates:

```
//: concurrency/Daemons.java
// Daemon threads spawn other daemon threads.
import java.util.concurrent.*;
import static net.mindview.util.Print.*;

class Daemon implements Runnable {
  private Thread[] t = new Thread[10];
  public void run() {
    for(int i = 0; i < t.length; i++) {
      t[i] = new Thread(new DaemonSpawn());
      t[i].start();
      printnb("DaemonSpawn " + i + " started, ");
    }
    for(int i = 0; i < t.length; i++)
      printnb("t[" + i + "].isDaemon() = " +
        t[i].isDaemon() + ", ");
    while(true)
      Thread.yield();
  }
}

class DaemonSpawn implements Runnable {
  public void run() {
    while(true)
      Thread.yield();
  }
}

public class Daemons {
  public static void main(String[] args) throws Exception {
    Thread d = new Thread(new Daemon());
    d.setDaemon(true);
```

```
    d.start();
    printnb("d.isDaemon() = " + d.isDaemon() + ", ");
    // Allow the daemon threads to
    // finish their startup processes:
    TimeUnit.SECONDS.sleep(1);
  }
} /* Output: (Sample)
d.isDaemon() = true, DaemonSpawn 0 started, DaemonSpawn 1
started, DaemonSpawn 2 started, DaemonSpawn 3 started,
DaemonSpawn 4 started, DaemonSpawn 5 started, DaemonSpawn 6
started, DaemonSpawn 7 started, DaemonSpawn 8 started,
DaemonSpawn 9 started, t[0].isDaemon() = true,
t[1].isDaemon() = true, t[2].isDaemon() = true,
t[3].isDaemon() = true, t[4].isDaemon() = true,
t[5].isDaemon() = true, t[6].isDaemon() = true,
t[7].isDaemon() = true, t[8].isDaemon() = true,
t[9].isDaemon() = true,
*///:~
```

The **Daemon** thread is set to daemon mode. It then spawns a bunch of other threads—which are *not* explicitly set to daemon mode—to show that they are daemons anyway. Then **Daemon** goes into an infinite loop that calls **yield( )** to give up control to the other processes.

You should be aware that daemon threads will terminate their **run( )** methods without executing **finally** clauses:

```
//: concurrency/DaemonsDontRunFinally.java
// Daemon threads don't run the finally clause
import java.util.concurrent.*;
import static net.mindview.util.Print.*;

class ADaemon implements Runnable {
  public void run() {
    try {
      print("Starting ADaemon");
      TimeUnit.SECONDS.sleep(1);
    } catch(InterruptedException e) {
      print("Exiting via InterruptedException");
    } finally {
      print("This should always run?");
    }
  }
}
```

```
public class DaemonsDontRunFinally {
  public static void main(String[] args) throws Exception {
    Thread t = new Thread(new ADaemon());
    t.setDaemon(true);
    t.start();
  }
} /* Output:
Starting ADaemon
*///:~
```

When you run this program, you'll see that the **finally** clause is not executed, but if you comment out the call to **setDaemon( )**, you'll see that the **finally** clause *is* executed.

This behavior is correct, even if you don't expect it based on the previous promises given for **finally**. Daemons are terminated "abruptly" when the last of the non-daemons terminates. So as soon as **main( )** exits, the JVM shuts down all the daemons immediately, without any of the formalities you might have come to expect. Because you cannot shut daemons down in a nice fashion, they are rarely a good idea. Non-daemon **Executor**s are generally a better approach, since all the tasks controlled by an **Executor** can be shut down at once. As you shall see later in the chapter, shutdown in this case proceeds in an orderly fashion.

Exercise 7: (2) Experiment with different sleep times in **Daemons.java** to see what happens.

Exercise 8: (1) Modify **MoreBasicThreads.java** so that all the threads are daemon threads, and verify that the program ends as soon as **main( )** is able to exit.

Exercise 9: (3) Modify **SimplePriorities.java** so that a custom **ThreadFactory** sets the priorities of the threads.

Coding variations

In the examples that you've seen so far, the task classes all implement **Runnable**. In very simple cases, you may want to use the alternative approach of inheriting directly from **Thread**, like this:

```
//: concurrency/SimpleThread.java
// Inheriting directly from the Thread class.

public class SimpleThread extends Thread {
```

```java
  private int countDown = 5;
  private static int threadCount = 0;
  public SimpleThread() {
    // Store the thread name:
    super(Integer.toString(++threadCount));
    start();
  }
  public String toString() {
    return "#" + getName() + "(" + countDown + "), ";
  }
  public void run() {
    while(true) {
      System.out.print(this);
      if(--countDown == 0)
        return;
    }
  }
  public static void main(String[] args) {
    for(int i = 0; i < 5; i++)
      new SimpleThread();
  }
} /* Output:
#1(5), #1(4), #1(3), #1(2), #1(1), #2(5), #2(4), #2(3),
#2(2), #2(1), #3(5), #3(4), #3(3), #3(2), #3(1), #4(5),
#4(4), #4(3), #4(2), #4(1), #5(5), #5(4), #5(3), #5(2),
#5(1),
*///:~
```

You give the **Thread** objects specific names by calling the appropriate **Thread** constructor. This name is retrieved in **toString( )** using **getName( )**.

Another idiom that you may see is that of the self-managed **Runnable**:

```java
//: concurrency/SelfManaged.java
// A Runnable containing its own driver Thread.

public class SelfManaged implements Runnable {
  private int countDown = 5;
  private Thread t = new Thread(this);
  public SelfManaged() { t.start(); }
  public String toString() {
    return Thread.currentThread().getName() +
      "(" + countDown + "), ";
  }
}
```

Thinking in Java   *Bruce Eckel*

```
  public void run() {
    while(true) {
      System.out.print(this);
      if(--countDown == 0)
        return;
    }
  }
  public static void main(String[] args) {
    for(int i = 0; i < 5; i++)
      new SelfManaged();
  }
} /* Output:
Thread-0(5), Thread-0(4), Thread-0(3), Thread-0(2), Thread-
0(1), Thread-1(5), Thread-1(4), Thread-1(3), Thread-1(2),
Thread-1(1), Thread-2(5), Thread-2(4), Thread-2(3), Thread-
2(2), Thread-2(1), Thread-3(5), Thread-3(4), Thread-3(3),
Thread-3(2), Thread-3(1), Thread-4(5), Thread-4(4), Thread-
4(3), Thread-4(2), Thread-4(1),
*///:~
```

This is not especially different from inheriting from **Thread** except that the syntax is slightly more awkward. However, implementing an interface does allow you to inherit from a different class, whereas inheriting from **Thread** does not.

Notice that **start( )** is called within the constructor. This example is quite simple and therefore probably safe, but you should be aware that starting threads inside a constructor can be quite problematic, because another task might start executing before the constructor has completed, which means the task may be able to access the object in an unstable state. This is yet another reason to prefer the use of **Executor**s to the explicit creation of **Thread** objects.

Sometimes it makes sense to hide your threading code inside your class by using an inner class, as shown here:

```
//: concurrency/ThreadVariations.java
// Creating threads with inner classes.
import java.util.concurrent.*;
import static net.mindview.util.Print.*;

// Using a named inner class:
class InnerThread1 {
  private int countDown = 5;
```

```
    private Inner inner;
    private class Inner extends Thread {
      Inner(String name) {
        super(name);
        start();
      }
      public void run() {
        try {
          while(true) {
            print(this);
            if(--countDown == 0) return;
            sleep(10);
          }
        } catch(InterruptedException e) {
          print("interrupted");
        }
      }
      public String toString() {
        return getName() + ": " + countDown;
      }
    }
  public InnerThread1(String name) {
    inner = new Inner(name);
  }
}

// Using an anonymous inner class:
class InnerThread2 {
  private int countDown = 5;
  private Thread t;
  public InnerThread2(String name) {
    t = new Thread(name) {
      public void run() {
        try {
          while(true) {
            print(this);
            if(--countDown == 0) return;
            sleep(10);
          }
        } catch(InterruptedException e) {
          print("sleep() interrupted");
        }
      }
      public String toString() {
```

```
        return getName() + ": " + countDown;
      }
    };
    t.start();
  }
}

// Using a named Runnable implementation:
class InnerRunnable1 {
  private int countDown = 5;
  private Inner inner;
  private class Inner implements Runnable {
    Thread t;
    Inner(String name) {
      t = new Thread(this, name);
      t.start();
    }
    public void run() {
      try {
        while(true) {
          print(this);
          if(--countDown == 0) return;
          TimeUnit.MILLISECONDS.sleep(10);
        }
      } catch(InterruptedException e) {
        print("sleep() interrupted");
      }
    }
    public String toString() {
      return t.getName() + ": " + countDown;
    }
  }
  public InnerRunnable1(String name) {
    inner = new Inner(name);
  }
}

// Using an anonymous Runnable implementation:
class InnerRunnable2 {
  private int countDown = 5;
  private Thread t;
  public InnerRunnable2(String name) {
    t = new Thread(new Runnable() {
      public void run() {
```

```
        try {
          while(true) {
            print(this);
            if(--countDown == 0) return;
            TimeUnit.MILLISECONDS.sleep(10);
          }
        } catch(InterruptedException e) {
          print("sleep() interrupted");
        }
      }
      public String toString() {
        return Thread.currentThread().getName() +
          ": " + countDown;
      }
    }, name);
    t.start();
  }
}

// A separate method to run some code as a task:
class ThreadMethod {
  private int countDown = 5;
  private Thread t;
  private String name;
  public ThreadMethod(String name) { this.name = name; }
  public void runTask() {
    if(t == null) {
      t = new Thread(name) {
        public void run() {
          try {
            while(true) {
              print(this);
              if(--countDown == 0) return;
              sleep(10);
            }
          } catch(InterruptedException e) {
            print("sleep() interrupted");
          }
        }
        public String toString() {
          return getName() + ": " + countDown;
        }
      };
      t.start();
```

```
      }
    }
  }

public class ThreadVariations {
  public static void main(String[] args) {
    new InnerThread1("InnerThread1");
    new InnerThread2("InnerThread2");
    new InnerRunnable1("InnerRunnable1");
    new InnerRunnable2("InnerRunnable2");
    new ThreadMethod("ThreadMethod").runTask();
  }
} /* (Execute to see output) *///:~
```

InnerThread1 creates a named inner class that extends **Thread**, and makes an instance of this inner class inside the constructor. This makes sense if the inner class has special capabilities (new methods) that you need to access in other methods. However, most of the time the reason for creating a thread is only to use the **Thread** capabilities, so it's not necessary to create a named inner class. **InnerThread2** shows the alternative: An anonymous inner subclass of **Thread** is created inside the constructor and is upcast to a **Thread** reference **t**. If other methods of the class need to access **t**, they can do so through the **Thread** interface, and they don't need to know the exact type of the object.

The third and fourth classes in the example repeat the first two classes, but they use the **Runnable** interface rather than the **Thread** class.

The **ThreadMethod** class shows the creation of a thread inside a method. You call the method when you're ready to run the thread, and the method returns after the thread begins. If the thread is only performing an auxiliary operation rather than being fundamental to the class, this is probably a more useful and appropriate approach than starting a thread inside the constructor of the class.

Exercise 10:   (4) Modify Exercise 5 following the example of the **ThreadMethod** class, so that **runTask( )** takes an argument of the number of Fibonacci numbers to sum, and each time you call **runTask( )** it returns the **Future** produced by the call to **submit( )**.

Terminology

As the previous section shows, you have choices in how you implement concurrent programs in Java, and these choices can be confusing. Often the problem comes from the terminology that's used in describing concurrent program technology, especially where threads are involved.

You should see by now that there's a distinction between the task that's being executed and the thread that drives it; this distinction is especially clear in the Java libraries because you don't really have any control over the **Thread** class (and this separation is even clearer with executors, which take care of the creation and management of threads for you). You create tasks and somehow attach a thread to your task so that the thread will drive that task.

In Java, the **Thread** class by itself does nothing. It drives the task that it's given. Yet threading literature invariably uses language like "the thread performs this or that action." The impression that you get is that the thread *is* the task, and when I first encountered Java threads, this impression was so strong that I saw a clear "is-a" relationship, which said to me that I should obviously inherit a task from a **Thread**. Add to this the poor choice of name for the **Runnable** interface, which I think would have been much better named "**Task**." If the interface is clearly nothing more than a generic encapsulation of its methods, then the "it-does-this-thing-**able**" naming approach is appropriate, but if it intends to express a higher concept, like **Task**, then the concept name is more helpful.

The problem is that the levels of abstraction are mixed together. Conceptually, we want to create a task that runs independently of other tasks, so we ought to be able to define a task, and then say "go," and not worry about details. But physically, threads can be expensive to create, so you must conserve and manage them. Thus it makes sense *from an implementation standpoint* to separate tasks from threads. In addition, Java threading is based on the low-level pthreads approach which comes from C, where you are immersed in, and must thoroughly understand, the nuts and bolts of everything that's going on. Some of this low-level nature has trickled through into the Java implementation, so to stay at a higher level of abstraction, you must use discipline when writing code (I will try to demonstrate that discipline in this chapter).

To clarify these discussions, I shall attempt to use the term "task" when I am describing the work that is being done, and "thread" only when I am referring to the specific mechanism that's driving the task. Thus, if you are discussing a system at a conceptual level, you could just use the term "task" without mentioning the driving mechanism at all.

Joining a thread

One thread may call **join( )** on another thread to wait for the second thread to complete before proceeding. If a thread calls **t.join( )** on another thread **t**, then the calling thread is suspended until the target thread **t** finishes (when **t.isAlive( )** is **false**).

You may also call **join( )** with a timeout argument (in either milliseconds or milliseconds and nanoseconds) so that if the target thread doesn't finish in that period of time, the call to **join( )** returns anyway.

The call to **join( )** may be aborted by calling **interrupt( )** on the calling thread, so a **try-catch** clause is required.

All of these operations are shown in the following example:

```
//: concurrency/Joining.java
// Understanding join().
import static net.mindview.util.Print.*;

class Sleeper extends Thread {
  private int duration;
  public Sleeper(String name, int sleepTime) {
    super(name);
    duration = sleepTime;
    start();
  }
  public void run() {
    try {
      sleep(duration);
    } catch(InterruptedException e) {
      print(getName() + " was interrupted. " +
        "isInterrupted(): " + isInterrupted());
      return;
    }
    print(getName() + " has awakened");
  }
}

class Joiner extends Thread {
```

```
    private Sleeper sleeper;
    public Joiner(String name, Sleeper sleeper) {
      super(name);
      this.sleeper = sleeper;
      start();
    }
    public void run() {
      try {
        sleeper.join();
      } catch(InterruptedException e) {
        print("Interrupted");
      }
      print(getName() + " join completed");
    }
  }

public class Joining {
  public static void main(String[] args) {
    Sleeper
      sleepy = new Sleeper("Sleepy", 1500),
      grumpy = new Sleeper("Grumpy", 1500);
    Joiner
      dopey = new Joiner("Dopey", sleepy),
      doc = new Joiner("Doc", grumpy);
    grumpy.interrupt();
  }
} /* Output:
Grumpy was interrupted. isInterrupted(): false
Doc join completed
Sleepy has awakened
Dopey join completed
*///:~
```

A **Sleeper** is a thread that goes to sleep for a time specified in its constructor. In **run( )**, the call to **sleep( )** may terminate when the time expires, but it may also be interrupted. Inside the **catch** clause, the interruption is reported, along with the value of **isInterrupted( )**. When another thread calls **interrupt( )** on this thread, a flag is set to indicate that the thread has been interrupted. However, this flag is cleared when the exception is caught, so the result will always be **false** inside the **catch** clause. The flag is used for other situations where a thread may examine its interrupted state apart from the exception.

A **Joiner** is a task that waits for a **Sleeper** to wake up by calling **join( )** on the **Sleeper** object. In **main( )**, each **Sleeper** has a **Joiner**, and you can see in the output that if the **Sleeper** either is interrupted or ends normally, the **Joiner** completes in conjunction with the **Sleeper**.

Note that the Java SE5 **java.util.concurrent** libraries contain tools such as **CyclicBarrier** (demonstrated later in this chapter) that may be more appropriate than **join( )**, which was part of the original threading library.

Creating responsive user interfaces

As stated earlier, one of the motivations for using threading is to create a responsive user interface. Although we won't get to *graphical* interfaces until the *Graphical User Interfaces* chapter, the following example is a simple mock-up of a console-based user interface. The example has two versions: one that gets stuck in a calculation and thus can never read console input, and a second that puts the calculation inside a task and thus can be performing the calculation *and* listening for console input.

```
//: concurrency/ResponsiveUI.java
// User interface responsiveness.
// {RunByHand}

class UnresponsiveUI {
  private volatile double d = 1;
  public UnresponsiveUI() throws Exception {
    while(d > 0)
      d = d + (Math.PI + Math.E) / d;
    System.in.read(); // Never gets here
  }
}

public class ResponsiveUI extends Thread {
  private static volatile double d = 1;
  public ResponsiveUI() {
    setDaemon(true);
    start();
  }
  public void run() {
    while(true) {
      d = d + (Math.PI + Math.E) / d;
    }
  }
}
```

```
    public static void main(String[] args) throws Exception {
      //! new UnresponsiveUI(); // Must kill this process
      new ResponsiveUI();
      System.in.read();
      System.out.println(d); // Shows progress
    }
  } ///:~
```

UnresponsiveUI performs a calculation inside an infinite **while** loop, so it can obviously never reach the console input line (the compiler is fooled into believing that the input line is reachable by the **while** conditional). If you uncomment the line that creates an **UnresponsiveUI**, you'll have to kill the process to get out.

To make the program responsive, put the calculation inside a **run( )** method to allow it to be preempted, and when you press the Enter key, you'll see that the calculation has indeed been running in the background while waiting for your user input.

Thread groups

A *thread group* holds a collection of threads. The value of thread groups can be summed up by a quote from Joshua Bloch,[8] the software architect who, while he was at Sun, fixed and greatly improved the Java collections library in JDK 1.2 (among other contributions):

> *"Thread groups are best viewed as an unsuccessful experiment, and you may simply ignore their existence."*

If you've spent time and energy trying to figure out the value of thread groups (as I have), you may wonder why there was not some more official announcement from Sun on the topic—the same question can be asked about any number of other changes that have happened to Java over the years. The Nobel laureate economist Joseph Stiglitz has a philosophy of life that would seem to apply here.[9] It's called *The Theory of Escalating Commitment*:

---

[8] *Effective Java™ Programming Language Guide*, by Joshua Bloch (Addison-Wesley, 2001), p. 211.

[9] And in a number of other places throughout the experience of Java. Well, why stop there? I've consulted on more than a few projects where this has applied.

"The cost of continuing mistakes is borne by others, while the cost of admitting mistakes is borne by yourself."

Catching exceptions

Because of the nature of threads, you can't catch an exception that has escaped from a thread. Once an exception gets outside of a task's **run( )** method, it will propagate out to the console unless you take special steps to capture such errant exceptions. Before Java SE5, you used thread groups to catch these exceptions, but with Java SE5 you can solve the problem with **Executor**s, and thus you no longer need to know *anything* about thread groups (except to understand legacy code; see *Thinking in Java, 2nd Edition*, downloadable from *www.MindView.net*, for details about thread groups).

Here's a task that always throws an exception which propagates outside of its **run( )** method, and a **main( )** that shows what happens when you run it:

```
//: concurrency/ExceptionThread.java
// {ThrowsException}
import java.util.concurrent.*;

public class ExceptionThread implements Runnable {
  public void run() {
    throw new RuntimeException();
  }
  public static void main(String[] args) {
    ExecutorService exec = Executors.newCachedThreadPool();
    exec.execute(new ExceptionThread());
  }
} ///:~
```

The output is (after trimming some qualifiers to fit):

```
java.lang.RuntimeException
        at ExceptionThread.run(ExceptionThread.java:7)
        at ThreadPoolExecutor$Worker.runTask(Unknown Source)
        at ThreadPoolExecutor$Worker.run(Unknown Source)
        at java.lang.Thread.run(Unknown Source)
```

Encompassing the body of main within a **try-catch** block is unsuccessful:

```
//: concurrency/NaiveExceptionHandling.java
// {ThrowsException}
import java.util.concurrent.*;
```

```java
public class NaiveExceptionHandling {
  public static void main(String[] args) {
    try {
      ExecutorService exec =
        Executors.newCachedThreadPool();
      exec.execute(new ExceptionThread());
    } catch(RuntimeException ue) {
      // This statement will NOT execute!
      System.out.println("Exception has been handled!");
    }
  }
} ///:~
```

This produces the same result as the previous example: an uncaught exception.

To solve the problem, we change the way the **Executor** produces threads. **Thread.UncaughtExceptionHandler** is a new interface in Java SE5; it allows you to attach an exception handler to each **Thread** object. **Thread.UncaughtExceptionHandler.uncaughtException( )** is automatically called when that thread is about to die from an uncaught exception. To use it, we create a new type of **ThreadFactory** which attaches a new **Thread.UncaughtExceptionHandler** to each new **Thread** object it creates. We pass that factory to the **Executors** method that creates a new **ExecutorService**:

```java
//: concurrency/CaptureUncaughtException.java
import java.util.concurrent.*;

class ExceptionThread2 implements Runnable {
  public void run() {
    Thread t = Thread.currentThread();
    System.out.println("run() by " + t);
    System.out.println(
      "eh = " + t.getUncaughtExceptionHandler());
    throw new RuntimeException();
  }
}

class MyUncaughtExceptionHandler implements
Thread.UncaughtExceptionHandler {
  public void uncaughtException(Thread t, Throwable e) {
    System.out.println("caught " + e);
  }
```

```
    }

class HandlerThreadFactory implements ThreadFactory {
  public Thread newThread(Runnable r) {
    System.out.println(this + " creating new Thread");
    Thread t = new Thread(r);
    System.out.println("created " + t);
    t.setUncaughtExceptionHandler(
      new MyUncaughtExceptionHandler());
    System.out.println(
      "eh = " + t.getUncaughtExceptionHandler());
    return t;
  }
}

public class CaptureUncaughtException {
  public static void main(String[] args) {
    ExecutorService exec = Executors.newCachedThreadPool(
      new HandlerThreadFactory());
    exec.execute(new ExceptionThread2());
  }
} /* Output: (90% match)
HandlerThreadFactory@de6ced creating new Thread
created Thread[Thread-0,5,main]
eh = MyUncaughtExceptionHandler@1fb8ee3
run() by Thread[Thread-0,5,main]
eh = MyUncaughtExceptionHandler@1fb8ee3
caught java.lang.RuntimeException
*///:~
```

Additional tracing has been added to verify that the threads created by the factory are given the new **UncaughtExceptionHandler**. You can see that the uncaught exceptions are now being captured by **uncaughtException**.

The above example allows you to set the handler on a case-by-case basis. If you know that you're going to use the same exception handler everywhere, an even simpler approach is to set the *default* uncaught exception handler, which sets a **static** field inside the **Thread** class:

```
//: concurrency/SettingDefaultHandler.java
import java.util.concurrent.*;

public class SettingDefaultHandler {
  public static void main(String[] args) {
```

```
      Thread.setDefaultUncaughtExceptionHandler(
        new MyUncaughtExceptionHandler());
      ExecutorService exec = Executors.newCachedThreadPool();
      exec.execute(new ExceptionThread());
    }
} /* Output:
caught java.lang.RuntimeException
*///:~
```

This handler is only called if there is no per-thread uncaught exception handler. The system checks for a per-thread version, and if it doesn't find one it checks to see if the thread group specializes its **uncaughtException( )** method; if not, it calls the **defaultUncaughtExceptionHandler**.

Sharing resources

You can think of a single-threaded program as one lonely entity moving around through your problem space and doing one thing at a time. Because there's only one entity, you never have to think about the problem of two entities trying to use the same resource at the same time: problems such as two people trying to park in the same space, walk through a door at the same time, or even talk at the same time.

With concurrency, things aren't lonely anymore, but you now have the possibility of two or more tasks interfering with each other. If you don't prevent such a collision, you'll have two tasks trying to access the same bank account at the same time, print to the same printer, adjust the same valve, and so on.

Improperly accessing resources

Consider the following example, where one task generates even numbers and other tasks consume those numbers. Here, the only job of the consumer tasks is to check the validity of the even numbers.

First we'll define **EvenChecker**, the consumer task, since it will be reused in all the subsequent examples. To decouple **EvenChecker** from the various types of generators that we will experiment with, we'll create an abstract class called **IntGenerator**, which contains the minimum necessary methods that **EvenChecker** must know about: that it has a **next( )** method and that it can be canceled. This class doesn't implement the **Generator** interface, because it must produce an **int**, and generics don't support primitive parameters.

```
//: concurrency/IntGenerator.java

public abstract class IntGenerator {
  private volatile boolean canceled = false;
  public abstract int next();
  // Allow this to be canceled:
  public void cancel() { canceled = true; }
  public boolean isCanceled() { return canceled; }
} ///:~
```

IntGenerator has a **cancel( )** method to change the state of a **boolean canceled** flag and **isCanceled( )** to see whether the object has been canceled. Because the **canceled** flag is a **boolean**, it is *atomic*, which means that simple operations like assignment and value return happen without the possibility of interruption, so you can't see the field in an intermediate state in the midst of those simple operations. The **canceled** flag is also **volatile** in order to ensure *visibility*. You'll learn about atomicity and visibility later in this chapter.

Any **IntGenerator** can be tested with the following **EvenChecker** class:

```
//: concurrency/EvenChecker.java
import java.util.concurrent.*;

public class EvenChecker implements Runnable {
  private IntGenerator generator;
  private final int id;
  public EvenChecker(IntGenerator g, int ident) {
    generator = g;
    id = ident;
  }
  public void run() {
    while(!generator.isCanceled()) {
      int val = generator.next();
      if(val % 2 != 0) {
        System.out.println(val + " not even!");
        generator.cancel(); // Cancels all EvenCheckers
      }
    }
  }
  // Test any type of IntGenerator:
  public static void test(IntGenerator gp, int count) {
    System.out.println("Press Control-C to exit");
    ExecutorService exec = Executors.newCachedThreadPool();
```

```
      for(int i = 0; i < count; i++)
        exec.execute(new EvenChecker(gp, i));
      exec.shutdown();
    }
    // Default value for count:
    public static void test(IntGenerator gp) {
      test(gp, 10);
    }
  } ///:~
```

Note that in this example the class that can be canceled is not **Runnable**. Instead, all the **EvenChecker** tasks that depend on the **IntGenerator** object test it to see whether it's been canceled, as you can see in **run( )**. This way, the tasks that share the common resource (the **IntGenerator**) watch that resource for the signal to terminate. This eliminates the so-called race condition, where two or more tasks race to respond to a condition and thus collide or otherwise produce inconsistent results. You must be careful to think about and protect against all the possible ways a concurrent system can fail. For example, a task cannot depend on another task, because task shutdown order is not guaranteed. Here, by making tasks depend on a non-task object, we eliminate the potential race condition.

The **test( )** method sets up and performs a test of any type of **IntGenerator** by starting a number of **EvenCheckers** that use the same **IntGenerator**. If the **IntGenerator** causes a failure, **test( )** will report it and return; otherwise, you must press Control-C to terminate it.

EvenChecker tasks constantly read and test the values from their associated **IntGenerator**. Note that if **generator.isCanceled( )** is **true**, **run( )** returns, which tells the **Executor** in **EvenChecker.test( )** that the task is complete. Any **EvenChecker** task can call **cancel( )** on its associated **IntGenerator**, which will cause all other **EvenCheckers** using that **IntGenerator** to gracefully shut down. In later sections, you'll see that Java contains more general mechanisms for termination of threads.

The first **IntGenerator** we'll look at has a **next( )** that produces a series of even values:

```
//: concurrency/EvenGenerator.java
// When threads collide.

public class EvenGenerator extends IntGenerator {
  private int currentEvenValue = 0;
```

```
  public int next() {
    ++currentEvenValue; // Danger point here!
    ++currentEvenValue;
    return currentEvenValue;
  }
  public static void main(String[] args) {
    EvenChecker.test(new EvenGenerator());
  }
} /* Output: (Sample)
Press Control-C to exit
89476993 not even!
89476993 not even!
*///:~
```

It's possible for one task to call **next( )** after another task has performed the first increment of **currentEvenValue** but not the second (at the place in the code commented "Danger point here!"). This puts the value into an "incorrect" state. To prove that this can happen, **EvenChecker.test( )** creates a group of **EvenChecker** objects to continually read the output of an **EvenGenerator** and test to see if each one is even. If not, the error is reported and the program is shut down.

This program will eventually fail because the **EvenChecker** tasks are able to access the information in **EvenGenerator** while it's in an "incorrect" state. However, it may not detect the problem until the **EvenGenerator** has completed many cycles, depending on the particulars of your operating system and other implementation details. If you want to see it fail much faster, try putting a call to **yield( )** between the first and second increments. This is part of the problem with multithreaded programs—they can appear to be correct even when there's a bug, if the probability for failure is very low.

It's important to note that the increment operation itself requires multiple steps, and the task can be suspended by the threading mechanism in the midst of an increment—that is, increment is not an atomic operation in Java. So even a single increment isn't safe to do without protecting the task.

Resolving shared resource contention

The previous example shows a fundamental problem when you are using threads: You never know when a thread might be run. Imagine sitting at a table with a fork, about to spear the last piece of food on a platter, and as your fork reaches for it, the food suddenly vanishes—because your thread was

---

suspended and another diner came in and ate the food. That's the problem you're dealing with when writing concurrent programs. For concurrency to work, you need some way to prevent two tasks from accessing the same resource, at least during critical periods.

Preventing this kind of collision is simply a matter of putting a lock on a resource when one task is using it. The first task that accesses a resource must lock it, and then the other tasks cannot access that resource until it is unlocked, at which time another task locks and uses it, and so on. If the front seat of the car is the limited resource, the child who shouts "shotgun!" acquires the lock (for the duration of that trip).

To solve the problem of thread collision, virtually all concurrency schemes *serialize access to shared resources*. This means that only one task at a time is allowed to access the shared resource. This is ordinarily accomplished by putting a clause around a piece of code that only allows one task at a time to pass through that piece of code. Because this clause produces *mutual exclusion*, a common name for such a mechanism is *mutex*.

Consider the bathroom in your house; multiple people (tasks driven by threads) may each want to have exclusive use of the bathroom (the shared resource). To access the bathroom, a person knocks on the door to see if it's available. If so, they enter and lock the door. Any other task that wants to use the bathroom is "blocked" from using it, so those tasks wait at the door until the bathroom is available.

The analogy breaks down a bit when the bathroom is released and it comes time to give access to another task. There isn't actually a line of people, and we don't know for sure who gets the bathroom next, because the thread scheduler isn't deterministic that way. Instead, it's as if there is a group of blocked tasks milling about in front of the bathroom, and when the task that has locked the bathroom unlocks it and emerges, the one that happens to be nearest the door at the moment goes in. As noted earlier, suggestions can be made to the thread scheduler via **yield( )** and **setPriority( )**, but these suggestions may not have much of an effect, depending on your platform and JVM implementation.

To prevent collisions over resources, Java has built-in support in the form of the **synchronized** keyword. When a task wishes to execute a piece of code guarded by the **synchronized** keyword, it checks to see if the lock is available, then acquires it, executes the code, and releases it.

The shared resource is typically just a piece of memory in the form of an object, but may also be a file, an I/O port, or something like a printer. To control access to a shared resource, you first put it inside an object. Then any method that uses the resource can be made **synchronized**. If a task is in a call to one of the **synchronized** methods, all other tasks are blocked from entering *any* of the **synchronized** methods of that object until the first task returns from its call.

In production code, you've already seen that you should make the data elements of a class **private** and access that memory only through methods. You can prevent collisions by declaring those methods **synchronized**, like this:

```
synchronized void f() { /* ... */ }
synchronized void g() { /* ... */ }
```

All objects automatically contain a single lock (also referred to as a *monitor*). When you call any **synchronized** method, that object is locked and no other **synchronized** method of that object can be called until the first one finishes and releases the lock. For the preceding methods, if **f( )** is called for an object by one task, a different task cannot call **f( )** or **g( )** for the same object until **f( )** is completed and releases the lock. Thus, there is a single lock that is shared by all the **synchronized** methods of a particular object, and this lock can be used to prevent object memory from being written by more than one task at a time.

Note that it's especially important to make fields **private** when working with concurrency; otherwise the **synchronized** keyword cannot prevent another task from accessing a field directly, and thus producing collisions.

One task may acquire an object's lock multiple times. This happens if one method calls a second method on the same object, which in turn calls another method on the same object, etc. The JVM keeps track of the number of times the object has been locked. If the object is unlocked, it has a count of zero. As a task acquires the lock for the first time, the count goes to one. Each time the same task acquires another lock on the same object, the count is incremented. Naturally, multiple lock acquisition is only allowed for the task that acquired the lock in the first place. Each time the task leaves a **synchronized** method, the count is decremented, until the count goes to zero, releasing the lock entirely for use by other tasks.

There's also a single lock *per class* (as part of the **Class** object for the class), so that **synchronized static** methods can lock each other out from simultaneous access of **static** data on a class-wide basis.

When should you synchronize? Apply *Brian's Rule of Synchronization:*[10]

> *If you are writing a variable that might next be read by another thread, or reading a variable that might have last been written by another thread, you must use synchronization, and further, both the reader and the writer must synchronize using the same monitor lock.*

If you have more than one method in your class that deals with the critical data, you must synchronize all relevant methods. If you synchronize only one of the methods, then the others are free to ignore the object lock and can be called with impunity. This is an important point: Every method that accesses a critical shared resource must be **synchronized** or it won't work right.

Synchronizing the **EvenGenerator**

By adding **synchronized** to **EvenGenerator.java**, we can prevent the undesirable thread access:

```
//: concurrency/SynchronizedEvenGenerator.java
// Simplifying mutexes with the synchronized keyword.
// {RunByHand}

public class
SynchronizedEvenGenerator extends IntGenerator {
  private int currentEvenValue = 0;
  public synchronized int next() {
    ++currentEvenValue;
    Thread.yield(); // Cause failure faster
    ++currentEvenValue;
    return currentEvenValue;
  }
  public static void main(String[] args) {
    EvenChecker.test(new SynchronizedEvenGenerator());
  }
} ///:~
```

---

[10] From Brian Goetz, author of *Java Concurrency in Practice*, by Brian Goetz, Tim Peierls, Joshua Bloch, Joseph Bowbeer, David Holmes, and Doug Lea (Addison-Wesley, 2006).

A call to **Thread.yield( )** is inserted between the two increments, to raise the likelihood of a context switch while **currentEvenValue** is in an odd state. Because the mutex prevents more than one task at a time in the critical section, this will not produce a failure, but calling **yield( )** is a helpful way to promote a failure if it's going to happen.

The first task that enters **next( )** acquires the lock, and any further tasks that try to acquire the lock are blocked from doing so until the first task releases the lock. At that point, the scheduling mechanism selects another task that is waiting on the lock. This way, only one task at a time can pass through the code that is guarded by the mutex.

Exercise 11: (3) Create a class containing two data fields, and a method that manipulates those fields in a multistep process so that, during the execution of that method, those fields are in an "improper state" (according to some definition that you establish). Add methods to read the fields, and create multiple threads to call the various methods and show that the data is visible in its "improper state." Fix the problem using the **synchronized** keyword.

Using explicit **Lock** objects

The Java SE5 **java.util.concurrent** library also contains an explicit mutex mechanism defined in **java.util.concurrent.locks**. The **Lock** object must be explicitly created, locked and unlocked; thus, it produces less elegant code than the built-in form. However, it is more flexible for solving certain types of problems. Here is **SynchronizedEvenGenerator.java** rewritten to use explicit **Lock**s:

```
//: concurrency/MutexEvenGenerator.java
// Preventing thread collisions with mutexes.
// {RunByHand}
import java.util.concurrent.locks.*;

public class MutexEvenGenerator extends IntGenerator {
  private int currentEvenValue = 0;
  private Lock lock = new ReentrantLock();
  public int next() {
    lock.lock();
    try {
      ++currentEvenValue;
      Thread.yield(); // Cause failure faster
      ++currentEvenValue;
      return currentEvenValue;
```

```
        } finally {
          lock.unlock();
        }
      }
    }
    public static void main(String[] args) {
      EvenChecker.test(new MutexEvenGenerator());
    }
  } ///:~
```

MutexEvenGenerator adds a mutex called **lock** and uses the **lock( )** and **unlock( )** methods to create a critical section within **next( )**. When you are using **Lock** objects, it is important to internalize the idiom shown here: Right after the call to **lock( )**, you must place a **try-finally** statement with **unlock( )** in the **finally** clause—this is the only way to guarantee that the lock is always released. Note that the **return** statement must occur inside the **try** clause to ensure that the **unlock( )** doesn't happen too early and expose the data to a second task.

Although the **try-finally** requires more code than using the **synchronized** keyword, it also represents one of the advantages of explicit **Lock** objects. If something fails using the **synchronized** keyword, an exception is thrown, but you don't get the chance to do any cleanup in order to maintain your system in a good state. With explicit **Lock** objects, you can maintain proper state in your system using the **finally** clause.

In general, when you are using **synchronized**, there is less code to write, and the opportunity for user error is greatly reduced, so you'll usually only use the explicit **Lock** objects when you're solving special problems. For example, with the **synchronized** keyword, you can't try and fail to acquire a lock, or try to acquire a lock for a certain amount of time and then give up—to do this, you must use the **concurrent** library:

```
//: concurrency/AttemptLocking.java
// Locks in the concurrent library allow you
// to give up on trying to acquire a lock.
import java.util.concurrent.*;
import java.util.concurrent.locks.*;

public class AttemptLocking {
  private ReentrantLock lock = new ReentrantLock();
  public void untimed() {
    boolean captured = lock.tryLock();
    try {
```

```
        System.out.println("tryLock(): " + captured);
      } finally {
        if(captured)
          lock.unlock();
      }
    }
  }
  public void timed() {
    boolean captured = false;
    try {
      captured = lock.tryLock(2, TimeUnit.SECONDS);
    } catch(InterruptedException e) {
      throw new RuntimeException(e);
    }
    try {
      System.out.println("tryLock(2, TimeUnit.SECONDS): " +
        captured);
    } finally {
      if(captured)
        lock.unlock();
    }
  }
  public static void main(String[] args) {
    final AttemptLocking al = new AttemptLocking();
    al.untimed(); // True -- lock is available
    al.timed();   // True -- lock is available
    // Now create a separate task to grab the lock:
    new Thread() {
      { setDaemon(true); }
      public void run() {
        al.lock.lock();
        System.out.println("acquired");
      }
    }.start();
    Thread.yield(); // Give the 2nd task a chance
    al.untimed(); // False -- lock grabbed by task
    al.timed();   // False -- lock grabbed by task
  }
} /* Output:
tryLock(): true
tryLock(2, TimeUnit.SECONDS): true
acquired
tryLock(): false
tryLock(2, TimeUnit.SECONDS): false
*///:~
```

A **ReentrantLock** allows you to try and fail to acquire the lock, so that if someone else already has the lock, you can decide to go off and do something else rather than waiting until it is free, as you can see in the **untimed( )** method. In **timed( )**, an attempt is made to acquire the lock which can fail after 2 seconds (note the use of the Java SE5 **TimeUnit** class to specify units). In **main( )**, a separate **Thread** is created as an anonymous class, and it acquires the lock so that the **untimed( )** and **timed( )** methods have something to contend with.

The explicit **Lock** object also gives you finer-grained control over locking and unlocking than does the built-in **synchronized** lock. This is useful for implementing specialized synchronization structures, such as *hand-over-hand locking* (also called *lock coupling*), used for traversing the nodes of a linked list—the traversal code must capture the lock of the next node before it releases the current node's lock.

Atomicity and volatility

An incorrect piece of lore that is often repeated in Java threading discussions is, "Atomic operations do not need to be synchronized." An *atomic operation* is one that cannot be interrupted by the thread scheduler; if the operation begins, then it will run to completion before the possibility of a context switch. Relying on atomicity is tricky and dangerous—you should only try to use atomicity instead of synchronization if you are a concurrency expert, or you have help from such an expert. If you think you're smart enough to play with this kind of fire, take this test:

> *The Goetz Test*[11]: If you can write a high-performance JVM for a modern microprocessor, then you are qualified to *think about* whether you can avoid synchronizing.[12]

It's useful to *know* about atomicity, and to know that, along with other advanced techniques, it was used to implement some of the more clever

---

[11] After the previously mentioned Brian Goetz, a concurrency expert who helped with this chapter, based on only partially tongue-in-cheek comments from him.

[12] A corollary to this test is, "If someone implies that threading is easy and straightforward, make sure that person is not making important decisions about your project. If that person already is, then you've got trouble."

java.util.concurrent library components. But strongly resist the urge to rely on it yourself; see Brian's Rule of Synchronization, presented earlier.

Atomicity applies to "simple operations" on primitive types except for **long**s and **double**s. Reading and writing primitive variables other than **long** and **double** is guaranteed to go to and from memory as indivisible (atomic) operations. However, the JVM is allowed to perform reads and writes of 64-bit quantities (**long** and **double** variables) as two separate 32-bit operations, raising the possibility that a context switch could happen in the middle of a read or write, and then different tasks could see incorrect results (this is sometimes called *word tearing*, because you might see the value after only part of it has been changed). However, you do get atomicity (for simple assignments and returns) if you use the **volatile** keyword when defining a **long** or **double** variable (note that **volatile** was not working properly before Java SE5). Different JVMs are free to provide stronger guarantees, but you should not rely on platform-specific features.

Atomic operations are thus not interruptible by the threading mechanism. Expert programmers can take advantage of this to write *lock-free code*, which does not need to be synchronized. But even this is an oversimplification. Sometimes, even when it seems like an atomic operation should be safe, it may not be. Readers of this book will typically not be able to pass the aforementioned Goetz Test, and will thus not be qualified to try to replace synchronization with atomic operations. Trying to remove synchronization is usually a sign of premature optimization, and will cause you a lot of trouble, probably without gaining much, or anything.

On multiprocessor systems (which are now appearing in the form of *multicore* processors—multiple CPUs on a single chip), *visibility* rather than atomicity is much more of an issue than on single-processor systems. Changes made by one task, even if they're atomic in the sense of not being interruptible, might not be visible to other tasks (the changes might be temporarily stored in a local processor cache, for example), so different tasks will have a different view of the application's state. The synchronization mechanism, on the other hand, forces changes by one task on a multiprocessor system to be visible across the application. Without synchronization, it's indeterminate when changes become visible.

The **volatile** keyword also ensures visibility across the application. If you declare a field to be **volatile**, this means that as soon as a write occurs for that field, all reads will see the change. This is true even if local caches are involved—**volatile** fields are immediately written through to main memory, and reads occur from main memory.

It's important to understand that atomicity and volatility are distinct concepts. An atomic operation on a non-**volatile** field will not necessarily be flushed to main memory, and so another task that reads that field will not necessarily see the new value. If multiple tasks are accessing a field, that field should be **volatile**; otherwise, the field should only be accessed via synchronization. Synchronization also causes flushing to main memory, so if a field is completely guarded by **synchronized** methods or blocks, it is not necessary to make it **volatile**.

Any writes that a task makes will be visible to that task, so you don't need to make a field **volatile** if it is only seen within a task.

volatile doesn't work when the value of a field depends on its previous value (such as incrementing a counter), nor does it work on fields whose values are constrained by the values of other fields, such as the **lower** and **upper** bound of a **Range** class which must obey the constraint **lower <= upper**.

It's typically only safe to use **volatile** instead of **synchronized** if the class has only one mutable field. Again, your first choice should be to use the **synchronized** keyword—that's the safest approach, and trying to do anything else is risky.

What qualifies as an atomic operation? Assignment and returning the value in a field will usually be atomic. However, in C++ even the following *might* be atomic:

```
i++;      // Might be atomic in C++
i += 2;  // Might be atomic in C++
```

But in C++, this depends on the compiler and processor. You're unable to write cross-platform code in C++ that relies on atomicity, because C++ doesn't have a consistent *memory model*, as Java does (in Java SE5).[13]

In Java, the above operations are definitely *not* atomic, as you can see from the JVM instructions produced by the following methods:

```
//: concurrency/Atomicity.java
```

------

[13] This is being remedied in the upcoming C++ standard.

```
// {Exec: javap -c Atomicity}

public class Atomicity {
  int i;
  void f1() { i++; }
  void f2() { i += 3; }
} /* Output: (Sample)
...
void f1();
  Code:
    0:          aload_0
    1:          dup
    2:          getfield        #2; //Field i:I
    5:          iconst_1
    6:          iadd
    7:          putfield        #2; //Field i:I
    10:          return

void f2();
  Code:
    0:          aload_0
    1:          dup
    2:          getfield        #2; //Field i:I
    5:          iconst_3
    6:          iadd
    7:          putfield        #2; //Field i:I
    10:          return
*///:~
```

Each instruction produces a "get" and a "put," with instructions in between. So in between getting and putting, another task could modify the field, and thus the operations are not atomic.

If you blindly apply the idea of atomicity, you see that **getValue( )** in the following program fits the description:

```
//: concurrency/AtomicityTest.java
import java.util.concurrent.*;

public class AtomicityTest implements Runnable {
  private int i = 0;
  public int getValue() { return i; }
  private synchronized void evenIncrement() { i++; i++; }
  public void run() {
    while(true)
```

```
      evenIncrement();
    }
    public static void main(String[] args) {
      ExecutorService exec = Executors.newCachedThreadPool();
      AtomicityTest at = new AtomicityTest();
      exec.execute(at);
      while(true) {
        int val = at.getValue();
        if(val % 2 != 0) {
          System.out.println(val);
          System.exit(0);
        }
      }
    }
  }
} /* Output: (Sample)
191583767
*///:~
```

However, the program will find non-even values and terminate. Although **return i** is indeed an atomic operation, the lack of synchronization allows the value to be read while the object is in an unstable intermediate state. On top of this, since **i** is also not **volatile**, there will be visibility problems. Both **getValue( )** *and* **evenIncrement( )** must be **synchronized**. Only concurrency experts are qualified to attempt optimizations in situations like this; again, you should apply Brian's Rule of Synchronization.

As a second example, consider something even simpler: a class that produces serial numbers.[14] Each time **nextSerialNumber( )** is called, it must return a unique value to the caller:

```
//: concurrency/SerialNumberGenerator.java

public class SerialNumberGenerator {
  private static volatile int serialNumber = 0;
  public static int nextSerialNumber() {
    return serialNumber++; // Not thread-safe
  }
} ///:~
```

---

[14] Inspired by Joshua Bloch's *Effective Java™ Programming Language Guide* (Addison-Wesley, 2001), p. 190.

SerialNumberGenerator is about as simple a class as you can imagine, and if you're coming from C++ or some other low-level background, you might expect the increment to be an atomic operation, because a C++ increment can often be implemented as a microprocessor instruction (although not in any reliable, cross-platform fashion). As noted before, however, a Java increment is *not* atomic and involves both a read and a write, so there's room for threading problems even in such a simple operation. As you shall see, volatility isn't actually the issue here; the real problem is that **nextSerialNumber( )** accesses a shared, mutable value without synchronizing.

The **serialNumber** field is **volatile** because it is possible for each thread to have a local stack and maintain copies of some variables there. If you define a variable as **volatile**, it tells the compiler not to do any optimizations that would remove reads and writes that keep the field in exact synchronization with the local data in the threads. In effect, reads and writes go directly to memory, and are not cached. **volatile** also restricts compiler reordering of accesses during optimization. However, **volatile** doesn't affect the fact that an increment isn't an atomic operation.

Basically, you should make a field **volatile** if that field could be simultaneously accessed by multiple tasks, and at least one of those accesses is a write. For example, a field that is used as a flag to stop a task must be declared **volatile**; otherwise, that flag could be cached in a register, and when you make changes to the flag from outside the task, the cached value wouldn't be changed and the task wouldn't know it should stop.

To test **SerialNumberGenerator**, we need a set that doesn't run out of memory, in case it takes a long time to detect a problem. The **CircularSet** shown here reuses the memory used to store **int**s, with the assumption that by the time you wrap around, the possibility of a collision with the overwritten values is minimal. The **add( )** and **contains( )** methods are **synchronized** to prevent thread collisions:

```
//: concurrency/SerialNumberChecker.java
// Operations that may seem safe are not,
// when threads are present.
// {Args: 4}
import java.util.concurrent.*;

// Reuses storage so we don't run out of memory:
class CircularSet {
```

```java
    private int[] array;
    private int len;
    private int index = 0;
    public CircularSet(int size) {
      array = new int[size];
      len = size;
      // Initialize to a value not produced
      // by the SerialNumberGenerator:
      for(int i = 0; i < size; i++)
        array[i] = -1;
    }
    public synchronized void add(int i) {
      array[index] = i;
      // Wrap index and write over old elements:
      index = ++index % len;
    }
    public synchronized boolean contains(int val) {
      for(int i = 0; i < len; i++)
        if(array[i] == val) return true;
      return false;
    }
  }

  public class SerialNumberChecker {
    private static final int SIZE = 10;
    private static CircularSet serials =
      new CircularSet(1000);
    private static ExecutorService exec =
      Executors.newCachedThreadPool();
    static class SerialChecker implements Runnable {
      public void run() {
        while(true) {
          int serial =
            SerialNumberGenerator.nextSerialNumber();
          if(serials.contains(serial)) {
            System.out.println("Duplicate: " + serial);
            System.exit(0);
          }
          serials.add(serial);
        }
      }
    }
    public static void main(String[] args) throws Exception {
      for(int i = 0; i < SIZE; i++)
```

```
      exec.execute(new SerialChecker());
    // Stop after n seconds if there's an argument:
    if(args.length > 0) {
      TimeUnit.SECONDS.sleep(new Integer(args[0]));
      System.out.println("No duplicates detected");
      System.exit(0);
    }
  }
}
} /* Output: (Sample)
Duplicate: 8468656
*///:~
```

SerialNumberChecker contains a **static CircularSet** that holds all the serial numbers that have been produced, and a nested **SerialChecker** class that ensures the serial numbers are unique. By creating multiple tasks to contend over serial numbers, you'll discover that the tasks eventually get a duplicate serial number, if you let it run long enough. To solve the problem, add the **synchronized** keyword to **nextSerialNumber( )**.

The atomic operations that are supposed to be safe are the reading and assignment of primitives. However, as seen in **AtomicityTest.java**, it's still easily possible to use an atomic operation that accesses your object while it's in an unstable intermediate state. Making assumptions about this issue is tricky and dangerous. The most sensible thing to do is just to follow Brian's Rule of Synchronization.

Exercise 12:   (3) Repair **AtomicityTest.java** using the **synchronized** keyword. Can you demonstrate that it is now correct?

Exercise 13:   (1) Repair **SerialNumberChecker.java** using the **synchronized** keyword. Can you demonstrate that it is now correct?

Atomic classes

Java SE5 introduces special atomic variable classes such as **AtomicInteger**, **AtomicLong**, **AtomicReference**, etc. that provide an atomic conditional update operation of the form:

```
boolean compareAndSet(expectedValue, updateValue);
```

These are for fine-tuning to use machine-level atomicity that is available on some modern processors, so you generally don't need to worry about using them. Occasionally they come in handy for regular coding, but again when

---

performance tuning is involved. For example, we can rewrite
AtomicityTest.java to use **AtomicInteger**:

```
//: concurrency/AtomicIntegerTest.java
import java.util.concurrent.*;
import java.util.concurrent.atomic.*;
import java.util.*;

public class AtomicIntegerTest implements Runnable {
  private AtomicInteger i = new AtomicInteger(0);
  public int getValue() { return i.get(); }
  private void evenIncrement() { i.addAndGet(2); }
  public void run() {
    while(true)
      evenIncrement();
  }
  public static void main(String[] args) {
    new Timer().schedule(new TimerTask() {
      public void run() {
        System.err.println("Aborting");
        System.exit(0);
      }
    }, 5000); // Terminate after 5 seconds
    ExecutorService exec = Executors.newCachedThreadPool();
    AtomicIntegerTest ait = new AtomicIntegerTest();
    exec.execute(ait);
    while(true) {
      int val = ait.getValue();
      if(val % 2 != 0) {
        System.out.println(val);
        System.exit(0);
      }
    }
  }
} ///:~
```

Here we've eliminated the **synchronized** keyword by using
AtomicInteger instead. Because the program doesn't fail, a **Timer** is added
to automatically abort after 5 seconds.

Here is **MutexEvenGenerator.java** rewritten to use **AtomicInteger**:

```
//: concurrency/AtomicEvenGenerator.java
// Atomic classes are occasionally useful in regular code.
// {RunByHand}
```

```
import java.util.concurrent.atomic.*;

public class AtomicEvenGenerator extends IntGenerator {
  private AtomicInteger currentEvenValue =
    new AtomicInteger(0);
  public int next() {
    return currentEvenValue.addAndGet(2);
  }
  public static void main(String[] args) {
    EvenChecker.test(new AtomicEvenGenerator());
  }
} ///:~
```

Again, all other forms of synchronization have been eliminated by using **AtomicInteger**.

It should be emphasized that the **Atomic** classes were designed to build the classes in **java.util.concurrent**, and that you should use them in your own code only under special circumstances, and even then only when you can ensure that there are no other possible problems. It's generally safer to rely on locks (either the **synchronized** keyword or explicit **Lock** objects).

Exercise 14: (4) Demonstrate that **java.util.Timer** scales to large numbers by creating a program that generates many **Timer** objects that perform some simple task when the timeout completes.

Critical sections

Sometimes, you only want to prevent multiple thread access to part of the code inside a method instead of the entire method. The section of code you want to isolate this way is called a *critical section* and is created using the **synchronized** keyword. Here, **synchronized** is used to specify the object whose lock is being used to synchronize the enclosed code:

```
synchronized(syncObject) {
  // This code can be accessed
  // by only one task at a time
}
```

This is also called a *synchronized block*; before it can be entered, the lock must be acquired on **syncObject**. If some other task already has this lock, then the critical section cannot be entered until the lock is released.

The following example compares both synchronization approaches by showing how the time available for other tasks to access an object is significantly increased by using a **synchronized** block instead of synchronizing an entire method. In addition, it shows how an unprotected class can be used in a multithreaded situation if it is controlled and protected by another class:

```java
//: concurrency/CriticalSection.java
// Synchronizing blocks instead of entire methods. Also
// demonstrates protection of a non-thread-safe class
// with a thread-safe one.
package concurrency;
import java.util.concurrent.*;
import java.util.concurrent.atomic.*;
import java.util.*;

class Pair { // Not thread-safe
  private int x, y;
  public Pair(int x, int y) {
    this.x = x;
    this.y = y;
  }
  public Pair() { this(0, 0); }
  public int getX() { return x; }
  public int getY() { return y; }
  public void incrementX() { x++; }
  public void incrementY() { y++; }
  public String toString() {
    return "x: " + x + ", y: " + y;
  }
  public class PairValuesNotEqualException
  extends RuntimeException {
    public PairValuesNotEqualException() {
      super("Pair values not equal: " + Pair.this);
    }
  }
  // Arbitrary invariant -- both variables must be equal:
  public void checkState() {
    if(x != y)
      throw new PairValuesNotEqualException();
  }
}

// Protect a Pair inside a thread-safe class:
```

```java
abstract class PairManager {
  AtomicInteger checkCounter = new AtomicInteger(0);
  protected Pair p = new Pair();
  private List<Pair> storage =
    Collections.synchronizedList(new ArrayList<Pair>());
  public synchronized Pair getPair() {
    // Make a copy to keep the original safe:
    return new Pair(p.getX(), p.getY());
  }
  // Assume this is a time consuming operation
  protected void store(Pair p) {
    storage.add(p);
    try {
      TimeUnit.MILLISECONDS.sleep(50);
    } catch(InterruptedException ignore) {}
  }
  public abstract void increment();
}

// Synchronize the entire method:
class PairManager1 extends PairManager {
  public synchronized void increment() {
    p.incrementX();
    p.incrementY();
    store(getPair());
  }
}

// Use a critical section:
class PairManager2 extends PairManager {
  public void increment() {
    Pair temp;
    synchronized(this) {
      p.incrementX();
      p.incrementY();
      temp = getPair();
    }
    store(temp);
  }
}

class PairManipulator implements Runnable {
  private PairManager pm;
  public PairManipulator(PairManager pm) {
```

```
      this.pm = pm;
    }
    public void run() {
      while(true)
        pm.increment();
    }
    public String toString() {
      return "Pair: " + pm.getPair() +
        " checkCounter = " + pm.checkCounter.get();
    }
  }
}

class PairChecker implements Runnable {
  private PairManager pm;
  public PairChecker(PairManager pm) {
    this.pm = pm;
  }
  public void run() {
    while(true) {
      pm.checkCounter.incrementAndGet();
      pm.getPair().checkState();
    }
  }
}

public class CriticalSection {
  // Test the two different approaches:
  static void
  testApproaches(PairManager pman1, PairManager pman2) {
    ExecutorService exec = Executors.newCachedThreadPool();
    PairManipulator
      pm1 = new PairManipulator(pman1),
      pm2 = new PairManipulator(pman2);
    PairChecker
      pcheck1 = new PairChecker(pman1),
      pcheck2 = new PairChecker(pman2);
    exec.execute(pm1);
    exec.execute(pm2);
    exec.execute(pcheck1);
    exec.execute(pcheck2);
    try {
      TimeUnit.MILLISECONDS.sleep(500);
    } catch(InterruptedException e) {
      System.out.println("Sleep interrupted");
```

```
    }
    System.out.println("pm1: " + pm1 + "\npm2: " + pm2);
    System.exit(0);
  }
  public static void main(String[] args) {
    PairManager
      pman1 = new PairManager1(),
      pman2 = new PairManager2();
    testApproaches(pman1, pman2);
  }
} /* Output: (Sample)
pm1: Pair: x: 15, y: 15 checkCounter = 272565
pm2: Pair: x: 16, y: 16 checkCounter = 3956974
*///:~
```

As noted, **Pair** is not thread-safe because its invariant (admittedly arbitrary) requires that both variables maintain the same values. In addition, as seen earlier in this chapter, the increment operations are not thread-safe, and because none of the methods are **synchronized**, you can't trust a **Pair** object to stay uncorrupted in a threaded program.

You can imagine that someone hands you the non-thread-safe **Pair** class, and you need to use it in a threaded environment. You do this by creating the **PairManager** class, which holds a **Pair** object and controls all access to it. Note that the only **public** methods are **getPair( )**, which is **synchronized**, and the **abstract increment( )**. Synchronization for **increment( )** will be handled when it is implemented.

The structure of **PairManager**, where functionality implemented in the base class uses one or more **abstract** methods defined in derived classes, is called a *Template Method* in *Design Patterns* parlance.[15] Design patterns allow you to encapsulate change in your code; here, the part that is changing is the method **increment( )**. In **PairManager1** the entire **increment( )** method is **synchronized**, but in **PairManager2** only part of **increment( )** is **synchronized** by using a **synchronized** block. Note that the **synchronized** keyword is not part of the method signature and thus may be added during overriding.

---

[15] See *Design Patterns*, by Gamma et al. (Addison-Wesley, 1995).

The **store( )** method adds a **Pair** object to a **synchronized ArrayList**, so this operation is thread safe. Thus, it doesn't need to be guarded, and is placed outside of the **synchronized** block in **PairManager2**.

PairManipulator is created to test the two different types of **PairManager**s by calling **increment( )** in a task while a **PairChecker** is run from another task. To trace how often it is able to run the test, **PairChecker** increments **checkCounter** every time it is successful. In **main( )**, two **PairManipulator** objects are created and allowed to run for a while, after which the results of each **PairManipulator** are shown.

Although you will probably see a lot of variation in output from one run to the next, in general you will see that **PairManager1.increment( )** does not allow the **PairChecker** nearly as much access as **PairManager2.increment( )**, which has the **synchronized** block and thus provides more unlocked time. This is typically the reason to use a **synchronized** block instead of synchronizing the whole method: to allow other tasks more access (as long as it is safe to do so).

You can also use explicit **Lock** objects to create critical sections:

```
//: concurrency/ExplicitCriticalSection.java
// {ThrowsException} on a multiprocessor machine
// Using explicit Lock objects to create critical sections.
package concurrency;
import java.util.concurrent.locks.*;

// Synchronize the entire method:
class ExplicitPairManager1 extends PairManager {
  private Lock lock = new ReentrantLock();
  public void increment() {
    lock.lock();
    try {
      p.incrementX();
      p.incrementY();
      store(getPair());
    } finally {
      lock.unlock();
    }
  }
}

// Use a critical section:
```

```
class ExplicitPairManager2 extends PairManager {
  private Lock lock = new ReentrantLock();
  public void increment() {
    Pair temp;
    lock.lock();
    try {
      p.incrementX();
      p.incrementY();
      temp = getPair();
    } finally {
      lock.unlock();
    }
    store(temp);
  }
}

public class ExplicitCriticalSection {
  public static void main(String[] args) throws Exception {
    PairManager
      pman1 = new ExplicitPairManager1(),
      pman2 = new ExplicitPairManager2();
    CriticalSection.testApproaches(pman1, pman2);
  }
} ///:~
```

This reuses most of **CriticalSection.java** and creates new **PairManager** types that use explicit **Lock** objects. **ExplicitPairManager2** creates a critical section using a **Lock** object; the call to **store( )** is outside of the critical section. *But this example fails on a multiprocessor machine* – can you figure out why?

Synchronizing on other objects

A **synchronized** block must be given an object to synchronize upon, and usually the most sensible object to use is just the current object that the method is being called for: **synchronized(this)**, which is the approach taken in **PairManager2**. That way, when the lock is acquired for the **synchronized** block, other **synchronized** methods and critical sections in the object cannot be called. So the effect of the critical section, when synchronizing on **this**, is simply to reduce the scope of synchronization.

Sometimes you must synchronize on another object, but if you do this you must ensure that all relevant tasks are synchronizing on the same object. The following example demonstrates that two tasks can enter an object when the methods in that object synchronize on different locks:

```java
//: concurrency/SyncObject.java
// Synchronizing on another object.
import static net.mindview.util.Print.*;

class DualSynch {
  private Object syncObject = new Object();
  public synchronized void f() {
    for(int i = 0; i < 5; i++) {
      print("f()");
      Thread.yield();
    }
  }
  public void g() {
    synchronized(syncObject) {
      for(int i = 0; i < 5; i++) {
        print("g()");
        Thread.yield();
      }
    }
  }
}

public class SyncObject {
  public static void main(String[] args) {
    final DualSynch ds = new DualSynch();
    new Thread() {
      public void run() {
        ds.f();
      }
    }.start();
    ds.g();
  }
} /* Output: (Sample)
g()
f()
g()
f()
g()
f()
g()
f()
```

```
g()
f()
*///:~
```

DualSync.f( ) synchronizes on **this** (by synchronizing the entire method), and **g( )** has a **synchronized** block that synchronizes on **syncObject**. Thus, the two synchronizations are independent. This is demonstrated in **main( )** by creating a **Thread** that calls **f( )**. The **main( )** thread is used to call **g( )**. You can see from the output that both methods are running at the same time, so neither one is blocked by the synchronization of the other.

Exercise 15: (1) Create a class with three methods containing critical sections that all synchronize on the same object. Create multiple tasks to demonstrate that only one of these methods can run at a time. Now modify the methods so that each one synchronizes on a different object and show that all three methods can be running at once.

Exercise 16: (1) Modify Exercise 15 to use explicit **Lock** objects.

Thread local storage

A second way to prevent tasks from colliding over shared resources is to eliminate the sharing of variables. *Thread local storage* is a mechanism that automatically creates different storage for the same variable, for each different thread that uses an object. Thus, if you have five threads using an object with a variable **x**, thread local storage generates five different pieces of storage for **x**. Basically, they allow you to associate state with a thread.

The creation and management of thread local storage is taken care of by the **java.lang.ThreadLocal** class, as seen here:

```
//: concurrency/ThreadLocalVariableHolder.java
// Automatically giving each thread its own storage.
import java.util.concurrent.*;
import java.util.*;

class Accessor implements Runnable {
  private final int id;
  public Accessor(int idn) { id = idn; }
  public void run() {
    while(!Thread.currentThread().isInterrupted()) {
      ThreadLocalVariableHolder.increment();
      System.out.println(this);
      Thread.yield();
```

```
        }
      }
    public String toString() {
      return "#" + id + ": " +
        ThreadLocalVariableHolder.get();
    }
  }

public class ThreadLocalVariableHolder {
  private static ThreadLocal<Integer> value =
    new ThreadLocal<Integer>() {
      private Random rand = new Random(47);
      protected synchronized Integer initialValue() {
        return rand.nextInt(10000);
      }
    };
  public static void increment() {
    value.set(value.get() + 1);
  }
  public static int get() { return value.get(); }
  public static void main(String[] args) throws Exception {
    ExecutorService exec = Executors.newCachedThreadPool();
    for(int i = 0; i < 5; i++)
      exec.execute(new Accessor(i));
    TimeUnit.SECONDS.sleep(3);   // Run for a while
    exec.shutdownNow();          // All Accessors will quit
  }
} /* Output: (Sample)
#0: 9259
#1: 556
#2: 6694
#3: 1862
#4: 962
#0: 9260
#1: 557
#2: 6695
#3: 1863
#4: 963
...
*///:~
```

ThreadLocal objects are usually stored as **static** fields. When you create a **ThreadLocal** object, you are only able to access the contents of the object using the **get( )** and **set( )** methods. The **get( )** method returns a copy of the object that is associated with that thread, and **set( )** inserts its argument into the object stored for that thread, returning the old object that was in storage. The **increment( )** and **get( )** methods demonstrate this in **ThreadLocalVariableHolder**. Notice that **increment( )** and **get( )** are not **synchronized**, because **ThreadLocal** guarantees that no race condition can occur.

When you run this program, you'll see evidence that the individual threads are each allocated their own storage, since each one keeps its own count even though there's only one **ThreadLocalVariableHolder** object.

Terminating tasks

In some of the previous examples, **cancel( )** and **isCanceled( )** methods are placed in a class that is seen by all tasks. The tasks check **isCanceled( )** to determine when to terminate themselves. This is a reasonable approach to the problem. However, in some situations the task must be terminated more abruptly. In this section, you'll learn about the issues and problems of such termination.

First, let's look at an example that not only demonstrates the termination problem but also is an additional example of resource sharing.

The ornamental garden

In this simulation, the garden committee would like to know how many people enter the garden each day through its multiple gates. Each gate has a turnstile or some other kind of counter, and after the turnstile count is incremented, a shared count is incremented that represents the total number of people in the garden.

```
//: concurrency/OrnamentalGarden.java
import java.util.concurrent.*;
import java.util.*;
import static net.mindview.util.Print.*;

class Count {
  private int count = 0;
  private Random rand = new Random(47);
  // Remove the synchronized keyword to see counting fail:
  public synchronized int increment() {
    int temp = count;
```

```java
        if(rand.nextBoolean()) // Yield half the time
          Thread.yield();
        return (count = ++temp);
      }
    public synchronized int value() { return count; }
  }

  class Entrance implements Runnable {
    private static Count count = new Count();
    private static List<Entrance> entrances =
      new ArrayList<Entrance>();
    private int number = 0;
    // Doesn't need synchronization to read:
    private final int id;
    private static volatile boolean canceled = false;
    // Atomic operation on a volatile field:
    public static void cancel() { canceled = true; }
    public Entrance(int id) {
      this.id = id;
      // Keep this task in a list. Also prevents
      // garbage collection of dead tasks:
      entrances.add(this);
    }
    public void run() {
      while(!canceled) {
        synchronized(this) {
          ++number;
        }
        print(this + " Total: " + count.increment());
        try {
          TimeUnit.MILLISECONDS.sleep(100);
        } catch(InterruptedException e) {
          print("sleep interrupted");
        }
      }
      print("Stopping " + this);
    }
    public synchronized int getValue() { return number; }
    public String toString() {
      return "Entrance " + id + ": " + getValue();
    }
    public static int getTotalCount() {
      return count.value();
    }
```

```
    public static int sumEntrances() {
      int sum = 0;
      for(Entrance entrance : entrances)
        sum += entrance.getValue();
      return sum;
    }
  }

  public class OrnamentalGarden {
    public static void main(String[] args) throws Exception {
      ExecutorService exec = Executors.newCachedThreadPool();
      for(int i = 0; i < 5; i++)
        exec.execute(new Entrance(i));
      // Run for a while, then stop and collect the data:
      TimeUnit.SECONDS.sleep(3);
      Entrance.cancel();
      exec.shutdown();
      if(!exec.awaitTermination(250, TimeUnit.MILLISECONDS))
        print("Some tasks were not terminated!");
      print("Total: " + Entrance.getTotalCount());
      print("Sum of Entrances: " + Entrance.sumEntrances());
    }
  } /* Output: (Sample)
Entrance 0: 1 Total: 1
Entrance 2: 1 Total: 3
Entrance 1: 1 Total: 2
Entrance 4: 1 Total: 5
Entrance 3: 1 Total: 4
Entrance 2: 2 Total: 6
Entrance 4: 2 Total: 7
Entrance 0: 2 Total: 8
...
Entrance 3: 29 Total: 143
Entrance 0: 29 Total: 144
Entrance 4: 29 Total: 145
Entrance 2: 30 Total: 147
Entrance 1: 30 Total: 146
Entrance 0: 30 Total: 149
Entrance 3: 30 Total: 148
Entrance 4: 30 Total: 150
Stopping Entrance 2: 30
Stopping Entrance 1: 30
Stopping Entrance 0: 30
Stopping Entrance 3: 30
```

```
Stopping Entrance 4: 30
Total: 150
Sum of Entrances: 150
*///:~
```

A single **Count** object keeps the master count of garden visitors, and is stored as a **static** field in the **Entrance** class. **Count.increment( )** and **Count.value( )** are **synchronized** to control access to the **count** field. The **increment( )** method uses a **Random** object to cause a **yield( )** roughly half the time, in between fetching **count** into **temp** and incrementing and storing **temp** back into **count**. If you comment out the **synchronized** keyword on **increment( )**, the program breaks because multiple tasks will be accessing and modifying **count** simultaneously (the **yield( )** causes the problem to happen more quickly).

Each **Entrance** task keeps a local value **number** containing the number of visitors that have passed through that particular entrance. This provides a double check against the **count** object to make sure that the proper number of visitors is being recorded. **Entrance.run( )** simply increments **number** and the **count** object and sleeps for 100 milliseconds.

Because **Entrance.canceled** is a **volatile boolean** flag which is only read and assigned (and is never read in combination with other fields), it's possible to get away without synchronizing access to it. If you have any doubts about something like this, it's always better to use **synchronized**.

This program goes to quite a bit of extra trouble to shut everything down in a stable fashion. Part of the reason for this is to show just how careful you must be when terminating a multithreaded program, and part of the reason is to demonstrate the value of **interrupt( )**, which you will learn about shortly.

After 3 seconds, **main( )** sends the **static cancel( )** message to **Entrance**, then calls **shutdown( )** for the **exec** object, and then calls **awaitTermination( )** on **exec**. **ExecutorService.awaitTermination( )** waits for each task to complete, and if they all complete before the timeout value, it returns **true**, otherwise it returns **false** to indicate that not all tasks have completed. Although this causes each task to exit its **run( )** method and therefore terminate as a task, the **Entrance** objects are still valid because, in the constructor, each **Entrance** object is stored in a **static** **List<Entrance>** called **entrances**. Thus, **sumEntrances( )** is still working with valid **Entrance** objects.

As this program runs, you will see the total count and the count at each entrance displayed as people walk through a turnstile. If you remove the **synchronized** declaration on **Count.increment( )**, you'll notice that the total number of people is not what you expect it to be. The number of people counted by each turnstile will be different from the value in **count**. As long as the mutex is there to synchronize access to the **Count**, things work correctly. Keep in mind that **Count.increment( )** exaggerates the potential for failure by using **temp** and **yield( )**. In real threading problems, the possibility for failure may be statistically small, so you can easily fall into the trap of believing that things are working correctly. Just as in the example above, there are likely to be hidden problems that haven't occurred to you, so be exceptionally diligent when reviewing concurrent code.

Exercise 17: (2) Create a radiation counter that can have any number of remote sensors.

Terminating when blocked

Entrance.run( ) in the previous example includes a call to **sleep( )** in its loop. We know that **sleep( )** will eventually wake up and the task will reach the top of the loop, where it has an opportunity to break out of that loop by checking the **cancelled** flag. However, **sleep( )** is just one situation where a task is blocked from executing, and sometimes you must terminate a task that's blocked.

Thread states

A thread can be in any one of four states:

1. *New*: A thread remains in this state only momentarily, as it is being created. It allocates any necessary system resources and performs initialization. At this point it becomes eligible to receive CPU time. The scheduler will then transition this thread to the runnable or blocked state.

2. *Runnable*: This means that a thread can be run when the time-slicing mechanism has CPU cycles available for the thread. Thus, the thread might or might not be running at any moment, but there's nothing to prevent it from being run if the scheduler can arrange it. That is, it's not dead or blocked.

3. *Blocked*: The thread can be run, but something prevents it. While a thread is in the blocked state, the scheduler will simply skip it and not

give it any CPU time. Until a thread reenters the runnable state, it won't perform any operations.

4. *Dead*: A thread in the dead or *terminated* state is no longer schedulable and will not receive any CPU time. Its task is completed, and it is no longer runnable. One way for a task to die is by returning from its **run( )** method, but a task's thread can also be interrupted, as you'll see shortly.

Becoming blocked

A task can become blocked for the following reasons:

- You've put the task to sleep by calling **sleep(milliseconds)**, in which case it will not be run for the specified time.

- You've suspended the execution of the thread with **wait( )**. It will not become runnable again until the thread gets the **notify( )** or **notifyAll( )** message (or the equivalent **signal( )** or **signalAll( )** for the Java SE5 **java.util.concurrent** library tools). We'll examine these in a later section.

- The task is waiting for some I/O to complete.

- The task is trying to call a **synchronized** method on another object, and that object's lock is not available because it has already been acquired by another task.

In old code, you may also see **suspend( )** and **resume( )** used to block and unblock threads, but these are deprecated in modern Java (because they are deadlock-prone), and so will not be examined in this book. The **stop( )** method is also deprecated, because it doesn't release the locks that the thread has acquired, and if the objects are in an inconsistent state ("damaged"), other tasks can view and modify them in that state. The resulting problems can be subtle and difficult to detect.

The problem we need to look at now is this: Sometimes you want to terminate a task that is in a blocked state. If you can't wait for it to get to a point in the code where it can check a state value and decide to terminate on its own, you have to force the task out of its blocked state.

Thinking in Java   *Bruce Eckel*

Interruption

As you might imagine, it's much messier to break out of the middle of a **Runnable.run( )** method than it is to wait for that method to get to a test of a "cancel" flag, or to some other place where the programmer is ready to leave the method. When you break out of a blocked task, you might need to clean up resources. Because of this, breaking out of the middle of a task's **run( )** is more like throwing an exception than anything else, so in Java threads, exceptions are used for this kind of abort.[16] (This walks the fine edge of being an inappropriate use of exceptions, because it means you are often using them for control flow.) To return to a known good state when terminating a task this way, you must carefully consider the execution paths of your code and write your **catch** clause to properly clean everything up.

So that you can terminate a blocked task, the **Thread** class contains the **interrupt( )** method. This sets the interrupted status for that thread. A thread with its interrupted status set will throw an **InterruptedException** if it is already blocked or if it attempts a blocking operation. The interrupted status will be reset when the exception is thrown or if the task calls **Thread.interrupted( )**. As you'll see, **Thread.interrupted( )** provides a second way to leave your **run( )** loop, without throwing an exception.

To call **interrupt( )**, you must hold a **Thread** object. You may have noticed that the new **concurrent** library seems to avoid the direct manipulation of **Thread** objects and instead tries to do everything through **Executor**s. If you call **shutdownNow( )** on an **Executor**, it will send an **interrupt( )** call to each of the threads it has started. This makes sense because you'll usually want to shut down all the tasks for a particular **Executor** at once, when you've finished part of a project or a whole program. However, there are times when you may want to only interrupt a single task. If you're using **Executor**s, you can hold on to the context of a task when you start it by calling **submit( )** instead of **execute( )**. **submit( )** returns a generic **Future<?>**, with an unspecified parameter because you won't ever call **get( )** on it—the point of holding this kind of **Future** is that you can call **cancel( )** on it and thus use it to interrupt a particular task. If you pass **true**

---

[16] However, exceptions are never delivered asynchronously. Thus, there is no danger of something aborting mid-instruction/method call. And as long as you use the **try-finally** idiom when using object mutexes (vs. the **synchronized** keyword), those mutexes will be automatically released if an exception is thrown.

to **cancel( )**, it has permission to call **interrupt( )** on that thread in order to stop it; thus **cancel( )** is a way to interrupt individual threads started with an **Executor**.

Here's an example that shows the basics of **interrupt( )** using **Executor**s:

```
//: concurrency/Interrupting.java
// Interrupting a blocked thread.
import java.util.concurrent.*;
import java.io.*;
import static net.mindview.util.Print.*;

class SleepBlocked implements Runnable {
  public void run() {
    try {
      TimeUnit.SECONDS.sleep(100);
    } catch(InterruptedException e) {
      print("InterruptedException");
    }
    print("Exiting SleepBlocked.run()");
  }
}

class IOBlocked implements Runnable {
  private InputStream in;
  public IOBlocked(InputStream is) { in = is; }
  public void run() {
    try {
      print("Waiting for read():");
      in.read();
    } catch(IOException e) {
      if(Thread.currentThread().isInterrupted()) {
        print("Interrupted from blocked I/O");
      } else {
        throw new RuntimeException(e);
      }
    }
    print("Exiting IOBlocked.run()");
  }
}

class SynchronizedBlocked implements Runnable {
  public synchronized void f() {
    while(true) // Never releases lock
```

```
            Thread.yield();
    }
    public SynchronizedBlocked() {
        new Thread() {
            public void run() {
                f(); // Lock acquired by this thread
            }
        }.start();
    }
    public void run() {
        print("Trying to call f()");
        f();
        print("Exiting SynchronizedBlocked.run()");
    }
}

public class Interrupting {
    private static ExecutorService exec =
        Executors.newCachedThreadPool();
    static void test(Runnable r) throws InterruptedException{
        Future<?> f = exec.submit(r);
        TimeUnit.MILLISECONDS.sleep(100);
        print("Interrupting " + r.getClass().getName());
        f.cancel(true); // Interrupts if running
        print("Interrupt sent to " + r.getClass().getName());
    }
    public static void main(String[] args) throws Exception {
        test(new SleepBlocked());
        test(new IOBlocked(System.in));
        test(new SynchronizedBlocked());
        TimeUnit.SECONDS.sleep(3);
        print("Aborting with System.exit(0)");
        System.exit(0); // ... since last 2 interrupts failed
    }
} /* Output: (95% match)
Interrupting SleepBlocked
InterruptedException
Exiting SleepBlocked.run()
Interrupt sent to SleepBlocked
Waiting for read():
Interrupting IOBlocked
Interrupt sent to IOBlocked
Trying to call f()
Interrupting SynchronizedBlocked
```

```
Interrupt sent to SynchronizedBlocked
Aborting with System.exit(0)
*///:~
```

Each task represents a different kind of blocking. **SleepBlock** is an example of interruptible blocking, whereas **IOBlocked** and **SynchronizedBlocked** are uninterruptible blocking.[17] The program proves that I/O and waiting on a **synchronized** lock are not interruptible, but you can also anticipate this by looking at the code—no **InterruptedException** handler is required for either I/O or attempting to call a **synchronized** method.

The first two classes are straightforward: The **run( )** method calls **sleep( )** in the first class and **read( )** in the second. To demonstrate **SynchronizedBlocked**, however, we must first acquire the lock. This is accomplished in the constructor by creating an instance of an anonymous **Thread** class that acquires the object lock by calling **f( )** (the thread must be different from the one driving **run( )** for **SynchronizedBlock** because one thread can acquire an object lock multiple times). Since **f( )** never returns, that lock is never released. **SynchronizedBlock.run( )** attempts to call **f( )** and is blocked waiting for the lock to be released.

You'll see from the output that you can interrupt a call to **sleep( )** (or any call that requires you to catch **InterruptedException**). However, you cannot interrupt a task that is trying to acquire a **synchronized** lock or one that is trying to perform I/O. This is a little disconcerting, especially if you're creating a task that performs I/O, because it means that I/O has the potential of locking your multithreaded program. Especially for Web-based programs, this is a concern.

A heavy-handed but sometimes effective solution to this problem is to close the underlying resource on which the task is blocked:

```
//: concurrency/CloseResource.java
// Interrupting a blocked task by
// closing the underlying resource.
// {RunByHand}
import java.net.*;
```

---

[17] Some releases of the JDK also provided support for **InterruptedIOException**. However, this was only partially implemented, and only on some platforms. If this exception is thrown, it causes IO objects to be unusable. Future releases are unlikely to continue support for this exception.

```
import java.util.concurrent.*;
import java.io.*;
import static net.mindview.util.Print.*;

public class CloseResource {
  public static void main(String[] args) throws Exception {
    ExecutorService exec = Executors.newCachedThreadPool();
    ServerSocket server = new ServerSocket(8080);
    InputStream socketInput =
      new Socket("localhost", 8080).getInputStream();
    exec.execute(new IOBlocked(socketInput));
    exec.execute(new IOBlocked(System.in));
    TimeUnit.MILLISECONDS.sleep(100);
    print("Shutting down all threads");
    exec.shutdownNow();
    TimeUnit.SECONDS.sleep(1);
    print("Closing " + socketInput.getClass().getName());
    socketInput.close(); // Releases blocked thread
    TimeUnit.SECONDS.sleep(1);
    print("Closing " + System.in.getClass().getName());
    System.in.close(); // Releases blocked thread
  }
} /* Output: (85% match)
Waiting for read():
Waiting for read():
Shutting down all threads
Closing java.net.SocketInputStream
Interrupted from blocked I/O
Exiting IOBlocked.run()
Closing java.io.BufferedInputStream
Exiting IOBlocked.run()
*///:~
```

After **shutdownNow( )** is called, the delays before calling **close( )** on the
two input streams emphasize that the tasks unblock once the underlying
resource is closed. It's interesting to note that the **interrupt( )** appears when
you are closing the **Socket** but not when closing **System.in**.

Fortunately, the **nio** classes introduced in the I/O chapter provide for more
civilized interruption of I/O. Blocked **nio** channels automatically respond to
interrupts:

```
//: concurrency/NIOInterruption.java
// Interrupting a blocked NIO channel.
```

```java
import java.net.*;
import java.nio.*;
import java.nio.channels.*;
import java.util.concurrent.*;
import java.io.*;
import static net.mindview.util.Print.*;

class NIOBlocked implements Runnable {
  private final SocketChannel sc;
  public NIOBlocked(SocketChannel sc) { this.sc = sc; }
  public void run() {
    try {
      print("Waiting for read() in " + this);
      sc.read(ByteBuffer.allocate(1));
    } catch(ClosedByInterruptException e) {
      print("ClosedByInterruptException");
    } catch(AsynchronousCloseException e) {
      print("AsynchronousCloseException");
    } catch(IOException e) {
      throw new RuntimeException(e);
    }
    print("Exiting NIOBlocked.run() " + this);
  }
}

public class NIOInterruption {
  public static void main(String[] args) throws Exception {
    ExecutorService exec = Executors.newCachedThreadPool();
    ServerSocket server = new ServerSocket(8080);
    InetSocketAddress isa =
      new InetSocketAddress("localhost", 8080);
    SocketChannel sc1 = SocketChannel.open(isa);
    SocketChannel sc2 = SocketChannel.open(isa);
    Future<?> f = exec.submit(new NIOBlocked(sc1));
    exec.execute(new NIOBlocked(sc2));
    exec.shutdown();
    TimeUnit.SECONDS.sleep(1);
    // Produce an interrupt via cancel:
    f.cancel(true);
    TimeUnit.SECONDS.sleep(1);
    // Release the block by closing the channel:
    sc2.close();
  }
} /* Output: (Sample)
```

```
Waiting for read() in NIOBlocked@7a84e4
Waiting for read() in NIOBlocked@15c7850
ClosedByInterruptException
Exiting NIOBlocked.run() NIOBlocked@15c7850
AsynchronousCloseException
Exiting NIOBlocked.run() NIOBlocked@7a84e4
*///:~
```

As shown, you can also close the underlying channel to release the block, although this should rarely be necessary. Note that using **execute( )** to start both tasks and calling **e.shutdownNow( )** will easily terminate everything; capturing the **Future** in the example above was only necessary to send the interrupt to one thread and not the other.[18]

Exercise 18: (2) Create a non-task class with a method that calls **sleep( )** for a long interval. Create a task that calls the method in the non-task class. In **main( )**, start the task, then call **interrupt( )** to terminate it. Make sure that the task shuts down safely.

Exercise 19: (4) Modify **OrnamentalGarden.java** so that it uses **interrupt( )**.

Exercise 20: (1) Modify **CachedThreadPool.java** so that all tasks receive an **interrupt( )** before they are completed.

Blocked by a mutex

As you saw in **Interrupting.java**, if you try to call a **synchronized** method on an object whose lock has already been acquired, the calling task will be suspended (blocked) until the lock becomes available. The following example shows how the same mutex can be multiply acquired by the same task:

```
//: concurrency/MultiLock.java
// One thread can reacquire the same lock.
import static net.mindview.util.Print.*;

public class MultiLock {
  public synchronized void f1(int count) {
    if(count-- > 0) {
      print("f1() calling f2() with count " + count);
      f2(count);
```

---

[18] Ervin Varga helped research this section.

```
      }
    }
    public synchronized void f2(int count) {
      if(count-- > 0) {
        print("f2() calling f1() with count " + count);
        f1(count);
      }
    }
    public static void main(String[] args) throws Exception {
      final MultiLock multiLock = new MultiLock();
      new Thread() {
        public void run() {
          multiLock.f1(10);
        }
      }.start();
    }
} /* Output:
f1() calling f2() with count 9
f2() calling f1() with count 8
f1() calling f2() with count 7
f2() calling f1() with count 6
f1() calling f2() with count 5
f2() calling f1() with count 4
f1() calling f2() with count 3
f2() calling f1() with count 2
f1() calling f2() with count 1
f2() calling f1() with count 0
*///:~
```

In **main( )**, a **Thread** is created to call **f1( )**, then **f1( )** and **f2( )** call each other until the **count** becomes zero. Since the task has already acquired the **multiLock** object lock inside the first call to **f1( )**, that same task is reacquiring it in the call to **f2( )**, and so on. This makes sense because one task should be able to call other **synchronized** methods within the same object; that task already holds the lock.

As observed previously with uninterruptible I/O, anytime that a task can be blocked in such a way that it cannot be interrupted, you have the potential to lock up a program. One of the features added in the Java SE5 concurrency libraries is the ability for tasks blocked on **ReentrantLock**s to be interrupted, unlike tasks blocked on **synchronized** methods or critical sections:

```
//: concurrency/Interrupting2.java
```

```java
// Interrupting a task blocked with a ReentrantLock.
import java.util.concurrent.*;
import java.util.concurrent.locks.*;
import static net.mindview.util.Print.*;

class BlockedMutex {
  private Lock lock = new ReentrantLock();
  public BlockedMutex() {
    // Acquire it right away, to demonstrate interruption
    // of a task blocked on a ReentrantLock:
    lock.lock();
  }
  public void f() {
    try {
      // This will never be available to a second task
      lock.lockInterruptibly(); // Special call
      print("lock acquired in f()");
    } catch(InterruptedException e) {
      print("Interrupted from lock acquisition in f()");
    }
  }
}

class Blocked2 implements Runnable {
  BlockedMutex blocked = new BlockedMutex();
  public void run() {
    print("Waiting for f() in BlockedMutex");
    blocked.f();
    print("Broken out of blocked call");
  }
}

public class Interrupting2 {
  public static void main(String[] args) throws Exception {
    Thread t = new Thread(new Blocked2());
    t.start();
    TimeUnit.SECONDS.sleep(1);
    System.out.println("Issuing t.interrupt()");
    t.interrupt();
  }
} /* Output:
Waiting for f() in BlockedMutex
Issuing t.interrupt()
Interrupted from lock acquisition in f()
```

```
Broken out of blocked call
*///:~
```

The class **BlockedMutex** has a constructor that acquires the object's own **Lock** and never releases it. For that reason, if you try to call **f( )** from a second task (different from the one that created the **BlockedMutex**), you will always be blocked because the **Mutex** cannot be acquired. In **Blocked2**, the **run( )** method will be stopped at the call to **blocked.f( )**. When you run the program, you'll see that, unlike an I/O call, **interrupt( )** can break out of a call that's blocked by a mutex.[19]

Checking for an interrupt

Note that when you call **interrupt( )** on a thread, the only time that the interrupt occurs is when the task enters, or is already inside, a blocking operation (except, as you've seen, in the case of uninterruptible I/O or blocked **synchronized** methods, in which case there's nothing you can do). But what if you've written code that may or may not make such a blocking call, depending on the conditions in which it is run? If you can only exit by throwing an exception on a blocking call, you won't always be able to leave the **run( )** loop. Thus, if you call **interrupt( )** to stop a task, your task needs a second way to exit in the event that your **run( )** loop doesn't happen to be making any blocking calls.

This opportunity is presented by the *interrupted status*, which is set by the call to **interrupt( )**. You check for the interrupted status by calling **interrupted( )**. This not only tells you whether **interrupt( )** has been called, it also clears the interrupted status. Clearing the interrupted status ensures that the framework will not notify you twice about a task being interrupted. You will be notified via either a single **InterruptedException** or a single successful **Thread.interrupted( )** test. If you want to check again to see whether you were interrupted, you can store the result when you call **Thread.interrupted( )**.

The following example shows the typical idiom that you should use in your **run( )** method to handle both blocked and non-blocked possibilities when the interrupted status is set:

---

[19] Note that, although it's unlikely, the call to **t.interrupt( )** could actually happen before the call to **blocked.f( )**.

Thinking in Java   *Bruce Eckel*

```
//: concurrency/InterruptingIdiom.java
// General idiom for interrupting a task.
// {Args: 1100}
import java.util.concurrent.*;
import static net.mindview.util.Print.*;

class NeedsCleanup {
  private final int id;
  public NeedsCleanup(int ident) {
    id = ident;
    print("NeedsCleanup " + id);
  }
  public void cleanup() {
    print("Cleaning up " + id);
  }
}

class Blocked3 implements Runnable {
  private volatile double d = 0.0;
  public void run() {
    try {
      while(!Thread.interrupted()) {
        // point1
        NeedsCleanup n1 = new NeedsCleanup(1);
        // Start try-finally immediately after definition
        // of n1, to guarantee proper cleanup of n1:
        try {
          print("Sleeping");
          TimeUnit.SECONDS.sleep(1);
          // point2
          NeedsCleanup n2 = new NeedsCleanup(2);
          // Guarantee proper cleanup of n2:
          try {
            print("Calculating");
            // A time-consuming, non-blocking operation:
            for(int i = 1; i < 2500000; i++)
              d = d + (Math.PI + Math.E) / d;
            print("Finished time-consuming operation");
          } finally {
            n2.cleanup();
          }
        } finally {
          n1.cleanup();
        }
```

```
      }
      print("Exiting via while() test");
    } catch(InterruptedException e) {
      print("Exiting via InterruptedException");
    }
  }
}

public class InterruptingIdiom {
  public static void main(String[] args) throws Exception {
    if(args.length != 1) {
      print("usage: java InterruptingIdiom delay-in-mS");
      System.exit(1);
    }
    Thread t = new Thread(new Blocked3());
    t.start();
    TimeUnit.MILLISECONDS.sleep(new Integer(args[0]));
    t.interrupt();
  }
} /* Output: (Sample)
NeedsCleanup 1
Sleeping
NeedsCleanup 2
Calculating
Finished time-consuming operation
Cleaning up 2
Cleaning up 1
NeedsCleanup 1
Sleeping
Cleaning up 1
Exiting via InterruptedException
*///:~
```

The **NeedsCleanup** class emphasizes the necessity of proper resource cleanup if you leave the loop via an exception. Note that all **NeedsCleanup** resources created in **Blocked3.run( )** must be immediately followed by **try-finally** clauses to guarantee that the **cleanup( )** method is always called.

You must give the program a command-line argument which is the delay time in milliseconds before it calls **interrupt( )**. By using different delays, you can exit **Blocked3.run( )** at different points in the loop: in the blocking **sleep( )** call, and in the non-blocking mathematical calculation. You'll see that if **interrupt( )** is called after the comment "point2" (during the non-blocking operation), first the loop is completed, then all the local objects are destroyed, and finally the loop is exited at the top via the **while** statement. However, if **interrupt( )** is called between "point1" and "point2" (after the **while** statement but before or during the blocking operation **sleep( )**), the task exits via the **InterruptedException**, the first time a blocking operation is attempted. In that case, only the **NeedsCleanup** objects that have been created up to the point where the exception is thrown are cleaned up, and you have the opportunity to perform any other cleanup in the **catch** clause.

A class designed to respond to an **interrupt( )** must establish a policy to ensure that it will remain in a consistent state. This generally means that the creation of all objects that require cleanup must be followed by **try-finally** clauses so that cleanup will occur regardless of how the **run( )** loop exits. Code like this can work well, but alas, due to the lack of automatic destructor calls in Java, it relies on the client programmer to write the proper **try-finally** clauses.

Cooperation between tasks

As you've seen, when you use threads to run more than one task at a time, you can keep one task from interfering with another task's resources by using a lock (mutex) to synchronize the behavior of the two tasks. That is, if two tasks are stepping on each other over a shared resource (usually memory), you use a mutex to allow only one task at a time to access that resource.

With that problem solved, the next step is to learn how to make tasks cooperate with each other, so that multiple tasks can work together to solve a problem. Now the issue is not about interfering with one another, but rather about working in unison, since portions of such problems must be solved before other portions can be solved. It's much like project planning: The footings for the house must be dug first, but the steel can be laid and the concrete forms can be built in parallel, and both of those tasks must be finished before the concrete foundation can be poured. The plumbing must be in place before the concrete slab can be poured, the concrete slab must be in place before you start framing, and so on. Some of these tasks can be done in parallel, but certain steps require all tasks to be completed before you can move ahead.

The key issue when tasks are cooperating is handshaking between those tasks. To accomplish this handshaking, we use the same foundation: the mutex, which in this case guarantees that only one task can respond to a signal. This eliminates any possible race conditions. On top of the mutex, we add a way for a task to suspend itself until some external state changes (e.g., "The plumbing is now in place"), indicating that it's time for that task to move forward. In this section, we'll look at the issues of handshaking between tasks, which is safely implemented using the **Object** methods **wait( )** and **notifyAll( )**. The Java SE5 concurrency library also provides **Condition** objects with **await( )** and **signal( )** methods. We'll see the problems that can arise, and their solutions.

wait( ) and notifyAll( )

wait( ) allows you to wait for a change in some condition that is outside the control of the forces in the current method. Often, this condition will be changed by another task. You don't want to idly loop while testing the condition inside your task; this is called *busy waiting*, and it's usually a bad use of CPU cycles. So **wait( )** suspends the task while waiting for the world to change, and only when a **notify( )** or **notifyAll( )** occurs—suggesting that something of interest may have happened—does the task wake up and check for changes. Thus, **wait( )** provides a way to synchronize activities between tasks.

It's important to understand that **sleep( )** *does not* release the object lock when it is called, and neither does **yield( )**. On the other hand, when a task enters a call to **wait( )** inside a method, that thread's execution is suspended, and the lock on that object is released. Because **wait( )** releases the lock, it means that the lock can be acquired by another task, so other **synchronized** methods in the (now unlocked) object can be called during a **wait( )**. This is essential, because those other methods are typically what cause the change that makes it interesting for the suspended task to reawaken. Thus, when you call **wait( )**, you're saying, "I've done all I can right now, so I'm going to wait right here, but I want to allow other **synchronized** operations to take place if they can."

There are two forms of **wait( )**. One version takes an argument in milliseconds that has the same meaning as in **sleep( )**: "Pause for this period of time." But unlike with **sleep( )**, with **wait(pause)**:

1. The object lock is released during the **wait( )**.

2. You can also come out of the **wait( )** due to a **notify( )** or **notifyAll( )**, in addition to letting the clock run out.

The second, more commonly used form of **wait( )** takes no arguments. This **wait( )** continues indefinitely until the thread receives a **notify( )** or **notifyAll( )**.

One fairly unique aspect of **wait( )**, **notify( )**, and **notifyAll( )** is that these methods are part of the base class **Object** and not part of **Thread**. Although this seems a bit strange at first—to have something that's exclusively for threading as part of the universal base class—it's essential because these methods manipulate the lock that's also part of every object. As a result, you can put a **wait( )** inside any **synchronized** method, regardless of whether that class extends **Thread** or implements **Runnable**. In fact, the *only* place you can call **wait( )**, **notify( )**, or **notifyAll( )** is within a **synchronized** method or block (**sleep( )** can be called within non-**synchronized** methods since it doesn't manipulate the lock). If you call any of these within a method that's not **synchronized**, the program will compile, but when you run it, you'll get an **IllegalMonitorStateException** with the somewhat nonintuitive message "current thread not owner." This message means that the task calling **wait( )**, **notify( )**, or **notifyAll( )** must "own" (acquire) the lock for the object before it can call any of those methods.

You can ask another object to perform an operation that manipulates its own lock. To do this, you must first capture that object's lock. For example, if you want to send **notifyAll( )** to an object **x**, you must do so inside a **synchronized** block that acquires the lock for **x**:

```
synchronized(x) {
  x.notifyAll();
}
```

Let's look at a simple example. **WaxOMatic.java** has two processes: one to apply wax to a **Car** and one to polish it. The polishing task cannot do its job until the application task is finished, and the application task must wait until the polishing task is finished before it can put on another coat of wax. Both **WaxOn** and **WaxOff** use the **Car** object, which uses **wait( )** and **notifyAll( )** to suspend and restart tasks while they're waiting for a condition to change:

```
//: concurrency/waxomatic/WaxOMatic.java
// Basic task cooperation.
package concurrency.waxomatic;
import java.util.concurrent.*;
import static net.mindview.util.Print.*;
```

```
class Car {
  private boolean waxOn = false;
  public synchronized void waxed() {
    waxOn = true; // Ready to buff
    notifyAll();
  }
  public synchronized void buffed() {
    waxOn = false; // Ready for another coat of wax
    notifyAll();
  }
  public synchronized void waitForWaxing()
  throws InterruptedException {
    while(waxOn == false)
      wait();
  }
  public synchronized void waitForBuffing()
  throws InterruptedException {
    while(waxOn == true)
      wait();
  }
}

class WaxOn implements Runnable {
  private Car car;
  public WaxOn(Car c) { car = c; }
  public void run() {
    try {
      while(!Thread.interrupted()) {
        printnb("Wax On! ");
        TimeUnit.MILLISECONDS.sleep(200);
        car.waxed();
        car.waitForBuffing();
      }
    } catch(InterruptedException e) {
      print("Exiting via interrupt");
    }
    print("Ending Wax On task");
  }
}

class WaxOff implements Runnable {
  private Car car;
  public WaxOff(Car c) { car = c; }
```

```
    public void run() {
        try {
            while(!Thread.interrupted()) {
                car.waitForWaxing();
                printnb("Wax Off! ");
                TimeUnit.MILLISECONDS.sleep(200);
                car.buffed();
            }
        } catch(InterruptedException e) {
            print("Exiting via interrupt");
        }
        print("Ending Wax Off task");
    }
}

public class WaxOMatic {
    public static void main(String[] args) throws Exception {
        Car car = new Car();
        ExecutorService exec = Executors.newCachedThreadPool();
        exec.execute(new WaxOff(car));
        exec.execute(new WaxOn(car));
        TimeUnit.SECONDS.sleep(5); // Run for a while...
        exec.shutdownNow(); // Interrupt all tasks
    }
} /* Output: (95% match)
Wax On! Wax Off! Wax On! Wax Off! Wax On! Wax Off! Wax On!
Wax Off! Wax On! Wax Off! Wax On! Wax Off! Wax On! Wax Off!
Wax On! Wax Off! Wax On! Wax Off! Wax On! Wax Off! Wax On!
Wax Off! Wax On! Wax Off! Wax On! Exiting via interrupt
Ending Wax On task
Exiting via interrupt
Ending Wax Off task
*///:~
```

Here, **Car** has a single boolean **waxOn**, which indicates the state of the waxing-polishing process.

In **waitForWaxing( )**, the **waxOn** flag is checked, and if it is **false**, the calling task is suspended by calling **wait( )**. It's important that this occur in a **synchronized** method, where the task has acquired the lock. When you call **wait( )**, the thread is suspended and the lock is released. It is essential that the lock be released because, to safely change the state of the object (for example, to change **waxOn** to **true**, which must happen if the suspended task is to ever continue), that lock must be available to be acquired by some other task. In this example, when another task calls **waxed( )** to indicate that it's time to do something, the lock must be acquired in order to change **waxOn** to **true**. Afterward, **waxed( )** calls **notifyAll( )**, which wakes up the task that was suspended in the call to **wait( )**. In order for the task to wake up from a **wait( )**, it must first reacquire the lock that it released when it entered the **wait( )**. The task will not wake up until that lock becomes available.[20]

WaxOn.run( ) represents the first step in the process of waxing the car, so it performs its operation: a call to **sleep( )** to simulate the time necessary for waxing. It then tells the car that waxing is complete, and calls **waitForBuffing( )**, which suspends this task with a **wait( )** until the **WaxOff** task calls **buffed( )** for the car, changing the state and calling **notifyAll( )**. **WaxOff.run( )**, on the other hand, immediately moves into **waitForWaxing( )** and is thus suspended until the wax has been applied by **WaxOn** and **waxed( )** is called. When you run this program, you can watch this two-step process repeat itself as control is handed back and forth between the two tasks. After five seconds, **interrupt( )** halts both threads; when you call **shutdownNow( )** for an **ExecutorService**, it calls **interrupt( )** for all the tasks it is controlling.

The previous example emphasizes that you must surround a **wait( )** with a **while** loop that checks the condition(s) of interest. This is important because:

- You may have multiple tasks waiting on the same lock for the same reason, and the first task that wakes up might change the situation (even if you don't do this someone might inherit from your class and do it). If that is the case, this task should be suspended again until its condition of interest changes.

---

[20] On some platforms there's a third way to come out of a **wait( )**: the so-called *spurious wake-up*. A spurious wake-up essentially means that a thread may prematurely stop blocking (while waiting on a condition variable or semaphore) without being prompted by a **notify( )** or **notifyAll( )** (or their equivalents for the new **Condition** objects). The thread just wakes up, seemingly by itself. Spurious wake-ups exist because implementing POSIX threads, or the equivalent, isn't always as straightforward as it should be on some platforms. Allowing spurious wake-ups makes the job of building a library like pthreads easier for those platforms.

- By the time this task awakens from its **wait( )**, it's possible that some other task will have changed things such that this task is unable to perform or is uninterested in performing its operation at this time. Again, it should be resuspended by calling **wait( )** again.

- It's also possible that tasks could be waiting on your object's lock *for different reasons* (in which case you *must* use **notifyAll( )**). In this case, you need to check whether you've been woken up for the right reason, and if not, call **wait( )** again.

Thus, it's essential that you check for your particular condition of interest, and go back into **wait( )** if that condition is not met. This is idiomatically written using a **while**.

Exercise 21: (2) Create two **Runnable**s, one with a **run( )** that starts and calls **wait( )**. The second class should capture the reference of the first **Runnable** object. Its **run( )** should call **notifyAll( )** for the first task after some number of seconds have passed so that the first task can display a message. Test your classes using an **Executor**.

Exercise 22: (4) Create an example of a *busy wait*. One task sleeps for a while and then sets a flag to **true**. The second task watches that flag inside a **while** loop (this is the busy wait) and when the flag becomes **true**, sets it back to **false** and reports the change to the console. Note how much wasted time the program spends inside the busy wait, and create a second version of the program that uses **wait( )** instead of the busy wait.

Missed Signals

When two threads are coordinated using **notify( )/wait( )** or **notifyAll( )/wait( )**, it's possible to miss a signal. Suppose **T1** is a thread that notifies **T2**, and that the two threads are implemented using the following (flawed) approach:

```
T1:
synchronized(sharedMonitor) {
  <setup condition for T2>
  sharedMonitor.notify();
}

T2:
while(someCondition) {
  // Point 1
  synchronized(sharedMonitor) {
```

```
      sharedMonitor.wait();
    }
}
```

The *<setup condition for T2>* is an action to prevent **T2** from calling **wait( )**, if it hasn't already.

Assume that **T2** evaluates **someCondition** and finds it true. At **Point 1**, the thread scheduler might switch to **T1**. **T1** executes its setup, and then calls **notify( )**. When **T2** continues executing, it is too late for **T2** to realize that the condition has been changed in the meantime, and it will blindly enter **wait( )**. The **notify( )** will be missed and **T2** will wait indefinitely for the signal that was already sent, producing deadlock.

The solution is to prevent the race condition over the **someCondition** variable. Here is the correct approach for **T2**:

```
synchronized(sharedMonitor) {
  while(someCondition)
    sharedMonitor.wait();
}
```

Now, if **T1** executes first, when control returns back to **T2** it will figure out that the condition has changed, and will *not* enter **wait( )**. Conversely, if **T2** executes first, it will enter **wait( )** and later be awakened by **T1**. Thus, the signal cannot be missed.

notify() vs. notifyAll()

Because more than one task could technically be in a **wait( )** on a single **Car** object, it is safer to call **notifyAll( )** rather than just **notify( )**. However, the structure of the above program is such that only one task will actually be in a **wait( )**, so you could use **notify( )** instead of **notifyAll( )**.

Using **notify( )** instead of **notifyAll( )** is an optimization. Only one task of the possible many that are waiting on a lock will be awoken with **notify( )**, so you must be certain that the right task will wake up if you try to use **notify( )**. In addition, all tasks must be waiting on the same condition in order for you to use **notify( )**, because if you have tasks that are waiting on different conditions, you don't know if the right one will wake up. If you use **notify( )**, only one task must benefit when the condition changes. Finally, these constraints must always be true for all possible subclasses. If any of these rules cannot be met, you must use **notifyAll( )** rather than **notify( )**.

One of the confusing statements often made in discussions of Java threading is that **notifyAll( )** wakes up "all waiting tasks." Does this mean that any task that is in a **wait( )**, anywhere in the program, is awoken by any call to **notifyAll( )**? In the following example, the code associated with **Task2** shows that this is not true—in fact, only the tasks that are waiting on a particular lock are awoken when **notifyAll( )** is called *for that lock*:

```java
//: concurrency/NotifyVsNotifyAll.java
import java.util.concurrent.*;
import java.util.*;

class Blocker {
  synchronized void waitingCall() {
    try {
      while(!Thread.interrupted()) {
        wait();
        System.out.print(Thread.currentThread() + " ");
      }
    } catch(InterruptedException e) {
      // OK to exit this way
    }
  }
  synchronized void prod() { notify(); }
  synchronized void prodAll() { notifyAll(); }
}

class Task implements Runnable {
  static Blocker blocker = new Blocker();
  public void run() { blocker.waitingCall(); }
}

class Task2 implements Runnable {
  // A separate Blocker object:
  static Blocker blocker = new Blocker();
  public void run() { blocker.waitingCall(); }
}

public class NotifyVsNotifyAll {
  public static void main(String[] args) throws Exception {
    ExecutorService exec = Executors.newCachedThreadPool();
    for(int i = 0; i < 5; i++)
      exec.execute(new Task());
    exec.execute(new Task2());
    Timer timer = new Timer();
```

```
          timer.scheduleAtFixedRate(new TimerTask() {
            boolean prod = true;
            public void run() {
              if(prod) {
                System.out.print("\nnotify() ");
                Task.blocker.prod();
                prod = false;
              } else {
                System.out.print("\nnotifyAll() ");
                Task.blocker.prodAll();
                prod = true;
              }
            }
          }, 400, 400); // Run every .4 second
    TimeUnit.SECONDS.sleep(5); // Run for a while...
    timer.cancel();
    System.out.println("\nTimer canceled");
    TimeUnit.MILLISECONDS.sleep(500);
    System.out.print("Task2.blocker.prodAll() ");
    Task2.blocker.prodAll();
    TimeUnit.MILLISECONDS.sleep(500);
    System.out.println("\nShutting down");
    exec.shutdownNow(); // Interrupt all tasks
  }
} /* Output: (Sample)
notify() Thread[pool-1-thread-1,5,main]
notifyAll() Thread[pool-1-thread-1,5,main] Thread[pool-1-
thread-5,5,main] Thread[pool-1-thread-4,5,main]
Thread[pool-1-thread-3,5,main] Thread[pool-1-thread-
2,5,main]
notify() Thread[pool-1-thread-1,5,main]
notifyAll() Thread[pool-1-thread-1,5,main] Thread[pool-1-
thread-2,5,main] Thread[pool-1-thread-3,5,main]
Thread[pool-1-thread-4,5,main] Thread[pool-1-thread-
5,5,main]
notify() Thread[pool-1-thread-1,5,main]
notifyAll() Thread[pool-1-thread-1,5,main] Thread[pool-1-
thread-5,5,main] Thread[pool-1-thread-4,5,main]
Thread[pool-1-thread-3,5,main] Thread[pool-1-thread-
2,5,main]
notify() Thread[pool-1-thread-1,5,main]
notifyAll() Thread[pool-1-thread-1,5,main] Thread[pool-1-
thread-2,5,main] Thread[pool-1-thread-3,5,main]
```

```
Thread[pool-1-thread-4,5,main] Thread[pool-1-thread-
5,5,main]
notify() Thread[pool-1-thread-1,5,main]
notifyAll() Thread[pool-1-thread-1,5,main] Thread[pool-1-
thread-5,5,main] Thread[pool-1-thread-4,5,main]
Thread[pool-1-thread-3,5,main] Thread[pool-1-thread-
2,5,main]
notify() Thread[pool-1-thread-1,5,main]
notifyAll() Thread[pool-1-thread-1,5,main] Thread[pool-1-
thread-2,5,main] Thread[pool-1-thread-3,5,main]
Thread[pool-1-thread-4,5,main] Thread[pool-1-thread-
5,5,main]
Timer canceled
Task2.blocker.prodAll() Thread[pool-1-thread-6,5,main]
Shutting down
*///:~
```

Task and Task2 each have their own **Blocker** object, so each **Task** object blocks on **Task.blocker**, and each **Task2** object blocks on **Task2.blocker**. In **main( )**, a **java.util.Timer** object is set up to execute its **run( )** method every 4/10 of a second, and that **run( )** alternates between calling **notify( )** and **notifyAll( )** on **Task.blocker** via the "prod" methods.

From the output, you can see that even though a **Task2** object exists and is blocked on **Task2.blocker**, none of the **notify( )** or **notifyAll( )** calls on **Task.blocker** causes the **Task2** object to wake up. Similarly, at the end of **main( )**, **cancel( )** is called for the **timer**, and even though the timer is canceled, the first five tasks are still running and still blocked in their calls to **Task.blocker.waitingCall( )**. The output from the call to **Task2.blocker.prodAll( )** does *not* include any of the tasks waiting on the lock in **Task.blocker**.

This also makes sense if you look at **prod( )** and **prodAll( )** in **Blocker**. These methods are **synchronized**, which means that they acquire their own lock, so when they call **notify( )** or **notifyAll( )**, it's logical that they are only calling it for that lock—and thus only wake up tasks that are waiting on that particular lock.

Blocker.waitingCall( ) is simple enough that you could just say **for(;;)** instead of **while(!Thread.interrupted( ))**, and achieve the same effect in this case, because in this example there's no difference between leaving the loop with an exception and leaving it by checking the **interrupted( )** flag— the same code is executed in both cases. As a matter of form, however, this example checks **interrupted( )**, because there are two different ways of leaving the loop. If, sometime later, you decide to add more code to the loop, you risk introducing an error if you don't cover both paths of exit from the loop.

Exercise 23: (7) Demonstrate that **WaxOMatic.java** works successfully when you use **notify( )** instead of **notifyAll( )**.

Producers and consumers

Consider a restaurant that has one chef and one waitperson. The waitperson must wait for the chef to prepare a meal. When the chef has a meal ready, the chef notifies the waitperson, who then gets and delivers the meal and goes back to waiting. This is an example of task cooperation: The chef represents the *producer*, and the waitperson represents the *consumer*. Both tasks must handshake with each other as meals are produced and consumed, and the system must shut down in an orderly fashion. Here is the story modeled in code:

```
//: concurrency/Restaurant.java
// The producer-consumer approach to task cooperation.
import java.util.concurrent.*;
import static net.mindview.util.Print.*;

class Meal {
  private final int orderNum;
  public Meal(int orderNum) { this.orderNum = orderNum; }
  public String toString() { return "Meal " + orderNum; }
}

class WaitPerson implements Runnable {
  private Restaurant restaurant;
  public WaitPerson(Restaurant r) { restaurant = r; }
  public void run() {
    try {
      while(!Thread.interrupted()) {
        synchronized(this) {
          while(restaurant.meal == null)
            wait(); // ... for the chef to produce a meal
        }
        print("Waitperson got " + restaurant.meal);
        synchronized(restaurant.chef) {
          restaurant.meal = null;
          restaurant.chef.notifyAll(); // Ready for another
```

```
        }
      }
    } catch(InterruptedException e) {
      print("WaitPerson interrupted");
    }
  }
}

class Chef implements Runnable {
  private Restaurant restaurant;
  private int count = 0;
  public Chef(Restaurant r) { restaurant = r; }
  public void run() {
    try {
      while(!Thread.interrupted()) {
        synchronized(this) {
          while(restaurant.meal != null)
            wait(); // ... for the meal to be taken
        }
        if(++count == 10) {
          print("Out of food, closing");
          restaurant.exec.shutdownNow();
        }
        printnb("Order up! ");
        synchronized(restaurant.waitPerson) {
          restaurant.meal = new Meal(count);
          restaurant.waitPerson.notifyAll();
        }
        TimeUnit.MILLISECONDS.sleep(100);
      }
    } catch(InterruptedException e) {
      print("Chef interrupted");
    }
  }
}

public class Restaurant {
  Meal meal;
  ExecutorService exec = Executors.newCachedThreadPool();
  WaitPerson waitPerson = new WaitPerson(this);
  Chef chef = new Chef(this);
  public Restaurant() {
    exec.execute(chef);
    exec.execute(waitPerson);
```

```
  }
  public static void main(String[] args) {
    new Restaurant();
  }
} /* Output:
Order up! Waitperson got Meal 1
Order up! Waitperson got Meal 2
Order up! Waitperson got Meal 3
Order up! Waitperson got Meal 4
Order up! Waitperson got Meal 5
Order up! Waitperson got Meal 6
Order up! Waitperson got Meal 7
Order up! Waitperson got Meal 8
Order up! Waitperson got Meal 9
Out of food, closing
WaitPerson interrupted
Order up! Chef interrupted
*///:~
```

The **Restaurant** is the focal point for both the **WaitPerson** and the **Chef**. Both must know what **Restaurant** they are working for because they must place or fetch the meal from the restaurant's "meal window," **restaurant.meal**. In **run( )**, the **WaitPerson** goes into **wait( )** mode, stopping that task until it is woken up with a **notifyAll( )** from the **Chef**. Since this is a very simple program, we know that only one task will be waiting on the **WaitPerson**'s lock: the **WaitPerson** task itself. For this reason, it's theoretically possible to call **notify( )** instead of **notifyAll( )**. However, in more complex situations, multiple tasks may be waiting on a particular object lock, so you don't know which task should be awakened. Thus, it's safer to call **notifyAll( )**, which wakes up all the tasks waiting on that lock. Each task must then decide whether the notification is relevant.

Once the **Chef** delivers a **Meal** and notifies the **WaitPerson**, the **Chef** waits until the **WaitPerson** collects the meal and notifies the **Chef**, who can then produce the next **Meal**.

Notice that the **wait( )** is wrapped in a **while( )** statement that is testing for the same thing that is being waited for. This seems a bit strange at first—if you're waiting for an order, once you wake up, the order must be available, right? As noted earlier, the problem is that in a concurrent application, some other task might swoop in and grab the order while the **WaitPerson** is waking up. The only safe approach is to *always* use the following idiom for a

wait( ) (within proper synchronization, of course, and programming against the possibility of missed signals):

```
while(conditionIsNotMet)
  wait();
```

This guarantees that the condition will be met before you get out of the wait loop, and if you have been notified of something that doesn't concern the condition (as can happen with **notifyAll( )**), or the condition changes before you get fully out of the wait loop, you are guaranteed to go back into waiting.

Observe that the call to **notifyAll( )** must first capture the lock on **waitPerson**. The call to **wait( )** in **WaitPerson.run( )** automatically releases the lock, so this is possible. Because the lock must be owned in order for **notifyAll( )** to be called, it's guaranteed that two tasks trying to call **notifyAll( )** on one object won't step on each other's toes.

Both **run( )** methods are designed for orderly shutdown by enclosing the entire **run( )** with a **try** block. The **catch** clause closes right before the closing brace of the **run( )** method, so if the task receives an **InterruptedException**, it ends immediately after catching the exception.

In **Chef**, note that after calling **shutdownNow( )** you *could* simply **return** from **run( )**, and normally that's what you should do. However, it's a little more interesting to do it this way. Remember that **shutdownNow( )** sends an **interrupt( )** to all the tasks that the **ExecutorService** started. But in the case of the **Chef**, the task doesn't shut down immediately upon getting the **interrupt( )**, because the interrupt only throws **InterruptedException** as the task attempts to enter an (interruptible) blocking operation. Thus, you'll see "Order up!" displayed first, and then the **InterruptedException** is thrown when the **Chef** attempts to call **sleep( )**. If you remove the call to **sleep( )**, the task will get to the top of the **run( )** loop and exit because of the **Thread.interrupted( )** test, without throwing an exception.

The preceding example has only a single spot for one task to store an object so that another task can later use that object. However, in a typical producer-consumer implementation, you use a first-in, first-out queue in order to store the objects being produced and consumed. You'll learn more about such queues later in this chapter.

Exercise 24: (1) Solve a single-producer, single-consumer problem using **wait( )** and **notifyAll( )**. The producer must not overflow the receiver's buffer, which can happen if the producer is faster than the consumer. If the consumer is faster than the producer, then it must not read the same data more than once. Do not assume anything about the relative speeds of the producer or consumer.

Exercise 25: (1) In the **Chef** class in **Restaurant.java**, **return** from **run( )** after calling **shutdownNow( )** and observe the difference in behavior.

Exercise 26: (8) Add a **BusBoy** class to **Restaurant.java**. After the meal is delivered, the **WaitPerson** should notify the **BusBoy** to clean up.

Using explicit **Lock** and **Condition** objects

There are additional, explicit tools in the Java SE5 **java.util.concurrent** library that can be used to rewrite **WaxOMatic.java**. The basic class that uses a mutex and allows task suspension is the **Condition**, and you can suspend a task by calling **await( )** on a **Condition**. When external state changes take place that might mean that a task should continue processing, you notify the task by calling **signal( )**, to wake up one task, or **signalAll( )**, to wake up all tasks that have suspended themselves on that **Condition** object (as with **notifyAll( )**, **signalAll( )** is the safer approach).

Here's **WaxOMatic.java** rewritten to contain a **Condition** that it uses to suspend a task inside **waitForWaxing( )** or **waitForBuffing( )**:

```
//: concurrency/waxomatic2/WaxOMatic2.java
// Using Lock and Condition objects.
package concurrency.waxomatic2;
import java.util.concurrent.*;
import java.util.concurrent.locks.*;
import static net.mindview.util.Print.*;

class Car {
  private Lock lock = new ReentrantLock();
  private Condition condition = lock.newCondition();
  private boolean waxOn = false;
  public void waxed() {
    lock.lock();
    try {
      waxOn = true; // Ready to buff
      condition.signalAll();
```

```
    } finally {
      lock.unlock();
    }
  }
  public void buffed() {
    lock.lock();
    try {
      waxOn = false; // Ready for another coat of wax
      condition.signalAll();
    } finally {
      lock.unlock();
    }
  }
  public void waitForWaxing() throws InterruptedException {
    lock.lock();
    try {
      while(waxOn == false)
        condition.await();
    } finally {
      lock.unlock();
    }
  }
  public void waitForBuffing() throws InterruptedException{
    lock.lock();
    try {
      while(waxOn == true)
        condition.await();
    } finally {
      lock.unlock();
    }
  }
}

class WaxOn implements Runnable {
  private Car car;
  public WaxOn(Car c) { car = c; }
  public void run() {
    try {
      while(!Thread.interrupted()) {
        printnb("Wax On! ");
        TimeUnit.MILLISECONDS.sleep(200);
        car.waxed();
        car.waitForBuffing();
      }
```

```java
        } catch(InterruptedException e) {
          print("Exiting via interrupt");
        }
        print("Ending Wax On task");
      }
    }

class WaxOff implements Runnable {
  private Car car;
  public WaxOff(Car c) { car = c; }
  public void run() {
    try {
      while(!Thread.interrupted()) {
        car.waitForWaxing();
        printnb("Wax Off! ");
        TimeUnit.MILLISECONDS.sleep(200);
        car.buffed();
      }
    } catch(InterruptedException e) {
      print("Exiting via interrupt");
    }
    print("Ending Wax Off task");
  }
}

public class WaxOMatic2 {
  public static void main(String[] args) throws Exception {
    Car car = new Car();
    ExecutorService exec = Executors.newCachedThreadPool();
    exec.execute(new WaxOff(car));
    exec.execute(new WaxOn(car));
    TimeUnit.SECONDS.sleep(5);
    exec.shutdownNow();
  }
} /* Output: (90% match)
Wax On! Wax Off! Wax On! Wax Off! Wax On! Wax Off! Wax On!
Wax Off! Wax On! Wax Off! Wax On! Wax Off! Wax On! Wax Off!
Wax On! Wax Off! Wax On! Wax Off! Wax On! Wax Off! Wax On!
Wax Off! Wax On! Wax Off! Wax On! Exiting via interrupt
Ending Wax Off task
Exiting via interrupt
Ending Wax On task
*///:~
```

In **Car**'s constructor, a single **Lock** produces a **Condition** object which is used to manage inter-task communication. However, the **Condition** object contains no information about the state of the process, so you need to manage additional information to indicate process state, which is the **boolean waxOn**.

Each call to **lock( )** must immediately be followed by a **try-finally** clause to guarantee that unlocking happens in all cases. As with the built-in versions, a task must own the lock before it can call **await( )**, **signal( )** or **signalAll( )**.

Notice that this solution is more complex than the previous one, and the complexity doesn't gain you anything in this case. The **Lock** and **Condition** objects are only necessary for more difficult threading problems.

Exercise 27: (2) Modify **Restaurant.java** to use explicit **Lock** and **Condition** objects.

Producer-consumers and queues

The **wait( )** and **notifyAll( )** methods solve the problem of task cooperation in a rather low-level fashion, handshaking every interaction. In many cases, you can move up a level of abstraction and solve task cooperation problems using a *synchronized queue*, which only allows one task at a time to insert or remove an element. This is provided for you in the **java.util.concurrent.BlockingQueue** interface, which has a number of standard implementations. You'll usually use the **LinkedBlockingQueue**, which is an unbounded queue; the **ArrayBlockingQueue** has a fixed size, so you can only put so many elements in it before it blocks.

These queues also suspend a consumer task if that task tries to get an object from the queue and the queue is empty, and resume when more elements become available. Blocking queues can solve a remarkable number of problems in a much simpler and more reliable fashion than **wait( )** and **notifyAll( )**.

Here's a simple test that serializes the execution of **LiftOff** objects. The consumer is **LiftOffRunner**, which pulls each **LiftOff** object off the **BlockingQueue** and runs it directly. (That is, it uses its own thread by calling **run( )** explicitly rather than starting up a new thread for each task.)

```
//: concurrency/TestBlockingQueues.java
// {RunByHand}
```

```java
import java.util.concurrent.*;
import java.io.*;
import static net.mindview.util.Print.*;

class LiftOffRunner implements Runnable {
  private BlockingQueue<LiftOff> rockets;
  public LiftOffRunner(BlockingQueue<LiftOff> queue) {
    rockets = queue;
  }
  public void add(LiftOff lo) {
    try {
      rockets.put(lo);
    } catch(InterruptedException e) {
      print("Interrupted during put()");
    }
  }
  public void run() {
    try {
      while(!Thread.interrupted()) {
        LiftOff rocket = rockets.take();
        rocket.run(); // Use this thread
      }
    } catch(InterruptedException e) {
      print("Waking from take()");
    }
    print("Exiting LiftOffRunner");
  }
}

public class TestBlockingQueues {
  static void getkey() {
    try {
      // Compensate for Windows/Linux difference in the
      // length of the result produced by the Enter key:
      new BufferedReader(
        new InputStreamReader(System.in)).readLine();
    } catch(java.io.IOException e) {
      throw new RuntimeException(e);
    }
  }
  static void getkey(String message) {
    print(message);
    getkey();
  }
```

```
  static void
  test(String msg, BlockingQueue<LiftOff> queue) {
    print(msg);
    LiftOffRunner runner = new LiftOffRunner(queue);
    Thread t = new Thread(runner);
    t.start();
    for(int i = 0; i < 5; i++)
      runner.add(new LiftOff(5));
    getkey("Press 'Enter' (" + msg + ")");
    t.interrupt();
    print("Finished " + msg + " test");
  }
  public static void main(String[] args) {
    test("LinkedBlockingQueue", // Unlimited size
      new LinkedBlockingQueue<LiftOff>());
    test("ArrayBlockingQueue", // Fixed size
      new ArrayBlockingQueue<LiftOff>(3));
    test("SynchronousQueue", // Size of 1
      new SynchronousQueue<LiftOff>());
  }
} ///:~
```

The tasks are placed on the **BlockingQueue** by **main( )** and are taken off
the **BlockingQueue** by the **LiftOffRunner**. Notice that **LiftOffRunner**
can ignore synchronization issues because they are solved by the
BlockingQueue.

Exercise 28: (3) Modify **TestBlockingQueues.java** by adding a new
task that places **LiftOff** on the **BlockingQueue**, instead of doing it in
main( ).

BlockingQueues of toast

As an example of the use of **BlockingQueues**, consider a machine that has
three tasks: one to make toast, one to butter the toast, and one to put jam on
the buttered toast. We can run the toast through **BlockingQueues** between
processes:

```
//: concurrency/ToastOMatic.java
// A toaster that uses queues.
import java.util.concurrent.*;
import java.util.*;
import static net.mindview.util.Print.*;

class Toast {
```

```
      public enum Status { DRY, BUTTERED, JAMMED }
      private Status status = Status.DRY;
      private final int id;
      public Toast(int idn) { id = idn; }
      public void butter() { status = Status.BUTTERED; }
      public void jam() { status = Status.JAMMED; }
      public Status getStatus() { return status; }
      public int getId() { return id; }
      public String toString() {
        return "Toast " + id + ": " + status;
      }
    }

    class ToastQueue extends LinkedBlockingQueue<Toast> {}

    class Toaster implements Runnable {
      private ToastQueue toastQueue;
      private int count = 0;
      private Random rand = new Random(47);
      public Toaster(ToastQueue tq) { toastQueue = tq; }
      public void run() {
        try {
          while(!Thread.interrupted()) {
            TimeUnit.MILLISECONDS.sleep(
              100 + rand.nextInt(500));
            // Make toast
            Toast t = new Toast(count++);
            print(t);
            // Insert into queue
            toastQueue.put(t);
          }
        } catch(InterruptedException e) {
          print("Toaster interrupted");
        }
        print("Toaster off");
      }
    }

    // Apply butter to toast:
    class Butterer implements Runnable {
      private ToastQueue dryQueue, butteredQueue;
      public Butterer(ToastQueue dry, ToastQueue buttered) {
        dryQueue = dry;
        butteredQueue = buttered;
```

```
    }
  public void run() {
    try {
      while(!Thread.interrupted()) {
        // Blocks until next piece of toast is available:
        Toast t = dryQueue.take();
        t.butter();
        print(t);
        butteredQueue.put(t);
      }
    } catch(InterruptedException e) {
      print("Butterer interrupted");
    }
    print("Butterer off");
  }
}

// Apply jam to buttered toast:
class Jammer implements Runnable {
  private ToastQueue butteredQueue, finishedQueue;
  public Jammer(ToastQueue buttered, ToastQueue finished) {
    butteredQueue = buttered;
    finishedQueue = finished;
  }
  public void run() {
    try {
      while(!Thread.interrupted()) {
        // Blocks until next piece of toast is available:
        Toast t = butteredQueue.take();
        t.jam();
        print(t);
        finishedQueue.put(t);
      }
    } catch(InterruptedException e) {
      print("Jammer interrupted");
    }
    print("Jammer off");
  }
}

// Consume the toast:
class Eater implements Runnable {
  private ToastQueue finishedQueue;
  private int counter = 0;
```

```
    public Eater(ToastQueue finished) {
      finishedQueue = finished;
    }
    public void run() {
      try {
        while(!Thread.interrupted()) {
          // Blocks until next piece of toast is available:
          Toast t = finishedQueue.take();
          // Verify that the toast is coming in order,
          // and that all pieces are getting jammed:
          if(t.getId() != counter++ ||
             t.getStatus() != Toast.Status.JAMMED) {
            print(">>>> Error: " + t);
            System.exit(1);
          } else
            print("Chomp! " + t);
        }
      } catch(InterruptedException e) {
        print("Eater interrupted");
      }
      print("Eater off");
    }
  }
}

public class ToastOMatic {
  public static void main(String[] args) throws Exception {
    ToastQueue dryQueue = new ToastQueue(),
               butteredQueue = new ToastQueue(),
               finishedQueue = new ToastQueue();
    ExecutorService exec = Executors.newCachedThreadPool();
    exec.execute(new Toaster(dryQueue));
    exec.execute(new Butterer(dryQueue, butteredQueue));
    exec.execute(new Jammer(butteredQueue, finishedQueue));
    exec.execute(new Eater(finishedQueue));
    TimeUnit.SECONDS.sleep(5);
    exec.shutdownNow();
  }
} /* (Execute to see output) *///:~
```

Toast is an excellent example of the value of **enum**s. Note that there is no explicit synchronization (using **Lock** objects or the **synchronized** keyword) because the synchronization is implicitly managed by the queues (which synchronize internally) and by the design of the system—each piece of **Toast** is only operated on by one task at a time. Because the queues block, processes suspend and resume automatically. You can see that the simplification produced by **BlockingQueue**s can be quite dramatic. The coupling between the classes that would exist with explicit **wait( )** and **notifyAll( )** statements is eliminated because each class communicates only with its **BlockingQueue**s.

Exercise 29: (8) Modify **ToastOMatic.java** to create peanut butter and jelly on toast sandwiches using two separate assembly lines (one for peanut butter, the second for jelly, then merging the two lines).

Using pipes for I/O between tasks

It's often useful for tasks to communicate with each other using I/O. Threading libraries may provide support for inter-task I/O in the form of *pipes*. These exist in the Java I/O library as the classes **PipedWriter** (which allows a task to write into a pipe) and **PipedReader** (which allows a different task to read from the same pipe). This can be thought of as a variation of the producer-consumer problem, where the pipe is the canned solution. The pipe is basically a blocking queue, which existed in versions of Java before **BlockingQueue** was introduced.

Here's a simple example in which two tasks use a pipe to communicate:

```
//: concurrency/PipedIO.java
// Using pipes for inter-task I/O
import java.util.concurrent.*;
import java.io.*;
import java.util.*;
import static net.mindview.util.Print.*;

class Sender implements Runnable {
  private Random rand = new Random(47);
  private PipedWriter out = new PipedWriter();
  public PipedWriter getPipedWriter() { return out; }
  public void run() {
    try {
      while(true)
        for(char c = 'A'; c <= 'z'; c++) {
          out.write(c);
          TimeUnit.MILLISECONDS.sleep(rand.nextInt(500));
        }
    } catch(IOException e) {
      print(e + " Sender write exception");
    } catch(InterruptedException e) {
```

```
          print(e + " Sender sleep interrupted");
      }
    }
  }

class Receiver implements Runnable {
  private PipedReader in;
  public Receiver(Sender sender) throws IOException {
    in = new PipedReader(sender.getPipedWriter());
  }
  public void run() {
    try {
      while(true) {
        // Blocks until characters are there:
        printnb("Read: " + (char)in.read() + ", ");
      }
    } catch(IOException e) {
      print(e + " Receiver read exception");
    }
  }
}

public class PipedIO {
  public static void main(String[] args) throws Exception {
    Sender sender = new Sender();
    Receiver receiver = new Receiver(sender);
    ExecutorService exec = Executors.newCachedThreadPool();
    exec.execute(sender);
    exec.execute(receiver);
    TimeUnit.SECONDS.sleep(4);
    exec.shutdownNow();
  }
} /* Output: (65% match)
Read: A, Read: B, Read: C, Read: D, Read: E, Read: F, Read:
G, Read: H, Read: I, Read: J, Read: K, Read: L, Read: M,
java.lang.InterruptedException: sleep interrupted Sender
sleep interrupted
java.io.InterruptedIOException Receiver read exception
*///:~
```

Sender and **Receiver** represent tasks that need to communicate with each other. **Sender** creates a **PipedWriter**, which is a standalone object, but inside **Receiver** the creation of **PipedReader** must be associated with a **PipedWriter** in the constructor. The **Sender** puts data into the **Writer**

and sleeps for a random amount of time. However, **Receiver** has no **sleep( )** or **wait( )**. But when it does a **read( )**, the pipe automatically blocks when there is no more data.

Notice that the **sender** and **receiver** are started in **main( )**, *after* the objects are completely constructed. If you don't start completely constructed objects, the pipe can produce inconsistent behavior on different platforms. (Note that **BlockingQueue**s are more robust and easier to use.)

An important difference between a **PipedReader** and normal I/O is seen when **shutdownNow( )** is called—the **PipedReader** is interruptible, whereas if you changed, for example, the **in.read( )** call to **System.in.read( )**, the **interrupt( )** would fail to break out of the **read( )** call.

Exercise 30: (1) Modify **PipedIO.java** to use a **BlockingQueue** instead of a pipe.

Deadlock

Now you understand an object can have **synchronized** methods or other forms of locking that prevent tasks from accessing that object until the mutex is released. You've also learned that tasks can become blocked. Thus it's possible for one task to get stuck waiting for another task, which in turn waits for another task, and so on, until the chain leads back to a task waiting on the first one. You get a continuous loop of tasks waiting on each other, and no one can move. This is called *deadlock*.[21]

If you try running a program and it deadlocks right away, you can immediately track down the bug. The real problem is when your program seems to be working fine but has the hidden potential to deadlock. In this case, you may get no indication that deadlocking is a possibility, so the flaw will be latent in your program until it unexpectedly happens to a customer (in a way that will almost certainly be difficult to reproduce). Thus, preventing deadlock through careful program design is a critical part of developing concurrent systems.

---

[21] You can also have *livelock* when two tasks are able to change their state (they don't block) but they never make any useful progress.

The *dining philosophers* problem, invented by Edsger Dijkstra, is the classic demonstration of deadlock. The basic description specifies five philosophers (but the example shown here will allow any number). These philosophers spend part of their time thinking and part of their time eating. While they are thinking, they don't need any shared resources, but they eat using a limited number of utensils. In the original problem description, the utensils are forks, and two forks are required to get spaghetti from a bowl in the middle of the table, but it seems to make more sense to say that the utensils are chopsticks. Clearly, each philosopher will require two chopsticks in order to eat.

A difficulty is introduced into the problem: As philosophers, they have very little money, so they can only afford five chopsticks (more generally, the same number of chopsticks as philosophers). These are spaced around the table between them. When a philosopher wants to eat, that philosopher must pick up the chopstick to the left and the one to the right. If the philosopher on either side is using a desired chopstick, our philosopher must wait until the necessary chopsticks become available.

```java
//: concurrency/Chopstick.java
// Chopsticks for dining philosophers.

public class Chopstick {
  private boolean taken = false;
  public synchronized
  void take() throws InterruptedException {
    while(taken)
      wait();
    taken = true;
  }
  public synchronized void drop() {
    taken = false;
    notifyAll();
  }
} ///:~
```

No two **Philosopher**s can successfully **take( )** the same **Chopstick** at the same time. In addition, if the **Chopstick** has already been taken by one **Philosopher**, another can **wait( )** until the **Chopstick** becomes available when the current holder calls **drop( )**.

When a **Philosopher** task calls **take( )**, that **Philosopher** waits until the **taken** flag is **false** (until the **Philosopher** currently holding the **Chopstick** releases it). Then the task sets the **taken** flag to **true** to indicate that the new

Philosopher now holds the **Chopstick**. When this **Philosopher** is finished with the **Chopstick**, it calls **drop( )** to change the flag and **notifyAll( )** any other **Philosopher**s that may be **wait( )**ing for the **Chopstick**.

```
//: concurrency/Philosopher.java
// A dining philosopher
import java.util.concurrent.*;
import java.util.*;
import static net.mindview.util.Print.*;

public class Philosopher implements Runnable {
  private Chopstick left;
  private Chopstick right;
  private final int id;
  private final int ponderFactor;
  private Random rand = new Random(47);
  private void pause() throws InterruptedException {
    if(ponderFactor == 0) return;
    TimeUnit.MILLISECONDS.sleep(
      rand.nextInt(ponderFactor * 250));
  }
  public Philosopher(Chopstick left, Chopstick right,
    int ident, int ponder) {
    this.left = left;
    this.right = right;
    id = ident;
    ponderFactor = ponder;
  }
  public void run() {
    try {
      while(!Thread.interrupted()) {
        print(this + " " + "thinking");
        pause();
        // Philosopher becomes hungry
        print(this + " " + "grabbing right");
        right.take();
        print(this + " " + "grabbing left");
        left.take();
        print(this + " " + "eating");
        pause();
        right.drop();
        left.drop();
      }
```

```
    } catch(InterruptedException e) {
      print(this + " " + "exiting via interrupt");
    }
  }
}
  public String toString() { return "Philosopher " + id; }
} ///:~
```

In **Philosopher.run( )**, each **Philosopher** just thinks and eats
continuously. The **pause( )** method **sleeps( )** for a random period if the
ponderFactor is nonzero. Using this, you see the **Philosopher** thinking
for a randomized amount of time, then trying to **take( )** the right and left
Chopsticks, eating for a randomized amount of time, and then doing it
again.

Now we can set up a version of the program that will deadlock:

```
//: concurrency/DeadlockingDiningPhilosophers.java
// Demonstrates how deadlock can be hidden in a program.
// {Args: 0 5 timeout}
import java.util.concurrent.*;

public class DeadlockingDiningPhilosophers {
  public static void main(String[] args) throws Exception {
    int ponder = 5;
    if(args.length > 0)
      ponder = Integer.parseInt(args[0]);
    int size = 5;
    if(args.length > 1)
      size = Integer.parseInt(args[1]);
    ExecutorService exec = Executors.newCachedThreadPool();
    Chopstick[] sticks = new Chopstick[size];
    for(int i = 0; i < size; i++)
      sticks[i] = new Chopstick();
    for(int i = 0; i < size; i++)
      exec.execute(new Philosopher(
        sticks[i], sticks[(i+1) % size], i, ponder));
    if(args.length == 3 && args[2].equals("timeout"))
      TimeUnit.SECONDS.sleep(5);
    else {
      System.out.println("Press 'Enter' to quit");
      System.in.read();
    }
    exec.shutdownNow();
  }
}
```

```
} /* (Execute to see output) *///:~
```

You will observe that if the **Philosopher**s spend very little time thinking, they will all be competing for the **Chopstick**s while they try to eat, and deadlock will happen much more quickly.

The first command-line argument adjusts the **ponder** factor, to affect the amount of time each **Philosopher** spends thinking. If you have lots of **Philosopher**s or they spend a lot of time thinking, you may never see deadlock even though it remains a possibility. A command-line argument of zero tends to make the program deadlock fairly quickly.

Note that the **Chopstick** objects do not need internal identifiers; they are identified by their position in the array **sticks**. Each **Philosopher** constructor is given a reference to a left and right **Chopstick** object. Every **Philosopher** except the last one is initialized by situating that **Philosopher** between the next pair of **Chopstick** objects. The last **Philosopher** is given the zeroth **Chopstick** for its right **Chopstick**, so the round table is completed. That's because the last **Philosopher** is sitting right next to the first one, and they both share that zeroth **Chopstick**. Now it's possible for all the **Philosopher**s to be trying to eat, waiting on the **Philosopher** next to them to put down its **Chopstick**. This will make the program deadlock.

If your **Philosopher**s are spending more time thinking than eating, then they have a much lower probability of requiring the shared resources (**Chopstick**s), and thus you can convince yourself that the program is deadlock free (using a nonzero **ponder** value, or a large number of **Philosopher**s), even though it isn't. This example is interesting precisely because it demonstrates that a program can appear to run correctly but actually be able to deadlock.

To repair the problem, you must understand that deadlock can occur if four conditions are simultaneously met:

1. Mutual exclusion. At least one resource used by the tasks must not be shareable. In this case, a **Chopstick** can be used by only one **Philosopher** at a time.

2. At least one task must be holding a resource and waiting to acquire a resource currently held by another task. That is, for deadlock to occur, a **Philosopher** must be holding one **Chopstick** and waiting for another one.

---

3. A resource cannot be preemptively taken away from a task. Tasks only release resources as a normal event. Our **Philosopher**s are polite and they don't grab **Chopstick**s from other **Philosopher**s.

4. A circular wait can happen, whereby a task waits on a resource held by another task, which in turn is waiting on a resource held by another task, and so on, until one of the tasks is waiting on a resource held by the first task, thus gridlocking everything. In **DeadlockingDiningPhilosophers.java**, the circular wait happens because each **Philosopher** tries to get the right **Chopstick** first and then the left.

Because *all* these conditions must be met to cause deadlock, you only need to prevent one of them from occurring to prohibit deadlock. In this program, the easiest way to prevent deadlock is to break the fourth condition. This condition happens because each **Philosopher** is trying to pick up its **Chopstick**s in a particular sequence: first right, then left. Because of that, it's possible to get into a situation where each of them is holding its right **Chopstick** and waiting to get the left, causing the circular wait condition. However, if the last **Philosopher** is initialized to try to get the left chopstick first and then the right, that **Philosopher** will never prevent the **Philosopher** on the immediate right from picking up their its chopstick. In this case, the circular wait is prevented. This is only one solution to the problem, but you could also solve it by preventing one of the other conditions (see advanced threading books for more details):

```
//: concurrency/FixedDiningPhilosophers.java
// Dining philosophers without deadlock.
// {Args: 5 5 timeout}
import java.util.concurrent.*;

public class FixedDiningPhilosophers {
  public static void main(String[] args) throws Exception {
    int ponder = 5;
    if(args.length > 0)
      ponder = Integer.parseInt(args[0]);
    int size = 5;
    if(args.length > 1)
      size = Integer.parseInt(args[1]);
    ExecutorService exec = Executors.newCachedThreadPool();
    Chopstick[] sticks = new Chopstick[size];
    for(int i = 0; i < size; i++)
```

```
        sticks[i] = new Chopstick();
      for(int i = 0; i < size; i++)
        if(i < (size-1))
          exec.execute(new Philosopher(
            sticks[i], sticks[i+1], i, ponder));
        else
          exec.execute(new Philosopher(
            sticks[0], sticks[i], i, ponder));
      if(args.length == 3 && args[2].equals("timeout"))
        TimeUnit.SECONDS.sleep(5);
      else {
        System.out.println("Press 'Enter' to quit");
        System.in.read();
      }
      exec.shutdownNow();
    }
} /* (Execute to see output) *///:~
```

By ensuring that the last **Philosopher** picks up and puts down the left **Chopstick** before the right, we remove the deadlock, and the program will run smoothly.

There is no language support to help prevent deadlock; it's up to you to avoid it by careful design. These are not comforting words to the person who's trying to debug a deadlocking program.

Exercise 31: (8) Change **DeadlockingDiningPhilosophers.java** so that when a philosopher is done with its chopsticks, it drops them into a bin. When a philosopher wants to eat, it takes the next two available chopsticks from the bin. Does this eliminate the possibility of deadlock? Can you reintroduce deadlock by simply reducing the number of available chopsticks?

New library components

The **java.util.concurrent** library in Java SE5 introduces a significant number of new classes designed to solve concurrency problems. Learning to use these can help you produce simpler and more robust concurrent programs.

This section includes a representative set of examples of various components, but a few of the components—ones that you may be less likely to use and encounter—are not discussed here.

Because these components solve various problems, there is no clear way to organize them, so I shall attempt to start with simpler examples and proceed through examples of increasing complexity.

CountDownLatch

This is used to synchronize one or more tasks by forcing them to wait for the completion of a set of operations being performed by other tasks.

You give an initial count to a **CountDownLatch** object, and any task that calls **await( )** on that object will block until the count reaches zero. Other tasks may call **countDown( )** on the object to reduce the count, presumably when a task finishes its job. A **CountDownLatch** is designed to be used in a one-shot fashion; the count cannot be reset. If you need a version that resets the count, you can use a **CyclicBarrier** instead.

The tasks that call **countDown( )** are not blocked when they make that call. Only the call to **await( )** is blocked until the count reaches zero.

A typical use is to divide a problem into n independently solvable tasks and create a **CountDownLatch** with a value of n. When each task is finished it calls **countDown( )** on the latch. Tasks waiting for the problem to be solved call **await( )** on the latch to hold themselves back until it is completed. Here's a skeleton example that demonstrates this technique:

```
//: concurrency/CountDownLatchDemo.java
import java.util.concurrent.*;
import java.util.*;
import static net.mindview.util.Print.*;

// Performs some portion of a task:
class TaskPortion implements Runnable {
  private static int counter = 0;
  private final int id = counter++;
  private static Random rand = new Random(47);
  private final CountDownLatch latch;
  TaskPortion(CountDownLatch latch) {
    this.latch = latch;
  }
  public void run() {
    try {
      doWork();
      latch.countDown();
```

```
      } catch(InterruptedException ex) {
        // Acceptable way to exit
      }
    }
    public void doWork() throws InterruptedException {
      TimeUnit.MILLISECONDS.sleep(rand.nextInt(2000));
      print(this + "completed");
    }
    public String toString() {
      return String.format("%1$-3d ", id);
    }
  }

  // Waits on the CountDownLatch:
  class WaitingTask implements Runnable {
    private static int counter = 0;
    private final int id = counter++;
    private final CountDownLatch latch;
    WaitingTask(CountDownLatch latch) {
      this.latch = latch;
    }
    public void run() {
      try {
        latch.await();
        print("Latch barrier passed for " + this);
      } catch(InterruptedException ex) {
        print(this + " interrupted");
      }
    }
    public String toString() {
      return String.format("WaitingTask %1$-3d ", id);
    }
  }

  public class CountDownLatchDemo {
    static final int SIZE = 100;
    public static void main(String[] args) throws Exception {
      ExecutorService exec = Executors.newCachedThreadPool();
      // All must share a single CountDownLatch object:
      CountDownLatch latch = new CountDownLatch(SIZE);
      for(int i = 0; i < 10; i++)
        exec.execute(new WaitingTask(latch));
      for(int i = 0; i < SIZE; i++)
        exec.execute(new TaskPortion(latch));
```

```
        print("Launched all tasks");
        exec.shutdown(); // Quit when all tasks complete
    }
} /* (Execute to see output) *///:~
```

TaskPortion sleeps for a random period to simulate the completion of part of the task, and **WaitingTask** indicates a part of the system that must wait until the initial portion of the problem is complete. All tasks work with the same single **CountDownLatch**, which is defined in **main( )**.

Exercise 32: (7) Use a **CountDownLatch** to solve the problem of correlating the results from the **Entrances** in **OrnamentalGarden.java**. Remove the unnecessary code from the new version of the example.

Library thread safety

Notice that **TaskPortion** contains a **static Random** object, which means that multiple tasks may be calling **Random.nextInt( )** at the same time. Is this safe?

If there is a problem, it can be solved in this case by giving **TaskPortion** its own **Random** object—that is, by removing the **static** specifier. But the question remains for Java standard library methods in general: Which ones are thread-safe and which ones aren't?

Unfortunately, the JDK documentation is not forthcoming on this point. It happens that **Random.nextInt( )** *is* thread-safe, but alas, you shall have to discover this on a case-by-case basis, using either a Web search or by inspecting the Java library code. This is not a particularly good situation for a programming language that was, at least in theory, designed to support concurrency.

CyclicBarrier

A **CyclicBarrier** is used in situations where you want to create a group of tasks to perform work in parallel, and then wait until they are all finished before moving on to the next step (something like **join( )**, it would seem). It brings all the parallel tasks into alignment at the barrier so you can move forward in unison. This is very similar to the **CountDownLatch**, except that a **CountDownLatch** is a one-shot event, whereas a **CyclicBarrier** can be reused over and over.

I've been fascinated with simulations from the beginning of my experience with computers, and concurrency is a key factor of making simulations possible. The very first program that I can remember writing[22] was a simulation: a horse-racing game written in BASIC called (because of the file name limitations) HOSRAC.BAS. Here is the object-oriented, threaded version of that program, utilizing a **CyclicBarrier**:

```java
//: concurrency/HorseRace.java
// Using CyclicBarriers.
import java.util.concurrent.*;
import java.util.*;
import static net.mindview.util.Print.*;

class Horse implements Runnable {
  private static int counter = 0;
  private final int id = counter++;
  private int strides = 0;
  private static Random rand = new Random(47);
  private static CyclicBarrier barrier;
  public Horse(CyclicBarrier b) { barrier = b; }
  public synchronized int getStrides() { return strides; }
  public void run() {
    try {
      while(!Thread.interrupted()) {
        synchronized(this) {
          strides += rand.nextInt(3); // Produces 0, 1 or 2
        }
        barrier.await();
      }
    } catch(InterruptedException e) {
      // A legitimate way to exit
    } catch(BrokenBarrierException e) {
      // This one we want to know about
      throw new RuntimeException(e);
    }
  }
  public String toString() { return "Horse " + id + " "; }
  public String tracks() {
    StringBuilder s = new StringBuilder();
```

---

[22] As a freshman in high school; the classroom had an ASR-33 teletype with a 110-baud acoustic-coupler modem accessing an HP-1000.

```
        for(int i = 0; i < getStrides(); i++)
          s.append("*");
        s.append(id);
        return s.toString();
      }
    }

    public class HorseRace {
      static final int FINISH_LINE = 75;
      private List<Horse> horses = new ArrayList<Horse>();
      private ExecutorService exec =
        Executors.newCachedThreadPool();
      private CyclicBarrier barrier;
      public HorseRace(int nHorses, final int pause) {
        barrier = new CyclicBarrier(nHorses, new Runnable() {
          public void run() {
            StringBuilder s = new StringBuilder();
            for(int i = 0; i < FINISH_LINE; i++)
              s.append("="); // The fence on the racetrack
            print(s);
            for(Horse horse : horses)
              print(horse.tracks());
            for(Horse horse : horses)
              if(horse.getStrides() >= FINISH_LINE) {
                print(horse + "won!");
                exec.shutdownNow();
                return;
              }
            try {
              TimeUnit.MILLISECONDS.sleep(pause);
            } catch(InterruptedException e) {
              print("barrier-action sleep interrupted");
            }
          }
        });
        for(int i = 0; i < nHorses; i++) {
          Horse horse = new Horse(barrier);
          horses.add(horse);
          exec.execute(horse);
        }
      }
      public static void main(String[] args) {
        int nHorses = 7;
        int pause = 200;
```

```
      if(args.length > 0) { // Optional argument
        int n = new Integer(args[0]);
        nHorses = n > 0 ? n : nHorses;
      }
      if(args.length > 1) { // Optional argument
        int p = new Integer(args[1]);
        pause = p > -1 ? p : pause;
      }
      new HorseRace(nHorses, pause);
    }
} /* (Execute to see output) *///:~
```

A **CyclicBarrier** can be given a "barrier action," which is a **Runnable** that is automatically executed when the count reaches zero—this is another distinction between **CyclicBarrier** and **CountdownLatch**. Here, the barrier action is created as an anonymous class that is handed to the constructor of **CyclicBarrier**.

I tried having each horse print itself, but then the order of display was dependent on the task manager. The **CyclicBarrier** allows each horse to do whatever it needs to do in order to move forward, and then it has to wait at the barrier until all the other horses have moved forward. When all horses have moved, the **CyclicBarrier** automatically calls its **Runnable** barrier-action task to display the horses in order, along with the fence.

Once all the tasks have passed the barrier, it is automatically ready for the next round.

To give it the effect of very simple animation, make the size of your console window small enough so that only the horses show.

DelayQueue

This is an unbounded **BlockingQueue** of objects that implement the **Delayed** interface. An object can only be taken from the queue when its delay has expired. The queue is sorted so that the object at the head has a delay that has expired for the longest time. If no delay has expired, then there is no head element and **poll( )** will return **null** (because of this, you cannot place **null** elements in the queue).

Here's an example where the **Delayed** objects are themselves tasks, and the **DelayedTaskConsumer** takes the most "urgent" task (the one that has been expired for the longest time) off the queue and runs it. Note that **DelayQueue** is thus a variation of a priority queue.

```java
//: concurrency/DelayQueueDemo.java
import java.util.concurrent.*;
import java.util.*;
import static java.util.concurrent.TimeUnit.*;
import static net.mindview.util.Print.*;

class DelayedTask implements Runnable, Delayed {
  private static int counter = 0;
  private final int id = counter++;
  private final int delta;
  private final long trigger;
  protected static List<DelayedTask> sequence =
    new ArrayList<DelayedTask>();
  public DelayedTask(int delayInMilliseconds) {
    delta = delayInMilliseconds;
    trigger = System.nanoTime() +
      NANOSECONDS.convert(delta, MILLISECONDS);
    sequence.add(this);
  }
  public long getDelay(TimeUnit unit) {
    return unit.convert(
      trigger - System.nanoTime(), NANOSECONDS);
  }
  public int compareTo(Delayed arg) {
    DelayedTask that = (DelayedTask)arg;
    if(trigger < that.trigger) return -1;
    if(trigger > that.trigger) return 1;
    return 0;
  }
  public void run() { printnb(this + " "); }
  public String toString() {
    return String.format("[%1$-4d]", delta) +
      " Task " + id;
  }
  public String summary() {
    return "(" + id + ":" + delta + ")";
  }
  public static class EndSentinel extends DelayedTask {
    private ExecutorService exec;
    public EndSentinel(int delay, ExecutorService e) {
      super(delay);
```

```
          exec = e;
        }
      public void run() {
        for(DelayedTask pt : sequence) {
          printnb(pt.summary() + " ");
        }
        print();
        print(this + " Calling shutdownNow()");
        exec.shutdownNow();
      }
    }
  }
}

class DelayedTaskConsumer implements Runnable {
  private DelayQueue<DelayedTask> q;
  public DelayedTaskConsumer(DelayQueue<DelayedTask> q) {
    this.q = q;
  }
  public void run() {
    try {
      while(!Thread.interrupted())
        q.take().run(); // Run task with the current thread
    } catch(InterruptedException e) {
      // Acceptable way to exit
    }
    print("Finished DelayedTaskConsumer");
  }
}

public class DelayQueueDemo {
  public static void main(String[] args) {
    Random rand = new Random(47);
    ExecutorService exec = Executors.newCachedThreadPool();
    DelayQueue<DelayedTask> queue =
      new DelayQueue<DelayedTask>();
    // Fill with tasks that have random delays:
    for(int i = 0; i < 20; i++)
      queue.put(new DelayedTask(rand.nextInt(5000)));
    // Set the stopping point
    queue.add(new DelayedTask.EndSentinel(5000, exec));
    exec.execute(new DelayedTaskConsumer(queue));
  }
} /* Output:
```

```
[128 ] Task 11 [200 ] Task 7 [429 ] Task 5 [520 ] Task 18
[555 ] Task 1 [961 ] Task 4 [998 ] Task 16 [1207] Task 9
[1693] Task 2 [1809] Task 14 [1861] Task 3 [2278] Task 15
[3288] Task 10 [3551] Task 12 [4258] Task 0 [4258] Task 19
[4522] Task 8 [4589] Task 13 [4861] Task 17 [4868] Task 6
(0:4258) (1:555) (2:1693) (3:1861) (4:961) (5:429) (6:4868)
(7:200) (8:4522) (9:1207) (10:3288) (11:128) (12:3551)
(13:4589) (14:1809) (15:2278) (16:998) (17:4861) (18:520)
(19:4258) (20:5000)
[5000] Task 20 Calling shutdownNow()
Finished DelayedTaskConsumer
*///:~
```

DelayedTask contains a **List<DelayedTask>** called **sequence** that
preserves the order in which the tasks were created, so that we can see that
sorting does in fact take place.

The **Delayed** interface has one method, **getDelay( )**, which tells how long it
is until the delay time expires or how long ago the delay time has expired.
This method forces us to use the **TimeUnit** class because that's the
argument type. This turns out to be a very convenient class because you can
easily convert units without doing any calculations. For example, the value of
delta is stored in milliseconds, but the Java SE5 method
System.nanoTime( ) produces time in nanoseconds. You can convert the
value of **delta** by saying what units it is in and what units you want it to be in,
like this:

```
NANOSECONDS.convert(delta, MILLISECONDS);
```

In **getDelay( )**, the desired units are passed in as the **unit** argument, and
you use this to convert the time difference from the trigger time to the units
requested by the caller, without even knowing what those units are (this is a
simple example of the *Strategy* design pattern, where part of the algorithm is
passed in as an argument).

For sorting, the **Delayed** interface also inherits the **Comparable** interface,
so **compareTo( )** must be implemented so that it produces a reasonable
comparison. **toString( )** and **summary( )** provide output formatting, and
the nested **EndSentinel** class provides a way to shut everything down by
placing it as the last element in the queue.

Note that because **DelayedTaskConsumer** is itself a task, it has its own
Thread which it can use to run each task that comes out of the queue. Since

the tasks are being performed in queue priority order, there's no need in this example to start separate threads to run the **DelayedTask**s.

You can see from the output that the order in which the tasks are created has no effect on execution order—instead, the tasks are executed in delay order as expected.

PriorityBlockingQueue

This is basically a priority queue that has blocking retrieval operations. Here's an example where the objects in the priority queue are tasks that emerge from the queue in priority order. A **PrioritizedTask** is given a priority number to provide this order:

```
//: concurrency/PriorityBlockingQueueDemo.java
import java.util.concurrent.*;
import java.util.*;
import static net.mindview.util.Print.*;

class PrioritizedTask implements
Runnable, Comparable<PrioritizedTask>  {
  private Random rand = new Random(47);
  private static int counter = 0;
  private final int id = counter++;
  private final int priority;
  protected static List<PrioritizedTask> sequence =
    new ArrayList<PrioritizedTask>();
  public PrioritizedTask(int priority) {
    this.priority = priority;
    sequence.add(this);
  }
  public int compareTo(PrioritizedTask arg) {
    return priority < arg.priority ? 1 :
      (priority > arg.priority ? -1 : 0);
  }
  public void run() {
    try {
      TimeUnit.MILLISECONDS.sleep(rand.nextInt(250));
    } catch(InterruptedException e) {
      // Acceptable way to exit
    }
    print(this);
  }
  public String toString() {
```

```
      return String.format("[%1$-3d]", priority) +
        " Task " + id;
    }
    public String summary() {
      return "(" + id + ":" + priority + ")";
    }
    public static class EndSentinel extends PrioritizedTask {
      private ExecutorService exec;
      public EndSentinel(ExecutorService e) {
        super(-1); // Lowest priority in this program
        exec = e;
      }
      public void run() {
        int count = 0;
        for(PrioritizedTask pt : sequence) {
          printnb(pt.summary());
          if(++count % 5 == 0)
            print();
        }
        print();
        print(this + " Calling shutdownNow()");
        exec.shutdownNow();
      }
    }
  }
}

class PrioritizedTaskProducer implements Runnable {
  private Random rand = new Random(47);
  private Queue<Runnable> queue;
  private ExecutorService exec;
  public PrioritizedTaskProducer(
    Queue<Runnable> q, ExecutorService e) {
    queue = q;
    exec = e; // Used for EndSentinel
  }
  public void run() {
    // Unbounded queue; never blocks.
    // Fill it up fast with random priorities:
    for(int i = 0; i < 20; i++) {
      queue.add(new PrioritizedTask(rand.nextInt(10)));
      Thread.yield();
    }
    // Trickle in highest-priority jobs:
    try {
```

```
        for(int i = 0; i < 10; i++) {
          TimeUnit.MILLISECONDS.sleep(250);
          queue.add(new PrioritizedTask(10));
        }
        // Add jobs, lowest priority first:
        for(int i = 0; i < 10; i++)
          queue.add(new PrioritizedTask(i));
        // A sentinel to stop all the tasks:
        queue.add(new PrioritizedTask.EndSentinel(exec));
      } catch(InterruptedException e) {
        // Acceptable way to exit
      }
      print("Finished PrioritizedTaskProducer");
    }
}

class PrioritizedTaskConsumer implements Runnable {
  private PriorityBlockingQueue<Runnable> q;
  public PrioritizedTaskConsumer(
    PriorityBlockingQueue<Runnable> q) {
    this.q = q;
  }
  public void run() {
    try {
      while(!Thread.interrupted())
        // Use current thread to run the task:
        q.take().run();
    } catch(InterruptedException e) {
      // Acceptable way to exit
    }
    print("Finished PrioritizedTaskConsumer");
  }
}

public class PriorityBlockingQueueDemo {
  public static void main(String[] args) throws Exception {
    ExecutorService exec = Executors.newCachedThreadPool();
    PriorityBlockingQueue<Runnable> queue =
      new PriorityBlockingQueue<Runnable>();
    exec.execute(new PrioritizedTaskProducer(queue, exec));
    exec.execute(new PrioritizedTaskConsumer(queue));
  }
} /* (Execute to see output) *///:~
```

As with the previous example, the creation sequence of the **PrioritizedTask** objects is remembered in the **sequence List**, for comparison with the actual order of execution. The **run( )** method sleeps for a short random time and prints the object information, and the **EndSentinel** provides the same functionality as before while guaranteeing that it is the last object in the queue.

The **PrioritizedTaskProducer** and **PrioritizedTaskConsumer** connect to each other through a **PriorityBlockingQueue**. Because the blocking nature of the queue provides all the necessary synchronization, notice that no explicit synchronization is necessary—you don't have to think about whether the queue has any elements in it when you're reading from it, because the queue will simply block the reader when it is out of elements.

The greenhouse controller with ScheduledExecutor

The *Inner Classes* chapter introduced the example of a control system applied to a hypothetical greenhouse, turning various facilities on or off or otherwise adjusting them. This can be seen as a kind of concurrency problem, with each desired greenhouse event as a task that is run at a predefined time. The **ScheduledThreadPoolExecutor** provides just the service necessary to solve the problem. Using either **schedule( )** (to run a task once) or **scheduleAtFixedRate( )** (to repeat a task at a regular interval), you set up **Runnable** objects to be executed at some time in the future. Compare the following with the approach used in the *Inner Classes* chapter to notice how much simpler it is when you can use a predefined tool like **ScheduledThreadPoolExecutor**:

```
//: concurrency/GreenhouseScheduler.java
// Rewriting innerclasses/GreenhouseController.java
// to use a ScheduledThreadPoolExecutor.
// {Args: 5000}
import java.util.concurrent.*;
import java.util.*;

public class GreenhouseScheduler {
  private volatile boolean light = false;
  private volatile boolean water = false;
  private String thermostat = "Day";
  public synchronized String getThermostat() {
```

```java
      return thermostat;
    }
    public synchronized void setThermostat(String value) {
      thermostat = value;
    }
    ScheduledThreadPoolExecutor scheduler =
      new ScheduledThreadPoolExecutor(10);
    public void schedule(Runnable event, long delay) {
      scheduler.schedule(event,delay,TimeUnit.MILLISECONDS);
    }
    public void
    repeat(Runnable event, long initialDelay, long period) {
      scheduler.scheduleAtFixedRate(
        event, initialDelay, period, TimeUnit.MILLISECONDS);
    }
    class LightOn implements Runnable {
      public void run() {
        // Put hardware control code here to
        // physically turn on the light.
        System.out.println("Turning on lights");
        light = true;
      }
    }
    class LightOff implements Runnable {
      public void run() {
        // Put hardware control code here to
        // physically turn off the light.
        System.out.println("Turning off lights");
        light = false;
      }
    }
    class WaterOn implements Runnable {
      public void run() {
        // Put hardware control code here.
        System.out.println("Turning greenhouse water on");
        water = true;
      }
    }
    class WaterOff implements Runnable {
      public void run() {
        // Put hardware control code here.
        System.out.println("Turning greenhouse water off");
        water = false;
      }
```

```java
  }
  class ThermostatNight implements Runnable {
    public void run() {
      // Put hardware control code here.
      System.out.println("Thermostat to night setting");
      setThermostat("Night");
    }
  }
  class ThermostatDay implements Runnable {
    public void run() {
      // Put hardware control code here.
      System.out.println("Thermostat to day setting");
      setThermostat("Day");
    }
  }
  class Bell implements Runnable {
    public void run() { System.out.println("Bing!"); }
  }
  class Terminate implements Runnable {
    public void run() {
      System.out.println("Terminating");
      scheduler.shutdownNow();
      // Must start a separate task to do this job,
      // since the scheduler has been shut down:
      new Thread() {
        public void run() {
          for(DataPoint d : data)
            System.out.println(d);
        }
      }.start();
    }
  }
  // New feature: data collection
  static class DataPoint {
    final Calendar time;
    final float temperature;
    final float humidity;
    public DataPoint(Calendar d, float temp, float hum) {
      time = d;
      temperature = temp;
      humidity = hum;
    }
    public String toString() {
      return time.getTime() +
```

```
          String.format(
            " temperature: %1$.1f humidity: %2$.2f",
            temperature, humidity);
      }
    }
    private Calendar lastTime = Calendar.getInstance();
    { // Adjust date to the half hour
      lastTime.set(Calendar.MINUTE, 30);
      lastTime.set(Calendar.SECOND, 00);
    }
    private float lastTemp = 65.0f;
    private int tempDirection = +1;
    private float lastHumidity = 50.0f;
    private int humidityDirection = +1;
    private Random rand = new Random(47);
    List<DataPoint> data = Collections.synchronizedList(
      new ArrayList<DataPoint>());
    class CollectData implements Runnable {
      public void run() {
        System.out.println("Collecting data");
        synchronized(GreenhouseScheduler.this) {
          // Pretend the interval is longer than it is:
          lastTime.set(Calendar.MINUTE,
            lastTime.get(Calendar.MINUTE) + 30);
          // One in 5 chances of reversing the direction:
          if(rand.nextInt(5) == 4)
            tempDirection = -tempDirection;
          // Store previous value:
          lastTemp = lastTemp +
            tempDirection * (1.0f + rand.nextFloat());
          if(rand.nextInt(5) == 4)
            humidityDirection = -humidityDirection;
          lastHumidity = lastHumidity +
            humidityDirection * rand.nextFloat();
          // Calendar must be cloned, otherwise all
          // DataPoints hold references to the same lastTime.
          // For a basic object like Calendar, clone() is OK.
          data.add(new DataPoint((Calendar)lastTime.clone(),
            lastTemp, lastHumidity));
        }
      }
    }
    public static void main(String[] args) {
      GreenhouseScheduler gh = new GreenhouseScheduler();
```

```
        gh.schedule(gh.new Terminate(), 5000);
        // Former "Restart" class not necessary:
        gh.repeat(gh.new Bell(), 0, 1000);
        gh.repeat(gh.new ThermostatNight(), 0, 2000);
        gh.repeat(gh.new LightOn(), 0, 200);
        gh.repeat(gh.new LightOff(), 0, 400);
        gh.repeat(gh.new WaterOn(), 0, 600);
        gh.repeat(gh.new WaterOff(), 0, 800);
        gh.repeat(gh.new ThermostatDay(), 0, 1400);
        gh.repeat(gh.new CollectData(), 500, 500);
    }
} /* (Execute to see output) *///:~
```

This version reorganizes the code and adds a new feature: collecting temperature and humidity readings in the greenhouse. A **DataPoint** holds and displays a single piece of data, while **CollectData** is the scheduled task that generates simulated data and adds it to the **List<DataPoint>** in **Greenhouse** each time it is run.

Notice the use of both **volatile** and **synchronized** in appropriate places to prevent tasks from interfering with each other. All the methods in the **List** that holds **DataPoint**s are **synchronized** using the **java.util.Collections** utility **synchronizedList( )** when the **List** is created.

Exercise 33: (7) Modify **GreenhouseScheduler.java** so that it uses a **DelayQueue** instead of a **ScheduledExecutor**.

Semaphore

A normal lock (from **concurrent.locks** or the built-in **synchronized** lock) only allows one task at a time to access a resource. A *counting semaphore* allows *n* tasks to access the resource at the same time. You can also think of a semaphore as handing out "permits" to use a resource, although no actual permit objects are used.

As an example, consider the concept of the *object pool*, which manages a limited number of objects by allowing them to be checked out for use, and then checked back in again when the user is finished. This functionality can be encapsulated in a generic class:

```
//: concurrency/Pool.java
// Using a Semaphore inside a Pool, to restrict
// the number of tasks that can use a resource.
import java.util.concurrent.*;
```

```
import java.util.*;

public class Pool<T> {
  private int size;
  private List<T> items = new ArrayList<T>();
  private volatile boolean[] checkedOut;
  private Semaphore available;
  public Pool(Class<T> classObject, int size) {
    this.size = size;
    checkedOut = new boolean[size];
    available = new Semaphore(size, true);
    // Load pool with objects that can be checked out:
    for(int i = 0; i < size; ++i)
      try {
        // Assumes a default constructor:
        items.add(classObject.newInstance());
      } catch(Exception e) {
        throw new RuntimeException(e);
      }
  }
  public T checkOut() throws InterruptedException {
    available.acquire();
    return getItem();
  }
  public void checkIn(T x) {
    if(releaseItem(x))
      available.release();
  }
  private synchronized T getItem() {
    for(int i = 0; i < size; ++i)
      if(!checkedOut[i]) {
        checkedOut[i] = true;
        return items.get(i);
      }
    return null; // Semaphore prevents reaching here
  }
  private synchronized boolean releaseItem(T item) {
    int index = items.indexOf(item);
    if(index == -1) return false; // Not in the list
    if(checkedOut[index]) {
      checkedOut[index] = false;
      return true;
    }
    return false; // Wasn't checked out
```

```
      }
    } ///:~
```

In this simplified form, the constructor uses **newInstance( )** to load the pool with objects. If you need a new object, you call **checkOut( )**, and when you're finished with an object, you hand it to **checkIn( )**.

The **boolean checkedOut** array keeps track of the objects that are checked out, and is managed by the **getItem( )** and **releaseItem( )** methods. These, in turn, are guarded by the **Semaphore available**, so that, in **checkOut( )**, **available** blocks the progress of the call if there are no more semaphore permits available (which means there are no more objects in the pool). In **checkIn( )**, if the object being checked in is valid, a permit is returned to the semaphore.

To create an example, we can use **Fat**, a type of object that is expensive to create because its constructor takes time to run:

```
//: concurrency/Fat.java
// Objects that are expensive to create.

public class Fat {
  private volatile double d; // Prevent optimization
  private static int counter = 0;
  private final int id = counter++;
  public Fat() {
    // Expensive, interruptible operation:
    for(int i = 1; i < 10000; i++) {
      d += (Math.PI + Math.E) / (double)i;
    }
  }
  public void operation() { System.out.println(this); }
  public String toString() { return "Fat id: " + id; }
} ///:~
```

We'll pool these objects to limit the impact of this constructor. We can test the **Pool** class by creating a task that will check out **Fat** objects, hold them for a while, and then check them back in:

```
//: concurrency/SemaphoreDemo.java
// Testing the Pool class
import java.util.concurrent.*;
import java.util.*;
import static net.mindview.util.Print.*;
```

```java
// A task to check a resource out of a pool:
class CheckoutTask<T> implements Runnable {
  private static int counter = 0;
  private final int id = counter++;
  private Pool<T> pool;
  public CheckoutTask(Pool<T> pool) {
    this.pool = pool;
  }
  public void run() {
    try {
      T item = pool.checkOut();
      print(this + "checked out " + item);
      TimeUnit.SECONDS.sleep(1);
      print(this +"checking in " + item);
      pool.checkIn(item);
    } catch(InterruptedException e) {
      // Acceptable way to terminate
    }
  }
  public String toString() {
    return "CheckoutTask " + id + " ";
  }
}

public class SemaphoreDemo {
  final static int SIZE = 25;
  public static void main(String[] args) throws Exception {
    final Pool<Fat> pool =
      new Pool<Fat>(Fat.class, SIZE);
    ExecutorService exec = Executors.newCachedThreadPool();
    for(int i = 0; i < SIZE; i++)
      exec.execute(new CheckoutTask<Fat>(pool));
    print("All CheckoutTasks created");
    List<Fat> list = new ArrayList<Fat>();
    for(int i = 0; i < SIZE; i++) {
      Fat f = pool.checkOut();
      printnb(i + ": main() thread checked out ");
      f.operation();
      list.add(f);
    }
    Future<?> blocked = exec.submit(new Runnable() {
      public void run() {
        try {
```

```
        // Semaphore prevents additional checkout,
        // so call is blocked:
        pool.checkOut();
      } catch(InterruptedException e) {
        print("checkOut() Interrupted");
      }
    }
  });
  TimeUnit.SECONDS.sleep(2);
  blocked.cancel(true); // Break out of blocked call
  print("Checking in objects in " + list);
  for(Fat f : list)
    pool.checkIn(f);
  for(Fat f : list)
    pool.checkIn(f); // Second checkIn ignored
  exec.shutdown();
  }
} /* (Execute to see output) *///:~
```

In **main( )**, a **Pool** is created to hold **Fat** objects, and a set of
CheckoutTasks begins exercising the **Pool**. Then the **main( )** thread
begins checking out **Fat** objects, *and not checking them back in*. Once it has
checked out all the objects in the pool, no more checkouts will be allowed by
the **Semaphore**. The **run( )** method of **blocked** is thus blocked, and after
two seconds the **cancel( )** method is called to break out of the **Future**. Note
that redundant checkins are ignored by the **Pool**.

This example relies on the client of the **Pool** to be rigorous and to voluntarily
check items back in, which is the simplest solution when it works. If you
cannot always rely on this, *Thinking in Patterns* (at *www.MindView.net*)
contains further explorations of ways to manage the objects that have been
checked out of object pools.

Exchanger

An **Exchanger** is a barrier that swaps objects between two tasks. When the
tasks enter the barrier, they have one object, and when they leave, they have
the object that was formerly held by the other task. **Exchanger**s are typically
used when one task is creating objects that are expensive to produce and
another task is consuming those objects; this way, more objects can be
created at the same time as they are being consumed.

To exercise the **Exchanger** class, we'll create producer and consumer tasks which, via generics and **Generator**s, will work with any kind of object, and then we'll apply these to the **Fat** class. The **ExchangerProducer** and **ExchangerConsumer** use a **List<T>** as the object to be exchanged; each one contains an **Exchanger** for this **List<T>**. When you call the **Exchanger.exchange( )** method, it blocks until the partner task calls its **exchange( )** method, and when both **exchange( )** methods have completed, the **List<T>** has been swapped:

```java
//: concurrency/ExchangerDemo.java
import java.util.concurrent.*;
import java.util.*;
import net.mindview.util.*;

class ExchangerProducer<T> implements Runnable {
  private Generator<T> generator;
  private Exchanger<List<T>> exchanger;
  private List<T> holder;
  ExchangerProducer(Exchanger<List<T>> exchg,
  Generator<T> gen, List<T> holder) {
    exchanger = exchg;
    generator = gen;
    this.holder = holder;
  }
  public void run() {
    try {
      while(!Thread.interrupted()) {
        for(int i = 0; i < ExchangerDemo.size; i++)
          holder.add(generator.next());
        // Exchange full for empty:
        holder = exchanger.exchange(holder);
      }
    } catch(InterruptedException e) {
      // OK to terminate this way.
    }
  }
}

class ExchangerConsumer<T> implements Runnable {
  private Exchanger<List<T>> exchanger;
  private List<T> holder;
  private volatile T value;
  ExchangerConsumer(Exchanger<List<T>> ex, List<T> holder){
    exchanger = ex;
```

```
      this.holder = holder;
    }
  public void run() {
    try {
      while(!Thread.interrupted()) {
        holder = exchanger.exchange(holder);
        for(T x : holder) {
          value = x; // Fetch out value
          holder.remove(x); // OK for CopyOnWriteArrayList
        }
      }
    } catch(InterruptedException e) {
      // OK to terminate this way.
    }
    System.out.println("Final value: " + value);
  }
}

public class ExchangerDemo {
  static int size = 10;
  static int delay = 5; // Seconds
  public static void main(String[] args) throws Exception {
    if(args.length > 0)
      size = new Integer(args[0]);
    if(args.length > 1)
      delay = new Integer(args[1]);
    ExecutorService exec = Executors.newCachedThreadPool();
    Exchanger<List<Fat>> xc = new Exchanger<List<Fat>>();
    List<Fat>
      producerList = new CopyOnWriteArrayList<Fat>(),
      consumerList = new CopyOnWriteArrayList<Fat>();
    exec.execute(new ExchangerProducer<Fat>(xc,
      BasicGenerator.create(Fat.class), producerList));
    exec.execute(
      new ExchangerConsumer<Fat>(xc,consumerList));
    TimeUnit.SECONDS.sleep(delay);
    exec.shutdownNow();
  }
} /* Output: (Sample)
Final value: Fat id: 29999
*///:~
```

In **main( )**, a single **Exchanger** is created for both tasks to use, and two
CopyOnWriteArrayLists are created for swapping. This particular variant

---

of **List** can tolerate the **remove( )** method being called while the list is being traversed, without throwing a **ConcurrentModificationException**. The **ExchangerProducer** fills a **List**, then swaps the full list for the empty one that the **ExchangerConsumer** hands it. Because of the **Exchanger**, the filling of one list and consuming of the other list can happen simultaneously.

Exercise 34: (1) Modify **ExchangerDemo.java** to use your own class instead of **Fat**.

Simulation

One of the most interesting and exciting uses of concurrency is to create simulations. Using concurrency, each component of a simulation can be its own task, and this makes a simulation much easier to program. Many video games and CGI animations in movies are simulations, and **HorseRace.java** and **GreenhouseScheduler.java**, shown earlier, could also be considered simulations.

Bank teller simulation

This classic simulation can represent any situation where objects appear randomly and require a random amount of time to be served by a limited number of servers. It's possible to build the simulation to determine the ideal number of servers.

In this example, each bank customer requires a certain amount of service time, which is the number of time units that a teller must spend on the customer to serve that customer's needs. The amount of service time will be different for each customer and will be determined randomly. In addition, you won't know how many customers will be arriving in each interval, so this will also be determined randomly.

```
//: concurrency/BankTellerSimulation.java
// Using queues and multithreading.
// {Args: 5}
import java.util.concurrent.*;
import java.util.*;

// Read-only objects don't require synchronization:
class Customer {
  private final int serviceTime;
  public Customer(int tm) { serviceTime = tm; }
```

```java
    public int getServiceTime() { return serviceTime; }
    public String toString() {
      return "[" + serviceTime + "]";
    }
  }

// Teach the customer line to display itself:
class CustomerLine extends ArrayBlockingQueue<Customer> {
  public CustomerLine(int maxLineSize) {
    super(maxLineSize);
  }
  public String toString() {
    if(this.size() == 0)
      return "[Empty]";
    StringBuilder result = new StringBuilder();
    for(Customer customer : this)
      result.append(customer);
    return result.toString();
  }
}

// Randomly add customers to a queue:
class CustomerGenerator implements Runnable {
  private CustomerLine customers;
  private static Random rand = new Random(47);
  public CustomerGenerator(CustomerLine cq) {
    customers = cq;
  }
  public void run() {
    try {
      while(!Thread.interrupted()) {
        TimeUnit.MILLISECONDS.sleep(rand.nextInt(300));
        customers.put(new Customer(rand.nextInt(1000)));
      }
    } catch(InterruptedException e) {
      System.out.println("CustomerGenerator interrupted");
    }
    System.out.println("CustomerGenerator terminating");
  }
}

class Teller implements Runnable, Comparable<Teller> {
  private static int counter = 0;
  private final int id = counter++;
```

```
    // Customers served during this shift:
    private int customersServed = 0;
    private CustomerLine customers;
    private boolean servingCustomerLine = true;
    public Teller(CustomerLine cq) { customers = cq; }
    public void run() {
      try {
        while(!Thread.interrupted()) {
          Customer customer = customers.take();
          TimeUnit.MILLISECONDS.sleep(
            customer.getServiceTime());
          synchronized(this) {
            customersServed++;
            while(!servingCustomerLine)
              wait();
          }
        }
      } catch(InterruptedException e) {
        System.out.println(this + "interrupted");
      }
      System.out.println(this + "terminating");
    }
    public synchronized void doSomethingElse() {
      customersServed = 0;
      servingCustomerLine = false;
    }
    public synchronized void serveCustomerLine() {
      assert !servingCustomerLine:"already serving: " + this;
      servingCustomerLine = true;
      notifyAll();
    }
    public String toString() { return "Teller " + id + " "; }
    public String shortString() { return "T" + id; }
    // Used by priority queue:
    public synchronized int compareTo(Teller other) {
      return customersServed < other.customersServed ? -1 :
        (customersServed == other.customersServed ? 0 : 1);
    }
}

class TellerManager implements Runnable {
  private ExecutorService exec;
  private CustomerLine customers;
  private PriorityQueue<Teller> workingTellers =
```

```
      new PriorityQueue<Teller>();
    private Queue<Teller> tellersDoingOtherThings =
      new LinkedList<Teller>();
    private int adjustmentPeriod;

    public TellerManager(ExecutorService e,
      CustomerLine customers, int adjustmentPeriod) {
      exec = e;
      this.customers = customers;
      this.adjustmentPeriod = adjustmentPeriod;
      // Start with a single teller:
      Teller teller = new Teller(customers);
      exec.execute(teller);
      workingTellers.add(teller);
    }
    public void adjustTellerNumber() {
      // This is actually a control system. By adjusting
      // the numbers, you can reveal stability issues in
      // the control mechanism.
      // If line is too long, add another teller:
      if(customers.size() / workingTellers.size() > 2) {
          // If tellers are on break or doing
          // another job, bring one back:
          if(tellersDoingOtherThings.size() > 0) {
            Teller teller = tellersDoingOtherThings.remove();
            teller.serveCustomerLine();
            workingTellers.offer(teller);
            return;
          }
        // Else create (hire) a new teller
        Teller teller = new Teller(customers);
        exec.execute(teller);
        workingTellers.add(teller);
        return;
      }
      // If line is short enough, remove a teller:
      if(workingTellers.size() > 1 &&
        customers.size() / workingTellers.size() < 2)
          reassignOneTeller();
      // If there is no line, we only need one teller:
      if(customers.size() == 0)
        while(workingTellers.size() > 1)
          reassignOneTeller();
    }
```

```java
    // Give a teller a different job or a break:
    private void reassignOneTeller() {
      Teller teller = workingTellers.poll();
      teller.doSomethingElse();
      tellersDoingOtherThings.offer(teller);
    }
    public void run() {
      try {
        while(!Thread.interrupted()) {
          TimeUnit.MILLISECONDS.sleep(adjustmentPeriod);
          adjustTellerNumber();
          System.out.print(customers + " { ");
          for(Teller teller : workingTellers)
            System.out.print(teller.shortString() + " ");
          System.out.println("}");
        }
      } catch(InterruptedException e) {
        System.out.println(this + "interrupted");
      }
      System.out.println(this + "terminating");
    }
    public String toString() { return "TellerManager "; }
}

public class BankTellerSimulation {
  static final int MAX_LINE_SIZE = 50;
  static final int ADJUSTMENT_PERIOD = 1000;
  public static void main(String[] args) throws Exception {
    ExecutorService exec = Executors.newCachedThreadPool();
    // If line is too long, customers will leave:
    CustomerLine customers =
      new CustomerLine(MAX_LINE_SIZE);
    exec.execute(new CustomerGenerator(customers));
    // Manager will add and remove tellers as necessary:
    exec.execute(new TellerManager(
      exec, customers, ADJUSTMENT_PERIOD));
    if(args.length > 0) // Optional argument
      TimeUnit.SECONDS.sleep(new Integer(args[0]));
    else {
      System.out.println("Press 'Enter' to quit");
      System.in.read();
    }
    exec.shutdownNow();
  }
```

```
} /* Output: (Sample)
[429][200][207] { T0 T1 }
[861][258][140][322] { T0 T1 }
[575][342][804][826][896][984] { T0 T1 T2 }
[984][810][141][12][689][992][976][368][395][354] { T0 T1
T2 T3 }
Teller 2 interrupted
Teller 2 terminating
Teller 1 interrupted
Teller 1 terminating
TellerManager interrupted
TellerManager terminating
Teller 3 interrupted
Teller 3 terminating
Teller 0 interrupted
Teller 0 terminating
CustomerGenerator interrupted
CustomerGenerator terminating
*///:~
```

The **Customer** objects are very simple, containing only a **final int** field.
Because these objects never change, they are *read-only* objects and they do
not require synchronization or the use of **volatile**. On top of that, each
Teller task only removes one **Customer** at a time from the input queue, and
works on that **Customer** until it is complete, so a **Customer** will only be
accessed by one task at a time, anyway.

CustomerLine represents a single line that the customers wait in before
being served by a **Teller**. This is just an **ArrayBlockingQueue** that has a
toString( ) that prints the results in the desired fashion.

A **CustomerGenerator** is attached to a **CustomerLine** and puts
Customers onto the queue at randomized intervals.

A **Teller** takes **Customer**s off of the **CustomerLine** and processes them
one at a time, keeping track of the number of **Customer**s it has served
during that particular shift. It can be told to **doSomethingElse( )** when
there aren't enough customers, and to **serveCustomerLine( )** when lots of
customers show up. To choose the next teller to put back on the line, the
compareTo( ) method looks at the number of customers served so that a
PriorityQueue can automatically put the least-worked teller at the
forefront.

The **TellerManager** is the hub of activity. It keeps track of all the tellers and what's going on with the customers. One of the interesting things about this simulation is that it attempts to discover the optimum number of tellers for a given customer flow. You can see this in the **adjustTellerNumber( )**, which is a control system to add and remove tellers in a stable fashion. All control systems have stability issues; if they react too quickly to a change, they are unstable, and if they react too slowly, the system moves to one of its extremes.

Exercise 35: (8) Modify **BankTellerSimulation.java** so that it represents Web clients making requests of a fixed number of servers. The goal is to determine the load that the group of servers can handle.

The restaurant simulation

This simulation fleshes out the simple **Restaurant.java** example shown earlier in this chapter by adding more simulation components, such as **Order**s and **Plate**s, and it reuses the **menu** classes from the *Enumerated Types* chapter.

It also introduces the Java SE5 **SynchronousQueue**, which is a blocking queue that has no internal capacity, so each **put( )** must wait for a **take( )**, and vice versa. It's as if you were handing an object to someone—there's no table to put it on, so it only works if that person is holding a hand out, ready to receive the object. In this example, the **SynchronousQueue** represents the place setting in front of a diner, to enforce the idea that only one course can be served at a time.

The rest of the classes and functionality of this example either follow from the structure of **Restaurant.java** or are intended to be a fairly direct mapping from the operations of an actual restaurant:

```
//: concurrency/restaurant2/RestaurantWithQueues.java
// {Args: 5}
package concurrency.restaurant2;
import enumerated.menu.*;
import java.util.concurrent.*;
import java.util.*;
import static net.mindview.util.Print.*;

// This is given to the waiter, who gives it to the chef:
class Order { // (A data-transfer object)
   private static int counter = 0;
```

```
  private final int id = counter++;
  private final Customer customer;
  private final WaitPerson waitPerson;
  private final Food food;
  public Order(Customer cust, WaitPerson wp, Food f) {
    customer = cust;
    waitPerson = wp;
    food = f;
  }
  public Food item() { return food; }
  public Customer getCustomer() { return customer; }
  public WaitPerson getWaitPerson() { return waitPerson; }
  public String toString() {
    return "Order: " + id + " item: " + food +
      " for: " + customer +
      " served by: " + waitPerson;
  }
}

// This is what comes back from the chef:
class Plate {
  private final Order order;
  private final Food food;
  public Plate(Order ord, Food f) {
    order = ord;
    food = f;
  }
  public Order getOrder() { return order; }
  public Food getFood() { return food; }
  public String toString() { return food.toString(); }
}

class Customer implements Runnable {
  private static int counter = 0;
  private final int id = counter++;
  private final WaitPerson waitPerson;
  // Only one course at a time can be received:
  private SynchronousQueue<Plate> placeSetting =
    new SynchronousQueue<Plate>();
  public Customer(WaitPerson w) { waitPerson = w; }
  public void
  deliver(Plate p) throws InterruptedException {
    // Only blocks if customer is still
    // eating the previous course:
```

```
        placeSetting.put(p);
    }
  public void run() {
    for(Course course : Course.values()) {
      Food food = course.randomSelection();
      try {
        waitPerson.placeOrder(this, food);
        // Blocks until course has been delivered:
        print(this + "eating " + placeSetting.take());
      } catch(InterruptedException e) {
        print(this + "waiting for " +
          course + " interrupted");
        break;
      }
    }
    print(this + "finished meal, leaving");
  }
  public String toString() {
    return "Customer " + id + " ";
  }
}

class WaitPerson implements Runnable {
  private static int counter = 0;
  private final int id = counter++;
  private final Restaurant restaurant;
  BlockingQueue<Plate> filledOrders =
    new LinkedBlockingQueue<Plate>();
  public WaitPerson(Restaurant rest) { restaurant = rest; }
  public void placeOrder(Customer cust, Food food) {
    try {
      // Shouldn't actually block because this is
      // a LinkedBlockingQueue with no size limit:
      restaurant.orders.put(new Order(cust, this, food));
    } catch(InterruptedException e) {
      print(this + " placeOrder interrupted");
    }
  }
  public void run() {
    try {
      while(!Thread.interrupted()) {
        // Blocks until a course is ready
        Plate plate = filledOrders.take();
        print(this + "received " + plate +
```

```
                 " delivering to " +
                 plate.getOrder().getCustomer());
              plate.getOrder().getCustomer().deliver(plate);
          }
      } catch(InterruptedException e) {
        print(this + " interrupted");
      }
      print(this + " off duty");
    }
    public String toString() {
      return "WaitPerson " + id + " ";
    }
}

class Chef implements Runnable {
  private static int counter = 0;
  private final int id = counter++;
  private final Restaurant restaurant;
  private static Random rand = new Random(47);
  public Chef(Restaurant rest) { restaurant = rest; }
  public void run() {
    try {
      while(!Thread.interrupted()) {
        // Blocks until an order appears:
        Order order = restaurant.orders.take();
        Food requestedItem = order.item();
        // Time to prepare order:
        TimeUnit.MILLISECONDS.sleep(rand.nextInt(500));
        Plate plate = new Plate(order, requestedItem);
        order.getWaitPerson().filledOrders.put(plate);
      }
    } catch(InterruptedException e) {
      print(this + " interrupted");
    }
    print(this + " off duty");
  }
  public String toString() { return "Chef " + id + " "; }
}

class Restaurant implements Runnable {
  private List<WaitPerson> waitPersons =
    new ArrayList<WaitPerson>();
  private List<Chef> chefs = new ArrayList<Chef>();
  private ExecutorService exec;
```

```
    private static Random rand = new Random(47);
    BlockingQueue<Order>
      orders = new LinkedBlockingQueue<Order>();
    public Restaurant(ExecutorService e, int nWaitPersons,
      int nChefs) {
      exec = e;
      for(int i = 0; i < nWaitPersons; i++) {
        WaitPerson waitPerson = new WaitPerson(this);
        waitPersons.add(waitPerson);
        exec.execute(waitPerson);
      }
      for(int i = 0; i < nChefs; i++) {
        Chef chef = new Chef(this);
        chefs.add(chef);
        exec.execute(chef);
      }
    }
    public void run() {
      try {
        while(!Thread.interrupted()) {
          // A new customer arrives; assign a WaitPerson:
          WaitPerson wp = waitPersons.get(
            rand.nextInt(waitPersons.size()));
          Customer c = new Customer(wp);
          exec.execute(c);
          TimeUnit.MILLISECONDS.sleep(100);
        }
      } catch(InterruptedException e) {
        print("Restaurant interrupted");
      }
      print("Restaurant closing");
    }
  }

public class RestaurantWithQueues {
  public static void main(String[] args) throws Exception {
    ExecutorService exec = Executors.newCachedThreadPool();
    Restaurant restaurant = new Restaurant(exec, 5, 2);
    exec.execute(restaurant);
    if(args.length > 0) // Optional argument
      TimeUnit.SECONDS.sleep(new Integer(args[0]));
    else {
      print("Press 'Enter' to quit");
      System.in.read();
```

```
        }
      exec.shutdownNow();
    }
} /* Output: (Sample)
WaitPerson 0 received SPRING_ROLLS delivering to Customer 1
Customer 1 eating SPRING_ROLLS
WaitPerson 3 received SPRING_ROLLS delivering to Customer 0
Customer 0 eating SPRING_ROLLS
WaitPerson 0 received BURRITO delivering to Customer 1
Customer 1 eating BURRITO
WaitPerson 3 received SPRING_ROLLS delivering to Customer 2
Customer 2 eating SPRING_ROLLS
WaitPerson 1 received SOUP delivering to Customer 3
Customer 3 eating SOUP
WaitPerson 3 received VINDALOO delivering to Customer 0
Customer 0 eating VINDALOO
WaitPerson 0 received FRUIT delivering to Customer 1
...
*///:~
```

One very important thing to observe about this example is the management of complexity using queues to communicate between tasks. This single technique greatly simplifies the process of concurrent programming by inverting the control: The tasks do not directly interfere with each other. Instead, the tasks send objects to each other via queues. The receiving task handles the object, treating it as a message rather than having the message inflicted upon it. If you follow this technique whenever you can, you stand a much better chance of building robust concurrent systems.

Exercise 36: (10) Modify **RestaurantWithQueues.java** so there's one **OrderTicket** object per table. Change **order** to **orderTicket**, and add a **Table** class, with multiple **Customer**s per table.

Distributing work

Here's a simulation example that brings together many of the concepts in this chapter. Consider a hypothetical robotic assembly line for automobiles. Each **Car** will be built in several stages, starting with chassis creation, followed by the attachment of the engine, drive train, and wheels.

```
//: concurrency/CarBuilder.java
// A complex example of tasks working together.
import java.util.concurrent.*;
import java.util.*;
```

```
import static net.mindview.util.Print.*;

class Car {
  private final int id;
  private boolean
    engine = false, driveTrain = false, wheels = false;
  public Car(int idn)  { id = idn; }
  // Empty Car object:
  public Car()  { id = -1; }
  public synchronized int getId() { return id; }
  public synchronized void addEngine() { engine = true; }
  public synchronized void addDriveTrain() {
    driveTrain = true;
  }
  public synchronized void addWheels() { wheels = true; }
  public synchronized String toString() {
    return "Car " + id + " [" + " engine: " + engine
      + " driveTrain: " + driveTrain
      + " wheels: " + wheels + " ]";
  }
}

class CarQueue extends LinkedBlockingQueue<Car> {}

class ChassisBuilder implements Runnable {
  private CarQueue carQueue;
  private int counter = 0;
  public ChassisBuilder(CarQueue cq) { carQueue = cq; }
  public void run() {
    try {
      while(!Thread.interrupted()) {
        TimeUnit.MILLISECONDS.sleep(500);
        // Make chassis:
        Car c = new Car(counter++);
        print("ChassisBuilder created " + c);
        // Insert into queue
        carQueue.put(c);
      }
    } catch(InterruptedException e) {
      print("Interrupted: ChassisBuilder");
    }
    print("ChassisBuilder off");
  }
}
```

```java
class Assembler implements Runnable {
  private CarQueue chassisQueue, finishingQueue;
  private Car car;
  private CyclicBarrier barrier = new CyclicBarrier(4);
  private RobotPool robotPool;
  public Assembler(CarQueue cq, CarQueue fq, RobotPool rp){
    chassisQueue = cq;
    finishingQueue = fq;
    robotPool = rp;
  }
  public Car car() { return car; }
  public CyclicBarrier barrier() { return barrier; }
  public void run() {
    try {
      while(!Thread.interrupted()) {
        // Blocks until chassis is available:
        car = chassisQueue.take();
        // Hire robots to perform work:
        robotPool.hire(EngineRobot.class, this);
        robotPool.hire(DriveTrainRobot.class, this);
        robotPool.hire(WheelRobot.class, this);
        barrier.await(); // Until the robots finish
        // Put car into finishingQueue for further work
        finishingQueue.put(car);
      }
    } catch(InterruptedException e) {
      print("Exiting Assembler via interrupt");
    } catch(BrokenBarrierException e) {
      // This one we want to know about
      throw new RuntimeException(e);
    }
    print("Assembler off");
  }
}

class Reporter implements Runnable {
  private CarQueue carQueue;
  public Reporter(CarQueue cq) { carQueue = cq; }
  public void run() {
    try {
      while(!Thread.interrupted()) {
        print(carQueue.take());
      }
```

```
      } catch(InterruptedException e) {
        print("Exiting Reporter via interrupt");
      }
      print("Reporter off");
    }
  }

  abstract class Robot implements Runnable {
    private RobotPool pool;
    public Robot(RobotPool p) { pool = p; }
    protected Assembler assembler;
    public Robot assignAssembler(Assembler assembler) {
      this.assembler = assembler;
      return this;
    }
    private boolean engage = false;
    public synchronized void engage() {
      engage = true;
      notifyAll();
    }
    // The part of run() that's different for each robot:
    abstract protected void performService();
    public void run() {
      try {
        powerDown(); // Wait until needed
        while(!Thread.interrupted()) {
          performService();
          assembler.barrier().await(); // Synchronize
          // We're done with that job...
          powerDown();
        }
      } catch(InterruptedException e) {
        print("Exiting " + this + " via interrupt");
      } catch(BrokenBarrierException e) {
        // This one we want to know about
        throw new RuntimeException(e);
      }
      print(this + " off");
    }
    private synchronized void
    powerDown() throws InterruptedException {
      engage = false;
      assembler = null; // Disconnect from the Assembler
      // Put ourselves back in the available pool:
```

```
      pool.release(this);
      while(engage == false)   // Power down
        wait();
  }
  public String toString() { return getClass().getName(); }
}

class EngineRobot extends Robot {
  public EngineRobot(RobotPool pool) { super(pool); }
  protected void performService() {
    print(this + " installing engine");
    assembler.car().addEngine();
  }
}

class DriveTrainRobot extends Robot {
  public DriveTrainRobot(RobotPool pool) { super(pool); }
  protected void performService() {
    print(this + " installing DriveTrain");
    assembler.car().addDriveTrain();
  }
}

class WheelRobot extends Robot {
  public WheelRobot(RobotPool pool) { super(pool); }
  protected void performService() {
    print(this + " installing Wheels");
    assembler.car().addWheels();
  }
}

class RobotPool {
  // Quietly prevents identical entries:
  private Set<Robot> pool = new HashSet<Robot>();
  public synchronized void add(Robot r) {
    pool.add(r);
    notifyAll();
  }
  public synchronized void
  hire(Class<? extends Robot> robotType, Assembler d)
  throws InterruptedException {
    for(Robot r : pool)
      if(r.getClass().equals(robotType)) {
        pool.remove(r);
```

```
      r.assignAssembler(d);
      r.engage(); // Power it up to do the task
      return;
    }
    wait(); // None available
    hire(robotType, d); // Try again, recursively
  }
  public synchronized void release(Robot r) { add(r); }
}

public class CarBuilder {
  public static void main(String[] args) throws Exception {
    CarQueue chassisQueue = new CarQueue(),
             finishingQueue = new CarQueue();
    ExecutorService exec = Executors.newCachedThreadPool();
    RobotPool robotPool = new RobotPool();
    exec.execute(new EngineRobot(robotPool));
    exec.execute(new DriveTrainRobot(robotPool));
    exec.execute(new WheelRobot(robotPool));
    exec.execute(new Assembler(
      chassisQueue, finishingQueue, robotPool));
    exec.execute(new Reporter(finishingQueue));
    // Start everything running by producing chassis:
    exec.execute(new ChassisBuilder(chassisQueue));
    TimeUnit.SECONDS.sleep(7);
    exec.shutdownNow();
  }
} /* (Execute to see output) *///:~
```

The **Car**s are transported from one place to another via a **CarQueue**, which is a type of **LinkedBlockingQueue**. A **ChassisBuilder** creates an unadorned **Car** and places it on a **CarQueue**. The **Assembler** takes the **Car** off a **CarQueue** and hires **Robot**s to work on it. A **CyclicBarrier** allows the **Assembler** to wait until all the **Robot**s are finished, at which time it puts the **Car** onto the outgoing **CarQueue** to be transported to the next operation. The consumer of the final **CarQueue** is a **Reporter** object, which just prints the **Car** to show that the tasks have been properly completed.

The **Robot**s are managed in a pool, and when work needs to be done, the appropriate **Robot** is hired from the pool. After the work is completed, the **Robot** returns to the pool.

In **main( )**, all the necessary objects are created and the tasks are initialized, with the **ChassisBuilder** begun last to start the process. (However, because of the behavior of the **LinkedBlockingQueue**, it wouldn't matter if it were started first.) Note that this program follows all the guidelines regarding object and task lifetime presented in this chapter, and so the shutdown process is safe.

You'll notice that **Car** has all of its methods **synchronized**. As it turns out, *in this example* this is redundant, because within the factory the **Car**s move through the queues and only one task can work on a car at a time. Basically, the queues force serialized access to the **Car**s. But this is exactly the kind of trap you can fall into—you can say "Let's try to optimize by not synchronizing the **Car** class because it doesn't look like it needs it here." But later, when this system is connected to another which *does* need the **Car** to be **synchronized**, it breaks.

Brian Goetz comments:

> It's much easier to say, "**Car** might be used from multiple threads, so let's make it thread-safe in the obvious way." The way I characterize this approach is: At public parks, you will find guard rails where there is a steep drop, and you may find signs that say, "Don't lean on the guard rail." Of course, the real purpose of this rule is not to prevent you from leaning on the rail—it is to prevent you from falling off the cliff. But "Don't lean on the rail" is a much easier rule to follow than "Don't fall off the cliff."

Exercise 37: (2) Modify **CarBuilder.java** to add another stage to the car-building process, whereby you add the exhaust system, body, and fenders. As with the second stage, assume these processes can be performed simultaneously by robots.

Exercise 38: (3) Using the approach in **CarBuilder.java**, model the house-building story that was given in this chapter.

Performance tuning

A significant number of classes in Java SE5's **java.util.concurrent** library exist to provide performance improvements. When you peruse the **concurrent** library, it can be difficult to discern which classes are intended for regular use (such as **BlockingQueue**s) and which ones are only for improving performance. In this section we will look at some of the issues and classes surrounding performance tuning.

Comparing mutex technologies

Now that Java includes the old **synchronized** keyword along with the new Java SE5 **Lock** and **Atomic** classes, it is interesting to compare the different approaches so that we can understand more about the value of each and where to use them.

The naïve approach is to try a simple test on each approach, like this:

```
//: concurrency/SimpleMicroBenchmark.java
// The dangers of microbenchmarking.
import java.util.concurrent.locks.*;

abstract class Incrementable {
  protected long counter = 0;
  public abstract void increment();
}

class SynchronizingTest extends Incrementable {
  public synchronized void increment() { ++counter; }
}

class LockingTest extends Incrementable {
  private Lock lock = new ReentrantLock();
  public void increment() {
    lock.lock();
    try {
      ++counter;
    } finally {
      lock.unlock();
    }
  }
}

public class SimpleMicroBenchmark {
  static long test(Incrementable incr) {
    long start = System.nanoTime();
    for(long i = 0; i < 10000000L; i++)
      incr.increment();
    return System.nanoTime() - start;
  }
```

```
    public static void main(String[] args) {
        long synchTime = test(new SynchronizingTest());
        long lockTime = test(new LockingTest());
        System.out.printf("synchronized: %1$10d\n", synchTime);
        System.out.printf("Lock:         %1$10d\n", lockTime);
        System.out.printf("Lock/synchronized = %1$.3f",
            (double)lockTime/(double)synchTime);
    }
} /* Output: (75% match)
synchronized:   244919117
Lock:           939098964
Lock/synchronized = 3.834
*///:~
```

You can see from the output that calls to the **synchronized** method appear to be faster than using a **ReentrantLock**. What's happened here?

This example demonstrates the dangers of so-called "microbenchmarking."[23] This term generally refers to performance testing a feature in isolation, out of context. Of course, you must still write tests to verify assertions like "**Lock** is much faster than **synchronized**." But you need an awareness of what's really happening during compilation and run time when you write these kinds of tests.

There are a number of problems with the above example. First and foremost, we will only see the true performance difference if the mutexes are *under contention*, so there must be multiple tasks trying to access the mutexed code sections. In the above example, each mutex is tested by the single **main( )** thread, in isolation.

Secondly, it's possible that the compiler can perform special optimizations when it sees the **synchronized** keyword, and perhaps even notice that this program is single-threaded. The compiler might even identify that the **counter** is simply being incremented a fixed number of times, and just pre-calculate the result. Different compilers and runtime systems vary, so it's hard to know exactly what will happen, but we need to prevent the possibility that the compiler can predict the outcome.

---

[23] Brian Goetz was very helpful in explaining these issues to me. See his article at *www-128.ibm.com/developerworks/library/j-jtp12214* for more about performance measurement.

To create a valid test, we must make the program more complex. First we need multiple tasks, and not just tasks that change internal values, but also tasks that read those values (otherwise the optimizer may recognize that the values are never being used). In addition, the calculation must be complex and unpredictable enough that the compiler will have no chance to perform aggressive optimizations. This will be accomplished by pre-loading a large array of random **int**s (pre-loading to reduce the impact of calls to **Random.nextInt( )** on the main loops) and using those values in a summation:

```
//: concurrency/SynchronizationComparisons.java
// Comparing the performance of explicit Locks
// and Atomics versus the synchronized keyword.
import java.util.concurrent.*;
import java.util.concurrent.atomic.*;
import java.util.concurrent.locks.*;
import java.util.*;
import static net.mindview.util.Print.*;

abstract class Accumulator {
  public static long cycles = 50000L;
  // Number of Modifiers and Readers during each test:
  private static final int N = 4;
  public static ExecutorService exec =
    Executors.newFixedThreadPool(N*2);
  private static CyclicBarrier barrier =
    new CyclicBarrier(N*2 + 1);
  protected volatile int index = 0;
  protected volatile long value = 0;
  protected long duration = 0;
  protected String id = "error";
  protected final static int SIZE = 100000;
  protected static int[] preLoaded = new int[SIZE];
  static { // Load the array of random numbers:
    Random rand = new Random(47);
    for(int i = 0; i < SIZE; i++)
      preLoaded[i] = rand.nextInt();
  }
  public abstract void accumulate();
  public abstract long read();
  private class Modifier implements Runnable {
    public void run() {
      for(long i = 0; i < cycles; i++)
        accumulate();
```

```java
          try {
            barrier.await();
          } catch(Exception e) {
            throw new RuntimeException(e);
          }
        }
      }
    }
    private class Reader implements Runnable {
      private volatile long value;
      public void run() {
        for(long i = 0; i < cycles; i++)
          value = read();
        try {
          barrier.await();
        } catch(Exception e) {
          throw new RuntimeException(e);
        }
      }
    }
    public void timedTest() {
      long start = System.nanoTime();
      for(int i = 0; i < N; i++) {
        exec.execute(new Modifier());
        exec.execute(new Reader());
      }
      try {
        barrier.await();
      } catch(Exception e) {
        throw new RuntimeException(e);
      }
      duration = System.nanoTime() - start;
      printf("%-13s: %13d\n", id, duration);
    }
    public void report(Accumulator acc2) {
      printf("%-22s: %.2f\n", this.id + "/" + acc2.id,
        (double)this.duration/(double)acc2.duration);
    }
  }

  class SynchronizedTest extends Accumulator {
    { id = "synch"; }
    public synchronized void accumulate() {
      value += preLoaded[index++];
      if(index >= SIZE) index = 0;
```

```
    }
  public synchronized long read() {
    return value;
  }
}

class LockTest extends Accumulator {
  { id = "Lock"; }
  private Lock lock = new ReentrantLock();
  public void accumulate() {
    lock.lock();
    try {
      value += preLoaded[index++];
      if(index >= SIZE) index = 0;
    } finally {
      lock.unlock();
    }
  }
  public long read() {
    lock.lock();
    try {
      return value;
    } finally {
      lock.unlock();
    }
  }
}

class AtomicTest extends Accumulator {
  { id = "Atomic"; }
  private AtomicInteger index = new AtomicInteger(0);
  private AtomicLong value = new AtomicLong(0);
  // Relying on more than one Atomic at a time doesn't
  // work, so we still have to synchronize. But it gives
  // a performance indicator:
  public synchronized void accumulate() {
    int i;
    i = index.getAndIncrement();
    value.getAndAdd(preLoaded[i]);
    if(++i >= SIZE)
      index.set(0);
  }
  public synchronized long read() { return value.get(); }
  public void report(Accumulator acc2) {
```

```
        printf("%-22s: %.2f\n", "synch/(Atomic-synch)",
          (double)acc2.duration/
            ((double)this.duration - (double)acc2.duration));
    }
}

public class SynchronizationComparisons {
  static SynchronizedTest synch = new SynchronizedTest();
  static LockTest lock = new LockTest();
  static AtomicTest atomic = new AtomicTest();
  static void test() {
    print("=============================");
    printf("%-12s : %13d\n", "Cycles", Accumulator.cycles);
    synch.timedTest();
    lock.timedTest();
    atomic.timedTest();
    synch.report(lock);
    atomic.report(synch);
  }
  public static void main(String[] args) {
    int iterations = 5; // Default
    if(args.length > 0) // Optionally change iterations
      iterations = new Integer(args[0]);
    // The first time fills the thread pool:
    print("Warmup");
    synch.timedTest();
    // Now the initial test doesn't include the cost
    // of starting the threads for the first time.
    // Produce multiple data points:
    for(int i = 0; i < iterations; i++) {
      test();
      Accumulator.cycles *= 2;
    }
    Accumulator.exec.shutdown();
  }
} /* Output: (Sample) using JDK6u10
Warmup
synch          :    129868038
=============================
Cycles         :        50000
synch          :    126407922
Lock           :     51207369
Atomic         :    141845223
synch/Lock        : 2.47
```

```
synch/(Atomic-synch)   : 8.19
=============================
Cycles          :          100000
synch           :       251174061
Lock            :       105338114
Atomic          :       279503250
synch/Lock             : 2.38
synch/(Atomic-synch)   : 8.87
=============================
Cycles          :          200000
synch           :       508778006
Lock            :       214398402
Atomic          :       574464795
synch/Lock             : 2.37
synch/(Atomic-synch)   : 7.75
=============================
Cycles          :          400000
synch           :      1027003521
Lock            :       428342577
Atomic          :      1115667617
synch/Lock             : 2.40
synch/(Atomic-synch)   : 11.58
=============================
Cycles          :          800000
synch           :      2179255097
Lock            :       877216314
Atomic          :      2371504710
synch/Lock             : 2.48
synch/(Atomic-synch)   : 11.34
*///:~
```

The code you see here, in the sixth printing of the book, is significantly different than the original code in this edition, and therein lies a morality tale about concurrency.

Threading: Always more surprises

I have spent years studying and struggling with concurrency. Just this chapter and the one in *Thinking in C++, Volume 2* each took many months of work. In the process I've learned that you can never believe that a program using shared-memory concurrency (which is what threading uses) is working correctly—you can only discover that it's wrong, but you can never prove that it's right. This is one of the well-know maxims of threading.

However, I've met numerous people who have an impressive amount of confidence in their ability to write correct threaded programs. I occasionally start thinking that I can get it right, too. This program was an example.

When I wrote it, I had a single-CPU machine, but I was able to convince myself that, because of the promises that I thought I understood about the new library tools in Java 5, the program was correct. And it didn't fail on my single-CPU machine.

Fast forward to the sixth printing of the book, and most new machines have at least two cores on them, as did the machine I was using. And I was surprised when it broke, but that's one of the problems. It's not Java's fault; "write once, run everywhere" cannot possibly extend to threading on single vs. multicore machines. It's a fundamental problem with threading. You *can* actually discover some threading problems on a single-CPU machine, but there are other problems that will not appear until you try it on a multi-CPU machine, where your threads are actually running in parallel.

And most important: you can never let yourself become too confident about your programming abilities when it comes to shared-memory concurrency. I would not be surprised if, sometime in the future, someone comes up with a proof to show that shared-memory concurrency programming is only possible in theory, but not in practice. It's the position I've adopted.

Program description

This program uses the *Template Method* design pattern[24] to put all the common code in the base class and isolate all the varying code in the derived-class implementations of **accumulate( )** and **read( )**. In each of the derived classes **SynchronizedTest**, **LockTest**, and **AtomicTest**, you can see how **accumulate( )** and **read( )** express different ways of implementing mutual exclusion.

In this program, tasks are executed via a **FixedThreadPool** in an attempt to keep all the thread creation at the beginning, and prevent any extra cost during the tests. Just to make sure, the initial test is duplicated and the first result is discarded because it includes the initial thread creation.

---

[24] See *Thinking in Patterns* at *www.MindView.net*.

A **CyclicBarrier** is necessary because we want to make sure all the tasks have completed before declaring each test complete.

A **static** clause pre-loads the array of random numbers, before any tests begin. This way, if there is any overhead to generating random numbers, we won't see it during the test.

Each time **accumulate( )** is called, it moves to the next place in the array **preLoaded** (wrapping to the beginning of the array) and adds another randomly generated number to **value**. The multiple **Modifier** and **Reader** tasks provide contention on the **Accumulator** object.

In **AtomicTest**, the situation is too complex to try to use **Atomic** objects— basically, if more than one **Atomic** object is involved, are forced to give up and use more conventional mutexes (the JDK documentation specifically states that using **Atomic** objects only works when the critical updates for an object are confined to a single variable). Thus, you can only rely on a single atomic object, and for consistency with the other tests, there are two. This is one place that the program broke on the dual-core machine in the pre-sixth printings. However, the test is left in place so that you can still get a feel for the performance benefit of **Atomic** objects.

To fix the problem, **accumulate( )** is **synchronized**. **AtomicTest.read( )** is also **synchronized** even though it doesn't have to be because **value.get( )** is a guarded operation and **return** is atomic. By subtracting the **SynchronizedTest** time from the **AtomicTest** time, we might get an indication of how long the un-synchronized **AtomicTest** might be. But the compiler and runtime might also optimize this away, so it's rather a wild guess.

In **main( )**, the **test( )** is run repeatedly and you can decide to ask for more than five repetitions (the default). For each repetition, the number of **test( )** cycles is doubled, so you can see how the different mutexes behave when running for longer and longer times.

As you can see from the output (produced on a modern, dual-core machine using update 10 of JDK6), **Lock** is consistently more efficient than **synchronized**; but that's why **Lock** was created.

Even more interesting is the way JDK6, update 10 differs from Java 5 which produced the original results. In the original results, for the first four iterations, the **synchronized** keyword seemed to be more efficient than using a **Lock** or an **Atomic**. But then a threshold was crossed and **synchronized** became quite inefficient, while **Lock** and **Atomic** seemed to roughly maintain their proportions, and therefore became much more efficient than **synchronized**. Java 6 produces fairly consistent results, which suggests that the compiler and runtime system have been tuned up since Java 5 (which is, in fact, just what Sun said had happened). So that's one more place where uncertainty can arise.

Keep in mind that this program only gives an *indication* of the differences between the various mutex approaches, and the output above only indicates these differences on my particular machine under my particular circumstances. As you can see if you experiment with it, there can be significant shifts in behavior when different numbers of threads are used and when the program is run for longer periods of time. Some hotspot runtime optimizations are not invoked until a program has been running for several minutes, and in the case of server programs, several hours.

That said, it is fairly clear that using **Lock** is usually significantly more efficient than using **synchronized**, and it also appears that the overhead of **synchronized** varies widely, while **Lock**s are relatively consistent.

Does this mean you should never use the **synchronized** keyword? There are two factors to consider: First, in **SynchronizationComparisons.java**, the bodies of the mutexed methods are extremely small. In general, this is a good practice—only mutex the sections that you absolutely must. However, in practice the mutexed sections may be larger than those in the above example, and so the percentage of time in the body will probably be significantly bigger than the overhead of entering and exiting the mutex, and could overwhelm any benefit of speeding up the mutex. Of course, the only way to know is— when you're tuning for performance, no sooner—to try the different approaches and see what impact they have.

Second, it's clear from reading the code in this chapter that the **synchronized** keyword produces much more readable code than the lock-**try/finally**-unlock idiom that **Lock**s require, and that's why this chapter primarily uses the **synchronized** keyword. As I've stated elsewhere in this book, code is read much more than it is written—when programming, it is more important to communicate with other humans than it is to communicate with the computer—and so readability of code is critical. As a result, it makes sense to start with the **synchronized** keyword and only change to **Lock** objects when you are tuning for performance.

Finally, it's nice when you can use the **Atomic** classes in your concurrent program, but be aware that, as we saw in **SynchronizationComparisons.java**, **Atomic** objects are only useful in very simple cases, generally when you only have one **Atomic** object that's being modified and when that object is independent from all other objects. It's safer to start with more traditional mutexing approaches and only attempt to change to **Atomic** later, if performance requirements dictate.

Lock-free containers

As emphasized in the *Holding Your Objects* chapter, containers are a fundamental tool in all programming, and this includes concurrent programming. For this reason, early containers like **Vector** and **Hashtable** had many **synchronized** methods, which caused unacceptable overhead when they were not being used in multithreaded applications. In Java 1.2, the new containers library was unsynchronized, and the **Collections** class was given various **static** "synchronized" decoration methods to synchronize the different types of containers. Although this was an improvement because it gave you a choice about whether you use synchronization with your container, the overhead is still based on **synchronized** locking. Java SE5 has added new containers specifically to increase thread-safe performance, using clever techniques to eliminate locking.

The general strategy behind these lock-free containers is this: Modifications to the containers can happen at the same time that reads are occurring, as long as the readers can only see the results of *completed* modifications. A modification is performed on a separate copy of a portion of the data structure (or sometimes a copy of the whole thing), and this copy is invisible during the modification process. Only when the modification is complete is the modified structure atomically swapped with the "main" data structure, and after that readers will see the modification.

In **CopyOnWriteArrayList**, a write will cause a copy of the entire underlying array to be created. The original array is left in place so that reads can safely occur while the copied array is being modified. When the modification is complete, an atomic operation swaps the new array in so that new reads will see the new information. One of the benefits of **CopyOnWriteArrayList** is that it does not throw **ConcurrentModificationException** when multiple iterators are traversing and modifying the list, so you don't have to write special code to protect against such exceptions, as you've had to do in the past.

CopyOnWriteArraySet uses **CopyOnWriteArrayList** to achieve its lock-free behavior.

ConcurrentHashMap and **ConcurrentLinkedQueue** use similar techniques to allow concurrent reads and writes, but only portions of the container are copied and modified rather than the entire container. However, readers will still not see any modifications before they are complete. **ConcurrentHashMap** doesn't throw **ConcurrentModificationException**s.

Performance issues

As long as you are primarily reading from a lock-free container, it will be much faster than its **synchronized** counterpart because the overhead of acquiring and releasing locks is eliminated. This is still true for a small number of writes to a lock-free container, but it would be interesting to get an idea of what "small" means. This section will produce a rough idea of the performance differences of these containers under different conditions.

I'll start with a generic framework for performing tests on any type of container, including **Map**s. The generic parameter **C** represents the container type:

```
//: concurrency/Tester.java
// Framework to test performance of concurrency containers.
import java.util.concurrent.*;
import net.mindview.util.*;

public abstract class Tester<C> {
  static int testReps = 10;
  static int testCycles = 1000;
  static int containerSize = 1000;
  abstract C containerInitializer();
  abstract void startReadersAndWriters();
  C testContainer;
  String testId;
  int nReaders;
  int nWriters;
  volatile long readResult = 0;
  volatile long readTime = 0;
  volatile long writeTime = 0;
  CountDownLatch endLatch;
  static ExecutorService exec =
    Executors.newCachedThreadPool();
```

```java
    Integer[] writeData;
    Tester(String testId, int nReaders, int nWriters) {
      this.testId = testId + " " +
        nReaders + "r " + nWriters + "w";
      this.nReaders = nReaders;
      this.nWriters = nWriters;
      writeData = Generated.array(Integer.class,
        new RandomGenerator.Integer(), containerSize);
      for(int i = 0; i < testReps; i++) {
        runTest();
        readTime = 0;
        writeTime = 0;
      }
    }
  void runTest() {
    endLatch = new CountDownLatch(nReaders + nWriters);
    testContainer = containerInitializer();
    startReadersAndWriters();
    try {
      endLatch.await();
    } catch(InterruptedException ex) {
      System.out.println("endLatch interrupted");
    }
    System.out.printf("%-27s %14d %14d\n",
      testId, readTime, writeTime);
    if(readTime != 0 && writeTime != 0)
      System.out.printf("%-27s %14d\n",
        "readTime + writeTime =", readTime + writeTime);
  }
  abstract class TestTask implements Runnable {
    abstract void test();
    abstract void putResults();
    long duration;
    public void run() {
      long startTime = System.nanoTime();
      test();
      duration = System.nanoTime() - startTime;
      synchronized(Tester.this) {
        putResults();
      }
      endLatch.countDown();
    }
  }
  public static void initMain(String[] args) {
```

```
        if(args.length > 0)
          testReps = new Integer(args[0]);
        if(args.length > 1)
          testCycles = new Integer(args[1]);
        if(args.length > 2)
          containerSize = new Integer(args[2]);
        System.out.printf("%-27s %14s %14s\n",
          "Type", "Read time", "Write time");
      }
    } ///:~
```

The **abstract** method **containerInitializer( )** returns the initialized container to be tested, which is stored in the field **testContainer**. The other **abstract** method, **startReadersAndWriters( )**, starts the reader and writer tasks that will read and modify the container under test. Different tests are run with varying number of readers and writers to see the effects of lock contention (for the **synchronized** containers) and writes (for the lock-free containers).

The constructor is given various information about the test (the argument identifiers should be self-explanatory), then it calls the **runTest( )** method **repetitions** times. **runTest( )** creates a **CountDownLatch** (so the test can know when all the tasks are complete), initializes the container, then calls **startReadersAndWriters( )** and waits until they all complete.

Each "Reader" or "Writer" class is based on **TestTask**, which measures the duration of its **abstract test( )** method, then calls **putResults( )** inside a **synchronized** block to store the results.

To use this framework (in which you'll recognize the Template Method design pattern), we must inherit from **Tester** for the particular container type we wish to test, and provide appropriate **Reader** and **Writer** classes:

```
//: concurrency/ListComparisons.java
// {Args: 1 10 10} (Fast verification check during build)
// Rough comparison of thread-safe List performance.
import java.util.concurrent.*;
import java.util.*;
import net.mindview.util.*;

abstract class ListTest extends Tester<List<Integer>> {
  ListTest(String testId, int nReaders, int nWriters) {
    super(testId, nReaders, nWriters);
  }
```

```java
  class Reader extends TestTask {
    long result = 0;
    void test() {
      for(long i = 0; i < testCycles; i++)
        for(int index = 0; index < containerSize; index++)
          result += testContainer.get(index);
    }
    void putResults() {
      readResult += result;
      readTime += duration;
    }
  }
  class Writer extends TestTask {
    void test() {
      for(long i = 0; i < testCycles; i++)
        for(int index = 0; index < containerSize; index++)
          testContainer.set(index, writeData[index]);
    }
    void putResults() {
      writeTime += duration;
    }
  }
  void startReadersAndWriters() {
    for(int i = 0; i < nReaders; i++)
      exec.execute(new Reader());
    for(int i = 0; i < nWriters; i++)
      exec.execute(new Writer());
  }
}

class SynchronizedArrayListTest extends ListTest {
  List<Integer> containerInitializer() {
    return Collections.synchronizedList(
      new ArrayList<Integer>(
        new CountingIntegerList(containerSize)));
  }
  SynchronizedArrayListTest(int nReaders, int nWriters) {
    super("Synched ArrayList", nReaders, nWriters);
  }
}

class CopyOnWriteArrayListTest extends ListTest {
  List<Integer> containerInitializer() {
    return new CopyOnWriteArrayList<Integer>(
```

```
        new CountingIntegerList(containerSize));
  }
  CopyOnWriteArrayListTest(int nReaders, int nWriters) {
    super("CopyOnWriteArrayList", nReaders, nWriters);
  }
}

public class ListComparisons {
  public static void main(String[] args) {
    Tester.initMain(args);
    new SynchronizedArrayListTest(10, 0);
    new SynchronizedArrayListTest(9, 1);
    new SynchronizedArrayListTest(5, 5);
    new CopyOnWriteArrayListTest(10, 0);
    new CopyOnWriteArrayListTest(9, 1);
    new CopyOnWriteArrayListTest(5, 5);
    Tester.exec.shutdown();
  }
} /* Output: (Sample)
Type                           Read time        Write time
Synched ArrayList 10r 0w      232158294700               0
Synched ArrayList 9r 1w       198947618203     24918613399
readTime + writeTime =        223866231602
Synched ArrayList 5r 5w       117367305062    132176613508
readTime + writeTime =        249543918570
CopyOnWriteArrayList 10r 0w      758386889               0
CopyOnWriteArrayList 9r 1w       741305671       136145237
readTime + writeTime =           877450908
CopyOnWriteArrayList 5r 5w       212763075     67967464300
readTime + writeTime =          68180227375
*///:~
```

In **ListTest**, the **Reader** and **Writer** classes perform the specific actions for a **List<Integer>**. In **Reader.putResults( )**, the **duration** is stored but so is the **result**, to prevent the calculations from being optimized away. **startReadersAndWriters( )** is then defined to create and execute the specific **Readers** and **Writers**.

Once **ListTest** is created, it must be further inherited to override **containerInitializer( )** to create and initialize the specific test containers.

In **main( )**, you can see variations on the tests with different numbers of readers and writers. You can change the test variables using command-line arguments because of the call to **Tester.initMain(args)**.

The default behavior is to run each test 10 times; this helps stabilize the output, which can change because of JVM activities like hotspot optimization and garbage collection.[25] The sample output that you see has been edited to show only the last iteration from each test. From the output, you can see that a **synchronized ArrayList** has roughly the same performance regardless of the number of readers and writers—readers contend with other readers for locks in the same way that writers do. The **CopyOnWriteArrayList**, however, is dramatically faster when there are no writers, and is still significantly faster when there are five writers. It would appear that you can be fairly liberal with the use of **CopyOnWriteArrayList**; the impact of writing to the list does not appear to overtake the impact of synchronizing the entire list for a while. Of course, you must try the two different approaches in your specific application to know for sure which one is best.

Again, note that this isn't close to being a good benchmark for absolute numbers, and your numbers will almost certainly be different. The goal is just to give you an idea of the relative behaviors of the two types of container.

Since **CopyOnWriteArraySet** uses **CopyOnWriteArrayList**, its behavior will be similar and it doesn't need a separate test here.

Comparing **Map** implementations

We can use the same framework to get a rough idea of the performance of a **synchronized HashMap** compared to a **ConcurrentHashMap**:

```
//: concurrency/MapComparisons.java
// {Args: 1 10 10} (Fast verification check during build)
// Rough comparison of thread-safe Map performance.
import java.util.concurrent.*;
import java.util.*;
import net.mindview.util.*;

abstract class MapTest
extends Tester<Map<Integer,Integer>> {
  MapTest(String testId, int nReaders, int nWriters) {
    super(testId, nReaders, nWriters);
  }
  class Reader extends TestTask {
```

---

[25] For an introduction to benchmarking under the influence of Java's dynamic compilation, see *www-128.ibm.com/developerworks/library/j-jtp12214*.

```java
        long result = 0;
        void test() {
          for(long i = 0; i < testCycles; i++)
            for(int index = 0; index < containerSize; index++)
              result += testContainer.get(index);
        }
        void putResults() {
          readResult += result;
          readTime += duration;
        }
      }
      class Writer extends TestTask {
        void test() {
          for(long i = 0; i < testCycles; i++)
            for(int index = 0; index < containerSize; index++)
              testContainer.put(index, writeData[index]);
        }
        void putResults() {
          writeTime += duration;
        }
      }
      void startReadersAndWriters() {
        for(int i = 0; i < nReaders; i++)
          exec.execute(new Reader());
        for(int i = 0; i < nWriters; i++)
          exec.execute(new Writer());
      }
    }

    class SynchronizedHashMapTest extends MapTest {
      Map<Integer,Integer> containerInitializer() {
        return Collections.synchronizedMap(
          new HashMap<Integer,Integer>(
            MapData.map(
              new CountingGenerator.Integer(),
              new CountingGenerator.Integer(),
              containerSize)));
      }
      SynchronizedHashMapTest(int nReaders, int nWriters) {
        super("Synched HashMap", nReaders, nWriters);
      }
    }

    class ConcurrentHashMapTest extends MapTest {
```

```
  Map<Integer,Integer> containerInitializer() {
    return new ConcurrentHashMap<Integer,Integer>(
      MapData.map(
        new CountingGenerator.Integer(),
        new CountingGenerator.Integer(), containerSize));
  }
  ConcurrentHashMapTest(int nReaders, int nWriters) {
    super("ConcurrentHashMap", nReaders, nWriters);
  }
}

public class MapComparisons {
  public static void main(String[] args) {
    Tester.initMain(args);
    new SynchronizedHashMapTest(10, 0);
    new SynchronizedHashMapTest(9, 1);
    new SynchronizedHashMapTest(5, 5);
    new ConcurrentHashMapTest(10, 0);
    new ConcurrentHashMapTest(9, 1);
    new ConcurrentHashMapTest(5, 5);
    Tester.exec.shutdown();
  }
} /* Output: (Sample)
Type                           Read time       Write time
Synched HashMap 10r 0w        306052025049              0
Synched HashMap 9r 1w         428319156207    47697347568
readTime + writeTime =        476016503775
Synched HashMap 5r 5w         243956877760   244012003202
readTime + writeTime =        487968880962
ConcurrentHashMap 10r 0w       23352654318              0
ConcurrentHashMap 9r 1w        18833089400     1541853224
readTime + writeTime =         20374942624
ConcurrentHashMap 5r 5w        12037625732    11850489099
readTime + writeTime =         23888114831
*///:~
```

The impact of adding writers to a **ConcurrentHashMap** is even less
evident than for a **CopyOnWriteArrayList**, but the
ConcurrentHashMap uses a different technique that clearly minimizes the
impact of writes.

Optimistic locking

Although **Atomic** objects perform atomic operations like **decrementAndGet( )**, some **Atomic** classes also allow you to perform what is called "optimistic locking." This means that you do not actually use a mutex when you are performing a calculation, but after the calculation is finished and you're ready to update the **Atomic** object, you use a method called **compareAndSet( )**. You hand it the old value and the new value, and if the old value doesn't agree with the value it finds in the **Atomic** object, the operation fails—this means that some other task has modified the object in the meantime. Remember that we would ordinarily use a mutex (**synchronized** or **Lock**) to prevent more than one task modifying an object at the same time, but here we are "optimistic" by leaving the data unlocked and hoping that no other task comes along and modifies it. Again, all this is done in the name of performance—by using an **Atomic** instead of **synchronized** or **Lock**, you might gain performance benefits.

What happens if the **compareAndSet( )** operation fails? This is where it gets tricky, and where you are limited in applying this technique only to problems that can be molded to the requirements. If **compareAndSet( )** fails, you must decide what to do; this is very important because if you can't do something to recover, then you cannot use this technique and must use conventional mutexes instead. Perhaps you can retry the operation and it will be OK if you get it the second time. Or perhaps it's OK just to ignore the failure—in some simulations, if a data point is lost, it will eventually be made up in the grand scheme of things (of course, you must understand your model well enough to know whether this is true).

Consider a fictitious simulation that consists of 100,000 "genes" of length 30; perhaps this is the beginning of some kind of genetic algorithm. Suppose that for each "evolution" of the genetic algorithm, some very expensive calculations take place, so you decide to use a multiprocessor machine to distribute the tasks and improve performance. In addition, you use **Atomic** objects instead of **Lock** objects to prevent mutex overhead. (Naturally, you only produced this solution after first writing the code in the simplest way that could possibly work, using the **synchronized** keyword. Once you had the program running, only then did you discover that it was too slow, and begin applying performance techniques!) Because of the nature of your model, if there's a collision during a calculation, the task that discovers the collision can just ignore it and not update its value. Here's what it looks like:

```
//: concurrency/FastSimulation.java
import java.util.concurrent.*;
import java.util.concurrent.atomic.*;
import java.util.*;
import static net.mindview.util.Print.*;

public class FastSimulation {
  static final int N_ELEMENTS = 100000;
  static final int N_GENES = 30;
  static final int N_EVOLVERS = 50;
  static final AtomicInteger[][] GRID =
    new AtomicInteger[N_ELEMENTS][N_GENES];
  static Random rand = new Random(47);
  static class Evolver implements Runnable {
    public void run() {
      while(!Thread.interrupted()) {
        // Randomly select an element to work on:
        int element = rand.nextInt(N_ELEMENTS);
        for(int i = 0; i < N_GENES; i++) {
          int previous = element - 1;
          if(previous < 0) previous = N_ELEMENTS - 1;
          int next = element + 1;
          if(next >= N_ELEMENTS) next = 0;
          int oldvalue = GRID[element][i].get();
          // Perform some kind of modeling calculation:
          int newvalue = oldvalue +
            GRID[previous][i].get() + GRID[next][i].get();
          newvalue /= 3; // Average the three values
          if(!GRID[element][i]
            .compareAndSet(oldvalue, newvalue)) {
            // Policy here to deal with failure. Here, we
            // just report it and ignore it; our model
            // will eventually deal with it.
            print("Old value changed from " + oldvalue);
          }
        }
      }
    }
  }
  public static void main(String[] args) throws Exception {
    ExecutorService exec = Executors.newCachedThreadPool();
    for(int i = 0; i < N_ELEMENTS; i++)
      for(int j = 0; j < N_GENES; j++)
        GRID[i][j] = new AtomicInteger(rand.nextInt(1000));
```

```
      for(int i = 0; i < N_EVOLVERS; i++)
        exec.execute(new Evolver());
      TimeUnit.SECONDS.sleep(5);
      exec.shutdownNow();
  }
} /* (Execute to see output) *///:~
```

The elements are all placed inside an array with the assumption that this will help performance (this assumption will be tested in an exercise). Each **Evolver** object averages its value with the one before and after it, and if there's a failure when it goes to update, it simply prints the value and goes on. Note that no mutexes appear in the program.

Exercise 39: (6) Does **FastSimulation.java** make reasonable assumptions? Try changing the array to ordinary **int**s instead of **AtomicInteger** and using **Lock** mutexes. Compare the performance between the two versions of the program.

ReadWriteLocks

ReadWriteLocks optimize the situation where you write to a data structure relatively infrequently, but multiple tasks read from it often. The **ReadWriteLock** allows you to have many readers at one time as long as no one is attempting to write. If the write lock is held, then no readers are allowed until the write lock is released.

It's completely uncertain whether a **ReadWriteLock** will improve the performance of your program, and it depends on issues like how often data is being read compared to how often it is being modified, the time of the read and write operations (the lock is more complex, so short operations will not see the benefits), how much thread contention there is, and whether you are running on a multiprocessor machine. Ultimately, the only way to know whether a **ReadWriteLock** will benefit your program is to try it out.

Here's an example showing only the most basic use of **ReadWriteLock**s:

```
//: concurrency/ReaderWriterList.java
import java.util.concurrent.*;
import java.util.concurrent.locks.*;
import java.util.*;
import static net.mindview.util.Print.*;

public class ReaderWriterList<T> {
  private ArrayList<T> lockedList;
```

```
   // Make the ordering fair:
   private ReentrantReadWriteLock lock =
     new ReentrantReadWriteLock(true);
   public ReaderWriterList(int size, T initialValue) {
     lockedList = new ArrayList<T>(
       Collections.nCopies(size, initialValue));
   }
   public T set(int index, T element) {
     Lock wlock = lock.writeLock();
     wlock.lock();
     try {
       return lockedList.set(index, element);
     } finally {
       wlock.unlock();
     }
   }
   public T get(int index) {
     Lock rlock = lock.readLock();
     rlock.lock();
     try {
       // Show that multiple readers
       // may acquire the read lock:
       if(lock.getReadLockCount() > 1)
         print(lock.getReadLockCount());
       return lockedList.get(index);
     } finally {
       rlock.unlock();
     }
   }
   public static void main(String[] args) throws Exception {
     new ReaderWriterListTest(30, 1);
   }
}

class ReaderWriterListTest {
   ExecutorService exec = Executors.newCachedThreadPool();
   private final static int SIZE = 100;
   private static Random rand = new Random(47);
   private ReaderWriterList<Integer> list =
     new ReaderWriterList<Integer>(SIZE, 0);
   private class Writer implements Runnable {
     public void run() {
       try {
         for(int i = 0; i < 20; i++) { // 2 second test
```

```
          list.set(i, rand.nextInt());
          TimeUnit.MILLISECONDS.sleep(100);
        }
      } catch(InterruptedException e) {
        // Acceptable way to exit
      }
      print("Writer finished, shutting down");
      exec.shutdownNow();
    }
  }
  private class Reader implements Runnable {
    public void run() {
      try {
        while(!Thread.interrupted()) {
          for(int i = 0; i < SIZE; i++) {
            list.get(i);
            TimeUnit.MILLISECONDS.sleep(1);
          }
        }
      } catch(InterruptedException e) {
        // Acceptable way to exit
      }
    }
  }
  public ReaderWriterListTest(int readers, int writers) {
    for(int i = 0; i < readers; i++)
      exec.execute(new Reader());
    for(int i = 0; i < writers; i++)
      exec.execute(new Writer());
  }
} /* (Execute to see output) *///:~
```

A **ReaderWriterList** can hold a fixed number of any type. You must give
the constructor the desired size of the list and an initial object to populate the
list with. The **set( )** method acquires the write lock in order to call the
underlying **ArrayList.set( )**, and the **get( )** method acquires the read lock
in order to call **ArrayList.get( )**. In addition, **get( )** checks to see if more
than one reader has acquired the read lock and, if so, displays that number to
demonstrate that multiple readers may acquire the read lock.

To test the **ReaderWriterList**, **ReaderWriterListTest** creates both
reader and writer tasks for a **ReaderWriterList<Integer>**. Notice that
there are far fewer writes than reads.

If you look at the JDK documentation for **ReentrantReadWriteLock**, you'll see that there are a number of other methods available, as well as issues of "fairness" and "policy decisions." This is a rather sophisticated tool, and one to use only when you are casting about for ways to improve performance. Your first draft of your program should use straightforward synchronization, and only if necessary should you introduce **ReadWriteLock**.

Exercise 40: (6) Following the example of **ReaderWriterList.java**, create a **ReaderWriterMap** using a **HashMap**. Investigate its performance by modifying **MapComparisons.java**. How does it compare to a **synchronized HashMap** and a **ConcurrentHashMap**?

Active objects

After working your way through this chapter, you may observe that threading in Java seems very complex and difficult to use correctly. In addition, it can seem a bit counterproductive—although tasks work in parallel, you must invest great effort to implement techniques that prevent those tasks from interfering with each other.

If you've ever written assembly language, writing threaded programs has a similar feel: Every detail matters, you're responsible for everything, and there's no safety net in the form of compiler checking.

Could there be a problem with the threading model itself? After all, it comes relatively unchanged from the world of procedural programming. Perhaps there is a different model for concurrency that is a better fit for object-oriented programming.

One alternative approach is called *active objects* or *actors*.[26] The reason the objects are called "active" is that each object maintains its own worker thread and message queue, and all requests to that object are enqueued, to be run one at a time. So with active objects, we *serialize messages rather than methods*, which means we no longer need to guard against problems that happen when a task is interrupted midway through its loop.

When you send a message to an active object, that message is transformed into a task that goes on the object's queue to be run at some later point. The

---

[26] Thanks to Allen Holub for taking the time to explain this to me.

Java SE5 **Future** comes in handy for implementing this scheme. Here's a simple example that has two methods which enqueue method calls:

```
//: concurrency/ActiveObjectDemo.java
// Can only pass constants, immutables, "disconnected
// objects," or other active objects as arguments
// to asynch methods.
import java.util.concurrent.*;
import java.util.*;
import static net.mindview.util.Print.*;

public class ActiveObjectDemo {
  private ExecutorService ex =
    Executors.newSingleThreadExecutor();
  private Random rand = new Random(47);
  // Insert a random delay to produce the effect
  // of a calculation time:
  private void pause(int factor) {
    try {
      TimeUnit.MILLISECONDS.sleep(
        100 + rand.nextInt(factor));
    } catch(InterruptedException e) {
      print("sleep() interrupted");
    }
  }
  public Future<Integer>
  calculateInt(final int x, final int y) {
    return ex.submit(new Callable<Integer>() {
      public Integer call() {
        print("starting " + x + " + " + y);
        pause(500);
        return x + y;
      }
    });
  }
  public Future<Float>
  calculateFloat(final float x, final float y) {
    return ex.submit(new Callable<Float>() {
      public Float call() {
        print("starting " + x + " + " + y);
        pause(2000);
        return x + y;
      }
    });
```

```java
    }
    public void shutdown() { ex.shutdown(); }
    public static void main(String[] args) {
      ActiveObjectDemo d1 = new ActiveObjectDemo();
      // Prevents ConcurrentModificationException:
      List<Future<?>> results =
        new CopyOnWriteArrayList<Future<?>>();
      for(float f = 0.0f; f < 1.0f; f += 0.2f)
        results.add(d1.calculateFloat(f, f));
      for(int i = 0; i < 5; i++)
        results.add(d1.calculateInt(i, i));
      print("All asynch calls made");
      while(results.size() > 0) {
        for(Future<?> f : results)
          if(f.isDone()) {
            try {
              print(f.get());
            } catch(Exception e) {
              throw new RuntimeException(e);
            }
            results.remove(f);
          }
      }
      d1.shutdown();
    }
} /* Output: (85% match)
All asynch calls made
starting 0.0 + 0.0
starting 0.2 + 0.2
0.0
starting 0.4 + 0.4
0.4
starting 0.6 + 0.6
0.8
starting 0.8 + 0.8
1.2
starting 0 + 0
1.6
starting 1 + 1
0
starting 2 + 2
2
starting 3 + 3
4
```

```
starting 4 + 4
6
8
*///:~
```

The "single thread executor" produced by the call to
Executors.newSingleThreadExecutor( ) maintains its own unbounded
blocking queue, and has only one thread taking tasks off the queue and
running them to completion. All we need to do in **calculateInt( )** and
calculateFloat( ) is to **submit( )** a new **Callable** object in response to a
method call, thus converting method calls into messages. The method body is
contained within the **call( )** method in the anonymous inner class. Notice
that the return value of each active object method is a **Future** with a generic
parameter that is the actual return type of the method. This way, the method
call returns almost immediately, and the caller uses the **Future** to discover
when the task completes and to collect the actual return value. This handles
the most complex case, but if the call has no return value, then the process is
simplified.

In **main( )**, a **List<Future<?>>** is created to capture the **Future** objects
returned by the **calculateFloat( )** and **calculateInt( )** messages sent to the
active object. This list is polled using **isDone( )** for each **Future**, which is
removed from the **List** when it completes and its results are processed.
Notice that the use of **CopyOnWriteArrayList** removes the need to copy
the **List** in order to prevent **ConcurrentModificationException**s.

In order to inadvertently prevent coupling between threads, any arguments to
pass to an active-object method call must be either read-only, other active
objects, or *disconnected objects* (my term), which are objects that have no
connection to any other task (this is hard to enforce because there's no
language support for it).

With active objects:

1. Each object has its own worker thread.

2. Each object maintains total control of its own fields (which is somewhat
    more rigorous than normal classes, which only have the *option* of
    guarding their fields).

3. All communication between active objects happens in the form of
    messages between those objects.

---

4. All messages between active objects are enqueued.

The results are quite compelling. Since a message from one active object to another can only be blocked by the delay in enqueuing it, and because that delay is always very short and is not dependent on any other objects, the sending of a message is effectively unblockable (the worst that will happen is a short delay). Since an active-object system only communicates via messages, two objects cannot be blocked while contending to call a method on another object, and this means that deadlock cannot occur, which is a big step forward. Because the worker thread within an active object only executes one message at a time, there is no resource contention and you don't have to worry about synchronizing methods. Synchronization still happens, but it happens on the message level, by enqueuing the method calls so that only one can happen at a time.

Unfortunately, without direct compiler support, the coding approach shown above is too cumbersome. However, progress is occurring in the field of active objects and actors, and more interestingly, in the field called *agent-based* programming. Agents are effectively active objects, but agent systems also support transparency across networks and machines. It would not surprise me if agent-based programming becomes the eventual successor to object-oriented programming, because it combines objects with a relatively easy concurrency solution.

You can find more information about active objects, actors and agents by searching the Web. In particular, some of the ideas behind active objects come from C.A.R. Hoare's *theory of Communicating Sequential Processes* (CSP).

Exercise 41: (6) Add a message handler to **ActiveObjectDemo.java** that has no return value, and call this within **main( )**.

Exercise 42: (7) Modify **WaxOMatic.java** so that it implements active objects.

Project:[27] Use annotations and Javassist to create a class annotation **@Active** that transforms the target class into an active object.

---

[27] Projects are suggestions to be used (for example) as term projects. Solutions to projects are not included in the solution guide.

Summary

The goal of this chapter was to give you the foundations of concurrent programming with Java threads, so that you understand that:

1. You can run multiple independent tasks.

2. You must consider all the possible problems when these tasks shut down.

3. Tasks can interfere with each other over shared resources. The mutex (lock) is the basic tool used to prevent these collisions.

4. Tasks can deadlock if they are not carefully designed.

It is vital to learn when to use concurrency and when to avoid it. The main reasons to use it are:

- To manage a number of tasks whose intermingling will use the computer more efficiently (including the ability to transparently distribute the tasks across multiple CPUs).

- To allow better code organization.

- To be more convenient for the user.

The classic example of resource balancing is to use the CPU during I/O waits. Better code organization is typically seen in simulations. The classic example of user convenience is to monitor a "stop" button during long downloads.

An additional advantage to threads is that they provide "light" execution context switches (on the order of 100 instructions) rather than "heavy" process context switches (thousands of instructions). Since all threads in a given process share the same memory space, a light context switch changes only program execution and local variables. A process change—the heavy context switch—must exchange the full memory space.

The main drawbacks to multithreading are:

1. Slowdown occurs while threads are waiting for shared resources.

2. Additional CPU overhead is required to manage threads.

3. Unrewarded complexity arises from poor design decisions.

4. Opportunities are created for pathologies such as starving, racing, deadlock, and livelock (multiple threads working individual tasks that the ensemble can't finish).

5. Inconsistencies occur across platforms. For instance, while developing some of the examples for this book, I discovered race conditions that quickly appeared on some computers but that wouldn't appear on others. If you develop a program on the latter, you might get badly surprised when you distribute it.

One of the biggest difficulties with threads occurs because more than one task might be sharing a resource—such as the memory in an object—and you must make sure that multiple tasks don't try to read and change that resource at the same time. This requires judicious use of the available locking mechanisms (for example, the **synchronized** keyword). These are essential tools, but they must be understood thoroughly because they can quietly introduce deadlock situations.

In addition, there's an art to the application of threads. Java is designed to allow you to create as many objects as you need to solve your problem—at least in theory. (Creating millions of objects for an engineering finite-element analysis, for example, might not be practical in Java without the use of the *Flyweight* design pattern.) However, it seems that there is an upper bound to the number of threads you'll want to create, because at some number, threads seem to become balky. This critical point can be hard to detect and will often depend on the OS and JVM; it can be less than a hundred or in the thousands. As you will often create only a handful of threads to solve a problem, this is typically not much of a limit, but in a more general design it becomes a constraint that might force you to add a cooperative concurrency scheme.

Regardless of how simple threading can seem using a particular language or library, consider it a black art. There's always something that can bite you when you least expect it. The reason that the dining philosophers problem is interesting is that it can be adjusted so that deadlock rarely happens, giving you the impression that everything is copacetic.

In general, use threading carefully and sparingly. If your threading issues get large and complex, consider using a language like *Erlang*. This is one of several *functional* languages that are specialized for threading. It may be possible to use such a language for the portions of your program that demand threading, if you are doing lots of it, and if it's complicated enough to justify this approach.

Further reading

Unfortunately, there is a lot of misleading information about concurrency—this emphasizes how confusing it can be, and how easy it is to think that you understand the issues (I know, because I've been under the impression that I've understood threading numerous times in the past, and I have no doubt that there will be more epiphanies for me in the future). There's always a bit of sleuthing required when you pick up a new document about concurrency, to try to understand how much the writer does and doesn't understand. Here are some books that I think I can safely say are reliable:

Java Concurrency in Practice, by Brian Goetz, Tim Peierls, Joshua Bloch, Joseph Bowbeer, David Holmes, and Doug Lea (Addison-Wesley, 2006). Basically, the "who's who" in the Java threading world.

Concurrent Programming in Java, Second Edition, by Doug Lea (Addison-Wesley, 2000). Although this book significantly predates Java SE5, much of Doug's work became the new **java.util.concurrent** libraries, so this book is essential for a complete understanding of concurrency issues. It goes beyond Java concurrency and discusses current thinking across languages and technologies. Although it can be obtuse in places, it merits rereading several times (preferably with months in between in order to internalize the information). Doug is one of the few people in the world who actually understand concurrency, so this is a worthwhile endeavor.

The Java Language Specification, Third Edition (Chapter 17), by Gosling, Joy, Steele, and Bracha (Addison-Wesley, 2005). The technical specification, conveniently available as an electronic document: *http://java.sun.com/docs/books/jls*.

Solutions to selected exercises can be found in the electronic document *The Thinking in Java Annotated Solution Guide*, available for sale from *www.MindView.net*.

Graphical User Interfaces

A fundamental design guideline is "Make simple things easy, and difficult things possible."[1]

The original design goal of the graphical user interface (GUI) library in Java 1.0 was to allow the programmer to build a GUI that looks good on all platforms. That goal was not achieved. Instead, the Java 1.0 *Abstract Windowing Toolkit* (AWT) produced a GUI that looked equally mediocre on all systems. In addition, it was restrictive; you could use only four fonts and you couldn't access any of the more sophisticated GUI elements that exist in your operating system. The Java 1.0 AWT programming model was also awkward and non-object-oriented. A student in one of my seminars (who had been at Sun during the creation of Java) explained why: The original AWT had been conceived, designed, and implemented in a month. Certainly a marvel of productivity, and also an object lesson in why design is important.

The situation improved with the Java 1.1 AWT event model, which takes a much clearer, object-oriented approach, along with the addition of JavaBeans, a component programming model that is oriented toward the easy creation of visual programming environments. Java 2 (JDK 1.2) finished the transformation away from the old Java 1.0 AWT by essentially replacing everything with the *Java Foundation Classes* (JFC), the GUI portion of which is called "Swing." These are a rich set of easy-to-use, easy-to-understand JavaBeans that can be dragged and dropped (as well as hand programmed) to create a reasonable GUI. The "revision 3" rule of the software industry (a product isn't good until revision 3) seems to hold true with programming languages as well.

---

[1] A variation on this is called "the principle of least astonishment," which essentially says, "Don't surprise the user."

This chapter introduces the modern Java Swing library and makes the reasonable assumption that Swing is Sun's final destination GUI library for Java.[2] If for some reason you need to use the original "old" AWT (because you're supporting old code or you have browser limitations), you can find that introduction in the 1st edition of this book, downloadable at *www.MindView.net*. Note that some AWT components remain in Java, and in some situations you must use them.

Please be aware that this is not a comprehensive glossary of either all the Swing components or all the methods for the described classes. What you see here is intended to be a simple introduction. The Swing library is vast, and the goal of this chapter is only to get you started with the essentials and comfortable with the concepts. If you need to do more than what you see here, then Swing can probably give you what you want if you're willing to do the research.

I assume here that you have downloaded and installed the JDK documentation from *http://java.sun.com* and will browse the **javax.swing** classes in that documentation to see the full details and methods of the Swing library. You can also search the Web, but the best place to start is Sun's own Swing Tutorial at *http://java.sun.com/docs/books/tutorial/uiswing*.

There are numerous (rather thick) books dedicated solely to Swing, and you'll want to go to those if you need more depth, or if you want to modify the default Swing behavior.

As you learn about Swing, you'll discover:

1.   Swing is a much improved programming model compared to many other languages and development environments (not to suggest that it's perfect, but a step forward on the path). JavaBeans (introduced toward the end of this chapter) is the framework for that library.

2.   "GUI builders" (visual programming environments) are a *de rigueur* aspect of a complete Java development environment. JavaBeans and Swing allow the GUI builder to write code for you

---

[2] Note that IBM created a new open-source GUI library for their Eclipse editor (*www.Eclipse.org*), which you may want to consider as an alternative to Swing. This will be introduced later in the chapter.

as you place components onto forms using graphical tools. This rapidly speeds development during GUI building, and also allows for greater experimentation and thus the ability to try out more designs and presumably come up with better ones.

3. Because Swing is reasonably straightforward, even if you do use a GUI builder rather than coding by hand, the resulting code should still be comprehensible. This solves a big problem with GUI builders from the past, which could easily generate unreadable code.

Swing contains all the components that you expect to see in a modern UI: everything from buttons that contain pictures to trees and tables. It's a big library, but it's designed to have appropriate complexity for the task at hand; if something is simple, you don't have to write much code, but as you try to do more complex things, your code becomes proportionally more complex.

Much of what you'll like about Swing might be called "orthogonality of use." That is, once you pick up the general ideas about the library, you can usually apply them everywhere. Primarily because of the standard naming conventions, while I was writing these examples I could usually guess successfully at the method names. This is certainly a hallmark of good library design. In addition, you can generally plug components into other components and things will work correctly.

Keyboard navigation is automatic; you can run a Swing application without using the mouse, and this doesn't require any extra programming. Scrolling support is effortless; you simply wrap your component in a **JScrollPane** as you add it to your form. Features such as tool tips typically require a single line of code to use.

For portability, Swing is written entirely in Java.

Swing also supports a rather radical feature called "pluggable look and feel," which means that the appearance of the UI can be dynamically changed to suit the expectations of users working under different platforms and operating systems. It's even possible (albeit difficult) to invent your own look and feel. You can find some of these on the Web.[3]

Despite all of its positive aspects, Swing is not for everyone nor has it solved all the user interface problems that its designers intended. At the end of the chapter, we'll look at two alternative solutions to Swing: the IBM-sponsored SWT, developed for the Eclipse editor but freely available as an open-source, standalone GUI library, and Macromedia's Flex tool for developing Flash client-side front ends for Web applications.

Applets

When Java first appeared, much of the brouhaha around the language came from the *applet*, a program that can be delivered across the Internet to run (inside a so-called *sandbox*, for security) in a Web browser. People foresaw the Java applet as the next stage in the evolution of the Internet, and many of the original books on Java assumed that the reason you were interested in the language was that you wanted to write applets.

For various reasons, this revolution never happened. A large part of the problem was that most machines don't include the necessary Java software to run applets, and downloading and installing a 10 MB package in order to run something you've casually encountered on the Web is not something most users are willing to do. Many users are even frightened by the idea. Java applets as a client-side application delivery system never achieved critical mass, and although you will still occasionally see an applet, they have generally been relegated to the backwaters of computing.

This doesn't mean that applets are not an interesting and valuable technology. If you are in a situation where you can ensure that users have a JRE installed (such as inside a corporate environment), then applets (or JNLP/Java Web Start, described later in this chapter) might be the perfect way to distribute client programs and automatically update everyone's machine without the usual cost and effort of distributing and installing new software.

---

[3] My favorite example of this is Ken Arnold's "Napkin" look and feel, which makes the windows look like they were scribbled on a napkin. See *http://napkinlaf.sourceforge.net*.

You'll find an introduction to the technology of applets in the online supplements to this book at *www.MindView.net*.

Swing basics

Most Swing applications will be built inside a basic **JFrame**, which creates the window in whatever operating system you're using. The title of the window can be set using the **JFrame** constructor, like this:

```
//: gui/HelloSwing.java
import javax.swing.*;

public class HelloSwing {
  public static void main(String[] args) {
    JFrame frame = new JFrame("Hello Swing");
    frame.setDefaultCloseOperation(JFrame.EXIT_ON_CLOSE);
    frame.setSize(300, 100);
    frame.setVisible(true);
  }
} ///:~
```

setDefaultCloseOperation( ) tells the **JFrame** what to do when the user executes a shutdown maneuver. The **EXIT_ON_CLOSE** constant tells it to exit the program. Without this call, the default behavior is to do nothing, so the application wouldn't close.

setSize( ) sets the size of the window in pixels.

Notice the last line:

```
frame.setVisible(true);
```

Without this, you won't see anything on the screen.

We can make things a little more interesting by adding a **JLabel** to the **JFrame**:

```
//: gui/HelloLabel.java
import javax.swing.*;
import java.util.concurrent.*;

public class HelloLabel {
  public static void main(String[] args) throws Exception {
    JFrame frame = new JFrame("Hello Swing");
    JLabel label = new JLabel("A Label");
```

```
    frame.add(label);
    frame.setDefaultCloseOperation(JFrame.EXIT_ON_CLOSE);
    frame.setSize(300, 100);
    frame.setVisible(true);
    TimeUnit.SECONDS.sleep(1);
    label.setText("Hey! This is Different!");
  }
} ///:~
```

After one second, the text of the **JLabel** changes. While this is entertaining and safe for such a trivial program, it's really not a good idea for the **main( )** thread to write directly to the GUI components. Swing has its own thread dedicated to receiving UI events and updating the screen. If you start manipulating the screen with other threads, you can have the collisions and deadlock described in the *Concurrency* chapter.

Instead, other threads—like **main( )**, here—should submit tasks to be executed by the Swing *event dispatch thread*.[4] You do this by handing a task to **SwingUtilities.invokeLater( )**, which puts it on the *event queue* to be (eventually) executed by the event dispatch thread. If we do this with the previous example, it looks like this:

```
//: gui/SubmitLabelManipulationTask.java
import javax.swing.*;
import java.util.concurrent.*;

public class SubmitLabelManipulationTask {
  public static void main(String[] args) throws Exception {
    JFrame frame = new JFrame("Hello Swing");
    final JLabel label = new JLabel("A Label");
    frame.add(label);
    frame.setDefaultCloseOperation(JFrame.EXIT_ON_CLOSE);
    frame.setSize(300, 100);
    frame.setVisible(true);
    TimeUnit.SECONDS.sleep(1);
    SwingUtilities.invokeLater(new Runnable() {
      public void run() {
        label.setText("Hey! This is Different!");
      }
    });
```

---

[4] Technically, the event dispatch thread comes from the AWT library.

```
    }
} ///:~
```

Now you are no longer manipulating the **JLabel** directly. Instead, you submit a **Runnable**, and the event dispatch thread will do the actual manipulation, when it gets to that task in the event queue. And when it's executing this **Runnable**, it's not doing anything else, so there won't be any collisions—*if* all the code in your program follows this approach of submitting manipulations through **SwingUtilities.invokeLater( )**. This includes starting the program itself—**main( )** should not call the Swing methods as it does in the above program, but instead should submit a task to the event queue.[5] So the properly written program will look something like this:

```
//: gui/SubmitSwingProgram.java
import javax.swing.*;
import java.util.concurrent.*;

public class SubmitSwingProgram extends JFrame {
  JLabel label;
  public SubmitSwingProgram() {
    super("Hello Swing");
    label = new JLabel("A Label");
    add(label);
    setDefaultCloseOperation(JFrame.EXIT_ON_CLOSE);
    setSize(300, 100);
    setVisible(true);
  }
  static SubmitSwingProgram ssp;
  public static void main(String[] args) throws Exception {
    SwingUtilities.invokeLater(new Runnable() {
      public void run() { ssp = new SubmitSwingProgram(); }
    });
    TimeUnit.SECONDS.sleep(1);
    SwingUtilities.invokeLater(new Runnable() {
      public void run() {
        ssp.label.setText("Hey! This is Different!");
      }
    });
  }
```

---

[5] This practice was added in Java SE5, so you will see lots of older programs that don't do it. That doesn't mean the authors were ignorant. The suggested practices seem to be constantly evolving.

```
} ///:~
```

Notice that the call to **sleep( )** is *not* inside the constructor. If you put it there, the original **JLabel** text never appears, for one thing, because the constructor doesn't complete until after the **sleep( )** finishes and the new label is inserted. But if **sleep( )** is inside the constructor, or inside any UI operation, it means that you're halting the event dispatch thread during the **sleep( )**, which is generally a bad idea.

Exercise 1: (1) Modify **HelloSwing.java** to prove to yourself that the application will not close without the call to **setDefaultCloseOperation( )**.

Exercise 2: (2) Modify **HelloLabel.java** to show that label addition is dynamic, by adding a random number of labels.

A display framework

We can combine the ideas above and reduce redundant code by creating a display framework for use in the Swing examples in the rest of this chapter:

```
//: net/mindview/util/SwingConsole.java
// Tool for running Swing demos from the
// console, both applets and JFrames.
package net.mindview.util;
import javax.swing.*;

public class SwingConsole {
  public static void
  run(final JFrame f, final int width, final int height) {
    SwingUtilities.invokeLater(new Runnable() {
      public void run() {
        f.setTitle(f.getClass().getSimpleName());
        f.setDefaultCloseOperation(JFrame.EXIT_ON_CLOSE);
        f.setSize(width, height);
        f.setVisible(true);
      }
    });
  }
} ///:~
```

This is a tool you may want to use yourself, so it's placed in the library **net.mindview.util**. To use it, your application must be in a **JFrame** (which all the examples in this book are). The **static run( )** method sets the title of the window to the simple class name of the **JFrame**.

Exercise 3: (3) Modify **SubmitSwingProgram.java** so that it uses **SwingConsole**.

Making a button

Making a button is quite simple: You just call the **JButton** constructor with the label you want on the button. You'll see later that you can do fancier things, like putting graphic images on buttons.

Usually, you'll want to create a field for the button inside your class so that you can refer to it later.

The **JButton** is a component—its own little window—that will automatically get repainted as part of an update. This means that you don't explicitly paint a button or any other kind of control; you simply place them on the form and let them automatically take care of painting themselves. You'll usually place a button on a form inside the constructor:

```
//: gui/Button1.java
// Putting buttons on a Swing application.
import javax.swing.*;
import java.awt.*;
import static net.mindview.util.SwingConsole.*;

public class Button1 extends JFrame {
  private JButton
    b1 = new JButton("Button 1"),
    b2 = new JButton("Button 2");
  public Button1() {
    setLayout(new FlowLayout());
    add(b1);
    add(b2);
  }
  public static void main(String[] args) {
    run(new Button1(), 200, 100);
  }
} ///:~
```

Something new has been added here: Before any elements are placed on the **JFrame**, it is given a "layout manager," of type **FlowLayout**. The layout manager is the way that the pane implicitly decides where to place controls on a form. The normal behavior of a **JFrame** is to use the **BorderLayout**, but that won't work here because (as you will learn later in this chapter) it

---

defaults to covering each control entirely with every new one that is added. However, **FlowLayout** causes the controls to flow evenly onto the form, left to right and top to bottom.

Exercise 4: (1) Verify that without the **setLayout( )** call in **Button1.java**, only one button will appear in the resulting program.

Capturing an event

If you compile and run the preceding program, nothing happens when you press the buttons. This is where you must step in and write some code to determine what will happen. The basis of event-driven programming, which comprises a lot of what a GUI is about, is connecting events to the code that responds to those events.

The way this is accomplished in Swing is by cleanly separating the interface (the graphical components) from the implementation (the code that you want to run when an event happens to a component). Each Swing component can report all the events that might happen to it, and it can report each kind of event individually. So if you're not interested in, for example, whether the mouse is being moved over your button, you don't register your interest in that event. It's a very straightforward and elegant way to handle event-driven programming, and once you understand the basic concepts, you can easily use Swing components that you haven't seen before—in fact, this model extends to anything that can be classified as a JavaBean (discussed later in the chapter).

At first, we will just focus on the main event of interest for the components being used. In the case of a **JButton**, this "event of interest" is that the button is pressed. To register your interest in a button press, you call the **JButton**'s **addActionListener( )** method. This method expects an argument that is an object that implements the **ActionListener** interface. That interface contains a single method called **actionPerformed( )**. So to attach code to a **JButton**, implement the **ActionListener** interface in a class, and register an object of that class with the **JButton** via **addActionListener( )**. The **actionPerformed( )** method will then be called when the button is pressed (this is normally referred to as a *callback*).

But what should the result of pressing that button be? We'd like to see something change on the screen, so a new Swing component will be introduced: the **JTextField**. This is a place where text can be typed by the end user or, in this case, inserted by the program. Although there are a number of ways to create a **JTextField**, the simplest is just to tell the constructor how wide you want that field to be. Once the **JTextField** is placed on the form, you can modify its contents by using the **setText( )** method (there are many other methods in **JTextField**, but you must look these up in the JDK documentation from *http://java.sun.com*). Here is what it looks like:

```
//: gui/Button2.java
// Responding to button presses.
import javax.swing.*;
import java.awt.*;
import java.awt.event.*;
import static net.mindview.util.SwingConsole.*;

public class Button2 extends JFrame {
  private JButton
    b1 = new JButton("Button 1"),
    b2 = new JButton("Button 2");
  private JTextField txt = new JTextField(10);
  class ButtonListener implements ActionListener {
    public void actionPerformed(ActionEvent e) {
      String name = ((JButton)e.getSource()).getText();
      txt.setText(name);
    }
  }
  private ButtonListener bl = new ButtonListener();
  public Button2() {
    b1.addActionListener(bl);
    b2.addActionListener(bl);
    setLayout(new FlowLayout());
    add(b1);
    add(b2);
    add(txt);
  }
  public static void main(String[] args) {
    run(new Button2(), 200, 150);
  }
} ///:~
```

Creating a **JTextField** and placing it on the canvas takes the same steps as for **JButton**s or for any Swing component. The difference in the preceding program is in the creation of the aforementioned **ActionListener** class **ButtonListener**. The argument to **actionPerformed( )** is of type

ActionEvent, which contains all the information about the event and where it came from. In this case, I wanted to describe the button that was pressed; **getSource( )** produces the object where the event originated, and I assumed (using a cast) that the object is a **JButton. getText( )** returns the text that's on the button, and this is placed in the **JTextField** to prove that the code was actually called when the button was pressed.

In the constructor, **addActionListener( )** is used to register the **ButtonListener** object with both the buttons.

It is often more convenient to code the **ActionListener** as an anonymous inner class, especially since you tend to use only a single instance of each listener class. **Button2.java** can be modified to use an anonymous inner class as follows:

```
//: gui/Button2b.java
// Using anonymous inner classes.
import javax.swing.*;
import java.awt.*;
import java.awt.event.*;
import static net.mindview.util.SwingConsole.*;

public class Button2b extends JFrame {
  private JButton
    b1 = new JButton("Button 1"),
    b2 = new JButton("Button 2");
  private JTextField txt = new JTextField(10);
  private ActionListener bl = new ActionListener() {
    public void actionPerformed(ActionEvent e) {
      String name = ((JButton)e.getSource()).getText();
      txt.setText(name);
    }
  };
  public Button2b() {
    b1.addActionListener(bl);
    b2.addActionListener(bl);
    setLayout(new FlowLayout());
    add(b1);
    add(b2);
    add(txt);
  }
  public static void main(String[] args) {
    run(new Button2b(), 200, 150);
  }
```

```
} ///:~
```

The approach of using an anonymous inner class will be preferred (when possible) for the examples in this book.

Exercise 5: (4) Create an application using the **SwingConsole** class. Include one text field and three buttons. When you press each button, make different text appear in the text field.

Text areas

A **JTextArea** is like a **JTextField** except that it can have multiple lines and has more functionality. A particularly useful method is **append( )**; with this you can easily pour output into the **JTextArea**. Because you can scroll backwards, this is an improvement over command-line programs that print to standard output. As an example, the following program fills a **JTextArea** with the output from the **Countries** generator in the *Containers in Depth* chapter:

```
//: gui/TextArea.java
// Using the JTextArea control.
import javax.swing.*;
import java.awt.*;
import java.awt.event.*;
import java.util.*;
import net.mindview.util.*;
import static net.mindview.util.SwingConsole.*;

public class TextArea extends JFrame {
  private JButton
    b = new JButton("Add Data"),
    c = new JButton("Clear Data");
  private JTextArea t = new JTextArea(20, 40);
  private Map<String,String> m =
    new HashMap<String,String>();
  public TextArea() {
    // Use up all the data:
    m.putAll(Countries.capitals());
    b.addActionListener(new ActionListener() {
      public void actionPerformed(ActionEvent e) {
        for(Map.Entry me : m.entrySet())
          t.append(me.getKey() + ": "+ me.getValue()+"\n");
      }
    });
```

```
      c.addActionListener(new ActionListener() {
        public void actionPerformed(ActionEvent e) {
          t.setText("");
        }
      });
      setLayout(new FlowLayout());
      add(new JScrollPane(t));
      add(b);
      add(c);
    }
    public static void main(String[] args) {
      run(new TextArea(), 475, 425);
    }
} ///:~
```

In the constructor, the **Map** is filled with all the countries and their capitals. Note that for both buttons, the **ActionListener** is created and added without defining an intermediate variable, since you never need to refer to that listener again during the program. The "Add Data" button formats and appends all the data, and the "Clear Data" button uses **setText( )** to remove all the text from the **JTextArea**.

As the **JTextArea** is added to the **JFrame**, it is wrapped in a **JScrollPane** to control scrolling when too much text is placed on the screen. That's all you must do in order to produce full scrolling capabilities. Having tried to figure out how to do the equivalent in some other GUI programming environments, I am very impressed with the simplicity and good design of components like **JScrollPane**.

Exercise 6: (7) Turn **strings/TestRegularExpression.java** into an interactive Swing program that allows you to put an input string in one **JTextArea** and a regular expression in a **JTextField**. The results should be displayed in a second **JTextArea**.

Exercise 7: (5) Create an application using **SwingConsole**, and add all the Swing components that have an **addActionListener( )** method. (Look these up in the JDK documentation from *http://java.sun.com*. Hint: Search for **addActionListener( )** using the index.) Capture their events and display an appropriate message for each inside a text field.

Exercise 8: (6) Almost every Swing component is derived from **Component**, which has a **setCursor( )** method. Look this up in the JDK documentation. Create an application and change the cursor to one of the stock cursors in the **Cursor** class.

Controlling layout

The way that you place components on a form in Java is probably different from any other GUI system you've used. First, it's all code; there are no "resources" that control placement of components. Second, the way components are placed on a form is controlled not by absolute positioning but by a "layout manager" that decides how the components lie based on the order that you **add( )** them. The size, shape, and placement of components will be remarkably different from one layout manager to another. In addition, the layout managers adapt to the dimensions of your applet or application window, so if the window dimension is changed, the size, shape, and placement of the components can change in response.

JApplet, **JFrame**, **JWindow**, **JDialog**, **JPanel**, etc., can all contain and display **Component**s. In **Container**, there's a method called **setLayout( )** that allows you to choose a different layout manager. In this section we'll explore the various layout managers by placing buttons in them (since that's the simplest thing to do). These examples won't capture the button events because they are only intended to show how the buttons are laid out.

BorderLayout

Unless you tell it otherwise, a **JFrame** will use **BorderLayout** as its default layout scheme. Without any other instruction, this takes whatever you **add( )** to it and places it in the center, stretching the object all the way out to the edges.

BorderLayout has the concept of four border regions and a center area. When you add something to a panel that's using a **BorderLayout**, you can use the overloaded **add( )** method that takes a constant value as its first argument. This value can be any of the following:

BorderLayout.NORTH	Top
BorderLayout.SOUTH	Bottom
BorderLayout.EAST	Right
BorderLayout.WEST	Left
BorderLayout.CENTER	Fill the middle, up to the other components or to the edges

If you don't specify an area to place the object, it defaults to **CENTER**.

In this example, the default layout is used, since **JFrame** defaults to **BorderLayout**:

```
//: gui/BorderLayout1.java
// Demonstrates BorderLayout.
import javax.swing.*;
import java.awt.*;
import static net.mindview.util.SwingConsole.*;

public class BorderLayout1 extends JFrame {
  public BorderLayout1() {
    add(BorderLayout.NORTH, new JButton("North"));
    add(BorderLayout.SOUTH, new JButton("South"));
    add(BorderLayout.EAST, new JButton("East"));
    add(BorderLayout.WEST, new JButton("West"));
    add(BorderLayout.CENTER, new JButton("Center"));
  }
  public static void main(String[] args) {
    run(new BorderLayout1(), 300, 250);
  }
} ///:~
```

For every placement but **CENTER**, the element that you add is compressed to fit in the smallest amount of space along one dimension while it is stretched to the maximum along the other dimension. **CENTER**, however, spreads out in both dimensions to occupy the middle.

FlowLayout

This simply "flows" the components onto the form, from left to right until the top space is full, then moves down a row and continues flowing.

Here's an example that sets the layout manager to **FlowLayout** and then places buttons on the form. You'll notice that with **FlowLayout**, the components take on their "natural" size. A **JButton**, for example, will be the size of its string.

```
//: gui/FlowLayout1.java
// Demonstrates FlowLayout.
import javax.swing.*;
import java.awt.*;
import static net.mindview.util.SwingConsole.*;

public class FlowLayout1 extends JFrame {
```

```
  public FlowLayout1() {
    setLayout(new FlowLayout());
    for(int i = 0; i < 20; i++)
      add(new JButton("Button " + i));
  }
  public static void main(String[] args) {
    run(new FlowLayout1(), 300, 300);
  }
} ///:~
```

All components will be compacted to their smallest size in a **FlowLayout**, so you might get a little bit of surprising behavior. For example, because a **JLabel** will be the size of its string, attempting to right-justify its text yields an unchanged display when using **FlowLayout**.

Notice that if you resize the window, the layout manager will reflow the components accordingly.

GridLayout

A **GridLayout** allows you to build a table of components, and as you add them, they are placed left to right and top to bottom in the grid. In the constructor, you specify the number of rows and columns that you need, and these are laid out in equal proportions.

```
//: gui/GridLayout1.java
// Demonstrates GridLayout.
import javax.swing.*;
import java.awt.*;
import static net.mindview.util.SwingConsole.*;

public class GridLayout1 extends JFrame {
  public GridLayout1() {
    setLayout(new GridLayout(7,3));
    for(int i = 0; i < 20; i++)
      add(new JButton("Button " + i));
  }
  public static void main(String[] args) {
    run(new GridLayout1(), 300, 300);
  }
} ///:~
```

In this case there are 21 slots but only 20 buttons. The last slot is left empty because no "balancing" goes on with a **GridLayout**.

GridBagLayout

The **GridBagLayout** provides you with tremendous control in deciding exactly how the regions of your window will lay themselves out and reformat themselves when the window is resized. However, it's also the most complicated layout manager, and is quite difficult to understand. It is intended primarily for automatic code generation by a GUI builder (GUI builders might use **GridBagLayout** instead of absolute placement). If your design is so complicated that you feel you need to use **GridBagLayout**, then you should be using a GUI builder tool to generate that design. If you feel you must know the intricate details, I'll refer you to one of the dedicated Swing books as a starting point.

As an alternative, you may want to consider **TableLayout**, which is *not* part of the Swing library but which can be downloaded from *http://java.sun.com*. This component is layered on top of **GridBagLayout** and hides most of its complexity, so it can greatly simplify this approach.

Absolute positioning

It is also possible to set the absolute position of the graphical components:

1. Set a **null** layout manager for your **Container**: **setLayout(null)**.

2. Call **setBounds( )** or **reshape( )** (depending on the language version) for each component, passing a bounding rectangle in pixel coordinates. You can do this in the constructor or in **paint( )**, depending on what you want to achieve.

Some GUI builders use this approach extensively, but this is usually not the best way to generate code.

BoxLayout

Because people had so much trouble understanding and working with **GridBagLayout**, Swing also includes **BoxLayout**, which gives you many of the benefits of **GridBagLayout** without the complexity. You can often use it when you need to do hand-coded layouts (again, if your design becomes too complex, use a GUI builder that generates layouts for you). **BoxLayout** allows you to control the placement of components either vertically or horizontally, and to control the space between the components using something called "struts and glue." You can find some basic examples of **BoxLayout** in the online supplements for this book at *www.MindView.net*.

The best approach?

Swing is powerful; it can get a lot done with a few lines of code. The examples shown in this book are quite simple, and for learning purposes it makes sense to write them by hand. You can actually accomplish quite a bit by combining simple layouts. At some point, however, it stops making sense to hand-code GUI forms; it becomes too complicated and is not a good use of your programming time. The Java and Swing designers oriented the language and libraries to support GUI-building tools, which have been created for the express purpose of making your programming experience easier. As long as you understand what's going on with layouts and how to deal with events (described next), it's not particularly important that you actually know the details of how to lay out components by hand; let the appropriate tool do that for you (Java is, after all, designed to increase programmer productivity).

The Swing event model

In the Swing event model, a component can initiate ("fire") an event. Each type of event is represented by a distinct class. When an event is fired, it is received by one or more "listeners," which act on that event. Thus, the source of an event and the place where the event is handled can be separate. Since you typically use Swing components as they are, but need to write custom code that is called when the components receive an event, this is an excellent example of the separation of interface from implementation.

Each event listener is an object of a class that implements a particular type of listener interface. So as a programmer, all you do is create a listener object and register it with the component that's firing the event. This registration is performed by calling an **addXXXListener( )** method in the event-firing component, in which "**XXX**" represents the type of event listened for. You can easily know what types of events can be handled by noticing the names of the "addListener" methods, and if you try to listen for the wrong events, you'll discover your mistake at compile time. You'll see later in the chapter that JavaBeans also use the names of the "addListener" methods to determine what events a Bean can handle.

All of your event logic, then, will go inside a listener class. When you create a listener class, the sole restriction is that it must implement the appropriate interface. You can create a global listener class, but this is a situation in which inner classes tend to be quite useful, not only because they provide a logical grouping of your listener classes inside the UI or business logic classes they are serving, but also because an inner-class object keeps a reference to its parent object, which provides a nice way to call across class and subsystem boundaries.

All the examples so far in this chapter have been using the Swing event model, but the remainder of this section will fill out the details of that model.

Event and listener types

All Swing components include **addXXXListener( )** and **removeXXXListener( )** methods so that the appropriate types of listeners can be added and removed from each component. You'll notice that the "**XXX**" in each case also represents the argument for the method, for example, **addMyListener(MyListener m)**. The following table includes the basic associated events, listeners, and methods, along with the basic components that support those particular events by providing the **addXXXListener( )** and **removeXXXListener( )** methods. You should keep in mind that the event model is designed to be extensible, so you may encounter other events and listener types that are not covered in this table.

Event, listener interface, and add- and remove-methods	Components supporting this event
ActionEvent **ActionListener** **addActionListener( )** **removeActionListener( )**	**JButton, JList, JTextField, JMenuItem** and its derivatives including **JCheckBoxMenuItem, JMenu,** and **JRadioButtonMenuItem**
AdjustmentEvent **AdjustmentListener** **addAdjustmentListener( )** **removeAdjustmentListener( )**	**JScrollbar** and anything you create that implements the **Adjustable** interface
ComponentEvent **ComponentListener** **addComponentListener( )** **removeComponentListener( )**	*****Component** and its derivatives, including **JButton, JCheckBox, JComboBox, Container, JPanel, JApplet, JScrollPane, Window, JDialog, JFileDialog, JFrame, JLabel, JList, JScrollbar, JTextArea,** and **JTextField**
ContainerEvent	**Container** and its derivatives,

Event, listener interface, and add- and remove-methods	Components supporting this event
addContainerListener( ) removeContainerListener( )	**JScrollPane, Window, JDialog, JFileDialog**, and **JFrame**
FocusEvent FocusListener addFocusListener( ) removeFocusListener( )	**Component** and **derivatives***
KeyEvent KeyListener addKeyListener( ) removeKeyListener( )	**Component** and **derivatives***
MouseEvent (for both clicks and motion) **MouseListener addMouseListener( ) removeMouseListener( )**	**Component** and **derivatives***
MouseEvent[6] (for both clicks and motion) **MouseMotionListener addMouseMotionListener( ) removeMouseMotionListener( )**	**Component** and **derivatives***
WindowEvent WindowListener addWindowListener( ) removeWindowListener( )	**Window** and its derivatives, including **JDialog, JFileDialog**, and **JFrame**
ItemEvent ItemListener addItemListener( ) removeItemListener( )	**JCheckBox, JCheckBoxMenuItem, JComboBox, JList**, and anything that implements the **ItemSelectable** interface
TextEvent TextListener addTextListener( ) removeTextListener( )	Anything derived from **JTextComponent**, including **JTextArea** and **JTextField**

---

[6] There is no **MouseMotionEvent** even though it seems like there ought to be. Clicking and motion is combined into **MouseEvent**, so this second appearance of **MouseEvent** in the table is not an error.

You can see that each type of component supports only certain types of events. It turns out to be rather tedious to look up all the events supported by each component. A simpler approach is to modify the **ShowMethods.java** program from the *Type Information* chapter so that it displays all the event listeners supported by any Swing component that you enter.

The *Type Information* chapter introduced *reflection* and used that feature to look up methods for a particular class—either the entire list of methods or a subset of those whose names match a keyword that you provide. The magic of reflection is that it can automatically show you *all* the methods for a class without forcing you to walk up the inheritance hierarchy, examining the base classes at each level. Thus, it provides a valuable timesaving tool for programming; because the names of most Java methods are made nicely verbose and descriptive, you can search for the method names that contain a particular word of interest. When you find what you think you're looking for, check the JDK documentation.

Here is the more useful GUI version of **ShowMethods.java**, specialized to look for the "addListener" methods in Swing components:

```
//: gui/ShowAddListeners.java
// Display the "addXXXListener" methods of any Swing class.
import javax.swing.*;
import java.awt.*;
import java.awt.event.*;
import java.lang.reflect.*;
import java.util.regex.*;
import static net.mindview.util.SwingConsole.*;

public class ShowAddListeners extends JFrame {
  private JTextField name = new JTextField(25);
  private JTextArea results = new JTextArea(40, 65);
  private static Pattern addListener =
    Pattern.compile("(add\\w+?Listener\\(.*?\\))");
  private static Pattern qualifier =
    Pattern.compile("\\w+\\.");
  class NameL implements ActionListener {
    public void actionPerformed(ActionEvent e) {
      String nm = name.getText().trim();
      if(nm.length() == 0) {
        results.setText("No match");
        return;
      }
```

```
    Class<?> kind;
    try {
      kind = Class.forName("javax.swing." + nm);
    } catch(ClassNotFoundException ex) {
      results.setText("No match");
      return;
    }
    Method[] methods = kind.getMethods();
    results.setText("");
    for(Method m : methods) {
      Matcher matcher =
        addListener.matcher(m.toString());
      if(matcher.find())
        results.append(qualifier.matcher(
          matcher.group(1)).replaceAll("") + "\n");
    }
  }
}
public ShowAddListeners() {
  NameL nameListener = new NameL();
  name.addActionListener(nameListener);
  JPanel top = new JPanel();
  top.add(new JLabel("Swing class name (press Enter):"));
  top.add(name);
  add(BorderLayout.NORTH, top);
  add(new JScrollPane(results));
  // Initial data and test:
  name.setText("JTextArea");
  nameListener.actionPerformed(
    new ActionEvent("", 0 ,""));
}
public static void main(String[] args) {
  run(new ShowAddListeners(), 500, 400);
}
} ///:~
```

You enter the Swing class name that you want to look up in the **name
JTextField**. The results are extracted using regular expressions, and
displayed in a **JTextArea**.

You'll notice that there are no buttons or other components to indicate that
you want the search to begin. That's because the **JTextField** is monitored by
an **ActionListener**. Whenever you make a change and press Enter, the list
is immediately updated. If the text field isn't empty, it is used inside

---

Class.forName( ) to try to look up the class. If the name is incorrect, **Class.forName( )** will fail, which means that it throws an exception. This is trapped, and the **JTextArea** is set to "No match." But if you type in a correct name (capitalization counts), **Class.forName( )** is successful, and **getMethods( )** will return an array of **Method** objects.

Two regular expressions are used here. The first, **addListener**, looks for "add" followed by any word characters, followed by "Listener" and the argument list in parentheses. Notice that this whole regular expression is surrounded by non-escaped parentheses, which means it will be accessible as a regular expression "group" when it matches. Inside **NameL.ActionPerformed( )**, a **Matcher** is created by passing each **Method** object to the **Pattern.matcher( )** method. When **find( )** is called for this **Matcher** object, it returns **true** only if a match occurs, and in that case you can select the first matching parenthesized group by calling **group(1)**. This string still contains qualifiers, so to strip them off, the **qualifier Pattern** object is used just as it was in **ShowMethods.java**.

At the end of the constructor, an initial value is placed in **name** and the action event is run to provide a test with initial data.

This program is a convenient way to investigate the capabilities of a Swing component. Once you know which events a particular component supports, you don't need to look anything up to react to that event. You simply:

1. Take the name of the event class and remove the word "**Event**." Add the word "**Listener**" to what remains. This is the listener interface you must implement in your inner class.

2. Implement the interface above and write out the methods for the events you want to capture. For example, you might be looking for mouse movements, so you write code for the **mouseMoved( )** method of the **MouseMotionListener** interface. (You must implement the other methods, of course, but there's often a shortcut for this, which you'll see soon.)

3. Create an object of the listener class in Step 2. Register it with your component with the method produced by prefixing "**add**" to your listener name. For example, **addMouseMotionListener( )**.

Here are some of the listener interfaces:

Listener interface w/ adapter	Methods in interface
ActionListener	actionPerformed(ActionEvent)
AdjustmentListener	adjustmentValueChanged(AdjustmentEvent)
ComponentListener ComponentAdapter	componentHidden(ComponentEvent) componentShown(ComponentEvent) componentMoved(ComponentEvent) componentResized(ComponentEvent)
ContainerListener ContainerAdapter	componentAdded(ContainerEvent) componentRemoved(ContainerEvent)
FocusListener FocusAdapter	focusGained(FocusEvent) focusLost(FocusEvent)
KeyListener KeyAdapter	keyPressed(KeyEvent) keyReleased(KeyEvent) keyTyped(KeyEvent)
MouseListener MouseAdapter	mouseClicked(MouseEvent) mouseEntered(MouseEvent) mouseExited(MouseEvent) mousePressed(MouseEvent) mouseReleased(MouseEvent)
MouseMotionListener MouseMotionAdapter	mouseDragged(MouseEvent) mouseMoved(MouseEvent)
WindowListener WindowAdapter	windowOpened(WindowEvent) windowClosing(WindowEvent) windowClosed(WindowEvent) windowActivated(WindowEvent) windowDeactivated(WindowEvent) windowIconified(WindowEvent) windowDeiconified(WindowEvent)
ItemListener	itemStateChanged(ItemEvent)

This is not an exhaustive listing, partly because the event model allows you to create your own event types and associated listeners. Thus, you'll regularly come across libraries that have invented their own events, and the knowledge gained in this chapter will allow you to figure out how to use these events.

Using listener adapters for simplicity

In the table above, you can see that some listener interfaces have only one method. These are trivial to implement. However, the listener interfaces that have multiple methods can be less pleasant to use. For example, if you want to capture a mouse click (that isn't already captured for you, for example, by a button), then you need to write a method for **mouseClicked( )**. But since **MouseListener** is an interface, you must implement all of the other methods even if they don't do anything. This can be annoying.

To solve the problem, some (but not all) of the listener interfaces that have more than one method are provided with *adapters*, the names of which you can see in the table above. Each adapter provides default empty methods for each of the interface methods. When you inherit from the adapter, you override only the methods you need to change. For example, the typical **MouseListener** you'll use looks like this:

```
class MyMouseListener extends MouseAdapter {
  public void mouseClicked(MouseEvent e) {
    // Respond to mouse click...
  }
}
```

The whole point of the adapters is to make the creation of listener classes easy.

There is a downside to adapters, however, in the form of a pitfall. Suppose you write a **MouseAdapter** like the previous one:

```
class MyMouseListener extends MouseAdapter {
  public void MouseClicked(MouseEvent e) {
    // Respond to mouse click...
  }
}
```

This doesn't work, but it will drive you crazy trying to figure out why, since everything will compile and run fine—except that your method won't be called for a mouse click. Can you see the problem? It's in the name of the method: **MouseClicked( )** instead of **mouseClicked( )**. A simple slip in capitalization results in the addition of a completely new method. However, this is not the method that's called when the mouse is clicked, so you don't get the desired results. Despite the inconvenience, an interface will guarantee that the methods are properly implemented.

An improved alternative way to guarantee that you are in fact overriding a method is to use the built-in **@Override** annotation in the code above.

Exercise 9: (5) Starting with **ShowAddListeners.java**, create a program with the full functionality of **typeinfo.ShowMethods.java**.

Tracking multiple events

To prove to yourself that these events are in fact being fired, it's worth creating a program that tracks behavior in a **JButton** beyond whether it has been pressed. This example also shows you how to inherit your own button object from **JButton**.[7]

In the code below, the **MyButton** class is an inner class of **TrackEvent**, so **MyButton** can reach into the parent window and manipulate its text fields, which is necessary in order to write the status information into the fields of the parent. Of course, this is a limited solution, since **MyButton** can be used only in conjunction with **TrackEvent**. This kind of code is sometimes called "highly coupled":

```
//: gui/TrackEvent.java
// Show events as they happen.
import javax.swing.*;
import java.awt.*;
import java.awt.event.*;
import java.util.*;
import static net.mindview.util.SwingConsole.*;

public class TrackEvent extends JFrame {
  private HashMap<String,JTextField> h =
    new HashMap<String,JTextField>();
  private String[] event = {
    "focusGained", "focusLost", "keyPressed",
    "keyReleased", "keyTyped", "mouseClicked",
    "mouseEntered", "mouseExited", "mousePressed",
    "mouseReleased", "mouseDragged", "mouseMoved"
  };
  private MyButton
    b1 = new MyButton(Color.BLUE, "test1"),
```

---

[7] In Java 1.0/1.1 you could *not* usefully inherit from the button object. This was only one of numerous fundamental design flaws.

```
        b2 = new MyButton(Color.RED, "test2");
     class MyButton extends JButton {
       void report(String field, String msg) {
         h.get(field).setText(msg);
       }
       FocusListener fl = new FocusListener() {
         public void focusGained(FocusEvent e) {
           report("focusGained", e.paramString());
         }
         public void focusLost(FocusEvent e) {
           report("focusLost", e.paramString());
         }
       };
       KeyListener kl = new KeyListener() {
         public void keyPressed(KeyEvent e) {
           report("keyPressed", e.paramString());
         }
         public void keyReleased(KeyEvent e) {
           report("keyReleased", e.paramString());
         }
         public void keyTyped(KeyEvent e) {
           report("keyTyped", e.paramString());
         }
       };
       MouseListener ml = new MouseListener() {
         public void mouseClicked(MouseEvent e) {
           report("mouseClicked", e.paramString());
         }
         public void mouseEntered(MouseEvent e) {
           report("mouseEntered", e.paramString());
         }
         public void mouseExited(MouseEvent e) {
           report("mouseExited", e.paramString());
         }
         public void mousePressed(MouseEvent e) {
           report("mousePressed", e.paramString());
         }
         public void mouseReleased(MouseEvent e) {
           report("mouseReleased", e.paramString());
         }
       };
       MouseMotionListener mml = new MouseMotionListener() {
         public void mouseDragged(MouseEvent e) {
           report("mouseDragged", e.paramString());
```

```
        }
      public void mouseMoved(MouseEvent e) {
        report("mouseMoved", e.paramString());
      }
    };
    public MyButton(Color color, String label) {
      super(label);
      setBackground(color);
      addFocusListener(fl);
      addKeyListener(kl);
      addMouseListener(ml);
      addMouseMotionListener(mml);
    }
  }
  public TrackEvent() {
    setLayout(new GridLayout(event.length + 1, 2));
    for(String evt : event) {
      JTextField t = new JTextField();
      t.setEditable(false);
      add(new JLabel(evt, JLabel.RIGHT));
      add(t);
      h.put(evt, t);
    }
    add(b1);
    add(b2);
  }
  public static void main(String[] args) {
    run(new TrackEvent(), 700, 500);
  }
} ///:~
```

In the **MyButton** constructor, the button's color is set with a call to **SetBackground( )**. The listeners are all installed with simple method calls.

The **TrackEvent** class contains a **HashMap** to hold the strings representing the type of event and **JTextField**s where information about that event is held. Of course, these could have been created statically rather than putting them in a **HashMap**, but I think you'll agree that it's a lot easier to use and change. In particular, if you need to add or remove a new type of event in **TrackEvent**, you simply add or remove a string in the **event** array—everything else happens automatically.

When **report( )** is called, it is given the name of the event and the parameter string from the event. It uses the **HashMap h** in the outer class to look up the actual **JTextField** associated with that event name and then places the parameter string into that field.

This example is fun to play with because you can really see what's going on with the events in your program.

Exercise 10: (6) Create an application using **SwingConsole**, with a **JButton** and a **JTextField**. Write and attach the appropriate listener so that if the button has the focus, characters typed into it will appear in the **JTextField**.

Exercise 11: (4) Inherit a new type of button from **JButton**. Each time you press this button, it should change its color to a randomly selected value. See **ColorBoxes.java** (later in this chapter) for an example of how to generate a random color value.

Exercise 12: (4) Monitor a new type of event in **TrackEvent.java** by adding the new event-handling code. You'll need to discover on your own the type of event that you want to monitor.

A selection of Swing components

Now that you understand layout managers and the event model, you're ready to see how Swing components can be used. This section is a non-exhaustive tour of the Swing components and features that you'll probably use most of the time. Each example is intended to be reasonably small so that you can easily lift the code and use it in your own programs.

Keep in mind:

1. You can easily see what each of these examples looks like during execution by compiling and running the downloadable source code for this chapter (*www.MindView.net*).

2. The JDK documentation from *http://java.sun.com* contains all of the Swing classes and methods (only a few are shown here).

3. Because of the naming convention used for Swing events, it's fairly easy to guess how to write and install a handler for a particular type of event. Use the lookup program **ShowAddListeners.java** from earlier in this chapter to aid in your investigation of a particular component.

4. When things start to get complicated you should graduate to a GUI builder.

Buttons

Swing includes a number of different types of buttons. All buttons, check boxes, radio buttons, and even menu items are inherited from **AbstractButton** (which, since menu items are included, would probably have been better named "AbstractSelector" or something equally general). You'll see the use of menu items shortly, but the following example shows the various types of buttons available:

```
//: gui/Buttons.java
// Various Swing buttons.
import javax.swing.*;
import javax.swing.border.*;
import javax.swing.plaf.basic.*;
import java.awt.*;
import static net.mindview.util.SwingConsole.*;

public class Buttons extends JFrame {
  private JButton jb = new JButton("JButton");
  private BasicArrowButton
    up = new BasicArrowButton(BasicArrowButton.NORTH),
    down = new BasicArrowButton(BasicArrowButton.SOUTH),
    right = new BasicArrowButton(BasicArrowButton.EAST),
    left = new BasicArrowButton(BasicArrowButton.WEST);
  public Buttons() {
    setLayout(new FlowLayout());
    add(jb);
    add(new JToggleButton("JToggleButton"));
    add(new JCheckBox("JCheckBox"));
    add(new JRadioButton("JRadioButton"));
    JPanel jp = new JPanel();
    jp.setBorder(new TitledBorder("Directions"));
    jp.add(up);
    jp.add(down);
    jp.add(left);
    jp.add(right);
    add(jp);
  }
  public static void main(String[] args) {
    run(new Buttons(), 350, 200);
  }
}
```

```
} ///:~
```

This begins with the **BasicArrowButton** from **javax.swing.plaf.basic**, then continues with the various specific types of buttons. When you run the example, you'll see that the toggle button holds its last position, in or out. But the check boxes and radio buttons behave identically to each other, just clicking on or off (they are inherited from **JToggleButton**).

Button groups

If you want radio buttons to behave in an "exclusive or" fashion, you must add them to a "button group." But, as the following example demonstrates, any **AbstractButton** can be added to a **ButtonGroup**.

To avoid repeating a lot of code, this example uses reflection to generate the groups of different types of buttons. This is seen in **makeBPanel( )**, which creates a button group in a **JPanel**. The second argument to **makeBPanel( )** is an array of **String**. For each **String**, a button of the class represented by the first argument is added to the **JPanel**:

```
//: gui/ButtonGroups.java
// Uses reflection to create groups
// of different types of AbstractButton.
import javax.swing.*;
import javax.swing.border.*;
import java.awt.*;
import java.lang.reflect.*;
import static net.mindview.util.SwingConsole.*;

public class ButtonGroups extends JFrame {
  private static String[] ids = {
    "June", "Ward", "Beaver", "Wally", "Eddie", "Lumpy"
  };
  static JPanel makeBPanel(
    Class<? extends AbstractButton> kind, String[] ids) {
    ButtonGroup bg = new ButtonGroup();
    JPanel jp = new JPanel();
    String title = kind.getName();
    title = title.substring(title.lastIndexOf('.') + 1);
    jp.setBorder(new TitledBorder(title));
    for(String id : ids) {
      AbstractButton ab = new JButton("failed");
      try {
        // Get the dynamic constructor method
```

```
        // that takes a String argument:
        Constructor ctor =
          kind.getConstructor(String.class);
        // Create a new object:
        ab = (AbstractButton)ctor.newInstance(id);
      } catch(Exception ex) {
        System.err.println("can't create " + kind);
      }
      bg.add(ab);
      jp.add(ab);
    }
    return jp;
  }
  public ButtonGroups() {
    setLayout(new FlowLayout());
    add(makeBPanel(JButton.class, ids));
    add(makeBPanel(JToggleButton.class, ids));
    add(makeBPanel(JCheckBox.class, ids));
    add(makeBPanel(JRadioButton.class, ids));
  }
  public static void main(String[] args) {
    run(new ButtonGroups(), 500, 350);
  }
} ///:~
```

The title for the border is taken from the name of the class, stripping off all the path information. The **AbstractButton** is initialized to a **JButton** that has the label "failed," so if you ignore the exception message, you'll still see the problem on the screen. The **getConstructor( )** method produces a **Constructor** object that takes the array of arguments of the types in the list of **Class**es passed to **getConstructor( )**. Then all you do is call **newInstance( )**, passing it a list of arguments—in this case, just the **String** from the **ids** array.

To get "exclusive or" behavior with buttons, you create a button group and add each button for which you want that behavior to the group. When you run the program, you'll see that all the buttons except **JButton** exhibit this "exclusive or" behavior.

Icons

You can use an **Icon** inside a **JLabel** or anything that inherits from **AbstractButton** (including **JButton**, **JCheckBox**, **JRadioButton**, and the different kinds of **JMenuItem**). Using **Icon**s with **JLabel**s is quite straightforward (you'll see an example later). The following example explores all the additional ways you can use **Icon**s with buttons and their descendants.

You can use any **GIF** files you want, but the ones used in this example are part of this book's code distribution, available at *www.MindView.net*. To open a file and bring in the image, simply create an **ImageIcon** and hand it the file name. From then on, you can use the resulting **Icon** in your program.

```java
//: gui/Faces.java
// Icon behavior in JButtons.
import javax.swing.*;
import java.awt.*;
import java.awt.event.*;
import static net.mindview.util.SwingConsole.*;

public class Faces extends JFrame {
  private static Icon[] faces;
  private JButton jb, jb2 = new JButton("Disable");
  private boolean mad = false;
  public Faces() {
    faces = new Icon[]{
      new ImageIcon(getClass().getResource("Face0.gif")),
      new ImageIcon(getClass().getResource("Face1.gif")),
      new ImageIcon(getClass().getResource("Face2.gif")),
      new ImageIcon(getClass().getResource("Face3.gif")),
      new ImageIcon(getClass().getResource("Face4.gif")),
    };
    jb = new JButton("JButton", faces[3]);
    setLayout(new FlowLayout());
    jb.addActionListener(new ActionListener() {
      public void actionPerformed(ActionEvent e) {
        if(mad) {
          jb.setIcon(faces[3]);
          mad = false;
        } else {
          jb.setIcon(faces[0]);
          mad = true;
        }
        jb.setVerticalAlignment(JButton.TOP);
        jb.setHorizontalAlignment(JButton.LEFT);
      }
    });
```

```
      jb.setRolloverEnabled(true);
      jb.setRolloverIcon(faces[1]);
      jb.setPressedIcon(faces[2]);
      jb.setDisabledIcon(faces[4]);
      jb.setToolTipText("Yow!");
      add(jb);
      jb2.addActionListener(new ActionListener() {
        public void actionPerformed(ActionEvent e) {
          if(jb.isEnabled()) {
            jb.setEnabled(false);
            jb2.setText("Enable");
          } else {
            jb.setEnabled(true);
            jb2.setText("Disable");
          }
        }
      });
      add(jb2);
    }
  public static void main(String[] args) {
    run(new Faces(), 250, 125);
  }
} ///:~
```

An **Icon** can be used as an argument for many different Swing component constructors, but you can also use **setIcon( )** to add or change an **Icon**. This example also shows how a **JButton** (or any **AbstractButton**) can set the various different sorts of icons that appear when things happen to that button: when it's pressed, disabled, or "rolled over" (the mouse moves over it without clicking). You'll see that this gives the button a nice animated feel.

Tool tips

The previous example added a "tool tip" to the button. Almost all of the classes that you'll be using to create your user interfaces are derived from **JComponent**, which contains a method called **setToolTipText(String)**. So, for virtually anything you place on your form, all you need to do is say (for an object **jc** of any **JComponent**-derived class):

```
jc.setToolTipText("My tip");
```

When the mouse stays over that **JComponent** for a predetermined period of time, a tiny box containing your text will pop up next to the mouse.

Text fields

This example shows what **JTextField**s can do:

```
//: gui/TextFields.java
// Text fields and Java events.
import javax.swing.*;
import javax.swing.event.*;
import javax.swing.text.*;
import java.awt.*;
import java.awt.event.*;
import static net.mindview.util.SwingConsole.*;

public class TextFields extends JFrame {
  private JButton
    b1 = new JButton("Get Text"),
    b2 = new JButton("Set Text");
  private JTextField
    t1 = new JTextField(30),
    t2 = new JTextField(30),
    t3 = new JTextField(30);
  private String s = "";
  private UpperCaseDocument ucd = new UpperCaseDocument();
  public TextFields() {
    t1.setDocument(ucd);
    ucd.addDocumentListener(new T1());
    b1.addActionListener(new B1());
    b2.addActionListener(new B2());
    t1.addActionListener(new T1A());
    setLayout(new FlowLayout());
    add(b1);
    add(b2);
    add(t1);
    add(t2);
    add(t3);
  }
  class T1 implements DocumentListener {
    public void changedUpdate(DocumentEvent e) {}
    public void insertUpdate(DocumentEvent e) {
      t2.setText(t1.getText());
      t3.setText("Text: "+ t1.getText());
    }
    public void removeUpdate(DocumentEvent e) {
      t2.setText(t1.getText());
```

```java
      }
    }
    class T1A implements ActionListener {
      private int count = 0;
      public void actionPerformed(ActionEvent e) {
        t3.setText("t1 Action Event " + count++);
      }
    }
    class B1 implements ActionListener {
      public void actionPerformed(ActionEvent e) {
        if(t1.getSelectedText() == null)
          s = t1.getText();
        else
          s = t1.getSelectedText();
        t1.setEditable(true);
      }
    }
    class B2 implements ActionListener {
      public void actionPerformed(ActionEvent e) {
        ucd.setUpperCase(false);
        t1.setText("Inserted by Button 2: " + s);
        ucd.setUpperCase(true);
        t1.setEditable(false);
      }
    }
    public static void main(String[] args) {
      run(new TextFields(), 375, 200);
    }
}

class UpperCaseDocument extends PlainDocument {
  private boolean upperCase = true;
  public void setUpperCase(boolean flag) {
    upperCase = flag;
  }
  public void
  insertString(int offset, String str, AttributeSet attSet)
  throws BadLocationException {
    if(upperCase) str = str.toUpperCase();
    super.insertString(offset, str, attSet);
  }
} ///:~
```

The **JTextField t3** is included as a place to report when the action listener for the **JTextField t1** is fired. You'll see that the action listener for a **JTextField** is fired only when you press the Enter key.

The **JTextField t1** has several listeners attached to it. The **T1** listener is a **DocumentListener** that responds to any change in the "document" (the contents of the **JTextField**, in this case). It automatically copies all text from **t1** into **t2**. In addition, **t1**'s document is set to a derived class of **PlainDocument**, called **UpperCaseDocument**, which forces all characters to uppercase. It automatically detects backspaces and performs the deletion, adjusting the caret and handling everything as you expect.

Exercise 13:   (3) Modify **TextFields.java** so that the characters in **t2** retain the original case that they were typed in, instead of automatically being forced to uppercase.

Borders

JComponent contains a method called **setBorder( )**, which allows you to place various interesting borders on any visible component. The following example demonstrates a number of the different borders that are available, using a method called **showBorder( )** that creates a **JPanel** and puts on the border in each case. Also, it uses RTTI to find the name of the border that you're using (stripping off all the path information), then puts that name in a **JLabel** in the middle of the panel:

```
//: gui/Borders.java
// Different Swing borders.
import javax.swing.*;
import javax.swing.border.*;
import java.awt.*;
import static net.mindview.util.SwingConsole.*;

public class Borders extends JFrame {
  static JPanel showBorder(Border b) {
    JPanel jp = new JPanel();
    jp.setLayout(new BorderLayout());
    String nm = b.getClass().toString();
    nm = nm.substring(nm.lastIndexOf('.') + 1);
    jp.add(new JLabel(nm, JLabel.CENTER),
      BorderLayout.CENTER);
    jp.setBorder(b);
    return jp;
```

```
    }
  public Borders() {
    setLayout(new GridLayout(2,4));
    add(showBorder(new TitledBorder("Title")));
    add(showBorder(new EtchedBorder()));
    add(showBorder(new LineBorder(Color.BLUE)));
    add(showBorder(
      new MatteBorder(5,5,30,30,Color.GREEN)));
    add(showBorder(
      new BevelBorder(BevelBorder.RAISED)));
    add(showBorder(
      new SoftBevelBorder(BevelBorder.LOWERED)));
    add(showBorder(new CompoundBorder(
      new EtchedBorder(),
      new LineBorder(Color.RED))));
  }
  public static void main(String[] args) {
    run(new Borders(), 500, 300);
  }
} ///:~
```

You can also create your own borders and put them inside buttons, labels, etc.—anything derived from **JComponent**.

A mini-editor

The **JTextPane** control provides a great deal of support for editing, without much effort. The following example makes very simple use of this component, ignoring the bulk of its functionality:

```
//: gui/TextPane.java
// The JTextPane control is a little editor.
import javax.swing.*;
import java.awt.*;
import java.awt.event.*;
import net.mindview.util.*;
import static net.mindview.util.SwingConsole.*;

public class TextPane extends JFrame {
  private JButton b = new JButton("Add Text");
  private JTextPane tp = new JTextPane();
  private static Generator sg =
    new RandomGenerator.String(7);
  public TextPane() {
    b.addActionListener(new ActionListener() {
```

```
      public void actionPerformed(ActionEvent e) {
        for(int i = 1; i < 10; i++)
          tp.setText(tp.getText() + sg.next() + "\n");
      }
    });
    add(new JScrollPane(tp));
    add(BorderLayout.SOUTH, b);
  }
  public static void main(String[] args) {
    run(new TextPane(), 475, 425);
  }
} ///:~
```

The button adds randomly generated text. The intent of the **JTextPane** is to allow text to be edited in place, so you will see that there is no **append( )** method. In this case (admittedly, a poor use of the capabilities of **JTextPane**), the text must be captured, modified, and placed back into the pane using **setText( )**.

Elements are added to the **JFrame** using its default **BorderLayout**. The **JTextPane** is added (inside a **JScrollPane**) without specifying a region, so it just fills the center of the pane out to the edges. The **JButton** is added to the **SOUTH**, so the component will fit itself into that region; in this case, the button will nest down at the bottom of the screen.

Notice the built-in features of **JTextPane**, such as automatic line wrapping. There are numerous other features that you can look up using the JDK documentation.

Exercise 14: (2) Modify **TextPane.java** to use a **JTextArea** instead of a **JTextPane**.

Check boxes

A check box provides a way to make a single on/off choice. It consists of a tiny box and a label. The box typically holds a little "x" (or some other indication that it is set) or is empty, depending on whether that item was selected.

You'll normally create a **JCheckBox** using a constructor that takes the label as an argument. You can get and set the state, and also get and set the label if you want to read or change it after the **JCheckBox** has been created.

Whenever a **JCheckBox** is set or cleared, an event occurs, which you can capture the same way you do a button: by using an **ActionListener**. The following example uses a **JTextArea** to enumerate all the check boxes that have been checked:

```
//: gui/CheckBoxes.java
// Using JCheckBoxes.
import javax.swing.*;
import java.awt.*;
import java.awt.event.*;
import static net.mindview.util.SwingConsole.*;

public class CheckBoxes extends JFrame {
  private JTextArea t = new JTextArea(6, 15);
  private JCheckBox
    cb1 = new JCheckBox("Check Box 1"),
    cb2 = new JCheckBox("Check Box 2"),
    cb3 = new JCheckBox("Check Box 3");
  public CheckBoxes() {
    cb1.addActionListener(new ActionListener() {
      public void actionPerformed(ActionEvent e) {
        trace("1", cb1);
      }
    });
    cb2.addActionListener(new ActionListener() {
      public void actionPerformed(ActionEvent e) {
        trace("2", cb2);
      }
    });
    cb3.addActionListener(new ActionListener() {
      public void actionPerformed(ActionEvent e) {
        trace("3", cb3);
      }
    });
    setLayout(new FlowLayout());
    add(new JScrollPane(t));
    add(cb1);
    add(cb2);
    add(cb3);
  }
  private void trace(String b, JCheckBox cb) {
    if(cb.isSelected())
      t.append("Box " + b + " Set\n");
    else
      t.append("Box " + b + " Cleared\n");
  }
```

```
  public static void main(String[] args) {
    run(new CheckBoxes(), 200, 300);
  }
} ///:~
```

The **trace( )** method sends the name of the selected **JCheckBox** and its current state to the **JTextArea** using **append( )**, so you'll see a cumulative list of the check boxes that were selected, along with their state.

Exercise 15: (5) Add a check box to the application created in Exercise 5, capture the event, and insert different text into the text field.

Radio buttons

The concept of radio buttons in GUI programming comes from pre-electronic car radios with mechanical buttons: When you push one in, any other buttons pop out. Thus, it allows you to force a single choice among many.

To set up an associated group of **JRadioButton**s, you add them to a **ButtonGroup** (you can have any number of **ButtonGroup**s on a form). One of the buttons can be optionally set to **true** (using the second argument in the constructor). If you try to set more than one radio button to **true**, then only the last one set will be **true**.

Here's a simple example of the use of radio buttons, showing event capture using an **ActionListener**:

```
//: gui/RadioButtons.java
// Using JRadioButtons.
import javax.swing.*;
import java.awt.*;
import java.awt.event.*;
import static net.mindview.util.SwingConsole.*;

public class RadioButtons extends JFrame {
  private JTextField t = new JTextField(15);
  private ButtonGroup g = new ButtonGroup();
  private JRadioButton
    rb1 = new JRadioButton("one", false),
    rb2 = new JRadioButton("two", false),
    rb3 = new JRadioButton("three", false);
  private ActionListener al = new ActionListener() {
    public void actionPerformed(ActionEvent e) {
      t.setText("Radio button " +
```

```
          ((JRadioButton)e.getSource()).getText());
      }
    };
    public RadioButtons() {
      rb1.addActionListener(al);
      rb2.addActionListener(al);
      rb3.addActionListener(al);
      g.add(rb1); g.add(rb2); g.add(rb3);
      t.setEditable(false);
      setLayout(new FlowLayout());
      add(t);
      add(rb1);
      add(rb2);
      add(rb3);
    }
    public static void main(String[] args) {
      run(new RadioButtons(), 200, 125);
    }
} ///:~
```

To display the state, a text field is used. This field is set to non-editable
because it's used only to display data, not to collect it. Thus it is an alternative
to using a **JLabel**.

Combo boxes (drop-down lists)

Like a group of radio buttons, a drop-down list is a way to force the user to
select only one element from a group of possibilities. However, it's a more
compact way to accomplish this, and it's easier to change the elements of the
list without surprising the user. (You can change radio buttons dynamically,
but that tends to be visibly jarring.)

By default, **JComboBox** box is not like the combo box in Windows, which
lets you select from a list *or* type in your own selection. To produce this
behavior you must call **setEditable( )**. With a **JComboBox** box, you choose
one and only one element from the list. In the following example, the
JComboBox box starts with a certain number of entries, and then new
entries are added to the box when a button is pressed.

```
//: gui/ComboBoxes.java
// Using drop-down lists.
import javax.swing.*;
import java.awt.*;
import java.awt.event.*;
```

```
import static net.mindview.util.SwingConsole.*;

public class ComboBoxes extends JFrame {
  private String[] description = {
    "Ebullient", "Obtuse", "Recalcitrant", "Brilliant",
    "Somnescent", "Timorous", "Florid", "Putrescent"
  };
  private JTextField t = new JTextField(15);
  private JComboBox c = new JComboBox();
  private JButton b = new JButton("Add items");
  private int count = 0;
  public ComboBoxes() {
    for(int i = 0; i < 4; i++)
      c.addItem(description[count++]);
    t.setEditable(false);
    b.addActionListener(new ActionListener() {
      public void actionPerformed(ActionEvent e) {
        if(count < description.length)
          c.addItem(description[count++]);
      }
    });
    c.addActionListener(new ActionListener() {
      public void actionPerformed(ActionEvent e) {
        t.setText("index: "+ c.getSelectedIndex() + "    " +
          ((JComboBox)e.getSource()).getSelectedItem());
      }
    });
    setLayout(new FlowLayout());
    add(t);
    add(c);
    add(b);
  }
  public static void main(String[] args) {
    run(new ComboBoxes(), 200, 175);
  }
} ///:~
```

The **JTextField** displays the "selected index," which is the sequence number of the currently selected element, as well as the text of the selected item in the combo box.

List boxes

List boxes are significantly different from **JComboBox** boxes, and not just in appearance. While a **JComboBox** box drops down when you activate it, a **JList** occupies some fixed number of lines on a screen all the time and doesn't change. If you want to see the items in a list, you simply call **getSelectedValues( )**, which produces an array of **String** of the items that have been selected.

A **JList** allows multiple selection; if you control-click on more than one item (holding down the Control key while performing additional mouse clicks), the original item stays highlighted and you can select as many as you want. If you select an item, then shift-click on another item, all the items in the span between the two are selected. To remove an item from a group, you can control-click it.

```
//: gui/List.java
import javax.swing.*;
import javax.swing.border.*;
import javax.swing.event.*;
import java.awt.*;
import java.awt.event.*;
import static net.mindview.util.SwingConsole.*;

public class List extends JFrame {
  private String[] flavors = {
    "Chocolate", "Strawberry", "Vanilla Fudge Swirl",
    "Mint Chip", "Mocha Almond Fudge", "Rum Raisin",
    "Praline Cream", "Mud Pie"
  };
  private DefaultListModel lItems = new DefaultListModel();
  private JList lst = new JList(lItems);
  private JTextArea t =
    new JTextArea(flavors.length, 20);
  private JButton b = new JButton("Add Item");
  private ActionListener bl = new ActionListener() {
    public void actionPerformed(ActionEvent e) {
      if(count < flavors.length) {
        lItems.add(0, flavors[count++]);
      } else {
        // Disable, since there are no more
        // flavors left to be added to the List
        b.setEnabled(false);
```

```
        }
      }
    };
  private ListSelectionListener ll =
    new ListSelectionListener() {
      public void valueChanged(ListSelectionEvent e) {
        if(e.getValueIsAdjusting()) return;
        t.setText("");
        for(Object item : lst.getSelectedValues())
          t.append(item + "\n");
      }
    };
  private int count = 0;
  public List() {
    t.setEditable(false);
    setLayout(new FlowLayout());
    // Create Borders for components:
    Border brd = BorderFactory.createMatteBorder(
      1, 1, 2, 2, Color.BLACK);
    lst.setBorder(brd);
    t.setBorder(brd);
    // Add the first four items to the List
    for(int i = 0; i < 4; i++)
      lItems.addElement(flavors[count++]);
    add(t);
    add(lst);
    add(b);
    // Register event listeners
    lst.addListSelectionListener(ll);
    b.addActionListener(bl);
  }
  public static void main(String[] args) {
    run(new List(), 250, 375);
  }
} ///:~
```

You can see that borders have also been added to the lists.

If you just want to put an array of **Strings** into a **JList**, there's a much simpler solution; you pass the array to the **JList** constructor, and it builds the list automatically. The only reason for using the "list model" in the preceding example is so that the list can be manipulated during the execution of the program.

JLists do not automatically provide direct support for scrolling. Of course, all you need to do is wrap the **JList** in a **JScrollPane**, and the details are automatically managed for you.

Exercise 16: (5) Simplify **List.java** by passing the array to the constructor and eliminating the dynamic addition of elements to the list.

Tabbed panes

The **JTabbedPane** allows you to create a "tabbed dialog," which has file-folder tabs running across one edge. When you press a tab, it brings forward a different dialog.

```java
//: gui/TabbedPane1.java
// Demonstrates the Tabbed Pane.
import javax.swing.*;
import javax.swing.event.*;
import java.awt.*;
import static net.mindview.util.SwingConsole.*;

public class TabbedPane1 extends JFrame {
  private String[] flavors = {
    "Chocolate", "Strawberry", "Vanilla Fudge Swirl",
    "Mint Chip", "Mocha Almond Fudge", "Rum Raisin",
    "Praline Cream", "Mud Pie"
  };
  private JTabbedPane tabs = new JTabbedPane();
  private JTextField txt = new JTextField(20);
  public TabbedPane1() {
    int i = 0;
    for(String flavor : flavors)
      tabs.addTab(flavors[i],
        new JButton("Tabbed pane " + i++));
    tabs.addChangeListener(new ChangeListener() {
      public void stateChanged(ChangeEvent e) {
        txt.setText("Tab selected: " +
          tabs.getSelectedIndex());
      }
    });
    add(BorderLayout.SOUTH, txt);
    add(tabs);
  }
  public static void main(String[] args) {
    run(new TabbedPane1(), 400, 250);
```

```
  }
} ///:~
```

When you run the program, you'll see that the **JTabbedPane** automatically stacks the tabs if there are too many of them to fit on one row. You can see this by resizing the window when you run the program from the console command line.

Message boxes

Windowing environments commonly contain a standard set of message boxes that allow you to quickly post information to the user or to capture information from the user. In Swing, these message boxes are contained in **JOptionPane**. You have many different possibilities (some quite sophisticated), but the ones you'll most commonly use are probably the message dialog and confirmation dialog, invoked using the **static JOptionPane.showMessageDialog( )** and **JOptionPane.showConfirmDialog( )**. The following example shows a subset of the message boxes available with **JOptionPane**:

```
//: gui/MessageBoxes.java
// Demonstrates JOptionPane.
import javax.swing.*;
import java.awt.*;
import java.awt.event.*;
import static net.mindview.util.SwingConsole.*;

public class MessageBoxes extends JFrame {
  private JButton[] b = {
    new JButton("Alert"), new JButton("Yes/No"),
    new JButton("Color"), new JButton("Input"),
    new JButton("3 Vals")
  };
  private JTextField txt = new JTextField(15);
  private ActionListener al = new ActionListener() {
    public void actionPerformed(ActionEvent e) {
      String id = ((JButton)e.getSource()).getText();
      if(id.equals("Alert"))
        JOptionPane.showMessageDialog(null,
          "There's a bug on you!", "Hey!",
          JOptionPane.ERROR_MESSAGE);
      else if(id.equals("Yes/No"))
        JOptionPane.showConfirmDialog(null,
          "or no", "choose yes",
```

```
            JOptionPane.YES_NO_OPTION);
        else if(id.equals("Color")) {
          Object[] options = { "Red", "Green" };
          int sel = JOptionPane.showOptionDialog(
              null, "Choose a Color!", "Warning",
              JOptionPane.DEFAULT_OPTION,
              JOptionPane.WARNING_MESSAGE, null,
              options, options[0]);
          if(sel != JOptionPane.CLOSED_OPTION)
            txt.setText("Color Selected: " + options[sel]);
        } else if(id.equals("Input")) {
          String val = JOptionPane.showInputDialog(
              "How many fingers do you see?");
          txt.setText(val);
        } else if(id.equals("3 Vals")) {
          Object[] selections = {"First", "Second", "Third"};
          Object val = JOptionPane.showInputDialog(
              null, "Choose one", "Input",
              JOptionPane.INFORMATION_MESSAGE,
              null, selections, selections[0]);
          if(val != null)
            txt.setText(val.toString());
        }
      }
    }
  };
  public MessageBoxes() {
    setLayout(new FlowLayout());
    for(int i = 0; i < b.length; i++) {
      b[i].addActionListener(al);
      add(b[i]);
    }
    add(txt);
  }
  public static void main(String[] args) {
    run(new MessageBoxes(), 200, 200);
  }
} ///:~
```

To write a single **ActionListener**, I've used the somewhat risky approach of checking the **String** labels on the buttons. The problem with this is that it's easy to get the label a little bit wrong, typically in capitalization, and this bug can be hard to spot.

Note that **showOptionDialog( )** and **showInputDialog( )** provide return objects that contain the value entered by the user.

Exercise 17: (5) Create an application using **SwingConsole**. In the JDK documentation from *http://java.sun.com*, find the **JPasswordField** and add this to the program. If the user types in the correct password, use **JOptionPane** to provide a success message to the user.

Exercise 18: (4) Modify **MessageBoxes.java** so that it has an individual **ActionListener** for each button (instead of matching the button text).

Menus

Each component capable of holding a menu, including **JApplet**, **JFrame**, **JDialog**, and their descendants, has a **setJMenuBar( )** method that accepts a **JMenuBar** (you can have only one **JMenuBar** on a particular component). You add **JMenu**s to the **JMenuBar**, and **JMenuItem**s to the **JMenus**. Each **JMenuItem** can have an **ActionListener** attached to it, to be fired when that menu item is selected.

With Java and Swing you must hand assemble all the menus in source code. Here is a very simple menu example:

```
//: gui/SimpleMenus.java
import javax.swing.*;
import java.awt.*;
import java.awt.event.*;
import static net.mindview.util.SwingConsole.*;

public class SimpleMenus extends JFrame {
  private JTextField t = new JTextField(15);
  private ActionListener al = new ActionListener() {
    public void actionPerformed(ActionEvent e) {
      t.setText(((JMenuItem)e.getSource()).getText());
    }
  };
  private JMenu[] menus = {
    new JMenu("Winken"), new JMenu("Blinken"),
    new JMenu("Nod")
  };
  private JMenuItem[] items = {
    new JMenuItem("Fee"), new JMenuItem("Fi"),
    new JMenuItem("Fo"),  new JMenuItem("Zip"),
```

```
      new JMenuItem("Zap"), new JMenuItem("Zot"),
      new JMenuItem("Olly"), new JMenuItem("Oxen"),
      new JMenuItem("Free")
  };
  public SimpleMenus() {
    for(int i = 0; i < items.length; i++) {
      items[i].addActionListener(al);
      menus[i % 3].add(items[i]);
    }
    JMenuBar mb = new JMenuBar();
    for(JMenu jm : menus)
      mb.add(jm);
    setJMenuBar(mb);
    setLayout(new FlowLayout());
    add(t);
  }
  public static void main(String[] args) {
    run(new SimpleMenus(), 200, 150);
  }
} ///:~
```

The use of the modulus operator in "**i%3**" distributes the menu items among the three **JMenu**s. Each **JMenuItem** must have an **ActionListener** attached to it; here, the same **ActionListener** is used everywhere, but you'll usually need an individual one for each **JMenuItem**.

JMenuItem inherits **AbstractButton**, so it has some button-like behaviors. By itself, it provides an item that can be placed on a drop-down menu. There are also three types inherited from **JMenuItem**: **JMenu**, to hold other **JMenuItem**s (so you can have cascading menus); **JCheckBoxMenuItem**, which produces a check mark to indicate whether that menu item is selected; and **JRadioButtonMenuItem**, which contains a radio button.

As a more sophisticated example, here are the ice cream flavors again, used to create menus. This example also shows cascading menus, keyboard mnemonics, **JCheckBoxMenuItem**s, and the way that you can dynamically change menus:

```
//: gui/Menus.java
// Submenus, check box menu items, swapping menus,
// mnemonics (shortcuts) and action commands.
import javax.swing.*;
import java.awt.*;
```

```
import java.awt.event.*;
import static net.mindview.util.SwingConsole.*;

public class Menus extends JFrame {
  private String[] flavors = {
    "Chocolate", "Strawberry", "Vanilla Fudge Swirl",
    "Mint Chip", "Mocha Almond Fudge", "Rum Raisin",
    "Praline Cream", "Mud Pie"
  };
  private JTextField t = new JTextField("No flavor", 30);
  private JMenuBar mb1 = new JMenuBar();
  private JMenu
    f = new JMenu("File"),
    m = new JMenu("Flavors"),
    s = new JMenu("Safety");
  // Alternative approach:
  private JCheckBoxMenuItem[] safety = {
    new JCheckBoxMenuItem("Guard"),
    new JCheckBoxMenuItem("Hide")
  };
  private JMenuItem[] file = { new JMenuItem("Open") };
  // A second menu bar to swap to:
  private JMenuBar mb2 = new JMenuBar();
  private JMenu fooBar = new JMenu("fooBar");
  private JMenuItem[] other = {
    // Adding a menu shortcut (mnemonic) is very
    // simple, but only JMenuItems can have them
    // in their constructors:
    new JMenuItem("Foo", KeyEvent.VK_F),
    new JMenuItem("Bar", KeyEvent.VK_A),
    // No shortcut:
    new JMenuItem("Baz"),
  };
  private JButton b = new JButton("Swap Menus");
  class BL implements ActionListener {
    public void actionPerformed(ActionEvent e) {
      JMenuBar m = getJMenuBar();
      setJMenuBar(m == mb1 ? mb2 : mb1);
      validate(); // Refresh the frame
    }
  }
  class ML implements ActionListener {
    public void actionPerformed(ActionEvent e) {
      JMenuItem target = (JMenuItem)e.getSource();
```

```java
        String actionCommand = target.getActionCommand();
        if(actionCommand.equals("Open")) {
          String s = t.getText();
          boolean chosen = false;
          for(String flavor : flavors)
            if(s.equals(flavor))
              chosen = true;
          if(!chosen)
            t.setText("Choose a flavor first!");
          else
            t.setText("Opening " + s + ". Mmm, mm!");
        }
      }
    }
    class FL implements ActionListener {
      public void actionPerformed(ActionEvent e) {
        JMenuItem target = (JMenuItem)e.getSource();
        t.setText(target.getText());
      }
    }
    // Alternatively, you can create a different
    // class for each different MenuItem. Then you
    // don't have to figure out which one it is:
    class FooL implements ActionListener {
      public void actionPerformed(ActionEvent e) {
        t.setText("Foo selected");
      }
    }
    class BarL implements ActionListener {
      public void actionPerformed(ActionEvent e) {
        t.setText("Bar selected");
      }
    }
    class BazL implements ActionListener {
      public void actionPerformed(ActionEvent e) {
        t.setText("Baz selected");
      }
    }
    class CMIL implements ItemListener {
      public void itemStateChanged(ItemEvent e) {
        JCheckBoxMenuItem target =
          (JCheckBoxMenuItem)e.getSource();
        String actionCommand = target.getActionCommand();
        if(actionCommand.equals("Guard"))
```

```java
          t.setText("Guard the Ice Cream! " +
            "Guarding is " + target.getState());
        else if(actionCommand.equals("Hide"))
          t.setText("Hide the Ice Cream! " +
            "Is it hidden? " + target.getState());
      }
    }
    public Menus() {
      ML ml = new ML();
      CMIL cmil = new CMIL();
      safety[0].setActionCommand("Guard");
      safety[0].setMnemonic(KeyEvent.VK_G);
      safety[0].addItemListener(cmil);
      safety[1].setActionCommand("Hide");
      safety[1].setMnemonic(KeyEvent.VK_H);
      safety[1].addItemListener(cmil);
      other[0].addActionListener(new FooL());
      other[1].addActionListener(new BarL());
      other[2].addActionListener(new BazL());
      FL fl = new FL();
      int n = 0;
      for(String flavor : flavors) {
        JMenuItem mi = new JMenuItem(flavor);
        mi.addActionListener(fl);
        m.add(mi);
        // Add separators at intervals:
        if((n++ + 1) % 3 == 0)
          m.addSeparator();
      }
      for(JCheckBoxMenuItem sfty : safety)
        s.add(sfty);
      s.setMnemonic(KeyEvent.VK_A);
      f.add(s);
      f.setMnemonic(KeyEvent.VK_F);
      for(int i = 0; i < file.length; i++) {
        file[i].addActionListener(ml);
        f.add(file[i]);
      }
      mb1.add(f);
      mb1.add(m);
      setJMenuBar(mb1);
      t.setEditable(false);
      add(t, BorderLayout.CENTER);
      // Set up the system for swapping menus:
```

```
    b.addActionListener(new BL());
    b.setMnemonic(KeyEvent.VK_S);
    add(b, BorderLayout.NORTH);
    for(JMenuItem oth : other)
      fooBar.add(oth);
    fooBar.setMnemonic(KeyEvent.VK_B);
    mb2.add(fooBar);
  }
  public static void main(String[] args) {
    run(new Menus(), 300, 200);
  }
} ///:~
```

In this program I placed the menu items into arrays and then stepped through each array, calling **add( )** for each **JMenuItem**. This makes adding or subtracting a menu item somewhat less tedious.

This program creates two **JMenuBar**s to demonstrate that menu bars can be actively swapped while the program is running. You can see how a **JMenuBar** is made up of **JMenu**s, and each **JMenu** is made up of **JMenuItem**s, **JCheckBoxMenuItem**s, or even other **JMenu**s (which produce submenus). When a **JMenuBar** is assembled, it can be installed into the current program with the **setJMenuBar( )** method. Note that when the button is pressed, it checks to see which menu is currently installed by calling **getJMenuBar( )**, then it puts the other menu bar in its place.

When testing for "Open," notice that spelling and capitalization are critical, but Java signals no error if there is no match with "Open." This kind of string comparison is a source of programming errors.

The checking and unchecking of the menu items is taken care of automatically. The code handling the **JCheckBoxMenuItem**s shows two different ways to determine what was checked: string matching (the less-safe approach, although you'll see it used) and matching on the event target object. As shown, the **getState( )** method can be used to reveal the state. You can also change the state of a **JCheckBoxMenuItem** with **setState( )**.

The events for menus are a bit inconsistent and can lead to confusion: **JMenuItem**s use **ActionListener**s, but **JCheckBoxMenuItem**s use **ItemListener**s. The **JMenu** objects can also support **ActionListener**s, but that's not usually helpful. In general, you'll attach listeners to each **JMenuItem**, **JCheckBoxMenuItem**, or **JRadioButtonMenuItem**, but the example shows **ItemListener**s and **ActionListener**s attached to the various menu components.

Swing supports mnemonics, or "keyboard shortcuts," so you can select anything derived from **AbstractButton** (button, menu item, etc.) by using the keyboard instead of the mouse. These are quite simple; for **JMenuItem**, you can use the overloaded constructor that takes, as a second argument, the identifier for the key. However, most **AbstractButton**s do not have constructors like this, so the more general way to solve the problem is to use the **setMnemonic( )** method. The preceding example adds mnemonics to the button and some of the menu items; shortcut indicators automatically appear on the components.

You can also see the use of **setActionCommand( )**. This seems a bit strange because in each case, the "action command" is exactly the same as the label on the menu component. Why not just use the label instead of this alternative string? The problem is internationalization. If you retarget this program to another language, you want to change only the label in the menu, and not change the code (which would no doubt introduce new errors). By using **setActionCommand( )**, the "action command" can be immutable, but the menu label can change. All the code works with the "action command," so it's unaffected by changes to the menu labels. Note that in this program, not all the menu components are examined for their action commands, so those that aren't do not have their action command set.

The bulk of the work happens in the listeners. **BL** performs the **JMenuBar** swapping. In **ML**, the "figure out who rang" approach is taken by getting the source of the **ActionEvent** and casting it to a **JMenuItem**, then getting the action command string to pass it through a cascaded **if** statement.

The **FL** listener is simple even though it's handling all the different flavors in the flavor menu. This approach is useful if you have enough simplicity in your logic, but in general, you'll want to take the approach used with **FooL**, **BarL**, and **BazL**, in which each is attached to only a single menu component, so no extra detection logic is necessary, and you know exactly who called the listener. Even with the profusion of classes generated this way, the code inside tends to be smaller, and the process is more foolproof.

You can see that menu code quickly gets long-winded and messy. This is another case where the use of a GUI builder is the appropriate solution. A good tool will also handle the maintenance of the menus.

Exercise 19: (3) Modify **Menus.java** to use radio buttons instead of check boxes on the menus.

Exercise 20: (6) Create a program that breaks a text file into words. Distribute those words as labels on menus and submenus.

Pop-up menus

The most straightforward way to implement a **JPopupMenu** is to create an inner class that extends **MouseAdapter**, then add an object of that inner class to each component that you want to produce pop-up behavior:

```
//: gui/Popup.java
// Creating popup menus with Swing.
import javax.swing.*;
import java.awt.*;
import java.awt.event.*;
import static net.mindview.util.SwingConsole.*;

public class Popup extends JFrame {
  private JPopupMenu popup = new JPopupMenu();
  private JTextField t = new JTextField(10);
  public Popup() {
    setLayout(new FlowLayout());
    add(t);
    ActionListener al = new ActionListener() {
      public void actionPerformed(ActionEvent e) {
        t.setText(((JMenuItem)e.getSource()).getText());
      }
    };
    JMenuItem m = new JMenuItem("Hither");
    m.addActionListener(al);
    popup.add(m);
    m = new JMenuItem("Yon");
    m.addActionListener(al);
    popup.add(m);
    m = new JMenuItem("Afar");
    m.addActionListener(al);
    popup.add(m);
    popup.addSeparator();
    m = new JMenuItem("Stay Here");
    m.addActionListener(al);
    popup.add(m);
    PopupListener pl = new PopupListener();
    addMouseListener(pl);
```

```
    t.addMouseListener(pl);
  }
  class PopupListener extends MouseAdapter {
    public void mousePressed(MouseEvent e) {
      maybeShowPopup(e);
    }
    public void mouseReleased(MouseEvent e) {
      maybeShowPopup(e);
    }
    private void maybeShowPopup(MouseEvent e) {
      if(e.isPopupTrigger())
        popup.show(e.getComponent(), e.getX(), e.getY());
    }
  }
  public static void main(String[] args) {
    run(new Popup(), 300, 200);
  }
} ///:~
```

The same **ActionListener** is added to each **JMenuItem**. It fetches the text from the menu label and inserts it into the **JTextField**.

Drawing

In a good GUI framework, drawing should be reasonably easy—and it is, in the Swing library. The problem with any drawing example is that the calculations that determine where things go are typically a lot more complicated than the calls to the drawing routines, and these calculations are often mixed together with the drawing calls, so it can seem that the interface is more complicated than it actually is.

For simplicity, consider the problem of representing data on the screen— here, the data will be provided by the built-in **Math.sin( )** method, which produces a mathematical sine function. To make things a little more interesting, and to further demonstrate how easy it is to use Swing components, a slider will be placed at the bottom of the form to dynamically control the number of sine wave cycles that are displayed. In addition, if you resize the window, you'll see that the sine wave refits itself to the new window size.

Although any **JComponent** may be painted and thus used as a canvas, if you just want a straightforward drawing surface, you will typically inherit from a **JPanel**. The only method you need to override is **paintComponent( )**,

---

which is called whenever that component must be repainted (you normally don't need to worry about this, because the decision is managed by Swing). When it is called, Swing passes a **Graphics** object to the method, and you can then use this object to draw or paint on the surface.

In the following example, all the intelligence concerning painting is in the **SineDraw** class; the **SineWave** class simply configures the program and the slider control. Inside **SineDraw**, the **setCycles( )** method provides a hook to allow another object—the slider control, in this case—to control the number of cycles.

```java
//: gui/SineWave.java
// Drawing with Swing, using a JSlider.
import javax.swing.*;
import javax.swing.event.*;
import java.awt.*;
import static net.mindview.util.SwingConsole.*;

class SineDraw extends JPanel {
  private static final int SCALEFACTOR = 200;
  private int cycles;
  private int points;
  private double[] sines;
  private int[] pts;
  public SineDraw() { setCycles(5); }
  public void paintComponent(Graphics g) {
    super.paintComponent(g);
    int maxWidth = getWidth();
    double hstep = (double)maxWidth / (double)points;
    int maxHeight = getHeight();
    pts = new int[points];
    for(int i = 0; i < points; i++)
      pts[i] =
        (int)(sines[i] * maxHeight/2 * .95 + maxHeight/2);
    g.setColor(Color.RED);
    for(int i = 1; i < points; i++) {
      int x1 = (int)((i - 1) * hstep);
      int x2 = (int)(i * hstep);
      int y1 = pts[i-1];
      int y2 = pts[i];
      g.drawLine(x1, y1, x2, y2);
    }
  }
  public void setCycles(int newCycles) {
```

```
        cycles = newCycles;
        points = SCALEFACTOR * cycles * 2;
        sines = new double[points];
        for(int i = 0; i < points; i++) {
          double radians = (Math.PI / SCALEFACTOR) * i;
          sines[i] = Math.sin(radians);
        }
        repaint();
      }
    }

    public class SineWave extends JFrame {
      private SineDraw sines = new SineDraw();
      private JSlider adjustCycles = new JSlider(1, 30, 5);
      public SineWave() {
        add(sines);
        adjustCycles.addChangeListener(new ChangeListener() {
          public void stateChanged(ChangeEvent e) {
            sines.setCycles(
              ((JSlider)e.getSource()).getValue());
          }
        });
        add(BorderLayout.SOUTH, adjustCycles);
      }
      public static void main(String[] args) {
        run(new SineWave(), 700, 400);
      }
    } ///:~
```

All of the fields and arrays are used in the calculation of the sine wave points; **cycles** indicates the number of complete sine waves desired, **points** contains the total number of points that will be graphed, **sines** contains the sine function values, and **pts** contains the y-coordinates of the points that will be drawn on the **JPanel**. The **setCycles( )** method creates the arrays according to the number of points needed and fills the **sines** array with numbers. By calling **repaint( )**, **setCycles( )** forces **paintComponent( )** to be called so the rest of the calculation and redraw will take place.

The first thing you must do when you override **paintComponent( )** is to call the base-class version of the method. Then you are free to do whatever you like; normally, this means using the **Graphics** methods that you can find in the documentation for **java.awt.Graphics** (in the JDK documentation from *http://java.sun.com*) to draw and paint pixels onto the **JPanel**. Here, you can see that almost all the code is involved in performing the calculations; the only two method calls that actually manipulate the screen are **setColor( )** and **drawLine( )**. You will probably have a similar experience when creating your own program that displays graphical data; you'll spend most of your time figuring out what it is you want to draw, but the actual drawing process will be quite simple.

When I created this program, the bulk of my time was spent in getting the sine wave to display. Once I did that, I thought it would be nice to dynamically change the number of cycles. My programming experiences when trying to do such things in other languages made me a bit reluctant to try this, but it turned out to be the easiest part of the project. I created a **JSlider** (the arguments are the leftmost value of the **JSlider**, the rightmost value, and the starting value, respectively, but there are other constructors as well) and dropped it into the **JFrame**. Then I looked at the JDK documentation and noticed that the only listener was the **addChangeListener**, which was triggered whenever the slider was changed enough for it to produce a different value. The only method for this was the obviously named **stateChanged( )**, which provided a **ChangeEvent** object so that I could look backward to the source of the change and find the new value. Calling the **sines** object's **setCycles( )** enabled the new value to be incorporated and the **JPanel** to be redrawn.

In general, you will find that most of your Swing problems can be solved by following a similar process, and you'll find that it's generally quite simple, even if you haven't used a particular component before.

If your problem is more complex, there are other, more sophisticated alternatives for drawing, including third-party JavaBeans components and the Java 2D API. These solutions are beyond the scope of this book, but you should look them up if your drawing code becomes too onerous.

Exercise 21:   (5) Modify **SineWave.java** to turn **SineDraw** into a JavaBean by adding "getter" and "setter" methods.

Exercise 22:   (7) Create an application using **SwingConsole**. This should have three sliders, one each for the red, green, and blue values in **java.awt.Color**. The rest of the form should be a **JPanel** that displays the color determined by the three sliders. Also include non-editable text fields that show the current RGB values.

Exercise 23: (8) Using **SineWave.java** as a starting point, create a program that displays a rotating square on the screen. One slider should control the speed of rotation, and a second slider should control the size of the box.

Exercise 24: (7) Remember the "sketching box" toy with two knobs, one that controls the vertical movement of the drawing point, and one that controls the horizontal movement? Create a variation of this toy, using **SineWave.java** to get you started. Instead of knobs, use sliders. Add a button that will erase the entire sketch.

Exercise 25: (8) Starting with **SineWave.java**, create a program (an application using the **SwingConsole** class) that draws an animated sine wave that appears to scroll past the viewing window like an oscilloscope, driving the animation with a **java.util.Timer**. The speed of the animation should be controlled with a **javax.swing.JSlider** control.

Exercise 26: (5) Modify the previous exercise so that multiple sine wave panels are created within the application. The number of sine wave panels should be controlled by command-line parameters.

Exercise 27: (5) Modify Exercise 25 so that the **javax.swing.Timer** class is used to drive the animation. Note the difference between this and **java.util.Timer**.

Exercise 28: (7) Create a dice class (just a class, without a GUI). Create five dice and throw them repeatedly. Draw the curve showing the sum of the dots from each throw, and show the curve evolving dynamically as you throw more and more times.

Dialog boxes

A dialog box is a window that pops up out of another window. Its purpose is to deal with some specific issue without cluttering the original window with those details. Dialog boxes are commonly used in windowed programming environments.

To create a dialog box, you inherit from **JDialog**, which is just another kind of **Window**, like a **JFrame**. A **JDialog** has a layout manager (which defaults to **BorderLayout**), and you add event listeners to deal with events. Here's a very simple example:

```
//: gui/Dialogs.java
// Creating and using Dialog Boxes.
import javax.swing.*;
```

```
import java.awt.*;
import java.awt.event.*;
import static net.mindview.util.SwingConsole.*;

class MyDialog extends JDialog {
  public MyDialog(JFrame parent) {
    super(parent, "My dialog", true);
    setLayout(new FlowLayout());
    add(new JLabel("Here is my dialog"));
    JButton ok = new JButton("OK");
    ok.addActionListener(new ActionListener() {
      public void actionPerformed(ActionEvent e) {
        dispose(); // Closes the dialog
      }
    });
    add(ok);
    setSize(150,125);
  }
}

public class Dialogs extends JFrame {
  private JButton b1 = new JButton("Dialog Box");
  private MyDialog dlg = new MyDialog(null);
  public Dialogs() {
    b1.addActionListener(new ActionListener() {
      public void actionPerformed(ActionEvent e) {
        dlg.setVisible(true);
      }
    });
    add(b1);
  }
  public static void main(String[] args) {
    run(new Dialogs(), 125, 75);
  }
} ///:~
```

Once the **JDialog** is created, **setVisible(true)** must be called to display and
activate it. When the dialog window is closed, you must release the resources
used by the dialog's window by calling **dispose( )**.

The following example is more complex; the dialog box is made up of a grid
(using **GridLayout**) of a special kind of button that is defined here as class
ToeButton. This button draws a frame around itself and, depending on its
state, a blank, an "x," or an "o" in the middle. It starts out blank, and then

---

Graphical User Interfaces   1365 depending on whose turn it is, changes to an "x" or an "o." However, it will also flip back and forth between "x" and "o" when you click on the button, to provide an interesting variation on the tic-tac-toe concept. In addition, the dialog box can be set up for any number of rows and columns by changing numbers in the main application window.

```java
//: gui/TicTacToe.java
// Dialog boxes and creating your own components.
import javax.swing.*;
import java.awt.*;
import java.awt.event.*;
import static net.mindview.util.SwingConsole.*;

public class TicTacToe extends JFrame {
  private JTextField
    rows = new JTextField("3"),
    cols = new JTextField("3");
  private enum State { BLANK, XX, OO }
  static class ToeDialog extends JDialog {
    private State turn = State.XX; // Start with x's turn
    ToeDialog(int cellsWide, int cellsHigh) {
      setTitle("The game itself");
      setLayout(new GridLayout(cellsWide, cellsHigh));
      for(int i = 0; i < cellsWide * cellsHigh; i++)
        add(new ToeButton());
      setSize(cellsWide * 50, cellsHigh * 50);
      setDefaultCloseOperation(DISPOSE_ON_CLOSE);
    }
    class ToeButton extends JPanel {
      private State state = State.BLANK;
      public ToeButton() { addMouseListener(new ML()); }
      public void paintComponent(Graphics g) {
        super.paintComponent(g);
        int
          x1 = 0, y1 = 0,
          x2 = getSize().width - 1,
          y2 = getSize().height - 1;
        g.drawRect(x1, y1, x2, y2);
        x1 = x2/4;
        y1 = y2/4;
        int wide = x2/2, high = y2/2;
        if(state == State.XX) {
          g.drawLine(x1, y1, x1 + wide, y1 + high);
          g.drawLine(x1, y1 + high, x1 + wide, y1);
```

```
        }
        if(state == State.OO)
          g.drawOval(x1, y1, x1 + wide/2, y1 + high/2);
      }
      class ML extends MouseAdapter {
        public void mousePressed(MouseEvent e) {
          if(state == State.BLANK) {
            state = turn;
            turn =
              (turn == State.XX ? State.OO : State.XX);
          }
          else
            state =
              (state == State.XX ? State.OO : State.XX);
          repaint();
        }
      }
    }
    class BL implements ActionListener {
      public void actionPerformed(ActionEvent e) {
        JDialog d = new ToeDialog(
          new Integer(rows.getText()),
          new Integer(cols.getText()));
        d.setVisible(true);
      }
    }
    public TicTacToe() {
      JPanel p = new JPanel();
      p.setLayout(new GridLayout(2,2));
      p.add(new JLabel("Rows", JLabel.CENTER));
      p.add(rows);
      p.add(new JLabel("Columns", JLabel.CENTER));
      p.add(cols);
      add(p, BorderLayout.NORTH);
      JButton b = new JButton("go");
      b.addActionListener(new BL());
      add(b, BorderLayout.SOUTH);
    }
    public static void main(String[] args) {
      run(new TicTacToe(), 200, 200);
    }
} ///:~
```

Because **static**s can only be at the outer level of the class, inner classes cannot have **static** data or nested classes.

The **paintComponent( )** method draws the square around the panel and the "x" or the "o." This is full of tedious calculations, but it's straightforward.

A mouse click is captured by the **MouseListener**, which first checks to see if the panel has anything written on it. If not, the parent window is queried to find out whose turn it is, which establishes the state of the **ToeButton**. Via the inner-class mechanism, the **ToeButton** then reaches back into the parent and changes the turn. If the button is already displaying an "x" or an "o," then that is flopped. You can see in these calculations the convenient use of the ternary **if-else** described in the *Operators* chapter. After a state change, the **ToeButton** is repainted.

The constructor for **ToeDialog** is quite simple: It adds into a **GridLayout** as many buttons as you request, then resizes it for 50 pixels on a side for each button.

TicTacToe sets up the whole application by creating the **JTextField**s (for inputting the rows and columns of the button grid) and the "go" button with its **ActionListener**. When the button is pressed, the data in the **JTextField**s must be fetched, and, since they are in **String** form, turned into **int**s using the **Integer** constructor that takes a **String** argument.

File dialogs

Some operating systems have a number of special built-in dialog boxes to handle the selection of things such as fonts, colors, printers, and the like. Virtually all graphical operating systems support the opening and saving of files, so Java's **JFileChooser** encapsulates these for easy use.

The following application exercises two forms of **JFileChooser** dialogs, one for opening and one for saving. Most of the code should by now be familiar, and all the interesting activities happen in the action listeners for the two different button clicks:

```
//: gui/FileChooserTest.java
// Demonstration of File dialog boxes.
import javax.swing.*;
import java.awt.*;
import java.awt.event.*;
import static net.mindview.util.SwingConsole.*;
```

```java
public class FileChooserTest extends JFrame {
  private JTextField
    fileName = new JTextField(),
    dir = new JTextField();
  private JButton
    open = new JButton("Open"),
    save = new JButton("Save");
  public FileChooserTest() {
    JPanel p = new JPanel();
    open.addActionListener(new OpenL());
    p.add(open);
    save.addActionListener(new SaveL());
    p.add(save);
    add(p, BorderLayout.SOUTH);
    dir.setEditable(false);
    fileName.setEditable(false);
    p = new JPanel();
    p.setLayout(new GridLayout(2,1));
    p.add(fileName);
    p.add(dir);
    add(p, BorderLayout.NORTH);
  }
  class OpenL implements ActionListener {
    public void actionPerformed(ActionEvent e) {
      JFileChooser c = new JFileChooser();
      // Demonstrate "Open" dialog:
      int rVal = c.showOpenDialog(FileChooserTest.this);
      if(rVal == JFileChooser.APPROVE_OPTION) {
        fileName.setText(c.getSelectedFile().getName());
        dir.setText(c.getCurrentDirectory().toString());
      }
      if(rVal == JFileChooser.CANCEL_OPTION) {
        fileName.setText("You pressed cancel");
        dir.setText("");
      }
    }
  }
  class SaveL implements ActionListener {
    public void actionPerformed(ActionEvent e) {
      JFileChooser c = new JFileChooser();
      // Demonstrate "Save" dialog:
      int rVal = c.showSaveDialog(FileChooserTest.this);
      if(rVal == JFileChooser.APPROVE_OPTION) {
```

```
        fileName.setText(c.getSelectedFile().getName());
        dir.setText(c.getCurrentDirectory().toString());
      }
      if(rVal == JFileChooser.CANCEL_OPTION) {
        fileName.setText("You pressed cancel");
        dir.setText("");
      }
    }
  }
  public static void main(String[] args) {
    run(new FileChooserTest(), 250, 150);
  }
} ///:~
```

Note that there are many variations you can apply to **JFileChooser**, including filters to narrow the file names that you will allow.

For an "open file" dialog, you call **showOpenDialog( )**, and for a "save file" dialog, you call **showSaveDialog( )**. These commands don't return until the dialog is closed. The **JFileChooser** object still exists, so you can read data from it. The methods **getSelectedFile( )** and **getCurrentDirectory( )** are two ways you can interrogate the results of the operation. If these return **null**, it means the user canceled out of the dialog.

Exercise 29: (3) In the JDK documentation for **javax.swing**, look up the **JColorChooser**. Write a program with a button that brings up the color chooser as a dialog.

HTML on Swing components

Any component that can take text can also take HTML text, which it will reformat according to HTML rules. This means you can very easily add fancy text to a Swing component. For example:

```
//: gui/HTMLButton.java
// Putting HTML text on Swing components.
import javax.swing.*;
import java.awt.*;
import java.awt.event.*;
import static net.mindview.util.SwingConsole.*;

public class HTMLButton extends JFrame {
  private JButton b = new JButton(
    "<html><b><font size=+2>" +
```

```
    "<center>Hello!<br><i>Press me now!");
  public HTMLButton() {
    b.addActionListener(new ActionListener() {
      public void actionPerformed(ActionEvent e) {
        add(new JLabel("<html>" +
          "<i><font size=+4>Kapow!"));
        // Force a re-layout to include the new label:
        validate();
      }
    });
    setLayout(new FlowLayout());
    add(b);
  }
  public static void main(String[] args) {
    run(new HTMLButton(), 200, 500);
  }
} ///:~
```

You must start the text with "<html>," and then you can use normal HTML tags. Note that you are not forced to include the normal closing tags.

The **ActionListener** adds a new **JLabel** to the form, which also contains HTML text. However, this label is not added during construction, so you must call the container's **validate( )** method in order to force a re-layout of the components (and thus the display of the new label).

You can also use HTML text for **JTabbedPane**, **JMenuItem**, **JToolTip**, **JRadioButton**, and **JCheckBox**.

Exercise 30: (3) Write a program that shows the use of HTML text on all the items from the previous paragraph.

Sliders and progress bars

A slider (which has already been used in **SineWave.java**) allows the user to input data by moving a point back and forth, which is intuitive in some situations (volume controls, for example). A progress bar displays data in a relative fashion from "full" to "empty" so the user gets a perspective. My favorite example for these is to simply hook the slider to the progress bar so when you move the slider, the progress bar changes accordingly. The following example also demonstrates the **ProgressMonitor**, a more full-featured pop-up dialog:

```
//: gui/Progress.java
```

```
// Using sliders, progress bars and progress monitors.
import javax.swing.*;
import javax.swing.border.*;
import javax.swing.event.*;
import java.awt.*;
import static net.mindview.util.SwingConsole.*;

public class Progress extends JFrame {
  private JProgressBar pb = new JProgressBar();
  private ProgressMonitor pm = new ProgressMonitor(
    this, "Monitoring Progress", "Test", 0, 100);
  private JSlider sb =
    new JSlider(JSlider.HORIZONTAL, 0, 100, 60);
  public Progress() {
    setLayout(new GridLayout(2,1));
    add(pb);
    pm.setProgress(0);
    pm.setMillisToPopup(1000);
    sb.setValue(0);
    sb.setPaintTicks(true);
    sb.setMajorTickSpacing(20);
    sb.setMinorTickSpacing(5);
    sb.setBorder(new TitledBorder("Slide Me"));
    pb.setModel(sb.getModel()); // Share model
    add(sb);
    sb.addChangeListener(new ChangeListener() {
      public void stateChanged(ChangeEvent e) {
        pm.setProgress(sb.getValue());
      }
    });
  }
  public static void main(String[] args) {
    run(new Progress(), 300, 200);
  }
} ///:~
```

The key to hooking the slider and progress bar components together is in sharing their model, in the line:

```
pb.setModel(sb.getModel());
```

Of course, you could also control the two using a listener, but using the model is more straightforward for simple situations. The **ProgressMonitor** does not have a model and so the listener approach is required. Note that the **ProgressMonitor** only moves forward, and once it reaches the end it closes.

The **JProgressBar** is fairly straightforward, but the **JSlider** has a lot of options, such as the orientation and major and minor tick marks. Notice how straightforward it is to add a titled border.

Exercise 31: (8) Create an "asymptotic progress indicator" that gets slower and slower as it approaches the finish point. Add random erratic behavior so it will periodically look like it's starting to speed up.

Exercise 32: (6) Modify **Progress.java** so that it does not share models, but instead uses a listener to connect the slider and progress bar.

Selecting look & feel

"Pluggable look & feel" allows your program to emulate the look and feel of various operating environments. You can even dynamically change the look and feel while the program is executing. However, you generally just want to do one of two things: either select the "cross-platform" look and feel (which is Swing's "metal"), or select the look and feel for the system you are currently on so your Java program looks like it was created specifically for that system (this is almost certainly the best choice in most cases, to avoid confounding the user). The code to select either of these behaviors is quite simple, but you must execute it *before* you create any visual components, because the components will be made based on the current look and feel, and will not be changed just because you happen to change the look and feel midway during the program (that process is more complicated and uncommon, and is relegated to Swing-specific books).

Actually, if you want to use the cross-platform ("metal") look and feel that is characteristic of Swing programs, you don't have to do anything—it's the default. But if you want instead to use the current operating environment's look and feel,[8] you just insert the following code, typically at the beginning of your **main( )**, but at least before any components are added:

```
try {
  UIManager.setLookAndFeel(
    UIManager.getSystemLookAndFeelClassName());
} catch(Exception e) {
  throw new RuntimeException(e);
```

---

[8] You may argue about whether the Swing rendering does justice to your operating environment.

}

You don't actually need anything in the **catch** clause because the **UIManager** will default to the cross-platform look and feel if your attempts to set up any of the alternatives fail. However, during debugging, the exception can be quite useful, so you may at least want to see some results via the **catch** clause.

Here is a program that takes a command-line argument to select a look and feel, and shows how several different components look under the chosen look and feel:

```
//: gui/LookAndFeel.java
// Selecting different looks & feels.
// {Args: motif}
import javax.swing.*;
import java.awt.*;
import static net.mindview.util.SwingConsole.*;

public class LookAndFeel extends JFrame {
  private String[] choices =
    "Eeny Meeny Minnie Mickey Moe Larry Curly".split(" ");
  private Component[] samples = {
    new JButton("JButton"),
    new JTextField("JTextField"),
    new JLabel("JLabel"),
    new JCheckBox("JCheckBox"),
    new JRadioButton("Radio"),
    new JComboBox(choices),
    new JList(choices),
  };
  public LookAndFeel() {
    super("Look And Feel");
    setLayout(new FlowLayout());
    for(Component component : samples)
      add(component);
  }
  private static void usageError() {
    System.out.println(
      "Usage:LookAndFeel [cross|system|motif]");
    System.exit(1);
  }
  public static void main(String[] args) {
    if(args.length == 0) usageError();
```

```
        if(args[0].equals("cross")) {
          try {
            UIManager.setLookAndFeel(UIManager.
              getCrossPlatformLookAndFeelClassName());
          } catch(Exception e) {
            e.printStackTrace();
          }
        } else if(args[0].equals("system")) {
          try {
            UIManager.setLookAndFeel(UIManager.
              getSystemLookAndFeelClassName());
          } catch(Exception e) {
            e.printStackTrace();
          }
        } else if(args[0].equals("motif")) {
          try {
            UIManager.setLookAndFeel("com.sun.java."+
              "swing.plaf.motif.MotifLookAndFeel");
          } catch(Exception e) {
            e.printStackTrace();
          }
        } else usageError();
        // Note the look & feel must be set before
        // any components are created.
        run(new LookAndFeel(), 300, 300);
    }
} ///:~
```

You can see that one option is to explicitly specify a string for a look and feel,
as seen with **MotifLookAndFeel**. However, that one and the default
"metal" look and feel are the only ones that can legally be used on any
platform; even though there are look-and-feel strings for Windows and
Macintosh, those can only be used on their respective platforms (these are
produced when you call **getSystemLookAndFeelClassName( )** and
you're on that particular platform).

It is also possible to create a custom look and feel package, for example, if you
are building a framework for a company that wants a distinctive appearance.
This is a big job and is far beyond the scope of this book (in fact, you'll
discover it is beyond the scope of many dedicated Swing books!).

Graphical User Interfaces

Trees, tables & clipboard

You can find a brief introduction and examples for these topics in the online supplements for this chapter at *www.MindView.net*.

JNLP and Java Web Start

It's possible to *sign* an applet for security purposes. This is shown in the online supplement for this chapter at *www.MindView.net*. Signed applets are powerful and can effectively take the place of an application, but they must run inside a Web browser. This requires the extra overhead of the browser running on the client machine, and also means that the user interface of the applet is limited and often visually confusing. The Web browser has its own set of menus and toolbars, which will appear above the applet.[9]

The *Java Network Launch Protocol* (JNLP) solves the problem without sacrificing the advantages of applets. With a JNLP application, you can download and install a standalone Java application onto the client's machine. This can be run from the command prompt, a desktop icon, or the application manager that is installed with your JNLP implementation. The application can even be run from the Web site from which it was originally downloaded.

A JNLP application can dynamically download resources from the Internet at run time, and can automatically check the version if the user is connected to the Internet. This means that it has all of the advantages of an applet together with the advantages of standalone applications.

Like applets, JNLP applications need to be treated with some caution by the client's system. Because of this, JNLP applications are subject to the same sandbox security restrictions as applets. Like applets, they can be deployed in signed JAR files, giving the user the option to trust the signer. Unlike applets, if they are deployed in an unsigned JAR file, they can still request access to certain resources of the client's system by means of services in the JNLP API. The user must approve these requests during program execution.

JNLP describes a protocol, not an implementation, so you will need an implementation in order to use it. Java Web Start, or JAWS, is Sun's freely available official reference implementation and is distributed as part of Java

---

[9] Jeremy Meyer developed this section.

SE5. If you are using it for development, you must ensure that the JAR file (**javaws.jar**) is in your classpath; the easiest solution is to add **javaws.jar** to your classpath from its normal Java installation path in **jre/lib**. If you are deploying your JNLP application from a Web server, you must ensure that your server recognizes the MIME type **application/x-java-jnlp-file**. If you are using a recent version of the Tomcat server (*http://jakarta.apache.org/tomcat*) this is pre-configured. Consult the user guide for your particular server.

Creating a JNLP application is not difficult. You create a standard application that is archived in a JAR file, and then you provide a launch file, which is a simple XML file that gives the client system all the information it needs to download and install your application. If you choose not to sign your JAR file, then you must use the services supplied by the JNLP API for each type of resource you want to access on the user's machine.

Here is a variation of **FileChooserTest.java** using the JNLP services to open the file chooser, so that the class can be deployed as a JNLP application in an unsigned JAR file.

```
//: gui/jnlp/JnlpFileChooser.java
// Opening files on a local machine with JNLP.
// {Requires: javax.jnlp.FileOpenService;
// You must have javaws.jar in your classpath}
// To create the jnlpfilechooser.jar file, do this:
// cd ..
// cd ..
// jar cvf gui/jnlp/jnlpfilechooser.jar gui/jnlp/*.class
package gui.jnlp;
import javax.jnlp.*;
import javax.swing.*;
import java.awt.*;
import java.awt.event.*;
import java.io.*;

public class JnlpFileChooser extends JFrame {
  private JTextField fileName = new JTextField();
  private JButton
    open = new JButton("Open"),
    save = new JButton("Save");
  private JEditorPane ep = new JEditorPane();
  private JScrollPane jsp = new JScrollPane();
  private FileContents fileContents;
```

```java
public JnlpFileChooser() {
  JPanel p = new JPanel();
  open.addActionListener(new OpenL());
  p.add(open);
  save.addActionListener(new SaveL());
  p.add(save);
  jsp.getViewport().add(ep);
  add(jsp, BorderLayout.CENTER);
  add(p, BorderLayout.SOUTH);
  fileName.setEditable(false);
  p = new JPanel();
  p.setLayout(new GridLayout(2,1));
  p.add(fileName);
  add(p, BorderLayout.NORTH);
  ep.setContentType("text");
  save.setEnabled(false);
}
class OpenL implements ActionListener {
  public void actionPerformed(ActionEvent e) {
    FileOpenService fs = null;
    try {
      fs = (FileOpenService)ServiceManager.lookup(
        "javax.jnlp.FileOpenService");
    } catch(UnavailableServiceException use) {
      throw new RuntimeException(use);
    }
    if(fs != null) {
      try {
        fileContents = fs.openFileDialog(".",
          new String[]{"txt", "*"});
        if(fileContents == null)
          return;
        fileName.setText(fileContents.getName());
        ep.read(fileContents.getInputStream(), null);
      } catch(Exception exc) {
        throw new RuntimeException(exc);
      }
      save.setEnabled(true);
    }
  }
}
class SaveL implements ActionListener {
  public void actionPerformed(ActionEvent e) {
    FileSaveService fs = null;
```

```
        try {
          fs = (FileSaveService)ServiceManager.lookup(
            "javax.jnlp.FileSaveService");
        } catch(UnavailableServiceException use) {
          throw new RuntimeException(use);
        }
        if(fs != null) {
          try {
            fileContents = fs.saveFileDialog(".",
              new String[]{"txt"},
              new ByteArrayInputStream(
                ep.getText().getBytes()),
              fileContents.getName());
            if(fileContents == null)
              return;
            fileName.setText(fileContents.getName());
          } catch(Exception exc) {
            throw new RuntimeException(exc);
          }
        }
      }
    }
    public static void main(String[] args) {
      JnlpFileChooser fc = new JnlpFileChooser();
      fc.setSize(400, 300);
      fc.setVisible(true);
    }
} ///:~
```

Note that the **FileOpenService** and the **FileSaveService** classes are imported from the **javax.jnlp** package and that nowhere in the code is the **JFileChooser** dialog box referred to directly. The two services used here must be requested using the **ServiceManager.lookup( )** method, and the resources on the client system can only be accessed via the objects returned from this method. In this case, the files on the client's file system are being written to and read from using the **FileContent** interface, provided by the JNLP. Any attempt to access the resources directly by using, say, a **File** or a **FileReader** object would cause a **SecurityException** to be thrown in the same way that it would if you tried to use them from an unsigned applet. If you want to use these classes and not be restricted to the JNLP service interfaces, you must sign the JAR file.

The commented **jar** command in **JnlpFileChooser.java** will produce the necessary JAR file. Here is an appropriate launch file for the preceding example.

```
//:! gui/jnlp/filechooser.jnlp
<?xml version="1.0" encoding="UTF-8"?>
<jnlp spec = "1.0+"
  codebase="file:C:/AAA-TIJ4/code/gui/jnlp"
  href="filechooser.jnlp">
  <information>
    <title>FileChooser demo application</title>
    <vendor>Mindview Inc.</vendor>
    <description>
      Jnlp File chooser Application
    </description>
    <description kind="short">
      Demonstrates opening, reading and writing a text file
    </description>
    <icon href="mindview.gif"/>
    <offline-allowed/>
  </information>
  <resources>
    <j2se version="1.3+"
      href="http://java.sun.com/products/autodl/j2se"/>
    <jar href="jnlpfilechooser.jar" download="eager"/>
  </resources>
  <application-desc
    main-class="gui.jnlp.JnlpFileChooser"/>
</jnlp>
///:~
```

You'll find this launch file in the source-code download for this book (from *www.MindView.net*) saved as **filechooser.jnlp** without the first and last lines, in the same directory as the JAR file. As you can see, it is an XML file with one **<jnlp>** tag. This has a few sub-elements, which are mostly self-explanatory.

The **spec** attribute of the **jnlp** element tells the client system what version of the JNLP the application can be run with. The **codebase** attribute points to the URL where this launch file and the resources can be found. Here, it points to a directory on the local machine, which is a good means of testing the application. *Note that you'll need to change this path so that it indicates the* *appropriate directory on your machine, in order for the program to load successfully.* The **href** attribute must specify the name of this file.

The **information** tag has various sub-elements that provide information about the application. These are used by the Java Web Start administrative console or equivalent, which installs the JNLP application and allows the user to run it from the command line, make shortcuts, and so on.

The **resources** tag serves a similar purpose as the applet tag in an HTML file. The **j2se** sub-element specifies the J2SE version required to run the application, and the **jar** sub-element specifies the JAR file in which the class is archived. The **jar** element has an attribute **download**, which can have the values "eager" or "lazy" that tell the JNLP implementation whether or not the entire archive needs to be downloaded before the application can be run.

The **application-desc** attribute tells the JNLP implementation which class is the executable class, or entry point, to the JAR file.

Another useful sub-element of the **jnlp** tag is the **security** tag, not shown here. Here's what a **security** tag looks like:

```
<security>
    <all-permissions/>
<security/>
```

You use the **security** tag when your application is deployed in a signed JAR file. It is not needed in the preceding example because the local resources are all accessed via the JNLP services.

There are a few other tags available, the details of which can be found in the specification at *http://java.sun.com/products/javawebstart/download-spec.html.*

To launch the program, you need a download page containing a hypertext link to the **.jnlp** file. Here's what it looks like (without the first and last lines):

```
//:! gui/jnlp/filechooser.html
<html>
Follow the instructions in JnlpFileChooser.java to
build jnlpfilechooser.jar, then:
<a href="filechooser.jnlp">click here</a>
</html>
///:~
```

Once you have downloaded the application once, you can configure it by using the administrative console. If you are using Java Web Start on Windows, then you will be prompted to make a shortcut to your application the second time you use it. This behavior is configurable.

Only two of the JNLP services are covered here, but there are seven services in the current release. Each is designed for a specific task such as printing, or cutting and pasting to the clipboard. You can find more information at *http://java.sun.com.*

Concurrency & Swing

When you program with Swing you're using threads. You saw this at the beginning of this chapter when you learned that everything should be submitted to the Swing event dispatch thread through **SwingUtilities.invokeLater( )**. However, the fact that you don't have to explicitly create a **Thread** object means that threading issues can catch you by surprise. You must keep in mind that there is a Swing event dispatch thread, which is always there, handling all the Swing events by pulling each one out of the event queue and executing it in turn. By remembering the event dispatch thread you'll help ensure that your application won't suffer from deadlocking or race conditions.

This section addresses threading issues that arise when working with Swing.

Long-running tasks

One of the most fundamental mistakes you can make when programming with a graphical user interface is to accidentally use the event dispatch thread to run a long task. Here's a simple example:

```
//: gui/LongRunningTask.java
// A badly designed program.
import javax.swing.*;
import java.awt.*;
import java.awt.event.*;
import java.util.concurrent.*;
import static net.mindview.util.SwingConsole.*;

public class LongRunningTask extends JFrame {
  private JButton
    b1 = new JButton("Start Long Running Task"),
```

```
      b2 = new JButton("End Long Running Task");
    public LongRunningTask() {
      b1.addActionListener(new ActionListener() {
        public void actionPerformed(ActionEvent evt) {
          try {
            TimeUnit.SECONDS.sleep(3);
          } catch(InterruptedException e) {
            System.out.println("Task interrupted");
            return;
          }
          System.out.println("Task completed");
        }
      });
      b2.addActionListener(new ActionListener() {
        public void actionPerformed(ActionEvent evt) {
          // Interrupt yourself?
          Thread.currentThread().interrupt();
        }
      });
      setLayout(new FlowLayout());
      add(b1);
      add(b2);
    }
    public static void main(String[] args) {
      run(new LongRunningTask(), 200, 150);
    }
} ///:~
```

When you press **b1**, the event dispatch thread is suddenly occupied in performing the long-running task. You'll see that the button doesn't even pop back out, because the event dispatch thread that would normally repaint the screen is busy. And you cannot do anything else, like press **b2**, because the program won't respond until **b1**'s task is complete and the event dispatch thread is once again available. The code in **b2** is a flawed attempt to solve the problem by interrupting the event dispatch thread.

The answer, of course, is to execute long-running processes in separate threads. Here, the single-thread **Executor** is used, which automatically queues pending tasks and executes them one at a time:

```
//: gui/InterruptableLongRunningTask.java
// Long-running tasks in threads.
import javax.swing.*;
import java.awt.*;
```

```
import java.awt.event.*;
import java.util.concurrent.*;
import static net.mindview.util.SwingConsole.*;

class Task implements Runnable {
  private static int counter = 0;
  private final int id = counter++;
  public void run() {
    System.out.println(this + " started");
    try {
      TimeUnit.SECONDS.sleep(3);
    } catch(InterruptedException e) {
      System.out.println(this + " interrupted");
      return;
    }
    System.out.println(this + " completed");
  }
  public String toString() { return "Task " + id; }
  public long id() { return id; }
};

public class InterruptableLongRunningTask extends JFrame {
  private JButton
    b1 = new JButton("Start Long Running Task"),
    b2 = new JButton("End Long Running Task");
  ExecutorService executor =
    Executors.newSingleThreadExecutor();
  public InterruptableLongRunningTask() {
    b1.addActionListener(new ActionListener() {
      public void actionPerformed(ActionEvent e) {
        Task task = new Task();
        executor.execute(task);
        System.out.println(task + " added to the queue");
      }
    });
    b2.addActionListener(new ActionListener() {
      public void actionPerformed(ActionEvent e) {
        executor.shutdownNow(); // Heavy-handed
      }
    });
    setLayout(new FlowLayout());
    add(b1);
    add(b2);
  }
```

```
    public static void main(String[] args) {
      run(new InterruptableLongRunningTask(), 200, 150);
    }
} ///:~
```

This is better, but when you press **b2**, it calls **shutdownNow( )** on the
ExecutorService, thereby disabling it. If you try to add more tasks, you get
an exception. Thus, pressing **b2** makes the program inoperable. What we'd
like to do is to shut down the current task (and cancel pending tasks) without
stopping everything. The Java SE5 **Callable/Future** mechanism described
in the *Concurrency* chapter is just what we need. We'll define a new class
called **TaskManager**, which contains *tuple*s that hold the **Callable**
representing the task and the **Future** that comes back from the **Callable**.
The reason the tuple is necessary is because it allows us to keep track of the
original task, so that we may get extra information that is not available from
the **Future**. Here it is:

```
//: net/mindview/util/TaskItem.java
// A Future and the Callable that produced it.
package net.mindview.util;
import java.util.concurrent.*;

public class TaskItem<R,C extends Callable<R>> {
  public final Future<R> future;
  public final C task;
  public TaskItem(Future<R> future, C task) {
    this.future = future;
    this.task = task;
  }
} ///:~
```

In the **java.util.concurrent** library, the task is not available via the **Future**
by default because the task would not necessarily still be around when you get
the result from the **Future**. Here, we force the task to stay around by storing
it.

TaskManager is placed in **net.mindview.util** so it is available as a
general-purpose utility:

```
//: net/mindview/util/TaskManager.java
// Managing and executing a queue of tasks.
package net.mindview.util;
import java.util.concurrent.*;
import java.util.*;
```

```
public class TaskManager<R,C extends Callable<R>>
extends ArrayList<TaskItem<R,C>> {
  private ExecutorService exec =
    Executors.newSingleThreadExecutor();
  public void add(C task) {
    add(new TaskItem<R,C>(exec.submit(task),task));
  }
  public List<R> getResults() {
    Iterator<TaskItem<R,C>> items = iterator();
    List<R> results = new ArrayList<R>();
    while(items.hasNext()) {
      TaskItem<R,C> item = items.next();
      if(item.future.isDone()) {
        try {
          results.add(item.future.get());
        } catch(Exception e) {
          throw new RuntimeException(e);
        }
        items.remove();
      }
    }
    return results;
  }
  public List<String> purge() {
    Iterator<TaskItem<R,C>> items = iterator();
    List<String> results = new ArrayList<String>();
    while(items.hasNext()) {
      TaskItem<R,C> item = items.next();
      // Leave completed tasks for results reporting:
      if(!item.future.isDone()) {
        results.add("Cancelling " + item.task);
        item.future.cancel(true); // May interrupt
        items.remove();
      }
    }
    return results;
  }
} ///:~
```

TaskManager is an **ArrayList** of **TaskItem**. It also contains a single-thread **Executor**, so when you call **add( )** with a **Callable**, it submits the **Callable** and stores the resulting **Future** along with the original task. This way, if you need to do anything with the task, you have a reference to that task. As a simple example, in **purge( )** the task's **toString( )** is used.

This can now be used to manage the long-running tasks in our example:

```
//: gui/InterruptableLongRunningCallable.java
// Using Callables for long-running tasks.
import javax.swing.*;
import java.awt.*;
import java.awt.event.*;
import java.util.concurrent.*;
import net.mindview.util.*;
import static net.mindview.util.SwingConsole.*;

class CallableTask extends Task
implements Callable<String> {
  public String call() {
    run();
    return "Return value of " + this;
  }
}

public class
InterruptableLongRunningCallable extends JFrame {
  private JButton
    b1 = new JButton("Start Long Running Task"),
    b2 = new JButton("End Long Running Task"),
    b3 = new JButton("Get results");
  private TaskManager<String,CallableTask> manager =
    new TaskManager<String,CallableTask>();
  public InterruptableLongRunningCallable() {
    b1.addActionListener(new ActionListener() {
      public void actionPerformed(ActionEvent e) {
        CallableTask task = new CallableTask();
        manager.add(task);
        System.out.println(task + " added to the queue");
      }
    });
    b2.addActionListener(new ActionListener() {
      public void actionPerformed(ActionEvent e) {
        for(String result : manager.purge())
          System.out.println(result);
      }
    });
    b3.addActionListener(new ActionListener() {
```

```
      public void actionPerformed(ActionEvent e) {
        // Sample call to a Task method:
        for(TaskItem<String,CallableTask> tt :
            manager)
          tt.task.id(); // No cast required
        for(String result : manager.getResults())
          System.out.println(result);
      }
    });
    setLayout(new FlowLayout());
    add(b1);
    add(b2);
    add(b3);
  }
  public static void main(String[] args) {
    run(new InterruptableLongRunningCallable(), 200, 150);
  }
} ///:~
```

As you can see, **CallableTask** does exactly the same thing as **Task** except that it returns a result—in this case a **String** identifying the task.

Non-Swing utilities (not part of the standard Java distribution) called **SwingWorker** (from the Sun Web site) and *Foxtrot* (from *http://foxtrot.sourceforge.net*) were created to solve a similar problem, but at this writing, those utilities had not been modified to take advantage of the Java SE5 **Callable/Future** mechanism.

It's often important to give the end user some kind of visual cue that a task is running, and of its progress. This is normally done through either a **JProgressBar** or a **ProgressMonitor**. This example uses a **ProgressMonitor**:

```
//: gui/MonitoredLongRunningCallable.java
// Displaying task progress with ProgressMonitors.
import javax.swing.*;
import java.awt.*;
import java.awt.event.*;
import java.util.concurrent.*;
import net.mindview.util.*;
import static net.mindview.util.SwingConsole.*;

class MonitoredCallable implements Callable<String> {
  private static int counter = 0;
```

```java
      private final int id = counter++;
      private final ProgressMonitor monitor;
      private final static int MAX = 8;
      public MonitoredCallable(ProgressMonitor monitor) {
        this.monitor = monitor;
        monitor.setNote(toString());
        monitor.setMaximum(MAX - 1);
        monitor.setMillisToPopup(500);
      }
      public String call() {
        System.out.println(this + " started");
        try {
          for(int i = 0; i < MAX; i++) {
            TimeUnit.MILLISECONDS.sleep(500);
            if(monitor.isCanceled())
              Thread.currentThread().interrupt();
            final int progress = i;
            SwingUtilities.invokeLater(
              new Runnable() {
                public void run() {
                  monitor.setProgress(progress);
                }
              }
            );
          }
        } catch(InterruptedException e) {
          monitor.close();
          System.out.println(this + " interrupted");
          return "Result: " + this + " interrupted";
        }
        System.out.println(this + " completed");
        return "Result: " + this + " completed";
      }
      public String toString() { return "Task " + id; }
    };

public class MonitoredLongRunningCallable extends JFrame {
  private JButton
    b1 = new JButton("Start Long Running Task"),
    b2 = new JButton("End Long Running Task"),
    b3 = new JButton("Get results");
  private TaskManager<String,MonitoredCallable> manager =
    new TaskManager<String,MonitoredCallable>();
  public MonitoredLongRunningCallable() {
```

```
    b1.addActionListener(new ActionListener() {
      public void actionPerformed(ActionEvent e) {
        MonitoredCallable task = new MonitoredCallable(
          new ProgressMonitor(
            MonitoredLongRunningCallable.this,
            "Long-Running Task", "", 0, 0)
        );
        manager.add(task);
        System.out.println(task + " added to the queue");
      }
    });
    b2.addActionListener(new ActionListener() {
      public void actionPerformed(ActionEvent e) {
        for(String result : manager.purge())
          System.out.println(result);
      }
    });
    b3.addActionListener(new ActionListener() {
      public void actionPerformed(ActionEvent e) {
        for(String result : manager.getResults())
          System.out.println(result);
      }
    });
    setLayout(new FlowLayout());
    add(b1);
    add(b2);
    add(b3);
  }
  public static void main(String[] args) {
    run(new MonitoredLongRunningCallable(), 200, 500);
  }
} ///:~
```

The **MonitoredCallable** constructor takes a **ProgressMonitor** as an argument, and its **call( )** method updates the **ProgressMonitor** every half second. Notice that a **MonitoredCallable** is a separate task and thus should not try to control the UI directly, so **SwingUtilities.invokeLater( )** is used to submit the progress change information to the **monitor**. Sun's Swing Tutorial (on *http://java.sun.com*) shows an alternate approach of using a Swing **Timer**, which checks the status of the task and updates the monitor.

If the "cancel" button is pressed on the monitor, **monitor.isCanceled( )** will return **true**. Here, the task just calls **interrupt( )** on its own thread, which will land it in the **catch** clause where the **monitor** is terminated with the **close( )** method.

The rest of the code is effectively the same as before, except for the creation of the **ProgressMonitor** as part of the **MonitoredLongRunningCallable** constructor.

Exercise 33: (6) Modify **InterruptableLongRunningCallable.java** so that it runs all the tasks in parallel rather than sequentially.

Visual threading

The following example makes a **Runnable JPanel** class that paints different colors on itself. This application is set up to take values from the command line to determine how big the grid of colors is and how long to **sleep( )** between color changes. By playing with these values, you may discover some interesting and possibly inexplicable features in the threading implementation on your platform:

```
//: gui/ColorBoxes.java
// A visual demonstration of threading.
import javax.swing.*;
import java.awt.*;
import java.util.concurrent.*;
import java.util.*;
import static net.mindview.util.SwingConsole.*;

class CBox extends JPanel implements Runnable {
  private int pause;
  private static Random rand = new Random();
  private Color color = new Color(0);
  public void paintComponent(Graphics g) {
    g.setColor(color);
    Dimension s = getSize();
    g.fillRect(0, 0, s.width, s.height);
  }
  public CBox(int pause) { this.pause = pause; }
  public void run() {
    try {
      while(!Thread.interrupted()) {
        color = new Color(rand.nextInt(0x1000000));
        repaint(); // Asynchronously request a paint()
        TimeUnit.MILLISECONDS.sleep(pause);
      }
```

```
      } catch(InterruptedException e) {
        // Acceptable way to exit
      }
    }
  }
}

public class ColorBoxes extends JFrame {
  private int grid = 12;
  private int pause = 50;
  private static ExecutorService exec =
    Executors.newCachedThreadPool();
  public void setUp() {
    setLayout(new GridLayout(grid, grid));
    for(int i = 0; i < grid * grid; i++) {
      CBox cb = new CBox(pause);
      add(cb);
      exec.execute(cb);
    }
  }
  public static void main(String[] args) {
    ColorBoxes boxes = new ColorBoxes();
    if(args.length > 0)
      boxes.grid = new Integer(args[0]);
    if(args.length > 1)
      boxes.pause = new Integer(args[1]);
    boxes.setUp();
    run(boxes, 500, 400);
  }
} ///:~
```

ColorBoxes configures a **GridLayout** so that it has **grid** cells in each dimension. Then it adds the appropriate number of **CBox** objects to fill the grid, passing the **pause** value to each one. In **main( )** you can see how **pause** and **grid** have default values that can be changed if you pass in command-line arguments.

CBox is where all the work takes place. This is inherited from **JPanel** and it implements the **Runnable** interface so that each **JPanel** can also be an independent task. These tasks are driven by a thread pool **ExecutorService**.

The current cell color is **color**. Colors are created using the **Color** constructor that takes a 24-bit number, which in this case is created randomly.

paintComponent( ) is quite simple; it just sets the color to **color** and fills the entire **JPanel** with that color.

In **run( )**, you see the infinite loop that sets the **color** to a new random color and then calls **repaint( )** to show it. Then the thread goes to **sleep( )** for the amount of time specified on the command line.

The call to **repaint( )** in **run( )** deserves examination. At first glance, it may seem like we're creating a lot of threads, each of which is forcing a paint. It might appear that this is violating the principle that you should only submit tasks to the event queue. However, these threads are not actually modifying the shared resource. When they call **repaint( )**, it doesn't force a paint at that time, but only sets a "dirty flag" indicating that the next time the event dispatch thread is ready to repaint things, this area is a candidate for repainting. Thus the program doesn't cause Swing threading problems.

When the event dispatch thread actually does perform a **paint( )**, it first calls **paintComponent( )**, then **paintBorder( )** and **paintChildren( )**. If you need to override **paint( )** in a derived component, you must remember to call the base-class version of **paint( )** so that the proper actions are still performed.

Precisely because this design is flexible and threading is tied to each **JPanel** element, you can experiment by making as many threads as you want. (In reality, there is a restriction imposed by the number of threads your JVM can comfortably handle.)

This program also makes an interesting benchmark, since it can show dramatic performance and behavioral differences between one JVM threading implementation and another, as well as on different platforms.

Exercise 34: (4) Modify **ColorBoxes.java** so that it begins by sprinkling points ("stars") across the canvas, then randomly changes the colors of those "stars."

Visual programming and JavaBeans

So far in this book you've seen how valuable Java is for creating reusable pieces of code. The "most reusable" unit of code has been the class, since it comprises a cohesive unit of characteristics (fields) and behaviors (methods) that can be reused either directly via composition or through inheritance.

Inheritance and polymorphism are essential parts of object-oriented programming, but in the majority of cases when you're putting together an application, what you really want is *components* that do exactly what you need. You'd like to drop these parts into your design like the chips an electronic engineer puts on a circuit board. It seems that there should be some way to accelerate this "modular assembly" style of programming.

"Visual programming" first became successful—*very* successful—with Microsoft's Visual BASIC (VB), followed by a second-generation design in Borland's Delphi (which was the primary inspiration for the JavaBeans design). With these programming tools the components are represented visually, which makes sense since they usually display some kind of visual component such as a button or a text field. The visual representation, in fact, is often exactly the way the component will look in the running program. So part of the process of visual programming involves dragging a component from a palette and dropping it onto your form. The Application Builder Integrated Development Environment (IDE) writes code as you do this, and that code will cause the component to be created in the running program.

Simply dropping the component onto a form is usually not enough to complete the program. Often, you must change the characteristics of a component, such as its color, the text that's on it, the database it's connected to, etc. Characteristics that can be modified at design time are referred to as *properties*. You can manipulate the properties of your component inside the IDE, and when you create the program, this configuration data is saved so that it can be rejuvenated when the program is started.

By now you're probably used to the idea that an object is more than characteristics; it's also a set of behaviors. At design time, the behaviors of a visual component are partially represented by *events*, meaning "Here's something that can happen to the component." Ordinarily, you decide what you want to happen when an event occurs by tying code to that event.

Here's the critical part: The IDE uses reflection to dynamically interrogate the component and find out which properties and events the component supports. Once it knows what they are, it can display the properties and allow you to change them (saving the state when you build the program), and also display the events. In general, you do something like double-clicking on an event, and the IDE creates a code body and ties it to that particular event. All you must do at that point is write the code that executes when the event occurs.

All this adds up to a lot of work that's done for you by the IDE. As a result, you can focus on what the program looks like and what it is supposed to do, and rely on the IDE to manage the connection details for you. The reason that visual programming tools have been so successful is that they dramatically speed up the process of building an application—certainly the user interface, but often other portions of the application as well.

What is a JavaBean?

After the dust settles, then, a component is really just a block of code, typically embodied in a class. The key issue is the ability for the IDE to discover the properties and events for that component. To create a VB component, the programmer originally had to write a fairly complicated piece of code following certain conventions to expose the properties and events (it got easier as the years passed). Delphi was a second-generation visual programming tool, and the language was actively designed around visual programming, so it was much easier to create a visual component. However, Java has brought the creation of visual components to its most advanced state with JavaBeans, because a Bean is just a class. You don't have to write any extra code or use special language extensions in order to make something a Bean. The only thing you need to do, in fact, is slightly modify the way that you name your methods. It is the method name that tells the IDE whether this is a property, an event, or just an ordinary method.

In the JDK documentation, this naming convention is mistakenly termed a "design pattern." This is unfortunate, since design patterns (see *Thinking in Patterns* at *www.MindView.net*) are challenging enough without this sort of confusion. It's not a design pattern, it's just a naming convention, and it's fairly simple:

1. For a property named **xxx**, you typically create two methods: **getXxx( )** and **setXxx( )**. The first letter after "get" or "set" will automatically be lowercased by any tools that look at the methods, in order to produce the property name. The type produced by the "get" method is the same as the type of the argument to the "set" method. The name of the property and the type for the "get" and "set" are not related.

2. For a **boolean** property, you can use the "get" and "set" approach above, but you can also use "is" instead of "get."

3. Ordinary methods of the Bean don't conform to the above naming convention, but they're **public**.

4. For events, you use the Swing "listener" approach. It's exactly the same as you've been seeing: **addBounceListener(BounceListener)** and **removeBounceListener(BounceListener)** to handle a **BounceEvent**. Most of the time, the built-in events and listeners will satisfy your needs, but you can also create your own events and listener interfaces.

We can use these guidelines to create a simple Bean:

```
//: frogbean/Frog.java
// A trivial JavaBean.
package frogbean;
import java.awt.*;
import java.awt.event.*;

class Spots {}

public class Frog {
  private int jumps;
  private Color color;
  private Spots spots;
  private boolean jmpr;
  public int getJumps() { return jumps; }
  public void setJumps(int newJumps) {
    jumps = newJumps;
  }
  public Color getColor() { return color; }
  public void setColor(Color newColor) {
    color = newColor;
  }
  public Spots getSpots() { return spots; }
  public void setSpots(Spots newSpots) {
    spots = newSpots;
  }
  public boolean isJumper() { return jmpr; }
  public void setJumper(boolean j) { jmpr = j; }
  public void addActionListener(ActionListener l) {
```

```
      //...
    }
    public void removeActionListener(ActionListener l) {
      // ...
    }
    public void addKeyListener(KeyListener l) {
      // ...
    }
    public void removeKeyListener(KeyListener l) {
      // ...
    }
    // An "ordinary" public method:
    public void croak() {
      System.out.println("Ribbet!");
    }
} ///:~
```

First, you can see that it's just a class. Usually, all your fields will be **private**
and accessible only through methods and properties. Following the naming
convention, the properties are **jumps**, **color**, **spots**, and **jumper** (notice
the case change of the first letter in the property name). Although the name of
the internal identifier is the same as the name of the property in the first
three cases, in **jumper** you can see that the property name does not force you
to use any particular identifier for internal variables (or, indeed, to even *have*
any internal variables for that property).

The events this Bean handles are **ActionEvent** and **KeyEvent**, based on the
naming of the "add" and "remove" methods for the associated listener.
Finally, you can see that the ordinary method **croak( )** is still part of the
Bean simply because it's a **public** method, not because it conforms to any
naming scheme.

Extracting **BeanInfo**
with the **Introspector**

One of the most critical parts of the JavaBean scheme occurs when you drag a
Bean off a palette and drop it onto a form. The IDE must be able to create the
Bean (which it can do if there's a default constructor) and then, without
access to the Bean's source code, extract all the necessary information to
create the property sheet and event handlers.

Part of the solution is already evident from the *Type Information* chapter: Java *reflection* discovers all the methods of an unknown class. This is perfect for solving the JavaBean problem without requiring extra language keywords like those in other visual programming languages. In fact, one of the prime reasons that reflection was added to Java was to support JavaBeans (although reflection also supports object serialization and Remote Method Invocation, and is helpful in ordinary programming). So you might expect that the creator of the IDE would have to reflect each Bean and hunt through its methods to find the properties and events for that Bean.

This is certainly possible, but the Java designers wanted to provide a standard tool, not only to make Beans simpler to use, but also to provide a standard gateway to the creation of more complex Beans. This tool is the **Introspector** class, and the most important method in this class is the **static getBeanInfo( )**. You pass a **Class** reference to this method, and it fully interrogates that class and returns a **BeanInfo** object which you can dissect to find properties, methods, and events.

Usually, you won't care about any of this; you'll probably get most of your Beans off the shelf, and you won't need to know all the magic that's going on underneath. You'll simply drag Beans onto your form, then configure their properties and write handlers for the events of interest. However, it's an educational exercise to use the **Introspector** to display information about a Bean. Here's a tool that does it:

```java
//: gui/BeanDumper.java
// Introspecting a Bean.
import javax.swing.*;
import java.awt.*;
import java.awt.event.*;
import java.beans.*;
import java.lang.reflect.*;
import static net.mindview.util.SwingConsole.*;

public class BeanDumper extends JFrame {
  private JTextField query = new JTextField(20);
  private JTextArea results = new JTextArea();
  public void print(String s) { results.append(s + "\n"); }
  public void dump(Class<?> bean) {
    results.setText("");
    BeanInfo bi = null;
    try {
```

```
      bi = Introspector.getBeanInfo(bean, Object.class);
    } catch(IntrospectionException e) {
      print("Couldn't introspect " +  bean.getName());
      return;
    }
    for(PropertyDescriptor d: bi.getPropertyDescriptors()){
      Class<?> p = d.getPropertyType();
      if(p == null) continue;
      print("Property type:\n  " + p.getName() + "\n" +
        "Property name:\n  " + d.getName());
      Method readMethod = d.getReadMethod();
      if(readMethod != null)
        print("Read method:\n  " + readMethod);
      Method writeMethod = d.getWriteMethod();
      if(writeMethod != null)
        print("Write method:\n  " + writeMethod);
      print("====================");
    }
    print("Public methods:");
    for(MethodDescriptor m : bi.getMethodDescriptors())
      print(m.getMethod().toString());
    print("=======================");
    print("Event support:");
    for(EventSetDescriptor e: bi.getEventSetDescriptors()){
      print("Listener type:\n  " +
        e.getListenerType().getName());
      for(Method lm : e.getListenerMethods())
        print("Listener method:\n  " + lm.getName());
      for(MethodDescriptor lmd :
          e.getListenerMethodDescriptors() )
        print("Method descriptor:\n  " + lmd.getMethod());
      Method addListener= e.getAddListenerMethod();
      print("Add Listener Method:\n  " + addListener);
      Method removeListener = e.getRemoveListenerMethod();
      print("Remove Listener Method:\n  "+ removeListener);
      print("====================");
    }
  }
  class Dumper implements ActionListener {
    public void actionPerformed(ActionEvent e) {
      String name = query.getText();
      Class<?> c = null;
      try {
        c = Class.forName(name);
```

```
    } catch(ClassNotFoundException ex) {
      results.setText("Couldn't find " + name);
      return;
    }
    dump(c);
  }
}
public BeanDumper() {
  JPanel p = new JPanel();
  p.setLayout(new FlowLayout());
  p.add(new JLabel("Qualified bean name:"));
  p.add(query);
  add(BorderLayout.NORTH, p);
  add(new JScrollPane(results));
  Dumper dmpr = new Dumper();
  query.addActionListener(dmpr);
  query.setText("frogbean.Frog");
  // Force evaluation
  dmpr.actionPerformed(new ActionEvent(dmpr, 0, ""));
}
public static void main(String[] args) {
  run(new BeanDumper(), 600, 500);
}
} ///:~
```

BeanDumper.dump( ) does all the work. First it tries to create a
BeanInfo object, and if successful, calls the methods of **BeanInfo** that
produce information about properties, methods, and events. In
Introspector.getBeanInfo( ), you'll see there is a second argument that
tells the **Introspector** where to stop in the inheritance hierarchy. Here, it
stops before it parses all the methods from **Object**, since we're not interested
in seeing those.

For properties, **getPropertyDescriptors( )** returns an array of
PropertyDescriptors. For each **PropertyDescriptor**, you can call
getPropertyType( ) to find the class of object that is passed in and out via
the property methods. Then, for each property, you can get its pseudonym
(extracted from the method names) with **getName( )**, the method for
reading with **getReadMethod( )**, and the method for writing with
getWriteMethod( ). These last two methods return a **Method** object that
can actually be used to invoke the corresponding method on the object (this is
part of reflection).

For the **public** methods (including the property methods), **getMethodDescriptors( )** returns an array of **MethodDescriptors**. For each one, you can get the associated **Method** object and print its name.

For the events, **getEventSetDescriptors( )** returns an array of **EventSetDescriptors**. Each of these can be queried to find out the class of the listener, the methods of that listener class, and the add- and remove-listener methods. The **BeanDumper** program displays all of this information.

Upon startup, the program forces the evaluation of **frogbean.Frog**. The output, after unnecessary details have been removed, is:

```
Property type:
  Color
Property name:
  color
Read method:
  public Color getColor()
Write method:
  public void setColor(Color)
====================
Property type:
  boolean
Property name:
  jumper
Read method:
  public boolean isJumper()
Write method:
  public void setJumper(boolean)
====================
Property type:
  int
Property name:
  jumps
Read method:
  public int getJumps()
Write method:
  public void setJumps(int)
====================
Property type:
  frogbean.Spots
Property name:
  spots
```

```
Read method:
  public frogbean.Spots getSpots()
Write method:
  public void setSpots(frogbean.Spots)
======================
Public methods:
public void setSpots(frogbean.Spots)
public void setColor(Color)
public void setJumps(int)
public boolean isJumper()
public frogbean.Spots getSpots()
public void croak()
public void addActionListener(ActionListener)
public void addKeyListener(KeyListener)
public Color getColor()
public void setJumper(boolean)
public int getJumps()
public void removeActionListener(ActionListener)
public void removeKeyListener(KeyListener)
======================
Event support:
Listener type:
  KeyListener
Listener method:
  keyPressed
Listener method:
  keyReleased
Listener method:
  keyTyped
Method descriptor:
  public abstract void keyPressed(KeyEvent)
Method descriptor:
  public abstract void keyReleased(KeyEvent)
Method descriptor:
  public abstract void keyTyped(KeyEvent)
Add Listener Method:
  public void addKeyListener(KeyListener)
Remove Listener Method:
  public void removeKeyListener(KeyListener)
====================
Listener type:
  ActionListener
Listener method:
  actionPerformed
```

```
Method descriptor:
  public abstract void actionPerformed(ActionEvent)
Add Listener Method:
  public void addActionListener(ActionListener)
Remove Listener Method:
  public void removeActionListener(ActionListener)
=====================
```

This reveals most of what the **Introspector** sees as it produces a **BeanInfo** object from your Bean. You can see that the type of the property and its name are independent. Notice the lowercasing of the property name. (The only time this doesn't occur is when the property name begins with more than one capital letter in a row.) And remember that the method names you're seeing here (such as the read and write methods) are actually produced from a **Method** object that can be used to invoke the associated method on the object.

The **public** method list includes the methods that are not associated with a property or an event, such as **croak( )**, as well as those that are. These are all the methods that you can call programmatically for a Bean, and the IDE can choose to list all of these while you're making method calls, to ease your task.

Finally, you can see that the events are fully parsed out into the listener, its methods, and the add- and remove-listener methods. Basically, once you have the **BeanInfo**, you can find out everything of importance for the Bean. You can also call the methods for that Bean, even though you don't have any other information except the object (again, a feature of reflection).

A more sophisticated Bean

This next example is slightly more sophisticated, albeit frivolous. It's a **JPanel** that draws a little circle around the mouse whenever the mouse is moved. When you press the mouse, the word "Bang!" appears in the middle of the screen, and an action listener is fired.

The properties you can change are the size of the circle as well as the color, size, and text of the word that is displayed when you press the mouse. A **BangBean** also has its own **addActionListener( )** and **removeActionListener( )**, so you can attach your own listener that will be fired when the user clicks on the **BangBean**. You should recognize the property and event support:

```
//: bangbean/BangBean.java
```

```
// A graphical Bean.
package bangbean;
import javax.swing.*;
import java.awt.*;
import java.awt.event.*;
import java.io.*;
import java.util.*;

public class
BangBean extends JPanel implements Serializable {
  private int xm, ym;
  private int cSize = 20; // Circle size
  private String text = "Bang!";
  private int fontSize = 48;
  private Color tColor = Color.RED;
  private ActionListener actionListener;
  public BangBean() {
    addMouseListener(new ML());
    addMouseMotionListener(new MML());
  }
  public int getCircleSize() { return cSize; }
  public void setCircleSize(int newSize) {
    cSize = newSize;
  }
  public String getBangText() { return text; }
  public void setBangText(String newText) {
    text = newText;
  }
  public int getFontSize() { return fontSize; }
  public void setFontSize(int newSize) {
    fontSize = newSize;
  }
  public Color getTextColor() { return tColor; }
  public void setTextColor(Color newColor) {
    tColor = newColor;
  }
  public void paintComponent(Graphics g) {
    super.paintComponent(g);
    g.setColor(Color.BLACK);
    g.drawOval(xm - cSize/2, ym - cSize/2, cSize, cSize);
  }
  // This is a unicast listener, which is
  // the simplest form of listener management:
  public void addActionListener(ActionListener l)
```

```
    throws TooManyListenersException {
      if(actionListener != null)
        throw new TooManyListenersException();
      actionListener = l;
    }
    public void removeActionListener(ActionListener l) {
      actionListener = null;
    }
    class ML extends MouseAdapter {
      public void mousePressed(MouseEvent e) {
        Graphics g = getGraphics();
        g.setColor(tColor);
        g.setFont(
          new Font("TimesRoman", Font.BOLD, fontSize));
        int width = g.getFontMetrics().stringWidth(text);
        g.drawString(text, (getSize().width - width) /2,
          getSize().height/2);
        g.dispose();
        // Call the listener's method:
        if(actionListener != null)
          actionListener.actionPerformed(
            new ActionEvent(BangBean.this,
              ActionEvent.ACTION_PERFORMED, null));
      }
    }
    class MML extends MouseMotionAdapter {
      public void mouseMoved(MouseEvent e) {
        xm = e.getX();
        ym = e.getY();
        repaint();
      }
    }
    public Dimension getPreferredSize() {
      return new Dimension(200, 200);
    }
} ///:~
```

The first thing you'll notice is that **BangBean** implements the **Serializable**
interface. This means that the IDE can "pickle" all the information for the
BangBean by using serialization after the program designer has adjusted
the values of the properties. When the Bean is created as part of the running
application, these "pickled" properties are restored so that you get exactly
what you designed.

When you look at the signature for **addActionListener( )**, you'll see that it can throw a **TooManyListenersException**. This indicates that it is *unicast*, which means it notifies only one listener when the event occurs. Ordinarily, you'll use *multicast* events so that many listeners can be notified of an event. However, that runs into threading issues, so it will be revisited in the next section, "JavaBeans and synchronization." In the meantime, a unicast event sidesteps the problem.

When you click the mouse, the text is put in the middle of the **BangBean**, and if the **actionListener** field is not **null**, its **actionPerformed( )** is called, creating a new **ActionEvent** object in the process. Whenever the mouse is moved, its new coordinates are captured and the canvas is repainted (erasing any text that's on the canvas, as you'll see).

Here is the **BangBeanTest** class to test the Bean:

```
//: bangbean/BangBeanTest.java
// {Timeout: 5} Abort after 5 seconds when testing
package bangbean;
import javax.swing.*;
import java.awt.*;
import java.awt.event.*;
import java.util.*;
import static net.mindview.util.SwingConsole.*;

public class BangBeanTest extends JFrame {
  private JTextField txt = new JTextField(20);
  // During testing, report actions:
  class BBL implements ActionListener {
    private int count = 0;
    public void actionPerformed(ActionEvent e) {
      txt.setText("BangBean action "+ count++);
    }
  }
  public BangBeanTest() {
    BangBean bb = new BangBean();
    try {
      bb.addActionListener(new BBL());
    } catch(TooManyListenersException e) {
      txt.setText("Too many listeners");
    }
    add(bb);
    add(BorderLayout.SOUTH, txt);
  }
```

```
    public static void main(String[] args) {
        run(new BangBeanTest(), 400, 500);
    }
} ///:~
```

When a Bean is used in an IDE, this class will not be used, but it's helpful to provide a rapid testing method for each of your Beans. **BangBeanTest** places a **BangBean** within the **JFrame**, attaching a simple **ActionListener** to the **BangBean** to print an event count to the **JTextField** whenever an **ActionEvent** occurs. Usually, of course, the IDE would create most of the code that uses the Bean.

When you run the **BangBean** through **BeanDumper** or put the **BangBean** inside a Bean-enabled development environment, you'll notice that there are many more properties and actions than are evident from the preceding code. That's because **BangBean** is inherited from **JPanel**, and **JPanel** is also a Bean, so you're seeing its properties and events as well.

Exercise 35: (6) Locate and download one or more of the free GUI builder development environments available on the Internet, or use a commercial product if you own one. Discover what is necessary to add **BangBean** to this environment and to use it.

JavaBeans and synchronization

Whenever you create a Bean, you must assume that it will run in a multithreaded environment. This means that:

1. Whenever possible, all the **public** methods of a Bean should be **synchronized**. Of course, this incurs the **synchronized** runtime overhead (which has been significantly reduced in recent versions of the JDK). If that's a problem, methods that will not cause problems in critical sections can be left un**synchronized**, but keep in mind that such methods are not always obvious. Methods that qualify tend to be small (such as **getCircleSize( )** in the following example) and/or "atomic"; that is, the method call executes in such a short amount of code that the object cannot be changed during execution (but review the *Concurrency* chapter— what you may think is atomic might not be). Making such methods un**synchronized** might not have a significant effect on the execution speed of your program. You're better off making all **public** methods of a Bean **synchronized** and removing the

synchronized keyword on a method only when you know for sure that it makes a difference and that you can safely remove the keyword.

2.   When firing a multicast event to a bunch of listeners interested in that event, you must assume that listeners might be added or removed while moving through the list.

The first point is fairly straightforward, but the second point requires a little more thought. **BangBean.java** ducked out of the concurrency question by ignoring the **synchronized** keyword and making the event unicast. Here is a modified version that works in a multithreaded environment and uses multicasting for events:

```java
//: gui/BangBean2.java
// You should write your Beans this way so they
// can run in a multithreaded environment.
import javax.swing.*;
import java.awt.*;
import java.awt.event.*;
import java.io.*;
import java.util.*;
import static net.mindview.util.SwingConsole.*;

public class BangBean2 extends JPanel
implements Serializable {
  private int xm, ym;
  private int cSize = 20; // Circle size
  private String text = "Bang!";
  private int fontSize = 48;
  private Color tColor = Color.RED;
  private ArrayList<ActionListener> actionListeners =
    new ArrayList<ActionListener>();
  public BangBean2() {
    addMouseListener(new ML());
    addMouseMotionListener(new MM());
  }
  public synchronized int getCircleSize() { return cSize; }
  public synchronized void setCircleSize(int newSize) {
    cSize = newSize;
  }
  public synchronized String getBangText() { return text; }
  public synchronized void setBangText(String newText) {
    text = newText;
```

```java
    }
    public synchronized int getFontSize(){ return fontSize; }
    public synchronized void setFontSize(int newSize) {
      fontSize = newSize;
    }
    public synchronized Color getTextColor(){ return tColor;}
    public synchronized void setTextColor(Color newColor) {
      tColor = newColor;
    }
    public void paintComponent(Graphics g) {
      super.paintComponent(g);
      g.setColor(Color.BLACK);
      g.drawOval(xm - cSize/2, ym - cSize/2, cSize, cSize);
    }
    // This is a multicast listener, which is more typically
    // used than the unicast approach taken in BangBean.java:
    public synchronized void
    addActionListener(ActionListener l) {
      actionListeners.add(l);
    }
    public synchronized void
    removeActionListener(ActionListener l) {
      actionListeners.remove(l);
    }
    // Notice this isn't synchronized:
    public void notifyListeners() {
      ActionEvent a = new ActionEvent(BangBean2.this,
        ActionEvent.ACTION_PERFORMED, null);
      ArrayList<ActionListener> lv = null;
      // Make a shallow copy of the List in case
      // someone adds a listener while we're
      // calling listeners:
      synchronized(this) {
        lv = new ArrayList<ActionListener>(actionListeners);
      }
      // Call all the listener methods:
      for(ActionListener al : lv)
        al.actionPerformed(a);
    }
    class ML extends MouseAdapter {
      public void mousePressed(MouseEvent e) {
        Graphics g = getGraphics();
        g.setColor(tColor);
        g.setFont(
```

```
          new Font("TimesRoman", Font.BOLD, fontSize));
        int width = g.getFontMetrics().stringWidth(text);
        g.drawString(text, (getSize().width - width) /2,
          getSize().height/2);
        g.dispose();
        notifyListeners();
      }
    }
    class MM extends MouseMotionAdapter {
      public void mouseMoved(MouseEvent e) {
        xm = e.getX();
        ym = e.getY();
        repaint();
      }
    }
    public static void main(String[] args) {
      BangBean2 bb2 = new BangBean2();
      bb2.addActionListener(new ActionListener() {
        public void actionPerformed(ActionEvent e) {
          System.out.println("ActionEvent" + e);
        }
      });
      bb2.addActionListener(new ActionListener() {
        public void actionPerformed(ActionEvent e) {
          System.out.println("BangBean2 action");
        }
      });
      bb2.addActionListener(new ActionListener() {
        public void actionPerformed(ActionEvent e) {
          System.out.println("More action");
        }
      });
      JFrame frame = new JFrame();
      frame.add(bb2);
      run(frame, 300, 300);
    }
} ///:~
```

Adding **synchronized** to the methods is an easy change. However, notice in
addActionListener( ) and **removeActionListener( )** that the
ActionListeners are now added to and removed from an **ArrayList**, so you
can have as many as you want.

You can see that the method **notifyListeners( )** is *not* **synchronized**. It can be called from more than one thread at a time. It's also possible for **addActionListener( )** or **removeActionListener( )** to be called in the middle of a call to **notifyListeners( )**, which is a problem because it traverses the **ArrayList actionListeners**. To alleviate the problem, the **ArrayList** is duplicated inside a **synchronized** clause, using the **ArrayList** constructor which copies the elements of its argument, and the duplicate is traversed. This way, the original **ArrayList** can be manipulated without impact on **notifyListeners( )**.

The **paintComponent( )** method is also not **synchronized**. Deciding whether to synchronize overridden methods is not as clear as when you're just adding your own methods. In this example, it turns out that **paintComponent( )** seems to work OK whether it's **synchronized** or not. But the issues you must consider are:

1. Does the method modify the state of "critical" variables within the object? To discover whether the variables are "critical," you must determine whether they will be read or set by other threads in the program. (In this case, the reading or setting is virtually always accomplished via **synchronized** methods, so you can just examine those.) In the case of **paintComponent( )**, no modification takes place.

2. Does the method depend on the state of these "critical" variables? If a **synchronized** method modifies a variable that your method uses, then you might very well want to make your method **synchronized** as well. Based on this, you might observe that **cSize** is changed by **synchronized** methods, and therefore **paintComponent( )** should be **synchronized**. Here, however, you can ask, "What's the worst thing that will happen if **cSize** is changed during a **paintComponent( )**?" When you see that it's nothing too bad, and a transient effect at that, you can decide to leave **paintComponent( )** un**synchronized** to prevent the extra overhead from the **synchronized** method call.

3. A third clue is to notice whether the base-class version of **paintComponent( )** is **synchronized**, which it isn't. This isn't an airtight argument, just a clue. In this case, for example, a field that *is* changed via **synchronized** methods (that is, **cSize**) has been mixed into the **paintComponent( )** formula and might

have changed the situation. Notice, however, that **synchronized** doesn't inherit; that is, if a method is **synchronized** in the base class, then it *is not* automatically **synchronized** in the derived-class overridden version.

4. **paint( )** and **paintComponent( )** are methods that must be as fast as possible. Anything that takes processing overhead out of these methods is highly recommended, so if you think you need to synchronize these methods it may be an indicator of bad design.

The test code in **main( )** has been modified from that seen in **BangBeanTest** to demonstrate the multicast ability of **BangBean2** by adding extra listeners.

Packaging a Bean

Before you can bring a JavaBean into a Bean-enabled IDE, it must be put into a Bean container, which is a JAR file that includes all the Bean classes as well as a "manifest" file that says, "This is a Bean." A manifest file is simply a text file that follows a particular form. For the **BangBean**, the manifest file looks like this:

```
Manifest-Version: 1.0

Name: bangbean/BangBean.class
Java-Bean: True
```

The first line indicates the version of the manifest scheme, which until further notice from Sun is 1.0. The second line (empty lines are ignored) names the **BangBean.class** file, and the third says, "It's a Bean." Without the third line, the program builder tool will not recognize the class as a Bean.

The only tricky part is that you must make sure that you get the proper path in the "Name:" field. If you look back at **BangBean.java**, you'll see it's in **package bangbean** (and thus in a subdirectory called **bangbean** that's off of the classpath), and the name in the manifest file must include this package information. In addition, you must place the manifest file in the directory *above* the root of your package path, which in this case means placing the file in the directory above the "bangbean" subdirectory. Then you must invoke **jar** from the same directory as the manifest file, as follows:

```
jar cfm BangBean.jar BangBean.mf bangbean
```

This assumes that you want the resulting JAR file to be named **BangBean.jar**, and that you've put the manifest in a file called **BangBean.mf**.

You might wonder, "What about all the other classes that were generated when I compiled **BangBean.java**?" Well, they all ended up inside the **bangbean** subdirectory, and you'll see that the last argument for the above **jar** command line is the **bangbean** subdirectory. When you give **jar** the name of a subdirectory, it packages that entire subdirectory into the JAR file (including, in this case, the original **BangBean.java** source-code file—you might not choose to include the source with your own Beans). In addition, if you turn around and unpack the JAR file you've just created, you'll discover that your manifest file isn't inside, but that **jar** has created its own manifest file (based partly on yours) called **MANIFEST.MF** and placed it inside the subdirectory **META-INF** (for "meta-information"). If you open this manifest file, you'll also notice that digital signature information has been added by **jar** for each file, of the form:

```
Digest-Algorithms: SHA MD5
SHA-Digest: pDpEAG9NaeCx8aFtqPI4udSX/O0=
MD5-Digest: O4NcS1hE3Smnzlp2hj6qeg==
```

In general, you don't need to worry about any of this, and if you make changes, you can just modify your original manifest file and reinvoke **jar** to create a new JAR file for your Bean. You can also add other Beans to the JAR file simply by adding their information to your manifest.

One thing to notice is that you'll probably want to put each Bean in its own subdirectory, since when you create a JAR file you hand the **jar** utility the name of a subdirectory, and it puts everything in that subdirectory into the JAR file. You can see that both **Frog** and **BangBean** are in their own subdirectories.

Once you have your Bean properly inside a JAR file, you can bring it into a Beans-enabled IDE. The way you do this varies from one tool to the next, but Sun provides a freely available test bed for JavaBeans in its "Bean Builder." (Download from *http://java.sun.com/beans*.) You place a Bean into the Bean Builder by simply copying the JAR file into the correct subdirectory.

Exercise 36: (4) Add **Frog.class** to the manifest file in this section and run **jar** to create a JAR file containing both **Frog** and **BangBean**. Now either download and install the Bean Builder from Sun, or use your own

Beans-enabled program builder tool and add the JAR file to your environment so you can test the two Beans.

Exercise 37: (5) Create your own JavaBean called **Valve** that contains two properties: a **boolean** called "on" and an **int** called "level." Create a manifest file, use **jar** to package your Bean, then load it into the Bean Builder or into a Beans-enabled program builder tool so that you can test it.

More complex Bean support

You can see how remarkably simple it is to make a Bean, but you aren't limited to what you've seen here. The JavaBeans architecture provides a simple point of entry but can also scale to more complex situations. These situations are beyond the scope of this book, but they will be briefly introduced here. You can find more details at *http://java.sun.com/beans*.

One place where you can add sophistication is with properties. The examples you've seen here have shown only single properties, but it's also possible to represent multiple properties in an array. This is called an *indexed property*. You simply provide the appropriate methods (again following a naming convention for the method names), and the **Introspector** recognizes an indexed property so that your IDE can respond appropriately.

Properties can be *bound*, which means that they will notify other objects via a **PropertyChangeEvent**. The other objects can then choose to change themselves based on the change to the Bean.

Properties can be *constrained*, which means that other objects can veto a change to that property if it is unacceptable. The other objects are notified by using a **PropertyChangeEvent**, and they can throw a **PropertyVetoException** to prevent the change from happening and to restore the old values.

You can also change the way your Bean is represented at design time:

1. You can provide a custom property sheet for your particular Bean. The ordinary property sheet will be used for all other Beans, but yours is automatically invoked when your Bean is selected.

2. You can create a custom editor for a particular property, so the ordinary property sheet is used, but when your special property is being edited, your editor will automatically be invoked.

3. You can provide a custom **BeanInfo** class for your Bean that produces information different from the default created by the **Introspector**.

4. It's also possible to turn "expert" mode on and off in all **FeatureDescriptor**s to distinguish between basic features and more complicated ones.

More to Beans

There are a number of books about JavaBeans; for example, *JavaBeans* by Elliotte Rusty Harold (IDG, 1998).

Alternatives to Swing

Although the Swing library is the GUI sanctioned by Sun, it is by no means the only way to create graphical user interfaces. Two important alternatives are *Macromedia Flash*, using Macromedia's *Flex* programming system, for client-side GUIs over the Web, and the open-source Eclipse *Standard Widget Toolkit* (SWT) library for desktop applications.

Why would you consider alternatives? For Web clients, you can make a fairly strong argument that applets have failed. Considering how long they've been around (since the beginning) and the initial hype and promise around applets, coming across a Web application that uses applets is still a surprise. Even Sun doesn't use applets everywhere. Here's an example:

http://java.sun.com/developer/onlineTraining/new2java/javamap/intro.html

An interactive map of Java features on the Sun site seems a very likely candidate for a Java applet, and yet they did it in Flash. This appears to be a tacit acknowledgement that applets have not been a success. More importantly, the Flash Player is installed on upwards of 98 percent of computing platforms, so it can be considered an accepted standard. As you'll see, the Flex system provides a very powerful client-side programming environment, certainly more powerful than JavaScript and with a look and feel that is often preferable to an applet. If you want to use applets, you must still convince the client to download the JRE, whereas the Flash Player is small and fast to download by comparison.

For desktop applications, one problem with Swing is that users *notice* that they are using a different kind of application, because the look and feel of

---

Swing applications is different from the normal desktop. Users are not generally interested in new looks and feels in an application; they are trying to get work done and prefer that an application look and feel like all their other applications. SWT creates applications that look like native applications, and because the library uses native components as much as possible, the applications tend to run faster than equivalent Swing applications.

Building Flash Web clients with Flex

Because the lightweight Macromedia Flash virtual machine is so ubiquitous, most people will be able to use a Flash-based interface without installing anything, and it will look and behave the same way across all systems and platforms.[10]

With *Macromedia Flex*, you can develop Flash user interfaces for Java applications. Flex consists of an XML- and script-based programming model, similar to programming models such as HTML and JavaScript, along with a robust library of components. You use the MXML syntax to declare layout management and widget controls, and you use dynamic scripting to add event-handling and service invocation code which links the user interface to Java classes, data models, Web services, etc. The Flex compiler takes your MXML and script files and compiles them into bytecode. The Flash virtual machine on the client operates like the Java Virtual Machine in that it interprets compiled bytecode. The Flash bytecode format is known as SWF, and SWF files are produced by the Flex compiler.

Note that there's an open-source alternative to Flex at *http://openlaszlo.org*; this has a structure that's similar to Flex but may be a preferable alternative for some. Other tools also exist to create Flash applications in different ways.

Hello, Flex

Consider this MXML code, which defines a user interface (note that the first and last lines will not appear in the code that you download as part of this book's source-code package):

---

[10] Sean Neville created the core of the material in this section.

```
//:! gui/flex/helloflex1.mxml
<?xml version="1.0" encoding="utf-8"?>
<mx:Application
  xmlns:mx="http://www.macromedia.com/2003/mxml"
  backgroundColor="#ffffff">
  <mx:Label id="output" text="Hello, Flex!" />
</mx:Application>
///:~
```

MXML files are XML documents, so they begin with an XML version/encoding directive. The outermost MXML element is the **Application** element, which is the topmost visual and logical container for a Flex user interface. You can declare tags representing visual controls, such as the **Label** element above, inside the **Application** element. Controls are always placed within a container, and containers encapsulate layout managers, among other mechanisms, so they manage the layout of the controls within them. In the simplest case, as in the above example, the **Application** acts as the container. The **Application**'s default layout manager merely places controls vertically down the interface in the order in which they are declared.

ActionScript is a version of ECMAScript, or JavaScript, which looks quite similar to Java and supports classes and strong typing in addition to dynamic scripting. By adding a script to the example, we can introduce behavior. Here, the MXML **Script** control is used to place ActionScript directly into the MXML file:

```
//:! gui/flex/helloflex2.mxml
<?xml version="1.0" encoding="utf-8"?>
<mx:Application
  xmlns:mx="http://www.macromedia.com/2003/mxml"
  backgroundColor="#ffffff">
  <mx:Script>
    <![CDATA[
    function updateOutput() {
      output.text = "Hello! " + input.text;
    }
    ]]>
  </mx:Script>
  <mx:TextInput id="input" width="200"
    change="updateOutput()" />
  <mx:Label id="output" text="Hello!" />
</mx:Application>
```

```
///:~
```

A **TextInput** control accepts user input, and a **Label** displays the data as it is being typed. Note that the **id** attribute of each control becomes accessible in the script as a variable name, so the script can reference instances of the MXML tags. In the **TextInput** field, you can see that the **change** attribute is connected to the **updateOutput( )** function so that the function is called whenever any kind of change occurs.

Compiling MXML

The easiest way to get started using Flex is with the free trial, which you can download at *www.macromedia.com/software/flex/trial*.[11] The product is packaged in a number of editions, from free trials to enterprise server versions, and Macromedia offers additional tools for developing Flex applications. Exact packaging is subject to change, so check the Macromedia site for specifics. Also note that you may need to modify the **jvm.config** file in the Flex installation **bin** directory.

To compile the MXML code into Flash bytecode, you have two options:

1. You can place the MXML file in a Java Web application, alongside JSP and HTML pages in a WAR file, and have requests for the **.mxml** file compiled at run time whenever a browser requests the MXML document's URL.

2. You can compile the MXML file using the Flex command-line compiler, **mxmlc**.

The first option, Web-based runtime compilation, requires a servlet container (such as Apache Tomcat) in addition to Flex. The servlet container's WAR file(s) must be updated with Flex configuration information, such as servlet mappings which are added to the **web.xml** descriptor, and it must include the Flex JAR files—these steps are handled automatically when you install Flex. After the WAR file is configured, you can place the MXML files in the Web application and request the document's URL through any browser. Flex will compile the application upon the first request, similar to the JSP model, and will thereafter deliver the compiled and cached SWF within an HTML shell.

---

[11] Note that you must download Flex, and not FlexBuilder. The latter is an IDE design tool.

The second option does not require a server. When you invoke the Flex **mxmlc** compiler on the command line, you produce SWF files. You can deploy these as you desire. The **mxmlc** executable is located in the **bin** directory of a Flex installation, and invoking it with no arguments will provide a list of valid command-line options. Typically, you'll specify the location of the Flex client component library as the value of the **-flexlib** command-line option, but in very simple examples like the two that we've seen so far, the Flex compiler will assume the location of the component library. So you can compile the first two examples like this:

```
mxmlc.exe helloflex1.mxml
mxmlc.exe helloflex2.mxml
```

This produces a **helloflex2.swf** file which can be run in Flash, or placed alongside HTML on any HTTP server (once Flash has been loaded into your Web browser, you can often just double-click on the SWF file to start it up in the browser).

For **helloflex2.swf**, you'll see the following user interface running in the Flash Player:

```
This was not too hard to do...|
```

Hello! This was not too hard to do...

In more complex applications, you can separate MXML and ActionScript by referencing functions in external ActionScript files. From MXML, you use the following syntax for the **Script** control:

```
<mx:Script source="MyExternalScript.as" />
```

This code allows the MXML controls to reference functions located in a file named **MyExternalScript.as** as if they were located within the MXML file.

MXML and ActionScript

MXML is declarative shorthand for ActionScript classes. Whenever you see an MXML tag, there exists an ActionScript class of the same name. When the Flex compiler parses MXML, it first transforms the XML into ActionScript and loads the referenced ActionScript classes, and then compiles and links the ActionScript into an SWF.

You can write an entire Flex application in ActionScript alone, without using any MXML. Thus, MXML is a convenience. User interface components such as containers and controls are typically declared using MXML, while logic such as event handling and other client logic is handled through ActionScript and Java.

You can create your own MXML controls and reference them using MXML by writing ActionScript classes. You may also combine existing MXML containers and controls in a new MXML document that can then be referenced as a tag in another MXML document. The Macromedia Web site contains more information about how to do this.

Containers and controls

The visual core of the Flex component library is a set of containers which manage layout, and an array of controls which go inside those containers. Containers include panels, vertical and horizontal boxes, tiles, accordions, divided boxes, grids, and more. Controls are user interface widgets such as buttons, text areas, sliders, calendars, data grids, and so forth.

The remainder of this section will show a Flex application that displays and sorts a list of audio files. This application demonstrates containers, controls, and how to connect to Java from Flash.

We start the MXML file by placing a **DataGrid** control (one of the more sophisticated Flex controls) within a **Panel** container:

```
//:! gui/flex/songs.mxml
<?xml version="1.0" encoding="utf-8"?>
<mx:Application
  xmlns:mx="http://www.macromedia.com/2003/mxml"
  backgroundColor="#B9CAD2" pageTitle="Flex Song Manager"
  initialize="getSongs()">
  <mx:Script source="songScript.as" />
  <mx:Style source="songStyles.css"/>
  <mx:Panel id="songListPanel"
    titleStyleDeclaration="headerText"
    title="Flex MP3 Library">
    <mx:HBox verticalAlign="bottom">
      <mx:DataGrid id="songGrid"
        cellPress="selectSong(event)" rowCount="8">
        <mx:columns>
          <mx:Array>
```

```
                <mx:DataGridColumn columnName="name"
                   headerText="Song Name" width="120" />
                <mx:DataGridColumn columnName="artist"
                   headerText="Artist" width="180" />
                <mx:DataGridColumn columnName="album"
                   headerText="Album" width="160" />
            </mx:Array>
          </mx:columns>
        </mx:DataGrid>
        <mx:VBox>
          <mx:HBox height="100" >
            <mx:Image id="albumImage" source=""
               height="80" width="100"
               mouseOverEffect="resizeBig"
               mouseOutEffect="resizeSmall" />
            <mx:TextArea id="songInfo"
               styleName="boldText" height="100%" width="120"
               vScrollPolicy="off" borderStyle="none" />
          </mx:HBox>
          <mx:MediaPlayback id="songPlayer"
             contentPath=""
             mediaType="MP3"
             height="70"
             width="230"
             controllerPolicy="on"
             autoPlay="false"
             visible="false" />
        </mx:VBox>
      </mx:HBox>
      <mx:ControlBar horizontalAlign="right">
        <mx:Button id="refreshSongsButton"
           label="Refresh Songs" width="100"
           toolTip="Refresh Song List"
           click="songService.getSongs()" />
      </mx:ControlBar>
    </mx:Panel>
    <mx:Effect>
      <mx:Resize name="resizeBig" heightTo="100"
         duration="500"/>
      <mx:Resize name="resizeSmall" heightTo="80"
         duration="500"/>
    </mx:Effect>
    <mx:RemoteObject id="songService"
       source="gui.flex.SongService"
```

```
      result="onSongs(event.result)"
      fault="alert(event.fault.faultstring, 'Error')">
    <mx:method name="getSongs"/>
  </mx:RemoteObject>
</mx:Application>
///:~
```

The **DataGrid** contains nested tags for its array of columns. When you see an attribute or a nested element on a control, you know that it corresponds to some property, event, or encapsulated object in the underlying ActionScript class. The **DataGrid** has an **id** attribute with the value **songGrid**, so ActionScript and MXML tags can reference the grid programmatically by using **songGrid** as a variable name. The **DataGrid** exposes many more properties than those shown here; the complete API for MXML controls and containers can be found online at *http://livedocs.macromedia.com/flex/15/asdocs_en/index.html*.

The **DataGrid** is followed by a **VBox** containing an **Image** to show the front of the album along with song information, and a **MediaPlayback** control that will play MP3 files. This example streams the content in order to reduce the size of the compiled SWF. When you embed images, audio, and video files into a Flex application instead of streaming them, the files become part of the compiled SWF and are delivered along with your user interface assets instead of streamed on demand at run time.

The Flash Player contains embedded codecs for playing and streaming audio and video in a variety of formats. Flash and Flex support the use of the Web's most common image formats, and Flex also has the ability to translate *scalable vector graphics* (SVG) files into SWF resources that can be embedded in Flex clients.

Effects and styles

The Flash Player renders graphics using vectors, so it can perform highly expressive transformations at run time. Flex *effects* provide a small taste of these sorts of animations. Effects are transformations that you can apply to controls and containers using MXML syntax.

The **Effect** tag shown in the MXML produces two results: The first nested tag dynamically grows an image when the mouse hovers over it, and the second dynamically shrinks that image when the mouse moves away. These effects are applied to the mouse events available on the **Image** control for **albumImage**.

Flex also provides effects for common animations like transitions, wipes, and modulating alpha channels. In addition to the built-in effects, Flex supports the Flash drawing API for truly innovative animations. Deeper exploration of this topic involves graphic design and animation, and is beyond the scope of this section.

Standard styling is available through Flex's support for Cascading Style Sheets (CSS). If you attach a CSS file to an MXML file, the Flex controls will follow those styles. For this example, **songStyles.css** contains the following CSS declaration:

```
//:! gui/flex/songStyles.css
.headerText {
  font-family: Arial, "_sans";
  font-size: 16;
  font-weight: bold;
}

.boldText {
  font-family: Arial, "_sans";
  font-size: 11;
  font-weight: bold;
}
///:~
```

This file is imported and used in the song library application via the **Style** tag in the MXML file. After the style sheet is imported, its declarations can be applied to Flex controls in the MXML file. As an example, the style sheet's **boldText** declaration is used by the **TextArea** control with the **songInfo id**.

Events

A user interface is a state machine; it performs actions as state changes occur. In Flex, these changes are managed through events. The Flex class library contains a wide variety of controls with extensive events covering all aspects of mouse movement and keyboard usage.

The **click** attribute of a **Button**, for example, represents one of the events available on that control. The value assigned to **click** can be a function or an inline bit of script. In the MXML file, for example, the **ControlBar** holds the **refreshSongsButton** to refresh the list of songs. You can see from the tag that when the **click** event occurs, **songService.getSongs( )** is called. In this example, the **click** event of the **Button** refers to the **RemoteObject** which corresponds to the Java method.

Connecting to Java

The **RemoteObject** tag at the end of the MXML file sets up the connection to the external Java class, **gui.flex.SongService**. The Flex client will use the **getSongs( )** method in the Java class to retrieve the data for the **DataGrid**. To do so, it must appear as a *service*—an endpoint with which the client can exchange messages. The service defined in the **RemoteObject** tag has a **source** attribute which denotes the Java class of the **RemoteObject**, and it specifies an ActionScript callback function, **onSongs( )**, to be invoked when the Java method returns. The nested **method** tag declares the method **getSongs( )**, which makes that Java method accessible to the rest of the Flex application.

All invocations of services in Flex return asynchronously, through events fired to these callback functions. The **RemoteObject** also raises an alert dialog control in the event of an error.

The **getSongs( )** method may now be invoked from Flash using ActionScript:

```
songService.getSongs();
```

Because of the MXML configuration, this will call **getSongs( )** in the **SongService** class:

```
//: gui/flex/SongService.java
package gui.flex;
import java.util.*;

public class SongService {
  private List<Song> songs = new ArrayList<Song>();
  public SongService() { fillTestData(); }
  public List<Song> getSongs() { return songs; }
  public void addSong(Song song) { songs.add(song); }
  public void removeSong(Song song) { songs.remove(song); }
  private void fillTestData() {
    addSong(new Song("Chocolate", "Snow Patrol",
```

```
        "Final Straw", "sp-final-straw.jpg",
        "chocolate.mp3"));
    addSong(new Song("Concerto No. 2 in E", "Hilary Hahn",
        "Bach: Violin Concertos", "hahn.jpg",
        "bachviolin2.mp3"));
    addSong(new Song("'Round Midnight", "Wes Montgomery",
        "The Artistry of Wes Montgomery",
        "wesmontgomery.jpg", "roundmidnight.mp3"));
  }
} ///:~
```

Each **Song** object is just a data container:

```
//: gui/flex/Song.java
package gui.flex;

public class Song implements java.io.Serializable {
  private String name;
  private String artist;
  private String album;
  private String albumImageUrl;
  private String songMediaUrl;
  public Song() {}
  public Song(String name, String artist, String album,
  String albumImageUrl, String songMediaUrl) {
    this.name = name;
    this.artist = artist;
    this.album = album;
    this.albumImageUrl = albumImageUrl;
    this.songMediaUrl = songMediaUrl;
  }
  public void setAlbum(String album) { this.album = album;}
  public String getAlbum() { return album; }
  public void setAlbumImageUrl(String albumImageUrl) {
    this.albumImageUrl = albumImageUrl;
  }
  public String getAlbumImageUrl() { return albumImageUrl;}
  public void setArtist(String artist) {
    this.artist = artist;
  }
  public String getArtist() { return artist; }
  public void setName(String name) { this.name = name; }
  public String getName() { return name; }
  public void setSongMediaUrl(String songMediaUrl) {
    this.songMediaUrl = songMediaUrl;
```

```
  }
  public String getSongMediaUrl() { return songMediaUrl; }
} ///:~
```

When the application is initialized or you press the **refreshSongsButton**, **getSongs( )** is called, and upon returning, the ActionScript **onSongs(event.result)** is called to populate the **songGrid**.

Here is the ActionScript listing, which is included with the MXML file's **Script** control:

```
//: gui/flex/songScript.as
function getSongs() {
  songService.getSongs();
}

function selectSong(event) {
  var song = songGrid.getItemAt(event.itemIndex);
  showSongInfo(song);
}

function showSongInfo(song) {
  songInfo.text = song.name + newline;
  songInfo.text += song.artist + newline;
  songInfo.text += song.album + newline;
  albumImage.source = song.albumImageUrl;
  songPlayer.contentPath = song.songMediaUrl;
  songPlayer.visible = true;
}

function onSongs(songs) {
  songGrid.dataProvider = songs;
} ///:~
```

To handle **DataGrid** cell selections, we add the **cellPress** event attribute to the **DataGrid** declaration in the MXML file:

```
cellPress="selectSong(event)"
```

When the user clicks on a song in the **DataGrid**, this will call **selectSong( )** in the ActionScript above.

Data models and data binding

Controls can directly invoke services, and ActionScript event callbacks give you a chance to programmatically update the visual controls when services return data. While the script which updates the controls is straightforward, it can get verbose and cumbersome, and its functionality is so common that Flex handles the behavior automatically, with data binding.

In its simplest form, data binding allows controls to reference data directly instead of requiring glue code to copy data into a control. When the data is updated, the control which references it is also automatically updated without any need for programmer intervention. The Flex infrastructure correctly responds to the data change events, and updates all controls which are bound to the data.

Here is a simple example of data binding syntax:

```
<mx:Slider id="mySlider"/>
<mx:Text text="{mySlider.value}"/>
```

To perform data binding, you place references within curly braces: **{}**. Everything within those curly braces is deemed an expression for Flex to evaluate.

The value of the first control, a **Slider** widget, is displayed by the second control, a **Text** field. As the **Slider** changes, the **Text** field's **text** property is automatically updated. This way, the developer does not need to handle the **Slider**'s change events in order to update the **Text** field.

Some controls, such as the **Tree** control and the **DataGrid** in the song library application, are more sophisticated. These controls have a **dataprovider** property to facilitate binding to collections of data. The ActionScript **onSongs( )** function shows how the **SongService.getSongs( )** method is bound to the **dataprovider** of the Flex **DataGrid**. As declared in the **RemoteObject** tag in the MXML file, this function is the callback that ActionScript invokes whenever the Java method returns.

A more sophisticated application with more complex data modeling, such as an enterprise application making use of Data Transfer Objects or a messaging application with data conforming to complex schemas, may encourage further decoupling of the source of data from the controls. In Flex

---

development, we perform this decoupling by declaring a "Model" object, which is a generic MXML container for data. The model contains no logic. It mirrors the Data Transfer Object found in enterprise development, and the structures of other programming languages. By using the model, we can databind our controls to the model, and at the same time have the model databind its properties to service inputs and outputs. This decouples the sources of data, the services, from the visual consumers of the data, facilitating use of the *Model-View-Controller* (MVC) pattern. In larger, more sophisticated applications, the initial complexity caused by inserting a model is often only a small tax compared to the value of a cleanly decoupled MVC application.

In addition to Java objects, Flex can also access SOAP-based Web services and RESTful HTTP services using the **WebService** and **HttpService** controls, respectively. Access to all services is subject to security authorization constraints.

Building and deploying

With the earlier examples, you could get away without a -**flexlib** flag on the command line, but to compile this program, you must specify the location of the **flex-config.xml** file using the -**flexlib** flag. For my installation, the following command works, but you'll have to modify it for your own configuration (the command is a single line, which has been wrapped):

```
//:! gui/flex/build-command.txt
mxmlc -flexlib C:/"Program
Files"/Macromedia/Flex/jrun4/servers/default/flex/WEB-
INF/flex songs.mxml
///:~
```

This command will build the application into an SWF file which you can view in your browser, but the book's code distribution file contains no MP3 files or JPG files, so you won't see anything but the framework when you run the application.

In addition, you must configure a server in order to successfully talk to the Java files from the Flex application. The Flex trial package comes with the JRun server, and you can start this through your computer's menus once Flex is installed, or via the command line:

```
jrun -start default
```

You can verify that the server has been successfully started by opening *http://localhost:8700/samples* in a Web browser and viewing the various samples (this is also a good way to get more familiar with the abilities of Flex).

Instead of compiling the application on the command line, you can compile it via the server. To do this, drop the song source files, CSS style sheet, etc., into the **jrun4/servers/default/flex** directory and access them in a browser by opening *http://localhost:8700/flex/songs.mxml*.

To successfully run the app, you must configure both the Java side and the Flex side.

Java: The compiled **Song.java** and **SongService.java** files must be placed in your **WEB-INF/classes** directory. This is where you drop WAR classes according to the J2EE specification. Alternatively, you can JAR the files and drop the result in **WEB-INF/lib**. It must be in a directory that matches its Java package structure. If you're using JRun, these would be placed in **jrun4/servers/default/flex/WEB-INF/classes/gui/flex/Song.class** and **jrun4/servers/default/flex/WEB-INF/classes/gui/flex/SongService.class**. You also need the image and MP3 support files available in the Web app (for JRun, **jrun4/servers/default/flex** is the Web app root).

Flex: For security reasons, Flex cannot access Java objects unless you give permission by modifying your **flex-config.xml** file. For JRun, this is located at **jrun4/servers/default/flex/WEB-INF/flex/flex-config.xml**. Go to the **<remote-objects>** entry in that file, look at the **<whitelist>** section within, and see the following note:

> *<!--*
> *For security, the whitelist is locked down by default. Uncomment the source element below to enable access to all classes during development.*
>
> *We strongly recommend not allowing access to all source files in production, since this exposes Java and Flex system classes.*
> *<source>*</source>*
> *-->*

Uncomment that **<source>** entry to allow access, so that it reads **<source>*</source>**. The meaning of this and other entries is described in the Flex configuration docs.

Exercise 38: (3) Build the "simple example of data binding syntax" shown above.

Exercise 39: (4) The code download for this book does not include the MP3s or JPGs shown in **SongService.java**. Find some MP3s and JPGs, modify **SongService.java** to include their file names, download the Flex trial and build the application.

Creating SWT applications

As previously noted, Swing took the approach of building all the UI components pixel-by-pixel, in order to provide every component desired whether the underlying OS had those components or not. SWT takes the middle ground by using native components if the OS provides them, and synthesizing components if it doesn't. The result is an application that feels to the user like a native application, and often has noticeably faster performance than the equivalent Swing program. In addition, SWT tends to be a less complex programming model than Swing, which can be desirable in a large portion of applications.[12]

Because SWT uses the native OS to do as much of its work as possible, it can automatically take advantage of OS features that may not be available to Swing—for example, Windows has "subpixel rendering" that makes fonts on LCD screens clearer.

It's even possible to create applets using SWT.

This section is not meant to be a comprehensive introduction to SWT; it's just enough to give you a flavor of it, and to see how SWT contrasts with Swing. You'll discover that there are lots of SWT widgets and that they are all reasonably straightforward to use. You can explore the details in the full documentation and many examples that can be found at *www.eclipse.org*. There are also a number of books on programming with SWT, and more on the way.

---

[12] Chris Grindstaff was very helpful in translating SWT examples and providing SWT information.

Installing SWT

SWT applications require downloading and installing the SWT library from the Eclipse project. Go to *www.eclipse.org/downloads/* and choose a mirror. Follow the links to the current Eclipse build and locate a compressed file with a name that begins with "swt" and includes the name of your platform (for example, "win32"). Inside this file you'll find **swt.jar**. The easiest way to install the **swt.jar** file is to put it into your **jre/lib/ext** directory (that way you don't have to make any modifications to your classpath). When you decompress the SWT library, you may find additional files that you need to install in appropriate places for your platform. For example, the Win32 distribution comes with DLL files that need to be placed somewhere in your **java.library.path** (this is usually the same as your PATH environment variable, but you can run **object/ShowProperties.java** to discover the actual value of **java.library.path**). Once you've done this, you should be able to transparently compile and execute an SWT application as if it were any other Java program.

The documentation for SWT is in a separate download.

An alternative approach is just to install the Eclipse editor, which includes both SWT and the SWT documentation that you can view through the Eclipse help system.

Hello, SWT

Let's start with the simplest possible "hello world"-style application:

```
//: swt/HelloSWT.java
// {Requires: org.eclipse.swt.widgets.Display; You must
// install the SWT library from http://www.eclipse.org }
import org.eclipse.swt.widgets.*;

public class HelloSWT {
  public static void main(String [] args) {
    Display display = new Display();
    Shell shell = new Shell(display);
    shell.setText("Hi there, SWT!"); // Title bar
    shell.open();
    while(!shell.isDisposed())
      if(!display.readAndDispatch())
        display.sleep();
    display.dispose();
```

```
    }
} ///:~
```

If you download the source code from this book, you'll discover that the "Requires" comment directive ends up in the Ant **build.xml** as a prerequisite for building the **swt** subdirectory; all the files that import **org.eclipse.swt** require that you install the SWT library from *www.eclipse.org*.

The **Display** manages the connection between SWT and the underlying operating system—it is part of a *Bridge* between the operating system and SWT. The **Shell** is the top-level main window, within which all the other components are built. When you call **setText( )**, the argument becomes the label on the title bar of the window.

To display the window and thus the application, you must call **open( )** on the **Shell**.

Whereas Swing hides the event-handling loop from you, SWT forces you to write it explicitly. At the top of the loop, you check to see whether the shell has been disposed—note that this gives you the option of inserting code to perform cleanup activities. But this means that the **main( )** thread *is* the user interface thread. In Swing, a second event-dispatching thread is created behind the scenes, but in SWT your **main( )** thread is what handles the UI. Since by default there's only one thread and not two, this makes it somewhat less likely that you'll clobber the UI with threads.

Notice that you don't have to worry about submitting tasks to the user interface thread like you do in Swing. SWT not only takes care of this for you, it throws an exception if you try to manipulate a widget with the wrong thread. However, if you need to spawn other threads to perform long-running operations, you still need to submit changes in the same way that you do with Swing. For this, SWT provides three methods which can be called on the **Display** object: **asyncExec(Runnable)**, **syncExec(Runnable)** and **timerExec(int, Runnable)**.

The activity of your **main( )** thread at this point is to call **readAndDispatch( )** on the **Display** object (this means that there can only be one **Display** object per application). The **readAndDispatch( )** method returns **true** if there are more events in the event queue, waiting to be processed. In that case, you want to call it again, immediately. However, if nothing is pending, you call the **Display** object's **sleep( )** to wait for a short time before checking the event queue again.

Once the program is complete, you must explicitly **dispose( )** of your **Display** object. SWT often requires you to explicitly dispose of resources, because these are usually resources from the underlying operating system, which may otherwise become exhausted.

To prove that the **Shell** is the main window, here's a program that makes a number of **Shell** objects:

```
//: swt/ShellsAreMainWindows.java
import org.eclipse.swt.widgets.*;

public class ShellsAreMainWindows {
  static Shell[] shells = new Shell[10];
  public static void main(String [] args) {
    Display display = new Display();
    for(int i = 0; i < shells.length; i++) {
      shells[i] = new Shell(display);
      shells[i].setText("Shell #" + i);
      shells[i].open();
    }
    while(!shellsDisposed())
      if(!display.readAndDispatch())
        display.sleep();
    display.dispose();
  }
  static boolean shellsDisposed() {
    for(int i = 0; i < shells.length; i++)
      if(shells[i].isDisposed())
        return true;
    return false;
  }
} ///:~
```

When you run it, you'll get ten main windows. The way the program is written, if you close any one of the windows, it will close all of them.

SWT also uses layout managers—different ones than Swing, but the same idea. Here's a slightly more complex example that takes the text from **System.getProperties( )** and adds it to the shell:

```
//: swt/DisplayProperties.java
import org.eclipse.swt.*;
import org.eclipse.swt.widgets.*;
import org.eclipse.swt.layout.*;
```

```
import java.io.*;

public class DisplayProperties {
  public static void main(String [] args) {
    Display display = new Display();
    Shell shell = new Shell(display);
    shell.setText("Display Properties");
    shell.setLayout(new FillLayout());
    Text text = new Text(shell, SWT.WRAP | SWT.V_SCROLL);
    StringWriter props = new StringWriter();
    System.getProperties().list(new PrintWriter(props));
    text.setText(props.toString());
    shell.open();
    while(!shell.isDisposed())
      if(!display.readAndDispatch())
        display.sleep();
    display.dispose();
  }
} ///:~
```

In SWT, all widgets must have a parent object of the general type
Composite, and you must provide this parent as the first argument in the
widget constructor. You see this in the **Text** constructor, where **shell** is the
first argument. Virtually all constructors also take a flag argument that allows
you to provide any number of style directives, depending on what that
particular widget accepts. Multiple style directives are bitwise-ORed together
as seen in this example.

When setting up the **Text( )** object, I added style flags so that it wraps the
text, and automatically adds a vertical scroll bar if it needs to. You'll discover
that SWT is very constructor-based; there are many attributes of a widget
that are difficult or impossible to change except via the constructor. Always
check a widget constructor's documentation for the accepted flags. Note that
some constructors require a flag argument even when they have no
"accepted" flags listed in the documentation. This allows future expansion
without modifying the interface.

Eliminating redundant code

Before going on, notice that there are certain things you do for every SWT
application, just like there were duplicate actions for Swing programs. For
SWT, you always create a **Display**, make a **Shell** from the **Display**, create a
readAndDispatch( ) loop, etc. Of course, in some special cases, you may

not do this, but it's common enough that it's worth trying to eliminate the duplicate code as we did with **net.mindview.util.SwingConsole**.

We'll need to force each application to conform to an interface:

```
//: swt/util/SWTApplication.java
package swt.util;
import org.eclipse.swt.widgets.*;

public interface SWTApplication {
  void createContents(Composite parent);
} ///:~
```

The application is handed a **Composite** object (**Shell** is a subclass) and must use this to create all of its contents inside **createContents( )**. **SWTConsole.run( )** calls **createContents( )** at the appropriate point, sets the size of the shell according to what the user passes to **run( )**, opens the shell and then runs the event loop, and finally disposes of the shell at program exit:

```
//: swt/util/SWTConsole.java
package swt.util;
import org.eclipse.swt.widgets.*;

public class SWTConsole {
  public static void
  run(SWTApplication swtApp, int width, int height) {
    Display display = new Display();
    Shell shell = new Shell(display);
    shell.setText(swtApp.getClass().getSimpleName());
    swtApp.createContents(shell);
    shell.setSize(width, height);
    shell.open();
    while(!shell.isDisposed()) {
      if(!display.readAndDispatch())
        display.sleep();
    }
    display.dispose();
  }
} ///:~
```

This also sets the title bar to the name of the **SWTApplication** class, and sets the **width** and **height** of the **Shell**.

We can create a variation of **DisplayProperties.java** that displays the machine environment, using **SWTConsole**:

```
//: swt/DisplayEnvironment.java
import swt.util.*;
import org.eclipse.swt.*;
import org.eclipse.swt.widgets.*;
import org.eclipse.swt.layout.*;
import java.util.*;

public class DisplayEnvironment implements SWTApplication {
  public void createContents(Composite parent) {
    parent.setLayout(new FillLayout());
    Text text = new Text(parent, SWT.WRAP | SWT.V_SCROLL);
    for(Map.Entry entry: System.getenv().entrySet()) {
      text.append(entry.getKey() + ": " +
        entry.getValue() + "\n");
    }
  }
  public static void main(String [] args) {
    SWTConsole.run(new DisplayEnvironment(), 800, 600);
  }
} ///:~
```

SWTConsole allows us to focus on the interesting aspects of an application rather than the repetitive code.

Exercise 40: (4) Modify **DisplayProperties.java** so that it uses **SWTConsole**.

Exercise 41: (4) Modify **DisplayEnvironment.java** so that it does *not* use **SWTConsole**.

Menus

To demonstrate basic menus, this example reads its own source code and breaks it into words, then populates the menus with these words:

```
//: swt/Menus.java
// Fun with menus.
import swt.util.*;
import org.eclipse.swt.*;
import org.eclipse.swt.widgets.*;
import java.util.*;
import net.mindview.util.*;
```

```
public class Menus implements SWTApplication {
  private static Shell shell;
  public void createContents(Composite parent) {
    shell = parent.getShell();
    Menu bar = new Menu(shell, SWT.BAR);
    shell.setMenuBar(bar);
    Set<String> words = new TreeSet<String>(
      new TextFile("Menus.java", "\\W+"));
    Iterator<String> it = words.iterator();
    while(it.next().matches("[0-9]+"))
      ; // Move past the numbers.
    MenuItem[] mItem = new MenuItem[7];
    for(int i = 0; i < mItem.length; i++) {
      mItem[i] = new MenuItem(bar, SWT.CASCADE);
      mItem[i].setText(it.next());
      Menu submenu = new Menu(shell, SWT.DROP_DOWN);
      mItem[i].setMenu(submenu);
    }
    int i = 0;
    while(it.hasNext()) {
      addItem(bar, it, mItem[i]);
      i = (i + 1) % mItem.length;
    }
  }
  static Listener listener = new Listener() {
    public void handleEvent(Event e) {
      System.out.println(e.toString());
    }
  };
  void
  addItem(Menu bar, Iterator<String> it, MenuItem mItem) {
    MenuItem item = new MenuItem(mItem.getMenu(),SWT.PUSH);
    item.addListener(SWT.Selection, listener);
    item.setText(it.next());
  }
  public static void main(String[] args) {
    SWTConsole.run(new Menus(), 600, 200);
  }
} ///:~
```

A **Menu** must be placed on a **Shell**, and **Composite** allows you to fetch its shell with **getShell( )**. **TextFile** is from **net.mindview.util** and has been described earlier in the book; here a **TreeSet** is filled with words so they will appear in sorted order. The initial elements are numbers, which are discarded. Using the stream of words, the top-level menus on the menu bar are named, then the submenus are created and filled with words until there are no more words.

In response to selecting one of the menu items, the **Listener** simply prints the event so you can see what kind of information it contains. When you run the program, you'll see that part of the information includes the label on the menu, so you can base the menu response on that—or you can provide a different listener for each menu (which is the safer approach, for internationalization).

Tabbed panes, buttons, and events

SWT has a rich set of controls, which they call *widgets*. Look at the documentation for **org.eclipse.swt.widgets** to see the basic ones, and **org.eclipse.swt.custom** to see fancier ones.

To demonstrate a few of the basic widgets, this example places a number of sub-examples inside tabbed panes. You'll also see how to create **Composite**s (roughly the same as Swing **JPanel**s) in order to put items within items.

```java
//: swt/TabbedPane.java
// Placing SWT components in tabbed panes.
import swt.util.*;
import org.eclipse.swt.*;
import org.eclipse.swt.widgets.*;
import org.eclipse.swt.events.*;
import org.eclipse.swt.graphics.*;
import org.eclipse.swt.layout.*;
import org.eclipse.swt.browser.*;

public class TabbedPane implements SWTApplication {
  private static TabFolder folder;
  private static Shell shell;
  public void createContents(Composite parent) {
    shell = parent.getShell();
    parent.setLayout(new FillLayout());
    folder = new TabFolder(shell, SWT.BORDER);
    labelTab();
    directoryDialogTab();
    buttonTab();
    sliderTab();
```

```
      scribbleTab();
      browserTab();
   }
   public static void labelTab() {
      TabItem tab = new TabItem(folder, SWT.CLOSE);
      tab.setText("A Label"); // Text on the tab
      tab.setToolTipText("A simple label");
      Label label = new Label(folder, SWT.CENTER);
      label.setText("Label text");
      tab.setControl(label);
   }
   public static void directoryDialogTab() {
      TabItem tab = new TabItem(folder, SWT.CLOSE);
      tab.setText("Directory Dialog");
      tab.setToolTipText("Select a directory");
      final Button b = new Button(folder, SWT.PUSH);
      b.setText("Select a Directory");
      b.addListener(SWT.MouseDown, new Listener() {
         public void handleEvent(Event e) {
            DirectoryDialog dd = new DirectoryDialog(shell);
            String path = dd.open();
            if(path != null)
               b.setText(path);
         }
      });
      tab.setControl(b);
   }
   public static void buttonTab() {
      TabItem tab = new TabItem(folder, SWT.CLOSE);
      tab.setText("Buttons");
      tab.setToolTipText("Different kinds of Buttons");
      Composite composite = new Composite(folder, SWT.NONE);
      composite.setLayout(new GridLayout(4, true));
      for(int dir : new int[]{
            SWT.UP, SWT.RIGHT, SWT.LEFT, SWT.DOWN
         }) {
         Button b = new Button(composite, SWT.ARROW | dir);
         b.addListener(SWT.MouseDown, listener);
      }
      newButton(composite, SWT.CHECK, "Check button");
      newButton(composite, SWT.PUSH, "Push button");
      newButton(composite, SWT.RADIO, "Radio button");
      newButton(composite, SWT.TOGGLE, "Toggle button");
      newButton(composite, SWT.FLAT, "Flat button");
```

```
      tab.setControl(composite);
    }
  private static Listener listener = new Listener() {
      public void handleEvent(Event e) {
        MessageBox m = new MessageBox(shell, SWT.OK);
        m.setMessage(e.toString());
        m.open();
      }
    };
  private static void newButton(Composite composite,
    int type, String label) {
    Button b = new Button(composite, type);
    b.setText(label);
    b.addListener(SWT.MouseDown, listener);
  }
  public static void sliderTab() {
    TabItem tab = new TabItem(folder, SWT.CLOSE);
    tab.setText("Sliders and Progress bars");
    tab.setToolTipText("Tied Slider to ProgressBar");
    Composite composite = new Composite(folder, SWT.NONE);
    composite.setLayout(new GridLayout(2, true));
    final Slider slider =
      new Slider(composite, SWT.HORIZONTAL);
    final ProgressBar progress =
      new ProgressBar(composite, SWT.HORIZONTAL);
    slider.addSelectionListener(new SelectionAdapter() {
        public void widgetSelected(SelectionEvent event) {
          progress.setSelection(slider.getSelection());
        }
      });
    tab.setControl(composite);
  }
  public static void scribbleTab() {
    TabItem tab = new TabItem(folder, SWT.CLOSE);
    tab.setText("Scribble");
    tab.setToolTipText("Simple graphics: drawing");
    final Canvas canvas = new Canvas(folder, SWT.NONE);
    ScribbleMouseListener sml= new ScribbleMouseListener();
    canvas.addMouseListener(sml);
    canvas.addMouseMoveListener(sml);
    tab.setControl(canvas);
  }
  private static class ScribbleMouseListener
    extends MouseAdapter implements MouseMoveListener {
```

```
      private Point p = new Point(0, 0);
      public void mouseMove(MouseEvent e) {
        if((e.stateMask & SWT.BUTTON1) == 0)
          return;
        GC gc = new GC((Canvas)e.widget);
        gc.drawLine(p.x, p.y, e.x, e.y);
        gc.dispose();
        updatePoint(e);
      }
      public void mouseDown(MouseEvent e) { updatePoint(e); }
      private void updatePoint(MouseEvent e) {
        p.x = e.x;
        p.y = e.y;
      }
    }
  public static void browserTab() {
    TabItem tab = new TabItem(folder, SWT.CLOSE);
    tab.setText("A Browser");
    tab.setToolTipText("A Web browser");
    Browser browser = null;
    try {
      browser = new Browser(folder, SWT.NONE);
    } catch(SWTError e) {
      Label label = new Label(folder, SWT.BORDER);
      label.setText("Could not initialize browser");
      tab.setControl(label);
    }
    if(browser != null) {
      browser.setUrl("http://www.mindview.net");
      tab.setControl(browser);
    }
  }
  public static void main(String[] args) {
    SWTConsole.run(new TabbedPane(), 800, 600);
  }
} ///:~
```

Here, **createContents( )** sets the layout and then calls the methods that
each create a different tab. The text on each tab is set with **setText( )** (you
can also create buttons and graphics on a tab), and each one also sets its tool
tip text. At the end of each method, you'll see a call to **setControl( )**, which
places the control that the method created into the dialog space of that
particular tab.

labelTab( ) demonstrates a simple text label. **directoryDialogTab( )** holds a button which opens a standard **DirectoryDialog** object so the user can select a directory. The result is set as the button's text.

buttonTab( ) shows the different basic buttons. **sliderTab( )** repeats the Swing example from earlier in the chapter of tying a slider to a progress bar.

scribbleTab( ) is a fun example of graphics. A drawing program is produced from only a few lines of code.

Finally, **browserTab( )** shows the power of the SWT **Browser** component—a full-featured Web browser in a single component.

Graphics

Here's the Swing **SineWave.java** program translated to SWT:

```
//: swt/SineWave.java
// SWT translation of Swing SineWave.java.
import swt.util.*;
import org.eclipse.swt.*;
import org.eclipse.swt.widgets.*;
import org.eclipse.swt.events.*;
import org.eclipse.swt.layout.*;

class SineDraw extends Canvas {
  private static final int SCALEFACTOR = 200;
  private int cycles;
  private int points;
  private double[] sines;
  private int[] pts;
  public SineDraw(Composite parent, int style) {
    super(parent, style);
    addPaintListener(new PaintListener() {
      public void paintControl(PaintEvent e) {
        int maxWidth = getSize().x;
        double hstep = (double)maxWidth / (double)points;
        int maxHeight = getSize().y;
        pts = new int[points];
        for(int i = 0; i < points; i++)
          pts[i] = (int)((sines[i] * maxHeight / 2 * .95)
            + (maxHeight / 2));
        e.gc.setForeground(
          e.display.getSystemColor(SWT.COLOR_RED));
```

```
            for(int i = 1; i < points; i++) {
                int x1 = (int)((i - 1) * hstep);
                int x2 = (int)(i * hstep);
                int y1 = pts[i - 1];
                int y2 = pts[i];
                e.gc.drawLine(x1, y1, x2, y2);
            }
        }
    });
    setCycles(5);
    }
    public void setCycles(int newCycles) {
        cycles = newCycles;
        points = SCALEFACTOR * cycles * 2;
        sines = new double[points];
        for(int i = 0; i < points; i++) {
            double radians = (Math.PI / SCALEFACTOR) * i;
            sines[i] = Math.sin(radians);
        }
        redraw();
    }
}

public class SineWave implements SWTApplication {
    private SineDraw sines;
    private Slider slider;
    public void createContents(Composite parent) {
        parent.setLayout(new GridLayout(1, true));
        sines = new SineDraw(parent, SWT.NONE);
        sines.setLayoutData(
            new GridData(SWT.FILL, SWT.FILL, true, true));
        sines.setFocus();
        slider = new Slider(parent, SWT.HORIZONTAL);
        slider.setValues(5, 1, 30, 1, 1, 1);
        slider.setLayoutData(
            new GridData(SWT.FILL, SWT.DEFAULT, true, false));
        slider.addSelectionListener(new SelectionAdapter() {
            public void widgetSelected(SelectionEvent event) {
                sines.setCycles(slider.getSelection());
            }
        });
    }
    public static void main(String[] args) {
        SWTConsole.run(new SineWave(), 700, 400);
```

```
    }
} ///:~
```

Instead of **JPanel**, the basic drawing surface in SWT is **Canvas**.

If you compare this version of the program with the Swing version, you'll see that **SineDraw** is virtually identical. In SWT, you get the graphics context **gc** from the event object that's handed to the **PaintListener**, and in Swing the **Graphics** object is handed directly to the **paintComponent( )** method. But the activities performed with the graphics object are the same, and **setCycles( )** is identical.

createContents( ) requires a bit more code than the Swing version, to lay things out and set up the slider and its listener, but again, the basic activities are roughly the same.

Concurrency in SWT

Although AWT/Swing is single-threaded, it's easily possible to violate that single-threadedness in a way that produces a non-deterministic program. Basically, you don't want to have multiple threads writing to the display because they will write over each other in surprising ways.

SWT doesn't allow this—it throws an exception if you try to write to the display using more than one thread. This will prevent a novice programmer from accidentally making this mistake and introducing hard-to-find bugs into a program.

Here is the translation of the Swing **ColorBoxes.java** program in SWT:

```
//: swt/ColorBoxes.java
// SWT translation of Swing ColorBoxes.java.
import swt.util.*;
import org.eclipse.swt.*;
import org.eclipse.swt.widgets.*;
import org.eclipse.swt.events.*;
import org.eclipse.swt.graphics.*;
import org.eclipse.swt.layout.*;
import java.util.concurrent.*;
import java.util.*;
import net.mindview.util.*;

class CBox extends Canvas implements Runnable {
  class CBoxPaintListener implements PaintListener {
```

```java
      public void paintControl(PaintEvent e) {
        Color color = new Color(e.display, cColor);
        e.gc.setBackground(color);
        Point size = getSize();
        e.gc.fillRectangle(0, 0, size.x, size.y);
        color.dispose();
      }
    }
    private static Random rand = new Random();
    private static RGB newColor() {
      return new RGB(rand.nextInt(255),
        rand.nextInt(255), rand.nextInt(255));
    }
    private int pause;
    private RGB cColor = newColor();
    public CBox(Composite parent, int pause) {
      super(parent, SWT.NONE);
      this.pause = pause;
      addPaintListener(new CBoxPaintListener());
    }
    public void run() {
      try {
        while(!Thread.interrupted()) {
          cColor = newColor();
          getDisplay().asyncExec(new Runnable() {
            public void run() {
                try { redraw(); } catch(SWTException e) {}
                // SWTException is OK when the parent
                // is terminated from under us.
            }
          });
          TimeUnit.MILLISECONDS.sleep(pause);
        }
      } catch(InterruptedException e) {
        // Acceptable way to exit
      } catch(SWTException e) {
        // Acceptable way to exit: our parent
        // was terminated from under us.
      }
    }
  }

public class ColorBoxes implements SWTApplication {
  private int grid = 12;
```

```
   private int pause = 50;
   public void createContents(Composite parent) {
     GridLayout gridLayout = new GridLayout(grid, true);
     gridLayout.horizontalSpacing = 0;
     gridLayout.verticalSpacing = 0;
     parent.setLayout(gridLayout);
     ExecutorService exec = new DaemonThreadPoolExecutor();
     for(int i = 0; i < (grid * grid); i++) {
       final CBox cb = new CBox(parent, pause);
       cb.setLayoutData(new GridData(GridData.FILL_BOTH));
       exec.execute(cb);
     }
   }
   public static void main(String[] args) {
     ColorBoxes boxes = new ColorBoxes();
     if(args.length > 0)
       boxes.grid = new Integer(args[0]);
     if(args.length > 1)
       boxes.pause = new Integer(args[1]);
     SWTConsole.run(boxes, 500, 400);
   }
} ///:~
```

As in the previous example, painting is controlled by creating a
PaintListener with a **paintControl( )** method that is called when the SWT
thread is ready to paint your component. The **PaintListener** is registered in
the **CBox** constructor.

What's notably different in this version of **CBox** is the **run( )** method, which
cannot just call **redraw( )** directly but must submit the **redraw( )** to the
asyncExec( ) method on the **Display** object, which is roughly the same as
SwingUtilities.invokeLater( ). If you replace this with a direct call to
redraw( ), you'll see that the program just stops.

When running the program, you will see little visual artifacts—horizontal
lines occasionally running through a box. This is because SWT is *not* double-
buffered by default, while Swing is. Try running the Swing version side by
side with the SWT version and you'll see it more clearly. You can write code to
double-buffer SWT; you'll find examples on the *www.eclipse.org* Web site.

Exercise 42: (4) Modify **swt/ColorBoxes.java** so that it begins by
sprinkling points ("stars") across the canvas, then randomly changes the
colors of those "stars."

SWT vs. Swing?

It's hard to get a complete picture from such a short introduction, but you should at least start to see that SWT, in many situations, can be a more straightforward way to write code than Swing. However, GUI programming in SWT can still be complex, so your motivation for using SWT should probably be, first, to give the user a more transparent experience when using your application (because the application looks/feels like the other applications on that platform), and second, if the responsiveness provided by SWT is important. Otherwise, Swing may be an appropriate choice.

Exercise 43: (6) Choose any one of the Swing examples that wasn't translated in this section, and translate it to SWT. (Note: This makes a good homework exercise for a class, since the solutions are *not* in the solution guide.)

Summary

The Java GUI libraries have seen some dramatic changes during the lifetime of the language. The Java 1.0 AWT was roundly criticized as being a poor design, and while it allowed you to create portable programs, the resulting GUI was "equally mediocre on all platforms." It was also limiting, awkward, and unpleasant to use compared with the native application development tools available for various platforms.

When Java 1.1 introduced the new event model and JavaBeans, the stage was set—now it was possible to create GUI components that could easily be dragged and dropped inside a visual IDE. In addition, the design of the event model and JavaBeans clearly shows strong consideration for ease of programming and maintainable code (something that was not evident in the 1.0 AWT). But it wasn't until the JFC/Swing classes appeared that the transition was complete. With the Swing components, cross-platform GUI programming can be a civilized experience.

IDEs are where the real revolution lies. If you want a commercial IDE for a proprietary language to get better, you must cross your fingers and hope that the vendor will give you what you want. But Java is an open environment, so not only does it allow for competing IDEs, it encourages them. And for these tools to be taken seriously, they must support JavaBeans. This means a leveled playing field; if a better IDE comes along, you're not tied to the one you've been using. You can pick up and move to the new one and increase your productivity. This kind of competitive environment for GUI IDEs has not been seen before, and the resulting marketplace can generate very positive results for programmer productivity.

This chapter was only meant to give you an introduction to the power of GUI programming and to get you started so that you can see how relatively simple it is to feel your way through the libraries. What you've seen so far will probably suffice for a good portion of your UI design needs. However, there's a lot more to Swing, SWT and Flash/Flex; these are meant to be fully powered UI design toolkits. There's probably a way to accomplish just about everything you can imagine.

Solutions to selected exercises can be found in the electronic document *The Thinking in Java Annotated Solution Guide*, available for sale from *www.MindView.net*.

A: Supplements

There are a number of supplements to this book, including the items, seminars, and services available through the MindView Web site.

This appendix describes these supplements so that you can decide if they will be helpful to you.

Note that although the seminars are often held as public events, they may be given as private, in-house seminars at your location.

Downloadable supplements

The code for this book is available for download from *www.MindView.net*. This includes the Ant build files and other support files necessary to do a successful build and execution of all the examples in the book.

In addition, a few portions of the book were moved to electronic form. The subjects include:

- Cloning Objects

- Passing & Returning Objects

- Analysis and Design

- Portions of other chapters from *Thinking in Java, 3rd Edition* that were not relevant enough to put in the print version of the 4th edition of this book.

Thinking in C: Foundations for Java

At *www.MindView.net*, you will find the *Thinking in C* seminar as a free download. This presentation, created by Chuck Allison and developed by MindView, is a multimedia Flash course which gives you an introduction to the C syntax, operators and functions that Java syntax is based upon.

Note that you must have the Flash Player from *www.Macromedia.com* installed on your system in order to play *Thinking in C*.

Thinking in Java seminar

My company, MindView, Inc., provides five-day, hands-on, public and in-house training seminars based on the material in this book. Formerly called the *Hands-On Java* seminar, this is our main introductory seminar that provides the foundation for our more advanced seminars. Selected material from each chapter represents a lesson, which is followed by a monitored exercise period so that each student receives personal attention. You can find schedule and location information, testimonials, and details at *www.MindView.net*.

Hands-On Java seminar-on-CD

The *Hands-On Java CD* contains an extended version of the material from the *Thinking in Java* seminar and is based on this book. It provides at least some of the experience of the live seminar without the travel and expense. There is an audio lecture and slides corresponding to every chapter in the book. I created the seminar and I narrate the material on the CD. The material is in Flash format, so it should run on any platform that supports the Flash Player. The *Hands-On Java CD* is for sale at *www.MindView.net*, where you can find trial demos of the product.

Thinking in Objects seminar

This seminar introduces the ideas of object-oriented programming from the standpoint of the designer. It explores the process of developing and building a system, primarily focusing on so-called "Agile Methods" or "Lightweight Methodologies," especially Extreme Programming (XP). I introduce methodologies in general, small tools like the "index-card" planning techniques described in *Planning Extreme Programming* by Beck and Fowler (Addison-Wesley, 2001), CRC cards for object design, pair programming, iteration planning, unit testing, automated building, source-code control, and similar topics. The course includes an XP project that will be developed throughout the week.

If you are starting a project and would like to begin using object-oriented design techniques, we can use your project as the example and produce a first-cut design by the end of the week.

Visit *www.MindView.net* for schedule and location information, testimonials, and details.

Thinking in Enterprise Java

This book has been spawned from some of the more advanced chapters in earlier editions of *Thinking in Java*. This book isn't a second volume of *Thinking in Java*, but rather focused coverage of the more advanced topic of enterprise programming. It is currently available (in some form, likely still in development) as a free download from *www.MindView.net*. Because it is a separate book, it can expand to fit the necessary topics. The goal, like *Thinking in Java*, is to produce a very understandable introduction to the basics of the enterprise programming technologies so that the reader is prepared for more advanced coverage of those topics.

The list of topics will include, but is not limited to:

- Introduction to Enterprise Programming
- Network Programming with Sockets and Channels
- Remote Method Invocation (RMI)
- Connecting to Databases
- Naming and Directory Services
- Servlets
- Java Server Pages
- Tags, JSP Fragments and Expression Language
- Automating the Creation of User Interfaces
- Enterprise JavaBeans
- XML
- Web Services
- Automated Testing

You can find the current state of *Thinking in Enterprise Java* at *www.MindView.net*.

Thinking in Patterns (with Java)

One of the most important steps forward in object-oriented design is the "design patterns" movement, chronicled in *Design Patterns*, by Gamma, Helm, Johnson & Vlissides (Addison-Wesley, 1995). That book shows 23 general classes of problems and their solutions, primarily written in C++. The *Design Patterns* book is a source of what has now become an essential, almost mandatory, vocabulary for OOP programmers. *Thinking in Patterns* introduces the basic concepts of design patterns along with examples in Java. The book is not intended to be a simple translation of *Design Patterns*, but rather a new perspective with a Java mindset. It is not limited to the traditional 23 patterns, but also includes other ideas and problem-solving techniques as appropriate.

This book began as the last chapter in *Thinking in Java, 1st Edition*, and as ideas continued to develop, it became clear that it needed to be its own book. At the time of this writing, it is still in development, but the material has been worked and reworked through numerous presentations of the *Objects & Patterns* seminar (which has now been split into the *Designing Objects & Systems* and *Thinking in Patterns* seminars).

You can find out more about this book at *www.MindView.net*.

Thinking in Patterns seminar

This seminar has evolved from the *Objects & Patterns* seminar that Bill Venners and I gave for the past several years. That seminar grew too full, so we've split it into two seminars: this one, and the *Designing Objects & Systems* seminar, described earlier in this appendix.

The seminar strongly follows the material and presentation in the *Thinking in Patterns* book, so the best way to find out what's in the seminar is to learn about the book from *www.MindView.net*.

Much of the presentation emphasizes the design evolution process, starting with an initial solution and moving through the logic and process of evolving the solution to more appropriate designs. The last project shown (a trash recycling simulation) has evolved over time, and you can look at that evolution as a prototype for the way your own design can start as an adequate solution to a particular problem and evolve into a flexible approach to a class of problems.

This seminar will help you:

- Dramatically increase the flexibility of your designs.
- Build in extensibility and reusability.
- Create denser communications about designs using the language of patterns.

Following each lecture there will be a set of patterns exercises for you to solve, where you are guided to write code to apply particular patterns to the solution of programming problems.

Visit *www.MindView*.net for schedule and location information, testimonials, and details.

Design consulting and reviews

My company also provides consulting, mentoring, design reviews and implementation reviews to help guide your project through its development cycle, including your company's first Java project. Visit *www.MindView*.net for availability and details.

B: Resources

Software

The JDK from *http://java.sun.com*. Even if you choose to use a third-party development environment, it's always a good idea to have the JDK on hand in case you come up against what might be a compiler error. The JDK is the touchstone, and if there is a bug in it, chances are it will be well known.

The JDK documentation from *http://java.sun.com*, in HTML. I have never found a reference book on the standard Java libraries that wasn't out of date or missing information. Although the JDK documentation from Sun is shot through with small bugs and is sometimes unusably terse, all the classes and methods are at least *there*. Sometimes people are initially uncomfortable using an online resource rather than a printed book, but it's worth your while to get over this and open the HTML docs so you can at least get the big picture. If you can't figure it out at that point, then reach for the printed books.

Editors & IDEs

There is a healthy competition in this arena. Many offerings are free (and the non-free ones usually have free trials), so your best bet is to simply try them out yourself and see which one fits your needs. Here are a few:

JEdit, Slava Pestov's free editor, is written in Java, so you get the bonus of seeing a desktop Java application in action. This editor is based heavily on plug-ins, many of which have been written by the active community. Download from *www.jedit.org*.

NetBeans, a free IDE from Sun, at *www.netbeans.org*. Designed for drag-and-drop GUI building, code editing, debugging, and more.

Eclipse, an open-source project backed by IBM, among others. The Eclipse platform is also designed to be an extensible foundation, so you can build your own standalone applications on top of Eclipse. This project created the SWT described in the *Graphical User Interfaces* chapter. Download from *www.Eclipse.org*.

IntelliJ IDEA, the payware favorite of a large faction of Java programmers, many of whom claim that IDEA is always a step or two ahead of Eclipse, possibly because IntelliJ is not creating both an IDE and a development platform, but just sticking to creating an IDE. You can download a free trial from *www.jetbrains.com*.

Books

***Effective Java*^{TM}** by Joshua Bloch (Addison-Wesley 2001). A must-have book by the man who fixed the Java collections library, modeled after Scott Meyer's classic *Effective C++*.

***Core Java*^{TM} 2, 7th Edition, Volumes I & II**, by Horstmann & Cornell (Prentice Hall, 2005). Huge, comprehensive, and the first place I go when I'm hunting for answers. The book I recommend when you've completed *Thinking in Java* and need to cast a bigger net.

***The Java*^{TM} Class Libraries: An Annotated Reference**, by Patrick Chan and Rosanna Lee (Addison-Wesley, 1997). Although sadly out of date and out of print, this is what the JDK reference *should* have been: enough description to make it usable. It's big, it's expensive, and the quality of the examples doesn't satisfy me. *But* it's a place to look when you're stuck, and it seems to have more depth (and sheer size) than most alternatives. However, *Core Java 2* has more recent coverage of many of the library components.

Java Network Programming, 2nd Edition, by Elliotte Rusty Harold (O'Reilly, 2000). I didn't begin to understand Java networking (or networking in general, for that matter) until I found this book. I also find his Web site, Café au Lait, to be a stimulating, opinionated, and up-to-date perspective on Java developments, unencumbered by allegiances to any vendors. His regular updates keep up with fast-changing news about Java. See *www.cafeaulait.org*.

Design Patterns, by Gamma, Helm, Johnson and Vlissides (Addison-Wesley, 1995). The seminal book that started the patterns movement in programming, mentioned numerous places in this book.

Refactoring to Patterns, by Joshua Kerievsky (Addison-Wesley, 2005). Marries refactoring and design patterns. The most valuable thing about this book is that it shows you how to evolve a design by folding in patterns as they are needed.

The Art of UNIX Programming, by Eric Raymond (Addison-Wesley, 2004). Although Java is a cross-platform language, the prevalence of Java on the server has made knowledge of Unix/Linux important. Eric's book is an excellent introduction to the history and philosophy of this operating system, and is a fascinating read if you just want to understand some of the roots of computing.

Analysis & design

Extreme Programming Explained, 2nd Edition, by Kent Beck with Cynthia Andres. (Addison-Wesley, 2005). I've always felt that there might be a much different, much better program development process, and I think XP comes pretty darn close. The only book that has had a similar impact on me was _Peopleware_ (described later), which talks primarily about the environment and dealing with corporate culture. _Extreme Programming Explained_ talks about programming and turns most things, even recent "findings," on their ear. They even go so far as to say that pictures are OK as long as you don't spend too much time on them and are willing to throw them away. (You'll notice that the book does _not_ have the "UML stamp of approval" on its cover.) I could see deciding to work for a company based solely on whether they used XP. Small book, small chapters, effortless to read, exciting to think about. You start imagining yourself working in such an atmosphere, and it brings visions of a whole new world.

UML Distilled, 2nd Edition, by Martin Fowler (Addison-Wesley, 2000). When you first encounter UML, it is daunting because there are so many diagrams and details. According to Fowler, most of this stuff is unnecessary, so he cuts through to the essentials. For most projects, you only need to know a few diagramming tools, and Fowler's goal is to come up with a good design rather than worry about all the artifacts of getting there. In fact, the first half of the book is all that most people will need. A nice, thin, readable book; the first one you should get if you need to understand UML.

Domain-Driven Design, by Eric Evans (Addison-Wesley, 2004). This book focuses on the _domain model_ as the primary artifact of the design process. I have found this to be an important shift in emphasis that helps keep designers at the right level of abstraction.

The Unified Software Development Process, by Ivar Jacobsen, Grady Booch, and James Rumbaugh (Addison-Wesley, 1999). I went in fully prepared to dislike this book. It seemed to have all the makings of a boring college text. I was pleasantly surprised—although there are a few parts that have explanations that seem as if those concepts aren't clear to the authors. The bulk of the book is not only clear, but enjoyable. And best of all, the process makes a lot of practical sense. It's not Extreme Programming (and does not have their clarity about testing), but it's also part of the UML juggernaut; even if you can't get XP through the door, most people have climbed aboard the "UML is good" bandwagon (regardless of their *actual* level of experience with it), so you can probably get it adopted. I think this book should be the flagship of UML, and the one you can read after Fowler's *UML Distilled* when you want more detail.

Before you choose any method, it's helpful to gain perspective from those who are not trying to sell you one. It's easy to adopt a method without really understanding what you want out of it or what it will do for you. Others are using it, which seems a compelling reason. However, humans have a strange little psychological quirk: If they want to believe something will solve their problems, they'll try it. (This is experimentation, which is good.) But if it doesn't solve their problems, they may redouble their efforts and begin to announce loudly what a great thing they've discovered. (This is denial, which is not good.) The assumption here may be that if you can get other people in the same boat, you won't be lonely, even if it's going nowhere (or sinking).

This is not to suggest that all methodologies go nowhere, but that you should be armed to the teeth with mental tools that help you stay in experimentation mode ("It's not working; let's try something else") and out of denial mode ("No, that's not really a problem. Everything's wonderful, we don't need to change"). I think the following books, read *before* you choose a method, will provide you with these tools.

Software Creativity, by Robert L. Glass (Prentice Hall, 1995). This is the best book I've seen that discusses *perspective* on the whole methodology issue. It's a collection of short essays and papers that Glass has written and sometimes acquired (P.J. Plauger is one contributor), reflecting his many years of thinking and study on the subject. They're entertaining and only long enough to say what's necessary; he doesn't ramble and bore you. He's not just blowing smoke, either; there are hundreds of references to other papers and studies. All programmers and managers should read this book before wading into the methodology mire.

Software Runaways: Monumental Software Disasters, by Robert L. Glass (Prentice Hall, 1998). The great thing about this book is that it brings to the forefront what we don't talk about: the number of projects that not only fail, but fail spectacularly. I find that most of us still think, "That can't happen to me" (or "That can't happen *again*"), and I think this puts us at a disadvantage. By keeping in mind that things can always go wrong, you're in a much better position to make them go right.

Peopleware, 2nd Edition, by Tom DeMarco and Timothy Lister (Dorset House, 1999). You *must* read this book. It's not only fun, it rocks your world and destroys your assumptions. Although DeMarco and Lister have backgrounds in software development, this book is about projects and teams in general. But the focus is on the *people* and their needs, rather than the technology and its needs. They talk about creating an environment where people will be happy and productive, rather than deciding what rules those people should follow to be adequate components of a machine. This latter attitude, I think, is the biggest contributor to programmers smiling and nodding when XYZ method is adopted, and then quietly doing whatever they've always done.

Secrets of Consulting: A Guide to Giving & Getting Advice Successfully, by Gerald M. Weinberg (Dorset House, 1985). A superb book, one of my all-time favorites. It's perfect if you are trying to be a consultant *or* if you're using consultants and trying to do a better job. Short chapters, filled with stories and anecdotes that teach you how to get to the core of the issue with minimal struggle. Also see *More Secrets of Consulting*, published in 2002, or most any other Weinberg book.

Complexity, by M. Mitchell Waldrop (Simon & Schuster, 1992). This chronicles the coming together in Santa Fe, New Mexico, of a group of scientists from different disciplines to discuss real problems that their individual disciplines couldn't solve (the stock market in economics, the initial formation of life in biology, why people do what they do in sociology, etc.). By crossing physics, economics, chemistry, math, computer science, sociology, and others, a multidisciplinary approach to these problems is developing. But more important, a different way of *thinking* about these ultra-complex problems is emerging: away from mathematical determinism and the illusion that you can write an equation that predicts all behavior, and toward first *observing* and looking for a pattern and trying to emulate that pattern by any means possible. (The book chronicles, for example, the emergence of genetic algorithms.) This kind of thinking, I believe, is useful as we observe ways to manage more and more complex software projects.

Python

Learning Python, 2nd Edition, by Mark Lutz and David Ascher (O'Reilly, 2003). A nice programmer's introduction to my favorite language, an excellent companion to Java. The book includes an introduction to Jython, which allows you to combine Java and Python in a single program (the Jython interpreter is compiled to pure Java bytecodes, so there is nothing special you need to add to accomplish this). This language union promises great possibilities.

My own list of books

Not all of these are currently available, but some can be found through used-book outlets.

Computer Interfacing with Pascal & C (self-published under the Eisys imprint, 1988. Available for sale only from *www.MindView.net*). An introduction to electronics from back when CP/M was still king and DOS was an upstart. I used high-level languages and often the parallel port of the computer to drive various electronic projects. Adapted from my columns in the first and best magazine I wrote for, *Micro Cornucopia*. Alas, Micro C was lost long before the Internet appeared. Creating this book was an extremely satisfying publishing experience.

Using C++ (Osborne/McGraw-Hill, 1989). One of the first books out on C++. This is out of print and replaced by its 2nd edition, the renamed *C++ Inside & Out*.

C++ Inside & Out (Osborne/McGraw-Hill, 1993). As noted, actually the 2nd edition of *Using C++*. The C++ in this book is reasonably accurate, but it's circa 1992 and *Thinking in C++* is intended to replace it. You can find out more about this book and download the source code at *www.MindView.net*.

Thinking in C++, 1st Edition (Prentice Hall, 1995). This won the *Software Development Magazine* Jolt Award for best book of the year.

Thinking in C++, 2nd Edition, Volume 1 (Prentice Hall, 2000). Downloadable from *www.MindView.net*. Updated to follow the finalized language standard.

Thinking in C++, 2nd Edition, Volume 2, coauthored with Chuck Allison (Prentice Hall, 2003). Downloadable from *www.MindView.net*.

Black Belt C++: The Master's Collection, Bruce Eckel, editor (M&T Books, 1994). Out of print. A collection of chapters by various C++ luminaries based on their presentations in the C++ track at the Software Development Conference, which I chaired. The cover on this book stimulated me to gain control over all future cover designs.

Thinking in Java, 1st Edition (Prentice Hall, 1998). The 1st edition of this book won the *Software Development Magazine* Productivity Award, the *Java Developer's Journal* Editor's Choice Award, and the *JavaWorld* Reader's Choice Award for best book. Downloadable from *www.MindView.net*.

Thinking in Java, 2nd Edition (Prentice Hall, 2000). This edition won the *JavaWorld* Editor's Choice Award for best book. Downloadable from *www.MindView.net*.

Thinking in Java, 3rd Edition, (Prentice Hall, 2003). This edition won the *Software Development Magazine* Jolt Award for best book of the year, along with other awards listed on the back cover. Downloadable from *www.MindView.net*.

Index

Please note that some names will be duplicated in capitalized form. Following Java style, the capitalized names refer to Java classes, while lowercase names refer to a general concept.

!

! · 105
!= · 103

&

& · 111
&& · 105
&= · 111

.

.NET · 57
.new syntax · 350
.this syntax · 350

@

@ symbol, for annotations · 1059
@author · 86
@Deprecated, annotation · 1060
@deprecated, Javadoc tag · 87
@docRoot · 85
@inheritDoc · 85
@interface, and extends keyword · 1070
@link · 85
@Override · 1059
@param · 86
@Retention · 1061
@return · 86
@see · 85
@since · 86
@SuppressWarnings · 1060
@Target · 1061
@Test · 1060
@Test, for @Unit · 1084
@TestObjectCleanup, @Unit tag · 1092
@TestObjectCreate, for @Unit · 1089
@throws · 87
@Unit · 1084; using · 1084
@version · 85

[

[ ], indexing operator · 193

^

^ · 111
^= · 111

|

| · 111
|| · 105
|= · 111

+

+ · 101; String conversion with operator + · 95, 118, 504

<

< · 103
<< · 112
<<= · 112
<= · 103

=

== · 103

>

> · 103
>= · 103
>> · 112
>>= · 112

A

abstract: class · 311; inheriting from abstract classes · 312; keyword · 312; vs. interface · 328
Abstract Window Toolkit (AWT) · 1303
AbstractButton · 1333
abstraction · 24
AbstractSequentialList · 859
AbstractSet · 793
access: class · 229; control · 210, 234; control, violating with reflection · 607; inner classes & access rights · 348; package access and friendly · 221; specifiers · 31, 210, 221; within a directory, via the default package · 223
action command · 1358
ActionEvent · 1358, 1406
ActionListener · 1316
ActionScript, for Macromedia Flex · 1417
active objects, in concurrency · 1295
Adapter design pattern · 325, 334, 434, 630, 733, 737, 795
Adapter Method idiom · 434
adapters, listener · 1328
add( ), ArrayList · 390
addActionListener( ) · 1403, 1410
addChangeListener · 1363
addition · 98

addListener · 1321
Adler32 · 975
agent-based programming · 1299
aggregate array initialization · 193
aggregation · 32
aliasing · 97; and String · 504; arrays · 194
Allison, Chuck · 4, 18, 1449, 1460
allocate( ) · 948
allocateDirect( ) · 948
alphabetic sorting · 418
alphabetic vs. lexicographic sorting · 783
AND: bitwise · 120; logical (&&) · 105
annotation · 1059; apt processing tool · 1074; default element values · 1062, 1063, 1065; default value · 1069; elements · 1061; elements, allowed types for · 1065; marker annotation · 1061; processor · 1064; processor based on reflection · 1071
anonymous inner class · 356, 904, 1314; and table-driven code · 859; generic · 645
application: builder · 1394; framework · 375
applying a method to a sequence · 728
apt, annotation processing tool · 1074
argument: constructor · 156; covariant argument types · 706; final · 266, 904; generic type argument inference · 632; variable argument lists (unknown quantity and type of arguments) · 198
Arnold, Ken · 1306
array: array of generic objects · 850; associative array · 394; bounds checking · 194; comparing arrays · 777; comparison with container · 748; copying an array · 775; covariance · 677; dynamic aggregate initialization syntax · 752; element comparisons · 778; first-class objects · 749; initialization · 193; length · 194, 749; multidimensional · 754; not Iterable · 433; of objects · 749; of primitives · 749; ragged · 755; returning an array · 753
ArrayBlockingQueue · 1215
ArrayList · 401, 817; add( ) · 390; get( ) · 390; size( ) · 390
Arrays: asList( ) · 396, 436, 816; binarySearch( ) · 784; class, container utility · 775
asCharBuffer( ) · 950
aspect-oriented programming (AOP) · 714

constant values · 335; implicit constants, and String · 504

constrained properties · 1414

constructor · 155; and anonymous inner classes · 356; and concurrency · 1137; and exception handling · 481, 483; and finally · 483; and overloading · 158; and polymorphism · 293; arguments · 156; base-class constructor · 294; behavior of polymorphic methods inside constructors · 301; calling base-class constructors with arguments · 245; calling from other constructors · 170; Constructor class for reflection · 589; default · 166; initialization during inheritance and composition · 249; instance initialization · 359; name · 156; no-arg · 156, 166; order of constructor calls with inheritance · 293; return value · 157; static construction clause · 190; static method · 189; synthesized default constructor access · 592

consulting & training provided by MindView, Inc. · 1450

container · 44; class · 389; *classes* · 389; comparison with array · 748; performance test · 859

containers: basic behavior · 398; lock-free · 1281; type-safe and generics · 390

contention, lock, in concurrency · 1272

context switch · 1112

continue keyword · 144

contravariance, and generics · 682

control framework, and inner classes · 375

control, access · 31, 234

conversion: automatic · 239; narrowing conversion · 120; widening conversion · 121

Coplien, Jim: curiously recurring template pattern · 702

copying an array · 775

CopyOnWriteArrayList · 1252, 1281

CopyOnWriteArraySet · 1282

copyright notice, source code · 19

CountDownLatch, for concurrency · 1230

covariant · 565; argument types · 706; arrays · 677; return types · 303, 583, 706

CRC32 · 975

critical section, and synchronized block · 1169

CSS (Cascading Style Sheets), and Macromedia Flex · 1423

curiously recurring: generics · 702; template pattern in C++ · 702

CyclicBarrier, for concurrency · 1232

D

daemon threads · 1130

data: final · 262; primitive data types and use with operators · 123; static initialization · 186

Data Transfer Object · 621, 797

Data Transfer Object (Messenger idiom) · 860

data type, equivalence to class · 27

database table, SQL generated via annotations · 1066

DatagramChannel · 971

DataInput · 926

DataInputStream · 920, 924, 929

DataOutput · 926

DataOutputStream · 921, 925

deadlock, in concurrency · 1223

decode( ), character set · 953

decompiler, javap · 505, 610, 660

Decorator design pattern · 717

decoupling, via polymorphism · 41, 277

decrement operator · 101

default constructor · 166; access the same as the class · 592; synthesizing a default constructor · 245

default keyword, in a switch statement · 151

default package · 211, 223

defaultReadObject( ) · 995

defaultWriteObject( ) · 994

DeflaterOutputStream · 973

Delayed · 1238

DelayQueue, for concurrency · 1235

delegation · 246, 716

Delphi, from Borland · 1394

DeMarco, Tom · 1459

deque, double-ended queue · 410, 829

derived: derived class · 281; derived class, initializing · 244; types · 34

design · 307; adding more methods to a design · 235; and composition · 304; and inheritance · 304; and mistakes · 234; library design · 210

design pattern: Adapter · 325, 334, 630, 733, 737, 795; Adapter method · 434; Chain of Responsibility · 1036;

flip( ), nio · 948

float: floating point true and false · 106; literal value marker (F) · 109

FlowLayout · 1318

flushing output files · 931

Flyweight design pattern · 800, 1301

focus traversal · 1305

folding, constant · 262

for keyword · 138

foreach · 141, 145, 199, 200, 219, 376, 393, 422, 429, 545, 629, 631, 694, 1011, 1036; and Adapter Method · 434; and Iterable · 431

format: precision · 517; specifiers · 516; string · 514; width · 516

format( ) · 514

Formatter · 515

forName( ) · 558, 1326

FORTRAN programming language · 110

forward referencing · 184

Fowler, Martin · 209, 495, 1457

framework, control framework and inner classes · 375

function: member function · 29; overriding · 36

function object · 737

functional languages · 1113

Future · 1125

G

garbage collection · 173, 175; and cleanup · 251; how the collector works · 178; order of object reclamation · 254; reachable objects · 889

Generator · 285, 627, 636, 645, 695, 732, 763, 780, 794, 1021, 1042; filling a Collection · 636; general purpose · 637

generics: @Unit testing · 1094; and type-safe containers · 390; anonymous inner classes · 645; array of generic objects · 850; basic introduction · 390; bounds · 653, 673; cast via a generic class · 699; casting · 697; Class references · 565; contravariance · 682; curiously recurring · 702; erasure · 650, 696; example of a framework · 1282; exceptions · 711; explicit type argument specification for generic methods · 398, 635; inner classes · 645; instanceof · 663, 697; isInstance( ) · 663; methods ·

631, 795; overloading · 699; reification · 655; self-bounded types · 701; simplest class definition · 413; supertype wildcards · 682; type tag · 663; unbounded wildcard · 686; varargs and generic methods · 635; wildcards · 677

get( ): ArrayList · 390; HashMap · 420; no get( ) for Collection · 811

getBeanInfo( ) · 1398

getBytes( ) · 929

getCanonicalName( ) · 560

getChannel( ) · 948

getClass( ) · 459, 558

getConstructor( ) · 1335

getConstructors( ) · 592

getenv( ) · 433

getEventSetDescriptors( ) · 1401

getInterfaces( ) · 560

getMethodDescriptors( ) · 1401

getMethods( ) · 592

getName( ) · 1400

getPropertyDescriptors( ) · 1400

getPropertyType( ) · 1400

getReadMethod( ) · 1400

getSelectedValues( ) · 1347

getSimpleName( ) · 560

getState( ) · 1357

getSuperclass( ) · 561

getWriteMethod( ) · 1400

Glass, Robert · 1458

glue, in BoxLayout · 1321

Goetz Test, for avoiding synchronization · 1160

Goetz, Brian · 1156, 1160, 1272, 1302

goto, lack of in Java · 146

graphical user interface (GUI) · 375, 1303

graphics · 1368; Graphics class · 1361

greater than (>) · 103

greater than or equal to (>=) · 103

greedy quantifiers · 529

GridBagLayout · 1320

GridLayout · 1319, 1392

Grindstaff, Chris · 1430

group, thread · 1146

groups, regular expression · 534

guarded region, in exception handling · 447

GUI: graphical user interface · 375, 1303; GUI builders · 1304

GZIPInputStream · 973

GZIPOutputStream · 973

H

handler, exception · 448

Harold, Elliotte Rusty · 1415, 1456; XOM XML library · 1003

has-a · 32; relationship, composition · 258

hash function · 847

hashCode( ) · 833, 839, 847; and hashed data structures · 843; equals( ) · 822; issues when writing · 851; recipe for generating decent · 853

hashing · 844, 847; and hash codes · 839; external chaining · 848; perfect hashing function · 848

HashMap · 834, 877, 1287, 1331

HashSet · 415, 821, 872

Hashtable · 877, 895

hasNext( ), Iterator · 407

Hexadecimal · 109

hiding, implementation · 228

Holub, Allen · 1295

HTML on Swing components · 1370

I

I/O: available( ) · 930; basic usage, examples · 927; between tasks using pipes · 1221; blocking, and available( ) · 930; BufferedInputStream · 920; BufferedOutputStream · 921; BufferedReader · 483, 924, 927; BufferedWriter · 924, 930; ByteArrayInputStream · 916; ByteArrayOutputStream · 917; characteristics of files · 912; CharArrayReader · 923; CharArrayWriter · 923; CheckedInputStream · 973; CheckedOutputStream · 973; close( ) · 928; compression library · 973; controlling the process of serialization · 986; DataInput · 926; DataInputStream · 920, 924, 929; DataOutput · 926; DataOutputStream · 921, 925; DeflaterOutputStream · 973; directory lister · 902; directory, creating directories and paths · 912; Externalizable · 986; File · 916, 925; File class · 901; File.list( ) · 901; FileDescriptor · 916; FileReader · 927; FileInputStream · 916; FilenameFilter · 901; FileOutputStream · 917; FileReader · 483, 923; FileWriter · 923, 930; FilterInputStream · 916; FilterOutputStream · 917; FilterReader · 924; FilterWriter · 924; from standard input · 941; GZIPInputStream · 973; GZIPOutputStream · 973; InflaterInputStream · 973; input · 914; InputStream · 914; InputStreamReader · 922, 923; internationalization · 923; interruptible · 1189; library · 901; lightweight persistence · 980; LineNumberInputStream · 920; LineNumberReader · 924; mark( ) · 926; mkdirs( ) · 914; network I/O · 946; new nio · 946; ObjectOutputStream · 981; output · 914; OutputStream · 914, 917; OutputStreamWriter · 922, 923; pipe · 915; piped streams · 936; PipedInputStream · 916; PipedOutputStream · 916, 917; PipedReader · 923; PipedWriter · 923; PrintStream · 921; PrintWriter · 924, 930, 932; PushbackInputStream · 920; PushbackReader · 924; RandomAccessFile · 925, 926, 934; read( ) · 914; readDouble( ) · 934; Reader · 914, 922, 923; readExternal( ) · 986; readLine( ) · 485, 924, 931, 942; readObject( ) · 981; redirecting standard I/O · 942; renameTo( ) · 914; reset( ) · 926; seek( ) · 926, 934; SequenceInputStream · 916, 925; Serializable · 986; setErr(PrintStream) · 943; setIn(InputStream) · 943; setOut(PrintStream) · 943; StreamTokenizer · 924; StringBuffer · 916; StringBufferInputStream · 916; StringReader · 923, 928; StringWriter · 923; System.err · 941; System.in · 941; System.out · 941; transient · 991; typical I/O configurations · 927; Unicode · 923; write( ) · 914; writeBytes( ) · 933; writeChars( ) · 933; writeDouble( ) · 934; writeExternal( ) · 986; writeObject( ) · 981; Writer · 914, 922, 923; ZipEntry · 977; ZipInputStream · 973; ZipOutputStream · 973

Icon · 1335

IdentityHashMap · 834, 877

if-else statement · 116, 135

isInstance( ) · 578; and generics · 663
isInterface( ) · 560
is-like-a · 307
Iterable · 629, 797; and array · 433; and
    foreach · 431
Iterator · 406, 409, 427; hasNext( ) · 407;
    next( ) · 407
Iterator design pattern · 349

J

Jacobsen, Ivar · 1457
JApplet · 1317; menus · 1352
JAR · 1412; file · 212; jar files and classpath
    · 216; utility · 978
Java: and set-top boxes · 111; AWT · 1303;
    bytecodes · 506; compiling and running
    a program · 80; Java Foundation
    Classes (JFC/Swing) · 1303; Java
    Virtual Machine (JVM) · 556; Java Web
    Start · 1376; public Java seminars · 15
Java standard library, and thread-safety ·
    1232
JavaBeans, see Beans · 1393
javac · 81
javadoc · 82
javap decompiler · 505, 610, 660
Javassist · 1104
JButton · 1335; Swing · 1311
JCheckBox · 1335, 1342
JCheckBoxMenuItem · 1353, 1357
JComboBox · 1345
JComponent · 1337, 1360
JDialog · 1364; menus · 1352
JDK 1.1 I/O streams · 922
JDK, downloading and installing · 80
JFC, Java Foundation Classes (Swing) ·
    1303
JFileChooser · 1368
JFrame · 1317; menus · 1352
JIT, just-in-time compilers · 181
JLabel · 1340
JList · 1347
JMenu · 1352, 1357
JMenuBar · 1352, 1358
JMenuItem · 1336, 1352, 1357, 1358, 1360
JNLP, Java Network Launch Protocol ·
    1376
join( ), threading · 1143
JOptionPane · 1350
Joy, Bill · 103

JPanel · 1334, 1360, 1392
JPopupMenu · 1359
JProgressBar · 1373
JRadioButton · 1335, 1344
JScrollPane · 1316, 1349
JSlider · 1373
JTabbedPane · 1349
JTextArea · 1315
JTextField · 1312, 1338
JTextPane · 1341
JToggleButton · 1334
JUnit, problems with · 1083
JVM (Java Virtual Machine) · 556

K

keyboard: navigation, and Swing · 1305;
    shortcuts · 1358
keySet( ) · 877

L

label · 146
labeled: break · 147; continue · 147
late binding · 40, 277, 281
latent typing · 721, 733
layout, controlling layout with layout
    managers · 1317
lazy initialization · 239
least-recently-used (LRU) · 838
left-shift operator (<<) · 112
length: array member · 194; for arrays ·
    749
less than (<) · 103
less than or equal to (<=) · 103
lexicographic: sorting · 418; vs. alphabetic
    sorting · 783
library: creator, vs. client programmer ·
    209; design · 210; use · 210
LIFO (last-in, first-out) · 412
lightweight: object · 406; persistence · 980
LineNumberInputStream · 920
LineNumberReader · 924
LinkedBlockingQueue · 1215
LinkedHashMap · 834, 838, 877
LinkedHashSet · 416, 821, 872, 874
LinkedList · 401, 410, 423, 817
linking, class · 563
list: boxes · 1347; drop-down list · 1345

multiple implementation inheritance · 371
multiple inheritance, in C++ and Java · 326
multiplication · 98
multiply nested class · 368
multitasking · 1112
mutual exclusion (mutex), concurrency · 1154
MXML, Macromedia Flex input format · 1416
mxmlc, Macromedia Flex compiler · 1418

N

name: clash · 211; collisions · 217; collisions when combining interfaces · 330; creating unique package names · 214; qualified · 560
namespaces · 211
narrowing conversion · 120
natural logarithms · 110
nested class (static inner class) · 364
nesting interfaces · 336
net.mindview.util.SwingConsole · 1310
network I/O · 946
Neville, Sean · 1416
new I/O · 946
new operator · 173; and primitives, array · 195
newInstance( ) · 1335; reflection · 561
next( ), Iterator · 407
nio · 946; and interruption · 1189; buffer · 946; channel · 946; performance · 967
no-arg constructor · 156, 166
North, BorderLayout · 1317
not equivalent (!=) · 103
NOT, logical (!) · 105
notifyAll( ) · 1198
notifyListeners( ) · 1411
null · 67
Null Iterator design pattern · 598
Null Object design pattern · 598
NullPointerException · 469
numbers, binary · 109

O

object · 25; aliasing · 97; arrays are first-class objects · 749; assigning objects by copying references · 96; Class object · 556, 998, 1156; creation · 156; equals( ) · 104; equivalence · 103; equivalence vs. reference equivalence · 104; final · 263; getClass( ) · 558; hashCode( ) · 833; interface to · 26; lock, for concurrency · 1155; member · 32; object-oriented programming · 553; process of creation · 189; serialization · 980; standard root class, default inheritance from · 241; wait( ) and notifyAll( ) · 1199; web of objects · 981
object pool · 1246
object-oriented, basic concepts of object-oriented programming (OOP) · 23
ObjectOutputStream · 981
Octal · 109
ones complement operator · 111
OOP: basic characteristics · 25; basic concepts of object-oriented programming · 23; protocol · 316; Simula-67 programming language · 26; substitutability · 25
OpenLaszlo, alternative to Flex · 1416
operating system, executing programs from within Java · 944
operation, atomic · 1160
operator · 94; + and += overloading for String · 242; +, for String · 504; binary · 111; bitwise · 111; casting · 120; comma operator · 140; common pitfalls · 119; indexing operator [ ] · 193; logical · 105; logical operators and short-circuiting · 106; ones-complement · 111; operator overloading for String · 504; overloading · 118; precedence · 95; relational · 103; shift · 112; String conversion with operator + · 95, 118; ternary · 116; unary · 101, 111
optional methods, in the Java containers · 813
OR · 120; (||) · 105
order: of constructor calls with inheritance · 293; of initialization · 185, 272, 302
ordinal( ), for enum · 1012
organization, code · 221
OSExecute · 944
OutputStream · 914, 917
OutputStreamWriter · 922, 923
overflow, and primitive types · 133
overloading: and constructors · 158; distinguishing overloaded methods ·

160; generics · 699; lack of name hiding during inheritance · 255; method overloading · 158; on return values · 165; operator + and += overloading for String · 242, 504; operator overloading · 118; vs. overriding · 255

overriding: and inner classes · 383; function · 36; private methods · 290; vs. overloading · 255

P

package · 210; access, and friendly · 221; and directory structure · 220; creating unique package names · 214; default · 211, 223; names, capitalization · 75; package access, and protected · 258

paintComponent( ) · 1360, 1368

painting on a JPanel in Swing · 1360

parameter, collecting · 713, 742

parameterized types · 617

parseInt( ) · 1368

pattern, regular expression · 527

perfect hashing function · 848

performance: and final · 271; nio · 967; test, containers · 859; tuning, for concurrency · 1270

persistence · 996; lightweight persistence · 980

PhantomReference · 889

philosophers, dining, example of deadlock in concurrency · 1224

pipe · 915

piped streams · 936

PipedInputStream · 916

PipedOutputStream · 916, 917

PipedReader · 923, 1221

PipedWriter · 923, 1221

pipes, and I/O · 1221

Plauger, P.J. · 1458

pluggable look & feel · 1373

pointer, Java exclusion of pointers · 372

polymorphism · 38, 277, 310, 554, 613; and constructors · 293; and multiple dispatching · 1048; behavior of polymorphic methods inside constructors · 301

pool, object · 1246

portability in C, C++ and Java · 123

position, absolute, when laying out Swing components · 1320

possessive quantifiers · 529

post-decrement · 102

postfix · 102

post-increment · 102

pre-decrement · 102

preferences API · 1006

prefix · 102

pre-increment · 102

prerequisites, for this book · 23

primitive: comparison · 104; data types, and use with operators · 123; final · 263; final static primitives · 264; initialization of class fields · 182; types · 65

primordial class loader · 556

printf( ) · 514

printStackTrace( ) · 458, 461

PrintStream · 921

PrintWriter · 924, 930, 932; convenience constructor in Java SE5 · 937

priority, concurrency · 1127

PriorityBlockingQueue, for concurrency · 1239

PriorityQueue · 425, 827

private · 31, 210, 221, 224, 258, 1155; illusion of overriding private methods · 268; inner classes · 377; interfaces, when nested · 339; method overriding · 290; methods · 303

problem space · 24

process control · 944

process, concurrent · 1112

ProcessBuilder · 944

ProcessFiles · 1100

producer-consumer, concurrency · 1208

programmer, client · 30

programming: basic concepts of object-oriented programming (OOP) · 23; event-driven programming · 1312; Extreme Programming (XP) · 1457; multiparadigm · 25; object-oriented · 553

progress bar · 1371

promotion, to int · 122, 132

property · 1394; bound properties · 1414; constrained properties · 1414; custom property editor · 1414; custom property sheet · 1414; indexed property · 1414

PropertyChangeEvent · 1414

PropertyDescriptors · 1400

PropertyVetoException · 1414

protected · 31, 210, 221, 225, 258; and package access · 258; is also package access · 227
protocol · 316
proxy: and java.lang.ref.Reference · 890; for unmodifiable methods in the Collections class · 817
Proxy design pattern · 593
public · 31, 210, 221, 222; and interface · 316; class, and compilation units · 211
pure substitution · 37, 307
PushbackInputStream · 920
PushbackReader · 924
pushdown stack · 412; generic · 625
Python · 1, 5, 9, 53, 60, 722, 787, 1113, 1460

Q

qualified name · 560
quantifier: greedy · 529; possessive · 529; regular expression · 529; reluctant · 529
queue · 389, 410, 423, 827; performance · 863; synchronized, concurrency · 1215
queuing discipline · 425

R

race condition, in concurrency · 1152
RAD (Rapid Application Development) · 588
radio button · 1344
ragged array · 755
random selection, and enum · 1021
random( ) · 419
RandomAccess, tagging interface for containers · 441
RandomAccessFile · 925, 926, 934, 948
raw type · 651
reachable objects and garbage collection · 889
read( ) · 914; nio · 948
readDouble( ) · 934
Reader · 914, 922, 923
readExternal( ) · 986
reading from standard input · 941
readLine( ) · 485, 924, 931, 942
readObject( ) · 981; with Serializable · 992
ReadWriteLock · 1292

recursion, unintended via toString( ) · 509
redirecting standard I/O · 942
ReentrantLock · 1160, 1192
refactoring · 209
reference: assigning objects by copying references · 96; final · 263; finding exact type of a base reference · 555; null · 67; reference equivalence vs. object equivalence · 104
reference counting, garbage collection · 178
Reference, from java.lang.ref · 889
referencing, forward · 184
reflection · 588, 1324, 1398; and Beans · 1394; and weak typing · 496; annotation processor · 1064, 1071; breaking encapsulation with · 607; difference between RTTI and reflection · 589; example · 1334; latent typing and generics · 726
regex · 527
Registered Factories, variation of Factory Method design pattern · 582
regular expressions · 523
rehashing · 878
reification, and generics · 655
relational operators · 103
reluctant quantifiers · 529
removeActionListener( ) · 1403, 1410
removeXXXListener( ) · 1322
renameTo( ) · 914
reporting errors in book · 21
request, in OOP · 27
reset( ) · 926
responsive user interfaces · 1145
resume( ), and deadlocks · 1184
resumption, termination vs. resumption, exception handling · 449
re-throwing an exception · 461
return: an array · 753; and finally · 476; constructor return value · 157; covariant return types · 303, 706; overloading on return value · 165; returning multiple objects · 621
reusability · 32
reuse: code reuse · 237; reusable code · 1393
rewind( ) · 953
right-shift operator (>>) · 112
rollover · 1337
RoShamBo · 1048
Rumbaugh, James · 1457

running a Java program · 80
runtime binding · 282; polymorphism · 277
runtime type information (RTTI) · 308; Class object · 556, 1335; ClassCastException · 570; Constructor class for reflection · 589; Field · 589; getConstructor( ) · 1335; instanceof keyword · 569; isInstance( ) · 578; Method · 589; misuse · 613; newInstance( ) · 1335; reflection · 588; reflection, difference between · 589; shape example · 553; type-safe downcast · 569
RuntimeException · 469, 498
rvalue · 95

S

ScheduledExecutor, for concurrency · 1242
scheduler, thread · 1117
scope: inner class nesting within any arbitrary scope · 355; inner classes in methods & scopes · 354
scrolling in Swing · 1316
searching: an array · 784; sorting and searching Lists · 884
section, critical section and synchronized block · 1169
seek( ) · 926, 934
self-bounded types, in generics · 701
semaphore, counting · 1246
seminars: public Java seminars · 15; training, provided by MindView, Inc. · 1450
sending a message · 27
sentinel, end · 626
separation of interface and implementation · 31, 228, 1321
sequence, applying a method to a sequence · 728
SequenceInputStream · 916, 925
Serializable · 980, 986, 991, 1001, 1405; readObject( ) · 992; writeObject( ) · 992
serialization: and object storage · 996; and transient · 991; controlling the process of serialization · 986; defaultReadObject( ) · 995; defaultWriteObject( ) · 994; Versioning · 995

Set · 389, 394, 415, 821; mathematical relationships · 641; performance comparison · 872
setActionCommand( ) · 1358
setBorder( ) · 1340
setErr(PrintStream) · 943
setIcon( ) · 1337
setIn(InputStream) · 943
setLayout( ) · 1317
setMnemonic( ) · 1358
setOut(PrintStream) · 943
setToolTipText( ) · 1337
shape: example · 34, 282; example, and runtime type information · 553
shift operators · 112
short-circuit, and logical operators · 106
shortcut, keyboard · 1358
shuffle( ) · 885
side effect · 94, 103, 166
sign extension · 112
signals, missed, in concurrency · 1203
signature, method · 72
signed twos complement · 116
Simula-67 programming language · 26
simulation · 1253
sine wave · 1360
single dispatching · 1047
SingleThreadExecutor · 1123
Singleton design pattern · 232
size( ), ArrayList · 390
size, of a HashMap or HashSet · 878
sizeof( ), lack of in Java · 122
sleep( ), in concurrency · 1126
slider · 1371
Smalltalk · 25
SocketChannel · 971
SoftReference · 889
Software Development Conference · 14
solution space · 24
SortedMap · 837
SortedSet · 825
sorting · 778; alphabetic · 418; and searching Lists · 884; lexicographic · 418
source code · 18; copyright notice · 19
South, BorderLayout · 1317
space: namespaces · 211; problem space · 24; solution space · 24
specialization · 258
specification, exception specification · 457, 493
specifier, access · 31, 210, 221

split( ), String · 322, 525
sprintf( ) · 521
SQL generated via annotations · 1066
stack · 410, 412, 895; generic pushdown ·
   625
standard input, reading from · 941
standards, coding · 21
State design pattern · 306
state machines, and enum · 1041
stateChanged( ) · 1363
static · 316; and final · 263; block · 190;
   construction clause · 190; data
   initialization · 186; final static primitives
   · 264; import, and enum · 1013;
   initialization · 274, 558; initializer · 582;
   inner classes · 364; keyword · 76, 172;
   method · 172, 282; strong type checking
   · 492; synchronized static · 1156; type
   checking · 615; vs. dynamic type
   checking · 814
STL, C++ · 900
stop( ), and deadlocks · 1184
Strategy design pattern · 322, 332, 737,
   764, 778, 780, 903, 910, 1036, 1238
stream, I/O · 914
StreamTokenizer · 924
String: CASE_INSENSITIVE_ORDER
   Comparator · 884; class methods · 503;
   concatenation with operator += · 118;
   conversion with operator + · 95, 118;
   format( ) · 521; immutability · 503;
   indexOf( ) · 592; lexicographic vs.
   alphabetic sorting · 783; methods · 511;
   operator + and += overloading · 242;
   regular expression support in · 524;
   sorting, CASE_INSENSITIVE_ORDER
   · 902; split( ) method · 322; toString( ) ·
   238
StringBuffer · 916
StringBufferInputStream · 916
StringBuilder, vs. String, and toString( ) ·
   506
StringReader · 923, 928
StringWriter · 923
strong static type checking · 492
Stroustrup, Bjarne · 207
structural typing · 721, 733
struts, in BoxLayout · 1321
Stub · 606
style: coding style · 88; of creating classes ·
   228
subobject · 244, 256

substitutability, in OOP · 25
substitution: inheritance vs. extension ·
   306; principle · 37
subtraction · 98
suites, @Unit vs. JUnit · 1095
super · 245; and inner classes · 383;
   keyword · 243
superclass · 243; bounds · 568
supertype wildcards · 682
suspend( ), and deadlocks · 1184
SWF, Flash bytecode format · 1416
Swing · 1303; and concurrency · 1382;
   component examples · 1332;
   components, using HTML with · 1370;
   event model · 1321
switch: and enum · 1016; keyword · 151
switch, context switching in concurrency ·
   1112
synchronized · 1155; and inheritance · 1411;
   and wait( ) & notifyAll( ) · 1198; block,
   and critical section · 1169; Brian's Rule
   of Synchronization · 1156; containers ·
   887; deciding what methods to
   synchronize · 1411; queue · 1215; static ·
   1156
SynchronousQueue, for concurrency · 1259
System.arraycopy( ) · 775
System.err · 450, 941
System.in · 941
System.out · 941
System.out, changing to a PrintWriter ·
   942
systemNodeForPackage( ), preferences
   API · 1007

T

tabbed dialog · 1349
table-driven code · 1033; and anonymous
   inner classes · 859
task vs. thread, terminology · 1142
tearing, word tearing · 1161
Template Method design pattern · 375,
   573, 666, 859, 969, 1173, 1279, 1284
templates, C++ · 618, 652
termination condition, and finalize( ) · 176
termination vs. resumption, exception
   handling · 449
ternary operator · 116

U

V

W

X

Y

Z